Unfair Dismissal

Employment Law Handbook

August 2010

IDS

THOMSON REUTERS

Unfair Dismissal

Employment Law Handbook

Previous edition 2005

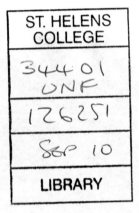
Incomes Data Services Ltd
Finsbury Tower, 103-105 Bunhill Row, London EC1Y 8LZ.
Tel: 0845 303 7217 Fax: 0845 310 5517
Website: www.incomesdata.co.uk

ISBN 978-1-847-03989-7

IDS Employment Law Handbook, 'Unfair Dismissal', is published by Incomes Data Services Limited (Registered in England & Wales, Company No 913794. Registered Office and address for service: 100 Avenue Road, London NW3 3PF).

No natural forests were destroyed to make this product: only farmed timber was used and re-planted.

A CIP catalogue record for this book is available from the British Library.

Printed by St Austell Printing Co, 41 Truro Road, St Austell, Cornwall PL25 5JE

Contents

9 Retirement

10 Automatically unfair dismissals

Abbreviations

Courts

ECJ	European Court of Justice
ECHR	European Court of Human Rights
PC	Privy Council
HL	House of Lords
CA	Court of Appeal
Ct Sess	Court of Session
NICA	Northern Ireland Court of Appeal
QBD	Queen's Bench Division
Div Ct	(Queen's Bench) Divisional Court
KBD	King's Bench Division
ChD	Chancery Division
NIRC	National Industrial Relations Court
EAT	Employment Appeal Tribunal
ET	Employment Tribunal

Case references

AC	Law Reports, Appeal Cases
All ER	All England Law Reports
BNIL	Bulletin of Northern Ireland Law
Ch	Law Reports, Chancery Division
CMLR	Common Market Law Reports
COET	Employment Tribunal folio number
EAT	EAT unreported case number
ECR	European Case Reports
ET	Employment Tribunal unreported case number
EWCA	Court of Appeal unreported case number
ICR	Industrial Cases Reports
IRLR	Industrial Relations Law Reports
ITR	Industrial Tribunal Reports
KB	Law Reports, King's Bench Division
QB	Law Reports, Queen's Bench Division
SCOET	Scottish Employment Tribunal folio number
TLR	Times Law Reports
WLR	Weekly Law Reports

Legislation

DDA	Disability Discrimination Act 1995
EqA	Equality Act 2010
EqPA	Equal Pay Act 1970
ERA	Employment Rights Act 1996
ERelA 1999	Employment Relations Act 1999
ERelA 2004	Employment Relations Act 2004
ETA	Employment Tribunals Act 1996
RRA	Race Relations Act 1976
SDA	Sex Discrimination Act 1975
TULR(C)A	Trade Union and Labour Relations (Consolidation) Act 1992

Statutory references, unless otherwise stated, are to the Employment Rights Act 1996 (ERA), except in Chapter 20 where references are to the 'Recoupment Regulations'.

Many cases in this Handbook were decided under legislation that preceded the ERA. Reference in made throughout to the corresponding provisions in the later consolidation statute and not to their antecedents in repealed legislation.

Introduction

In Addison v Babcock FATA Ltd 1987 ICR 805, CA, Sir John Donaldson, then Master of the Rolls, who had in 1972–74 been President of the National Industrial Relations Court when the right not to be unfairly dismissed was introduced, referred to a decision of that court and said that 'in those far-off days we fondly hoped and imagined that a few such decisions would finally settle the law and that the National Industrial Relations Court could then retire as an appellate court'.

Things have not worked out quite like that, however, and although the National Industrial Relations Court was retired as an appellate court in 1974, it was replaced in due course by the Employment Appeal Tribunal. The flood of decisions on unfair dismissal law has continued unabated and there have been innumerable statutory amendments to the law as first set out in the Industrial Relations Act 1971.

The law, as amended, is now contained in the Employment Rights Act 1996 (ERA). This Act consolidated various statutes concerned with individual employment rights, such as the Employment Protection (Consolidation) Act 1978 and the Wages Act 1986, into a single statutory code. The law has not stood still, however, and the ERA itself has been amended many times. Two recent changes of particular significance were the introduction of 'retirement' as a potentially fair reason for dismissal in October 2006 and the repeal of the statutory dispute resolution procedures in April 2009.

Retirement dismissals

On 1 October 2006 the Employment Equality (Age) Regulations 2006 SI 2006/1031 came into force, making it unlawful for employers to discriminate against a person on the ground of his or her age. While this did not sound the death knell for compulsory retirement – which remains lawful where the employee has reached the 'default retirement age' of 65 and the employer has followed the statutory retirement procedure set out in the Regulations – employees now enjoy the right to request working beyond their intended retirement date. Not surprisingly, this important change necessitated corresponding amendments to the law on unfair dismissal. As a result, the upper age limit for claiming unfair dismissal was removed and retirement – i.e. retiring an employee in accordance with the statutory retirement procedure set out in the Regulations – was added as the sixth potentially fair reason for dismissal under S.98 ERA. Retirement dismissals are discussed in detail in Chapter 9.

Repeal of statutory dispute resolution procedures

The other recent change of note was the repeal of the statutory dispute resolution procedures (SDRPs) on 6 April 2009 by the Employment Act 2008.

i

The SDRPs, which were introduced just four and a half years previously by the Employment Act 2002 (with much of the detail contained in the Employment Act (Dispute Resolution) Regulations 2004 SI 2004/752), established statutory dismissal and disciplinary procedures for the first time. Where these procedures applied – which was in the majority of cases – the employer was expected to go through defined steps whenever a dismissal or disciplinary action was contemplated. The employee was expected to cooperate and to take certain steps him or herself. A failure by an employer to comply with the procedures prior to dismissing an employee rendered that dismissal automatically unfair under S.98A(1) ERA. Furthermore, any compensation awarded by a tribunal could be reduced or increased by between 10 and 50 per cent to reflect a failure on the part of employer or employee to comply with any aspect of the procedures.

The repeal of the SDRPs, and S.98A ERA, has had a major impact on unfair dismissal law, although contrary to some reports, the law did not simply revert to the 'good old days'. Instead, a revised Acas Code of Practice on Disciplinary and Grievance Procedures was introduced. This Code is relevant to the question of liability and will be taken into account by a tribunal when determining the reasonableness of a dismissal in accordance with S.98(4) ERA. Furthermore, under new S.207A of the Trade Union and Labour Relations (Consolidation) Act 1992, if the dismissal is found to be unfair, the tribunal can increase or decrease an award of compensation by up to 25 per cent for an unreasonable failure to follow the Code if it considers it just and equitable to do so.

That said, the situation with regard to procedurally unfair dismissals is once again governed by the House of Lords' decision in Polkey v AE Dayton Services Ltd 1988 ICR 142, HL. In that case their Lordships ruled that employers could not argue that a procedurally improper dismissal was nevertheless fair because it would have made no difference to the outcome if the employer had followed a fair procedure. In their view, an employer's actions in dispensing with a fair procedure were highly relevant to the question of whether the employer acted reasonably in dismissing, and therefore tribunals were not entitled to take into account, when determining the fairness or otherwise of a dismissal, whether a proper procedure would have made any difference to the employer's decision to dismiss.

Under the SDRP scheme, S.98A(2) ERA provided that failure to follow a procedure other than one required by the SDRPs would not be regarded as by itself making the employer's action unreasonable if the employer could show that it would have decided to dismiss the employee even if the procedure had been followed. Now that S.98A has been repealed, tribunals are again prevented from asking whether procedural failings would have made any difference to the decision to dismiss in determining the reasonableness of a dismissal. That question is only relevant when calculating the compensatory award at the remedies stage, at which point the tribunal may reduce such an award proportionately to reflect the chance that the employee would have been fairly dismissed in any event had a proper procedure been complied with. The procedural steps an employer should follow when dismissing an employee are discussed in Chapter 6, while the so-called 'Polkey reductions' to compensation are considered in detail in Chapter 18.

Scope of Handbook

This Handbook aims to provide a clear and accurate statement of the law of unfair dismissal as at 1 July 2010. However, it does not cover every ground of unfair dismissal contained in the ERA. Unfair redundancy dismissals are dealt with in IDS Employment Law Handbook, 'Redundancy' (2008); dismissals relating to pregnancy, maternity, family leave and flexible working rights in IDS Employment Law Handbook, 'Maternity and Parental Rights' (2009); working time dismissals in IDS Employment Law Handbook, 'Working Time' (2009); dismissals for reasons relating to the minimum wage in IDS Employment Law Handbook, 'Wages' (2003); dismissals made in connection with part-time workers' rights in IDS Employment Law Supplement, 'Part-time and Atypical Workers' (2001); and dismissals for reasons relating to fixed-term workers' rights in IDS Employment Law Supplement, 'Fixed-Term Work' (2003). Furthermore, dismissals made in connection with a transfer of an undertaking are covered in IDS Employment Law Handbook, 'Transfer of Undertakings' (2007), while industrial action and trade union dismissals are covered in IDS Employment Law Handbooks, 'Industrial Action' (2010) and 'Trade Unions' (2000) respectively.

The scheme of this Handbook is as follows:

- Chapter 1 covers the legal definition of dismissal

- Chapter 2 deals with the various exclusions from the right to claim that exist – e.g. where the claimant is not an employee or has insufficient qualifying service

- Chapter 3 tackles the central issue of unfairness in the statutory definition and explains how the reason for dismissal must be established and how tribunals approach the question of reasonableness

- Chapters 4 to 8 then explain the application of the general principles discussed in Chapter 3 to the potentially fair reasons for dismissal that may be put forward – capability and qualifications, ill health, conduct, statutory ban and 'some other substantial reason'

- Chapter 9 deals with the special procedures that apply to retirement dismissals

iii

- Chapters 10 to 13 are concerned with automatically unfair dismissals, discussing the special rules that apply to such dismissals before focusing on particular types of automatically unfair dismissal, including Sunday working dismissals, dismissals of occupational pension scheme trustees and employee representatives, dismissals relating to trade union blacklists, health and safety dismissals, dismissals for asserting a statutory right and dismissals for making a protected disclosure ('whistleblowing')

- Chapters 14 to 19 consider the remedies available in unfair dismissal cases – reinstatement, re-engagement and compensation. Chapter 19 also covers interim relief orders

- Chapter 20 examines the mechanism for recoupment from compensation awards of social security benefits received by applicants

- Finally, Chapter 21 looks at the right of employees to receive a written statement of the reasons for dismissal.

It should be noted that many of the decisions cited in this Handbook are decisions of employment tribunals. These are intended to be illustrative only and are not binding on other tribunals, even if the facts and circumstances of the two cases appear to be identical.

The law is stated as at 1 July 2010. This Handbook completely replaces IDS Employment Law Handbook, 'Unfair Dismissal' (2005), which should now be discarded.

This publication aims to provide accurate, authoritative information and comment on the subjects it covers. It is offered to subscribers on the understanding that the publisher is not in business as a lawyer or consultant.

1 Dismissal

Express dismissal

Non-renewal of limited-term contracts

Constructive dismissal

Non-dismissals

An employee who wishes to claim unfair dismissal must first show that he or she has been dismissed within the meaning of S.95 of the Employment Rights Act 1996 (ERA). S.95 states that an employee will be treated as dismissed if: **1.1**

- his or her contract of employment is terminated by the employer with or without notice – S.95(1)(a)

- he or she is employed under a limited-term contract and the contract expires by virtue of the limiting event without being renewed under the same terms – S.95(1)(b), or

- he or she has been constructively dismissed – S.95(1)(c). A constructive dismissal occurs when an employee resigns, with or without notice, because of a repudiatory breach of contract by the employer.

There is also a dismissal where an employee under notice of dismissal from the employer resigns on a date earlier than the date on which the employer's notice is due to expire – S.95(2).

Note that if an employee is dismissed but that sanction is reduced on appeal to, for example, demotion, the effect of the decision on appeal is to revive the contract of employment so as to treat the employee as if he or she had never been dismissed for the purposes of an unfair dismissal claim – Roberts v West Coast Trains Ltd 2005 ICR 254.

Dismissal on the ground of redundancy – which may give rise to an unfair dismissal claim – is defined separately in S.136(1) in almost identical terms to those in S.95. However, there are two special cases where an employee is treated as not having been dismissed for the purposes of the statutory redundancy scheme: **1.2**

- an employee who has been locked out by the employer and has resigned without notice cannot claim constructive dismissal on account of redundancy even though the employer's conduct might ordinarily have entitled him or her to do so – S.136(2)

- when an employee accepts a renewal of his or her contract or a re-engagement to take effect within four weeks of the old contract ending, there is no dismissal for redundancy purposes – S.138(1). The offer may be

1

from the original employer or from an associated employer – S.146. (Note that S.138(1) applies only for the purposes of the statutory redundancy scheme and does not prevent an employee who has been re-employed from bringing an unfair dismissal claim – Jones v Governing Body of Burdett Coutts School 1997 ICR 390, EAT.)

There are also two special cases where there is a dismissal under the ERA for the purposes of the statutory redundancy scheme only:

- certain events causing implied termination of the contract by operation of law (e.g. dissolution of partnership, death of an individual employer or appointment of a receiver by the court) – S.136(5)

- special cases of termination of 'employment' by statute (involving termination of membership of certain bodies covered by regulations – e.g. police forces and fire brigades). This applies even though the individuals concerned are not employees but statutory office-holders – S.172.

1.3 Finally, it should be noted that the rules for giving counter-notice are stricter in relation to redundancy dismissals than in other cases. In an ordinary S.95 dismissal, an employee who is dismissed with notice and who then gives counter-notice to leave on a date before the expiry of the employer's notice is still treated as having been dismissed by the employer, and the reason for dismissal is taken to be the reason for which the employer's notice was given – S.95(2). In redundancy cases, however, the employee is treated as dismissed only if the counter-notice is given in writing within the 'obligatory period' of the employer's notice. This is the period, ending on the date of expiry of the employer's notice, which equates to the statutory notice period under S.86 or to the employee's contractual notice entitlement, whichever is the longer. If the employee gives notice before the obligatory period – where, for instance, the employer has been generous in giving a long notice period – he or she is not treated as having been dismissed for redundancy – S.136(3).

Redundancy dismissals are discussed fully in IDS Employment Law Handbook, 'Redundancy' (2008), Chapter 1. The remainder of this chapter deals with the three categories of dismissal defined in S.95(1) – express dismissal by the employer, non-renewal of a limited-term contract and constructive dismissal – which apply in unfair dismissal cases. We also deal briefly with non-dismissals – i.e. ways of terminating an employment contract, such as resignation by the employee, that do not rank as dismissals. These 'non-dismissals' are considered in greater detail in IDS Employment Law Handbook, 'Contracts of Employment' (2009), Chapters 9 and 10.

Note that the concepts discussed in this chapter apply to dismissals under both the ERA and the Trade Union and Labour Relations (Consolidation) Act 1992 (TULR(C)A), unless otherwise stated.

2

Express dismissal

A preliminary question that often arises, particularly in claims of unfair dismissal, is whether there has in fact been a dismissal at all. In these circumstances the burden of proof falls on the employee to show a dismissal. The standard of proof is that of the 'balance of probabilities' as normally applied in civil courts: the tribunal must consider whether it was more likely than not that the contract was terminated by dismissal rather than, for example, by resignation or by mutual agreement between employer and employee.

Doubt may arise as to whether a dismissal has taken place when the words or actions of the employer or employee give rise to ambiguity, either by their nature or because of the circumstances in which they took place. Furthermore, an apparent resignation may be treated as a dismissal if it was the result of an ultimatum along the lines of 'resign or you'll be fired', or if the resignation was induced by deceit or trickery on the part of the employer. These problems are discussed below.

Note that because a dismissal arises when the contract of employment is terminated, it is possible for there to be a dismissal even before the employee has actually started work pursuant to the contract. A person engaged under a contract of employment to start work at a future date can claim unfair dismissal if the contract was terminated by the employer for an inadmissible reason (for which no period of qualifying service is necessary) before that date – Sarkar v South Tees Acute Hospitals NHS Trust 1997 IRLR 328, EAT. Inadmissible reasons for dismissal are discussed in Chapter 10, 'Automatically unfair dismissals'.

Ambiguous words

Words that are capable of being interpreted as a resignation or a dismissal may not necessarily amount to such in the circumstances. When an employer tells an employee to 'get out' or says 'you are finished', the question arises as to whether this amounts to an express dismissal or a mere rebuke. (Note, however, that a rebuke may in some circumstances amount to a constructive dismissal – see below under 'Constructive dismissal'.) Conversely, when an employee storms out of a meeting shouting 'I'm off', without stating whether this is a temporary or a permanent move, it may be unclear whether or not the employee has actually resigned.

Broadly speaking, the test as to whether ostensibly ambiguous words amount to a dismissal or a resignation is an objective one:

- all the surrounding circumstances must be considered

- if the words are still ambiguous, the tribunal should ask itself how a reasonable employer or employee would have understood them in light of those circumstances.

1.6   When considering ambiguous words in their proper context, tribunals will look at events both preceding and subsequent to the incident in question and take account of the nature of the workplace in which the misunderstanding arose:

- **Norrie v Munro's Transport (Aberdeen) Ltd** EAT 437/88: N, a lorry driver, was promoted to assistant transport manager with a firm of hauliers. Later, following a reorganisation of the firm's transport routes, N was directed to drive vehicles again for a trial period until new work could be found for him in the Transport Office. On the day these duties were about to start, N refused to do the job. After attempts to persuade him failed a director said, 'The job is there for you,' upon which N asked if he was being dismissed. He was told that he was not, but he maintained his stance until the director said, 'You might as well put your jacket on.' N left the premises and claimed unfair dismissal. The EAT took the words 'You might as well put your jacket on' to be ambiguous and endorsed the tribunal's approach of considering the surrounding circumstances – e.g. the fact that N had received express assurances that he would maintain his promoted status and that he was not being dismissed – to arrive at its decision that the words did not constitute a dismissal

- **Hogan v ACP Heavy Fabrications Ltd** EAT 340/92: the employee, given a 'take it or leave it' ultimatum by his employer in respect of a proposed change in terms and conditions, rejected the proposal and walked out of the meeting. Later that evening he got very drunk, sought out the managing director in a public house and abused him in a violent and aggressive manner. The EAT took the view that the employee's actions at the meeting, taken in isolation, could be regarded as comments made 'in the heat of the moment', to which he ought not to be held until he had had time to reconsider his position. But his subsequent behaviour at the public house made it obvious that he regarded his employment as being at an end

- **Peebles Publishing Group Ltd v Black EAT** 179/91: B was given unpaid compassionate leave when her husband was dying of cancer. On her return to work a few weeks later she was told that she owed the company money. As she left the premises in a distressed state, she passed the managing director and told him that she could not cope and was leaving. She handed him her car keys. B called to apologise the next day and then went to see her employer but was told that she had resigned and could only be re-employed on different terms. On the question of whether or not B had been dismissed, a tribunal noted that B had never clearly said that she was resigning so it felt entitled to look at the surrounding circumstances. It found that B was 'stunned' when she was told she owed the company money and that she was going through a very difficult time and was acting out of character. It further found that her employer was well aware of the stress that she was under and that the decision to 're-employ' B was not based on a genuine or

4

reasonable belief that she had resigned. The tribunal held that she had in fact been dismissed

- **Futty v D and D Brekkes Ltd 1974** IRLR 130, ET: F was a fish-filleter and his foreman, fed up with F's banter, said, 'If you do not like the job, fuck off.' F claimed this was a dismissal and found himself another job. The company saw it differently: it thought F would come back when over his 'huff' and denied dismissing him. With other fish-filleters' help the tribunal interpreted the words used, not in isolation, but against a background of the fish dock and found the words were not dismissal but a 'general exhortation to get on with the job'.

If an employer subsequently seeks clarification of whether an employee's words or conduct amount to a resignation, this could indicate that the employee in question has not resigned. In Goodwill Incorporated (Glasgow) Ltd v Ferrier EAT 157/89, for example, the EAT pointed out that the employer had written to the employee to ask whether she really intended to resign. This was taken as evidence that the employer did not genuinely believe that the employee's ambiguous words amounted to a resignation. A similar view was taken in Tom Cobleigh plc v Young EAT 292/97, where an employee's manner of leaving the office one afternoon gave many indications of an intention to resign. The employer subsequently purported to accept that 'resignation'. In holding that the employer had in fact dismissed the employee, the tribunal pointed out that the employer had written to the employee for clarification of his intentions. This ran counter to the employer's subsequent claim that it considered the employee's actions to have amounted to an unequivocal resignation.

1.7

The same objective test applies when the ambiguity occurs in correspondence between employer and employee. Where an employee has received an ambiguous letter, the EAT has said that the interpretation 'should not be a technical one but should reflect what an ordinary, reasonable employee... would understand by the words used'. It added that 'the letter must be construed in the light of the facts known to the employee at the date he receives the letter' – see Chapman v Letheby and Christopher Ltd 1981 IRLR 440, EAT.

It is a well established principle in the construction of commercial contracts that any ambiguity will be construed against the party seeking to rely on it and in Graham Group plc v Garratt EAT 161/97 the EAT held that this principle should also be applied to ambiguous words or acts in the context of a dismissal or resignation. In that case G was selected for redundancy. On 26 February he was told that he was entitled to nine weeks' notice commencing on that day and that if he did not work the notice he would not have to pay tax on his money. G decided to stay at home. On 29 February he was telephoned and told that the nine weeks began on that day. He then received a letter which confirmed the new date and that he would be given nine weeks' pay in lieu of notice. A tribunal had to determine whether G had been dismissed with or without notice

1.8

5

for the purpose of determining the effective date of termination of his contract. The tribunal, directing itself in accordance with Chapman v Letheby and Christopher Ltd (above), asked itself how a reasonable employee in G's position would have interpreted the terms of his dismissal. It concluded that he would have understood that he was dismissed in February with nine weeks' notice but that he did not have to work during that period.

The tribunal added, however, that, even if its construction was wrong, the letter was ambiguous and should be interpreted against the employer. In its view, where an employer wants to rely on a notice served by him as having a particular meaning, he should be required to show that it unambiguously has that meaning. Employers should not be able to rely on their own ambiguities if the employee is in doubt as to the true position and may lose his or her statutory rights. The EAT held that the tribunal had asked the right questions and was entitled to construe the communications to G in the way that it did. It confirmed that ambiguities should be construed against those relying upon them.

1.9 Unambiguous words

The general rule is that unambiguous words of dismissal or resignation may be taken at their face value without the need for any analysis of the surrounding circumstances. The leading case is Sothern v Franks Charlesly and Co 1981 IRLR 278, CA. S was office manager for a firm of solicitors. After some months of mutual friction she attended a partnership meeting and said 'I am resigning'. The firm took her at her word, accepted the oral statement of resignation and recruited a replacement the next day. The Court of Appeal held that, on the facts, these were unambiguous words of resignation and were understood as such by the employer. That concluded the matter: there was no room to consider what the employee actually intended or what a reasonable employer might have assumed she intended. As Lord Justice Fox put it: 'The natural meaning of the words and the fact that the employers understood them to mean that the employee was resigning cannot be overridden by appeals to what a reasonable employer might have assumed. The non-disclosed intention of a person using language as to his intended meaning is not properly to be taken into account in determining what the true meaning is.'

There are, however, important qualifications to the general rule in the Sothern case that plain words are to be taken at their face value. Fox LJ thought that there might be an exception in the case of an immature employee, or a decision taken in the heat of the moment, or an employee being jostled into a decision by the employer. Dame Elizabeth Lane confirmed this view by referring to exceptions in the case of 'idle words or words spoken under emotional stress which the employers knew or ought to have known were not meant to be taken seriously... [or] a case of employers anxious to be rid of an employee who seized upon her words and gave them a meaning which she did not intend'. In such cases it may be appropriate to investigate the context in which the words were spoken in order to ascertain what was really intended and understood.

Some cases where the exception has been applied:

- **Barclay v City of Glasgow District Council** 1983 IRLR 313, EAT: a mentally disabled employee's unambiguous words of resignation after a row with his superiors were held as not to amount to a notice of termination. The EAT said that there is 'a duty on employers... in an appropriate case to take into account the special circumstances of an employee'

- **Rugby Travel Specialists Ltd v Spender** EAT 307/97: the EAT ruled that a tribunal was entitled to take account of an employee's health and well-being on the day a meeting was held to discuss his future employment. This was a relevant factor in determining whether his subsequent resignation, which was promptly withdrawn, was a true resignation or merely a response to the managing director's statement that if he did not resign he would be dismissed. The EAT refused to interfere with the tribunal's finding that he had, in fact, been dismissed

- **Peebles Publishing Group Ltd v Black** EAT 179/91: the EAT upheld the tribunal's ruling that even if the words B had used did constitute unambiguous words of resignation, the fact that she was acting shortly after a bereavement placed her case within the exceptions to the rule in Sothern v Franks Charlesly (above).

Another example is Greater Glasgow Health Board v MacKay EAT 742/87, where an employee said that she was leaving and wrote out an apparently unequivocal letter of resignation. However, she then sent in sick notes and attempted to withdraw her resignation. The EAT upheld a tribunal finding that she was suffering from stress and anxiety, that she did not rationally and genuinely tender her resignation, and that the employer must have been aware that she was suffering from stress when she put in her resignation. These factors added up to special circumstances which turned an apparently unambiguous resignation into an unfair dismissal. **1.10**

The existence of exceptions to the rule in the Sothern case received higher support in Sovereign House Security Services Ltd v Savage 1989 IRLR 115, CA, where the Court of Appeal confirmed that, while unambiguous words should normally be taken at their face value, in special circumstances the tribunal would be entitled to decide that there was no resignation despite appearances to the contrary. In that case unambiguous words of resignation spoken in the heat of the moment did not amount to a resignation.

In Kwik-Fit (GB) Ltd v Lineham 1992 ICR 183, EAT, the EAT followed the Sovereign House case but drew back from saying that where these special circumstances exist the employer is under a duty to reconsider events so that failure to satisfy that duty will necessarily lead to a finding that a dismissal has

7

occurred. Here L reacted angrily to receiving a humiliating warning from his employer. Under some provocation he then threw down his keys and drove off from the workplace. His employer treated his employment as terminated. A tribunal held that the facts were consistent with there having been an unambiguous resignation but added that as this was an exceptional case where people were acting in the heat of the moment there was an onus on the employer to check the employee's true intention in order to ascertain whether a resignation had occurred. Applying this logic, the tribunal found that the employer's failure to reconsider events sufficiently in order to discover L's true intentions meant that his 'resignation' should in fact be viewed as a dismissal. On appeal, the EAT ordered the case to be remitted because the tribunal had gone too far in placing an 'onus' or 'duty' on the employer to investigate the true intention of the employee in such circumstances. However, Mr Justice Wood confirmed that where special circumstances arise, apparently unambiguous words can be considered in the light of the surrounding circumstances so that it may be risky for an employer simply to accept what seems to be a 'resignation'. He added that in such cases a prudent employer will allow a reasonable period of time to elapse before accepting a supposed resignation. If, during this period, facts arise which require further investigation, an employer who does not investigate would risk the tribunal drawing an inference of 'dismissal' from the evidence.

1.11   The EAT emphasised in Denham v United Glass Ltd EAT 581/98 that it is only when there is doubt as to whether the employee intended to resign that the tribunal can go on to consider whether there were 'special circumstances'. In that case, D handed a letter to his supervisor on 20 March and asked him to give it to the personnel department. The supervisor passed the letter on to personnel but it was not opened until 24 March. By that time D had changed his mind and had told his supervisor on 23 March that he wanted to retract his resignation. When D received a letter from the company accepting his resignation he wrote back asking to be reinstated. When his request was refused, D claimed that he had been unfairly dismissed. D contended that his case fell into the category of 'special circumstances'. In particular, he pointed to a medical report which indicated that at the time of the purported resignation he was under stress and was not, therefore, acting rationally. The EAT held that D had resigned in clear and unambiguous terms. Since there could be no doubt that he had really intended to resign, there were no grounds for considering any 'special circumstances', such as the fact that he was under a lot of stress at the time. Similarly, in Ali v Birmingham City Council EAT 0313/08 A handed a resignation letter to his manager, E. Having received advice from Human Resources, E offered him a cooling-off period to reconsider his decision. She also asked him whether he would reconsider, but he reaffirmed his decision to resign. She then left him for approximately 30 minutes to think about it, after which he confirmed that he still wished to resign. Four days later, M asked for his resignation to be rescinded. The EAT held that during the four-day period following his resignation, A was clearly indicating that he wished to resign either by his positive conduct or by failing to inform the employer otherwise. His resignation was 'far from being an impulsive decision made and implemented in the heat of the moment'. He therefore had no claim for unfair dismissal.

What applies to an angry or emotional resignation may also apply – but more rarely – to an angry dismissal. In Martin v Yeomen Aggregates Ltd 1983 IRLR 49, EAT, the employer angrily dismissed M but within five minutes realised he had been over-hasty and varied the penalty to one of two days' suspension. M, however, insisted that he had been dismissed and claimed unfair dismissal. The EAT held that, in the circumstances, there had been no dismissal. Mr Justice Kilner Brown said that it was desirable, as a matter of common sense and good industrial relations, that an employer (or employee) should – in special circumstances – have the opportunity of withdrawing words spoken in the heat of the moment. If words spoken in anger were immediately withdrawn, there was no dismissal.

The circumstances will need to be exceptional – as they were in the Martin case – to justify a finding of no dismissal. The general rule is that once notice to terminate a contract of employment has been given it cannot be withdrawn unilaterally but only by agreement between the parties – Harris and Russell Ltd v Slingsby 1973 ICR 454, NIRC. In William Hill Organisation Ltd v Rainbird EAT 1406/96, for example, the employer summarily dismissed R on a Friday but phoned her the following Monday to invite her back. The EAT held that this was too late to revoke the dismissal. Similarly, in Vardy v Davidson EAT 513/98 V, the proprietor of the company for which D worked, visited D at home and summarily dismissed her. A subsequent visit by a director of the company who purported to withdraw the dismissal could not remedy the situation. It should be noted, however, that even if an employer's attempt to withdraw a dismissal is held to be ineffective, the employee may well be left with an empty remedy. This is because an offer to withdraw a dismissal is equivalent to an offer of reinstatement and the employee's refusal of reinstatement may well be treated as a total failure to mitigate loss, disentitling him or her from a compensatory award – see Chapter 18.

Ambiguous conduct   1.12
As noted above, the conduct of the parties is one of the surrounding circumstances to be taken into account when alleged words of dismissal or resignation are ambiguous. Occasionally, however, there are no direct words at all on either side but it is nonetheless argued that a dismissal (or resignation) can be inferred from the actions of the parties. If the employer's conduct is at issue, this will normally be a case of constructive dismissal – see below – but sometimes it may be an express dismissal. In Kirklees Metropolitan Council v Radecki 2009 ICR 1244, CA, for example, the Court of Appeal held that removing an employee from the payroll while he was suspended and

9

negotiating a compromise agreement was a sufficiently unequivocal statement of the employer's intention to terminate employment. Two further examples:

- **Hogg v Dover College** 1990 ICR 39, EAT: the EAT held that the college's letter to a teacher removing him as head of history and offering him new terms amounted to an express dismissal. The new terms were so different from the old that the situation could only be described as the termination of one contract and the formation of a new one. That case was followed in Alcan Extrusions v Yates and ors 1996 IRLR 327, EAT, where the imposition of a new and more demanding shift system on an employee was held to amount to a dismissal

- **Frederick Ray Ltd v Davidson** EAT 678/79: D was off sick but sent in a medical certificate and continued to be paid. The employer told D's wife that he was still employed if he had not received his P45. Some days later D was sent his P45 and claimed that this was an unfair dismissal. The EAT held that sending the P45 would not by itself amount to a dismissal but, in the circumstances, there was a dismissal because of what the employer had said to D's wife.

However, employees should not rush to infer from the circumstances that they have been dismissed. In Leeman v Johnson Gibbons (Tools) Ltd 1976 IRLR 11, ET, a tribunal said that removal of an employee's clock card was not a dismissal but simply an indication that the employee should see the management before starting work. Similarly, in Devlin v Craigon Agriculture Ltd 1976 ITR 116 (NI), ET, a tribunal held that the replacement of an employee during a long illness was not a circumstance from which the employee's dismissal could be inferred because it was still possible for him to be taken back upon his becoming fit. That case may be contrasted with Glenboig Union Fireclay Co Ltd v Stewart 1971 ITR 14, Ct Sess (Inner House), in which the permanent closure of an employee's workplace during his sickness did mean dismissal because he could not be taken back on becoming well.

1.13 Equally, an employee's conduct may sometimes lead to a finding that he or she has resigned. In Harrison v George Wimpey and Co Ltd 1972 ITR 188, NIRC, H became sick at Christmas and stayed away for four months without communicating with his employer, although he was in fact obtaining sick notes every two weeks. Sir John Donaldson said: 'Where an employee so conducts himself as to lead a reasonable employer to believe that the employee has terminated the contract of employment, the contract is then terminated.' The NIRC upheld a tribunal's finding of implied resignation by H, but also pointed out that the employer was under a duty to make enquiries and to warn the employee of his intentions. Similarly, in Oram v Initial Contract Services Ltd EAT 1279/98 O failed to return to work after a disciplinary penalty had been reduced from dismissal to a final written warning because the company had not answered concerns she had raised. ICS Ltd was of the view that the terms of her return were clear and that any matters of concern would be discussed once she had come back. The EAT upheld the tribunal's finding that O had resigned. ICS Ltd had not imposed any conditions on O's return, failure to perform which would be regarded as a resignation; rather, she had attempted to challenge its control of the disciplinary process by imposing conditions of her own. When she refused to confirm that she would return to work, the company assumed that she had decided to resign.

That said, employers should not act too hastily in assuming from an employee's failure to respond to correspondence or to turn up for work that he or she has terminated the contract, particularly if the employee is on suspension. In Hassan v Odeon Cinemas Ltd 1998 ICR 127, EAT, H was suspended on 22 September 1995. The following day the company wrote to him confirming the suspension but received no reply. On 2 November the company again wrote to H saying that, as it had still not heard from him, it assumed that he had terminated his employment. The letter stated that, if nothing was heard from him within seven days, his P45 would be posted to him. The company made a number of other unsuccessful attempts to get in touch with H until, on 16 March 1996, he turned up and asked to start work. He was told that as far as the company was concerned his employment was terminated and he was handed his P45. H brought a claim of unfair dismissal. The EAT said that H had not breached his contract of employment by failing to turn up for work since he was not obliged to do so until the suspension was lifted. The employer's letter written in November purporting to accept the employee's supposed breach of contract could not, therefore, constitute a dismissal. The EAT decided that the employee was not dismissed until he was handed his P45 on 16 March.

In practice, it is only in exceptional circumstances that resignation will be the proper inference to draw from an employee's conduct. It used to be open to an employer to argue that, if resignation could not be inferred, the employee's conduct nevertheless amounted to a fundamental breach of the employment contract and had ended the contract automatically. This concept of 'constructive resignation', or 'self-dismissal', was firmly refuted by a majority of the Court of Appeal in London Transport Executive v Clarke 1981 ICR 355, CA, which held that a repudiatory breach by an employee – such as taking a seven-week holiday without permission – did not bring the contract to an end automatically. The contract would only end when the employer accepted the employee's breach – i.e. by dismissing the employee. If an employer refuses to have the employee back after an act of misconduct, the employer cannot claim that the employee has dismissed him or herself: this will be a dismissal by the employer.

The Court of Appeal's judgment in Clarke was followed in Brockley v Hursthouse EAT 762/87. After receiving a warning about her work, B, a solicitor's secretary, returned her files and office keys to her employer and retrieved the deeds to her house from the office to deposit with another solicitor. She then failed to attend work for two days and offered no

1.14

explanation for her absence. Her employer wrote to her enclosing her P45 and outstanding pay, and said that he concluded from her actions that she wished to terminate her employment. The EAT held that the tribunal had misdirected itself in finding that B had dismissed herself. The case was remitted for the tribunal to consider whether she had resigned, or whether her employer had accepted her repudiatory breach of contract and dismissed her.

1.15 **Enforced resignation**

It has long been established that if an employee is told that he or she has no future with an employer and is expressly invited to resign, then that employee is to be regarded as having been dismissed – see, for example, East Sussex County Council v Walker 1972 ITR 280, NIRC.

The principles to be considered in such circumstances were set out by the Court of Appeal in Martin v Glynwed Distribution Ltd 1983 ICR 511, CA. Sir John Donaldson MR said that: 'Whatever the respective actions of the employer and employee at the time when the contract of employment is terminated, at the end of the day the question always remains the same, "Who really terminated the contract of employment?". If the answer is the employer, there was a dismissal.' He went on to hold that this question was one of fact for the tribunal to decide in the circumstances of the particular case.

The invitation made to the employee to resign need not amount to a threat or coercion but, when the employer's behaviour is particularly heavy-handed, tribunals are more likely to find that there has been a dismissal. In Bickerton v Inver House Distillers Ltd EAT 656/91 an employee was told that she had no future with her employer and that she would be dismissed at the end of the week. If, however, she chose to resign she would be allowed to remain in employment for a further four months and would then receive a lump sum by way of compensation. She was given no time to consider this offer and her employer insisted that she write the resignation letter immediately. The EAT held that this amounted to an express dismissal. Similarly, in Rentokil Ltd v Morgan EAT 703/95 the employee was told he was going to be dismissed with immediate effect but was offered a non-negotiable severance package that included one year's pay in lieu of notice on condition that he sign a letter of resignation. The EAT upheld the tribunal's finding that it was the employer's decision to dismiss, not the letter of resignation, that had terminated the employment.

1.16 It is quite common for employees who are facing disciplinary proceedings to resign rather than suffer the ignominy of dismissal. In such circumstances it will usually be the employee who is held to have terminated the contract, provided it can be said that the resignation came about through his or her genuine choice. In Staffordshire County Council v Donovan 1981 IRLR 108, EAT, for example, D agreed to resign while disciplinary proceedings were in progress:

12

the terms included a compensatory payment and a testimonial from the employer. The proceedings might have resulted in D's dismissal but were subject to a right of appeal. The EAT held that there was no dismissal and no threat of dismissal: the alternative to resignation was simply the completion of the disciplinary proceedings. Mr Justice Slynn said: 'It seems to us that it would be most unfortunate if, in a situation where parties are seeking to negotiate in the course of disciplinary proceedings and an agreed form of resignation is worked out by the parties, one of the parties should be able to say subsequently that the fact that agreement was reached in the course of disciplinary proceedings entitles the employee thereafter to say that there was a dismissal.'

In SAS Service Partners v Whalley EAT 561/91, however, the EAT held that an employee who resigned when it became clear that his appeal against dismissal would fail had, in fact, been dismissed. This was not a case in which there was no way of telling how the disciplinary proceedings would turn out; a dismissal had already taken place and the only question was whether the employer was going to reverse the original decision. When the employee 'resigned', the original dismissal came into effect.

What starts off as an enforced resignation – i.e. a dismissal – may become a voluntary one if the employee negotiates satisfactory financial terms and leaves because of them. Two examples:

- **Sheffield v Oxford Controls Co Ltd** 1979 IRLR 133, EAT: the director of a company was threatened with dismissal if he did not resign. Negotiations over a severance payment followed and an agreement was drawn up and initialled. The EAT held that there had been no dismissal. Satisfactory terms of resignation had emerged, so that the threat of dismissal was no longer the operative factor in the director's decision to resign. (Contrast this case with that of Bickerton v Inver House Distillers (above), where resignation in a 'take it or leave it' situation was a dismissal despite a lump sum payment being made to the employee)

- **Crowley v Ashland UK Chemicals Ltd** EAT 31/79: C was told that the company had lost confidence in him as a personnel manager and that he should resign. Negotiations over severance pay followed and he did resign four days later in return for a lump sum of £5,670. The EAT held that there had been no dismissal. The four days during which proper negotiations took place indicated a genuine agreement to terminate.

However, not all negotiated termination payments will give rise to a voluntary resignation. In Sandhu v Jan de Rijk Transport Ltd 2007 ICR 1137, CA, the Court of Appeal held that an employment tribunal had reached a perverse decision in finding that an employee had voluntarily resigned after agreeing severance terms at the same meeting at which the employer told him that he was being dismissed. The company had decided that S should be dismissed following misconduct allegations and, for this

1.17

13

purpose, S was summoned to attend a meeting, although he was not informed in advance about the allegations against him or the purpose of the meeting. The company's managing director opened the meeting by telling S that he was being dismissed. S then negotiated three months' extra salary and the short-term retention of his company car. Lord Justice Wall, giving the leading judgment, said that the tribunal had misdirected itself when deciding that the case was 'on all fours' with the Sheffield and Crowley cases. Neither of those cases bore any resemblance to the facts of the present case. Wall LJ emphasised the 'highly unusual' facts in Sheffield and that Crowley contained a number of critical features wholly absent from the instant case – for example, the negotiations were free from pressure and took place over a four-day period. Moreover, in both cases the terms of the severance were plainly advantageous to the employee – £10,000 for Mr Sheffield and one year's salary for Mr Crowley. Significantly, Wall LJ noted, in no reported judgment had an employee legally resigned during the same meeting or interview at which the employer had first raised the possibility of dismissing the employee.

Note that in the Crowley and Nightingale cases, not only was there held to be no dismissal, there was no resignation either. Instead, the contracts were terminated by agreement. Termination by mutual agreement is dealt with below under 'Non-dismissals'.

1.18 ## Warning of future dismissal

A warning that dismissal is on the cards or is inevitable by a certain date will not amount to a dismissal and an employee who leaves his or her employment in such circumstances will be taken to have resigned. In Morton Sundour Fabrics Ltd v Shaw 1967 ITR 84, Div Ct, Mr Justice Widgery said that an employer could not dismiss an employee by saying 'I intend to dispense with your services at some time in the coming months'. Notice to terminate a contract of employment must either state the date of termination or contain material from which the date can be positively ascertained. In that case S was warned of impending redundancy but no specific date was mentioned. He then got another job, gave in his notice and left. It was held that the employer had never given him notice to terminate, so he was not entitled to a redundancy payment. Although a redundancy case, its principle is equally applicable to unfair dismissal law.

This rule that a statement of intent does not amount to a valid notice of dismissal has been strictly applied by the EAT. For example, letters stating that dismissal for redundancy would take effect 'no later than 26 December' were in the EAT's eyes insufficiently certain to constitute notices of dismissal in Burton Group Ltd v Smith 1977 IRLR 351, EAT, even though the dismissals did actually take place on 26 December. Similarly, a letter from the employer warning the employee that his employment would be terminated if he did not turn up for work on a specified date did not constitute a dismissal with notice in Rai v Somerfield Stores Ltd 2004 IRLR 124, EAT. Indeed, a notice to employees that 'all production will cease at the Brentford plant on 15 February' was held by the EAT not to be sufficient to amount to a valid notice of dismissal in Doble v Firestone Tyre and Rubber Co Ltd 1981 IRLR 300, EAT.

The same principles apply when an employee gives notice of an intention to resign but does not specify the date. In Ely v YKK Fasteners (UK) Ltd 1994 ICR 164, CA, E obtained a job in Australia and told his employer he would be resigning in due course. His employer went about arranging for his replacement, even though E at no stage gave formal notice indicating his final day of employment. The employer later told E that if he did not pinpoint a date his employment would be treated as terminated from 21 December. When the job in Australia fell through, E informed his employer (on 21 December) that he was no longer going to emigrate and wished to continue working. However, the employer chose to treat E as having resigned and would only consider re-employing him on different terms. The Court of Appeal upheld a tribunal decision that E had been (fairly) dismissed because he had merely given notice of his intention to resign at some time in the future. The employer had terminated the employment when choosing to treat it as coming to an end on 21 December.

Resignation induced by deception

1.19

A resignation obtained by dishonesty or deception will be a dismissal, since there is no genuine consent to the termination on the part of the employee. Two examples:

- **Greens Motors (Bridport) Ltd v Makin**, unreported 16.4.86, CA: M, a sales manager, claimed that he went to see his managing director with a 28-day medical certificate. He signed a note, typed by the managing director's wife, which he was told was a formality connected with sick pay and which he did not read because it was partly covered by other papers. This proved to be a note giving two months' notice of resignation and in due course the employer sent M his P45 with a letter thanking him for his loyal service. A tribunal found this to be a dismissal. The Court of Appeal held that on the facts found by the tribunal, M was expressly dismissed by the employer when he was sent his P45. The employer could not rely on a 'resignation' that had been obtained by fraudulent misrepresentation (nor could the employer have relied on one that had been obtained by an innocent misrepresentation)

- **Caledonian Mining Co Ltd v Bassett and anor** 1987 ICR 425, EAT: employees of a contractor at an NCB colliery were told that there would be a reduction in the workforce at that colliery and were asked if they would accept work with the employer at other sites. They replied

15

affirmatively but no offer of alternative work was forthcoming from the employer. Over three months later the employees were offered jobs, for which they had not applied, by the NCB. Although work with the NCB meant a substantial drop in earnings, they accepted the offers and changed their employment. A tribunal found that the offers from the NCB had been orchestrated by the employer to inveigle the employees into resigning so that the employer could avoid having to make redundancy payments. On appeal, the employer argued that there had been no dismissals. The EAT held that on the tribunal's finding that the employees had been dishonestly persuaded to resign, their contracts had been terminated by dismissal rather than by the employees' resignations. It was the deceitful actions of the employer that had brought about the terminations so it was the employer who really terminated the contracts.

1.20   **Partial termination of employment**

Terminating a divisible part of an employee's contract is not a dismissal if the employer gives reasonable notice. In Land and anor v West Yorkshire Metropolitan County Council 1981 ICR 334, CA, the employees were full-time firefighters who were also retained for additional duties in their spare time, for which they were paid extra. The employer, in conjunction with the Fire Brigades Union, decided to abolish part-time duties and gave the employees due notice of this. The employees continued to do their full-time jobs but complained that they had been unfairly dismissed from their part-time employment. The Court of Appeal held that there was only a single contract of employment: it could be divided into two parts which could be terminated separately. Since the employer had terminated the part of the contract covering part-time work with due notice, there was no breach of contract and there had been no dismissal because the single contract was still in existence (even if in an attenuated form).

Matters are different if there are two (or more) separate contracts with the same employer. In such a case, termination of any one contract by the employer is a dismissal as far as that contract is concerned. The House of Lords held in Lewis v Surrey County Council 1987 ICR 982, HL, that separate contracts must be looked at separately. Their Lordships did, however, suggest (obiter) that there might be two exceptions:

- where the arrangements are simply a sham and the purported multiple contracts are in reality a single contract

- where, even though there were separate contracts, there was also a unifying collateral contract which could be described as an 'umbrella' contract – i.e. the reality was that there was a single contract, although there was no deliberate sham on the part of the employer.

16

Non-renewal of limited-term contracts 1.21

Termination of a limited-term contract (LTC) without renewal is deemed to be a dismissal by virtue of S.95(1)(b) ERA. Employers who fail to renew LTCs are liable, therefore, to unfair dismissal claims in the same way as if they had actively ended the contracts. S.235(2A) ERA states that a contract of employment is a 'limited-term contract' if:

- the employment under the contract is not intended to be permanent, and

- provision is accordingly made in the contract for it to terminate by virtue of a limiting event.

Subsection (2B) goes on to define a 'limiting event' as:

- in the case of a contract for a fixed term, the expiry of the term

- in the case of a contract made in contemplation of the performance of a specific task, the performance of the task, and

- in the case of a contract which provides for its termination on the occurrence of an event (or the failure of an event to occur), the occurrence of the event (or the failure of the event to occur).

The expiry of a limited-term contract without renewal amounts to a dismissal even if the employee knew at the outset that it would not be renewed or that it was unlikely to be renewed – Nottinghamshire County Council v Lee 1980 ICR 635, CA. There is an exception in the case of a contract of training or apprenticeship. In North East Coast Shiprepairers Ltd v Secretary of State for Employment 1978 IRLR 149, EAT, an apprentice's contract expired and he was not taken on as a journeyman fitter. The EAT held that the contract of apprenticeship was strictly a one-off contract which was incapable of being renewed, since engagement as a journeyman would have been under a completely new contract. There was no dismissal – only a failure to employ following the cessation of previous employment of a quite different nature.

Despite the fact that the wording of S.95(1)(b) appears to cover all non-renewals of limited-term contracts whether instigated by the employer, by the employee or by agreement, it seems that the non-renewal of a limited-term contract by mutual consent will not amount to a dismissal. This is illustrated by two cases which arose under the previous statutory regime relating to fixed-term contracts. In Manson and anor v (1) University of Strathclyde (2) Automated Microscopy Systems Ltd EAT 356/87, M and J, two research fellows, agreed to the non-renewal of their fixed-term contracts with the university which had employed them because they wanted to take up jobs with a company set up for the commercial exploitation of their research. On the particular facts of this case, the EAT was not prepared to view the non-renewal as a dismissal but rather as a termination by mutual agreement (thus barring 1.22

the two from claiming redundancy payments from the university). The EAT was swayed by the fact that there was no redundancy situation and that M and J could have stayed in the employ of the university if they had wished. However, in Thames Television Ltd v Wallis 1979 IRLR 136, EAT, a researcher who had been employed on a series of fixed-term contracts was held to have been dismissed when her contract was not renewed; the fact that she had received an ex gratia payment because of that non-renewal did not mean that the contract was terminated by mutual agreement.

For further details on the rights of limited-term employees under the 2002 Regulations, see IDS Employment Law Supplement, 'Fixed-Term Work' (2003).

1.23 Constructive dismissal

Section 95(1)(c) states that there is a dismissal when the *employee* terminates the contract, with or without notice, in circumstances such that he or she is entitled to terminate it without notice by reason of the employer's conduct. This form of dismissal is commonly referred to as 'constructive dismissal'.

In the leading case on this subject, Western Excavating (ECC) Ltd v Sharp 1978 ICR 221, CA, the Court of Appeal ruled that the employer's conduct which gives rise to a constructive dismissal must involve a *repudiatory breach of contract*. As Lord Denning MR put it: 'If the employer is guilty of conduct which is a significant breach going to the root of the contract of employment, or which shows that the employer no longer intends to be bound by one or more of the essential terms of the contract, then the employee is entitled to treat himself as discharged from any further performance. If he does so, then he terminates the contract by reason of the employer's conduct. He is constructively dismissed.'

In order to claim constructive dismissal, the employee must establish:

● that there was a fundamental breach of contract on the part of the employer

● that the employer's breach caused the employee to resign

● that the employee did not delay too long before resigning, thus affirming the contract and losing the right to claim constructive dismissal.

Note that a constructive dismissal is not necessarily an unfair one – Savoia v Chiltern Herb Farms Ltd 1982 IRLR 166, CA.

1.24 Fundamental breach
In order to identify a fundamental breach of contract on the part of the employer, it is first necessary to establish what the terms of the contract are. Individual actions by an employer that do not in themselves constitute fundamental breaches of any contractual term may have the cumulative effect

18

of, for example, undermining the trust and confidence inherent in every contract of employment. A course of conduct can cumulatively amount to a fundamental breach of contract entitling an employee to resign and claim constructive dismissal following a 'last straw' incident even though the last straw by itself does not amount to a breach of contract – Lewis v Motorworld Garages Ltd 1986 ICR 157, CA.

Terms of the contract. Contractual terms may be either express or implied. **1.25** Express terms are those which have been specifically agreed between the parties, whether in writing or under an oral agreement. Implied terms are those that exist either because of the nature and circumstances of the contract itself, or because the law states that such a term is to be implied in the particular circumstances.

The grounds on which a term may be implied into a contract are very limited. It is not sufficient for the proposed term to be a reasonable one in all the circumstances. A term can only be implied if:

- it is necessary to give the contract 'business efficacy', or

- it represents the custom and practice in that employment and is 'reasonable, certain and notorious' – Devonald v Rosser and Sons 1906 2 KB 728, CA, or

- it is an inherent legal duty central to the relationship between employer and employee – for example, the duty to provide a safe system of work, or the duty not to undermine trust and confidence.

A term may also be implied from the conduct of the parties or because it is so obvious the parties are assumed to have intended it.

For a full treatment of express and implied terms in employment contracts, see IDS Employment Law Handbook, 'Contracts of Employment' (2009), Chapter 2.

Actual breach and anticipatory breach. A fundamental breach of contract by **1.26** the employer may be an actual or an anticipatory breach. An actual breach of contract arises when the employer refuses or fails to carry out an obligation imposed by the contract at a time when performance is due. An anticipatory breach arises when, before performance is due, the employer intimates to the employee, by words or conduct, that he does not intend to honour an essential term or terms of the contract when the time for performance arrives. For example, a reduction of 25 per cent without warning in an employee's monthly pay cheque is an actual breach, whereas a letter at the beginning of the month stating that 'With effect from the end of this month your salary will be reduced by 25 per cent' would be an anticipatory breach.

The danger faced by employees who resign in the light of an anticipatory breach is that they may be held to have acted too hastily. Vague or conditional proposals of a change in terms, conditions or working practices will not

19

amount to an anticipatory breach and will not justify an employee's resigning and claiming constructive dismissal. In Sangarapillai v Scottish Homes EAT 420/91, for example, S was given a different job title in a salary review and resigned before the completion of that review. The EAT upheld the tribunal's finding that there had been no fundamental breach of contract at the time of the dismissal. Although S had been given a different job title, that did not amount to a clear indication from his employer that his salary or status was to be downgraded.

On the other hand, where the employer clearly indicates that an employee's contract is to be breached, the employee is not obliged to 'wait and see' whether the employer carries out the threat – see Wellworthy Ltd v Ellis EAT 915/83. Note, though, that there will be no constructive dismissal if the employee resigns after a threat to breach the contract is withdrawn – Norwest Holst Group Administration Ltd v Harrison 1985 ICR 668, CA.

1.27 An anticipatory breach must be a fundamental breach for an employee to be entitled to act upon it by resigning and claiming constructive dismissal. In Nelson v Kingston Cables Distributors Ltd EAT 662/99 N's employer wrote to her while she was on maternity leave telling her that the accountancy function that she used to perform had significantly diminished and that on her return she would be required to join a different team. In the EAT's view, there was no reason in principle why an employer who, instead of waiting until the woman's actual return to work to spring such a change on her, gives a clear indication in advance that the old conditions of her job will no longer be available to her and that she must accept a fundamental change if and when she does return, should not be found to have evinced an intention not to be bound by the contract. This would be capable of amounting to an anticipatory repudiation of the contract entitling the employee to treat the contract as brought to an end. However, the case had to be remitted for the tribunal to consider whether the employer's proposed change to N's role was a fundamental change in the terms of her employment.

Either way, as the Court of Appeal in Western Excavating (ECC) Ltd v Sharp (above) emphasised, there must actually be a breach of contract by the employer (actual or anticipatory) for the employee to claim constructive dismissal. This created problems in Greenaway Harrison Ltd v Wiles 1994 IRLR 380, EAT, where the employer informed W of a rearrangement of her hours of work, to be implemented in four weeks' time. When she objected she was told that the change was essential and that if she did not agree to it she would be given notice of dismissal. She was told that she could speak to the managing director but that there was little possibility of his changing his mind. W resigned and a tribunal upheld her claim that she had been constructively dismissed. On appeal, the employer argued that there had been no anticipatory breach because no final decision on the change in hours had yet been taken – the final decision was for the managing director, and W had been offered a meeting with him. The EAT gave short shrift to this argument, holding that the

20

decision to dismiss W if she did not accept the change in terms and conditions was a final one. The fact that W had been given an opportunity to persuade the company to change its mind did not prevent there being an anticipatory breach.

A further argument of the employer caused the EAT more difficulty, however. This was that there had been no breach of contract, anticipatory or otherwise, since all the employer had threatened was to terminate the original contract on notice, which it was lawfully entitled to do. That termination might give rise to a claim of unfair dismissal, but it did not involve or threaten any breach of contract.

The EAT observed that this was 'a far-reaching submission' which, if accepted, would seriously call into question many of the previously decided cases. It chose to reject the argument, stating that it stretched the principle of the Western Excavating case beyond its proper limits. The EAT concluded that the tribunal had been entitled on the facts to hold that a threat to terminate W's contract by giving notice of termination was a significant breach amounting to a repudiation which she was entitled to accept.

1.28

With respect, the EAT's legal analysis on this point is far from satisfactory. Simply to conclude, as it does, that the threat to give notice to terminate the contract of employment was in itself a repudiatory breach (even though an actual termination in these circumstances will never amount to a breach) avoids rather than solves the problem. A better approach might have been to hold that the employer's threat amounted to a breach of the term of mutual trust and confidence that is implied into every contract of employment.

Disputes over contractual interpretation. An employee may not be able to show a breach of contract by the employer if the time for performance of the contract is not yet due and the parties genuinely dispute the meaning of the contractual term in question. In Financial Techniques (Planning Services) Ltd v Hughes 1981 IRLR 32, CA, there was a dispute over the interpretation of a profit-sharing scheme and H resigned and claimed constructive dismissal on the ground that his employer had indicated that money would be deducted from his next quarterly payment. The Court of Appeal rejected his claim, holding that when there is a genuine dispute about the terms of a contract it is not an anticipatory breach for one party to do no more than argue his or her point of view. The employer in this case had not repudiated the contract but had simply offered a different and genuinely held view of the obligations that it imposed.

1.29

However, Lord Justice Templeman stressed that this did not mean that an employer could invariably insist on a plausible but mistaken view of his or her contractual obligations without being held to have repudiated the contract. In the case of an actual breach, the employer's mistaken belief as to his contractual liability would not prevent his conduct from amounting to a repudiation. There could also be cases of anticipatory breach, his Lordship indicated, in which it would be 'unreasonable to force the other party to go on and either to accept

21

the mistaken view of the contract or to litigate without knowing what he was going to get at the end of it'.

Yet there have been some cases suggesting that where there is a genuine dispute about the meaning of a contract's terms, an employer's insistence on performing the contract according to a genuine but incorrectly held belief may prevent those actions from constituting a repudiatory breach, and may do so even in cases of actual (as opposed to anticipatory) breach. In Bridgen v Lancashire County Council 1987 IRLR 58, CA, for instance, Sir John Donaldson MR said: 'The mere fact that a party to a contract takes a view of its construction which is ultimately shown to be wrong, does not of itself constitute repudiatory conduct. It has to be shown that he did not intend to be bound by the contract as properly construed.' It should be stressed, however, that Sir John Donaldson's comments did not form the basis of the final decision in that case and so are not binding on lower courts (although they have been accepted without comment by the EAT on a number of occasions – see, for example, O'Kelly v GMBATU EAT 396/87 and Haberdasher's Monmouth School for Girls v Turner EAT 0922/03).

1.30 The relevance of an employer's mistaken belief as to the true contractual position was considered by the EAT in Brown v JBD Engineering Ltd 1993 IRLR 568, EAT. In that case B was a director and shareholder in JBD Ltd who ceased all direct communication with the other directors after an incident at a board meeting. There followed a period of negotiations through solicitors about the company's purchase of his shares and the terms on which his employment should cease. During this period B attended the company premises only rarely. One day he attended work to find that the locks had been changed, that the company had appointed a replacement, and that all his clients had been informed that he was no longer working there. A tribunal rejected his complaint of constructive dismissal on the ground that the company had genuinely believed that B would not be returning. The EAT held that the tribunal had erred in holding that actions of an employer taken in good faith upon a genuine belief of fact can never amount to a repudiation of contract. Nevertheless, although the fact that an employer acted on a genuine but mistaken belief is not enough by itself to prevent the conduct from amounting to a repudiation, it may be treated as a relevant factor in determining whether the breach amounted to a repudiation, at least in cases in which the belief was reasonable and was brought about, in whole or in part, by the conduct of the employee. The tribunal should have asked itself whether, given the whole circumstances of the case, including the stage reached in the negotiations and the fact that the employee had not attended work for some time, the employer's actions amounted to a fundamental breach going to the root of the contract.

1.31 **Is the breach fundamental?** As the Brown case above suggests, once a tribunal has established that the relevant contractual term exists and that a breach (actual or anticipatory) has occurred, it must then consider whether the breach is fundamental. This is essentially a question of fact and degree and the tribunal's decision will not be interfered with unless there is a misdirection in law or it is perverse. A key factor for the tribunal to take into account is the effect that the breach has on the employee concerned. Thus a £5 pay cut is clearly a more serious matter for an employee earning £100 per week than it is for an employee earning £500 and is therefore more likely to constitute a fundamental breach with regard to the former. Note, however, that where an employer breaches the implied term of trust and confidence, the breach is 'inevitably' fundamental – Morrow v Safeway Stores plc 2002 IRLR 9, EAT.

It makes no difference to the issue of whether or not there has been a fundamental breach that the employer did not intend to end the contract – Bliss v South East Thames Regional Health Authority 1987 ICR 700, CA. Similarly, the circumstances that induced the employer to act in breach of contract are irrelevant to the issue of whether a fundamental breach has occurred – Wadham Stringer Commercials (London) Ltd v Brown EAT 322/82. Here B, a fleet sales director, was demoted in status and moved into a cramped and unventilated office. The employer argued that economic circumstances impelled the company to treat B in this way, but the EAT stressed that the test of fundamental breach is a purely contractual one and that the surrounding circumstances are not relevant.

Reasonableness. In Western Excavating (ECC) Ltd v Sharp (above) the Court of Appeal expressly rejected the argument that S.95(1)(c) ERA introduces a concept of reasonable behaviour by employers into contracts of employment. This means that an employee is not justified in leaving employment and claiming constructive dismissal merely because the employer has acted unreasonably. However, in a number of more recent cases the EAT seemed to take the view that the reasonableness or otherwise of the employer's behaviour is relevant to the question of whether the employer is in *fundamental breach* of contract. Of course, the implied term of mutual trust and confidence found in every contract of employment is now so broad that unreasonable conduct on an employer's part will often amount to a breach of that term and give rise to a claim of constructive dismissal. However, the EAT appeared to curtail the scope of the implied term by applying the 'range of reasonable responses' test developed in respect of unfair dismissal claims to the question of whether there has been a breach of contract (see, for example, Abbey National plc v Fairbrother 2007 IRLR 320, EAT, and Claridge v Daler Rowney Ltd 2008 ICR 1267, EAT).

1.32

This approach has now been roundly rejected by the Court of Appeal in Bournemouth University Higher Education Corporation v Buckland 2010 ICR 908, CA, where the Court upheld the decision of the EAT that the question of whether the employer's conduct fell within the range of reasonable responses is not relevant when determining whether there is a constructive dismissal. Rather, it is something to be considered by the tribunal if the employer puts forward a potentially fair reason for dismissal when deciding whether dismissal for that reason was fair. In the words of Mr Justice Clark in the EAT: the 'question of dismissal, whether actual or constructive, is quite distinct from the separate questions of reason for dismissal and its fairness as a matter of statutory construction'.

1.33   **Can the breach be cured?** In the Buckland case, B, a university professor, had alleged breach of trust and confidence when the university overturned marks he had given on students' exam papers without discussing it with him. The EAT found that although this was a fundamental breach, it had been negated by an inquiry that upheld B's complaint. By the time he resigned, therefore, there was no breach of contract for him to accept and he was not constructively dismissed. On appeal, the Court of Appeal rejected this notion that a repudiatory breach of contract can be cured unilaterally by the party in default, taking away the innocent party's option of acceptance (by resigning – see 'Resignation' below). It did, however, encourage a robust approach to affirmation in these circumstances. As Lord Justice Sedley explained: 'A wronged party, particularly if it fails to make its position entirely clear at the outset, cannot ordinarily expect to continue with the contract for very long without losing the option of termination, at least where the other party has offered to make suitable amends.' Affirmation of the contract is discussed below.

Examples of the types of breach that commonly give rise to constructive dismissal claims are given in IDS Employment Law Handbook, 'Contracts of Employment' (2009), Chapter 8.

1.34   ## Resignation

Once it has been established that the employer has committed a repudiatory breach of contract, the employee must go on to show that he or she accepted the repudiation. This means that the employee must terminate the contract by resigning, either with or without notice. In Triton Oliver (Special Products) Ltd v Bromage EAT 709/91 the employer withdrew B's company car and petrol allowance when he was absent with a long-term illness. B's solicitors wrote to the employer stating that the withdrawal of the car was a breach of contract and that they were currently considering whether it amounted to a constructive dismissal. The EAT held that this letter fell far short of an acceptance by the employee of the employer's breach.

A contract will not actually come to an end until the employee has communicated to the employer, either by words or by conduct, the fact that he or she is terminating the employment – Edwards v Surrey Police 1999 IRLR 456, EAT. However, a resignation need not be expressed in a formal way. The fact of the employee's resignation may be inferred from his or her conduct and the surrounding circumstances – Johnson v Monty Smith Garages Ltd EAT 657/79. But simply presenting a claim for unfair dismissal to a tribunal will not be sufficient, even though the tribunal would have forwarded a copy of the complaint to the employer and the employer would have thus found out that the employee was not coming back – Rai v Somerfield Stores Ltd 2004 IRLR 124, EAT.

Usually it is not difficult to recognise a resignation but there are circumstances in which the situation may not be so clear. An example: **1.35**

- **McDonald v Lowndes Queensway Group Ltd** EAT 651/90: McD was on sick leave when he was demoted. In the midst of McD's dispute with his employer, his solicitors wrote stating that if he were not offered a satisfactory solution by a given date he would initiate proceedings for constructive dismissal. The date passed and McD brought his action. The EAT held that the solicitors' letter was sufficiently explicit to indicate that McD had resigned.

Although an employee cannot submit a claim of unfair constructive dismissal before actually resigning, he or she may give notice and claim constructive dismissal before the notice expires – Presley v Llanelli Borough Council 1979 ICR 419, EAT. The date the notice expires then becomes the effective date of termination.

Employee already in breach of contract. One issue that remains unclear is whether an employee who is him or herself in fundamental breach can rely on the employer's repudiatory breach to resign and claim constructive dismissal. This question has arisen primarily in restrictive covenant cases but is of more general application and may be particularly relevant where the employee is taking industrial action. In RDF Media Group plc and anor v Clements 2008 IRLR 207, QBD, the High Court suggested that where an employee was him or herself in repudiatory breach of his or her contract of employment he or she could not accept the breach by the employer to bring the contract to an end. However, the Court there was clearly concerned with *mutual* obligations – in that case, the implied obligation not to destroy mutual trust and confidence – and it is arguable that an employee would not be prevented from pursuing a constructive dismissal claim where the employer sought to unilaterally impose a contractual variation – such as, for example, the removal of the contractual bonus. **1.36**

In any event, the proposition put forward in the RDF case has since been doubted in another High Court case – Tullett Prebon plc and ors v BGC Brokers LP and ors 2010 EWHC 484, QBD – where Mr Justice Jack stated that: 'The ordinary position is that, if there is a breach of a contract by one party which entitles the other to terminate the contract but he does not do so, then the contract both remains in being and may be terminated by the first party if the second party has himself committed a repudiatory breach of the contract.' Turning to consider the issue of mutual trust and confidence, Jack J made it clear that damage to the one party's trust and confidence in the other does not entitle that party to damage the other's trust and confidence in him or her. He did conclude, however, that the employee's conduct may be relevant to the

25

question of whether the employer's conduct has sufficiently damaged the trust and confidence to amount to a breach of contract and to this extent he acknowledged that there may in practice be little difference between his approach and that suggested in the RDF case.

1.37 Causation

An employee will be regarded as having accepted the employer's repudiation only if his or her resignation has been caused by the breach of contract in issue. This means that if there is an underlying (or ulterior) reason for the employee's resignation, such that he or she would have left anyway irrespective of the employer's conduct, then there has not been a constructive dismissal. In Walker v Josiah Wedgwood and Sons Ltd 1978 ICR 744, EAT, W was subjected to a number of slights by his employer and handed in his resignation. When asked why he was leaving he replied that he had got a better job. He also said that what the employer was doing was right for the company but that he would have no part in it. The EAT said that this indicated no more than that W had a better job to go to and did not like the employer's management style: there was no indication that he was leaving because of any breach of contract on the part of the employer. Similarly, in McAllen v Torlane Transport Ltd EAT 692/96 M, a van driver, resigned and claimed constructive dismissal. He told a tribunal that he walked out because he was asked to drive an unsafe vehicle. The EAT upheld the tribunal's decision that the real reason for M's resignation was a dispute over pay and he was not leaving because of any breach of contract by the employer.

Sometimes there is more than one reason why an employee leaves a job. For instance, he or she may feel some dissatisfaction with the present job and have received an offer of something that promises to be better. Where there are mixed motives, a tribunal must determine the effective cause of the resignation. In Jones v F Sirl and Son (Furnishers) Ltd 1997 IRLR 493, EAT, J had been subjected to a number of fundamental breaches of contract in the space of a few months. Three weeks after the last of these breaches she resigned, having been offered another job. A tribunal took the view that, since the employee's departure had been prompted by the offer of alternative employment, the employer's breach had not caused her resignation. The EAT overruled this, holding that the correct approach in such a case was to ask what was the effective cause of the resignation. The tribunal had not found that in the absence of the job offer J would have stayed and the EAT held that, considering J's long service (30 years) and the fact that she took another job only three weeks after her contract was fundamentally breached, the breaches – not the job offer – were the effective cause of her resignation.

1.38

Certain comments made by the EAT in the Walker case (above) suggest that employees must tell their employer why they are resigning if they are to establish the cause of the resignation. This decision was endorsed by the EAT in Holland v Glendale Industries Ltd 1998 ICR 493, EAT, where it stated that the general principle is that where one party by his or her conduct repudiates the contract and the other party wishes to rely upon that repudiation, the latter must by words and/or conduct make it plain that he or she is accepting the repudiation and leaving because of the conduct.

However, the Holland decision has since been overruled by the Court of Appeal in Weathersfield Ltd t/a Van and Truck Rentals v Sargent 1999 IRLR 94, CA. In that case the Court of Appeal held that it was not necessary for an employee, in order to prove that a resignation was caused by a breach of contract, to inform the employer immediately of the reasons for his or her resignation. It was for the tribunal in each case to determine, as a matter of fact, whether or not the employee resigned in response to the employer's breach rather than for some other reason.

In the light of the above judgment, the position now seems to be that an employee need not expressly inform the employer of his or her reasons for resigning in order to prove that he or she resigned because of the employer's breach. The reason (or lack of reason) given by the employee is merely one piece of evidence for the tribunal to consider when reaching a conclusion as to the true reason for the employee's resignation.

Affirmation of the contract   1.39

We have already dealt with the situation where an employee's premature resignation defeats a claim of constructive dismissal (see 'Fundamental breach – actual breach and anticipatory breach' above). If, on the other hand, the employee waits too long after the employer's breach of contract before resigning, he or she may be taken to have affirmed the contract with the same result – loss of the right to claim constructive dismissal. In the words of Lord Denning MR in Western Excavating (ECC) Ltd v Sharp 1978 ICR 221, CA, the employee 'must make up his mind soon after the conduct of which he complains: for, if he continues for any length of time without leaving, he will lose his right to treat himself as discharged'. This was emphasised again more recently by the Court of Appeal in Bournemouth University Higher Education Corporation v Buckland 2010 ICR 908, CA, although Lord Justice Jacob did point out that, given the pressure on the employee in these circumstances, the law looks very carefully at the facts before deciding whether there has really been an affirmation.

An employee may continue to perform the employment contract under protest for a period without necessarily being taken to have affirmed the contract. In Cantor Fitzgerald International v Bird and ors 2002 IRLR 867, QBD, for example, the High Court held that three brokers had not affirmed their contracts by waiting more than two months before resigning with immediate effect. They had clearly indicated their discontent with the employment and

27

given clear signs of their intention to leave. 'Affirmation,' said Mr Justice McCombe, 'is essentially the legal embodiment of the everyday concept of "letting bygones be bygones".'

There comes a point, however, when delay will indicate affirmation. In WE Cox Toner (International) Ltd v Crook 1981 IRLR 443, EAT, for example, C, a company director, was accused of gross dereliction of duty on insubstantial grounds by his fellow directors and was threatened with dismissal. Six months of angry correspondence, largely conducted through solicitors, followed before the employer finally refused to withdraw the accusation and threats. A month later, C tendered his resignation and claimed that he had been unfairly constructively dismissed. A tribunal considered that C could not be said to have affirmed the contract because he had never accepted the position but instead had protested vigorously. When it finally became clear that the company would not withdraw the allegations, it was not unreasonable for C to take time to look around for another job before he resigned. C had been unfairly dismissed and his claim was not ruled out by the seven-month delay. The EAT held that the tribunal had misdirected itself. Mere delay by itself did not constitute an affirmation of the contract, but if the delay went on for too long it could be very persuasive evidence of an affirmation. The tribunal should have adverted to the fact that throughout the seven-month period C had continued to work and be paid under the contract. Even if it were arguable that he was working under protest for six months, the delay for a further month after the company had finally made its intentions clear was fatal to C's claim that he had not affirmed the contract.

1.40   If the employee is able to point to special circumstances, this may justify a delay in resigning. Three examples:

- **Ginns v Leon Motor Services Ltd** ET Case No.27872/78: where an employee was suffering from mental illness and was unable to make a positive decision, a delay of nine months was excused

- **Post Office v Roberts** 1980 IRLR 347, EAT: where an employee continued working while her union representative was attempting to investigate the true position with her employer, a delay of six weeks was acceptable. The EAT held that the 'real point of time' at which the employee had to make a decision did not arrive until the full facts became clear and attempts to solve the problem had failed

- **Bliss v South East Thames Regional Health Authority** 1987 ICR 700, CA: a delay of two months was held not to constitute affirmation because the employer had specifically given the employee time to make up his mind whether he wished to return following the employer's breach and had continued to pay him while he came to his decision. In these circumstances there was no need for the employee expressly to reserve his position.

Special circumstances also arise when an employer imposes new terms on an employee at short or no notice. The employee is not obliged to make up his or her mind whether or not to accept the change at once. A reasonable trial period is permitted so that the employee can try working under the new terms before deciding what course to take. This common law trial period is often confused with the statutory trial period which applies when a redundant employee is offered alternative work. The two are, however, quite separate. The statutory trial period is for a maximum of four weeks. The common law trial period, on the other hand, has no fixed duration. It may, depending on the circumstances, be more than four weeks, or it may be less – see, for example, Bevan v CTC Coaches Ltd EAT 107/88.

An employee's *absence from work* during the time he or she was alleged to have affirmed the contract may be a pointer against a genuine affirmation. In Bashir v Brillo Manufacturing Co 1979 IRLR 295, EAT, the EAT held that an employee's delay of ten weeks before resigning following his disciplinary demotion was not too long when he had been off sick during that period. It was important that the amount of sick pay was the same both for his original post and for the demoted post, so that acceptance of sick pay could not be treated as acquiescence in demotion. B had in any case made it clear that he did not accept the demotion. Similarly, in Burton v Northern Business Systems Ltd EAT 608/92 B was demoted while off sick. He informed his employer that he did not accept his demotion but that he wanted time to think. He resigned several months later (while still off sick). In upholding the employee's right to bring a claim of constructive dismissal, the EAT stressed that mere delay does not of itself amount to affirmation unless it is coupled with acts from which it can be inferred that the employee is affirming the contract. There were no such acts of affirmation in the instant case; on the contrary, the employee had insisted that he was keeping his position open.

1.41

The EAT reached a similar conclusion in El-Hoshi v Pizza Express Restaurants Ltd EAT 0857/03, holding that there had to be some express or implied event indicating affirmation. Mere delay was neutral and was not itself capable of amounting to affirmation, and nor was the acceptance of sick pay. The sending in of sick notes merely affirmed the existence of a contract. Affirmation of the existence of a contract did not mean acceptance of the employer's actions. In the instant case the tribunal had added a neutral factor (delay) to another neutral factor (the claiming and acceptance of sick pay, supported by sick notes) and determined that those factors together constituted affirmation. That was an error. Two neutral factors could not add up to a positive factor defeating the employee's claim. However, an employee who applied for and received statutory sick pay after he claimed that he had been constructively dismissed was held to have affirmed the contract – Greensmith v Toton Plant Hire Ltd ET Case No.08532/84.

1.42   **Continuing breaches.** An employee can exercise his or her right to accept the breach at any time while it is continuing. In Reid v Camphill Engravers 1990 ICR 435, EAT, R claimed that over a period of three years his employer had paid him a lower salary than the statutory (and therefore contractual) minimum set by a Wages Council. The tribunal held that because R did not resign when he discovered that he was being underpaid, he had affirmed the contract and could no longer use the breach as a basis for his claim. The EAT overturned this decision. The employer had been in continuing breach of contract. Even if R had not reacted to the first breach, it was open to him to rely on it when his employer committed further breaches.

A further illustration of this point can be found in Lewis v Motorworld Garages Ltd 1986 ICR 157, CA, where L was demoted and then not given a salary increase which other employees received. However, he did not resign. There followed a series of criticisms of his performance, which he considered to be unjustified, culminating in a final warning which prompted him to resign and complain that he had been constructively dismissed. A tribunal held that the demotion and the withholding of the salary increase were repudiatory breaches, but that L could not rely on them because of his delay in resigning. The Court of Appeal disagreed. L was relying on a course of conduct by the employer which breached the implied contractual duty of trust and confidence. The tribunal should have taken account of the earlier breaches, both as background material and as part of a series of actions down to the final warning which caused L to resign, in order to see whether there was a course of conduct which cumulatively amounted to a breach of the implied duty of trust and confidence.

1.43   **'Last straw' cases.** In so-called 'last straw' cases, the question of affirmation of contract can become somewhat complicated. Before looking at the issues, however, it is necessary to give a brief explanation of what is meant by 'last straw' in this context. Basically, a course of conduct can cumulatively amount to a fundamental breach of contract entitling an employee to resign and claim constructive dismissal following a 'last straw' incident, even though the last straw by itself does not amount to a breach of contract – see Lewis v Motorworld Garages Ltd (above). The Court of Appeal in that case stressed that it is immaterial that one of the events in the course of conduct was serious enough in itself to amount to a repudiatory breach and that the employee did not treat the breach as such by resigning. This principle was applied by the EAT in Abbey National plc v Robinson EAT 743/99, where it upheld a tribunal's decision that an employee was entitled to claim constructive dismissal almost a year after a breach of contract by the employer. The employee resigned as a result of the cumulative effect of a course of events and the fact that one of those events amounted to a repudiatory breach did not mean that she had affirmed the contract.

In Omilaju v Waltham Forest London Borough Council 2005 ICR 481, CA, the Court of Appeal explained that the act constituting the last straw does not have

30

to be of the same character as the earlier acts, nor must it constitute unreasonable or blameworthy conduct, although in most cases it will do so. But the last straw must contribute, however slightly, to the breach of the implied term of trust and confidence. An entirely innocuous act on the part of the employer cannot be a final straw, even if the employee genuinely, but mistakenly, interprets the act as hurtful and destructive of his or her trust and confidence in the employer. The test of whether the employee's trust and confidence has been undermined is objective. And while it is not a prerequisite of a last straw case that the employer's act should be unreasonable, it will be an unusual case where conduct which is perfectly reasonable and justifiable satisfies the last straw test.

Such cases should be contrasted with those where there is a *one-off act* by the employer which merely has *ongoing consequences*. Thus, where an employee is demoted, allegedly in breach of contract, that employee should act promptly upon being demoted rather than wait and then seek to rely at a later date on a continuing drop in wages as representing an ongoing breach.

It should be noted that in Thornton Print v Morton EAT 0090/08 the EAT discouraged focusing too heavily on the last straw, lamenting that the expression itself was 'in danger of becoming a term of art in employment cases,' noting for example the tribunal's reference to it in this case as a 'doctrine'. It commented that the principle of a 'last straw', as explained by the Court of Appeal in Omilaju, 'means no more than that the final matter that leads to the acceptance of a repudiatory breach of contract when taken together and cumulatively with earlier conduct entitles a party to accept a repudiatory breach, whether that last matter is in itself a breach of contract or not'. In the instant case the tribunal had found that the treatment of M by his manager amounted to a fundamental breach of the implied term of trust and confidence. It went on to hold that a letter inviting M to a disciplinary meeting was sufficient to meet the test of the 'final straw doctrine'. **1.44**

The EAT thought it unfortunate that the question of whether the letter was a 'last straw' had taken such prominence. Looking at the tribunal's decision as a whole, it was quite clear that it had found there to have been a repudiatory breach of contract that had never been affirmed. A repudiatory breach had to be accepted if a contract was to be brought to an end, and until that acceptance was communicated to the other party it had no effect. The letter was merely a trigger for the acceptance of the breach. The fact that it might also have been an additional breach did not matter, as the repudiatory breach had already happened.

Moving on to the issue of affirmation of contract, one question that arises in cases where the employee resigns as a result of a last straw incident is whether, by continuing to work after each incident, the employee has waived the breach and affirmed the contract. The EAT offered guidance to tribunals on this question in JV Strong and Co Ltd v Hamill EAT 1179/99. In that case H, a groundsman, was mistreated at the first site at which he worked and the treatment resumed after he voluntarily transferred to a different site. The EAT held that the tribunal had been entitled to find that the cumulative effect of all the incidents amounted to a fundamental breach of the implied term of trust and confidence. The common thread running through all the incidents was the employer's failure to give H the support he was entitled to expect.

1.45 The EAT said that where there is a series of unpleasant incidents about which the employer does nothing, it could not see how the breach of contract by the employer could be permanently waived simply by the employee continuing to work. The EAT acknowledged that such behaviour is normally an example of waiver, but in cases where there has been a course of conduct the tribunal must consider whether the last straw incident is a sufficient trigger to revive the earlier ones. In doing so, it must take account of the nature of the incidents, the overall time span, the length of time between the incidents, and any factor that may have amounted to a waiver of any earlier breaches. The EAT added that the tribunal must also consider the nature of the alleged waiver. It is not enough that the facts give rise to either an express or an implied waiver. The tribunal must also consider whether it was a 'once and for all' waiver or one that was conditional on there being no repetition of the same conduct. Identifying this would involve an examination of the evidence and impressions as to the general working atmosphere and the significance of the incidents. The EAT found no error in the tribunal's view that H's taking advantage of an opportunity to transfer to a different site was his way of finding a solution to the problem and that, in doing so, he had not waived the breach.

Support for this approach can be found in Logan v Commissioners of Customs and Excise 2004 ICR 1, CA, where the Court of Appeal held that where an employee is complaining about an employer's course of conduct culminating with an act alleged to constitute the last straw, there is no need for there to be 'proximity in time or in nature' between the last straw and the previous act of the employer. The first incident occurred in April 1997 when L's line manager, H, allegedly subjected her to a 'verbal assault'. L's complaint about the incident was rejected by her employer and L, nervous of encountering H again in her employment, went on long-term sick leave with stress. Much later, in meetings taking place in January and May 1999, L was told by her manager, B, that, if she would not return to work, she had to choose between medical retirement and dismissal. L resigned following the second meeting. The Court of Appeal rejected the tribunal's finding that the last straw doctrine could not apply because there was insufficient proximity in time between the acts that took place in 1997 and those that occurred in 1999.

32

Non-dismissals 1.46

So far this chapter has dealt with the various ways of bringing an employment contract to an end that amount to a dismissal in the context of unfair dismissal claims. There are also a number of ways in which a contract can be terminated that do not count as a dismissal in law:

- resignation of the employee
- termination by agreement between the employer and the employee
- termination by operation of law, including frustration of contract.

These are considered briefly below. For a fuller treatment, see IDS Employment Law Handbook, 'Contracts of Employment' (2009), Chapters 9 and 10.

Resignation 1.47

A resignation is the termination of a contract of employment by the employee. It need not be expressed in a formal way, and may be inferred from the employee's conduct and the surrounding circumstances – Johnson v Monty Smith Garages Ltd EAT 657/79.

Usually it is not difficult to recognise a resignation, but there are circumstances in which the situation may not be so clear. In McDonald v Lowndes Queensway Group Ltd EAT 651/90, for example, McD was on sick leave when he was demoted. In the midst of a dispute with his employer, McD's solicitors wrote stating that if he were not offered a satisfactory solution by a given date he would initiate proceedings for constructive dismissal. The date passed and McD brought his action. The EAT held that the solicitors' letter was sufficiently explicit to indicate that McD had resigned.

Note that situations where a contract comes to an end in ambiguous circumstances are considered above under 'Express dismissal'.

Notice. Section 86(2) ERA provides that an employee who has been continuously employed for one month or more is obliged to give at least one week's notice of termination. It should be stressed that this is a *minimum* period of notice. If the contract provides for more notice, it is the longer notice period which prevails. If the contract is silent on the matter, then the courts will imply a reasonable notice period, which may be considerably longer than the statutory minimum, depending on the nature of the employment concerned. A resignation given without notice will effectively terminate the employment but – unless the situation is one of constructive dismissal – it will also amount to a breach of contract. It is rare, however, for employers to sue ex-employees in such circumstances. 1.48

If the employer cuts short an employee's notice period, this will convert the resignation into a dismissal:

33

- **John Brignell and Co (Builders) Ltd v Bishop** 1974 IRLR 157, CA: B gave a week's notice and the employer promptly gave him his cards. This converted the resignation into an unfair summary dismissal

- **British Midland Airways Ltd v Lewis** 1978 ICR 782, EAT: L said that he wanted to resign on 28 January and was told that he would have to give three months' notice. L asked if he could leave a month early but no agreement was reached. The employer then told him that he would have to go on 4 February because a replacement had been found. This was an unfair dismissal because L was made to go on a date to which he had not agreed.

1.49 An employer may by his response to a resignation turn it into a constructive dismissal. In Ford v Milthorn Toleman Ltd 1980 IRLR 30, CA, for example, F gave three months' notice and the employer promptly demoted him and changed the basis of his remuneration. He resigned immediately and the Court of Appeal upheld his claim that he had been unfairly constructively dismissed.

Some divisions of the EAT used to apply a legal doctrine known as 'constructive resignation', holding that, where an employee had been guilty of gross misconduct in fundamental breach of contract, the employee's breach automatically brought the contract to an end without the need for any intervention by the employer. The employee was taken to have 'constructively resigned' or 'dismissed him or herself'. However, this doctrine was firmly refuted by the majority of the Court of Appeal in London Transport Executive v Clarke 1981 ICR 355, CA. They held that a repudiatory breach by an employee – such as taking a seven-week holiday without permission – did not bring the contract to an end automatically. The contract would only end when the employer accepted the employee's breach – i.e. by dismissing the employee. If an employer refuses to have an employee back after an act of misconduct, he cannot claim that the employee has dismissed him or herself: this will be a dismissal by the employer which he may have to justify to a tribunal.

Finally, note that an enforced resignation or one that is obtained by deception on the part of the employer will amount to a dismissal – see 'Express dismissal' above.

1.50 **Termination by agreement**

Parties to an employment contract are free to agree between themselves to terminate it. Both sides are then released from further performance of their obligations under the contract and the contract is discharged by mutual consent. When this happens there is no dismissal, the effect being similar to that of a resignation by the employee (although where there has been a resignation the employee may still potentially be able to claim constructive dismissal).

Since the effect of a termination by agreement is to deny the employee statutory employment protection rights, courts and tribunals are reluctant to make such a finding unless there is very clear evidence that an entirely voluntary agreement has been entered into. This is particularly so when the agreement is reached after notice of dismissal has already been given – CPS Recruitment Ltd t/a Blackwood Associates v Bowen and anor 1982 IRLR 54, EAT. Nevertheless, a genuine termination by agreement may well stem from the employer's initiative, as where the employer suggests that the employee should look for another job. However, in Hart v British Veterinary Association EAT 145/78 the EAT said that tribunals should look at such situations with care to see whether the employer's words really amount to a dismissal. The intention of the employer and the attitude of the employee need to be considered: if there is no threat of dismissal and the employee acts voluntarily, termination is by agreement.

An agreement that a contract will automatically terminate on the happening **1.51** of a future event is unlikely to be a valid termination by mutual agreement. In Igbo v Johnson Matthey Chemicals Ltd 1986 ICR 505, CA, an employee was granted extended leave of absence to visit her family in Nigeria. Before she left she signed a document stating that a failure to return to work on a certain date would result in automatic termination of the employment contract. In the event, she returned to England on time but did not attend for work on the relevant date because of sickness. The employer treated her employment as having been terminated consensually in accordance with the holiday agreement. The Court of Appeal, however, ruled that the employee had been dismissed. The automatic termination clause in the employee's contract was an attempt to avoid or limit the operation of the unfair dismissal provisions and as such was void under S.203(1) ERA. Lord Justice Parker further pointed out that illness was an unforeseen eventuality when the agreement was entered into. The automatic termination of the employment contract in such circumstances would have been a harsh result. (Note that this case should now be read in light of the changes made to Ss.235 and 95(1)(b) ERA by the Fixed-term Employees (Prevention of Less Favourable Treatment) Regulations 2002 SI 2002/2034. These sections now make it clear that a contract of employment that provides for its termination on the occurrence of an event (or the failure of an event to occur) is a 'limited-term contract' (LTC), non-renewal of which amounts to a dismissal – see 'Non-renewal of limited-term contracts' above. That said, given the facts in Igbo, it is unlikely that the employee's contract would actually constitute an LTC. Such a contract must satisfy various conditions, including that employment under the contract is not intended to be permanent, which it clearly was in Igbo.)

Voluntary redundancy and early retirement. In general, courts and tribunals **1.52** have been willing to hold that a voluntary redundancy will still be a dismissal if it is in response to a genuine redundancy situation – Burton, Allton and Johnson Ltd v Peck 1975 ICR 193, QBD. It has even been held that an

35

employee who actively seeks to be made redundant will still be regarded as having been dismissed – Walley v Morgan 1969 ITR 122, Div Ct. However, each case will turn on its own facts and it is for tribunals to decide whether there has been a consensual termination of employment or whether the employee has volunteered to be dismissed as redundant. Two contrasting examples:

- **Optare Group Ltd v Transport and General Workers' Union** 2007 IRLR 931, EAT: the EAT upheld a tribunal's decision that three employees who volunteered to leave their posts at the start of a redundancy exercise were dismissed. It was immaterial that the employees might have accepted a similar package even in the absence of a redundancy situation. However, the EAT noted that the result would have been different had there been evidence that the employees were anxious to leave and had expressed this wish independently of, or prior to, a redundancy situation arising

- **Kaaba and anor v Hackney Community College and ors** EAT 283/97: the EAT upheld the tribunal's finding that there had been no dismissal. K's employer asked for volunteers for its 'voluntary redundancy scheme'. K, a lecturer who felt she had been shabbily treated, volunteered for the scheme and received a substantial payment. She later claimed that she had been unfairly constructively dismissed. The EAT held that K had not been forced to leave but had carefully considered her situation, including the generous payment on offer, and had freely resigned, although in form it was a dismissal through redundancy.

1.53 It would seem that early retirement, however, is *not* a dismissal unless it is clearly involuntary. This is the case even when circumstances are such that the employer would otherwise have had to make redundancies. In Birch and anor v University of Liverpool 1985 ICR 470, CA, the employer was forced to make a substantial reduction in staff and circulated letters inviting employees to take advantage of an early retirement scheme. Applications were subject to the employer's final approval and the scheme was expressly stated not to be a redundancy scheme. B applied for, and was granted, early retirement – but he then went on to claim a redundancy payment. The Court of Appeal held that this was not a dismissal but a termination by mutual agreement.

The position is not entirely clear, however, particularly in cases where the employee has already been issued with a notice of dismissal for redundancy and later takes early retirement instead. In Scott and ors v Coalite Fuels and Chemicals Ltd 1988 ICR 355, EAT, a group of employees agreed to early retirement when they were already under notice of dismissal for redundancy. The EAT, following the Birch case, held that they had not been dismissed. The tribunal had been entitled to find that the agreement to terminate superseded the original redundancy notice. By contrast, in Gateshead Metropolitan Borough Council v Mills EAT 610/92 M was given one year's notice of redundancy. He applied, and was accepted, for early retirement. A tribunal decided that he was also entitled to a redundancy payment on the ground that M had been dismissed and the notice had never been withdrawn. The Council relied on Scott v Coalite (above) and argued that, once the agreement to take early retirement had been reached, it had impliedly withdrawn the notice. The EAT rejected this argument, holding that the notice could not be withdrawn without the consent of the employee. There was no express consent by M and no evidence that he had impliedly consented. The agreement to take early retirement was not inconsistent with a dismissal for redundancy and the tribunal had been correct to find that there had been a dismissal.

As noted above, the cases in this area tend to suggest that the courts and tribunals are more likely to make a finding of no dismissal (either on the basis of agreement to terminate or termination by the employee) in cases of voluntary early retirement than in cases of voluntary redundancy, even when the circumstances are such that the employer would otherwise have had to make redundancies. However, courts and tribunals are not bound to do so and much will still depend upon the facts of the individual case, as illustrated by the Mills case (above).

Termination by operation of law

1.54

Contracts of employment may terminate at common law when certain supervening events take place or where the contract is frustrated. These are terminations by operation of law, not by dismissal or resignation. The effect at common law is that the contracts automatically come to an end and the obligations of the parties cease. However, in certain situations statute law intervenes to preserve employee rights that would otherwise vanish.

Supervening events. The general common law rule is that contracts of employment are automatically terminated on the happening of certain events, normally as a result of some act on the part of the employer. Where there is a term in the contract, express or implied, which shows that the parties have agreed that certain events will not have the effect of ending the contract, the courts will give effect to that term. What is stated below reflects the general position in the absence of any agreement between the parties to the contrary.

1.55

The supervening events that will normally terminate a contract of employment automatically at common law are:

- death of the employer (where the contract is with an individual employer) or employee. (The death of either party might also be categorised as a frustrating event – see further below)

- dissolution or major reconstruction of a partnership

- appointment of a receiver by the court (but not the appointment of a receiver out of court by debenture holders)

- compulsory winding up by court order (but not a voluntary winding-up)

- permanent closure of the employee's workplace

- transfer of employer's business – at common law the transfer of an employer's business to another person automatically terminates all existing contracts of employment. However, this rule has been superseded to a large extent by the Transfer of Undertakings (Protection of Employment) Regulations 2006 SI 2006/246.

1.56 It seems that at common law such terminations (apart from one caused by the death of the employee) are treated as wrongful terminations by the employer on the basis that he has put it out of his power to continue to perform the contract. As a result, the employees may be able to sue for damages.

Certain statutory provisions may also have the effect of automatically terminating employment contracts. There is a general principle that when further performance of a contract becomes impossible because of legislation, e.g. when a particular office is abolished by statute, then the contract is discharged – Reilly v The King 1934 AC 176, PC. In Tarnesby v Kensington and Chelsea and Westminster Area Health Authority (Teaching) 1981 ICR 615, HL, the House of Lords held that the suspension of T's doctor's registration for disciplinary reasons automatically terminated his employment as a hospital consultant. This was because S.28(1) of the Medical Act 1956 provided that no unregistered doctor should hold an appointment as a hospital medical officer.

1.57 **Statutory protection.** Employment protection legislation mitigates the effects of the common law in many of the above situations. For instance, S.136(5) ERA provides that any act on the part of the employer or any event affecting him (including, in the case of an individual, his death) which operates to terminate a contract of employment will be deemed to be a dismissal by reason of redundancy for the purposes of claiming redundancy pay. There is no corresponding provision for unfair dismissals, however. Furthermore, employees have a number of rights, exercisable against the Secretary of State for Trade and Industry, on the insolvency of their employer.

1.58 **Frustration**

Frustration occurs when, through neither party's fault, some reasonably unforeseeable event occurs which makes the contract impossible or unlawful to perform, or radically different from what the parties originally intended – Davis Contractors v Fareham UDC 1956 AC 696, HL. When a contract is frustrated it comes to an end automatically by operation of law, without a dismissal on the part of the employer or a resignation on the part of the employee, and the parties are discharged from futher obligations under it. The employee cannot therefore claim unfair dismissal and is not

38

entitled to any notice or payment in lieu – GF Sharp and Co Ltd v McMillan 1998 IRLR 632, EAT.

Frustration is an objective question and it is irrelevant that the parties believed or intended that the contract should continue – GF Sharp and Co Ltd v McMillan (above). The burden of proof, which is a high one, is on the party who seeks to argue that the contract has been frustrated. Where the frustrating event has been caused by the fault of either party, that party will not be entitled to rely on it to treat the contract as being at an end – FC Shepherd and Co Ltd v Jerrom 1986 ICR 802, CA; Williams v Watsons Luxury Coaches Ltd 1990 ICR 536, EAT.

The doctrine of frustration is discussed at some length in IDS Employment Law Handbook, 'Contracts of Employment' (2009), Chapter 10. Here, we give a brief overview of the circumstances in which frustration normally arises.

Employee's illness. An employee's prolonged or sudden serious illness or disability is capable of frustrating the employment contract. Whether or not it does so will depend on a number of factors. The EAT in Egg Stores (Stamford Hill) Ltd v Leibovici 1977 ICR 260, EAT, set out the following relevant considerations: **1.59**

- the length of previous employment

- the expected future duration of employment

- the nature of the job

- the nature, length and effect of the illness or disabling event

- the employer's need for the work to be done and need for a replacement to do it

- the risk to the employer of acquiring employment protection obligations towards a replacement employee

- whether the employee has continued to be paid

- the acts and statements of the employer in relation to the employment, including the dismissal of, or failure to dismiss, the employee

- whether a reasonable employer could be expected to wait any longer for the employee to return.

The EAT in Williams v Watsons Luxury Coaches Ltd (above) added two further factors to be taken into account: the contractual terms as to sick pay and the prospects of recovery.

In James v Greytree Trust EAT 699/95 the EAT emphasised the difficulty of applying the doctrine of frustration, which has developed over many years through the common law, to employment situations that are largely governed   **1.60** by statute. In that case a tribunal held that the contract of employment of an employee who had already been off sick for four months was frustrated when she produced a sick note for a further six months. In overturning that decision, the EAT pointed out that the relationship of employer and employee is increasingly seen as one of status rather than one of contract. Moreover, some statutory provisions – for example, those on maternity leave – envisage that employees may be absent from work for long periods while the employment contract continues. The EAT also took into account the fact that the provisions on sickness absence in the employee's contract appeared to envisage the possibility of prolonged absence from work. In the EAT's view, the employee's sickness absence was not excessively long in relation to her length of service. At the stage at which it was claimed frustration had occurred, many employers would only just be beginning to bring into play the ordinary investigation procedures for long-term incapacity. The EAT concluded that the contract of employment had not been frustrated and that the employee had been dismissed.

As was made clear by the EAT in the James case, where the contract expressly or impliedly makes provision for sickness absence or long-term or permanent incapacity for illness and envisages that the contract will continue to subsist, it will be harder to show that it has been frustrated. This is especially so in the case of long-serving employees whose contracts are expected to continue indefinitely. In Villella v MFI Furniture Centres Ltd 1999 IRLR 468, QBD, the High Court emphasised that for frustration to occur there must be some outside event not foreseen or provided for by the parties at the time of contracting. Since the employee's contract in that case expressly foresaw and provided for long-term incapacity for illness, it followed that the fact that the employee subsequently became incapacitated was incapable of frustrating the contract.

1.61 **Imprisonment of employee.** Imprisonment of an employee is also capable of frustrating the employment contract – FC Shepherd and Co Ltd v Jerrom 1986 ICR 802, CA. Whether or not it does so will depend on such factors as the likely length of absence of the employee, how necessary it is to replace him or her, and whether it is necessary to find a permanent, rather than temporary, replacement. In the Jerrom case it was held that an indeterminate Borstal sentence of between six months and two years, which was expected to last for nine months, did frustrate the four-year contract of the single apprentice in a fairly small company. But such a sentence would not necessarily frustrate the contract of a general labourer in a very large company with a tradition of hiring temporary labour.

Restrictive bail conditions or a remand in custody may amount to a frustrating event in the same way as a custodial sentence. It will depend on the employee's ability to perform the contract and the surrounding circumstances. In Four Seasons Healthcare Ltd (formerly Cotswold Spa Retirement Hotels Ltd) v Maughan 2005 IRLR 324, EAT M was employed by FSH Ltd as a nurse at a care home. He was suspended without pay following an allegation that he had abused a patient and was subsequently convicted and sentenced to two years' imprisonment. He brought an unauthorised deduction from wages claim relating to the period of unpaid suspension but FSH Ltd argued that the fact that M's bail conditions prevented his attending work meant that his contract of employment had been frustrated. The EAT rejected this argument. It noted that FSH Ltd had not been able to cite any case in which it was suggested that a period of bail, even if preventing an employee from attending work, might frustrate an employment contract. In any event, the EAT found that FSH Ltd had the power under M's contract to require him to work somewhere other than the care home, but had chosen not to do so. Further, in suspending M rather than dismissing him, FSH Ltd had shown itself willing to continue the contract until the conclusion of the Crown Court proceedings.

Exclusion from place of work by third party. The employee's exclusion from his or her place of work by a third party may also frustrate the employment contract. In Stanley Wattam Ltd v Rippin EAT 355/98, for example, R was employed by SW Ltd as a chicken sexer. From 1993 she had been seconded to work at the employer's most important customer, P. A dispute between R and P arose on a day when P's most important supplier was due to make a visit to watch R at work. Fearful of the potential embarrassment that R might cause, P decided to ban her for good from its premises. With no other possibility of seconding R to another site, SW Ltd eventually sent her her P45. In her claim of unfair dismissal, legal argument was based on whether R had been dismissed or her contract frustrated. The tribunal found the former. On appeal, the EAT ruled that the tribunal had erred. Since R had been excluded from her place of work by a third party (P), there were no alternative ways of continuing R's contract. It was a classic case of frustration of contract.

1.62

2 Exclusions from right to claim

Employees only

Continuous service threshold

Illegality

Diplomatic and state immunity

Working abroad

Special categories of worker

Settlements and contracting out

Time limits

The right to bring a claim of unfair dismissal under the Employment Rights Act **2.1** 1996 (ERA) applies only to employees. Moreover, employees must have at least one year's continuous employment in order to qualify for the right (unless the dismissal is for an 'inadmissible reason' to which this requirement does not apply). In this chapter we first consider these two basic requirements for bringing an unfair dismissal claim. We then look at a number of other reasons which may preclude an individual from being able to make a claim.

Certain exclusions from the right to claim unfair dismissal arise under general law:

- illegality in the employment contract may bar a claimant

- diplomatic or state immunity may exclude the right to claim

- claims that relate to employment abroad may fall outside the territorial jurisdiction of the employment tribunals.

In addition, various specified categories of worker, such as police officers and certain mariners, are excluded under specific provisions of the ERA. However, S.109 ERA, which prevented employees from claiming unfair dismissal where they had reached the 'normal retiring age' (NRA) for their job or, in the absence of an NRA, where they had reached the age of 65, has been repealed by the Employment Equality (Age) Regulations 2006 SI 2006/1031. There is now no age limit on the right to claim unfair dismissal. However, employers may fairly dismiss for retirement if they follow the statutory retirement procedure contained in the Age Regulations – see Chapter 9.

The ERA also allows the parties to exclude the jurisdiction of a tribunal by an **2.2** agreement between themselves, in the following circumstances:

43

- when there is a settlement under the auspices of an Acas conciliator

- when there is a settlement under the auspices of the tribunal itself

- when there is a 'compromise agreement'

- when there has been collective contracting out through a dismissal procedures agreement.

Unfair dismissal claims are frequently challenged at the outset on the ground that one or more of the above exclusions operate to deprive the tribunal of jurisdiction to hear the claim. Finally, the tribunal's jurisdiction may also be challenged on the ground that the claim was presented out of time.

2.3   Industrial action dismissals

Special rules apply to industrial action dismissals that have the effect of depriving employees dismissed for taking part in a strike or other industrial action of the right to claim unfair dismissal except in very limited circumstances. These rules, which are contained in the Trade Union and Labour Relations (Consolidation) Act 1992 (TULR(C)A), are discussed at length in IDS Employment Handbook, 'Industrial Action' (2010), Chapter 8. Briefly, the relevant provisions provide that:

- an employee has no right to complain of unfair dismissal if at the time of dismissal he or she was taking part in unofficial industrial action unless the reason for the dismissal was one of certain protected reasons such as health and safety – S.237 TULR(C)A

- an employee who is dismissed for taking part in protected industrial action (i.e. lawfully organised official action) will be treated as having been automatically unfairly dismissed if the dismissal took place during the protected period, or after the end of that period where certain specified conditions are met – S.238A

- an employee who is selectively dismissed when taking part in official industrial action or locked out by his or her employer, in circumstances where S.238A does not apply, is entitled to claim unfair dismissal – S.238.

2.4   National security

Section 10(1) of the Employment Tribunals Act 1996 provides that an employment tribunal 'shall dismiss' an unfair dismissal complaint if 'it is shown that the action complained of [in other words, the dismissal] was taken for the purpose of safeguarding national security'. This has generally been taken to mean that dismissal for the purpose of safeguarding national security was *automatically fair*. However, in B v BAA plc 2005 ICR 1530, EAT, the EAT held that an employment tribunal should not reject an employee's unfair dismissal claim simply on the basis that the dismissal was carried out for the purpose of safeguarding national security. The tribunal should go on to consider whether dismissal was within the range of reasonable responses available to the employer. This case is dealt with in more detail in Chapter 3 under 'Automatically fair and unfair dismissals'.

Bankruptcy

2.5

It is worth noting that bankruptcy – which deprives a person of the right to bring or pursue legal proceedings to recover money or property in which his or her creditors will have an interest – does *not* prevent an employee from pursuing a claim for unfair dismissal. This is because unfair dismissal is a cause of action personal to the employee. In Grady v HM Prison Service 2003 ICR 753, CA, the Court of Appeal held that unlike a claim of wrongful dismissal, which is a monetary claim and therefore vests in the trustee in bankruptcy, a claim of unfair dismissal is primarily directed at the restoration of a contractual relationship in which the claimant's skill and labour are the essential commodity. Under the ERA an employment tribunal must first consider the reinstatement or re-engagement of an employee who is found to have been unfairly dismissed before turning to consider the question of compensation. A claim for reinstatement or re-engagement, and indeed a significant element of the compensation that can be awarded in lieu of these, does not form part of a bankrupt's estate, even though the eventual fund (if an award is made) may. It is a claim of a unique kind that provides for the restoration of something that can only be done by the claimant. For more on remedies for unfair dismissal, see Chapter 14.

Employees only

2.6

Only employees can claim unfair dismissal rights. An employee is defined in S.230(1) ERA as 'an individual who has entered into or works under (or, where the employment has ceased, worked under) a contract of employment'. 'Contract of employment' is in turn defined as a 'contract of service or apprenticeship, whether express or implied, and (if it is express) whether oral or in writing' – S.230(2). This raises the question of when it can be said that someone is employed under a 'contract of *service*', as opposed to a contract for *services*. In the latter case, he or she would be self-employed, i.e. an 'independent contractor'.

There is no precise and uniformly applied legal definition of a contract of employment. As Lord Justice Denning put it in Stevenson Jordan and Harrison Ltd v Macdonald and Evans 1952 1 TLR 101, CA: '[I]t is almost impossible to give a precise definition... It is often easy to recognise a contract of service when you see it, but difficult to say wherein the difference lies.' In practice, it is obvious enough in the great majority of cases whether a worker is an employee or an independent contractor, but there is a grey area between the two and borderline cases have generated a large body of case law. Over the years the courts have developed a number of tests of employment status and have viewed a variety of factors as

45

relevant in particular cases. This area of law is dealt with in considerable detail in IDS Employment Law Handbook, 'Contracts of Employment' (2009), Chapter 1. Here we simply provide a brief outline of the important cases and consider the various factors that are generally regarded as relevant.

2.7   The tendency in recent years has been to take a broad and flexible approach to the question of who is an employee and the courts and tribunals have adopted what has become known as the *multiple* or *mixed* test. This involves the proposition that no single test is conclusive and that what the tribunal or court must do is weigh up all the relevant factors and decide whether, on balance, the relationship between the parties is governed by a contract of employment. The test seems originally to have been formulated by Mr Justice MacKenna in Ready Mixed Concrete (South East) Ltd v Minister of Pensions and National Insurance 1968 2 QB 497, QBD, but has been developed in a number of subsequent cases. Following the decisions in Carmichael and anor v National Power plc 1999 ICR 1226, HL; Express and Echo Publications Ltd v Tanton 1999 IRLR 367, CA; and Hewlett Packard Ltd v O'Murphy 2002 IRLR 4, EAT, it is clear that four essential elements *must* be fulfilled for a contract of employment to exist. There must be:

- a contract (between the worker and the alleged employer)
- an obligation on the worker to provide work personally
- mutuality of obligation
- an element of control over the work by the employer.

2.8   **Requirement of a contract.** In order for an individual to have 'employee' status, there must be a contract in existence and it must be between the party doing the work and the party for whom the work is done. This can be a problem in cases where a third party, such as an agency, is involved, as often no express agreement will exist between the individual (the agency worker) and the party for whom that individual is carrying out the work (the client). However, the courts have acknowledged that a contractual relationship may be implied between the client and agency worker in certain limited circumstances – see Dacas v Brook Street Bureau (UK) Ltd 2004 ICR 1437, CA, and James v Greenwich Borough Council 2008 ICR 545, CA.

A prerequisite for a contract is an *intention to create legal relations*. In Roberts v Major Read on behalf of the Salvation Army and anor ET Case No.1304316/08 a tribunal found that a religious officer of the Salvation Army was not an employee for the purpose of an unfair dismissal claim, as he had entered into an agreement which expressly excluded legal relations. The agreement was valid as its purpose was not to avoid obligations imposed by employment legislation but to give effect to the spiritual nature of the working arrangement. By contrast, in New Testament Church of God v Stewart 2008 ICR 282, CA, the Court of Appeal considered that, on the facts, a minister of religion could proceed with his unfair dismissal claim, despite a line of authorities indicating that the duties of a minister of religion are inconsistent with an intention to create legal relations. The minister was subject to various standards and guidelines laid down by the Church, the Church deducted income tax and national insurance from his salary, and it described him as an employee.

Note that, even where an individual's formal contract of employment is *void*, he or she may still be an employee in practice and thus entitled to pursue an unfair dismissal claim– see Shrewsbury and Telford Hospital NHS Trust v Lairikyengbam 2010 ICR 66, EAT. In that case an NHS Trust which had employed a locum consultant on a series of fixed-term contracts spanning almost four years had acted beyond its powers as it had not sought the committee approval required by the relevant regulations. Consequently, the consultant's formal contract of employment was void. Nevertheless, the EAT held that the continued performance of his duties meant he was still an 'employee' within the meaning of the ERA.

Personal performance. It is the essence of a contract of service that an individual undertakes to supply his or her services personally – Express and Echo Publications Ltd v Tanton (above). However, a limited or occasional power of delegation may not be fatal to the existence of a contract of service – see MacFarlane and anor v Glasgow City Council 2001 IRLR 7, EAT, and Byrne Bros (Formwork) Ltd v Baird and ors 2002 ICR 667, EAT. **2.9**

Mutuality of obligation. The requirement that there be mutuality of obligation is usually expressed as an obligation on the employer to provide work and a corresponding obligation on the employee to accept and perform any work offered. So, an unpaid volunteer who worked for a Citizens Advice Bureau for one or two days a week was not an employee for the purpose of bringing a claim of unfair dismissal. There could be no contract of employment where the volunteer was not obliged to attend work and received no remuneration. Travelling expenses and free training were not sufficient to amount to remuneration – Melhuish v Redbridge Citizens Advice Bureau, 2005 IRLR 419, EAT. Other relevant considerations include whether there are any notice requirements or whether a worker is free to leave at any time. **2.10**

Whether there is sufficient mutuality of obligation is most often at issue in cases where an individual has carried out work on a casual, irregular or sporadic basis over a period of time. The question then is whether mutuality of obligation subsists during those periods when the individual is not working, so as to give rise to a continuous 'global' contract of employment spanning the separate engagements. The required obligation generally consists of an exchange of mutual promises of future performance. Where there has been a regular pattern of work over a period of time, a court or tribunal is more likely to infer the existence of a continuing overriding arrangement.

47

In the absence of a global contract it may still be possible to establish that a contract of employment exists in relation to each individual assignment, with the result that the individual is regarded as an employee in respect of each individual engagement (although in these circumstances the employee may find it difficult to establish the necessary one year's continuous service for bringing an unfair dismissal claim – see 'Continuous service threshold' below.) In Little v BMI Chiltern Hospital EAT 0021/09 L accepted that there was no overriding global contract of employment and that between engagements there was no mutuality of obligation. However, he contended instead that each separate period of work for BMI represented a separate contract of employment during which the necessary mutuality of obligations existed. The EAT held that he was not an employee because there was no obligation to provide him with work – nor indeed to pay him – for the whole of any assignment. There was no mutuality of obligation even on the basis of a succession of individual assignments. While there was a contract in place when L worked, it was in fact and law a contract for freelance services and not one of employment.

2.11 **Control.** While it is uncertain exactly how much control by the alleged employer over the worker is necessary in order for there to be a contract of service, it is clear from the case law that the work does not have to be carried out under the employer's actual supervision or control. However, indirect control in the form of the employer's right to terminate the contract if the individual fails to meet the required standards is not by itself sufficient. Some element of direct control over what the individual does is required. The requirement of control is often a problem in the context of agency work.

2.12 **Surrounding circumstances.** If all of these elements (a contract, personal service, mutuality of obligation and control) are present, the contract may be one of employment. The next step is to consider the surrounding circumstances of the case. While it is impossible to draw up a complete list of the factors that should be weighed in the balance, as every case will depend upon its own facts, the kinds of detail which may be relevant include:

- whether the person doing the work provides his or her own equipment
- whether he or she hires staff
- the degree of financial risk taken by the individual doing the work
- whether he or she has responsibility for investment and management
- whether the work done by the individual is an integral part of the employer's business
- the intentions of the parties.

As a general rule, the greater the degree of personal responsibility an individual takes in any of the matters set out above, the more likely it is that he or she will be an independent contractor rather than an employee.

Miscellaneous factors that may indicate the existence of a contract of employment include:

- any prohibition on working for other companies or individuals
- control by a disciplinary code laid down by the employer
- remuneration by way of payment of wages or salary
- payment during absence for illness
- paid holidays
- membership of a company pension scheme.

2.13

As indicated above, it is often atypical workers such as casual workers and homeworkers who are most likely to have difficulty in establishing employee status. These and other special categories of workers are discussed in detail in IDS Employment Law Handbook, 'Contracts of Employment' (2009), Chapter 1 under 'Specific categories of workers', and in IDS Employment Law Supplement, 'Part-time and Atypical Workers' (2001), Chapter 1.

Finally, note that the issue of employment status was categorised by the Privy Council in Lee Ting Sang v Chung Chi-Keung and anor 1990 ICR 409, PC, as a mixed question of fact and law. The tribunal's interpretation of a set of circumstances is a question of fact and is not open to appeal unless it involves an error of law or is perverse. However, if an individual's employment status turns upon the interpretation of a contractual document, that is a question of law and is open to appeal. In Clark v Oxfordshire Health Authority 1998 IRLR 125, CA, the Court of Appeal pointed out that only in exceptional cases will the question of employment status turn solely upon the construction of written documents. In the majority of cases, held the Court, the question will also involve the tribunal in an investigation and evaluation of the factual circumstances in which the work is performed. This approach appears, broadly speaking, to have been affirmed by the House of Lords in Carmichael and anor v National Power plc 1999 ICR 1226, HL.

Continuous service threshold

2.14

The normal rule is that in order to qualify to bring an unfair dismissal claim an employee must have been *continuously employed for not less than one year* ending with the effective date of termination – S.108(1) ERA. There are a number of exceptions to this rule – see 'Exceptions to continuous service threshold' below – but for the great majority of unfair dismissal cases the qualifying period is one year's continuous employment. 'Year' means a year of 12 calendar months and 'month' means a calendar month – S.210(2) ERA. In Pacitti Jones v O'Brien 2005 IRLR 888, Ct Sess (Inner House), the

49

Court of Session held that the date on which an employee started work is included when computing his or her period of continuous employment for unfair dismissal purposes. Thus an employee who worked from 8 April 2002 until 7 April 2003 had the necessary one year's continuous service to bring a claim.

Clearly, there are two essential dates for the purposes of computing an employee's period of continuous employment. These are the date employment began (see below) and the effective date of termination (EDT). The EDT is discussed in IDS Employment Law Handbook, 'Contracts of Employment' (2009), Chapter 11.

2.15 A period of continuous employment *begins* with the day on which an employee starts work – S.211(1)(a); Pacitti Jones v O'Brien (above). In General of the Salvation Army v Dewsbury 1984 ICR 498, EAT, the EAT held that this refers to the beginning of the employee's employment under the relevant contract of employment and not to when the employee first turns up physically to start work. In that case D, a teacher, accepted a post expressed as starting on May 1, which was a Saturday. However, because of the weekend and the May Day Bank Holiday, she did not actually start her duties until May 4, the following Tuesday. The EAT held that she must be treated as having 'started work' on May 1, with the result that she just qualified to bring an unfair dismissal claim.

In Convergent Telecom Ltd v Swann and anor EAT 534/02 the EAT distinguished Dewsbury on its facts. That case concerned S.218(6), which allows for continuity of employment to be preserved when an employee moves from one employer to an associated employer and permits the employee to count the period of employment with the first employer as part of his or her employment with the second employer for the purpose of bringing an unfair dismissal claim. The EAT upheld a tribunal's decision that an employee who moved from one employer to another could rely upon S.218(6) to preserve continuity of employment in circumstances in which the two employers were not associated employers at the time S accepted the new job, but were at the time he actually commenced the new job. In reaching this conclusion, the EAT held that it could see no basis for overriding the wording of S.211(1)(a) and the common sense approach that 'continuous employment begins with the date on which the employee starts work', which may be, as in the Dewsbury case, 'a day or so before the actual commencement of work if the start date is a bank holiday or weekend'.

2.16 There are two cases in which an artificial adjustment is made retrospectively to the start date which may affect the qualifying period of continuous service in unfair dismissal cases – S.211(3):

- if an employee is absent from work because he or she has been taking part in a strike or because of a lock-out by the employer, the start of employment is deemed to have been postponed by the number of days (not working days) between the last working day before the strike or lock-out and the day on which work is resumed – S.216(2)

- there is a similar postponement of the start date if an employee is absent because of military service – S.217(2).

'Continuous employment' is a technical term. It means a period of continuous employment computed in accordance with the rules set out in Ss.210–219 ERA, which provide a complete definition of what is meant by 'continuously employed' – Wood v York City Council 1978 ICR 840, CA. These rules deal with three main issues:

2.17

- when a week worked under a contract of employment does and does not count as a week of continuous employment

- breaks in employment and when these count as periods of continuous employment even though there is no employment contract in existence

- when continuity is preserved after a change of employer (for example, in Da Silva v Composite Mouldings and Design Ltd 2009 ICR 416, EAT, an employee who was dismissed on the voluntary liquidation of one company and employed by another retained his continuity of service under S.218, since both companies had the same owner who had retained control throughout the relevant period).

These issues are considered in detail in IDS Employment Law Handbook, 'Continuity of Employment' (2001), to which reference should be made regarding all aspects of continuous employment.

Exceptions to continuous service threshold

2.18

There are a number of exceptions to the normal rule that one year's continuous service must be shown.

Automatically unfair dismissals. Most importantly, *no* period of qualifying service is required to bring a claim of automatically unfair dismissal for one of the 'inadmissible' reasons (with three exceptions noted below) – see S.108 ERA, Ss.154 and 239(1) TULR(C)A, para 164 of Schedule A1 to the TULR(C)A, S.12(4) of the Employment Relations Act 1999, Reg 16(4) of the Flexible Working (Procedural Requirements) Regulations 2002 SI 2002/3207, and Reg 18(4) of the Employee Study and Training (Procedural Requirements) Regulations 2010 SI 2010/155. These inadmissible reasons are listed in Chapter 10 under 'List of automatically unfair reasons'. Therefore, in cases where an employee has less than one year's service, it is crucial to determine at the outset whether or not his or her dismissal was for one of the inadmissible reasons.

2.19

As noted above, there are three grounds of automatically unfair dismissal where the one-year qualifying limit in S.108(1) *does* apply:

- retirement dismissals where an employer has failed to comply with the statutory retirement procedure – see Chapter 9

- dismissals because of a spent conviction, and

- dismissals where there is a transfer of an undertaking.

2.20 **Redundancy.** The one-year qualifying limit does not apply to dismissals for redundancy where selection for redundancy was for one of the inadmissible reasons listed in Chapter 10 – see S.108(3)(h) ERA, S.154 TULR(C)A, and para 164, Schedule A1, TULR(C)A. Note, though, that there are a few automatically unfair reasons for dismissal listed in Chapter 10 for which no provision is made in respect of selection for redundancy – see under 'List of automatically unfair reasons – selection for redundancy' in that chapter.

2.21 **Other exceptions.** There are a couple of further limited exceptions to the general rule that an employee must show one year's continuous employment in order to claim unfair dismissal:

- the qualifying period is *one month* where the employee is dismissed in circumstances in which he or she would qualify for paid suspension on medical grounds – S.108(2) ERA. The medical suspension provisions, which are rarely used, are set out in Ss.64–65 ERA and cover a limited range of occupations – basically those involving lead, certain dangerous chemicals and radiation

- the one-year qualifying limit does *not* apply in relation to the dismissal of office holders who have fair dismissal rights under Reg 33 of the Ecclesiastical Offices (Terms of Service) Regulations 2009 SI 2009/2108 – Reg 33(3) of those Regulations.

2.22 ## Illegality

Illegality in employment contracts is dealt with in IDS Employment Law Handbook, 'Contracts of Employment' (2009), Chapter 4, which should be referred to for a full treatment of the subject. Here we merely outline the main points.

Briefly, the general rule is that an illegal contract is unenforceable and that no statutory employment rights – including the right to complain of unfair dismissal – can be enforced under it. However, depending on the type of illegality, the knowledge and intent of the parties may be significant. An innocent party *may* be able to claim under the contract, but it is necessary to distinguish the different kinds of illegality.

52

Statutory illegality
2.23

In certain circumstances employment is directly prohibited by legislation. For example, there is a variety of restrictions on the employment of children and young persons. And health and safety legislation prohibits the employment of pregnant women or employees with certain medical conditions in specified circumstances. Immigrants may also be subject to strict controls in respect of taking up employment in the United Kingdom.

If an employment contract is illegal by statute from its inception, it will be void and unenforceable by either party, whether or not they were aware of the illegality. An employee under such a contract will be left without any employment protection rights. Where, however, an employment contract *becomes* illegal during the course of its performance because of a statutory provision, and the employee is dismissed as a result, he or she will *not* be barred from claiming unfair dismissal – and may indeed be successful in doing so if he or she can demonstrate that the employer acted unreasonably in dismissing for this reason – see Chapter 7, 'Statutory ban'.)

Illegality at common law
2.24

An employment contract whose object or purpose involves criminality or immorality is unenforceable as being contrary to public policy. Provided both parties have the same object in mind, this will apply even if both parties honestly believe that no breach of the law is involved – JM Allan (Merchandising) Ltd v Cloke 1963 2 WLR 899, CA. The object of the contract will depend on what was contemplated when the contract was entered into.

However, a contract involving criminal or immoral activities will not necessarily be unenforceable if such activities do not form a term of the contract. In Coral Leisure Group Ltd v Barnett 1981 IRLR 204, EAT, a public relations executive who was claiming unfair dismissal said that part of his job was procuring prostitutes for clients. The EAT said that a contract for sexually immoral purposes would have been contrary to public policy and unenforceable. But the claimant did not enter employment with the intention of procuring and this had not been the purpose of the contract, but had simply become part of the way in which he carried out the contract. That was not enough to make the contract unenforceable.

Illegality in performance
2.25

A contract that is prohibited by statute or that is for a criminal or immoral purpose cannot be performed legally – it is illegal by its very nature. But the question of illegality in an employment contract normally arises when the contract is perfectly legal on its face but is being performed in an illegal way, normally through some kind of tax fraud in the way the employee is paid. Whether or not an illegal act in the performance of an otherwise lawful contract

53

has the effect of rendering that contract unenforceable is an imprecise area of the law. In Colen and anor v Cebrian (UK) Ltd 2004 ICR 568, CA, Lord Justice Waller, with whom the other members of the Court agreed, pointed out that, even if the employer in that case had been able to demonstrate some illegality of performance, it did not necessarily follow that the employees' claims for unfair dismissal and unpaid wages would have failed. In order to resist those claims, he suggested, the employer would have had to show that the illegal performance had been sufficient to turn a 'valid contract into an illegal contract', or that the employees 'needed to rely on their illegality to succeed in their claim'. The Court held that the burden of proof in such cases is on the employer to show that it had either contracted with the employee with the object (for example) of defrauding the Inland Revenue, or had performed the contracts in a way which had this result.

The degree of knowledge of the parties may be crucial. The principle that the courts will not enforce a contract that is performed in an illegal manner is strictly applied where both the employer and the employee know about the illegality and are party to it. In Napier v National Business Agency Ltd 1951 2 All ER 264, CA, the Court of Appeal said that a contract which the parties know to involve a fraud on the Inland Revenue is wholly unenforceable at common law. This principle was extended to statutory rights in Tomlinson v Dick Evans U Drive Ltd 1978 IRLR 77, EAT, where T complained of unfair dismissal, but it came to light that she had been paid £15 a week in cash as 'expenses' against the submission of false vouchers. The EAT said that this was a joint fraud on the Revenue by employer and employee and that 'both were in it up to the neck'. It made no difference that T was trying to enforce a statutory right and not a contractual one: because the contract was illegal it was a nullity and she lost her statutory rights.

2.26 Where an employee's wages have been deliberately misrepresented to the Inland Revenue for the purpose of evading tax and national insurance contributions, the employer is nearly always party to the illegality because it is the employer's statutory duty to deduct tax and national insurance from the employee's salary and account for the same to the Revenue. In these circumstances, having acted illegally, the *employer* will not be able to rely on the contract. (Note though that illegality will only be made out in such cases if it is established that there has been misrepresentation of the facts: wrongly categorising an individual's employment status – as self-employed rather than as an employee – is not enough – Enfield Technical Services Ltd v Payne; BF Components Ltd v Grace 2008 ICR 1423, CA.) An *employee*, on the other hand, will only be prevented from enforcing a contract that has been performed illegally, and thus from bringing a claim of unfair dismissal, if, in addition to knowing about the facts that make the performance illegal, he or she *actively participated* in the illegal performance –Hall v Woolston Hall Leisure Ltd 2000 IRLR 578, CA.

54

It is a question of fact in each case whether there has been a sufficient degree of participation by the employee. Take the following contrasting cases:

- **Hewcastle Catering Ltd v Ahmed and anor** 1991 IRLR 473, CA: two waiters were instructed by their employer to issue a different kind of bill to customers who indicated an intention to pay by cash. Such payments were not declared for VAT purposes. When VAT inspectors found out about this fraud, they questioned staff and obtained a statement from one of the waiters which described what had been going on. Both were later dismissed and claimed unfair dismissal. The Court of Appeal held that their contracts of employment were not void. Even though by assisting their employer in the VAT fraud both employees were acting illegally, and were doing so as a regular part of the performance of their duties, in the particular circumstances of the case they were entitled to proceed with their unfair dismissal claims. The Court placed particular emphasis on the fact that the obligation to make VAT returns lay with the employer, that the employees were not specifically employed on the basis that they would assist in the VAT fraud, and that the employees did not benefit in any way from the fraud, which was perpetrated entirely at the instigation of the employer. The Court also held that it was in the public interest to encourage the disclosure of VAT fraud. To prevent employees who had been instrumental in the uncovering of such a fraud from being able to claim unfair dismissal would operate against this principle. The Court concluded that courts and tribunals should take a pragmatic approach to different factual situations, seeking to right genuine wrongs, so long as they do not appear to be assisting or encouraging employees to commit illegal acts

- **Soteriou v Ultrachem and ors** EAT 0250/01: S began working for U as an accountant in 1987. He worked at U's head office and rendered invoices monthly in arrears. In 1998 S registered for VAT and thereafter invoiced U using the name AGS services. At the end of that year the Contributions Agency launched an investigation into S's employment status. At the interview that followed, S made a number of claims supporting his self-employed status, which led to the Department of Social Security (DSS) ultimately accepting that he was self-employed. S's relationship with U subsequently broke down and he brought a claim, among other things, of unfair dismissal. The tribunal found, as a preliminary point, that S had become an employee of U's some time in 1996. It further found that S was well aware of the difference between employee and self-employed status and the tax implications thereof and that he had made fraudulent statements to the DSS in order to maintain his self-employed status. It concluded that he had knowingly committed a fraud in relation to the employment contract and therefore could not rely on that contract to claim unfair dismissal. On appeal, the EAT upheld the tribunal's decision, holding that S had 'knowingly and actively participated' in a deception on the Contributions

55

Agency, with the result that his contract of employment was tainted with illegality and thus unenforceable. The EAT rejected S's attempt to argue that his position was akin to that of the employees in the Hewcastle case, holding that his situation was completely different. In addition to deciding that he had 'knowingly and actively participated' in the deception, it further held that he had told a 'string of lies' for his own benefit.

Contracts may be performed illegally for only part of their duration. This will mean that the contract would be illegal and unenforceable for that period only. But this may have unfortunate effects for an employee's continuity of employment, as 'continuously employed' means continuously employed under a legal contract of employment – Hyland v JH Barker (North West) Ltd 1985 ICR 861, EAT.

2.27 Diplomatic and state immunity

The general rule of international law is that foreign (including Commonwealth) states and all emanations of their governments are entitled to immunity in civil actions unless they are engaging in purely commercial transactions or they elect to waive that immunity. This meant that, prior to the State Immunity Act 1978, employees of foreign and Commonwealth missions in the United Kingdom were unable to claim unfair dismissal in the UK courts.

The State Immunity Act 1978 changed that position. The general immunity of foreign states from the jurisdiction of UK courts is preserved by S.1(1), but S.4(1) removes that immunity in respect of proceedings relating to a contract of employment between a foreign state and an individual if:

- the contract was made in the United Kingdom, or

- the work is to be wholly or partly performed in the United Kingdom.

2.28 But there are important exceptions to this. For a start, under S.16 members of foreign missions within the meaning of Article 1 of the Vienna Convention on Diplomatic Relations 1961 are excluded. S.16 further provides that S.4 does not apply to members of a consular post within the meaning of the Vienna Convention on Consular Relations 1963. The exclusion in relation to members of foreign missions can apply to fairly lowly employees of the mission. For example, in Arab Republic of Egypt v Gamal-Eldin and anor 1996 ICR 13, EAT, two drivers at the Embassy's Medical Office were held to come within the S.16 exclusion. And in Government of the United Kingdom of Saudi Arabia v Nasser EAT 672/99 the EAT held that a driver employed by the Embassy to transport Saudi nationals arriving by air to hospitals, hotels or shops and to act as their translator was a member of the 'administrative and technical staff' of the Saudi Arabian mission for the purposes of the S.16 exclusion, with the result that the Embassy had state immunity and the employee could not claim unfair dismissal. The S.16 exclusion has even been held to extend to British nationals – see Ahmed v Government of the Kingdom of Saudi Arabia 1996 ICR 25, CA.

Further exceptions to the loss of state immunity are contained in S.4(2) and turn on whether or not a commercial activity is involved. If the employee was employed by the foreign state for *non-commercial* purposes – e.g. he or she was a diplomat or other embassy employee – then S.4(1) does not apply to remove immunity if:

- the employee is a national of the foreign state at the time he or she starts proceedings – S.4(2)(a), or

- at the time when the contract was made the employee was neither a national of the United Kingdom nor habitually resident in the United Kingdom – S.4(2)(b).

A 'national of the United Kingdom' in this context is defined as a British citizen, a British Overseas Territories citizen, a British National (Overseas) citizen, a British Overseas citizen, a British subject under the British Nationality Act 1981 or a British protected person under that Act – S.4(5).

2.29

If, however, the work performed under the contract is for an office, agency or establishment maintained by the foreign state in the United Kingdom for *commercial* purposes, then the foreign state may not rely on the two exceptions in S.4(2) unless the individual was habitually resident in the employing state at the time the contract was made – S.4(3).

Section 4(2) also provides that immunity will not be lost if the parties agree in writing that the foreign state shall enjoy immunity – S.4(2)(c). However, this can never form the basis for immunity in respect of tribunal proceedings because UK statutory employment rights can only be enforced in UK tribunals and, by virtue of S.4(4), any written agreement by the parties to bestow immunity is void where the substantive law entitles a claimant to bring proceedings only before a UK court or tribunal.

Waiver of immunity

2.30

A foreign state may be held to have waived its immunity if it has submitted to the jurisdiction of the courts – S.2(1). A state is deemed to have so submitted 'if it has intervened or taken any step in the proceedings' – S.2(3). In London Branch of the Nigerian Universities Commission v Bastians 1995 ICR 358, EAT, B was dismissed from his job at the Commission and brought proceedings for unfair dismissal. When it received a copy of the employee's claim form from the tribunal office, the Nigerian High Commission sent a note to the Foreign and Commonwealth Office, marked 'for transmission to the appropriate authority', which contained a statement of the reasons why the employee was dismissed and a comment that B's allegations were 'grossly incorrect'. The note

57

was forwarded by the Foreign and Commonwealth Office to the regional office of the employment tribunals. The tribunal hearing B's claim treated this note as the entering of a Notice of Appearance (now known as the 'response form') by the employer and therefore concluded that immunity had been waived. Overruling the tribunal, the EAT acknowledged that the service of a defence or the taking of any other steps to defend the case on the merits will normally be construed as a submission to the jurisdiction of the tribunal. But all that had occurred in this case was a diplomatic communication between representatives of foreign states, which contained none of the characteristics required of a Notice of Appearance. Accordingly, immunity had not been waived. Nor was immunity waived in Arab Republic of Egypt v Gamal-Eldin and anor (above) when the medical counsellor at the Egyptian Embassy wrote to the tribunal explaining the situation. The letter did not constitute the taking of steps in the proceedings or a submission to jurisdiction. Furthermore, the counsellor did not have authority to submit to jurisdiction. (Note that while these cases remain relevant to the question of whether a foreign state has intervened or taken steps in the proceedings, it should be borne in mind that employers wishing to enter a response must now use the mandatory response form (ET3) prescribed by the Secretary of State.)

The question of who is authorised to waive immunity was considered by the Court of Appeal in Aziz v Republic of Yemen 2005 EWCA Civ 745, CA. A was employed as an accounts assistant at the London Embassy of the Republic of Yemen until his dismissal. He brought a claim of unfair dismissal and the Republic submitted a response, stating that it intended to resist the claim. In the course of the tribunal hearing, the Republic argued that it had not taken any steps in the proceedings because any steps taken by its solicitors had not been properly authorised by the Republic. S.2(7) provides that the head of a State's diplomatic mission in the United Kingdom, or the person for the time being performing his or her functions, is deemed to have authority to submit on behalf of the State in respect of any proceedings. The EAT admitted evidence from the Yemeni Ambassador in London, who claimed that he did not authorise the taking of any step in the proceedings before the tribunal, and did not authorise the waiver of immunity. Taking the Ambassador's evidence at face value, the EAT therefore allowed the appeal. On further appeal by A, the Court of Appeal confirmed that any action taken by a member of the diplomatic mission (or solicitors instructed by the mission) must be taken with the authority of the head of mission or the person for the time being performing his or her functions. A solicitor acting without such authority cannot waive immunity. However, the head of mission's deemed authority under S.2(7) includes authority to delegate. Authority can therefore be conferred on solicitors either directly or indirectly by a member of the mission authorised by the head of mission to do so. The EAT should not have concluded that it was so obvious that immunity applied that it was unnecessary to inquire into the facts and should have remitted the point as to whether immunity had been waived to the fact-finding tribunal.

International organisations   2.31

The International Organisations Act 1968 provides that Orders in Council may be made to confer various forms of legal immunity on a number of international organisations with a UK base. A number of orders have been made in consequence. Other legislation may also apply to such organisations. For example, the Commonwealth Secretariat Act 1966 conferred immunity from civil action on the Secretariat and this operated to bar a tribunal's jurisdiction to hear an unfair dismissal claim in Gadhok v Commonwealth Secretariat EAT 171/77. The Act did, however, provide for disputes over contracts to be referred to arbitration and employees of international bodies may well have some such alternative to tribunal proceedings open to them.

For a more detailed discussion on the law governing state and diplomatic immunity see IDS Employment Law Handbook, 'Employment Tribunal Practice and Procedure' (2006), Chapter 1.

Working abroad   2.32

Section 196 ERA used to exclude employees who ordinarily worked outside Great Britain from the right to claim unfair dismissal and from other protections contained in that Act. However, it was repealed by the Employment Relations Act 1999 and was not replaced with alternative wording, leaving the ERA silent with regard to its territorial scope. This left the tribunals and the appeal courts to struggle with the question of whether, and if so to what extent, ERA rights applied to employees working outside Great Britain.

After a number of conflicting decisions on the matter, the issue finally came before the House of Lords in Lawson v Serco Ltd and two other cases 2006 ICR 250, HL, where their Lordships heard three conjoined appeals which all raised similar issues as to the circumstances in which employees working overseas have the right to bring claims of unfair dismissal under the ERA. In Lawson v Serco Ltd L, who is of British nationality and domiciled in England, worked as a security supervisor for S Ltd, a company registered in the United Kingdom and based in England. The job required L to carry out all his work on Ascension Island in the South Atlantic, where the company was contracted to provide security services to the Royal Air Force. In the second case, Botham v Ministry of Defence, B was a British national employed by the MoD in Germany. He was considered part of the 'civil component' of the British Forces in Germany; he paid UK tax on his earnings; and his contract of employment was expressly stated to be governed by the law of England and Wales. Furthermore, his statement of employment particulars

59

described him as 'UK-based'. In the third case, Crofts and ors v Veta Ltd and ors, C was employed as a pilot by V Ltd, a wholly-owned subsidiary of CPA Ltd. Both V Ltd and CPA Ltd were registered in Hong Kong. C's contract was governed by Hong Kong law and his flight instructions were issued from Hong Kong. However, his 'permanent home base' – where his flight cycle would start and end – was Heathrow Airport. Each of these employees brought unfair dismissal claims in a UK employment tribunal, and all three cases made their way to the House of Lords on the question of jurisdiction.

2.33   Lord Hoffmann, who delivered the leading judgment in the case, emphasised that it would be 'a mistake to try to formulate an ancillary rule of territorial scope, in the sense of a verbal formula such as S.196 used to provide'. Nevertheless, his Lordship accepted that Parliament must have intended, as a general principle, for the unfair dismissal rules to apply to 'the employee who was working in Great Britain'. His Lordship divided employees into three categories for the purpose of establishing whether a UK employment tribunal has territorial jurisdiction to hear a claim of unfair dismissal:

- in the standard case, the question will depend on whether the employee was *working in Great Britain at the time of dismissal*

- in the case of peripatetic employees, the *employee's base* – the place at which he or she started and ended assignments – should be treated as his or her place of employment. The question then is whether the base was in Great Britain at the time of dismissal

- employees working and based abroad may in exceptional circumstances be entitled to claim unfair dismissal, even though they are not employed in Great Britain at the time of dismissal, provided their employment has *sufficiently strong connections with Great Britain and British employment law*.

The question of whether a case falls within the territorial scope of S.94(1) ERA is a question of law – although clearly one in relation to which the facts found by a tribunal will be critical.

2.34   ## Enforcing EU-derived rights

Given the confusion over the territorial scope of the unfair dismissal legislation following the repeal of S.196 ERA, the House of Lords' decision in Lawson (above) was greeted with considerable relief by practitioners and commentators. At last there appeared to be some definitive guidance as to whether an employee working abroad should be able to bring a claim for unfair dismissal within the UK tribunal system.

This degree of certainty was, however, thrown into some doubt by the Court of Appeal's decision in Duncombe and ors v Secretary of State for Children, Schools and Families 2010 IRLR 331, CA. In that case D was employed by what was then the Department for Education and Skills to work under a succession of fixed-term contracts in a European School in Karlsruhe in Germany. D's contract stated that it 'shall be governed by English law and the English courts shall have exclusive jurisdiction in all matters regarding it'. Teaching posts in European Schools were subject to a maximum of nine years' duration by virtue of regulations governing the schools (the Nine Year Rule). D brought tribunal proceedings arising out of the expiry of his last contract, claiming wrongful dismissal and unfair dismissal. It was accepted that these claims could only get off the ground if Reg 8 of the Fixed-term Employees (Prevention of Less Favourable Treatment) Regulations 2002 SI 2002/2034 applied to convert his succession of fixed-term contracts into a permanent one. The claims were dismissed by the tribunal at a pre-hearing review on the basis that they relied on Reg 8, from whose scope D was excluded according to the territorial jurisdiction test set out in Lawson. Therefore, his claims had no reasonable prospect of success.

D's appeal against the ruling on unfair dismissal failed at an EAT preliminary hearing on the basis that, following Lawson, it had no reasonable prospect of success. However, he went on to successfully challenge the wrongful dismissal aspect of the tribunal's decision on the basis of a new point of appeal; namely, the effect of Bleuse v MBT Transport Ltd and anor 2008 ICR 488, EAT, in which judgment was handed down after the EAT's preliminary hearing of the unfair dismissal point. That decision was authority for the proposition that the limitations on territorial scope set down in Lawson have to be modified where necessary to give effect to a claimant's directly effective rights under EU law. In that case, Mr Justice Elias, then President of the EAT, permitted the claimant to rely on the Working Time Regulations 1998 SI 1998/1833 in an employment tribunal, even though he worked abroad. D argued that, assuming the Fixed-term Work Directive (No.99/70) is directly enforceable, no distinction could be drawn between his case and that of Bleuse. Thus he should, by analogy, be entitled to rely on the Fixed-term Employees Regulations. The EAT allowed D's appeal and declared that the tribunal had jurisdiction, in hearing the wrongful dismissal claim, to apply the relevant provisions of the Regulations to determine the question of whether the employer could justify employing D under fixed-term contracts.

D appealed against the unfair dismissal part of the EAT's judgment and the Secretary of State appealed against the EAT's decision on wrongful dismissal. Dealing first with D's wrongful dismissal claim, the Court of Appeal agreed with the Secretary of State that D would not be able to satisfy the Lawson test if it applied to the Regulations as it did to the right not to be unfairly dismissed under S.94 ERA. However, the Court accepted D's 'simple' and 'beguiling' argument that he still had a cause of action for wrongful dismissal based on the fact that the parties had chosen English law as the law of the contract. The Fixed-term Employees Regulations apply to all fixed-term employment contracts governed by English law regardless of where those contracts are performed – there is no territorial limitation in the Regulations themselves. On that basis, the Court decided, the Lawson principles became irrelevant. The result was that D's fixed-

2.35

term contract was converted into a permanent one. Furthermore, the availability of a remedy for breach of a contract, whether or not modified by the operation of the Regulations, was founded in common law and was not dependent upon the ERA. D's claim for wrongful dismissal could therefore proceed and the Secretary of State's appeal was dismissed. The Court of Appeal went on to say that, had it been necessary to do so, it would have applied the Bleuse principle (of which more below) to L's wrongful dismissal claim.

2.36 As to D's appeal in respect of the unfair dismissal claim, the Court acknowledged that different considerations applied. Whereas the choice of English law as the law of the contract meant that D's contract claim could be brought in the tribunal, a claim of unfair dismissal had to be brought under the ERA and so was subject to the territorial limitation imposed by Lawson. The Court agreed with the Secretary of State that, on a straight application of Lawson, D would not be able to establish the right to bring an employment claim in Great Britain. On this point, at least, the tribunal had made no error of law. However, the Court went on to endorse Bleuse, holding, moreover, that, in accordance with the EU principle of effectiveness, it should be applied to permit an unfair dismissal claim to be made where that was necessary for the effective vindication of a right derived from EU law – in this case, the Fixed-term Employees Regulations. To that extent, the implied territorial limitation on the right not to be unfairly dismissed, as identified in Lawson, should be modified. The Court noted that D's EU-derived right to a permanent contract would be denied if he could be dismissed on the basis that he was employed on a fixed-term contract that had expired, as in such a situation he would have no remedy for unfair dismissal. The Court therefore allowed his appeal and directed that his unfair dismissal claim should be allowed to proceed.

At the time of writing, the Court's judgment is under appeal to the Supreme Court. However, until the Supreme Court gives its judgment, it remains the unsatisfactory position that Lawson should be followed when determining questions of territorial jurisdiction over unfair dismissal claims – unless to do so would deprive a claimant of an effective remedy for his or her directly effective EU rights, in which case the Lawson test must be modified to give effect to those rights.

2.37 Special categories of worker

There are a number of provisions in the ERA that deal with unfair dismissal rights in relation to specific categories of worker such as crown employees, the police and mariners.

2.38 Crown employees

The question of whether Crown employees work under contracts of employment is dealt with in IDS Employment Law Handbook, 'Contracts of Employment' (2009), Chapter 1. In practice, the issue is irrelevant in the context of unfair dismissal, because S.191(1) expressly applies the unfair dismissal provisions to 'persons in Crown employment' in the same way as to other employees – with the exception of S.101, which makes it automatically unfair to dismiss certain shop workers and betting workers who refuse to work on Sundays (a provision unlikely to apply to many Crown employees in any event).

Members of the armed forces. Service in the armed forces is regarded as   2.39
'Crown employment'. At first glance, the rights of members of the armed forces are set out in S.192. This applies the provisions dealing with Crown employment to members of the armed forces, but with certain exceptions. However, S.192 has yet to be brought into force. Instead, the 'transitory provisions' set out in para 16 of Schedule 2 to the Act continue to apply. These provide (through the substitution of modified text) that unless and until S.192 is brought into effect, it should be read as if the provisions in S.191 – which apply the unfair dismissal provisions to persons in Crown employment – do not apply to service as a member of the armed forces. Thus members of the armed forces are currently excluded from the right to claim unfair dismissal. (Note that in McQuade v Secretary of State for Defence, unreported 7/10/03, Ct Sess (Outer House), the Court of Session held that the exclusion of members of the armed forces from the unfair dismissal scheme did not breach their rights under the European Convention on Human Rights.)

National security. It used to be the case that, subject to a limited number of   2.40
exceptions relating to automatically unfair dismissals, unfair dismissal rights were generally excluded in the case of Crown employees in respect of whom a Minister had issued a certificate to certify that employment of a particular description or the employment of a particular person should be excluded from protection for the purpose of safeguarding national security. That exception no longer exists (although there remains a question over whether members of the security services are excluded from the protection conferred by S.103A ERA against being unfairly dismissed on the ground of making a protected disclosure – see Chapter 13).

House of Commons and House of Lords staff   2.41
Sections 194 and 195 provide that unfair dismissal rights apply to relevant members of the House of Lords staff and the House of Commons staff as they apply in relation to other employment, subject to two exceptions:

- S.101 – automatically unfair dismissal for Sunday working (see Chapter 10)

- S.102 – automatically unfair dismissal of an occupational pension scheme trustee in connection with his or her duties in that capacity (see Chapter 10).

'Relevant member of the House of Lords staff' means any person who is employed under a contract of employment with the Corporate Officer of the House of Lords – S.194(6). 'Relevant member of the House of Commons staff'

63

means any person who was appointed by the House of Commons Commission or is employed in the refreshment department or who is a member of the Speaker's personal staff – S.195(5).

2.42 **Police**

People employed in the police service are generally excluded from unfair dismissal rights – S.200(1). 'Police service' means service as a member of a constabulary or service in any capacity by virtue of which a person has 'the powers or privileges of a constable' – S.200(2). Prison staff are not covered by this section and may therefore bring unfair dismissal claims – S.126 of the Criminal Justice and Public Order Act 1994. So, too, may police employees in supporting roles.

There are two important exceptions to the general rule that persons employed in the police service are excluded from bringing unfair dismissal claims. These relate to:

• health and safety dismissals under S.100 (see Chapter 11), and

• dismissals for making a protected disclosure under S.103A (see Chapter 13) – S.200(1).

Where either of these provisions applies, a person who holds the office of constable or an appointment as a police cadet will be treated as employed by the relevant officer (as defined) under a contract of employment – Ss.43KA and 134A.

2.43 **Share fishermen and women**

The master and crew of a fishing vessel who are remunerated only by a share in the profits or gross earnings of the vessel on which they are employed are excluded from unfair dismissal rights – S.199(2). In Goodeve v Gilsons 1985 ICR 401, CA, the Court of Appeal considered the case of a fisherman who had been remunerated by a share in the profits of the whole fleet of vessels operated by his employer. It held that the singular could not be read as including the plural in the words 'the vessel', so that S.199(2) did not apply. The employee was not a share fisherman as defined and he was not, therefore, excluded from the right to claim unfair dismissal.

2.44 **Mariners**

Persons employed on board a ship registered in the United Kingdom under S.8 of the Merchant Shipping Act 1995 can only bring a claim of unfair dismissal if:

• the ship is registered as belonging to a port in Great Britain

• under his or her contract of employment, the person employed does not work *wholly* outside Great Britain, and

• he or she is ordinarily resident in Great Britain – S.199(7) and (8).

64

(Great Britain means England, Scotland and Wales; the United Kingdom means Great Britain and Northern Ireland. Neither expression includes the Channel Islands or the Isle of Man.)

2.45 The rules governing the right of mariners to bring unfair dismissal claims used to be contained in S.196(5), which was repealed by the Employment Relations Act 1999. However, very similar wording is used in S.199, which was inserted by the same Act, with the result that the case law interpreting S.196(5) is likely to be relevant to the interpretation of S.199. Much of the case law concerned with S.196(5) centred on the phrases 'wholly outside Great Britain' and 'ordinarily resident in Great Britain'. In Royle v Globtik Management Ltd 1977 ICR 552, EAT, the employer managed three tankers, two of which were registered in London and one in the Bahamas. R, who was resident in Great Britain, worked only on the London-registered ships. However, he worked only on voyages between the Persian Gulf and the Far East, although he had been on a three-day course in Liverpool during his employment. The EAT held that he was not entitled to bring an unfair dismissal claim on two grounds:

- he worked wholly outside Great Britain (the three days in Liverpool being too trivial to count)

- he could not be said to have been employed to work on a UK-registered ship because he could at any time have been transferred to the Bahamas-registered ship (which seemed to involve reading the word 'exclusively' into S.196(5)).

2.46 In Wood v Cunard Line Ltd 1990 IRLR 281, CA, W worked exclusively on a UK-registered ship based in Puerto Rico. He had been recruited at, and was paid by, the head office in Southampton and his standard form contract stated that each voyage terminated in Great Britain. In practice, however, the ship never entered UK waters. The Court held that employment was wholly outside Great Britain even though the employee travelled to the ship from Great Britain and was paid the appropriate rate of pay during the trip. Employment is wholly outside Great Britain if the *work on board the ship* is performed wholly outside Great Britain – even if the employment technically begins when the employee is in Great Britain.

In Huggins v Geest Transportation Group COET 818/200 H worked exclusively on a UK-registered ship and his employment was not wholly outside Great Britain. However, he was not ordinarily resident in Great Britain because his home was in the West Indies. It followed that he was disqualified from presenting an unfair dismissal claim.

2.47 **Foreign-registered ships.** Section 199(7) and (8) apply only to those who are employed on ships registered under S.8 of the Merchant Shipping Act 1995, i.e. on UK-registered ships. Mariners employed on foreign-registered ships are covered by the more general principles governing territorial jurisdiction under the

65

ERA established by the House of Lords in Lawson v Serco Ltd and two other cases 2006 ICR 250, HL (see 'Working abroad' above) – Diggins v Condor Marine Crewing Services Ltd 2010 ICR 213, CA. In that case, D was employed by CMCS Ltd as chief officer on a ship which, although registered in the Bahamas, operated between the Channel Islands and Portsmouth. D was required to stay on board throughout his fortnightly rosters, but otherwise his home was in Lowestoft. In April 2007 he was dismissed, and his subsequent unfair dismissal claim was rejected by the employment tribunal as D did not meet the conditions set down in S.199(7). The EAT allowed D's appeal, holding that the tribunal did have jurisdiction notwithstanding his failure to meet the criteria in S.199(7), as D was a 'peripatetic employee' based in Great Britain. CMCS Ltd appealed to the Court of Appeal, arguing that only S.199(7) determines the right of those who work on ships to claim unfair dismissal. The Court disagreed. That subsection only applies to those who are employed on ships registered under S.8 of the Merchant Shipping Act 1995. However, if they were not so employed, a tribunal would still have jurisdiction under the Lawson principles. The Court then went on to consider whether, on the facts, the employment tribunal had jurisdiction to hear D's case. It held that D was a peripatetic employee under the Lawson principles. CMCS Ltd may have been based in Guernsey but D 'had no real connection with that place and he had even less so with the Bahamas, where the ship was registered'. It supported the EAT's conclusion that his tours of duty started and finished in Portsmouth. Therefore he was based in Great Britain, and accordingly CMCS Ltd's appeal was dismissed.

2.48 Settlements and contracting out

The general rule is that nobody can contract out of unfair dismissal rights and obligations: any purported agreement to this effect will be void, whether or not it is contained in a contract of employment – S.203(1). Statute, however, expressly provides for a number of exceptions to this general rule. These are: settlements reached under the auspices of an Acas conciliator, compromise agreements, and collective contracting out under a dismissal procedures agreement. In addition, a settlement recorded by the tribunal may effectively bar a claim.

2.49 Tribunal settlements

Where a settlement has been incorporated into a tribunal decision dismissing the application upon withdrawal by the claimant, the claimant will be prevented or 'estopped' from bringing another claim in respect of the same facts or issues – unless the decision to dismiss is successfully reviewed or appealed. This is because the doctrine of 'res judicata' – which bars the reopening of a legal issue or cause of action which has already been decided – is not restricted to cases where a tribunal has given a reasoned decision on the substantive issues in the case. A tribunal's order dismissing a claim upon the claimant's withdrawal is also a judicial decision and not a mere administrative act – Barber v Staffordshire County Council 1996 IRLR 209, CA. However, a withdrawal of a claim in and of itself does not create an issue or cause of action estoppel, since it does not involve a judicial act – Khan v Heywood and Middleton Primary Care Trust 2007 ICR 24, CA. In Ako v Rothschild Asset Management Ltd 2002 ICR 899, CA, the Court of Appeal held that a claimant who withdrew her tribunal application was not estopped from bringing the same claim again when her intention had been to discontinue the application – and replace it with a new application naming an additional respondent – rather than abandon it altogether. The Court recommended that tribunals, on being notified of the withdrawal of an application, should ask the claimant for a statement of the circumstances of the withdrawal before deciding whether to make an order dismissing the proceedings.

For more detail on estoppel and res judicata, see IDS Employment Law Handbook, 'Employment Tribunal Practice and Procedure' (2006), Chapter 1.

Acas settlements   2.50

There is an exception to the general rule against contracting out where an Acas conciliator has taken action and an agreement has been reached that the employee will refrain from instituting or continuing with a complaint – S.203(2)(e). The agreement will be binding if the conciliator has 'taken action' under S.18 of the Employment Tribunals Act 1996. This says that where a claimant has presented a claim, it is the conciliator's duty 'to endeavour to promote a settlement of the proceedings without their being determined by an employment tribunal'. A conciliator also has the power to promote a settlement under the Acas pre-claim conciliation service *before* proceedings have been instituted, although there is no duty to do so in these circumstances. The conciliator must in particular seek to promote the reinstatement or re-engagement of the employee but, if the employee does not want this or it is not practicable, he or she must seek to promote agreement as to a sum of money to be paid to the employee as compensation.

The case law suggests that a conciliator's involvement in an individual case need not be particularly extensive for a binding settlement to be reached. In Slack v Greenham (Plant Hire) Ltd and anor 1983 ICR 617, EAT, for example, the EAT said that a conciliator is under no obligation to explain unfair dismissal (or other) rights to an employee, particularly where the employee is keen on a quick settlement and does not have it in mind to complain of unfair dismissal. Further, in Moore v Duport Furniture Products Ltd 1982 ICR 84, HL, the House of Lords held that simply recording a settlement's terms on a COT3 form (the standard form used for this purpose) constituted taking action under S.18 and barred any unfair dismissal complaint by the employee. This was so even though the conciliator took no part in arriving at the settlement because it was agreed by the parties in his absence. (Note, however, that there

67

has since been a policy shift on Acas's part and it now seems unlikely that a conciliator would simply rubber-stamp a settlement to which the parties to an employment dispute have already agreed.)

2.51   In Slack v Greenham (Plant Hire) Ltd the EAT expressed the opinion that a conciliated settlement could be set aside if a conciliator acted in bad faith, adopted unfair methods or was not impartial. One tribunal set aside a settlement on the ground that it was based on a mutual mistake of the parties, who both erroneously believed that the employee's pension was worth a good deal more than was actually the case – O'Rourke v Airport Catering Services ET Case No.31930/83. And in Trafford Carpets Ltd v Barker EAT 206/90 the EAT held that a conciliated agreement was a sham and did not deprive the tribunal of jurisdiction where its terms wrongly indicated that no payment in lieu of notice had been made and did so with a view to misleading a Government Department about the employee's eligibility for an Enterprise Allowance.

Conciliated settlements are usually recorded on COT3 forms, but there is *no requirement that they should be in writing*. Provided there is clear evidence of an oral agreement between the parties in which a conciliator has been an intermediary, this will constitute a binding settlement which will bar the employee from bringing an unfair dismissal claim – Gilbert v Kembridge Fibres Ltd 1984 ICR 188, EAT. It will be immaterial that the employee may change his or her mind when the oral agreement is reduced to writing.

However, although an agreement to settle a claim does not have to be in writing, the parties must have entered into a contractually binding agreement. In Duru v Granada Retail Catering Ltd EAT 281/00 GRC Ltd asked the conciliator to offer D a settlement payment of £250 in respect of his alleged unfair dismissal. D told the conciliator during a telephone call that he would accept the offer, adding that he would contact her on receipt of the draft COT3. The same day the conciliator phoned GRC Ltd to say that the offer had been accepted. GRC Ltd stated that it had some standard wording it would like to use on the COT3, but would be prepared to see D's document first. The conciliator than faxed a COT3 to the employer, who decided that the wording on the document was satisfactory. Later that day D rang the conciliator and left a message stating that he wanted the employer to put the offer in writing before he accepted it. However, GRC Ltd refused, stating that it had already sent back a signed COT3. A tribunal found that at the end of D's first telephone conversation with the conciliator there was an enforceable oral agreement to settle the claim, with the result that D was barred from pursuing his claim of unfair dismissal. The EAT, however, overruled this decision, holding among other things that when GRC Ltd told the conciliator to offer D £250, it was not making an offer in the contractual sense because it did not intend to be bound by that offer as soon as D 'accepted' it. Rather, it was the employer's intention that the agreement would become binding when recorded in writing on the draft COT3 in terms that it found satisfactory. The facts also supported the view that D had not accepted an offer to settle the claim because he was expecting to see the offer set out in a draft COT3. The contractual principles of offer and acceptance had not been satisfied because there had never been a meeting of minds between the parties as to what exactly was being agreed.

Compromise agreements

2.52

Compromise agreements represent another exception to the general rule in S.203(1) that individuals cannot contract out of unfair dismissal rights. By virtue of S.203(2)(f), S.203(1) does not apply where a compromise agreement is entered into, thereby making it possible for parties to settle an employment dispute between themselves without the intervention of an Acas conciliator. In order to be binding, however, such agreements must:

- be in writing

- relate to the particular proceedings

- only be made where the employee has received advice from a relevant (and fully insured) independent adviser as to the terms and effect of the proposed agreement and in particular its effect on his or her ability to pursue his or her rights before a tribunal

- identify the adviser, and

- state that the conditions regulating compromise agreements have been satisfied – S.203(3).

A person is a relevant independent adviser if he or she:

2.53

- is a qualified lawyer (i.e. in England and Wales, a person authorised to exercise a right of audience or to conduct litigation within the meaning of the Legal Services Act 2007; in Scotland, an advocate or a solicitor who holds a practising certificate – S.203(4))

- is an officer, official, employee or member of an independent trade union who has been certified in writing by the trade union as competent to give advice and as authorised to do so on behalf of the trade union

- works at an advice centre (whether as an employee or as a volunteer) and has been certified in writing by the centre as competent to give advice and as authorised to do so on behalf of the centre, or

- is a person of a description specified in an order made by the Secretary of State – S.203(3A). (Note that the Compromise Agreements (Description of Person) Order 2004/754 extends the type of person who can give legal advice in relation to compromise agreements to Fellows of the Institute of Legal Executives employed by a solicitors' practice, although many such

69

Fellows are in fact authorised to conduct litigation or have rights of audience and will count as qualified lawyers within the meaning of S.203(4).)

2.54 Section 203(3B) adds that a person is *not* a relevant independent adviser in relation to the employee (or worker) if he or she is –

- employed by or is acting in the matter for the employer or an associated employer

- a trade union or advice centre adviser and the trade union or advice centre is the employer or an associated employer

- an advice centre adviser and the employee (or worker) makes a payment for the advice received

- a person specified in an order made by the Secretary of State under S.203(3A) and any condition specified in the order in relation to the giving of advice by persons of that description is not satisfied.

The terms of S.203(3) will be strictly enforced by tribunals and a failure to comply with any of the above requirements is likely to render the agreement void. There is, however, some uncertainty as to what is needed in order for the agreement to '*relate to the particular proceedings*'. In Hinton v University of East London 2005 ICR 1260, CA, the Court of Appeal ruled that the parties needed to identify expressly the particular proceedings to which the compromise agreement relates, either by a generic description (e.g. 'unfair dismissal') or by referring to the section of the relevant statute (e.g. S.98 ERA – general right to complain of unfair dismissal). It was not enough to use a rolled-up expression such as 'all statutory rights', or to refer merely to the title of a statute – e.g. 'the Employment Rights Act 1996' – and assume that such a reference would effectively settle all and any claims under that Act.

2.55 Having dealt with the statutory requirements, the Appeal Court went on to make some observations on an obiter basis about good practice when drafting compromise agreements, suggesting that employers should not use standard form agreements that seek to compromise every conceivable employment right irrespective of whether it is relevant to the particular circumstances. But despite this guidance, a comprehensive list of employment protection claims (without further detail) was sufficient to compromise claims in Topping v ABP Meat Processors Ltd ET Case No.2900133/07. T brought claims for unfair dismissal and disability discrimination, despite having signed a compromise agreement listing specific jurisdictions that included unfair dismissal and disability discrimination. He argued that the agreement was not effective to compromise these claims because it did not contain brief particulars of them, as required by Hinton. However, the tribunal disagreed, holding that the inclusion of such particulars was merely best practice and not a statutory requirement. In any event, the tribunal recognised that, where

70

proceedings have not commenced and are not even contemplated at the time the compromise agreement is signed, giving particulars is not always easy. Accordingly, the claims had been validly compromised.

There is also some uncertainty as to whether the agreement has to *identify the adviser* in the body of the agreement in order for it to be valid. In Lambert v Croydon College ET Case No.35472/96 the agreement failed to state the name of the legal adviser. Although it was clear from the surrounding correspondence who that adviser was, the tribunal held that the agreement had failed to satisfy the requirements of S.203(3). In Sankyo Pharma (UK) Ltd v Bartlett EAT 687/99, on the other hand, there was no reference to the employee's adviser, a solicitor, in the body of the compromise agreement, although a covering letter with the agreement did identify the adviser. The tribunal found that the conditions regulating compromise agreements had not been complied with. However, in the course of allowing the appeal and remitting the case to a freshly constituted tribunal, the EAT commented that it was not aware of there being an EAT authority suggesting that a solicitor's signature must be on the document containing the agreement itself.

Once a valid compromise agreement has been reached, the employee is barred **2.56** from bringing a claim of unfair dismissal, even if the terms of the agreement are subsequently breached by the employer. However, a tribunal may be able to hear the employee's claim for breach of the agreement by virtue of its contractual jurisdiction under the Employment Tribunals Extension of Jurisdiction (England and Wales) Order 1994 SI 1994/1623. Note, however, that tribunals have jurisdiction in contractual matters only in respect of a claim that 'arises or is outstanding on the termination of the employee's employment'. A tribunal was able to hear a claim for breach of a compromise agreement in Rock-It Cargo Ltd v Green 1997 IRLR 581, EAT, since the agreement in that case was concerned with the terms upon which the employee's employment was to be brought to an end. Most compromise agreements, however, are likely to be made some time after termination when a tribunal hearing of the unfair dismissal complaint is pending. Such agreements, if broken, will have to be enforced in the ordinary courts – see, for example, Miller Bros and FP Butler Ltd v Johnston 2002 ICR 744, EAT.

For further details of conciliated settlements and compromise agreements, see IDS Employment Law Handbook, 'Employment Tribunal Practice and Procedure' (2006), Chapter 9.

Dismissal procedures agreements
2.57

Section 110(1) ERA states that the right to claim unfair dismissal will be excluded where there is a valid dismissal procedures agreement between the parties. The agreement must be approved by the Secretary of State: if this is done, rights under the agreement are substituted for statutory unfair dismissal rights. Various criteria must be met before an agreement can be approved – e.g. the remedies provided for unfair dismissal must be on the whole as beneficial as those provided by the ERA and the procedures must include a right to arbitration or, at the very least, the right to arbitration on a point of law – S.110(3).

Time limits

2.58

Employees who have the right to claim unfair dismissal will generally lose that right if they fail to present their claim to a tribunal before the end of three months beginning with the effective date of termination – S.111(2)(a) ERA. (For discussion of the effective date of termination (EDT), see IDS Employment Law Handbook, 'Contracts of Employment' (2009), Chapter 11.) Tribunals have a discretion to extend the time limit if the claimant can show that it was not reasonably practicable to put the claim in on time *and* that the claim has been submitted within a reasonable time of its becoming practicable to present the complaint – S.111(2)(b). (Note that there is one exception to this that applies to 'blacklisting' dismissals under S.104F. Where a complaint under that provision is presented out of time, the tribunal has a discretion to extend the time limit if, in all the circumstances of the case, it considers it 'just and equitable' to do so – S.111(5). This is the same test that applies in discrimination cases and is wider than the 'not reasonably practicable' test set out in S.111(2)(a). A full explanation of both tests can be found in IDS Employment Law Handbook, 'Employment Tribunal Practice and Procedure' (2006), Chapter 3.)

2.59   **Effect of internal appeals.** In general, the fact that a claimant is pursuing an internal appeal against dismissal does not mean that he or she will be given extra time within which to present an unfair dismissal claim. Before its repeal on 6 April 2009, Reg 15(2) of the Employment Act 2002 (Dispute Resolution) Regulations 2004 SI 2004/752 automatically extended time by three months if, at the date when the normal time limit expired, the employee had reasonable grounds for believing that a dismissal or disciplinary procedure was being followed. In Ashcroft v Haberdashers' Aske's Boys' School 2008 ICR 613, EAT, the EAT considered a situation where there was an internal appeal but time was not automatically extended under the Dispute Resolution Regulations (because the result of the appeal was communicated to the claimant six hours *before* the expiry of the time limit). The EAT observed the Regulations' objective of promoting dispute resolution over litigation, and held that in such circumstances, when assessing whether it was reasonably practicable for the claim to have been brought in time under S.111(2)(b), tribunals should look at the period *after* the conclusion of the appeal and *before* the expiry of the time limit, rather than at the entire three-month period. Applying those principles, the EAT held that it was not reasonably practicable for A to have presented his claim in the six hours between the conclusion of his internal appeal and the expiry of the time limit, and remitted the case to the tribunal to decide whether the claim had been submitted within a reasonable period after the expiry of the time limit.

However, it should be stressed that the conclusion reached in Ashcroft should be treated with some caution following the repeal of the Dispute Resolution Regulations. In Palmer and anor v Southend-on-Sea Borough Council 1984 ICR 372, CA, decided well before the Regulations were enacted in 2004, the Court of Appeal held that the existence of an internal appeal cannot by itself justify extending the time limit. The EAT in Ashcroft suggested that the 2004 Regulations effectively repealed the Court's decision on this point but, following the repeal of those Regulations, we suggest that tribunals should once again follow Palmer. Having said that, the existence of an internal appeal may nevertheless be one of a number of factors a tribunal takes into account in determining whether it was reasonably practicable for an employee to submit his or her claim within the three-month time limit.

Retrospective claims. It would seem that the fact that an employee was unaware of having a legal right to bring a claim of unfair dismissal is not a ground for the tribunal to exercise its discretion under S.111(2)(b). This issue was particularly significant in the light of European-led changes, which have removed, or threaten to remove, previous restrictions on the right to bring a claim. Most important of these was the abolition of the minimum hours threshold that had previously prevented many part-time employees from claiming unfair dismissal. The removal of the hours threshold created problems for employees who were dismissed prior to its abolition and who were unable to claim unfair dismissal as a result. Can employees in these circumstances bring proceedings retrospectively under the new law, or are such claims out of time?   **2.60**

This question arose in Biggs v Somerset County Council 1996 IRLR 203, CA, where B presented a claim for unfair dismissal 18 years after her dismissal from her part-time post, but within three months of the House of Lords' decision in R v Secretary of State for Employment ex parte Equal Opportunities Commission and anor 1994 ICR 317, HL, which held that the hours threshold was unlawful. The Court of Appeal, taking a highly restrictive approach, dismissed her claim on the ground that it was 'reasonably practicable' within the meaning of S.111(2)(b) ERA for B to have presented her claim within three months of her dismissal. The Court's reasoning was that the decision in the EOC case, rather than changing the law, was declaratory of what the law had always been, since the primacy of European law had been established by the European Communities Act 1972. The words 'reasonably practicable' are directed to difficulties faced by an individual claimant – for example, illness. There was no legal impediment to prevent someone who claimed to be unfairly dismissed in 1976 from

73

presenting a claim and arguing that the restriction on claims by part-time workers was indirectly discriminatory. In addition, B could not rely upon Article 157 of the Treaty on the Functioning of the European Union (then Article 119 of the EC Treaty) – which enshrines the principle of equal pay in EU law – to claim unfair dismissal and disapply UK time limits, since Article 157 did not confer a separate right to compensation for unfair dismissal.

For full details of time limits and all other aspects of bringing an unfair dismissal claim, see IDS Employment Law Handbook, 'Employment Tribunal Practice and Procedure' (2006).

3 Unfairness

> **Reason for dismissal**
>
> **Reasonableness of dismissal**
>
> **Fairness of internal procedure**
>
> **Automatically fair and unfair dismissals**

When a claim for unfair dismissal is being heard by a tribunal, there are various matters that need to be established. As the previous two chapters have explained, the employee will have to show that he or she was employed under a contract of employment and that he or she was, indeed, dismissed. The tribunal will also have to ascertain whether there is anything, such as the lack of one year's continuous service, that excludes the employee from bringing a claim. In this chapter we consider the central issue – the fairness or unfairness of the dismissal.

3.1

Section 98 of the Employment Rights Act 1996 (ERA) sets out how a tribunal should approach the question of whether a dismissal is fair. There are two stages:

- first, the employer must show the reason for the dismissal and that it is one of the potentially fair reasons set out in S.98(1) and (2) (which now include retirement by virtue of the Employment Equality (Age) Regulations 2006 SI 2996/1031)

- if the employer is successful at the first stage, the tribunal must then determine whether the dismissal was fair or unfair under S.98(3A) and (4). With the exception of retirement dismissals, this requires the tribunal to consider whether the employer acted reasonably in dismissing the employee for the reason given. Where the reason for the dismissal is retirement, this requires the tribunal to consider whether the employer has complied with various procedural obligations set out in Schedule 6 to the 2006 Regulations – S.98ZG (see Chapter 9 for further details).

In addition, there are a number of reasons for dismissal which are deemed to be 'automatically unfair'. If an employee is able to show that he or she was dismissed for one of these 'inadmissible' reasons, then the question of reasonableness does not arise.

In this chapter, we:

3.2

- deal with the general considerations that apply to showing the reason for dismissal: who has to show what; what happens if the employer puts forward the wrong reason; what happens if there is more than one reason for dismissal; and what happens if information comes to the attention of the employer after the decision to dismiss has been made

- consider the general approach taken by tribunals to the question of reasonableness

- look at the question of procedural unfairness – i.e. did the employer act unreasonably in failing to follow a fair procedure when dismissing the employee; and

- briefly discuss the automatically fair and unfair reasons for dismissal contained in the ERA (automatically unfair dismissals are discussed in greater depth in Chapter 10).

Note that this chapter is concerned with unfairness generally. Later chapters deal with the specific reasons for dismissal provided for in S.98(1) and (2) and consider fairness in those contexts. For purported retirement dismissals, separate statutory rules – and therefore separate considerations – apply, both to establishing whether the reason for dismissal was retirement and then to determining whether or not the dismissal was fair. These are discussed separately in Chapter 9.

3.3 Reason for dismissal

There are six potentially fair reasons for dismissal set out in S.98. These are:

- a reason related to the *capability or qualifications* of the employee for performing work of the kind which he or she was employed by the employer to do (see Chapters 4 and 5)

- a reason related to the *conduct* of the employee (see Chapter 6)

- the *retirement* of the employee (see Chapter 9)

- that the employee was redundant (see IDS Employment Law Handbook, 'Redundancy' (2008), Chapter 8)

- that the employee could not continue to work in the position he or she held without contravening (either on the employee's part or on that of the employer) *a duty or restriction imposed by or under an enactment* (see Chapter 7)

- *'some other substantial reason'* of a kind such as to justify the dismissal of an employee holding the position which that employee held (see Chapter 8).

It is up to the employer to show the reason for dismissal and that it was a potentially fair one – i.e. one that fell within the scope of S.98(1) and (2) and was capable of justifying the dismissal of the employee. The employer does not have to prove that it actually did justify the dismissal because that is a matter for the tribunal to assess when considering the question of reasonableness. As Lord Justice Griffiths put it in Gilham and ors v Kent County Council (No.2) 1985 ICR 233, CA: 'The hurdle over which the employer has to jump at this stage of an inquiry into an unfair dismissal complaint is designed to deter employers from dismissing employees for some trivial or unworthy reason. If he does so, the dismissal is deemed unfair without the need to look further into its merits. But if on the face of it the reason could justify the dismissal, then it passes as a substantial reason, and the inquiry moves on to [S.98(4)], and the question of reasonableness.'

The burden of proof on employers at this stage is not a heavy one. A 'reason for dismissal' has been described as: 'a set of facts known to the employer, or it may be of beliefs held by him, which cause him to dismiss the employee' – Abernethy v Mott, Hay and Anderson 1974 ICR 323, CA. In cases of dismissal for capability or conduct, where the statute only refers to a reason which 'relates to' either of these grounds, it is sufficient that the employer genuinely believed on reasonable grounds that the employee was incompetent or guilty of misconduct. The employer does not have to prove the offence or inadequacy – Alidair Ltd v Taylor 1978 ICR 445, CA. Furthermore, an honest belief held on reasonable grounds will be enough, even if it is wrong.   **3.4**

If, on the other hand, the dismissal is asserted to be for redundancy or because of a statutory ban on continued employment, the employer must show that what is being asserted is true – i.e. that the employee was in fact redundant as defined by statute or that an enactment did in fact prohibit continued employment. However, a genuine belief that redundancy or a statutory ban applies may, in certain circumstances, amount to 'some other substantial reason' justifying the dismissal of the employee – see, for example, Hounslow London Borough Council v Klusova 2008 ICR 396, CA.

The question of whether dismissal is 'by reason of retirement' must be determined in accordance with special procedural requirements set down in S.98ZA–98ZF ERA. Different considerations therefore apply – see Chapter 9.

Identification of reason   **3.5**

Employers sometimes incorrectly identify their reason for dismissal. This may be due to a genuine mistake about the law or may amount to a deliberate attempt to conceal the true reason. They may, for instance, be acting out of kindness, as where an employer dismisses for 'redundancy' when the real reason is incompetence or, less kindly, when the real reason relates to, for example, anti-union attitudes. A distinction must be drawn here between the facts (or beliefs) that caused the dismissal – crucial to ascertaining the reason for dismissal – and the label that the employer has attached to them, which is not normally determinative (although see 'Wrong label affecting fairness' below).

77

The general approach taken by tribunals is to discover the real reason behind the dismissal by examining all the facts (and beliefs) that caused it. They do not have to accept the employer's stated reason where supporting evidence is poor or where they suspect that there was an ulterior motive. For example, in Associated Society of Locomotive Engineers and Firemen v Brady 2006 IRLR 576, EAT, B, the General Secretary of the respondent trade union, was dismissed after a fracas at a workplace barbecue. The union argued that the dismissal was for misconduct. However, the EAT held that the tribunal had been entitled to find on the facts that the real reason for the dismissal was the employer's political antipathy towards B, irrespective of the fact that his misconduct might well have justified dismissal.

However, where the employer fails to show a potentially fair reason for dismissal, tribunals are not obliged to ascertain the real reason for dismissal if there is insufficient evidence to do so – Hertz (UK) Ltd v Ferrao EAT 0570/05. In these circumstances the dismissal will be unfair.

3.6 **Wrong label – same facts/beliefs.** Where the employer has made a genuine mistake and where the facts (or beliefs) that led the employer to dismiss were known to the employee at the time of the dismissal and those facts (or beliefs) were fully aired in the tribunal proceedings, the tribunal may ignore the wrong label. The leading case is:

- **Abernethy v Mott, Hay and Anderson** 1974 ICR 323, CA: A, a civil engineer, refused to work away from head office and was dismissed on the ground of 'redundancy'. When he brought an unfair dismissal claim, the employer stated that the reason for dismissal was redundancy and/or incapability. The tribunal held that A was not redundant and that there was no redundancy situation, but that he had been fairly dismissed on the ground of incapability. On appeal, A argued that the employer, having ostensibly dismissed him for redundancy, should not have been allowed to rely on a different reason before the tribunal. The Court of Appeal held that the employer was entitled to rely on the set of facts which led to A's dismissal. Since these facts were made clear to A at the time of dismissal, it did not matter that the employer attached the wrong legal label to them

In Jocic v London Borough of Hammersmith and Fulham and ors EAT 0194/07 it was the tribunal, not the employer, who introduced a different reason for the dismissal ('some other substantial reason' instead of redundancy). The EAT held that this substitution was no more than the attachment of a different label to precisely the same set of facts and had not caused any prejudice to J. It therefore upheld the tribunal's conclusion that the dismissal was fair on the basis of some other substantial reason. The EAT stated that if the difference between the reason relied upon by the employer and the reason found by the tribunal goes to facts and substance and might have made some substantial or significant difference to the way in which the hearing was conducted or in the material that would have been put before the tribunal, then the tribunal's substitution will be an error of law. Otherwise, the difference should be seen as one of relabelling, which is perfectly acceptable at law.

Wrong label – different facts/beliefs. Where the employee has not been confronted with the full and true nature of the allegations against him or her, nor had adequate opportunity to consider and answer those allegations, the dismissal is likely to be unfair. Two examples:

    3.7

- **Hotson v Wisbech Conservative Club** 1984 ICR 859, EAT: the stated reason for the dismissal of a club barmaid was gross inefficiency in handling bar takings (which related to her capability to perform her job). During the tribunal hearing of her unfair dismissal complaint the tribunal chairman (now called judge) suggested, and the employer's representative agreed, that the employer was really alleging dishonesty rather than inefficiency (in other words, misconduct). The tribunal proceeded to find the dismissal fair on the ground of suspected dishonesty. The EAT held that the difference between inefficiency and dishonesty was more than a mere change of label. The charge of dishonesty should have been stated at the outset or not stated at all: at the very least the employee should have had the fullest opportunity to consider the implications of the charge and to answer it. Here, therefore, the change of reason went to the very substance of the allegations leading to dismissal. It was not simply a matter of changing the label from capability to conduct since there was also a fundamental shift in the facts/beliefs leading to dismissal

- **Murphy v Epsom College** 1985 ICR 80, CA: M was dismissed on the ground of redundancy. A tribunal found that this was a fair dismissal either for redundancy or for 'some other substantial reason', without specifying what that reason was and despite the fact that the employer had never argued the latter as a ground for dismissal before the tribunal. The EAT agreed that this was a fair dismissal for redundancy, but said that the tribunal should not have found 'some other substantial reason' as this had been neither pleaded nor expressly raised at the tribunal: natural justice required that no party should have a case decided against them on a ground on which they have not had an opportunity to be heard. The Court of Appeal upheld the EAT's decision.

Wrong label affecting fairness. Although the label assigned to a particular set of facts will not normally be crucial, there will be situations in which it can affect the tribunal's assessment of fairness. It might, for example, make a significant difference to the way in which the hearing is conducted or to the material that is put before the tribunal – see Jocic v London Borough of Hammersmith and Fulham and ors (above). In London Borough of Hackney v Benn 1996 EWCA Civ 561, CA, the employer had, in accordance with a detailed disciplinary code, classified B's manifest failure to do her job properly

    3.8

79

as gross misconduct and dismissed her without warning. The tribunal found that B was actually dismissed for incapacity and that she should therefore have been given a warning about the standard of her work. The Court of Appeal held that the tribunal had substituted its own view for that of a reasonable employer. In a case where such a detailed disciplinary code was followed so carefully, a tribunal should be slow to find that the employer had misdescribed the reason for dismissal. While the label to be attached to a particular set of facts leading to dismissal was not normally crucial, in this case it had impeded the tribunal in considering what the range of reasonable responses to that particular set of facts was. A finding of fair dismissal was substituted.

Two contrasting cases:

- **Wilson v Post Office** 2000 IRLR 834, CA: W was dismissed for unacceptable levels of short-term absence. In its response to W's tribunal claim for unfair dismissal, the Post Office cited 'incapability by reason of unsatisfactory attendance record' as the reason for dismissal. The tribunal went on to find that the reason for dismissal was incapability on the ground of ill health and that the dismissal was unfair. The Court of Appeal remitted the case, ruling that the real reason for dismissal had not been capability but W's failure to comply with the Post Office's attendance procedure, which fell within 'some other substantial reason'. Therefore, different factors needed to be taken into account when judging the reasonableness of the dismissal, with W's future health prospects carrying less weight than they would in a capability dismissal

- **Williams v Cheshire Fire and Rescue Service** EAT 0621/07: W was dismissed because of his poor absence record and the EAT held that the tribunal was entitled to find that the reason for dismissal was conduct. The fact that the Rescue Service had submitted that the dismissal was for capability or some other substantial reason did not oblige the tribunal to accept that analysis. Once it had identified the reason, the tribunal had considered the totality of the circumstances in deciding whether the dismissal was within the band of reasonable responses. This, said the EAT, was 'markedly different' to the situation in Wilson (above) where the tribunal had concentrated on the state of the claimant's health when looking at the question of reasonableness.

3.9 **Reason expressly rejected by employer.** Tribunals are not entitled to find a dismissal fair for a reason that the employer could have relied on but expressly decided against. In Trico-Folberth Ltd v Devonshire 1989 ICR 747, CA, D had a very bad record of sickness absences, had received formal verbal and written warnings and, after a final absence of seven weeks, was dismissed because of her attendance record. At an internal appeal the employer rescinded the dismissal and instead decided to terminate D's employment on medical grounds. A tribunal said that dismissal because of D's attendance record would

80

have been perfectly fair: the employer had taken the appropriate procedural steps and could not be expected to tolerate D's attendance record any longer. But the employer had deliberately chosen not to dismiss D on that ground. Instead she had been dismissed on medical grounds and this was wholly unfair because there had been no medical investigation of D's condition and no consultation with her. It was immaterial that the employer could have dismissed D fairly for another reason because the employer had made it plain that she was not going to be dismissed for that other reason. Both the EAT and the Court of Appeal upheld the tribunal's decision.

Change of reason by employer on appeal to the EAT. An employer will not generally be allowed to change its pleaded reason for dismissal on appeal from a tribunal decision. The leading case here is:

3.10

- **Nelson v BBC (No.1)** 1977 ICR 649, CA: N was a BBC radio producer who was dismissed on the ground of redundancy. A tribunal found this a fair dismissal for redundancy but the EAT, on appeal, thought that there was probably no redundancy but instead a fair dismissal for 'some other substantial reason', saying that the difference in labels was 'only a very technical point'. N appealed further. The Court of Appeal held that N was not redundant as argued by the BBC. Redundancy had been the only defence pleaded before the tribunal and there had been no application to amend the defence. The BBC should not have been allowed to raise a quite different ground for dismissal on appeal and this was not merely a technical point. The EAT had erred in applying the tribunal's findings of fact, made in the context of a redundancy dismissal, as if they had been found in relation to a dismissal for some other substantial reason which was a completely different defence. The BBC had not established its pleaded reason for dismissal, so N's dismissal was unfair.

In fact, in the Nelson case the employer's argument rested on a very narrow and legally mistaken interpretation of N's contract: the conduct of the case on both sides would have been quite different if the employer had argued 'some other substantial reason' as the reason for dismissal or indeed if the tribunal of its own accord had decided that the dismissal was for some other substantial reason, as happened in Hannan v TNT-IPEC (UK) Ltd 1986 IRLR 165, EAT. In that case, the EAT held that the difference was simply and genuinely one of labels; that all the facts and issues had been fully canvassed at the tribunal hearing; and, most importantly, that the complainant would not have conducted his case differently in any significant way if he had known the course that the tribunal was going to take. No injustice had been suffered and the EAT refused to interfere with the tribunal's decision.

In summary, employers should be careful to plead the right reason for dismissal. If in doubt, they should plead in the alternative – e.g. 'dismissal was because of redundancy or, alternatively, for some other substantial reason

81

resulting from the reorganisation of the business'. Tribunals may find dismissal to have been for an unpleaded reason – i.e. they may correct the employer's label – but only if all the issues have been ventilated at the hearing and there has been no prejudice to the complainant. Further, as the Nelson case shows, if the tribunal fails to correct the label, the employer will generally be unable to introduce a new label upon appeal.

3.11 Multiple reasons for dismissal

Employers may have more than one reason for dismissal: indeed, in the case of a particularly unsatisfactory employee, they may have several. The statute, however, requires them to show the reason or, if there was more than one, the principal reason for the dismissal – S.98(1)(a).

This provision is aimed at preventing employers from putting forward multiple reasons under different headings in the hope that one or two might be accepted by the tribunal, a tactic used in Smith v Glasgow City District Council 1987 ICR 796, HL. In that case S was a senior deputy director in the Council's Works Department who was dismissed after an internal investigation by a special committee. In a letter to S from the committee, four reasons for dismissal were set out, all relating to conduct or capability. A tribunal found that the employer had not established the second charge against S (which was agreed to have been a particularly serious one); it also indicated that it viewed the fourth charge as less serious than the others. Nevertheless, the tribunal held that dismissal was fair in all the circumstances and the EAT agreed. The House of Lords, upholding the Court of Session, held that the tribunal had found that one serious charge against S was neither established in fact nor believed to be true on reasonable grounds. The Council had failed to show what the principal reason for dismissal was and, in any case, it was not shown that the charge which was not established was neither the principal reason for dismissal nor formed part of the principal reason. Since what was at least an important part of the reason for dismissal was not made out at all, the tribunal should have found that the Council had failed to show a reason and that S's dismissal was consequently unfair.

The decision in Smith's case will apply when the employer is alleging a composite reason for dismissal and fails to establish a significant element. But if the employer is alleging different grounds for dismissal and that each ground justified dismissal independently of the others, it will probably be sufficient if at least one of the grounds is established (provided the tribunal agrees that it was the principal reason for dismissal and that it would justify dismissal independently of the other grounds) – Carlin v St Cuthbert's Co-operative Association Ltd 1974 IRLR 188, NIRC.

3.12

It will be different if the employer simply categorises the same matters in two different ways as reasons for dismissal. In Shakespeare and anor v National Coal Board, unreported 30.3.88, CA, two miners were dismissed for aggressive and threatening behaviour towards colleagues who had worked during the miners' strike. The NCB gave as reasons for dismissal contraventions of S.90 of the Mines and Quarries Act 1954 and Reg 9 of the General Duties and Conduct Regulations 1956. It was later conceded that S.90 was not a proper ground for dismissal and had been cited in error. It was argued that since it was unknown whether or not S.90 formed the principal reason for dismissal, the NCB had failed to show a valid reason for dismissal. The Court of Appeal rejected this argument, saying that it was perfectly clear what the reason for dismissal was – the alleged conduct of the two miners. The fact that the NCB had tried to pin two different labels on it was immaterial. Therefore, the Court of Appeal upheld the tribunal's decision that the dismissals were fair.

Employers will clearly fail, however, if they allege two different grounds as the reason for dismissal and the tribunal rejects both. In O'Grady v Cookshop Supplies ET Case No.31001/83, for example, the employer dismissed a shop assistant to make economies but found that the shop could not do without her and a (lower-paid) replacement was recruited a month later. The employer pleaded redundancy and/or 'some other substantial reason' for dismissal. The tribunal said that there was no redundancy, simply an unsuccessful experiment that proved that the requirement for employees had not diminished. Nor was there a substantial reason for dismissal because the saving in wages was insignificant in relation to the shop's turnover. It followed that no reason for dismissal had been shown.

Constructive dismissal 3.13

Constructive dismissals can pose problems for employers when explaining their reasons for dismissal. When an employee claims that he or she has been unfairly constructively dismissed, there has not in fact been any 'dismissal' at all by the employer. The employee has resigned as a result of the employer's fundamental breach of contract and a kind of legal fiction converts this into a dismissal. However, despite the fact that the employer has not expressly dismissed the employee he must still show the reason for dismissal.

In this situation, the reason for dismissal is the reason for which the employer breached the contract of employment – see Lord Justice Browne-Wilkinson in Berriman v Delabole Slate Ltd 1985 ICR 546, CA. Typically, the employer's reason for dismissal will be 'some other substantial reason' – see Chapter 8. For example, in Genower v Ealing, Hammersmith and Hounslow Area Health Authority 1980 IRLR 297, EAT, the employer moved G to a different job in breach of contract. The reason for doing so was 'some other substantial reason' – the fact that the employer was carrying out a reorganisation of the business. Since the tribunal had found that the employer had good reason for moving staff around and that it had adopted a fair procedure, the EAT upheld the tribunal's decision that the dismissal was fair.

83

3.14   If an employer does not attempt to show a potentially fair reason at all in a constructive dismissal case but instead simply relies on the argument that there was no dismissal, a tribunal will be under no obligation to investigate the reason for dismissal (or its reasonableness) for itself – Derby City Council v Marshall 1979 ICR 731, EAT. This essentially means that the dismissal, if shown, will be automatically unfair because no reason for dismissal has been given.

Therefore, it will always be the safest course for employers to plead a reason for dismissal even if they are denying that the employee was ever dismissed – i.e. denying that they were in fundamental breach of contract. The new Response Form (ET3) – introduced in April 2009 following the repeal of the statutory disciplinary and grievance procedures – no longer requires the respondent to specifically answer the question: 'Was the claimant dismissed?' However, in Section 5 of the form – which requires the respondent to set out the grounds of resistance – the employer should start by denying that the employee was dismissed, setting out the grounds for so doing. He should then put forward an alternative ground of resistance, i.e. on the basis that the employee was dismissed, using some form of words such as: 'Alternatively, if, which is denied, the claimant was dismissed, the dismissal was for some other substantial reason justifying dismissal and was not unfair in all the circumstances.' Tribunals often do find constructive dismissals to be fair, but only if the employer has shown the reason for dismissal and is found to have acted reasonably.

3.15   **Reason must apply at the time of the dismissal**
In determining the reason for a dismissal, the tribunal may only take account of those facts (or beliefs) that were known to the employer *at the time of the dismissal*. This means that no account will be taken of matters coming to light or occurring after the dismissal has taken place – W Devis and Sons Ltd v Atkins 1977 ICR 662, HL. Thus, if an employee is dismissed on the employer's whim for no reason at all, the dismissal will not be made retrospectively fair if the employer later finds out that the employee had been engaged in long-standing and large-scale embezzlement from the company that would have amply justified the dismissal if it had been discovered earlier. But such matters will be very relevant in assessing compensation – see Chapters 16 and 18.

That said, where an employee is dismissed with notice the dismissal does not take place until the notice expires, so a tribunal may take account of events which occurred during the notice period, as well as the reason stated in the notice, in order to establish the real reason for dismissal – Parkinson v March Consulting Ltd 1998 ICR 276, CA. In Williamson v Alcan (UK) Ltd 1978 ICR 104, EAT, the employee was dismissed because of his chronic ill health, but there was medical evidence from a specialist that he had made a spontaneous recovery during the notice period. The case was remitted to a different tribunal to reconsider in light of the new evidence. In doing so, the EAT stated that if –

84

after the date notice of dismissal was given and before the contract had actually come to an end – the employer acquired information which would indicate that it ought not to have dismissed the employee, that dismissal could well become unfair if it did not withdraw the notice.

That case was followed in Stacey v Babcock Power Ltd 1986 ICR 221, EAT, where the employee was fairly dismissed for redundancy with three months' notice. During the notice period the employer obtained a new contract for which a number of new workers were recruited. However, the dismissed employee was not offered a job. The EAT held that the events during the notice period turned what was initially a fair dismissal into an unfair one.

Evidence of events after dismissal may, exceptionally, serve as **3.16** corroboration of an employer's reason for dismissal. In W Devis and Sons Ltd v Atkins 1976 ICR 196, QBD, Mr Justice Phillips gave the example of an employee dismissed for drunkenness at work and thought that subsequent evidence of habitual insobriety would be relevant in corroborating evidence of earlier drunkenness.

An employer cannot use information obtained during an internal appeal hearing against dismissal to substitute a *different* reason for dismissal – Monie v Coral Racing Ltd 1981 ICR 109, CA. However, the House of Lords held in West Midlands Co-operative Society Ltd v Tipton 1986 ICR 192, HL, that information revealed in the course of an internal appeal that relates to the original reason for dismissal should be taken into account when considering the fairness of that dismissal, irrespective of whether the internal appeal takes place before or after the dismissal has been effected. This case is dealt with further under 'Reasonableness of dismissal' and 'Fairness of internal procedure' below. (For more information on internal appeals see Chapter 6 under 'Disciplinary proceedings'.)

Industrial pressure to dismiss
3.17
An employer can be faced with a situation in which the workforce demands, for whatever reason, that a certain employee be dismissed, and backs up this demand by taking, or threatening to take, industrial action. S.107 ERA states that in such a case an employer who responds to the action by dismissing the employee in question will not be able to rely on the industrial pressure as the reason for the dismissal if the employee subsequently brings a claim before a tribunal. Questions as to the main reason for dismissal and whether it was reasonable to dismiss for that reason will be decided as if no such pressure had been exerted.

Section 107, therefore, creates a legal fiction whereby the real reason for dismissal has to be ignored. So, if the only reason for the dismissal the employer can show is pressure from industrial action, the tribunal is bound to find the dismissal unfair because the employer has failed to establish a

85

potentially fair reason as required by S.98(1) ERA. Thus, in Hazells Offset Ltd v Luckett 1977 IRLR 430, EAT, a studio manager was dismissed because union representatives indicated to the employer that they would not work with him. The EAT agreed with the tribunal that the real reason for the dismissal was union pressure accompanied by threats of industrial action. But S.107 prevented the employer from saying so and prevented the tribunal from taking account of the real reason for dismissal. Since the real reason could not be put forward, the employer was unable to show a reason at all and the dismissal was therefore unfair.

If, however, the employer had another reason for dismissal – even if it was not the principal reason – the tribunal will ignore the industrial pressure and determine the fairness of the dismissal on the merits of the subsidiary reason. But the very fact that it was a subsidiary reason may mean that it is unlikely to have had sufficient bearing on the decision to dismiss to make the decision for the subsidiary reason fair.

For further information on industrial pressure to dismiss, see IDS Employment Law Handbook, 'Industrial Action' (2010), Chapter 10.

3.18 **Written reasons for dismissal**

Dismissed employees with one year's continuous service have the right to ask their employers for a written statement giving particulars of the reasons for their dismissal. These statements are admissible in tribunal proceedings as evidence of the employer's reasons for dismissal. Employees dismissed while they are pregnant or during ordinary or additional maternity or adoption leave are entitled to such a statement without having to request it and regardless of their length of service – see Chapter 21 for further details.

3.19 ## Reasonableness of dismissal

Once an employer has shown a potentially fair reason for dismissal, the tribunal must go on to decide whether the dismissal for that reason was fair or unfair. In respect of retirement dismissals, the fairness or otherwise of the dismissal must be determined in accordance with S.98ZG ERA – see Chapter 9 for further details. In respect of the five other potentially fair reasons (i.e. capability or qualifications, conduct, redundancy, statutory duty or 'some other substantial reason'), the tribunal must decide whether the employer acted reasonably or unreasonably in dismissing for the reason given in accordance with S.98(4).

Section 98(4) provides that: 'the determination of the question whether the dismissal is fair or unfair (having regard to the reason shown by the employer) – (a) depends on whether in the circumstances (including the size and administrative resources of the employer's undertaking) the employer acted reasonably or unreasonably in treating it as a sufficient reason for dismissing

86

the employee, and (b) shall be determined in accordance with equity and the substantial merits of the case'.

In other words, it is not enough that the employer has a reason that is capable **3.20** of justifying dismissal. The tribunal must be satisfied that, in all the circumstances, the employer was actually justified in dismissing for that reason. In this regard, there is no burden of proof on either party, and the issue of whether the dismissal was reasonable is a neutral one for the tribunal to decide – Boys and Girls Welfare Society v Macdonald 1997 ICR 693, EAT. Thus in Makro Self Service Wholesalers Ltd v Rees EAT 0559/07, where R was dismissed for sexual harassment at work, the EAT held that a tribunal had erred in law by finding that the employer had failed to establish that there were reasonable grounds for believing that R was guilty of the alleged misconduct, since this wrongly placed the burden of proof on the employer.

Whether or not an employer has acted reasonably is not a question of law. The wording of S.98(4) has the effect of giving tribunals a wide discretion to base their decisions on the facts of the case before them and in the light of good industrial relations practice – Union of Construction, Allied Trades and Technicians v Brain 1981 ICR 542, CA. But while the question is essentially one of fact, the appellate courts have nevertheless developed certain general principles, some of which have crystallised into principles of law. Chapters 4 to 8 deal with the different potentially fair grounds for dismissal whose fairness is determined under S.98(4) and the principles that are applied in those particular contexts, e.g. sickness, misconduct, etc.

The important point to note about the reasonableness test is that it is the **3.21** employer's conduct which the tribunals have to assess, not the unfairness or injustice to the employee. An example:

- **Chubb Fire Security Ltd v Harper** 1983 IRLR 311, EAT: H was dismissed for refusing to accept a considerable drop in income on the reorganisation of his employer's business. A tribunal decided that the employer had acted unreasonably. The EAT held that the tribunal had applied S.98(4) incorrectly. It had made no finding as to the advantages to the employer of the reorganisation and the reasonableness of its implementation and appeared to have concentrated its approach on the reasonableness of H's belief that the change to his terms and conditions would be disadvantageous to him. It had erred in not asking the right question – did the employer act reasonably in dismissing H for his refusal to accept the new term? In answering that question the tribunal should have considered whether the employer was acting reasonably in deciding that the advantages to the company of implementing the proposed reorganisation outweighed any disadvantage which H might suffer. The mere fact that an employee is reasonable in refusing disadvantageous

87

changes does not, therefore, mean that an employer is unreasonable in dismissing for that refusal.

As the Chubb case itself demonstrates, injustice to the employee is not completely ignored and will be balanced against the benefits gained by the employer when considering whether the employer acted reasonably. However, in another case on similar facts – Richmond Precision Engineering Ltd v Pearce 1985 IRLR 179, EAT – the EAT stated that the task of weighing the advantages to the employer against the disadvantages to the employee is merely one factor which tribunals have to take into account when asking whether the employer acted reasonably. The tribunal in that case should also have considered whether the offer to P of less favourable terms was one which a reasonable employer could have made in the circumstances which faced RPE Ltd and whether RPE Ltd acted unreasonably in treating P's refusal of the offer as a reason for dismissing him.

3.22   **Tribunals must not substitute their own views**
The test of whether or not the employer acted reasonably is usually expressed as an objective one – i.e. tribunals must use their own collective wisdom as industrial juries to determine 'the way in which a reasonable employer in those circumstances, in that line of business, would have behaved' – NC Watling and Co Ltd v Richardson 1978 IRLR 255, EAT. Nonetheless, there is also a subjective element involved inasmuch as tribunals must also take account of the honest beliefs of the employer at the time of the dismissal.

What tribunals must not do is put themselves in the position of the employer and consider what they themselves would have done in the circumstances. They must not usurp a function which is properly that of management. What a tribunal must decide is not what it would have done if it had been management, but whether the employer acted reasonably – Grundy (Teddington) Ltd v Willis 1976 ICR 323, QBD. As the Court of Appeal explained in Foley v Post Office; HSBC Bank plc (formerly Midland Bank plc) v Madden 2000 ICR 1283, CA, although members of the tribunal can substitute their decision for that of the employer, that decision must not be reached by a process of substituting themselves for the employer and forming an opinion of what they would have done had they been the employer.

3.23   In London Ambulance Service NHS Trust v Small 2009 IRLR 563, CA, the Court of Appeal held that a tribunal had slipped into the 'substitution mindset' and wrongly substituted its own view for that of the employer regarding the reasonableness of S's dismissal for misconduct. When determining the issue of liability, the tribunal should have confined its consideration of the facts to those found by the Trust at the time of dismissal. Instead, it had referred to its own findings of fact about S's conduct, including facts that had been disputed at the disciplinary hearing. Although the tribunal was bound to come to its own view for the purpose of deciding the extent to which S *contributed* to his dismissal, that was a different issue. The decision on contributory fault was one for the

88

tribunal to make if it decided that the dismissal was unfair. However, the decision to dismiss was for the Trust to make. Lord Justice Mummery suggested that, as a general rule, it might be better practice for the tribunal to keep its findings of fact relevant to the employer's decision to dismiss separate from its findings of facts that are only relevant to other issues such as contributory fault.

Another example of a tribunal wrongly substituting its opinion for that of the employer can be found in The North West London Hospitals NHS Trust v Bowater EAT 0144/09. B, a staff nurse, was dismissed for gross misconduct following a comment she made while straddling the naked genitals of a patient who was suffering from a fit, the comment being: 'It's been a few months since I have been in this position with a man underneath me.' The tribunal held that B was unfairly dismissed. It found that at worst the comment could have been described as lewd but a large proportion of the population would have considered it to be merely humorous. The EAT allowed the employer's appeal, holding that – in finding that the employee's remark would have been regarded as merely humorous by some – the tribunal had taken into account an irrelevant factor. Instead, it should have considered how that comment would have been treated by a reasonable NHS Trust, and whether the decision to dismiss, when it was made, had been outside the band of responses of a reasonable Trust in those circumstances.

Tribunals should be careful not to substitute their own judgment where an employee is dismissed for breach of an employer's policy, such as a substance abuse policy. They should not attempt to determine whether the employee was actually in breach. Instead they should assess whether the employer's interpretation and application of the policy was reasonable in the circumstances – BP Chemicals v Fitzpatrick EAT 67/05.

The 'band (or range) of reasonable responses' test   3.24
Employers often have at their disposal a range of reasonable responses to matters such as the misconduct or incapability of an employee, which may span summary dismissal down to an informal warning. It is inevitable that different employers will choose different options. In recognition of this fact, and in order to provide a 'standard' of reasonableness that tribunals can apply, the 'band of reasonable responses' approach was formulated. This requires tribunals to ask: Did the employer's action fall within the band (or range) of reasonable responses open to an employer?

This approach was approved by the Court of Appeal in British Leyland (UK) Ltd v Swift 1981 IRLR 91, CA, where Lord Denning MR said: 'The correct test is: Was it reasonable for the employers to dismiss him? If no reasonable employer would have dismissed him, then the dismissal was unfair. But if a reasonable employer might reasonably have dismissed him, then the dismissal was fair. It must be remembered that in all these cases there is a band of reasonableness, within which one employer might reasonably take one view: another quite reasonably take a different view.'

3.25 The test was applied in Iceland Frozen Foods Ltd v Jones 1983 ICR 17, EAT, where a tribunal had phrased its finding of unfair dismissal as follows: '*in our view* neither of the applicant's faults, either singly or taken together, came anywhere near being sufficiently serious to make it reasonable to dismiss him applying the provisions of [S.98(4)]' (our stress). The EAT held that the tribunal had misdirected itself by substituting its own opinion for the objective test of the band of reasonable responses. Mr Justice Browne-Wilkinson summarised the law concisely and his summary is frequently quoted and applied by tribunals:

'Since the present state of the law can only be found by going through a number of different authorities, it may be convenient if we should seek to summarise the present law. We consider that the authorities establish that in law the correct approach for the… tribunal to adopt in answering the question posed by [S.98(4)] is as follows:

(1) the starting point should always be the words of [S.98(4)] themselves;

(2) in applying the section [a] tribunal must consider the reasonableness of the employer's conduct, not simply whether they (the members of the… tribunal) consider the dismissal to be fair;

(3) in judging the reasonableness of the employer's conduct [a] tribunal must not substitute its decision as to what was the right course to adopt for that of the employer;

(4) in many (though not all) cases there is a band of reasonable responses to the employee's conduct within which one employer might reasonably take one view, another quite reasonably take another;

(5) the function of the… tribunal, as an industrial jury, is to determine whether in the particular circumstances of each case the decision to dismiss the employee fell within the band of reasonable responses which a reasonable employer might have adopted. If the dismissal falls within the band the dismissal is fair: if the dismissal falls outside the band it is unfair.'

3.26 Following a number of cases that challenged the primacy of the 'band of reasonable responses' test, it was emphatically reaffirmed by the Court of Appeal in Foley v Post Office; HSBC Bank plc (formerly Midland Bank plc) v Madden 2000 ICR 1283, CA. Lord Justice Mummery confirmed that the test as expounded in Iceland Frozen Foods remained binding on employment tribunals. He explained further that cases involving extreme facts did not render the 'range of reasonable responses' test perverse or unhelpful. It is simply that the approach will not be required in every case. He said: 'There will be cases in which there is no band or range to consider. If, for example, an employee, without good cause, deliberately sets fire to his employer's factory and it is burnt to the ground, dismissal is the only reasonable response. If an employee is dismissed for politely saying "good morning" to his line manager,

90

that would be an unreasonable response. But in between these extreme cases there will be cases where there is room for reasonable disagreement among reasonable employers as to whether dismissal for the particular misconduct is a reasonable or an unreasonable response. In those cases it is helpful for the tribunal to consider "the range of reasonable responses".'

A case where dismissal fell just inside the range of reasonable responses:

- **Rawley v National Car Parks** ET Case No.2205017/06: R and some of her colleagues were invited to a drinks party by Westminster City Council, which was in negotiations for a contract with NCP. A colleague had concerns about R's behaviour during the party and rang her manager, who texted R's mobile phone saying she needed to go home and he would speak to her the next day. She replied that she would go when she wished. When he advised her strongly to go home, she sent a text saying, 'sack me I don't care'. She was called to a disciplinary hearing, where she admitted to being 'happily drunk and the life and soul of the party'. She was summarily dismissed for acting in a discourteous manner to a client and bringing NCP into disrepute. The tribunal considered that the decision to dismiss was somewhat severe and that it would have imposed a written warning. However, it reminded itself that it could not substitute its view for that of the employer. It held that the decision to dismiss was close to the boundary of the range of reasonable responses, but was just within it.

In Royal Bank of Scotland Group plc v Wilson EAT 0363/08 the EAT cautioned against the use of emotive language by tribunals when considering the reasonableness of dismissal. W, a personal mortgage adviser, had arranged a mortgage with a customer on behalf of her son and daughter-in-law. Without seeing the couple or obtaining their signed consent, W submitted an electronic mortgage application to the Bank's mortgage department with instructions that, contrary to its normal practice, it was not to withdraw the application fee from the prospective mortgagors' account. However, the department did withdraw the fee from the account. The couple decided not to proceed with the application and complained that the fee had been withdrawn without their consent. W was subsequently dismissed for gross misconduct. The tribunal held that this fell 'well outside' the range of reasonable responses, being a 'gross over-reaction' to a technical error, which had no serious consequences. The tribunal had 'little sympathy' for the Bank, considering that it only had itself to blame for any embarrassment which arose.

In the EAT's judgment, the tribunal's reasoning demonstrated that, while endorsing the 'range of reasonable responses' test, in reality it had substituted its own decision for that of the employer. The tribunal's conclusion that W's was 'an error of a technical nature' and that he did no more than 'cut a bureaucratic corner' was plainly not how the Bank viewed the matter. The

3.27

91

question for the tribunal was whether it was reasonable for the Bank to take the view that it was a serious and not a technical matter: and this depended, at least in part, on whether the Bank had brought home to W by its training and procedures what his role was and why the Bank placed importance on the training and procedures it had implemented. The EAT noted the 'unusually robust' language used by the tribunal and observed that a tribunal is always wise to look with particular care at its reasoning and findings of fact before it expresses criticism in emotive language. Expressions of indignation were not a substitute for, and were often inimical to, careful findings of fact and application of the law.

3.28   As the cases show, the application of the range of reasonable responses test is not an exact science and, certainly in borderline cases, there is scope for different tribunals to apply the test differently. Therefore the decisions they reach will be difficult to challenge unless the tribunal has, while purporting to apply the test, clearly substituted its own judgment – see 'Appeals to EAT' below.

Note that the 'range of reasonable responses' test applies not only to the decision to dismiss but also to the procedure by which that decision is reached – J Sainsbury plc v Hitt 2003 ICR 111, CA; Whitbread plc (t/a Whitbread Medway Inns) v Hall 2001 ICR 699, CA. See 'Fairness of internal procedure – general factors' below for further details.

3.29   **Reasonableness test applies at the time of dismissal**
In determining the reasonableness of an employer's decision to dismiss, the tribunal may only take account of those facts (or beliefs) that were known to the employer at the time of the dismissal. (The same applies when determining the actual reason for dismissal – see above.) A dismissal will not be made reasonable by events which occur after the dismissal has taken place – W Devis and Sons Ltd v Atkins 1977 ICR 662, HL.

It is therefore important for employers to establish 'the time of the dismissal'. In Alboni v Ind Coope Retail Ltd 1998 IRLR 131, CA, the Court of Appeal said that legislation made it plain that a dismissal means the actual termination of employment, and not the giving of notice. Therefore, when determining the reasonableness of a dismissal, a tribunal must have regard to what occurred between the date the employee was given notice and the date on which dismissal took effect, and not simply to the facts known to the employer when notice was given.

There may be occasions where an employee is summarily dismissed but has a right to an internal appeal. If the appeal is successful, then the employee is retrospectively reinstated as if there were no dismissal, whereas if the appeal is unsuccessful then the dismissal stands. The question of how to treat information gained during an internal appeal was dealt with in West Midlands

Co-operative Society Ltd v Tipton 1986 ICR 192, HL. In that case the House of Lords said, in relation to contracts of employment providing an appeals procedure, that both the original and the appellate decision by an employer to dismiss are necessary elements in the overall process of dismissal. To separate them and to consider only one half of the process in determining whether the employer acted reasonably in dismissing an employee is artificial. Therefore, although it would be wrong for an employer to dismiss an employee for a reason which only surfaced during the appeals process, a tribunal should consider facts which came to light during the appeal in considering whether the employer's decision to dismiss was reasonable.

Size and administrative resources of the employer's undertaking   3.30
In determining whether the employer acted reasonably in the circumstances, the tribunal must have regard to the 'size and administrative resources of the employer's undertaking' – S.98(4)(a) ERA. There are two situations in which these factors are particularly significant in determining reasonableness:

- when assessing what kind of disciplinary procedure and, particularly, internal appeals machinery is practicable for the employer

- when there is a question as to whether suitable alternative work should have been provided for the employee, for example in redundancy cases or in cases where the employee is no longer capable of doing his or her current job but could perform less onerous tasks.

Some examples: 3.31

- **Royal Naval School v Hughes** 1979 IRLR 383, EAT: a tribunal had criticised a girls' boarding-school for not providing a mechanism to appeal beyond the board of governors who took the decision to dismiss. The EAT thought this criticism unfounded and pointed out that it could be impossible to provide an apparatus for higher appeals in a small organisation

- **Appleyard v FM Smith (Hull) Ltd** 1972 IRLR 19, ET: it was fair to dismiss a maintenance fitter/driver who lost his driving licence in a small firm with only three fitters – although it might not have been in a large firm

- **MacKellar v Bolton** 1979 IRLR 59, EAT: the dismissal of a doctor's receptionist was held to be fair. The EAT pointed out that a GP 'is not armed with an elaborate personnel department and a number of subsidiary commanders between him and [his receptionist]'. Nor, when patients complain, is it reasonable to expect him to arrange a formal disciplinary hearing with witnesses

- **Bevan Harris Ltd (t/a The Clyde Leather Co) v Gair** 1981 IRLR 520, EAT: the dismissal of a foreman on the ground of capability was found to be fair. The EAT held that it was unreasonable, in view of the small size of the business, to expect the employers to demote instead of dismissing, even if an alternative job was available.

Size and administrative resources will not, however, excuse a total absence of proper procedural steps. In De Grasse v Stockwell Tools Ltd 1992 IRLR 269, EAT, a small firm dismissed a machinist for redundancy with no warning, consultation or consideration of alternative employment. The EAT held that the fact that an employer is a small undertaking may affect the nature or formality of the consultation process – i.e. it may be informal – but it cannot excuse a total lack of consultation.

3.32 Equity

Section 98(4)(b) requires tribunals to determine the reasonableness of a dismissal 'in accordance with equity and the substantial merits of the case'. Equity, in this context, is equivalent to 'fair play' and is invoked particularly when a dismissed employee complains that his or her employer has dealt more leniently with other employees in similar circumstances.

Inconsistency of punishment for misconduct may give rise to a finding of unfair dismissal, as the Court of Appeal recognised in Post Office v Fennell 1981 IRLR 221, CA. In that case F had been dismissed for striking a colleague during a quarrel in the canteen. A tribunal found the dismissal unfair, pointing out that the Post Office had acted differently in comparable cases, and ordered re-engagement. In the Court of Appeal Lord Justice Brandon cited the words 'having regard to equity and the substantial merits of the case' contained in S.57(3) of the Employment Protection (Consolidation) Act 1978 (the precursor to S.98(4) ERA) and said: 'It seems to me that the expression "equity" as there used comprehends the concept that employees who misbehave in much the same way should have meted out to them much the same punishment, and it seems to me that [a] tribunal is entitled to say that, where that is not done, and one man is penalised much more heavily than others who have committed similar offences in the past, the employer has not acted reasonably in treating whatever the offence is as a sufficient reason for dismissal.'

Brandon LJ made two further observations. First, it is for the tribunal to decide whether, on the facts, there was sufficient evidence of inconsistent treatment. As he pointed out, the tribunal would have less detailed information regarding other cases allegedly dealt with more leniently by the employer than the information in the case before it. His second point stressed that while a degree of consistency was necessary, there must also be considerable latitude in the way in which an individual employer deals with particular cases.

3.33

Another leading case in this area was decided by the EAT within two months of the Court of Appeal's decision in Fennell. The EAT also recognised the importance of consistency of treatment but placed more emphasis on the employer's ability to be flexible in such matters – Hadjioannou v Coral Casinos Ltd 1981 IRLR 352, EAT. On the facts of that particular case it was found that there had been no evidence of inconsistent treatment. Nevertheless, and without reference to the Fennell case, the EAT stated that a complaint of unreasonableness by an employee based on inconsistency of treatment would only be relevant in limited circumstances:

- where employees have been led by an employer to believe that certain conduct will not lead to dismissal

- where evidence of other cases being dealt with more leniently supports a complaint that the reason stated for dismissal by the employer was not the real reason

- where decisions made by an employer in truly parallel circumstances indicate that it was not reasonable for the employer to dismiss.

The third of these circumstances appears slightly more restrictive than that envisioned in the Fennell case, particularly since the EAT added the comment that, in its view, there would not be many cases where the evidence would show truly similar circumstances. The EAT also stressed the danger inherent in attaching too much weight to consistency of treatment when the proper emphasis when applying S.98(4) is on the 'particular circumstances of the individual employee's case'. Moreover, the EAT deprecated the idea of a 'tariff' approach to misconduct cases.

3.34 The EAT's decision in Hadjioannou was subsequently endorsed by the Court of Appeal in Paul v East Surrey District Health Authority 1995 IRLR 305, CA, in a judgment that did not refer to the decision in Fennell. Nor was Fennell referred to in Securicor Ltd v Smith 1989 IRLR 356, CA, where the Court of Appeal held that where two employees, C and S, were dismissed for the same incident and C was successful on appeal but S was not, the question to be asked was whether the appeal panel's decision was so irrational that no employer could reasonably have accepted it. The Court of Appeal held S's dismissal to be fair on the ground that there was a clear and rational basis for distinguishing between the cases of C and S, namely that S was more to blame for the incident than C.

The Securicor decision was relied upon by the EAT in London Borough of Harrow v Cunningham 1996 IRLR 256, EAT, a case in which two employees, S and W, undertook a private job for personal gain in breach of the employer's disciplinary code. S was dismissed for gross misconduct whereas W was not. The employer – taking into account W's seven years of service, together with his satisfactory work performance and disciplinary record – felt able to stop short of dismissal and instead issued a final written warning. C, on the other hand, was already subject to a final written warning relating to his conduct. The EAT overturned the tribunal's finding that C's dismissal was unfair because he had been treated differently to W: the tribunal had failed to ask whether the distinction made between the two employees was irrational and had instead substituted its own view for that of the employer.

Although the Fennell decision was not referred to in any of these subsequent cases, they do not contradict it but merely put a different emphasis on the same rule. Employers, while retaining flexibility of response to employee behaviour, have to act reasonably in the sanctions they choose to apply. Any change of punishment policy without warning; any dismissal for faults previously condoned; or any unjustified difference in treatment of employees in similar positions will help to make the dismissal unfair.

3.35   Three recent examples of how the rule has been applied:

* **East Riding of Yorkshire Council v Cowton** EAT 0432/08: C worked as a care worker at a home for adults with severe learning difficulties. In 2006 a complaint was made about her standard of care and she was taken through the employer's capability procedure, by the end of which her capability issues were resolved. However, she was warned that any further issues would be dealt with under the employer's disciplinary procedure. In June 2007 she was invited to a disciplinary meeting to face an allegation that she had given a resident mashed, instead of puréed, potato contrary to what was specified in the resident's care plan, causing her to choke and putting her at risk of further complications. Two workers had fed mashed food to the same resident and other residents had also wrongly been fed mashed food. The employer dismissed C but did not discipline or dismiss any other worker who had served mashed food. The tribunal held that the dismissal of C was unfair because she had been treated differently to the other workers. The EAT held that the tribunal had wrongly substituted its own view and that it should have asked whether it was reasonable for the employer to have reached the view that C's position was different. Plainly it was, because unlike the other care workers, C had gone through a capability procedure and been expressly warned that any further issues would be dealt with under a disciplinary procedure

* **Epstein v Royal Borough of Windsor and Maidenhead** EAT 0250/07: E and B were lifeguards at a swimming pool. They were both on duty when a swimmer suffered an epileptic fit and nearly drowned. E had assumed from the movement of the swimmer's hands and feet that he was playing a breath-holding game and so took no action. B did not notice the swimmer at all. Luckily one of the swimmer's friends eventually raised the alarm, which caused E to enter the water and assist. E was dismissed for a gross error of judgement whereas B was not even disciplined. The EAT held that it was reasonable for the employer to conclude that B had not been in a position to see the swimmer, and therefore was not at fault. Further, even if

there had been some failure of omission by B, that would not excuse E's offence of commission and would not render E's dismissal unfair

- **Mist v TK Maxx** ET Case No.1802500/06: M was summarily dismissed for selling counterfeit goods on the employer's premises after being seen placing DVDs in staff pigeon holes and admitting that he had copied DVDs for colleagues. M pointed out that some of his customers were managers – including his own line manager – and others were in responsible posts including the loss prevention team. Further, he said that he had been pressured by some staff, including managers, to provide the DVDs. The employer's rules, however, made it clear that employees were responsible for their own actions, and any illegal or wrongful act could not be justified on the basis that it was ordered by a superior. The tribunal held that M could reasonably have been expected to conclude that his actions had been condoned. Regardless of the statement in the employer's rules, it was not in accordance with equity for an employee to be dismissed for conduct in which his own line manager and 16 other managers were actively colluding.

As is clear from the cases above, where several employees are involved in the misconduct, employers should consider their respective culpability, their individual circumstances and any mitigating/aggravating factors when deciding whether it is reasonable to differentiate between them. This should be done *before* deciding on the penalty to be imposed, otherwise dismissal of only one of the employees is likely to fall outside the range of reasonable responses – see, for example, Jones v Wrekin Housing Trust Ltd ET Case No.2900634/06. **3.36**

Employers can also fall foul of S.98(4) if they attempt to treat employees in a consistent manner but without regard to the circumstances of each individual employee. In Merseyside Passenger Transport Executive v Millington EAT 232/89 M worked on a passenger ferry. During one of his shifts he went to a pub to have lunch. He was joined by two other employees, H and W. The employer had a strict rule that employees should not enter licensed premises while working. A member of management went to the pub and immediately suspended all three employees. There was no suggestion that M was drunk – he had merely gone to the most convenient place to obtain food – but H and W acted in a way consistent with their being drunk. On the following day, all three were summarily dismissed. Management believed that it risked an unfair dismissal claim if it did not treat all three alike for breaching the same rule. However, the tribunal took the view that there were enough differences between M's conduct and that of H and W, coupled with mitigating factors on M's behalf, to make a reasonable employer distinguish between them and treat M more leniently. The EAT agreed. It added that to treat all employees the same as a matter of course, without considering the particular circumstances of each individual, simply could not be done.

3.37 The concept of equity will also come into play where the employer had led the employee to believe that he or she would not be dismissed for certain conduct – see Hadjioannou v Coral Casinos Ltd (above). Some examples:

- **Sarkar v West London Mental Health NHS Trust** 2010 IRLR 508, CA: the Court of Appeal upheld a tribunal's decision that the Trust had unfairly dismissed S for gross misconduct through its formal disciplinary procedure, when it had initially taken the view that the misconduct could be dealt with under its 'Fair Blame Policy' (FBP) – a dispute resolution procedure designed to deal with less serious matters. The tribunal was entitled to regard the initial use of the FBP as an indication of the Trust's view that the misconduct alleged against S was relatively minor and that it was prepared to deal with it under a procedure that could not result in his dismissal. The tribunal did not err in law in concluding that it was inconsistent of the Trust to then charge S with gross misconduct based on the same matters

- **Ryan v Helpline Group plc** ET Case No.3302226/07: R, who delivered and collected cars for HG plc, caused damage to two cars on 3 March 2007. The employer took no immediate action. Then, in May, one of the employer's clients complained that R had damaged a wall when delivering a car. R was called to a disciplinary hearing on 28 June in relation to both incidents. The employer decided not to take any further action regarding the incident in May but dismissed him for the incident in March on the basis that this constituted gross misconduct. The tribunal, by a majority, held that the employer's failure to take action after the March incident gave a clear indication to R that he was not going to be disciplined and it was contrary to equity to dismiss him after such a lapse of time

- **Wilson v Security Plus Ltd** ET Case No.1902594/08: W worked as a member of a cash and valuable transit crew. On 4 September 2008 he entered a building society wearing his safety helmet, as he was required to do, but shortly after entering the premises he removed the helmet to wipe his forehead. He was subsequently summarily dismissed for gross misconduct. He had taken his helmet off some four weeks earlier when he went to the toilet, and had been told by the employer that failing to wear his helmet at all times was regarded as gross misconduct and could result in his dismissal. He was given no disciplinary sanction on that occasion. The tribunal held that dismissal was outside the range of reasonable responses. The incidents in August and September were materially similar, yet on the first occasion he was not even given a warning. This gave W a 'false sense of security'. The employer's handbook and training procedures stressed the importance of wearing the helmet at all times but had not made it clear that failure to wear the helmet for whatever reason would lead to dismissal.

Contractual rights and duties

3.38

Contractual obligations are, of course, of great significance in many unfair dismissal cases but they are not necessarily decisive. The test remains the overall test of reasonableness and employers may well be acting reasonably even if they are in breach of contract. Equally, they may be acting unreasonably if they adhere to the letter of their contractual rights.

Thus, a wrongful dismissal – e.g. a dismissal without notice in a case not involving gross misconduct – is not unfair if the employer would otherwise be reasonable in dismissing – Treganowan v Robert Knee and Co Ltd 1975 ICR 405, QBD. The High Court added that statutory unfair dismissal protection had in no way altered the scope to claim wrongful dismissal. The statute merely required a tribunal to consider whether an employer had acted reasonably in treating the reason for dismissal as a sufficient basis for dismissal. The correct test was whether it was reasonable to dismiss, and the length of notice given was a completely different issue.

As the EAT pointed out in Roberts and ors v Mid-Glamorgan County Council EAT 193/76, 'the whole of the legislation from the 1971 Act onwards on fair and unfair dismissal is designed to apply *irrespective of the law of contract*' (our stress). The distinction was explained by the EAT in BSC Sports and Social Club v Morgan 1987 IRLR 391, EAT, where M was instantly dismissed when, after repeated warnings, he failed in his capacity as club steward of the employer's club to maintain an adequate standard of hygiene and cleanliness. A tribunal found that, while the employer was fully justified in dismissing him for misconduct, the fact that his dismissal was summary (i.e. without notice) rendered it unfair. The EAT, following Treganowan, allowed the employer's appeal, stating that 'the factor of summary dismissal can only be considered in the context of whether or not it was reasonable to dismiss at all. In other words a summary dismissal may be evidence of a failure to show that the dismissal itself was a reasonable response. No doubt there have been many occasions when Industrial Tribunals have relied on a summary dismissal as a material consideration when assessing the reasonableness of the act of dismissal. If this Industrial Tribunal had approached the case in that way we should not have been able to interfere. However… it was an error in point of law to say that it was reasonable to terminate the employment and that the fact of instant dismissal made it unfair dismissal. Once a decision to dismiss has been reached on reasonable grounds, it is for the employer to decide whether or not to dismiss with notice or summarily. If he does so without notice the employer may be open to an action for wrongful dismissal. It seems to us that in preserving the remedy of wrongful dismissal the legislature recognises that there are cases in which instant dismissal, though not unfair, is nevertheless wrongful.'

3.39

An example:

99

- **MPI Ltd v Woodland** EAT 0548/06: W was summarily dismissed for various performance failures and for taking unauthorised leave, which the tribunal found to be a dismissal related to capability. The tribunal went on to hold that instant dismissal of W was not within the band of reasonable responses: although a need to improve his performance had been brought to W's attention, no formal warning had been given to him. However, dismissal on notice would have been a reasonable response. The EAT overturned the tribunal's decision on the basis that it had expressly found that dismissal on notice would have been reasonable. Having reached the conclusion that it was reasonable and fair to dismiss, the tribunal ought in law to have found the dismissal to have been fair irrespective of the fact that it believed that the dismissal should have been on notice.

3.40   **Impact of the Human Rights Act**

Section 6 of the Human Rights Act 1998 (HRA) makes it unlawful for a *public* authority to act in a way that is incompatible with the rights laid down in the European Convention on Human Rights (ECHR). Although it is not directly unlawful for a *private* employer to act in a manner incompatible with the ECHR, S.3 HRA requires that courts and tribunals must, so far as possible, read and give effect to UK legislation in a way compatible with Convention rights. This interpretative obligation applies to all domestic legislation, including the ERA, and draws no distinction between legislation governing public authorities and that governing private individuals. Further, as noted by the Court of Appeal in X v Y 2004 ICR 1634, CA, an employment tribunal is a 'public authority' within the meaning of S.6(3) HRA. The effect of this, said the Court, is to reinforce the tribunal's 'extremely strong interpretative obligation' imposed by S.3 when dealing with a case involving a private employer.

In X v Y, the Court of Appeal commented that as tribunals have to take account of fairness, the reasonable response of the reasonable employer, equity and the substantial merits of the case in the normal course of deciding an unfair dismissal claim under S.98, it would be reasonable to expect that a decision in favour of the employer would not involve a breach of an employee's Convention rights in any event. However, the Court acknowledged the possibility that this might not always be the case and went on to suggest a framework of questions for tribunals dealing with unfair dismissal claims involving *private* employers in which HRA issues arise:

- do the circumstances of the dismissal fall within the ambit of one or more of the Articles of the ECHR? If they do not, the Convention is not engaged and need not be considered

- if they do, does the state have a positive obligation to secure enjoyment of the relevant Convention right between private persons? If it does not, the Convention right is unlikely to affect the outcome of an unfair dismissal claim against a private employer. (Note that both Article 8 – the right to

100 ───────────────────────────────

privacy and family life – and Article 14, which requires the state to secure to individuals the enjoyment of their rights under the Convention without discrimination, do impose such an obligation on the state but were found not to be engaged on the facts of X v Y – see below)

- if it does, is the interference with the employee's Convention right by dismissal justified?

- if it is not, was there a permissible reason for the dismissal under the ERA that does not involve unjustified interference with a Convention right? If there was not, the dismissal will be unfair for the absence of a permissible reason to justify it

- if there was, is the dismissal fair, tested by the provisions of S.98 ERA, reading and giving effect to them under S.3 HRA so as to be compatible with the Convention right?

Where public employers are involved, the questions for the tribunal will be similar, although step two can be bypassed. As noted above, S.6 HRA makes it unlawful for a public authority to act in a way which is incompatible with ECHR rights. However, in X v Y, the Court of Appeal noted that an employment tribunal does not have jurisdiction to hear a claim under S.6. Therefore, if an employee dismissed by a public authority wishes to argue that his dismissal was unfair under S.98 ERA because one of his Convention rights has been breached, he will need to rely on S.3 HRA, rather than S.6, to claim that S.98 should be read in a way which is compatible with the Convention right in question. S.6 may not, however, be completely irrelevant to unfair dismissal claims: tribunals are likely to take their interpretative duties under S.3 even more seriously when public authorities are involved. In Pay v Lancashire Probation Service 2004 ICR 187, EAT, the EAT, exercising its interpretative obligations under S.3 HRA, accepted that a public authority employer will not act reasonably under S.98 if it violates employees' Convention rights. The EAT thought that, at least as far as public authority employers were concerned, the words 'reasonably or unreasonably' in S.98(4) should be interpreted as including the phrase 'having regard to the applicant's Convention rights'. In this context, a public authority employer would not have acted 'reasonably' under S.98(4) where it was found to have unjustifiably breached an employee's Convention rights.

Interestingly, in neither of the above cases was a Convention right found to have been breached on the facts. The employee in X v Y had been dismissed after his employer discovered that the police had cautioned him for engaging in sexual activity with another man in a public toilet. Upholding the tribunal's decision that the dismissal was fair, the Court of Appeal concluded that since the activity that led to the dismissal did not take place in private, the employee's Article 8 right to respect for his private life, and thus his right under Article 14 not to suffer discrimination in relation to his Convention rights, had not been engaged. It followed that the tribunal's duty under S.3 HRA to interpret S.98(4)

101

ERA in a way compatible with Convention rights had not been triggered. The fact that the employee wished to keep the matter private did not make it part of his private life or deprive it of its public aspect.

3.42   In the Pay case, P – a probation officer specialising in the treatment of sex offenders – was dismissed following his employer's discovery that he was director of a business involved in sadomasochistic activities and that he performed acts of domination over women at a private members' club (as evidenced in photographs published on the internet). The EAT agreed with the tribunal that P's activities were in the public domain and therefore could not be described as part of his private life. It followed that Article 8 was not relevant to the claim. The EAT also endorsed the tribunal's view that Article 10 (which protects freedom of expression) had not been infringed: the employer's action had been justified under Article 10(2) (which places limitations on the right to freedom of expression) in view of the risk of damage to the reputation of the probation service that P's activities posed.

P subsequently took his case to the European Court of Human Rights (see Pay v United Kingdom 2009 IRLR 139, ECtHR), which was prepared to proceed on the assumption that P's activities were *not* in the public domain and that, therefore, Article 8 was applicable. This was because P's activities took place in a nightclub that was likely to be frequented only by like-minded people, and the photographs of him published on the internet had been anonymised. However, in light of the sensitive nature of P's work, the interference with P's right to privacy was justified in accordance with Article 8(2) since his activities, if they became widely known, would compromise his work with sex offenders and damage the reputation of the Service. For the same reason the interference with his Article 10 right was justified under Article 10(2).

3.43   Article 8 was also found to be engaged in McGowan v Scottish Water 2005 IRLR 167, EAT, but the employer's action was held to be justified in the circumstances. A public sector employee had been dismissed after his employer obtained evidence through covert surveillance of his house that he was falsifying time sheets. The employee claimed that he had been unfairly dismissed because his right to respect for his private and family life under Article 8 had been breached. The EAT accepted that covert surveillance which involved tracking the movements of all of the inhabitants of a home 'raises... a strong presumption that the right to have one's private life respected is being infringed'. However, in rejecting the employee's claim, it held that the employer's action was justified as it was protecting its assets and was investigating what was effectively a criminal activity.

Note that the Court of Appeal has held that Article 6 of the ECHR, which provides that an individual has the right to a fair hearing, may in certain circumstances provide employees with the right to legal representation at disciplinary hearings – Kulkarni v Milton Keynes Hospital NHS Foundation

Trust and anor 2010 ICR 101, CA; R (on the application of G) v Governors of X School v and anor 2010 IRLR 222, CA. These cases, which did not involve unfair dismissal claims, are discussed further in Chapter 4 under 'Procedural factors'.

Appeals to EAT

Tribunal decisions on reasonableness are essentially findings of fact and an appeal to the EAT or a higher appellate court will lie only on a question of law. Appeals will therefore succeed only in the following circumstances:

- *where the tribunal misdirected itself as to the law.* The most common instance of this is where the tribunal has substituted its own view of what an employer should have done, instead of asking whether what the employer did fell within the range of reasonable responses open to him. Similarly, it is a misdirection in law to misapply the onus of proof: it is not for the employer to prove that a dismissal was reasonable – that is a matter for the tribunal to decide. Also, the standard of proof in unfair dismissal proceedings is the civil one of the 'balance of probabilities' – i.e. 'was it more likely than not that...?' The criminal law standard of proof – 'beyond reasonable doubt' – has no place in unfair dismissal cases

- *where the tribunal misdirected itself on the undisputed facts* or ignored important factual considerations which it should have taken into account. In British Leyland (UK) Ltd v Swift 1981 IRLR 91, CA, S was dismissed after a company road fund licence was found on his own vehicle and he pleaded guilty to its fraudulent use in a magistrate's court. Despite abundant evidence of gross misconduct a tribunal found the dismissal unfair. However, in giving its decision the tribunal took no account of the fact that S had persistently lied both to the police and to his employer: neglect of this highly significant consideration was one reason for setting aside the decision

- *where the decision was perverse* in the sense that it was one that no reasonable tribunal could have reached on the evidence before it. In Williams and ors v Whitbread Beer Co Ltd, unreported 19.6.96, CA, the Court of Appeal said that a tribunal decision should only be set aside on the ground that it is perverse if the decision was not a permissible option on the facts found. For example, in London Transport Executive v Clarke 1981 ICR 355, CA, C asked for six weeks' leave to go to Jamaica in 1979. The employer refused: C had had long periods of absence in the previous three years and had taken leave in Jamaica in 1977. C defied the employer by going to Jamaica for seven weeks anyway. The employer dismissed him while he was away and a tribunal held that the dismissal was unfair on the ground that the employer should have waited to discuss matters on his return. The majority of the Court of Appeal held this finding to be perverse as it 'outrages common sense'.

3.45

Fairness of internal procedure

The interpretation given to the wording of S.98(4) by the courts has had the effect of introducing the concept of a procedurally unfair dismissal – i.e. a dismissal that is unfair because the employer has failed to follow a fair procedure, even though a potentially fair ground for dismissal has been established. The concept, which does not appear in the legislation, was developed in the early 1970s and approved by the House of Lords in W Devis and Sons Ltd v Atkins 1977 ICR 662, HL. It became a dominant feature of employment relations in that decade but waned in the early 1980s following the widespread application of the 'no difference rule' – first formulated in British Labour Pump Co Ltd v Byrne 1979 ICR 347, EAT. This rule basically meant that where there was a proven procedural irregularity in an otherwise fair dismissal – e.g. a failure to consult over redundancy – but it could be shown that carrying out the proper procedure would have made no difference, then the dismissal would be fair.

The House of Lords resoundingly rejected this approach in Polkey v AE Dayton Services Ltd 1988 ICR 142, HL. In that case P was summarily dismissed for redundancy with no warning or consultation and the tribunal hearing his unfair dismissal claim said that: 'There could be no more heartless disregard of the provisions of the code of practice than that.' It was referring to the (now repealed) 1972 Industrial Relations Code of Practice, para 46 of which said: 'If redundancy becomes necessary, management in consultation, as appropriate, with employees or their representatives, should: (i) give as much warning as practicable to the employees concerned…' The tribunal, however, went on to hold that if the employer had acted in accordance with the Code of Practice, the result would not have been any different. The House of Lords unanimously condemned this approach on the grounds that it was contrary to the decision in Devis (above) and contrary to the plain wording of S.98(4). That section simply directs tribunals to consider whether the employer acted reasonably when dismissing. Their Lordships reasoned, therefore, that the employer's actions in dispensing with a fair procedure were highly relevant to the question of whether a dismissal is fair. With this landmark decision, the pendulum swung back in favour of proper procedure.

3.46

The position changed again with the enactment of the Employment Act 2002, which introduced the (now-repealed) statutory dispute resolution procedures (SDRPs) in 2004 and inserted a new S.98A into the ERA, making a dismissal automatically unfair if the employer had failed to follow a relevant statutory dismissal or disciplinary procedure (DDP). S.98A(2) brought about a partial reversal of Polkey, providing that a failure by the employer to follow a fair procedure *other than the applicable DDP* would not be regarded by itself as making a dismissal unfair if the employer could show, on the balance of

104

probabilities, that he would have decided to dismiss the employee if that additional procedure had been followed. If the employer could overcome this hurdle – and there was no issue of substantive unfairness – the dismissal would be deemed fair despite the procedural failures committed by the employer. Thus, the 'no difference' rule was reinstated, albeit only in circumstances where the minimum obligations of the SDRPs had been observed.

Section 98A was repealed by the Employment Act 2008, with the result that the law has returned to the Polkey position, and employers will no longer be able to invoke the 'no difference' argument when defending a failure to adopt a fair procedure, except in exceptional cases (see under 'Exception to Polkey' below). The SDRPs were also repealed by the 2008 Act but, despite what many commentators have said, their abolition has not simply meant a return to the pre-2004 regime since parties are now expected to comply with a revised Acas Code of Practice on Discipline and Grievance Procedures. A failure to comply with the Code will be taken into account by tribunals when assessing liability. However, unlike the SDRPs, it will not *automatically* render a dismissal unfair. This new Code is considered in more detail below.

It should be noted that the SDRPs did not disappear overnight and continue to **3.47** apply to disputes that arose before 6 April 2009 but are awaiting a tribunal hearing, as well as to those that started before 6 April but continued after that date. In such cases, the old rules, including the partial reversal of Polkey, still apply – see IDS Employment Law Supplement, 'Disciplinary and Grievance Procedures' (2009), Chapter 1 for further details of the transitional provisions. For an explanation of the old SDRPs, reference should be had to IDS Employment Law Supplement, 'Statutory Disciplinary and Grievance Procedures' (2004).

General factors   3.48
Polkey v AE Dayton Services Ltd (above) firmly establishes procedural fairness as an integral part of the reasonableness test under S.98(4). As stated by Lord Bridge in that case, where an employer fails to take the appropriate procedural steps, the one question a tribunal is not permitted to ask in applying the reasonableness test is whether it would have made any difference if the right procedure had been followed. That question was simply irrelevant to the issue of reasonableness (although very relevant to the issue of compensation). Thus, if there is a failure to adopt a fair procedure at the time of the dismissal, whether set out in the Acas Code or otherwise – for example, in the employer's disciplinary rules – the dismissal will not be rendered fair simply because the unfairness did not affect the end result. However, any compensation will be substantially reduced – see Chapter 18.

While a failure to comply with procedural safeguards will not *automatically* render a dismissal unfair, Lord Bridge itemised the procedural steps that will be necessary in the great majority of cases if an employer is to be considered to have acted reasonably in dismissing:

105

- in a case of incapacity, giving an employee fair warning and a chance to improve

- in a case of misconduct, investigating fully and fairly and hearing what the employee wants to say in explanation or mitigation

- in a case of redundancy, warning and consulting affected employees, adopting a fair basis for selection and taking reasonable steps to redeploy affected employees.

In addition, when determining the question of reasonableness, the tribunal should have regard to the procedures set out in the revised Acas Code of Practice, which is discussed below.

3.49 **Relevance of employer's reason for dismissal.** In Westminster City Council v Cabaj 1996 ICR 960, CA, the Court of Appeal stated that although employers should follow the agreed procedures, a failure to do so would not necessarily mean that a dismissal is unfair. The question a tribunal must decide in cases of unfair dismissal is not whether in all the circumstances the employer acted reasonably, but the narrower question under S.98(4) of whether the employer acted reasonably in treating the reason shown as a sufficient reason for dismissing the employee. In remitting the case, the Court of Appeal said that the tribunal should first ask whether the failure to convene a properly constituted appeal panel impeded the employee in demonstrating that the real reason for his dismissal was not sufficient. It should also consider the employer's reason (if any) for deciding to dismiss C without observing the requirements of the disciplinary code.

The Cabaj judgement makes clear the importance of a proper procedure in helping to ensure that the employer's decision to dismiss is reasonable. For example, in many misconduct cases it will be difficult for the employer to establish that his belief in the employee's guilt – and therefore any subsequent dismissal – is reasonable without having first held an investigation. However, if an employee is caught red-handed in the course of serious misconduct, an investigation may not be as crucial. This was confirmed in Taylor v OCS Group Ltd 2006 ICR 1602, CA, where the Court of Appeal stressed that the tribunal's task under S.98(4) is not only to assess the fairness of the disciplinary process as a whole but also to consider the employer's reason for the dismissal as the two impact upon each other. It stated that where an employee is dismissed for serious misconduct, a tribunal might well decide that, notwithstanding some procedural imperfections, the employer acted reasonably in treating the reason as sufficient to dismiss the employee. Conversely, the Court considered that where the misconduct is of a less serious nature, so that the decision to dismiss is nearer the borderline, the tribunal might well conclude that a procedural deficiency had such impact that the employer did not act reasonably in dismissing the employee.

106

Range of reasonable responses test applies. When assessing whether the 3.50
employer adopted a reasonable procedure, tribunals should use the range of
reasonable responses test that applies to substantive unfair dismissal claims (see
'Reasonableness of dismissal' above) – J Sainsbury plc v Hitt 2003 ICR 111,
CA; Whitbread plc (t/a Whitbread Medway Inns) v Hall 2001 ICR 699, CA.

An example:

- **McAlney v E.on UK plc** ET Case No.2406839/08: M was employed by E
  UK plc as a customer services representative. He also worked as a private
  taxi driver and the employer was fully aware of this. M was dismissed
  following an allegation by a fellow employee, G, that he had picked up a
  fare in his taxi while he was on sick leave. The tribunal held that the way the
  employer carried out the subsequent investigation and disciplinary
  procedure fell outside the range of reasonable responses in that the
  employer had interviewed M without giving him full details of G's
  allegations, depriving M of the opportunity to put forward a substantive
  and meaningful response; did not allow external witnesses to give evidence;
  and refused to consider any evidence that might exculpate M – for example,
  a written statement that had been produced by a member of the public.
  Although satisfied that the employer had an honest belief in M's guilt, the
  tribunal concluded that this belief had been formed hastily without the
  appropriate inquiries being made, without relevant evidence being taken
  into account, and without proper consideration being given to the evidence
  that was before it. This meant the decision to dismiss fell outside the range
  of reasonable responses and was unfair.

Exception to Polkey

3.51

In Polkey v AE Dayton Services Ltd (above) it was stated that if an employer
could reasonably have concluded that a proper procedure would be 'utterly
useless' or 'futile', he might well be acting reasonably in ignoring it. This was a
matter for the tribunal to consider in the light of the circumstances known to
the employer at the time of the dismissal. Lord Bridge expressed the view that
such cases would be 'exceptional' and, because of this, the appellate courts have
been cautious about finding dismissals fair where the proper procedure has
been ignored on the ground that to follow it would have been futile.
Nonetheless, there have been cases where the EAT has held that the
circumstances were exceptional enough to 'excuse' the employer from
following the proper disciplinary procedure. Two examples:

- **MacLeod v Murray Quality Foods Ltd** EAT 290/90: M worked in MQF's
  factory, which was struggling financially. The factory received a large order
  from a new customer and it was a matter of some urgency that the order be
  executed on time. Tea breaks were cancelled until the order was completed.
  M ignored this instruction and, after being warned that he would be
  dismissed if he did not return to work, was dismissed. The tribunal found

107

that the circumstances were sufficiently urgent to justify the employer issuing the instruction, even though tea breaks were provided for in M's contract. It found the dismissal fair. The EAT accepted that the procedure was flawed in that no investigation had been carried out. Nonetheless, it agreed with the tribunal's finding on the basis that M knew why he was being dismissed and he had the opportunity to make representations to the managing director. Referring to Polkey, the EAT said that the circumstances of the case were 'exceptional'

- **Ellis v Hammond and anor t/a Hammond and Sons** EAT 1257/95: E had received several warnings, including three formal written warnings, about her conduct and her work. Matters came to a head when she was asked to work harder and, in response, swore at her supervisor and started throwing things at another employee. After a further warning, she swore at everybody and left. She did not report for work the following week and was dismissed without the benefit of a final disciplinary hearing. The EAT upheld a tribunal's decision that E had been fairly dismissed, even though the employer had decided to dispense with a final disciplinary hearing. The EAT stressed that the correct question for the tribunal to ask was whether the decision not to hold a final disciplinary hearing was justified at the time of the dismissal, not in the light of being wise after the event.

The test for tribunals to use is an objective test. They must ask whether an employer, acting reasonably, could have made the decision that it would have been futile to follow proper procedures – Duffy v Yeomans and Partners Ltd 1995 ICR 1, CA.

3.52 The Acas Code of Practice

The revised Acas Code of Practice on Disciplinary and Grievance Procedures ('the Code'), issued under S.199 of the Trade Union and Labour Relations (Consolidation) Act 1992 (TULR(C)A), came into effect on 6 April 2009. The Code, which is available on the Acas website (www.acas.org.uk/drr), contains a section on handling disciplinary issues and sets out six steps employers should normally follow, namely:

- establish the facts of each case (paras 5–8)

- inform the employee of the problem (paras 9–10)

- hold a meeting with the employee to discuss the problem (paras 11–12)

- allow the employee to be accompanied at the meeting (paras 13–16)

- decide on appropriate action (paras 17–24)

- provide employees with an opportunity to appeal (paras 25–28).

The Introduction to the Code also states that it is important to 'deal with issues fairly' whenever a disciplinary process is being followed. This includes dealing

108

with issues promptly and without unreasonable delay; acting consistently; carrying out any necessary investigations; and giving employees the opportunity to put their case before any decisions are made (see para 4).

A failure to follow the Code is relevant to the question of *liability* and will be taken into account by a tribunal when determining the reasonableness of a dismissal in accordance with S.98(4) – S.207 TULR(C)A. However, it will not render the dismissal automatically unfair and the tribunal will take all the circumstances into account. Para 3 of the Code makes it clear that 'tribunals will take the size and resources of an employer into account when deciding on relevant cases and it may sometimes not be practicable for all employers to take all of the steps set out in this Code'. However, there is a risk in departing from the Code since employers will be banking on an employment tribunal agreeing that such departure was reasonable.

3.53

Failure to comply with the Code played a part in rendering dismissal unfair in Singh v Borgers Ltd ET Case No.1312543/09. S was dismissed after admitting that he was responsible for supplying defective parts to the employer's major customer. A tribunal held that the dismissal was procedurally unfair. The employer had failed to comply with the Code in a number of ways: the investigation and hearing were carried out by the same person; S was not notified of the hearing in writing, or provided with reasonable time to prepare his case before the hearing, or advised of his right to be accompanied at the meeting; and, finally, the appeal was not 'heard' as envisaged by para 25 of the Code – the employer had simply carried out a desk exercise and informed S that his appeal was not upheld. Furthermore, and irrespective of the Acas Code, the disciplinary procedure operated by the employer contravened both natural justice and established good industrial relations practice in that, for example, it did not allow S a proper opportunity to prepare his case in advance of the disciplinary hearing and failed to provide S with an effective appeal process.

The Code states that 'a fair disciplinary process should always be followed before dismissing for gross misconduct' (para 22). Thus, unless the misconduct is so heinous as to require instant dismissal – e.g. where there is a danger to life or immediate severe harm to the business – even serious conduct cases should be dealt with in the normal way. However, where immediate dismissal is deemed necessary, it is arguable that the lack of a fair procedure would not render it unfair as the exception in Polkey v AE Dayton Services Ltd 1988 ICR 142, HL, would apply – see above. Further, cases such as Taylor v OCS Group Ltd 2006 ICR 1602, CA, suggest that the more serious the misconduct alleged, the more likely it is that a dismissal tainted by procedural irregularities would nonetheless be fair.

3.54

A failure to follow the Code is not only relevant to the question of liability, but also to assessment of *compensation*. Assuming the dismissal is found to be unfair, compliance with the Code by both employer and employee will be taken into account when determining whether there should be an adjustment to any

109

award – S.207A TULR(C)A. This section applies to most tribunal claims, including unfair dismissal, and provides that the tribunal can increase an award of compensation by up to 25 per cent if it finds that the employer has unreasonably failed to follow the Code, or decrease it by up to 25 per cent if the employee has unreasonably failed to follow the Code, if it considers it just and equitable in all the circumstances to do so. It is difficult to envisage a situation in which a tribunal could find that an employer has acted unreasonably in failing to comply with the Code when deciding on unfair dismissal liability but then go on to hold that that failure was reasonable when it comes to deciding whether there should be an uplift in compensation. Such adjustments are therefore likely to be fairly common in practice.

3.55   **The Code's ambit.** The Acas Code expressly covers disciplinary issues relating to 'misconduct' and 'poor performance', both of which are potentially fair reasons for dismissal under the ERA: the former on grounds of 'conduct' under S.98(2)(b); the latter on grounds of 'capability or qualifications' under S.98(2)(a). Although the Code sets out one disciplinary procedure to deal with both conduct and performance issues, many employers are likely to have a separate capability procedure in place to deal with the latter. This is recognised in the Introduction to the Code which provides that 'if employers have a separate capability procedure they may prefer to address performance issues under this procedure' – para 1. However, it goes on to emphasise that 'the basic principles of fairness set out in this Code should still be followed, albeit that they may need to be adapted'.

Not all dismissals fall within the Code's ambit: redundancy dismissals and the non-renewal of fixed-term contracts are specifically excluded. Further, there are a number of types of dismissal that do not sit easily within the Code's reach. For example, the category 'capability or qualifications' in S.98(2)(a) ERA encompasses more than simply poor performance, and it is unclear how the Code applies to the broader issues of incapability on grounds of sickness absence or lack of qualification that are embraced by it. Arguably the Code does not apply, since in most such cases, there is an absence of 'fault' on the part of the employee, taking them outside the 'disciplinary' area. The same applies to dismissals by reason of statutory ban or for some other substantial reason. However, Appendix 4 of the non-statutory and non-binding Guide to the Acas Code – 'Discipline and grievances at work' – envisages that the Code will apply in cases of ill health, although it recommends a 'more sympathetic and considerate approach' and emphasises the need to be aware of the requirements of the Disability Discrimination Act 1995.

3.56   But even if the Code does not apply, an employer cannot simply dispense with procedural fairness. Polkey and related case law will still be relevant and tribunals will need to be satisfied that the employer has followed a fair and appropriate procedure in the circumstances. For example, in a redundancy case the employer should warn and consult affected employees, adopt a fair basis for selection and take reasonable steps to redeploy affected employees. Moreover, in many cases the reasons for dismissal may overlap and employers should be wary of abandoning the Code altogether. Indeed, the Code sets out general standards of good practice that may be relevant in circumstances not covered by the Code: S.207 TULR(C)A is widely drafted and obliges tribunals to take into account a provision of the Code whenever they consider it to be relevant.

For further information on the Acas Code of Practice on Disciplinary and Grievance Procedures, reference should be made to IDS Employment Law Supplement, 'Disciplinary and Grievance Procedures' (2009).

Internal policies and procedures   3.57

In considering the fairness of a dismissal the tribunal will also consider whether an employer has complied with its own internal policies and procedures. In Sinclair v Wandsworth Council EAT 0145/07, for example, S was found to be unfit for work because of drink and was suspended. Following disciplinary action, he was dismissed. The tribunal was satisfied that the Council had conducted a full and reasonable investigation into the events and that, in view of an earlier written warning given to S, and of the limited steps he had taken to address his alcohol problem, dismissal was within the range of reasonable responses available to the employer. Nevertheless, the majority of the tribunal (comprising the two lay members) found that S's dismissal was procedurally unfair under S.98(4) ERA because of two material defaults on the Council's part in the application of its alcohol policy. First, the policy had not been provided to S or his supervisors until immediately before the disciplinary hearing that resulted in his dismissal. Secondly, the Council had failed to spell out precisely what S would need to do in order to stop the disciplinary action, and had not made it clear that, if he did not seek treatment, the action would continue.

The employment judge disagreed with the majority. In his view, the message of the alcohol policy – if not the policy itself – had been made plain to S, in that he was sufficiently informed that disciplinary action could be put on hold if he underwent treatment. In any event, the employment judge felt that any unfairness prior to the disciplinary hearing was cured on appeal. Nevertheless, owing to the views of the majority, the tribunal concluded that S had been unfairly dismissed. The EAT held that the tribunal was entitled to find that the employer's failure to implement its alcohol policy when disciplining an employee with an alcohol problem rendered the dismissal unfair. While conceding that it was possible for an appeal hearing to cure earlier deficiencies in an employer's procedure, the EAT decided that the majority had been entitled to find that the deficiencies identified had not been cured. Accordingly, it declined to disturb the tribunal's decision that S had been unfairly dismissed.

Internal appeals   3.58

The Acas Code recommends that employees be provided with an opportunity to appeal against any disciplinary action taken against them, such as dismissal.

111

As this recommendation is part of the Code, an unreasonable failure to provide an appeal risks incurring liability and/or an adjustment to any compensation award in related tribunal proceedings.

In terms of general fairness, the courts have established that defects in the original disciplinary hearing and pre-dismissal procedures can be remedied on appeal. In a case that was subsequently followed on a number of occasions – Whitbread and Co plc v Mills 1988 ICR 776, EAT – the EAT suggested that in order for that to happen the appeal must be in the nature of a full rehearing of the case rather than a mere review of the original decision. However, in Taylor v OCS Group Ltd 2006 ICR 1602, CA, the Court of Appeal held that the EAT in Whitbread had not established a rule of law that only a rehearing – as opposed to a review – was capable of curing earlier defects. Such a rule would fetter a tribunal's discretion when considering the fairness of the dismissal under S.98(4). It was evident, said the Court, that Whitbread had not always been properly understood and that tribunals had been tempted to categorise appeal hearings either as rehearings or reviews. In view of the confusion surrounding Whitbread, the Court suggested that it would be advisable not to cite it in future cases. The tribunal's task under S.98(4), the Court stressed, is to assess the fairness of the disciplinary process as a whole. Where procedural deficiencies occur at an early stage, the tribunal should examine the subsequent appeal hearing, particularly its procedural fairness and thoroughness, and the open-mindedness of the decision-maker.

An appeal may, therefore, cure earlier defects. Conversely, the way in which an appeal is carried out may make the dismissal unfair, particularly if the employee has a contractual right of appeal. In West Midlands Co-operative Society Ltd v Tipton 1986 ICR 192, HL, the House of Lords held that a dismissal may be unfair where the employer has refused to entertain an appeal to which the employee was contractually entitled on the basis that the employee was thereby denied the opportunity of showing that the employer's reason for dismissing him could not reasonably be treated as sufficient.

3.59 In Evans v Wolverhampton City Council ET Case No.1307237/07 E, who was dismissed because of his absence record, had a contractual right of appeal. The tribunal was satisfied that the employer had carried out a reasonable investigation and that dismissal was within the range of reasonable responses. However, bearing in mind Tipton – which held that, where an employment contract provided an appeals procedure, both the employer's original and appellate decisions to dismiss are necessary elements in the overall process of dismissal – the tribunal found that E's dismissal was unfair because of the way in which the appeal hearing was conducted. For example, a number of new matters were raised on appeal but the employer provided no documentary evidence as to why the appeal was rejected. The employer's 'considerable and largely unexplained delay' in determining the appeal – over four months after

112

the decision to dismiss was made – added to the tribunal's concerns regarding the conduct and outcome of the appeal process.

If the evidence indicates that the employer closed its mind to anything other than upholding the dismissal on appeal, this will render the dismissal procedurally unfair. See, for example, Bidwell v Havering Primary Care Trust ET Case No.3202420/05, where the person who heard B's appeal believed that to uphold the appeal and impose a lesser sanction would have been to condone B's actions.

For a more detailed consideration of what amounts to a fair procedure in a given set of circumstances see Chapters 4 to 8, which consider each of the potentially fair reasons for dismissal in turn. In particular, Chapter 6, 'Conduct', deals with disciplinary proceedings and the conduct of internal appeals.

Overlapping grievance and disciplinary issues

3.60

It is common for grievance and disciplinary matters to overlap but this can cause problems for employers deciding how to proceed. It is likely to prove difficult to resolve a grievance at the same time as pursuing disciplinary proceedings. If the employee is dismissed while the grievance procedure is ongoing, he or she may argue that the way the grievance was handled rendered the dismissal procedurally unfair. However, the employer may not wish to postpone disciplinary action indefinitely until the employee is satisfied that the grievance has been dealt with, particularly if the grievance is protracted. The Acas Code of Practice provides little guidance. It gives the example of an employee who raises a grievance during a disciplinary process, stating that the disciplinary process 'may be temporarily suspended' to deal with the grievance. It then goes on to state that where the disciplinary and grievance issues are related, it may be appropriate to deal with them 'concurrently' (para 44).

The Acas Guide, 'Discipline and grievances at work', while non-binding, provides examples of where it may be appropriate to consider suspending the disciplinary procedure to deal with a grievance, namely:

- where the grievance relates to a conflict of interest that the manager holding the disciplinary hearing is alleged to have
- where bias is alleged in the conduct of the disciplinary meeting
- where management has been selective with the evidence it has supplied to the manager holding the meeting
- where there is possible discrimination.

There is no guidance (either in the Code or its Guide) as to how long it might be appropriate to suspend proceedings for.

The following case provides some useful clarification on dealing with concurrent disciplinary and grievance issues:

3.61

113

- **Samuel Smith Old Brewery (Tadcaster) v Marshall and anor** EAT 0488/09:
M and his wife (W) managed a pub for the employer. The employer
informed M and W that staffing hours had to be reduced for financial
reasons. M and W refused to implement the proposed reduction and raised
a grievance. Following a grievance hearing the employer revised its
proposed reduction of hours. It provided an opportunity to appeal the
decision but stated that in the meantime the employees were required to
implement the change, failing which disciplinary action might be taken.
However, M and W refused to comply and appealed against the grievance
hearing decision. The employer instigated disciplinary proceedings but M
and W refused to attend any disciplinary hearings until the grievance
procedure had been exhausted. The employer proceeded with a hearing in
their absence, following which it dismissed M and W for gross misconduct;
namely, a 'deliberate refusal to carry out lawful instructions'. The
employment tribunal concluded that the dismissal was within the range of
reasonable responses but found that as M and W had been deprived of their
right to pursue the grievance appeal, they had been unfairly dismissed.

The EAT overturned the tribunal's decision, holding that there was no authority
for the proposition that it was necessary to complete the entire grievance
procedure before a disciplinary hearing could take place. Further, it was only in
the rarest of cases that it would be outside the range of reasonable responses for
an employer to proceed with a disciplinary process before hearing a grievance
appeal, at least in the absence of clear evidence of unfairness or prejudice to the
employee. The decision that no reasonable employer would have arranged for
the grievance appeal to be heard until after the disciplinary hearing where there
had been a repeated and ill-advised refusal to comply with a reasonable
instruction was wrong in law and amounted to a substitution of the tribunal's
views for those of the employer. The tribunal reached its decision with the
benefit of hindsight, i.e. knowing that M and W would have complied with the
instruction if their grievance was unsuccessful.

This decision will come as some relief to employers. However, it does not mean that
they can rush headlong to dismissal when grievance issues are outstanding. They
will generally need to be sensitive to the issues raised in the grievance and to have
gone some way towards dealing with it. For example, in the above case the
grievance procedure was well under way before disciplinary action was taken and
the EAT acknowledged that the fact that the employer had already held a grievance
hearing made its case stronger. Further, the employees' grievance had been quite
protracted and they had continued to ignore the employer's instruction (which was
found to be lawful) for about three months, at some significant cost to the
employer. The EAT also noted that neither the management agreement nor the
employer's disciplinary procedure contained a 'standstill' provision, providing that
where a grievance has been raised in relation to a change in the status quo, the
status quo is to be preserved until the determination of the grievance.

114

The EAT did suggest that an employer might be expected to complete a **3.62** grievance procedure before starting or continuing disciplinary proceedings where not to do so would cause clear prejudice to the employee. This might be the case where, for example, the grievance relates to discrimination or bullying or where bias is alleged in the conduct of the disciplinary or grievance hearing, or indeed in any other of the examples set out in the Acas Guide (see above).

Where grievance and disciplinary procedures are being run concurrently, the issues should generally be dealt with separately to prevent one from influencing or overshadowing the other. In Tweedle v Mid-Yorkshire Hospitals NHS Trust ET Case No.1801749, for example, T raised a grievance about a number of work-related issues, including bullying and an unmanageable workload. However, the subsequent investigation and grievance hearing focused on T's performance and capability, rather than on her complaints. T resigned, complaining about the manner in which her grievance had been dealt with, in particular that the employer had failed to take it seriously. A tribunal subsequently upheld her claim for constructive unfair dismissal, concluding that T was entitled to take the view that her complaints were being side-stepped. It noted that the investigatory report concentrated on her performance and capability and gave no explanation as to how this related to her complaints of bullying and harassment, etc.

Automatically fair and unfair dismissals **3.63**

In the section headed 'Reason for dismissal' we listed the potentially fair reasons for dismissal set out in the ERA: if the employer establishes one of these reasons, the tribunal must then go on to consider whether it acted reasonably in dismissing for that reason. There are, however, certain reasons for dismissal which can be described as *automatically* fair or unfair in the sense that if one of these reasons is established the tribunal must find the dismissal fair or unfair (as the case may be). The question of reasonableness does not arise.

Automatically fair dismissals. There are two situations where dismissal may **3.64** be described as automatically fair:

- where the employee was taking part in unofficial industrial action – S.237 TULR(C)A (see IDS Employment Law Handbook, 'Industrial Action' (2010), Chapter 8). In these circumstances, employees do not have the right to complain of unfair dismissal at all. However, S.237 does not apply where the reason for dismissal (or selection for redundancy) is shown to be one of the following automatically unfair reasons: jury service; maternity and family leave; health and safety; employee representatives; protected disclosures; flexible working; assertion of the statutory right to time off to care for dependants; or time off for study or training – S.237(1A)

- where the employer was conducting a lock-out or the employee was taking part in official industrial action and the employer dismisses all relevant

115

employees and does not re-employ any of them within three months – S.238 TULR(C)A (see IDS Employment Law Handbook, 'Industrial Action' (2010), Chapter 8). In these circumstances tribunals will be prohibited from considering whether the dismissals were fair or unfair. However, S.238 does not apply where S.238A renders a dismissal automatically unfair (i.e. where an employee is dismissed because he or she took lawful industrial action in certain circumstances). Nor does it apply where the reason for dismissal (or selection for redundancy) is shown to be one of the following automatically unfair reasons: jury service; pregnancy and family leave; health and safety; employee representatives; flexible working; assertion of the statutory right to time off to care for dependants; or time off for study or training – S.238(2A).

3.65 Until fairly recently, it was generally accepted that dismissal for the purpose of safeguarding national security was also automatically fair. S.10(1) of the Employment Tribunals Act 1996 provides that an employment tribunal 'shall dismiss' an unfair dismissal complaint if 'it is shown that the action complained of was taken for the purpose of safeguarding national security'. However, in B v BAA plc 2005 ICR 1530, EAT, the EAT held that an employment tribunal should not reject an employee's unfair dismissal claim simply on the basis that the dismissal was carried out for the purpose of safeguarding national security. The tribunal should go on to consider whether dismissal was within the range of reasonable responses available to the employer. Mr Justice Burton, giving the EAT's judgment, stated that, in order to invoke S.10(1), an employer must prove, first, its reason for an employee's dismissal and, secondly, that dismissal for such reason was for the purpose of – and not necessarily that it had the effect of – safeguarding national security. In doing so, the employer is not required to prove the underlying facts and show that a threat to national security existed. The EAT went on to conclude, however, that a proper construction of S.10(1) requires a tribunal, notwithstanding a national security reason for dismissal, to consider whether the employer's decision to dismiss, as opposed to taking some other action such as redeployment, was reasonable. In the EAT's view, imposing such a reasonableness test upon national security dismissals would accord with a tribunal's obligation under the Human Rights Act 1998 to read S.10(1) in a way which gives effect to an individual's right to a fair trial under Article 6 of the European Convention on Human Rights.

The EAT's decision to import the 'reasonableness' test in S.98(4) of the Employment Rights Act 1996 into S.10(1) ETA seems a touch contrived, notwithstanding the argument that S.10(1) might otherwise offend Article 6 of the European Convention. Up to now, it has been generally accepted that S.10(1) exists specifically to ensure that questions of reasonableness do not arise when dismissals are shown to be for the purpose of safeguarding national security. Arguably, therefore, the EAT's interpretation of S.10(1) ascribes a meaning to the provision which is diametrically opposed to its intended purpose.

116

In the circumstances, it is perhaps unsurprising that parts of the EAT's **3.66** reasoning are somewhat unclear. In the last paragraph of the judgment, Mr Justice Burton seems to suggest that if a tribunal concludes that a national security dismissal is unreasonable, it should go on to consider whether the action complained of – i.e. the unfair dismissal – was itself for the purpose of safeguarding national security. Yet surely this is a question that the tribunal will already have answered in the affirmative at a much earlier stage of the proceedings when trying to establish whether S.10(1) is relevant to the case. Furthermore, Burton P does not make it clear what the effect of an unreasonable national security dismissal would be. One of the EAT's concerns was that, in the above circumstances, justice required the tribunal to consider whether the employer should have redeployed the employee as an alternative to dismissal. Rather than requiring the reasonableness test, however, this issue arguably turns on the original question of whether the employer's reason for dismissing the employee – as opposed to removing her from her post – was for the purpose of safeguarding national security, or for some other reason.

Automatically unfair dismissals. There are now numerous categories of **3.67** automatically unfair dismissals (subject to various qualifications and exceptions). These are discussed in Chapter 10.

4 Capability and qualifications

Definitions

Establishing lack of capability

Reasonableness

Procedural factors

Section 98(1)(b) and (2) of the Employment Rights Act 1996 (ERA) sets out **4.1** the potentially fair reasons for dismissing an employee. One such reason is where the dismissal 'relates to the capability or qualifications of the employee for performing work of the kind which he was employed... to do' – S.98(2)(a).

In this chapter we look first at the definitions of the two key words in the statutory provision – 'capability' and 'qualifications'. We then consider what an employer has to do to establish lack of capability or qualifications as a reason for dismissal. Finally, we deal with assessing the reasonableness of a dismissal on the ground of incapability and with the procedural factors involved.

Definitions
4.2

Section 98(2)(a) focuses on two key concepts: capability and qualifications, which, if lacking, can amount to potentially fair reasons for dismissal.

Capability
4.3
Capability is defined in S.98(3)(a) ERA as 'capability assessed by reference to skill, aptitude, health or any other physical or mental quality'. Examples of employees who have been held to be lacking in capability include:

- an inflexible and unadaptable worker – Abernethy v Mott, Hay and Anderson 1974 ICR 323, CA

- an employee who failed to reach the employer's standards, even if those standards were higher than those of similar employers – Fletcher v St Leonard's School EAT 25/87

- workers who could not meet management's raised standards – Gozdzik and Scopigno v Chlidema Carpet Co Ltd EAT 598/78

- an employee who, although efficient, was difficult and abrasive and so affected the quality of the staff's work generally – Bristow v ILEA EAT 602/79.

In addition to these examples there are many cases in which incapability has stemmed from sickness or disability. These are dealt with separately in Chapter 5.

4.4 **Work of the kind which the employee was employed to do.** The employee's alleged incapability must relate to the 'work of the kind which [the employee] was employed by the employer to do' – S.98(2)(a) ERA. Whether an employee is capable of doing the work which he or she was employed to do must be determined in accordance with the employee's current contractual obligations. This is particularly relevant where there has been a variation in the original employment contract, either by oral or written agreement, or by conduct. An example:

- **Plessey Military Communications Ltd v Brough** EAT 518/84: B was taken on as a miller. Shortly after starting work, he developed dermatitis and was taken off 'wet work' and put on 'dry work' as a vibro miller. Six months later he returned to wet work and suffered from dermatitis again and the employer transferred him back to dry work, where he remained for some 18 months until he was dismissed. The employer argued that B was contractually employed to do wet work, which he was incapable of doing. On the facts, the employment tribunal found that the employer had transferred B permanently to dry work. On appeal, the EAT said that this showed that the terms of B's contract, and therefore his contractual position, had changed and that his capacity had to be assessed in accordance with that change.

However, a dismissal for incapacity may be fair even though the employee can still perform some of the contractual duties. In Shook v Ealing London Borough Council 1986 ICR 314, EAT, the claimant was employed as a social worker. Her appointment letter gave the employer the right to vary the duties and designation of the post. Back troubles prevented the claimant from continuing her social work and she was dismissed when the employer was unable to find alternative work for her. The EAT rejected the employee's argument that the test for incapacity was to look not only at what the employee was actually doing at the time, but also at what the employee might potentially be called upon to do within the terms of the contract. The EAT said that the employer did not have to show that the employee was incapable of performing every activity that she might be called upon to do – the reason for dismissal had to 'relate' to the employee's capability. However widely the claimant's contract was construed, her disabilities related to the performance of her duties, even though they may well not have affected all of them.

4.5 **Intransigent, inflexible or difficult employees.** Such employees are covered by the 'aptitude' or 'mental quality' part of the statutory definition, in so far as these shortcomings affect performance or relations with colleagues or customers. Where, however, an employee's personality leads to defiant clashes with management or supervisors, or affects fellow employees' morale, the reason for dismissal may shade into conduct, or the resultant disharmony may be classed as 'some other substantial reason' justifying dismissal. In practice, employers get over these labelling problems by making a 'plea in the alternative' and citing alternative reasons on the ET3 (Response to Employment Tribunal Claim) form.

Where mental qualities clearly affect performance and efficiency or relations with clients and customers, dismissal is most appropriately regarded as dismissal for lack of capability. In AJ Dunning and Sons (Shopfitters) Ltd v Jacomb 1973 ICR 448, NIRC, the claimant was regarded as 'competent, experienced, had a detailed knowledge of building law and was loyal, conscientious and meticulous'. But his uncooperative and unbending nature meant that he got on badly with clients. Indeed, several contractors refused to have him on their sites. As he clearly lacked the necessary aptitude and mental quality for the job of contracts manager, he was fairly dismissed for incapability.

Physical qualities or characteristics. Any physical quality may constitute a
potentially fair reason for dismissal if it means that someone is incapable of doing the job he or she was employed to do. In Bradley v Business Press International Ltd ET Case No.20265/83 the claimant started work in a photographic processing laboratory. Shortly afterwards an eye test revealed that he was colour-blind, which meant that he was physically unsuited to the work. His dismissal was therefore fair. And in Raymond v Dorset County Council ET Case No.426/79 the claimant was a fireman who wore spectacles. Health and Safety Regulations were introduced that prohibited firemen with spectacles wearing breathing apparatus. As the claimant's vision was well below the minimum recommended by the Home Office, he was fairly dismissed for lack of capability.

4.6

Note that care must be taken when dealing with disabled workers, since the Disability Discrimination Act 1995 (incorporated into the Equality Act 2010 from a date to be appointed) makes it unlawful to discriminate against disabled people and imposes a duty on employers to take reasonable steps to make certain types of adjustments to accommodate disabled workers. For further information, see IDS Employment Law Handbook, 'Disability Discrimination' (2002) (due to be updated in autumn 2010).

Overlap with misconduct. Some cases of incapability may really be cases of
misconduct. This was recognised by the EAT in Sutton and Gates (Luton) Ltd v Boxall 1979 ICR 67, EAT, when it said that 'capability' should be treated as applying to those cases in which the incapability is due to inherent incapacity. Where someone fails to come up to standard through his or her own carelessness, negligence or idleness, this is not incapability but misconduct. The main significance of the distinction is in respect of assessment of the employee's

4.7

121

contribution to the dismissal, but it is also relevant in determining the steps that a reasonable employer ought to take before dismissing the employee – see below under 'Procedural factors'.

In some cases conduct and capability can overlap as reasons for dismissal and it may prove difficult to distinguish between the two – especially for employers filling in their response forms. If the reasons for dismissal do overlap, all that is required of employers is that they identify which in their own mind was the principal reason for dismissal – Hart v Sussex Group Training Association EAT 239/78. Failure to state accurately the precise statutory reason will not be fatal where the facts reveal a substantial reason under the ERA. An example:

- **Wood v Agnew Stores (Holdings)** Ltd EAT 582/85: an off-licence manager was dismissed for 'misconduct' because of large stock deficits. The employment tribunal preferred to regard this as a reason relating to capability but found that any mistake in nomenclature did not make the dismissal unfair. The EAT agreed that this was 'simply a matter of label' and that there was an evidential basis for the dismissal either way.

4.8　It will not necessarily matter, therefore, that the true reason for dismissal is found to be different from the one proffered by the employer, provided there is no change in the facts relied on and the employee is not disadvantaged in meeting the employer's case – see Chapter 3 under 'Reason for dismissal – identification of reason' for further details. Nevertheless, as discussed in Chapter 3, in some cases a failure to attach the correct label may be fatal for the employer. For example, in Home Charm Retail Ltd v Smith EAT 137/82 a store manager was dismissed for 'gross incompetence', even though he had made the store extremely profitable. The EAT upheld a finding of unfair dismissal because it could not see how the employee could have been incapable. The employer's concern centred on the manager's failure to follow strict paperwork procedure, and the EAT acknowledged that if the problem had been treated as one of misconduct the employer might have escaped unfair dismissal liability. However, the employer did not present the evidence which would have supported such a ruling.

Similarly, in Cobb v The Governing Body of Tadcaster Grammar School ET Case No.1803914/06 a tribunal held that the school had unfairly dismissed C, the head of science, for gross misconduct when the real reason was a fairly minor issue of capability. Each February C voluntarily took the school sixth form on a skiing trip. In 2006 C stayed in separate accommodation. The trip passed without incident, but the school believed that his staying in separate accommodation amounted to a serious failure in his duty of care as party leader and dismissed him for gross misconduct. The tribunal held that C's failing was due to capability not misconduct, but that it did not affect his ability to carry out his role of Head of Science. An appropriate course of action would have been to suspend him from leading school trips until he had completed retraining in this area.

If an employee reacts badly to capability issues raised by his or her employer, this reaction can itself become a misconduct issue. This happened in Lewis v Blue Arrow Ltd ET Case No.2901344/06 after L was called to a capability meeting to discuss his reluctance to work in aircraft tanks, as required by his employer, because he suffered from claustrophobia. The next day his partner phoned the employer to say that L was ill. When L's manager called to find out the nature of his illness, L became very angry and was abusive towards him. A tribunal upheld the employer's decision to dismiss L for gross misconduct.

Purported redundancy dismissals. Employers are often tempted to make **4.9** dismissals by reason of an employee's incapability more palatable by asserting 'redundancy' as the reason for dismissal. However, such good intentions can backfire. If challenged in the employment tribunal, an employer who has put forward redundancy as the sole reason for dismissal will be expected to show that the dismissal meets the statutory definition of redundancy in S.139(1) ERA. If it transpires that there was no cessation of the business or cessation or diminution in the requirements of the business for employees to carry out work of a particular kind, then the dismissal cannot be for redundancy and may well be unfair on the basis that the employer has not made out the true reason for dismissal.

That said, an employer who has implemented capability procedures in dealing with an under-performing employee may escape the sanction of unfair dismissal if the only error it commits is labelling the reason for dismissal 'redundancy' rather than 'capability'. In Barbeary v John Laing Services Ltd ET Case No.2204621/97, for example, B was an Operations Director for JLS Ltd, with overall responsibility for a number of contracts, including a substantial one with Anglian Water. Serious problems arose with that contract, as a result of which Anglian Water informed B that it was imposing a time penalty. Two months later, Anglian Water suspended the contract on safety grounds, and shortly afterwards terminated it, alleging fundamental breach of contract by JLS Ltd. B was told that the loss of the contract made his continued employment untenable, and he was dismissed – ostensibly by reason of redundancy – and paid six months' salary in lieu of notice. A tribunal dismissed his claim for unfair dismissal, holding that the reason for dismissal was lack of capability rather than redundancy. In the circumstances, and in view of B's seniority, the employer was entitled to hold him responsible for the loss of the contract. The economic loss this caused, the safety implications and the fact that B had been put on notice about the various problems during the progress of the contract, brought dismissal within the range of reasonable responses.

Some other substantial reason? As noted in Chapter 8, 'Some other **4.10** substantial reason' (SOSR) is a catch-all category that can be used by employers to justify dismissal. However, given the general nature of this category, it is not surprising that tribunals have sometimes found that a purported dismissal for SOSR was, in fact, for a more specific reason, such as capability. Two examples:

- **Lauffer v Barking, Havering and Redbridge University Hospitals NHS Trust** 2009 EWHC 2360, QBD: L, who had been employed by the Trust since 1998 as a consultant general surgeon, was involved in a number of operations that resulted in injury to the patients and, on a few occasions, in their death. L was suspended from practice and, following a meeting on 25 June 2009, was dismissed on the basis that the Trust had lost trust and confidence in him. The Trust stressed that the dismissal was not for misconduct or capability. L contended that the Trust should have followed its capability procedure, which provided for a detailed pre-hearing procedure, including retraining, counselling and performance review. L applied to the High Court for an interim injunction to restore him to the position he was in prior to the June meeting to enable him to engage in the capability pre-hearing process. The Trust argued that L had been dismissed for SOSR and that the contractual capability procedure was therefore not engaged. In granting L's injunction the Court noted that a loss of trust and confidence could fall under the category of 'some other substantial reason' (see Chapter 8 under 'Miscellaneous reasons' for further details). However, in this case, the evidence indicated that it was L's lack of judgement and insight which gave rise to the Trust's concern. It was strongly arguable, said the Court, that this lack went to L's capability to perform his role as a surgeon and that what was relied upon as the cause for the loss of trust and confidence was actually an adverse view of L's capability. The Court therefore granted L's interim injunction and restored him to the position he was in prior to the meeting on 25 June when, as contended by L, the pre-hearing process under the Trust's capability procedure would be contractually available to him

- **Logan v Siemens Medical Solutions** ET Case No.1804973/06: the employer attempted to argue SOSR when L was summarily dismissed following a number of concerns raised by customers. The tribunal noted that third-party pressure to dismiss could amount to 'some other substantial reason' (see Chapter 8 for further details). However, no such pressure had been exerted in this case. The tribunal considered that the reason could be more appropriately categorized as capability (as it involved L's performance and attitude). Therefore, the information received from the customers should either have been investigated to see if specific problems could be identified or dealt with as a capability issue with a view to seeing if L's performance could be improved. It certainly did not justify the employer dismissing L without notice.

4.11 **Qualifications**

'Qualifications' for the purposes of S.98(2)(a) ERA are defined as 'any degree, diploma or other academic, technical or professional qualification relevant to the position which [the employee] held' – S.98(3)(b). In Blue Star Ship Management Ltd v Williams 1978 ICR 770, EAT, the EAT held that

124

'qualifications', as defined, are concerned with 'matters relating to aptitude and ability' and that a 'mere licence, permit or authorisation' is not a qualification unless it is substantially concerned with the aptitude or ability of the employee to do the job. Thus, holding a driving licence is a qualification, because it relates to aptitude or ability to do a job which necessitates driving. But simply being registered as a seafarer or holding a union card would not be a qualification as defined.

The statutory definition of qualifications not only covers certificates of qualification that can be taken from one employer to another as evidence of an employee's authoritatively recognised ability to do a particular job but also includes in-house aptitude tests devised by an employer, provided they are relevant to the particular job – Blackman v Post Office 1974 ICR 151, NIRC.

4.12 Qualification requirements need not necessarily be expressly stated in the contract of employment. They may be inferred from the job advertisement or implied from the nature of the job itself. Thus, in Tayside Regional Council v McIntosh 1982 IRLR 272, EAT, M was recruited as a motor mechanic. The job advertisement stated that possession of a clean current driving licence was essential, but M's contract made no mention of this. The EAT held that possession of a driving licence was clearly an essential and continuing condition of M's employment, so that he was fairly dismissed when he was disqualified from driving.

Qualification dismissals usually arise where someone is engaged on the understanding that he or she will acquire a particular qualification and then fails to do so. In Blackman v Post Office (above), for instance, B was employed as an unestablished post and telegraph officer who had to take an aptitude test after satisfactorily completing a trial period. He was allowed three attempts but failed each time (although only narrowly on the last occasion). Although there were no complaints about his practical work, his dismissal for lack of qualifications was held to be fair.

Change in employer's requirements. Qualifications that the employee had or 4.13 should have had at the outset of the employment relationship are not to be regarded as fixed and unchanging. In a fast-developing world they easily become outmoded as a result of new techniques or reorganisation, or the company's changing pattern of work. In Rooney v Davic Engineering Ltd ET Case No.14518/79, for example, the claimant had passed the company's trade test and successfully completed a three-month probationary period. When one side of the business declined, a particular customer began to represent 90–95 per cent of the company's business. This contractor insisted that only those welders who had obtained a particular qualification be allowed to work on components intended for him. The claimant, who had been warned of the consequences of failure, took the test three times and failed each time. When the contractor refused to waive the regulations and give him another chance,

125

the company did not have enough work to keep him fully occupied. The employment tribunal found the dismissal fair.

Similarly, in Owen v Rhymney Valley District Council ET Case No.10316/87 the claimant's contract of employment did not originally require that swimming-pool attendants had to renew their life-saving qualification periodically. However, the tribunal held that the employer acted reasonably in varying the claimant's contract to include this requirement and so his dismissal for failing to renew his qualification was fair.

Although employers may change their policy regarding staff qualifications, they must act reasonably towards those serving employees who do not meet the new criteria. In Evans v Bury Football Club Co Ltd EAT 185/81 E was a professional footballer on a fixed-term contract when injury brought his playing career to an end. He was offered and accepted a job with the same club as assistant physiotherapist. A new manager was then appointed who required a qualified physiotherapist and did not consider E suitable because of his lack of experience and qualifications. E was given a week's notice of non-renewal before the expiry of his contract. A tribunal found his dismissal fair. The EAT upheld E's appeal, holding that, although the employer had changed the policy for good reason, it was not reasonable to dismiss the employee when contrary expectations had been raised in his mind.

4.14 **Lapse or loss of qualifications.** If an employee loses qualifications that are needed for his or her job, then dismissal is likely to be fair if no alternative employment is available. Loss of qualifications arises most frequently in relation to driving licences, as in Tayside Regional Council v McIntosh (above), where holding a licence was an 'essential and continuing condition' of M's employment and so dismissal was fair. A similar conclusion was reached in respect of an otherwise exemplary employee employed as a sales representative who lost his driving licence after failing a breathalyser test while driving outside of work duties – Anderson v Safety Kleen UK Ltd EAT 306/90. In that case, the matter was not treated as a disciplinary offence but as the loss of an essential qualification for the job which the employee was employed to do. (See also Chapter 7 under 'Driving bans'.) Likewise, in Cowell v Hayward Tyler Ltd ET Case No.1152/87 the employee's qualification as a 'coded welder' lapsed when he was assigned to do work outside his field. After failing the requisite exams three times he was dismissed fairly by his employer.

Even if an employee subsequently regains the relevant qualification, this will not automatically render him or her capable of performing his or her duties. In Mathews v DHL Air Ltd EAT 0089/05 M, a pilot, had his Civil Aviation Authority (CAA) medical licence revoked because he was suffering from an anxiety-related disorder. Such a licence is a prerequisite for all working pilots. The employer subsequently decided that it had no option but to dismiss M given there was no assurance that he would regain his licence and he had refused an offer of alternative employment involving ground duties. By the time of M's appeal hearing against dismissal, the CAA had restored his medical licence. M argued that this meant that he had regained the capability to perform flying duties. However, the employer considered that M would not be operationally fit to fly until he had successfully completed a period of ground duties. Since M refused to undertake ground duties, his appeal against dismissal failed. A tribunal dismissed M's unfair dismissal claim, holding that the employer had a right to insist upon M performing ground duties as a means of rehabilitation. The EAT upheld the tribunal's decision, noting that while M had regained the necessary qualification for flying, the tribunal was entitled to find that he had not yet regained the necessary capability.

Ill health. If the employee loses his or her qualification due to ill health, the reason for dismissal will be capability (i.e. loss of the relevant qualification) rather than sickness. This may have implications for the steps an employer should follow prior to dismissal. An example:

4.15

- **Sayers v Loganair Ltd** EAT 0084/04: S had worked as a pilot on the basis that he was the sole aircrew. He became ill after being splashed by a disinfectant. As the result of a medical examination, a limitation was placed on his pilot's licence by the Civil Aviation Authority, such that it was only valid if he was accompanied by a co-pilot. It was envisaged that the limitation would remain in place for approximately six months. However, the restriction was extended following a further medical examination. S was subsequently dismissed on the basis that the restriction on his licence had not been lifted. He was advised by the employer that no alternative employment was available, such as vacancies on multi-crew aircraft. An employment tribunal held that S had been dismissed for a potentially fair reason, namely the fact that he had ceased to hold the necessary licence to do the job for which he had been employed. However, it went on to conclude that S's dismissal was unfair because the employer should have obtained an up-to-date assessment of his state of health before deciding to dismiss him. The EAT held that this conclusion was flawed: a further medical examination would have made no difference to the restriction on S's licence since the employer's doctor had no power to alter the restriction. Further, the employer had not been presented with any medical evidence or advice by or on behalf of the employee that his medical condition was likely to improve in the near future to the extent that the restriction would be lifted. Had the tribunal found dismissal to be on the grounds of ill health, an up-to-date medical examination by the employer might have been required prior to dismissal. However, that was not the case here.

4.16 Establishing lack of capability

Where an employer seeks to rely on incapability or lack of qualifications as the ground for dismissal, the onus is on it to show that this was the actual reason or principal reason for dismissal. The employer does not have to establish in detail the correctness of the belief in the employee's incompetence, only that it has reasonable grounds for that belief and has taken reasonable steps to verify its conclusions. As Lord Denning MR put it in Alidair Ltd v Taylor 1978 ICR 445, CA: 'Whenever a man is dismissed for incapacity or incompetence it is sufficient that the employer honestly believes on reasonable grounds that the man is incapable or incompetent. It is not necessary for the employer to prove that he is in fact incapable or incompetent.'

Put another way by Lord Justice Geoffrey Lane in the same case, the Court of Appeal's test of a fair capability dismissal (aside from procedure) has two elements:

- does the employer honestly believe this employee is incompetent or unsuitable for the job?

- are the grounds for that belief reasonable?

What the tribunal has to decide is whether there was material in front of the employer that satisfied the employer of the employee's inadequacy or unsuitability and on which it was reasonable to dismiss. It is for the employer to set the standards asked of employees; tribunals cannot substitute their own view of an employee's competence. Employers can insist on levels of performance that are higher than those at comparable institutions. In Fletcher v St Leonard's School EAT 25/87, for example, the EAT said that an independent school was entitled to set its own standards of teaching, even if they were higher than those in a local state school, and so its dismissal of a teacher who failed to conform to the higher standards was fair.

4.17 Satisfying the test

The Alidair test (above) means that an employer has to produce evidence of poor performance and show that this was the real reason for dismissing the employee. In Kent County Council v Maidment EAT 3/87 a teacher was dismissed following complaints about his competence by the school's headmistress. The teacher was given no reason for his dismissal and when he claimed unfair dismissal the Council produced no evidence from the members of the disciplinary subcommittee that took the decision to dismiss. The EAT upheld a tribunal finding that the employer had failed to prove the reason or principal reason for dismissal and that the dismissal was therefore unfair. It noted that the evidence tendered suggested that the reason for dismissal was 'a clash of personalities' and held that the tribunal was correct to find that there was insufficient evidence to establish the true reason for dismissal.

128

The availability of evidence of an employee's incapability will vary from job to job. In Fletcher v St Leonard's School (above), for example, the employer could point to evidence that pupils' grades had fallen below the normal rate of success. Similarly, the incompetence of sales people can be shown by their failure to reach targets set by the employer. The incompetence of a piece-worker can be measured in the same way. However, failure to meet such targets does not always justify dismissal. The tribunal will take into account all the surrounding circumstances: whether the target was realistic; the reasons for the employee not attaining the target; how other sales staff fared and the employee's length of service. For example, in Sibun v Modern Telephones Ltd 1976 IRLR 81, ET, S had been selling satisfactorily for 20 years. However, over a period of 15 months, his sales missed targets by 25 per cent. After several warnings he was dismissed. A tribunal held that it was unreasonable to judge him on results over the last 15–18 months after his long period of satisfactory service. In the circumstances, a three-year period should have been given before it was fair to dismiss.

The incompetence of managers is often more difficult to measure and prove. In Cook v Thomas Linnell and Sons Ltd 1977 ICR 770, EAT, the EAT said that if an employer has genuinely come to believe over a period of time that a manager is incompetent, that is in itself evidence of incapability. However, it will be necessary to see whether there is supporting evidence. Supporting evidence may include evidence of a fall-off in trade or complaints from customers or colleagues. In Queensway Discount Warehouses Ltd v McNeall EAT 569/85 the employer established incapability as the reason for dismissal based on a genuine belief that the manager was unable to motivate staff or deal with customers' orders and that his store presented a poor image. The tribunal's decision of fair dismissal was upheld by the EAT.

Single acts of negligence or incompetence. Incapability is usually established **4.18** over a period of time, during which the employee's incompetence or inability to meet reasonable standards becomes apparent. However, in rare cases, a one-off act can sometimes be relied upon by employers to establish incapability, particularly if the act so undermines confidence in the employee that the employer is justified in dismissing for it. In Alidair Ltd v Taylor (above), for example, a pilot put the lives of many passengers at risk when he landed his aircraft negligently. This amounted to a sufficient reason for dismissal in view of his gross incompetence and the potentially calamitous consequences of his actions. And in Clark v Airflow Streamlines plc ET Case No.29621/83 an experienced car mechanic negligently left an old oil seal in place during a pre-sale service. As a result, the purchaser of the car drove only 11 miles before the engine seized up and the rear wheels locked. The majority of the tribunal, while sympathising with the mechanic, looked at the potential danger and at the damage to the employer's reputation and found the dismissal fair.

129

In general, however, tribunals are unlikely to be sympathetic to an employer who dismisses an employee – particularly a long-serving employee – on account of a single error of judgement in circumstances where that error, although perhaps costly, is not potentially calamitous. In Day v Diemer and Reynolds Ltd 1975 IRLR 298, ET, a tribunal held the dismissal of a print machine operator to be unfair where he had been dismissed because he failed to follow a procedure designed to ensure that the gathering of various sections of a book was done properly and in the right order. Although his error led to a print run of more than 7,000 faulty books, the tribunal ruled that the sanction of dismissal was out of all proportion to the employee's mistake. A similar conclusion was reached by the tribunal in Jones v London Co-Operative Society 1975 IRLR 110, ET, where a till operator was dismissed for ringing up the wrong amount on the till and failing to give the customer a receipt. Although such errors were classified as grounds for summary dismissal in the Staff Code, the tribunal held that the employer had not acted reasonably in dismissing the employee for a one-off mistake, honestly made, in circumstances where she had an unblemished career and had been operating under considerable pressure on the day of the incident.

4.19 The fact that a serious incident has occurred while on an employee's 'watch' is not necessarily evidence of incapability and all the circumstances need to be taken into account. An example:

● **Mezey v South West London and St George's Mental Health NHS Trust** 2010 EWCA Civ 293, CA: M, a consultant psychiatrist since 1991, allowed B, a patient suffering from a persistent delusional disorder, one hour's unsupervised leave in the hospital grounds. However, he absconded during this time and the next day attacked and killed a stranger. An investigating panel was convened to look into M's care and management of B. The panel's report found that it was not appropriate for M to grant B unescorted ground leave before she had personally assessed him. Nevertheless, it concluded that this did not amount to serious professional incompetence. The Trust proposed to convene a capability hearing to consider the report's findings but M sought an injunction from the High Court to prevent the Trust from holding the hearing which, she argued, would be in breach of contract. She submitted that the purpose of the contractual capability procedure was to improve future performance but the report had found that there was no issue of lack of capability. The Court agreed, holding that it was not open to the Trust on the basis of the report to impose any capability sanction under the Department of Health (DoH) capability procedure.

The Court of Appeal dismissed the Trust's appeal against the injunction. Although the investigating panel had found that M had failed to deliver an adequate standard of care, a capability issue would only arise under the DoH capability procedure if that failure was caused by 'lack of knowledge, ability or consistently poor performance' and M's capability to practice had

130

been called into question. The findings of the report precluded such a judgment being made, having concluded that M's decision to grant unescorted leave, while inappropriate, was not likely to put other patients or the public at risk in the future and might well have been made by other competent practitioners. It also emphasised that M was an obviously conscientious and competent consultant psychiatrist. Therefore, far from being called into question, her capability to practice had been vindicated. In the light of those findings, the threshold for invoking the capability procedure had not been crossed and the High Court had been right to conclude that to hold a capability hearing was a breach of contract which could be restrained by injunction.

Small but persistent errors. A number of small incidents, by themselves relatively unimportant, may add up over a period of time to a sufficient reason for dismissal. Miller v Executors of John C Graham 1978 IRLR 309, EAT, concerned a farm manager whose technical qualifications and abilities were not questioned by his employer. However, following a number of small incidents the employer concluded that he was not capable of performing his managerial duties. He was warned about this but, after some initial improvements, matters deteriorated again. The EAT upheld the tribunal's finding of a fair dismissal. **4.20**

Systems of assessment. Appraisal systems or performance management reviews often form the basis for initiating procedures that may eventually lead to dismissal on the ground of incapability. However, tribunals will often expect to see other evidence of incompetence in addition to the view of the manager responsible for conducting the employee's appraisal before accepting that it was reasonable to dismiss by reason of incapability. **4.21**

Sometimes, the introduction of a new appraisal system reveals a lack of capability in employees whose performance had not hitherto been called into serious question. In Gozdzik and Scopigno v Chlidema Carpet Co Ltd EAT 598/78, for example, the inefficiency of two employees was not fully revealed until a new bonus system was introduced. Their dismissal was held to be fair even though the employer had previously tolerated their lack of productivity.

Inconsistent evidence. An employer's case that an employee is (or has become) incapable of doing his or her job, or has failed to reach the requisite standards, can be undermined by evidence to the contrary. For example, the employee may seek to rebut the employer's claim by citing his or her track record in recent performance reviews or appraisals or by showing that he or she has been in receipt of discretionary benefits (such as bonuses) as evidence that the employer's contention is not valid. **4.22**

Employers should, therefore, be careful to ensure that any dismissal is for a genuine capability reason and is not motivated by age discrimination. In Burke

131

v Up Design Ltd ET Case No.3203091/07 B, aged 59, was hired via a recruitment consultant as an experienced garment technologist and product developer. Shortly after she started work, the employer began to have concerns about her performance. Matters came to a head when she was asked to send some information to a client in order to prevent a contract being cancelled, and she failed to provide adequate assistance to the client concerned. When the employer raised its concerns with B, she was defensive and the conversation became heated. B was then dismissed. B's direct discrimination claim failed, the tribunal holding that age 'played no part whatsoever' in her dismissal. Further, the tribunal accepted the employer's evidence that it did not know B's age prior to the commencement of tribunal proceedings.

4.23 Reasonableness

Once the reason for dismissal has been established, the question of whether the dismissal was fair or unfair in the particular circumstances of the case will be judged according to the 'reasonableness' test set out in S.98(4) ERA, which is discussed in detail in Chapter 3. Under that test, the tribunal will consider not only what steps a reasonable employer would have taken when faced with an employee who does not come up to scratch, but also what steps the employer should have taken at the very start to minimise the risk of poor performance and to create the conditions that allow an employee to carry out his or her duties satisfactorily.

Proper training, supervision and encouragement are essential, especially where the employee has been promoted to a new job. If the employer fails to provide instruction and support at the outset, or sets unrealistic standards for an employee, then a subsequent dismissal for incompetence may be unfair. Three examples:

- **Fowler v Hertfordshire County Council** ET Case No.1501047/06: F, a teacher, was invited to a meeting to discuss some concerns the head teacher had about her. At the outset of the meeting the head announced that it was an informal capability meeting and gave F a letter listing 13 concerns, none of which were about F's teaching ability. The nature of the meeting and the number of concerns came as a complete surprise to F. The head had prepared a list of targets, including that one of F's lessons be observed each week for a four-week period. Two days later, when the head informed F that she would observe a lesson the following Monday, F resigned. The tribunal, by a majority, found that F had been unfairly constructively dismissed, holding that it was difficult to see how an employee could have any trust and confidence in an employer who initiated a capability procedure, even an informal one, when there were no grounds for doing so, set onerous targets for which there was no justification, and invited an employee to attend one meeting but then without warning turned it into something different and more serious

- **Mansfield Hosiery Mills Ltd v Bromley** 1977 IRLR 301, EAT: B was first employed as a boiler service fitter. The employer's advertisement for the job stated that he would receive training but in fact he received none. He did his job well at first and was promoted to plant maintenance supervisor. However, a number of complaints were made about his lack of enthusiasm (rather than technical competence). The EAT upheld the tribunal's finding that the employer's failure to supervise, train and encourage a new or newly promoted employee or to warn the employee of likely dismissal are circumstances to be taken into account when considering reasonableness and may outweigh the employee's shortcomings

- **Steelprint Ltd v Haynes** EAT 467/95: S Ltd introduced a new computer system and, as a result, H's workload changed from proofreading to inputting orders onto the computer system. She failed to meet the speed and accuracy targets for inputting information and was dismissed. The EAT agreed with the tribunal's finding of unfair dismissal. H had not received any training to raise her typing performance and S Ltd had shown no flexibility in allowing her to do other tasks at which she may have excelled.

4.24 By contrast, in Queensway Discount Warehouses Ltd v McNeall EAT 569/85 a salesman was promoted to a managerial position, only to be dismissed after two disastrous trial periods. The employee claimed that the dismissal was unfair because he had not received the company's management training programme and so the employer had not fulfilled the company's responsibilities to someone newly promoted. The tribunal rejected this argument on the grounds that the employee was an experienced assistant manager and his failings were not due to lack of training.

Alternative employment

4.25 Despite adequate training and support, some employees still fail to make the grade. In such cases there is no obligation upon the employer to offer employment in a subsidiary position. Even where the employee has reached his or her position through promotion, that employee has no automatic right to return to his or her old job (unless there is provision to that effect in the contract). The employer's duty to consider redeploying the employee will depend on the circumstances of each particular case, although the size and administrative resources of the business will be especially important – see Bevan Harris Ltd (t/a The Clyde Leather Co) v Gair 1981 IRLR 520, EAT, a case which involved a small family business where redeployment was impracticable.

133

However, even a multinational company may not necessarily be acting unreasonably if it fails to offer a long-serving employee alternative work. In Tyndall v Burmah Oil Trading Ltd EAT 655/83 an employee with a good work record became incompetent and was retired early. He claimed unfair dismissal on the ground that the company should have found a niche for him. The EAT, however, thought early retirement was a reasonable response as there was a recession and the employee was nearing retiring age. And in Sonvadi v Superdrug Stores plc ET Case No.57554/94 the claimant was dismissed in July 1994 from his post as manager of one of the employer's stores by reason of incapability. The main grounds were his lack of communication with his staff and his failure to motivate them. He had joined the company as a trainee manager, been promoted to assistant manager, and then promoted to the post of manager in April 1993. His principal ground of complaint was that, in so far as he was perceived to be incapable, dismissal was not a reasonable response. At most, he should have been demoted in line with a provision in the company handbook that demotion could be used as an alternative to dismissal. In rejecting his claim of unfair dismissal the tribunal held that there is no rule of law that demotion should automatically be considered in capability dismissals. The employer was entitled in the circumstances of the instant case to come to the view that the claimant's appointment as an assistant manager would not work. Further, in Bevan Harris Ltd (t/a The Clyde Leather Co) v Gair (above), the EAT emphasised that the correct test is whether the dismissal fell within the range of options open to a reasonable employer in the circumstances and held that a tribunal had therefore applied the wrong test in deciding that the dismissal was unfair because a reasonable employer would have considered demotion rather than dismissal.

4.26 Employers will never be expected to create a post for an employee artificially but, in borderline cases, if a job is available and the employer has not offered it, the scales may be tipped in favour of the employee. There is a limit, however, to how far an employer will be expected to accommodate an employee who is incapable of mastering the skills of the particular job that he or she is employed to do. In Watson v Commissioners of Inland Revenue ET Case No.2105124/03 the question arose as to whether an employer had failed to act reasonably when declining to move W into a job that did not require the specific skills in respect of which the employee was especially weak. W accepted that the employer had reasonably reached a view that he was incapable of carrying out his duties to a satisfactory standard and conceded that the procedure leading to his dismissal had been fair. However, he contended that his dismissal was nonetheless unfair in that, given the large number of duties that someone in his grade could be called upon to undertake, he should have been moved sideways into a post that did not require him to perform the duties that he was incapable of carrying out satisfactorily. The tribunal rejected this argument and held that W had not been unfairly dismissed. There was no duty on the employer to move the employee

134

sideways: were it otherwise, the employer might never be able to dismiss an employee such as the claimant fairly for lack of capability, since the employer would have to exhaust every potential post first.

Procedural factors   4.27

It has long been recognized that employers should follow a fair procedure before dismissing an employee for incapability. In Lewis Shops Group v Wiggins 1973 ICR 335, NIRC – approved by the EAT in Littlewoods Organisation Ltd v Egenti 1976 ICR 516, EAT – the NIRC commented that 'the general concept of fair play inherent in the disciplinary procedures should also guide management in considering a dismissal for inefficiency'. This means that in general an employer should be slow to dismiss an employee for incapability 'without first telling the employee of the respects in which he is failing to do his job adequately, warning him of the possibility or likelihood of dismissal on this ground, and giving him an opportunity of improving his performance' – James v Waltham Holy Cross UDC 1973 ICR 398, NIRC. This can be broken down into the following basic steps:

- proper investigation/appraisal of the employee's performance and identification of the problem

- warning of the consequences of failing to improve

- a reasonable chance to improve.

In Burns v Turboflex Ltd EAT 377/96 the EAT emphasised the fact that employers should allow employees to answer allegations of poor performance. In that case the claimant was dismissed while he was out of the country. The EAT held that it was contrary to the rules of natural justice to deny him the chance to respond to the allegations made against him.

If an employer fails to follow these steps it is very likely that a tribunal will rule that it acted unreasonably and unfairly. And where the Acas Code of Practice on Disciplinary and Grievance Procedures applies, the tribunal may well increase the compensation it awards by up to 25 per cent.

The Acas Code of Practice   4.28

As explained in Chapter 3, the revised Acas Code of Practice on Disciplinary and Grievance Procedures ('The Code') sets out principles for handing disciplinary and grievance procedures in the workplace with which employers and employees are expected to comply. The Code is relevant to the question of liability and will be taken into account by a tribunal when determining the reasonableness of a dismissal in accordance with S.98(4) – S.207 TULR(C)A. Further, if the dismissal is found to be unfair, the tribunal can increase (or indeed decrease) an award of compensation by up to 25 per cent for an

135

unreasonable failure to follow the Code if it considers it just and equitable to do so – S.207A TULR(C)A.

The Code contains a section on handling disciplinary issues (pages 5–8) which sets out the steps employers must normally follow, namely:

- establish the facts of each case

- inform the employee of the problem

- hold a meeting with the employee to discuss the problem

- allow the employee to be accompanied at the meeting

- decide on appropriate action

- provide employees with an opportunity to appeal.

4.29　**Scope of Code.** The Introduction to the Code states that it is designed to help employers and employees deal with disciplinary and grievance situations in the workplace and confirms that 'disciplinary situations' include 'poor performance'. This clearly embraces many of the situations considered above; for example, where the employee is inflexible and unadaptable or has simply failed to meet the employer's targets. However, it does not appear to cover 'qualification' cases, since in most of these there is an absence of 'fault' on the part of the employee. Nevertheless, an employer will still need to follow a fair and appropriate procedure in such cases and the Code establishes general standards of good practice that may prove helpful.

The Code sets out one disciplinary procedure to deal with both 'conduct' and 'poor performance'. This is somewhat surprising given that they have traditionally been viewed as best dealt with under separate procedures – disciplinary (for misconduct) and capability (for poor performance). In Littlewoods Organisation Ltd v Egenti (above), for example, the EAT stated that 'the same fairly strict requirement of various steps of procedure, which exists in cases of dismissal for misconduct, where it is a disciplinary measure, is or may be different from a situation in which the dismissal is on the ground of lack of competence or lack of capability'. Indeed, a tribunal could find that an employer has acted unfairly if a performance issue is treated in exactly the same way as a conduct issue. For example, the employer may need to be more sensitive to the needs of an employee with a performance issue, since he or she may be trying his or her best but simply not be up to the job. Further, giving an employee the opportunity to improve is more important in performance cases.

4.30　Many employers do have a separate capability procedure in place. This is recognised in the Introduction to the Code, which provides that, 'if employers have a separate capability procedure they may prefer to address performance issues under this procedure'. It goes on to state that 'the basic principles of fairness set out in this Code should still be followed, albeit that they may need to be adapted'.

The Code implies that where an employer does have a separate capability procedure, the employer may choose which to follow. However, employers should be cautious in doing so as tribunals may find dismissal to be unfair if there are capability procedures in place that were not adhered to. Similarly, switching from one to the other without good reason may be unwise. In Bennett v Cornwall County Council and ors ET Case No.1701815/06, for example, the tribunal held that a switch by the employer from a capability to a disciplinary procedure without any reason or explanation was unfair. It meant that the 'whole push' of the procedure was radically different, although the subject matter was substantially the same. It was not reasonable to expect B to properly meet the concerns presented in a different framework and with a different intention.

Investigation/appraisal

4.31

The Introduction to the Acas Code states that 'employers should carry out any necessary investigations, to establish the facts of the case'. As mentioned under 'Establishing lack of capability' above, the onus is on the employer to show a potentially fair reason for dismissal. This may be difficult to do in relation to capability dismissals if the employer has not carried out a proper investigation of the employee's failings in performance. Investigation may highlight the reason for the employee's poor performance and may bring to light management's own failings. This in turn may determine what a reasonable response by management should be. Since complaints about an employee's incapability must relate to 'work of the kind which he was employed by the employer to do' (S.98(2)(a) ERA), investigation and appraisal must obviously take place in the context of the job the employee was employed to do. Further, if the employer's complaint is that the employee lacks a relevant qualification, this should be investigated to ensure, for example, that the qualification is necessary for the employee to carry out his or her duties.

If the employer fails to investigate, dismissal may be unfair in two ways: first, because no potentially fair grounds were shown; and secondly, because the dismissal was not handled properly. The employer must ensure that the employee is aware of the charges being levelled and allow him or her the opportunity to state his or her case. In British Midland Airways Ltd v Gilmore EAT 173/81 a pilot was only made aware of the charges against him at his disciplinary hearing and he was not aware that the company had any intention of dismissing him. In addition, the findings of the hearing were never communicated to him. Instead he was merely told that he was dismissed. The EAT held the dismissal to be unfair because of these breaches of natural justice. It said that procedural requirements could not be waived merely because the employee was involved in a job where death could result

137

from incompetence. (Note that the dismissal of an airline pilot for a single act of incompetence is likely to be fair in principle – see Alidair Ltd v Taylor 1978 ICR 445, CA. However, in that case the employee was given a full opportunity to hear what was said against him and to state his case.) In SMT Sales and Service Co Ltd v Irwin EAT 485/79 a branch manager with 27 years' service was dismissed instantly when he refused to resign. His results were below targeted levels but there was no investigation into the reason. The dismissal was therefore held to be unfair.

4.32 **More than one suspect.** Where one of two employees is suspected of being responsible for acts or omissions meriting dismissal and the employer, despite reasonable investigation, cannot discover which of them is to blame, it may be fair to dismiss both of them. This rule is not confined to dismissals for misconduct and can apply equally to dismissals for incapability – Guberman v Augustus Barnett (Scotland) Ltd EAT 152/85. However, this rule is not applied lightly. In another EAT decision, it was made clear that suspicion must have been narrowed to the point of certainty that it was one of two employees who was guilty of the act complained of – Leyland Vehicles Ltd v Wright EAT 712/81.

4.33 **Probationers.** Employees on probation are a special case because tribunals and courts consider it particularly important that reasonable steps are taken to maintain appraisal of probationers throughout the probationary period. This was stressed by the EAT in Post Office v Mughal 1977 ICR 763, EAT, where it said that: 'The question for the... tribunal is: have the employers shown that they took reasonable steps to maintain appraisal of the probationer throughout the period of probation, giving guidance by advice or warning when such was likely to be useful or fair; and that an appropriate officer made an honest effort to determine whether the probationer came up to the required standard, having informed himself of the appraisals made by supervising officers and any other facts recorded about the probationer? If this procedure is followed, it is only if the officer responsible for deciding upon selection of probationers then arrives at a decision which no reasonable assessment could dictate, that [a] tribunal should hold the dismissal to be unfair.'

Insufficient appraisal and training rendered the dismissal of a probationer unfair in Herity v Ashbury Confectionery Ltd ET Case No.1902731/03. In that case H, a machine operator, was summarily dismissed for lack of capability during his probationary period. A tribunal held his dismissal to be unfair. The employer had failed to provide adequate training and, as a probationer, H was in a special category of employee in respect of whom it was especially important to carry out regular appraisals. The lack of appraisal and proper training was probably enough to make the dismissal unfair; but coupled with the way that the dismissal was carried out, with little or no formal procedure, the decision to dismiss certainly fell outside the band of reasonable responses.

In White v London Transport Executive 1981 IRLR 261, EAT, it was argued, on the basis of the principle laid down in Mughal (above), that there is an implied term in every probationary contract of employment that the employer is bound to support, assist, offer guidance to and train the probationary employee. The EAT rejected this argument, but said that 'the right term to imply is... an obligation on the employer to take reasonable steps to maintain an appraisal of a probationer during a trial period, giving guidance by advice or warning where necessary'. A failure to guide and train may render an otherwise fair dismissal unfair – ILEA v Lloyd 1981 IRLR 394, CA.

Hearing   4.34

The Acas Code requires a 'disciplinary hearing' to be held for the employee to answer any allegations of poor performance. However, many employers may prefer to have a capability hearing for performance issues, reserving disciplinary hearings for conduct issues. As noted above, the Code allows employers to use their own capability procedures to address performance issues, provided the 'basic principles of fairness' set out in the Code are still followed. An example:

- **Buckley v Barker and Stonehouse Ltd** ET Case No.2500923/05: on 16 November 2004 B, an assistant store manager at Darlington, was invited by the Managing Director's secretary to attend a meeting on 18 November. Having no idea what the meeting was to be about, B asked the Company Director for clarification but he said that she would find out on the day. The meeting took place with the two directors and B (who was unrepresented). She was informed that they had several fundamental concerns about her performance which they wanted to discuss with her; for example, her lack of commercial awareness. B was given two options: to move from Darlington to Middlesbrough as an assistant manager for a period of retraining; or to stay and face a disciplinary/capability hearing. B asked for two or three days to think about the situation but was told that they would like to get a decision that day. B telephoned the Company Director later that day to tell him she was going to resign. The tribunal upheld B's claim for unfair constructive dismissal. It held that although the employer was within its rights to have a meeting to discuss B's perceived shortcomings, the way it had gone about it was unfair. It had called her to a meeting without giving her any details or advising her of her right to be accompanied (see below). Although retraining in Darlington might have been an option further down the line, it should first have clearly informed her of the improvements required in her performance and given her a time limit in which to comply.

This case indicates that what an employer sees as an 'informal chat' may in fact be a disciplinary/capability hearing with the added procedural requirements that entails, such as the right to be accompanied (see below). It also highlights the fact that if an employer does not follow the correct procedure, not only is there a risk

139

of a finding of unfair dismissal at a later date, but, more immediately, an employee may be entitled to resign and claim constructive dismissal.

4.35 **Right to be accompanied.** Under S.10 of the Employment Relations Act 1999 (ERelA), where a worker 'reasonably requests' to be accompanied at a 'disciplinary hearing', the employer must permit the worker to be accompanied by a 'companion'. The companion – chosen by the worker – may be a trade union representative or a fellow worker – S.10(2A).

A disciplinary hearing is defined in the ERelA as a hearing that could result in:

- the administration of a formal warning – S.13(4)(a)

- the taking of some other action – S.13(4)(b)

- the confirmation of a warning issued or some other action taken – S.13(4)(c) (this applies to appeal hearings).

Therefore, even if the employer is holding what it terms a 'capability' hearing to discuss performance issues, the statutory right to be accompanied would still apply if it is likely to result in a formal warning or some other action.

As the Acas Code emphasises, to exercise the statutory right to be accompanied workers must make a *reasonable* request – para 15. According to the Code, what is reasonable will depend on the circumstances of each case but it will not normally be reasonable for the employee to insist on being accompanied 'by a companion whose presence would prejudice the hearing'.

4.36 **Right to legal representation.** It is generally accepted that neither the ERelA nor the Acas Code confers an entitlement to have a *legal* representative present at the hearing. However, it appears in certain circumstances that Article 6 of the European Convention on Human Rights (ECHR) – which provides that an individual has the right to a fair hearing in the determination of his or her civil rights or of any criminal charge – may do so. This is despite the fact that Article 6(3) provides that only in the case of a *criminal* charge does an individual have the right to legal assistance. This is likely to be particularly relevant for public authority employers who are required by the Human Rights Act 1996 (HRA) to observe Convention obligations. Two key Court of Appeal cases on this issue:

- **Kulkarni v Milton Keynes Hospital NHS Foundation Trust and anor** 2010 ICR 101, CA: K, a junior doctor accused of misconduct involving inappropriate touching of a patient, sought legal representation at his disciplinary hearing. His main argument, that he had a contractual right to legal representation, succeeded before the Court of Appeal. Although not strictly necessary for its decision, Lady Justice Smith – giving the leading judgment – went on to note that where an employee is facing what is 'in effect a criminal charge', Article 6 of the ECHR implies a right to legal representation. Case law of the European Court of Human Rights (ECtHR) indicated that Article 6 would not apply where all that was at stake was the loss of a specific job. However, where the outcome of the proceedings is potentially more serious, such as the loss of the right to practise a particular profession, Article 6 would then be engaged. In the instant case, K was facing an accusation of serious sexual misconduct and, if found guilty, would effectively be barred from employment in the NHS. It did not matter that the right to legal representation was being requested in the context of civil proceedings because K was effectively facing a criminal charge. Therefore, the Court said, had it been necessary to make a decision on this issue, it would have held that Article 6 was engaged

- **R (on the application of G) v Governors of X School and anor** 2010 IRLR 222, CA: G, a music teaching assistant at X school, was suspended in October 2007 pending an investigation into allegations that he had formed an inappropriate relationship with a 15-year-old boy. No criminal proceedings were brought but the school instigated disciplinary proceedings. G was permitted representation at the hearing by either a trade union representative or a colleague, but not by a solicitor. Following the hearing, M was summarily dismissed for an abuse of trust amounting to gross misconduct. The school reported his dismissal to the Secretary of State so that he might determine whether to place G on a 'barred list' preventing him from working with children in future. G appealed against the decision to dismiss and requested legal representation at the appeal. This request was also refused. The High Court granted G's application for judicial review, holding that Article 6 entitled G to legal representation at the disciplinary and appeal hearings. The School appealed. Lord Justice Laws, giving the leading judgment of the Court of Appeal, held that since the disciplinary proceedings were determinative of G's civil right to practise his profession, they attracted Article 6 protection. He went on to consider whether Article 6 imported a right to legal representation in these circumstances. He noted that Article 6 does not necessarily entail a right of representation in *civil* proceedings (unlike criminal proceedings) but it was 'well established' by ECtHR case law that it may do so. Smith LJ's comments in Kulkarni (above) reinforced this view. Although she had expressly justified the right to representation by reference to the allegation against K being in the nature of a criminal charge, it was clear from the context both that she was considering the scope of the Article's *civil* protection and that the possibility of K effectively being barred from the NHS was uppermost in her mind. The level of civil procedural protection guaranteed by Article 6, therefore, depended on the gravity of issue at stake. Given that G's right to practise his profession was at stake, he was entitled under Article 6 to be afforded the opportunity of legal representation in the disciplinary proceedings.

4.37 Although both the above cases concerned issues of serious misconduct, the same reasoning is likely to apply in respect of an employee who is facing serious performance issues, such that if found guilty, he or she might lose the right to

141

practise in his or her given field. Laws LJ did not intend to create a 'hard and fast rule' on public authority employers' obligations in internal disciplinary hearings. Entitlement to legal representation will depend on all the facts, including the nature of the right affected and the capacity of a reviewing court or tribunal to 'reach back' into factual findings made at the disciplinary stage (which is limited where an employment tribunal is concerned, as its jurisdiction in an unfair dismissal case would not comprise a full review of the merits of the underlying facts, but rather would address the issue of whether dismissal by the employer was within the range of reasonable responses).

These Court of Appeal decisions suggest that wherever disciplinary proceedings could, in the event of an adverse outcome, end an employee's ability to practise a profession, it will be difficult to refute the argument that legal representation should be permitted. Neither of these cases was initiated in an employment tribunal or indeed involved a claim of unfair dismissal. However, employment tribunals are likely to interpret the requirement for reasonableness under S.98(4) ERA in accordance with Article 6, bearing in mind their obligation under S.3 HRA to interpret UK legislation (including the ERA) in a way compatible with ECHR rights. Therefore, failure – at least by public sector employers – to allow for legal representation, when appropriate to do so, could render the dismissal procedurally unfair. This could well apply even to *private* employers, given the framework of questions for tribunals dealing with unfair dismissal claims in which HRA issues arise set out by the Court of Appeal in X v Y 2004 ICR 1634, CA – see Chapter 3 under 'Reasonableness of dismissal – impact of the Human Rights Act' for details. Further, in Kulkarni v Milton Keynes Hospital NHS Foundation Trust and anor (above), Smith LJ stated that the issue could be framed in terms of natural justice under domestic law, as well as breach of Article 6 – although this was not picked up by Laws LJ in Governors of X School v R (above).

4.38 **Right to call witnesses.** Para 12 of the Acas Code states that both employees and employers should be able to call relevant witnesses. This has raised some eyebrows, not least because case law is somewhat ambiguous on this point. However, the rules of natural justice, in so far as they apply to disciplinary hearings, require that an employee know precisely what the accusations against him or her are and have a full opportunity of stating his or her case. It seems appropriate, therefore, that the question of whether or not it is reasonable to allow a witness to be called in a particular case should be decided in light of these principles. The right to call witnesses is discussed in greater detail in Chapter 6 under 'Disciplinary proceedings – disciplinary hearings'.

4.39 **Warnings**
In Polkey v AE Dayton Services Ltd 1988 ICR 142, HL, Lord Bridge observed that in the great majority of cases employers will not be considered to have acted reasonably in dismissing for incapability unless they have given the

employee fair warning and a chance to improve. In practice, most employers will have already incorporated a system of warnings into their dismissal procedures. Even before Polkey, warnings were considered a necessary procedural requirement, particularly in cases of misconduct, and this requirement was applied to dismissals for capability as early as 1973 – Winterhalter Gastronom Ltd v Webb 1973 ICR 245, NIRC.

The Acas Code confirms the importance of warnings as part of the disciplinary or capability process, stating at Para 18: 'Where misconduct is confirmed or the employee is found to be performing unsatisfactorily it is usual to give the employee a written warning. A further act of misconduct or failure to improve performance within a set period would normally result in a final written warning.'

In the context of incapability, warnings are most appropriate where it is in the **4.40** employee's power to improve his or her performance. Warnings give incompetent employees the opportunity to improve their performance and management a chance to pinpoint the reason for poor performance, be it insufficient training, weak support from colleagues, personality problems, lack of effort or a genuine inability to perform the job competently. However, there is no hard-and-fast rule that a dismissal must be unfair unless a formal warning is given. The Acas Code itself merely states that it is 'usual' to give a written warning, implying that there are some cases where a warning will not be needed. The important question is whether the employee was aware of the employer's dissatisfaction with his or her work – Laycock v Jones Buckie Shipyard Ltd EAT 395/81. Clearly, though, such an awareness will usually be brought home by a formal warning, and in practice warnings of some kind should be given in most cases (but see further below). This is particularly so in light of the fact that employers now risk any award of compensation for unfair dismissal being increased by up to 25 per cent if the tribunal considers that they unreasonably failed to comply with the Code (see Chapter 18).

Employers should make it clear to employees that they are warning them and the consequences of a failure to improve performance should be set out in clear terms – for instance, that it 'may result in dismissal or some other contractual penalty such as demotion or loss of seniority' (Para 20 of the Code). An example:

- **British Sulphur Corporation v Lawrie** EAT 159/86: L, a researcher, acquitted herself well in most aspects of her job but her written work for the company journal was substandard. She told her departmental head that she did not want to write any more articles and shortly afterwards she was dismissed. The EAT (by a majority) upheld a tribunal decision that she was unfairly dismissed. The company had given her no warning about the consequences of a failure to improve and an insufficient period of time during which any improvement could be assessed. If L had been formally

143

warned that failure to improve would mean dismissal she might have agreed to write articles and with instruction might have improved.

After a warning has been given, the employer should abide by its terms. For example, a warning of possible demotion might make it unfair to dismiss for incompetence demonstrated during the period of warning – Marks and Spencer plc v Williams EAT 528/81.

4.41 An employer wishing to dismiss an employee for not performing his or her duties properly following an earlier warning should ensure that the warning is relevant to the current problem; otherwise, dismissal may be unfair. For example, in Eccles v Ribble Motor Services Ltd EAT 609/90 the EAT held that an employer who dismissed an employee for fundamental incompetence was not entitled to take into account a prior warning for carelessness. Similarly, a warning given when someone is recruited or promoted will not generally be sufficient if it later becomes necessary to dismiss the employee for incompetence unless the employee had been expressly put on probation – Eddels v Anna French Ltd EAT 848/93.

In some circumstances a warning can be implied. In Judge International Ltd v Moss 1973 IRLR 208, NIRC, for example, the failure to review an employee's salary was held to be sufficient to put him on his guard. Similarly, a warning can be implied from the deterioration of a close working relationship, such as that which pertains between a managing director and his personal secretary – Brown v Hall Advertising Ltd 1978 IRLR 246, EAT. However, given the importance attached to warnings in the Acas Guide, such cases are likely to be few and far between.

The Lord Chancellor in Polkey v AE Dayton Services Ltd (above) emphasised that there would be some occasions where the failure to warn employees about their shortcomings would not render a dismissal unfair. The following are the main categories of capability dismissal where warnings have successfully been dispensed with. It must, however, be stressed that there is no hard-and-fast rule that warnings are unnecessary – each case must be considered on its own facts. Further, the Acas Code states that 'if an employee's first misconduct or unsatisfactory performance is sufficiently serious, it may be appropriate to move directly to a final written warning. This might occur where the employee's actions have had, or are liable to have, a serious or harmful impact on the organisation' (Para 19). This implies that a warning should only be dispensed with altogether in exceptional circumstances.

4.42 **Gross incompetence or unsuitability.** It may be fair to dismiss without warning where the employee's continued employment is against the interests of the business, either because of gross inadequacy or where the employee would not have changed his or her ways in any case – James v Waltham Holy Cross UDC 1973 ICR 398, NIRC. As Sir John Donaldson said, 'cases can arise in which the inadequacy of performance is so extreme that there must be an

144

irredeemable incapability. In such circumstances, exceptional though they no doubt are, a warning and opportunity for improvement are of no benefit to the employee and may constitute an unfair burden on the business.'

The EAT applied this principle in Littlewoods Organisation Ltd v Egenti 1976 ICR 516, EAT. A costs clerk responsible for the company's audits was dismissed without being given an explicit warning that he would be treated this way if there was no improvement, although his work had been unfavourably assessed more than once. A tribunal found the dismissal to be unfair. On appeal the EAT remitted the case, reminding the tribunal that there may be cases in which a person may be so incompetent that warnings are not necessary, and a person in the clerk's position must, in all the circumstances, have been aware that dismissal was on the cards.

It may also be unnecessary to warn an employee who refuses to admit that his or her performance is not up to scratch. Here a tribunal may infer that a warning would have been of no avail.

Intransigent or inflexible attitudes. It may, in some circumstances, also be pointless warning an employee whose attitude towards his or her work or workplace is intransigent or inflexible. This is particularly true where it is clear that the employee is constitutionally incapable of changing or unwilling to do so. In AJ Dunning and Sons (Shopfitters) Ltd v Jacomb 1973 ICR 448, NIRC, the NIRC allowed an appeal from a tribunal finding of unfair dismissal based on lack of specific warning of dismissal. What the tribunal should have done, the NIRC said, was to ask whether the nature of the employee's incapacity – in this case, his unbending and uncooperative nature and inability to get on with clients – was such that, had he received a warning, he might have been able or was likely to improve. **4.43**

Single acts of gross incompetence/negligence. The potentially disastrous consequences of one mistake may excuse an employer for dismissing without a prior warning where those consequences are so serious that the employer cannot be expected to suffer the risk of the employee's continuing employment (although this does not negate the need to investigate the matter and give the employee an opportunity to state his or her case). In Alidair Ltd v Taylor 1978 ICR 445, CA, the Court of Appeal approved the following statement made by the EAT: 'In our judgement there are activities in which the degree of professional skill which must be required is so high, and the potential consequences of the smallest departure [from] that high standard are so serious, that one failure to perform in accordance with those standards is enough to justify dismissal. The passenger-carrying airline pilot, the scientist operating the nuclear reactor, the chemist in charge of research into the possible effects of, for example, thalidomide, the driver of the Manchester to London express, the driver of an articulated lorry full of sulphuric acid, are all in the situation in **4.44**

which one failure to maintain the proper standard of professional skill can bring about a major disaster.'

But just because, in some job contexts, the consequences of making a single mistake can be potentially calamitous does not mean that a rare mistake by an experienced employee carrying out such jobs will always justify dismissal. In Boxall v Surrey and Sussex Healthcare NHS Trust ET Case No.3101155/99, for example, B had 30 years' experience in midwifery. During that time, she had been disciplined only once as a result of a cot death following a home delivery. Part of the disciplinary sanction applied on that occasion comprised six months' supervised practice in the community. The incident that resulted in B's dismissal concerned the birth of a stillborn child to a patient in her care. The Trust concluded that she had been negligent in that she had not read a CTG trace properly and had failed to follow up the patient's complaints about a particular pain. It accepted that her negligence was due to lack of skill rather than reckless disregard of duty, but decided that retraining would not be recommended in this case in view of the fact that the claimant had recently undergone a period of supervised practice and because she failed to acknowledge her incompetence. In holding that B's dismissal was outside the band of reasonable options open to the employer, the tribunal concluded that the Trust had attached disproportionate weight to the fact that the claimant had undergone supervised practice in the community. This was not relevant to the issue of retraining in a hospital labour ward where the stillbirth had taken place. Furthermore, B's perceived inability to recognise her own failings was something that could have been addressed by training.

4.45 **Employees in senior positions.** Senior employees and managers may not need to be warned that they are failing to achieve the standards of performance required of them. By the very nature of their jobs, said the NIRC in James v Waltham Holy Cross UDC (above), they may be aware of what is required of them and fully capable of judging for themselves whether they are achieving that requirement. It is true that three years later the EAT in McPhail v Gibson 1977 ICR 42, EAT, took a contrary view and suggested that an explicit warning for senior employees is particularly important. However, these views are not necessarily contradictory. The important question is whether the manager, as with all grades of employee, was aware that his or her job was in jeopardy. In Laycock v Jones Buckie Shipyard Ltd EAT 395/81 the EAT acknowledged that, although such an awareness will usually be brought home by a formal warning, 'as a matter of common sense, the higher someone is in the managerial scale the more likely it is that he will be conscious of the satisfaction or lack of satisfaction that his performance is giving'.

The relationship between status and capability was considered by the EAT in Burns v Turboflex Ltd EAT 377/96. In that case B, a managing director, was dismissed having failed to take adequate steps to devise and implement a business plan following the takeover of the company for which he worked. By a majority, a tribunal found his dismissal to be fair, notwithstanding that B had been out of the country when he was dismissed and had never received anything in writing regarding the employer's concerns over his progress in developing the business plan. The majority thought that, as a senior executive, B should have been aware that his failure to make sufficient progress with the business objectives put his job at risk. On appeal, the EAT held that the tribunal's decision was fundamentally flawed in that it failed to distinguish between the need to provide a warning of dismissal and the need to give an employee an opportunity to meet the criticisms as to his or her capability. The failure by the employer to accord such an opportunity to B vitiated the tribunal's decision that B's dismissal was fair.

In the course of giving judgment the EAT made the following observations regarding the necessity of issuing warnings in capability dismissal cases: 'We do not consider that it is possible to lay down as a proposition of law any general rule that is dependent upon the status or the nature of the job. A van driver employed at a modest salary does not need to be warned that he should not drink before he drives; the personnel director of a large company does not need to be told that he should not make racist or sexist comments about or to members of his staff; a pilot does not need to be warned that he should not crash the plane. There can in our view be no absolute rule as to when warnings are or are not inappropriate. All must depend upon the facts of the case.'

Reasonable opportunity to improve

4.46

Providing the employee with an opportunity to improve was identified by Lord Bridge in Polkey v AE Dayton Services Ltd (above) as being necessary in the great majority of cases if the employer is to act reasonably. Para 20 of the Acas Code states that a warning should set out the improvement in performance required, together with a timescale. Obviously, if an employer warns an employee that his or her job is in danger but fails to provide that employee with a reasonable opportunity to improve, or to provide itself with an opportunity of assessing whether improvement has taken place, a dismissal may be found to be unfair.

In Steelprint Ltd v Haynes EAT 467/95 the EAT upheld an employment tribunal's finding of unfair dismissal in respect of an employee, H, who had been denied training as a means of helping her to improve defects in her performance. H had originally been employed as a proof-reader, but following the introduction of computer technology, she was required to undertake computer inputting tasks for which she had to learn to touch-type. She failed to master this new skill and, having initiated a period of monitoring, the employer issued a series of warnings over a three-month period, which culminated in her dismissal. A tribunal held the dismissal to be unfair, primarily on account of the lack of any offer of training on the employer's part or any consideration of moving H onto other tasks at which she was more adept. In upholding that finding, the EAT observed: 'The tribunal came to the conclusion that to expect someone to take on what is effectively a new job without considering the full training was outside the range of responses that a reasonable employer would contemplate before going on to dismiss. We cannot see anything in that conclusion [that could] remotely [be] said to be unfounded on the evidence.'

Employment tribunals' definitions of a reasonable improvement period will differ greatly and depend on the circumstances of each case. In Evans v George Galloway and Co Ltd 1974 IRLR 167, ET, a man with six years' service was thought to deserve six months, rather than five weeks, while in Winterhalter Gastronom Ltd v Webb 1973 ICR 245, NIRC, three months was thought suitable for a sales director with two years' service. And in Clark v Johnson EAT 484/78 the EAT extended a long-serving butcher's improvement period from one to nine months.

4.47 In Sibun v Modern Telephones Ltd 1976 IRLR 81, ET, the tribunal thought that important factors in determining a reasonable period were length of service, performance during that service and the extent to which the employee's results were falling below the expected. An additional factor might be how long the employee had known of the employer's dissatisfaction before a formal warning was given – Leighton v British Industrial Fastenings Ltd COET 1161/202.

Longer periods to improve are often appropriate in situations where the employee has been asked to do new kinds of work. In British Sulphur Corporation v Lawrie EAT 159/86 (see under 'Warnings' above) the EAT's faith in the employee improving as a writer was partly fuelled by the fact that she had very recently been switched from pure research work to writing for the company journal. She was given insufficient instruction and an insufficient period of time over which her journalism could be assessed. And in Playle v Turmeric Ltd COET 813/215 the employee inherited a long-standing accounting system which was harshly criticised by auditors. Dismissal was unfair because the employee was entitled to more time to remedy the system.

Employers should not set unrealistic targets during the improvement period, particularly if they have waited for some time before acting and kept their doubts about the employee to themselves. However, an employee cannot complain if he or she has freely agreed to the target – Bach-Price v International Equipment and Services Exhibition Organisation Ltd EAT 453/79.

4.48 It is important that an employer is not seen as merely going through the motions when presenting an employee with an opportunity to improve his or her performance. In this regard, the employer may come unstuck if the evidence at a tribunal shows that the capability procedure put in place lacks any objective basis by which improvement could be measured. In Williams v Pembrokeshire County Council ET Case No.1602049/03, for example, W began working for the Council in 1974 and in 1997 was promoted to the post of Home Manager of a residential home. From 1999 onwards concerns were expressed about her managerial capability, which led to the Council's capability procedure being invoked. As part of that procedure she was transferred in 2002 to a different residential home, but still in the capacity of Home Manager. W's line manager retained an office at the home and had responsibility for her in relation to the capability procedure. In March 2003 she was called to a hearing under the procedure and told that as she had shown no improvement she was to be dismissed. A tribunal held the dismissal to be unfair. It found that there had been a 'self-fulfilling prophecy' that W would fail from the time of her transfer in 2002. The Council had failed to take proper account of her length of service and had failed to give her a correspondingly lengthy and supported period for consolidation and improvement. In supervising her during the improvement period, the line manager had adopted a remote, backseat role. The action plan did not contain any fair or objective measurement by which any improvement could be judged. Instead, the manager had merely relied on hearsay and speculative reports from other staff.

Lapsed warnings. The Acas Code explicitly provides that employees should be   **4.49**
told how long a warning will remain current – para 20. However, it cannot be assumed that warnings automatically lapse at the end of an improvement period. Whether it can be inferred that the warning has lapsed will depend on the circumstances. This was made clear in Kraft Foods Ltd v Fox 1978 ICR 311, EAT, where the EAT said: 'There is sometimes a tendency for a warning to be regarded as having lapsed if a period of time has gone by. In certain circumstances, of course, that may be true. Here, however, the company were dealing with a man who, in the end, was not capable of doing the job; he fell short of the requirements. It seems to us that it is wrong to say that, where a man has been given six months in which to improve, if the employer gives him a further period of time beyond the six months, the employer is to be criticised thereafter for saying that the employee did not act in accordance with the warning at the end of the period of time. It may well be that the employer is being over-generous; but being over-generous is not the same thing as being unreasonable.'

Furthermore, the Court of Appeal has further held – albeit in the context of a misconduct dismissal – that it is not necessarily unfair for an employer to take into account an 'expired' warning – Airbus UK Ltd v Webb 2008 ICR 561, CA (discussed further in Chapter 6). All will depend on the circumstances and if, for example, an employee has been led to believe that his performance is no longer being monitored at the end of an improvement period, it may then be unfair to dismiss him for poor performance, at least without a further warning.

Monitoring progress. The employer should monitor the employee's progress   **4.50**
during the improvement period. The fact that an employee has shown at least some capacity to improve may be taken into account by a tribunal when determining whether the dismissal for failing to make sufficient improvement falls within the band of reasonable responses. An example:

149

- **Tufail v Scottish Life Assurance Co** ET Case No.28133/95: T had begun working for the employer in 1987 and had had a satisfactory record until 1993, when she was transferred to a new department. Her annual appraisal for 1994 graded her work as unsatisfactory, as a result of which she was given a written warning. Two months after that, her Divisional Manager reported that her standard of work had improved to the extent that he was now satisfied with her performance. At her next appraisal her work was again graded as unsatisfactory and she was given another warning – this time described as being a 'first and final warning'. Her performance was then monitored weekly. The employer's assessment was that, while her performance had improved, the degree of improvement was not sufficient to bring her up to the required standard and she was dismissed. In holding her dismissal to be unfair, the tribunal observed that the fact that T had shown the requisite improvement a year earlier proved that she had it within her ability to improve to an acceptable standard. A reasonable employer would have considered her previous good service and her demonstrated ability to improve, and would have allowed her more time.

4.51 **'No difference' rule**

In Polkey v AE Dayton Services Ltd 1988 ICR 142, HL, the House of Lords ruled that employers could not argue that a procedurally improper dismissal was nevertheless fair because it would have made no difference if the employer had followed a fair procedure. Their Lordships held that an employer's actions in dispensing with a fair procedure were highly relevant to the question of whether an employer acted reasonably in dismissing, and that tribunals were not entitled to take into account, when determining the fairness or otherwise of a dismissal, whether a proper procedure would have made any difference to the employer's decision to dismiss. Only in wholly exceptional cases where it could be shown that carrying out a proper procedure would have been 'utterly useless' or 'futile' would procedural failures be overlooked when considering reasonableness for the purposes of S.98(4). Lord Bridge in Polkey itemised the procedural steps which will be necessary in the great majority of cases if an employee is to be considered to have acted reasonably. Speaking of capability dismissals in particular, he mentioned that giving an employee fair warning and a chance to improve would generally be expected. Polkey and the so-called 'no difference' rule is discussed further in Chapter 3 under 'Fairness of internal procedure'.

4.52 **Right of appeal**

Denying an employee a right of appeal against the decision to dismiss on the ground of capability or lack of qualifications is likely to lead to the conclusion that the dismissal is unfair, particularly if the right of appeal was contractual – see West Midlands Co-operative Society Ltd v Tipton 1986 ICR 192, HL. Indeed, the Acas Code recommends that employees be provided with an

150

opportunity to appeal and an unreasonable failure to provide an appeal therefore risks an uplift to any compensation awarded – see para 25 (see Chapter 18).

As stated at para 26 of the Code, an appeal should be dealt with impartially and, wherever possible, by a manager who has not previously been involved in the case. Ideally, the appeal should be heard by a higher level of management. However, as was recognised by the EAT in Royal Naval School v Hughes 1979 IRLR 383, EAT, in smaller organisations this may not always be practicable. Furthermore, dismissal is likely to be unfair on procedural grounds if the rules of natural justice are not observed. In a capability context, this means that the employer must inform the employee of his or her shortcomings, give him or her a chance to be heard, and act honestly. In Campion v Hamworthy Engineering Ltd 1987 ICR 966, CA, C was dismissed for poor workmanship following a disciplinary hearing held by the works manager. C appealed to the company's welfare officer, who listened to arguments from both sides and then adjourned. Following a private discussion with the works manager in another room, the welfare officer announced that the dismissal was upheld. The Court of Appeal restored an employment tribunal's finding of unfair dismissal and agreed that there had been a serious breach of natural justice when the welfare officer retired with the works manager to deliberate over C's case.

For more on the conduct of internal appeal hearings, see Chapter 6 under 'Disciplinary proceedings'.

5 Ill health

Long-term ill health

Persistent short-term absences

Alternative employment

Ill-health benefits

Factors affecting reasonableness

Particular types of sickness

Dismissal for ill health is a potentially fair reason for dismissal as it relates to the employee's capability of performing the work which he or she was employed to do – S.98(2)(a) Employment Rights Act 1996 (ERA). As stated in Chapter 4, capability is assessed by reference to skill, aptitude, *health or any other physical or mental quality* – S.98(3)(a) ERA. However, different considerations apply to *ill health*-related capability dismissals to those that apply to *performance*-related capability dismissals (discussed in the previous chapter).

5.1

It is not normally difficult to show that the reason for dismissal was ill health as it tends to result in either long-term absence, as in the case of a serious illness or injury, or in frequent short absences over a long period. However, absenteeism *per se* will not be sufficient to show incapability on ill-health grounds and the employer will also need to establish that there is an underlying medical condition. This is almost always the case where long-term absence is concerned and may well be the case where there are frequent short-term absences. However, short-term absences may also be caused by a number of different and unconnected minor illnesses, in which case different considerations apply. This is dealt with under 'Persistent short-term absences' below.

Employees with underlying health problems may struggle into work rather than take sick leave. This could well affect their performance or behaviour at work and should be taken into account by an employer when deciding what action to take. In such circumstances, whether the matter is treated as relating to performance/conduct or ill health will depend on a number of factors, including the employer's awareness of the health problem, the extent to which it is actually causing the employee's poor performance/misconduct and the nature of the poor performance/misconduct in question. This issue is most likely to arise where the employee suffers from mental health problems and is discussed further under 'Particular types of sickness – mental illness' below.

If an employee's ill health causes him or her to lose a qualification required to perform his or her job, the reason for dismissal is likely to be loss of the relevant

5.2

153

qualification, rather than ill health. While still a capability issue, different considerations may apply – Sayers v Loganair Ltd EAT 0084/04. If the employer is uncertain as to which reason to rely on, it is probably sensible to deal with the matter, at least initially, as a potential ill-health dismissal, as such dismissals require employers to follow more rigorous procedural steps. (Capability issues arising out of poor performance and lack of qualifications are dealt with in Chapter 4.)

Once it is established that the reason for the employee's dismissal was ill health, the second limb of the fairness test under S.98(4) comes into play: did the employer act reasonably in treating ill health as a sufficient ground for dismissal? Much will depend on the procedure the employer followed as consultation with the employee and expert medical advice are often crucial to the question of reasonableness. Procedural factors are dealt with under 'Long-term absence' and 'Persistent short-term absences' below.

If the employer has followed a fair procedure, whether or not its decision to dismiss is fair will depend on a number of factors – considered under 'Factors affecting reasonableness' below. Certain types of sickness or disability – in particular, pregnancy- and maternity-related illnesses, drink- and drugs-related illnesses, mental illnesses and HIV/AIDS – need to be handled with especial care and are considered in more detail under 'Particular types of sickness' below.

5.3 As discussed in Chapter 3, the 'range of reasonable responses' test of fairness will apply both to the decision to dismiss and to the procedure that was followed in reaching that decision – see Pinnington v City and County of Swansea and anor EAT 0561/03 where the EAT stated that the test should apply to the way employers inform themselves of the true medical position, applying the Court of Appeal's decision in J Sainsbury plc v Hitt 2003 ICR 111, CA. (The Pinnington case was appealed to the Court of Appeal but not on this point – Pinnington v Swansea City and County Council and anor 2005 ICR 685, CA.) As the EAT found in Yorkshire Bus Group Ltd v Kahut EAT 344/96 and 851/96, a tribunal will err in law if it finds 'something completely outside the band of reasonableness, when demonstrably it is not'. In that case, K had been absent for more than 12 months with back pain. There was medical evidence that K was unfit for work, he had been regularly consulted, and K himself had told his employer he had no intention of coming back to work. The EAT found that it was perverse of a tribunal to hold that dismissal of K in these circumstances did not fall within the band of reasonable responses.

5.4 **Acas Code of Practice on Disciplinary and Grievance Procedures.** It is not entirely clear whether the revised Acas Code of Practice on Disciplinary and Grievance Procedures ('the Code') applies to ill-health dismissals. While the Code does not specifically refer to sickness absence, the accompanying non-statutory Acas Guide, 'Discipline and grievances at work' ('the Guide') devotes a considerable amount of space to the issue (see Appendix 4: 'Dealing with absence'). The Guide makes a distinction between persistent short-term absences – suggesting that in some circumstances these may be dealt with as a disciplinary matter, in which case the Code would apply – and longer-term absence where 'employers need to take a more sympathetic and considerate approach'.

In practice, application of the Code may depend on whether an employee is being dismissed for ill health, in which case it will be a capability issue and the Code will not apply, or for a poor attendance record (which is more akin to a conduct issue), in which case employers should follow the Code. This distinction is dealt with more fully. However, as we make clear under 'Persistent short-term absences' below, it can be a difficult distinction to make and employers should carry out the necessary investigations, including obtaining medical evidence where appropriate, before any action is taken. Since the purpose of an investigation is to establish the facts, this is the equivalent of the first step recommended in the Acas Code. A properly conducted investigation should then establish the next appropriate step to be taken.

Disability discrimination
5.5

It is important to note from the outset that if the underlying illness amounts to a disability under the Disability Discrimination Act 1995 (to be incorporated into the Equality Act 2010 (EqA) from a date to be appointed), a dismissal may amount to unlawful discrimination even if it is found to be fair under the ERA. Liability for disability discrimination and for unfair dismissal must be considered separately: a disability-related dismissal that cannot be justified under the DDA/EqA will not be automatically unfair as separate consideration must be given to the matters contained in S.98(4) ERA – Heinz Co Ltd v Kenrick 2000 ICR 491, EAT. However, the Court of Appeal has acknowledged that the approach to justification under the DDA/EqA is similar, though not identical, to that taken to determination of whether or not an employer has acted reasonably in treating the reason for dismissal as a sufficient reason to dismiss for the purposes of an unfair dismissal claim – Post Office v Jones 2001 ICR 805, CA.

Disability discrimination is discussed in depth in IDS Employment Law Handbook, 'Disability Discrimination' (2002), which is due to be updated at the end of 2010.

Frustration
5.6

Before turning to consider ill-health dismissals in more detail, it is worth noting that an employee's prolonged or sudden serious injury or disability is capable of *frustrating the employment contract*. Frustration of a contract occurs where, through no fault of either party, some reasonably unforeseeable event takes place which makes future performance of the contract either impossible or something radically different from what was initially contemplated. The effect of frustration is that the contract, together with all the rights and obligations of the parties under it, terminates automatically without a dismissal.

155

Tribunals are generally reluctant to find that an employment contract has been frustrated as this means that the employee loses all employment rights, including the right to claim unfair dismissal. Employers should therefore be cautious in invoking the doctrine of frustration. The best view would seem to be that employers should only rely on frustration where the unforeseen event renders all further employment permanently impossible. Even then, they should also plead an alternative defence – that if there was a dismissal (i.e. the contract was not frustrated) it was a fair dismissal on the ground of the employee's prolonged incapability through sickness. But before doing this, they need to make sure that they have followed the correct procedures for sickness dismissals (see below), and have complied with any obligations imposed by the DDA/EqA.

The doctrine of frustration is discussed at some length in IDS Employment Law Handbook, 'Contracts of Employment' (2009), Chapter 10.

5.7 Long-term ill health

The key to a fair dismissal for long-term illness or injury, which invariably involves long-term absence from work, is a fair procedure. A fair procedure requires, in particular:

- consultation with the employee

- a thorough medical investigation (to establish the nature of the illness or injury and its prognosis), and

- consideration of other options, in particular alternative employment within the employer's business.

An employee's entitlement, if any, to enhanced ill-health benefit will also be highly relevant – see 'Ill-health benefits' below. A booklet produced jointly by the Department for Work and Pensions (DWP) and Acas – 'Managing attendance and employee turnover' (available at www.acas.org.uk) – states that employees on long-term sick leave can be dismissed 'only as a last resort once all other options have been considered'.

The revised Acas Code of Practice on Disciplinary and Grievance Procedures (and its accompanying Guide) may provide some useful guidance when it comes to the procedure an employer should follow prior to dismissal, although as discussed in the introduction to this chapter, it is not certain that the Code applies to sickness absence situations, particularly long-term absence.

5.8 Employers will also need to consider their additional obligations under the disability discrimination legislation since, where long-term ill health is concerned, it is highly likely that the underlying illness will amount to a disability under the DDA/EqA. In its Guide to the Acas Code, Acas recommends that employers 'take a more sympathetic and considerate

156

approach, particularly if the employee is disabled and where reasonable adjustments at the workplace might enable them to return to work' (see Appendix 4). The impact of the DDA on unfair dismissal law is considered under 'Relevance of the DDA/EqA' below.

Consultation with the employee 5.9

In the context of long-term sickness absence, consultation has a number of purposes, which include: establishing the true medical position; keeping the employer abreast of the employee's progress; and keeping the employee up to date with the employer's position, which is particularly important if the employer is considering dismissal. Since warnings are not normally considered to be appropriate in cases of long-term sickness, given a total absence of fault on the employee's part, consultation assumes greater importance. As Lord McDonald stated in Taylorplan Catering (Scotland) Ltd v McInally 1980 IRLR 53, EAT: 'It would be absurd to apply a procedure of formal warnings to cases of genuine ill health.' This reinforces the view that the Acas Code of Practice, with its in-built warnings, does not apply to long-term ill-health dismissals.

The EAT stressed the importance of consultation and discovering the true medical position in the leading case of East Lindsey District Council v Daubney 1977 ICR 566, EAT, where Mr Justice Phillips said: 'Unless there are wholly exceptional circumstances, before an employee is dismissed on the ground of ill health it is necessary that he should be consulted and the matter discussed with him, and that in one way or another steps should be taken by the employer to discover the true medical position. We do not propose to lay down detailed principles to be applied in such cases, for what will be necessary in one case may not be appropriate in another. But if in every case employers take such steps as are sensible according to the circumstances to consult the employee and to discuss the matter with him, and to inform themselves upon the true medical position, it will be found in practice that all that is necessary has been done. Discussions and consultation will often bring to light facts and circumstances of which the employers were unaware, and which will throw new light on the problem. Or the employee may wish to seek medical advice on his own account, which, brought to the notice of the employers' medical advisers, will cause them to change their opinion. There are many possibilities. Only one thing is certain, and that is that if the employee is not consulted, and given an opportunity to state his case, an injustice may be done.' In Taylorplan Catering (Scotland) Ltd v McInally (above), the EAT added that consultation is also necessary to balance the employer's need for the work to be done against the employee's need for time to recover.

Where the employee suffers from a disability for the purposes of the DDA/EqA, the 'Code of Practice – Employment and Occupation', published by the Disability Rights Commission (now incorporated into the Equality and Human Rights Commission), advises that the employer should consult the disabled employee at

157

appropriate stages, not only about the effects of his or her disability on future employment but also on adjustments that could be made (para 8.16).

5.10   Proper consultation with the employee, for the purposes of unfair dismissal law, should include:

● discussions at the start of the illness and periodically throughout its duration and informing the employee if the stage when dismissal may be considered is approaching

● personal contact between the employer and the employee

● consideration of the medical evidence – see 'Medical investigation' below

● consideration of the employee's opinion on his or her condition

● consideration of what can be done to get the employee back to work

● consideration of offering alternative employment, if any, in the employer's business – see 'Alternative employment' below

● consideration of an employee's entitlement to enhanced ill-health benefits, if available – see 'Ill-health benefits' below.

There have been a number of cases where a failure to consult the employee has resulted in a finding of unfair dismissal. The East Lindsey District Council v Daubney case above is a good example. D was dismissed on the ground of ill health. The Council had acted upon a report prepared by its physician. The report was based on an examination carried out by another doctor and merely stated that D was 'unfit to carry out the duties of his post and should be retired on the grounds of permanent ill health'. The dismissal was found unfair by a tribunal because D had not had an opportunity to state his case or to obtain an independent medical opinion. The EAT noted that the physician's report was 'verging on the inadequate' because it was lacking in detail. However, it held that the Council would have been entitled to act upon the report, 'brief as it was', if it had consulted D and discussed the matter with him.

5.11   **Discussions.** Discussions should be held periodically throughout the period of absence – from the onset of the illness up to and including the decision to dismiss. The Acas Guide recommends that where an employee is on long-term sick leave, the employee and employer should keep in regular contact and the employee should be kept fully informed if there is any risk to employment (page 73). Even if an employer has obtained medical evidence, it is important to consult the employee before a decision to dismiss is taken to keep the employee informed and to ensure that the medical report has not been misinterpreted. An example:

● **WM Computer Services Ltd v Passmore** EAT 721/86: P suffered from severe depression and took a number of months' sick leave. During his absence his employer kept in close contact with him, refused to accept his resignation on one occasion, and extended his sickness benefit. However, when the decision to dismiss was taken, the employer failed to consult P, relying only on a medical report prepared by the company medical adviser. Both the tribunal and the EAT held the dismissal to be unfair. Even though the procedure had been perfectly adequate at earlier stages, when the decision to dismiss was made the employer had failed to consult P personally. The EAT emphasised that while the medical evidence 'loomed large' in the case, the decision whether or not to dismiss P was an employment one, not a medical one. In addition, the EAT criticised the employer for failing to seek clarification from the medical adviser and upheld the tribunal's finding that the employer had misconstrued the medical report, wrongly concluding that it recommended that P should not return to work.

Personal contact. When employees are on long-term sick leave, a certain amount of written correspondence will be inevitable. However, employers should try to ensure regular personal contact with the employee to avoid any argument that there was no proper consultation prior to dismissal. In Post Office v Stones EAT 390/80, for example, the EAT upheld a tribunal's decision that the employer's 'paper consideration' of S's attendance record prior to dismissing her was not enough. Had the employer carried out a fuller analysis, based on closer personal contact with S, it would have reached a different decision.　　5.12

At the same time, an employer should be sensitive to the employee's need for space to convalesce and should consider the employee's right to privacy under Article 8(1) of the European Convention on Human Rights – see Chapter 3, 'Impact of the Human Rights Act' for further details. Where the employee's condition makes him or her effectively house-bound, an employer wishing to meet for the purposes of consultation will need to visit him or her at home. An employer should ideally gain the employee's consent, explaining the reason for the visit and who will be attending. An employer should also consider less intrusive options, such as contact by telephone or even e-mail, since face-to-face meetings will not always be necessary. Much will depend on the circumstances of the particular employee and an employer would be well advised to establish the employee's preferred form of communication in the initial stages of consultation. An employer should certainly not push an employee to attend a return-to-work meeting before he or she is ready to do so – Alexander v Downland Retirement Management Ltd ET Case No.3103380/03 (see 'Ill-health benefits' below).

Employee's opinion. The employee's opinion as to his or her likely date of return and what work he or she will be capable of performing should be considered. Two examples:　　5.13

- **Bennett v Safeway Stores Ltd** ET Case No.2101807/04: B went on sick leave on 11 November 2003, suffering from carpal tunnel syndrome, a disability for the purposes of the DDA. On 2 March her employer, SS Ltd, received a medical report stating that she had undergone an operation six weeks

─── 159

previously, and recovery was likely to take six to eight weeks; thereafter a return to work on light duties was recommended for two to three weeks. However, on 5 April B was signed off work for a further six weeks due to post-operative problems. B confirmed on 19 April that there was no change in her condition. At that stage SS Ltd discussed with her in detail possible alternative vacancies but B made it clear that she would not be able to undertake any of the available alternatives. On 28 April, SS Ltd dismissed her, since it was difficult to continue to cover her absence by getting other staff to work additional hours, and the difficulty would only be exacerbated with the approach of summer. A tribunal dismissed her claim for unfair dismissal (and her claim for disability discrimination). SS Ltd had fully considered the possibility of B returning to her own position with any adjustments and the possibility of alternative work. It had reasonably concluded that there was no possibility of any of these options in the foreseeable future and B appeared to be in agreement with this at the time. Although an employer would normally be expected to obtain an up-to-date medical report before deciding to dismiss, it was reasonable for SS Ltd to conclude that a further medical report would provide no fresh information, given B's own belief (consistent with the medical certificates still being issued) that she would not be fit to return in the foreseeable future. In addition, it had a pressing business need to appoint someone permanently to her post

- **Portman v Bromley Hospitals NHS Trust** EAT 1300/96: P, a hospital ward manager, was off sick for a long time with Hodgkin's disease. When she returned, her work was poor and she had intermittent relapses. P insisted that her work was not affected by her illness. The hospital went on to invoke a capability procedure against P, eventually giving her the choice between demotion or dismissal for incompetence. P then requested early retirement on ill-health grounds (although this was subsequently rejected). The doctor who examined her for retirement purposes reported that she had severe depression and would never again be fit for work. P was dismissed solely on the ground of incompetence. The appeal panel upheld this decision although it found that ill health was a contributory factor. The EAT upheld the tribunal's finding of fair dismissal on the basis that the hospital had reasonably concluded that P did not meet the required standards of competence and P had consistently denied – until just prior to her dismissal – that her health had affected her performance.

However, an employer should not place too much reliance on an employee's opinion, particularly when the employee is suffering from mental illness. This also applies in the case of physical ill health, as the following case illustrates:

- **Jones v Nightfreight (Holdings) Ltd** ET Case No. 26813/87: J was absent from work because of cartilage trouble. When asked when he would be able to return, J told his employer that he would be fit for work in eight weeks.

When he failed to attend work on the due date he was dismissed. The tribunal found that the employer had been over-reliant on J's opinion and had forced him to be precise when a medical report should have been obtained instead. Accordingly, the dismissal was unfair.

Fit notes. Since 6 April 2010, when the Social Security (Medical Evidence) and Statutory Sick Pay (Medical Evidence) (Amendment) Regulations 2010 SI 2010/137 came into force, sick notes have been replaced by 'statements of fitness for work', known colloquially as 'fit notes'. These may (and indeed are intended to) promote discussion at an earlier stage in an employee's illness as to what can be done to get the employee back to work as soon as possible. The most significant change is that as well as declaring that the patient is 'not fit for work', a doctor now has the option of stating that the patient 'may be fit for work taking account of the following advice'. The form then gives a list of four typical examples of modifications that could be appropriate, which the doctor can tick – namely, a phased return, amended duties, altered hours and/or workplace adaptations – and a space in which he or she can add comments. On receiving a fit note giving advice of modifications that could enable an employee to return to work or continue in work, the employer should first discuss the matter with the employee – given that GPs or other doctors do not necessarily understand the workplace or job involved, employers should be wary of following the advice without discussing the practical implications. **5.14**

Right to be accompanied. Under S.10 of the Employment Relations Act 1999 (ERelA), where a worker 'reasonably requests' to be accompanied at a 'disciplinary hearing', the employer must permit the worker to be accompanied by a 'companion'. The companion – chosen by the worker – may be a trade union representative or a fellow worker – S.10(2A). **5.15**

A disciplinary hearing is defined in the ERelA as a hearing that could result in:

- the administration of a formal warning – S.13(4)(a)

- the taking of some other action – S.13(4)(b)

- the confirmation of a warning issued or some other action taken – S.13(4)(c) (this applies to appeal hearings).

Therefore, even if the employer is holding what it terms a 'capability' meeting to discuss the employee's ill health, the statutory right to be accompanied would still apply if it is likely to result in dismissal.

Circumstances in which consultation is not required. The EAT in East Lindsey District Council v Daubney (above) envisaged that consultation could only be dispensed with if there were 'wholly exceptional circumstances'. Not surprisingly then, the number of cases where a failure to consult properly has not resulted in a finding of unfair dismissal is small. **5.16**

161

However, in the following case special circumstances were held to exist which excused the employer's failure to consult:

● **Eclipse Blinds Ltd v Wright** 1992 IRLR 133, Ct Sess (Inner House): W, a registered disabled person with a heart complaint, was a full-time receptionist. After nine years' employment her health had deteriorated to the point where she had to become part time and she then went sick for a further 13 weeks. She told the company that she thought her health was improving and gave it permission to contact her GP. The GP wrote to say that W's health was not good and that there was no possibility of her returning to work in the near future. W, however, had informed the employer that she thought her health was improving. Therefore, it appeared that she did not realise the seriousness of her illness. The employer had to replace W but concerned that she was unaware of the true medical position, decided simply to write a letter rather than consult her personally over her dismissal in case it inadvertently slipped out. The Court of Session held that the employer had a genuine concern to avoid giving W information about her health and in these special circumstances had not acted unreasonably.

Taking this decision to its logical conclusion, an employer may be acting reasonably in not consulting an employee where this might result in disclosure of information contained in a medical report which would be likely to cause serious harm to the employee's physical or mental health. (Note that S.7 of the Access to Medical Reports Act 1988 provides an exemption from the employee's right to access a medical report concerning him or her in such circumstances – see under 'Access to medical reports' below.) An employer may also be acting reasonably in not consulting where the employee is suffering from mental ill health which renders him or her delusional – Wright v Commissioners of Inland Revenue EAT 385/79.

5.17 There also appears to be an exception to the need to consult where the employment is of a special nature requiring, for example, a higher than usual level of attendance or that employees be of robust health, particularly where there is a contractual term to that effect:

● **Leonard v Fergus and Haynes Civil Engineering Ltd** 1979 IRLR 235, Ct Sess (Inner House): L was a steel fixer on a North Sea oil platform working to a fixed deadline in severe conditions. His contract contained a term, agreed with his union, that any man absent for two shifts in a 14-day period would be classed as unsuitable for North Sea work. The Court held that dismissal for breach of this term was fair because the relationship between the employer and employee was of an 'exceptional and special nature'. It said that L had not been dismissed merely on the ground of ill health but for failing to meet an essential requirement of his contract that he must not be frequently absent on medical grounds. The

Daubney guidelines had 'no relevance whatever' given the exceptional and special nature of the employment in this case. (The Court here appears to be suggesting that there was some other substantial reason (SOSR) for the dismissal, meaning that the more prolonged procedural requirements for ill-health dismissals did not apply. SOSR is dealt with in Chapter 8)

- **Taylorplan Catering (Scotland) Ltd v McInally** 1980 IRLR 53, EAT: M was a barman at a workman's camp in the Shetlands, a job which was 'arduous' and involved 'unusual working conditions'. He became depressed and was advised by his doctor that he was unsuited to the working conditions in such an isolated environment. He was not consulted before being dismissed. The EAT, overturning a tribunal's finding of unfair dismissal, agreed that in normal cases a measure of consultation was needed before dismissing an employee for ill-health reasons. It noted, however, that in some cases employers will have an express clause, such as the one in Leonard (above), to the effect that after a specified number of absences an employee will be deemed unsuitable for the work and his or her employment will be terminated. Although there was no such express clause in this case, the employer's need for employees of robust health was 'patent' and it was 'clearly established' that M was medically unsuited to the work. Further, M knew that this was the medical view before he was dismissed. Consultation would have served no useful purpose since its dual aims – of balancing an employer's and employee's needs and establishing the true medical position – had already been met.

5.18 It could be argued that in Taylorplan, as in Leonard, the unusual working conditions could have amounted to SOSR for dismissal. However, the EAT did treat it as an ill-health dismissal and relied on the decision in British Labour Pump Co Ltd v Byrne 1979 ICR 347, EAT. This laid down a rule that where there was a proven procedural irregularity in an otherwise fair dismissal but it could be shown that carrying out the proper procedure would have made no difference, then the dismissal would be fair. However, the Byrne case was subsequently overturned by the House of Lords in Polkey v AE Dayton Services Ltd 1988 ICR 142, HL, and for this reason, the Taylorplan decision should be treated with some caution. Under Polkey, only if an employer could reasonably have concluded that a proper procedure would be 'utterly useless' or 'futile' might it be acting reasonably in ignoring it. It will be rare for a tribunal to find that consultation prior to an ill-health dismissal would be futile, particularly as consultation is recognised as being an integral part of such dismissals (effectively taking the place of warnings). Even if there is little prospect of the employee returning to work, the general requirement for employers to take a sympathetic and considerate approach would normally dictate that some manner of consultation should take place. Polkey and its implications are discussed in detail in Chapter 3 under 'Fairness of internal procedure'.

5.19   **Medical investigation**

Mr Justice Phillips in East Lindsey District Council v Daubney (above) stated that 'in one way or another steps should be taken by the employer to discover the true medical position' prior to any dismissal. In most cases this will involve consultation with doctors. A failure to seek proper medical advice (where this is appropriate) is likely to result in a finding of unfair dismissal. Three examples:

- **Parsons and Co Ltd v Kidney** EAT 788/87: after K had been absent for several weeks her doctor informed the employer that she was suffering either from back strain or from a slipped disc. Recovery from the former would take about six weeks, and from the latter about 12. The employer arbitrarily chose to accept the more serious of the two diagnoses and dismissed K instead of attempting to clarify the complaint. The EAT found the dismissal unfair. Not only had there been a failure to consult with K, there had also been a failure to establish clearly the nature of her disability and the likely length of her absence

- **Fry v Russell Williams Textiles Ltd** ET Case No.28250/94: F's employer gave her time off for an operation, believing that it was for medical reasons. After the operation, the company found out that it was for cosmetic surgery, which it did not consider to be a medical reason at all. F was dismissed for conduct on the basis that she had deceived the company that her operation was for medical reasons. A tribunal found that the company had failed to establish conduct as a proper reason to dismiss. F had had the operation on the advice of a physician to remove an overlarge stomach. It was clear from F's evidence that over the years this had had a psychological as well as a physiological effect on her: psychological because it caused her stress and physiological because her job was made difficult by her inability to bend down. In the tribunal's view, these reasons came under the general banner of 'medical'. The tribunal held that the employer was not acting within a range of reasonable responses when concluding that cosmetic surgery was not medical. Medical advice should have been obtained

- **Millington v Wandsworth Council** ET Case No.2302863/06: M went on long-term sick leave on 31 October 2005 suffering from stress. She wrote to the Council on 16 January saying she had been given a fit to return to work certificate by her GP, and she was planning to return on 6 February. On 26 January she was called to a sickness review meeting and was told that a possible outcome might be dismissal. At the end of the meeting she was dismissed, the Council having concluded that M had said nothing to convince them that her attendance would improve upon her return to work. A tribunal held that in the absence of medical evidence to support its view, the Council had no reasonable grounds for its belief that her attendance would not improve in the future.

164 ——————————————————————————————

The first medical opinion sought should normally be that of the employee's own GP. However, he or she should not be approached without the employee's consent because of the doctor's duty of confidentiality to the patient. Further, the employer will need to comply with its obligations under the Access to Medical Reports Act 1988 when requesting information (see 'Access to Medical reports' below). If consent is received, the GP should be asked the nature of the illness, the expected period of absence and the type of work the employee will be capable of doing on his or her return.

5.20

The new 'fit note' system (under which GPs have the option of stating that the patient 'may be fit for work') could prompt an earlier medical investigation in which GPs are likely to play a greater role. If the employer receives a GP fit note suggesting that the employee 'may be fit for work', it may need to seek clarification, either from the GP or from a specialist. Simply ignoring such suggestions or failing properly to consider them could render any subsequent dismissal unfair. Recommendations in a fit note may also amount to reasonable adjustments for the purposes of the DDA/EqA. Furthermore, if the employer fails to implement advice in a fit note on the employee's return to work and his or her condition gets worse, the fit note might be put forward as evidence that this was foreseeable for the purposes of any personal injury claim against the employer.

Examination by specialists. A decision to dismiss on medical grounds will not be reasonable unless the employer has all the relevant facts which are either known or could reasonably be discovered at the time the decision is made. Where there is any doubt, a specialist's report may be necessary and any decision to dismiss without one may be unfair, especially if a specialist report is pending or has been recommended. Two examples:

5.21

- **Edwards v Curtis of Burnham Ltd** ET Case No.17694/95: E had been off work for a long time with RSI. At the company's request her GP sent it a report stating that he was unable to say when E would be able to work and that he would recommend that she seek the advice of a consultant. The employer invited E to come in to work to discuss matters. During the meeting, E told them that she had an appointment to see a consultant in two days' time. E was nonetheless dismissed. The dismissal was held to be unfair: the employer should have waited for the consultant's opinion before dismissing

- **Airbus UK Ltd v Wilson** EAT 0061/06: W suffered a serious accident at work in February 2003 in which he injured his back. The employer, AUK Ltd, was provided with a medical report in June 2004 that stated that W had a phobic anxiety about returning to the one place that would allow the process of rehabilitation to begin. The report also suggested obtaining a specialist's opinion but was pessimistic that W would ever be fit to return to work. Subsequently W was assessed by a clinical psychologist. However, the employer dismissed W without waiting for the psychologist's report because

165

it had experienced a significant upturn in business but had strict rules about headcount, meaning that W could not be replaced, even on a temporary basis, while he was still on the books. The EAT upheld a tribunal's finding that W was unfairly dismissed because of AUK Ltd's failure to seek further information about the assessment carried out by the psychologist. The employer had been selective in its interpretation of the first medical report, choosing to ignore the 'less palatable' part recommending a specialist opinion, which 'did not fit in with the requirements of the business'.

5.22 **Acting in accordance with medical advice.** Provided an employer consults the employee and allows the employee to state his or her case, he will not normally be criticised for dismissing in accordance with proper medical advice. Employers are not under a duty to evaluate medical advice unless it is plainly inaccurate or based on inadequate examination – Liverpool Area Health Authority (Teaching) Central and Southern District v Edwards 1977 IRLR 471, EAT. The test is whether the employer knew the advice was flawed in this way, or ought reasonably to have known it, *and* that no reasonable employer would have been entitled to rely upon the report – First Manchester Ltd v Kennedy EAT 0818/04 and 0027/05.

In East Lindsey District Council v Daubney 1977 ICR 566, EAT, D's employer asked the district community physician whether D should be retired early on ill-health grounds. The doctor's response was in the affirmative and so D was dismissed without the employer obtaining a full medical report or an independent medical opinion and without personally consulting him. The EAT found the dismissal unfair because of the lack of consultation, but also gave some sound advice regarding medical enquiries. It is not the function of employers, the EAT said, to turn themselves into some sort of medical appeal tribunal to review the opinions and advice of their medical advisers. Employers should not set themselves up as medical experts – the decision to dismiss is not a medical question but an employment question to be answered by the employer in the light of available medical advice.

The advice sought in each case will depend on the individual circumstances. In Daubney, the EAT criticised the employer for being too restrictive in the advice it sought, which explained why the medical opinion stated only that the employee was 'unfit to carry out the duties of his post and should be retired on the grounds of permanent ill health'. This, said the EAT was 'verging on the inadequate' because 'the employer may well need more detailed information before being able to make a rational and informed decision whether to dismiss'. However, it considered on balance that the employer would have been entitled to act on the opinion, brief as it was, had it consulted D.

Employers should, so far as possible, ensure that they remain neutral when requesting information to avoid appearing to favour a particular outcome. Further, employers should be careful not to 'pick and choose' which parts of

166

the advice to rely upon, especially if ignoring advice that is more favourable to the employee – Airbus UK Ltd v Wilson EAT 0061/06. Finally, employers should, if requested, give employees reasonable opportunity to counter the medical evidence with a further report – Liverpool Area Health Authority (Teaching) Central and Southern District v Edwards (above).

Prognosis. When deciding whether or not to dismiss an employee for lack of capability, an employer must take into account not only the employee's current level of fitness but also his or her likely future level of fitness. If there is evidence that an employee's condition will worsen should he or she return to work, that may make dismissal fair, even if the employee is currently fit to do his or her job. In House v Greene King Services Ltd ET Case No.1500987/07, for example, H sustained a knee injury in 1991, before he began working for GKS Ltd. In April 2006 he had to undergo emergency surgery on his knee and was signed off work. A medical report produced in December 2006 said that his work as a drayman for GKS Ltd had accelerated the wear and tear on his knee, but the knee had responded well to surgery and H's consultant fully supported his return to work as a drayman. The employer was concerned that H's work could contribute to a recurrence of his knee problem, and wrote to the consultant for further information but received no reply. It then obtained a further occupational health opinion which stated that H's work would have a negative impact on his knee and bring forward the time when he would require a knee replacement operation. While H was fit to return to work, the report said that ideally he should be provided with a role without significant lifting. Since GKS Ltd had no alternative work to offer, H was dismissed on capability grounds. A tribunal held that although H was fit for work at the time of his dismissal, his employer had genuine concerns, based on medical evidence, that if H returned to work he would suffer further damage to his knee. The likelihood of further injury was sufficiently serious and substantial to make dismissal a reasonable response.

5.23

Conflicting medical reports. If two medical reports conflict, the failure to investigate further (perhaps by way of a third opinion) could render dismissal unfair, particularly where there is a substantial difference of opinion. An example:

5.24

- **Fearnley v Initial Healthcare Services** ET Case No.21959/95: F, who suffered from a mild form of epilepsy, had epileptic seizures on three occasions in 1994. She lost consciousness on two occasions for a few seconds and then carried on normally. Her GP stated that her epilepsy was stable but the doctor instructed by the employer stated that her epileptic seizures represented a significant risk to herself and others. The employer tried, to no avail, to find alternative work for F. In the meantime, she produced a letter from a neurological registrar at the University of Wales which contradicted the opinion of the employer's doctor. The employer considered investigating the discrepancy between the reports but did not do so. A tribunal found her subsequent dismissal unfair on the basis that had the employer investigated

167

further, it was 'almost certain' that F would not have been dismissed. This was underlined by the fact that following her dismissal she was examined by another doctor who confirmed the opinion of the neurological registrar. However, it was not a question of 'being wise after the event'. The employer had recognised that there was a substantial difference of opinion which put it on notice that further investigation was required.

In Liverpool Area Health Authority (Teaching) Central and Southern District v Edwards 1977 IRLR 471, EAT, the EAT suggested that where there were conflicting medical reports, the matter should be remitted to the doctor who issued the first report, who may or may not be persuaded of the other doctor's view on a further examination. It also suggested that where a second (or indeed third) medical opinion is being sought, that doctor should have sight of the previous medical report(s) to ensure consistency and that all relevant issues are covered.

5.25　If an employer relies on one medical opinion in preference to another that is more favourable to the employee, it should have good reason for doing so. In Evers v Doncaster Monk Bridge Ltd ET Case No.26661/78 a tribunal thought it reasonable for the employer to rely on the company doctor's report instead of that of E's doctor, as the company doctor was aware of the dangers inherent in E's working environment, whereas E's doctor was not. If the report of the employer's own doctor suggests that the only way to reconcile conflicting diagnoses or prognoses is to obtain a report from an independent consultant, failure to do so will almost certainly be unfair – British Gas plc v Breeze EAT 503/87. And in Brammel v North West Regional Railways Ltd ET Case No.70014/95 a tribunal found that where the employer's doctor thought B – who had contracted viral meningitis and been off work for almost a year after being released from hospital into the care of his GP under the advice of a hospital consultant – was fit to work and his GP disagreed, an independent report should have been commissioned from the hospital consultant.

5.26　**Employee's refusal to cooperate.** Any attempt by an employer to compel an employee to undergo a medical examination may entitle the employee to resign and claim unfair constructive dismissal unless the contract of employment expressly provides for such power. An example:

● **Bliss v South East Thames Regional Health Authority** 1987 ICR 700, CA: B, a consultant at an NHS hospital, was involved in an acrimonious and protracted dispute with a colleague. As a result, the regional medical officer asked him to undergo a medical examination by a psychiatric consultant. B refused and resigned, suing for damages for breach of contract. It was common ground before the Court of Appeal that there was an implied term in B's contract of employment that the employer was entitled to require him to undergo a medical examination if it had reasonable grounds for believing that he might be suffering from physical or mental disability that might cause harm to patients. However, since the committee whose duty it was to investigate such cases did not find any

168 ───────────────────────────

mental or pathological illness, the employer had no reasonable grounds for requiring the examination and was in breach of trust and confidence when it unreasonably insisted upon it.

However, if an employee refuses to cooperate in providing medical evidence the employer is entitled to base its decision on the relevant facts available, even if those facts are insufficient to give the full medical position. The Acas Guide, at page 72, recommends that, in such circumstances, the employee should be informed in writing that a decision will be taken on the basis of the information available and that it could result in dismissal. Dismissal may then be fair. An example:

- **Tahir v Sainsbury's Supermarkets Ltd** ET Case No.1801002/07: T injured his back on 31 May and went off work sick. He provided sick notes from his GP but withheld his consent to the release of his GP records to SS Ltd's occupational health service. It dismissed him on 3 November believing, on the basis of their consultation, that he was unlikely to be fit to return to work in the near future. His unfair dismissal claim was rejected by a tribunal, which held that SS Ltd could not safely allow T to return to work in the face of a medical certificate saying he was unfit for work, and given the employer's own observations of T's physical state. The employer had to make a decision on whether it was appropriate to dismiss on the limited information it had, having made reasonable attempts to obtain further information. Given the duration of T's sickness absence, it was entitled to dismiss when it did

Access to medical reports. The Access to Medical Reports Act 1988 gives individuals certain rights in respect of reports relating to their health that have been prepared by a medical practitioner 'who is or has been responsible for the clinical care of the individual'. Under that Act: **5.27**

- an employer who wishes to contact an employee's doctor must notify the employee in writing and must secure his or her written consent before doing so

- in giving such notification, the employer must inform the employee of his or her right to withhold consent; to have access to the report and to then withhold consent for it to be supplied; and to request amendments to the report

- if the employee states that he or she wishes to have access to the report, the employer must tell the doctor when making the application and at the same time let the employee know that the report has been requested

- the employee must contact the doctor within 21 days of the date of the application to make arrangements to see the report

- if the employee considers the report to be incorrect or misleading, he or she can make a written request to have it amended

169

- if the doctor refuses to amend the report, the employee has the right to ask him or her to attach a statement to the report reflecting the employee's view on any matters of disagreement

- the employee has the right to withhold consent to the report being supplied to the employer.

There is an exemption from the rights to access under the 1988 Act where 'disclosure would in the opinion of the practitioner be likely to cause serious harm to the physical or mental health of the individual or others or would indicate the intentions of the practitioner in respect of the individual' – S.7. Failure by an employer to consult with the employee in such circumstances may fall into the range of reasonable responses – see under 'Consultation with the employee – exceptions' above.

Note that the 1988 Act only covers reports prepared by a medical practitioner responsible for the worker's care. If a report is requested by an occupational health consultant instructed by the employer, for example, the individual's rights to access will be limited to those provided by the Data Protection Act 1998.

5.28 **Data protection.** When dealing with employees' health records, employers should pay heed to the Data Protection Act 1998, as medical information will constitute 'sensitive personal data' under that Act. The Information Commissioner has issued a Data Protection Code covering this area, the 'Employment Practices Data Protection Code Part 4: Information about Workers' Health', together with supplementary guidance, to which employers should refer (see www.ico.gov.uk).

5.29 **Exceptions.** In East Lindsey District Council v Daubney 1977 ICR 566, EAT, the EAT appeared to envisage that only in 'wholly exceptional circumstances' would an employer not be required to take steps to discover the true medical position. This might possibly apply where the employment is of a special nature, requiring, for example, a higher than usual level of attendance – Leonard v Fergus and Haynes Civil Engineering Ltd 1979 IRLR 235, Ct Sess (Inner House). There, the employer's failure to inquire into the nature of L's incapacity did not make his dismissal unfair – see 'Consultation with the employee – exceptions' above for further details.

Note that the 'Polkey exception' – whereby an employer might exceptionally be entitled to dispense with a proper procedure if it could reasonably have concluded that this would have been 'utterly useless' or 'futile' – may be even less likely to apply in the case of medical investigation. In Millington v Wandsworth Council ET Case No.2302863/06, for example, the tribunal found that without an up-to-date medical report as at the time of M's dismissal, it was unable to carry out the investigation required under Polkey to establish whether M would have been dismissed in any event. To do so would be to 'embark on a sea of speculation based on the very failure to obtain a medical report and investigate [the] true medical position which we find to be one of the reasons for the unfairness of [M's] dismissal'.

Relevance of the DDA/EqA

The medical investigation may reveal or confirm that the employee's illness amounts to a disability under the DDA/EqA. If this is the case, the employer will need to tread particularly carefully since dismissal could amount to unlawful discrimination even if it is found to be fair under the ERA. Liability for disability discrimination under the DDA/EqA must be considered separately from liability for unfair dismissal under the ERA. For example, a dismissal may amount to unlawful 'disability-related discrimination' under the DDA unless it can be justified. However, a dismissal that cannot be justified does not automatically fail the reasonableness test under S.98(4) ERA – HJ Heinz Co Ltd v Kenrick 2000 ICR 491, EAT. Conversely, there may be situations where a dismissal is unfair under the ERA (for example, because there is some procedural defect) but nonetheless justified under the disability discrimination legislation. The EAT confirmed in Royal Liverpool Children's NHS Trust v Dunsby 2006 IRLR 351, EAT (discussed under 'Persistent short-term absences – unconnected minor ailments' below) that the disability discrimination legislation does not impose an absolute obligation on an employer to refrain from dismissing an employee who is absent wholly or in part on the ground of ill health due to disability – it simply requires such a dismissal to be justified. (Note that from a date to be appointed the EqA will replace 'disability-related discrimination' with 'discrimination arising from disability', whereby a person (A) discriminates against a disabled person (B) if A treats B unfavourably 'because of something arising in consequence of B's disability' and A cannot objectively justify the treatment.)

The disability discrimination legislation also imposes on employers a separate duty to make reasonable adjustments for disabled workers, giving rise to a stand-alone discrimination claim. If an employer fails to make a reasonable adjustment that would have avoided the need to dismiss an employee, the dismissal may well fall foul of the reasonableness test set out in S.98(4) ERA. A failure to make a reasonable adjustment may also amount to an unfair constructive dismissal. In Meikle v Nottinghamshire County Council 2005 ICR 1, CA, the Court of Appeal held that failing to implement certain reasonable adjustments to the working conditions of a disabled worker amounted to a constructive dismissal. M suffered from an eye condition and the Court held that the employer's persistent and long-term failure either to enlarge her written materials or to amend her timetable breached the implied term of trust and confidence and rendered her dismissal unfair.

171

Persistent short-term absences

5.31

Employers dealing with persistent short-term absenteeism should first establish the reasons for the absences. There are a number of possible reasons for such absences – for example, they could be caused by a series of minor unconnected ailments, such as colds and stomach upsets; by recurrent conditions such as back problems or asthma; or by family, personal or childcare problems. In addition to absence for genuine reasons, there is also the possibility of employees 'skiving' by, for example, taking advantage of the self-certification scheme or abusing agreed time-off arrangements.

Where the sickness absences are genuine they may be due to a series of unconnected, minor ailments or, even if seemingly unconnected, be caused by an underlying medical condition (which could also amount to a disability under the DDA/EqA). Determining the cause will make a crucial difference to the procedure that must be followed.

5.32 ### Unconnected minor ailments

Employers wishing to dismiss for persistent short-term absenteeism will not generally be expected to follow the procedure required in cases of long-term illnesses (see 'Long-term ill health' above). As stated by the EAT in International Sports Co Ltd v Thomson 1980 IRLR 340, EAT, where an employer is concerned with an employee's unacceptable level of intermittent absences due to unconnected minor ailments, it would be placing too heavy a burden on the employer to require it to carry out a formal medical investigation. The EAT went on to say that, in any event, such an investigation would 'rarely be fruitful because of the transient nature of the employee's symptoms and complaints'. In such cases there comes a time when a reasonable employer is entitled to say 'enough is enough' and, so long as warnings have been given, treating the frequent absences as a sufficient reason for dismissing is likely to fall within the band of reasonable responses – Post Office v Jones 1977 IRLR 422, EAT.

In Rolls-Royce Ltd v Walpole 1980 IRLR 343, EAT, for example, W's absenteeism record averaged about 50 per cent for the last three years of his employment. Most of the absences were certified by a doctor, being the result of, for example, injuries sustained while playing rugby. The employer gave him warnings that the absences – which followed no particular pattern – were getting out of hand and followed company procedure meticulously. Since there seemed no reason to anticipate any improvement, W was eventually dismissed for capability. The EAT, by a majority, allowed the employer's appeal against a tribunal's finding that the dismissal was unfair in light of the fact that W's poor attendance extended over a period of three years and there was no suggestion that the employee was suffering from any underlying condition that rendered him more susceptible to illness than his fellow employees. In the

172

circumstances, a medical examination, for example, by the employer's own doctor would have been of no assistance.

In International Sports Co Ltd v Thomson (above) the EAT stated that in cases of persistent intermittent absenteeism an employer should:

- carry out a fair review of the attendance record and the reasons for absence

- give the employee an opportunity to make representations; and

- give appropriate warnings of dismissal if things do not improve.

If there is no adequate improvement in the attendance record, then, said the EAT, dismissal will be justifiable. This will be so regardless of whether or not the reasons for the absences are genuine. An example: **5.33**

- **Davis v Tibbett and Britten Group plc** EAT 460/99: D was dismissed following persistent short-term absences that were all caused by genuine though unconnected medical reasons, such as a broken ankle, food poisoning, a sleep disorder and a muscle injury. D appealed against a tribunal's finding that he had not been unfairly dismissed, submitting that the employer's belief that the absences were not genuine played a part in his dismissal. The EAT, however, dismissed the appeal, holding that there was no evidence that the employer had questioned the authenticity of D's ill-health reasons. It was, said the EAT, possible for absences to be unreasonable, even if genuine. The EAT held that it was well established that persistent absenteeism may be an admissible reason for dismissal and in those circumstances whether or not the employee is at fault is immaterial. The employer in this case was entitled to look at the whole history and decide whether or not it was prepared to continue to shoulder the burden of an employee who had been absent on so many occasions. This was not a case where it would have been helpful to seek medical evidence since there had been a large number of unconnected ailments. The EAT cited with approval the comments made in the International Sports case where the absences were also for genuine but unconnected illnesses.

'Enough is enough'. It is impossible to say with absolute precision at what point an employee's absenteeism will reach the level where 'enough is enough'. Previous case law may be of some use: **5.34**

- **International Sports Co Ltd v Thomson** (above): T's absence had reached a level of about 25 per cent in the last 18 months of her employment

- **Davis v Tibbett** (above): D had taken a total of 217 days' sick leave in the three years prior to his dismissal.

However, much will depend on the particular circumstances of the case. For example, in some industries absences may be particularly damaging and employers may not be expected to tolerate such a high level of absenteeism:

173

- **Patval v London Borough of Camden** ET Case No.2203464/07: the tribunal accepted that there were often ongoing issues affecting the users of IT services for which there needed to be a flexible and reliable response from IT support. Any absences in IT support, therefore, caused the employer severe disruption

- **Davis v Tibbett** (above): the regular attendance of employees such as D was an important factor in the employer's transport business, given the stringent demands placed on it by its principal customer.

If the employer has a sickness absence policy in place (with triggers and warnings), this will alert employees to what the employer considers an unacceptable level of absence. Provided the policy is consistently applied, it will generally be reasonable for the employer to rely on this.

5.35 **Opportunity to make representations.** An employee should always be given a chance to explain his or her absences. Ideally, an employer should ensure that someone speaks to an employee after every absence. This will give the employee a chance to discuss any problems he or she may be having either domestically or with the job. It could also reveal the existence of an underlying medical condition (see below). At the very least, an employee should be consulted at the point when his or her record is causing concern so that he or she has an opportunity to explain the absences. An example:

- **Backhouse v Coleman's of Stamford** ET Case No.19865/95: B was dismissed for absenteeism after being absent for 38 days in 11 months. She had received five verbal warnings and had been given a written warning six months before her dismissal. Following an absence of three weeks, the employer dismissed B without holding a disciplinary meeting or giving her any opportunity to state her case. The tribunal found that B's dismissal was unfair.

It is important that an employer does not make assumptions about an employee's absences, since treating genuine sickness absence as misconduct can lead to a finding of unfair dismissal. In Leeson v Makita Manufacturing Europe Ltd EAT 0911/00 L had been signed off work for a week and prescribed antibiotics. He went to play golf on the fifth day of his sick leave to get some fresh air and exercise after being confined indoors all week. The EAT held that the fact that L was well enough to do some recreational activity did not justify the employer's conclusion that he was fit enough to work.

5.36 **Warnings.** Although 'warnings' or 'cautions' may seem inappropriate to cases of absence caused by genuine illness, they are a necessary step given that such absences can lead to dismissal. Formal warnings were certainly viewed as factors going to the reasonableness, and hence fairness, of the dismissals in International Sports Co Ltd v Thomson (above) and Rolls-Royce Ltd v Walpole (above). Further, the Acas Guide advises that in all cases of persistent short-term absence the employee should be told what improvement in attendance is expected and warned of the likely consequences if this does not happen. This adds weight to the argument that the Acas Code applies to cases of short-term absenteeism, at least in cases where the ailments are minor and unrelated (see the introduction to this chapter under 'Acas Code of Practice on Disciplinary and Grievance Procedures'). It is therefore instructive to set out in full the recommendations made in the Acas Guide (at pages 71–72):

- unexpected absences should be investigated promptly and the employee asked for an explanation at a return-to-work interview

- if there are no acceptable reasons then the employer may wish to treat the matter as a conduct issue and deal with it under the disciplinary procedure – see Chapter 6

- where there is no medical certificate to support frequent short-term, self-certified absences, then the employee should be asked to see a doctor to establish whether treatment is necessary and whether the underlying reason for the absence is work-related. If no medical support is forthcoming, the employer should consider whether to take action under the disciplinary procedure

- in all cases the employee should be told what improvement in attendance is expected and warned of the likely consequences if this does not happen

- if there is no improvement, the employee's length of service, performance, the likelihood of a change in attendance, the availability of suitable alternative work where appropriate and the effect of past and future absences on the organisation should all be taken into account in deciding appropriate action.

The Guide also advises employers to keep absence records so that absence can be monitored and any problems addressed at an early stage, and to deal with persistent absence promptly, firmly and consistently in order to show both the employee concerned and other employees that absence is regarded as a serious matter. However, employers should avoid reaching decisions that are primarily intended to communicate a message to the rest of the workforce: in Leeson v Makita Manufacturing Europe Ltd EAT 0911/00 a tribunal held that the reason for L's dismissal was the employer's desire to 'be seen to be tackling the absenteeism problem'. The EAT held that this was not a fair reason for dismissal because it had more to do with the employer's wish to make an example of the employee to deter others than with dealing with his genuine sickness absence.

5.37

The language used in warnings for absenteeism should be appropriate to the circumstances. Two examples:

- **Lynock v Cereal Packaging Ltd** 1988 ICR 670, EAT: the EAT emphasised that where there was genuine illness it should not be treated as a disciplinary

175

matter and that employers had to treat each case individually with 'sympathy, understanding and compassion'. However, it said the purpose of a 'warnings' system was to give a 'caution' that the stage had been reached where, with the best will in the world, continued employment would become impossible

- **Davis v Tibbett and Britten Group plc** EAT 460/99: the EAT criticised the warnings that had been issued on the basis that they were couched in language appropriate for disciplinary matters, rather than persistent absenteeism on account of genuine ill health. Even so, it did not consider that the use of inappropriate language in itself tainted the employer's procedure with unfairness.

5.38 If the employer does issue a warning, it must abide by its terms. In Scott v Birmingham City Council ET Case No.1303486/04 S had taken an exceptional amount of sick leave. His employer made it clear that any further period of sustained period of sickness within the following six months would trigger a capability hearing to consider his future employment. Following a further period of absence S was invited to attend the capability hearing. At that stage the employer made the decision to dismiss S. However, following the meeting it sent a letter to S stating that he had six months in which to improve his attendance. Some two months after sending that letter, the employer dismissed S following another capability hearing. The tribunal held that had the employer dismissed S following the first capability meeting, that dismissal would have been fair. However, by sending the letter giving him six months to improve, the employer had effectively invoked the absence procedure again, confusing the position and misleading C. Therefore, C's dismissal was unfair.

Further, a warning in respect of persistent absences should not be combined with a warning for other matters to justify dismissal. An example:

- **Adan v Asda Stores Ltd** ET Case No.1202390/08: A had an exemplary attendance record for the first two years of his employment. However, on a number of occasions after November 2006 he was spoken to and counselled about his absences and lateness. On 20 November 2007 he was given a verbal warning for taking an unauthorised break. On 19 March he was given a final written warning for refusing to obey a reasonable management instruction. The next month he was off work on certificated sickness absence for two weeks, which triggered the employer's absence procedure. He was called to an investigatory meeting and then a disciplinary hearing, following which he was issued with a verbal warning. However, the employer's disciplinary procedure provided that an employee who had a live final written warning and commits a further offence will be dismissed. Therefore, the employer felt compelled to dismiss A. His unfair dismissal claim was upheld by a tribunal on the basis that no reasonable employer would 'tot up' a final written warning for misconduct with a verbal warning issued for breach of an absence policy when the absence was by reason of genuine certified sickness absence.

Triggers. Many absence policies specify certain procedures, such as oral and written warnings, that will be triggered when the number of absences reaches a particular level. Employers should ensure that any absence procedure is applied consistently and that the consequences of failing to comply with the procedure are properly communicated to employees. In Connorton v British Steel plc ET Case No.2502634/99 C had the worst attendance record at the plant in which he worked. Although he had been given two written warnings, one in November 1995 and one in July 1997, his absences had in general been treated leniently. After absences from work on 23 and 24 April 1999 C was called to a meeting at which he disclosed, for the first time, that he had an alcohol problem, that this was the reason for his absences, and that he had now resumed counselling. However, the employer decided that C's claim to have an alcohol problem could not be accepted as a way of avoiding disciplinary action and dismissed him. The tribunal held that the dismissal was unfair. C had never been given a final warning and had no reason to believe that his employer would not continue to treat him with the same leniency it had shown in the past. When he went to the meeting he had no idea that it might result in his dismissal.

5.39

However, employers should not adhere too rigidly to absence procedures where this would result in unfairness to the employee. Other factors may also be relevant. In Stiles v Post Office ET Case No.4343/95, for example, the tribunal noted that when making the original decision to dismiss, the employer had failed to pay sufficient attention to the improvement in S's attendance record and to his good work record generally. However, both of these factors were considered on appeal, which amounted to a full rehearing and cured the defects in the original procedure. S's dismissal was therefore fair.

Disability-related absences. Employers may need to be more flexible about the way schemes designed to improve attendance are operated in respect of employees who have a disability. The fact that some of the absences are related to a disability does not necessarily mean, however, that dismissal for persistent absence will be unfair (or indeed discriminatory).

5.40

In Royal Liverpool Children's NHS Trust v Dunsby 2006 IRLR 351, EAT, repeated sickness absence ultimately led to D's dismissal after the Trust's four-stage sickness absence procedure had been exhausted. At the 'stage four' hearing, D contended for the first time that two of her absences had been due not merely to headaches, as previously recorded, but to migraines caused by gynaecological problems, which would not recur since her medication had been changed. At a subsequent tribunal hearing it was assumed that D's gynaecological problems amounted to a disability under the DDA. In the tribunal's view, if the disability-related absences had been disregarded, the 'stage two' review would not have taken place, and the review in June 2004 would therefore have been stage three

177

rather than stage four, meaning that D would not have been at risk of dismissal. The tribunal consequently allowed the unfair dismissal claim, finding that it had not been reasonable for the Trust to treat disability-related absences as part of the 'totting-up' review process. The tribunal also held that the dismissal was not justified under the DDA because D would not have been at risk of dismissal in June 2004 had it not been for the disability-related absences. The EAT overturned the tribunal's decision, holding that there was no absolute rule that an employer acts unreasonably if it treats disability-related absences as part of a 'totting-up' review process or as part of a reason for dismissal on the ground of repeated short-term absence. If, however, the tribunal considered that it was unreasonable to do so in this case, it should have explained why. D's assertion for the first time at the fourth stage of the sickness absence procedure that just two absences nearly a year before should be left out of account did not necessarily make it unreasonable for the Trust, looking at the whole pattern, to dismiss. There was no rule that an employer, in operating a sickness absence procedure, must discount disability-related absences.

5.41   The EAT also held that the DDA does not impose an absolute obligation on an employer to refrain from dismissing an employee who is absent wholly or in part on the ground of ill health due to disability – it simply requires such a dismissal to be justified. Accordingly, a tribunal cannot conclude that a dismissal is not justified merely because the employee was absent on the ground of disability. Accordingly, it allowed the Trust's appeal and ordered that the case be remitted to a fresh tribunal for rehearing. In doing so, however, it noted the apparent strength of the employer's case, based on D's 'appalling' absence record and the fact that periodic and repeated absence caused the Trust severe operational difficulties.

The EAT in Dunsby did not consider the question of whether D's disability-related absences should have been discounted as a reasonable adjustment under the DDA. Nevertheless, the tone of the EAT's judgment suggests that it is not automatically the case that failure to discount such absences will amount to a failure to make reasonable adjustments. The fact that only a small proportion of D's absences were disability-related appears crucial to the EAT's decision. Where the vast majority of short-term absences are caused by a disability, there would be an underlying medical condition and the employer should implement its long-term sickness procedure with a view (once all other options have been explored) to dismissing by reason of ill health rather than for persistent absenteeism – see 'Underlying medical condition' below.

5.42   **Factors to be taken into account if no improvement.** The Acas Guide states that if there is no improvement in the employee's absence record, the following factors should 'all be taken into account in deciding appropriate action': the employee's length of service; performance; the likelihood of a change in attendance; the availability of suitable alternative work where appropriate; and the effect of past and future absences on the organisation.

178 ⎯⎯⎯⎯⎯⎯⎯⎯⎯⎯⎯⎯⎯⎯⎯⎯⎯⎯⎯⎯⎯⎯⎯⎯⎯⎯⎯⎯

In addition, the employer should consider: 'the nature of the illness; the likelihood of it recurring or some other illness arising; the length of the various absences and the spaces of good health between them; the need of the employer for the work done by the particular employee; the impact of the absences on others who work with the employee; the adoption and the carrying out of the policy; the important emphasis on a personal assessment in the ultimate decision and of course, the extent to which the difficulty of the situation and the position of the employer has been made clear to the employee so that the employee realises that the point of no return, the moment when the decision was ultimately being made may be approaching' – Lynock v Cereal Packaging Ltd 1988 ICR 670, EAT.

Both the Acas Code and Lynock suggest that the likelihood of future illnesses/ **5.43** absences is a factor to be taken into account and in Davis v Tibbett and Britten Group plc EAT 460/99 the EAT endorsed the tribunal's finding that it was reasonable for the employer to conclude, given D's past absenteeism, that he was unlikely to meet an acceptable standard of attendance in the future. However, Lynock also makes it clear that if the employer has justifiably reached the point where 'enough is enough' (due to the sheer number of absences) it will not then need to investigate the likelihood of a change in attendance: the EAT said 'it seems to us to be impossible to give a reasonable prognosis or projection of the possibility of what will happen in the future. Whilst an employer may make enquiries… it is in no way… an obligation on the employer so to do because the results may produce nothing of assistance to him.' For that very reason, the EAT held that the employer was not required to seek further medical advice. Nor will the fact that the employee happens to be fit and working at that point make any difference. As stated by the EAT in Lynock, 'there is no principle that the mere fact that an employee is fit at the time of dismissal makes his dismissal unfair; one has to look at the whole history and the whole picture'.

Although length of service may also be a factor, it is not determinative. In Regan v Magnetti Marelli UK Ltd EAT 577/99 the EAT upheld a tribunal's decision that R had been fairly dismissed for persistent absenteeism, despite his having been employed there for almost 30 years. The employer had given a number of warnings and essentially reached the point where 'enough was enough'.

Underlying medical condition
5.44

If it becomes clear that there is an underlying medical condition that has been the cause of a significant number of an employee's short-term absences, the employer would be well advised to seek a medical opinion in order to determine the extent and likely duration of the medical condition, and whether, and if so how soon, treatment will bring the absenteeism down to an acceptable level. Particular thought should be given to whether the underlying condition amounts to a disability under the DDA/EqA since the employer would then have a duty to consider whether there are any reasonable adjustments that

179

could be made to help the employee. The employer should also be aware that any dismissal might amount to disability discrimination.

If an underlying condition does come to light, the employer may need to treat past absences more leniently and, especially if there is unlikely to be any improvement, should regard the case as one of long-term illness rather than short-term absenteeism (see under 'Long-term absence' above). After all, it might be considered unfair to treat an employee who takes persistent short-term absences for an underlying medical condition differently to an employee who takes long-term absence for an underlying medical condition.

Two illustrations:

- **Smith v Van Den Berghs and Jurgens Ltd** ET Case No.11351/79: the employer argued that S had been dismissed on account of his 'absenteeism', which was classed as 'misconduct' and not sickness, even though all S's absences were apparently because of genuine illness. The tribunal heard that all the disciplinary procedures had been followed before S was dismissed, including written warnings and suspension, but it nevertheless held the dismissal to be unfair. The tribunal said that such disciplinary action had been an inappropriate method of dealing with the situation since there was not a 'shred of evidence' that any of the absences were not genuine, and so to call those absences 'misconduct' was a 'misconception and unreasonable'. The majority of S's absences were related to recurrent trouble with an abscess and its treatment, about which no medical evidence had been sought. The tribunal made it clear that its decision might well have been different if the employer – basing its dismissal of S on his persistent ill health – had investigated the medical position and obtained a medical opinion supporting S's dismissal on medical grounds

- **Asafu-Adaye v London Borough of Camden** ET Case No.2201504/07: Over the course of about two years A took a considerable amount of sick leave. It transpired that this was because he suffered from chronic back pain. The employer's own occupational health advisers had made it clear on a number of occasions that A's good health could be restored following physiotherapy but the employer eventually dismissed A for capability, contending that it had done everything that could reasonably be expected. A tribunal accepted that the employer had 'conscientiously' followed the correct procedure for long-term illness over a 'sympathetically extensive period of time'. Further, the employer had sought medical advice, adjusted A's duties and looked at redeployment. Nevertheless, the tribunal held that A's dismissal for ill-health reasons was unfair. In fairness to A's 22 years of service, any reasonable employer would have awaited the outcome of the medically recommended though 'much overdue' physiotherapy (either through the NHS or at the employer's expense) – provided that the treatment took place in the reasonably near future and A agreed to participate fully.

Label for dismissal

5.45

As explained above, where ill health is involved, there are at least two potential reasons for dismissal: the ill health itself (where there is an underlying medical condition) or the resultant absenteeism (where this has reached the point where 'enough is enough', provided the illnesses are minor and unconnected). The cases demonstrate that the distinction is crucial when it comes to the procedure that must be followed. It is less obvious, however, what statutory label should be attached to the dismissal when it comes to tribunal proceedings. As noted in Chapter 3, there are six potentially fair reasons for dismissal set out in S.98. The three most relevant for our purposes are capability, 'some other substantial reason' (SOSR) and conduct.

It is clear that where an employee is being dismissed on the ground of ill health, the correct label will be *capability*. The courts and tribunals have, however, been less certain about what category absenteeism falls into: the EAT in International Sports Co Ltd v Thomson 1980 IRLR 340, EAT, considered it amounted to 'conduct' but could also be SOSR; in Davis v Tibbett and Britten Group plc EAT 460/99 the EAT described it as 'incapacity'; in Williams v Cheshire Fire and Rescue Service EAT 0621/07 it was considered to be 'conduct'; and in Lynock v Cereal Packaging Ltd 1988 ICR 670, EAT, the EAT considered it to be 'capability', but felt it 'might possibly have been a question of conduct'. It admitted that 'neither word is entirely apposite to the situation'.

The Court of Appeal has provided some clarification on the issue in Wilson v Post Office 2000 IRLR 834, CA. In that case W was dismissed for unacceptable levels of short-term absence. In its response to W's tribunal claim for unfair dismissal, the Post Office cited 'incapability by reason of unsatisfactory attendance record' as the reason for dismissal. The tribunal went on to find that the reason for dismissal was incapability on the ground of ill health and that the dismissal was unfair. The Court of Appeal remitted the case, ruling that the real reason for dismissal had not been capability but W's failure to comply with the Post Office's attendance procedure, which fell within 'some other substantial reason'. Therefore, different factors needed to be taken into account when judging the reasonableness of the dismissal, with W's future health prospects carrying less weight than they would in a capability dismissal.

It seems clear from this that an employer who wishes to dismiss an employee for persistent absenteeism will be dismissing for SOSR, rather than capability. This appears logical since the employer is less concerned with the employee's capability to do the job per se, but with his or her past absenteeism. Further 'conduct' does not seem an appropriate label given the EAT's emphasis in cases such as Lynock v Cereal Packaging Ltd (above) that absenteeism should not be treated as a disciplinary matter.

5.46

Wilson was applied in Millington v Wandsworth Council ET Case No.2302863/06 where the tribunal noted that there were two 'quite distinct'

181

processes an employer must follow if it is dismissing for poor attendance on the one hand or capability on the other. The tribunal was 'much more comfortable' with the Court of Appeal's categorisation of the former in Wilson as 'SOSR' rather than as 'conduct', especially where all absences were certified. The tribunal did not consider that certified absences can be viewed as misconduct save in circumstances where the employee has deliberately or negligently put him or herself at risk of injury or ill health.

5.47   As noted in Chapter 3, the label assigned to dismissal is not normally crucial *unless* it affects the fairness of dismissal. If an employer makes it clear that the reason for dismissal is persistent absenteeism, dismissal will not be rendered unfair merely because the dismissal letter states it is 'on the ground of capability'. However, if an employer, perhaps for compassionate reasons, leads the employee to believe that the reason for his or her dismissal is capability, rather than persistent absenteeism, it will not then be able to rely on SOSR at tribunal. Dismissal will then be unfair if the employer did not investigate the medical position, as required for capability dismissals. An example:

- **Devonshire v Trico-Folberth Ltd** 1989 ICR 747, CA: D had a number of sickness-related absences from work. After several warnings she was dismissed for her 'unacceptable attendance record'. An internal appeal panel decided, on compassionate grounds, that her employment ought to be terminated, not for poor attendance, but because she was medically unfit to do the job. A tribunal said that, had D been dismissed for the original reason – poor attendance – the dismissal would have been fair, but once the reason became medical unfitness 'the whole picture changed'. It held that the dismissal was unfair because the employer had carried out insufficient investigation into D's medical condition and insufficient consultation with the employee and her GP to warrant dismissal for ill health. The employer appealed, arguing that the tribunal should not have awarded D any compensation given that the employer could have dismissed her fairly on the ground of poor attendance. She had, therefore, suffered no loss as the result of her dismissal. The EAT and the Court of Appeal, however, affirmed the tribunal's decision regarding compensation. The Court of Appeal held that there was no evidence that had the employer known of the legal consequences of its compassionate approach, it would instead have dismissed D for poor attendance.

Of course if an employer dismisses an employee for absenteeism (i.e. SOSR), when it clearly should have been treated as ill-health capability, that will also be unfair. However, there may well be circumstances where the dividing line between SOSR and capability is unclear. For example, the employee may have an appalling absence record, some of which is due to an underlying medical condition and some of which is due to minor and unconnected ailments. In these circumstances, it is a matter of judgement whether the dismissal is for SOSR or capability, depending perhaps on what proportion of the absences are unconnected and what proportion are based on an underlying condition. This difficulty is highlighted in the Millington case:

- **Millington v Wandsworth Council** (above): M had what was described by the tribunal as an 'appalling' absence record, all due to certified illness. Some of those illnesses were caused by anxiety and depression but some were completely unrelated. The tribunal noted that running through the history of the case (and during the tribunal proceedings themselves) there had been confusion as to whether M was being considered for dismissal on the ground of her past attendance record (SOSR) or on the ground of her medical capability for future employment. Therefore, on balance, the tribunal held that the principal reason for dismissal was related to her capability. Accordingly M's dismissal was unfair since the employer had failed to follow the Daubney guidelines for capability/ill health dismissals (see under 'Long-term absence' above), notably in failing to obtain an up-to-date medical report relevant to M's most recent absence.

5.48   If an employer is in any doubt about whether it is a capability or absenteeism issue, it should initially deal with it as a capability matter since this involves the most prolonged and detailed procedure to be followed. Where the employer believes that the employee is taking sick leave dishonestly or, perhaps, as suggested in Millington, that the employee has deliberately or negligently put him or herself at risk of injury or ill health, the employer could treat it as a conduct issue. This requires more detailed investigation than is generally necessary for a SOSR dismissal – for example, evidence will be needed to substantiate the employer's belief that the employee was not sick or that he or she was negligent. However, the employer would not need to show that the employee's absenteeism had reached such a level that it was entitled to say 'enough is enough'.

Given the myriad of circumstances that can arise, and given that there is still some legal uncertainty over the appropriate label – for example, in Williams v Cheshire Fire and Rescue Service EAT 0621/07 the EAT held that, notwithstanding the Court of Appeal's decision in Wilson v Post Office (above), a tribunal was correct to categorise the employee's poor attendance record as 'conduct' – it is probably sensible to plead in the alternative, i.e. 'dismissal was because of some other substantial reason or, alternatively, for capability or alternatively for conduct'. However, employers should make it clear, both at the time of dismissal and in their response, that, for example, the actual reason for dismissal was persistent absenteeism.

Conduct dismissals are discussed in detail in Chapter 6, while dismissals for SOSR are considered in Chapter 8.

5.49 Alternative employment

Employers have a duty to consider redeploying employees who are not able to carry out some or all of their former duties due to ill health where alternative work exists that the employee may be able to do. However, there is no onus on employers to create a special job where none exists – Merseyside and North Wales Electricity Board v Taylor 1975 ICR 185, QBD. Unless the medical evidence indicates that there is no possibility of an employee being fit to return to work in any capacity, a failure on an employer's part to consider the question of alternative employment may be sufficient to render a dismissal unfair. An example:

- **Dick v Boots the Chemist Ltd** EAT 68/91: D, a store detective, was severely assaulted by a shoplifter she had apprehended. She was absent from work 'indefinitely'. Almost three years later a doctor reported that it was unlikely that she would ever be fit for her job again. The tribunal was satisfied that there had been sufficient consultation – with the employee, her medical advisers and the company's welfare services manager – and was prepared to excuse the employer's failure to consider alternative employment on the ground that, on the basis of the doctor's report, this would have been futile. The EAT disagreed and said the tribunal had erred. The company's procedure had been seriously flawed by the complete failure to consider the question of alternative employment.

While employers are not obliged to create jobs, they must be prepared to be somewhat flexible. Two examples:

- **Garricks (Caterers) Ltd v Nolan** 1980 IRLR 259, EAT: a maintenance fitter was dismissed when heart trouble meant he could no longer work shifts, only days. The EAT upheld the tribunal's decision of unfair dismissal. Fairness, it said, does not require the employer to go to unreasonable lengths to accommodate an employee who is not able to carry out his job to the full extent. However, there is a duty to investigate existing possibilities and establish whether arrangements could be made to accommodate the employee in the jobs available (in this case, providing some assistance with lifting)

- **Silver v Royal Borough of Windsor and Maidenhead** ET Case No.2536/88: the employer was criticised for not having discussed the possibility of alternative employment fully with the employee. The employer had failed to offer her alternative employment as a telephonist/receptionist, even on a trial basis, and had failed to discuss the possibility of alternative employment fully with her. This was not excused by the employer's belief that S had an unsuitable temperament for such work.

5.50 Where the ill health arises because of the nature of the work itself, employers may be acting unreasonably if they do not take reasonable steps to remove the cause. Three examples:

184

- **Jagdeo v Smiths Industries Ltd** 1982 ICR 47, EAT: J became ill when moved to a new factory department that required her to do more soldering than before. She became allergic to solder fumes. Unsuccessful attempts were made to alleviate the problem by the use of three different types of mask. No alternative work was available for her. However, an officer of the Health and Safety Executive had suggested that the problem had been successfully eliminated at other factories by the use of an extractor fan. The EAT held that in the absence of any explanation from the company as to what steps, if any, had been taken to install extractor fans, it was impossible for the tribunal to decide whether the employer had acted reasonably. The case was remitted to be heard on that point

- **Thanet District Council v Websper** EAT 1090/01: the EAT upheld a tribunal's decision that, in refusing to transfer W to an alternative role to alleviate work stress, the Council had breached an implied term that it should provide a safe place to work, leading to a finding of unfair constructive dismissal, based on W's resignation in response

- **Rubery Owen-Rockwell Ltd v Goode** EAT 112/80: G, a machine operator, was allergic to a particular coolant used by the machine which he operated, resulting in his suffering considerable sinus problems. On the basis of a medical report he was dismissed. The EAT found the dismissal unfair as there were other machines he could have operated which either used other coolants or used no coolant at all. These alternatives should have been explored even if they would have involved demotion, lower pay or lower status.

'Suitable vacancy', therefore, may involve a demotion, lower pay or lower status. In British Gas Services Ltd v McCaull 2001 IRLR 60, EAT, the EAT held that a tribunal had erred in finding a dismissal unfair on the ground that an offer of alternative employment involved a reduction in pay of between 23 and 30 per cent. The job was the only suitable alternative employment available and was offered at the going rate. This could not be said to be outside the range of reasonable responses open to the reasonable employer.

5.51 As the fairness of a dismissal is assessed at the time of dismissal, alternative employment that arises during the notice period should be considered. In Portals Ltd v Gates EAT 202/80 G was certified unfit for work by the company's doctor after being absent for over a year and given nine months' notice. His dismissal duly took effect nine months later. However, during that time a suitable vacancy had arisen but had not been offered to G. The EAT found the dismissal unfair as events happening between the giving of notice and the effective date of termination must be considered (see Chapter 3, 'Reasonableness of dismissal – reasonableness test applies at the time of dismissal' for further details).

An employer's duty to assist employees by offering alternative employment is reinforced by the disability discrimination legislation. For example, in Ferguson v London Borough of Barnet ET Case No.3300322/05 a tribunal held that the employer's failure to consider F for alternative employment amounted to a failure to make a reasonable adjustment under the DDA, which was 'inextricably linked' with the decision to dismiss her. The failure to take account of its duties under the DDA meant F had been unfairly dismissed.

If as a reasonable adjustment an employee is transferred to a new job, he or she should be given time to adjust. This could involve a trial period, allowing the employee to work from home, a gradual build-up to full-time hours or additional training for an employee with learning disabilities who moves to another workplace. Additional job coaching may also be necessary to enable a disabled person to take up the new job. These factors, which are relevant to the reasonableness of an adjustment, may well be taken into account by the tribunal when assessing the reasonableness of an employer's decision to dismiss.

Ill-health benefits

5.52

The purpose of enhanced ill-health retirement benefits, permanent health insurance (PHI) or other contractual sickness and disability schemes would be defeated if an employer could end or deny entitlements under such a scheme by dismissing employees when they become unfit for work. As a result, case law has established that there is an implied *contractual* term that an employee will not be dismissed without good cause if the effect or intention is to deny his or her rights under a PHI or similar scheme – see, for example, Aspden v Webbs Poultry and Meat Group (Holdings) Ltd 1996 IRLR 521, QBD, and Villella v MFI Furniture Centres Ltd 1999 IRLR 468, QBD. (For further details, see Employment Law Handbook, 'Contracts of Employment' (2009), Chapter 2.)

This principle was extended to unfair dismissal law in First West Yorkshire Ltd t/a First Leeds v Haigh 2008 IRLR 182, EAT, where the EAT held that it was unreasonable, and thus unfair, for an employer to dismiss an employee by reason of long-term ill health without first considering whether he or she was contractually entitled to be medically 'retired' and granted an ill-health pension. Given this, the tribunal had been fully entitled to find that the employer should have waited for a medical specialist to report back on whether or not H was likely to be permanently incapacitated before dismissing him for incapacity.

5.53

Clearly, an employer who dismisses an employee for ill-health reasons merely by virtue of the fact that he or she has applied for a permanent ill-health pension will be acting unfairly. In Langley-Ingress v Governing Body, The Grove School ET Case No.2901908/06 the employer maintained that since L had applied for a permanent ill-health pension, she had thereby self-declared herself as unfit for further work. The tribunal held that equating an application for ill-health retirement with de facto incapacity was very unfair indeed. It stated that employees must be allowed to sound out the possibility of ill-health retirement without fear of being estopped from asserting their capability for work thereafter if their application for ill-health retirement did not succeed. The tribunal also criticised the employer for relying on medical reports prepared in the context of L applying for ill-health retirement, remarking that there was 'little wonder' that they were pessimistic about her prospects of returning to work. A fair process demanded provision of more up-to-date medical reports, and a proper examination of the employee at a time when she was no longer motivated by a desire to obtain ill-health retirement benefits.

If it transpires that an employee is entitled to an ill-health pension and he or she freely elects to take it, there will be no dismissal as termination will be by mutual agreement. The employer should, however, be careful not to pressure the employee into choosing between ill-health early retirement and dismissal since a tribunal might find that there was no genuine mutual agreement in these circumstances and conclude that the employee was actually dismissed – see Chapter 1 under 'Express dismissal – enforced resignation'.

Factors affecting reasonableness   5.54

For a decision to dismiss to be fair, it must be balanced and informed in the light of the particular facts relating to the employee concerned. As noted above, where an employee is suffering from an underlying medical condition (leading to either long-term absence or persistent short-term absences), the procedure used will be paramount to the question of fairness. If a full and fair procedure is not followed (in particular, consultation, medical investigation and the consideration of other options, such as alternative employment) dismissal is likely to be unfair. However, procedure is not the only consideration and there are a number of other factors that are commonly taken into account by tribunals when assessing the fairness of a dismissal.

Nature, length and effect of illness   5.55

As discussed in Chapter 4 under 'Definitions', the employee's alleged incapability must relate to 'work of the kind which [the employee] was employed by the employer to do' – S.98(2)(a) ERA. This is determined in accordance with the employee's current contractual obligations – see, for example, Plessey Military Communications Ltd v Brough EAT 518/84. Employers do not have to prove that an employee's illness renders him or her incapable of performing *all* the duties under the contract. They only have to show that the ill health relates to the employee's capability and that it was a sufficient reason to dismiss – Shook v Ealing London Borough Council 1986 ICR 314, EAT. Nevertheless, the proportion of work an employee is still able to carry out at the time of dismissal will be relevant to the issue of reasonableness.

If the employer concludes, following consultation with the employee and a medical investigation, that the condition is unlikely to improve and there is no

187

prospect of a return to work in the foreseeable future even if adjustments are made, dismissal may be fair. For example, in Smith v Post Office ET Case No.7707/95 a tribunal took account of the fact that the chances of a clinically depressed employee on three types of medication achieving satisfactory attendance in the future were remote when considering the fairness of his dismissal for persistent short-term absences.

Full consideration must, however, be given to any recent improvement in the employee's condition and/or attendance record. In Scott v Secretary of State for Scotland EAT 196/88 S, who had taken a significant amount of sick leave (largely due to a neck injury) in the past, was only absent for six out of the last 185 days. The EAT thought that this factor, along with the lack of consultation and medical investigation, made her dismissal unfair. Similarly, in Post Office v Stones EAT 390/80 (see under 'Long-term absence – consultation with the employee' above) there was evidence that the employee's marital difficulties, the cause of much of her ill-health absence, were behind her when she was dismissed. The EAT upheld a tribunal's finding that any reasonable employer would have concluded that there had been a distinct improvement in the employee's attendance record and that there were good prospects for the future.

5.56 If an employer reasonably reaches the conclusion (following consultation and medical advice) that the employee will not be fit for work for a prolonged period of time, the fact that following his or her dismissal, he or she recovers quicker than anticipated will not render the dismissal unfair – Arriva Scotland v Weir EAT 0068/05. That said, where an employee is dismissed with notice the dismissal does not actually take place until the notice expires, so a tribunal may take account of any changes that occur during the notice period. In Williamson v Alcan (UK) Ltd 1978 ICR 104, EAT, the employee was dismissed because of his chronic ill health, but there was medical evidence from a specialist that he had made a spontaneous recovery during the notice period. The case was remitted to a different tribunal to reconsider in light of the new evidence. In remitting, the EAT stated that if – after the date notice of dismissal was given and before the contract had actually come to an end – the employer acquired information which would indicate that it ought not to have dismissed the employee, that dismissal could well become unfair if it did not withdraw the notice.

Further, the House of Lords held in West Midlands Co-operative Society Ltd v Tipton 1986 ICR 192, HL, that information revealed in the course of an internal appeal that relates to the original reason for dismissal should be taken into account when considering the fairness of that dismissal, irrespective of whether the internal appeal takes place before or after the dismissal has been effected.

5.57 **Illness caused by employer**

If the employer was in any way responsible for the employee's illness that led to the dismissal, this may be a factor that is taken into account by a tribunal when deciding on the fairness of the dismissal – Royal Bank of Scotland v McAdie 2008 ICR 1087, CA. In reaching this decision the Court of Appeal endorsed the EAT's decisions in Edwards v Governors of Hanson School 2001 IRLR 733, EAT, and Frewin v Consignia plc EAT 0981/02, and overruled the decision in London Fire and Civil Defence Authority v Betty 1994 IRLR 384, EAT, in so far as it held that the employer's responsibility for the incapacity was irrelevant to the issue of whether the dismissal was fair. The Court accepted that it may be necessary to 'go the extra mile' in such circumstances; for example, being more proactive in finding alternative employment for the employee or putting up with a longer period of sickness absence.

The Court also emphasised, however, that the fact that an employer is at fault for causing the incapacity does not *necessarily* mean that a resulting dismissal will be unfair. Indeed, in the case before it it upheld the EAT's decision (overruling the tribunal) that M – whose stress-related illness had been caused by the Bank – had not been unfairly dismissed. The Court approved the EAT's view that there was in truth no alternative to dismissal. The medical evidence was unequivocal, both that M was unfit for work and that there was no prospect of recovery. Further, M had expressly stated that she would never be able to return to work. This was not, therefore, a case where there was something more that the Bank, having caused the illness, could and should have done to try to save M's employment.

Neither the EAT nor the Court of Appeal felt it necessary to consider what the effect of an employer maliciously causing an employee's ill health would be in cases of unfair dismissal. The EAT did, however, have some difficulty with the implication in Edwards v Governors of Hanson School (above) that in such a case there could never be a fair dismissal.

Employee's length of service   5.58

In general, more tolerance should be shown towards a hardworking, long-serving employee, particularly where his or her period of absence is comparatively short. In Ginns v Leon Motor Services Ltd ET Case No.27872/78, for example, a tribunal thought that the ill-health absence of a long-serving employee should be treated in a different manner to that of a short-term employee. An employee with only one or two years' service may not, it said, expect the same beneficial treatment as might an employee with ten years' service. This meant that G, an employee with a total of 29 years' service, was entitled to expect more consideration and even better treatment.

Two further examples:

- **Clarke v Pickering Kenyon** ET Case No.47091/93: a tribunal held that an absence of three and a half months because of illness did not give rise to a reasonable cause for dismissal where the employee had 18 and a half years' service. The tribunal noted that her job could have been filled by temporary

189

staff without difficulty and at no extra expense as C was not being paid her salary during that period

- **Alexander v Downland Retirement Management Ltd** ET Case No.3103380/03 (considered under 'Ill-health benefits' above): the tribunal noted that the decision to dismiss A appeared to have ignored her good record and 17 years' service, which the tribunal considered should have been a significant factor to weigh in the balance.

5.59 Importance of the job

The importance of the job and the feasibility of employing a temporary replacement may be assessed by a tribunal when considering fairness. In Patval v London Borough of Camden ET Case No.2203464/07 the importance of P's position in IT support to the employer's operation was taken into account when deciding that his dismissal was fair. IT support was critical to the employer's operation generally and was vital for all departments and service users.

The possibility of engaging a temporary replacement should generally be explored before action is taken. However, the nature of the job may make this impracticable. And, as demonstrated in the Patval case, if the employee is taking frequent short-term absences for his condition, this may not be feasible.

5.60 Effect on other employees

The effect of continued absence or illness on other employees may also be relevant. Two examples:

- **Ali v Tillotsons Containers Ltd** 1975 IRLR 272, ET: A was a member of a production team whose bonuses depended on its output. As a consequence of A's absences through ill health and the employer's inability to find an adequate replacement for him, the other members of the team lost money. A tribunal found this a relevant consideration in the decision to dismiss A

- **Patval v London Borough of Camden** ET Case No.2203464/07: to avoid delay in a fast-moving industry, P's work in IT support had to be done by one of his colleagues. This meant they had less time for their own duties, which further impacted on service users. The tribunal found that it was reasonable to expect an employee who had started a task to complete it to prevent repetition. Furthermore, some tasks could not be simply handed over part-way though without incurring a substantial amount of work. After a number of both short- and long-term absences, the employer was entitled to say 'enough is enough' and dismiss.

5.61 Effect on output or sales

The general effect on output or sales may also be considered, especially in smaller concerns where there may be no possibility of arranging cover. Further, if the industry in which the employee works is particularly fast-moving, absence could cause the employer serious disruption – see, for example, Patval v London Borough of Camden (above).

Size of employer   5.62
Section 98(4) ERA states that tribunals should take account of the 'size and administrative resources of the employer's undertaking' in assessing reasonableness. Thus, for example, a large company may be expected to have greater resources to cover absences for a longer period and to help employees get back to work than a small family firm. In Ferguson v London Borough of Barnet ET Case No.3300322/05 the tribunal noted that the employer was a comparatively large undertaking with a human resources department and a legal department. This made the employer's failure to make reasonable adjustments under the DDA all the more inexcusable and dismissal was unfair.

Nature of employment   5.63
Where employment is of a special nature that requires a higher than usual level of attendance or that employees be of robust health, dismissal for absenteeism may be fair, particularly if there is an express or implied term in the contract covering the situation. Two examples:

- **Leonard v Fergus and Haynes Civil Engineering Ltd** 1979 IRLR 235, Ct Sess (Inner House): L was a steel fixer on a North Sea oil platform working to a fixed deadline in severe conditions. His contract contained a term, agreed with his union, that any man absent for two shifts in a 14-day period would be classed as unsuitable for North Sea work. The Court of Session held that dismissal for breach of this term was fair because the relationship between the employer and employee was of an 'exceptional and special nature'. It said that L had not been dismissed merely on the ground of ill health but for failing to meet an essential requirement of his contract

- **Taylorplan Catering (Scotland) Ltd v McInally** 1980 IRLR 53, EAT: the employee was a barman in a workmen's camp at Sullom Voe, Shetland, a job that was 'arduous' and involved 'unusual working conditions'. After several months T developed behavioural problems and depression, apparently caused by the stress of working in these conditions. The EAT found his dismissal fair because the employer's need for employees of robust health was 'patent' and it was 'clearly established' that M was medically unsuited to this sort of work.

However, it should be noted that the working conditions in both these cases were extreme. If a term similar to that in the Leonard case was inserted into the contract of an employee working in a more normal environment, a dismissal for breach of it without more would in all likelihood be unfair, as unfair dismissal is a question of 'reasonableness', not 'breach of contract'. (These cases

191

are also discussed under 'Long-term absence – consultation with the employee – exceptions' above.)

5.64 There are also other, less extreme, circumstances where the effect of an employee's absence can be particularly damaging and may be a persuasive factor when assessing a dismissal's fairness. Some examples:

- **Betteridge v St Helens Council** ET Case No.2102835/04: B worked in one of the Council's schools. During 2003 the school was made subject to 'special measures' and the management of the school was transferred from the head teacher to the Council's Senior Assistant Director of Education. Without improvement, this might have been the first step towards closure of the school. B suffered from chronic back pain and depression and was disabled for DDA purposes. In October 2003, she went on sick leave suffering from depression. By March 2004 the Council's consultant occupational physician reported that he doubted whether B would be able to cope with the pressures occasioned by the school being on special measures and said that, although he was confident that she would improve greatly in the future, in practical terms it looked as if she might not return to work. The Council wanted to make a decision about B's continued employment before the date of the next medical review in order to be able to make arrangements for the following academic year and arranged for the physician to see B again after five weeks. He reported that he did not think she would return to work in the foreseeable future and she was dismissed in May. A tribunal rejected B's unfair dismissal claim, noting that she had effectively been absent for an academic year and the school was in the degrading position of being subject to special measures – a 'devastating blow' for which strong action was urgently needed. It held that the Council was entitled to take the view that effective and swift action was called for, to provide pupils with certainty and continuity in the following year and to save the reputation of the school and ensure its continuance

- **Patval v London Borough of Camden** ET Case No.2203464/07: P was employed in IT support. The tribunal accepted that there were often ongoing issues affecting the users of IT services for which there needed to be a flexible and reliable response from IT support. Any absences in IT support, therefore, caused the employer severe disruption

- **Davis v Tibbett and Britten Group plc** EAT 460/99: the regular attendance of employees such as D was an important factor in the employer's transport business, given the stringent demands placed on them by its principal customer.

5.65 **Health and safety**

A dismissal may be fair if the employee's continued employment poses a health or safety risk to the employee or to third parties. For example, in Harper v

National Coal Board 1980 IRLR 260, EAT, H, an epileptic, attacked and displayed violence towards some of his fellow employees during occasional fits. The EAT acknowledged the employer's duty to exercise reasonable care for the safety of other employees and reluctantly found the dismissal fair. And in Singh-Deu v Chloride Metals Ltd 1976 IRLR 56, ET, S's job in a lead smelting factory was not particularly skilled but demanded that he constantly had his wits about him, since it involved filtering toxic dust and fumes. There was a difference of medical opinion as to whether it would be safe to let him return to work after he had been diagnosed as having schizophrenia. However, the tribunal was satisfied that to allow S to return to work was a risk nobody could take in this 'highly dangerous industry'.

Sick pay
5.66

The fact that sick pay is provided is merely one of the factors to be considered. Dismissal effected during the currency of sick pay arrangements will not necessarily be unfair. Nor will it necessarily be fair to dismiss once sick pay entitlements are exhausted. In Hardwick v Leeds Area Health Authority 1975 IRLR 319, ET, a tribunal held it unfair to dismiss H as soon as her sick pay entitlement had been exhausted in accordance with an established Health Service rule, particularly as she had indicated that she would be returning to work just one week later. The employer acted unreasonably in following an established but outmoded rule irrespective of the circumstances. In Coulson v Felixstowe Dock and Railway Co 1975 IRLR 11, ET, on the other hand, the tribunal held that the dismissal of an employee before his sick pay entitlement had run out was fair since his absence had caused a good deal of inconvenience. The sick pay scheme, it said, was only a financial arrangement and did not indicate the amount of sickness absence to which the employee was entitled.

An employer should not assume that just because an employee is receiving sick pay there is no need to consider alternative employment. In Konczak v BAE Systems (Operations) Ltd ET Case No.2405642/06, a disability discrimination claim, a tribunal held that the employer should have investigated K's ill-health absence before she had exhausted her entitlement to sick pay (almost one year after her sick leave began). Had the employer addressed the issue sooner there was a possibility, said the tribunal, that it would have been able to find suitable alternative employment for her. Certainly, it would have had longer in which to do so.

Employers should note, however, that it may be unfair to dismiss an employee by reason of long-term ill health without first considering whether he or she was contractually entitled to be medically 'retired' and granted an ill-health pension – First West Yorkshire Ltd t/a First Leeds v Haigh 2008 IRLR 182, EAT (see 'Ill-health benefit' above). Furthermore, a failure to pay sick pay may amount to a breach of contract sufficient to found a constructive dismissal. For example, in Summer Bridge Doors Ltd v Pickering EAT 1088/02 the EAT found that a failure to pay even statutory sick pay to a disabled woman amounted to a fundamental breach of contract.

5.67 Fit notes

It is too early to do anything other than speculate about the significance of the new 'fit notes' scheme (under which doctors now have the option of stating that a patient 'may be fit for work'). Nevertheless, if a doctor signs off an employee indefinitely, ignoring the 'may be fit for work' option, this may justifiably lead an employer to conclude that there is no alternative but to consider dismissing the employee. However, the employer should certainly not dismiss an employee purely on this basis and should investigate the medical position further. Nor, of course, should it simply ignore any suggestions made in a fit note. For more discussion on medical investigations, see 'Long-term absence – medical investigation' above.

5.68 Particular types of sickness

There are many types of illness or disability that can cause problems at work. In this section we consider briefly some of the more common ones that arise.

5.69 Pregnancy and maternity dismissals

It is automatically unfair to dismiss a woman if 'the reason or principal reason for the dismissal is of a prescribed kind, or the dismissal takes place in prescribed circumstances' – S.99 ERA. The prescribed reasons or circumstances are set out in Reg 20 of the Maternity and Parental Leave etc Regulations 1999 SI 1999/3312 ('MPL Regulations') and include reasons connected with:

- the pregnancy of the employee – Reg 20(3)(a)

- the fact that the employee has given birth to the child (but only where the dismissal ends the employee's ordinary or additional maternity leave) – Reg 20(3)(b) and (4)

- the fact that the employee took, sought to take or availed herself of the benefits of any terms and conditions preserved during ordinary maternity leave or additional maternity leave – Reg 20(3)(d)

- the fact that she failed to return to work after a period of ordinary or additional maternity leave where the employer failed to notify her of the date on which the period would end and she reasonably believed that the period had not ended, or the employer gave her less than 28 days' notice and it was not reasonably practicable for her to return on that date – Reg 20(3)(ee)

- the fact that she undertook, considered undertaking or refused to undertake work as part of a 'keeping-in-touch' day – Reg 20(3)(eee).

For ill-health purposes, the most relevant prescribed reason is that **5.70** 'connected with the pregnancy of the employee'. The phrase is to be construed widely – Clayton v Vigers 1989 ICR 713, EAT, applying the House of Lords decision in Brown v Stockton-on-Tees Borough Council 1988 ICR 410, HL. It would certainly cover pregnancy-related illnesses and miscarriages. It may also cover IVF treatment – Kaveri v Birmingham Power Ltd ET Case No.08037/95.

Employers should be cautious about dismissing employees for absenteeism occasioned by pregnancy as tribunals tend to treat such dismissals as pregnancy dismissals – and so automatically unfair. Some examples:

- **Bonnar v Swindells** ET Case No.2400514/99: B was off work sick from 20 November 1998 because of complications arising from her pregnancy. She telephoned her employer on 5 December to say that she had been given a further sick note for two weeks by her GP but had been advised that she would feel better after the first three months of pregnancy had passed. Her employment was terminated. The tribunal held that B had been unfairly dismissed on the ground of pregnancy. She was dismissed because it would be some time before she could return to work

- **Davis v Hampton Coaches (Westminster) Ltd** ET Case No.2300181/98: D was off sick on five occasions during her first four months of employment and away for medical appointments on three further occasions. On 20 October 1997 D told her employer that she was pregnant. On 30 October she was certified unfit for work for two weeks owing to a pregnancy-related condition. The employer wrote D a letter dated 3 November dismissing her for being absent and failing to make contact. According to the employer, the medical certificate was not received until 4 November. The tribunal held that D was unfairly dismissed on the ground of pregnancy. The employer took no action on D's absences until after being informed of her pregnancy and the letter dated 3 November was actually postmarked 8.15 pm on 4 November

- **Hill v The Old Rectory Nursing Home Ltd** ET Case No.2100018/07: H began working as a care assistant on 1 May 2005. On 20 February 2006, after eight episodes of sickness absence, she was given a final written warning that if her attendance did not improve she would be dismissed. In early June she informed her employer that she was pregnant. During June and July, H was off work on four occasions with pregnancy-related sickness. She was dismissed on 14 August because of her level of sickness absence. The tribunal found her dismissal automatically unfair

- **Louis v INP Ltd t/a Initial City Link** ET Case No.1501415/03: L had a number of pregnancy-related absences that led to her dismissal. The reason given by her employer was that she had failed to keep the company properly informed of her absences, which in turn had severely affected INP Ltd's delivery business. The tribunal held that the impact on the business, no

195

matter how harsh, did not affect the fact that L had been dismissed due to her pregnancy-related absences. The dismissal was thus automatically unfair and also amounted to sex discrimination.

However, all cases must be considered on their own particular facts. In Wright v DHSS ET Case No.1448/77 W was dismissed while absent due to being both sick and pregnant, but a tribunal found that it was the sickness and not the pregnancy that was the real reason for dismissal. W had a long record of absences caused by anxiety neurosis and depression. There was nothing to connect them with her pregnancy, although they might have been aggravated by it. The tribunal said that W's symptoms were 'a long-standing and underlying matter' and that the reason for dismissal was her mental condition and not her pregnancy. (This meant only that the dismissal was not automatically unfair: the tribunal went on to hold that it was unfair under S.98.)

5.71 **Illness at end of maternity leave.** Particular difficulties have arisen where employees have been dismissed after the date on which they were due to return to work at the end of their maternity leave period when suffering from an illness which was caused by, or had its basis in, pregnancy. The question then arises as to whether the protection from dismissal offered to pregnant employees under Reg 20(3)(a) extends beyond the end of a woman's maternity leave period – i.e. whether the dismissal is automatically unfair or whether it is an 'ordinary' dismissal subject to the reasonableness test in S.98(4) ERA. In Caledonia Bureau Investment and Property v Caffrey 1998 IRLR 110, EAT, the EAT took the view that the protection contained in S.99(1)(a) ERA (the precursor to Reg 20(3)(a)) could apply after the end of a period of statutory maternity leave. In that case the employee failed to return to work at the end of her ordinary maternity leave because of post-natal depression. Her employer dismissed her a few months later. The EAT held that the dismissal constituted a pregnancy-related dismissal and was automatically unfair.

However, the Caffrey case was decided prior to the introduction of Reg 20(3)(b) of the MPL Regulations, which appears to overrule it. Reg 20(3)(b) contains the right not to be dismissed for a reason connected with the fact that the employee has given birth to a child, but is expressly restricted by Reg 20(4) to situations in which the dismissal ends the employee's ordinary or additional maternity leave. In other words, an employee is not protected under Reg 20(3)(b) from a childbirth-related dismissal that occurs *after* the end of her maternity leave period. This provision reflects the position under European law, which gives special protection to women during the period running from the beginning of their pregnancy to the end of their maternity leave. The effect of Reg 20(4) is that any dismissal after the end of an employee's maternity leave for an illness that relates to childbirth will not be automatically unfair but the fairness or otherwise of the dismissal will be considered under the ordinary unfair dismissal principles.

At the time when the Caffrey case was decided, S.99 did not outlaw dismissals connected to the fact that employee had given birth to a child – it only referred to dismissals connected with pregnancy. The EAT was therefore only able to find in the employee's favour by treating her post-natal depression as a reason connected with pregnancy under Reg 20(3)(a), which has no express limitation in time. However, since the introduction of Reg 20(3)(b), it seems unlikely that post-natal depression would be treated as 'pregnancy-related' when it so obviously falls fairly and squarely within the scope of that provision, i.e. is connected with the fact that the employee has given birth to a child – after all, 'post-natal' means after-birth. Clarification from a higher court would be welcome.

Employer's knowledge of pregnancy. The EAT has held that if a claim of unfair dismissal for pregnancy under Reg 20(3)(a) is to succeed it is essential that the employer knew or believed that the woman was pregnant or that she was being dismissed for a reason connected with her pregnancy – Del Monte Foods Ltd v Mundon 1980 ICR 694, EAT. In that case M had been warned repeatedly about her absences due to gastroenteritis and similar complaints. Eventually the decision was taken to dismiss her. One day later she telephoned to say that she was pregnant but the employer went ahead with the dismissal. The EAT said that it was essential to show the employer's knowledge of M's pregnancy at the time of dismissal: if the employer simply found out about the pregnancy afterwards and did not change the decision to dismiss, this would not be a dismissal for pregnancy reasons. Such a dismissal would not necessarily be fair, however: the tribunal would still have to consider whether the employer acted reasonably in dismissing under S.98(4).   **5.72**

Doubt was thrown on the Mundon decision by comments made by the EAT in HJ Heinz Co Ltd v Kenrick 2000 ICR 491, EAT. However, it was upheld by the EAT in Ramdoolar v Bycity Ltd 2005 ICR 368, EAT, the Appeal Tribunal observing that actual knowledge was necessary and 'it is not enough that symptoms of pregnancy existed which arguably or in fact [the employer] ought to have realised meant that the employee was pregnant'. The only possible exception that the EAT could see was if the employer detected symptoms of pregnancy and, fearing the consequences, dismissed the employee because it suspected her of being pregnant.

Pregnancy and maternity dismissals are considered in detail in IDS Employment Law Handbook, 'Maternity and Parental Rights' (2009), Chapter 12.

Sex discrimination. Less favourable treatment on the ground of illness suffered as a consequence of pregnancy can amount to sex discrimination under S.3A(3)(b) of the Sex Discrimination Act 1975 (incorporated into the Equality Act 2010 from a date to be appointed). So, in Hill v The Old Rectory Nursing Home Ltd (above) the tribunal found that H had been discriminated against contrary to S.3A(3)(b) where she had been dismissed because of her level of sickness absence during her pregnancy, some of which was pregnancy-related. However, where a woman falls   **5.73**

ill with a pregnancy-related illness, such as post-natal depression, *after* she returns from maternity leave, the illness will be treated the same as any other illness – Brown v Rentokil Ltd 1998 ICR 790, ECJ. For further details see IDS Employment Law Handbook, 'Maternity and Parental Rights' (2009), Chapter 13, 'Direct sex discrimination – pregnancy-related illness'.

5.74 Drink and drugs

There is a trend towards treating long-term alcoholism and, to a lesser extent, dependence on illegal drugs as serious illnesses, with many employers adopting special policies allowing time off for medical treatment and counselling. Bodies such as the Chartered Institute of Personnel and Development (CIPD) and Alcohol Concern recommend that employees with a drink or drug dependency should be regarded as sick, and that employers should therefore focus on rehabilitation rather than dismissal. This is backed up by the Acas Guide, which states that employers should consider whether it is appropriate to treat the problem as a medical rather than a disciplinary matter (page 75). However, there will be times when the employer feels it has no option but to dismiss an employee who has been drinking or taking drugs (either on or off duty). The employer will then need to decide whether to approach the issue as one of capability or misconduct.

5.75 **Capability or misconduct?** Generally speaking, an employer should treat alcohol or drug dependency as a capability issue. This could be evidenced by diminished performance coupled with long bouts of certified sickness. Conduct, on the other hand, is usually relied on when the employee has committed an isolated act related to drink or drugs. Occasional absence or occasional on-duty drinking suggests irregular drinking and is therefore likely to be a conduct issue.

When the drink/drug problem first comes to the employer's attention, it will need to decide whether to deal with it as a capability or conduct issue, since the procedural requirements are different in each case. If the employer chooses the wrong label at this stage, it could result in a finding of unfair dismissal. An example:

- **Mather v Tayside Regional Council** SCOET S/1842/78: M's poor attendance was because of alcoholism. Attempts were made to have him retired on medical grounds but he was certified fit. Following a warning, M was dismissed for uncertified absenteeism. The dismissal was unfair. In the tribunal's view the employer should not have treated it as a disciplinary issue but as a sickness problem and should have obtained medical advice on the prospects of treatment and recovery.

In this chapter we concentrate on alcoholism and drug addiction as illnesses and, therefore, as capability issues. Chapter 6 deals with the conduct issues that arise from drinking and taking drugs.

Alcoholism. Alcoholism can be a free-standing condition or may stem from a **5.76** separate underlying illness. In either case, it should normally be treated as a capability issue, although where there is an underlying illness, employers may be expected to show more tolerance. In Strathclyde Regional Council v Syme EAT 233/79 S was a school janitor for ten years. During the last two there were complaints that he drank and at a disciplinary interview he promised to resign if found drunk again. Later he had hospital treatment but after another incident he was held to that promise and resigned. The tribunal found this to be a dismissal. The EAT, upholding the tribunal's finding of unfairness, considered that S's problem should have been treated as medical, not disciplinary, and independent medical evidence should have been obtained since there was evidence before the tribunal to show that he suffered from bi-polar disorder and that this was the cause of his drinking. So while dismissal might have been fair in a straight case of alcoholism (bearing in mind the employer's duties to pupils and other staff), in the circumstances it was unfair.

Employers would therefore be well advised to seek medical advice on an employee's health where drinking is concerned, particularly where there is reason to believe that the employee's alcohol problem has an underlying medical cause. Once an employer has established that an employee's drinking is associated with a medical condition, it should follow the guidelines set down in East Lindsey District Council v Daubney 1977 ICR 566, EAT – see under 'Long-term absence' above. Misdemeanours such as lateness, erratic behaviour or poor performance may well be symptoms of that medical problem and should be treated accordingly. The employer should also seek to ascertain whether the underlying illness amounts to a disability for the purposes of the DDA/EqA (although alcoholism itself does not amount to a disability for the purposes of the Act).

In some cases, the danger of relapse and the nature of the employee's job may make dismissal a reasonable response. For example, employers in the drink trade could argue that dismissal of an alcoholic employee falls within the range of reasonable responses because he or she should not be allowed easy access to alcohol. Two further examples:

- **Singh v NEI International Combustion Ltd** ET Case No.5288/80: S, who had received treatment for alcoholism, was passed fit for work but with the proviso that he would need constant supervision. This was impracticable because he was an overhead crane-driver. His dismissal for capability was fair because there was no alternative work available

- **Strathclyde Regional Council v Syme** (above): the EAT suggested that had the school janitor been suffering purely from alcoholism (and not from the underlying bi-polar disorder), dismissal might have been fair, in view of the employer's duties to pupils and other staff.

199

5.77 Tribunals take a strict view where health and safety is involved. This is hardly surprising, since employers have obligations under common law and various statutes, notably the Health and Safety at Work etc Act 1974, to keep their employees (and others) safe. Employers are obliged to take reasonable steps to ensure that employees are not acting under the influence of alcohol or drugs if this is likely to risk the health and safety of others. Further, there may be an absolute prohibition on the possession of alcohol (and drugs) where safety considerations are paramount, for example, on ships and oil rigs. Dismissal for alcoholism is more likely to be fair in these circumstances.

Despite the tendency to regard alcoholism as an illness, there will still be occasions where it will be reasonable to treat it as a conduct issue. For example, if an employee fails to undergo treatment, dismissal for misconduct may be a reasonable response. In Carter v Plevshire Ltd ET Case No.21893/81 C was warned that he would be dismissed if he made no effort to overcome his drink problem. His refusal to attend Alcoholics Anonymous or to seek medical help finally made the employer realise that it would be impossible to continue to employ him. In the circumstances the dismissal was fair, even though C was medically certified as suffering from 'nervous debility' at the time. Misconduct, i.e. failure to give up the drinking and to be reliable and come to work, was the reason for his dismissal, not his illness.

Further, manifestations of the illness in the form of gross misconduct are usually viewed as such. An illustration:

- **Evans v Bass North Ltd** EAT 715/86: E, an alcoholic, had been employed as a chef for 11 years. His employer had always taken a sympathetic view of his problem, but he was dismissed on Christmas Eve for gross misconduct after breaking a prohibition against drinking in the kitchen and for later threatening the manager. The EAT found the dismissal fair for misconduct, even though it acknowledged that E was suffering from a disease.

The Acas Guide indicates, at page 31, that serious *incapability* at work brought on by alcohol or illegal drugs may also amount to gross misconduct.

5.78 **Drug dependency.** Drug addiction, like alcoholism, should in theory be treated as an illness. However, tribunals have almost invariably regarded drug-related dismissals as a conduct issue – see Chapter 6 under 'Drinking, drugs and smoking'. One reason for this could be the fact that most incidents of drug abuse at work involve cannabis. While 'hard' drugs like heroin are known to be addictive, there is a school of thought that holds that 'softer' drugs like cannabis do not form a clinical dependency. An argument based on ill health for the use of cannabis might, therefore, be difficult to sustain, although there is always the possibility that an employee takes cannabis because of an underlying medical condition, such as Parkinson's disease, or for pain relief.

Another, more obvious, factor explaining the different approach taken to drug-related dismissals is that the use of non-prescription drugs amounts to a criminal offence. Furthermore, employers themselves can commit an offence under the Misuse of Drugs Act 1971 if they know that illegal drugs are being used or distributed on their premises. Despite this, the Acas Guide has bracketed drink and drug abuse together, encouraging employers to treat both matters in the same way (pages 74–75). It remains to be seen whether tribunals will similarly equate the two issues. Two contrasting cases:

- **Walton v TAC Construction Materials Ltd** EAT 526/80: W was dismissed when his employer discovered that he was a registered drug addict, despite the fact that he was being successfully treated for his heroin addiction. The EAT held that dismissal in pursuance of a company policy against employing drug addicts was within the range of reasonable responses open to an employer

- **Davis v British Airways Board** EAT 139/80: D was dismissed after receiving a conditional discharge for forging prescriptions for amphetamines, which he used to counteract fatigue. A major reason for dismissal was the employer's view that the drugs rendered him incapable of working. The EAT upheld a tribunal's decision that dismissal was unfair because the employer should have properly investigated the effect of the drugs on D's capability.

As noted above, there is a distinction to be drawn between the use of drugs proscribed by the criminal law and other drugs. The Acas Guide cites serious incapability brought on by the use of *illegal* drugs as an example of misconduct (page 31), suggesting that the abuse of legal drugs should be treated differently. In Chappell v SYP Ltd ET Case No.2800461/02 C took an overdose of paracetamol while at work. She was dismissed for misuse of drugs. In finding her dismissal unfair, the tribunal commented that it was unreasonable of the employer to accuse her of 'misusing drugs' as the phrase invariably connotes the use of drugs such as ecstasy and cannabis. **5.79**

Where illegal drug use has led to a separate and distinct medical condition, the issue becomes one of ill-health capability, particularly if there is no evidence that the employee is continuing to take drugs – see, for example, McDonald v Cape Contracts Ltd SCOET S/2085/84 (discussed under 'Mental illness' below). Further, although drug addiction itself is not a disability for the purposes of the DDA/EqA, it may, like alcoholism, be a *symptom* of an underlying disability that is protected.

Alcohol and drug policies. Some employers have alcohol and drug policies in place that are more comprehensive than the minimum procedure required by statute. Generally, the more detailed the policy, the more effective it will be in dealing with the problem. When determining the fairness of a dismissal the **5.80**

201

tribunal will consider any relevant internal policy and the extent to which it has been adhered to. An example:

- **Angus Council v Edgley** EAT 289/99: the employer had a policy on alcohol abuse whereby employees with drinking problems would be given the opportunity to seek diagnosis and specialist help. The EAT upheld a tribunal's decision that the failure to implement that policy in respect of an employee who had been found drinking in a pub during working hours led to the employee's dismissal being unfair. Since it was clear from the disciplinary history of the employee that he had an alcohol problem, it was unreasonable of the employer to treat the pub incident as a one-off that could be dealt with under its normal disciplinary procedures.

5.81   **Mental illness**

Mental illness covers a whole range of conditions such as stress and depression, bipolar disorder, schizophrenia, and eating and obsessive compulsive disorders, as well as personality disorders and some self-harming behaviour. Such conditions can give rise to a number of difficulties at work: poor performance, long or frequent periods of absence, and erratic or irrational behaviour. Dismissal may therefore have to be considered. Dismissal on the ground of mental ill health is, like other ill-health dismissal, an employment and not a medical question, but one that should be answered in the light of medical advice – WM Computer Services Ltd v Passmore EAT 721/86. However, as Lord McDonald pointed out in Thompson v Strathclyde Regional Council EAT 628/83, incapacity on this ground is 'an exceptionally delicate and sensitive field'. Therefore, cases involving mental ill health should be approached in a similar manner to other types of illness but handled perhaps with greater tolerance and support. Employers should also consider that mental illness may constitute a disability for the purposes of the DDA/EqA.

5.82   **Fair procedure.** Consultation with the employee, medical investigation and consideration of alternative employment are just as important where the employee suffers from a mental illness as where he or she suffers from a physical illness. Employers must do their utmost to discover what the true medical position is.

However, given the nature of mental illness, greater reliance may have to be placed on medical advice than on consultation (although it may be difficult, if not impossible, for doctors to predict the duration of the symptoms and when the employee may be fit to resume work). Indeed, in some cases, consultation may give a very misleading impression, especially where, for example, the employee is suffering from paranoia or where a depressive illness is attributed by the employee to the stresses and strains of the working environment itself.

There have been many instances where a dismissal on the ground of mental illness has been held to be unfair through lack of, or inadequate, medical investigation or consultation. Two examples:

- **WM Computer Services Ltd v Passmore** EAT 721/86: P was dismissed after prolonged absences associated with depression. He returned to work after being certified fit by his own psychiatrist. He was asked to see the company doctor, who reported more pessimistically on P's fitness although he did not certify P unfit. The employer decided to dismiss P on the basis of the company doctor's report and only sought the doctor's further advice on how best to terminate the employment. P's absence had been substantial, his work poor, his conduct unstable and he might have made a second suicide attempt. Nevertheless, the EAT upheld a tribunal's finding of unfair dismissal since the employer had misconstrued its doctor's report – written without knowledge of the employer's intention to dismiss – as recommending that P should not return to work. In addition, there had been a failure to consult P and no real consideration of possible redeployment

- **Peacock v Vi-Seal Tapes Ltd** ET Case No.20821/80: P was under warning for absenteeism and lateness. His depression and drinking were known to the company. His dismissal for a week's absence without sending in a medical certificate was unfair. The employer had been informed that he was suffering another bout of depression and should have investigated further.

Performance and behavioural problems. If an employer recruits someone suffering from a mental illness, the employee's performance should be judged by standards which make appropriate allowances for the condition. Should performance drop below that standard, then a dismissal is potentially fair. If the illness first manifests itself during employment, employers will still be expected to show tolerance and take the illness into account when judging an employee's performance and conduct. It may also need to change tack and treat it as an ill-health capability issue. Two examples:

5.83

- **McDonald v Cape Contracts Ltd** SCOET S/2085/84: McD, an apprentice engineer, was involved in a violent incident at work which resulted in his being hospitalised for schizophrenia. Seven months later he submitted a medical certificate to his employer declaring that he was fully fit to return to work. His employer subsequently wrote to his GP for his medical history. Her reply, which set out a positive prognosis, mentioned that his illness was drug-induced. The employer subsequently dismissed McD for gross misconduct. A tribunal found the dismissal unfair. The employer had ignored the fact that McD had been suffering from a very acute psychotic illness and had concentrated instead on the conduct itself and the fact that it was drug-induced. Having regard to the medical advice available at the time, it was not within the range of reasonable responses for the employer to treat the matter as one of misconduct for which McD should be held responsible. Instead it should have treated it as a capability matter relating to his health. Therefore, it should have been concerned not with the incident some nine months earlier, disturbing as it was, but with the question of whether McD was fit to resume his apprenticeship

- **Dolan v Chief Constable of Avon and Somerset Constabulary** ET Case No.1402819/06: D joined the Constabulary as a police officer in 1975 and by May 2003 had been promoted to the post of Detective Inspector in the Criminal Investigation Department (CID). However, in March 2004 he began to suffer stress relating to matters outside work and in September he went on sick leave until the following January. The deterioration in his mental health coincided with concerns about his performance at work and in February he was moved from the CID to a uniformed duty inspector role. The Constabulary put in place measures to improve D's performance but in August 2005 it commenced a formal procedure in respect of unsatisfactory performance and eventually D resigned in October 2006. A tribunal upheld his claim for unfair constructive dismissal and disability discrimination. The employer never questioned whether the sudden deterioration in D's performance might be due to the fact that he was still suffering from mental illness. It should have deferred its unsatisfactory performance procedure until it was established that the problems did not arise from his medical condition. In failing to do so, and subjecting M to comments about his performance, the employer had not only failed to make reasonable adjustments under the DDA but had also engaged in conduct likely or calculated to destroy trust and confidence.

5.84 As the Dolan case demonstrates, if the illness amounts to a disability, the employer will also be required to make reasonable adjustments under the DDA/ EqA. However, even where the illness does not amount to a disability, any adjustments made by the employer in an attempt to avoid dismissal will be taken into account by a tribunal when assessing whether or not it was fair.

Mental illness may render an employee unsuitable for continued employment when it results in unacceptable behaviour or an inability to perform adequately. In some cases behaviour may be violent, in other cases unreliable, and erratic behaviour could be hazardous. In all these situations, once investigation and consultation has taken place, the reasonableness of a decision to dismiss will ultimately depend on the facts. Some examples:

- **Wright v Commissioners of Inland Revenue** EAT 385/79: the Inland Revenue knew that W was a schizophrenic when he was appointed to his job. After two years he started suffering delusions, claiming that he was under surveillance by MI5 agents, with whom his doctor was in league, all of which disrupted work in the office. W refused medication and was reluctant to go into hospital. After lengthy interviews and medical investigations, he was dismissed on the ground that his condition rendered him incapable of carrying out his duties. The EAT affirmed the tribunal's finding of fair dismissal

- **Halton Borough Council v Hollett** EAT 559/87: during the course of his employment, it came to light that H suffered from a psychotic illness for which he was taking medication. His behaviour at work became increasingly rash and the employer received a complaint. During a disciplinary hearing H admitted that he had reduced his medication because his GP had said that he could do so if he felt fit enough. The employer did not investigate this further but issued a final written warning, saying it was up to H to take the full medication as recommended. Shortly before the written warning was due to lapse, the employer received another complaint about H's behaviour. As the written warning was still current, H was dismissed. On appeal a consultant psychiatrist's report was produced stating that H's eccentric behaviour was perhaps due to too low a dosage and recommending that it be increased. The EAT upheld a tribunal's finding of unfair dismissal, holding that some sort of medical investigation should have taken place. H was 'trying his best' and his mental illness should have been taken into account. The tribunal had before it clear evidence to suggest that the employer had used a relatively trivial complaint about H as an excuse for dismissing him

- **Singh-Deu v Chloride Metals Ltd** 1976 IRLR 56, ET: S was employed at a lead smelting factory. His job was not particularly skilled but demanded that he constantly had his wits about him, since it involved filtering toxic dust and fumes. The effect of a mistake could be disastrous, not only for the rest of the workforce but for the whole neighbourhood. S was diagnosed by his own doctor and by the company doctor as having paranoid schizophrenia. His subsequent dismissal was fair even though there was a difference of medical opinion as to whether it would be safe to let him return to work. The tribunal was satisfied that to allow S to return to work was a risk nobody could take in this 'highly dangerous industry.'

Capability or conduct? If an employee relies on a mental illness to explain or excuse misconduct, the employer should investigate the matter further before dismissing (or confirming the decision to dismiss). It may then need to treat the issue as one of capability, rather than conduct. In City of Edinburgh Council v Dickson EAT 0038/09, for example, the EAT held that the dismissal of an employee for watching pornography on a school computer was unfair. His employer had rejected his claim that his uncharacteristic behaviour was the result of a hypoglycaemic episode caused by his diabetes without investigating or understanding his medical condition. **5.85**

Interestingly, in Dickson the EAT concluded that once the tribunal had found that D was not responsible for his conduct, it's 'heinousness' then became irrelevant for misconduct purposes. This was not a case, said the EAT, where

205

the employee's actions, although involuntary, were so extreme that it was unreasonable for him to return to his previous post, nor did the Council argue that the inappropriate behaviour might recur. Had that been the case, the Council might have been entitled to dismiss D for capability, rather than conduct, provided a fair procedure was followed.

5.86 Where the conduct is serious and the employee's mental condition is not such that his or her actions were involuntary, the employer may be entitled to dismiss for misconduct even though the conduct was linked to some extent to the employee's mental health. An example:

- **Frost v West Midlands Police Authority** ET Case No.1303344/06: F was involved in a road traffic accident in 1997, which resulted in him suffering pain and discomfort from that time on. He maintained that the pain caused him to become agitated or irritable from time to time. In October 2005 he was alleged to have behaved inappropriately by making homophobic comments to a representative of the employer's Lesbian, Gay, Bisexual and Transgender Forum. At the subsequent disciplinary hearing he said that he was suffering discomfort, and he could only put his behaviour down to his 'head being bad'. He was dismissed as he was already on a final written warning for inappropriate sexual behaviour. His doctor produced a report for his appeal stating that his physical condition and associated pain might lead to irritability and agitation, resulting in him making comments that might seem inappropriate, and asking the employer to look at his case in a sympathetic light. Although a tribunal held that it was unfair to dismiss F for the conduct in question, it accepted in principle that the employer was entitled to treat it as a conduct issue and concluded that F had contributed to his dismissal by 20 per cent. The medical evidence indicated that, despite his physical and mental impairments, he should be regarded as responsible for his actions.

Therefore, when deciding whether dismissal should be for conduct or capability, much will depend on the seriousness of the conduct and the severity of the employee's condition. In Scott v South Thames Corporation EAT 157/96 the EAT made the point that there is no legal rule or principle which lays down mutually exclusive procedures for dealing with health problems and with problems arising out of an employee's conduct. In each case, the question of whether the employer acted reasonably will depend on the circumstances.

5.87 **Refusal to undergo examination or treatment.** An employer cannot dismiss an employee simply for refusing to undergo a psychiatric or medical examination, especially where it does not have the contractual power to insist that the employee does so – Bliss v South East Thames Regional Health Authority 1987 ICR 700, CA (see under 'Long-term absence – medical investigation' above). However, where an employee exhibits performance- or behaviour-related problems at work and refuses to undergo an examination, the employer is entitled to base its decisions on the information available. In Petch v DHSS EAT 851/86 P was dismissed after the Civil Service Medical Advisory Service certified him incapable of working properly due to his depression. His own doctor had certified him fit shortly before, but P withheld permission for consultation between the doctors. His unfair dismissal claim failed on the ground that he himself had prevented a full medical investigation and that the decision had to be made on the available evidence

Similarly, an employee's refusal to take medication may justify dismissal if this causes his or her condition to worsen (or there is a risk that it will do so). In Gillies v Scottish Equitable Life Assurance Society EAT 295/88, for example, G, an actuary, had a history of paranoid schizophrenia. In a conversation with his employer he stated that he believed he was being drugged or poisoned through the office ventilation system. The employer was aware of the employee's earlier mental illness and sought medical advice. Medical reports suggested that his health was deteriorating owing to his refusal to take medication and that no reliance should be placed on his work until he had been treated. However, he absolutely refused treatment and the employer, concerned about the safety risk posed by his continued employment, eventually dismissed him, following a period of suspension. The EAT held that his dismissal was fair despite the fact that the quality of G's work up until his suspension was high. On the evidence before it, it was reasonable for the Society to consider G unfit for work, given the risk of continuing deterioration and his disruptive behaviour.

Illness caused by stress at work. Note that where the mental illness has been caused by stress at work, it may be necessary for the employer to 'go the extra mile' by, for example, being more proactive in finding alternative employment for the employee or putting up with a longer period of sickness absence – see Royal Bank of Scotland v McAdie 2008 ICR 1087, CA (discussed under 'Factors affecting reasonableness – illness caused by employer' above).

5.88

Alternative work. The possibility of alternative work should be discussed with an employee who would otherwise be dismissed, although there is no obligation to create a new job (see under 'Alternative employment' above).

5.89

Employers should not assume that a mentally ill employee no longer wants or can cope with the pressure of the job; consultation is still necessary. Two examples:

- **Ginns v Leon Motor Services Ltd** COET 846/79: G had worked well for the employer for 29 years, latterly as a foreman, before suffering a nervous breakdown. His employer wrote to him after he had been absent for four weeks saying that it would be unfair to subject him to the same pressure so he would be relieved of his foreman's duties. The employer did not mention either his new duties or whether his pay would be affected and failed to answer his letters. G successfully claimed unfair constructive dismissal, the tribunal holding it had rarely seen such a clear case of repudiatory conduct by an employer. It also criticised the complete lack of consultation, which was an 'elementary requirement of fairness and good practice' when an employer is contemplating ill-health dismissal

- **Marriott v Rolle Medical Partnership** ET Case No.1700920/06: M worked for her employer for almost 16 years, latterly as office manager. She went on sick leave in October 2005, suffering from stress resulting from her obsessive compulsive disorder (OCD). Her GP reported in March 2006 that she was making good progress, and that a structured, graded return to work would enable her to return to being a useful and productive member of staff. The employer, however, considered that M's OCD meant that she was not able to return to her old role as office manager given that the work was inherently pressured. It therefore offered her the role of secretary on less pay but M accepted voluntary redundancy rather than take up the new post. A tribunal held that M had been forced into taking voluntary redundancy when her role was not redundant. This meant redundancy could not be a potentially fair reason for dismissal and she had therefore been unfairly dismissed. The employer had effectively made an assumption that because of her condition M should be denied the opportunity to return to her previous level of responsibility and in so doing had gone against the advice of M's GP.

5.90 **HIV/AIDS**

Dismissal of an employee simply because he or she is HIV positive is likely to be unfair unless it is a rare case where the job involves a real danger of infecting fellow employees or the public, such as certain healthcare jobs. Even in these circumstances the employer would almost certainly be expected to have considered alternative employment before dismissing. Employers should also bear in mind that any dismissal may well amount to disability discrimination under the DDA/EqA if not handled properly, as individuals who suffer from HIV are deemed to have a disability from the point of diagnosis without having to show that they have an impairment that has (or is likely to have) a substantial adverse long-term effect on their ability to carry out day-to-day activities.

Employers must be alive to the possibility of bullying of employees with HIV, given the stigma and ignorance that still exists. If measures are not put in place to combat this, the employer runs the risk of constructive dismissal claims, disability discrimination claims and claims for sexual orientation discrimination under the Employment Equality (Sexual Orientation) Regulations 2003/1661 (incorporated into the Equality Act 2010 from a date to be appointed). Furthermore, an HIV-positive employee who is stigmatised or discriminated against at work may well suffer from stress and depression, which may lay the employer open to personal injury claims.

In certain fields, such as health care work, an HIV-positive employee can pose a health risk to others. The employer's duty to make reasonable

208

adjustments under the DDA/EqA means that measures must be put in place to negate those risks to enable the employee to keep working (either in his or her normal job with modifications or in an alternative job where there is less risk involved). However, if an employer has done all it reasonably can and the employee still poses a significant risk, the employer may be entitled to dismiss him or her fairly for health and safety reasons (which may amount to SOSR). Conversely, if the employee either wilfully or carelessly neglects the health and safety measures put in place by the employer, it may then be fair to dismiss him or her for misconduct.

Capability dismissals. Dismissal of an employee who is suffering from an illness associated with AIDS is potentially fair when the reason relates to the employee's ability to do the job. However, the fact that someone has become ill as a result of being infected with the HIV virus does not mean that he or she should be treated differently from any other employee with a non-contagious life-threatening illness. Accordingly, where an infected employee is absent from work for long or short periods of time, the employer must follow the normal sickness procedure: investigation, consultation and consideration of alternative employment.

5.91

A person who has developed full-blown AIDS may not be fit enough to work again and in that situation a dismissal for capability might be fair. It is also possible that the contract has been frustrated – see IDS Employment Law Handbook, 'Contracts of Employment' (2009), Chapter 10.

SOSR dismissals. Employers are sometimes faced with strong pressure from members of the workforce or customers to dismiss or transfer an employee who is, or is believed to be, HIV positive. The pressure may originate from a fear of being infected themselves or from personal prejudices. However, apart from a few identifiable risk areas such as healthcare work, an HIV-infected person poses no risk to others through normal work or social contact. Most of the potential areas of conflict can therefore be resolved through education and consultation.

5.92

In so far as other employees are concerned, employers have an implied contractual duty to render reasonable support to an employee who is being harassed by colleagues – Wigan Borough Council v Davies 1979 ICR 411, EAT. Failure to do so may entitle the employee to resign and claim constructive dismissal, depending on the seriousness of the breach. It is the responsibility of employers to take appropriate action to remedy the situation. They should allay the fears of employees who are concerned about the transmission of HIV, primarily through informing and educating them. If these measures have no effect, an employer may have to consider transferring one or more of them to a different location. In certain circumstances the employer may also need to consider disciplining or dismissing employees who harass a work colleague. In Philpott v North Lambeth Law Centre ET Case No.11212–13/86, for example, the tribunal held that the dismissal of two solicitors who refused to work with

209

H, a newly engaged solicitor who had worked for Gay Switchboard, on the ground that he would introduce AIDS into the law centre, was fair. They were dismissed for a number of reasons, including the malicious manner in which they had brought the issue of AIDS to the attention of their fellow employees and members of the public.

However, it may not be practicable for an employer to dismiss employees for refusing to work with an infected person as this could lead to widespread disruption of the workforce. In this situation the employer may be left with no option but to transfer or dismiss the employee who has, or is suspected of having, HIV or AIDS. Such a dismissal is likely to be for SOSR but employers should be aware that they cannot justify such a dismissal by reference to any pressure involving the calling or organising of a strike or other industrial action – S.107 ERA. But if the pressure takes other forms, whether the dismissal was fair will depend on all the circumstances, although tribunals will not expect employers to crumble too easily under pressure, particularly if it is from a relatively small group of employees. It will be of fundamental importance that the employer did everything possible to resolve the situation, distanced itself from the views and actions of the employees, and explained the situation fully to the HIV-infected employee before taking action. In Buck v The Letchworth Palace Ltd ET Case No.36488/86 B, a homosexual cinema projectionist, was dismissed without notice after he was convicted of an indecency offence in a public toilet and his colleagues refused to work with him, fearing that they might catch AIDS, even though B did not himself have AIDS. Although a tribunal found the dismissal fair, this was because the reason for dismissal was B's off-duty criminal conduct rather than the pressure imposed by his colleagues and their 'unreasonable prejudices'. The tribunal was critical of the employer's handling of the matter and its complete failure to consult with B.

5.93 **Disclosure and confidentiality.** Confidentiality is of particular concern to many employees who are HIV positive or have Aids. The National Aids Trust (NAT) has produced a resource pack, 'HIV at Work', which states that while disclosure may be beneficial, there is no justification for asking an employee to disclose HIV-related information, unless their infection is affecting their ability to perform their job or there is an occupational risk of transmission. It recommends selective disclosure to HR, occupational health or whoever it is felt is most appropriate to be entrusted with the information. If the employer breaches confidentiality in respect of that disclosure, this may found a claim for unfair constructive dismissal. Two contrasting cases:

• **Dos Santos v Fitch Ratings Ltd** ET Case No.2203907/08: following a few periods of sick leave DS arranged to have a blood test, the results of which indicated that he was HIV positive. He informed his line managers, M and G, but emphasised how important it was to him that the information should be kept confidential. M and G felt genuine concern for DS and sought to provide support. They persuaded him to inform HR but he stressed the importance that the information should not be divulged any further. However, a few days later M passed the information on to her line manager, P, as she felt he needed to understand the seriousness of the condition underlying DS's frequent absences. P then called DS into a meeting to express his support. DS was extremely upset to discover that his confidence had been broken and felt so betrayed that he resigned in response. A tribunal upheld DS's claim for unfair constructive dismissal. It considered that M's disclosure involved a breach of the implied term of trust and confidence: although it was not *calculated* to destroy that relationship, the tribunal considered it was *likely* to do so. DS disclosed highly personal information under strict terms of confidence, which was breached. The tribunal also upheld DS's claim for unlawful harassment under the DDA. The employer's action in disclosing the information was unwanted by him and it had the *effect* of violating his dignity or creating an intimidating, hostile, degrading, humiliating or offensive environment, even if it did not have that purpose

- **Tucker v Burgess (trading as Ferndown Fruit Market)** ET Case No.3103296/06: T began working for B, a sole trader, as a shop assistant in 2003, having been diagnosed as being HIV positive some seven years earlier. In 2006, T told B of her condition and subsequently gave B a letter from the hospital saying that she had been prescribed new medication that could cause unpleasant side effects within the first four weeks. B showed the letter to an employee who was in charge of the shop when he was not there, so she could keep an eye on T. When T discovered that B had shown the letter to her colleague, she was shocked and upset by the 'breach of trust and confidentiality' and resigned. However, a tribunal rejected her claim for unfair constructive dismissal on this ground, holding that disclosure of the hospital letter was a proper management decision and not a breach of confidentiality.

5.94 Failing to respect an employee's confidentiality may also amount to a breach of his or her right to privacy under Article 8(1) of the European Convention of Human Rights, which can be taken into account by a tribunal under S.98(4) ERA when assessing the fairness of dismissal – see Chapter 3, under 'Reasonableness of dismissal – impact of the Human Rights Act' for further details. Furthermore, employers have a legal duty to safeguard the confidentiality of an employee's personal and medical information under the Data Protection Act 1998.

5.95 **HIV testing.** Sometimes employers wish to introduce HIV testing of their employees. However, they should be aware that, in the absence of an express term governing HIV screening, an order by the employer that members of the workforce submit to an HIV test against their will could amount to a fundamental breach of the implied term of trust and confidence, entitling the employees to resign and claim unfair constructive dismissal.

A right to test employees might be implied where the employee has life-and-death responsibilities for others; for example, a train driver. This is because, in some cases, people with the AIDS virus develop dementia. Another situation might be where the job involves travel to countries where restrictions on entry are imposed. Similarly, where the nature of the employee's job entails a greater risk of transmission, for example, health-care work, there may be a right to test. The NAT resource pack states that mandatory HIV testing of healthcare workers involved in surgical procedures may be justified. However, in the vast majority of cases the employer will need to obtain the individual's express consent to testing and any dismissal for refusal to give consent is likely to be unfair.

Even where there is a contractual term governing HIV screening, this will not entitle the employer to carry out tests in all circumstances. Nor can an employer necessarily dismiss an employee for refusing to take a test, even if technically he or she is in breach of contract. The employer would need to have a valid reason for requiring the test and should explain to the employee what the consequences of persistent refusal to take the test might be. Some of the issues relevant to drug and alcohol testing are likely to be relevant here – see Chapter 6 under 'Drinking, drugs and smoking'.

6 Conduct

Misconduct is a potentially fair reason for dismissal under S.98(2)(b) of the Employment Rights Act 1996 (ERA). In this chapter, we look at some of the more general considerations applicable to conduct dismissals – such as establishing conduct as the reason for dismissal and the requirements of the reasonableness test – before moving on to the main categories of misconduct into which most cases fall. We then look at the specific additional issues that potentially arise where the misconduct in question constitutes a criminal offence, whether perpetrated within or outside of the workplace. Finally, we set out the procedural steps that employers should ordinarily follow during disciplinary proceedings when dealing with employee misconduct.

General considerations   6.1

An employer faced with the possibility of dismissing an employee by reason of misconduct will have to consider a number of issues in order to ensure that any resulting dismissal is not unfair. Clearly, specific forms of misconduct will raise

213

their own particular issues. But before examining these, it is appropriate to discuss the general considerations that apply to all cases irrespective of the nature of the misconduct in question. These include:

- establishing conduct as a potentially fair reason for dismissal

- relevant considerations affecting the 'reasonableness' of dismissing for misconduct under S.98(4) ERA

- the concept of 'gross misconduct', which, if made out, entitles the employer to dismiss an employee summarily (i.e. without notice)

- how the Human Rights Act 1998 may affect the fairness or unfairness of dismissals for certain types of misconduct.

6.2   Establishing the reason for dismissal

It is the employer who must show that misconduct was the reason for dismissal. According to the EAT in British Home Stores Ltd v Burchell 1980 ICR 303, EAT, a three-fold test applies. The employer must show that:

- it believed the employee was guilty of misconduct

- it had in mind reasonable grounds upon which to sustain that belief, and

- at the stage at which that belief was formed on those grounds, it had carried out as much investigation into the matter as was reasonable in the circumstances.

This means that the employer need not have conclusive direct proof of the employee's misconduct – only a genuine and reasonable belief, reasonably tested. The Burchell test was approved by the Court of Appeal in W Weddel and Co Ltd v Tepper 1980 ICR 286, CA, and, more recently, in Panama v London Borough of Hackney 2003 IRLR 278, CA.

Although the Burchell case was concerned with a suspicion of dishonesty, the principles laid down by the EAT in that case have become the established test for determining the sufficiency of the reason for dismissal in other types of conduct cases where the employer has no direct proof of the employee's misconduct, but only a strong suspicion. However, the test is clearly not appropriate to all misconduct cases: take 'appearance' cases, for example. Here it is usually easy to tell whether the employee is breaking a dress rule or not. In such cases the focus is more on whether the decision to dismiss falls within the range of reasonable responses under S.98(4), not whether the employer has shown a statutorily acceptable reason for the dismissal under S.98(2).

6.3   Employee's own assessment of behaviour irrelevant. Once the Burchell test is satisfied, and the employer has shown a reasonable belief that the employee was guilty of misconduct, it is irrelevant that the employee did not consider the behaviour inappropriate him or herself. In Cunliffe v Primagraphics Ltd ET

214

Case No.1500499/06 the employee put forward the – in the tribunal's view – 'novel and ambitious' argument that, since he did not personally regard the e-mail he had sent round the office to be offensive and inflammatory, the employer did not have grounds for the belief that he had breached the company's e-mail and internet policy. As the tribunal said: 'If pushed to its logical conclusion, this would amount to a submission that an employee could distribute material which was plainly and objectively offensive and which had caused great offence to its recipients but that this would not constitute the commission of a disciplinary offence if the employee personally did not find it offensive.' Such an interpretation had to be rejected. Here, there was no doubt that the e-mail – calling for immigrants who were 'complaining [about] our way of life' to leave the country – was objectively offensive, and the employee should reasonably have been aware that it was such; indeed, he acknowledged as much in cross-examination when he said that the e-mail 'would not offend a white, British patriot'. The dismissal had been fair.

Two or more suspects. Where more than one employee is suspected of misconduct, the Burchell requirements of 'genuine belief on reasonable grounds after reasonable investigation' do not apply. This rule was laid down by the Court of Appeal in Monie v Coral Racing Ltd 1981 ICR 109, CA – a case of suspected theft where more than one employee was under suspicion but the culprit was unidentifiable. The Court held that where two employees are suspected of misconduct and the employer, despite investigation, cannot discover which of them is to blame, it may be fair to dismiss both on reasonable suspicion short of actual belief. It is not clear, however, just what degree of suspicion of one or the other's guilt is necessary. Sir David Cairns referred to 'virtual certainty', Lord Justice Dunn to 'a reasonable suspicion' and Lord Justice Stephenson to 'reasonable belief'. **6.4**

The Monie case has since been followed in a range of other circumstances; for example, where one of two employees was to blame for fighting – British Aerospace v Mafe EAT 565/80, and where damage was due to faulty servicing by one of two workers – McPhie and anor v Wimpey Waste Management Ltd 1981 IRLR 316, EAT. It was distinguished, however, in Leyland Vehicles Ltd v Wright EAT 712/81, where the EAT held that there was 'no reasonable conclusive proof' that one of the two dismissed employees must have been guilty of theft.

The Monie principle is also capable of being applied to cases where three or more employees are under suspicion. In Parr v Whitbread and Co plc 1990 ICR 427, EAT, the EAT set out five guidelines to be considered by tribunals in cases of 'group' or 'blanket' dismissals for both misconduct and incapability. If a tribunal is able to find on the evidence before it: **6.5**

- that an act had been committed which if committed by an individual would justify dismissal

- that the employer had made a reasonable – i.e. a sufficiently thorough – investigation into the matter and with appropriate procedures

- that as a result of that investigation the employer reasonably believed that more than one person could have committed the act

- that the employer had acted reasonably in identifying the group of employees who could have committed the act and that each member of the group was individually capable of so doing

- that as between the members of the group the employer could not reasonably identify the individual perpetrator

then, provided that the beliefs are held on solid and sensible grounds at the date of dismissal, the employer is entitled to dismiss each member of that group.

Where any one of a group of employees could have committed a particular offence, the fact that one or more members of that group are not dismissed does not render dismissal of the others unfair provided that the employer is able to show solid and sensible grounds (which do not have to be related to the relevant offence) for differentiating between members of the suspected group. There is no 'all or none' principle applying to group dismissals – Frames Snooker Centre v Boyce 1992 IRLR 472, EAT.

6.6 **Where conduct is admitted.** The Burchell guidelines are clearly most appropriate where misconduct is suspected. Little purpose would be served by an investigation where the misconduct is admitted – Royal Society for the Protection of Birds v Croucher 1984 ICR 604, EAT. Indeed, the Court of Appeal has said that where an employee has either pleaded guilty to, or been convicted of, a criminal offence, it would be 'ridiculous' to conclude that the employer did not have reasonable grounds for believing that the offence had been committed – P v Nottinghamshire County Council 1992 ICR 706, CA. However, the reasonableness test contained in S.98(4) (see below) must still be applied and the employer must consider whether that particular conduct warranted dismissal. There may also be special circumstances in which the reasonable employer would still be expected to carry out his own investigation – e.g. where new matters came to light. The last two points were stressed by the EAT in Secretary of State for Scotland v Campbell 1992 IRLR 263, EAT.

6.7 **Nature of conduct and relevance of timeframe.** Conduct does not have to be blameworthy to fall within the ambit of S.98(2), although blameworthiness could be relevant when considering the dismissal's fairness. Nor will mere lapse of time necessarily prevent the misconduct from being a prescribed reason for dismissal where there is a clear causal link between the two. Both these aspects were stressed by the EAT in Jury v ECC Quarries Ltd EAT 241/80, where the Appeal Tribunal rejected J's arguments that behaviour could not be 'conduct' unless it was reprehensible; and that the lapse of time (he was dismissed five months after his refusal to retrain as a Class 2 HGV driver when all Class 3 vehicles went out of service) prevented his refusal from being the reason for the dismissal. That said, the EAT in Kilduff v Mind in Bradford EAT 0568/04 made it clear that an honest or reasonable mistake was a relevant factor when considering the question as to what conduct took place and how criticisable that conduct was.

Third-party allegations. The extent to which an employer can rely on allegations made by a third party when reaching a decision on whether to dismiss was considered in Henderson v Granville Tours Ltd 1982 IRLR 494, EAT, where the EAT found it unreasonable to dismiss on customers' complaints alone, no matter how truthful and reliable the complainants might be. Further investigation is needed, even by small firms, before reasonable belief in the misconduct is established.   6.8

More than one potentially fair reason. It is generally accepted that more than one potentially fair reason under S.98 ERA can apply to an employee's dismissal. For example, in Perkin v St George's Healthcare NHS Trust 2006 ICR 617, CA, the employee's style of management seriously undermined the proper running of the trust at a most senior level, and adversely reflected on the trust both internally and externally. The Court of Appeal said that his dismissal could have been for the potentially fair reasons of 'conduct', 'capability' or 'some other substantial reason'. Consequently, it is not necessarily incumbent on the employer to restrict himself to just one potentially fair reason before the tribunal. However, categorisation will certainly affect the steps that the employer will need to take prior to dismissal in order to ensure fairness. For this reason, an employer would be well advised to settle on a single category of potentially fair reason to ensure that he follows the correct procedure prior to taking any disciplinary action.   6.9

Reasonableness of a conduct dismissal   6.10

Establishing that the reason for dismissal relates to the employee's conduct under S.98(2)(b) ERA is simply the first stage in the process. While the Burchell test is relevant to establishing the employer's belief in the employee's guilt – and, therefore, to establishing the reason for dismissal – it applies equally to the question of whether it was reasonable for the employer to treat that reason as a sufficient reason to dismiss in the circumstances under S.98(4) ERA – see Foley v Post Office; HSBC Bank plc (formerly Midland Bank plc) v Madden 2000 ICR 1283, CA. However, as explained in Chapter 3, the burden of proof is neutral when it comes to reasonableness.

When assessing whether the Burchell test has been met, the tribunal must ask itself whether what occurred fell within the 'range of reasonable responses' of a reasonable employer. The Court of Appeal has held that the 'range of reasonable responses' test applies in a conduct case both to the decision to dismiss and to the procedure by which that decision was reached. In J Sainsbury plc v Hitt 2003 ICR 111, CA, the Court of Appeal found that a tribunal had

217

substituted its own decision as to whether or not an investigation into alleged misconduct was reasonable. This, said the Court of Appeal, was an error of law. The relevant question was whether it was an investigation that fell within the range of reasonable responses that a reasonable employer might have adopted. In Whitbread plc (t/a Whitbread Medway Inns) v Hall 2001 ICR 699, CA, a similar result was reached in relation to admitted misconduct. Note, however, that in certain circumstances there will be no 'range' of reasonable responses. For example, if an employee deliberately sets fire to his employer's factory, dismissal is the only reasonable response. Conversely, if an employee is dismissed for politely saying 'good morning', this would be unreasonable – see Foley, above.

The procedural steps most usually required of an employer in conduct cases are discussed at the end of this chapter under 'Disciplinary proceedings'. However, it is important to note at this stage that the procedural steps required of employers have undergone a fair amount of change in recent years. In October 2004 the Government introduced the statutory dispute resolution procedures (SDRPs), with the primary aim of encouraging parties to seek early resolution of disputes in the workplace. They also set out minimum procedural steps – contained in the statutory dismissal and disciplinary procedures (DDPs) – that employers were required to follow prior to contemplating taking any disciplinary action. Failure to follow the DDPs meant that any dismissal was automatically unfair under S.98A(1) ERA. However, a new S.98A(2) provided that failure to follow a procedure other than one required by the statutory DDPs would not be regarded as by itself making the employer's action unreasonable if the employer could show that he would have decided to dismiss the employee if he had followed the procedure.

6.11 Given the repeal of the SDRPs and S.98A ERA on 6 April 2009, the compulsory dismissal and disciplinary procedure has vanished. In its place, employers are expected to have regard to the principles for handling disciplinary and grievance procedures in the workplace set out in the revised Acas Code of Practice on Disciplinary and Grievance Procedures. The Code is relevant to the question of liability and will be taken into account by a tribunal when determining the reasonableness of a dismissal in accordance with S.98(4) – S.207 TULR(C)A 1992. Further, if the dismissal is found to be unfair, the tribunal can increase (or indeed decrease) an award of compensation by up to 25 per cent for an unreasonable failure to follow the Code if it considers it just and equitable to do so – S.207A TULR(C)A.

The effect of the repeal of the statutory DDPs and, in particular, S.98A(2) ERA, is that, in determining the reasonableness of a dismissal, tribunals are once again forbidden from asking whether procedural failings would have made any difference to the decision to dismiss. In other words, an employer is unable to argue in his defence that even if he had followed a fair procedure, he still would have dismissed the employee. This was the position that was first established by the House of Lords in Polkey v AE Dayton Services Ltd 1988 ICR 142, HL. That case, however, also made it clear that the issue of whether a failure to follow proper procedure made any difference to the decision to dismiss could be taken into account when calculating the compensatory award at the remedies stage. A tribunal may reduce such an award proportionately to the chance that the employee would have been fairly dismissed in any event had a proper procedure been complied with. These so-called 'Polkey reductions' to compensation are considered in detail in Chapter 18.

Finally, it should be noted that the SDRPs continue to apply to disputes that arose before 6 April 2009 but are awaiting a tribunal hearing, as well as those that started before 6 April 2009 but continued after that date – see IDS Employment Law Supplement, 'Statutory disciplinary and grievance procedures' (2009).

Gross misconduct 6.12

Whether an employee's behaviour amounts to misconduct or gross misconduct can have important consequences. Gross misconduct may result in summary dismissal, thus relieving the employer of the obligation to pay notice pay. Exactly what type of behaviour amounts to gross misconduct is difficult to pinpoint and will depend on the facts of the individual case. However, it is generally accepted that it must be an act which fundamentally undermines the employment contract (i.e. it must be repudiatory conduct by the employee going to the root of the contract) – Wilson v Racher 1974 ICR 428, CA. Moreover, the conduct must be a deliberate and wilful contradiction of the contractual terms or amount to gross negligence – Laws v London Chronicle (Indicator Newspapers Ltd) 1959 1 WLR 698, CA and Sandwell and anor v Westwood EAT 0032/09.

Paragraph 23 of the Acas Code states that the employer's disciplinary rules should give examples of what the employer regards as gross misconduct, i.e. conduct that he considers serious enough to justify summary dismissal. The Code suggests this might include theft or fraud, physical violence, gross negligence or serious insubordination. Although there are some types of misconduct that may be universally seen as gross misconduct, such as theft or violence, others may vary according to the nature of the organisation and what it does. In workplaces with significant health and safety risks, for example, any breach of a health and safety procedure may be viewed as gross misconduct justifying dismissal, whereas a similar breach in a workplace where workers are not exposed to the same level of risk may warrant only a warning. If an employer views certain behaviour as very serious and capable of amounting to gross misconduct because of the nature of the business but that behaviour might not be viewed in the same way elsewhere, it is particularly important to include it in the disciplinary rules so that employees are aware of that fact.

219

6.13 The Acas Guide, which accompanies the Acas Code, gives the following examples at page 31 of gross misconduct that might be included:

- theft or fraud

- physical violence or bullying

- deliberate and serious damage to property

- serious misuse of an organisation's property or name

- deliberately accessing internet sites containing pornographic, offensive or obscene material

- serious insubordination

- unlawful discrimination or harassment

- bringing the organisation into serious disrepute

- serious incapability at work brought on by alcohol or illegal drugs

- causing loss, damage or injury though serious negligence

- a serious breach of health and safety rules

- a serious breach of confidence.

Even where gross misconduct may justify summary dismissal, an employer suspecting an employee of such conduct should still follow a fair procedure, including a full investigation of the facts. If an employer does establish a reasonable belief that the employee is guilty of the misconduct in question, he must still hold a meeting and hear the employee's case, including any mitigating circumstances that might lead to a lesser sanction. Accordingly, even if the employee has committed an act of gross misconduct, the fairness or otherwise of any subsequent dismissal remains to be determined in accordance with the statutory test (see above).

6.14 **Impact of the Human Rights Act 1998**

Section 6 of the Human Rights Act 1998 (HRA) makes it unlawful for a *public* authority to act in a way that is incompatible with the rights laid down in the European Convention on Human Rights (ECHR). Although it is not directly unlawful for a *private* employer to act in a manner incompatible with the ECHR, S.3 HRA requires that tribunals must, so far as possible, read and give effect to UK legislation in a way compatible with Convention rights. This interpretative obligation applies to all domestic legislation, including the ERA, and draws no distinction between legislation governing public authorities and that governing private individuals. Further, as noted by the Court of Appeal in X v Y 2004 ICR 1634, CA, an employment tribunal is a 'public authority' within the meaning of S.6(3) HRA. The effect of this, said the Court, is to

220

reinforce the tribunal's 'extremely strong interpretative obligation' imposed by S.3 when dealing with a case involving a private employer.

In X v Y, the Court of Appeal commented that as tribunals have to take account of fairness, the reasonable response of the reasonable employer, equity and the substantial merits of the case in the normal course of deciding an unfair dismissal claim under S.98, it would be reasonable to expect that a decision in favour of the employer would not involve a breach of an employee's Convention rights in any event. However, the Court acknowledged the possibility that this might not always be the case and went on to suggest a framework of questions for tribunals dealing with unfair dismissal claims involving *private* employers in which HRA issues arise:

- do the circumstances of the dismissal fall within the ambit of one or more of the Articles of the ECHR? If they do not, the Convention is not engaged and need not be considered

- if they do, does the state have a positive obligation to secure enjoyment of the relevant Convention right between private persons? If it does not, the Convention right is unlikely to affect the outcome of an unfair dismissal claim against a private employer. (Note that both Article 8 – the right to privacy and family life – and Article 14, which requires the state to secure to individuals the enjoyment of their rights under the Convention without discrimination, do impose such an obligation on the state but were found not to be engaged on the facts of X v Y – see below)

- if it does, is the interference with the employee's Convention right by dismissal justified?

- if it is not, was there a permissible reason for the dismissal under the ERA that does not involve unjustified interference with a Convention right? If there was not, the dismissal will be unfair for the absence of a permissible reason to justify it

- if there was, is the dismissal fair, tested by the provisions of S.98 ERA, reading and giving effect to them under S.3 HRA so as to be compatible with the Convention right?

Where public employers are involved, the questions for the tribunal will be similar, although the second question identified above will be irrelevant. As noted above, S.6 HRA makes it unlawful for a public authority to act in a way that is incompatible with ECHR rights. However, in X v Y, the Court of Appeal noted that an employment tribunal does not have jurisdiction to hear a claim under S.6. Therefore, if an employee dismissed by a public authority wishes to argue that his dismissal was unfair under S.98 ERA because one of his Convention rights has been breached, he will need to rely on S.3 HRA, rather than S.6, to claim that S.98 should be read in a way that is compatible with the Convention right in question. S.6 may not, however, be completely irrelevant

6.15

221

to unfair dismissal claims: tribunals are likely to take their interpretative duties under S.3 even more seriously when public authorities are involved. In Pay v Lancashire Probation Service 2004 ICR 187, EAT, the EAT, exercising its interpretative obligations under S.3 HRA, accepted that a public authority employer will not act reasonably under S.98 if it violates employees' Convention rights. The EAT thought that, at least so far as public authority employers are concerned, the words 'reasonably or unreasonably' in S.98(4) should be interpreted as including the phrase 'having regard to the applicant's Convention rights'. In this context, a public authority employer would not have acted 'reasonably' under S.98(4) where it was found to have unjustifiably breached an employee's Convention rights.

Interestingly, in neither of the above cases was a Convention right found to have been breached on the facts. The employee in X v Y had been dismissed after his employer discovered that the police had cautioned him for engaging in sexual activity with another man in a public lavatory. Upholding the tribunal's decision that the dismissal was fair, the Court of Appeal concluded that, since the activity which led to the dismissal did not take place in private, the employee's Article 8 right to respect for his private life – and thus his right under Article 14 not to suffer discrimination in relation to his Convention rights – had not been engaged. It followed that the tribunal's duty under S.3 HRA to interpret S.98(4) ERA in a way compatible with Convention rights had not been triggered. The fact that the employee wished to keep the matter private did not make it part of his private life or deprive it of its public aspect.

6.16 In the Pay case, P – a probation officer specialising in the treatment of sex offenders – was dismissed following his employer's discovery that he was a director of a business involved in sadomasochistic activities and that he performed acts of domination over women at a private members' club (as evidenced in photographs published on the internet). The EAT agreed with the employment tribunal that P's activities were in the public domain and therefore could not be described as part of his private life. It followed that Article 8 was not relevant to the claim. The EAT also endorsed the tribunal's view that Article 10 (which protects freedom of expression) had not been infringed: the employer's action had been justified under Article 10(2) of the European Convention (which places limitations on the right to freedom of expression) in view of the risk of damage to the reputation of the probation service that P's activities posed.

P subsequently took his case to the European Court of Human Rights (see Pay v United Kingdom 2009 IRLR 139, EctHR), which was prepared to proceed on the assumption that P's activities were *not* in the public domain and that Article 8 was therefore applicable. This was because P's activities took place in a nightclub that was likely to be frequented only by like-minded people, and the photographs of him published on the internet had been anonymised. However, in light of the sensitive nature of P's work, the interference with P's right to privacy was justified in accordance with Article 8(2), since his activities, if they became widely known, would compromise his work with sex offenders and damage the reputation of the Service. For the same reason the interference with his Article 10 right was justified under Article 10(2).

Article 8 was found to be engaged in McGowan v Scottish Water 2005 IRLR 167, EAT, but the employer's action was also held to be justified in the circumstances. In that case, a public sector employee had been dismissed after his employer obtained evidence through covert surveillance of his home that he was falsifying time sheets. The employee claimed that he had been unfairly dismissed because his right to respect for his private and family life under Article 8 had been breached. The EAT accepted that covert surveillance that involved tracking the movements of all of the inhabitants of a home 'raises... a strong presumption that the right to have one's private life respected is being infringed'. However, in rejecting the employee's claim, it held that the employer's action was justified as it was protecting its assets and was investigating what was effectively a criminal activity.

6.17

Note that the Court of Appeal has held that Article 6 of the ECHR, which provides that an individual has the right to a fair hearing, may in certain circumstances provide employees with the right to legal representation at disciplinary hearings – Kulkarni v Milton Keynes Hospital NHS Foundation Trust and anor 2010 ICR 101, CA; R (on the application of G) v Governors of X School and anor 2010 IRLR 222, CA. These cases, which did not involve unfair dismissal claims, are discussed further in Chapter 4 under 'Procedural factors'.

Absenteeism and lateness

6.18

In general, absenteeism and lateness will not merit dismissal for a first offence. In such cases the recalcitrant employee should be warned of the consequences of further absences and be given the chance to explain before dismissal. However, there may be cases where the consequences of a first absence or a first lateness are serious enough to justify dismissal without warning. This was so in Galloway v K Miller (Contractors) ET Case No.S/2430/81, where the employers lost a valuable contract because of G's absence from work. His dismissal, despite his previous good record, was in the circumstances fair, said the tribunal. So too in Ward v Coincheck Electronics Ltd ET Case No.1805368/03, where W was dismissed for one day's absence. The employer was a small company and W's role was key to a busy production process. It was clearly stated in W's contract that unauthorised absence was gross misconduct.

Lateness

6.19

Where a warning has been given about lateness but the employee continues to be tardy, the employer should ask for an explanation and check the reasons

223

before dismissing. In one employee's case, dismissal for being late seven days out of 77, after being warned to improve his timekeeping, was unfair – because on three of these days he was held up by a railway dispute. But his colleague who had been late 12 times out of 88 was fairly dismissed – Hallett and anor v MAT Transport Ltd 1976 IRLR 5, ET.

6.20   **Absenteeism**

The 2010 Acas Advisory Booklet, 'Managing attendance and employee turnover', provides useful guidance to employers on how to handle persistent short-term absenteeism. It states, among other things, that:

- unexpected absences should be investigated promptly and the employee asked for an explanation at a return-to-work interview

- if there are no acceptable reasons then the matter should be treated as a conduct issue and dealt with under the disciplinary procedure

- where there is no medical certificate to support frequent short-term, self-certified absences, then the employee should be asked to see a doctor to establish whether treatment is necessary and whether the underlying reason for absence is work-related. If no medical support is forthcoming, the employer should consider whether to take action under the disciplinary procedure

- if the absence could be disability-related, the employer should consider what reasonable adjustments could be made in the workplace to help the employee (see IDS Employment Law Handbook, 'Disability Discrimination' (2002), Chapter 4)

- if the absence is because of temporary problems relating to dependants, the employee may be entitled to time off under the provisions of the ERA relating to time off for dependants (see IDS Employment Law Handbook, 'Maternity and Parental Rights' (2009), Chapter 10)

- if the absence is as a result of the employee's pregnancy, the employer should record this separately. Employers should tread carefully in cases of absenteeism occasioned by pregnancy because the employee has the right to take time off for ante-natal and other pregnancy-related care and enjoys special protection against detrimental treatment (see IDS Employment Law Handbook, 'Maternity and Parental Rights' (2009), for more information)

- if the absence is because the employee has difficulty managing both work and home responsibilities, then the employer should give serious consideration to more flexible ways of working. Employees with children under the age of 17 (or 18 in the case of parents of disabled children) have the right to request flexible working arrangements – including job-sharing, part-time working, flexi-time, working from home/teleworking and school-time contracts – and employers must have a good business reason for rejecting any application (see IDS Employment Law Handbook, 'Maternity and Parental Rights' (2009), Chapter 11)

- in all cases the employee should be told what improvement in attendance is expected and warned of the likely consequences if this does not happen

- if there is no improvement, the employee's length of service, performance, the likelihood of a change in attendance, the availability of suitable alternative work, and the effect of past and future absences on the organisation should all be taken into account in deciding appropriate action.

The Booklet goes on to state that it is very important to deal with persistent **6.21** absence promptly, firmly and consistently in order to show both the employee concerned and other employees that absence is regarded as a serious matter and may result in dismissal. An examination of records will identify those employees who are regularly absent and may disclose an absence pattern. In such cases employers should make sufficient enquiries to determine whether the absence is because of genuine illness or for other reasons. If the absence is because of a genuine illness, it should not be dealt with under the disciplinary procedure – Davis v Tibbett and Britten Group plc EAT 460/99. It is therefore important that an employer does not make assumptions about an employee's absences, since treating genuine sickness absence as misconduct can lead to a finding of unfair dismissal – see, for example, Millington v Wandsworth Council ET Case No.2302863/06, where the tribunal did not consider that certified absences could be considered as a 'conduct' issue save in circumstances where the employee has deliberately or negligently put him or herself at risk of injury or ill health.

Absenteeism will generally fall under the 'conduct' label where the employee is away from work unauthorised or where he or she is not genuinely off work sick. Ill health absence – both long- and short-term – is considered in detail in Chapter 5.

Unauthorised absence. Where an employee stays away from work without **6.22** the employer's permission, this is likely to found a fair dismissal, especially where he or she has been warned of the consequences. In Nestle (UK) Ltd v Thacker EAT 279/98 an employee who took a holiday despite having been refused permission and warned of possible dismissal if she went was fairly dismissed on her return despite her length of service and previous unblemished record. However, even when an employee has had prior warning that taking a holiday without permission will result in dismissal, the employer should still hold a disciplinary hearing to discuss the matter. In Heskey v Adwest Rearsby Ltd EAT 158/97 H's request to take an extended holiday was refused and he was told that he would be dismissed if he went on the holiday regardless. Nevertheless, H went on his extended holiday and was dismissed. AR Ltd dispensed with the disciplinary and appeal hearings as, owing to his absence, H was unable to attend and any hearing would therefore have been

225

useless. The EAT held that AR Ltd should have waited until H returned before holding a disciplinary hearing. The case was remitted for a rehearing before a different tribunal.

Employers should take care when framing disciplinary rules governing the taking of holiday and the need for prior approval. In George Ellison Ltd v Brown EAT 338/03 B was dismissed for going on holiday despite the express refusal of his managing director, who also wished to take holiday on the same dates. While finding that B's dismissal was unfair because the MD was the 'judge in his own cause', the EAT also noted that B was not acting in an unauthorised manner because the rules – which were contractual – stated that those employees who had not got approval for their holiday would be allocated the two weeks following 22 July. This was the period during which B was absent. The EAT dismissed the argument that the rule applied only to those who had not sought approval at all rather than to all employees who had not got approval, including those for whom approval had been refused.

6.23   Dismissal for unauthorised absences for religious purposes may also be fair, although in such circumstances an employer would normally be expected to warn the employee about the consequences of his or her continued absences before taking action and, where possible, do his best to find a more suitable alternative job – see, for example, Hill v BXL Plastics Ltd ET Case No.23340/81. However, employers should be careful not to contravene the Employment Equality (Religion or Belief) Regulations 2003 SI 2003/1660 – see IDS Employment Law Handbook, 'Race and Religion Discrimination' (2004).

Despite the employee obtaining prior permission for taking a period of annual leave, overstaying that leave may found a fair dismissal if the employment contract provides that such conduct would be likely to result in dismissal. In Ali v Joseph Dawson Ltd EAT 43/89 the employer employed a considerable number of people from Pakistan and India who often wanted to take extended leave to go home. In order to control the exercise of these long periods of leave, the company introduced a scheme that, if operated successfully, would benefit both the employees and the employer. However, it had to be strictly operated and failure to adhere to the arrangement would be likely to result in dismissal. The claimant took extended leave and was dismissed for overstaying his leave by one week. He had been delayed because of his failure to ensure that he had the necessary entry documents. He was dismissed after a five-minute hearing and the EAT upheld the tribunal's finding of fair dismissal. (On the question of whether the contract automatically terminates in these circumstances see Chapter 1 under 'Non-dismissals'.)

6.24   **'Phoney' sickness absences.** Obviously, 'phoney' sickness absences tend to justify tougher action by employers than absences occasioned by a recurrent illness – which might be better dealt with in the same way as long-term sickness absences – or absences caused by unrelated, minor ailments.

Two examples:

226

- **Nkengfack v London Borough of Southwark** 2002 EWCA Civ 711, CA: the Court of Appeal upheld the decision of a tribunal which found the dismissal of a teacher in a small school who was seen working in her own hair salon while purporting to be off sick with back pain to be fair. The dishonesty inherent in her conduct was an important factor

- **Shail v Swindon Pressings Ltd** EAT 0771/04: the EAT held that the employer fairly dismissed an employee who was observed carrying out building work at a residential property while off sick.

But before acting upon a mere suspicion that the employee is not genuinely ill, and risk a finding of unfair dismissal in the absence of reasonable grounds for believing that the employee is guilty of misconduct, the employer must conduct a reasonable investigation. In Leeson v Makita Manufacturing Europe Ltd EAT 0911/00 L had been signed off work for a week and prescribed antibiotics. He went to play golf on the fifth day of his sick leave to give him the benefit of some fresh air and exercise after being confined indoors all week. The EAT held that the fact that L was well enough for some recreational activity did not justify the employer's conclusion that he was fit enough to work.

Note that dismissal for absence because of imprisonment is not considered to be a 'conduct' dismissal but dismissal for 'some other substantial reason' (SOSR) – Kingston v British Railways Board 1984 ICR 781, CA (see Chapter 8).

Abusive language   6.25

The fairness of a dismissal for bad language must obviously depend on the individual circumstances of each case. It is almost always a question of context and degree – see Burnett v City of Glasgow District Council EAT 491/76, for instance, where it was fair to dismiss an employee who used foul and abusive language to his manager when refusing to obey a legitimate order. Most cases are not so clear-cut, however.

The problem of swearing and abuse usually arises in one of two ways: either as a history of foul-mouthed conduct (in which case warnings would be appropriate) or as a single serious outburst. In either case the real problem is probably a breakdown of the working relationship – of which bad language is a symptom, not a cause. Thus the tribunal should consider the abusive words in light of all the circumstances. Note that although most cases involve verbal outbursts, there are also cases where the abusive or obscene language is written down. In either type of case the relevant factors to be taken into account include:

- *the effect on discipline within the company* – especially on the authority of superiors. Dismissal for swearing at a superior can be fair if it constitutes a serious threat to management authority and undermines the employer/

employee relationship. In MacIsaac v James Ferries and Co Ltd EAT 1442/96, for instance, M was very abusive towards his superior, calling him 'a thief, a liar and a cheat' and 'the worst... disaster ever to join the company'. The EAT relied on the case of Wilson v Racher (below) and held that as M's behaviour had caused an irreparable breach in the working relationship between him and his superior, a continuation of that relationship was quite impossible. Insubordinate behaviour is something that tribunals and courts will never condone. In Bate v Samworth Brothers Ltd t/a Samworth Distribution ET Case No.1301113/06, for example, B was dismissed fairly when he subjected his superior to a barrage of verbal abuse because he was unhappy with an instruction he had been given. His superior had asked him three times to stop swearing at him. The employer has a duty to create a working environment in which managers and supervisors are able to issue instructions to the workforce with confidence. B's refusal to carry out a reasonable instruction was an aggravating feature. However, it is recognised that situations often develop where both parties are to blame and the dismissal of an employee provoked by the employer may be unfair (see Wilson v Racher below)

- *the status of the employee* – this can be relevant where, for instance, the employee using bad language is a member of management and the objects of his or her disfavour are his or her superiors. In Morris v Sperry Corporation EAT 51/81 M was fairly dismissed for reacting to a business reorganisation in terms which the tribunal could only describe as 'florid in the extreme'. He described his superiors as liars, used profanities and was overheard 'ranting and raving'. The EAT said his conduct was so much out of keeping with his position as a senior executive that he could no longer be employed.

However, a certain amount of workers' shop-floor language may well be considered acceptable. It will depend very much on the context and on its effect on the employment relationship. In Pepper v Webb 1969 1 WLR 514, CA – a wrongful, not unfair, dismissal complaint – a gardener's refusal, using four-letter words, to carry out an order amounted to a repudiatory breach of contract when seen in the light of his previous insolence and inefficiency. By contrast, in Wilson v Racher 1974 ICR 428, CA (also a wrongful dismissal case), more obscene phrases used by a gardener in exasperation at the employer's persistent and largely unfounded criticisms were not repudiatory. Lord Justice Edmund Davies suggested the test was whether in the circumstances 'the... use of this extremely bad language... made impossible the continuance of the master and servant relationship, and showed that the plaintiff was indeed resolved to follow a line of conduct which made the continuation of that relationship impossible'

- *employee relations* – the effect of bad language on relations at work may also be decisive. Where threatening or abusive language exacerbates an already sensitive situation it is likely to justify dismissal even though, under normal circumstances, such a drastic move might be considered unreasonable. In Shakespeare and anor v National Coal Board, unreported 30.3.88, CA, for instance, two employees returning to work after the 1984/85 miners' strike were dismissed for threatening and insulting three miners who had returned to work earlier. Their dismissal was held to be fair despite the fact that ordinarily such behaviour would not have warranted such harsh measures

- *workplace environment* – words which are acceptable on a construction site may be unacceptable in an office. Tribunals judge the offence complained of in the light of the commonly accepted standards of the particular work environment in which the language was used. Thus in Crewe v Dominion Garage Ltd COET 1164/158 the tribunal accepted that bad language is pervasive in a garage or workshop. However, where the employee's job brings him or her into contact with the public, customers or suppliers, the use of bad language could adversely affect the employer's business reputation and so justify dismissal – Sketchley v Kissoon EAT 514/79. In Guyers v Ashworth Hospital Authority ET Case No. 2103665/01, for example, a nurse was fairly dismissed for using profane language when describing a patient in a note to a colleague

- *provocation* – an employer's duty to act reasonably before dismissing someone means that he should investigate the events leading up to the use of bad language, as well as the incident itself. Provocation may excuse an employee's outburst and justify the reaction it caused. The context may well be an important factor – in Little v Greenhams Ltd ET Case No.1700135/02 a tribunal put weight on the fact that L swore in order to speed up evacuation during a fire drill for which he was responsible and found his later dismissal unfair. Heat-of-the-moment outbursts should also be treated with particular caution – the seriousness of the offence needs to be weighed against the likelihood of recurrence and the degree of provocation suffered – Charles Letts and Co Ltd v Howard 1976 IRLR 248, EAT. Quite often bad language is a symptom of a personality clash. In these circumstances, the reason for dismissal might be 'some other substantial reason' (SOSR), not 'conduct' – Lasharie v Brass and Alloy Pressings (Deritend) Ltd EAT 35/81 (see further Chapter 8)

- *chance to apologise* – the EAT said in Charles Letts and Co Ltd v Howard (above) that an opportunity to apologise for using abusive language is important, especially where the outburst was a sudden explosion of temper by an employee under the influence of drink. The person deciding whether

229

to dismiss should allow a cooling-off period and give the employee an opportunity to apologise before it is too late

- *mitigating circumstances* – in Townsend v Hereford and Worcester Ambulance Service NHS Trust ET Case No.5205700/99 T, an ambulance driver, called the call centre supervisor a 'shit-stirring bastard' when she made a complaint about his overstaying a break. During the formal investigation against T, the employer discovered that T's son had died four months earlier. However, the employer discounted this as a factor as T had used bad language in the past. Despite the fact that T wrote a letter of apology to the supervisor and said that he deeply regretted the incident, he was dismissed. The tribunal found this to be unfair as the employer had failed to ascertain the circumstances of his son's death so as to properly assess the effect on T; nor had the employer taken account of the fact that T had been off work for three months with stress and had only just returned. Dismissal was too harsh a sanction given his son's death, his illness, his apology and his long and unblemished service. Similarly, in Croucher v Royal Mail Group plc ET Case No.3301206/07 C, a postman, was summarily dismissed for calling a colleague a 'sneaky cunt' when he pressed him for parcels for delivery before they were meant to be ready. The tribunal found that the dismissal was unfair because the employer failed to take account of a number of mitigating factors. For instance, C had been provoked, he had apologised and offered to attend mediation, the day of the incident was the first anniversary of his father's death and he had had ongoing difficulties with his mother over the past year. The employer maintained that there was zero tolerance of bad language, but there was no evidence of this being communicated to the workforce. However, C's blameworthy conduct was assessed at 25 per cent and his compensation reduced accordingly

- *actual words used* – in Hunt v Royal Mail Group Ltd ET Case No.2702308/07 H, who took part in industrial action, used 'particularly unpleasant obscene language' against a colleague who was crossing the picket line. While the wording used was similar to that in Croucher (above), it seems that the context distinguished this case, with the effect that H's dismissal was fair. He had deliberately used the words with the clear purpose of causing offence. The context in which the abusive language is used is therefore important.

6.26 Employers should note that all employees are entitled to the same protection against abuse from other employees. In Morris v Network South Central EAT 8/97 an employee was dismissed for verbally abusing his ex-wife, who also worked on the company's premises. The EAT could find no fault with the tribunal's decision that all employees were entitled to equal protection and that the dismissal was therefore fair.

230

Disloyalty

6.27

Every employment contract has an implied term of fidelity and good faith, which means that the employee must not act in a manner contrary to the interests of the employer. Apart from underlining the element of personal commitment to the employer essential in a contract of service, the term may also apply outside strict working hours. It exists for so long as the employment subsists, whether or not the employee is actually turning up to work, and may continue after employment has been terminated.

Dismissal

6.28

Breach of the implied duty of fidelity and good faith will normally entitle the employer to dismiss the employee summarily for gross misconduct at common law – Boston Deep Sea Fishing and Ice Co v Ansell 1888 39 ChD 339, CA. A single act of misconduct will suffice where it is 'serious, wilful and obvious' and strikes at the root of the contract of employment – Bishop v Graham Group plc EAT 800/98. However, a breach of this term (or, indeed, an express 'loyalty' clause) will not necessarily render the dismissal fair under the ERA. The test that tribunals apply is not whether the employee was in breach of contract, but whether the employer acted reasonably in all the circumstances in dismissing the employee for being in breach.

The employer must show that he had a genuine and reasonable belief, based on reasonable investigation, that the employee was in breach of the duty of fidelity. Dismissal on the ground of suspicion alone will only be justifiable where that suspicion is great and the anticipated loss to the company large – but in such cases the dismissal would be for SOSR, not conduct, said the EAT in S and U Stores Ltd v Bessant EAT 8/82 (see further Chapter 8). However, in the vast majority of cases there must be sufficient evidence to sustain a reasonable belief in the employee's guilt. Once this is shown, the tribunal must consider whether the employer acted reasonably in dismissing. Different considerations will apply depending on the nature of the breach.

Dismissal for breach of the implied term of fidelity normally arises where the employee:

- discloses confidential information
- competes, or prepares to compete, with the employer, or
- 'moonlights' out of working hours.

Disclosure of confidential information

6.29

Where employees have access to confidential information and trade secrets, there is an implied duty not to use that information except for the purposes authorised by the employer. In Monk v Vine Products EAT 248/79 the

231

employee, a personnel and training manager, disclosed to shop stewards some figures for proposed wage increases, forcing the company to conclude a productivity deal different from that which it had intended. When the company was again disadvantaged by similar incidents, the managing director lost confidence in the employee and dismissed him. The EAT upheld the tribunal's decision that it was fair to do so.

Dismissal for the misuse or leaking of confidential information will usually fall within the range of reasonable responses – provided the employer has carried out a reasonable investigation and taken account of any mitigating factors. The importance of the information involved may be relevant to the tribunal's considerations. For example, trivial information leaked accidentally, or without gain in mind, may not give grounds for a fair dismissal – see, for example, Sullivan v Associated Heat Services Ltd ET Case No.5985/80. Similarly, the purpose for which the information is used may be taken into account. In Williams v Wrexham Maelor Hospital NHS Trust ET Case No.26079/96, for example, W was dismissed for obtaining the name and address of a patient from hospital records to enable her to pursue a claim for industrial injury with the Department of Social Security (now part of the Department for Work and Pensions). The tribunal found that dismissal was outside the range of reasonable responses because W had a clean disciplinary record, long service, and the employer had failed to take account of the purpose for which she had acquired the information.

6.30   **Public interest.** It is arguable that employees dismissed for disclosing confidential information may be able to challenge the dismissal on the basis that the disclosure was in the public interest. In Veitch v Broadgate Farm Co-operative Ltd ET Case No.2505366/01, for example, a care worker was dismissed for breaching her duty of confidentiality to someone in her care. The employee told a colleague that a volunteer worker she was allowing to use machinery was suffering from a depressive illness, had declined to take his medication and was prone to impulsive behaviour. The tribunal acknowledged her duty of confidentiality but said that serious consequences could follow when professionals fail to share information with those who 'need to know'. The dismissal was therefore unfair.

However, tribunals are not always so sympathetic to employees who claim to have acted in the public interest. In Byford v Film Finances Ltd EAT 804/86 the employee suspected that the directors of the company were carrying out illegal activities in connection with share transfers. She leaked confidential information to the minority shareholders of the company, who commenced legal action as a result. The EAT upheld the tribunal's decision that the employer had no option but to dismiss an employee who had gone behind her employer's back and been deceitful.

Note that certain disclosures are protected by law under the public interest disclosure provisions of the ERA, S.103A of which states that an employee who is dismissed for making a protected disclosure will be treated as automatically unfairly dismissed – see Chapter 13.

Risk of disclosure of confidential information. Dismissal of an employee who has a close relative or associate working for a competitor may be fair for SOSR if there is a conflict of interest or a real risk of trade secrets or confidential information being disclosed (even accidentally) as a result (see Chapter 8). Every case turns on its facts and much will depend on the position of both individuals, the level of access they have to confidential information and the importance of that information – Skyrail Oceanic Ltd v Coleman 1980 ICR 596, EAT.

6.31

Competing and preparing to compete

6.32

Employees who actively compete with their employers will be in breach of the implied duty of fidelity. The general rule here is that an employer is entitled to defend himself against unfair competition and to take whatever reasonable steps are necessary in order to achieve that end – RS Components Ltd v Irwin 1973 ICR 535, NIRC. The breach of trust does not have to result in severe damage for dismissal to be fair. What is important is the actual breach itself and not the extent of loss. In Mansard Precision Engineering Co Ltd v Taylor and anor 1978 ICR 44, EAT, the EAT held that two senior employees concerned in establishing a business in competition with their employer were fairly dismissed for breach of trust, even though the damage caused was slight. 'Once it is recognised,' the EAT said, 'as it must be, that there has to be mutual confidence and trust, the mere fact that it is breached at all seems to us to be a perfectly justifiable, reasonable and sufficient reason for the employer to say, "I no longer have trust in you, I no longer have confidence in you. You must go".'

Conversely, a mere desire on the part of the employee to 'go it alone', absent any concrete steps in that direction having been taken, is unlikely to adversely affect the employer's trust in the employee so as to justify the drastic sanction of dismissal. In Shortland v Certainty Group TFM Ltd ET Case No.2407033/04 the employer was fully aware of S's ambition to have her own business arranging corporate events and knew that she had formed a company to carry out such work. When G, the managing director of an important client, believed that C had come into possession of information from his company that she intended to use for the benefit of her own company, the employer investigated the matter. However, it found that there was insufficient evidence to charge her with gross misconduct; a warning about her conduct was appropriate but no more. G, who agreed that this was not a case of gross misconduct, was nevertheless dissatisfied with this outcome; he stated that his trust and confidence in C had evaporated and he wanted her removed from the site, which his company owned. There being no alternative employment available within the company, C was dismissed. The tribunal found that C had been unfairly dismissed. The employer was in a difficult position – in fact, both the employer and C were victims of G's

233

intransigence – but it had failed to challenge G's decision that he had lost trust and confidence in C with sufficient robustness. The extent of the injustice to C had not been properly taken into account.

6.33 It will be apparent from the above that a mere *intention* to set up in competition is not in itself a breach of the implied contractual duty of loyalty and fidelity justifying dismissal – Laughton and anor v Bapp Industrial Supplies Ltd 1986 ICR 634, EAT. To breach the duty the employee's acts must go beyond this. In Laughton the EAT took the view that, in the absence of an express term that is not in restraint of trade, there must be some evidence that the employee had done or was about to do some wrongful act – for example, misuse confidential information. In that case, two employees of a nuts and bolts manufacturer were summarily dismissed when their employer discovered that in their spare time they had written to ten of their employer's suppliers informing them of their intention to start up their own business and asking for lists of the suppliers' products and prices. The EAT held that the dismissals were unfair. It pointed out that the employees had not misused confidential information or otherwise abused their position. Their contact with the suppliers amounted to a mere enquiry. Moreover, the employees were still devoting their working time and talents to their employer's business.

However, the Laughton case should not be seen as a green light to employees to pursue their competitive plans while still employed. The case turned very much on its own facts and a different tribunal might have construed the approach made by the employees to the suppliers as solicitation of the employee's suppliers, which would have been a breach of the implied duty of fidelity – see below under 'Soliciting customers or suppliers'.

6.34 Two examples where the employees' preparatory activities did go beyond a mere intention to compete and thus justified dismissal:

- **Marshall v Industrial Systems and Control Ltd** 1992 IRLR 294, EAT: M, the managing director of ISC Ltd, formed a business plan with another manager to commence business in competition with ISC Ltd and, in particular, to obtain distribution rights from ISC Ltd's major client. They approached a third senior employee and invited him to join them. The EAT held that M's summary dismissal for gross misconduct was fair. This was not simply a matter of forming an intention to compete in the future, as was the position in the Laughton case (see above), since M had formed a concrete plan to obtain business from his employer's best client and had taken steps towards fulfilling that objective

- **Adamson v B and L Cleaning Services Ltd** 1995 IRLR 193, EAT: A was a foreman for a contract cleaning company. When the contract on which he was working came up for renewal, he informed his employer that he had asked for himself to be put on the tender list. The employer dismissed him when he refused to withdraw his tender. The EAT held that the dismissal was fair. The employee had not merely been testing the market with a view to competing with the employer; he had approached a customer with the intention of taking work and revenue away from his employer.

In general, the more concrete the preparatory steps taken, the more likely it is that the employee will have breached his or her duty of fidelity. However, whatever the circumstances, the employer should always investigate the matter and give the employee the opportunity to put his or her case before resorting to dismissal. Employees might repent if faced with the prospect of being dismissed before they are ready to start out on their own. It is always a question of fact whether or not an opportunity to cancel plans would have made a difference, and a warning should always be given if the employee's preparations are far from maturity – Ladbroke Racing Ltd v Mason and anor 1978 ICR 49, EAT.

Where an employer is aware that employees are aiding competitors, then it **6.35** is important not to ignore such behaviour. In Thorn (UK) Ltd v Little EAT 455/95 L was employed as a service engineer. It was common practice for the service engineers to hand out the business cards of competitors when the customers' machines were not covered by a warranty. T (UK) Ltd was aware of this practice but had done nothing to stop it. L was dismissed after a customer complained about receiving one of the business cards. The EAT upheld the tribunal's finding of unfair dismissal on the ground, inter alia, that the employer had failed to take any steps to stamp out what was a very old practice. Possible steps could involve surveillance, though employers should use a degree of caution before resorting to such action. However, in Haynes and anor v Daimler Chrysler (UK) Ltd t/a Mercedes Benz and ors ET Case No.2302821–2/02 the tribunal rejected an argument that in instructing private detectives to keep employees' homes under surveillance, the employer had in any way breached their human rights. The employer suspected that the employees might be working in competition by servicing and repairing cars for their own benefit and the surveillance revealed details of deliveries of motor parts and evidence of an employee test-driving customers' cars, which was strictly forbidden under company rules. The resulting dismissals were fair.

Note that simply seeking work with a competitor, or giving notice to work for one, is not generally an admissible reason for dismissal – unless there are grounds for believing that the employee was intending to abuse his or her confidential position and information – Harris and Russell Ltd v Slingsby 1973 ICR 454, NIRC.

Soliciting customers or suppliers. It is well established that soliciting an **6.36** employer's customers for the employee's own benefit, or for the benefit of a third party, will merit dismissal. Employers must not, however, act prematurely without having carried out a proper investigation and given the employee a chance to explain, as in Baxter v Wreyfield EAT 9/82. Here the employer

235

dismissed B without investigating further a customer's complaint that she had been approached to transfer her custom to a new business to be started by B and her husband. The EAT found that in light of the facts known to the employer at the time, dismissal was unfair. However, since the evidence disclosed that the employee was in fact guilty of misconduct that would justify dismissal, no compensation was awarded.

6.37 **Poaching staff/offering work to other employees.** There are different views on whether an employee who invites or persuades other employees to join him or her in a competing business is in breach of the implied duty of fidelity. In Marshall v Industrial Systems and Control Ltd (above) the EAT held that M drafted a business plan with another senior manager and together they had approached a third senior employee and invited him to join them. The EAT held that M had breached the duty of fidelity and that his subsequent summary dismissal was fair. By contrast, in Tithebarn Ltd v Hubbard EAT 532/89 H, a senior sales trainer, told P, another employee, that he intended to leave T Ltd and set up his own competing business and invited P to join him. The EAT held that T's actions did not amount to a breach of his implied duty of fidelity and his dismissal was therefore unfair. H had merely carried out preparatory acts and had simply invited P to work for him in due course.

6.38 ## 'Moonlighting'

Taking a job outside working hours is not in itself a breach of the implied duty of fidelity, even where that job involves working for a competitor. The general rule at common law is that, in the absence of an express term, employees are free to do what they want during their off-duty hours provided that these activities do not interfere with or harm the employer's legitimate business interests – Hivac Ltd v Park Royal Scientific Instruments Ltd 1946 1 Ch 169, CA. In determining whether the damage to the employer is such as to breach the employee's implied obligation of fidelity, regard will be had to the type of work involved, the position of the employee within the employer's organisation, the employee's hours of work, and the risk and extent of potential commercial harm to the employer.

Similar factors are taken into consideration when a tribunal considers the fairness of a dismissal for moonlighting. If spare-time working is directly damaging to the employer's interests, or creates a risk of serious harm, it may rank as straightforward gross misconduct and justify dismissal. Thus, employees who possess valuable commercial skills or have access to trade secrets will obviously have to be careful. But so too will other employees whose work is such that it cannot be properly performed if they engage in extra-mural activities. For example, it would be improper for a solicitor's trainee to work for another solicitor in his or her spare time. There might be a real risk of embarrassment to the main employer if the trainee were asked to act for a client in his or her spare time who was the other party in a case in which the main employer was engaged. In this situation there would be a genuine conflict of interest and a dismissal would probably be fair, provided the appropriate procedures had been followed.

As not all spare-time work, even for a competitor, will breach the implied term of fidelity, employers should tread cautiously before dismissing employees for engaging in spare-time work which does not harm their business interests. Two examples:

6.39

- **Nova Plastics Ltd v Froggatt** 1982 IRLR 146, EAT: F, an odd-job man, did spare-time work for a rival company which did not greatly affect his employer. The EAT thought the tribunal was entitled to conclude that he was not in breach of trust simply because he happened to work for a competitor in his spare time. The nature of F's work was such that it could not possibly amount to any serious aid to the rival as a competitor. His dismissal was therefore unfair

- **EETPU v Parnham and anor** EAT 378/78: Mr and Mrs P worked as kitchen assistant and cook at a trade union conference centre. Mrs P obtained a weekend job at a café and the couple were promptly dismissed for disloyalty. The EAT upheld a tribunal's finding that dismissal of the husband and wife was unfair. Mrs P's spare-time job had done nothing to harm the employer's interests. In addition, the employer had failed to warn them or give them a chance to explain, or even to provide an adequate grievance procedure.

Employers who dismiss on the ground that spare-time work is damaging their business interests must be sure of their ground. This means that employers must carry out a reasonable investigation in order to satisfy themselves that an employee's outside activities pose a threat to or undermine their business interests – EETPU v Parnham and anor (above). In Scottish Daily Record and Sunday Mail (1986) Ltd v Laird 1996 IRLR 665, Ct Sess (Inner House), L was the editor of a newspaper whose employment contract expressly prohibited him from having any interest in any competing business. He was dismissed when his employer discovered that he was involved in the publication of two free regional newspapers. A tribunal held that the dismissal was unfair, pointing out that the employer had made no enquiries into the circulation of the two free newspapers, the area which the papers covered or their advertising rates. Had the employer done so, it would have become clear that the employee's outside interests were of a relatively minor nature which could cause only minimal harm to his employer. The Court of Session agreed that no reasonable employer would have dismissed without making proper enquiries as to the extent and circumstances of L's involvement with the other newspapers.

6.40

In certain circumstances spare-time work may not harm the employer's business interests, but a dismissal may be rendered fair because of other aspects of the employee's conduct; where managers are involved, for example, or where

237

employees behave badly on being found out. In Casson v John Lewis and Co Ltd EAT 266/77 a manager failed to inform the employer of her own outside business activities as required by the rules, and then lied about it. Her dismissal was fair even though her extra-curricular activities did the employer no harm and were quite unconnected with the business.

6.41 Similarly, in Enterprise Liverpool plc v Bauress and anor EAT 0645/05, B and E were discovered using their employer's van and materials to moonlight during working hours while they should have been carrying out work for one of the employer's clients. The tribunal found that their subsequent dismissals were unfair: another employee, who was also found to have been moonlighting during working hours, had not been dismissed.

On appeal, however, the EAT overturned the tribunal's decision, holding that the employer had fairly dismissed in this case. It accepted that, in the absence of an established policy for dealing with this particular type of misconduct, the employer's decision not to dismiss an employee created a benchmark or point of reference against which the standards of a reasonable employer could thereafter be tested. Where the employer subsequently imposed a more serious disciplinary sanction in any case of sufficiently similar misconduct, the tribunal must ask itself whether the employer had good reason for departing from the set benchmark. With this in mind, the EAT held that there were good reasons for treating B and E differently from the other employee, who had been issued with a final written warning for the same offence. First, B and E had maintained, throughout the disciplinary process, that they had prior permission from their supervisor to be where they were, which was not true; the other employee had immediately admitted his guilt. Secondly, the other employee had 30 years' good service, whereas B and E had just finished their apprenticeship. The EAT held that it fell within the band of reasonable responses to regard these as sufficient reasons to depart from the benchmark.

6.42 **Express 'loyalty' terms**

Employers may enlarge and extend the basic duty of fidelity by including an express provision in the employment contract restricting breach of confidentiality, competition or even simply other work without written permission. On the whole, decisions in cases where such terms exist tend to go against the employee who flouts them. For example, in Winder v Commissioners of Inland Revenue ET Case No.1101770/97 W was dismissed for writing to a political organisation offering to reveal sensitive information. The employer's rules prohibited misuse of information acquired in the course of employment. Although no disclosure had taken place, the tribunal found that the employer was entitled to conclude that the offer was a breach of the duty to maintain confidence contained in the standing rules.

However, the existence of express terms is by no means decisive. Broad general clauses prohibiting any other engagement are probably too vague and sweeping

238

to justify dismissal for participating in a completely different occupation outside working hours. In Barratt v Co-operative Insurance Society Ltd ET Case No.9436/82, for instance, B was an insurance agent whose contract prohibited him from engaging 'in any other occupation'. He inherited a life interest in a run-down pub from his mother and gave his wife some help in sorting out the business. The employer dismissed him after hearing about this. A tribunal found that the dismissal was unfair. The contractual term was vague; there had been no adequate investigation; and B's interest in the pub was probably not an 'occupation' anyway.

Refusal to agree to restrictive covenants 6.43

Employers often try to protect their business interests by means of a restrictive covenant in their employees' contracts of employment, or in separate 'non-competition' or 'non-disclosure' agreements. An employee's refusal to accept such a covenant makes dismissal for that refusal potentially fair for SOSR. This is further discussed in Chapter 8, under 'Protecting employers' interests'.

Disobedience 6.44

Implied into every employment contract is the employee's obligation to obey the employer's lawful (i.e. contractual) and reasonable orders. Refusal to do so is a potentially fair reason to dismiss for misconduct.

However, the mere fact that an employee has disobeyed an instruction – even if he or she is in breach of contract – does not guarantee that a tribunal will find the dismissal fair. The question of whether the employee was in breach of contract in disobeying the order is a relevant, but not conclusive, factor. This stems from the fact that the fairness of a dismissal under S.98(4) ERA is based on the question of reasonableness. Accordingly, an employer may give an order that is perfectly legitimate under the contract only to find that the dismissal of an employee who disobeys it is unfair. On the other hand, an instruction may not fall within the terms of the contract but dismissal for failure to obey it may nonetheless be fair – provided the employer acted reasonably.

Tribunals faced with disobedience dismissals usually concentrate on three main issues:

- whether the order given was legitimate
- whether the order was reasonable
- the reasonableness of the employee's refusal.

Was the order legitimate? The answer normally depends upon whether the 6.45
order was one that the employer could give under the terms of the contract. If it was, then by disobeying that order the employee will usually be committing

239

an act of misconduct justifying dismissal; if not, then the employer's insistence on compliance will be in breach of contract (although see below).

To ascertain whether an employee is contractually bound to obey an instruction, tribunals will consider sources such as the contract of employment itself and any particulars of employment issued under S.1 ERA. These will identify express terms such as the nature of the job, the employee's workplace(s), hours, holiday entitlement, etc. Other relevant sources include such things as collective agreements and work rules. Terms will also be implied by common law, e.g. that employees will obey all legitimate and reasonable instructions and cooperate with the company in performing their jobs. Finally, other terms may derive from unwritten custom and practice operating in a particular trade or district.

6.46 Note that an employee's contractual obligation is sometimes wider than the ambit of the duties he or she usually performs. In Glitz v Watford Electric Co Ltd 1979 IRLR 89, EAT, the claimant was engaged as a copy typist/general clerical duties clerk. At the time of her engagement it was not contemplated that she would operate a duplicating machine, nor was she asked to do so during the following three years. However, the EAT held that in the context of a small clerical team working for a small employer, she was contractually obliged to operate the duplicator since it fell within the ambit of 'general clerical duties'.

In Redbridge London Borough Council v Fishman 1978 ICR 569, EAT, however, the EAT warned against paying too much attention to the contractual position. According to Mr Justice Phillips, 'many dismissals are unfair although the employer is contractually entitled to dismiss the employee. Contrariwise, some dismissals are not unfair although the employer was not contractually entitled to dismiss the employee.' This warning was heeded in Farrant v Woodroffe School 1998 ICR 184, EAT, when the employee in that case was dismissed for refusing to accept a change in his duties, even though it transpired that his employer had no right under the contract to insist on the change. The EAT said that where an employer relies upon a refusal to obey an instruction as the reason for the dismissal, the lawfulness of the instruction will be relevant to, but not determinative of, the fairness of the dismissal.

6.47 **Was the order reasonable?** Employees are not bound to obey all lawful instructions. While the contractual obligations are important, it is the reasonableness of the instruction (and whether the employer acted within the band of reasonable responses in dismissing) that is crucial in an unfair dismissal claim. At common law, employees have always been able to refuse lawful instructions that are dangerous or unreasonable and this rule now extends to unfair dismissal enquiries as well. Two examples:

- **Davies v Jack Troth t/a Richards Transport** EAT 81/87: D, an HGV driver, arrived at work and was told to collect a trailer from Sheffield and take it to Grimsby. After he collected the trailer a fault developed and it became clear that D would not get to Grimsby that day without breaking hours regulations. D rang his employer telling him that he had neither the clothes nor the money to stay overnight and so he wanted to return to the depot. His employer was incensed and dismissed him. The EAT found the dismissal unfair. It accepted that the employer could contractually require D to make for Grimsby and stay overnight but concluded that asking him to do so when he had no money or change of clothes was an unreasonable instruction

- **Whymark v Louis Reece Ltd** ET Case No.47043/95: LR Ltd was finding business difficult and decided to ask the staff to complete a questionnaire designed to test their awareness of the profit and turnover needed to survive. W thought the test a waste of time and refused to complete it. His dismissal for gross insubordination was held to be unfair. Although the tribunal understood the employer's concerns, it thought that the questionnaire was nothing short of juvenile.

Just as an employer may act unreasonably in giving a lawful instruction, dismissal of an employee for refusing to comply with an order which has no contractual basis may be fair. An example: **6.48**

- **Coward v John Menzies (Holdings) Ltd** 1977 IRLR 428, EAT: C, a branch manager at Letchworth, was considered not to be up to that post. As a result the employer offered him a transfer to Swansea (with no financial loss) for retraining as an assistant manager. He refused and was dismissed. The EAT held that, even if there were no contractual right to require C to transfer, the employer had acted reasonably in the interests of the business.

Reasonableness of the employee's refusal. In cases where an employee complains of being dismissed for refusing to comply with an order, it is not only the nature of the employer's order which is relevant under S.98(4) but also the reasonableness of the employee's refusal to carry it out – Union of Construction, Allied Trades and Technicians v Brain 1981 ICR 542, CA. In that case, the editor of the union's newspaper refused to sign an undertaking which effectively meant that he would be liable for any libels against a construction industry journal printed in the paper even though he had no way of controlling the content of articles written by senior officers. He was dismissed – unfairly, held the Court of Appeal. Lord Justice Donaldson said that when dismissal is for refusal to obey an instruction, 'the primary factor which falls to be considered by the reasonable employer deciding whether or not to dismiss his recalcitrant employee is the question, "Is the employee acting reasonably or could he be acting reasonably in refusing to obey my instruction?"' According to the Court, even if the employer had been acting reasonably in ordering the employee to sign the undertaking (which it doubted), the employee's refusal to sign was reasonable and so dismissal was unfair. **6.49**

The importance of the employee's reasons for disobeying are illustrated in the following examples:

- **Osborn Transport Services v Chrissanthou** EAT 412/77: the EAT declined to overturn a tribunal's conclusion that it was unfair to dismiss C for refusing to pick up a load from a specific customer. This was because he had had a previous bad experience with the customer and had been given an undertaking that he would not have to go there again. Factors like these outweighed the urgency of his employer sending a driver and the fact that no others were readily available

- **Intercity East Coast Ltd v McGregor** EAT 473/96: M stayed behind after work one evening to talk to the local union representative. His supervisor told him that he was trespassing on railway premises and that he should go home. The following day the train on which M was scheduled to work on was running late, with the result that M would have been obliged to remain on railway premises beyond his scheduled hours. He refused to work his shift on the basis of his supervisor's comments the previous evening. He was dismissed. The EAT upheld the tribunal's finding of unfair dismissal, subject to an element of contributory fault.

6.50 Tribunals will expect an employer to have investigated an employee's refusal and perhaps then to have reconsidered his own requirements. However, there is no absolute requirement on an employer to enquire further into reasons given by the employee, as long as the employee is given the opportunity to speak in his or her defence – Aitken v Weatherford UK Ltd 2005 1 SC 360, Ct Sess (Inner House).

In looking at the reasonableness of a refusal, the tribunal will look at factors such as the details of the employee's contract. For example, in Skelton v Biddles (Bookbinders) Ltd EAT 332/86 S's contract said that he was entitled to use of a company car 'for personal transport' but his employer forbade him to use the car for any holiday. He wanted to leave it at a friend's house near Luton Airport and was dismissed when he refused to obey the employer's order not to do so. The EAT held the dismissal to be unfair because the contract gave S exclusive use of the car – he was entitled to use it as his own personal property. In such circumstances, S was entitled to disregard his employer's contrary order. However, it should be remembered that the reasonableness of a disobedience dismissal does not depend on the contractual position alone – see Redbridge London Borough Council v Fishman (above).

We discuss some common scenarios in which employees may refuse to obey their employer's instructions below.

6.51 **Refusal to work overtime**

If an employee has been dismissed for refusing to work overtime, the tribunal will look initially at the contract to determine whether or not overtime was a

242

contractual requirement. Although the contractual position is not, as we have said, conclusive to the fairness of the dismissal, it is certainly a key starting point in many cases.

Even if there is no contractual term, dismissal of an employee for refusal to work overtime may be reasonable on the ground of business necessity. For example, in Horrigan v Lewisham London Borough Council 1978 ICR 15, EAT, a driver transporting disabled people for the social services department ended his hours at 4.30 pm and did voluntary overtime after that. Often his rounds did not end until 6 pm. After giving notice that he would not do the overtime on a daily basis he was dismissed. The EAT held that the dismissal was fair. Although the overtime was non-contractual, the Council could not be expected to tolerate a situation of not knowing from one day to the next whether the employee would be available to work the overtime necessary to finish his rounds.

This contrasts with Steels v Goldsmith Garage Ltd EAT 467/87 where the claimant, who had 20 years' service, suddenly refused to work on Saturday mornings, although he had done so for the past three years. This was due to a misunderstanding about safety factors. The employer dismissed him but the employee backtracked on realising that he had been dismissed. The tribunal found the dismissal fair because the employee was in breach of a contractual obligation. However, the EAT overruled this, saying that it was unfair to dismiss a man with 20 years' service who had never previously refused to work overtime and had indicated that he would work the shifts on learning that the alternative was dismissal.

Changing working hours   6.52
Problems often occur when an employer seeks to introduce contractual overtime, or in some other way to alter working hours. A unilateral change in working hours will almost inevitably be a breach of contract. If the employer imposes the change and the employee resigns, the employee can argue that he or she has been constructively dismissed. In some circumstances, however, the employer may simply dismiss the employee who refuses to accept the change. Merely because the employer is in the wrong contractually does not mean that the dismissal will be automatically unfair. The tribunal will look to see whether the employer had sound business reasons for the change in hours and will consider whether the employer had adequately consulted the employee to see whether his or her objections to a change could be sorted out. In many cases, dismissals in these circumstances may be fair for SOSR – see Chapter 8.

Refusal to retrain   6.53
If an employee refuses to retrain – when retraining is necessary to meet business contingencies or to improve the employee's performance – an employer may have no option but to dismiss.

243

Provided the retraining instruction is reasonable, dismissal may be fair even if there is no explicit warning of the consequences of non-compliance. In Jury v ECC Quarries Ltd EAT 241/80 the employee was dismissed when his employer's last HGV Class 3 vehicle went out of service. He had twice previously refused to train for Class 2 driving. The EAT held that the employee had refused to put himself in a position to drive other vehicles and although the offers of retraining were five and 12 months prior to dismissal the employee must have been aware he was putting his job at risk. Although he was not explicitly warned of dismissal, he ought to have understood that his job was in jeopardy as a result of his refusal. Similarly, in Minter v Wellingborough Foundries (BL Cars Ltd) EAT 105/80 it was fair for the employer to ask a professional employee – a nurse – to retrain, particularly as there were doubts about her capability, and it was fair to dismiss her when she refused without adequate reason.

6.54   **Refusal to transfer**

Dismissal for refusal to move to a different workplace frequently occurs where the employee's contract contains an express mobility clause that the employer is seeking to enforce. For instance, in Waton v Balfour Kilpatrick Ltd ET Case No.S/1172/90 W, an electrician, had an express mobility clause in his contract which said that he could be 'transferred to work on any job or site on which the company operates'. For 14 years W had worked in his native Scotland but he was dismissed when he refused to transfer to a job in England. Dismissal was fair, said a tribunal, because the mobility clause gave the employer a clear contractual right to move W. The tribunal thought that the employer was reasonable to enforce the clause because of the nature of the construction industry, the need for flexibility among staff and the common practice among builders of transferring their employees to different sites according to their needs.

However, because it is the reasonableness of the order that is important, dismissal of an employee can be unfair – even if the employer has a clear contractual right to transfer the employee. In Wilson v IDR Construction Ltd 1975 IRLR 260, ET, W refused to go to a new construction site on the following day, although the employer had a contractual right to order him to do so, and he was promptly dismissed. If the employer had investigated properly, it would have become clear that W was only refusing to move on that one day and that he had genuine reasons – his wife was ill and his car was being repaired. But W was not given a chance to explain and his dismissal was held to be unfair.

Therefore, even when equipped with an unambiguous mobility clause, employers should investigate the reasons underpinning an employee's refusal. They should also consider whether there are alternatives to relocating an employee. In Holman v Forestry Commission ET Case No.19474/86 a civil servant based in Cardiff was offered relocation to Edinburgh when his unit was closed down, but he had strong domestic reasons for wanting to stay in South

Wales. He was dismissed for being in breach of a contractual mobility obligation after refusing to relocate. The tribunal found that the claimant was a loyal, efficient employee who had been doing some useful temporary work. It also noted that 13 posts at his grade had become available in South Wales. It thought that the employer had acted unreasonably in not waiting another six months; had this been done, there was a 50 per cent chance that a post could have been found for the employee.

Implied terms. Note that tribunals will imply reasonable terms even into unambiguous express mobility clauses – United Bank Ltd v Akhtar 1989 IRLR 507, EAT. In that case A, a bank employee, worked in Leeds on a low salary. His contract contained a mobility clause which stated that he could be transferred to any of the bank's workplaces in the United Kingdom. A was told to move to the bank's Birmingham branch without notice. He was offered no relocation expenses and he refused on both financial and personal grounds (his wife had just suffered a miscarriage). He resigned and claimed unfair constructive dismissal. Before the tribunal, the bank argued that it could not have been in fundamental breach of A's contract and have constructively dismissed him because it had an absolute contractual right to transfer A and any payment of relocation expenses was purely discretionary. Mr Justice Knox, however, upheld the tribunal's finding of unfair dismissal. He said that the operation of a contractual mobility clause was subject to three overriding implied terms: 6.55

- reasonable notice must be given before exercising the power to transfer an employee

- a mobility clause must be operated in such a way as to make it feasible. An employee should not be required to do something which was, in practice, impossible

- a mobility clause is subject to the general duty not to behave in a way likely to destroy mutual trust and confidence between employer and employee.

The EAT confirmed that it was impossible for A to move at short notice without relocation money, and that the trust and confidence integral to the contract had been destroyed by the employer. The bank was in breach of the three overriding implied terms, and A had thus been unfairly constructively dismissed. (If A had been expressly dismissed, it would have been the reasonableness of the employer's order which would have been crucial, not the contractual mobility clause, and it seems likely that the employer would have been held unreasonable in enforcing the clause.) 6.56

Refusing change in duties
6.57
In some circumstances employees refuse to do a specific part of their job, or they object to a change in duties. An example:

245

- **Hood v Scotsman Publications Ltd** EAT 113/90: H, a very senior journalist, had been working for *The Scotsman* for nearly 30 years. He was an assistant editor who primarily edited the letters page but was also a chief leader writer. When a new editor, L, arrived, he decided that the paper should feature obituaries and insisted that H edit the new service. H persistently refused – even though he had been relieved of most of his other duties so that he could devote his energies to the obituaries service. H believed that he was being sidelined into a dead-end job and he regarded it as a demotion. This dispute continued and L did make some concessions, but he eventually dismissed H for refusing to take on the obituaries service. The tribunal held that dismissal was a reasonable response: before L became editor it was reasonably common for employees to be moved into different areas and throughout his career H himself had done various jobs on the paper. The tribunal said that there was no evidence that he had been demoted and the right of the editor to implement editorial policy had to be recognised. The EAT upheld the tribunal's finding.

But contrast the following two cases. In Wiggins Teape Fine Papers Ltd v Murchison EAT 322/89 M was dismissed for refusing to carry out stocktaking that he was contractually required to do. The EAT upheld the tribunal's finding of unfair dismissal. The tribunal took the view that dismissal was not a penalty open to the employer under the disciplinary procedure for M's offence. Furthermore, dismissal was excessive and unreasonable given the length of his service, although he had contributed to his dismissal by 50 per cent. And in London Probation Board v Lee EAT 0493/08 the employee was dismissed for refusing to carry out new duties following a transfer. He was asked to provide training for people, but refused because he believed that they would then take over his own job. As a disciplinary sanction, he was moved to a different job at a different location. The employee objected to the transfer and, when he refused to perform his new duties, was dismissed. The tribunal found the dismissal unfair, and the EAT agreed. Although his contract of employment contained a mobility clause, it did not permit the compulsory transfer to other duties. In any event, the use of any power to transfer as a disciplinary sanction was unlawful. The tribunal summarised the situation as follows: '[The employee] was given an unreasonable and unlawful order to move location and jobs and was then disciplined and dismissed for not having complied with that original unlawful order. No reasonable employer would act in such a manner.'

6.58 ### Short-term emergencies

Tribunals recognise that in times of emergency employers may have to ask employees to do work which they would not normally do. In Grigg v Daylay Eggs Ltd EAT 426/79 the EAT held that it was reasonable for the employer to expect a senior employee to help out in an emergency by working away from home for a fortnight, albeit in difficult conditions, and fair to dismiss him for refusing.

Similarly, in Tennent Caledonian Breweries Ltd v McKiddie EAT 674/86 M was a licensee of a pub that was owned by the company. Following several disorderly incidents and allegations of widespread drug use on the premises, the Licensing Board called a hearing to decide whether M or the company could continue to hold a licence. M had not been present at the pub when some of the incidents occurred and the employer instructed him to stay on the premises seven days a week until the Licensing Board had made its decision. When the employer found out that he was not present as instructed, he was dismissed. The EAT overturned a tribunal decision that the dismissal was unfair and held that dismissal was within the range of reasonable responses. It said that the loss of the licence was a very serious matter and M had disobeyed a clear instruction given in a crisis situation.

Flouting specific instructions 6.59
As stated earlier, tribunals will first consider whether the employer's instruction was legitimate and reasonable. In Payne v Spook Erection Ltd 1984 IRLR 219, EAT, an employee was unfairly dismissed for refusing to operate a system designed to keep tabs on the workforce. The EAT held that the scheme was 'obviously and intolerably unfair' and 'wholly unacceptable as a matter of good industrial relations practice' and the employee could not reasonably be expected to implement it.

Furthermore, an employer cannot reasonably ask an employee to do a dishonest or illegal act, even though it ostensibly falls within the scope of the employer's powers. Thus in Morrish v Henlys (Folkestone) Ltd 1973 ICR 482, NIRC, an employee's dismissal for refusing to connive at falsification of company records was unfair.

Tribunals will look at the way employers handle wilful or persistent disobedience to specific orders in deciding whether the dismissal was fair. As the EAT said in Kaye v Blackwell (Contracts) Ltd EAT 765/78, 'there may be circumstances where, there having been several requests followed by a repeated and settled refusal to do the work, it is right and proper for the employer to dismiss albeit there has been no previous written or oral warning'.

Wilful disobedience will not always merit dismissal, however. In Bluemink Ltd t/a Caledonia Crane Hire v Thomson EAT 291/85 the employee was unfairly dismissed for refusing to come to work one morning because of a hangover. The EAT held that such misconduct was only one of the material considerations the tribunal had to consider. Others included the employee's previous good conduct.

Flouting company rules/working practices 6.60
In Ladbroke Racing Ltd v Arnott and ors 1983 IRLR 154, Ct Sess (Inner House) the Court of Session stated that dismissal for breach of a company rule is not automatically fair – it still has to be decided whether dismissal was a reasonable response to a particular breach. Another case where an

'automatic' dismissal for breaching company rules was held to be unfair was Marks and Spencer plc v O'Connell EAT 230/95. In that case the employer failed to consider the circumstances surrounding an employee's breach of the smoking regulations.

One issue that may be relevant to the question of fairness is whether or not the employee was aware of the rule in question. In Donachie v Allied Suppliers Ltd EAT 46/80 the EAT held that it was unreasonable to dismiss an employee for failure to comply with a material term of the contract of which he was unaware and of which he could not reasonably have been aware.

6.61 **Minor, one-off or first breaches of company rules.** In Lock v Cardiff Railway Company Ltd 1998 IRLR 358, EAT, the claimant was dismissed for asking a teenage passenger on his train to leave because he did not have a ticket or the money to pay the fare. The boy was left in a strange area with no means of getting home. The dismissal was found to be unfair because it was a one-off act of misjudgement and the employee had never been warned that dismissal could result.

However, there may be circumstances where single breaches of the rules may found a fair dismissal. This was the case in Post Office t/a Royal Mail v Gallagher EAT 21/99, where after 12 years of blameless conduct an employee was dismissed for a first offence under the rules on failure to deliver mail. The dismissal was held to be fair by the EAT, which took account of the serious nature of the offence, the clear provisions of the employer's disciplinary code, the fact that those provisions were strictly adhered to and the proper investigation of the offence. Similarly, in AAH Pharmaceuticals v Carmichael EAT 0325/03 the employee was found to have been fairly dismissed for breaching company rules on leaving drugs in his delivery van overnight. The EAT commented: 'In any particular case, exceptions can be imagined where, for example, the penalty of dismissal might not be imposed, but equally, in our judgment, when a breach of a necessarily strict rule has been properly proved, exceptional service, previous long service and/or previous good conduct may properly not be considered sufficient to reduce a penalty of dismissal.'

6.62 **Repeated breaches of working practices.** Tribunals are increasingly being asked to rule on cases where employees refuse to perform a particular aspect of their overall duties, often for religious reasons. For instance, there was the well-publicised case of the Christian registrar – Islington London Borough Council v Ladele 2010 ICR 532, CA – who was subjected to disciplinary proceedings when she refused to conduct civil partnerships. She complained that the Council's treatment of her constituted unlawful discrimination on the ground of her religion or belief contrary to the Employment Equality (Religion or Belief) Regulations 2003 SI 2003/1660. Although this argument initially succeeded before the tribunal, both the EAT and the Court of Appeal held that she had not been discriminated against and that, accordingly, her various claims under the Religion or Belief Regulations failed.

Although unfair dismissal law played no role in the Ladele case (in which the claimant remained a Council employee), it is worth noting that this type of case could throw up questions of whether the employer can fairly dismiss the employee – either expressly or constructively – in these circumstances. In McFarlane v Relate Avon Ltd 2010 ICR 507, EAT, for instance, the employee's claim under the Religion or Belief Regulations was accompanied by a claim for unfair constructive dismissal. In that case, McF objected, on religious grounds, to providing sex therapy to same-sex couples. With regard to the unfair dismissal claim, RA Ltd argued that it had been reasonable to dismiss McF on the basis that he had given an assurance that he would work with same-sex clients, and thus comply with RA Ltd's equal opportunity and ethical practice policies, when, in fact, he had no intention of doing so. This argument failed before the tribunal because it found that McF had never actually given such an assurance. As a result, the employer had no reasonable belief that gross misconduct had been committed. However, RA Ltd succeeded with the alternative argument that this was a dismissal for SOSR, and that it was reasonable for it to dismiss an employee who was, to put it no higher, equivocal about his willingness to conduct himself in accordance with principles which – legitimately, as it had previously held – it regarded as of fundamental importance. This finding was upheld by the EAT on appeal. **6.63**

Although the employee's dismissal was found to have been fair for SOSR, it seems that similar considerations would have applied if the employer had been entitled to proceed with the 'conduct' ground for dismissal – i.e. on the basis that the employee had given an unequivocal assurance that he would abide by the employer's equal opportunity and ethical practice policies and that dismissal would, subject to any mitigating factors, have been a reasonable response to the employee's refusal to act in accordance with that assurance.

Disobedience for health and safety reasons

6.64

Employees sometimes refuse to carry out instructions because of health and safety fears. It is automatically unfair for an employer to dismiss an employee for an 'inadmissible reason' relating to health and safety under S.100 ERA (see Chapter 11, 'Health and safety dismissals'). In other words, the question of reasonableness does not arise. However, dismissals for health and safety reasons that fall outside the scope of S.100 are governed by the ordinary rules contained in S.98. In particular, the tribunal has to decide whether or not the employer acted reasonably in dismissing. It is an implied term in contracts of employment that the employer will provide employees with a safe system of work and take reasonable care for their safety. As part of this duty, employers must investigate 'promptly and sensibly' all bona fide complaints about safety drawn to their attention by employees – British Aircraft Corporation Ltd v

249

Austin 1978 IRLR 332, EAT. Failure to do so may entitle an employee to terminate his or her contract and claim unfair constructive dismissal.

In addition, employers are subject to numerous statutory health and safety regulations. However, because it is the reasonableness of an employer's orders that is crucial in unfair dismissal cases, his contractual and statutory health and safety obligations, although relevant, are not conclusive. In most cases tribunals will not need to make a finding on whether these statutory obligations have been contravened. Instead they will need to consider whether adequate precautions have been taken to ensure employees' safety and, if not, whether it was practicable to take such precautions. As a result, an employer could be in breach of a statutory duty regarding health and safety, but dismissal for an employee's refusal to work may still be fair. An example:

- **Lindsay v Dunlop Ltd** 1980 IRLR 93, EAT: L was employed in the tyres curing section where hot rubber tyres gave off fumes thought to be toxic. The employer was aware that there was no efficient local ventilation and so asked the employees to wear masks as a temporary measure pending a report from the Health and Safety Commission. Most employees accepted this but L did not and, when he persisted in refusing to work in the area until the fumes were dispersed, he was dismissed. A tribunal held that the dismissal was fair but L appealed on the grounds that the employer was in breach of the statutory duty under S.63 of the Factories Act 1961 and also the common law duty to provide a safe system of work. The EAT, however, rejected his appeal, holding that, although a tribunal may consider the employer's legal obligations when deciding whether the dismissal was reasonable, it was unnecessary to make findings on whether or not such obligations had been complied with. The EAT found that, although L had a genuine fear of injury from the fumes, the employer did not act unreasonably in requiring him to wear a mask while further advice was sought – especially since his fellow employees had agreed to work in those circumstances.

6.65 The Lindsay case should be contrasted with Smith Anderson and Co Ltd v MacGregor EAT 369/89, where M worked for 12-hour shifts on machinery that generated great heat and gave him throat infections. M complained about the conditions and the lack of ventilation in the workroom. The employees were not meant to leave the room during working hours and M was dismissed when he was seen outside the workroom four times during a shift. The EAT upheld the tribunal's finding that the employer had acted unreasonably. The instruction that M should not go outside the room during the shift was not reasonable in view of the conditions in the room and the need for the employees to get occasional breaths of fresh air.

6.66 **Investigating complaints.** If an employee objects to his or her working conditions, the employer should investigate the matter promptly and

250

communicate his findings to the employee. If an employer jumps the gun and dismisses employees for refusing to work when there are unresolved health and safety complaints, dismissal is likely to be unfair. This was the situation in Heaps, Collis and Harrison Ltd t/a Air Power Centre v Burt EAT 173/99 where the employee raised concerns about the levels of radioactivity on a barge on which he was working. His grievance had not been finally disposed of at the time of his suspension and summary dismissal. The EAT upheld the finding of unfair dismissal reached by the tribunal on the ground that the employer had been unduly precipitate.

Drinking, drugs and smoking 6.67

Employees whose performance or behaviour at work is affected by alcohol or drugs leave themselves open to fair dismissal on the ground of either capability or conduct. However, there is an increasing trend towards treating long-term alcoholism and, to a lesser extent, drug dependency as serious illnesses, with many employers having adopted specific policies allowing time off for medical treatment and counselling. Chronic abuse resulting in diminished performance and long bouts of absence from work is clearly a 'sickness' problem, and employers should take reasonable steps to investigate the true medical position and the prospects of rehabilitation before deciding whether the individual's employment can be continued (see Chapter 5). It may also be that a problem with alcohol or drugs is a symptom of a disability, in which case the employee may be protected under the Disability Discrimination Act 1995 (although addiction to drugs or alcohol as a free-standing condition is excluded from the definition of 'disability' contained in that Act). But, at the other end of the spectrum, there are straightforward cases of drink and drug misconduct where the employee recklessly or even deliberately disregards company rules or acceptable standards of conduct. Here, employers may be justified in adopting a less tolerant approach – especially where there is a company rule identifying drunkenness and drug use at work as meriting dismissal.

A simple example of a fair dismissal for being drunk at work is the case of Weir v Stephen Alans Jewellers EAT 550/97. The employee was the manager of a jeweller's shop who had gone to watch a football match in a nearby pub one afternoon. He had drunk three or four pints at the pub and failed to lock up the shop properly at the end of the day. He was dismissed for gross misconduct. The EAT could find no fault in the tribunal's finding of fair dismissal.

Drinking on or off duty 6.68

Disciplinary breaches such as drunkenness or possessing drink at work normally point to 'conduct' as the reason for dismissal, and are generally assumed to be a serious matter. To establish conduct as the reason for

251

dismissal, employers must satisfy the Burchell test (see 'General considerations – establishing the reason for dismissal' above) that stipulates that employers must have a genuine belief on reasonable grounds, after reasonable investigation, that an employee was guilty of the misconduct in question. However, even in cases where employers do have such a belief, Acas advises employers to consider whether it would be appropriate to treat the problem as a medical rather than a disciplinary matter (see the Acas Advisory Booklet, 'Health, work and wellbeing').

The need for investigation and medical advice is well illustrated in Martin v British Railways Board EAT 362/91. M was dismissed when his manager thought he was drunk at work – his eyes looked glazed and his speech was slurred. At his internal appeal, M told the employer that he had not been drunk but suffered from hypertension, the symptoms of which resembled drunkenness. His appeal was dismissed and the EAT in Scotland confirmed the tribunal's finding of unfair dismissal. The employer should have made further investigations to discover whether H's condition was in fact due to a medical cause.

6.69 Problems arise where it is not immediately clear whether a drinking (or drug) problem falls within the 'sickness' category or the 'misconduct' category. Choosing a wrong label, as we have seen, will not be fatal in itself. However, the confusion could lead to wrong steps being taken or right ones not being taken when they should be. Two examples:

- **Strathclyde Regional Council v Syme** EAT 233/79: S was a school janitor for ten years. During the last two there were complaints that he drank and at a disciplinary interview he promised to resign if found drunk again. Later he had hospital treatment but after another incident he was held to that promise and resigned. The tribunal found this to be a dismissal. The EAT, upholding the tribunal's finding of unfairness, considered that S's problem should have been treated as medical, not disciplinary, and independent medical evidence should have been obtained since there was evidence before the tribunal to show that he suffered from manic-depression and that this was the cause of his drinking. So while dismissal might have been fair in a straightforward case of alcoholism (bearing in mind the employer's duties to pupils and other staff), in the circumstances it was unfair

- **Preston v MBDA (UK) Ltd** ET Case No.2405916/02: the employer had known for some time that P had a serious drink problem. After an incident when he was believed to be smelling of alcohol, he admitted having been drinking at lunchtime and allegedly admitted to having had a drink on the premises. A disciplinary hearing was called and he was summarily dismissed for gross misconduct. The tribunal found the dismissal to be unfair, since, although the employer had accepted that P was suffering from an illness, it had dealt with it purely as a misconduct issue. However, P's compensatory award was limited because, had the employer correctly approached the matter on a capability basis, it would have made no difference to the decision to dismiss.

Where an employee's drinking is associated with a medical condition, misdemeanours such as lateness, erratic behaviour or poor performance will often be part of that medical problem. However, manifestations of the illness in the form of gross misconduct may still be treated as such, and tribunals recognise that employers can reach the point where they are entitled to say 'enough is enough'. In Evans v Bass North Ltd EAT 715/86 the employee, an alcoholic, had been employed as a chef for 11 years. His employer had always taken a sympathetic view of his problem, but he was dismissed on Christmas Eve after breaking a prohibition against drinking in the kitchen and for later threatening the manager. The EAT found the dismissal fair for misconduct, even though it acknowledged that the employee was suffering from a disease.

Alcohol rule/policy. Employers who have disciplinary rules against drinking at work are at an advantage when it comes to justifying their dismissals. The existence of a rule increases the likelihood of a tribunal finding that a dismissal, without warnings for an isolated incident, was fair – the rule itself operating as a warning. But to have that effect, the consequences of breach must also be clear. **6.70**

In Dairy Produce Packers Ltd v Beverstock 1981 IRLR 265, EAT, an employee was dismissed for drinking in a public house when he should have been working. He claimed that others who had been drinking during working hours had been subjected to less severe penalties. The company argued that it was reasonable to distinguish between the employee's case and the others as in the other instances the drinking had taken place on the premises. The EAT decided that if employers wished to impose different penalties in such circumstances, they had to make this clear in either their rules or the contract of employment. That had not been done in this case and the dismissal was therefore unfair.

However, any 'drinking' rule must be applied in a reasonable and not a rigid or inflexible way. In Charlery v Glendale Grounds Management ET Case No.6002920/98 the employer had a rule stating that employees under the influence of alcohol might be summarily dismissed. This rule was applied unwisely to an employee who was seen walking along a road outside the park at which he was an attendant holding a can of beer. His dismissal was found to be unfair on the basis that drinking half a can of beer during a lunch break where there had been no specific warning against so doing was not sufficient misconduct to justify dismissal. And in Scottish Grain Distillers Ltd v McNee and Lennox EAT 34/82 the employer had an inflexible rule that unauthorised possession of alcohol led to summary dismissal. In a locker search, jars with a small amount of liquid containing on analysis 1 per cent or less of ethyl alcohol were found in the two claimants' lockers. Both were dismissed. The EAT, upholding the tribunal's finding of unfair dismissal, considered that even if the liquid could fairly be described as alcohol, the breach was trivial. **6.71**

253

Just as the existence of clear disciplinary rules may help an employer defend a claim of unfair dismissal, so too the existence of an alcohol policy that states that an employee 'will' be given the opportunity to seek diagnosis and specialist help may affect how a reasonable employer should deal with an employee with an alcohol dependency. In Sinclair v Wandsworth Council EAT 0145/07 the EAT upheld a tribunal's finding that the dismissal of the employee was unfair because, despite having such a policy, the employer did not apply it; any reasonable employer would have informed the employee of the alcohol policy (he had only been provided with a copy immediately before the disciplinary hearing that resulted in his dismissal); and that disciplinary action could only be suspended if he actively sought to address his alcohol problem. The employee had not been given the opportunity of accepting treatment as an alternative to disciplinary action.

6.72 **Change in the rules.** Any change in the rules must be brought to the employees' attention. Failure to do so may result in a finding of unfair dismissal. In Claypotts Construction Ltd v McCallum EAT 699/81 the employee overstayed lunch in a pub by an hour and was dismissed. His written particulars of employment stated that such offences would be dealt with by a recorded warning but more recently employees had been orally informed that such conduct would not be tolerated. The EAT, upholding the tribunal's finding of unfair dismissal, said that the employer was not entitled to dismiss summarily, because any alteration in the rules had not been adequately drawn to the employee's attention. Note that where the new rules are brought in by formal agreement with the union the employer is generally entitled to assume that members are aware of them – Gray Dunn and Co Ltd v Edwards 1980 IRLR 23, EAT (but see W Brooks and Son v Skinner below).

If rules are introduced as a temporary measure – say, to prevent loss of production at Christmas – employers should tread carefully, especially if excesses have been condoned in the past. In W Brooks and Son v Skinner 1984 IRLR 379, EAT, an employee was dismissed under the provisions of a new rule for failing to report to work after over-indulging at the Christmas party. Although the rule had been agreed with the union, individual employees were not informed and a reasonable employee would not have expected dismissal to be the sanction given the employer's previous leniency in such matters.

6.73 **Give employee opportunity to explain.** Giving an employee a chance to respond fully and thoughtfully to the allegations may mean taking him or her off work and not holding an interview until he or she sobers up. The importance of this goes beyond simply establishing whether the employee was drinking: it is to allow the employee to put forward any explanation he or she may have.

Failure to give the employee an opportunity to apologise is particularly important in the case of a sudden loss of temper under the influence of drink. In Charles Letts and Co Ltd v Howard 1976 IRLR 248, EAT, a case where underlying tensions erupted into a row with the manager when the employee was drunk, the EAT said: 'In our view, particularly in a case of what appears to have been a sudden explosion and loss of temper by a man who was under the influence of drink, it must be important for an officer, weighing the pros and cons of dismissal or of lenience, to send for the man concerned and to give him every opportunity and encouragement to climb off his high horse and to apologise, so that matters can be put right before it is too late.'

The employee's explanation may also reveal that there are work-related reasons for their alcohol abuse. For example, the employee may explain that he or she has started drinking heavily because they feel unable to cope with their workload. The employer should further investigate any such claims and ensure that any problems at work are adequately addressed and that the employee receives the appropriate support. Failing this, a tribunal may find that dismissing the employee in these circumstances was unfair.

Mitigating circumstances. Even if a rule has been breached, there may be 6.74 mitigating circumstances that make a dismissal unfair. In Weetabix Ltd v Criggie and anor EAT 344/89 two employees contravened a clear company rule when they were caught drinking on an evening shift. However, their dismissals were held to be unfair as there were mitigating factors. The employees had not bought the alcohol to drink at work – one of them intended it for his fishing trip after the shift; they had finished their allotted work; neither was drunk; and one of them was suffering from a domestic upset, which they were discussing over the drink.

In Hepworth Pipe Co Ltd v Chahal EAT 611/80 the claimant had worked well as a crane driver for nine years. He was known by his employer to be a diabetic. One morning he arrived for work apparently drunk and was dismissed after admitting drinking the evening before. On appeal, he claimed his condition was aggravated by lack of insulin. The EAT, upholding the tribunal's finding of unfair dismissal, held that the tribunal had adopted the correct approach in finding the dismissal unfair on the ground that the employer ought to have investigated any possible circumstances mitigating the employee's apparently drunken state.

Drinking previously condoned. Where drinking has been previously condoned, 6.75 summary dismissal in most cases will be unfair. In such cases, a clear warning that an employee's job is in danger if such conduct is repeated is necessary. In Sandon and Co Ltd v Lundin EAT 421/76 a managing director had formed the habit of leaving work at 11.30 am to visit the pub and returning often as late as 3 pm, smelling of drink though not drunk. His chairman hinted that he should resign because of poor trading results but he refused to do so and was then dismissed by

255

the board for misconduct. The EAT agreed with the tribunal that the dismissal was unfair. There should have been a plain warning – instead of which the employee had been allowed to go on like this for two years.

6.76 **Health and safety.** Tribunals take a very strict view where health and safety is involved. This is hardly surprising, since employers have obligations under common law and various statutes, notably the Health and Safety at Work etc Act 1974, to keep their employees safe. Employers are obliged to take reasonable steps to ensure that their employees are not acting under the influence of alcohol or drugs if this is likely to risk the health and safety of others. Indeed, employees themselves have a duty under the Act to look after their colleagues. In Connor v George Wimpey ME and C Ltd EAT 387/82 it was held to be fair to dismiss an oil-rig scaffolder for being drunk when returning to work – work where safety on platforms and during transport thereto was heavily stressed. There were stringent rules in his contract that provided for possible dismissal in these circumstances but, even if there had been no specific reference to drinking and possible dismissal in the contract, the EAT would have found it well within the discretion of a prudent employer instantly to dismiss an employee found to be so much under the influence of alcohol as to be considered unsafe to let on board the transport plane. The safety requirements of North Sea platforms and transport needed no emphasis – particularly the strict control of alcohol.

Potential danger to others made it fair to dismiss a bus driver for drinking a pint of beer during a one-hour break between duties in Tait v South Yorkshire Passenger Transport Executive ET Case No.21644/79. The tribunal acknowledged that dismissal might be described as harsh after five years' service, but the employer had to enforce the rule strictly as laxity could lead to regular drinking by drivers. The dismissal was therefore fair. And in Douglas v Britannia Airways Ltd ET Case No.6956/87 an air stewardess was fairly dismissed for drinking on several flights. The tribunal stressed that the safety of the passengers, especially in an emergency situation, was central to her job and that in her condition she put lives at jeopardy.

If dismissals for potential danger are fair, dismissals for drunken negligence are even more likely to be so. In Richardson v Teesside Farmers Oils Ltd COET 335/116 R was drunk at a Christmas party and let a woman colleague, who had no driving licence, drive his loaded oil tanker. She hit a wall, causing minor damage. The tribunal found the dismissal to be fair, despite R's eight years' service and some procedural lapses by the employer. He was breaking the law and putting at risk fellow employees and the employer's operating licence.

6.77 Even where there is only evidence of off-duty drinking, a dismissal can still be fair. In McLean v McLane Ltd EAT 682/96 the claimant, a fork-lift truck driver, was dismissed after his employer read in a newspaper that he had been convicted of being drunk and disorderly and in possession of cannabis. Although there was no evidence of his ever having come to work under the influence of alcohol or drugs, his employer was concerned that it might happen and worried about the consequences if it did. The EAT held that the dismissal was fair.

Off-duty drinking and driving may well have repercussions on employment if the employee concerned loses his or her driving licence. This is dealt with in Chapter 7 under 'Driving bans'.

Note also that S.27 of the Transport and Works Act 1992 creates a number of criminal offences aimed at certain categories of railway worker who go to work under the influence of alcohol (or drugs). Operators who have failed to exercise all due diligence to prevent the commission of any such offence by those who work for them will also be guilty of an offence – S.28. Breath tests may be carried out by a constable who has reasonable cause to suspect that a railway worker has been drinking – S.29. It is also a criminal offence to drive a motor vehicle if under the influence of drink (or drugs) – the Road Traffic Act 1988.

Employer's reputation. One reason sometimes advanced by employers to justify dismissal for drinking is that their public reputation has been, or will be, damaged by the employee's actions. Such an argument was accepted in HB Raylor v McArdle EAT 573/84. The employee had been seen 'legless' on a building site, even though at the time he was off-duty. His dismissal was held to be fair, as the employer was acting reasonably in considering that his presence in such a state would undermine the confidence of the employer's site agents. **6.78**

Dismissal for other people's drinking. In some circumstances, employees may be dismissed as a result of other people's drinking. The most obvious instances involve schoolteachers. In West Sussex County Council v Bell EAT 60/86 the claimant's dismissal was, in the EAT's view, fair because he had, among other things, bought an under-age pupil a drink at a pub and allowed such pupils to drink whisky at his house, one of whom became intoxicated. Similarly, if a senior manager allowed employees to drink on the premises in breach of company rules, his or her dismissal may be fair – see Williams v Ciba-Geigy Plastics and Additives Co EAT 87/81. **6.79**

Drugs **6.80**

Drug addiction, like alcoholism, should in theory be treated as an illness. However, tribunals have almost invariably regarded drug-related dismissals as a misconduct issue. Perhaps the reason for the different approach is that the use of drugs, unlike alcohol, can amount to a criminal offence. Furthermore, employers themselves can commit an offence under the Misuse of Drugs Act 1971 if they know that illegal drugs are being used or distributed on their premises.

Note also that S.27 of the Transport and Works Act 1992 creates a number of criminal offences aimed at certain categories of railway worker who go to work under the influence of drugs. Operators who have failed to exercise all due diligence to prevent the commission of any such offence by those who work for them will also be guilty of an offence – S.28. It is also a criminal offence to drive a motor vehicle if under the influence of drugs – the Road Traffic Act 1988.

6.81 **Drugs policy.** Rules prohibiting the use of drugs at work are not particularly common, except in jobs that are involved in some way with the dispensing or manufacture of drugs such as work in pharmacies or hospitals. However, company rule or not, dismissal will usually be a reasonable response to drug use at work. In Anderson and anor v Oak Motor Works Ltd ET Case Nos.21967–68/81, for example, two employees were caught smoking cannabis in the workshop where they were rebuilding engines. The tribunal decided that the employer's fears about health and safety were justified and the dismissals fair. But employers must investigate properly. In Templeman v Freight and Repair Service (Taunton) Ltd ET Case No.21126/85 a tribunal found that the employer's grounds for supposing that T's erratic behaviour at work was due to smoking cannabis on duty were too vague.

Even if an employee is caught simply in possession of cannabis on company premises, dismissal may be a reasonable response. In Hawkes v Coca Cola Enterprises Ltd ET Case No.3300022/01 the dismissal of an employee for possession of cannabis at work was found to be fair. The tribunal found that the employee should have been aware of the employer's policy on illegal substances, but even if there had been no such policy, it believed that possession of illegal substances at work could amount to gross misconduct.

6.82 There is a distinction between the taking of drugs proscribed by the criminal law and other drugs. In Chappell v SYP Ltd ET Case No.2800461/02 the claimant took an overdose of paracetamol while at work. She was dismissed for misuse of drugs. In finding her dismissal unfair, the tribunal commented that it was unreasonable of the employer to accuse her of 'misusing drugs' as the phrase invariably connotes use of drugs such as ecstasy and cannabis. In deciding whether dismissal was within the 'range of reasonable responses', a tribunal will take into account a number of different factors including:

- whether the conduct was on or off duty
- whether the employer's confidence in the employee has been irredeemably undermined
- safety at work
- contact with children or young people

- the effect on the employer's reputation and business
- the illegality of the employee's actions
- any mitigating factors.

Off-duty drug use. Employees' conduct outside the workplace is not usually a sufficient ground for dismissal. The general attitude of tribunals to off-duty drug use – usually made known to the employer by a charge or conviction – is that it merits dismissal only if it adversely affects relationships with other employees, or with contacts the employee makes while doing his or her job, or the employer's reputation and thus the business. So said the EAT in Norfolk County Council v Bernard 1979 IRLR 220, EAT, upholding a tribunal's decision that dismissal of a teacher after his conviction for possession of cannabis was unfair. The employee was a drama specialist who spent most of his time instructing teachers, although he would sometimes teach teenagers in demonstration classes and was involved with church and other youth groups. He was convicted on guilty pleas and fined for possession and cultivation of cannabis after a few leaves were found in his car, following which he was dismissed. The tribunal accepted his evidence that he had been given them a few months before, smoked two or three cigarettes made from them, and had then forgotten about them. They also accepted evidence that he was highly competent and very well liked, had a high moral character and disapproved of drug use. Since the conviction arose from a single incident, the result of foolishness not vice, the tribunal felt that dismissal was excessive. The EAT agreed.

That case can be contrasted with McLean v McLane Ltd EAT 682/96, in which the claimant, a fork-lift truck driver, was dismissed after his employer read in a newspaper that he had been convicted of being drunk and disorderly and in possession of cannabis. Although there was no evidence of his ever having come to work under the influence of alcohol or drugs, his employer was concerned that, with two previous convictions for possession of cannabis, it might happen, and worried about the consequences if it did. The EAT held that the dismissal was fair.

Interview and prompt investigation are necessary even if there has been a conviction. A conviction is only proof that the employee is 'guilty as charged', but in the context of unfair dismissal there may still be explanations, mitigating factors or arguments that the employee wants to put forward in reaction to the employer's proposed sanction. For instance, despite a conviction, the employee may not actually smoke cannabis, as in Tabor v Mid Glamorgan County Council ET Case No.8353/81, where the employee knew that the plant was being grown in his garden but did not use it himself. Or there may have been only one isolated incident, as in Norfolk County Council v Bernard (above).

6.83

6.84

259

If criminal proceedings are pending, an employer does not necessarily have to await the outcome before deciding to dismiss provided he has acted reasonably in reaching that decision and has conducted a proper investigation (see below under 'Theft and dishonesty').

6.85 **Trust and confidence.** If an employer's trust and confidence in an employee is irredeemably undermined by an employee's drug use, a resulting dismissal could be fair. In Mathewson v RB Wilson Dental Laboratory Ltd 1989 IRLR 512, EAT, M was arrested and charged during his lunch break for being in possession of a small quantity of cannabis bought for personal use. After returning to work an hour late, he owned up to the offence and was promptly dismissed. Before the tribunal, the employer successfully argued that M had breached a company rule and, in any event, it was not possible to continue to employ someone 'involved in drugs'. The employer stressed that M was a skilled employee and expressed fears about the adverse impact an admitted drug user might have on young impressionable employees. While this decision seems harsh – M had not been convicted, there were procedural defects, and the employer had an obvious moral revulsion to drugs – the confidence integral to the employment relationship had clearly vanished after M's arrest.

6.86 **Safety factors.** Although tribunals do accept a proven safety risk as a good reason to dismiss, it does not relieve employers of their duty to investigate. In Davis v British Airways Board ET Case No.31890/79 the claimant had given eight years' satisfactory service as an airline steward before his employer found out that he had been using amphetamines and dismissed him for taking drugs which could incapacitate him for work and endanger the company's reputation. It was held that the employer was unreasonable in not inquiring further into the medical effects of the drug.

6.87 **Contact with children or young people.** Where the employee's work means that he or she regularly comes into contact with children or young people, this is seen as an important factor in drug abuse cases, especially where the employee is in a position to influence them as a teacher. In Norfolk County Council v Bernard (above) – a case in which dismissal was found to be unfair – stress was placed on the fact that the employee was not normally in contact with children, and that he took a strict moral attitude towards drug-taking and felt he would not be embarrassed in dealing with drug problems among pupils. In Tabor v Mid Glamorgan County Council (above), by contrast, the employee taught teenage pupils daily and his replies to the local authority committee showed that he did not agree with the law's approach to cannabis. Although he did not use the drug himself and had been fined only £10 by the magistrates for allowing others to grow it in his garden, the committee felt that it could not leave him in charge of children. The tribunal found the dismissal to be fair.

6.88 **Public image of the company is threatened.** The public's attitude to someone involved with drugs is often a potent factor in a tribunal's decision. Frequently, it comes down to a question of local publicity, although the attitude of tribunals to this tends to vary with the case. In Gunn v British Waterways Board EAT 138/81 a lock-keeper was demoted after a record of unreliability and cannabis convictions and then dismissed after he was convicted of stealing money and drugs and his employer's name was mentioned in the papers. The EAT held that this was a fair dismissal even though performance of the employee's duties, which were menial, would not be affected. The Board's reputation as a responsible employer was at stake. Similarly, in Morgan v Railtrack plc ET Case No.2305231/02 a signalman's dismissal for refusing to submit to a drugs test following a signalling error that resulted in a train being sent along the wrong track was found to be fair. The Eurostar train involved in the incident was carrying a number of tabloid journalists and, owing to the potential for adverse publicity, it had made sense for the employer to require the employee to take a drug test in order to protect the company's reputation.

Illegality. The fact that an employee has committed an illegal/criminal offence should be viewed as an additional rather than the major factor in the charge of misconduct. In Anderson and anor v Oak Motor Works Ltd (above), where the two employees had been caught smoking cannabis at work, the employment tribunal observed that the illegality was a consideration and that most employers would share this view. And in Tabor v Mid Glamorgan County Council (above) the tribunal shared the employer's concern that a teacher should show disrespect for the law – the employee in that case had told a committee that he did not agree with the outlawing of cannabis. **6.89**

Mitigating factors. In Davis v British Airways Board (above) the claimant had begun to take amphetamines because of fatigue and depression caused partly by the strain of long-haul flights. His resulting dismissal was held to be unfair since his employer had failed to investigate adequately the true medical effects of such drugs. And in Burns v Dart Pleasure Craft Ltd ET Case No.2095/80 the employee claimed that he had smoked cannabis because of matrimonial difficulties. The tribunal suggested that a reasonable employer would not have dismissed but would have given an ultimatum and waited to see if he gave up, especially as the boats he worked on were laid up for the winter and the only work to be done was on-shore. However, in Soulsbury v Connex South Eastern ET Case No.1100582/96 the tribunal found the employee's dismissal to be fair despite the fact that he maintained that the employer had failed to take account of the fact that he had suffered harassment at work having 'come out' as a homosexual. The tribunal held that it was within the range of reasonable responses for the employer to refuse to excuse drug-taking because of domestic or work difficulties. **6.90**

As mentioned above in relation to alcohol abuse, the employer should also proceed carefully where the employee asserts that his or her drug-taking is a direct result of problems at work, such as a heavy workload. The employer may be well advised to investigate and, if appropriate, provide support before making a decision whether to dismiss.

Finally, if an employer finds out about a previous drug offence and dismisses the employee as a result, the dismissal may be unfair under S.4(3)(b) of the Rehabilitation of Offenders Act 1974. If a conviction becomes 'spent' under that Act, dismissal for failing to disclose it is automatically unfair.

6.91 ## Drug and alcohol testing

As previously mentioned, employers have obligations under the common law and various statutes, most notably the Health and Safety at Work etc Act 1974, to keep their employees safe. For this reason, an employer's drug and alcohol policy may include provision for testing to ensure that employees are not acting under the influence of alcohol or drugs if this is likely to give rise to a risk to the health and safety of others. However, the extent to which employers have the right to require employees to undertake drug or alcohol testing is limited. Moreover, given the intrusiveness of the testing procedure, employers must tread carefully – the need to require the employee to submit to a drug or alcohol test must be balanced against the employee's right to respect for his or her privacy: the employer must not investigate drug or alcohol use (which, if it does take place, will usually occur away from work) unless there is real concern that, without such testing, safety or security at work may be compromised. Unreasonable requests to submit to a test may also leave the employer open to claims of unfair constructive dismissal on the ground that the employer's conduct has destroyed or seriously damaged the relationship of mutual trust and confidence between the employer and the employee. In addition, employers must not forget the need to comply with the provisions of the Data Protection Act 1998 when processing employees' health information – see IDS Employment Law Supplement, 'Data Protection' (2000), for more information.

Some employers reserve the contractual right to test their staff in contracts of employment. If an employee has accepted this and then refuses a test, he or she will be in breach of contract. Nevertheless, the employer should have regard to all the circumstances, including any mitigating factors, before dismissing the employee. In the absence of a contractual term, employers cannot require employees to take an alcohol or drug test unless there are legitimate safety concerns. Even where testing is justified, however, employers must get the employee's consent to obtain a sample each time a test is carried out. Otherwise this would constitute both assault and battery under the common law.

6.92 **'With cause' testing.** Testing for drug misuse or alcohol abuse in the workplace usually takes one of two forms: 'with cause' testing, where employers have a reasonable suspicion that an employee's performance is impaired through the use of alcohol or drugs that give rise to safety risks, or random testing – i.e. randomly testing a number of employees at regular intervals.

262

Where the employer has a reasonable suspicion that the employee has taken drugs or is intoxicated and that this impacts on safety at work, he may ask the employee to take a test. What amounts to 'reasonable suspicion' will obviously depend on the circumstances, but it is likely that there must be some signs to alert the employer that there may be substance abuse, e.g. lack of concentration, unusual irritability or aggression, a deterioration in relationships with colleagues, customers or management, increased short-term absenteeism, poor time-keeping or impaired job performance.

Even if the employer has evidence of alcohol or drug use, he should not make a hasty decision to dismiss where such use does not impact on work performance. The importance of a reasonable investigation in these circumstances is best illustrated by way of an example. In Nichols v Network Rail Infrastructure Ltd ET Case No.2802555/06, for instance, N, who started work at 8 am, was asked to take a breath test when a colleague noticed that his breath smelled of alcohol. In fact, N had drunk alcohol the previous evening. The test showed an alcohol level of 25mg per 100ml of blood, which was below the maximum permissible level of 29mg. Despite this, N was then asked to provide a urine sample. He agreed and was suspended pending the result. The urine sample was found to contain a level of alcohol in excess of the limit (55 mg). He was called to a hearing and dismissed.

An employment tribunal found that his dismissal was unfair. It noted that N's job was safety critical but found that there were mitigating factors – such as N's 'wholly worthy record of service' spanning 30 years – and that the employer failed to conduct a sufficient investigation. On the particular day in question, his conduct had not given any grounds for concern that he might be unfit for work and he had readily cooperated. Furthermore, the employer's rules provided that an alcohol level of 30–79mg may result in dismissal, whereas a level of 80mg or above will automatically result in dismissal. Thus, the employer was under an obligation to consider exercising discretion, but had failed to do so. It made no enquiry as to mitigating factors. It also failed to disclose to N the grounds the company had for believing that the disparity in the levels indicated by the breathalyser and the urine sample was not unusual. There was also a question as to whether the employer had the right to require a urine sample when the breath test was negative. All of these matters should have given the employer pause for thought. The sanction of dismissal was unreasonable.

6.93 But this case can be contrasted with McFarlane and ors v Alcoa Europe Flat Rolled Products ET Case No.1304583/05. There, the employer's drugs and alcohol policy, which was incorporated into employees' terms and conditions of employment, deemed impairment through drugs or alcohol to exist when employees were found to have consumed drugs or alcohol in an unsanctioned or unreported way (as determined by an appropriate test). Owing to this wording, the claimants, who tested positive for cannabis, were unable to argue that they were not impaired by drugs while at work. The tribunal found that,

263

on the employer's definition of 'impairment', the company was entitled to conclude that the claimants were impaired. Since they worked in a safety-critical environment, dismissal was within the band of reasonable responses.

This type of testing is also often carried out where has been a workplace accident or incident that has caused, or could have caused, a danger to health or safety at work and there is evidence that the employee's conduct has had some bearing on the incident. For example, in Morgan v Railtrack plc (above) the tribunal found that M's dismissal for refusing to submit to a drugs test following a signalling error was fair.

6.94   **Random testing.** Testing employees at random, usually for drugs, is particularly prevalent in safety-critical industries, such as transport or manufacturing. Even in industries where safety is paramount, however, employers must refrain from adopting a 'one-size-fits-all' approach to workplace testing. There is unlikely to be justification for testing the whole workforce where different employees pose different safety risks depending on the type of work they carry out. So says the Supplementary Guidance to the Information Commissioner's Employment Practices Code, intended to help employers comply with their obligations under the Data Protection Act 1998 (see under 'Data protection issues' below). This advises that: 'a train driver or signal engineer whose actions are impaired through exposure to alcohol or drugs would generally pose a significantly greater safety risk than would a ticket inspector or rail enquiries clerk. This difference in risk should be reflected in carrying out an impact assessment. Information about ticket inspectors or rail enquiries clerks should not be obtained through testing simply on the basis that "fairness" somehow requires that if drivers or signal engineers are tested, they should be tested as well' (Part 4.4.4).

The Code also notes that, as a general rule, testing should be designed to ensure safety at work. However, in exceptional circumstances, employers may be justified in testing to detect illegal use where this would 'breach the worker's contract of employment, conditions of employment or disciplinary rules, and cause serious damage to the employer's business, e.g. by substantially undermining public confidence in the integrity of a law enforcement agency' (Part 4.4.5 – Good Practice Recommendations). This may be relevant to some very senior employees, whose drug or alcohol use, if made public, would have serious implications for the employer's reputation or public standing.

6.95   An example of a straightforward fair dismissal for testing positive after a random drugs test is the EAT's decision in Roberts v British Railways Board EAT 648/96. There, the employer operated an alcohol and drugs policy which involved random testing of its staff – a policy which, the tribunal found, was 'of great importance so far as safety in the Railway network is concerned'. The policy stipulated that a positive test would result in the employee's dismissal. When the employee tested positive for cannabis in a random test, he was summarily dismissed. The tribunal ruled that the dismissal was fair, and the EAT later upheld that finding.

Although an employee dismissed as a result of being caught in this manner will normally be fairly dismissed, employers may still need to listen to his or her response and investigate the matter. In Gayle v Works 4 Ltd ET Case No.2300786/07 G, who is black and of Afro-Caribbean descent, was required by his employer, W4 Ltd, to periodically submit to random drugs tests. The result of one such test was negative, but the information supplied to W4 Ltd indicated that there were trace elements of cannabis and cocaine. Even though the information supplied by the testing company made clear that this did not equate to a positive test, W4 Ltd took the view that it indicated drug use, and required G to attend another test. The night before the second test, G was admitted to hospital and signed off work for two weeks. On his return, he was called to a disciplinary meeting for having failed to attend the second test. In a break from usual practice, R, W4 Ltd's managing director, dealt with the disciplinary hearing. Despite G producing an e-mail from the testing company confirming that the results of the first test were negative, a sick certificate and a letter from his GP explaining the condition that had caused his visit to hospital, R stated that he believed G was trying to avoid having the test because he had drugs in his system, and that G would have to be dismissed. R presented no evidence to back up his assertion, other than saying he had heard it through 'word of mouth'. Nor did he respond to the suggestion that his actions were influenced by G's race. The letter of dismissal that G eventually received not only referred to the missed test, but relied on the traces found in the original drugs test. The dismissal was found to be unfair (as well as discriminatory).

However, there may be circumstances where it is not necessary for the employer to hold formal disciplinary proceedings after a positive drug test. In Sutherland v Sonat Offshore (UK) Inc EAT 186/93 an employee who worked on an offshore rig was dismissed as a result of a positive drug screening without a formal disciplinary hearing. The EAT said that this was a case in which the employer was entitled to take the view that, from the time the urine sample was confirmed as positive, to hold a formal hearing would serve no useful purpose.

Human rights issues. Employers should be weary of unnecessarily invading the privacy of their employees as it can leave them open to legal challenges. The testing procedure itself is highly invasive. The obtaining of samples can be intrinsically degrading because employees will need to remove their outer clothing and urinate in secure rooms or lavatories in which the water supply has been turned off. Another person may have to be present at the test to ensure there is no specimen-tampering. Laboratory procedures can also entail invasions of personal privacy. Urinalysis reveals not only the presence of illegal drugs, but also the existence of many other physical and medical conditions, including genetic predisposition to disease, the use of prescription drugs and pregnancy. 6.96

As previously mentioned under 'General considerations – impact of the Human Rights Act 1998' above, since the introduction of the Human Rights Act 1998 (HRA), courts and tribunals have been required to interpret, so far as possible, Acts of Parliament and statutory instruments in a way that is compatible with the fundamental rights laid down in the European Convention on Human Rights (ECHR). This paves the way for claimants to argue before a tribunal that, where the circumstances of their dismissal fall within the ambit of a Convention right, the tribunal must consider, in determining the question of fairness under S.98(4) ERA, whether the employer unjustifiably interfered with the right in question. In the context of testing for alcohol or drugs at work, the Convention right most likely to be relied upon is the right to respect for private and family life in Article 8 of the ECHR. A tribunal might well have to consider whether the testing process undertaken by an employer interfered with the employee's right to respect for his or her private life under Article 8(1) and, if the answer is 'yes', go on to consider whether that interference was nevertheless justified by virtue of Article 8(2) in that it was necessary in a democratic society as being, for example, in the interests of public safety.

6.97 Given the possibility of such contentions, employers should ensure that their behaviour in the context of drink and drug testing is proportionate to the seriousness of the allegations against the employee, as any interference with the employee's private life will be permissible only if it is necessary to achieve a legitimate aim. This proposition is illustrated by the Privy Council's decision in Whitefield v General Medical Council 2003 IRLR 39, PC. In that case, the GMC had good reason to be concerned about a general practitioner's fitness to practice and accordingly required him to refrain from any drinking of alcohol whatsoever and to submit to random blood and urine testing as a condition of being permitted to continue practising as a GP. This, he argued, infringed his right under Article 8 of the Convention to respect for his private life, particularly in that it restricted his right to drink even in a social context. However, the Privy Council considered the requirement to refrain from drinking and to submit to random testing was not an interference under Article 8(1), as his right as a GP to an unrestricted social life had to give way to the wider public interest in ensuring that he did not present a risk to the public. Alternatively, even if the GMC's conditions did infringe the claimant's Article 8(1) rights, the Privy Council reasoned that, on the facts of the case, the infringement was a proportionate means of achieving a legitimate aim for the purposes of Article 8(2).

The impact of the HRA was also considered, albeit obiter, by the EAT in O'Flynn v Airlinks the Airport Coach Co Ltd EAT 0269/01. In that case, the claimant was a customer care assistant working in the private sector who was dismissed when she tested positive for cannabis following a random drug test – the employer operated a 'zero tolerance' policy with respect to drugs. The EAT held that the employee's claim of unfair dismissal was not affected by the HRA because the act she complained of took place before the HRA came into force. Nevertheless, the EAT went on to express its conclusions on what impact the HRA would have had if it had been in force and applicable to the case. In particular, the EAT thought that the policy only infringed the employee's private life to the extent that it required her to provide a urine sample as part of an established and unopposed random screening process, and also to the extent that the practical effects of the testing process meant that no drugs with persistent detectable characteristics could be taken by employees in their private time without jeopardising their employment. However, with regard to whether those infringements were 'proportionate' within the terms of Article 8(2), the EAT took the view that it was permissible for an employer to interfere with an employee's private life under the HRA to a degree that is in accordance with the law and necessary in a democratic society in the interests of, among other things, public safety. Where an employee has responsibility for public safety in the course of his or her employment, there could be no suggestion that drug or alcohol testing or a zero tolerance policy for safety reasons would be disproportionate.

Being obiter, the EAT's comments above are not binding on tribunals, though they are helpful in demonstrating the way that Article 8 issues may well interplay with the consideration of unfair dismissal in the context of drug and alcohol misconduct. As a general rule, employers should ensure that they do not use random drug testing as a means of policing private behaviour that is likely to have no discernible impact on job performance. Such behaviour may well amount to an interference with Article 8(1) that is not capable of justification under Article 8(2).

Smoking 6.98

Subject to some limited exemptions, smoking in enclosed or substantially enclosed workplaces became illegal anywhere in the United Kingdom on 1 July 2007. In addition to premises, the smoking ban applies to work vehicles that are used by more than one person and vehicles used by members of the public. The ban is provided for in the Health Act 2006 and accompanying regulations.

The Health Act 2006 creates two key offences, which incur criminal liability and are punishable by a fine. The first is committed by anyone who smokes in a smoke-free environment. The second may be committed by employers who fail to prevent smoking in a smoke-free place, although there are possible defences to this.

Given that employers are under a statutory obligation to prevent smoking in enclosed or substantially enclosed workplaces, taking disciplinary action against staff found to be flouting the smoking ban would seem to be important. However, the question of whether smoking in a smoke-free place of work justifies dismissal is not a foregone conclusion. Dismissal in these circumstances must be seen to have been within the range of reasonable responses of a reasonable employer. A number of questions are important in this context. First, is there a workplace smoking policy? If there is, is it explained in such a policy, or in the employees' contracts, that smoking in

267

a smoke-free place can amount to gross misconduct? Moreover, have the policy and its consequences been adequately explained to employees? If any of these questions is answered in the negative, an employer may have difficulty persuading a tribunal that a single instance of smoking warranted a dismissal without notice. An approach of giving a final written warning for a first offence, and dismissing if it is repeated, would seem less likely to lead to successful tribunal claims.

6.99 The following cases pre-date the introduction of the smoking ban but nonetheless provide useful examples of the factors tribunals will take into account when determining whether dismissal fell within the band of reasonable responses.

In Marks and Spencer plc v O'Connell EAT 230/95 an employee's summary dismissal for a single instance of smoking in front of a store, in contravention of staff regulations, was held to be unfair because the employer had not considered the individual circumstances of his case. This was so notwithstanding that the regulations provided for automatic dismissal for any employee found smoking in a prohibited area. Both the tribunal and the EAT dismissed the argument that the policy would be unworkable if exceptions were allowed, and held that, in circumstances where the employee was working a 12-hour night shift, the employer's response was unreasonable.

In Jones v B and Q plc ET Case No.1600705/05 C lit a cigar from the heat emanating from a toaster in a non-smoking room before retreating to the designated smoking area. The employer categorised this as gross misconduct and summarily dismissed him. A tribunal found that C was unfairly dismissed. It did not accept that his conduct had posed a significant risk of injury to other employees on the premises. Moreover, the smoking room was immediately next door to the designated non-smoking area, and there was no evidence of any actual harm or injury to any employee or damage to the premises having arisen from his action. Although smoking in the non-smoking area would have caused offence to a non-smoker, the amount of smoking that had taken place there was transitory. In all the circumstances, dismissal fell outside the band of reasonable responses.

That said, it may still be within the range of reasonable responses to dismiss a person for smoking in contravention of a ban even where there are strong mitigating factors. In Singh v Walkers Snack Foods Ltd EAT 412/97, for example, the claimant was fairly dismissed for smoking in a place where smoking was banned despite the fact that he had worked there for 18 years, had an unblemished record, had just heard news of his two brothers' ill health and was supported by a petition signed by 75 per cent of the workforce. The EAT said that although its sympathy lay with the claimant, the employer had taken all these mitigating factors into account and dismissal was within the range of reasonable responses – even if it was on the harsh side.

Health and safety. There are two specific situations in which a dismissal for smoking in a smoke-free place will inevitably be held to be fair – these are where smoking is banned for health and safety or for hygiene reasons. Some examples:

6.100

- **O'Hara v Avana Bakeries** ET Case No.711/86 (a case pre-dating the smoking ban): a bakery worker was dismissed after being caught smoking in contravention of a 'no smoking' rule. An employment tribunal found the dismissal to be fair, stressing that, in a company manufacturing fresh foods, it was a matter of great importance that foreign bodies such as cigarette ends did not find their way into the food. There were signs prominently displayed which prohibited smoking everywhere but in the canteen and notices had been issued stating that employees caught smoking would be instantly dismissed. Although the policy had been flouted in the past, the company had since moved to a strict observance of the ban; something, the tribunal said, that the employer should have made clear to employees. However, at the time of his misbehaviour, the employee had been well aware of the implications of illicit smoking and dismissal was fair

- **Newton v R Manners and Sons** ET Case No.2504125/06 (again, this case pre-dates the smoking ban): RM operated a very strict policy about smoking on company premises and in company vehicles, and the disciplinary procedures stated breach of the no-smoking policy constituted gross misconduct. One afternoon, N was seen smoking a cigarette in a company vehicle. Following an investigation, N was called to a disciplinary hearing and summarily dismissed for breach of the no-smoking policy, even though he insisted that it was the first and only time he had smoked in a vehicle. An employment tribunal found that N was fairly dismissed. Although this was undoubtedly a harsh policy, it seemed that any employee who took a single puff on a cigarette in a company vehicle would be liable for dismissal. As the company was a food-handling business, dismissal did not fall outside the range of reasonable responses

- **Smith v Michelin Tyre plc** ET Case No.100726/07: the employer's decision to dismiss a long-serving employee for a one-off breach of a workplace smoking policy was fair. The employer had always prohibited smoking, except in authorised areas, because of the use of flammable products in its production process. Weighing the employee's personal circumstances against the importance of the policy in preserving the employer's business, its property and the lives of the other staff, dismissal was a reasonable response.

Constructive dismissal. Prior to the introduction of the smoking ban, a number of employees raised the argument that, since they had been allowed to smoke for a considerable amount of time, they had an implied term in their contracts of employment allowing them to smoke. This issue was dealt with by the EAT in the constructive dismissal case of Dryden v Greater Glasgow Health

6.101

269

Board 1992 IRLR 469, EAT. There, it held that there was no implied term in the employee's contract entitling her to facilities enabling her to smoke at work, and that a total ban on smoking on the employer's premises was a 'works rule' within the scope of the employment contract, rather than a unilateral variation of that contract. Moreover, the EAT held that 'where a rule is introduced for a legitimate purpose, the fact that it bears hardly on a particular employee does not, in our view, justify an inference that the employer has acted in such a way as to repudiate the contract'.

The likely upshot of Dryden is that an employee who smokes will struggle to show that the introduction of a smoking ban amounts to his or her employer conducting itself in a manner calculated or likely to erode the trust and confidence between employee and employer. A constructive dismissal claim founded on the introduction of a smoking ban would be much more likely to succeed if it focused on an employer's method of implementation rather than on the ban itself. Even a total ban on smoking on the premises can be said to have a legitimate purpose, but if it is introduced without consultation or advance warning, and no provision is made for employees to adapt, the employer's conduct could be viewed as repudiatory.

6.102 While the contract of employment offers little relief to employees struggling to cope with the smoking ban, it does offer assistance to non-smokers. There is a well-established implied term in every contract of employment that an employer must provide a safe working environment. Extending this theme, the EAT in Waltons and Morse v Dorrington 1997 IRLR 488, EAT, has held that an implied term exists to the effect that an employer must provide a working environment that is reasonably tolerable – including the quality of air – for the performance of its employees' duties. Given that the dangers of passive smoking are substantial, an employee who is exposed to smoke in the workplace and whose employer does not respond to his or her concerns could rely on this implied term. In that particular case, D was a secretary who worked in offices where members of staff were allowed to smoke, and had communicated to her employer that she was not comfortable working in a smoky environment. Adjustments were made whereby the secretaries were only allowed to smoke in a designated room, and other staff only in their offices, but the location of the designated room meant that the changes did not reduce D's exposure to smoke. D resigned and claimed unfair constructive dismissal. Upholding her claim, the tribunal and the EAT both accepted that the employer's failure to remedy her situation had amounted to a repudiatory breach of its contractual obligations, and that D, having given the new arrangements a chance to work, had resigned in response to that breach.

While the factual circumstances of D's case – smoking taking place in an office – are not likely to recur following the introduction of the smoking ban, the case is likely to be of relevance to claims made by employees who either find themselves exposed to smoke which is entering their workplace from outdoors, or who perform their duties outdoors in a smoke-filled environment. As a result, employers need to think carefully about where to permit smoking in parts of the workplace that are not enclosed or substantially enclosed – for example, a designated smoking area that sits immediately below an open window could expose staff working near that window to a large amount of smoke.

Incapacity. Damage to health through smoking could result in an employee becoming unfit for work, thus providing grounds for dismissal for incapacity (see Chapter 5). Even where a dismissal for incapacity is found to be unfair, a tribunal may reduce the compensation on account of the employee's contributory fault in having brought the illness upon him or herself – Parrott v Yorkshire Electricity Board 1972 IRLR 75, ET. **6.103**

Employee's attitude **6.104**

The general rule as stated in the revised Acas Code of Practice on Discipline and Grievance Procedures is that, except in cases of gross misconduct, employees should never be dismissed for a first disciplinary offence. The House of Lords made it clear in Polkey v AE Dayton Services Ltd 1988 ICR 142, HL, that an exception will only be permitted when the employer has formed a considered and reasonable view that a warning would be 'utterly useless' or 'futile'.

Thus, where employees adopt an intransigent or bloody-minded attitude towards their employer, it will only be fair to dismiss without warning or a chance to explain where the attitude is a clear and considered view and not merely the result of a passing emotion. In such cases, said the NIRC in James v Waltham Holy Cross UDC 1973 ICR 398, NIRC, 'there can be no point in giving [the employee] an opportunity of restating a view the expression of which led to the decision to dismiss'. But the NIRC warned that employers 'should be slow to conclude that an opportunity to reflect and a subsequent opportunity to explain could in no circumstances produce a changed situation in which dismissal would be unnecessary'.

The giving of a warning may well focus the mind and lead to the adoption of a more realistic attitude to change on the part of the employee. As the EAT commented in Foster v Somerset County Council EAT 0355/03, attitude is 'something which was potentially capable of change, however unlikely it may have appeared to be'.

But sometimes warnings will have no effect whatsoever. In Mintoft v Armstrong Massey Ltd t/a UAC Motors of Scarborough EAT 516/80, for instance, an experienced sales manager, M, persistently refused to comply with his employer's paperwork procedures (detailed recording of faults and repairs in second-hand cars), introduced so that the garage could give warranties with some degree of confidence. In August and November 1979 he was sent letters requiring him to **6.105**

271

follow these procedures. In late March 1980 he received another letter stating that there had been no improvement and warning of dismissal if there was another occurrence. He went sick a few days later and when he returned was met with criticism about the state of the used cars. In the presence of the managing director M was abusive to his own branch manager, restated his dislike of the system and said in clear terms that he was not prepared to operate it. He was then dismissed. The tribunal found that M's attitude was such that he was never going to change his view about the system. The EAT upheld the tribunal's finding of fair dismissal. It rejected the argument that it was unfair not to give M an opportunity to change his ways in compliance with the March warning. This was because M had made it plain he was not going to operate the procedure: 'It is really upon that attitude at that meeting and previously that the company decided to dismiss. It seems to us, in the light of the status of these two men in the depot, that the... tribunal was perfectly entitled to conclude that a further period would not have achieved any result.'

Nor will the employer necessarily act unreasonably by not giving the employee a chance to improve. In Perkin v St George's Healthcare NHS Trust 2006 ICR 617, CA, the employee's style of management seriously undermined the proper running of the healthcare trust at a most senior level, and adversely reflected on the trust both internally and externally. A tribunal found – and the EAT and the Court of Appeal both subsequently agreed – that he was unlikely to change his behaviour. In the circumstances, dismissal was a reasonable response. (Note that the tribunal went on to find the dismissal procedurally unfair but, given that there was a 100 per cent chance that he would have been dismissed even if a fair procedure had been followed and that he was entirely to blame for his dismissal, his compensation was reduced to nil.) Another interesting point made in this case is that 'personality' is not a potentially fair reason for dismissal under S.98, although the person's personality can manifest itself in a way that can bring it within the 'conduct' category.

6.106 **Reason for intransigence or inflexibility.** Tribunals should have regard to the cause of the employee's intransigent attitude when deciding whether it was fair to dismiss him or her for adopting it. In Mock v Glamorgan Aluminium Co Ltd EAT 493/80 it was the managing director's initial fundamental breach of contract (assault on M) that triggered M's unyielding attitude; it was this that destroyed the trust and good faith essential in employment contracts, not M's attitude, so the dismissal was unfair. In such cases, however, the employee's non-conciliatory attitude might be a factor justifying a reduction in compensation.

6.107 **Attitude to customers.** Dismissal may be fair where an employee's non-cooperation with clients puts the business at risk, as in AJ Dunning and Sons (Shopfitters) Ltd v Jacomb 1973 ICR 448, NIRC, where a contracts manager fell out with a number of the company's major clients. A tribunal found the dismissal unfair for lack of warning. The NIRC disagreed on appeal. The evidence showed that the manager knew his conduct was putting his job in jeopardy, and that he was incapable of changing.

Non-cooperation between employees. Employers who are faced with the problem of employees who refuse to cooperate with each other should take reasonable steps to try to improve the relationship and satisfy themselves that the situation is irredeemable before deciding that dismissal is the only answer – Turner v Vestric Ltd 1980 ICR 528, EAT.

6.108

Where employers' attempts to conciliate fail, dismissal is likely to be fair, especially where the conflict manifests itself in an act of gross misconduct. Thus in Greaves v London Borough of Newham EAT 673/82 G's dismissal for sending her employer a list of serious and unsubstantiated allegations about her boss was fair, even though she was not totally to blame for the differences that had arisen between them.

Allegations of bullying, harassment or discriminatory conduct against an employee may lead to a fair dismissal on conduct grounds. Much will depend on the circumstances. In Vaux Breweries Ltd v McNaughton EAT 937/98 M was dismissed when he admitted to certain allegations of sexual harassment, such as saying 'squeeze me' to female members of staff who walked by and talking of 'thrashing' staff members if they did something wrong. The EAT held that it was within the range of reasonable responses for an employer, faced with such admissions in a case involving young female members of staff who left employment complaining of sexual harassment by a manager of a unit employing only women, to impose the sanction of dismissal. The fact that another employer might reasonably have issued a warning was beside the point.

Even one-off or relatively minor incidents of racist behaviour may be grounds for a fair dismissal. In Price v Uxbridge College ET Case No. 3318423/06 P was accused of using the expression 'monkey boy' three times when referring to an Asian colleague. She denied this, but the employer decided to dismiss, taking into account the fact that she had a propensity to use nicknames, discrepancies in her evidence and her conduct generally. P maintained that the dismissal was unfair, and pointed to the fact that a colleague who had placed racially offensive words on the employer's intranet was not dismissed. The tribunal found her dismissal fair: the employer had reasonable grounds for concluding that P was guilty of making the offending remark; it followed a fair procedure; and against the background of the culture of racial tolerance and equality of opportunity, which was the mainstay of the employer as an educational institution, it acted reasonably in treating the words used as racist and gross misconduct. Moreover, the employer had significant reasons for treating P differently from the way the other employee had been treated. That employee had not directed offensive remarks against a specific individual, and had recognised the impropriety of her conduct, made a remorseful admission and apologised. By contrast, P equivocated between denial and attempts at justification.

6.109

273

While an employee's unacceptable behaviour, in clear breach of workplace policies, may justify a decision to dismiss, an employer's failure to take account of mitigating factors is likely to take the employer's decision outside the range of reasonable responses open to it. So, in Heaney v Lloyds TSB Bank plc ET Case No.2402140/06 the tribunal found that the employer had unfairly dismissed H after four – out of a total of 11 – allegations of harassment against him were found proven. H had 31 years' unblemished service and the last matter complained of had taken place a year earlier and there had been no further blameworthy conduct since then. However, his compensation was reduced by 30 per cent to take account of H's contributory conduct.

6.110 Personal appearance

Employers are entitled to a large measure of discretion in controlling their company's image, including the appearance of staff, especially when their duties bring them into contact with the public or where their mode of dress affects hygiene or safety standards. Even if no rules are laid down about this, there is likely to be an implied term that employees wear suitable and acceptable clothes at work and no ornaments or articles of jewellery that endanger them or their fellow-workers or offend against commonly accepted standards.

A balance must be struck between the interests of the business and the reasonable freedom of the employee, said the EAT in Boychuk v HJ Symons Holdings Ltd 1977 IRLR 395, EAT. When striking that balance, tribunals will take into account factors such as:

● the employer's reasons for the requirements

● whether the requirements are spelled out in the contract

● the employee's reason for objecting

● the way the employer sets about enforcing the standard he insists on.

In every case the tribunal will examine the facts to see whether the needs of the business justify the appearance rule. Tribunals have been quite bold in asserting their own view of what is reasonable – and in some cases putting the employer's view down to mere prejudice or excessive fussiness. However, what they cannot do is dictate the standards they would have allowed had they been in the employer's shoes.

6.111 **Fitting the image to the business.** This is an area of commercial judgement and there will be a range of views a reasonable employer might take. In Eales v Halfords Ltd ET Case No.25468/80 E was told at his interview that there were strict dress rules – he must wear sensible black or brown shoes, dark trousers of conservative cut, collar and tie. He committed occasional minor transgressions by wearing light trousers or shoes, but the last straw came when he dyed his hair yellow. The tribunal thought the employer had rather over-estimated the smartness required to serve in a bicycle shop in Mansfield and found E's dismissal unfair. In Higham v International Stores COET 589/50, on the other hand, H wore sandals, no socks and no tie to work. After warnings he was dismissed on the ground that his standard of dress in a middle-class store was likely to alienate customers.

Uniform rules. Tribunals are likely to accept that in service or retail industries a uniform is reasonably necessary – either to ensure that the employee can be readily identified by the customer (e.g. flight attendants, hotel door-keepers, etc) or simply to project the image of the company. Refusal to wear the appropriate uniform may result in dismissal. In Mayor v Merseyside Passenger Transport Executive ET Case No.30017/86 M, a bus driver required to wear an authorised uniform, was given a final written warning for wearing a Father Christmas outfit at Christmas time. He was subsequently dismissed for wearing a non-regulation shirt with no collar and very short sleeves. The tribunal found the dismissal fair, holding that the employer was entitled to take into account his pattern of disobedience. However, exceptions may need to be made for individual employees. For example, in Malik v British Home Stores COET 987/12, a race discrimination case, the tribunal thought the department store should have permitted a Muslim woman to wear trousers instead of a skirt under the uniform overall.

6.112

Offending other employees or customers. In Lengthorn v RA Bird and Co Ltd ET Case No.11522/83 the claimant was fairly dismissed after his employer received complaints from shop customers about prominent lovebites on his neck. Despite warnings and suggestions that he wear a roll-neck sweater the employee refused to treat the matter seriously, leaving his employer with little alternative but to sack him.

6.113

Similarly, in the Boychuk case (above), the employee was dismissed after warnings and discussions for persisting in wearing lesbian badges. The EAT held that it was within the employer's discretion to forbid badges that could be expected to be offensive to fellow employees and customers. But, it continued, 'that does not mean that an employer, by a foolish or unreasonable judgement of what could be expected to be offensive, can impose some unreasonable restriction. It does mean that a reasonable employer, who after all is ultimately responsible for the interests of the business, can be allowed to decide what, upon reflection and mature consideration, could be offensive.' The employer can act on his judgement without waiting to see whether in fact offence is taken.

Safety and hygiene. Tribunals are sympathetic to employers seeking to impose safety rules. However, they must first investigate any complaints the

6.114

275

employee might have and, if possible, remedy such grievances before resorting to discipline – British Aircraft Corporation Ltd v Austin 1978 IRLR 332, EAT (where the employee complained about the safety glasses provided and refused to wear them). In Kirkcaldy District Council v Baxter EAT 540/78 the EAT held that it was unreasonable to expect a dustman to continue working in driving rain for which inadequate protective clothing was provided: his demands for a fresh set were reasonable and dismissal was unfair.

The standard of personal hygiene required of an employee may be influenced by a number of factors including the nature of the job; the product, if any; the process of production itself; and the reasonable demands of fellow employees. In Singh v RHM Bakeries (Southern) Ltd EAT 818/77 the EAT upheld the tribunal's decision that the employee, whose job involved handling food, was fairly dismissed for breaking a clear company rule against wearing beards imposed in the interests of hygiene. And in O'Boyle v British Telecommunications ET Case No.35813/81 the employee was fairly dismissed after failing to heed warnings to improve his personal hygiene. Other employees had made numerous complaints that they could no longer work with or alongside him because of his body odour, so something had to be done.

6.115 **Employee's objections.** In Catharell v Glyn Nuttall Ltd ET Case No.7935/81, where the employer's dismissal of an apprentice electrician for refusing to have his long hair cut was held to be unfair, the tribunal said 'as long as his hair length was not detrimental to the [employer's] business or his performance of his duties, [he] was entitled to determine for himself the personal question'. In general, the employee's objections have to be balanced against the employer's reasons for the rule in question and some objections weigh more heavily than others. Objections based on religious dress conventions, for instance, are taken very seriously indeed and may outweigh an employer's interest in uniformity. Any physical discomfort may also be a good reason for refusing to comply – Kirkcaldy District Council v Baxter (above).

6.116 **Handling appearance problems**
Employees' dress and appearance at work can be a sensitive issue (particularly as it is not merely restricted to clothing but may also cover, for example, styles and length of hair, piercings and make-up). Employers must therefore tread carefully when this issue arises in their workplace. The following procedural steps should be followed.

6.117 **Make the position clear.** Except in obvious cases, employees cannot be expected to realise that their appearance is unsuitable unless they are told what the company's policy is. An employee who refuses to comply should be told of the employer's reasons, or he or she may reasonably believe there is no good reason for the rules. In Catharell v Glyn Nuttall Ltd (above) the employer had conveyed the impression that the objection to long hair was on 'purely aesthetic grounds'.

Interpret the rules reasonably. In Kirkcaldy District Council v Baxter (above) the employer could not rely on a rule that dustmen would work in inclement weather if appropriate clothing was provided, because the protective clothing provided was in fact letting in water and had ceased to be 'appropriate'.

6.118

Consult on new rules. In Teagle v Whelton Sinclair COET 947/47 new rules were introduced only after the claimant had worked in the office for two years. That this was done by means of a notice, unheralded by any discussions, was a major factor leading to the finding of unfairness. Similarly, in Leaper and anor v Delta Hotels Ltd t/a Sheraton Inn ET Case Nos.S/3799/76 and 3835/76 a new uniform (which the employees thought hideous) was produced as a fait accompli after the employees had been promised they would not have to wear anything they disliked. Dismissal was held to be unfair.

6.119

Investigate alleged breaches. In Eales v Halfords Ltd (above) the district superintendent authorised dismissal for 'yellow' dyed hair without going to see the employee for himself. The tribunal called this lapse 'unforgivable'. If he had interviewed the employee, he would have discovered that he had permission to dye his hair blond and that he was prepared to re-dye it darker.

6.120

Warn and discuss before dismissing. It must be very rare that a clothing offence amounts to gross misconduct so that dismissal for a single offence is justified. On the other hand, a settled determination to disobey a reasonable rule is likely to justify dismissal in the absence of very good reasons for objecting. So this is an area where a procedure makes all the difference. Two examples:

6.121

- **Rowntree v Lakeside Country Club Ltd** ET Case No.16409/78: R had been employed as a barmaid (with no dress restrictions) for nearly a year before she was told to change out of her jeans, which she did. A few weeks later she wore them again and was dismissed. The tribunal said the order not to wear jeans was not within the terms of R's contract, but anyway she should not have been dismissed for a single offence

- **Gavin v Paul Dean (Football and Turf Accountant) Ltd** ET Case No.2406940/97: G was dismissed for not complying with the dress code, which she said was too expensive. The dismissal was unfair because the employer did not take full account of G's personal circumstances or consider making a financial contribution as it had with other employees. It also failed to warn her of the risk of dismissal and ignored a possible compromise she put forward.

Note that dress rules that discriminate, either directly or indirectly, on grounds of sex, race, disability, religion or belief, sexual orientation or age may fall foul of anti-discrimination legislation – see IDS Employment Law Handbooks, 'Sex Discrimination' (2008), 'Race and Religion Discrimination' (2004), and 'Disability Discrimination' (2002), and IDS Employment Law Supplements, 'Sexual Orientation Discrimination' (2004) and 'Age Discrimination' (2006).

277

6.122 Sleeping on duty

By itself, sleeping on duty, although misconduct, is usually insufficient to ground a fair dismissal, although it may attract a very severe warning – McDonagh v Johnson and Nephew (Manchester) Ltd EAT 140/78. Additional factors are taken into account by tribunals. These include whether the employer has a clear rule on the matter known to all those affected – see, for example, Ayub v Vauxhall Motors Ltd 1978 IRLR 428, ET – although the absence of such a rule will not necessarily render the dismissal unfair; all the circumstances must be considered. The following are all relevant factors in considering the reasonableness of a decision to dismiss for this type of misconduct.

6.123 **Consistency in applying the rule or practice.** In Olender and ors v IMI Yorkshire Imperial Ltd ET Case No.25296/80 a tribunal found it unfair to dismiss senior and otherwise satisfactory employees for sleeping on duty where another employee with less service had been treated differently.

6.124 **The employee's work record.** In Singh v British Railways Engineering Ltd COET 1025/217 it was not unfair to dismiss the employee for sleeping away from his workplace while on duty, particularly in view of his poor employment record. However, the employer's failure to take into account the employee's satisfactory service was an important consideration in the Olender case (above).

Note that sleeping on duty is sometimes the 'last straw' that, added to an indifferent record, puts an end to the employer's patience (see the Singh case above). However, previous disciplinary warnings will not necessarily have this cumulative effect. In Lonrho Textiles Ltd v Cryan EAT 737/78 a serious warning for dangerous skylarking which could, on its own, have justified dismissal, was not sufficient background for such a sanction when the same employee was caught sleeping on duty. His compensation was, however, cut by 50 per cent.

6.125 **Length of service.** An employee's long and unblemished service should always be considered by the employer before taking the decision to dismiss. In Vargich v Newage International Ltd ET Case No. 1900763/03 the dismissal of the claimant was unfair given his 18 years of unblemished service, a recent bereavement and the fact that no harm was caused. Similarly, in Newton and anor v Ryder plc ET Case Nos.2801633/06 and 2801676/06 the employer failed to take into account the claimants' length of service (17 years) and clean disciplinary record. However, the fact that an employee has long service and a clean work record may not render a dismissal for sleeping on duty unfair where serious damage is caused or safety is prejudiced – Crosby v United Molasses Co Ltd ET Case No.23761/81.

6.126 **Health and safety.** Employers should be wary of treating sleeping while on duty as automatically warranting dismissal without looking into all the

278

circumstances. In particular, the nature of the work and the employee's working hours may alert the employer that there are underlying health and safety issues that need to be addressed before any such decision can be taken. This is especially important where the employee in question is working at night. An example:

- **Newton and anor v Ryder plc** ET Case Nos.2801633/06 and 2801676/06: N and M, who worked as mechanics, were dismissed for sleeping while on duty – an offence specified in the employee handbook as gross misconduct. They admitted that they would occasionally nod off during the night, but maintained that they had not set out deliberately to sleep: when they stopped doing manual work and sat down to do paperwork, they would occasionally drop off for a few minutes or occasionally for up to 20 minutes. The tribunal found the dismissals unfair. A reasonable employer would have made a distinction between a premeditated plan to go to sleep – e.g. making up a bed or going off to a quiet corner – or simply dropping off while working. Moreover, N had previously raised with R plc the difficulty of working nights and the need to review arrangements for breaks. A reasonable employer would have tackled the issue primarily as a health and safety matter.

Conversely, where safety is prejudiced or serious damage is caused as a result of the employee falling asleep, the employee's dismissal is likely to be fair. So, for example, in Crosby v United Molasses Co Ltd ET Case No.23761/81 a tribunal found that it was fair to dismiss a good and willing employee with long service for falling asleep on duty when this caused some £10,000 worth of damage.

Theft, dishonesty and fraudulent conduct   6.127

It is generally accepted that theft and fraud is serious misconduct that justifies summary dismissal at common law. Another consideration is that such conduct may well be criminal behaviour, sometimes leading to a separate and parallel investigation by the police and possibly to criminal charges. Where this happens, an array of additional considerations come into play. These are considered under 'Criminal offences at work' below. In this section, we focus on the issues that are specifically relevant to ensuring that dismissal for theft and similar misconduct is fair.

Theft offences. Not all dismissals for theft will necessarily be fair. It depends   6.128
on the circumstances. In one case, an employee with 15 years' blameless service was seen wearing the supervisor's watch, which had gone missing some six months previously. His dismissal was held to be unfair partly because of his record, but also because a distinction was drawn between theft from the employer, which breaches the confidence between employer and employee, and other theft – for example, from a fellow employee – which will

279

not always call for such drastic action – Johnson Matthey Metals Ltd v Harding 1978 IRLR 248, EAT.

Although some dismissals for minor thefts will be unfair, there are circumstances where an employer would be justified in dismissing an employee for even the most petty of crimes. In Gamestec Leisure Ltd v Magee EAT 0419/02 the employer supplied fruit machines to the licensed retail trade. It was a cash-based business requiring the highest possible standards from employees who, like the claimant, had unsupervised access to the money in the machines. The employer was informed by two licensees that there was a cash discrepancy at two sites, of £8 and £3 respectively. The claimant was the service engineer responsible for both sites. He admitted taking £3 from one machine but claimed he put it back. He explained the £8 discrepancy on the presence of children who were fiddling with his tool box. On this basis, the employer disregarded the £8 discrepancy but considered that the £3 discrepancy amounted to either theft or gross negligence. M was dismissed. The EAT overturned the decision of the tribunal and found that dismissal was within the range of reasonable responses.

6.129 **Dishonesty.** Dishonest conduct may be less clear-cut than theft. In John Lewis plc v Coyne 2001 IRLR 139, EAT, the employee was dismissed for making personal calls without permission, which was characterised as dishonesty by the employer in resulting disciplinary proceedings. The employer's rules indicated that unauthorised personal calls would be treated very seriously. The EAT, however, stated that there are two aspects to dishonesty: one objective, one subjective. First, one must decide whether according to the ordinary standards of reasonable and honest people what was done was dishonest. Secondly, one must consider whether the person concerned must have realised that what he or she was doing was by those standards dishonest. In many cases, it will be obvious. However, it was not necessarily obvious that using the employer's phone for personal reasons was dishonest. Much would depend on the circumstances of the case, which the employer did not investigate in any way. Thus, the dismissal was unfair.

6.130 **Fraudulent conduct.** Almost all disciplinary procedures stipulate that clocking offences will be treated as gross misconduct likely to result in summary dismissal. In Rotherham Engineering Services Ltd v Harrison EAT 735/77 H, a charge-hand, left work 1½ hours early, even though he was well aware that his employer regarded such an offence as serious. He had arranged with his gang for them to clock him out at the proper time. The EAT held his dismissal fair, saying it was obliged to approach the case on the basis 'that clocking offences must be regarded by any employer and indeed by any tribunal as serious offences'.

But not all dismissals for fraudulent conduct will be automatically fair. Dishonesty at the 'lower end of the spectrum' might, in the light of surrounding circumstances, merit a warning instead. Tribunals must look at the equity of the case and at the individual facts involved before deciding what lies within the band of reasonable responses – Schering Chemicals Ltd v Maginn EAT 180/83. Despite this, tribunals must be careful not to fall into the trap of substituting their own decision for that of the reasonable employer. In Anglian Home Improvements Ltd v Kelly 2005 ICR 242, CA, the Court of Appeal overturned the decision of the tribunal for falling into this error. The tribunal had erred in holding that K's conduct in massaging financial records in order to meet his targets was not serious enough to merit dismissal, despite the fact that the employer's rules held that deliberate falsification of records was gross misconduct.

6.131 Even where the employee does not gain from his or her ostensibly fraudulent conduct, it may so undermine the employer's confidence that dismissal will be fair – AEI Cables Ltd v McLay 1980 IRLR 84, Ct Sess (Inner House). This is particularly true in those occupations where stringent rules regarding the use and control of monies are essential and relations between management and staff require trust and good faith. In Mecca Leisure Ltd v Haggerty and ors EAT 324–6/83, for example, it was fair to dismiss a bingo hall manager for transferring cash to another branch to cover a colleague's float shortage until it could be replaced after the weekend. He was a senior employee entrusted with considerable amounts of money and had breached his employer's trust and confidence. Where, however, the employee is unaware that what he or she is doing is dishonest it may be unreasonable to dismiss without a warning, although again much depends on the circumstances of the case – Rees v Borough of Afan EAT 461/82.

Employees often seem to treat fiddling expenses as a perk rather than gross misconduct. However, even if the employee genuinely believes he or she is entitled to the sums wrongly claimed, dismissal is often fair – especially if the employee is in a position of trust. In John Lewis and Co Ltd v Smith EAT 289/81 S was dismissed after she submitted an expenses slip for a sum in excess of the amount actually incurred, even though the employer accepted she might have genuinely believed that she was in some sense entitled to the extra money. The EAT asked 'how could the employer, after what [S] had allowed herself to do... trust her in a position in which not only was her own integrity of paramount importance, but in which she was responsible for the proper working of the machinery designed to ensure the integrity of others?' and held the dismissal fair.

Unauthorised use of computers

6.132

Given the widespread use of the internet and e-mail as work tools, employers would be well-advised to put in place rules regarding their use. This is particularly important as e-mails sent from work computers can expose the company to liability for discrimination and/or defamation. As is the case with all disciplinary rules, it is important that employees are made aware of them and told that dismissal can result from breach.

Acas has produced an advice leaflet, 'Internet and e-mail policies', which gives guidance on how to draw up an effective computer use policy. It stresses the importance of tailoring the policy to the needs and the culture of the individual workplace, setting out clearly the permitted uses of IT equipment at work as well as outlining the consequences for breach. The policy should also make transparent any monitoring or interception that might be lawfully undertaken and the reasons for such monitoring. For more information on the legal pitfalls to be avoided when drawing up a computer use policy, see IDS Employment Law Supplement, 'Employee Privacy in the Workplace' (2001), Chapter 5, 'Computer use, the Internet and e-mail'. This is also an area where human rights issues may come into play, notably Article 8 (the right to respect for private and family life) and Article 10 (the right to freedom of expression) of the European Convention on Human Rights. These issues are briefly mentioned under 'Social networking and "blogging"' below, but are discussed in more detail under 'General considerations – impact of the Human Rights Act 1988' above.

The most common types of unauthorised use of computers in the workplace that may, after a reasonable investigation, result in a fair dismissal are discussed below.

6.133   **Accessing pornographic material**
Unless it is of an obscene nature, the mere downloading of 'ordinary' pornography by an employee at work will not necessarily be regarded by an employment tribunal as amounting to gross misconduct justifying summary dismissal. However, if employees have been informed as part of a computer use policy that any time spent downloading or circulating pornography will be regarded as a dismissible offence, it is likely to be fair – subject to proper investigation and disciplinary procedures – to dismiss an employee, even for a first offence. Contrast the following two cases:

- **London Borough of Hillingdon v Thomas** EAT 1317/01: the EAT overturned the finding of the tribunal that the summary dismissal of T for accessing pornography on the employer's facilities and during work time was unfair. The categorisation of the offence as gross misconduct was within the range of reasonable responses. Although the employer had no IT policy in place and the disciplinary procedure generally characterised this type of conduct as misconduct and not gross misconduct, the disciplinary procedure went on to state that it may be viewed as gross misconduct 'according to the circumstances or the position which the employee held'

- **Royal Bank of Scotland v Goudie** EAT 0693/03: G was disciplined and dismissed for breaching the employer's IT security policy by sending via external e-mails certain images that the employer considered pornographic. The bank used an internal matrix to categorise images it considered offensive. Categories in the mid-range could be considered as either gross misconduct or misconduct. The matrix also set out certain mitigating factors that might be taken into account. However, the matrix was not disclosed to G and she did not have the opportunity to test the application of the criteria to the circumstances of her case during the disciplinary process. The EAT upheld the finding of a tribunal that her dismissal was unfair. The matrix had a direct impact on the outcome of the disciplinary process and it was clearly important for the employee to be aware of how the employer graded the material and the sanctions it applied, together with possible mitigating factors.

Even where there is evidence that the employee accessed pornographic material on a work computer in clear breach of the computer use policy, an employer who fails to conduct a reasonable investigation into the incident will do so at its own peril. In particular, the employer should not be distracted by the 'conduct' label into thinking that no medical evidence needs to be considered where the employee relies on a medical condition to explain or excuse his or her misconduct. **6.134**

In City of Edinburgh Council v Dickson EAT 0038/09 the employee, who was employed as a community learning and development worker, was found in the school's community computer suite watching pornographic images. A disciplinary investigation revealed that on the same morning he had visited a magazine website containing inappropriate sexual imagery. The employee said that he had no recollection of either incident but, if they had occurred, his behaviour must have been the result of a hypoglycaemic episode caused by his diabetes. At the disciplinary hearing, his explanation for his behaviour was rejected and he was summarily dismissed. An employment tribunal found that the employee had been unfairly dismissed, and the EAT agreed. The employer had rejected his explanation without investigating or understanding his medical condition (he had type one diabetes, which was poorly controlled). Furthermore, it had taken into account the uninformed opinion of a third party – namely, the HR adviser's pharmacist wife – and dismissed the informed opinion of the employer's occupational health doctor. By rejecting the evidence that was capable of explaining the employee's behaviour and memory loss, the employer had come to a decision that no reasonable employer could have reached.

Sending offensive images or jokes **6.135**

Employers should always be concerned about their employees' behaviour where it has the potential to cause upset either to a fellow employee or a client or customer, as it will be vicariously liable for any harassment caused. An employer's computer use policy should therefore clearly set out that, for example, the sending of images or jokes that could be considered offensive by the recipient will not be condoned. However, where there is evidence that the policy has not been applied stringently, it is unlikely to be of much assistance

283

to an employer in defending an unfair dismissal claim. In Robinson v Network IT Recruitment Ltd ET Case No.2901763/04, for example, the employee produced evidence that 'jokey' e-mails, some of which the tribunal found 'disgusting and offensive', were frequently circulated within the office without reprimand. Nor were there proper IT systems (including firewalls) in place to prevent adult images and jokes proliferating. In these circumstances, the tribunal found that a reasonable employer would not have regarded the sending of an image that depicted a young baby being held up in front of a mirror with a superimposed penis as a strict liability gross misconduct offence: the employee had sent it to two female colleagues with whom he was on good terms and the particular image related to a running joke between them. Furthermore, the tribunal found that the employer had used this incident to justify getting rid of a troublesome employee. However, the tribunal reduced the employee's compensation by 15 per cent by reason of contributory conduct.

It is worth pointing out that it would not be open to an employee accused of sending offensive material contrary to the employer's internet and e-mail policy to argue that he or she knew that the recipient would not regard it as obscene. The employer is entitled to take an objective approach, applying a 'man-on-the-Clapham-omnibus' test, to determine whether any particular image or text breaches the company's standards of e-mail use, provided the test is applied fairly and in a non-discriminatory way and the standards are well known and enforced through the company's policy.

6.136 ### Accessing confidential information
If an employee deliberately uses an unauthorised password to enter a computer known to contain confidential information to which he or she is not entitled, that of itself is gross misconduct that will usually justify summary dismissal. The employee's motive for gaining access is irrelevant to the question of whether the employer had substantial grounds for dismissal – Denco Ltd v Joinson 1991 ICR 172, EAT. Mr Justice Wood, in giving the judgment of the EAT, stressed the desirability of making it abundantly clear to employees that unauthorised interference with computers will carry severe penalties.

6.137 ### Excessive personal use
Most employers condone occasional, limited and appropriate personal use of the computer while at work. However, where the employee spends an excessive amount of time 'surfing' the web, he or she may have difficulty persuading a tribunal that any resulting dismissal was unfair. In McKinley v Secretary of State for Defence ET Case No.2302411/04, for example, the tribunal found that the employee was fairly dismissed when it was discovered that he spent between 10 and 15 per cent of daily working time on non-work-related internet use – although it thought that this conduct fell within the 'outer reaches of the definition of gross misconduct'. In reaching this conclusion, it took into account

that McK was employed in a senior position (he was the chief financial officer), that he was in charge of the company's IT policy and that, in an organisation without access to broadband internet, his extensive and persistent misuse of the internet had serious resource and cost implications for the employer.

Social networking and 'blogging' 6.138

The popularity of social networking sites, such as Facebook and Bebo, and the practice of 'blogging' – a form of publicly available on-line diary – has given rise to its own particular set of problems for employers. Some employers block access to social networking sites altogether, whereas others condone occasional use while at work. In any event, employers should always specifically address this issue in their IT policies, decide what is appropriate in their workplace and ensure that the policy is applied consistently. Discipline and dismissal will not necessarily be unreasonable in the absence of such a policy, but having a clear policy and procedures in place reduces the risk of unfairness in such proceedings. A prudent employer will also inform his employees that the use of personal blogs, even if they are written in their spare time, may give grounds for disciplinary action, including dismissal, in certain circumstances.

One word of caution, however. Even where dismissal may be a reasonable response in the circumstances, employers would be well advised to refrain from hastily making a decision to dismiss without considering the consequences. For example, the employer may want to consider issuing a warning to an employee who occasionally moans about his or her workplace in a personal blog that is not read by many people. By contrast, taking a heavy-handed approach and dismissing the employee, even if this is fair under S.98(4) ERA, may generate a fair amount of bad publicity for the employer.

It should be clear that any offensive, defamatory, discriminatory or other comments on any social network or blog will result in disciplinary action that may lead to dismissal. If an employee publishes in a public forum comments that are defamatory of his or her employer, libel proceedings may be taken by the employer in the same way as if the defamatory comments had been published anywhere else. If the comments damage the employer's reputation or are intended or likely to destroy the relationship of trust and confidence between employer and employee, discipline and dismissal will be legitimate courses of action. It is unlikely that employees will be able to hide behind pseudonyms to evade such action, as employers will generally be able to obtain an order for disclosure of the identity of the person who posted the libellous material from the host website – see Totalise plc v The Motley Fool Ltd and anor 2001 EWCA Civ 1897, CA.

It is not just the publication of untrue statements that employers should be 6.139
concerned about. Open access to online networks and discussion forums also raises the issue of potential breaches of confidentiality. Quite apart from any express restrictions, employees owe implied contractual duties of fidelity and confidentiality to their employer, and any information that an employee posts

285

on a public forum about the employer's business has the potential to give rise to breach of these duties. For example, if a disgruntled employee reveals his or her employer's trade secrets in a blog or a Facebook posting, the employer might seek an injunction ordering that the material be removed, and may be able to recover damages for any consequent loss based on the employee's breach of contract. Any such breach of confidentiality or fidelity would also be a disciplinary issue capable of leading to dismissal.

However, a distinction should be drawn between material that either defames the employer or breaches confidence on the one hand, and comments or opinions tending to disparage the employer or fellow employees or which the employer simply does not care for on the other hand. If the material is not actually damaging to the employer in any way, then it is unlikely that the relationship of trust and confidence will be so seriously undermined as to permit the employer to dismiss. Nonetheless, the employer may be entitled to treat comments bringing the business into disrepute as misconduct, in which case disciplinary action may be appropriate. The appropriateness of the employer's response in such situations will depend in part on whether such behaviour is covered by the disciplinary and/or computer use policy.

Whether dismissal will be fair will very much depend on the circumstances, including the nature of the employee's work, his or her position within the company, the nature of the comments made, and the damage, if any, caused to the employer as a result of the comments. An example:

- **Walters v Asda Stores Ltd** ET Case No. 2312748/08: A Ltd operated a policy, entitled 'Internet abuse – don't blog your way into trouble', which informed employees that complaints about the store on a social networking or blog site would be treated as misconduct, and that conduct which damaged the employer's trust and confidence in an employee would be deemed to be gross misconduct. On 7 November 2007 a message was posted on W's Facebook site saying that although she was supposed to love her customers, hitting them with a pickaxe would make her far happier. A Ltd investigated the matter, and W denied that she was the author of the comment. A Ltd did not accept her denial and because she was a manager decided that her action amounted to gross misconduct and she was dismissed. A majority of the tribunal found that the dismissal was unfair. It accepted that W had posted the message but, given that A Ltd had accepted that her conduct fell into the category of misconduct, rather than gross misconduct, a reasonable employer would not have regarded her position as a manager to be a factor of such importance as to outweigh the mitigating factors against dismissal. However, W contributed to her dismissal to the extent of 50 per cent and her compensation was reduced accordingly.

286

Human rights issues. This is another area where Convention rights, in particular the right to respect for private life (Article 8) and the right to freedom of expression (Article 10), may come into play. Briefly, employers who check up on a prospective employee's online profile might be interfering with that individual's Article 8 right to respect for his or her private life. It is questionable, however, whether information that an individual makes freely available on an openly accessible website could reasonably be considered part of his or her private life and whether Article 8 will be engaged in these circumstances – see Pay v United Kingdom 2009 IRLR 139, ECtHR. Where disciplinary action leads to dismissal, the question of whether dismissal was fair in accordance with S.98(4) ERA may have to be considered in the light of the employee's Article 10 right. This arguably includes the right to moan publicly about one's working conditions and/or colleagues, so long as it does not involve damaging or libellous statements. However, even where a Convention right has been interfered with, the employer's actions may be justified – for example, because of the risk of damage to the employer's reputation.

6.140

Violence and fighting

6.141

When deciding the fairness of a dismissal for fighting, tribunals should apply the test set out in British Home Stores Ltd v Burchell 1980 ICR 303, EAT, of genuine belief on reasonable grounds after reasonable investigation that the employee was guilty of misconduct – Ducal Ltd v McPherson EAT 466/80.

Investigation

6.142

What is reasonable by way of investigation will vary between cases and circumstances – Malik v National Plastics Ltd EAT 682/78. A failure to investigate or interview the participants will not always be unfair – if they fight in the office in front of a manager, for example, as in Reid v Giltspur Bullens Transport Services Ltd EAT 549/78. Neither does reasonableness demand that everyone in the vicinity of the fight should be questioned – particularly where large numbers are involved – Harkins v Scottish Region, British Gas Corporation EAT 593/80. However, if only a few employees are present, an employer who does not, without good reason, question them all will not usually be held to have acted reasonably, particularly where there are conflicting accounts over what actually happened. One good reason for not questioning all those present may be the fear of prejudicing the employees' trial – Malik v National Plastics Ltd (above). (For a fuller discussion on investigations pending trial, see 'Criminal offences at work' below.)

Where reasonable investigation leaves it uncertain who started the fight, employers may sack all the participants fairly, unless there are circumstances that make this unreasonable. In this they are supported by the EAT's statement in British Aerospace v Mafe EAT 565/80 that, in so far as spontaneous violence

287

is concerned, 'fighting is frequently regarded as justification for the dismissal of the participants without the employer being required to draw fine distinctions between the relative guilt of those involved'.

6.143 **Reasonableness of the decision to dismiss**
Fighting at work is generally regarded as gross misconduct justifying dismissal without prior warning. In serious cases this is so even though there is no disciplinary rule specifically forbidding it. In CA Parsons and Co Ltd v McLoughlin 1978 IRLR 65, EAT, the EAT said that 'in these days it ought not to be necessary for anybody... to have in black-and-white in the form of a rule that a fight is something which is going to be regarded very gravely by management'. However, employers should note that not all fighting is to be regarded as equally serious, and not all fights justify dismissal without prior warning.

Clear rules known to all employees, warning them of what they can expect, will be an important factor. Failure to provide such rules may tip the balance against an employer. In Meyer Dunmore International Ltd v Rogers 1978 IRLR 167, EAT, for instance, the employee was dismissed for fighting after a minor dispute which he did not start. The EAT upheld the tribunal's finding that the dismissal was unfair on the grounds that there was no clear rule about fighting, the employer's investigation was unsatisfactory, and, though there was some machinery about, there was no evidence that the fighting was particularly dangerous.

However, even where there is an express disciplinary rule, employers cannot rely on it to make dismissal for breach automatically fair. Such dismissals must still be reasonable in all the circumstances under S.98(4) ERA. This is illustrated by the EAT's decision in Taylor v Parsons Peebles NEI Bruce Peebles Ltd 1981 IRLR 119, EAT, where a tribunal was held to have erred in law in finding that the employer acted reasonably in dismissing an employee with long service and good conduct for striking a fellow worker – simply because the company's disciplinary rules laid down that such an offence would lead to dismissal. 'The proper test,' said the EAT, 'is not what the policy of the... employers was but what the reaction of a reasonable employer would have been in the circumstances. That reaction would have taken into account the long period of service and good conduct which the appellant was in a position to claim.'

Below, we discuss some of the factors tribunals take into account when determining the question of reasonableness.

6.144 **Proper procedure.** The form and adequacy of a disciplinary inquiry depends on the circumstances of the case, on which see further below under 'Disciplinary proceedings'.

6.145 **Consistency of punishment.** Employers who, without warning, act out of line with responses adopted in comparable cases of violence or fighting in the past may be held to have acted unreasonably. In Post Office v Fennell 1981 IRLR 221, CA, F was summarily dismissed for assaulting a fellow employee in the

288

canteen. When he complained of unfair dismissal he alleged that a number of employees had been treated differently in the past for similar offences. The tribunal found his dismissal unfair, partly because it felt that the Post Office had exaggerated the offence and partly because of the Post Office's inconsistent behaviour. Both the EAT and the Court of Appeal agreed with the tribunal's finding of inconsistency. The Court of Appeal held that there was evidence before the tribunal that the Post Office had departed from a previous course of conduct without warning, and this was sufficient material for the tribunal's conclusion that the dismissal was unfair.

Similarly, inconsistency of treatment between employees accused of the same offence is a factor tribunals will take into account, although the respective roles each employee played in the incident, their past records and their level of contrition may justify the different treatment. The guiding principle is whether the distinction made by the employer was within the band of reasonable responses open to it – Walpole v Vauxhall Motors Ltd 1998 EWCA Civ 706, CA.

Health and safety. Even modest incidents of fighting or violence, where close to machinery or where dangerous implements are to hand, will be treated extremely seriously by tribunals because of the potential consequences. In Greenwood v HJ Heinz and Co Ltd EAT 199/77 the EAT said: 'It seems to us that it is quite wrong to say that a management faced with fighting, even of a very modest nature, in a workplace where there is a large amount of machinery would be perverse in deciding that whoever started the fight must be dismissed. The potential for danger which any degree of violence involves in close proximity to machinery is blindingly obvious. It is difficult enough sometimes to keep people who have to operate machines safe from hurting themselves in the machinery, even in the absence of any violence at all. Add some violence, and the risk of serious injury to other people, let alone severe interference with the work, is clearly great. While circumstances must of course vary infinitely, in our judgment it certainly does not go without saying that to dismiss by reason of one blow, or even by reason of the threat of a blow, is by itself plainly wrong. It may be in some circumstances wrong. It may well be a perfectly proper thing for management to do.' 6.146

Status of the parties involved. Attacks on supervisors or managers by subordinates will normally result in a fair dismissal but not inevitably so – all the circumstances must be considered – Capps v Baxter and Down Ltd EAT 793/78. In London Borough of Ealing v Goodwin EAT 121/79 a disabled road-sweeper had been at odds with his supervisor for some time when matters came to a head. Following an argument, the employee struck the supervisor. The EAT held the dismissal unfair. Although the actual assault was quite a minor one, the EAT said it is never trivial for an employee to strike a superior. However, there were exceptional circumstances – the employee was disabled and had 23 years' unblemished service. 6.147

289

Attacks by supervisors on subordinate employees are no less serious. Even minor assaults may so destroy the relationship of trust and good faith between the employer and employee as to entitle the employee to treat the contract as at an end and claim unfair constructive dismissal – Mock v Glamorgan Aluminium Co Ltd EAT 493/80.

6.148 **Mitigating circumstances.** Matters such as provocation, long service and good conduct should always be taken into account. Tribunals will look at the severity of the provocation and whether the employee's response to it was proportionate. In Capps v Baxter and Down Ltd (above), for instance, the EAT recognised that the claimant, whose wife's fidelity had been called into question by a foreman, was acting under severe provocation when he struck the latter. In these circumstances, the EAT did not agree with the employer that dismissal was the inevitable consequence of his action. And in Stanton and Staveley Ltd v Ellis EAT 48/84 the employer acted unreasonably in dismissing an employee for assaulting a fellow employee who had racially abused him. The employer had taken the decision to dismiss in line with company policy without looking into the nature and degree of provocation involved.

Long service and good conduct may also be important mitigating factors. In Taylor v Parsons Peebles NEI Bruce Peebles Ltd (above), for example, the employee's dismissal in accordance with the company's disciplinary rules was unfair. The employer should have taken account of the employee's long service and good conduct before coming to a decision. It might be more reasonable in such circumstances to allow the employee a chance to calm down, apologise and give an undertaking to behave in the future – Taylor Woodrow Construction Ltd v Veale EAT 544/76.

6.149 **Threats of violence.** When considering dismissal for threats of violence, one of the factors employers should take into account is the atmosphere of fear and intimidation caused by the threat – British Communications Corporation Ltd t/a Racal BBC Ltd v Smart EAT 227/79. The employee's attitude afterwards and any apology he or she offers should also be taken into consideration – see Taylor v Tibbett and Britten UK ET Case No.2400283/00.

6.150 **Off-duty fighting and violence**
The important factor here is the link between the off-duty conduct and the workplace. In Malik v National Plastics Ltd EAT 682/78 the claimant and others were dismissed for engaging in serious fighting outside the workplace and after hours. It resulted in substantial injury to participants and 'discord, fear and even perhaps terror' throughout the workplace. The EAT held the dismissal fair. The incident had occurred sufficiently close to the works and sufficiently close to working hours as plainly to have an effect upon the industrial life of the factory. In another case, Eggleton v Kerry Foods Ltd EAT 938/95, the claimant had been warned about his behaviour towards another employee with whom there was some problem over a woman. He got into a

fight with the other employee and was dismissed. The dismissal was held to be fair even though the fight took place off-site because it affected working arrangements. Contrast Lanarkshire Health Board v McLeish EAT 22/91, however, where an employer attempted to establish an adverse connection between the employee's work as an auxiliary nurse and her assault upon a fellow employee outside working hours. The EAT concluded that in this case the assault was unrelated to the workplace and did not indicate that the employee was prone to violent behaviour or that she would, as a consequence, be a danger to her patients.

Criminal offences at work

6.151

Dismissal is an employment and not a criminal matter. In a case where the employee is believed to have committed misconduct in relation to his or her employment that also constitutes a criminal offence (e.g. theft, drug taking, physical assault or business fraud), an employer is not required to be sure 'beyond reasonable doubt' that the employee has actually committed the offence before dismissing. When deciding the sufficiency of the employer's reason for dismissal in such cases, employment tribunals will usually take into account the guidelines established in British Home Stores Ltd v Burchell 1980 ICR 303, EAT (see under 'General considerations – establishing the reason for dismissal' above). Under those guidelines, employers need only have a genuine belief on reasonable grounds after reasonable investigation that the employee committed the offence in question. Moreover, as we have seen, tribunals must not substitute their own view of whether dismissal was reasonable but should ask whether it fell within the range of reasonable responses open to the reasonable employer – British Leyland (UK) Ltd v Swift 1981 IRLR 91, CA.

More than one suspect

6.152

As we saw at the beginning of this chapter, where two or more employees are suspected of dishonesty and the employer, despite investigation, cannot discover who is to blame, it may be fair to dismiss all the suspects on reasonable suspicion short of actual belief. In Monie v Coral Racing Ltd 1981 ICR 109, CA, money was stolen from the employer's safe in circumstances such that only the manager or assistant manager could have taken it. Both were dismissed on the ground that at least one of them must be guilty of theft and there was no way of telling which. In such circumstances the Court of Appeal held the dismissal to be fair.

In the Monie case the employer's suspicion had been narrowed down to the point of certainty that a serious theft had been committed by one or both of two men, although it was impossible to tell which. Where the employer has no 'reasonable conclusive proof' that one of those dismissed was guilty, however,

291

the principle in Monie will not apply and actual belief must be shown – Leyland Vehicles Ltd v Wright EAT 712/81.

6.153 ## Criminal trial pending

The mere fact that an employee has been charged by the Crown Prosecution Service with a criminal offence is not sufficient on its own for the employer to conclude that the offence has been committed. In Scottish Special Housing Association v Cooke and ors 1979 IRLR 264, EAT, the EAT considered this to be a 'very dangerous doctrine'. It held that 'the mere fact of a charge of theft being preferred, standing by itself and without any further information available to the employer, is not sufficient to constitute reasonable grounds'.

However, employers need not wait until the outcome of the criminal trial before dismissing an employee. They must, though, obtain sufficient material to justify their decision to dismiss. The fact that a criminal court later acquits the employee will not affect the fairness or otherwise of the employer's decision made at the time of the dismissal – Harris (Ipswich) Ltd v Harrison 1978 ICR 1256, EAT.

6.154 Criminal proceedings and police involvement in the case can have an important bearing on the timing of dismissal and the kind of investigation an employer can properly carry out. On the one hand, the employer must make its own enquiries into alleged criminal acts. On the other, the fact that criminal charges have been made may limit what it can do. Only minimal investigation is likely to be necessary where the employee is caught red-handed or makes a confession to the police. Thus in Scottish Special Housing Association v Linnen 1979 IRLR 265, EAT, the claimant was fairly dismissed when copper belonging to his employer was found by the police in his garden. And in Parker v Clifford Dunn Ltd 1979 ICR 463, EAT, the EAT found it reasonable to rely on the employee's confession of theft to the police. In such cases, the EAT said, it is 'entirely reasonable for the company to depend upon what the police... put forward as the result of that investigation, rather than themselves intervening by way of independent inquiries'. (Such a dismissal must nonetheless be carried out fairly. Any procedural defect may otherwise render it unfair – Rumbelows Ltd v Ellis EAT 664/87.) Where the evidence is not so clear-cut, however, further investigation will be necessary and employers 'ought to take reasonable steps to obtain the proper material' on which to decide whether or not to dismiss – Chard and Hodge v Strand Hotels EAT 305/77.

Whether the employer puts its own internal investigation on hold while the police investigation is under way is essentially a matter for the employer to decide. In Secretary of State for Justice v Mansfield EAT 0539/09 the claimant, a prison officer, was unhappy about the employer's decision to suspend the disciplinary proceedings while the police investigation into his alleged misconduct was ongoing. He argued that the suspension resulted in unreasonable delay. The EAT rejected this argument, holding that the employer's decision to postpone the disciplinary hearing while the police were still gathering evidence and while a Crown Court prosecution was under way was entirely proper and could not be said to be unreasonable.

Police charges can inhibit an employer's enquiries. In Carr v Alexander Russell Ltd 1979 ICR 469, Ct Sess (Outer House) the Court of Session went so far as to say that it would be improper for employers to carry out any form of internal investigation into alleged dishonesty, or to question the employee, when a criminal prosecution is pending because of the risk of prejudicing the subsequent criminal trial. This remains the approach of Scottish tribunals. However, in Harris (Ipswich) Ltd v Harrison (above) the EAT in England expressly refrained from following the Carr case. It thought that the employer should discuss the matter with the employee, not only to give the employee a chance to put his or her side but also to discuss the action which the employer proposed to take.

6.155

Difficulties can arise where the employee stays silent in order to protect him or herself. An employee's refusal to take part in the employer's investigation – perhaps because of legal advice that participation may prejudice the criminal proceedings – does not mean that dismissal before the outcome of criminal proceedings will necessarily be unfair. In such a case 'the employer is entitled to consider whether the material which he has is strong enough to justify his dismissal without waiting. If there are doubts, then no doubt it would be fair to wait. On the other hand, if the evidence produced is, in the absence of an explanation, sufficiently indicative of guilt, then the employer may be entitled to act' – Harris and anor v Courage (Eastern) Ltd 1981 ICR 496, EAT (upheld by the Court of Appeal – 1982 ICR 530).

In the Harris case H and S were charged with the theft of beer from their employer. They had been told to take a company lorry from the depot to a garage. A similar lorry was later seen being loaded up with kegs of beer at a depot close to the garage. H was recognised, and a description of another man was consistent with his being S. The lorry was driven off at speed, grazing the depot gates as it went. Shortly afterwards, the vehicle was found by the police with H and S in it. The lorry had paint on it from the depot gate and had almost exactly the same registration number as given by one of the witnesses at the depot. The company set the disciplinary procedure in motion but the employees, on the advice of their lawyers, declined to take part. They were dismissed, but subsequently acquitted in the crown court. The Court of Appeal upheld the EAT's conclusion that the dismissals were fair. The Court considered that, in the absence of an explanation from H and S, the employer reasonably believed them to be involved in the theft.

No protestations of innocence. The above decision shows that one of the reasons for offering employees the chance to put their side is to strengthen the employer's case if they refuse to participate in the disciplinary process. In Carr

6.156

v Alexander Russell Ltd (above) Lord McDonald thought it significant that the employee had made no protestations of innocence and no attempt to use the grievance procedure, although he knew of it. His Lordship did not think the employer was under a duty to demand an explanation before deciding to dismiss: the employee should have proclaimed his innocence unbidden.

6.157 **Confessions retracted.** An employee may retract a confession given to the employer once he or she realises that criminal proceedings are to be commenced. However, this does not stop the employer being able to rely on that original confession if it is reasonable, in the circumstances, to do so – University College at Buckingham v Phillips 1982 ICR 318, EAT. In that case the EAT said, 'we think that, in the majority of cases, a later retraction will not substantially remove the force of the original confession. But it is not a matter on which we can lay down any general rule: it is a matter for the... tribunal to decide in each case.'

6.158 **Injunction to prevent dismissal.** As a general rule, the courts are unwilling to grant an injunction stopping an employer from dismissing employees. However, in R v British Broadcasting Corporation ex p Lavelle 1983 ICR 99, QBD, the High Court said that an employee could seek an injunction to stop a dismissal taking effect where this was necessary to prevent a real danger of miscarriage of justice in a criminal case. In that case the employee had sought an injunction to stop her employer proceeding with her internal appeal (against her dismissal for theft) because she thought her explanation to her employer might prejudice her criminal trial over the same offence. However, the High Court judge decided that on the facts of the case, there would be no miscarriage of justice if the employer continued hearing her appeal and the injunction was therefore refused.

6.159 **After the criminal trial**
Where an employer leads the employee to believe that it will be bound by the outcome of the criminal trial, it runs the risk of acting unfairly if it dismisses the employee after an acquittal. And since many acquittals are obtained on very technical grounds, employers may wish to reserve their position on whether or not to dismiss in the light of evidence that comes to light at the trial. If such a reservation is made, then the position should be made crystal-clear to the employee.

There is another reason why employers may wish to wait before making a decision on whether to dismiss. Further evidence, though not sufficient to secure a criminal conviction, may still reveal a serious breach of duty or discipline justifying dismissal. For example, a cashier charged with theft from a till, guilty or not, is often undoubtedly in breach of company rules in the way in which the till has been operated. And an employee who removes goods from the premises, whether criminally guilty or not, is often in breach of company rules by acting in this way – Harris (Ipswich) Ltd v Harrison 1978 ICR 1256, EAT. Where the employer decides that the evidence that has come to light at the trial gives it reasonable grounds to dismiss for a breach of company rules, it should make this clear to the employee concerned. In Greater Manchester Passenger Transport Executive v Sheikh unreported 28.6.76, EAT, a bus driver was suspended and later charged with theft. He was acquitted but the company decided to dismiss for breaches confirmed by the trial. The EAT upheld the finding of unfairness. In the EAT's view, where employers suspend and await the outcome of a trial, 'they need to make it very clear... that they are dismissing the employee, not for the offence which has been found not to be proved, but for the underlying failure to follow the procedure which had also given rise to the charge being made'.

Where an employee has been convicted of a dishonest act, this may well constitute **6.160** reasonable grounds for the employer's belief in the employee's guilt, but it is still necessary for the employer to carry out such investigations as are reasonable in the circumstances. So held the EAT in Secretary of State for Scotland v Campbell 1992 IRLR 263, EAT. In that case the claimant was convicted of embezzling club funds. He maintained that the way the club was run made it difficult for him to control the finances. He was only one member of a large committee involved in managing the club. The tribunal found that a reasonable employer would have made a detailed investigation into how the finances had got into such a state before dismissing and the EAT upheld the finding of unfair dismissal.

Once an employer has dealt with the matter, however, it is not then entitled to change its mind in light of a subsequent criminal conviction unless new evidence has come to light. In Central Nottinghamshire Area Health Authority v Shine EAT 562/82 the employee was given a written warning for neglecting her patients and misusing their money. Subsequently she was convicted of receiving stolen goods (i.e. goods bought with that money) and she was summarily dismissed. The EAT held that the dismissal was unfair because the employer had imposed a double penalty for the same offence. No new evidence had emerged to justify the employer's change of mind.

Employers do not have to await a criminal appeal and subsequent appeals will not affect fairness: once the outcome of the trial is known, a guilty verdict might well suffice to form an adequate basis for dismissal. In Kingston v British Railways Board 1984 ICR 781, CA, the employee was found guilty of assault. The facts had been fully investigated in the crown court and the employer was entitled to rely on the verdict without conducting independent investigations before dismissing (since the employee was in prison serving his sentence). This was so notwithstanding the fact that the conviction was subsequently quashed by the Court of Appeal.

When to dismiss
6.161
Delay in investigation may make the dismissal unfair. In Marley Homecare Ltd v Dutton 1981 IRLR 380, EAT, for instance, the dismissal of a cashier was found to be unfair because of too long a delay (one week) between test

295

purchases and confronting the employee. She could neither remember the incident nor put forward an explanation. However, lengthy inquiry may sometimes be needed to confirm a suspicion. In Refund Rentals Ltd v McDermott 1977 IRLR 59, EAT, the EAT held that 14 weeks' delay for investigation of a suspected theft could not be said to make dismissal unfair when the investigation provided reasonable grounds for the employer's suspicions – even though the employee might have been lulled into a belief that the incident was closed. The moral may be that, to avoid a finding of unfair dismissal, employers should be open about their suspicions from the start, make it plain what it is they are investigating, and suspend with pay (unless the contract allows for suspension without pay) while they look into things.

Where there is insufficient evidence to sustain a reasonable belief in an employee's guilt, it will generally be unfair to dismiss prior to a trial settling the matter. But if it is inappropriate to allow the employee to remain in his or her old post in the meantime, there are two possibilities open to the employer: suspension or temporary transfer.

6.162   **Suspension.** The employer must make it quite clear that an employee is being suspended pending the outcome of the trial and that only after this will a final decision about his or her future (including dismissal) be made. It may, however, be months before the trial. Unless the employer has a contractual right to suspend without pay, the employee must receive full wages for the entire period. If he or she is not paid, the employee may be entitled to bring a claim in the employment tribunal for unlawful deduction from wages, or even constructive dismissal. Any tribunal claim by the employee should be brought as soon as possible, as awaiting the outcome of the trial is likely to be an inadequate excuse for a late application – Trevelyans (Birmingham) Ltd v Norton 1991 ICR 488, EAT (see further Chapter 2, under 'Time limits'). Even if there is a contractual right to suspend without pay, the tribunal may imply a term to the effect that such suspension will only last for a reasonable period unless the contract expressly states the length of time employees can be thus suspended.

If the employer undertakes to wait, and to suspend the employee until after the criminal charge has been disposed of, dismissal in breach of that undertaking may be unfair unless the employee is told of the change in the employer's attitude and given a chance to make representations. In Harris (Ipswich) Ltd v Harrison 1978 ICR 1256, EAT, the claimant was charged with theft from his employer and was suspended on pay until the charge could be dealt with. However, when it was learnt that he had elected for a trial by jury that was not likely to take place for some time, he was dismissed. The EAT considered that it was the employer's duty 'before deciding to change their mind and to dismiss him without awaiting the result of the trial in the crown court, first to make some enquiry of him... [T]o dismiss him in those circumstances, without any enquiry at all, was unfair... [T]here was no reason... why they should not have communicated with his solicitors... [H]ad they sought to discuss the matter...

no doubt the matter could have been thrashed out, and it would have been difficult to say... that they had acted unfairly.'

Temporary transfer. Again, this option is only permissible where the employer   **6.163**
has the contractual right. However, where it is made clear that the transfer is only a temporary measure until the trial and that there is no loss of pay, then, even if the employee claims constructive dismissal, the employer may be able to persuade the tribunal that it was nonetheless fair. Indeed, it may even be arguable that a temporary job transfer with no loss of pay does not amount to a fundamental breach of contract entitling an employee to claim constructive dismissal anyway, in which case he or she will be taken to have been dismissed and the question of unfair dismissal will not arise – Scott v Aveling Barford Ltd 1978 ICR 214, EAT.

Employee on remand   6.164
Pending trial, an employee may be remanded in custody or on bail. Where an employee is remanded in custody, it should be remembered that he or she has not been convicted of any offence. Unless, therefore, the employer has carried out all reasonable investigation, and dismissal can be said to be a reasonable response in the circumstances, it would be unwise for him to dismiss for conduct reasons (except where the employee has pleaded guilty). It might, however, be reasonable to dismiss at an early stage for 'some other substantial reason' (SOSR) – see Chapter 8 – if the organisation cannot manage without a replacement and the prospects of a quick release are bleak.

Alternatively, the contract of employment may itself end by operation of law through the employee's inability to perform it while on remand – or where bail conditions substantially interfere with normal working – in which case there is no dismissal. Whether or not bail conditions or remand 'frustrate' the contract in this way will depend on the facts of each case, although, as a general rule, tribunals are reluctant to decide that there has been a frustration. See Chapter 1, under 'Non-dismissals', for further details.

Custodial sentences   6.165
If, at the end of criminal proceedings, an employee is sentenced to long-term imprisonment, the employer may decide to dismiss. It is likely to be a fair dismissal for conduct if the employee's offence was related to his or her work. It may also be a fair dismissal for SOSR if the circumstances of the imprisonment are such as to reflect adversely on the employer's image or to destroy trust and confidence in the employee. A custodial sentence may also 'frustrate' the contract – see Chapter 1, under 'Non-dismissals'.

Previous convictions   6.166
An employer, particularly one that is operating in a sector where honesty and integrity is seen as paramount, such as the financial services sector, may want to know whether an employee has any past criminal convictions for dishonesty.

297

The circumstances in which the employer is entitled to this type of information will largely depend on the nature of the work carried out.

6.167 **Spent convictions under the Rehabilitation of Offenders Act 1974.** An employee is under no obligation to disclose to any employer a conviction that is 'spent' under the Rehabilitation of Offenders Act 1974 (ROA 1974). A conviction is 'spent' after a period varying in length with the gravity of the original sentence, although the Act only applies in any case to minor offences – i.e. where convictions do not lead to a custodial sentence exceeding 30 months. Once a conviction is spent, the person is treated as having committed no offence at all and any questions about his or her past convictions or conduct (e.g. on an application form) are taken as not referring to a spent conviction – S.4(2) ROA 1974. Moreover, a spent conviction, or a failure to disclose it, is not a proper ground for dismissing an employee or prejudicing him or her in any way in the job – S.4(3)(b) ROA 1974.

Certain professions (doctors, dentists, solicitors and barristers, for example) and office-holders (applicants for judicial or law enforcement posts) are not protected by the 1974 Act; nor are holders of certain posts with local authorities, like teachers and social workers. Similarly, the Act does not apply to certain regulated occupations, including managers of abortion clinics, registered firearms dealers and anyone applying to work in an occupation regulated by the Gaming Board – see the Rehabilitation of Offenders Act 1974 (Exceptions) Orders SI 1975/1023, which is amended periodically.

Dismissal for having, or failing to disclose, a spent conviction is not one of the automatically fair reasons for dismissal listed in the ERA (see Chapter 10 for a full list of the reasons for dismissal that are automatically unfair). But it seems that the effect of S.4(3)(b) ROA 1974, read with S.4(2), ought to be that a tribunal need not consider general questions of fairness under S.98(4) ERA where a spent conviction, or failure to disclose it, has been relied on in the decision to dismiss.

6.168 This interpretation garners some support from case law. In Property Guards Ltd v Taylor and anor 1982 IRLR 175, EAT, the EAT upheld a tribunal's finding that two security guards were unfairly dismissed when their employer learnt that they both had minor spent convictions for dishonesty which they had failed to disclose. It is not clear, however, whether the EAT believed that it followed from S.4(3) ROA 1974 that the decision to dismiss on the basis of the spent conviction was not a proper ground for dismissal under S.98(1) or (2) ERA and was therefore necessarily unfair, or whether there was a justifiable reason for dismissal but that by virtue of S.4(3) the employer did not act reasonably in treating it as a sufficient reason for dismissing the employees.

In Hendry and anor v Scottish Liberal Club 1977 IRLR 5, ET a tribunal justified a finding of unfair dismissal on the basis of both these approaches. We would suggest that the correct view is that if the employer's reason for dismissal

298

is that the employee has, or has concealed, a spent conviction, the employer has not shown a justifiable reason for dismissal so as to satisfy S.98(1) or (2) ERA and the dismissal is therefore automatically unfair. Moreover, the spent conviction does not need to be the principal reason for dismissal for the ex-offender's claim to succeed: it will be sufficient for the spent conviction to play a material part in the decision to dismiss.

Where, however, an employee conceals convictions for dishonesty that are not spent, he or she forfeits the employer's trust on discovery of this deception and may be fairly dismissed despite satisfactory service. In Torr v British Railways Board 1977 ICR 785, EAT, the EAT rejected the argument that the Rehabilitation of Offenders Act was part of a wider public policy that made it unfair to dismiss a person because he or she has a previous conviction irrespective of other circumstances. 'It is of the utmost importance,' said the EAT, 'that an employer seeking an employee to hold a position of responsibility and trust should be able to select for employment a candidate in whom he can have confidence. It is fundamental to that confidence that the employee should truthfully disclose his history so far as it is sought by the intending employer.' In that case the employee's deliberate lie regarding his conviction had destroyed 'the foundation on which the requisite confidence of master and servant has to be built'. Therefore, although the employee had been working satisfactorily as a guard for 16 months, the dismissal was fair.

Adverse CRB disclosures. Under Part V of the Police Act 1997, **6.169** organisations that are recruiting for posts exempted from the terms of the ROA 1974 (for which, see above) may obtain information on employees' criminal records from the Criminal Records Bureau (CRB). For example, an employer may ask an individual applying for a position in the care sector to apply for an enhanced criminal record certificate, which will not only provide details of any convictions or cautions but could include any information that the chief officer of the relevant police force believes might be relevant. The same request would be made of an employee who moves into a new role that requires a CRB check. Any information thus disclosed, even if it amounts to unproven allegations, may be relied on by an employer in deciding whether or not to dismiss. However, in R (on the application of John Pinnington) v Chief Constable of Thames Valley Police 2008 EWHC 1870 (Admin) the High Court warned against employers applying a blanket policy of dismissing any individual who is unable to provide a 'clean' certificate.

In B v A EAT S/0029/06 B was dismissed from his post as a full-time support worker with a charity that provided care to extremely vulnerable young people. The dismissal followed the charity's receipt of an 'enhanced disclosure' letter from the Chief Constable, which disclosed an allegation that B had, in 1993, committed a serious sexual offence. B contended that

299

someone else had eventually been convicted of the offence, but his dismissal was upheld after an appeal. B had not persuaded the police to retract the disclosure, and the charity had not assisted B by asking the police to verify his contention. B brought an unfair dismissal claim against the charity. His claim was upheld on the basis that the charity's failure to assist B was outside the band of reasonable responses. On appeal, the EAT overturned that decision. Although the tribunal had regarded the charity's failure to ask the police to verify B's assertion as unreasonable, it had made no findings as to what would have happened if it had in fact asked, and had not found that B had requested such assistance. Furthermore, the tribunal had not made a finding that dismissal itself was outside the band of reasonable responses. In fact, the tribunal had stated that upon receipt of the disclosure from the Chief Constable, the charity had no choice but to dismiss. In light of this, the EAT was of the opinion that the tribunal's decision had been 'plainly wrong', and that 'the only conclusion that a reasonable tribunal could have arrived at... is that it was reasonable for the respondents not to have approached the police... and that, in the whole circumstances, the decision was a fair one'.

It should be noted that, in the V v A case above, rather than remitting the matter for reconsideration by the tribunal, the EAT itself substituted a finding that the dismissal was fair. While that was an outcome decided on the particular facts of the case, it is difficult to conceive of a situation where the result might be different: the upshot of the decision was that it was not for the employer but for the individual employee to challenge the police about the non-conviction information supplied.

6.170 ## Criminal offences outside of employment

The scope of 'conduct' as a potentially fair reason for dismissal in accordance with S.98(2)(b) ERA is not limited to conduct in the course, or within the scope, of employment. It also covers conduct outside of employment 'so long as in some respect or other it affects the employee, or could be thought to be likely to affect the employee, when he is doing his work' – Singh v London Country Bus Services Ltd 1976 IRLR 176, EAT.

6.171 **Adverse connection between the offence and the employment.** When dismissal is contemplated by the employer on the basis of a criminal offence committed outside employment, the tribunal will place particular emphasis on whether there is an adverse connection between the offence and the employment. The approach advocated by Acas is considered salient to such dismissals, and para 30 of its Code of Practice on Disciplinary and Grievance Procedures states that consideration needs to be given as to what effect the charge or conviction of a criminal offence has on the employee's suitability to do the job and his or her relationship with the employer, work colleagues and customers.

Nature of the employee's job. The types of criminal offence that most   **6.172** commonly affect the employment relationship are those involving sexual conduct, violence or dishonesty. The factors that persuade tribunals that there is an adverse connection between conduct and employment will obviously vary from case to case. A tribunal will pay attention to all the circumstances in each dismissal claim – including the employee's length of service, status, relations with fellow workers, influence over vulnerable groups and even the employee's effect on the business subsequent to a charge or conviction. In Lloyds Bank plc v Bardin EAT 38/89 a part-time cleaner was dismissed after she pleaded guilty to three charges of obtaining money by deception. The EAT decided that the issue was not whether the employee was actually a security risk but whether the bank acted reasonably in all the circumstances in treating her as one. On this basis, the EAT found an adequate link between the offence and the employee's type of work to warrant dismissal.

The nature of the employee's job was considered crucial by the EAT in Moore v C and A Modes 1981 IRLR 71, EAT. In that case, the claimant, a section leader in one of the employer's stores, was dismissed after 20 years' service for shoplifting at another store. The dismissal was held to be fair. On appeal, the EAT commented: 'It seems to us to be quite unreal to expect any employer in the retail trade not to dismiss someone who has, for 20 years, been a trusted employee, who is reasonably believed to have been stealing just down the road although not from the employers themselves, because nobody should be more alive than such an employee to the damage which is caused by what is commonly called shoplifting.'

Potential damage to an employer's reputation is also considered to be an important factor in these cases. This is particularly pertinent where public service employees are concerned. In Gunn v British Waterways Board EAT 138/81, for instance, the employee was dismissed after breaking into a surgery to steal some drugs. The EAT rejected a plea that his job was unaffected and pointed to the effect on the employer's reputation and the adverse reaction of the workforce.

However, the EAT has also held that the impact on an employee of allegations of serious criminal misbehaviour with regard to the loss of his or her job and the effect on his or her reputation and future employment prospects is relevant to whether a dismissal is fair. In A v B 2003 IRLR 405, EAT, a residential social worker was suspended pending an investigation into allegations that he had had an inappropriate relationship with a 14-year-old in his care. The EAT said that such allegations must always be the subject of the most careful investigations, given the potential effect that they could have on the employee.

301

Disciplinary proceedings

6.173

As explained in Chapter 3, a conduct dismissal will not normally be treated as fair unless certain procedural steps have been followed. Without following such steps, it will not in general be possible for an employer to show that he acted reasonably in treating the conduct reason as a sufficient reason to dismiss. In Polkey v AE Dayton Services Ltd 1988 ICR 142, HL, Lord Bridge itemised the procedural steps as follows:

- a full investigation of the conduct, and

- a fair hearing to hear what the employee wants to say in explanation or mitigation.

When assessing whether the employer adopted a reasonable procedure, tribunals will use the range of reasonable responses test that applies to substantive unfair dismissal claims. As Lord Justice Mummery said in J Sainsbury plc v Hitt 2003 ICR 111, CA: 'The range of reasonable responses test (or, to put it another way, the need to apply the objective standards of the reasonable employer) applies as much to the question whether the investigation into the suspected misconduct was reasonable in all the circumstances as it does to the reasonableness of the decision to dismiss for the conduct reason.'

6.174

In Taylor v OCS Group Ltd 2006 ICR 1602, CA, the Court of Appeal further stressed that a tribunal's task under S.98(4) ERA is not simply to assess the fairness of the disciplinary process as a whole but also to consider the employer's reason for the dismissal as the two impact upon each other. It stated that where an employee is dismissed for serious misconduct, a tribunal might well decide that, notwithstanding some procedural imperfections, the employer acted reasonably in treating the reason as sufficient to dismiss the employee. Conversely, the Court considered that where the misconduct is of a less serious nature, so that the decision to dismiss is nearer the borderline, the tribunal might well conclude that a procedural deficiency had such impact that the employer did not act reasonably in dismissing the employee.

Until April 2009, employers were required to follow, at a minimum, the procedural steps set out in the statutory dismissal and disciplinary procedures (DDPs). Failure to comply with the DDPs meant that a subsequent dismissal was automatically unfair by virtue of S.98A(1) ERA. The DDPs, and with them S.98A(1), were repealed with effect from 6 April 2009 (although they continue to apply in some circumstances – see 'General considerations – reasonableness of conduct dismissal' above). In their place, employers are expected to have regard to the matters set out in the revised Acas Code of Practice on Discipline and Grievance Procedures ('the Acas Code') when contemplating taking disciplinary action. The Acas Code is relevant to the question of liability and will be taken into account by a tribunal when determining the reasonableness

302

of a dismissal in accordance with S.98(4) – S.207 TULR(C)A. Furthermore, if the dismissal is found to be unfair, the tribunal can increase (or indeed decrease) an award of compensation by up to 25 per cent for an unreasonable failure to follow the Code if it considers it just and equitable to do so – S.207A TULR(C)A. For further details of these potential adjustments to compensation, see Chapter 18, under 'Adjustments for breach of Acas Code of Practice'.

Where the tribunal finds that the employer failed to adopt a fair procedure at the time of the dismissal, whether set out in the Acas Code or otherwise – for example, in the employer's disciplinary rules – the dismissal will not be rendered fair simply because the unfairness did not affect the end result. That, as the House of Lords established in Polkey (above), is an issue that is only relevant in determining the level of compensation – see Chapter 18, under '"Polkey reductions"'.

Acas Code of Practice

6.175

The Acas Code of Practice on Discipline and Grievance Procedures sets out basic requirements for fairness that will be applicable in most conduct cases. It is intended to provide the standard of reasonable behaviour in most instances. A failure to follow the Code can result in an adjustment in compensation of up to 25 per cent in a subsequent employment tribunal claim.

The Acas Code's section on handling disciplinary issues (paras 5–28) sets out the steps employers must normally follow, namely:

- carry out an *investigation* to establish the facts of each case
- *inform* the employee of the problem
- hold a *meeting* with the employee to discuss the problem
- allow the employee to be *accompanied* at the meeting
- decide on *appropriate action*
- provide employees with an opportunity to *appeal*.

We examine these basic steps in detail below.

The Code does acknowledge that it may sometimes not be practicable for all employers to take all of the steps set out in the Code. Dismissal, however, may still be reasonable. Conversely, even if all the steps have been followed, dismissal may be unfair.

6.176

In order to expand and explain these basic principles, a non-statutory and non-binding Acas Guide, 'Discipline and grievance at work', accompanies the Acas Code. It provides detailed practical advice on the formulation and operation of disciplinary procedures. Page 13 of the Guide states that procedures should:

303

- be in writing

- be non-discriminatory

- provide for matters to be dealt with speedily

- allow for information to be kept confidential

- tell employees what disciplinary action might be taken

- say what levels of management have the authority to take the various forms of disciplinary action

- require employees to be informed of the complaints against them and supporting evidence, before a disciplinary meeting

- give employees a chance to have their say before management reaches a decision

- provide employees with the right to be accompanied

- provide that no employee is dismissed for a first breach of discipline, except in cases of gross misconduct

- require management to investigate fully before any disciplinary action is taken

- ensure that employees are given an explanation for any sanction

- allow employees to appeal against a decision

- apply to all employees, irrespective of their length of service, status or number of hours worked

- ensure that any investigatory period of suspension is with pay, and specify how pay is to be calculated during such period. If, exceptionally, suspension is to be without pay, this must be provided for in the contract of employment

- ensure that any suspension is brief, and is never used as a sanction against the employee prior to a disciplinary meeting and decision. Keep the employee informed of progress

- ensure that the employee will be heard in good faith and that there is no pre-judgement of the issue

- ensure that, where the facts are in dispute, no disciplinary penalty is imposed until the case has been carefully investigated, and there is a reasonably held belief that the employee committed the act in question.

6.177   Although the Code of Practice is not, in itself, legally binding, it is admissible as evidence before a tribunal. In particular, a tribunal must take its provisions into account where they are relevant to the case in question – S.207 TULR(C)A.

Obviously, it is not possible to devise a procedure that is fully applicable in all circumstances. In this regard, it is recognised both in S.98(4) ERA and in the Acas Code that allowances must be made for the particular circumstances of each case and the size and administrative resources of the employer's undertaking. Furthermore, while application of the principle in the Polkey decision puts great emphasis on the importance of a fair procedure, the House of Lords in that case also stressed that a failure to comply with procedural safeguards would not automatically render a dismissal unfair as there would be cases where a proper disciplinary procedure would be 'utterly useless' or 'futile', in which case the employer might well be acting reasonably in ignoring it. However, Lord Bridge in Polkey expressed the view that such cases would be 'exceptional' (see under 'No difference rule' below).

For more information on the Acas Code, see IDS Employment Law Supplement, 'Disciplinary and Grievance Procedures' (June 2009).

Investigation
6.178

An employer should carry out a full investigation before deciding whether dismissal is a reasonable response in the circumstances. There are unlikely to be many cases in which an employer could successfully argue that investigation would have made no difference to the decision to dismiss. Applying the Burchell test, the employer should not act on the basis of mere suspicion: it must have a genuine belief that the employee is guilty, based on reasonable grounds, after having carried out as much investigation into the matter as was reasonable in all the circumstances of the case. The employer's task is to gather all the available evidence. Once in full possession of the facts, the employer will be in a position to make a reasonable decision about what action to take. It is also important that the employer puts itself into a position of being able to make specific rather than general allegations against the employee.

An employer who fails to establish all the facts risks a finding that a resulting dismissal was unfair both in respect of a failure to carry out a reasonable investigation and a failure to comply with the Acas Code, which carries an attendant risk that any compensation payable will be increased by up to 25 per cent (see Chapter 18).

Gross misconduct. The Acas Code states that 'a fair disciplinary process should always be followed before dismissing for gross misconduct' (para 22). Thus, unless the misconduct is so heinous as to require instant dismissal – e.g. where there is a danger to life or immediate severe harm to the business – even serious conduct cases should be dealt with in the normal way. (Where immediate dismissal is deemed necessary, it is arguable that the lack of a fair procedure would not render it unfair as the exception in Polkey v AE Dayton Services Ltd 1988 ICR 142, HL, would apply – see under 'No difference rule' below. But even if the dismissal was found to be unfair, a tribunal might find that the failure to comply with the Code was reasonable in the circumstances
6.179

and that it would not be just and equitable to make an uplift to any award of compensation.)

6.180 **What is a 'reasonable' investigation?** The extent of the investigation and the form that it takes will vary according to the particular circumstances. In some cases, as the Code explains, the investigation stage will only involve the employer collating evidence; in others, an investigatory meeting with the employee will be required (para 5). If the employer decides to hold an investigatory meeting, it is important that it should not result in disciplinary action (para 7). If it becomes clear during the course of such a meeting that disciplinary action is needed, the meeting should be adjourned and the employee given notice of a separate disciplinary hearing and told of his or her right to be accompanied. Note that an employee only has a statutory right to be accompanied at a disciplinary hearing but not an investigatory meeting, unless this is allowed by the employer's own procedure – see below, under 'Right to be accompanied'.

There is no hard-and-fast rule as to the level of inquiry the employer should conduct into the employee's (suspected) misconduct in order to satisfy the Burchell test. This will very much depend on the particular circumstances, including the nature and gravity of the case, the state of the evidence and the potential consequences of an adverse finding to the employee. In ILEA v Gravett 1988 IRLR 497, EAT, Mr Justice Wood (then President of the EAT) offered the following advice: 'at one extreme there will be cases where the employee is virtually caught in the act and at the other there will be situations where the issue is one of pure inference. As the scale moves towards the latter end, so the amount of inquiry and investigation which may be required, including questioning of the employee, is likely to increase.'

6.181 The Acas Guide emphasises that the more serious the allegations against the employee, the more thorough the investigation conducted by the employer ought to be (page 17). In A v B 2003 IRLR 405, EAT, the EAT said that the gravity of the charges and the potential effect on the employee will be relevant when considering what is expected of a reasonable investigation. In its view, an investigation leading to a warning need not be as rigorous as one likely to lead to dismissal. In that case the fact that the employee, if dismissed, would never again be able to work in his chosen field was by no means as irrelevant as the tribunal appeared to think. Serious criminal allegations must always be carefully investigated, and the investigator should put as much focus on evidence that may point towards innocence as on that which points towards guilt. This is particularly so where the employee has been suspended and cannot communicate with witnesses. Having said this, the EAT accepted that the standard of reasonableness will always be high where dismissal is a likely consequence, and so the serious effect on future employment and the fact that criminal charges are involved

306

may not in practice alter that standard. Such factors merely reinforce the need for a careful and conscientious inquiry.

The Court of Appeal picked up on this point in Salford Royal NHS Foundation Trust v Roldan 2010 IRLR 721, CA (perhaps unsurprisingly, since Lord Justice Elias, sitting in the Court of Appeal, had given judgment in A v B when he was President of the EAT). In that case, the employee, a nurse who was dismissed for gross misconduct, not only faced criminal charges but also the risk of deportation. The Court saw the threat of the employee's deportation, which might have resulted from her dismissal, equally as deserving of careful investigation as the potential criminal charges she faced. Accordingly, given the employment tribunal's conclusion that procedural errors meant that the employee's dismissal had been unfair, the potentially serious adverse consequences dismissal would have had on her reinforced the justification for the tribunal's finding. This case may therefore be taken as authority for the more general principle that, if a dismissal could 'blight' an employee's career in some significant way, tribunals will be required to scrutinise the employer's procedures all the more carefully.

Facts in dispute? An investigation should be carried out whenever there is a factual issue to be determined. In Scottish Daily Record and Sunday Mail (1986) Ltd v Laird 1996 IRLR 665, Ct Sess (Inner House), the claimant was dismissed for failing to inform his employer of some outside professional interests. Although there was no dispute that he should have informed his employer of these other interests and had not done so, the Court stated that an investigation should nonetheless have taken place because there was a dispute as to whether there was a conflict between the employee's job on the one hand and the employer's and his own other professional interests on the other. 6.182

Conversely, where an employee admits an act of gross misconduct and where the facts are not in dispute, it may not be necessary to carry out a full investigation. In Boys and Girls Welfare Society v Macdonald 1997 ICR 693, EAT, the claimant was employed as a residential social worker in a children's home. During an altercation, he spat at one of the children. He admitted doing so at the disciplinary hearing and was dismissed. The EAT said that it was not always necessary to apply the Burchell test where there was no real conflict on the facts. Therefore it was not necessary for the employer to interview the boy with whom the employee had the altercation or to consider the extreme provocation under which the employee was placed. Similarly, in Community Integrated Care Ltd v Smith EAT 0015/08, the EAT in Scotland held that it was reasonable for the employer to treat the employee's comment 'I'm not saying I didn't say it' when confronted with a complaint that she verbally abused a patient as an admission of her guilt. In these circumstances, the employer did not have to conduct any further investigation into the matter; there was no real dispute about the fundamental facts.

6.183   **Delay.** The investigation should be carried out *without unreasonable delay*. The Acas Code emphasises the importance of establishing the facts and putting allegations to the employee promptly before recollections fade. So, in RSPCA v Cruden 1986 ICR 205, EAT, for example, an unjustifiable delay of seven months before disciplinary proceedings were commenced against an RSPCA inspector made an otherwise fair dismissal unfair, even though the employee suffered no prejudice.

6.184   **Intervening police investigation.** The employer's investigation may be hampered where the alleged misconduct is also the subject of a police inquiry. However, tribunals will not necessarily regard this as a valid excuse for a delay in completing the disciplinary procedure. Much will depend on the individual circumstances of the case. In A v B 2003 IRLR 405, EAT, the employee was suspended in mid-1997 and a disciplinary hearing did not take place until December 1999. Even taking account of the fact that police investigations took place between October 1997 and October 1998, such delays were held by the EAT to be 'grossly improper'. However, in another case where an allegation against an employee became part of a wide-ranging police investigation into allegations of ill treatment of inmates at a prison, a delay of two years did not render the dismissal of the prison worker unfair where full written evidence had been taken at an early stage – Newman v HM Prison Service ET Case No.3104586/02.

6.185   **Impartiality.** The Acas Guide stresses that employers should keep an open mind when carrying out an investigation; their task is to look for evidence that weakens as well as supports the employee's case. If disciplinary action results in dismissal and there is an indication that the employer has pre-judged the outcome, that can be enough to make the dismissal unfair – see, for example, Sovereign Business Integration plc v Trybus EAT 0107/07.

Paragraph 6 of the Acas Code states that 'where practicable, different people should carry out the investigation and disciplinary hearing'. Such a division of functions is recognised by the courts as an important indicator of impartiality. An example:

- **Warren James Jewellers Ltd v Christy** EAT 1041/02: C was dismissed on suspicion of theft when the bank paying-in slip for a day when she was left in charge of the shop was short by £1,000. In holding that her dismissal was unfair, the employment tribunal found that there had been no reasonable investigation, pointing to the fact that, among other things, the area manager who acted as the investigating officer was also responsible for disciplining and dismissing C.

6.186   The same principle of impartiality extends to those acting as witnesses in an investigation. For example:

- **Moyes v Hylton Castle Working Men's Social Club and Institute Ltd** 1986 IRLR 482, EAT: M was dismissed from his job as club steward after two incidents in which he allegedly sexually harassed a barmaid, the second of which was observed by the chairman and the assistant secretary of the club. The investigation was carried out by a sub-committee of five, which included the two club officials who were witnesses. A subsequent meeting of the full committee, which again included the chairman and assistant secretary, made the decision to dismiss. Overturning the employment tribunal's decision that the involvement of the two officials in the capacity of both witness and judge did not make the dismissal unfair, the EAT held that this was a breach of natural justice and any reasonable observer would conclude that justice did not appear to have been done and had not been done. The EAT acknowledged that there could be cases where a witness to an incident would have to make the decision to dismiss but in the present case found that it was entirely unnecessary for the two officials to act in both roles.

However, as the EAT accepted in the Moyes case, it is not always possible in small organisations for functions to be separated in this way. In Barlow v Clifford and Co (Sidcup) Ltd EAT 0910/04 the EAT found that where there are a limited number of people available it is not necessarily unfair for the same people to be involved in the early stages of the disciplinary process and in the decision to dismiss.

It is for the tribunal to determine whether, on the facts of a particular case and after having regard to the nature of the allegations made, the manner of the investigation, the size and capacity of the employer's undertaking, and all other relevant circumstances, it was unfair in a particular case for the investigator to also chair the disciplinary meeting and be the dismissal-decision-taker – Premier International Foods Ltd v Dolan and anor EAT 0641/04.

Gathering the evidence. In conducting the investigation, an employer should interview witnesses, although employers need not interview every available witness once a fact has been clearly established. However, the investigation may be flawed if an obvious witness is overlooked. For example, where the employer relied on a second-hand account of a fight between two employees instead of interviewing the only eye-witness, the investigation was found to be flawed – Baxters (Butchers) Ltd v Hart EAT 934/83. **6.187**

Information supplied by third parties. It may be acceptable for the employer to rely on witness statements and related information, provided to it from other sources, notably the police. The extent to which this may permissibly limit the employer's own investigation into the matter will invariably depend on the particular circumstances. The following two cases provide useful examples of the extent to which employers may be able to rely on evidence garnered by the police. **6.188**

In Harding v Hampshire County Council EAT 0672/04 allegations of serious misconduct were made against H, who worked for the Council as a youth

309

project worker. The police investigated the allegations (which were of sexual offences against three young boys and accessing child pornography on his computer), but eventually decided that there was not enough evidence to proceed to criminal charges. In due course, the Council began its own investigation, which relied to a large extent on the material assembled during the police enquiry. The Council, after a lengthy review of the information compiled by the police, decided that there was sufficient evidence to conclude that H had committed acts of gross misconduct and, following a disciplinary hearing, he was summarily dismissed. An employment tribunal found the dismissal fair, and specifically rejected H's submission that the employer had not conducted a reasonable investigation because it had to a large extent relied on the police inquiry and not made further enquiries.

On appeal, the EAT could find no fault with the tribunal's conclusion. It noted that there is no general rule or principle of law as to whether it is sufficient in an individual case for an employer, where there has been a police investigation into alleged misconduct, to rely upon the product of that investigation and to make no further investigation of its own. Whether it is reasonable for the employer to conduct further investigation will depend on the facts of the individual case. In H's case, the police investigation had been 'manifestly detailed'. The material provided to the employer included numerous witness statements, the records of the interviews of the relevant children, reports from the police computer expert and H's computer expert, and three interviews the police had conducted with H himself. Absent any suggestion that any of the witness statements were no longer accurate, there was no obligation on the employer to reinterview the witnesses. Moreover, the employer had tried to conduct a further interview with H, which he had refused. Bearing in mind that the correct test is not whether there could have been further investigation but whether the investigation which was carried out was reasonable in all the circumstances, it was clear that, in this case, there were no further enquiries that the employer should have made.

6.189   In Rhondda Cynon Taf County Borough Council v Close 2008 IRLR 868, EAT, the employee, a care worker, sought to distinguish her situation from that of the claimant in the Hampshire County Council case (above) by arguing that the allegation that formed the basis of the police investigation against her differed from the allegations that were the subject of the employer's disciplinary investigation: the police had investigated a possible manslaughter charge following the death of a patient, whereas the employer had dismissed her for sleeping on duty and swearing in front of patients. The EAT was not convinced, however. It held that it was not outside the band of reasonableness for an employer to choose not to carry out its own independent questioning of witnesses in a disciplinary procedure but instead to rely on police witness statements, even though those statements had been made to the police in relation to a different investigation. Furthermore, where certain matters are raised and dealt with in witness statements on the ground that the evidence may be relevant to a subsequent trial, and these statements are confirmed, it is irrelevant that the focus of the criminal investigation was different. Another consideration in this instant case was that the police witness statements had been made close to the time of the alleged misconduct, which meant that there was every reason to suppose that they would have been more reliable than statements taken by the employer as part of a disciplinary investigation almost three years later. The EAT therefore concluded that: 'The council obtained evidence based on the witness statements; they confirmed that the witnesses still stood by those statements; they allowed cross-examination of two of those witnesses; and they assessed the evidence of the witnesses they heard, and concluded that they were more reliable than the claimant. That is essentially what the employers have to do in circumstances of this kind.'

Both the above decisions are helpful to employers: they say that investigations need not be started again from scratch where the police have already looked into the matter. Nonetheless, employers should make sure that, based on the matter that forms the basis of their investigation, they carefully evaluate the information received from the police, and consider whether any parts of that information need to be revisited and/or require additional investigation.

Occasionally, evidence of the employee's misconduct emerges from more unusual sources. In Banks v Inland Revenue Liverpool ET Case No.2102391/04 B brought discrimination claims against IR, which were dismissed by the tribunal. The tribunal was scathing in its criticism of B: it concluded that she was a bully who was given to manipulative conduct in order to get her own way, and that her claims had been made with malicious intent. On the basis of the tribunal's judgment, IR took disciplinary action against B, and dismissed her for serious and gross misconduct. B complained of unfair dismissal, alleging that her dismissal was procedurally unfair because IR failed to conduct its own inquiry into her alleged misconduct and impermissibly relied on the tribunal's judgment. The tribunal hearing her unfair dismissal claim rejected this allegation. In its view, IR was entitled to rely on the tribunal's findings of fact, which had been 'damning in respect of the way the claimant had conducted herself both within the actual proceedings, and during her employment with the respondent'. In these circumstances, there was no need for the employer to carry out an internal investigation in addition to the judgment of the tribunal, which had considered ten days of evidence before reaching its decision. However, the tribunal noted the 'unusual facts of this case' and stressed that its decision was 'not a green light for respondents to use judgments of the tribunal as justification for dismissing those employees who have been unsuccessful in... litigation' against their employer.

Criminal proceedings pending. Where criminal proceedings are pending, matters can become complicated. For example, internal inquiries will often be   6.190

311

hampered by the employee's reluctance to discuss the incident. Nevertheless, employers should do their best to satisfy themselves of the employee's guilt. If they can show that that they believed, after carrying out a reasonable investigation, that the employee was guilty of misconduct meriting dismissal, then a subsequent acquittal on a criminal charge arising out of the same events would not of itself make the dismissal unfair. In Ali v Sovereign Buses (London) Ltd EAT 0274/06 the EAT reviewed the authorities on the issue and concluded that there is no hard-and-fast rule as to what an employer should do when deciding whether to press ahead with disciplinary proceedings when there is a criminal trial pending. It will depend on the circumstances of the case, although the employer should not dismiss too easily.

For more on the effect of criminal proceedings on dismissal, see under 'Criminal offences at work' above.

6.191 **Suspension.** In some circumstances an employer may feel it necessary to suspend the employee while the investigation is being carried out – notably, in gross misconduct cases – and until any disciplinary action takes place. However, the Acas Code recommends that, if a suspension with pay is considered necessary, it should be as brief as possible and kept under review and it should be made clear to the employee that the suspension does not amount to disciplinary action (para 8). Suspension without pay will be in breach of contract unless there is a clear contractual term allowing it.

6.192 **Providing details of charges and possible consequences**
If, once the investigation has been completed, disciplinary action is considered necessary, the Acas Code states that the employer should inform the employee in writing of the charge(s) against him or her and the possible consequences of the disciplinary action (para 9). This should contain enough information to enable him or her to prepare an answer to the case. It would normally be appropriate to provide copies of any written evidence, including witness statements. The notification should also give details of the time and venue for the disciplinary hearing (para 10).

It is important that the employee knows the *full allegations* against him or her. The Court of Appeal has stated that disciplinary charges should be precisely framed and evidence limited to those particulars – Strouthos v London Underground Ltd 2004 IRLR 636, CA. It is not only fundamental that employees should know the case against them, but where there is evidence against them they should also know what that evidence is. However, there is no general rule that a failure to make the evidence available to an employee either before, or at the outset of, the hearing will always amount to a breach of natural justice. Statements should be disclosed where the essence of the case against the employee is contained therein and where he or she has not otherwise been informed of the nature of that case. However, where the employee is fully aware of that case and has a full opportunity to respond to the allegations and the obtained statements

312

are peripheral to the decision reached, the failure to disclose will not render a dismissal unfair – Hussain v Elonex plc 1999 IRLR 420, CA.

There are many examples of cases in which a failure to inform an employee of the full allegations against him or her or to disclose the relevant evidence has led to a finding of unfair dismissal. Two examples: **6.193**

- **Hotson v Wisbech Conservative Club** 1984 ICR 859, EAT: the stated reason for the dismissal of a club barmaid was gross inefficiency in handling bar takings. During the tribunal hearing of her unfair dismissal complaint the chairman suggested, and the employer's representative agreed, that the employer was really alleging dishonesty. The tribunal proceeded to find the dismissal fair on the ground of suspected dishonesty. The EAT held that the difference between inefficiency and dishonesty was more than a mere change of label. The charge of dishonesty should have been stated at the outset or not stated at all: at the very least the employee should have had the fullest opportunity to consider the implications of the charge and to answer it

- **A v B** 2003 IRLR 405, EAT: A, a residential social worker, was dismissed after the employer decided, after a disciplinary hearing, that allegations that he had had an inappropriate relationship with a 14-year-old in his care were well founded. The EAT held that the dismissal was unfair. It acknowledged that it will often be enough if an employee knows the gist of the evidence against him. Additionally, if an employer reasonably forms a view that certain evidence is immaterial and cannot assist the employee, then it need not necessarily be disclosed. However, in this case, the young girl's evidence was not entirely consistent – she had made allegations against a number of other people and others had given evidence which conflicted with hers. It was therefore important that all the documentation was made available.

Right to be accompanied   **6.194**

When informing the employee of the time and venue for the disciplinary meeting, the employer should advise the employee of his or her right to be accompanied (para 10). Under S.10 of the Employment Relations Act 1999 (ERelA), where a worker 'reasonably requests' to be accompanied at a 'disciplinary hearing', the employer must permit the worker to be accompanied by a 'companion'. The companion – chosen by the worker – may be a trade union representative or a fellow worker – S.10(2A).

A disciplinary hearing is defined in the ERelA as a hearing that could result in:

- the administration of a formal warning – S.13(4)(a)

- the taking of some other action – S.13(4)(b)

313

- the confirmation of a warning issued or some other action taken – S.13(4)(c) (this applies to appeal hearings).

6.195 The chosen companion may address the hearing in order to put the worker's case, sum up that case, and respond on the worker's behalf to any view expressed at the hearing – S.10(2B) ERelA. He or she may also confer with the worker. However, the companion may not answer questions on behalf of the worker, address the hearing if the worker does not wish it, prevent the employer from making his case or prevent any other person from making a contribution – S.10(2C). An employee has a statutory right to ask for a meeting to be rescheduled if necessary in order for his or her chosen companion to attend as long as the alternative date suggested is within five working days of that proposed by the employer.

As the Acas Code emphasises, to exercise the statutory right to be accompanied workers must make a *reasonable* request – para 15. According to the Code, what is reasonable will depend on the circumstances of each case but it will not normally be reasonable for the employee to insist on being accompanied 'by a companion whose presence would prejudice the hearing'.

6.196 **Right to legal representation.** It is generally accepted that neither the ERelA nor the Acas Code confers an entitlement to have a legal representative present at the hearing. However, it appears that in certain circumstances Article 6 of the European Convention on Human Rights (ECHR) – which provides that an individual has the right to a fair hearing in the determination of his or her civil rights or of any criminal charge – may do so. This is despite the fact that Article 6(3) provides that only in the case of a criminal charge does an individual have the right to legal assistance. This is likely to be particularly relevant for public authority employers who are required by the Human Rights Act 1996 (HRA) to observe Convention obligations. Two key Court of Appeal cases on this issue:

- **Kulkarni v Milton Keynes Hospital NHS Foundation Trust and anor** 2010 ICR 101, CA: K, a junior doctor accused of misconduct involving inappropriate touching of a patient, sought legal representation at his disciplinary hearing. His main argument, that he had a contractual right to legal representation, succeeded before the Court of Appeal. Although not strictly necessary for its decision, Lady Justice Smith – giving the leading judgment – went on to note that where an employee is facing what is 'in effect a criminal charge', Article 6 of the ECHR implies a right to legal representation. Case law of the European Court of Human Rights (ECtHR) indicated that Article 6 would not apply where all that was at stake was the loss of a specific job. However, where the outcome of the proceedings is potentially more serious, such as the loss of the right to practise a particular profession, Article 6 would then be engaged. In the instant case, K was facing an accusation of serious sexual misconduct and, if found guilty, would effectively be barred from employment in the NHS. It did not matter that the right to legal representation was being requested in the context of civil proceedings because K was effectively facing a criminal charge. Therefore, the Court said, had it been necessary to make a decision on this issue, it would have held that Article 6 was engaged

- **R (on the application of G) v Governors of X School and anor** 2010 IRLR 222, CA: G, a music teaching assistant at X school, was suspended in October 2007 pending an investigation into allegations that he had formed an inappropriate relationship with a 15-year-old boy. No criminal proceedings were brought but the school instigated disciplinary proceedings. G was permitted representation at the hearing by either a trade union representative or a colleague, but not by a solicitor. Following the hearing, M was summarily dismissed for an abuse of trust amounting to gross misconduct. The school reported his dismissal to the Secretary of State so that he might determine whether to place G on a 'barred list' preventing him from working with children in future. G appealed against the decision to dismiss and requested legal representation at the appeal. This request was also refused. The High Court granted G's application for judicial review, holding that Article 6 entitled G to legal representation at the disciplinary and appeal hearings. On the school's appeal the Court of Appeal held that, since the disciplinary proceedings were determinative of G's civil right to practise his profession, they attracted Article 6 protection. Article 6 does not necessarily entail a right of representation in civil proceedings (unlike criminal proceedings) but it was 'well established' by ECtHR case law that it may do so. The level of civil procedural protection guaranteed by Article 6 depended on the gravity of the issue at stake. Given that G's right to practise his profession was at risk, he was entitled under Article 6 to be afforded the opportunity of legal representation in the disciplinary proceedings.

6.197 In the second of the cases outlined above Lord Justice Laws noted that the Court was not intending to create a 'hard and fast rule' regarding public authority employers' obligations in internal disciplinary hearings. He made it clear that the entitlement to legal representation will depend on all the facts, including the nature of the right affected and the capacity of a reviewing court or tribunal to 'reach back' into factual findings made at the disciplinary stage. This is limited so far as an employment tribunal is concerned, as its jurisdiction in an unfair dismissal case would not comprise a full review of the merits of the underlying facts, but rather would address the issue of whether dismissal by the employer was within the range of reasonable responses.

The Court of Appeal decisions discussed above suggest that wherever disciplinary proceedings could, in the event of an adverse outcome, end an employee's ability to practise a profession, it will be difficult to refute the argument that legal representation should be permitted. Neither of these cases

— 315

was initiated in an employment tribunal or indeed involved a claim of unfair dismissal. However, employment tribunals are likely to interpret the requirement for reasonableness under S.98(4) ERA in accordance with Article 6, bearing in mind their obligation under S.3 HRA to interpret UK legislation (including the ERA) in a way compatible with ECHR rights. Therefore, failure – at least by public sector employers – to allow for legal representation, when appropriate to do so, could render the dismissal procedurally unfair. This could well apply even to private employers, given the framework of questions for tribunals dealing with unfair dismissal claims in which HRA issues arise set out by the Court of Appeal in X v Y 2004 ICR 1634, CA – see Chapter 3 under 'Reasonableness of dismissal – impact of the Human Rights Act' for details. Further, in Kulkarni v Milton Keynes Hospital NHS Foundation Trust and anor (above), Lady Justice Smith stated that the issue could be framed in terms of natural justice under domestic law, as well as breach of Article 6 – although this was not picked up by Laws LJ in R v Governors of X School (above).

6.198 The disciplinary hearing

The purpose of the disciplinary hearing is twofold: it allows the employer to find out whether or not the misconduct has been committed and it allows the employee to explain the conduct or any mitigating circumstances. The Acas Code states that the disciplinary hearing should be held 'without unreasonable delay whilst allowing the employee reasonable time to prepare their case' (para 11). Employers and employees (and their companions) should make every effort to attend the meeting (para 12).

The Acas Guide recommends that employers arrange for someone who is not involved in the case to attend the meeting to take a note and act as a witness to what was said (page 19). If the employee needs an interpreter or facilitator because of a language barrier or understanding difficulties, the Guide suggests that the employer consider providing one. The attendance of an individual in this role may be in addition to the employee's companion. Although the Guide says that 'ideally one person should carry out both roles', this will not necessarily be practical and employers should always remember that the overriding test in a case of unfair dismissal is one of reasonableness in the circumstances. Note that if the employee has a disability and needs an interpreter or other assistant at the meeting in order to remove any disadvantage faced by the employee as a result of that disability, an employer's refusal to allow one may be a breach of his duty to make reasonable adjustments under the Disability Discrimination Act 1995 – see IDS Employment Law Supplement, 'Disciplinary and Grievance Procedures', Chapter 5.

6.199 **Conduct of meeting.** The Acas Code sets out the following requirements:

- the employer should explain the complaint against the employee and go through the evidence that has been gathered

- the employee should be allowed to set out his or her case and answer any allegations that have been made

- the employee should be given a reasonable opportunity to ask questions, present evidence and call witnesses

- the employee should be given an opportunity to raise points about any information provided by witnesses

- where an employer or employee intends to call relevant witnesses they should give advance notice that they intend to do this (para 12).

The Acas Guide points out that the purpose of the meeting is to establish the facts rather than to catch people out, and suggests that it contain the following five elements:

6.200

- statement of the complaint by the employer outlining the complaint and the evidence

- the employee's reply answering any allegations that have been made

- general questioning and discussion, which should be a two-way process

- summing up

- adjournment before a decision (pages 20–22).

Even if misconduct is admitted, the employee should at least be given an opportunity to explain. If, however, the employee declines to offer any explanation, the employer will not be prevented from proceeding further and, if it is reasonable, dismissing the individual – W Weddel and Co Ltd v Tepper 1980 ICR 286, CA. However, the employer should be careful to make the employee fully aware of what is happening and of the possible consequences of a refusal to speak at the hearing.

A failure to ensure that the employee is given a fair chance to refute any allegations of misconduct against him or her may lead a tribunal to conclude that the decision to dismiss was a foregone conclusion. An example:

6.201

- **Sands v Duke Contractors Ltd** ET Case No.1100153/07: in July 2006, S went off sick with a broken ankle and produced medical certificates to that effect during the ensuing months. In November 2006, DC Ltd summarily dismissed him for gross misconduct; among other things, it questioned his inability to return to work. An employment tribunal upheld S's unfair dismissal claim, finding that DC Ltd failed to conduct a fair disciplinary hearing: it did not present the allegations against him clearly; withheld witness statements that were allegedly in its possession; adopted an accusatory manner during the hearing, which put S in the position of having to defend himself; asked him closed questions, which

317

inhibited his capacity to respond fully and openly; and failed to take S's responses into account.

6.202 **Absence of bias.** It is a cardinal principle of natural justice that the person conducting the proceedings should not be a 'judge in his own cause'. In other words, the decision-maker should not have a direct interest in the outcome of the proceedings and should not give any appearance of bias or partiality. Commonly cited evidence of bias is where a supervisor or manager involved in the disciplinary proceedings was also involved at an earlier stage in the case and so may already have formed an opinion. In order to minimise the possibility of bias, the procedure should separate the processes of investigation, decision-making and appeal wherever possible. In Whitbread plc (t/a Whitbread Medway Inns) v Hall 2001 ICR 699, CA, the claimant's dismissal was found to be unfair despite his admission of guilt because the manager holding the disciplinary meeting had initiated the investigation and was biased against him, as she had already made up her mind to dismiss. Similarly, in Perkin v St George's Healthcare NHS Trust 2006 ICR 617, CA, the person who had talked of wanting an 'exit strategy' for a difficult employee was the wrong person to chair his disciplinary hearing.

Although absence of bias is important, it has also been recognised that the requirement that there should be no possibility of bias cannot be applied in absolute terms in the employment field. It may be unreasonable – particularly with smaller concerns – to expect the different stages of investigation and adjudication to be conducted by different individuals, or to expect those individuals to be unaffected by daily contact with each other. As the EAT has said: 'In the end the only thing that matters is whether the disciplinary tribunal acted fairly and justly' – Haddow and ors v Inner London Education Authority 1979 ICR 202, EAT.

6.203 **Non-attendance of employee.** Paragraph 24 of the Code states that 'where an employee is persistently unable or unwilling to attend a disciplinary meeting without good cause the employer should make a decision on the evidence available'. There are obvious areas for dispute here over the definitions of 'persistently' and 'without good cause' and employers should exercise caution before proceeding with a disciplinary hearing in the employee's absence.

Before making a decision on how to proceed when an employee is repeatedly unable or unwilling to attend a meeting, the Acas Guide suggests that the employer take into account the following considerations:

• any rules the organisation has for dealing with failure to attend disciplinary meetings

• the seriousness of the disciplinary issue under consideration

• the employee's disciplinary record (including current warnings), general work record, work experience, position and length of service

- medical opinion on whether the employee is fit to attend the meeting

- how similar cases in the past have been dealt with (page 20).

In the following case the employer acted unfairly by jumping to conclusions   **6.204**
about an employee's fitness to attend a meeting:

- **William Hicks and Partners (A Firm) v Nadal** EAT 0164/05: N was suspended over a number of allegations including bullying and intimidation of staff and a couple of days later her doctor wrote to the employer to say that she was suffering from stress and was not fit to attend any hearing in the foreseeable future. Despite this the employer arranged a disciplinary hearing, but it was postponed on a couple of occasions following the receipt of further sick notes. Eventually, however, the hearing took place in N's absence after the employer discovered that she had been in negotiations with a new employer. The EAT upheld the tribunal's finding of unfair dismissal on the grounds that N's employer should not have ignored medical advice it had commissioned without 'compelling evidence' that N was 'pulling the wool over her own doctor's eyes' or in the absence of 'authoritative contrary medical evidence' about her fitness, neither of which it had. The EAT pointed out that the opportunity for an employee to put his or her side of matters had long been established as an essential part of a reasonable investigation. It accepted that there may be cases where an employer had made proper enquiries, including sufficient medical enquiries, to establish that the employee was fit to attend a hearing but had unreasonably declined to do so without just cause. However, it said that this must be an exception to the general rule that disciplinary hearings should always involve the presence of the employee.

Witnesses. Often employers will be faced with diametrically conflicting   **6.205**
accounts of an alleged incident with no, or very little, other evidence to
provide corroboration one way or the other. In these circumstances, said the
Court of Appeal in Salford Royal NHS Foundation Trust v Roldan 2010
IRLR 721, CA, although it is incumbent on employers to form a genuine
belief on reasonable grounds that the misconduct has occurred, they are not
obliged to believe one employee over another. Lord Justice Elias, giving the
judgment of the Court, explained that sometimes it may be proper for
employers to say that they cannot resolve the conflict and therefore do not
find the case proved against the accused employee, without coming down in
favour of one side or the other.

In the course of his judgment, Elias LJ also picked up on comments made by Lord
Justice Mummery in the earlier decision of London Ambulance Service NHS
Trust v Small 2009 IRLR 563, CA. There, Mummery LJ observed, without laying
down any fixed rule, that it would often be helpful for a tribunal when looking
at questions of fairness, contributory fault, Polkey and so forth, to set out their

319

relevant findings of fact separately with respect to each element. Elias LJ noted that, in his view, it will not normally be appropriate for tribunal witnesses to give their evidence in any such compartmentalised way; an economic and efficient approach, in line with the overriding objective, would normally require witnesses to deal with all relevant evidence on one occasion. The notion that the tribunal must hear all the witnesses twice (once on liability and then again on remedies) would unnecessarily add to the length and cost of the hearing without any obvious benefit. However, he did recognise that there will be exceptions to this, particularly in the case of small employers where the factual evidence to the different issues may be given by the same person. There it will generally be appropriate to leave some evidence to be given at a later date.

6.206   **Cross-examination of witnesses.** The inclusion in para 12 of the Code of a right to call witnesses (see above) has raised some eyebrows, not least because case law is more ambiguous on this point. In Santamera v Express Cargo Forwarding t/a IEC Ltd 2003 IRLR 273, EAT, the EAT stated that cross-examination will be an exception in employment disciplinary proceedings. On the facts, the allegations involved bullying and the witness felt intimidated by the claimant. The employer reasonably believed that the allegations were true. In these circumstances, the dismissal was not rendered unfair by the refusal to allow the employee to cross-examine the witness. However, although the rules on fairness contained in S.98(4) ERA do not require an employer to carry out 'a forensic or quasi-judicial investigation', it did not follow that an employer will never be obliged to allow an employee to cross-examine his or her accusers during disciplinary proceedings. The EAT emphasised that in each case a tribunal must decide with reference to the facts before it whether the employer's procedure had been fair and reasonable. The decision leaves open the question of when it is reasonable for an employer to allow cross-examination of witnesses and when it is not. Its effect is that, so long as a refusal to allow cross-examination falls within the band of reasonable responses open to the employer, it will not render a dismissal unfair.

Admittedly, the Acas Code does not specifically state that employees have the right to cross-examine witnesses, merely to call them. However, there would be little point in calling a witness to attend a hearing if questions could not be put to him or her and it has to be assumed that the intention behind the Code is to allow witnesses to be questioned. It is, of course, open to an employer to refuse to allow a witness to be called if it is reasonable in the circumstances, although there is no guidance as to what would be considered reasonable here. The rules of natural justice, in so far as they apply to disciplinary hearings, require that an employee know precisely what the accusations against him or her are and have a full opportunity of stating his or her case. It seems appropriate, therefore, that the question of whether or not it is reasonable to allow a witness to be called in a particular case should be decided in light of these principles.

320

In Rhondda Cynon Taf County Borough Council v Close 2008 IRLR 868,   **6.207**
EAT, the EAT rejected the employee's argument that her dismissal was
rendered unfair by the employer's failure to make all the witnesses available for
cross-examination. She had been able to challenge the evidence against her and
to cross-examine two witnesses who gave oral evidence at the disciplinary
hearing. In the end, however, the employer had assessed the evidence of the
witnesses and concluded that they were more reliable than her.

If an allegation has been made by, or evidence obtained from, an individual
who is not an employee of the employer's organisation (e.g. a customer), it may
not be practicable or desirable for that person to attend a disciplinary hearing.
In such cases, the Acas Guide recommends that the employer try to get a written
statement from that individual (page 19). If a witness – whether or not a fellow
employee – wants to remain anonymous, the Guide advises employers to take
written statements, seek corroborative evidence, and check that the person's
motives are genuine.

Protecting the identity of informants. Where an employer receives evidence   **6.208**
from an informant who wishes to remain anonymous, the employee is
potentially disadvantaged by not being able to challenge that person's evidence.
The EAT set out guidelines for employers to follow in these circumstances in
Linfood Cash and Carry Ltd v Thomson and anor 1989 ICR 518, EAT, with
the express purpose of trying to maintain a balance of interest between
protecting the anonymity of the informant and providing a fair hearing for the
employee. The EAT made the following suggestions:

- informants' statements should be reduced to writing (although they might
  need to be edited later to preserve anonymity)

- in taking statements it is important to note the date, time and place of each
  observation or incident; the informant's opportunity to observe clearly and
  accurately; circumstantial evidence, such as knowledge of a system, the
  reason for the informant's presence or any memorable small details; and
  whether the informant had any reason to fabricate evidence

- further investigation should then take place, corroboration being clearly
  desirable

- tactful enquiries into the character and background of the informant would
  be advisable

- a decision must then be taken whether to hold a disciplinary hearing,
  particularly when the employer is satisfied that the informant's fear is
  genuine

- if the disciplinary process is to continue, the responsible member of
  management at each stage of the procedure should personally interview the
  informant and decide what weight is to be given to his or her evidence

321

- the informant's written statement – if necessary with omissions to avoid identification – should be made available to the employee and his or her representative

- if the employee or his or her representative raise an issue that should be put to the informant, it may be desirable to adjourn the disciplinary proceedings so that the chairman can question the informant

- it is particularly important that full and careful notes should be taken at disciplinary hearings when informants are involved

- if evidence from an investigating officer is to be taken at a hearing it should where possible be prepared in writing. (Note that this final point is not limited to cases where an investigation has been started because of statements made by an informant.)

6.209 However, as the EAT itself noted: 'Every case must depend upon its own facts, and circumstances may vary widely.' In Ramsey and ors v Walkers Snack Foods Ltd and anor 2004 IRLR 754, EAT, the Linford guidelines were not followed fully. In particular, full statements were not taken from informants at the outset and the statements that were taken were heavily edited. In addition, informants were only interviewed by one manager, who was not involved in the disciplinary process. However, the EAT noted that the case involved multiple informants who were terrified of being identified because they worked in a factory with a close-knit community. They were thus unwilling to sign statements unless they had been sufficiently edited so as to remove any risk of identification. Nor did they wish to be exposed to further questioning that might risk their identities becoming known. In the circumstances, the risk of reprisals was real. The EAT stated that, when considering whether or not the approach taken was fair, the focus should be on the reasons for granting anonymity in the first place. On this basis, as the tribunal had made a clear finding that the offer of anonymity was reasonable and the employer genuinely believed that no information would be provided unless it was entirely confidential, the approach taken was fair, notwithstanding non-compliance with the Linford guidelines in some respects.

The same approach was followed in Surrey County Council v Henderson EAT 0326/05 where the employer had given anonymity to five complainants who accused the employee of having threatened them and their families with violence. The employee was not provided with copies of their statements. The tribunal found that his dismissal was unfair, but the EAT overturned that decision and remitted the case to be reconsidered by a different tribunal. In its view, the tribunal had failed to consider whether, having regard to the reasons why the complainants insisted on anonymity, the procedure adopted by the employer in the particular circumstances of this case fell within or outside the band of reasonable responses. That band may include some reasonable employers who would have disclosed the witness statements taken from the five complainants, either in full or in redacted form, or in some other summary form and others who would not, given the promises of confidentiality made by the employer to those complainants based on their fears and concerns for themselves and their families.

There is generally no breach of natural justice in relying on the evidence of an anonymous informant at a disciplinary hearing. It is well established that the rules of natural justice, in so far as they apply to disciplinary hearings, only require that an employee should know precisely what the accusations against him or her are and have a full opportunity of stating his or her case. There is no prescriptive right to be allowed to cross-examine witnesses (see above). In any case, witnesses other than anonymous informants – e.g. employees of other companies or members of the general public – may be unwilling to appear at internal disciplinary hearings and cannot be compelled to do so. The EAT's guidelines in the Linford case (above), appropriately amended, could be useful in all cases where a witness is reluctant to appear in person.

6.210

An employer will not always be able to guarantee the anonymity of an informant. In A v Company B Ltd 1997 IRLR 405, ChD, A's reputation in the industry in which he worked was destroyed when accusations were made against him by an anonymous informant. His employer, despite having lost a claim of unfair dismissal, refused to disclose either the nature of the allegations against him or the identity of the informant. As A was not in a position to counter the allegations, he was unable to repair his reputation and therefore unable to find a new job. The High Court granted his application for an order requiring B Ltd to reveal both the nature of the allegations and the identity of his accuser. The Court decided that it had discretion to order the disclosure of an informant's identity where this was necessary to enable an employee to know whether he had a civil action for defamation or malicious falsehood against the informant whose information led to the employee's dismissal. It was intolerable, the Court said, that an individual could be stained by serious allegations, the nature of which he had no means of discovering, and be left in a position where he could not even invoke the law to defend his reputation.

Grievance raised during disciplinary procedure. The Acas Code recommends (at para 44) that where an employee raises a grievance during a disciplinary process the disciplinary process may need to be temporarily suspended in order to deal with the matter. However, where the grievance and disciplinary cases are related, it may be appropriate to deal with both issues concurrently. The Code clearly intends employers to have a discretion to deal with the situation appropriately that was not available to them under the (now-repealed) statutory disciplinary procedures. The accompanying Guide suggests that a suspension of the disciplinary procedure may be appropriate where:

6.211

- the grievance relates to a conflict of interest that the manager holding the disciplinary meeting is alleged to have

323

- bias is alleged in the conduct of the disciplinary meeting

- management has been selective in the evidence it has supplied to the manager holding the meeting

- there is possible discrimination (page 22).

6.212 **The decision**

It is good practice for the employer to adjourn the disciplinary hearing in order to consider the case before coming to a decision. The Acas Code states that 'after the meeting' the employer should decide whether or not disciplinary or any other action is justified and inform the employee accordingly in writing (para 17).

In deciding whether disciplinary action is appropriate and, if so, what form it should take, the Acas Guide suggests that employers consider:

- whether the rules of the organisation indicate what the likely penalty will be as a result of the particular misconduct

- the penalty imposed in similar cases in the past

- whether standards of other employees are acceptable, and whether this employee is not being unfairly singled out

- the employee's disciplinary record (including current warnings), general work record, work experience, position and length of service

- any special circumstances which might make it appropriate to adjust the severity of the penalty

- whether the proposed penalty is reasonable in all the circumstances

- whether any training, additional support or adjustments to the work are necessary (page 27).

6.213 **Length of service.** The employee's length of service is relevant when deciding the appropriate sanction. In Strouthos v London Underground Ltd 2004 IRLR 636, CA, the Court held that the fact that S had been employed for 20 years with no relevant previous warnings was material. While acknowledging that there can be conduct so serious that dismissal is appropriate irrespective of length of service, the EAT had been wrong to say that length of service was not relevant.

6.214 **Prior disciplinary record.** Rarely will previous warnings be irrelevant when an employer is considering dismissal – see, for example, Cunliffe v Primagraphics Ltd ET Case No.1500499/06 (where the employer decided that the appropriate penalty was dismissal in circumstances where the employee, who was already subject to a final written warning for insulting and intimidatory behaviour to a colleague, sent an offensive e-mail around the office). In deciding the fairness of such a dismissal, tribunals will take into account the previous warnings issued,

324

even if such warnings related to different kinds of conduct from that for which the employee is ultimately dismissed – Auguste Noel Ltd v Curtis 1990 ICR 604, EAT. However, where a final warning was clearly unreasonable, and where that final warning contributes to a later dismissal, the dismissal may be unfair – Co-operative Retail Services Ltd v Lucas EAT 145/93.

Expired warnings. It is usual for expired warnings not to be taken into account **6.215** when deciding whether disciplinary action is appropriate. In Diosynth Ltd v Thomson 2006 IRLR 284, Ct Sess (Inner House), the Court of Session said that an employee was entitled to assume that a warning, which would cease to have effect after 12 months, meant exactly what it said. Accordingly, the employer acted unreasonably in taking the expired warning into account when deciding to dismiss the employee by reason of misconduct. The dismissal, which would not have been carried out had the warning not been on his file, was thus unfair.

That said, the Court of Appeal, in Airbus UK Ltd v Webb 2008 ICR 561, CA, subsequently distinguished the Diosynth decision, commenting that that case was not authority for a broad proposition that an expired warning must be ignored for *all* purposes. In that case, the claimant was the only one of four employees caught watching television outside the normal break time to be dismissed. The other three, who were given a final written warning, had no prior disciplinary record, whereas the claimant had previously been given a final written warning that had expired three weeks before. The Court held that the employer had been entitled to take the claimant's previous, though expired, warning into account when deciding whether it was reasonable to dismiss.

Although these decisions seem initially difficult to reconcile, on closer reading they should not pose any problems in practice for employers. As the Court of Appeal explained in the Airbus case, once the warning ceased to have effect as a penalty, it could not be relied on as the reason for dismissal. But this did not mean that the misconduct, in respect of which the penalty was imposed, could not be relevant to the consideration of the reasonableness of the employer's later action in dismissing the employee for similar misconduct. In the words of Lord Justice Mummery: 'The language of section 98(4) is wide enough to cover the employee's earlier misconduct as a relevant circumstance of the employer's later decision to dismiss the employee, whose later misconduct is shown by the employer to the employment tribunal to be the reason or principal reason for the dismissal.'

In the Diosynth case, the employer had not been entitled to dismiss the employee **6.216** by reason of the expired warning on his file in circumstances where his misconduct was not sufficient, on its own, to justify dismissal. In other words, the expired warning was not capable of 'tipping the balance' in favour of dismissal. By contrast, in the Airbus case, the employee was dismissed by reason of his misconduct, not because he had an expired final written warning on his file. The employer, having considered that the conduct of all four employees (including the claimant) was sufficiently serious to result in dismissal, had been entitled to take into account,

325

when considering any mitigating circumstances, that the claimant had a previous expired warning for misconduct whereas the other three had clean disciplinary records. In these circumstances, the employer's decision to dismiss only the claimant had been reasonably open to it.

It follows from this that the Airbus case does not give employers a free hand to treat expired warnings as still being in effect. Rather, it establishes that, once a warning for misconduct has expired, an employer does not artificially have to pretend that the previous misconduct never took place when dealing with further acts of misconduct on the part of the same employee. It still remains good practice to 'wipe the slate clean' after a warning has expired, but the Court's decision emphasises that just because something is contrary to notions of good practice does not invariably mean that it will be unreasonable. The question for tribunals is, as ever, whether the degree of reliance on the previous misconduct and/or the expired warning was reasonable in the circumstances.

Expired warnings are further discussed under 'Final written warning – time limits for warnings' below.

6.217   **Consistency of treatment.** As the Acas Guide points out, fairness does not mean that similar offences will always call for the same disciplinary action (page 28). Each case must be looked at in the context of its particular circumstances, which may include health or domestic problems, provocation, or justifiable ignorance of the rule or standard involved. The Acas Guide gives two scenarios based on an example involving disciplinary action taken against an employee who has made a series of mistakes concerning delivery dates with the result that a customer has threatened to take its business elsewhere. In the first scenario, the employee had received relevant training and her team leader and section manager had stressed to her the importance of agreeing delivery dates. In the second, she had received no training or guidance from her supervisor or manager. In the first scenario, a final written warning was deemed appropriate, whereas no disciplinary action was warranted in the second.

In Paul v East Surrey District Health Authority 1995 IRLR 305, CA, the Court of Appeal held that an employer is entitled to take into account not only the nature of the conduct and the surrounding facts but also any personal circumstances affecting the employee. That case concerned a nurse who was dismissed for drinking on duty. He argued that his dismissal was unfair since colleagues who had also been drinking on duty had not been dismissed. The Court found that the attitude of the employee to his or her conduct may be a relevant factor in deciding whether a repetition of it is likely and commented: 'Thus an employee who admits that the conduct proved is unacceptable and accepts advice and help to avoid a repetition may be regarded differently from one who refuses to accept responsibility for his actions, argues with

326 ——————————————————————————————

management or makes unfounded suggestions that his fellow employees have conspired to accuse him falsely.'

The employer must consider the circumstances of each individual employee. Two contrasting examples:

6.218

- **Merseyside Passenger Transport Executive v Millington** EAT 232/89: M worked on a passenger ferry. During one of his shifts he went to a pub to have lunch. He was joined by two other employees, H and W. The employer had a strict rule that employees should not enter licensed premises while working. A member of management went to the pub and immediately suspended all three employees. There was no suggestion that M was drunk – he had merely gone to the most convenient place to obtain food – but H and W acted in a way consistent with their being drunk. On the following day, all three were summarily dismissed. Management believed that it risked an unfair dismissal claim if it did not treat all three alike for breaching the same rule. However, an employment tribunal took the view that there were enough differences between M's conduct and that of H and W, coupled with mitigating factors on M's behalf, to make a reasonable employer distinguish between them and treat M more leniently. The EAT agreed. It added that to treat all employees the same as a matter of course, without considering each individual's particular circumstances, simply could not be done

- **Levenes Solicitors v Dalley** 2008 EWCA Civ 69, CA: the Court of Appeal found that the employer had not acted unreasonably in dismissing D for failing to issue a claim in time when another solicitor who had failed to serve proceedings in time on three occasions had not been dismissed. The fact that D was also facing a charge of being absent from work for no good reason justified the difference in treatment.

Reasonable penalty. Employers should ensure that any penalty imposed is commensurate to the misconduct committed by the employee or risk being in fundamental breach of the duty of trust and confidence. In Macaulay v Saga Publishing Ltd ET Case No.1103038/06 M was given a final written warning after playing a practical joke on a colleague. An employment tribunal found that the employer's penalty was too harsh, as it meant that he would not get a pay increase and bonus, and he had been entitled to treat himself as constructively dismissed. The maximum penalty for M's conduct would have been a verbal warning.

6.219

First written warning. Paragraph 18 of the Code states that where misconduct is confirmed it is usual to give the employee a written warning. The employee should also be given sufficient time in which to improve. However, it may not be necessary to give the employee an opportunity to improve where there is evidence

6.220

327

that he or she is unlikely to change their behaviour in future – Perkin v St George's Healthcare NHS Trust 2006 ICR 617, CA.

Employers may have as many stages in their procedures as they consider appropriate. For example, some procedures may include an 'informal' stage (although note that if such action results in a written record it may not be viewed as informal for the purpose of the right to be accompanied) and/or more than one formal warning stage before a final written warning is given. What is important is that parties are aware of which stage has been reached and its consequences. An example:

- **Sarkar v West London Mental Health NHS Trust** 2010 IRLR 508, CA: the Court of Appeal upheld an employment tribunal's decision that the Trust had unfairly dismissed S for gross misconduct through its formal disciplinary procedure, when it had initially taken the view that the misconduct could be dealt with under its 'Fair Blame Policy' (FBP) – a dispute resolution procedure designed to deal with less serious matters. The tribunal was entitled to regard the initial use of the FBP as an indication of the Trust's view that the misconduct alleged against S was relatively minor and that it was prepared to deal with it under a procedure that could not result in his dismissal. The tribunal did not err in law in concluding that it was inconsistent of the Trust to then charge S with gross misconduct based on the same matters.

6.221 A written warning, whether first or final, should set out the nature of the misconduct and the change to behaviour required, with a timescale (para 20). The employee should be told how long the warning will remain current and informed of the consequences of further misconduct within the set period – for instance, in the case of a final warning, that it may result in dismissal or some other contractual penalty such as demotion or loss of seniority. A failure by the employer to comply with any of these requirements may make it unreasonable to rely on the warning in any future disciplinary action.

A record of the warning should be kept, but it should be disregarded for disciplinary purposes after a specified period (e.g. six months). The Acas Guide also suggests that the warning should inform the employee of his or her right to appeal and the timescale within which an appeal must be made.

6.222 **Final written warning.** A further act of misconduct within a set period would normally result in a final written warning (para 18). However, where an employee's first misconduct is sufficiently serious – for example, it has had or may have had a serious harmful impact on the organisation – it may be appropriate to move directly to a final written warning (para 19).

A final written warning may also be used where misconduct is sufficiently serious to amount to gross misconduct justifying summary dismissal but the

328

circumstances are such that dismissal is not deemed appropriate, as illustrated by the following example taken from page 30 of the Acas Guide:

- a long-serving employee returns from a celebratory lunch having consumed too much alcohol. He is very apologetic and promises that it will not happen again. Although being unfit for work because of excessive alcohol is listed in the company rules as gross misconduct, taking into account his ten years' service and exemplary record, the employer decides not to dismiss but to give him a final written warning.

Time limits for warnings. There is no set time limit for a written warning: the Acas Code only requires that a timescale be included (para 20) and the example of six months given in the Acas Guide is purely that. The Guide recommends that, 'except in agreed special circumstances, any disciplinary action taken should be disregarded for disciplinary purposes after a specified period of satisfactory conduct' (page 33). It states that normal practice is for different types of warning to remain in force for different periods; for example, six months for a first written warning and 12 months for a final written warning (or more in exceptional circumstances). It suggests that the established period should be set out in the disciplinary procedure and that warnings should cease to be 'live' when that period has expired. However, the Guide does provide for exceptions. First, where there is a pattern of an employee's conduct improving during the period of a warning and lapsing shortly afterwards, it suggests that his or her previous record can be taken into account when deciding how long a future warning should last. Secondly, although stating that a decision to dismiss should not be based on an expired warning, the Guide accepts that the fact that there is an expired warning may explain an employer's decision not to substitute a lesser penalty.

6.223

Since an employee's prior disciplinary record is often a factor in deciding whether dismissal is an appropriate sanction, both parties will benefit from knowing whether a previous warning has expired.

Dismissal. Para 21 of the Acas Code makes it clear that a decision to dismiss should only be taken by a manager who has the authority to do so and that the employee should be informed as soon as possible of the reasons for the dismissal, the date on which the employment contract will end, the appropriate period of notice and the right of appeal.

6.224

An employee with at least a year's service at the effective date of termination has a statutory right under S.92 ERA to receive a written statement of the reasons for his or her dismissal if he or she requests one. If such a request is made, the employer must provide the statement within 14 days. An employee who is pregnant or who is on maternity or adoption leave which is brought to an end by the dismissal is entitled to written reasons for dismissal without having to make a request and regardless of length of service. A failure to

329

provide written reasons will result in an award of two weeks' pay to the employee – S.93 ERA (see Chapter 21).

6.225 **Other sanctions.** If the disciplinary rules provide for sanctions other than dismissal, such as transfer, demotion or suspension without pay, the employer should consider whether such an alternative is appropriate – see page 30 of the Acas Guide.

The question of alternative employment is normally considered relevant to an employer's reasonableness in dismissing where there has been little or no contributory behaviour on the part of the employee dismissed – for example, in situations of incapacity and redundancy. However, the Court of Appeal's decision in P v Nottinghamshire County Council 1992 ICR 706, CA, appears to have extended this duty to consider redeployment into certain misconduct cases. In that case the employee was dismissed from his position as an assistant groundsman at a girls' school run by Nottinghamshire County Council. He had pleaded guilty to a charge of indecent assault against his daughter and asked for two further offences of indecent conduct with two older daughters to be taken into account. At the time of his dismissal he was informed that an attempt would be made by the Council to redeploy him in the Highways Department. However, he was not accepted there on account of his sickness record. His complaint of unfair dismissal was upheld by a tribunal in a majority decision. When the matter reached the Court of Appeal, it stated that in an appropriate case, and where the size and administrative resources of the employer's undertaking permit, it may be unfair to dismiss an employee without first considering whether he or she could be redeployed in an alternative job, notwithstanding that it is clear that the employee could not be allowed to continue in his or her original job.

Unfortunately, the Court of Appeal in the Nottinghamshire case provided no real guidance as to what might constitute an 'appropriate case' when it comes to dismissals for misconduct. It may well be that in such cases alternative employment should only be investigated where the dismissal would not have been regarded as necessary in the first place if the employee had been employed in a different post.

6.226 **'No difference' rule**

In Polkey v AE Dayton Services Ltd 1988 ICR 142, HL, the House of Lords ruled that employers could not argue that a procedurally improper dismissal was nevertheless fair because it would have made no difference if the employer had followed a fair procedure. Their Lordships held that an employer's actions in dispensing with a fair procedure were highly relevant to the question of whether an employer acted reasonably in dismissing, and that tribunals were not entitled to take into account, when determining the fairness or otherwise of a dismissal, whether a proper procedure would have made any difference to the employer's decision to dismiss. Only in wholly exceptional cases where it could be shown that carrying out a proper procedure would have been 'utterly useless' or 'futile' would procedural failures be overlooked when considering reasonableness for the purposes of S.98(4) ERA. Polkey and the so-called 'no difference' rule is discussed further in Chapter 3 under 'Fairness of internal procedure'.

The appeal

6.227

Paragraph 25 of the Acas Code states that: 'Where an employee feels that disciplinary action taken against them is wrong or unjust they should appeal against the decision. Appeals should be heard without unreasonable delay and ideally at an agreed time and place. Employees should let employers know the grounds for their appeal in writing.' This makes it clear that the right to appeal applies to all disciplinary hearings, not just those resulting in dismissal, with the result that a refusal to allow an employee to appeal at any stage of the procedure could lead to an uplift in any compensation award if the employee subsequently brings a successful tribunal claim. It also imposes an obligation on the employee to appeal in writing, with the result that any failure to do so may be taken into account by an employment tribunal when determining any related claim and any resulting compensation may be reduced accordingly under S.207A TULR(C)A – see Chapter 18, under 'Adjustments for breach of Acas Code of Practice'. Delay by either party also has the potential to incur a penalty.

The Acas Guide states that the opportunity to appeal against a disciplinary decision is essential to natural justice and that an appeal may be raised on any number of grounds such as new evidence, undue severity or inconsistency of the penalty (page 33). It also says that an appeal can be either a review of the disciplinary sanction or a rehearing, which reflects the Court of Appeal's judgment in Taylor v OCS Group Ltd 2006 ICR 1602, CA. In that case the Court held that the task for an employment tribunal when considering whether the employer acted reasonably in dismissing is to assess the fairness of the disciplinary process as a whole. Where procedural deficiencies occur at an early stage, the tribunal should examine the subsequent appeal hearing, particularly its procedural fairness and thoroughness, and the open-mindedness of the decision-maker.

The Guide warns against using an appeal to punish the employee for appealing and recommends that it should not result in any increase in the penalty as this may deter individuals from appealing (page 34). The employee has a statutory right to be accompanied at an appeal hearing – Ss.10(1), (2) and 13(4)(c) ERelA 1999.

Once a decision has been made, employees should be informed in writing of the results of the appeal hearing 'as soon as possible' (Acas Code, para 28).

Internal appeals are part of dismissal process. Section 98(4) ERA requires employment tribunals to consider whether or not the employer acted reasonably

6.228

331

in treating the reason for dismissal as a sufficient reason. It was argued before the House of Lords in West Midlands Co-operative Society Ltd v Tipton 1986 ICR 192, HL, that tribunals should only consider the employer's actions in relation to matters known before and at the time of the dismissal. Their Lordships rejected this argument on the ground that injustice could result if an employer acts reasonably on the facts known at the time of the dismissal but quite unreasonably in maintaining that decision in the light of new facts established in the course of the appeal procedure. Accordingly, they held that the employer's actions at the appeal stage are relevant to the reasonableness of the whole dismissal process.

A failure to carry out a reasonable and proper procedure at each stage of the dismissal process, including the appeal stage, will be taken very seriously. An example:

- **Stoker v Lancashire County Council** 1992 IRLR 75, CA: S was dismissed for misconduct. The decision was then subject to two appeal hearings by different subcommittees of LCC. The first subcommittee confined its activities to reviewing the 'penalty' only, not the reason for the decision, despite the fact that S's contract clearly entitled him to full hearings before both subcommittees. The Court of Appeal held that a reasonable employer can be expected to comply with the full requirements of an appeal procedure set out in his own disciplinary code, and any failure to do so is a matter which must be considered when judging the reasonableness of the employer's action. Since neither the employment tribunal nor the EAT had considered the employer's failure to comply with the requirements of the contractual appeal procedure, the case was remitted to a differently constituted tribunal for reconsideration.

6.229 In Westminster City Council v Cabaj 1996 ICR 960, CA, the claimant was dismissed for irregular timekeeping. Although the disciplinary code stated that he was entitled to an appeal against his dismissal in front of a panel of three Council members, his appeal was heard by only two members. The Court of Appeal ruled that, although employers should follow the agreed procedure, not every plain and significant breach of agreed disciplinary procedures will inevitably render a dismissal unfair. The question that an employment tribunal must decide is not whether in all the circumstances the employer acted reasonably, but the narrower question under S.98(4) ERA of whether the employer acted reasonably in treating the reason shown as a sufficient reason for dismissing the employee. The relevance of an employer's failure to follow an agreed disciplinary procedure, therefore, lies in whether that failure denied the employee the opportunity of demonstrating that the reason for his or her dismissal was not sufficient. This is a question for the tribunal to decide on the facts. In the instant case the tribunal should have first decided whether the failure to have a full appeal panel was such that the claimant was denied the opportunity of demonstrating that the real reason for his dismissal was insufficient, and then considered the employer's reasons for the failure to observe the disciplinary code. Since it could not be said that the tribunal's answers to those questions would inevitably lead it to a conclusion that the dismissal was unfair, the case was remitted to a differently constituted tribunal to consider the matter afresh.

So, not every procedural defect will have the effect of rendering a dismissal unfair. Another example of this is Sartor v P and O European Ferries (Felixstowe) Ltd 1992 IRLR 271, CA. There, the employee's appeal was defective in that the two staff who heard the appeal had also been involved in the original investigation of the misconduct and could not be said to be independent. The Court of Appeal declined to overturn the tribunal's finding of fair dismissal as the employment tribunal had not erred in law in reaching its conclusion. However, a majority of the Court of Appeal said that they would have reached a different conclusion on the facts and employers are well advised to adhere carefully to their disciplinary procedures.

It is clear from these cases that what will affect fairness is the existence of a defect that renders the appeal process defective in the sense that that process should or could have found a flaw in the original decision to dismiss. Conversely, defects in the original disciplinary procedures may be remedied on appeal. For this purpose, it is (as we mentioned above) irrelevant as to whether the appeal hearing takes the form of a rehearing or a review as long as the appeal is sufficiently thorough to cure the earlier procedural shortcomings. This was established by the Court of Appeal in Taylor v OCS Group Ltd 2006 ICR 1602, CA, which finally laid to rest the notion, derived from the EAT's decision in Whitbread and Co plc v Mills 1988 ICR 776, EAT, that only a full rehearing of the case (rather than a mere review of the original decision) was capable of curing an earlier defect. After careful analysis of the decision in Whitbread, the Court in the Taylor case said that the Appeal Tribunal had used the words 'rehearing' and 'review' as mere illustrations of the kind of hearings that would be thorough enough to cure an earlier defect in the disciplinary process. It had not propounded a rule of law that only a rehearing – as opposed to a review – was capable of curing these defects. Such a rule would fetter a tribunal's discretion when considering the fairness of the dismissal under S.98(4). It was evident from other reported cases that Whitbread had not always been properly understood and that tribunals have been tempted to categorise appeal hearings either as rehearings or reviews. In view of the confusion surrounding Whitbread, the Court suggested that it would be advisable for it not to be cited in future cases.

However, if the appeal hearing is itself defective, it cannot remedy earlier **6.230** defects, as the following EAT decision made clear:

- **Byrne v BOC Ltd** 1992 IRLR 505, EAT: B was dismissed for falsifying overtime claims. The tribunal was satisfied that the procedural defects leading up to dismissal were sufficient to render the dismissal unfair – the initial hearing was convened with undue haste, only 30 minutes after B's return from holiday, and B was not told in advance that she was charged with an offence involving dishonesty. It found, however, that the appeal

333

hearing had remedied the earlier inadequacies. The EAT agreed that the appeal had remedied the defects but found that the appeal itself was unfair in that the person hearing it was 'judge in his own cause'. Since the appeal was unfair, it was incapable of curing earlier defects.

The conduct of the appeal hearing is therefore very important. The principles of natural justice should be observed so far as possible (see under 'Disciplinary hearings' above). However, there is one principle of natural justice that is, in the EAT's view, often too impracticable in the commercial context to be insisted on rigidly – that is the rule that there should be different people handling every stage of the disciplinary process and that they should avoid having contact with each other during that process. The EAT recognised that it was inevitable that those involved in the original decision to dismiss would be in daily contact with their superiors in line-management and that total disconnection cannot be achieved – Rowe v Radio Rentals Ltd (below). From the decided cases, what appears to be relevant is the degree of involvement by the same person at the different stages. Two examples:

- **Rowe v Radio Rentals Ltd** 1982 IRLR 177, EAT: R was dismissed for trading for personal gain when employed as a TV engineer. His immediate superior, L, made the decision to dismiss him. L reported this decision to W, the Regional Controller. R appealed against the dismissal and the appeal was heard by W. The appeal was dismissed and R complained to a tribunal that the dismissal was unfair. The EAT upheld the employment tribunal's decision that the dismissal was not unfair on the ground that W's earlier involvement in the dismissal process was simply to be informed of the decision to dismiss. W could not properly be regarded, when hearing the appeal, as being a 'judge in his own cause' and justice had therefore been done

- **Byrne v BOC Ltd 1992** IRLR 505, EAT: B's manager, P, had been involved in the investigation of B's overtime claims. He made the decision to bring charges and had consulted the personnel department to find out what the appropriate procedure and penalty would be. He also conducted the appeal hearing. These factors led the EAT to the 'inescapable conclusion' that P, when hearing the appeal, was a 'judge in his own cause'. Thus the appeal hearing was unfair.

6.231 While it is recognised that the person who investigated the offence might need to be present at the appeal hearing to give factual information, a tribunal is likely to take a dim view of that person remaining behind after the hearing to discuss matters with the ultimate decision-maker. Such a practice smacks of bias and may be sufficient to render a dismissal unfair. An illustration:

- **Lawton v Park Cake Bakeries** EAT 90/88: L, a charge-hand, was dismissed for assaulting another employee. The investigation was carried out by J, who also conducted the hearing at which L was dismissed. J attended the appeal hearing, which was conducted by B, and remained behind while B reached his decision. The EAT held that there was no breach of natural justice in J being involved in the appeal hearing, but it was 'highly undesirable' that J should have stayed behind afterwards. However, the employment tribunal had accepted the evidence of witnesses who said that the decision was B's and B's alone and this fact had not been challenged by L. The EAT upheld the tribunal's finding of fair dismissal but with the warning that, without such evidence, the dismissal might well have been unfair on procedural grounds.

Effective date of termination. If the employee is unsuccessful on appeal, then the effective date of termination of the employment contract will be the date of the original dismissal. If successful, then the employee will be treated as having been suspended pending the outcome of the appeal, and will obviously be entitled to receive full back pay for the period of the suspension – West Midlands Co-operative Society Ltd v Tipton 1986 ICR 192, HL. This means also that an employee will not have been dismissed for the purposes of an unfair dismissal claim – Roberts v West Coast Trains Ltd 2005 ICR 254, CA.   6.232

7 Statutory ban

Establishing the reason

Reasonableness

Driving bans

Work permits

7.1
'Statutory ban' is a convenient shorthand expression for the potentially fair reason for dismissal set out in S.98(2)(d) of the Employment Rights Act 1996 (ERA), which is that the employee could not continue to work in the position which he or she held without contravention (either on the employee's part or on that of the employer) of a duty or restriction imposed by or under an enactment.

It is for the employer to show that there is a statutory prohibition which makes it impossible for the employee to carry on in the same job. If successful, the employer will have established a *potentially* fair reason for dismissal, but that alone will not be conclusive of the issue of fairness. The tribunal will still have to consider whether the employer acted reasonably in dismissing under S.98(4): if the employer could, for example, easily have changed the employee's job so that he or she could do it legally, dismissal is likely to be unfair.

In this chapter we deal first with establishing the reason for dismissal, then with the general approach of tribunals to the issue of reasonableness in this context. Finally, we look at two common categories of statutory ban dismissals: cases involving loss of a driving licence and cases involving work permits.

Establishing the reason
7.2

The employer must show that continued employment of the employee does in fact contravene a statutory enactment. It is not enough to show – as it would be in the case of a conduct or capability dismissal – a genuine belief on reasonable grounds and after reasonable investigation that there would be such a contravention. This is because S.98(2)(a) and (b) refer to a reason which *relates to* capability or qualifications and conduct and this is wide enough to cover the employer's genuine and reasonable belief. But S.98(2)(d) does not contain the words 'relates to' and the employer must prove the actual existence of the statutory ban – Bouchaala v Trusthouse Forte Hotels Ltd 1980 ICR 721, EAT.

Failure to establish the existence of a statutory ban will not necessarily be fatal, however, as the employer may be able to establish a different reason for dismissal – see below under 'Overlapping reasons for dismissal'. But if the employer relies solely on a statutory ban that does not in fact apply it will fail to show a reason for dismissal at all – thus in effect making the dismissal automatically unfair. An illustration:

- **City of Birmingham District Council v Elson** EAT 609/78: the Schools Regulations 1959 provided that 'a person who is not a qualified teacher may be employed... if no qualified teacher is available to give the instruction'. E was an unqualified teacher and she was dismissed when a qualified teacher became available, the only reason for dismissal being the employer's belief that it would be illegal to retain her services. The EAT held that the employer's interpretation of the Regulations was wrong. In the context, 'employed' must mean 'taken on' or 'appointed'. The Regulations did not require an existing employee to be dismissed: they only meant that there should be no new appointment of an unqualified teacher if a qualified teacher was available. The employer could not rely on S.98(2)(d) and E's dismissal was therefore unfair.

7.3 If there is a statutory ban, tribunals and courts have no business considering whether the ban and the policy underlying it are reasonable: they are only concerned with whether the employer has established the existence of a statutory prohibition and that it applies to the employee's job. Whether or not the employer has applied the statutory ban reasonably affects the *reasonableness* of dismissal, but it cannot affect the *reason* for dismissal – Woodcock v University of Cambridge EAT 332/79.

'Enactment' for the purposes of S.98(2)(d) includes not only statutes but delegated legislation (statutory instruments) and regulations made under statutory instrument. In the Woodcock case (above) the enactment in issue was a university statute made by the University Commissioners under the Universities of Oxford and Cambridge Act 1923. The EAT stressed that the wording in S.98(2)(d) is 'restriction imposed by or under an enactment' so that the university statute was covered.

7.4 **Overlapping reasons for dismissal**

A genuine belief, reached on reasonable grounds and after reasonable investigation, that an employee's continued employment would be illegal is not enough to establish a valid reason for dismissal under S.98(2)(b) if that belief is erroneous. But it may amount to 'some other substantial reason' (SOSR) for dismissal under S.98(1)(b) and the dismissal may be fair – Bouchaala v Trusthouse Forte Hotels Ltd (above). In that case the company was told by the Department of Employment that it could no longer legally employ B (a Tunisian) because of work permit rules, so he was dismissed. In fact, B had been given indefinite leave to remain in the United Kingdom and did not need a work permit. The EAT held that a genuine belief that continued employment would be illegal could amount to SOSR and that the dismissal was fair in the circumstances.

338

The moral is that employers should *always* plead SOSR as an alternative reason for dismissal. The employer did so in the Bouchaala case and (unnecessarily as it turned out) in Woodcock v University of Cambridge (above). But in City of Birmingham District Council v Elson (above) the employer relied exclusively on a mistaken interpretation of statutory regulations and lost. The EAT noted that no question of reasonableness or reliance on legal advice had been argued before the tribunal.

In some cases there may well be more than one alternative ground for dismissal. For example, in Bryan v Kennerty Farm Dairies Ltd EAT 584/87 a distribution manager lost his driving licence and the employer pleaded capability (not statutory ban) as the reason for dismissal. A tribunal thought that the real reason for dismissal was one relating to conduct, but found the dismissal fair. The EAT upheld the decision, but thought that the tribunal could equally well have found SOSR to be the reason for dismissal. In that case the factual reason for dismissal was fully ventilated and argued by both sides before the tribunal so that the employee was not put at a disadvantage as a result of the employer using the wrong label – see Chapter 3 under 'Reason for dismissal'. For more on driving ban cases see below.

7.5

Automatic termination by statute

7.6

Certain statutory provisions may have the effect of automatically terminating employment contracts. There is a general principle that when further performance of a contract becomes impossible because of legislation, e.g. when a particular office is abolished by statute, then the contract is discharged – Reilly v The King 1934 AC 176, PC. In Tarnesby v Kensington and Chelsea and Westminster Area Health Authority (Teaching) 1981 ICR 615, HL, the House of Lords held that the suspension of T's doctor's registration for disciplinary reasons automatically terminated his employment as a hospital consultant. This was because S.28(1) of the Medical Act 1956 provided that no unregistered doctor should hold an appointment as a hospital medical officer. And while suspension no longer has this effect, the same would apply if a doctor's name was permanently removed from the register.

However, in Shrewsbury and Telford Hospital NHS Trust v Lairikyengbam 2010 ICR 66, EAT, an NHS Trust that had employed a locum consultant on a series of fixed-term contracts spanning almost four years had acted beyond its powers since it had not sought the committee approval required by the relevant Regulations. Consequently, the consultant's formal contract of employment was void. Nevertheless, the EAT holds that the continued performance of his duties meant that he was still an 'employee' within the meaning of the Employment Rights Act 1996, and thus entitled to pursue an unfair dismissal claim. The case was remitted to a new tribunal to decide whether the reason for his ultimate dismissal was the statutory ban on his employment.

339

7.7 Reasonableness

If the employer has made out the reason for dismissal – the existence of a statutory ban on the employee's continued employment in the job – a tribunal must then decide whether it was reasonable to dismiss for this reason. This will involve consideration of such matters as:

- the likely duration of the statutory ban

- whether it affects the whole or only part of the employee's work

- whether the employee can readily be redeployed.

7.8 Four cases illustrate how these factors are taken into account:

- **Madan v St Helens and Knowsley Community NHS Trust** ET Case No.2100813/01: M worked for the NHS Trust as a clinical medical officer. She also ran a slimming clinic separately from her work for the Trust. The Trust became aware that the General Medical Council (GMC) had referred complaints against her work at the slimming clinic to its Professional Conduct Committee. It agreed that she could continue to work, provided her work was monitored, pending the outcome of the GMC investigation. A few weeks later the GMC suspended M from practice and the Trust immediately terminated her employment because it would be illegal for her to continue working. She claimed unfair dismissal. The tribunal held that M was dismissed because of a statutory ban but that the dismissal was unfair because there was no consultation and no opportunity for her to explore alternatives

- **Yarrow v QIS Ltd** ET Case No.32972/76: Y was a radiographer whose employment was subject to the Ionisation Radiation (Sealed Sources) Regulations 1969, which made it unlawful to employ as a radiographer anybody who contracted one of a number of specified diseases. Y contracted psoriasis – a specified disease – and was dismissed. The tribunal found that the employer had considered suspension, but psoriasis was a recurrent condition with no known cure and Y had to be regarded as permanently unfit to work as a radiographer. There was no alternative work available and his dismissal was held to be fair

- **Balogun v Lucas Batteries Ltd** ET Case No.1270/79: B, a machine operator working on processes involving lead, began to suffer from hypertension. The Control of Lead at Work Regulations in force at the time made it an offence knowingly to employ a person with hypertension in lead processing. The employer went to a good deal of trouble to try to find an alternative job but none was available and B was dismissed. The tribunal held that the dismissal was a fair dismissal for statutory ban

340

- **Ascroft v Lancashire Magistrates' Courts Committee** COET 1138/10: A's duties were partly those of a magistrates' court clerk and partly administrative. New regulations – the Justices' Clerks (Qualification of Assistants) Rules 1979 – were issued in draft form in 1976 and A became aware that from October 1980 he would have to hold a valid training certificate, which involved passing some exams. In 1976 he failed the exams; in 1977 he did not resit because of a muddle about dates; in 1978 he refused to resit; in 1979 he failed again; and in 1980 he refused to resit. Since he had ceased to be qualified to sit as a court clerk he was dismissed. The tribunal held that there were no alternative vacancies and A could not be kept solely on administrative duties, and so his dismissal was fair.

In cases like Ascroft (above), where the statutory ban comes into operation when an employee fails to acquire the necessary qualifications, the employer's failure to assist the employee to qualify may be a factor making dismissal unfair. In Sandhu v Department of Education and Science and anor 1978 IRLR 208, EAT, S was a trainee teacher who was prohibited from teaching under the Schools Regulations 1959 when the DES declared him unsuitable as a teacher. A tribunal found his ensuing dismissal automatically fair because the employer had no option but to dismiss. The EAT held that this ignored S's case, which was that the DES decision was largely based on reports from S's employer and that the employer had discriminated against him and had treated him unreasonably during his probationary period. The EAT remitted the case to a new tribunal to look at the events leading up to S's dismissal and consider whether the employer had acted reasonably towards S. **7.9**

Precipitate dismissal may also be unfair. If there is a possibility of obtaining an extension of time to allow an employee a further opportunity to gain a qualification, it may be unreasonable to dismiss before it is known whether an extension will be granted. At any rate, the EAT thought so in the following case: **7.10**

- **Sutcliffe and Eaton Ltd v Pinney 1977** IRLR 349: the Hearing Aid Council Act 1968 prohibited the employment of hearing aid dispensers for more than five years unless they passed certain exams. P was a trainee hearing aid dispenser who failed the exams three times, the last time being just before the end of the five-year period. His name was removed from the register of hearing aid dispensers and it would have been a criminal offence, punishable by a fine of up to £100 a day, for the employer to continue to employ him. He was therefore dismissed, but P then successfully applied for an extension to sit the exam again. The EAT held that the fact that to continue to employ somebody could be a breach of statute was not conclusive of the reasonableness of his or her dismissal. In this case it was very unlikely that any proceedings would have been taken against the employer if P had been kept on and an extension of the training period had been applied for. The tribunal had been entitled to find that the employer had acted unreasonably and that P's dismissal was unfair.

This case should be treated with some caution, however, as the decision seems to be a particularly harsh one for the employer, who was faced with either dismissing the employee or committing a criminal offence. It was also decided before the 'range of reasonable responses' test was fully developed. It is certainly arguable that a different tribunal, faced with similar facts, might find dismissal in these circumstances to be fair. But having said that, a not dissimilar approach was taken by the EAT in Kelly v University of Southampton 2008 ICR 357, EAT, where K, an American citizen who was employed as a lecturer by the university, had her employment summarily terminated when her visa expired. She had applied for indefinite leave to remain in the United Kingdom and this was granted two weeks later. The EAT considered that even if the seriousness of an alleged contravention made it reasonable for an employer to dismiss speedily, there is no reason why provision should not be made for an appeal – particularly where the illegal state of affairs is disputed, or technical, or arises from an oversight which can be remedied by the time an appeal would have been heard.

7.11 Driving bans

Driving bans are the main cause of statutory ban dismissals. When an employee has lost his or her driving licence, tribunals will normally expect the employer to consider the following matters before deciding on dismissal:

- whether driving is an essential part of the job or whether the employee can satisfactorily carry on his or her duties without a driving licence

- whether retaining the employee will mean dislocation and inconvenience

- whether there is another job to which the employee could be redeployed

- whether the employee has been given an opportunity to express his or her views and whether any suggestions made have been reasonably considered.

7.12 Some examples:

- **Toase v Milk Marketing Board** ET Case No.24778/76: T was a mechanic fitter (who held an HGV licence) and his work involved driving an average of 139 miles a month on road tests, etc. When he lost his licence his foreman said that his six colleagues could cover for his driving duties, even though one of the other mechanic fitters did not hold a driving licence. However, T was dismissed. The tribunal held that the statutory ban was made out as the reason for dismissal, but that the employer acted unreasonably in dismissing because T could have continued his employment without driving

- **Riley v ADT Fire and Security plc** ET Case No.2403497/05: R, who had worked for the company for 22 years as an installation engineer, a job that required him to drive, was banned from driving for 2 years for a drink-driving offence. The company was initially able to team him up with an apprentice who could drive, but after about ten months the apprentice was no longer available. He was offered two alternative posts which he turned down, and his employment was terminated on notice. His claim for unfair dismissal was rejected. Some employers might have been prepared to wait for a further year for R to regain his driving licence, but the company was entitled to decide it could not wait for the remaining period of the driving ban to expire. Dismissal was within the band of reasonable responses

- **Roberts v Toyota (GB) Ltd** EAT 614/80: it was an implied term in the contract of an area sales manager that he should hold a driving licence. He received a 12-month driving ban for a drink-driving offence and was dismissed. Prior to his conviction he told the national sales manager that if he lost his licence he would be prepared to purchase a company car and provide a driver to drive him in the course of his work. This was put to the board of directors, who considered that it was impracticable. The EAT held that the tribunal was fully entitled to hold that the dismissal was fair in these circumstances.

The employee's conduct may be a factor in assessing the reasonableness of **7.13** the dismissal. For instance, in Handforth v Olaf Olsen (Newmillerdam) Ltd ET Case No.9012/79 H was a sales secretary who needed to drive. She held an Australian licence and obtained a provisional licence from the DVLC, but did not tell the employer that she was not qualified to drive on her own in the United Kingdom. This came to light when her company vehicle was damaged in a minor accident and an insurance claim was repudiated. The tribunal held that H's dismissal because of statutory ban was fair since she had misled her employer.

In a similar case, Morris v Haven Industrial Services Ltd ET Case No.04281/81, M, a foreman installation fitter, used a company vehicle. When his employer decided to check on driving qualifications M lied and said he had mislaid his licence. However, enquiries to the police showed that he had no licence at all. The tribunal held that he was fairly dismissed for gross misconduct, rather than for statutory ban.

Contrast these two cases with Arbuckle Smith and Co Ltd v Holmes EAT 178/87, where the employee was dismissed for misconduct after being charged by the police with driving an HGV without the appropriate licence and the EAT upheld the tribunal's decision that his dismissal was unfair. A proper investigation would have revealed that the management knew all along that H was only in possession of a provisional licence. There had been no deliberate deception on H's part and he could have been given other duties on a temporary basis until he obtained a full licence.

Employers will be expected to follow a fair procedure before dismissing an **7.14** employee who has been disqualified from driving. This will include

343

consultation with the employee to see if any alternative arrangements can be made during the period of the driving ban. In Ager v Inforex (UK) Ltd ET Case No.23962/79 A's contract expressly stated that dismissal would follow the loss of his driving licence. The employer rejected out of hand a suggestion that A's wife could do the necessary driving. A tribunal found the dismissal unfair because the employer should at least have given this arrangement a trial run (although it awarded only four weeks' pay in compensation to reflect the likelihood that the arrangement would not have worked). And in Mathieson v WJ Noble and Son Ltd 1972 IRLR 76, ET, a salesman who was disqualified from driving engaged a private chauffeur to drive him during the disqualification period and made arrangements to pay additional insurance premiums on his company car, with the agreement of the company chairman. The company, however, dismissed him before these arrangements could be put into operation. A tribunal did not think that M was contractually obliged to drive, so that no statutory ban applied to his continued employment. It would, however, also have found the dismissal unfair under S.98(4) because of the employer's unreasonableness.

But in Ashton Paper Mills Ltd v Haines EAT 361/79 a tribunal found dismissal of a timber inspector, for whom mobility was essential, unfair because the employer did not give serious consideration to his proposal to provide a driver. The EAT, however, thought that the tribunal should have given some consideration to the practicability of the scheme put forward (about which the EAT was clearly sceptical) and remitted the case for it to do so.

7.15 Employers should also adopt a consistent approach when deciding whether to dismiss. In Buckley v Alpha Catering Services Ltd ET Case No.3104588/99, for example, B was disqualified from driving for three years. It was his second driving ban. Agreement could not be reached on alternative duties and he was dismissed. The tribunal accepted the employer's argument that B was required to hold a licence and that the situation was not of the employer's making but arose from B's serious misbehaviour. However, the dismissal was unfair because another employee who could reasonably be required to drive from time to time was neither dismissed nor transferred when she was disqualified from driving. The employer did not carry out a sufficiently detailed investigation into the way other employees had been treated.

Premature action by the employer may make dismissal unfair. This may happen if the employer dismisses before it is certain that the employee will lose his or her licence or before it is known how long the driving ban will be. Some illustrations:

- **Greenhalgh v Nixdorf Computer** ET Case No.15839/82: G was dismissed after a positive breath analysis. The tribunal held that his dismissal was unfair because it was premature to dismiss before the outcome of the court hearing was known. But G was awarded only net pay to the date of the court hearing, since the tribunal found 100 per cent contributory conduct

- **Somerville v Ofrex Ltd** ET Case No.14908/82: S, a service engineer, was dismissed when it was found that his (New Zealand) driving licence was invalid in the United Kingdom. In fact, he obtained a valid licence five weeks later. The tribunal found that his dismissal was unfair because the employer had acted with unnecessary haste and should have investigated more thoroughly

- **Meehan v Chelmsford Star Co-operative Society Ltd** ET Case No.35769/81: M, a field TV engineer, was a diabetic but was certified fit to drive by his doctor. However, the DVLC revoked his licence subject to a right of appeal. His licence was in fact restored after about ten weeks, but the employer had dismissed him promptly as soon as he lost it. The tribunal held that his dismissal was unfair because the employer should have awaited the outcome of M's appeal.

Even when tribunals do find a dismissal unfair they are likely to find a substantial degree of contributory conduct if the ban was because of drink-driving or traffic offences. Thus, in Toase v Milk Marketing Board (above), for example, contribution was assessed at 50 per cent. 7.16

In Nairne v Highland and Islands Fire Brigade 1989 IRLR 366, Ct Sess, N was dismissed after a second drink-driving ban. A tribunal found the dismissal unfair on procedural grounds and concluded that N had contributed to it by 25 per cent. The EAT held that this was perverse and substituted a finding of 75 per cent contribution: N had been warned, it was his second offence in two years, he was a senior officer required to set an example, and he was required to hold a valid driving licence. The Court of Session upheld the EAT's judgment on appeal.

Where, however, the employee was not at fault, as in Meehan v Chelmsford Star Co-operative Society Ltd (above), where diabetes was the cause of the driving ban, there will obviously be no contributory fault.

Work permits 7.17

Since 1997 it has been a criminal offence for an employer to employ a person who is subject to immigration control and who is not legally entitled to work in the United Kingdom. This has caused considerable problems for both employers and employees (and their advisers), given the constant changes in immigration law in recent years which have made it very difficult to keep abreast with the rules. Furthermore, the question of whether a person has a right to remain in the United Kingdom is separate to that of whether they have a right to work here, and until comparatively recently, decisions on these matters were in the hands of two different government departments. This has led to considerable confusion and it is not uncommon for different departments to give differing advice. For example, in Bouchaala v Trusthouse Forte Hotels Ltd 1980 ICR 721, EAT, the company was told by the Department of

345

Employment that it could no longer legally employ B (a Tunisian) because of work permit rules, so he was dismissed. In fact, B had been given indefinite leave to remain in the United Kingdom by the Home Office and did not need a work permit. Two recent cases show the potential pitfalls.

- **Kelly v University of Southampton** 2008 ICR 357, EAT: K, an American citizen, was offered a job as a lecturer by the university, subject to her completing the necessary immigration processes. While she received permission from one government department to work for 60 months, the Home Office issued her with a visa granting her leave to remain in the United Kingdom for only 48 months. Concerned that it would be committing a criminal offence by continuing to employ her after the expiration of her visa, the university terminated her employment by letter backdated to the last day of her leave to remain. K was given no right of appeal as the university believed that her employment had terminated by operation of law. K obtained indefinite leave to remain in the United Kingdom two weeks later. The EAT held that the university would not have committed an offence by continuing to employ her, since she had lawful permission to work, so S.98(2)(d) did not apply. However, had the statutory ban been established, dismissal would nevertheless have been unreasonable. Even if the seriousness of an alleged contravention makes it reasonable for an employer to dismiss speedily, there is no reason why provision should not be made for an appeal – particularly where the illegal state of affairs is disputed, or technical, or arises from an oversight which can be remedied by the time an appeal would have been heard

- **Hounslow London Borough Council v Klusova** 2008 ICR 396, CA: K, a Russian national, was employed by the Council from 2000. She had leave to remain in the United Kingdom until May 2004. Before that leave expired she made various attempts to extend it which had not been finally determined even by the time her dismissal case reached the Court of Appeal. In March 2005 K was briefly detained by the immigration authorities, who released her subject to various conditions stated in an immigration officer's letter, one of which was that she could not work. In fact, K had a letter from the Home Office which indicated that she was entitled to work, pending the determination of her application to remain. The Council asked her for proof that she was entitled to work and her solicitors responded by asking for clarification of the Council's grounds for thinking she did not have such entitlement. Not having received the proof it had asked for, the Council dismissed her summarily. When K claimed unfair dismissal, the Council sought to rely on the statutory ban. The Court of Appeal held that K had official leave to remain and work in the United Kingdom from the Home Office at the time of her dismissal, and this could not be altered by an immigration officer's letter. In consequence, there was no statutory ban on her working and the Council could not rely on this ground.

These cases illustrate the importance of an employer arguing SOSR as an alternative to statutory ban, especially where immigration status is concerned. (SOSR was in fact argued in both cases but at the time the statutory dismissal and disciplinary procedures were in place and, because neither employer had followed the procedures, the dismissals were automatically unfair. The statutory dismissal and disciplinary procedures, which were abolished by the Employment Act 2008, did not apply to statutory ban cases but did apply to SOSR dismissals.)

7.18

8 Some other substantial reason

Business reorganisations

Protecting employers' interests

Third-party pressure to dismiss

Breakdown in trust and confidence

Expiry of a limited-term contract

Transfer of undertakings

Miscellaneous reasons

In the preceding chapters we have considered three of the six potentially fair **8.1**
reasons for dismissal specified in S.98(2) of the Employment Rights Act 1996
(ERA): capability or qualifications, conduct, and statutory ban. The other two
potentially fair reasons listed in S.98(2), retirement and redundancy, are
discussed in Chapter 9 of this Handbook and in IDS Employment Law
Handbook, 'Redundancy' (2008), Chapter 8, respectively. In this chapter we
focus on S.98(1)(b), which provides a sixth potentially fair reason for dismissal
– 'some other substantial reason' ('SOSR').

Section 98(1)(b) is a catch-all category covering dismissal for 'some other
substantial reason of a kind such as to justify the dismissal of an employee
holding the position which the employee held'. Sir John Brightman – in RS
Components Ltd v Irwin 1973 ICR 535, NIRC – stated that 'Parliament
may well have intended to set out in [S.98(2)] the common reasons for a
dismissal, but can hardly have hoped to produce an exhaustive catalogue of
all the circumstances in which an employer would be justified in terminating
the services of an employee'. S.98(1)(b) provides a residual potentially fair
reason for dismissal which employers can use if the reason for dismissal
does not fall within the five specific categories in S.98(2).

The employer is required to show only that the substantial reason for **8.2**
dismissal was a potentially fair one. Once the reason has been established, it
is then up to the tribunal to decide whether the employer acted reasonably
under S.98(4) in dismissing for that reason. As in all unfair dismissal claims
(with the exception of those based on retirement dismissals), a tribunal will
decide the fairness of the dismissal by asking whether the decision to dismiss
fell within the range of reasonable responses that a reasonable employer
might adopt. Depending on the circumstances, this may involve matters such
as whether the employee was consulted, warned and given a hearing, and/or
whether the employer searched for suitable alternative employment.

─── **349**

SOSR under S.98(1)(b) must be of a kind such as to justify the dismissal of *an employee holding the job in question*. In Cobley v Forward Technology Industries plc 2003 ICR 1050, CA, the Court of Appeal considered whether the dismissal of a chief executive following a successful company takeover could amount to SOSR. It held that although in most circumstances a change in the ownership of a company's shares will not affect the employment relationships between the company and its staff, different considerations apply to the dismissal of a chief executive than to that of a secretary or storeman. The employer was entitled in the circumstances to rely on SOSR.

8.3 To amount to a substantial reason to dismiss, there must be a finding that the reason *could* – but not necessarily does – justify dismissal – Mercia Rubber Mouldings Ltd v Lingwood 1974 ICR 256, NIRC. Indeed, tribunals that confuse the employer's burden of establishing SOSR as the reason for dismissal with the tribunal's overall assessment of the reasonableness of the dismissal under S.98(4) may find themselves overruled on appeal. In Gilham and ors v Kent County Council (No.2) 1985 ICR 233, CA, the County Council had to reduce expenditure in line with Government policy or face serious financial penalties. Consequently, G was offered a contract which meant less pay. She turned it down and complained that she had been unfairly dismissed. The tribunal held that the Council had not made out a substantial reason for dismissal because it did not consider the reason put forward as one that reasonably justified dismissal in the circumstances. However, the Court of Appeal held – obiter – that the tribunal had fallen into error in law by confusing the test for establishing a reason for dismissal with the test of reasonableness under S.98(4). The Court said that it was impossible to argue that the stated reason for dismissal – the Council's need to reduce its expenditure – was not SOSR that could potentially justify dismissal. And in Cobley (above) the Court of Appeal confirmed that identification of a substantial reason for dismissal does not require considerations of fairness, which falls to be considered at a later stage.

By its very nature, SOSR is not to be construed as meaning a reason that is of the same kind as those set out in S.98(2) – RS Components Ltd v Irwin (above). However, SOSR can include reasons containing elements of conduct or capability. In Huggins v Micrel Semiconductor (UK) Ltd EAT 0009/04, for example, the EAT upheld a finding that a dismissal was for SOSR when it was caused by a breakdown in trust and confidence related to the employee's conduct. And in Wilson v Post Office 2000 IRLR 834, CA, the Court of Appeal held that an employer had dismissed an employee for SOSR because his attendance record did not meet the requirements of the agreed procedure. Even though the employee's absences had been caused by ill-health, the Court held that the tribunal had erred when it characterised this as a capability dismissal. (Note, however, that in Perkin v St George's Healthcare NHS Trust 2006 ICR 617, CA, a tribunal held that the dismissal of a senior executive whose manner and attitude towards colleagues had led to a breakdown in the employer's

350

confidence in him and rendered it impossible for the senior executives to work together as a team was for 'conduct [or] some other substantial reason', adding that both were potentially fair reasons within the meaning of S.98(1). On appeal, the Court of Appeal held that the tribunal had not erred even though, in the Court's view, it would have been preferable if it had analysed the dismissal as being for SOSR rather than for conduct. However, the tribunal's failure to characterise the reason for dismissal as SOSR was not fatal to its reasoning or to the safety of its decision.)

As long as it is not a S.98(2) reason, any reason for dismissal, however obscure, **8.4** can be pleaded on grounds of SOSR – with the proviso that it is a *substantial* reason and thus not frivolous or trivial. However, while the reason for dismissal needs to be substantial, it need not be sophisticated – merely *genuine*. For example, in Harper v National Coal Board 1980 IRLR 260, EAT, H was dismissed because he sometimes attacked fellow employees during his epileptic seizures. The employer held inaccurate beliefs concerning epileptics in general. The tribunal found dismissal to be fair either on the ground of capability or for SOSR. The EAT said that an employer cannot claim that a reason for dismissal is substantial if it is a whimsical or capricious reason which no ordinary person would entertain. It stated that where, however, the belief is 'one which is genuinely held, and particularly is one which most employers would be expected to adopt, it may be a substantial reason even where modern sophisticated opinion can be adduced to suggest that it has no scientific foundation'. The EAT therefore upheld the tribunal's decision. (Note, though, that if these facts arose again, the Disability Discrimination Act 1995 could apply – see IDS Employment Law Handbook, 'Disability Discrimination' (2002).)

SOSR is most often invoked where: **8.5**

- the employer is trying to reorganise the business and/or change the terms and conditions of employment in some way

- the employer is trying to protect its interests either by preventing employees from setting up in competition, or by taking steps to avert a potential leakage of confidential information or damage being caused to its reputation

- there has been third-party pressure to dismiss the employee

- the trust and confidence necessary for the employment relationship to function has broken down irremediably

- a limited-term contract has expired; or

- dismissal for 'economic, technical or organisational' reasons, that falls short of redundancy, has followed a transfer of an undertaking.

This chapter deals with each of these scenarios in turn and also examines various miscellaneous reasons for dismissal that can be classified as SOSR.

351

8.6 **Automatically substantial reasons.** There are a number of circumstances where the ERA provides that the dismissal of a temporary replacement employee will be a potentially fair dismissal for a substantial reason. S.106 provides that a dismissal will be for SOSR where the replacement employee is dismissed to make way for the return of the original employee who has been absent for one of the following reasons:

- medical or maternity suspension

- pregnancy or childbirth

- adoption leave

- additional paternity leave following birth or adoption.

However, S.106 only applies if, when the temporary employee is engaged, the employer informs him or her in writing that the employment would be terminated on the return of the original employee. Furthermore, even if the dismissal of a temporary replacement employee is deemed to be potentially fair for SOSR under S.106, tribunals must still consider the reasonableness of such a dismissal under S.98(4) – S.106(4). If, for example, there are other positions that the temporary replacement employee could fill, it is likely that the employer will have acted unreasonably in dismissing, thereby rendering the dismissal unfair.

Note that temporary employees must have a year's continuous service in order to bring a claim for unfair dismissal under S.98 – S.108. However, now that maternity and adoption leave can last for up to a year, S.106 may become more relevant than it has been in the past when maternity leave was shorter and two years' continuous employment was required to bring an unfair dismissal claim.

8.7 **Contributory fault.** Most dismissals for SOSR do not involve any fault on the part of the employee. It follows that when a dismissal for SOSR is found to be unfair, it is rare for contributory conduct to be an issue in assessing compensation. Where contributory fault is found, it is most likely to be in cases involving a breakdown in trust and confidence for which the employee was at least partially to blame – see, for example, Perkin v St George's Healthcare NHS Trust (above), Butcher v Salvage Association EAT 988/01 and Huggins v Micrel Semiconductor (UK) Ltd (above).

8.8 ## Business reorganisations

Tribunals have long recognised the right of employers to dismiss employees who refuse to go along with a business reorganisation. As Lord Denning MR put it in Lesney Products and Co Ltd v Nolan and ors 1977 IRLR 77, CA: '[I]t is important that nothing should be done to impair the ability of employers to reorganise their workforce and their terms and conditions of work so as to improve efficiency.' Employees may, therefore, be dismissed either for refusing to

352 ————————————————————————

agree to changes arising out of a business reorganisation or because their services are no longer required owing, for example, to the introduction of new technology.

Where an employee is dismissed for refusing to agree to a change in working conditions that the employer is entitled to impose under the contract, the dismissal may be for misconduct. However, dismissals of employees who refuse to accept a business reorganisation are often pleaded under SOSR.

Of course, a dismissal in the context of a reorganisation may in fact be for **8.9** *redundancy*, not SOSR, if the statutory definition of redundancy is satisfied – see IDS Employment Law Handbook, 'Redundancy' (2008), Chapter 2. Occasionally, the distinction may be unclear. However, an employer should be wary of trying to disguise a genuine redundancy situation as a business reorganisation because, for example, it wants to avoid making redundancy payments. In Moore v Midas Precision Metalwork Ltd ET Case No.1200536/09, for example, a sheet metal worker claimed unfair dismissal when he refused to accept a change to his terms and conditions that meant that he would have been put on a three-day week. The employer had suffered badly as a result of a downturn in orders and feared that it would be unable to afford redundancy payments. It claimed that M's dismissal was not for redundancy, but for SOSR as a result of a business reorganisation. However, the tribunal found that M's dismissal was mainly attributable to the fact that the requirements of the business for employees to carry out sheet metalworking had diminished. M was therefore dismissed principally because he was redundant.

Establishing SOSR as the reason for dismissal
8.10

To establish SOSR as the reason for dismissal, an employer does *not* have to show that a reorganisation or rearrangement of working patterns was essential. In Hollister v National Farmers' Union 1979 ICR 542, CA, the Court of Appeal said that a 'sound, good business reason' for reorganisation was sufficient to establish SOSR for dismissing an employee who refused to accept a change in his or her terms and conditions. This reason is not one the tribunal considers sound, but one 'which management thinks on reasonable grounds is sound' – Scott and Co v Richardson EAT 0074/04.

It is not for the tribunal to make its own assessment of the advantages of the employer's business decision to reorganise or to change employees' working patterns. In fact, the employer need only show that there were 'clear advantages' in introducing a particular change, to pass the low hurdle of showing SOSR for dismissal. The employer does not need to show any particular 'quantum of improvement' achieved – Kerry Foods Ltd v Lynch 2005 IRLR 680, EAT. In that case, the advantage to the employer in introducing a new rota for managers was sufficient to show SOSR for dismissing a manager following his refusal to accept new terms and conditions that included a move to a six-day week and a reduction in his holiday entitlement (see below). And in Scott and Co v Richardson (above), the EAT held that the tribunal had erred not only by

353

substituting its own opinion of whether the employer's business decision to change to a shift system of work gave the employer a discernible advantage, but also in ruling that the advantage to the employer had to be so substantial that it mitigated the consequences of the dismissal. Having found that the employer had introduced the shift system to ensure that work done in the evenings would be done at normal rates of pay and not at overtime rates, thereby making the business more profitable, the tribunal should have concluded that the profit motive was a sound commercial reason for carrying out the reorganisation, and that S's dismissal for refusing the change was for SOSR.

8.11   That said, employers must do more than simply assert that there were 'good business reasons' for a reorganisation involving dismissals. A tribunal must be satisfied that changes in terms and conditions were not imposed for arbitrary reasons – Catamaran Cruisers Ltd v Williams and ors 1994 IRLR 386, EAT. Employers will also be expected to prove the reason for dismissal and, as a result, to submit evidence showing just what the business reasons were and that they were substantial. Some examples:

- **Banerjee v City and East London Area Health Authority** 1979 IRLR 147, EAT: the Health Authority had a policy of amalgamating part-time consultancies into full-time posts. When the part-timer with whom B shared duties left, the Health Authority scrapped both part-time posts and replaced them with a full-time post to which B was not appointed. He complained of unfair dismissal. The Health Authority produced no evidence of the advantages of the policy or the importance attached to it. The EAT held that in these circumstances no tribunal could conclude that there was a substantial reason for dismissal

- **Mukherjee v Kensington, Chelsea and Westminster Area Health Authority (Teaching)** EAT 284/80: the Health Authority carried out a merger of consultancy posts, with one of the consultants, M, losing her job as a result. The Health Authority submitted full evidence about its need to reorganise and about its genuine efforts to find alternative employment for M. M's dismissal was found to be fair for SOSR

- **Kerry Foods Ltd v Lynch** 2005 IRLR 680, EAT: the employer adduced a number of reasons for introducing a six-day week and a reduction in holiday entitlement for L, a manager. First, it did not want to operate a two-tier system with managers at different depots working different rotas; secondly, it wanted to rectify an historical situation whereby Saturday was not perceived as being a normal working day because there was no management presence; thirdly, the depots with managers working the same rota as their team showed an improvement in their Saturday trading performance; and finally, there was a need to improve the quality of the supervisory cover. It did not need to provide evidence either of the adverse impact or the quantum of improvement to satisfy the definition of SOSR.

354

Imposing contractual changes

8.12

The fact that an employee is contractually entitled to resist the change does not mean that his or her dismissal will be unfair – Bowater Containers Ltd v McCormack 1980 IRLR 50, EAT. Although, as a basic principle of contract law, variations to a contract of employment must be agreed by both parties in order to take effect, an employer can fairly dismiss an employee for refusing to accept detrimental changes to his or her terms and conditions where there is a sound business reason to do so. And, as the EAT pointed out in Catamaran Cruisers Ltd v Williams (above), 'sound business reasons' are not restricted to situations where the survival of the business is at stake.

Since any dismissal for refusal to carry out duties that *are* countenanced by the contract is likely to be for misconduct, employers will need to be clear as to whether the duties being imposed fall within the scope of the employment contract, or require a variation of that contract. If the latter is the case, a dismissal for misconduct for refusing to comply is likely to be unfair and may involve a breach of contract, whereas a dismissal with notice under the existing contract, coupled with an offer of employment on the varied terms, will be potentially fair for SOSR, assuming there is a legitimate business reason for the variation. In Rumani v Thyssenkrupp Materials (UK) Ltd ET Case No.1305900/06, for example, a tribunal found that R had been unfairly dismissed for misconduct for refusing to carry out accountancy work for a separate company that was not within the terms of his contract. It noted that had the employer analysed the matter properly, it could have required R to accept a variation 'in the circumstances of their poor trading position and the fact that [R] had the ability and time to carry out the duties'. The employer could have given R notice and offered employment on the varied terms, and if R refused, he would have been dismissed with notice for SOSR.

The fact that an employer with a sound business reason for imposing changes in fundamental breach of contract can dismiss fairly for SOSR led one claimant to argue that 'a contract of employment is not worth the paper it is written on' – Baker v Securicor Omega Express Ltd EAT 91/98. However, as the lay members of the EAT in Catamaran Cruisers Ltd v Williams and ors (above) were at pains to point out, 'the fact that the authorities show that an employer is not restricted, when offering less attractive terms and conditions of employment, to a situation where the survival of his business is at stake, does not provide an open door to change'. This fact is illustrated in UB (Ross Youngs) Ltd v Elsworthy EAT 264/91 where an employer attempted, as part of a reorganisation, to rearrange the shift pattern of an employee in such a way as to make it impossible for her to meet her obligations under her contract of employment. The employer had thus breached the implied term of trust and confidence between employer and employee and the EAT was unconvinced that there was SOSR for dismissal.

8.13

355

8.14 **Reasonableness of the change**

If there are good business reasons for the change in terms and conditions or working practices, the employer will invariably establish SOSR as the potentially fair reason for dismissal under S.98(1)(b) of an employee who refuses to accept the change. This is only part of the fairness test, however. Under S.98(4) the tribunal must also consider the reasonableness of the change and of the dismissal. This involves considering whether, in all the circumstances, including the employer's size and administrative resources, the employer acted reasonably in treating the business reason as a sufficient reason to dismiss. A tribunal will err in law if it substitutes its own view of whether or not the employer acted reasonably in the circumstances rather than asking whether the decision to dismiss for SOSR fell within the range of reasonable responses that a reasonable employer might adopt – William Cook Sheffield Ltd v Bramhall and ors EAT 0899/03. If there is a sound business reason for a reorganisation, the reasonableness of the employer's conduct must be judged in that context – St John of God (Care Services) Ltd v Brooks and ors 1992 IRLR 546, EAT.

8.15 **Balancing the needs of employer and employee.** Tribunals must focus on the statutory test under s.98(4) and resist the urge to promote one factor above all others as a crucial indicator of fairness. This is especially the case where the proposed new terms are worse than existing terms. In this situation, tribunals have fallen into error in focusing solely on the reasonableness of the employer in seeking to introduce the changes, or, alternatively, on the reasonableness of the employee in refusing them. The following cases illustrate the correct approach:

- **Richmond Precision Engineering Ltd v Pearce** 1985 IRLR 179, EAT: the new owner of the company proposed changes to terms and conditions of employment in order to harmonise them with those of his existing workforce. For P, the changes involved a reduction in his hourly pay rate, an increase in hours, a reduction in his holiday entitlement and loss of certain benefits. Despite extensive negotiations, during which the employer made some concessions, P refused to accept the changes and was dismissed. In considering the fairness of the dismissal for SOSR, the EAT held that the tribunal had wrongly considered the sole question of whether the employer had acted reasonably in deciding that the advantages to the company of implementing the proposed reorganisation outweighed any disadvantage the employee might suffer. This, said the EAT, was merely one factor to be considered in the circumstances. It did not follow that just because there were disadvantages to the employee, the employer had acted unreasonably in treating his refusal to accept the terms as sufficient reason to dismiss

- **St John of God (Care Services) Ltd v Brooks and ors** 1992 IRLR 546, EAT: a hospital faced with a severe cash crisis offered new, inferior terms to the workforce. 140 out of 170 employees accepted the new terms. Employees who did not accept the new terms were dismissed. The tribunal found the dismissals unfair on the ground that the terms and conditions offered were not terms that a reasonable employer would have offered in the circumstances. The EAT rejected the tribunal's approach, stressing that the reasonableness of a dismissal must be looked at in the full context of a business reorganisation: no one factor should be concentrated on to the exclusion of others. The reasonableness of the new terms on offer was not the crucial or sole test of fairness. Such an approach lent undue importance to the reasonableness of the employee's refusal and failed to acknowledge that both employer and employee may be acting reasonably according to their own legitimate interests, which may be irreconcilable

- **Catamaran Cruisers Ltd v Williams and ors** 1994 IRLR 386, EAT: following the purchase of a company, the new owners proposed new terms and conditions of employment to improve safety and efficiency. Although most employees accepted the changes, a few did not and they were dismissed for their refusal to accept the new contracts. In remitting the case to a tribunal to decide on the fairness of the dismissal, the EAT directed the tribunal to carry out a 'balancing process', considering the position from both the employees' and the employer's point of view. It approved comments made by the EAT in Chubb Fire Security Ltd v Harper 1983 IRLR 311, EAT, to the effect that even if it was reasonable for an employee to refuse to accept the new terms, it did not necessarily follow that it was unreasonable for the employer to dismiss

- **Copsey v WWB Devon Clays Ltd** 2005 ICR 1789, CA: C, a practising Christian, was dismissed following his refusal to work a seven-day shift pattern which might sometimes have required him to work on a Sunday. C brought a claim of unfair dismissal, contending that he had been dismissed on account of his religious beliefs. The tribunal found that C had been fairly dismissed for SOSR. It found that the employer had a sound business reason for requiring the change in C's working pattern – namely, significant increases in production requirements. Moreover, it had done everything it could to avoid dismissing C, including offering him other job opportunities within the company. The Court of Appeal held that the tribunal's failure to consider C's right to 'manifest his religion' under Article 9 of the European Convention on Human Rights did not affect the outcome of the case, since the same decision would have been reached if the tribunal had held that Article 9 applied. The change in shift patterns was an economic necessity for the employer, which had done all it could to avoid dismissing the employee and to accommodate his desire not to work on Sundays. (Note that the facts of this case took place before the Employment Equality (Religion or Belief) Regulations 2003 SI 2003/1660 came into force. Under those Regulations (which will be subsumed into the Equality Act 2010 from a date to be appointed), the employer's requirement that the employee work on Sundays would probably

357

amount to an act of indirect discrimination – see IDS Employment Law Handbook, 'Race and Religion Discrimination' (2004), Chapter 1.)

8.16 **Other factors.** A range of other factors may also be relevant to the question of reasonableness under S.98(4). These include:

- whether or not proposed new terms have been agreed with a recognised trade union. In the Catamaran case (above), the employer had agreed the new contracts with the recognised trade union. The EAT directed that this was relevant to the question of reasonableness

- consultation with both the trade union (where appropriate) and individual employees. In Trebor Bassett Ltd v (1) Saxby (2) Boorman EAT 658/91 the employer failed to explain to S and B how the proposed changes to their contracts would affect them. This meant that S and B were unaware that they faced a drop in pay when they signed the new contracts. The EAT upheld the tribunal's decision that, by not consulting the employees about the effect of the changes, the employer had not acted reasonably and the dismissals were therefore unfair. In Murray v Dewramet Ltd EAT 319/98 the EAT found that the degree of consultation required will vary with the circumstances, particularly in relation to rationalisation exercises. What is important is that employees have an opportunity to be involved in a meaningful way

- the number of employees who ultimately agree to accept the changes to terms and conditions. In the St John of God case (above), 140 out of 170 employees accepted the changes and the EAT held that this was relevant to fairness. The relevance of this factor was also expressly approved by the EAT in Catamaran (above).

It should be noted that in Trebor Bassett Ltd v (1) Saxby (2) Boorman (above) the proposed changes to the contracts of employment concerned the arrangements for overtime – to which there was no contractual entitlement. The EAT held that as the employees worked overtime on a very regular basis, such that it had become 'institutionalised', TB Ltd should have consulted the employees about changes to overtime arrangements.

8.17 **Constructive dismissal**

On the reorganisation of a business some employees may feel dissatisfied with their new terms and conditions or duties. Where a change in terms or working conditions is unilaterally imposed by the employer and the change amounts to a fundamental breach of contract, the employee is entitled to resign and claim unfair constructive dismissal. Where this happens, the employer will usually plead SOSR as the reason for dismissal. In this somewhat artificial situation, a tribunal must establish the principal reason for the fundamental breach of contract that led to the constructive dismissal – Genower v Ealing, Hammersmith and Hounslow Area Health Authority 1980 IRLR 297, EAT. If the imposed terms are part of a reorganisation for which the employer has a sound business reason, SOSR will be made out, following the test laid down in Hollister v National Farmers' Union 1979 ICR 542, CA, and discussed above. Two contrasting examples in which SOSR was pleaded in response to a constructive dismissal claim:

- **UB (Ross Youngs) Ltd v Elsworthy** EAT 264/91: an employer attempted, as part of a reorganisation, to rearrange the shift pattern of an employee in such a way as to make it impossible for her to meet her obligations under her contract of employment. (To have carried out her obligations would have meant that she and her husband, who also worked shifts, would never be at home at the same time.) The employee resigned and claimed unfair constructive dismissal. The employer was found to have breached the implied term of trust and confidence between employer and employee and the EAT was unconvinced that there was SOSR for dismissal

- **Lee v Total Convenience Stores UK Ltd** ET Case No.1201493/06, 1201712/06: L was employed at a petrol station to check stock, make orders and count money. In February 2006 the employer discovered a shortfall of £1,000 in its takings. Following an investigation L was completely exonerated. However, the employer noted that the site had failed to follow company policy and procedures. As a consequence, it decided that L would not be required to count cash from the main safe, as best practice specified that safe access should be limited to one person. L considered this a diminution in his role and he stopped attending work and claimed unfair constructive dismissal. The tribunal found that in altering L's duties, the employer had fundamentally breached L's contract and he was entitled to resign. However, it concluded that the employer took the action it did for sound commercial business reasons and that L's dismissal was potentially fair for SOSR.

8.18 Once a tribunal has found a potentially fair reason for dismissal – i.e. SOSR – it must go on to consider the question of reasonableness under S.98(4). A constructive dismissal is not automatically unfair – Savoia v Chiltern Herb Farms Ltd 1982 IRLR 166, CA. The principles governing reasonableness under S.98(4) apply to both express and constructive dismissals and are discussed above under 'Reasonableness of the change'. Two constructive dismissal examples:

- **Baker v Securicor Omega Express Ltd** EAT 91/98: SOE Ltd imposed a change from weekly to monthly pay. B objected and resigned, claiming that he had been unfairly constructively dismissed. It was accepted both that the company had acted in fundamental breach of contract in imposing the change and that it had a good business reason for doing so. At issue was the fairness of the dismissal. The EAT upheld the decision of the tribunal that the constructive dismissal was fair. The tribunal had taken into account all relevant factors, including the degree of consultation that took place between the employer and both the trade union and B individually; the

359

transitional arrangements offered (including an interest-free loan); the fact that over 8,000 employees finally accepted the change; and the fact that there was no reduction in earnings, merely a change to the method of payment. The tribunal had also rightly balanced the employer's need for uniformity with the disadvantage suffered by B, who was in debt and had to meet a number of weekly repayments to creditors

- **Avery Label Systems Ltd v Toal** EAT 243/91: ALS Ltd reorganised its business with the result that T was demoted from manager to 'team leader'. In this new role T's managerial salary was red-circled but he did not receive additional shift payments to compensate him for an enforced return to shift-working. The EAT held that in all the circumstances the tribunal was entitled to take the view that T was unfairly constructively dismissed.

8.19 Protecting employers' interests

Employers are entitled to protect their commercial interests against threats posed by their employees' actions and to take the necessary steps to achieve that end. If dismissal is the step taken, then assuming there has been no misconduct, SOSR will generally be relied on. There are three main motivations behind such dismissals: first, the employer is seeking to protect its confidential information; secondly, the employer wishes to restrict competition; and thirdly, the employer is seeking to protect its reputation against a risk posed by an employee's activities. We consider these in turn below (though in many cases they may overlap).

8.20 Protecting confidential information

If a breach of confidence has occurred already, that is a matter of conduct – see Chapter 6. But dismissal of an employee because of a suspicion that he or she may leak or use confidential information in the future is usually described as being for SOSR. Frequently such a suspicion arises where the employee has a close relative or associate working for a competitor.

In order for employers to establish a substantial reason for dismissal in such circumstances, they must show that a genuine commercial risk is posed by continuing to employ the employee. In Abey v R and E Holdings (Yorkshire) Ltd t/a Quick Pass School of Motoring ET Case No.14985/82 a driving school receptionist had a long-standing relationship with one of the instructors. When he left to set up in competition, it had a substantial effect on the employer's business. The tribunal held A's dismissal to be fair. However, in Weal v Insulpak Ltd ET Case No.1116/63 W was a quality controller whose father – the works director – moved to a competitor. A tribunal found her dismissal unfair, pointing out that she did not have much access to confidential information and that the relationship between a father and a grown-up daughter living at home was quite different from that of a husband and wife.

360

In Simmons v SD Graphics Ltd EAT 548/79 the EAT said that there is no rule **8.21** of law or general principle governing the situation where two employees with a close personal relationship both hold confidential information and work for competing companies. Whether or not dismissal in these circumstances is fair is a question of fact for the tribunal. In that case S was a telephonist/filing clerk with access to confidential information. She lived with a senior sales manager who moved to work for an aggressive competitor. S was dismissed. The EAT upheld the tribunal's finding that she had been fairly dismissed for SOSR. By contrast, in Skyrail Oceanic Ltd v Coleman 1980 ICR 596, EAT, C was dismissed from her job with a travel agent when she married a man employed by a rival travel agent and the EAT upheld the tribunal finding that this dismissal was unfair. The tribunal had rightly held that the dismissal was for SOSR, taking account of the level of access to confidential information by the two people, the importance of that information, and the positions they held. It was well known that industrial espionage was a particular problem with travel agents and C had access to most of the confidential information held by her employer. However, she had given an undertaking not to divulge confidential information and there was no evidence that she had leaked any. In these circumstances, fairness dictated that she be given sufficient warning to allow her to seek other employment.

Note that in cases where an employee is dismissed because of his or her relationship with a competitor's employee, he or she may also be in a position to bring a claim of direct discrimination on the ground of marital or civil partnership status under S.3 of the Sex Discrimination Act 1975 (or S.13 of the Equality Act 2010, when it comes into force). However, such a claim will fail unless the employee can demonstrate that he or she was dismissed as a result of his or her marital or civil partnership status, and that an employee in a different but equally close relationship would not have been dismissed. See further IDS Employment Law Handbook, 'Sex Discrimination' (2008), Chapter 4.

Restricting competition **8.22**

In RS Components Ltd v Irwin 1973 ICR 535, NIRC, the employer, which manufactured electrical components, found that employees were leaving, setting up in competition and soliciting former customers, which was very damaging to the business. The employer imposed a restrictive covenant on all sales staff to prevent them from soliciting customers for up to 12 months after leaving employment. I refused to agree to the new terms and was dismissed. The NIRC held that the dismissal was for SOSR and was reasonable. It added that it would also be reasonable for employers, when developing new technical processes, to require employees to agree to a restriction on the use of the knowledge they acquired of the new techniques and to dismiss them if they refused.

Even if the restriction an employer seeks to impose is unreasonably wide and therefore likely to be unenforceable, the dismissal of an employee for a refusal

361

to agree to it may well be potentially fair for SOSR. In Willow Oak Developments Ltd t/a Windsor Recruitment v Silverwood and ors 2006 ICR 1552, CA, W Ltd was experiencing loss of staff and confidential information to competitors. It sought to address this by asking a number of its employees to sign new employment contracts containing wide restraint clauses. These prohibited employees, first, from poaching W Ltd's employees and ex-employees for a period of 12 months after the termination of employment and, secondly, from working for a wholly or partly competing business for six months after termination. The employees were given little opportunity to consider the restraint clauses or to seek professional advice, and were not warned that they would be dismissed if they rejected the new terms. When they refused to sign, they were dismissed. They subsequently brought claims of unfair dismissal. The tribunal decided that W Ltd's reason for the dismissals – i.e. the employees' refusal to accept the new terms – could not amount to SOSR because at least one of the restrictions was unreasonably wide. However, the Court of Appeal held that this was wrong. The question asked by S.98(1) is whether the employer's reason is 'of a kind' to justify the dismissal. The Court said that this means that the reason should fall into a category that is not excluded by law as a ground for dismissal. Accordingly, if the reason is whimsical or capricious or dishonest or discriminatory, it will be excluded by S.98(1). But if the reason falls into a category that can legally form a ground for dismissal, then it can be potentially fair as SOSR under S.98(1). An employee's refusal to accept covenants proposed by the employer for the protection of his legitimate interests can legally be a ground for dismissal.

8.23   However, this does not give employers carte blanche to impose new restrictive covenants on existing employees. The reasonableness or otherwise of a proposed restriction will be one of the factors to be considered when the tribunal proceeds to the next stage of determining whether the employer acted reasonably in treating the employee's refusal as a sufficient reason to dismiss him or her. On the facts of the Willow Oak case, the reasonableness of the proposed covenants proved not to be relevant, since the manner in which the employer tried to force the employees to agree to the covenants made a finding of unfair dismissal inevitable. In other cases of this sort, however, the question of whether the covenants are legally enforceable may well be relevant to determining the fairness of a dismissal. Where this is so, the guidance given by Mr Justice Burton when the case was before the EAT may be useful. He suggested that, if the proposed covenant appears to be plainly unreasonable, or its excessively wide terms are not severable, that may make it easier for the tribunal to conclude that there was unfairness. If the proposed contract or covenant is arguably unenforceable, there will be a greater need to consider the approach of the employer, in particular the amount of time given to the employees to consider the proposals and whether they had the opportunity to obtain legal advice. If the covenant is plainly reasonable, then the fairness of the procedure will need to be considered, but the tribunal may well be satisfied that the dismissal was fair.

Note that the Court's decision in Willow Oak effectively (though not explicitly) overrules the EAT's decision in Forshaw and ors v Archcraft Ltd 2006 ICR 70, EAT, which held (on similar facts) that an employee's refusal to agree to an unreasonably wide restrictive covenant could not constitute SOSR for dismissal. However, the correct approach appears to have been adopted (in this respect) in Teknek Electronics Ltd v Munro EAT 1291/97, where the employer sought to impose an extremely onerous covenant upon M. When M refused to accept, he was dismissed. The employer told him he could have his job back if he agreed to the condition. The tribunal found that the reason for dismissal was SOSR in that it was legitimate for the employer to seek to protect the company's interests by imposing the covenant. However, dismissal was not reasonable in the circumstances. The EAT upheld this decision, commenting that the claimant was not contractually obliged to accept the covenant and the employer had essentially resorted to blackmail in attempting to impose a covenant that was so onerous it was probably unenforceable.

Preventing damage to reputation

8.24

An employer that dismisses an employee after receiving information that the employee has been engaged in activities that could seriously damage the employer's business or reputation may be able to show SOSR for the dismissal. This is so even if the employee's conduct is unproven, or not directly relevant to his or her working responsibilities.

In A v B 2010 ICR 849, EAT, A was employed in a senior position by B, a public authority. His job did not involve working with children or with issues specifically related to children, but child protection was one of B's responsibilities. In November 2007 the Metropolitan Police Child Abuse Investigation Command contacted B and made a number of allegations against A, one of which, in B's opinion, carried a 'significant risk of reputational damage' to B. In January 2008 A was asked to a disciplinary meeting and although he denied the disclosure, B concluded that it had to accept the police advice that A was a risk to children. It considered this to be a breach of the trust and confidence at the heart of the employment contract and dismissed A with immediate effect. A tribunal held that A had been fairly dismissed for SOSR. Given the nature of B's organisation, the allegations and A's role, dismissal was within the range of reasonable responses and there were no reasonable alternatives available.

On appeal, the EAT took the view that when an employer receives information under an official disclosure regime that an employee poses a risk to children, it must in principle be entitled to treat that information as reliable. An employer cannot be expected to carry out its own independent investigation to test the reliability of the information since it will typically have neither the expertise nor the resources to do so. However, an employer will not be acting reasonably for the purpose of S.98(4) ERA if it takes an uncritical view of the information disclosed, and if it is in a position to question the reliability of the information,

8.25

363

it ought to do so. Applying those principles to the instant case, the EAT held that the tribunal's finding that B had adopted an appropriately critical approach was unimpeachable. Turning to consider whether B was entitled to treat that information as a sufficient reason for dismissal, the EAT noted that in a case where the employee's job involves working with children, dismissal on the basis that he or she posed a risk to children would generally be justified. But that was not the situation here, and this was undoubtedly why B had put its case on the basis of a breakdown in trust and confidence. In the EAT's view, it was necessary to identify more particularly why the disclosure was said to have made it impossible for B to continue to employ A. B was a high-profile public authority whose responsibilities covered at least some aspects of child protection. A had a senior representative role on its behalf. If he were subsequently shown to have committed offences against children – particularly if he had done so while travelling for work – it would cause serious damage to B's reputation. That damage would be greatly exacerbated if it emerged that B had been warned about A's activities but had taken no action. As to whether the risk of such damage justified A's dismissal, the EAT noted that it had not been established that A was a danger to children and, even if he were, his dismissal would not significantly reduce that danger. The concern was solely for the employer's reputation. However, the EAT held that the tribunal was entitled to regard the dismissal as justified.

8.26 Third-party pressure to dismiss

In some circumstances an employer may feel compelled to dismiss an employee because of pressure from a third party. The pressure may come from a valued customer who threatens to withdraw his or her custom unless an employee is dismissed, or from a third party who wields influence over the employer. In such circumstances SOSR is often relied on as the reason for dismissal.

In Dobie v Burns International Security Services (UK) Ltd 1984 ICR 812, CA, a County Council had a contractual right to approve or disapprove the employment or continued employment of security staff provided by the employer at Liverpool Airport. Friction developed between a senior local authority employee and D, who was dismissed as a result. D brought a claim of unfair dismissal. The tribunal ruled that third-party pressure to dismiss can amount to SOSR and the Court of Appeal upheld this decision.

The employer does not have to establish the truth of any allegations made against the employee or agree with the request to dismiss in order to rely on third-party pressure as the reason for dismissal. In Edwards v Curtis t/a Arkive Computing EAT 845/95 E was dismissed at the insistence of C's only customer, who had complained about the standard of his work. E argued that he had been dismissed for lack of capability and sought to argue that he was capable of doing his job. The tribunal, rejecting E's suggestion, held that the dismissal had resulted from the pressure applied by the customer and was therefore fair. The EAT upheld the tribunal's decision.

Tribunals will accept customer pressure as SOSR if the evidence points to an **8.27** ultimatum having been served on the employer, such as in the Edwards case. But there does not have to be a direct instruction to dismiss, if the effect of the pressure amounts to the same thing. Sometimes a customer may simply demand a higher standard of work without naming anyone, but if the employer knows where the fault lies, and warnings are not heeded, there may be a good reason for dismissal.

However, the employer must show that *some* pressure was exerted by the customer. In Grootcon (UK) Ltd v Keld 1984 IRLR 302, EAT, K was dismissed because his employer – contractors on a North Sea oil rig belonging to BP – said that BP would not have him back on the rig because he was unfit. The only direct evidence was a telex from BP saying that K would have to be cleared by its medical department. The EAT held that to rely on third-party pressure as a cause of dismissal, the employer must adduce proper evidence of this.

In Securicor Guarding Ltd v R 1994 IRLR 633, EAT, the EAT held that it was **8.28** unfair of SG Ltd to dismiss R on the ground that R's pending prosecution for sexual offences against children would offend the sensibilities of the customer for whom R carried out his duties. SG Ltd should at least have asked that customer whether there was any objection to the continued employment of R at that site. Similarly, in Gray v Visual Statement EAT 171/95 VS was concerned about the number of hours that G was working. VS's funding came partly from Urban Aid, which had specified that only one person was to work full time. In an attempt to reduce the number of hours that G worked, VS took action that resulted in G's dismissal. The EAT said that although there was a suggestion that the Urban Aid funding might have been at risk, there did not appear to have been any attempt made to investigate what Urban Aid's response to the situation would have been. Therefore, there could have been no pressing necessity for VS to end G's employment.

It may not be sufficient for the employer simply to point to a decision taken by a third party as the reason for dismissal. In Pillinger v Manchester Area Health Authority 1979 IRLR 430, EAT, a research biochemist was dismissed because an outside organisation – a medical research body – withdrew funds from his research project. The EAT said that as the employer had not shown any reason for the third-party decision to withdraw funds, no substantial reason for dismissal had been established. It was not sufficient merely to say that the funds had been withdrawn, making it impossible to continue to employ P.

If the pressure put on the employer is improper, the employer may fail to establish **8.29** a reason for dismissal. In Lavelle v Alloa Brewery Co Ltd EAT 655/85, for example, L, a barman, was arrested in the bar where he worked and told that he would be charged with obstructing the police. No charges were preferred but the police

365

intimated to the pub that its licence would be at risk if L were not dismissed. The pub bent to this pressure. The employer argued that such pressure constituted SOSR but the EAT disagreed, holding that improper police pressure to dismiss an employee could not be SOSR and that therefore the employer had established no reason for dismissal. However, in Davenport v Taptonholme for Elderly People EAT 559/98 the EAT recognised that Lavelle was an exceptional and highly unusual case that laid down no general principle. In that case, the employer ran a registered care home for the local authority. The authority was therefore in a position to dictate to the employer in respect of those persons who should not be employed at the home. After allegations of abuse were made against D, the authority conducted an investigation and recommended that D should no longer be employed at the home. As a result, D was dismissed. Although the tribunal considered that the authority had treated D unjustly, this could not prevent the employer from relying on SOSR. If the authority's decision had been ignored, the home could have been closed. In contrast to the Lavelle case, the EAT found no evidence of improper pressure being brought to bear upon the employer.

In one unusual case – Parker v Stephens and Scown Solicitors ET Case No.1701281/98 – the employee was employed by a firm of solicitors as a caretaker. He became involved in a dispute with a client of the firm, who complained that P had access to his files and could use information to further the dispute. P was dismissed and the tribunal held that there was SOSR for the dismissal. In so doing, it noted that solicitors are in a unique position and their clients give them confidential information in trust. In view of the terms of a robust letter sent by P to the client, the client's concerns justified dismissal.

8.30   Reasonableness

Employers must act reasonably when dismissing as a result of third-party pressure. It is not enough for an employer to show that there was third-party pressure to dismiss an employee, thereby establishing SOSR as the reason for dismissal. The tribunal will also need to consider whether it was reasonable to dismiss the employee because of that pressure – S.98(4).

Two contrasting examples:

● **Rigblast Energy Services Ltd v Hogarth** EAT 665/93: H was employed on an oil rig by R Ltd, which, in turn, was engaged by T, the operator of the rig. The contract between R Ltd and T required R Ltd to remove any employee whom T considered unsuitable. Following an injury sustained by H and his ensuing absence from work, T, without giving any reason, refused to allow H to return to work. R Ltd had no other positions available for H and he was dismissed. The EAT upheld the tribunal's finding of unfair dismissal. H had never been warned that T had the contractual entitlement to stop any employee working on the rig and, more importantly, R Ltd had not taken sufficient steps to find out why T did not want H to return to work on the rig

366

- **SK v NOL** ET Case No.1401180/07: when SK applied to NOL for a job he disclosed the fact that he was an ex-offender and was on the sex offenders register. He was subsequently employed as a support worker assisting the police and probation service to monitor serious offenders, including sex offenders. However, a police officer recognised SK and the police decided they would not work with him, even though NOL made it clear that there were proper precautions and risk management arrangements in place. NOL offered SK an alternative job, which would not have involved him working with the police, but he did not accept it and he was dismissed. The tribunal found that the decision by the police not to work with SK amounted to SOSR justifying his dismissal. NOL made all reasonable efforts to persuade the police to change their view and its decision not to proceed with a joint meeting with the police was reasonable in all the circumstances.

In Dobie v Burns International Security Services (UK) Ltd 1984 ICR 812, CA, **8.31** the Court of Appeal said that, in considering reasonableness, tribunals should look at the conduct of the employer and, crucially, whether dismissal is an injustice to the employee. However, the Court also pointed out that an argument based on injustice is less likely to be sustainable if the employee's own contract warned that a third party may intervene to have him or her removed. Furthermore, a reasonable employer would be expected at least to consider whether the employee could be redeployed to a post in which there is no contact with the third party concerned – Norwest Construction Co Ltd v Higham EAT 278/82. In KCA Drilling Ltd v Breeds EAT 130/00, another oil rig case, the employee's contract of employment stated that the employer was required to comply with any request from the employer's client – the oil company that owned the oil rig on which it was contracted to work – to remove the employee from the rig. In this situation – and where the employee had refused offers of redeployment – the resulting dismissal was fair.

Two further examples:

- **Osanyinibi v Executive Group Ltd** ET Case No.6000556/00: O was dismissed from his job as a station cleaner following a call from the hygiene manager at the station to his employer. The employer was anxious to retain the contract for cleaning at the station and dismissed O after failing to persuade the station to change its mind. The tribunal found that as a result of real commercial pressure there was SOSR for dismissal. However, there was no evidence that the employer had taken any account of the injustice to O and the dismissal was therefore unfair

- **Greenwood v Whiteghyll Plastics Ltd** EAT 0219/07: WP Ltd employed G to carry out shop fittings at various stores. For some time, G worked at stores owned by M, one of WP Ltd's major customers. However, in July 2006 M made complaints about G's standard of work and subsequently told WP Ltd that G was barred from working in its stores. Unable to find G alternative work owing to 'no spare capacity', WP Ltd dismissed him. The tribunal concluded that WP Ltd had dismissed G for SOSR, and had acted reasonably in doing so. However, the EAT upheld G's appeal. There was no evidence before the tribunal to show that WP Ltd had considered the nature and extent of any injustice to G, and the tribunal had also fallen into error in failing to consider this matter. It may well have been the case, the EAT noted, that had the tribunal considered any injustice to G, it would have decided that it made no difference to the decision to dismiss. On the other hand, the injustice may have been so severe – and on this point the EAT thought it noteworthy that the tribunal made no finding criticising G's work or his capability – that the employer should have reorganised its business, enabling G to take another job within the company.

8.32 ## Difficulties with other employees

Third-party pressure to dismiss can often come from other employees who are in dispute with, or disapprove of, a colleague in some way. Disruption among employees is obviously harmful to an employer's business interests and, if it reaches a substantial level, such disruption may justify dismissal of the employee in question for SOSR. In Treganowan v Robert Knee and Co Ltd 1975 ICR 405, QBD, there was a severe personality clash between T and the other women in her office over the merits of a 'permissive society', and the atmosphere soured considerably when T boasted about a sexual liaison which she had with someone half her age. T was dismissed and the High Court affirmed that the employer had shown SOSR and the dismissal was fair.

The employer should, however, take steps to try to alleviate the situation and should not dismiss the employee until it can reasonably conclude that the breakdown in relationships is irremediable. Failure to take reasonable steps to improve relationships will make the dismissal unfair – Turner v Vestric Ltd 1980 ICR 528, EAT. In deciding on the ultimate reasonableness of such a dismissal, the tribunal will consider whether the relationships can be patched up and also whether the objections of the fellow employees are reasonable or motivated by blind prejudice.

8.33 ## Threat of industrial action

If the pressure coming from other employees, whether via their union or not, is in the form of industrial action, or the threat of industrial action, then special considerations apply. Under S.107 ERA employers are not allowed to invoke shop-floor pressure as a reason for dismissal, so SOSR cannot be argued in such circumstances. For example, in Simpson v Moore Paragon UK Ltd ET Case No.25097/85 S, a printer, was sent to prison for incest. His employer said that his job would be kept open for him but, when he returned, the workforce refused to work with him. S was dismissed. Before the tribunal, the employer denied that the workforce had actually threatened to take industrial action and pleaded SOSR as the reason for dismissal. However, the tribunal found that the whole workforce had informed their supervisors that they refused to work with S, and that such pressure was sufficient to come within S.107. Thus the employer had not established a potentially fair reason for dismissal.

Breakdown in trust and confidence 8.34

A commonly-cited SOSR for dismissal is 'loss of trust and confidence' between the parties. However, this terminology should be used with care. In A v B 2010 ICR 849, EAT (discussed under 'Protecting employers' interests – preventing damage to reputation' above), the EAT admonished the tendency of parties to assume that 'loss of trust and confidence' automatically brings obligations under an employment contract to an end, which it does not. The EAT emphasised the importance of identifying why the employer considered it impossible to continue to employ the employee – in that case, the employer's need to avert damage to its reputation.

Nevertheless, there will still be cases in which the employment relationship has broken down irremediably and where loss of trust and confidence will amount to SOSR for dismissal. For example, in Hutchinson v Calvert EAT 0205/06 H, who suffered from muscular dystrophy and was seriously disabled, employed C as a carer. The nature of this employment relationship was necessarily very intimate, and, as the EAT put it, had to be 'based on complete trust and confidence'. The relationship was satisfactory for more than two and a half years but then became frayed. The tribunal found that in May 2004 C mentioned to H that she needed to discuss with his mother details of holiday due and sick pay, and to satisfy herself as to whether her employer was H or his mother. A couple of days later they had another conversation, during which H became agitated and upset. He subsequently dismissed C as he did not want her to continue caring for him, on the basis that the relationship between them had broken down. C claimed unfair dismissal and a tribunal found that SOSR had not been made out and that the dismissal was procedurally unfair. On appeal, however, the EAT held that the tribunal had applied the wrong test in ascertaining the reason for dismissal. It noted that – following Harper v National Coal Board 1980 IRLR 260, EAT – so long as an employer can show a genuinely held belief that it had a fair reason for dismissal, that reason may be a substantial reason provided it is not whimsical or capricious, even where modern sophisticated opinion can be produced to suggest that it has no scientific foundation. The tribunal had failed to consider whether H genuinely believed that the relationship between himself and C had broken down and could not be retrieved. In addition, in determining whether the dismissal was fair under S.98(4), the tribunal had failed to take into account the very special circumstances of the case. The EAT remitted the case to be determined by a fresh tribunal.

8.35 In Perkin v St George's Healthcare NHS Trust 2006 ICR 617, CA, P worked for an NHS trust as its finance director. His responsibilities included managing a team of employees, liaising with senior colleagues and establishing working relationships with people outside the trust. When members of staff raised concerns about his personality and management style, the trust's chief executive asked him to resign. P refused. At a subsequent disciplinary hearing, the trust's chairman concluded that P's management style had led to a breakdown of confidence in his ability to fulfil his role among the executive team. He had also failed to establish the necessary relationships with stakeholders and external advisers to advance the Trust's interests. Moreover, his 'personal attacks' on colleagues, 'extending on occasions to abuse', had made it impossible for him to resume his previous role and re-establish an effective working relationship with them. As a result, he was summarily dismissed and brought a claim for unfair dismissal. The tribunal found that the reasons for dismissal were 'conduct [and] some other substantial reason' and held that the trust's action had been a reasonable response, but that the dismissal was procedurally unfair.

P appealed to the EAT, which upheld the tribunal's findings. On appeal to the Court of Appeal, P challenged the tribunal's decision on several grounds, including that he had effectively been dismissed on the ground of his personality. The Court agreed that personality, of itself, cannot be a ground for dismissal. For there to be a potentially fair reason for dismissal, an employee's personality must manifest itself in such a way as to bring the actions of the employee within S.98. In this case, the tribunal had concluded that P's unacceptable behaviour and the breakdown in confidence between him and the Trust, for which he was responsible and which had the potential of damaging the Trust's operations, amounted to the potentially fair reasons of conduct and SOSR. The Court acknowledged that the tribunal seemed to treat the case mainly as one of conduct, and although the Court itself would have properly classified it as falling within the category of SOSR, the tribunal's failure to do so was not fatal to its reasoning and did not affect the safety of its decision.

8.36 As the Perkin case suggests, there is a fine line between SOSR and conduct when it comes to cases involving personality clashes. In Huggins v Micrel Semiconductor (UK) Ltd EAT 0009/04 the relationship between H and management deteriorated to the point that a disciplinary meeting was arranged to discuss H's attitude. In the course of that meeting it became clear that the issue was more complex and that H had problems with his health. Management sought to investigate this further but H refused to disclose a medical report obtained from his GP. When H wrote an intemperate letter undermining the management of the company – while still refusing to disclose the report – he was dismissed. The EAT found no error of law when the tribunal characterised this dismissal as being for SOSR, in that H's conduct had caused or contributed to a breakdown in trust and confidence. The dismissal was fair in the circumstances, although no recognised orthodox procedure had been followed. The EAT noted that the employer's business was very small and that H had chosen not to help resolve the issues by refusing to disclose the medical report.

For the obligation of trust and confidence between employer and employee to break down, it appears that there must be some action on the part of one of the parties – Wadley v Eager Electrical Ltd 1986 IRLR 93, EAT. In that case, W was employed servicing and repairing domestic appliances principally in customers' homes. His wife worked as a shop assistant for the same business. She was suspected of misappropriating monies and convicted and sentenced for offences relating to 137 matters over a 22-year period, the total sum amounting to nearly £2,200. She was then dismissed, and the employer, convinced of W's complicity, dismissed him too, without informing him of any specific matters for which he was under suspicion. A tribunal found that the trust and confidence between employer and employee had completely broken down, and that W's dismissal was for SOSR and not unfair. The EAT, however, overturned the tribunal's decision, holding that it had not been the act of the employee that had caused any breakdown of trust and confidence and it was impossible to accept that the behaviour of W's wife could lead to a breach of confidence in the trust residing in W.

Expiry of a limited-term contract

8.37

As discussed in Chapter 1, when a limited-term contract expires and is not renewed, the employee is effectively dismissed – S.95(1)(b) ERA. This applies to contracts that are stated to be for a fixed term and to those that are limited by the completion of a task or by a particular event – S.235(2B).

The expiry of a limited-term contract can be a substantial reason for dismissal but this is not automatically the case – Terry v East Sussex County Council 1976 IRLR 332, EAT. In that case the EAT said that the expiry of a fixed-term contract could be SOSR for a dismissal but it was still up to the employer to show what the reason was and establish that it was substantial. If the expiry of a limited-term contract was automatically SOSR for dismissal, employers could hide behind pleas of SOSR simply by calling a contract limited-term when the real reason for termination was something else altogether.

Employers are expected to show clear evidence of a substantial reason for dismissal due to the expiry of a limited-term contract, as the following cases demonstrate:

8.38

- **Primary Fluid Power Ltd v Brislen** EAT 0611/04: the EAT upheld a tribunal's decision that the dismissal of an apprentice three months after the conclusion of his fixed-term apprenticeship was unfair. On 3 July 2000, B

— 371

started a three-year apprenticeship with PFP Ltd and this required him to work at PFP Ltd's premises as well as studying at college. By the time of the end of his apprenticeship in July 2003 he was still engaged on a City and Guilds course and had also started an NVQ Level 3 course. B's statement of terms and conditions of employment was varied on 21 July 2003 and signed by a senior manager to indicate that 'a successful probation/induction has been served'. PFP Ltd dismissed B on 25 November because there was no permanent position for him and B claimed unfair dismissal. PFP Ltd argued that B's employment had terminated at the end of his fixed-term apprenticeship, and this had been prolonged until the end of November when it had learned that the City and Guilds course was completed and B had started on the NVQ Level 3. It argued that the dismissal was for SOSR. The tribunal held that the contract made it clear that the apprenticeship came to an end in July 2003. There was no evidence to suggest that there was a consensual extension of the apprenticeship to November to take account of the courses B was undertaking. PFP Ltd tried to argue that it had a genuine and reasonable belief, albeit a mistaken one, that the fixed-term apprenticeship ended in November. But the EAT noted that PFP Ltd had in its possession all the relevant contractual documents and it could have clarified the position in July but did not do so

- **West Midlands Regional Health Authority v Guirguis** EAT 567/77: when G's fixed-term contract as a locum consultant radiologist was not renewed, the only evidence preferred was that the regional health officer thought it an undesirable policy to employ locums. The same evidence showed, however, that locums were often employed for a longer period than G had been employed for. The employer had therefore failed to show that it had any policy, let alone a policy which amounted to a substantial reason for G's dismissal. Thus it failed to establish a potentially fair reason for dismissal.

8.39 In Fay v North Yorkshire County Council 1986 ICR 133, CA, the Court of Appeal clarified the circumstances in which the expiry of a limited-term contract can amount to SOSR: where it is shown that the contract was adopted for a genuine purpose, which was known to the employee, and had ceased to be applicable. F, a teacher, was employed under four successive fixed-term contracts and when her last contract was not renewed she brought an unfair dismissal claim. The tribunal ruled that her dismissal was for SOSR and reasonable. The Court of Appeal upheld this. The tribunal had been entitled to conclude that the short-term contracts under which F had been successively employed were the ordinary kind of fixed-term contract and were for the genuine purpose of covering a period of temporary absence. The purpose of the contract had been brought to F's attention and, when that purpose came to an end and the post was filled by someone else, the short-term contract was not renewed.

372

Note the importance of communicating the purpose of the contract to the employee in such cases. In Adams v Coventry University ET Case No.1303464/07 A was initially employed by the University on a temporary contract. At the end of September 2005 she was offered a permanent job by the local Council, at which point the University offered her improved conditions in order to retain her services. A was left with the impression that she was to become a permanent employee, although on 10 October she accepted a fixed-term contract for one year. The contract was further extended, but A was dismissed after the person whose job she had been covering returned to work from maternity leave. The tribunal upheld A's claim for unfair dismissal. She had not been told that she was being employed only to cover an absent employee – the temporary contract she was offered did not mirror the maternity absence and she was never told that it did. She was offered it because the University wanted to persuade her to stay at a time when she had been offered a permanent job elsewhere. There were further extensions to her contract without any reference to the extensions covering maternity absence. The University should also have done more to look for suitable alternative employment.

8.40 The failure to look for suitable alternative employment was also a consideration in Rochdale Metropolitan Borough Council v Jentas EAT 494/01 where J, a temporary employee, was repeatedly re-engaged on a series of one-month contracts for a period of 20 months. When her final temporary contract came to an end, her employment terminated. A tribunal found that there was SOSR for the decision not to renew her contract but that the dismissal was unfair because the employer had not considered whether suitable temporary work was available in another department. J had a substantial period of service, had moved from position to position, and had sought to obtain a permanent position with the employer. The EAT upheld this decision, while commenting that it was a 'one-off case on particular facts'.

Where a permanent position is created to replace a temporary post, the employer may be expected to help the temporary incumbent apply for the permanent post. Two examples:

- **Gavin v Home Office Immigration and Nationality Directorate** ET Case No.1802566/01: G was unsuccessful in his application for the permanent post, which was filled by an external candidate. Although a Council order providing that permanent posts could only be filled by open competition established SOSR for the non-renewal of G's fixed-term contract, the tribunal held that the employer should have done more than simply tell G of the vacancy in a casual phone call. He should have been pointed in the right direction and told of the application procedure

- **Darbyshire v The Governing Body of All Saints CE Primary School** ET Case No.2405746/05: D was employed as a teacher on a temporary fixed-term contract from 1 September 2004 to 31 August 2005 or the return of the post holder from maternity leave, whichever was the sooner. There were no

373

problems over her abilities during the year, and she made it clear to the head teacher on a number of occasions that she would like to remain at the school should the teacher on maternity leave decide not to return. Early in July 2005 a teaching assistant in the school told the head teacher that she would like to apply for the post if the teacher did not return. The head teacher approached the governing body, who agreed the appointment. D was informed of the appointment on 12 July and her employment terminated on 31 August. A tribunal found that D had been unfairly dismissed. It was unreasonable for the school not to have given D the opportunity to be considered for the post or to take any steps to consult her before giving the post to another person. Had the governing body been made aware of D's wish to remain at the school it would have given serious consideration to her superior qualifications.

8.41   Note that the Fixed-term Employees (Prevention of Less Favourable Treatment) Regulations 2002 SI 2002/2034 now gives employees on limited-term contracts the right to be informed by their employer of all available vacancies within the establishment in which they work – Reg 3(6). It is likely that a failure by the employer to comply with this duty will be a factor in the consideration of the fairness of any dismissal. Furthermore, an employee on a limited-term contract that has previously been renewed, or who has been re-engaged on a limited-term contract before the start of the current contract, will be treated as a permanent employee if he or she has amassed four years' continuous service – Reg 8. The only exception is where employment for a limited term can be justified on objective grounds. Needless to say, termination of such a contract on the basis that it has expired will not be considered a substantial reason to dismiss, nor would it be fair.

For further discussion of the rights of limited-term employees, see IDS Employment Law Supplement, 'Fixed-Term Work' (2003).

8.42   Transfer of undertakings

SOSR is often cited as the reason for dismissal in cases where there has been a transfer of an undertaking. The Transfer of Undertakings (Protection of Employment) Regulations 2006 SI 2006/246 (TUPE) protect employees' employment in these circumstances, primarily by providing an effective remedy for those who are dismissed because of the transfer. That remedy is provided for at Reg 7 of TUPE, which renders *automatically unfair* dismissals where the sole or principal reason is either the transfer itself, or a reason connected with the transfer that is not an economic, technical or organisational reason ('an ETO reason') entailing changes in the workforce – Reg 7(1). This applies to dismissals of employees of either the transferor or the transferee, carried out either before or after the transfer – and irrespective of whether or not the employee in question is assigned to the organised grouping of resources or

374

employees that is, or will be, transferred – Reg 7(1) and (4). (For more on automatically unfair dismissals generally, see Chapter 10.)

Dismissals for a reason *unrelated* to the transfer, or for a reason connected with the transfer that is *an ETO reason entailing changes in the workforce*, are potentially fair, subject to the unfair dismissal rules contained in the ERA – Reg 7(2) and (3). If the sole or principal reason for the dismissal is wholly unconnected with the transfer, then whether or not this reason is potentially fair falls to be assessed in the normal way. If an ETO reason entailing changes in the workforce has been established, however, Reg 7(3) provides that the reason for dismissal will be taken to be SOSR, under S.98(1)(b) ERA, unless the reason established fulfils the definition of redundancy in S.98(2)(c), in which case redundancy will be taken to be the reason for dismissal. Having established whether the ETO reason entailing changes in the workforce is redundancy or SOSR, the tribunal then needs to assess the employer's reasonableness in treating that reason as justifying the employee's dismissal under S.98(4) in the normal way.

Economic, technical, or organisational reasons...

8.43

TUPE does not contain a definition of an ETO reason. The DTI Guide 'Employment rights on the transfer of an undertaking: a guide to the 2006 TUPE Regulations for employees, employers and representatives' suggests that ETO reasons are likely to include:

- a reason relating to the profitability or market performance of the transferee's business (i.e. an economic reason)

- a reason relating to the nature of the equipment or production processes which the transferee operates (i.e. a technical reason); or

- a reason relating to the management or organisational structure of the transferee's business (i.e. an organisational reason).

Tribunals have generally sought to give the ETO exception in Reg 7 a narrow meaning. In Wheeler v Patel and anor 1987 ICR 631, EAT, the EAT said that an economic reason for dismissal entailing a change in the workforce must relate to the conduct of the business concerned: broader economic reasons did not fall within the scope of the clause. Therefore, the transferor's desire to obtain an enhanced price for the business or to achieve a sale by capitulating to the transferee's demands to dismiss the workforce did not constitute an ETO reason. This approach was endorsed by the Court of Appeal in Whitehouse v Charles A Blatchford and Sons Ltd 2000 ICR 542, CA. It said that 'the words "economic, technical or organisational reason entailing changes in the workforce" clearly support the conclusion that the reason must be connected with the future conduct of the business as a going concern'. However, in that case the Court of Appeal held that there was evidence upon which the tribunal could conclude that there was an economic or organisational reason for the dismissal. During negotiation for the renewal of a contract to supply prosthetic

8.44

375

appliances to a hospital, the hospital imposed a condition that staff numbers would have to be reduced by one. This reduction was directly related to the provision of services and the conduct of any business that provided them; although the transfer was the occasion for the dismissal, it was not the reason for it. In no way, said the Court of Appeal, was the situation analogous to that of a vendor who dismisses his employees solely for the purpose of getting the best price for his business. Note, however, that the dismissal of an employee by the transferor prior to the transfer, for reasons that relate solely to the future conduct of the business by the *transferee* after the transfer, is not capable of being for an ETO reason – Hynd v Armstrong and ors 2007 IRLR 338, Ct Sess (Inner House). The Court of Session held in that case that the 'right' to dismiss for an ETO reason arises only where the employer dismisses the employee for a reason of its own relating to its own future conduct of the business and entailing a change in its own workforce, and not where the employer dismisses the employee for reasons unrelated to the future conduct of its own business.

8.45 An 'economic reason' is most likely to apply in the case of failing businesses and companies in administration. Genuine economic factors, such as where there is no money left in a business in administration to pay salaries, will amount to an economic reason for dismissal – Secretary of State for Employment v Spence and ors 1986 ICR 651, CA. Economic reasons have been found to exist where staff have been dismissed by a receiver in order to make the business viable – e.g. Warner v Adnet Ltd 1998 ICR 1056, CA, and Whitehouse (above); and where the transferee has had to make substantial economies owing to financial over-commitments – as in Meikle v McPhail (Charleston Arms) 1983 IRLR 351, EAT. However, where employees of a failing business are dismissed in order to make the business a more attractive proposition for sale as a going concern, this is more likely to be viewed as being by reason of the transfer itself, and therefore automatically unfair, especially if there is evidence of collusion between transferor and transferee. The fact that a relevant transfer is in the offing, however, does not necessarily make dismissals for economic reasons unlawful. In Honeycombe 78 Ltd v (1) Cummins and ors (2) Secretary of State for Trade and Industry EAT 100/99, for example, the EAT accepted that an administrator who dismissed staff immediately prior to a transfer did so because there were no assets remaining in the business with which to pay the staff, which was a valid economic reason. The EAT rejected the claimants' argument that the real reason for dismissal was to fit the business for sale as a going concern, even though the sale had been envisaged at the date of dismissal.

8.46 We are not aware of any cases on 'technical reasons' for dismissal but the phrase would presumably cover situations involving some sort of technological innovation, where, for example, an employer has adopted computerised equipment so that fewer employees are needed. Dismissals arising out of technical innovations could also be for economic or organisational reasons.

376

An 'organisational reason' might cover the relocation of a company where some staff are dismissed because it is not practical to relocate them. In Bannister and ors v Brasway plc ET Case No.27791/82 a tribunal held that where there is selective re-engagement by the transferee, so that employees whose skills are not needed by the new employer are dismissed, such dismissals will be for an organisational reason.

... entailing changes in the workforce

8.47

An ETO reason must involve 'changes in the workforce' if it is to be a potentially fair reason for dismissal. The Court of Appeal has held that this must amount to a reduction in the numbers or a change in the functions of the workforce. It is not sufficient merely that there has been a change in the identity of some of the staff, where, for instance, dismissals were followed by the engagement of new staff to replace the old – Berriman v Delabole Slate Ltd 1985 ICR 546, CA. Applying that decision, the EAT in Crawford v Swinton Insurance Brokers Ltd 1990 ICR 85, EAT, held that a reduction in numbers was not necessary as long as staff were given entirely different jobs to do. Engaging a workforce in a different occupation as the result of a reorganisation amounted to a change in the workforce.

In the Berriman case, the Court of Appeal also held that the transferor or transferee must show that the changes in the workforce were *necessary*. It is not enough simply to show an ETO reason for dismissal that incidentally involved changes in the workforce. The Court of Appeal construed the words 'economic, technical or organisational' to mean that the employer must show some sort of imperative behind the dismissal – i.e. that it was necessary and not merely desirable in the commercial interests of the business. According to Lord Justice Browne-Wilkinson, 'the phrase "economic, technical or organisational reason entailing changes in the workforce"... requires that the change in the workforce is part of the economic, technical or organisational reason. The employers' plan must be to achieve changes in the workforce. It must be an objective of the plan, not just a possible consequence of it.'

An example:

8.48

- **Burstal v Compass Cleaning Ltd** ET Case No.1402457/02: the claimant was employed as company secretary and MD's secretary by a company solely owned by her husband. The company lost its largest contract comprising 98 per cent of its work to CC Ltd and it was accepted that TUPE applied to transfer the employees to CC Ltd. When the claimant was dismissed by CC Ltd on the transfer, she complained to a tribunal of unfair dismissal. The tribunal rejected her claim, finding that, as the contract was subsumed into CC Ltd's operation, an MD was not needed, and so an assistant to the MD was also not necessary. This was an ETO reason entailing changes in the workforce, which was a fair reason for the claimant's dismissal.

377

8.49   **Constructive dismissal**

An employee's common law right, upon the employer's fundamental breach of contract, to resign and treat him or herself as dismissed is preserved in the context of a TUPE transfer by Reg 4(11). Constructive dismissal claims depend on the employee being able to establish that the employer committed a repudiatory breach of a fundamental term of the employment contract, and that he or she resigned because of that breach. Although a constructive dismissal is not necessarily unfair (as discussed under 'Business reorganisations – constructive dismissal' above), any fundamental breach of contract that is a result of the transfer – for example, unilateral changes to transferring employees' terms and conditions to align them with the transferee's existing workforce – will render a constructive dismissal automatically unfair.

Constructive dismissal claims are subject to the proviso that, if the employee remains in employment despite the alleged breach, he or she may be deemed to have affirmed the contract. Such claims can also be defeated by a clause in the employment contract permitting the employer to take the action in question. For example, there will be no breach of contract where an employee is required to change his or her place of work in circumstances where an employer is acting reasonably in enforcing a mobility clause in the contract of employment. This situation may, however, give rise to a claim for dismissal under the 'material detriment' right contained in Reg 4(9) – see below.

8.50   Employers who impose changes in the job functions of employees may have a defence to a claim of automatically unfair constructive dismissal if they can show an ETO reason entailing a change in the workforce. As mentioned above, the Court of Appeal in Berriman v Delabole Slate Ltd 1985 ICR 546, CA, construed the phrase 'entailing changes in the workforce' narrowly to mean changes in the overall numbers or functions of the employees looked at as a whole. A fundamental change in job functions may be sufficient to constitute a 'change in the workforce' for the purposes of Reg 7(2), so that, for example, a constructive dismissal brought about by a transferee's insistence that an acquired employee change his or her job function might be potentially fair. For example, in Crawford v Swinton Insurance Brokers Ltd 1990 ICR 85, EAT, C was told after the transfer that her work was to change from clerical work to selling and that her terms and conditions as to hours of work would change. The EAT held that the tribunal was correct in holding that there was a change in the workforce where the same people were kept on but given entirely different jobs. Thus, it seems, the more fundamental the change to the employees' functions, the more likely it is that the dismissal will be covered by Reg 7(2) and be potentially fair for SOSR (or redundancy).

8.51   **Material detriment dismissal**

Reg 4(9) provides a remedy for an employee who envisages being materially worse off as a result of a transfer, but not to such an extent that he or she can claim constructive dismissal. The employee does not have to show that there was a breach of contract, let alone a fundamental one. Reg 4(9) provides that where a transfer involves or would involve 'a substantial change in working conditions to the material detriment' of the employee, he or she can treat the contract as terminated by dismissal. There is nothing in TUPE to suggest that the rules in Reg 7(1) and (2) on the unfairness of TUPE-connected dismissals do not apply to a 'material detriment' dismissal just as much as they apply to other express and constructive dismissals. So, such a dismissal is liable to be automatically unfair unless it is found to be entirely unconnected to the transfer, or, if transfer-connected, for an ETO reason, in which case it will be potentially fair for SOSR (or redundancy).

Employee objection to transfer

8.52

Employees have the right to object to a transfer, in which case they will not automatically transfer – Reg 4(7). Where this happens, the transfer operates to terminate the contract of employment with the transferor, without the objecting employee being treated for any purposes as dismissed – Reg 4(8) – *except* where the transfer involves or would involve a substantial change in the employee's working conditions to his or her material detriment under Reg 4(9), or where the employee resigns and claims constructive dismissal under Reg 4(11) in response to a repudiatory breach of contract by the employer.

For more detail on unfair dismissal in the context of transfers, see IDS Employment Law Handbook, 'Transfer of Undertakings' (2007), Chapter 4.

Miscellaneous reasons

8.53

The open-ended nature of SOSR has meant that a wide variety of reasons have been held to be capable of falling within its ambit. Below are just some examples.

Persistent absences. In Wilson v Post Office 2000 IRLR 834, CA, the Court of Appeal held that the dismissal of an employee for his persistent absences was for SOSR. Although ill health had caused the absences, the employer's reason for dismissal was that W's attendance record did not meet the requirements of the agreed attendance procedure. The tribunal had erred in characterising the reason for dismissal as capability and assessing fairness accordingly.

8.54

Employers should be aware that although dismissals for short but persistent periods of absence may in some circumstances be fair for SOSR, issues may arise under the Disability Discrimination Act 1995 (to be subsumed into the Equality Act 2010 from a date to be appointed) if the underlying reason for the absences amounts to a disability – see IDS Employment Law Handbook, 'Disability Discrimination' (2002).

Inappropriate conduct in a private capacity. In Abiaefo v Enfield Community Care NHS Trust EAT 152/96 the EAT upheld a tribunal's finding

8.55

379

that a health visitor was fairly dismissed for SOSR when it was discovered that she had hit her small son with a stick.

Similarly, the fact that an employee has been charged with criminal offences may amount to SOSR. In A v City of Bradford Metropolitan District Council ET Case No.1800011/99 A was suspended after he was investigated and then charged by the police with sexual abuse of children. The Council then dismissed A rather than waste public money on continuing his suspension until the case came to trial. It did not investigate the allegations on the express instructions of the police. A tribunal found A's dismissal fair for SOSR. The decision to dismiss was within the band of reasonable responses; especially given the fact that A's job had brought him into contact with children. And in Pay v Lancashire Probation Service 2004 ICR 187, EAT, the EAT upheld a tribunal's decision that the dismissal of a probation officer responsible for treating sex offenders because of his links to a business involved in sadomasochistic activities was for SOSR under S.98(1) and also fair under S.98(4).

In the above cases the employees' conduct, though carried out in a private capacity, was inappropriate particularly with regard to the areas in which they respectively worked. We discuss above under 'Protecting employers' interests – preventing reputational damage' how private conduct can amount to SOSR even in circumstances where the nature of the conduct is not necessarily in direct conflict with the employee's working responsibilities, but poses a risk of serious damage to the employer's business or reputation. It is worth noting in this regard that when the Pay case (above) was referred to the European Court of Human Rights, it was held that his dismissal did not breach his right to respect for his private life under Article 8 of the European Convention on Human Rights because his dismissal was justified in view of the sensitive nature of his work with sex offenders – Pay v United Kingdom 2009 IRLR 139, ECtHR.

8.56 **Genuine but mistaken belief that continued employment would contravene the law.** In Hounslow London Borough Council v Klusova 2008 ICR 396, CA, the Court of Appeal held that an employer's genuine but mistaken belief in the unlawfulness of a Russian national's continued employment under immigration rules was SOSR for dismissal. The employer's failure to consult the employee over its concerns as to the lawfulness of her employment, and its failure to consider Home Office guidance on immigration checks, were not so serious as to evidence a lack of genuine belief in the unlawfulness of her continued employment.

8.57 **Imprisonment of an employee.** If a sentence is too short to frustrate the contract, and the employee is dismissed, SOSR can be invoked as the reason for dismissal – Kingston v British Railways Board 1984 ICR 781, CA. The nature of the offence as well as the length of service are relevant to the question of whether the dismissal was fair.

380 ————————————————————————————————

In Rangwani v Birmingham Heartlands and Solihull NHS Trust (Teaching) ET Case No.1302910/98 R, a GP, was charged with conspiring to murder his mistress. He was remanded in custody for two months and then released on bail pending his trial. Although R's contract was not frustrated – given his length of service and the employer's failure to investigate how long he was likely to be unavailable for work – a tribunal found that he had been dismissed for SOSR when the employer failed to renew his latest fixed-term contract. It held that patients would be very concerned that the doctor treating them was facing serious criminal charges allegedly involving the misuse of drugs.

Employed couples. Where a couple are employed together and one partner has been dismissed or has left the employment, the fairness of the dismissal of the remaining partner often depends on the extent to which the job was dependent on the partner who has left. In Kelman v GJ Oram 1983 IRLR 432, EAT, Mr K managed a pub with his wife as assistant. When Mr K was dismissed for stock deficiencies, Mrs K was also dismissed. The EAT agreed with the tribunal's finding that Mr K's dismissal was unfair, but that his wife's dismissal was fair. Her husband's dismissal meant that it was impracticable for her employment to continue and so dismissal was fair for SOSR. **8.58**

However, in Scottish and Newcastle Retail Ltd v Stanton and ors EAT 1126/96 the EAT held that where a joint contract provides that the dismissal of one partner will automatically result in the dismissal of the other, the employer is under a duty to both partners to investigate any allegations of misconduct. Therefore, when the employer failed to investigate Mr S's alleged misconduct, not only was his dismissal unfair but so too was his wife's. Her dismissal was inexorably linked to her husband's dismissal and the employer was therefore under a duty to Mrs S to investigate the allegation against her husband.

Another case that demonstrates the caution required when dismissing the remaining half of a couple is Great Mountain and Tumble Rugby Football Club v Howlett EAT 173/88. Mr and Mrs H were employed as a 'steward and wife to assist' and the contract stipulated that if one left, the other's contract would also be terminated. The marriage broke up and, after his wife left, Mr H was dismissed. The tribunal pointed out that Mrs H's duties were minimal and that her absence would make little difference to the running of the club. The reason for dismissal – Mrs H's departure – was not a sufficient reason. **8.59**

Note that a finding that such a dismissal is fair will not in itself prevent a tribunal from finding that it nevertheless amounts to sex discrimination or discrimination on the ground of marital or civil partnership status under the Sex Discrimination Act 1975 (or, when it comes into force, the Equality Act 2010) – see IDS Employment Law Handbook, 'Sex Discrimination' (2008), Chapter 4.

Dismissal to make room for an employer's son in a small family business. In Priddle v Dibble 1978 ICR 149, EAT, P, a farm labourer, was dismissed when the employer wanted his own son to take over. The tribunal found the **8.60**

dismissal fair for SOSR. It said that P had known from the start of his employment that the employer's son would eventually work on the farm, and that it was natural and in accordance with farming tradition for D to employ his son with a view to handing the farm over to him.

8.61 **Misrepresenting facts affecting employment.** If an employee conceals facts or lies about qualifications in order to get a job, this may be SOSR for dismissal. In Taylor-Pearce v Gwent Health Authority ET Case No.7281/86 T-P obtained a post as a senior registrar in geriatric medicine after exaggerating his qualifications. When this was discovered he was dismissed in spite of his claims that the mistake was made by the typist who typed his curriculum vitae. The tribunal found dismissal for SOSR and held that it was reasonable to dismiss having found that T-P had knowingly misstated details about his career.

In WH Smith Ltd v Kite EAT 562/95 the EAT held that an employee could be fairly dismissed for SOSR after he had failed to disclose that he had a previous conviction. Despite the fact that the company had not asked K whether he had previous convictions, when it eventually found out, there was a breakdown in trust and confidence, which, the EAT held, could be a fair reason for dismissal. See also 'Breakdown in trust and confidence' above.

8.62 **Switching to cashless pay.** In Millson v Associated Western Ltd ET Case No.9876/89 the employer received requests from supervisors and other employees to switch from paying wages in cash to paying by bank transfer or cheque. Further, the union conducted a ballot that was overwhelmingly in favour of the change. M, however, refused to accept the change and was dismissed. The tribunal rejected her unfair dismissal claim because it was satisfied that the employer had good and substantial reasons for changing the method of payment; namely, to satisfy the majority of employees.

8.63 **An erroneous belief that the employee has resigned.** In Ely v YKK Fasteners (UK) Ltd 1994 ICR 164, CA, the employee informed his employer that he intended to resign but never in fact did so. A few months later he changed his mind and said that he would not be leaving after all. The employer, however, insisted that he had resigned and that his change of heart did not alter this position. The tribunal held that E had not resigned but had merely given notice of his intention to resign at some future date. Thus, in informing E that his employment was at an end, the employer had dismissed him. However, the dismissal was for SOSR and was fair in the circumstances. This decision was upheld on appeal by both the EAT and the Court of Appeal.

A similar argument failed, however, in Harris v Cray Valley Ltd ET Case No.1804985/06. H became engaged over the Christmas break in 2005. She lived in Grimsby and her fiancé lived in Liverpool, and it was her intention to sell her house and move to Liverpool. However, she would only move if she was able to sell her house: if she could not sell it, her fiancé might move to Grimsby. Relying on H's stated intention to leave, her employer carried out a reorganisation and

382

her primary duties were reassigned within the company. On 5 June, her employer wrote to her asking her to formalise the details of her leaving date. She was upset by the letter and made it clear that she had not given notice to leave, and did not wish to do so. However, her employer insisted that she leave. A tribunal upheld her claim of unfair dismissal. The tribunal noted that it is possible for a dismissal based on an incorrect assumption that someone had resigned to be a fair dismissal for SOSR, but in this case H had made it clear that she had not resigned before her employer took action to terminate her contract.

Dismissal of chief executive following takeover. In Cobley v Forward Technology Industries plc 2003 ICR 1050, CA, C, the chief executive of FTI plc, was removed from the board of directors following a successful takeover. His position as chief executive was conditional on his remaining a director of the company and he was dismissed accordingly. The Court of Appeal found that his dismissal was for SOSR. The dismissal was fair given C's position and the commercial realities of the situation, of which he had been well aware. **8.64**

Cobley was followed by the EAT in Mountain Spring Water Co Ltd v Colesby EAT 0855/04. In that case a director of M Ltd, B, was wrongfully excluded from its management and shareholding for long periods of time, during which C effectively ran the company. After court proceedings B was restored to his position as a major shareholder and he then brought a resolution, which was passed, for C to be removed from the office of director of the company. Under the company articles of association, C's employment as an executive director was automatically terminated at the same time as she was removed from the office of director. However, the EAT noted that this did not resolve the issue of whether or not her dismissal was unfair, which depended not on contract law but on S.98 ERA. It concluded that the breakdown in trust and confidence between the company, following the re-establishment of B's shareholding, and C, who had run the company in his absence and been party to the opposition to his court proceedings, was capable of being SOSR and remitted the issue of unfair dismissal for reconsideration by the same tribunal. (See also 'Breakdown in trust and confidence' above.)

Refusal to work with a particular manager. In Driskel v Peninsula Business Services Ltd and ors 2000 IRLR 151, EAT, D was sexually harassed by her manager. Her internal complaint was rejected but she refused to return to her job unless the manager was moved elsewhere. The manager refused to move. An employment tribunal found that the employer had been manoeuvred into an impasse in which it had to dismiss either D or her manager. It chose to dismiss D and this decision was for SOSR. The EAT overturned the tribunal's decision that D had not been sexually harassed but upheld its decision that she had been fairly dismissed. It emphasised that the employer had made a genuine investigation of D's complaints; had genuinely tried to accommodate D with acceptable employment, even involving promotion; and had genuinely sought to persuade both parties to moderate their position. Even had the tribunal **8.65**

correctly identified sex discrimination, this could not mean that the manager's position was so weakened that D's demands would not still have posed an impasse soluble only by dismissal of one or the other. In these circumstances, the tribunal was entitled to hold that D's dismissal was fair.

Note that this case is likely to be confined to its very particular facts and that, in the vast majority of cases involving the dismissal of a victim of sexual harassment, the dismissal will be held to be unfair.

8.66   **Refusal to accept stop-and-search policy.** In Trotter v Grattan plc EAT 0179/03 G plc, a large mail order company, introduced a random stop-and-search policy after consultation with the workforce and trade unions. The policy was brought in because the company was worried about theft and about staff storing customer information on mobile phones. T resigned and brought a claim of unfair constructive dismissal because he objected to searches of the body and mobile phones. The tribunal found that the introduction of the policy had been a unilateral variation of T's contract of employment, and that there had been a breach of the implied term of trust and confidence entitling him to resign, but held that the dismissal was fair. The EAT upheld the tribunal's decision. The 'dismissal', which had been carried out for SOSR, had been reasonable in the circumstances. The policy had been introduced to deter employees from stealing, and such policies were common throughout industry. Accordingly, the introduction of the policy had fallen within the band of reasonable responses open to the employer.

9 Retirement

Retirement is a potentially fair reason for dismissal under S.98(2)(ba) of the 9.1
Employment Rights Act 1996 (ERA). Prior to the introduction of S.98(2)(ba),
employees at or over their 'normal retiring age' (or, in the absence of a normal
retiring age, the age of 65) were, with some exceptions, excluded from claiming
unfair dismissal by S.109 ERA. This was repealed (and S.98(2)(ba) introduced)
by the Employment Equality (Age) Regulations 2006 SI 2006/1031 ('the Age
Regulations') in October 2006. The position now is that there is no 'upper age
limit' to claiming unfair dismissal – but where an employer can show that the
reason, or principal reason, for dismissal was retirement, and that the statutory
obligations indicated in S.98ZG ERA (and contained in Schedule 6 to the Age
Regulations) were complied with, then any such dismissal will be deemed fair.

In this chapter we review the statutory rules governing retirement dismissals
contained in Schedule 6 to the Age Regulations, as the extent to which an
employer has complied with these rules affects whether a dismissal is by
reason of retirement and whether such a dismissal is fair. We then consider
precisely what is meant by a dismissal by reason of 'retirement', before
turning to look at how tribunals should determine the fairness of such a
dismissal. The test to determine the fairness of a retirement dismissal is
entirely distinct from the 'reasonableness' test set out in S.98(4) ERA that is
applicable to dismissals for any of the other five potentially fair reasons set
down in S.98(1)(b) and (2) ERA – for details of which, see Chapter 3. Finally,
we consider the justification for having a statutory 'default retirement age',
and the likelihood of reform in this area.

For the purposes of this Handbook, we are concentrating on retirement from
the point of view of the fair dismissal legislation. It is important to note,
though, that retirement dismissals also invariably raise the question of
potential liability for age discrimination. For a detailed discussion of retirement
(and non-retirement) dismissals from this perspective, please refer to IDS
Employment Law Supplement, 'Age Discrimination' (2006), Chapter 5.

9.2   **Equality Act 2010.** Note that although most of the Age Regulations will be revoked when the Equality Act 2010 comes into force, Schedule 6 (and Schedule 8) will remain, so the statutory retirement regime will stay the same for the purpose of assessing the fairness of retirement dismissals.

9.3   ## Overview

The statutory rules governing retirement dismissals are somewhat complicated, given that there are, in fact, two sets of interrelated rules – one to be used to determine whether a dismissal is 'by reason of retirement' and another setting out the statutory retirement procedure that employers must follow – each of which can impact upon an employer's potential liability for unfair dismissal. Before becoming immersed in the detail, we begin by giving a brief outline of how these rules fit together.

9.4   **Retirement as reason for dismissal.** The first key question that has to be considered in retirement dismissal cases is whether the dismissal is 'by reason of retirement', as S.98(2)(ba) ERA provides that dismissals carried out by reason of retirement are *potentially fair*. In other words, retirement is the sixth potentially fair reason for dismissal, along with capability, conduct, redundancy, statutory duty and 'some other substantial reason'.

The question of whether a dismissal is 'by reason of retirement' for the purposes of S.98(2)(ba) is determined in accordance with Ss.98ZA–98ZF ERA. These provisions deal with a number of different dismissal permutations but basically, provided that:

- the dismissed employee is at or over the age of 65

- the dismissed employee is at or over his or her normal retirement age (if there is one), which itself is 65 or over

- the employer follows the statutory retirement procedure, which involves matters such as considering an employee's request to continue working beyond retirement, having complied with the notification duty in para 2 of Schedule 6 to the Regulations between six and 12 months before the intended date of retirement, and

- the dismissal is carried out on the intended retirement date,

the reason for dismissal will be deemed by Ss.98ZA–98ZF to be retirement.

9.5   An employer's failure to comply with the notification duty under para 2 of Schedule 6 within the above timeframe will not necessarily render a retirement dismissal unfair. However, the notification duty must be complied with no later than the fourteenth day before the retirement dismissal is carried out – para 4, Sch 6. If it is not, the dismissal will be *automatically unfair* under S.98ZG.

386

Where an employee has a normal retiring age of *below* 65, his or her dismissal will not be potentially fair on the ground of retirement unless the NRA is itself objectively justified under Reg 3(1) of the Age Regulations as being a proportionate means of achieving a legitimate aim.

Fairness. Once it is established that the reason for dismissal was retirement, the question of whether the dismissal is fair or unfair will be determined in accordance with S.98ZG. This states that the dismissal will be *deemed fair* unless the employer has failed to comply with one of the following obligations laid down by the statutory retirement procedure:

9.6

- the duty to notify the employee (either between 12 and six months prior to dismissal under para 2 of Schedule 6 or, failing that, prior to the fourteenth day before dismissal under para 4 of Schedule 6) of his or her intended retirement date and of his or her right to request to continue working beyond that date

- in accordance with the rules laid down in paras 6 and 7 of Schedule 6, the duty to consider any request made by the employee not to be retired, and

- in accordance with the rules laid down in para 8 of Schedule 6, the duty to consider an employee's appeal against the employer's decision to refuse the employee's request not to be retired.

If the employer fails to comply with any of these obligations, S.98ZG provides that the retirement dismissal will be *automatically unfair*.

Note that, unlike many categories of automatically unfair dismissal, the one-year qualifying period of service applies where an employee claims that his or her dismissal is automatically unfair under S.98ZG – see further Chapter 10. However, employers should be wary of retiring an employee with less than one year's service without complying with the statutory retirement procedure, as there is no qualifying service barrier to bringing an age discrimination claim based on a failure to comply with that procedure.

Statutory retirement procedure

9.7

The statutory retirement procedure is contained in Schedule 6 to the Age Regulations and given effect by Reg 47. In broad summary, it requires the following:

- the employer must, no more than one year and no less than six months before the intended retirement date, notify the employee in writing of the date on which it intends the employee to retire and of the employee's right to request to continue working beyond that date – para 2

- if the employee wishes to make a request to continue working, he or she should do so more than three months but not more than six months before

387

the intended retirement date (or, if the employer has not given notification of the right to request by six months before the intended retirement date, at any time thereafter before the intended retirement date) – para 5

- if a request is made, the employer must hold a meeting with the employee to discuss the request within a reasonable period after receiving it, and must inform the employee of its decision as soon as is reasonably practicable after the meeting – para 7

- if the employee wishes to appeal against the employer's decision, he or she must give notice of appeal as soon as is reasonably practicable – para 8, and

- if an appeal is made, the employer must hold an appeal meeting with the employee within a reasonable period, and must inform the employee of its decision as soon as is reasonably practicable after the meeting – para 8.

9.8 Note that the statutory retirement procedure only applies to retirement 'dismissals' and not to retirements by mutual consent. However, the distinction is not always clear-cut and an employer would be prudent to follow the retirement procedure in any event to guard against the possibility that the employee might later claim that he or she was, in fact, dismissed. See Chapter 1 for a discussion of what amounts, or does not amount, to a dismissal.

Below, we examine the retirement procedure in greater detail, indicating at which stages a failure to comply may lead to a finding of unfair dismissal (on this point, see also 'Fairness of retirement dismissal' below). Although for unfair dismissal purposes the procedure must be followed in respect of retirement dismissals of *all* employees (whether over the age of 65 or not), for the sake of simplicity we assume in this section that the retirement dismissal in question involves an employee at or over the default retirement age of 65.

9.9 **Definitions.** The following definitions, found in S.98ZH ERA, are central to the statutory retirement rules:

- 'intended date of retirement' means the date specified by either the employer or the employee under the statutory retirement procedure as being the intended date of retirement in relation to the employee's dismissal

- 'operative date of termination' means the date on which the employee's employment is terminated, and

- 'normal retirement age' means the age at which employees in the employer's undertaking who hold, or have held, the same kind of position as the employee are normally required to retire.

The most difficult of these concepts is the 'normal retirement age', and we consider its meaning in some detail under 'Retirement as reason for dismissal – normal retirement age' below.

Confusingly, para 1 of Schedule 6 to the Age Regulations contains definitions of the 'operative date of termination' and of the 'intended date of retirement' that differ from those in S.98ZH. These are, however, effectively the same but much more detailed, making specific reference to the retirement procedure itself.

Duty to notify employee   9.10

Under para 2 of Schedule 6, an employer who wishes to carry out a retirement dismissal has a duty to notify the employee in question in writing of:

- the date on which it intends the employee to retire, and

- the employee's right to make a request to continue working beyond the intended retirement date.

The notice under para 2 must be given not more than one year and not less than six months before the intended retirement date.

Paragraph 2(2) makes it clear that the duty to notify applies regardless of whether there is a term in the employee's contract indicating when his or her retirement is expected to occur; any other notification of the employee's retirement date given by the employer; and any other information about the employee's right to make a request to continue working given by the employer. So an employer who has given an employee over one year's notice of the intended retirement will need to repeat the notification within the timeframe indicated above to avoid falling foul of this requirement.

As we discuss in 'Retirement as reason for dismissal' below, an employer's   9.11
compliance with the para 2 duty will go some way towards ensuring that the dismissal of an employee aged 65 or over will be considered to be for retirement and thus potentially fair – and is indeed also an important factor in determining whether a dismissal is in fact fair (see 'Fairness of retirement dismissal' below). It is important to note that tribunals have taken a strict approach to assessing compliance with the notification requirements – see, for example, the approach taken in Favell v Holford Engineering Ltd and Hodgetts v Middlesbrough Borough Council, considered under '"Continuing duty" to notify employee' below.

If, however, an employer fails to comply with the notification duty within the timescale set out in para 2, it may be able to avoid a finding that the dismissal was not by reason of retirement, and/or that it was unfair, by complying with the 'continuing duty' to notify the employee under para 4 of Schedule 6 (see below).

Note that quite apart from its effect with regard to liability for unfair dismissal (and age discrimination), an employer's failure to notify under para 2 can itself be the subject of a tribunal claim by the employee under para 11 of Schedule 6 – see IDS Employment Law Supplement, 'Age Discrimination' (2006), Chapter 5 under 'Statutory retirement procedure – the duty to consider'.

389

9.12 **'Continuing duty' to notify employee**

If an employee's intended retirement date is less than six months away and the employer has not yet complied with the notification duty under para 2, then para 4 of Schedule 6 places the employer under a 'continuing duty' to notify the employee in writing of the intended retirement date and of his or her right to request to continue working beyond that date. This duty expires 14 days before the operative date of dismissal.

Note that the employer must notify the employee of both the intended retirement date *and* the employee's right to request to continue working, if it is to avoid a finding of unfair dismissal. In Favell v Holford Engineering Ltd ET Case No.1500659/07 F's employer wrote to him in October 2006 informing him of its intention that he would retire on his upcoming 65th birthday. F did not make a request to work beyond that date. He attended a ceremony at which he was awarded a watch for his retirement and put up a notice thanking his colleagues and saying 'I shall remember you all and the good times I have had at Holford'. However, following his retirement he brought a grievance and subsequently tribunal proceedings. In considering his claim of unfair dismissal, the tribunal found that there was no doubt that the reason for dismissal was retirement. However, because of the employer's failure to notify F of his right to request not to retire on the intended date of retirement, the dismissal was unfair.

9.13 If the employer complies with the para 4 continuing duty, the dismissal will still potentially be 'by reason of retirement', and thus potentially fair, depending on whether the rest of the requirements of the statutory retirement procedure have been complied with. We discuss this further in 'Retirement as reason for dismissal' below.

If, however, the employer does not provide the requisite information prior to the fourteenth day before the intended date of dismissal, the dismissal, if it goes ahead, will be automatically unfair under S.98ZG ERA – see 'Fairness of retirement dismissal' below.

An employer's failure to comply with the continuing duty of notification was a critical issue in Hodgetts v Middlesbrough Borough Council ET Case No.2516138/06. H, aged 64, worked as a minibus driver, transporting children to and from school. When she enquired about the possibility of being able to continue in employment beyond retirement, her employer informed her that it was in the process of devising a policy in the light of the new legislation. On 18 October 2006 H's employer gave her a form, without explanation, which she could complete if she wanted to request to continue working beyond retirement. She did so, and on 24 October her employer telephoned her to terminate her employment on her 65th birthday, which fell on 28 October. She brought claims for unfair dismissal and age discrimination. The timing of H's dismissal meant that the transitional provisions in the Age Regulations applied to her dismissal, with the result that her employer had been under a continuing duty of

390 ────────────────────

notification. The tribunal found that the employer had failed at any time to notify H of her intended retirement date and of her right to work beyond that date. It followed that the employer had not established that retirement was the reason for dismissal, nor had it proved any other potentially fair reason for dismissal. The employment tribunal thus upheld H's unfair dismissal claim.

Employee's right to request to continue working 9.14

Paragraph 5 of Schedule 6 provides that an employee has the right to request not to be retired on the intended date of retirement. The request must be in writing and state that it is made 'under this paragraph' – para 5(3). In Holmes v Active Sensors Ltd ET Case No.3100214/07 H worked as an assembly technician for AS Ltd. In October 2006 he was informed that the company would be retiring him on 24 November – his 65th birthday. A letter confirmed this decision and informed H of his statutory right to make a request in writing to continue working beyond the age of 65. The following day H wrote a reply, stating that he would like to work until at least January 2007. The employer treated this letter as a request to reconsider its decision but after a couple of meetings between the production manager and H the company decided to stand by its original decision to retire H at 65. H made a number of complaints to a tribunal, including unfair dismissal. The tribunal agreed with the employer that it had correctly followed the retirement notification procedure. Since the employer had given the correct notice (which was reduced by virtue of the transitional provisions in the Age Regulations), H's unfair dismissal complaint turned on whether he had served a valid notice under para 5 requesting that his employment should continue after the intended date of retirement. H claimed that his letter of 25 October complied. However, the tribunal found that it did not do so because it failed, in accordance with para 5(3), to expressly state that the request was being 'made under this paragraph'. The wording of para 5(3) was very clear and the only possible interpretation was that for any notice under para 5 to be valid, it must state that it is made pursuant to that paragraph. It followed that H had been dismissed for retirement and the dismissal was not unfair. In reaching this conclusion the tribunal expressed its surprise that the Age Regulations require employees to refer specifically to them, as similarly stringent requirements are not placed on any notices served by the employer.

Paragraph 5(2) states that the employee must propose that his or her employment should continue beyond the proposed retirement date:

- indefinitely

- for a stated period, or

- until a stated date.

Where the employer has complied with the notification duty under para 2 – i.e. 9.15 has, less than one year but more than six months before the intended retirement date, informed the employee of that date and of his or her right to make a

391

request under para 5 – the employee's request must be made more than three months but not more than six months before the retirement date specified by the employer. Where the employer has not complied with para 2, the employee's request can be made right up to the proposed retirement date (though not more than six months before that date). This is so regardless of whether the employer has complied with the 'continuing duty' under para 4 (see '"Continuing duty" to notify employee' above) – para 5(5).

Where the employer has not complied with the notification duty in para 2, and has not yet complied with the continuing duty in para 4, the employee can take the initiative by making a para 5 request to continue working – para 5(2). In doing so, the employee must identify in the request the date on which he or she believes that the employer intends the retirement dismissal to take place. If the employee does so, the date identified by the employee in his or her request will become the 'intended date of retirement', regardless of whether the employer subsequently complies with the 'continuing duty' under para 4 and specifies a different date – para 1(2)(c).

9.16   **Employer's duty to consider a request**

Paragraph 6 of Schedule 6 states that an employer must consider an employee's request to continue working in accordance with paras 7–9. In summary, the employer must hold a meeting with the employee to discuss the request and notify the employee of its decision as soon as reasonably practicable thereafter. If the employee decides to appeal against this initial decision, the employer must hold a further meeting and notify the employee of its decision on the appeal as soon as reasonably practicable thereafter.

If the employer fails to comply with any aspect of para 7 (meeting to consider request) or para 8 (appeals), the retirement dismissal, if carried out, will be automatically unfair under S.98ZG – see 'Fairness of retirement dismissal' below.

9.17   **Meeting.** Unless the employer agrees to the employee's request to continue working, it is obliged by para 7 of Schedule 6 to hold a meeting with the employee (within a reasonable period after receiving the request) to discuss the request, and both parties must take all reasonable steps to attend the meeting. There is no indication of what a reasonable period might be, but employers should have regard to the employee's need to plan for retirement and to the fact that, if the request to continue working is refused, an appeal would ideally take place before the date of dismissal.

The duty to hold a meeting does *not* apply where:

- before the end of the period within which it would be reasonable for the meeting to be held, the parties agree that the employee's employment will continue indefinitely, or for a stipulated period, and the employer gives notice to the employee to that effect – para 7(3), or

392

- it is not practicable to hold a meeting within a reasonable period and the employer considers the employee's request without a meeting, considering any representations made by the employee – para 7(4) and (5).

Decision. As soon as is reasonably practicable after the meeting (or the employer's consideration of the employee's request), the employer must inform the employee of its decision in a written and dated notice – para 7(6) and (8). If the employer decides to agree to the request, para 7(7) provides that the notice must state: **9.18**

- that the employee's employment will continue indefinitely, or

- that the employee's employment will continue for a further period and specify the length of that period or the date on which the employment will end.

Where the employer decides to reject the employee's request, the notice must simply confirm 'that the employer wishes to retire the employee and the date on which the dismissal is to take effect' and inform the employee of his or her right to appeal. The employer does not have to give reasons for denying the employee's request to continue working.

Appeal. Where the employer rejects the employee's request, or allows the employee to continue working for a shorter period than requested, it must inform the employee of his or her right to appeal against the decision – para 7(7). Under para 8, the employee may appeal 'as soon as is reasonably practicable' after the date of the employer's decision under para 7 – para 8(1). The appeal notice should be in writing and dated – para 8(10). **9.19**

Under para 8(2) the employee is obliged to set out the 'grounds of appeal', which will in most cases be the reasons why the employee thinks he or she should be allowed to continue working – such as, for example, the employee's continuing contribution to a particular project or the value to the business of his or her experience.

Where an appeal is lodged, the employer is once again placed under an obligation to hold a meeting with the employee (within a reasonable period of the notice of appeal) and thereafter to tell the employee of the decision in a written and dated notice. There is no reason why the appeal meeting cannot take place after the retirement dismissal has taken place, as long as it is held within a reasonable period of the appeal notice. The rules governing the meeting and the decision are contained in para 8, and mirror those in para 7, which are discussed above. Again, there is no requirement, where the employer rejects the employee's appeal, for the employer to give reasons for its decision.

Right to be accompanied. By virtue of para 9 of Schedule 6, an employee has the right to be accompanied, by a single companion, to a meeting or an appeal **9.20**

393

meeting held under the statutory retirement procedure where he or she 'reasonably requests' it.

Paragraph 9(2) provides that the companion should be:

- chosen by the employee

- a 'worker' (as defined by S.230(3) ERA) employed by the same employer as the employee, and

- permitted to address the meeting (but not to answer questions on the employee's behalf) and to confer with the employee during the meeting.

Note that, unlike the general statutory right to be accompanied at disciplinary and grievance meetings (Ss.10–15 of the Employment Relations Act 1999), para 9 does not allow an employee to insist upon being accompanied by a trade union official who is not a co-worker.

9.21 If the employee's chosen companion is not available at the time proposed for the meeting by the employer, and the employee proposes an alternative time which is:

- convenient for employer, employee and companion, and

- falls before the end of the period of seven days beginning with the first day after the day proposed by the employer,

the employer must postpone the meeting to the time proposed by the employee – para 9(3) and (4).

The companion must be permitted to take paid time off during working hours for the purposes of accompanying the employee. If such time off is refused, the companion may, within three months of the employer's failure (or, where this was not reasonably practicable, within such further period as is reasonable), make a complaint to an employment tribunal seeking compensation – para 9(5) and (6).

Where an employee is denied the right to be accompanied by his or her chosen companion, he or she may, within three months of the employer's failure (or, where this was not reasonably practicable, within such further period as is reasonable), bring a tribunal claim for compensation of an amount not exceeding two weeks' pay under para 12.

Paragraph 13 contains provisions protecting the employee and the companion from being subjected to a detriment, or dismissed, in relation to the right to be accompanied. Dismissal in these circumstances will be automatically unfair – see Chapter 10 for more details on automatic unfair dismissal claims.

9.22 **Dismissal before employee notified of employer's decision**
Paragraph 10 of Schedule 6 deals with the situation where an employer, who is under a duty to consider an employee's request to continue working, dismisses

394

the employee on the intended retirement date on or before informing him or her in accordance with para 7(6) of its decision in respect of the employee's request. This state of affairs could arise, for example, where the employer does not initiate the retirement procedure more than six months in advance of the intended date of retirement in accordance with para 2, meaning that the employee is entitled to make his or her request to continue working under para 5 on any date thereafter up to the intended date of retirement (see above). If the employee makes his or her request, say, the day before the dismissal date, there will be no time for the employer to arrange a meeting and give a decision before the dismissal takes effect.

Paragraph 10(2) provides that, in these circumstances, the employee's contract of employment will continue in force for all purposes, including that of determining the length of the employee's continuous service, until the day following that on which the employer eventually gives notice of its decision under para 7(6). In other words, the dismissal of the employee on the initial intended retirement date does not actually take effect.

Paragraph 10(3) provides that the day after that on which the employer gives the employee notice of its decision under para 7(6) becomes the date on which the contract is terminated, and is also deemed to be the 'intended date of retirement' for the purposes of the statutory retirement rules. Thus, the dismissal date and the intended retirement date will be one and the same. This is important if an employer is to show under Ss.98ZA–98ZF ERA that retirement is the reason for dismissal (and thus potentially fair), as one of the determining factors is that the contract of employment is terminated on the intended retirement date – see 'Retirement as reason for dismissal' below.

9.23

The *initial* intended retirement date is almost completely ignored in these circumstances. However, para 10(4) states that it does remain the 'operative date of termination' for the purposes of Ss.98ZA–98ZH ERA. This effectively means that the employee will have to be at or over the age of 65 and/or at or over the normal retirement age at the *initial* retirement date if the dismissal is to be considered by reason of retirement for the purposes of the unfair dismissal rules. Again, see 'Retirement as reason for dismissal' below for details.

What happens if an employer, possibly ignoring an employee's request under the statutory retirement procedure altogether, never notifies the employee of its decision in accordance with para 7(6)? Since under para 7 the employer has to hold a meeting within a *reasonable period* and give the decision with regard to the employee's request as soon as is *reasonably practicable* thereafter, the delay need not be very long before the employer will be *incapable* of fulfilling its obligation under para 7(6). We suggest that once para 7(6) cannot be complied with, meaning that there can never be a new dismissal date put in place by para 10, para 10 ceases to take effect. At this point, the retirement dismissal will be

395

automatically unfair under S.98ZG on account of the employer's failure to comply with its procedural obligations.

9.24   **Agreement to change retirement date**

Paragraph 3 of Schedule 6 applies where an 'intended date of retirement' has been identified by the employer or the employee under the statutory retirement procedure and:

• the employer and employee agree under the procedure that retirement will take effect on a later date, or

• the employer and employee agree under the procedure that retirement will take effect on an earlier date – para 3(1).

Paragraph 3 provides that if the new, agreed retirement date falls six months or less after the original intended date, or falls before the original intended date, the statutory retirement procedure will not apply to the new retirement date – para 3(2). That is, the employer will not be placed under a fresh notification duty under para 2 and the employee will not be allowed to make another statutory request under para 5 to continue working. The employee will simply retire on the new, agreed date (which becomes the new 'intended date of retirement'), unless another change is agreed outside of the statutory procedure.

By implication, it follows that if a new, agreed retirement date is *more* than six months after the original intended retirement date, the statutory retirement procedure *will* apply all over again. The employer will be placed under a para 2 duty to notify the employee and the employee will be allowed to make another formal request in accordance with para 5 to continue working beyond the new, agreed retirement date.

9.25   ## Retirement as reason for dismissal

In order for a dismissal to be potentially fair under S.98(2)(ba) ERA, the reason (or principal reason) for dismissal must be the retirement of the employee. As with the other potentially fair reasons for dismissal in S.98, it is for the employer to show the reason for dismissal. However, in practice a dismissal will only be by reason of retirement if it falls within the extended statutory definition set out in Ss.98ZA–98ZF ERA and the extent to which the employer has complied with the statutory retirement procedure. We consider the statutory definition in detail below in two parts – 'Dismissal where there is no normal retirement age' and 'Dismissal where there is a normal retirement age' – before discussing what is meant by the 'normal retirement age' and how this may be judicially interpreted.

First, a brief overview. A dismissal will be by reason of retirement, and thus potentially fair under the ERA, where an employer ensures that:

396

- at the intended date of retirement, the employee will be aged 65 or over

- the normal retirement age for the position in question (if there is one) is 65 or over, and at the intended date of retirement the employee will be at or over that normal retirement age

- less than 12 months but more than six months before the intended retirement date, it initiates the statutory retirement procedure by notifying the employee in writing, in accordance with para 2 of Schedule 6 to the Age Regulations, of when he or she is to be retired and of his or her right to request to continue working beyond the intended retirement date (see 'Statutory retirement procedure – duty to notify employee' above), and

- it terminates the employee's contract on the intended date of retirement.

An employer's failure to comply with the notification duty under para 2 of Schedule 6 within the above timeframe will not necessarily render a retirement dismissal unfair. However, the notification duty must be complied with no later than the fourteenth day before the retirement dismissal is carried out – para 4, Sch 6. If it is not, the dismissal will be automatically unfair under S.98ZG. **9.26**

If an employee is dismissed *before* attaining the age of 65, retirement will nevertheless be the reason for dismissal, and the dismissal will thus be potentially fair, as long as:

- the employee has attained the normal retirement age for his or her position

- less than 12 months but more than six months before the intended retirement date, the employer initiates the statutory retirement procedure by complying with para 2 of Schedule 6

- the dismissal is carried out on the intended date of retirement, and

- the normal retirement age is objectively justified and therefore does not amount to age discrimination (see IDS Employment Law Supplement, 'Age Discrimination' (2006), Chapter 5 under 'Objective justification of retirement dismissals').

Relationship with other reasons for dismissal. Note that an employee dismissed for retirement at the age of 65 or over with proper notice under para 2 of Schedule 6, and on the intended date, will not be able to argue that, in reality, he or she was dismissed for a reason other than retirement – even for an otherwise automatically unfair reason such as making a protected disclosure. Ss.98ZB and 98ZD each state that in such circumstances 'retirement of the employee shall be taken to be the *only* reason for the dismissal... and any other reason shall be disregarded' (our stress). **9.27**

Where retirement is adduced as the reason or principal reason for dismissal, *other* reasons for dismissal may come into play only in one of the following two situations:

397

- where retirement is found, in fact, *not* to be the reason for dismissal under Ss.98ZA–98ZF. For example, under S.98ZA where the employee is dismissed before the age of 65 in circumstances where he or she does not have a normal retirement age – see 'Dismissal where no normal retirement age – dismissal before 65' below

- where the employer has failed to comply with the duty to notify the employee of his or her intended retirement date and of his or her right to request an extension under para 2 of Schedule 6, but has complied with the 'continuing duty' under para 4 of Schedule 6, and the tribunal finds that retirement was the principal reason for dismissal with reference to the matters set out in S.98ZF (which are set out under 'Dismissal where no normal retirement age – dismissal at 65 or over' below).

In the first scenario, where retirement is not the reason for dismissal, the employer will clearly have to show an alternative potentially fair reason for dismissal in order to avoid liability for unfair dismissal. As discussed in Chapter 3, if an employer cannot show a potentially fair reason for dismissal the dismissal is deemed to be unfair without the need to look further into its merits. In the second scenario, retirement is *not* statutorily deemed to be the *only* reason for dismissal, so the employee may be able to persuade a tribunal that he or she was dismissed for another, 'real', reason; or the employer may be able to plead another potentially fair reason for dismissal in the alternative.

9.28   **Dismissal where there is no normal retirement age**
Two scenarios are considered here: dismissal of an employee before the age of 65 and dismissal of an employee who is 65 or over.

9.29   **Dismissal before 65.** Under S.98ZA ERA retirement *will not* be the reason for dismissal where the employee in question has no normal retirement age (NRA), *and* the 'operative date of termination' occurs *before* he or she reaches the age of 65. The operative date of termination is the date on which the employee is *actually* dismissed, not any date on which he or she may be deemed to have been dismissed by para 10 of Schedule 6 to the Age Regulations – see 'Statutory retirement procedure – dismissal before employee notified of employer's decision' above.

It follows that such a dismissal will be unfair under the ERA if the employer cites retirement as the reason for it.

9.30   **Dismissal at 65 or over.** Where an employee with no NRA is dismissed aged 65 or over, such a dismissal will be deemed to be by reason of retirement where:

- less than 12 months but more than six months before the intended retirement date, the employer initiated the statutory retirement procedure by notifying the employee, in accordance with para 2 of Schedule 6 to the Regulations, of when he or she is to be retired and of the employee's right to request to continue working beyond the intended date of retirement, and

- the contract of employment terminates on the intended date of retirement – S.98ZB(1) and (2).

Section 98ZB applied in Holmes v Active Sensors Ltd ET Case No.3100214/07 (see 'Statutory retirement procedure – employee's right to request to continue working' above). As the employer did not have an expressly stated NRA and H was dismissed at 65, the procedure set out in S.98ZB applied. The employer gave H four weeks' contractual notice (as required at the time under the transitional provisions to the Age Regulations) and notified him of his right to apply for his employment to be extended. The employer had thus correctly adhered to the retirement notification procedure and H's dismissal was deemed to have been by reason of retirement.

Conversely, a dismissal of an employee aged 65 or over with no NRA will *not* be by reason of retirement where the contract terminates before the intended date of retirement, whether or not the employer has complied with its para 2 notification duty – S.98ZB(3) and (4). As explained under 'Statutory retirement procedure' above, the 'intended date of retirement' can be identified by the employer when complying with the notification duty under para 2 of Schedule 6; failing that, by the employer when complying with the continuing notification duty under para 4 of Schedule 6; or, failing that, by the employee when making his or her request under para 5 of Schedule 6 to work beyond that intended retirement date.

9.31

Finally, S.98ZB(5) sets out a situation in which the reason for a dismissal *might* be retirement, depending on the determination of the tribunal. This is where the employer has failed to comply with the notification duty under para 2 of Schedule 6 but does not make the mistake of dismissing the employee before the intended date of retirement. S.98ZB(5) states that a tribunal, in determining the reason (or principal reason) for dismissal in these circumstances, should have 'particular regard... to the matters in S.98ZF'. These matters relate to the statutory retirement procedure and are as follows:

- whether or not the employer, having failed to comply with the notification duty under para 2 of Schedule 6, complied with the 'continuing duty' to notify the employee under para 4 of that Schedule

- if the employer notified the employee in accordance with para 4, how long before the notified retirement date that notification was given

- if the employee made a request under para 5 to continue working beyond the intended date of retirement, whether or not the employer followed, or sought to follow, the procedures in para 7 – i.e. whether the employer, within an appropriate timeframe, held a meeting with the employee to

399

consider the request and informed the employee of its decision in accordance with the procedural requirements.

9.32 The upshot of S.98ZB(5) is that an employer is given an opportunity to rectify the situation where it has failed to initiate the statutory retirement procedure timeously.

Technically, S.98ZB(5) also applies where the employer has failed to notify the employee under para 2 and there is no intended retirement date at all. However, a dismissal in such circumstances could not be found to be for retirement under S.98ZF or any other provision.

9.33 **Dismissal where there is a normal retirement age**
This section covers: dismissals before the NRA; dismissals at or after an NRA of 65 or over; dismissals at or after an NRA of below 65; and dismissals after the intended retirement date.

9.34 **Dismissal before normal retirement age.** Where an employer dismisses an employee – whether or not the employee has attained the age of 65 – *before* his or her NRA, the dismissal will not be potentially fair by reason of retirement – S.98ZC. The employer will need to point to an alternative potentially fair reason for dismissal in order to avoid liability for unfair dismissal.

9.35 **Dismissal at or after normal retirement age of 65 or over.** The dismissal of an employee at or after his or her NRA of 65 or higher will be by reason of retirement where:

- the employer notified the employee in accordance with para 2 of Schedule 6 (see 'Statutory retirement procedure – duty to notify employee' above), and

- the contract of employment terminates on the intended date of retirement – S.98ZD(1) and (2).

However, as with S.98ZB, such a dismissal will *not* be by reason of retirement where, regardless of whether the employer has notified the employee in accordance with para 2, the employee's contract is terminated *before* the intended date of retirement – S.98ZD(3) and (4).

Finally, S.98ZD(5) provides that a dismissal *might* be by reason of retirement where the employer failed to comply with the notification duty under para 2 but did not make the mistake of dismissing the employee before the intended date of retirement. Here, the tribunal will determine the reason for dismissal, having particular regard to the matters set out in S.98ZF (see 'Dismissal where there is no normal retirement age – dismissal at 65 or over' above). Again, as with S.98ZB(5) (above), technically S.98ZD(5) also applies where the employer has failed to notify the employee under para 2 and there is no intended retirement date at all. However, a dismissal in such circumstances could not be found to be for retirement under S.98ZF or any other provision.

400

A case decided under S.98ZD:

9.36

- **Hodgetts v Middlesbrough Borough Council** ET Case No.2516138/06. H, aged 64, worked as a minibus driver, transporting children to and from school. On 18 October 2006 H's employer gave her a form, without explanation, which she could complete if she wanted to request to continue working beyond retirement. She did so, and on 24 October her employer telephoned her to terminate her employment on her 65th birthday, which fell on 28 October. She brought claims for unfair dismissal and age discrimination. The tribunal found that the employer had failed at any time to notify H of her intended retirement date and of her right to work beyond that date. It followed that the employer had not established that retirement was the reason for dismissal, nor had it proved any other potentially fair reason for dismissal. The employment tribunal thus upheld H's unfair dismissal claim.

Dismissal at or after normal retirement age of below 65. Section 98ZE is concerned with the situation in which an employee's NRA is below 65 and the employer dismisses him or her at or over that age (whether or not the employee is under or over 65 at the time of dismissal).

9.37

Section 98ZE(2) provides that 'if it is unlawful discrimination under the [Age] Regulations for the employee to have [an NRA of under 65], retirement of the employee shall not be taken to be the reason (or a reason) for dismissal'. What this appears to mean is that where an employee has an NRA of below 65, his or her dismissal will not be potentially fair on the ground of retirement unless the NRA is itself objectively justified under Reg 3(1) of the Age Regulations as being a proportionate means of achieving a legitimate aim. (For details of objective justification of retirement dismissals, see IDS Employment Law Supplement, 'Age Discrimination' (2006), Chapter 5. Note that the Equality Act 2010, which will revoke the Age Regulations once in force (with the exception of Schedules 6 and 8), retains the same test of objective justification for age-related dismissals in S.13(2).)

In Plewes v Adams Pork Produce Ltd ET Case No.2600842/07 the employer's policy of requiring employees to retire the day before their 65th birthday caused it to fall foul of the statutory retirement procedure by one day. P, aged 64, worked in the employer's food manufacturing business. In March and October of 2006, P enquired about working beyond his retirement date in December of that year. Although he was originally informed that his request had been granted in principle, the employer later changed its position and retired him on the day before his 65th birthday in accordance with the terms of his contract of employment. Defending P's subsequent unfair dismissal claim, the employer sought to rely on S.98ZD ERA to argue that the dismissal was fair, maintaining that it did not operate an NRA of below 65, but that it simply did not expect employees to work on their 65th birthday. However, upholding P's unfair

401

dismissal claim, the employment tribunal rejected the employer's argument. P's case fell squarely within S.98ZE ERA. The employer's requirement for employees to retire before 65 was discriminatory and could not be justified.

9.38   Where an NRA of under 65 *is* objectively justified – and therefore does not amount to unlawful discrimination under the Age Regulations – retirement will be considered to be the reason for dismissal of an employee at or over that NRA where:

- the employer has notified the employee in accordance with para 2 of Schedule 6 to the Age Regulations (see 'Statutory retirement procedure – duty to notify employee' above), and

- the contract of employment terminates on the intended date of retirement – S.98ZE(4).

Retirement will not be taken to be the reason for dismissal of an employee at or over an objectively justified NRA if the employee's contract is terminated *before* the intended date of retirement, even if the employer has notified the employee in accordance with para 2 – S.98ZE(5) and (6).

Finally, S.98ZE(7) provides that a dismissal *might* be by reason of retirement where the employer has failed to comply with the notification duty under para 2 of Schedule 6, but does not dismiss the employee before the intended date of retirement. Here, the reason for dismissal will be determined by the tribunal, which must have particular regard to the matters in S.98ZF (see 'Dismissal where there is no normal retirement age – dismissal at 65 or over' above). Technically S.98ZE(7) also applies if the employer has failed to comply with the notification duty under para 2 and there is no intended date of retirement at all. However, if there is no intended date of retirement, the reason for dismissal cannot be retirement.

9.39   **Dismissal after intended retirement date.** It is clear from the above provisions that in many cases where an employer dismisses an employee *on* the intended retirement date, the reason for dismissal will be deemed to be retirement. Furthermore, where an employer dismisses an employee *before* the intended retirement date, the reason for dismissal will be deemed *not* to be retirement. But what happens where the employer essentially complies with the procedure but then dismisses the employee *after* the intended date of retirement?

The ERA is silent on this point. However, according to the DTI's 'Notes on Age Regulations' (March 2006), where an employer has notified the employee in accordance with para 2 of Schedule 6 (see 'Statutory retirement procedure – duty to notify employee' above), and the dismissal takes effect after the intended date of retirement, it will be for the tribunal to determine whether retirement is, in fact, the reason for dismissal. The Notes further point out that in making the determination, the tribunal *may* take the matters listed in S.98ZF ERA into

402

account (paras 287–288) – see 'Dismissal where no normal retirement age – dismissal at 65 or over' above for a breakdown of the matters listed in S.98ZF.

Normal retirement age

9.40

As we noted above, following the repeal of S.109 ERA, employees at or over the 'normal retiring age' are no longer excluded from claiming unfair dismissal. However, the concept of a 'normal retirement age' remains relevant to establishing whether or not retirement is the reason for dismissal. The normal retirement age is defined in S.98ZH as 'the age at which employees in the employer's undertaking who hold, or have held, the same kind of position as the employee are normally required to retire'.

It seems likely that the case law on the 'normal retiring age' under the now-repealed S.109 is relevant to assist tribunals and courts in interpreting the statutory definition of the 'normal retirement age' in S.98ZH. The change in wording (from 'retiring' to 'retirement') does not seem to be substantive. Although 'normal retiring age' was not statutorily defined, the context in which it appeared in S.109 indicates that its meaning was similar: employees were excluded from the right to claim unfair dismissal when they reached the normal retiring age where 'in the undertaking in which the employee was employed there was a normal retiring age for an employee holding the position held by the employee'. In this chapter we use the acronym 'NRA' for both the old 'normal retiring age' and the new 'normal retirement age' on the assumption that they have the same or very similar meanings.

Below, we discuss how the concept of the 'normal retiring age' was judicially interpreted as a guide to how the courts are likely to approach the meaning of 'normal retirement age'. It should be borne in mind, however, that tribunals seeking to establish whether there is a normal retirement age – and, if so, what that age is – in the context of determining whether retirement is the reason for dismissal, should always take as their starting point the statutory definition in S.98ZH.

Relationship between normal retirement age and contractual retirement age. If there is a contractual retirement age (CRA), this creates a presumption that the NRA is the same – Waite v Government Communications Headquarters 1983 ICR 653, HL. However, the presumption can be rebutted. First, there may be evidence that the CRA is not uniformly enforced or is subject to variation. In Waite, the House of Lords held that:

9.41

- the overall criterion for determining the NRA is the reasonable expectation of employees holding the same position as the claimant at the effective date of termination of the claimant's contract (this is an objective test)

- if there is a CRA, this will be presumed to be the age at which employees reasonably expect to retire – i.e. the NRA. This presumption may be rebutted, however, if there is evidence that the CRA is regularly departed from or ignored

403

- if there is evidence that shows that the CRA has been replaced in practice by another precise and definite higher age, that age will be the NRA (but see 'Can the NRA be *lower* than the CRA?' below)

- if the evidence shows that the CRA has been abandoned, but that it has not been replaced by a definite alternative age – e.g. the employees have a CRA of 62, but in practice are allowed to stay on and retire as they choose at ages up to 70 – there is no NRA.

9.42 Statistics will be relevant in deciding whether the CRA has been abandoned in practice, although their Lordships stressed that the test is not solely a statistical one.

Even where the CRA is applicable to all or nearly all the employees in a group, the presumption that this CRA is the NRA is rebuttable. This is in part because the NRA falls to be determined by reference to the facts known *at the time of dismissal*, not at the time of contract (nor, as in Cross v British Airways plc, below, at the time the employees' undertaking was transferred) – see, for example, Barclays Bank plc v O'Brien and ors 1994 ICR 865, CA (considered below).

9.43 In the following cases, the CRA did *not* establish the NRA:

- **Cross and anor v British Airways plc** 2006 ICR 1239, CA: the employees' CRA of 60 had been preserved by statute following a transfer of an undertaking, whereas their NRA of 60 had not. Their CRA remained at 60, whereas their NRA became 55 in line with that of the other employees in the company who performed their role. What was 'transferred' was a right in general law not to be unfairly dismissed before reaching the NRA, whatever that might be at the time of dismissal

- **Alderton v Seismograph Service (England) Ltd** ET Case No.22220/87: a retirement age calculated according to a formula based on years of overseas service and giving different results for different employees was not an NRA. The tribunal held that an NRA must be an age in years identifiable by, and common to, all employees in the relevant group

- **Mauldon v British Telecommunications plc** 1987 ICR 450, EAT: the CRA was 60 but over 90 per cent of the relevant employees were retained beyond that age and a large proportion stayed on until they were 65. The EAT held that the CRA had been abandoned but had not been replaced by a definite NRA

- **Secretary of State for Scotland v Meikle** 1986 IRLR 208, EAT: Scottish prison officers had a CRA of 55, although in practice they were allowed to remain beyond that age, subject to health and efficiency. The Scottish Department introduced a new policy whereby officers, depending on their age and length of service, would retire either at 57½ or between 57½ and 60. The EAT held that there was evidence that the CRA had been departed from, but it had been replaced by a variety of higher ages, so there was no NRA.

404

In the latter case the EAT said that 'abandonment' of the CRA did not mean that it had to have been 'given up absolutely', but only that it had been regularly departed from.

Can the NRA be lower than the CRA? The House of Lords in Waite v Government Communications Headquarters (above) referred to the possibility of the CRA being substituted by 'some definite *higher*' NRA (our stress). Historically, many courts have adopted the principle that the NRA cannot be lower than the CRA. In Bratko v Beloit Walmsley Ltd 1996 ICR 76, EAT, the employer sought to reduce the retiring age of employees, not by varying the CRA but by unilaterally introducing a new, lower NRA. Prior to March 1992, there was a CRA of 65 which was universally applied and which therefore constituted the NRA. The employer had been in negotiation with the union for some time with a view to reducing the retirement age by agreement. When these negotiations broke down, the employer notified all employees in writing that with effect from 31 March 1992 the retirement age was reduced to 64. A tribunal accepted the employer's argument that the notice to the employees of a new retirement age was effective to change the employees' expectations, thereby introducing an NRA that was lower than the age at which employees were required to retire under their contracts of employment. The EAT overruled the tribunal. It held that, since the CRA established a presumption as to the NRA, it would be surprising in principle if the employer could change the NRA to the employee's disadvantage without taking the steps necessary to reduce the contractual age by agreement or by some other lawful and effective means. In the EAT's view, the House of Lords in Waite had accepted that the presumption in regard to the CRA could be rebutted by evidence of a higher NRA, but their Lordships had not envisaged the possibility of an NRA that was lower than the CRA. The EAT added that if the employer wished to reduce the CRA, the correct way to do so was either by a consensual variation or by terminating the employees' contracts and offering them new ones containing the revised provision as to retirement.

This interpretation of the House of Lords' decision in Waite was confirmed by the Court of Appeal in Wall v British Compressed Air Society 2004 ICR 408, CA, where Lord Justice Simon Brown held that the House of Lords did not contemplate that employees with a CRA could ever have an NRA lower than their CRA (unless, of course, their contractual terms were varied). And in Royal and Sun Alliance Insurance Group plc v Payne 2005 IRLR 848, EAT, an employer argued that there was an NRA of 62 for those in the claimant's position, meaning that under the law as it then stood, he was not entitled to claim unfair dismissal. Having decided that the employee's CRA was 65, the EAT concluded that an employee's NRA for unfair dismissal purposes can never be lower than his or her CRA. The presumption that the NRA and the CRA are the same can be rebutted only by evidence that the NRA is higher. Therefore the tribunal had been correct to allow the employee's unfair dismissal

9.44

405

claim to proceed. In so finding, the EAT departed from its decision in the earlier case of Cross and ors v British Airways plc 2005 IRLR 423, EAT, in which Burton P expressly stated that an employee may have an NRA either higher or lower than his or her CRA.

9.45 However, when Cross reached the Court of Appeal, the Court confirmed that the NRA in that case was 55 despite the CRA being 60 – Cross and anor v British Airways plc 2006 ICR 1239, CA. Unfortunately, the Court seems to have made its decision without hearing argument on the point in a case that was primarily concerned with the law on transfers of undertakings. Nevertheless, the Court clearly stated that 'the normal retiring age for a group of employees in the same employment may be lower than the contractual retiring age for a particular employee or employees in the group'.

There are thus conflicting decisions on this point. We suggest that tribunals faced with the question of whether the NRA can be lower than the CRA would be best advised to adopt the line taken by the Court of Appeal in Cross, for the following reasons. First, there is nothing in the statutory definition in S.98ZH (above) to indicate that the NRA may only be equivalent to or higher than any CRA. It simply refers to the age at which employees in the employer's undertaking who hold the same kind of position as the claimant are 'normally required to retire'. Secondly, it must not be forgotten that courts interpreting the NRA in the context of S.109 were, in effect, determining whether or not an aggrieved claimant had a right to claim unfair dismissal at all. Under the old law, claimants were excluded from the right to claim where they had reached the normal retiring age, or, if none existed, the age of 65. The courts would thus have been keenly aware of the injustice caused to an employee were they to hold that he or she could not bring an unfair dismissal claim once he or she had passed the age at which employees normally retired, but before the retirement age set out in their contracts. While an employee today may still be disadvantaged by being retired at an NRA lower than his or her CRA, at least he or she does not lose the right to claim unfair dismissal. And, where such an NRA is lower than 65, it will need to be objectively justified if dismissal at that age is to be fair (see 'Dismissal where normal retirement age – dismissal at or after normal retirement age of below 65' above).

9.46 **Changing the NRA.** It was made clear by the Court of Appeal in Brooks and ors v British Telecommunications plc 1992 IRLR 66, CA, that it was possible for an employer to alter employees' NRA provided such a course did not involve a breach of their contracts. This was confirmed in Patel v Nagesan 1995 IRLR 370, CA, where the Appeal Court held that an employer could not impose unilateral contractual changes in an attempt to change the NRA. In that case N was originally employed by SRN Homes as a matron in a rest home for the elderly. There was no retirement age specified in her contract of employment and it was the company's stated policy to consider retirement age on a case-by-case basis. N intended to retire at 65. In 1987 the home was

406

purchased by P but N continued to work under the same contractual terms. In July 1990, however, P wrote to all the staff telling them that he intended to introduce new contracts on 26 September 1990. One of the new terms was an NRA of 60. N refused to accept the new terms but P nevertheless wrote to her on 11 October 1990 saying that, because she would be 60 on 9 November 1990, he was giving her ten weeks' notice of dismissal. N brought a claim of unfair dismissal, which the employer contested on the ground that N had reached the NRA at the date her employment was terminated and was therefore excluded, under the now-repealed S.109, from bringing a claim. N argued that there was no NRA applicable to her. Her contract, originally made with SRN Homes, did not specify any particular age. She also had a letter from SRN Homes which said that the company dealt with retirement on a case-by-case basis. In her view, P's attempt to alter her contractual terms without her consent was a repudiatory breach entitling her to resign and claim constructive dismissal. The Court of Appeal agreed that there was no evidence of an NRA of 60 for N. It then applied the House of Lords' test in Waite (above) and asked what the reasonable expectation or understanding of the employees in N's position at the relevant time was. The Court said that it was clear that N did not expect to retire at 60 and added that, even if all the other employees had accepted 60 as their retiring age, N was in a unique position in the employer's undertaking, since she was the person in charge and had statutory responsibilities imposed upon her by virtue of her position. Any NRA of 60 did not, therefore, apply to her (see 'Employee holding a unique position' below).

A further example:

9.47

- **East v Baxenden Chemicals Ltd** ET Case No.1305892/06: employees of BC Ltd were eligible to receive their occupational pension at the age of 64, which was generally regarded as the NRA. Between 1997, when E joined, and 2006 no employees remained in employment beyond that age, except in two exceptional cases. On 19 May 2006 E was informed that his retirement date was 1 July, and he indicated that he wanted to continue working beyond that age. His request was refused on the ground that 64 was the NRA, and he claimed unfair dismissal. The tribunal upheld his claim. The NRA was 64 until 20 April 2006, but on that date BC Ltd had written to employees saying: 'After 6 April 2006 you will be able to take your benefits from the pension scheme but also carry on working.' The tribunal held that the plain meaning of that statement was that members of the pension scheme could continue to work beyond their 64th birthday, and so from that date there was no NRA.

Relevant class of employees. Section 98ZH defines the NRA by reference to employees holding the 'same kind of position' as the claimant. S.235(1), in turn, defines an employee's 'position' as the following matters 'taken as a whole':

9.48

- his or her status as an employee

407

- the nature of his or her work, and

- his or her terms and conditions of employment.

It is the position of the employee *at the time of dismissal* that counts – Hughes v DHSS 1985 ICR 419, HL.

In determining the group of employees holding the same kind of position as the claimant, regard must be had to all employees in the identified group, regardless of their proximity to retirement. In Brooks and ors v British Telecommunications plc 1992 IRLR 66, CA, 23 employees aged 60 to 65 were dismissed between May 1986 and March 1988. Their CRA was at all times 60. They complained of unfair dismissal, arguing that the presumption that the CRA of 60 was the NRA had been rebutted. The CRA had not been superseded by a specific higher retiring age and so there was no NRA for employees in their position. The tribunal examined the employer's retirement practice and found that, from 1982 to 1988, those employees in the relevant grade who were approaching 60 had a reasonable expectation of being retained beyond 60. However, there were proposals afoot to change the NRA for this grade to 60 and this had been communicated to employees. The tribunal held that the NRA for the grade as a whole was 60. The Court of Appeal upheld the tribunal's decision. In the Court's view, it was not permissible to subdivide a group of employees of a particular grade according to their age and proximity to retirement when determining the NRA. The relevant question was what, at the date of dismissal, was the age which all employees of all ages in the claimant's position could reasonably regard as the NRA applicable to the group.

9.49   The EAT followed this approach in Dormers Wells Infant School v Gill EAT 596/97, noting that the test is: What is the age which employees of all ages in the employee's position could reasonably regard as the NRA applicable to the group? It added that the fact that individuals within the group retire at different ages will not necessarily mean that there is no NRA. However, there must be a specific age at which those within the group reasonably expect to retire. Otherwise there will be no NRA. In other words, the fact that individuals within the group end up retiring at different ages does not prevent a finding that the NRA is different from the CRA, so long as there is one specific age that could reasonably be regarded as being the NRA for the group. (Note that this case has since been held by the Court of Appeal to have been wrongly decided on the question of whether an employee holding a unique position can have an NRA – see Wall v British Compressed Air Society 2004 ICR 408, CA, below. However, this aspect of the EAT's reasoning would appear to stand.)

In exceptional circumstances it may be permissible to define a group by reference to its particular terms and conditions relating to retirement. In Barber v Thames Television plc 1992 IRLR 410, CA, the employer's retirement policy was changed over a period of time to remove disparities in treatment of staff on the basis of their sex. All employees who joined the firm after 1978 were to retire at 60, but male employees who joined before 1978 were entitled to work until 65. The employer then informed employees who had started before 1978 that their retirement age would be reduced, initially to 64, with the aim of achieving a uniform retirement age of 60 by 1992. B, a male senior supervisor who had joined the company before 1978, was compulsorily retired on his 64th birthday and claimed unfair dismissal. The question was whether or not he was disqualified from claiming, under the law as it then stood, because he had reached his NRA. When the case reached the EAT, it was held that the correct group of employees was the totality of senior supervisors of equal status to B – including those who had joined after 1978 and whose NRA was 60. There was no common retirement age for this group as a whole. However, the Court of Appeal disagreed. In its view, there were two separate groups of supervisors: one consisting of those employed after 1978, whose NRA was 60, and the other consisting of those employed prior to 1978, whose retirement age was, as a result of the policy change, 64 at the date B retired. Since there was an NRA of 64 for those in B's position at the date of his retirement, he was precluded from bringing an unfair dismissal claim. A difference in retirement ages was capable of being the distinguishing factor between one group and another, the Court held.

9.50 The Barber case was distinguished, however, in Barclays Bank plc v O'Brien and ors 1994 ICR 865, CA. The facts of that case were that six people aged between 60 and 65 employed as messengers were dismissed in 1990. Their CRA was 60, but prior to 1987 there had been no NRA. This was because employees over 60 had been able to apply each year for an extension of their employment up to age 65. Such extensions had in practice been granted. In 1987 a circular was sent to employees stating that in future the NRA was to be 60. In practice, employees who were over 55 at that date were still allowed to apply for extensions to work beyond 60, subject to a maximum of five years from their next birthday. The EAT held that this was merely a 'measure of compassion' and that the NRA after 1987 was 60. In reaching this conclusion, it followed the Court of Appeal's judgment in Brooks and ors v British Telecommunications plc (above). In determining the NRA, it was necessary to look at the expectation of the group as a whole, irrespective of their ages. The Barber case was distinguished on a number of grounds. First, the parties in the instant case had agreed that the relevant group was 'the messengers' as a whole; no such concession had existed in Barber. Secondly, the Barber case had involved a fixed, non-discretionary phasing of retirement ages, whereas in the instant case the employer had discretion whether or not to allow extensions to those who applied after 1987. Thirdly, in the Barber case the differences in retiring age related to employees' dates of joining the company, and not to their age. Finally, if the Barber approach were adopted in the present case, it might lead to the creation of one-person

409

groups, which would be contrary to the intention of the legislative scheme. The EAT's decision was upheld by the Court of Appeal.

9.51   **Employee holding a unique position.** It has previously been held that where there are no other employees holding the position which the claimant holds, then no NRA can be established – Age Concern Scotland v Hines 1983 IRLR 477, EAT. See also Patel v Nagesan (above), where the Court of Appeal held that no NRA applied to the matron of a rest home for the elderly who was in a unique position. Moreover, in Dormers Wells Infant School v Gill EAT 596/97 the EAT rejected the claimant's argument that since he was the only maintenance officer in the school, and had been told that he could retire at the same time as his partner (which would have made him over 65 at the time of retiring), that older age was his NRA. The EAT, declining to depart from the Age Concern Scotland and Patel decisions, held that where an employee is in a unique position within the undertaking, he or she can have no NRA.

However, the Court of Appeal in Wall v British Compressed Air Society 2004 ICR 408, CA, held by a majority that the Age Concern Scotland and Dormers Wells Infant School cases had been wrongly decided. In the Wall case W was 67 years old when he was dismissed from his position as director general of BCAS. He claimed unfair dismissal. The parties agreed that W had a CRA of 70 and that as director general he had occupied a unique position within the undertaking. The tribunal, directing itself in accordance with the Dormers Wells Infant School case, decided that because W was in a unique position, no comparison could be made with employees in the same position as him and therefore, even assuming he had a CRA of 70, no NRA could be established. On appeal, however, the EAT overturned the tribunal's decision, holding that, assuming W had a contractual retiring age of 70, there was no reason why this should not also constitute his NRA, even though he was the only person holding his position. When the case reached the Court of Appeal, the majority distinguished the Court of Appeal's decision in Patel on the basis that, since the employee in that case did not have a CRA, the case had not addressed the issue of whether the CRA of an employee holding a unique position constitutes his or her NRA. The central issue in the instant case was whether the word 'normal' in S.109(1)(a) (as in 'normal retiring age') necessarily required the existence of one or more comparators, with the result that an employee in a unique position could never rely on his or her CRA to establish an NRA. The majority of the Court decided, in agreement with the EAT, that there appeared to be no good reason to discriminate in this way solely on the basis of there needing to be at least one other employee holding the same position. The majority went on to conclude that where the employee holding a unique position has a CRA, there is no need for comparisons to be made with other employees holding the same position in order to establish an NRA. It followed that W's NRA was 70.

9.52   As noted above, the majority of the Court of Appeal distinguished the decision in Patel v Nagesan on the basis that the claimant in that case did

410

not have a CRA. Thus, it would appear to remain the case that an employee holding a unique position in an undertaking who does not have a CRA, does not have an NRA either. This was certainly the view of the EAT in Tarbert (Loch Fyne) Harbour Authority v Currie EAT S/0033/05. In that case the claimant was employed as a harbour master. His written contract was silent as to his retirement age. When he brought an unfair dismissal claim at the age of 67, the tribunal found that it was an 'express oral term' of his contract that his retirement age was 70. The EAT, however, found that the tribunal had not been entitled to come to this conclusion on the evidence. The claimant had no CRA – and accordingly, no NRA. The EAT noted: 'in a case where an employee holds a unique position, there will usually be no question of considering his case in the light of retirement practices adopted by other employees and resort must be had to his contract of employment... It follows that, in such a case, if the contract is silent, there is no normal retiring age.'

Fairness of retirement dismissals 9.53

Once it is established that the reason for dismissal was retirement – and thus potentially fair – the question of whether the dismissal is actually fair or unfair must be determined in accordance with S.98ZG ERA. The effect of this provision is that the dismissal will be *deemed to be fair* unless the employer has failed to comply with one or more of the following obligations laid down by the statutory retirement procedure:

- the duty to notify the employee (either between 12 and six months prior to dismissal under para 2 of Schedule 6 to the Age Regulations or, failing that, prior to the fourteenth day before dismissal under para 4 of Schedule 6) of his or her intended retirement date and of his or her right to request to continue working beyond that date (see 'Statutory retirement procedure – duty to notify employee' and 'Statutory retirement procedure – "continuing duty" to notify employee' above)

- the duty to consider any request made by the employee not to be retired, in accordance with the rules laid down in paras 6 and 7 of Schedule 6 (see 'Statutory retirement procedure – employer's duty to consider a request' above), and

- the duty to consider the employee's appeal against the employer's decision to refuse his or her request not to be retired, in accordance with the rules laid down in para 8 of Schedule 6 (see 'Statutory retirement procedure – employer's duty to consider a request' above).

If the employer *fails* to comply with any of these obligations, the 9.54 retirement dismissal will be *automatically unfair* – S.98ZG. Note,

411

however, that if the *employee* has failed to comply properly with the statutory requirements in making a request to continue working, then his or her subsequent dismissal may be considered to be fair even if the employer has not properly complied with the duty to consider the employee's request – see, for example, Holmes v Active Sensors Ltd ET Case No.3100214/07, considered above under 'Statutory retirement procedure – employee's right to request to continue working'.

Where a dismissal is automatically unfair under S.98ZG and re-employment has been ordered, a tribunal may make an award of four weeks' pay – see Chapter 14 under 'Compensation'.

We observed in the opening paragraphs to this chapter that the test to determine the fairness of a retirement dismissal is entirely distinct from the 'reasonableness' test applicable to any of the other five potentially fair reasons for dismissal, which is discussed in Chapter 3. The fairness or unfairness of a retirement dismissal is entirely a matter of process: an employer's failure to comply with the statutory retirement procedure will lead to a finding of unfair dismissal, while an employer's compliance with that procedure will lead to a finding of fair dismissal, *regardless of questions of justice and equity*. Tribunals must therefore resist the temptation to consider the reasonableness of an employer's refusal to allow an employee to continue working in determining fairness. The only discretion open to tribunals is in determining whether retirement was in fact the reason for dismissal in accordance with the matters set out in S.98ZF – see 'Retirement as reason for dismissal' above.

9.55 Default retirement age

As discussed above, the statutory unfair dismissal regime makes it lawful for employers to retire staff at or above the age of 65, with no requirement to objectively justify the decision to dismiss or indeed to adduce reasons for doing so. This 'default retirement age' (DRA) – contained in Reg 30 of the Age Regulations (or para 8 of Schedule 9 to the Equality Act 2010 when it comes into force) – was challenged by the charity Age UK as being incompatible with the EU Equal Treatment Framework Directive (No.2000/78).

When the case first came before the High Court in December 2006, it referred several questions to the European Court of Justice. In R (Incorporated Trustees of the National Council on Ageing (Age Concern England)) v Secretary of State for Business, Enterprise and Regulatory Reform 2009 ICR 1080, ECJ, the ECJ held that the DRA in Reg 30 comes within the scope of the Equal Treatment Framework Directive and therefore falls to be justified by legitimate social policy objectives, such as those related to employment policy, the labour market or vocational training. However, it is for the national court to ascertain whether the legislation pursues such objectives and, if so, whether the means

412

used are appropriate and necessary. The case then returned to the High Court, as R (on the application of Age UK) v Secretary of State for Business, Innovation and Skills 2010 ICR 260, High Court (Admin), which held that the United Kingdom's default retirement age is lawful and that employers are entitled to retire staff at the age of 65. Having reviewed all the arguments for and against, the Court concluded that, on balance, setting the DRA at 65 was within the competence of the Government at the time it implemented the Directive. The judge went on to comment that he might have reached a different conclusion if the Government had not brought forward its review of the Regulations from 2011 to 2010. He also noted that he 'cannot presently see how 65 could remain as a DRA after the review'. Accordingly, the claims failed.

So the position remains that the DRA is lawful, and employers are entitled to retire staff at the age of 65 – so long as they follow the statutory procedure – without justification. However, given the High Court judge's comments, it seems likely that the Government will raise the DRA in the near future. Indeed, the Coalition Government elected in May 2010 has made it clear that it intends to phase out the DRA, although no timetable has yet been set. The explanatory notes to the Equality Act 2010 indicate that 'any changes' resulting from the review of the default retirement age (that was initiated by the previous government and was ongoing at the time of the election) 'will be implemented during 2011' (para 820). If, as seems likely, the DRA remains but is raised to, say, 70, any retirement dismissals below that age will have to be objectively justified if the employer is to avoid unfair dismissal liability. If the DRA was to be abolished altogether, employers would have to objectively justify all retirement dismissals in order to avoid unfair dismissal liability.

413

10 Automatically unfair dismissals

List of automatically unfair reasons

Different rules applicable to automatically unfair dismissals

Dismissal in connection with jury service

Dismissal for refusing to work on Sunday

Dismissal of employee representatives

Dismissal in connection with occupational pensions

Dismissal in connection with tax credits

Dismissal relating to study and training

Dismissal relating to trade union blacklists

Certain reasons for dismissal can be described as 'automatically unfair' in the sense that, if one of these reasons is established, the employment tribunal *must* find the dismissal unfair. Claims of ordinary unfair dismissal (i.e. those not based on automatically unfair reasons) require a tribunal to consider: (i) whether the employer's reason for dismissal is one of the potentially fair reasons set out in S.98(1) and (2) of the Employment Rights Act 1996 (ERA); and, if the reason is potentially fair, (ii) whether, in the circumstances of the case, the employer acted reasonably or unreasonably in treating that reason as a sufficient reason for dismissing the employee – S.98(4). However, consideration of the reasonableness of the decision to dismiss is entirely irrelevant when it comes to claims based on any of the statutory provisions that render a dismissal automatically unfair. In such cases, the focus of the tribunal's inquiry will be on establishing, on the evidence, whether the prohibited reason was the reason or principal reason for dismissal. If it was, then there is no option but for the tribunal to find the dismissal unfair.

10.1

This chapter starts by providing a list of the automatically unfair reasons for dismissal. We then outline the different rules that apply to automatically (as opposed to ordinary) unfair dismissals so far as qualifying for the right to claim, burden of proof and remedies are concerned. Finally, we examine in detail those categories of automatically unfair dismissal that are not dealt with elsewhere in this Handbook or in other IDS publications. 'Ordinary' unfair dismissals under S.98 are dealt with in Chapters 3–8.

————————————————————————— **415**

10.2 List of automatically unfair reasons

There are numerous categories of automatically unfair dismissals (subject to various qualifications and exceptions) which emanate from a number of different statutory sources. They are:

- dismissal for reasons relating to *jury service* – S.98B ERA (see below)

- *retirement* dismissals where the employer has failed to comply with its obligations under paras 4, 6, 7 or 8 of the statutory retirement procedure – S.98ZG ERA (see Chapter 9)

- dismissal in connection with the right to *time off for dependants* under S.57A ERA – S.99 ERA (see IDS Employment Law Handbook, 'Maternity and Parental Rights' (2009), Chapter 10)

- dismissal for a reason relating to *pregnancy, childbirth or family leave* (i.e. maternity, adoption, parental or paternity leave) under Reg 20 of the Maternity and Parental Leave etc Regulations 1999 SI 1999/3312 or Reg 29 of the Paternity and Adoption Leave Regulations 2002 SI 2002/2788 – S.99 ERA (see IDS Employment Law Handbook, 'Maternity and Parental Rights' (2009), Chapter 12)

- dismissal for a *health and safety* reason – S.100 ERA (see Chapter 11)

- *Sunday working* dismissals – S.101 ERA (see below)

- dismissal in connection with the entitlement to *paid annual leave and other rights* under the Working Time Regulations 1998 SI 1998/1833 – S.101A ERA (see IDS Employment Law Handbook, 'Working Time' (2009), Chapter 7)

- dismissal of an *occupational pension scheme trustee* in connection with his or her duties in that capacity – S.102 ERA (see below)

- dismissal of an *employee representative* in connection with his or her duties in that capacity – S.103 ERA (see below)

- dismissal for making a *protected disclosure* – S.103A ERA (see Chapter 13)

- dismissal for *asserting a statutory right* – S.104 ERA (see Chapter 12)

- dismissal in connection with the entitlement to the *national minimum wage* – S.104A ERA (see IDS Employment Law Handbook, 'Wages' (2003), Chapter 7)

- dismissal in connection with *working tax credits* to which the employee may be entitled – S.104B ERA (see below)

- dismissal in connection with the *right to request flexible working* – S.104C ERA and Reg 16(3) Flexible Working (Procedural Requirements)

416 —————————————————————————————

Regulations 2002 SI 2002/3207 (see IDS Employment Law Handbook, 'Maternity and Parental Rights' (2009), Chapter 11)

- dismissal in connection with the *right to request study and training* – S.104E ERA and Reg 18(3) Employee Study and Training (Procedural Requirements) Regulations 2010 SI 2010/155 (see below)

- dismissal for a reason relating to a *trade union blacklist* prohibited under the Employment Relations Act 1999 (Blacklists) Regulations 2010 SI 2010/493 – S.104F ERA (see below)

- dismissal because of a *'spent' conviction* within the terms of the Rehabilitation of Offenders Act 1974 (see S.4(3)(b) of that Act), unless the employee falls into a category excluded from the provisions of that Act by a statutory order (see Chapter 6 under 'Criminal offences at work – previous convictions')

- dismissal in connection with *trade union membership, activities or use of union services* – S.152 Trade Union and Labour Relations (Consolidation) Act 1992 (TULR(C)A) (see IDS Employment Law Handbook, 'Trade Unions' (2000), Chapter 10)

- dismissal in connection with an application or campaign for *trade union recognition or the securing of bargaining arrangements* – para 161, Sch A1 TULR(C)A (see IDS Employment Law Handbook, 'Trade Unions' (2000), Chapter 5, under 'Detriment and dismissal')

- dismissal for taking *official industrial action* in certain circumstances – S.238A TULR(C)A (see IDS Employment Law Handbook, 'Industrial Action' (2010), Chapter 8)

- dismissal in connection with the *right to be accompanied at disciplinary and grievance hearings* – S.12(3) Employment Relations Act 1999 (see IDS Employment Law Supplement, 'Disciplinary and Grievance Procedures' (2009), Chapter 6)

- dismissal in connection with the *right to be accompanied at a meeting under the statutory retirement procedure* – para 13(5), Schedule 6, Employment Equality (Age) Regulations 2006 SI 2006/1031 (see IDS Employment Law Supplement, 'Age Discrimination' (2006), Chapter 5)

- dismissal where there is a *transfer of an undertaking* and the transfer, or a reason connected with it, is the reason or principal reason for the dismissal – Reg 7(1) Transfer of Undertakings (Protection of Employment) Regulations 2006 SI 2006/246 (TUPE) (see IDS Employment Law Handbook, 'Transfer of Undertakings' (2007) , Chapter 4)

- dismissal relating to the performance of the functions of, or activities as, a member or representative (or candidate for election as a member or

417

representative) of a *European Works Council* or in relation to a request made for time off in order to perform such functions/activities – Reg 28 Transnational Information and Consultation of Employees Regulations 1999 SI 1999/3323 (see IDS Employment Law Supplement, 'Information and Consultation Rights' (2005)

- dismissal in connection with the rights of *part-time workers* under the Part-time Workers (Prevention of Less Favourable Treatment) Regulations 2000 SI 2000/1551 – Reg 7 (see IDS Employment Law Supplement, 'Part-time and Atypical Workers' (2001), Chapter 4)

- dismissal in connection with the rights of *fixed-term employees* under the Fixed-term Employees (Prevention of Less Favourable Treatment) Regulations 2002 SI 2002/2034 – Reg 6 (see IDS Employment Law Supplement, 'Fixed-term Work' (2003), Chapter 3)

- dismissal in connection with the establishment of a *European public limited liability company* under the European Public Limited-Liability Company Regulations 2004 SI 2004/2326 – Reg 42

- dismissal in connection with *information and consultation* rights under the Information and Consultation of Employees Regulations 2004 SI 2004/3426 – Reg 30 (see IDS Employment Law Supplement, 'Information and Consultation Rights' (2005))

- dismissal in connection with the information and consultation rights of *occupational or personal pension scheme members* under the Occupational and Personal Pension Schemes (Consultation by Employers and Miscellaneous Amendment) Regulations 2006 SI 2006/349 – para 5, Sch 1 (see below)

- dismissal in connection with the information and consultation rights of employees of *European cooperative societies* under the European Cooperative Society (Involvement of Employees) Regulations 2006 SI 2006/2059 – Reg 31

- dismissal in connection with the information, consultation and negotiation rights of employees involved in *cross-border mergers* under the Companies (Cross-Border Mergers) Regulations 2007 SI 2007/2974 – Regs 46 and 47

- dismissal in connection with the information, consultation and negotiation rights of employees of *European public limited liability companies* under the European Public Limited-Liability Company (Employee Involvement) (Great Britain) Regulations 2009 SI 2009/2401 – Reg 29.

10.3 **Future extension of reasons**

The list of automatically unfair reasons for a dismissal has grown substantially in recent years, as most new employment rights are accompanied by a right not

418 ────────────────────────────

to be unfairly dismissed for exercising that right. At the time of writing there are two additional automatically unfair reasons for dismissal that have been inserted into the ERA by other Acts of Parliament, but have not yet been brought into force by a commencement order. These are:

- dismissal of an employee under the age of 18 for exercising, or seeking to exercise, rights to participate in *education or training* under Ss.27–28 of the Education and Skills Act 2008 – S.101B ERA

- dismissal in connection with *pension enrolment* under the Pension Act 2008 – S.104D ERA.

Selection for redundancy   10.4

In the context of redundancy dismissals, by virtue of S.105(1) ERA, an employee who is dismissed by reason of redundancy will be regarded as having been automatically unfairly dismissed where: (i) the circumstances constituting the redundancy are shown to have applied equally to one or more other employees in the same undertaking who held positions similar to that held by the employee and who have not been dismissed by the employer; and (ii) the reason or principal reason for which the employee was selected for redundancy is one of the reasons set out in S.105(2A)–(7M). By virtue of S.153 and para 162 of Schedule A1 TULR(C)A, the same applies to dismissals in connection with trade union membership, activities or use of union services and dismissals in connection with trade union recognition or the securing of bargaining arrangements.

Effectively, this means that (subject to the exceptions below) it will be unfair to select an employee for redundancy for any of the reasons listed as automatically unfair reasons above. The exceptions are that:

- no provision is made in S.12 of the Employment Relations Act 1999 for a selection for redundancy to be automatically unfair if the reason relates to the statutory right to be accompanied at disciplinary or grievance hearings

- no specific provision is made to render selection for redundancy automatically unfair if the reason is connected with a transfer of an undertaking to which TUPE applies. (However, if an employee is selected for redundancy and dismissed solely by reason of the transfer or for a reason connected to the transfer that is not an 'economic, technical or organisational reason entailing changes in the workforce' (an ETO reason), the dismissal will fall within Reg 7(1) and be automatically unfair. If the employer can establish that the reason for the selection and subsequent dismissal was an ETO reason, the dismissal will be fair if the tribunal concludes that the employee's selection for redundancy and the application of the redundancy dismissal procedure fell within the band of reasonable responses available to the employer – Reg 7(3).)

Different rules applicable to automatically unfair dismissals

10.5

The rationale behind making some reasons for dismissal automatically unfair is a public policy one: there is a sufficient public interest in protecting employees who are dismissed for such reasons. This public policy is reflected in modifications made to the normal rules that apply to qualifying for the right to claim unfair dismissal, to the availability of interim relief and to the level of compensation that can be recovered, in respect of some (though not all) automatically unfair reasons. These rules are discussed below.

10.6 **Qualifying service**

Where an employee is dismissed (or selected for redundancy) for an automatically unfair reason, the one-year service requirement for the right to claim unfair dismissal does not apply – Ss.108 ERA; and Ss.154 and 239 TULR(C)A; para 164, Sch A1 TULR(C)A; and S.12(4) of the Employment Relations Act 1999. The exceptions to this are dismissals because of a spent conviction, dismissals that are by reason of retirement but automatically unfair due to a breach of the statutory retirement procedure, and dismissals where there is a transfer of an undertaking (see further Chapter 2).

10.7 **Burden of proof**

It is sometimes asserted that, in claims of automatic unfair dismissal, it is for the claimant to prove that the dismissal was for a prohibited reason. But this is not strictly accurate. As with ordinary unfair dismissal, the burden is technically on the employer to show the reason for dismissal. Usually, the employer seeks to discharge this by showing that, where dismissal is admitted, the reason for it was one of the potentially fair reasons under S.98(1) and (2) ERA. It will therefore normally be the employee who argues that the real reason for dismissal was an automatically unfair reason. In these circumstances, the employee acquires an evidential burden to show – without having to prove – that there is an issue which warrants investigation and which is capable of establishing the competing automatically unfair reason that he or she is advancing. However, once the employee satisfies the tribunal that there is such an issue, the burden reverts to the employer, who must prove, on the balance of probabilities, which one of the competing reasons was the principal reason for dismissal – Maund v Penwith District Council 1984 ICR 143, CA.

The Maund case was considered by the Court of Appeal in Kuzel v Roche Products Ltd 2008 ICR 799, CA, where the employee contended that, having rejected the employer's reason for dismissal, the tribunal was compelled to find that the real reason for dismissal was that put forward by the employee, in this case a reason falling within S.103A (protected disclosure). The Court, however, disagreed. If an employer does not show to the satisfaction of a tribunal that

420

the reason for dismissal was the one put forward by the employer, it is open to the tribunal to find that the real reason was that asserted by the employee. But it does not follow, either as a matter of law or logic, that the tribunal *must* find that, if the reason was not that put forward by the employer, then it must have been that asserted by the employee. It may be open to the tribunal to find that, on a consideration of all the evidence in the particular case, the true reason for dismissal was not advanced by either side.

There is one important qualification to the above. Where the employee lacks the requisite continuous service to claim ordinary unfair dismissal – i.e. one year – he or she will acquire the burden of proving, on the balance of probabilities, that the reason for dismissal was an automatically unfair reason – Smith v Hayle Town Council 1978 ICR 996, CA, and Tedeschi v Hosiden Besson Ltd EAT 959/95.

Interim relief   10.8

Interim relief is an emergency interlocutory procedure designed to ensure the preservation of the status quo – i.e. the employee's employment – pending the hearing of the unfair dismissal complaint. It is governed by Ss.128–132 ERA and is available in the following categories of automatically unfair dismissal:

- dismissal related to the carrying out of designated health and safety activities (S.100(1)(a) ERA)

- dismissal in connection with the performance of functions as a health and safety representative or member of a safety committee (S.100(1)(b) ERA)

- dismissal in connection with the performance of functions or activities as a working time representative or as a candidate for such a role (S.101A(d) ERA)

- dismissal in connection with the performance of functions as a trustee of a relevant occupational pension scheme (S.102(1) ERA)

- dismissal in connection with candidature or performance of functions or activities as an employee representative for the purposes of consultation on collective redundancies or proposed transfer of an undertaking (S.103 ERA)

- dismissal related to the making of a protected disclosure (S.103A ERA)

- dismissal related to trade union blacklists (S.104F ERA)

- dismissal in connection with the statutory right to be accompanied at a disciplinary or grievance hearing – S.12(5) Employment Relations Act 1999

- dismissal in connection with an employee's right to be accompanied at a meeting to consider a request to enter into study or training – Reg 18(5) Employee Study and Training (Procedural Requirements) Regulations 2010 SI 2010/155

- the reason for dismissal relates to trade union membership, activities or use of union services – S.161(1) TULR(C)A

421

- dismissal was for an impermissible reason connected with the statutory trade union recognition procedures (para 161(2), Schedule A1 TULR(C)A).

10.9 It should be noted that interim relief is not available in cases of selection for redundancy for any of the above inadmissible reasons. This is because the availability of interim relief hinges on the *reason* for dismissal. In a case where an employee claims to have been selected for redundancy due to an automatically unfair reason, the reason for dismissal remains redundancy – see McConnell and anor v Bombardier Aerospace/Short Brothers plc (No.2) 2009 IRLR 201, NICA.

Full details of the interim relief procedure are provided in Chapter 19.

10.10 **Compensation for automatically unfair dismissals**
Special rules governing the basic and compensatory awards apply to some automatically unfair dismissals

10.11 **Basic award.** In certain cases of automatically unfair dismissal, a minimum basic award applies – S.120 ERA. There are three different levels of minimum basic award depending on the reason for dismissal.

In respect of dismissals (or selection for redundancy) relating to:

- the carrying out of designated health and safety activities (S.100(1)(a))

- the performance of functions as a health and safety representative or member of a safety committee (S.100(1)(b))

- the performance of functions as an employee representative under the Working Time Regulations (S.101A(d))

- the performance of the functions of an occupational pension trustee (S.102(1))

- the performance of the functions of an employee representative (S.103)

- there is a minimum basic award (as from 1 February 2009) of £4,700 – S.120(1).

In respect of dismissals relating to trade union blacklists under S.104F there is a minimum basic award (as from 2 March 2010) of £5,000 – S.210(1C).

10.12 The third level of basic minimum award applies to retirement dismissals. As explained in Chapter 9, S.98ZG provides for a form of automatically unfair dismissal where an employer has failed to comply with certain obligations under the statutory retirement procedure. Under S.120(1A) and (1B), if a dismissal is rendered unfair by operation of S.98ZG and the amount of the basic award would be less than four weeks' pay, the tribunal shall substitute a basic award of four weeks' pay unless it would result in injustice to the employer.

422

Compensatory award. Section 214(1) ERA imposes a statutory cap on compensatory awards for unfair dismissal of £65,300 (as of 1 February 2010). However, S.124(1) does not apply where the reason for the dismissal was that the employee:

10.13

- carried out or proposed to carry out activities in connection with preventing or reducing risks to health and safety at work, having been designated by the employer to do so (S.100(1)(a) ERA)

- performed or proposed to perform the functions of a health and safety representative, or member of a safety committee, either in accordance with arrangements established by statute or after being recognised as such by the employer (S.100(1)(b))

- made a protected disclosure (S.103A), or

- was selected for redundancy and the reason for selection was one of the above reasons (S.105(3) and (6A)) – S.124(1A).

Where S.124(1A) applies, there is no limit on the amount of compensatory award that can be awarded.

The general rules relating to calculation of the basic award are discussed in Chapter 15, and those relating to the compensatory award are discussed in Chapters 16–18.

10.14

In the remaining sections of this chapter we consider those categories of automatically unfair dismissal not dealt with elsewhere in IDS Employment Law Handbooks and Supplements. These are dismissals:

- in connection with jury service

- for refusing to work on Sunday

- of employee representatives

- in connection with occupational pensions

- in connection with tax credit entitlement

- relating to study and training

- relating to trade union blacklists.

Dismissal in connection with jury service

10.15

Section 98B(1) ERA provides that an employee will be regarded as unfairly dismissed if the reason (or, if more than one, the principal reason) for the dismissal is that he or she has been summoned to attend for jury service under the Juries Act 1974, the Coroners Act 1988, the Court of Session Act 1988 or the Criminal Procedure (Scotland) Act 1995, or has been absent from work because he or she attended court in pursuance of being so summoned.

423

The employee will, however, lose the protection of S.98B(1) if the employer shows: (a) that the circumstances were such that the employee's absence in pursuance of being so summoned was likely to cause substantial injury to the employer's undertaking; (b) that the employer brought those circumstances to the attention of the employee; (c) that the employee refused or failed to apply to the appropriate officer for excusal from, or a deferral of, the obligation to attend court; and (d) that the refusal or failure was not reasonable – S.98B(2). The 'appropriate officer' for the above purposes is defined in S.98B(3), although in practice the officer will usually be identified in the letter accompanying the summons for jury service.

Section 98B(1) ERA came into force on 1 April 2005, but to the best of our knowledge, there have yet to be any claims of automatically unfair dismissal made under it.

10.16 Dismissal for refusing to work on Sunday

The provisions relating to Sunday trading that were previously contained in the Sunday Trading Act 1994 and the Betting, Gaming and Lotteries Act 1963 (as amended by Schedule 8 to the Deregulation and Contracting Out Act 1994) are now contained in the ERA. The purpose of the Sunday trading provisions is to safeguard the employment rights of shop and betting workers who object to working on Sunday. To that end, the ERA provides that shop or betting workers who enjoy 'protected' or 'opted-out' status have the right to refuse to do Sunday work and any agreement or provision of an employment contract is unenforceable in so far as it requires the employee to work on a Sunday – Ss.37 and 43. The employee also has the right not to suffer any detriment as a result of refusing to work on a Sunday – S.45. Furthermore, any dismissal for a refusal or threatened refusal to do Sunday work is deemed to be automatically unfair – S.101.

Under S.101 ERA, an employee is deemed to have been unfairly dismissed, regardless of his or her age, length of service or hours of work, if:

- the employee is a shop worker or a betting worker

- he or she enjoys 'protected' or 'opted-out' status, or proposes to give the employer an opting-out notice

- the reason or principal reason for the dismissal is that the employee refused, or was threatening to refuse, to work on Sundays or on a particular Sunday.

These requirements are considered in turn below.

10.17 'Shop' and 'betting' workers

In order to benefit from the protection of S.101, an employee must be either a 'shop worker' or a 'betting worker' as defined by Ss.232 and 233 ERA. Other workers are not covered.

424

Shop workers. A 'shop worker' is an employee who, under his or her contract of employment, is or may be required to do shop work – S.232(1). 'Shop work' is defined in S.232(2) as 'work in or about a shop... on a day on which the shop is open for the serving of customers'. S.232(3) states that a 'shop' includes any premises where any retail trade or business is carried on. 'Retail trade or business' includes the business of a barber or hairdresser, the business of hiring goods other than for use in the course of a trade or business, and retail sales by auction. However, it does not include catering businesses – i.e. the sale of meals, refreshments or intoxicating liquor for consumption on the premises on which they are sold, or the sale of meals or refreshments prepared to order for immediate consumption off the premises – or the sale of programmes, catalogues and similar items at theatres or other places of amusement – S.232(6) and (7).

10.18

It is clear from the wording of the statutory provisions that the definition of 'shop worker' extends beyond workers who are directly involved in serving customers (such as sales assistants and checkout operators). During the committee stage of the Sunday Trading Bill, the Minister (Mr Peter Lloyd) said that the definition of shop work and, consequently, shop workers, would include 'cleaners, storemen, shelf-fillers and trolley supervisors... The definition would also include clerical workers at the back or above the shop or doing work related to the shop. Staff of the shop and staff cafeterias and managers on or about the premises would also be covered... van drivers based at the store, who deliver goods to customers, would also be included. In fact, all those whose work is connected with and for a shop that decides to open on a Sunday will be covered' (Hansard, 9 February 1994, vol.237, cols.297–298).

The Minister's statement suggests that, while the definition of 'shop worker' should be construed broadly, it is necessary for the employee who claims to be a shop worker actually to be based at the store in question or to do a substantial amount of work at the store when it is open for serving customers. It is clear that a delivery driver taking goods from the store to customers may be a shop worker, but what of the delivery driver who brings goods to the store from a warehouse? In Williams v Asda Stores Ltd EAT 306/96 the claimant was employed by Asda as an HGV driver. He worked from a regional distribution centre. His HGV was loaded by warehouse staff at the distribution centre and he then drove to various Asda stores to make deliveries. The claimant was involved in unloading the goods at the stores and occasionally in transporting goods from one Asda store to another. He claimed that his work amounted to work 'in or about a shop' within the meaning of S.232(2). The employment tribunal looked to the statements of the Minister set out above, but also noted that the Minister had stated that he did not think that the definition of shop work covered drivers working for another company who deliver goods to a store but who do not work at or around the store. The tribunal could not see how the definition could exclude those working for a third party delivering to a store but include those working for the employer delivering to the store. On that basis, the tribunal found that the claimant was not a shop worker. The EAT,

10.19

in effect, upheld that conclusion following an appeal by the claimant against the tribunal's subsequent decision that he had not been dismissed for asserting a statutory right. In dismissing the appeal, the EAT held that the claimant did not have statutory protection in respect of refusing to undertake Sunday working because he was not a shop worker as defined.

As noted above, S.232(3) provides that a 'shop' includes any premises where any retail trade or business is carried on. The term is not restricted to traditional high street type stores and can include, for example, car repairers – see Rafiq v National Tyres Ltd ET Case No.5200977/99. In Horler and ors v Makro Self Service Wholesalers Ltd ET Case No.42131/95 and ors a tribunal had to decide whether a wholesale cash-and-carry business fell within that definition. The employer pointed out that there were restrictions on who could buy goods at the company's premises. Transactions could only be carried out on production of a 'Makro Tradecard' and individuals had to be registered under a business name and produce identification in order to obtain such a card. Invoices were issued in the name of the business and payment had to be made either by the person named on the card or by company cheque. However, the tribunal noted that in practice a large proportion of the public were able to obtain cards. Any of the cardholders – of whom there were some 200,000 – could make a purchase and any of their friends could come in as guests and arrange for purchases to be made for them by the cardholder. Many of the goods offered for sale were particularly suitable for customers' own personal use or consumption, and the store turned a blind eye to the purposes for which the goods were bought. In those circumstances, it was impossible to regard the store as anything other than an operation which included a significant proportion of retail sales. The tribunal concluded that the Sunday trading provisions applied.

10.20 The opposite conclusion was reached by the employment tribunal in Markall v Automobile Association ET Case No.2404839/99. In that case the claimant was employed by the AA to answer telephone calls from members about membership services. The tribunal rejected her claim that she was a shop worker because, although she was clearly involved in selling and had sales targets to meet, that was not a sufficient basis for concluding that she worked in a shop. The ordinary and everyday meaning of 'shop' did not extend to the premises in which the claimant worked and AA members would not for a moment consider that they were telephoning a shop when they rang to make enquires about their membership.

Specific statutory provision is made to cover the situation in which premises are used mainly for purposes other than those of retail trade or business and would not (apart from S.232(3)) be regarded as a shop. In those circumstances, only that part of the premises which is used wholly or mainly for the purposes of retail trade or business, or wholly or mainly for the purposes of both retail trade or business and wholesale trade, is to be regarded as a shop – S.232(4). 'Wholesale trade' means the sale of goods for use or resale in the course of a business or the hire of goods for use in the course of a business – S.232(5). This provision precludes the possibility

426

that the whole of a church or museum, for example, might be defined as a shop merely because there is a gift shop on part of the premises.

Betting workers. Betting workers as defined in S.233 ERA are also covered by the Sunday trading provisions. A 'betting worker' is an employee who, under his or her contract of employment, is or may be required to do betting work – S.233(1). 'Betting work' is defined as work at a track for a bookmaker on a day on which the bookmaker acts as such at the track, being work which consists of or includes dealing with betting transactions, and work in a licensed betting office on a day on which the office is open for use for the effecting of betting transactions – S.233(2). 'Betting transactions' include the collection or payment of winnings on a bet and any transaction in which one or more of the parties is acting as a bookmaker – S.233(3). A 'bookmaker' is defined as someone who, whether on his or her own account or as a servant or agent of another, carries on the business of receiving or negotiating bets or conducting pool betting operations, or holds him or herself out as doing so – S.233(4). **10.21**

Sunday work must involve shop work or betting work. Under S.101(1), the dismissal must be caused by the employee's refusal to do 'shop work' or 'betting work' on Sunday. As noted above, 'shop work' is defined in S.232(2) as 'work in or about a shop... on a day on which the shop is open for the serving of customers'. It follows that an employee will not be protected against dismissal, even though he or she is employed as a shop worker throughout the week, if the work that he or she is asked to do on a Sunday takes place when the shop is closed to customers. This would cover work such as shelf-stacking, stocktaking or other activities which take place when the shop is not open to the public. In Sands v Donlan ET Case No.3226/95 S was employed in the greetings cards section of a shop. She was asked to work on a Sunday in preparation for Christmas sales. The shop was not going to be open for the serving of customers on that day. S refused and was dismissed. A tribunal found that the principal reason for her dismissal was her refusal to work on the Sunday in question. However, the work that S was being asked to do on that Sunday was not 'shop work', as the shop would not be open to the public. Consequently, S had not been dismissed because of a refusal to do shop work on a Sunday and her dismissal was not unfair. **10.22**

Protected and opted-out status **10.23**
Only 'protected' or 'opted-out' shop or betting workers are covered by the unfair dismissal provisions set out in S.101. Essentially, a protected worker is a worker who was already employed as a shop or betting worker (but not solely to work on Sunday) when the Sunday trading provisions came into force, or a worker who cannot be contractually required to work on Sundays. An opted-out worker is a worker who has given his or her employer a written notice opting out of Sunday work.

Protected status. Under S.36 ERA a shop or betting worker will be a 'protected' worker if he or she meets one of two sets of criteria contained in **10.24**

427

S.36(2) and (3). The first set of criteria, which in effect applies only to long-serving employees, is as follows:

- the worker must have been in employment as a shop/betting worker on the day before the 'relevant commencement date' – S.36(2)(a). (The relevant commencement date is 26 August 1994 for shop workers and 3 January 1995 for betting workers – i.e. the respective dates on which the Sunday Trading Act 1994 and Schedule 8 to the Deregulation and Contracting Out Act 1994 came into force)

- on that day, he or she must not have been employed to work only on Sunday – S.36(2)(a)

- the worker must have been continuously employed during the period beginning with the day before the relevant commencement date and ending with the 'appropriate date' – S.36(2)(b). (The appropriate date means the effective date of termination for the purposes of S.101 – 101(4))

- he or she must have been a shop/betting worker throughout that period of continuous employment, or throughout every part of it during which his or her relations with the employer were governed by a contract of employment – S.36(2)(c).

10.25 Section 36(4) deems an employee to be a protected worker for the purposes of S.36(2)(a), despite the fact that the employment relationship had ceased by the day before the relevant commencement date, if:

- the employee's continuity of employment was preserved at the commencement date by virtue of S.212(3) or S.219 ERA (absence by reason of sickness, temporary cessation of work or arrangement or custom, or absence pending the reinstatement/re-engagement of a dismissed employee), *and*

- when the employment relationship ceased, that employee was a shop worker or betting worker and was not employed to work only on Sunday.

Alternatively, any shop or betting worker has protected status if, under the terms of his or her contract, he or she is not and cannot be required to work on Sundays, and could not be required to do so even if Part IV of the ERA (which deals with Sunday working) were disregarded – S.36(3). This provision applies regardless of whether the employee was in employment at the relevant commencement date. An employer's right to require an employee to work on Sunday is a question of construction of the relevant contract of employment.

10.26 **Opted-out status.** Section 40 ERA provides that an 'opted-out' shop or betting worker is an employee who, under his or her contract of employment, is or may be required to work on Sunday (whether or not as a result of previously giving an opting-in notice – see below), but who is not employed to work only on Sunday and who has given his or her employer a signed and dated 'opting-out' notice stating in writing that he or she objects to Sunday working. To satisfy

428

the statutory requirements, the worker must have been in continuous employment as a shop or betting worker during the period beginning with the day on which the opting-out notice was given and ending with the effective date of termination of the contract – Ss.41(1) and 101(4). Opted-out shop or betting workers do not obtain the protection afforded by S.101 (unfair dismissal for refusing to work on Sunday) until the expiry of three months after the opting-out notice was served – Ss.41(3) and 101(2).

An employer has a duty under S.42 to provide any shop or betting worker who is or may be required under his or her contract of employment to work on Sunday (whether or not as a result of previously giving an opting-in notice – see below), but who is not employed to work only on Sunday, with a statement in the prescribed statutory form explaining the employee's right to opt out of Sunday work and the consequences of such action, including the right not to be dismissed as a result of opting out – see S.42(4). The statement must be provided within two months of the worker becoming a shop or betting worker to whom this section applies. Failure to comply with this requirement has the effect, where the employee has given an opting-out notice, of reducing the three-month notice period specified in S.41(3), during which the worker cannot claim the protection of S.101 against unfair dismissal, to one month – S.42(2). However, an employer will not be treated as having failed to comply if the employee serves the opting-out notice within two months of becoming entitled to receive the statutory statement – S.42(3).

Loss of protected or opted-out status – opting in. A shop or betting worker   10.27
will lose protected status if he or she gives the employer an 'opting-in notice' and, after giving that notice, makes an 'express agreement' with the employer to do shop work or betting work on Sunday or on a particular Sunday – S.36(5). Similarly, under S.41(2) an opted-out shop or betting worker loses that status if he or she gives the employer an 'opting-in notice' after previously giving an opting-out notice, and then expressly agrees to do shop work or betting work on Sunday or a particular Sunday.

An opting-in notice for the above purposes is a written notice, signed and dated by the worker, in which he or she expressly states that he or she wishes to work on Sunday or does not object to Sunday working – S.36(6). As for the 'express agreement' by which the worker consents to work on Sundays or a particular Sunday, this is not defined in the statutory provisions. It would seem, however, to encompass verbal as well as written agreements: an employee who voluntarily turns up for work on a particular Sunday pursuant to a request made by the employer might, therefore, be regarded as having given 'express agreement'. This is in contrast to the prior opting-in notice, which must always be in writing (S.36(6)).

Once a worker becomes opted in, he or she will lose the specific protection of S.101 and will only reacquire it if he or she serves a further opting-out notice and waits three months.

10.28 **Reason for dismissal**
Finally, we turn to the circumstances in which shop and betting workers are protected against dismissal for refusing to work on a Sunday. S.101 provides that dismissal will be automatically unfair in the following circumstances:

- the employee is a protected shop worker or betting worker, or an opted-out shop or betting worker, and the reason for the dismissal (or, if more than one, the principal reason) is that the employee refused or proposed to refuse to do shop or betting work on Sunday or on a particular Sunday – S.101(1), or

- the employee is a shop worker or a betting worker and the reason or principal reason for dismissal is that he or she gave, or proposed to give, an opting-out notice to the employer – S.101(3).

10.29 **Selection for redundancy.** The dismissal of an employee who is selected for redundancy on either of the above grounds is also automatically unfair if the principal reason for the dismissal is that the employee was redundant but the redundancy situation applied equally to one or more other employees who held similar positions in the same undertaking and who were not dismissed – S.105(1) and (4).

10.30 **Principal reason for dismissal – showing causation.** An employee who claims that he or she has been dismissed either for refusing (or proposing to refuse) to do shop/betting work on a Sunday, or because he or she gave (or proposed to give) an opting-out notice, has to establish that the refusal or giving of notice was actually the reason or, if there was more than one, the principal reason for dismissal. A 'principal reason' is the reason that operated in the employer's mind at the time of dismissal – per Lord Denning MR in Abernethy v Mott, Hay and Anderson 1974 ICR 323, CA. If, on the evidence, a tribunal concludes that the objection to Sunday working or the serving of an opt-out notice was not the main reason for dismissal, the dismissal will not be automatically unfair. In these circumstances, if the employee has sufficient continuous service to claim ordinary unfair dismissal, the tribunal may go on to consider whether the dismissal was, in any event, unfair under S.98 ERA.

Two contrasting examples:

- **Thompson v Benny Dee (Wood Green) Ltd** EAT 637/98: T, who worked in a shop, voluntarily agreed to work some Sundays if required. When she asked for a Saturday off, the employer acceded to her request but placed her on the rota to work on the Sunday. When she asked if she could have that day off as well, she was told that it would be difficult but was not given a final answer. Her name remained on the rota for the Sunday but, without checking the rota again, she left work on the Friday and returned on the Monday morning. A disciplinary meeting was held at which T would only say that the employer had known she was not coming in on the Sunday. At the end of the meeting, she handed an envelope to the employer containing an opt-out notice and verbally stated that she was a Christian and did not want to work on Sundays. T was advised to return the following day, having given further thought to her absence on the Sunday. She arrived 20 minutes late, only to make it clear that she had nothing to add to what she had already said. She was then dismissed. On her claim for unfair dismissal, the employment tribunal found that the service of the opting-out notice was intended as a tactic to put pressure on the employer, but that she had not been dismissed by reason of serving the notice. Rather, her dismissal was because of her non-attendance on a Sunday when she was rostered to work. As she lacked the necessary qualifying service to claim ordinary unfair dismissal under S.98, her claim was dismissed. On appeal, the EAT upheld the tribunal's reasoning, confirming that T had not been dismissed for serving a notice opting out of Sunday working

- **Gregory v Park Garden Centre t/a Almondsbury Garden Centre** ET Case No.1402255/03: G began working for the employer as a trainee assistant manager in July 2002. He was appraised in September 2002 and told that the employer was impressed with his work. There were no problems identified to him as to his capability. He worked from Friday to Tuesday, having Wednesday and Thursday off. However, his wife worked from Monday to Friday, and their working patterns caused strains in their relationship. On 25 May 2003 G wrote to the employer saying that he had decided to exercise his right to object to working on Sundays, but by way of compromise offered to work every second Sunday. The employer did not reply formally to his letter, but on 29 June he was summoned to a meeting where he was summarily dismissed but given a month's pay in lieu of notice. The employer claimed that G had never shown competence in his job, and he was dismissed summarily to avoid his accruing the right to claim unfair dismissal. On his claim for automatically unfair dismissal, a tribunal held that G was dismissed because he had exercised his right to opt out of Sunday working. The dismissal was thus automatically unfair.

Refusal to work on a Sunday. It would appear that the reference in S.101(1) to   **10.31**
an employee's 'refusal' to work on a Sunday should be construed fairly broadly. In Gasking v The Sweater Shop plc ET Case No.65065/94, for example, G was employed as a supervisor in a shop. She qualified as a protected shop worker because she had been in employment on the day before the Sunday Trading Act 1994 came into force. Initially, G's employer required her to work every third Sunday. She was subsequently asked to work every Sunday but, after a few months working under the new arrangement, she expressed a wish to work on alternate Sundays instead. After receiving no response to her request, G said that she would prefer to be demoted to sales assistant rather than continue to work every Sunday. Shortly afterwards, she was dismissed. The tribunal had to decide whether the dismissal came about because G 'refused (or proposed to refuse) to do shop work... on Sunday or on a particular Sunday'. In the tribunal's view, it was necessary to adopt a broad construction of the verb 'to refuse'. 'To refuse'

431

meant 'to deny, to decline, to reject'. On that basis, the tribunal decided that a willingness to be demoted rather than to work every Sunday could amount to a refusal to work on Sunday.

The tribunal went on to find on the facts that it was G's refusal to work on a Sunday that was the reason or principal reason for her dismissal. It rejected the employer's argument that the real reason for the dismissal was that G was unsuitable for the post of supervisor and that there was no other position available for her in the store. In particular, the tribunal noted that G had received no warnings about her performance; she had been dismissed shortly after making the request for demotion; and the employer had given a number of evasive responses when G's mother enquired as to the reason for the dismissal.

10.32 **Assertion of Sunday working statutory rights.** A dismissal for asserting any of the rights contained in Part IV ERA (which sets out the provisions on Sunday trading) is rendered automatically unfair by virtue of S.104 ERA. An employee 'asserts' a statutory right by bringing proceedings against the employer to enforce such a right, or by alleging that the employer has infringed such a right. For further details see Chapter 12.

10.33 **Religious discrimination.** It should be noted that a provision, criterion or practice that staff must work on a Sunday could, in the absence of objective justification, amount to indirect discrimination on the grounds of religion or belief – see IDS Employment Law Handbook, 'Race and Religion Discrimination' (2003), Chapter 10.

10.34 Dismissal of employee representatives

Section 103 ERA provides that an employee will be regarded as unfairly dismissed if the reason (or, if more than one, the principal reason) for the dismissal is that the employee, being an employee representative for the purposes of collective consultation on redundancies or transfers of undertakings, or a candidate in an election for such representatives, performed or proposed to perform any functions or activities as such an employee representative or candidate.

It is also automatically unfair to select an employee representative (or candidate) for redundancy on the same basis where the reason (or principal reason) for the dismissal was redundancy but the redundancy situation applied equally to one or more other employees in the same undertaking who held positions similar to the employee and who were not dismissed – S.105(1) and (6).

10.35 **Identifying employee representatives.** For the purposes of S.103, 'employee representatives' are defined in Chapter II of Part IV TULR(C)A (in the case of redundancy consultation) and in Regs 13 and 14 of the Transfer of Undertakings (Protection of Employment) Regulations 2006 SI 2006/264 (TUPE) (in the case

432

of transfers of undertakings). So far as redundancy consultation is concerned, Chapter II of Part IV TULR(C)A – and, more specifically, S.188 of that Act – establishes that the 'appropriate representatives' are:

- where the employees are of a description in respect of which an independent trade union is recognised, the representatives of the trade union, or

- in any other case (i.e. where the employees are not members of a union recognised by the employer), either: (i) employee representatives who were appointed or elected by the affected employees for a purpose other than redundancy consultation but 'who (having regard to the purposes for and the method by which they were appointed or elected) have authority from those employees to receive information and to be consulted about the proposed dismissals on their behalf'; or (ii) employee representatives elected by the affected employees for the purposes of redundancy consultation in an election satisfying the statutory requirements set out in S.188A.

So far as consultation concerning a transfer of an undertaking is concerned, Reg 13(3) of the TUPE Regulations mirrors S.188 of the 1992 Act in its definition of appropriate representatives, save that the statutory requirements that need to be satisfied under the second head are those set out in Reg 14(1). **10.36**

The collective redundancy consultation provisions are contained in Ss.188–198 TULR(C)A and are discussed in detail in IDS Employment Law Handbook, 'Redundancy' (2008), Chapter 11. The provisions relating to consultation on the transfer of an undertaking are contained in Regs 13 and 14 of the TUPE Regulations, and are discussed in IDS Employment Law Handbook, 'Transfer of Undertakings' (2007), Chapter 8.

Note that the dismissal of an employee representative is one of the dismissals to which the minimum basic award in S.120(1) ERA (currently £4,700) applies – see Chapter 15. Such dismissals also allow the claimant to apply for interim relief – see Chapter 19.

Dismissal in connection with occupational pensions
10.37

In this section we consider the two forms of automatically unfair dismissal that are linked to occupational pensions: dismissal of occupational pension scheme trustees and dismissal in relation to employees' information and consultation rights in respect of occupational and personal pensions.

Dismissal of occupational pension scheme trustees
10.38

Section 102 ERA provides that an employee will be regarded as unfairly dismissed if the reason (or, if more than one, the principal reason) for the dismissal is that the employee performed, or proposed to perform, any of his or her functions as a

433

trustee of a relevant occupational pension scheme. S.102(1A) also makes it clear that the same protection extends to any director of a company who is a trustee of a relevant occupational pension scheme (i.e. a director of a corporate trustee).

It is also automatically unfair to select a trustee for redundancy on the same basis where the reason (or principal reason) for the dismissal was redundancy but the redundancy situation applied equally to one or more other employees in the same undertaking who held positions similar to the employee and who were not dismissed – S.105(1) and (5).

10.39   'Relevant occupational pension scheme' for the purposes of S.102 means an occupational pension scheme as defined in S.1 of the Pension Schemes Act 1993 and which is established under a trust. S.1 of the 1993 Act states that the term 'occupational pension scheme' means 'any scheme or arrangement which is comprised in one or more instruments or agreements and which has, or is capable of having, effect in relation to one or more descriptions or categories of employments so as to provide benefits, in the form of pensions or otherwise, payable on termination of service, or on death or retirement, to or in respect of earners with qualifying service in an employment of any such description or category'.

Note that any employee-trustee who presents a complaint of unfair dismissal under S.102(1) is entitled to apply for interim relief – see Chapter 19 for details. Dismissal of an employee-trustee also attracts a minimum basic award under S.120(1) (currently £4,700) – see Chapter 15.

10.40   **Pension consultation dismissals**
The Occupational and Personal Pension Schemes (Consultation by Employers and Miscellaneous Amendment) Regulations 2006 SI 2006/349 require employers to engage in an information and consultation process with employee representatives when seeking to make changes to occupational or personal pension schemes. A similar provision to S.103 ERA (see 'Dismissal of employee representatives' above) governing unfair dismissal in this context is found in para 5 of Schedule 1 to the Regulations.

Paragraphs 5(1) – 5(3) provide that an employee who is either a consulted representative or a candidate to be such a representative shall be regarded as unfairly dismissed if the reason for dismissal is either:

- that the employee performed or proposed to perform the functions of a representative under the Regulations, or

- that the employee exercised, proposed to exercise, or made a request to exercise, the right to paid time-off under paras 2 or 3 of the Schedule.

10.41   Paragraphs 5(1) and 5(4) provide that any employee who is an active or prospective member of an occupational or personal pension scheme, irrespective of whether or not he or she is a representative or candidate, shall

434

be regarded as unfairly dismissed if the reason for dismissal is one specified in para 5(5). The reasons specified in para 5(5) are that the employee:

- made, or proposed to make, a complaint to an employment tribunal to enforce a right or secure an entitlement under the Regulations. It is immaterial whether the employee actually had the right or entitlement, or whether it was infringed, provided the claim to the right, and (if applicable) the claim that it had been infringed was made in good faith – para 5(6). (For discussion of the concept of 'good faith' see Chapter 12, 'Dismissal for asserting a statutory right' under 'Requirement of good faith')

- complained, or proposed to complain, to the Pensions Regulator about the employer's failure to consult over changes in accordance with the Regulations

- stood as a candidate in an election for employee representatives

- attempted to influence by lawful means the voting in elections for representatives

- voted in such an election

- expressed doubts about whether such an election was properly conducted.

In respect of the last four of these reasons, para 5(5)(h) specifies that it will also be an automatically unfair reason for dismissal if the employee is dismissed for proposing to do, failing to do, or proposing to decline any of these things.

Dismissal in connection with tax credits 10.42

In April 2003, the Tax Credits Act 2002 introduced working tax credits. Tax credits comprise a payment designed to top up the earnings of working people (employed and self-employed) on low incomes, including those who do not have children. They are made up of a number of elements depending on the circumstances of the worker concerned, including elements to support the costs of approved or registered childcare and to help working households in which someone has a disability. Payment of tax credits is made via the employer through normal pay except in respect of the childcare element, which will be paid directly to the main carer.

With effect from 1 September 2002, Schedule 1 to the Tax Credits Act 2002 amended the ERA to introduce protection for employees against dismissal for claiming entitlement to working tax credits. S.104B(1) ERA provides that an employee will be regarded as unfairly dismissed if the reason (or, if more than one, the principal reason) for the dismissal is that:

- the employee is entitled, or will or may be entitled, to a working tax credit

435

- the employee (or someone on his or her behalf) took or proposed to take action with a view to securing the benefit of, or enforcing a right to, a working tax credit, or

- as a result of action taken by or on behalf of the employee to secure the benefit of, or enforce the right to, a working tax credit, the employer was fined or had proceedings brought against it pursuant to the 2002 Act.

10.43 Section 104B(2) makes it clear that, in respect of the second and third reasons listed above, it is irrelevant whether the employee actually has the right to a working tax credit or whether that right has been infringed. However, for either of those two reasons to apply, the employee's claim to the right and (if applicable) the claim that it has been infringed must have been made in good faith. (For discussion of the concept of 'good faith' see Chapter 12, 'Dismissal for asserting a statutory right' under 'Requirement of good faith'.)

It is also automatically unfair to select an employee for redundancy on any of the grounds specified in S.104B(1) where the reason (or principal reason) for the dismissal is that the employee was redundant and the redundancy situation applied equally to one or more other employees who held similar positions in the same undertaking and who were not dismissed – S.105(1) and (7A).

10.44 Dismissal relating to study and training

On 6 April 2010, the Government introduced a new right for employees to request to undertake study and training. The rules governing the operation of this right are found in Ss.63D–63K ERA; the Employee Study and Training (Eligibility, Complaints and Remedies) Regulations 2010 SI 2010/156 (the Eligibility Regulations); and the Employee Study and Training (Procedural Requirements) Regulations 2010 SI 2010/155 (the Procedural Regulations). A detailed discussion of the new right falls outside the scope of this Handbook, but a basic understanding of the process is necessary to put unfair dismissal provisions into context.

Note that the Government has opted to stagger the introduction of the study and training provisions. From 6 April 2010 the right to request study and training applies only to employees of companies employing over 250 people. From 6 April 2011, the right will be extended to all employees (provided they fulfil the basic qualifying conditions – see below).

10.45 **The right to request**
As the name implies, the right to request study and training is fairly limited in scope. An employee is not entitled to have his or her request granted, but merely to have it considered seriously and for rejections to be made on legitimate grounds. The right is very similar to the right to request flexible working that

436

applies to carers of children under the age of 17 (or 18 in the case of disabled children) – see IDS Employment Law Handbook, 'Maternity and Parental Rights' (2009).

The right to request study and training applies to employees aged 18 or over who have 26 weeks or more continuous employment – S.63D and Reg 2(1) Employee Study and Training (Qualifying Period of Employment) Regulations 2010 SI 2010/800. To begin the right to request process, the employee must make an application in writing to his or her employer, clearly identifying it as an application under S.63D. The application must be for the purpose of enabling the employee to undertake study or training (or both) the purpose of which is to improve:

- the employee's effectiveness in the employer's business, and

- the performance of the employer's business.

Once an employer has received an application, and assuming that it does not immediately agree to the terms of the request, it should convene a meeting with the employee to discuss the application. The employee is entitled to be accompanied to this meeting by a colleague of his or her choosing.

10.46

Following the meeting, the employer has 14 days in which to inform the employee of its decision. If the decision is to grant the request (in part or in full), then the employer should provide details of the agreed training; its location and provider; what qualification it will lead to; whether the time spent training will be paid; any changes to working hours; and how the tuition costs will be met. If the employer refuses the application, it must state which of the grounds for refusal listed in S.63F(7) it is relying on, explain why that reason (or reasons) applies and offer the chance of an appeal. The grounds for refusal (in part or in full) are: that the training would not improve the employee's effectiveness or the performance of the business; the burden of additional costs; the detrimental effect on ability to meet customer demand; inability to reorganise work among existing staff; inability to recruit additional staff; the detrimental impact on quality; the detrimental impact on performance; insufficiency of work during the periods the employee proposes to work; and planned structural changes.

Reason for dismissal

10.47

There are two provisions dealing with automatically unfair dismissal in relation to a request to undertake study and training: S.104E ERA and Reg 18 of the Procedural Regulations.

Section 104E ERA. Section 104E states that a dismissal will be regarded as unfair if the reason for dismissal is that the employee:

10.48

- made, or proposed to make, an application under S.63D

- exercised, or proposed to exercise, a right conferred by S.63F

- brought proceedings against the employer under S.63I, or

- alleged the existence of any circumstance which would constitute a ground for bringing such proceedings.

The 'proceedings under S.63I' referred to above are a claim that the employer has not complied with the provisions of the Procedural Regulations, a claim that the employer's reason for refusing the request is not one of those specified in S.63F(7), or a claim that the employer's refusal was based on incorrect facts.

To state that S.104E is clumsily drafted would be putting it mildly. The provision for dismissal to be unfair where the employee exercised a right conferred by S.63F appears to make little sense because S.63F is entitled 'Employer's duties in relation to application' and does not confer any positive rights on employees. However, the Procedural Regulations were made in accordance with S.63F, so we can assume that the tribunals and courts will take a purposive interpretation of S.104E and treat the rights conferred by S.63F as being those contained in the Procedural Regulations.

10.49 **Regulation 18 of the Procedural Regulations.** In addition to S.104E, there is a provision dealing with automatically unfair dismissal in the Procedural Regulations. Reg 18 relates exclusively to the right to be accompanied at a meeting under the right to request procedure, and states that an employee will be regarded as unfairly dismissed if the reason for dismissal is that the employee:

- exercised or sought to exercise his or her right to be accompanied under Reg 16, or

- having been asked by a colleague to accompany him or her to a meeting under Reg 16, accompanied or sought to accompany him to that meeting.

10.50 ## Dismissal relating to trade union blacklists

In March 2009 it emerged that a company had kept 'blacklists' of thousands of construction workers known to be trade union members and activists, and sold the information to employers in the construction industry. This led the Government to use an enabling power in S.3 of the Employment Relations Act 1999 to introduce Regulations designed to prevent the practice of blacklisting. These Regulations, the Employment Relations Act 1999 (Blacklists) Regulations 2010 SI 2010/493, came into force on 2 March 2010 and introduced a new ground of automatically unfair dismissal, the detail of which is now found in S.104F ERA. To understand the circumstances in which an employee can be unfairly dismissed, however, it is necessary first to outline the key features of the Regulations.

Prohibited lists

10.51

Regulation 3 sets out a general prohibition on blacklists, stating that no person shall compile, use, sell or supply a list which:

- contains details of persons who are or have been members of trade unions or persons who are taking part or have taken part in the activities of trade unions, and

- is compiled with a view to being used by employers or employment agencies for the purposes of discrimination in relation to recruitment or in relation to the treatment of workers.

Discrimination in this context does not refer to a breach of the various discrimination enactments, but to less favourable treatment on the grounds of trade union membership or trade union activities – Reg 3(3).

Regulation 4 sets out a number of exceptions to the general prohibition: where the person supplying a list could not be expected to know that it is a prohibited list; where the list is compiled, used or supplied in order to expose a breach of Reg 3; where the list is used to recruit to a post that reasonably requires either trade union membership or knowledge of trade union matters; where the list is required by law; or where the list is supplied in connection with legal proceedings.

10.52

Under Reg 5 a person may complain to an employment tribunal if he or she is refused employment by an employer who has either contravened Reg 3 or has used information that it ought reasonably to be expected to know is supplied in contravention of Reg 3.

Reason for dismissal

10.53

In addition to offering protection to persons refused employment as a result of an employer relying on a blacklist, the Regulations also provide protection from unfair dismissal for workers already employed. Under S.104F(1) ERA, an employee shall be regarded as unfairly dismissed if the reason, or principal reason, for the dismissal relates to a prohibited list and either:

- the employer contravenes Reg 3 in relation to that list, or

- the employer (i) relies on information supplied by a person who contravenes Reg 3 in relation to that list, and (ii) knows or ought reasonably to know that the information relied on is supplied in contravention of Reg 3.

Burden of proof. Given the difficulty employees are likely to face in showing a breach of Reg 3 by the employer, S.104F(2) provides for a partial reversal of the burden of proof along the lines of that seen in S.63A of the Sex Discrimination Act 1975 (see IDS Employment Law Handbook, 'Sex Discrimination' (2008), Chapter 7). S.104F(2) states that if there are facts from which the tribunal could conclude, in the absence of any other explanation, that the employer contravened Reg 3 or relied on information that was supplied in

10.54

439

contravention of Reg 3, the tribunal *must* find that such a contravention or reliance occurred, unless the employer shows otherwise.

As the blacklisting provisions only recently came into force, there is currently no case law to shed light on how they may operate in practice. It is, however, worth noting that the statutory language used is broader than that used in some of the other automatically unfair dismissal provisions examined in this chapter. The reason for dismissal need only *relate to* a prohibited list. This, coupled with the partial reversal of the burden of proof, surely means that any dismissal that arises from circumstances where a blacklist was used carries a substantial risk of being found to be automatically unfair.

11 Health and safety dismissals

Employees have the right not to be dismissed if they complain about, or refuse to work in, unsafe conditions. This right has its origins in, and must be interpreted in the light of, EU Directive No.89/391 on the introduction of measures to encourage improvements in the safety and health of workers at work ('the Directive'). It was inserted into the old Employment Protection (Consolidation) Act 1978 by the Trade Union Reform and Employment Rights Act 1993 and is now contained in S.100 of the Employment Rights Act 1996 (ERA). **11.1**

Section 100 provides that where an employer dismisses an employee for a prohibited health and safety reason, the dismissal is automatically unfair. This means that the reasonableness of the employer's action in dismissing is not a matter which is taken into consideration in deciding whether the dismissal was fair.

A number of special rules appertaining to S.100 dismissals should be borne in mind: **11.2**

- the right contained in S.100 applies to all employees regardless of their age or length of service – Ss.109(2)(c) and 108(3)(c)

- any health and safety representative or safety committee member who presents a complaint under S.100(1)(a) or (b) (see below under 'Scope of protection') is entitled to interim relief – S.128(1)

- dismissal of a health and safety representative or safety committee member under S.100(1)(a) or (b) is a category of dismissal that attracts a minimum basic award (£4,700 as from 1 February 2009) – S.120(1)

- there is no upper limit on the compensatory award for a dismissal that is automatically unfair for any of the reasons contained in S.100 – S.124(1A).

For more details see Chapters 15 and 16 on basic and compensatory awards and Chapter 19 on interim relief.

Scope of protection **11.3**

Section 100 provides that an employee is automatically unfairly dismissed if the reason, or principal reason, for dismissal is that he or she:

- carried out, or proposed to carry out, activities in connection with preventing or reducing risks to health and safety at work, having been designated by the employer to do so – S.100(1)(a)

441

- performed, or proposed to perform, any functions of a health and safety representative, or member of a safety committee, either in accordance with arrangements established by statute or after being acknowledged as such by the employer – S.100(1)(b)

- took part, or proposed to take part, in consultation with the employer pursuant to the Health and Safety (Consultation with Employees) Regulations 1996 SI 1996/1513 or in an election of safety representatives within the meaning of those Regulations, whether as a candidate or otherwise – S.100(1)(ba)

- brought to the employer's attention, by reasonable means, circumstances connected with his or her work which he or she reasonably believed were harmful or potentially harmful to health or safety – S.100(1)(c). (This only applies where there is either no health and safety representative or safety committee or it was not reasonably practicable for the employee to raise the matter by those means)

- in circumstances of danger which he or she reasonably believed to be serious and imminent and which he or she could not reasonably be expected to avert, left, proposed to leave or (while the danger persisted) refused to return to his or her place of work or any dangerous part of his or her place of work – S.100(1)(d)

- in circumstances of danger took, or proposed to take, appropriate steps to protect him or herself or other persons from danger which he or she reasonably believed to be serious and imminent – S.100(1)(e).

11.4   Whether an employee has taken, or proposed to take, appropriate steps for the purposes of this final ground is to be judged by reference to all the circumstances, including his or her knowledge and the facilities and advice available to him or her at the time – S.100(2). If, however, an employer shows that it was, or would have been, so negligent of the employee to take the steps that he or she took, or proposed to take, that a reasonable employer might have dismissed him or her, then the employee's dismissal will not be regarded as automatically unfair – S.100(3). In such cases the fairness of the dismissal will be determined according to the usual test under S.98(4).

11.5   **Redundancy selection**
Section 105 provides that an employee selected for redundancy on one of the grounds specified in S.100(1) will be treated as automatically unfairly dismissed where the reason (or principal reason) for the dismissal was redundancy but the redundancy situation applied equally to one or more other employees in the same undertaking who held positions similar to that of the employee and who were not dismissed. The special rules listed in the introduction to this chapter apply equally to selection for redundancy on health and safety grounds, save that interim relief is not available.

442 ————————————————————————————————————

Comparators. The requirement for comparators who have not been dismissed **11.6** is not merely cosmetic. In O'Dea v ISC Chemicals Ltd 1996 ICR 222, CA, the Court of Appeal dealt with similar provisions on selection for redundancy on trade union grounds under S.153 of the Trade Union and Labour Relations (Consolidation) Act 1992 (TULR(C)A). In rejecting the claimant's appeal, the Court emphasised that there must be other employees holding a similar position who were similarly at risk of redundancy but not dismissed. If no such comparators exist, the claim must fail. However, in identifying whether there were others who held similar positions to the claimant, the Court ruled that time spent working as a shop steward would not by itself distinguish a person from other employees for this purpose.

Selection criteria. While the fact that an employee has acted as a health and **11.7** safety representative or has taken some action in respect of a health and safety matter cannot be a fair reason for selecting that individual for redundancy, neither can it be a factor allowed to operate in the employee's favour in a selection exercise. As in cases of employees who have been engaged in trade union activities, an employer must take a neutral stance in relation to the skills and knowledge a health and safety representative has acquired when drawing up redundancy selection criteria.

In Smiths Industries Aerospace and Defence Systems v Rawlings 1996 IRLR 656, EAT, a health and safety representative was selected for redundancy on the basis of a points system relating to performance at work. He argued that he had been automatically unfairly dismissed because the points system did not recognise the skills that he had developed in his role as health and safety representative. The EAT rejected that argument. In the Appeal Tribunal's view, there was no evidence suggesting that his health and safety duties led to bias against him. Nor had his dismissal been unfair on ordinary principles under what is now S.98(4). Health and safety representatives were not entitled to receive more favourable treatment than their fellow employees in the pool for redundancy selection. Acting as a safety representative did not amount to a 'second job' and health and safety duties did not therefore form part of the duties performed under the contract of employment. Taking a representative's performance of health and safety duties into account when conducting a redundancy exercise would result in discrimination in that employee's favour.

This principle applies regardless of whether the employee is a trade union- **11.8** appointed safety representative under S.100(1)(b), or a person designated by the employer to carry out activities in connection with health and safety at work under S.100(1)(a). In Shipham and Co Ltd v Skinner EAT 840/00 the EAT found that although there were factual distinctions between the two roles – in particular that the employee's role as a designated health and safety adviser *could* be described as a 'second job' for which he received additional payment – this did not merit a difference in approach when considering the fairness of selection for redundancy under ordinary unfair dismissal principles.

443

11.9 **Who is protected?**

Sections 100 and 105 ERA apply to *employees* only – see Chapter 2. There is no specific power under the ERA to extend the right to non-employees (although under S.209 the Secretary of State has the power to extend the right not to suffer a detriment on health and safety grounds contained in S.44). There is a general power in S.23 of the Employment Relations Act 1999 allowing the Government to extend to non-employees the protection of any right contained in the ERA but no such order has yet been made under that provision. However, unless or until the right to claim unfair dismissal on health and safety grounds is extended to at least some categories of non-employee, there may be some conflict with the Directive, which aims to protect 'workers'. Although the Directive defines a 'worker' using the language of employment, it also uses the phrase 'employment relationship', which can be interpreted in a wider manner than a contract of employment in the United Kingdom.

In Costain Building and Civil Engineering Ltd v Smith and anor 2000 ICR 215, EAT, the EAT considered the position of S, an agency worker working at a building site, who was purportedly appointed by a trade union as a safety representative on the site. His contract was later cancelled at the behest of the client. When considering his complaint of automatic unfair dismissal under S.100(1)(b), the tribunal found that S was an employee of the client, ignoring several factors that weighed against such a finding. Overturning this decision, the EAT found that S was not an employee of the client as there was no contract between them. It noted that under the Safety Representatives and Safety Committees Regulations 1977 SI 1977/500, a person appointed by a trade union to be a safety representative must be an employee. As such, the purported appointment by the trade union was ineffective in law. The EAT stated that appointment as a safety representative did not automatically mean that S was an employee nor that he was thereby elevated to that status.

11.10 **Health and safety of third parties**

In Von Goetz v St George's Healthcare NHS Trust EAT 1395/97, EAT, the EAT saw no reason to limit the ambit of S.100 (and, in particular, subsections 1(c) and 1(e)) to harm, or the possibility of harm, to fellow employees, or to any employees, and could extend to the health and safety of third parties such as, for example, hospital patients. To this extent, the EAT had no problem in accepting that the domestic legislation went further than required by the Directive, the terms of which are expressly limited to the health and safety of workers.

11.11 **Reason for dismissal – burden of proof**

As noted above, S.100 provides that an employee is to be regarded as having been automatically unfairly dismissed if the reason or principal reason for

444

dismissal was one of the health and safety grounds listed above. S.105 extends protection to those who are selected for redundancy on those grounds. In such cases, there will often be a dispute between the employer and the employee as to the real reason for the dismissal.

In these circumstances, if the employee has sufficient qualifying service to bring an ordinary unfair dismissal claim (i.e. has at least one year's continuous service), the burden of proof is on the employer to prove the reason for the dismissal on the balance of probabilities. This was established by the Court of Appeal in Maund v Penwith District Council 1984 ICR 143, CA, in relation to a claim for automatically unfair dismissal on trade union grounds under S.152 TULR(C)A. The Court went on to hold that once the employer has shown a reason for dismissal, there is an evidential burden on the employee to produce some evidence to show that there is a real issue as to whether or not the reason given is true. Once this is done, the onus remains on the employer to prove the real reason for dismissal.

Where, however, an employee does not have enough qualifying service to bring an ordinary unfair dismissal claim, the burden of proof is on the employee to show an automatically unfair reason for dismissal for which no qualifying service is required. This was decided by the Court of Appeal (by a majority) in Smith v Hayle Town Council 1978 ICR 996, CA, again in relation to a claim under S.152 TULR(C)A, and was applied in relation to what is now S.100 in Tedeschi v Hosiden Besson Ltd EAT 959/95 and Parks v Lansdowne Club EAT 310/95. In the latter case the employee claimed that he had been dismissed for raising concerns about fire extinguishers at the premises where he worked while the employer said that he was dismissed for gross misconduct. The employee's claim failed as he had not discharged the burden of showing that his dismissal was for a health and safety reason. The EAT upheld this finding.

Reason for dismissal – causation   11.12

In seeking to establish the reason, or principal reason, for dismissal it is necessary to ask why the employer acted as it did. In Balfour Kilpatrick Ltd v Acheson and ors 2003 IRLR 683, EAT, a group of employees were dismissed for failing to attend work. The men left the site on which they worked and refused to return until the company had dealt with their health and safety concerns. The company argued that it had dismissed the men not on health and safety grounds but because of their absence. If they had been absent for other reasons, they would still have been dismissed, it said. Although the EAT ultimately found that the facts did not fall within any of the S.100 reasons, it nonetheless considered whether – if they had – the S.100 reason could be said to be the principal reason for dismissal. By analogy with Chief Constable of West Yorkshire Police v Khan 2001 ICR 1065, HL, a House of Lords case on victimisation under the Race Relations Act 1976, the EAT found that it was necessary to ask *why* a person acted as he or she did. If the employer had no

445

knowledge of the protected act (or S.100 reason) or dismissed for an independent reason, the dismissal will not be automatically unfair. A 'but for' test is inappropriate.

On the facts, however, the company was aware of the reason for the employees' absence and dismissed them for that reason even though it was unconcerned about it. It was irrelevant that it would have dismissed them for absences for a host of other reasons. The fact that the company was dismissing because of the failure to return to work and was indifferent to the reason why the men were not at work was immaterial. It knew what the employees were asserting the reason to be. Although it did not decide the point, the EAT commented that it was likely that an employer would equally be liable if it had the opportunity to find out the reason for the absence but chose not to take it.

11.13 Automatically unfair dismissal and industrial action

Where the principal reason for dismissal (or selection for redundancy) is one which falls within the scope of S.100, the employee is to be regarded as having been unfairly dismissed. But what if the actions of the employee amount to industrial action? S.237(1) TULR(C)A provides that an employee has no right to complain of unfair dismissal if at the time of dismissal he or she was taking part in an *unofficial* strike or other unofficial industrial action. S.238A protects employees taking part in *official* industrial action in certain specified circumstances but where this section does not apply, employees cannot complain of unfair dismissal if they were taking part in official industrial action unless the employer has selectively dismissed or re-engaged within three months of the date of the complainant's dismissal – S.238(2). However, Ss.237(1A) and 238(2A) state that the provisions barring individuals from the right to complain of unfair dismissal where they were taking part in industrial action at the time of dismissal *do not* apply where the reason for the dismissal is a health and safety reason under S.100. It is therefore no defence for the employer to argue that an employee's refusal to work in circumstances of danger amounted to industrial action.

However, industrial action may have a bearing on whether one of the automatically unfair reasons can be made out. This was highlighted in Balfour Kilpatrick Ltd v Acheson and ors (above), where employees took unofficial action because of widespread concerns about the adverse effects of the weather on working conditions. They sought to argue that their actions fell within S.100(1)(c) or (d). However, in the course of its decision, the EAT held that industrial action was not a reasonable means of bringing health and safety concerns to the attention of the employer for the purposes of S.100(1)(c). Although it would have been reasonable for the purposes of S.100(1)(d), any serious and imminent danger had ceased by the time the employer dismissed the employees and therefore S.100(1)(d) did not come into play. As no S.100 reason could be established, the men lost any right to compensation. They

446 ——————————————————————————

could not bring a claim for ordinary unfair dismissal because they were involved in unofficial industrial action at the time of their dismissal.

Constructive dismissal claims
11.14

Section 95(1) states that, for the purposes of Part X ERA (which includes S.100), an employee is dismissed by his or her employer 'if... the employee terminates the contract under which he [or she] is employed (with or without notice) in circumstances in which he [or she] is entitled to terminate it without notice by reason of the employer's conduct'. It is clear, therefore, that S.100 covers constructive dismissal claims.

It is well established that the type of conduct which gives rise to a constructive dismissal under the ordinary unfair dismissal rules must involve a *fundamental* breach of contract by the employer – Western Excavating (ECC) Ltd v Sharp 1978 ICR 221, CA. And it is clear that by punishing an employee in some way for his or her health and safety activities, an employer may be guilty of a fundamental breach, most usually of the implied duty of trust and confidence. What is less clear, however, is whether *any* breach of S.100 would entitle an employee to resign and claim that he or she has been constructively dismissed. To put it another way, did the legislators intend any breach of the health and safety provisions to be treated as a fundamental breach or is it a question of fact and degree in each case?

The answer to this question remains unclear, with conflicting decisions at tribunal level and no appellate authority on point. In Baddeley v Mehta t/a Supascoop ET Case No.46041/94 the tribunal held that the right to claim under what is now S.100 arises only where the employer dismisses the employee or fundamentally breaches the employee's contract as a punishment for the employee's health and safety activity. However, in Teasdale v Walker t/a Blaydon Packaging ET Case Nos.2505103/98 and 2500328/99 an employee raised a concern with his employer over the condition of ropes used to secure pallets to his lorry. The employer took no steps to deal with this complaint and required the employee to continue using the ropes. The employee treated himself as constructively dismissed, with the tribunal identifying a breach of the implied term to ensure the health and safety of the employee. In the tribunal's view, this breach was fundamental because the employer had failed to comply with S.100(1)(c) ERA.
11.15

It may be that this issue is largely academic anyway. In many cases that fall within S.100, tribunals have found breaches of the implied duty of trust and confidence or of the implied duty on employers to take reasonable care to ensure the health and safety of their employees. Furthermore, if an employee raises a health and safety concern as a grievance, he or she may be able to show a breach of trust and confidence if the employer fails to deal with the grievance adequately or at all. Moreover, in WA Goold (Pearmak) Ltd v McConnell and anor 1995 IRLR 516, EAT, it was held that an employer's failure to provide employees with a proper procedure for dealing with work-related grievances (in

447

this case about a drop in pay) was a breach of the implied term in their contracts of employment that the employer would reasonably and promptly afford a reasonable opportunity to the employees to obtain redress of any grievance they might have. The employees were therefore entitled to resign and claim that they had been constructively dismissed. Applying this approach, an employee can surely argue that if the employer ignores his or her grievance about a health and safety matter, the employer's actions would amount to a breach of contract sufficient to entitle the employee to resign and claim constructive dismissal.

11.16   Three cases involving claims of unfair constructive dismissal under S.100:

- **Skelton v Artel Services Ltd** ET Case No.3104190/99: S, who had raised a number of health and safety complaints with his employer over the years, was instructed to drive a truck with no near-side wing mirror. When S refused, his manager shouted at him and told S that he would have to stand in the yard all day as there was no other work for him to do. S walked out and did not return. A tribunal held that he had been constructively dismissed. Telling S to stand in the yard was demeaning and humiliating and in fundamental breach of the implied duty of trust and confidence. The dismissal was unfair as it fell within the scope of S.100(1)(c) – S had brought to his employer's attention matters that he reasonably believed were potentially harmful to health and safety

- **Bragg v Gilbert Foods** ET Case No.43924/96: B complained repeatedly to his employer about the company's failure to provide him with protective gloves. His job involved removing frozen meat from a vat full of ice-cold water. Without gloves, his hands became numb and B eventually contracted pneumonia. When he returned to work he made a further request for gloves and resigned when none were forthcoming. A tribunal found that the employer was in fundamental breach of the implied duty to provide and maintain a safe workplace and a safe system of work. The dismissal was unfair because it fell within S.100(1)(c) – S had brought the potentially harmful issue of the absence of gloves to his employer's attention and the employer had refused to provide them

- **Castell v Ian Williams Ltd** ET Case No.1701885/08: C, an electrician, attended a site where he assessed that he was going to have to work dangerously by handling live wires, or illegally by isolating the power without authority from the power company. Despite this his supervisor instructed him to carry out the work and when he refused he was sent to another of IW Ltd's sites. The work was subsequently carried out by another electrician, who isolated the power illegally. Over the next two days there were other instances relating to health and safety that caused C concern and on 24 July he decided to resign as he believed there was a culture of dishonesty and undertaking shortcuts and that if he stayed he would be forced to carry out tasks that would present a serious risk to

448

health and safety. Dismissing C's claim that he was dismissed for health and safety reasons, the tribunal concluded that, although his concerns about his employer's attitude to health and safety were justified, the circumstances giving rise to those concerns were not of such serious and imminent danger that he could not reasonably have been expected to avert them. The company did not exert significant pressure on him to work in circumstances of risk; when he refused to undertake work no action was taken against him and he was not criticised for the stand he took in relation to health and safety. Having resigned before taking steps to raise his concerns at a senior level, C had acted 'precipitately'.

Employee's own medical condition

11.17

Where employees are dismissed because of a medical condition – either because their own health or that of others might be put at risk by their continued employment – the matter does not fall within the scope of the health and safety provisions of S.100. The fairness of the decision to dismiss will be dealt with under the normal unfair dismissal provisions or, if relevant, the disability discrimination provisions – see Chapter 5, 'Ill health' and IDS Employment Law Handbook, 'Disability Discrimination' (2003) (due to be updated in autumn 2010). Three examples:

- **Lane Group plc and anor v Farmiloe** EAT 0352 and 0357/03: F, a warehouseman, suffered from psoriasis, a skin condition that made it impossible for him to wear the protective footwear provided by the employer. The employer investigated the possibility of finding alternative footwear but this was found to be medically unacceptable. A health and safety officer with the local council confirmed that the wearing of protective footwear was obligatory under health and safety regulations. F was dismissed. The EAT found that the employer was not in breach of the Disability Discrimination Act 1995 and remitted the case to the tribunal for a decision on whether the dismissal was unfair under normal unfair dismissal provisions, while suggesting that the employee's case had been seriously undermined by its findings that the requirement for protective footwear was absolute

- **Dixon v Gatwick Parking Service Ltd** ET Case No.37420/94: D, a part-time PSV driver, was absent for six weeks suffering from angina. The employer was concerned about the safety of passengers having a driver with a heart condition and spoke to a number of agencies, including the Health and Safety Executive and the DVLC. It became clear from the insurance brokers, however, that if an accident did occur the insurance would not cover the claim. D was therefore dismissed. A tribunal held that the dismissal was fair within the terms of S.98(4)

- **Walker v Unijet Group plc** ET Case No.57285/94: W, a reservation agent whose work required him to use a keyboard, was absent from work

449

suffering from RSI. He was asked to return on administrative duties but was unable to do so because even to hold a pen or piece of paper could have damaged him: he needed complete rest. W was dismissed on medical grounds and he claimed that the dismissal was in breach of S.100(1)(c) and (d). The tribunal held that, while it would have been dangerous for W to have worked at all, the danger related to W subjectively and the statutory test is an objective one. W was unfit for work and had been dismissed for that reason. However, the tribunal had no jurisdiction to hear W's unfair dismissal complaint under S.98 as he had less than two years' service (as required at the time).

11.18 Health and safety representatives

Section 100(1)(a) and (b) protect only those employees who are designated health and safety representatives. Their health and safety activities may well put them in conflict with the employer and the provisions are designed to offer some protection against their being penalised for carrying out their proper functions. As we discuss in Chapter 10, trade union representatives and employee representatives enjoy a similar protection from dismissal to that found in S.100(1)(a) and (b), with the result that case law decided under one provision can prove highly relevant in a claim brought under another.

The *manner* in which a health and safety representative carries out his or her designated functions may be relevant to a claim under S.100(1)(a). In Goodwin v Cabletel UK Ltd 1998 ICR 112, EAT, G, a construction manager, was responsible for ensuring that the employer's subcontractors complied with relevant statutory health and safety requirements. G complained of safety breaches by one particular subcontractor, recommending that it should not be given any further work. The employer did not approve of G's approach, which it found confrontational, and took the view that it was G's job to help the subcontractors improve their safety standards. Subsequent safety breaches led to further friction between the subcontractor and G and this prompted the employer to demote G to a position where he would not be in direct contact with the subcontractor. G resigned and claimed constructive dismissal under S.100(1)(a). The tribunal rejected G's claim on the ground that S.100(1)(a) does not protect a safety representative in the event of dismissal for the way in which he or she carries out health and safety duties. The employer had never sought to suppress or limit G's health and safety duties; G had merely been advised and admonished as to his method of discharging those duties.

11.19 The EAT held that the tribunal had erred in finding that S.100(1)(a) did not apply if the dismissal was due to the manner in which a safety representative carried out his or her duties. Applying a similar approach to that adopted by the Court of Appeal in Bass Taverns Ltd v Burgess 1995 IRLR 596, CA – a case involving dismissal for trade union activities – the EAT made it clear that the protection afforded to the manner in which a designated employee carries out health and safety activities should not be diluted by too easily finding acts done for that purpose to be a justification for dismissal. On the other hand, not every act, however malicious or irrelevant to the task in hand, must necessarily be treated as a protected act in circumstances where dismissal would be justified on legitimate grounds. In the instant case, the question which the tribunal should have asked was whether the manner in which the employee approached the health and safety problems took him outside the scope of the protected health and safety activities. The EAT remitted the case to a different tribunal for it to consider the matter afresh, although it commented that a finding adverse to G would be 'surprising' given that the tribunal had found G to be a man of competence and integrity who had acted in the best interests of the firm.

The case of Shillito v Van Leer (UK) Ltd 1997 IRLR 495, EAT, illustrates how difficult it can be to determine whether the acts of a health and safety representative fall within the scope of S.100(1)(a) and (b) in situations where he or she may have had mixed motives. In that case S was a senior shop steward and a health and safety representative for one particular area. A number of employees in a different area expressed concern about an odour given off by a solvent. S went to management and insisted that the affected employees receive medical attention. He was subsequently disciplined for not following the agreed procedures in the employer's safety manual. S claimed that this amounted to an unlawful detriment within the terms of S.44 ERA, which prohibits action short of dismissal for a health and safety reason.

11.20

A tribunal found that S had acted outside his duties as the safety representative for his designated area and had confused his role as shop steward with that of a safety representative. In its view, he had acted as a shop steward in trying to embarrass the employer over health and safety matters. On appeal, S argued that the tribunal had misdirected itself by considering his motives and whether he had acted reasonably, pointing out that the legislation did not require health and safety representatives to act reasonably in order for the statutory protection to apply. The EAT agreed that, if S had been disciplined for performing the functions of a health and safety representative, the reasonableness of his behaviour would have been irrelevant, even if his purpose was to embarrass the employer. However, it was clear that S had not been disciplined in connection with his duties as a safety representative because he was not the representative for that area. S's intention was not, therefore, to pursue a health and safety matter but to pursue a personal agenda to embarrass the company. Since his actions fell outside the scope of his duties as a safety representative and he acted in bad faith, he was not able to rely on the statutory protection.

Note that although the above case was decided under S.44, the decision is relevant to a claim brought under S.100. This is because the circumstances giving rise to a complaint under both sections are the same. Thus, any

451

interpretation of the acts protected by S.44 will apply to the same acts protected by S.100 and vice versa.

11.21   Some further examples:

- **Ratcliffe v Green Corns Ltd** ET Case No. 2401758/06: R, GC Ltd's Health and Safety Manager, prepared a report in which he expressed concerns about the level of assaults on staff. The report was not well received by management; it was thought to be over-critical and patronising, and in some respects stated the obvious. The Chief Executive said the report placed R 'in contempt of his colleagues', while the HR Director told R that there was no way back for him after the report. A few days later he offered R a 'dignified' exit by way of redundancy, and proposed a compromise agreement involving payment of £6,000 tax-free in lieu of notice. R refused to accept the compromise agreement, but his 'redundancy' was still put into effect. The tribunal found that there was no doubt that the report was central to R's dismissal, and that the production of the report – which raised genuine concerns – was part of his normal duties as health and safety manager. The reason for dismissal thus fell within S.100(1)(a)

- **South West Trains Ltd v McDonnell** EAT 0052/03 (a case concerned with similar provisions covering dismissals for trade union activities): a shop steward, McD, was seeking to speak to a colleague, E, about strike action and membership of a trade union. This was found to be within his trade union activities. However, E subsequently complained that in speaking to him McD had subjected him to intimidation and harassment. Such behaviour fell outside the bounds of legitimate activity. A tribunal found that regardless of what had actually happened between the two, the employer had believed that McD was guilty of harassment and intimidation. The principal reason for dismissal was therefore misconduct. The EAT held that it was open to the tribunal to reach this conclusion on the evidence

- **Sears v RS Cockerill (Farms) Ltd** ET Case No.1803943/98: S was appointed as a health and safety representative and continually raised health and safety concerns with the employer. He was dismissed for constantly pestering the employer. However, as the pestering was done in good faith in order to improve working conditions, the tribunal held that S was dismissed for performing his health and safety functions

- **Nicholls v St Helier NHS Trust** ET Case No.2305780/97: N was a designated health and safety representative accused by a colleague of harassment. N had supplied her with protective trousers that were too big and some bicycle clips with which to hold them up. He had also given her protective safety goggles with eyelashes painted on them. N was dismissed for harassing his colleague although he claimed that he had merely used unusual methods to encourage his colleague to take appropriate safety measures. The tribunal found that the real reason for dismissal was the employer's belief that N was guilty of harassment. In reaching this conclusion the tribunal made it clear that it had a duty in S.100 cases to look behind the employer's stated reason for dismissal in order to ascertain if the real reason was connected with health and safety.

Employees who are not health and safety representatives

11.22

Section 100(1)(ba), (c), (d) and (e) all protect individual employees who are not health and safety representatives. Each subsection will apply in different circumstances and has its own restrictions or limitations. For this reason, they need to be dealt with separately. However, there may be a degree of overlap. The fact that a matter falls within one subsection does not preclude its being protected by another – Balfour Kilpatrick Ltd v Acheson and ors 2003 IRLR 683, EAT.

Section 100(1)(ba)

11.23

This subsection protects employees who take part (or propose to take part) in consultations with employers under the Health and Safety (Consultation with Employees) Regulations 1996 S1 1996/1513 or in elections of safety representatives within the meaning of those Regulations (whether as a candidate or not). The 1996 Regulations, which came into force on 1 October 1996, require, *inter alia*, that employers inform and consult employees or safety representatives on matters relating to health and safety at work. As far as we are aware, there have been no decided cases under this subsection.

Section 100(1)(c)

11.24

This subsection provides that an employee will be regarded as automatically unfairly dismissed if the reason (or principal reason) for dismissal was that the employee brought to the employer's attention, by reasonable means, circumstances connected with his or her work which the employee reasonably believed were harmful or potentially harmful to health or safety. It only applies if there was no safety representative or safety committee at the employee's place of work or, if there was a safety representative or committee, it was not reasonably practicable for the employee to raise the matter by those means.

In Balfour Kilpatrick Ltd v Acheson and ors 2003 IRLR 683, EAT, the EAT identified three requirements that need to be satisfied for a claim under S.100(1)(c) to be made out. It must be established that:

- it was not reasonably practicable for the employee to raise the health and safety matters through the safety representative or safety committee
- the employee must have brought to the employer's attention by reasonable means the circumstances that he or she reasonably believes are harmful or potentially harmful to health or safety; and

453

- the reason, or principal reason, for the dismissal must be the fact that the employee was exercising his or her rights.

11.25 A distinction must be drawn between S.100(1)(c) – which protects the *raising* of a safety issue – and S.100(1)(d) and (e), which protect the safety of the employee. In ABC News Intercontinental Inc v Gizbert EAT 0160/06 a news reporter, G, had indicated to his employer an unwillingness to travel to war zones in Iraq and Afghanistan. When he was made redundant following budget cuts, G contended that the dismissal was automatically unfair under S.100(1)(c). An employment tribunal concurred, concluding that the principal reason for selecting G for redundancy was his refusal to travel to war zones. Allowing ABC's appeal, the EAT held that such a reason cannot fall within the purview of S.100(1)(c) because it does not relate to the employee bringing a health and safety matter to the employer's attention. On the tribunal's findings, the reason for G's dismissal was that he would not go to war zones, and ABC needed reporters who would. That reason was more closely related to S.100(1)(d) and (e), but G's dismissal could not be automatically unfair under either of those provisions because he had not been in imminent danger (see below).

11.26 **Appropriate channels.** Section 100(1)(c) covers any employee who, by reasonable means, brings a health and safety matter to the employer's attention. On the face of it, however, the employee must go through a safety committee or representative wherever possible. Several employees have lost tribunal claims because they did not go through the appropriate channels, preferring instead to take the matter into their own hands. However, in Balfour Kilpatrick Ltd v Acheson and ors (above) the EAT took a robust approach to its interpretation of this requirement. In that case, adverse weather conditions led to protective clothing and footwear becoming very wet in heavy rain. There was no means of drying it quickly. There were also large areas of standing water on the building site in question, increasing the dangers of working with electricity and the risk of disease. Employees chose to raise their concerns with union representatives rather than the appointed safety representatives. When the employer refused to resolve the situation, the men went home. They were dismissed when, a few days later, they still refused to return to work.

The EAT accepted that it would have been reasonably practicable for the men to approach the safety representatives but held that it was 'highly artificial' for employees to concern themselves with the appropriate route of communicating a matter of serious and imminent concern to the employer. The important thing is that the message is communicated quickly and succinctly. The EAT noted that Article 13(2)(d) of EU Directive No.89/391 obliges employees to 'immediately inform the employer and/or the workers with specific responsibility for the safety and health of workers of any work situation they have reasonable grounds for considering represents a serious and immediate danger to safety and health and of any shortcomings in the protection arrangements'. In order to ensure that S.100 was compatible with the Directive,

454

the EAT inserted a phrase into subsection (e) so that it read: 'in circumstances of danger which the employee reasonably believed to be serious and imminent, he took (or proposed to take) appropriate steps to protect himself or other persons from the danger *or to communicate these circumstances by any appropriate means to the employer*'. According to the EAT, this would in turn restrict the scope of S.100(1)(c), although it commented that 'there might be better ways of achieving the same result'. In any event, the EAT was clear that an employee performing his or her obligations under the Directive in immediately informing the employer of a serious danger could not be lawfully dismissed on that ground under English law. Therefore, the employees were entitled to raise their concerns with the trade union representatives.

On behalf of the employer it was then argued that although on the day the men walked out there was a serious and imminent danger to health, this was no longer the case a few days later when the men had still not returned to work and were dismissed accordingly. By this time, it was argued, the men should have sought to resolve the matter with the safety representatives. The EAT was unconvinced. Where the employer had continued without protest to discuss matters directly with the union representatives, the EAT held that those representatives should be treated as representatives of workers on matters of health and safety 'by reason of being acknowledged as such by the employer'. The employer's argument bore 'no relation to reality'. **11.27**

The impact of this case on the scope of S.100(1)(c) is not entirely clear. The EAT appears to be saying that the facts actually fell within S.100(1)(e) *as construed in light of the Directive*. If this is correct, then it may be that the requirement to use appropriate channels remains in cases that do not involve serious and imminent danger and therefore still fall within S.100(1)(c). However, in such cases, where the employer deals with trade union representatives rather than safety representatives without complaint, the trade union representatives may be treated as such for the purposes of the section. Alternatively, on the facts of this case at least, the EAT could be saying that in order to ensure compatibility with the Directive, the requirement for a tribunal to assess the reasonable practicability of communicating with safety representatives is effectively disapplied. In any event, the important message is that by virtue of the Directive, the courts and tribunals will take a robust approach to the interpretation of S.100 and employers will not be allowed to resort to technical legal arguments in order to circumvent the protection afforded by S.100.

Means of bringing concerns to employer's attention. In the Balfour Kilpatrick case, the employer also argued that taking industrial action could not be considered a reasonable means of bringing the men's health and safety concerns to the employer's attention. Here the EAT agreed, commenting that neither could it be said to amount to 'informing' the employer under Article 13 of the Directive. Although in some exceptional circumstances employees could **11.28**

455

communicate concerns to their employer by action rather than words (where, for example, an employee points out a hazard to an employer who is some distance away), this did not extend to the taking of industrial action.

Two further examples of means which were not considered reasonable:

- **Tate v Salvesen Logistics Ltd** EAT 226/97: T raised health and safety concerns in a casual conversation initiated by a director of an associated company of the employer. Although T asked for the conversation to be treated in confidence, the director refused and passed on details to the employer. T was dismissed. The EAT upheld a tribunal's decision that it was not reasonable for T to raise his concerns in this manner. He should have raised them with his line manager

- **Stephens v NFT Distribution Ltd** ET Case No.1201794/98: S persistently raised health and safety concerns in letters which his employer found to be offensive, continuing to do so even after he was instructed to desist. S was dismissed. A tribunal found that S had not used reasonable means to communicate his concerns. His letters were offensive, patronising, flippant and entirely lacking in respect. No employer could be expected to tolerate them.

11.29 **Reasonable grounds for belief.** The question of what amounts to reasonable grounds for believing that there were circumstances harmful to health and safety was considered in Kerr v Nathan's Wastesavers Ltd EAT 91/95. In that case K was dismissed because he refused to drive a vehicle which, in his opinion, might have become overloaded by the end of the working day. The tribunal dismissed his unfair dismissal claim because, although K's belief was genuine, it was not based on reasonable grounds. The employer had a procedure whereby employees could either return to the depot or telephone in to arrange for a second vehicle to meet them somewhere so that they could swap vehicles. K had not taken advantage of this practice and therefore did not have reasonable grounds for thinking that the request to drive the vehicle was potentially harmful to safety.

The EAT upheld the tribunal's decision and gave some guidance on the correct approach to take when deciding whether an employee has the reasonable belief required by S.100(1)(c). The EAT emphasised that not too onerous a duty of enquiry should be placed on the employee in this regard. The purpose of the legislation is to protect employees who raise matters of health and safety; the fact that concern might be allayed by further enquiry need not mean that the employee's concern is not reasonable. On a different point, the EAT also stated that it was irrelevant whether or not the employer had acted unreasonably when considering a claim under the subsection.

11.30 A case where the employee did not have reasonable grounds for believing that there were circumstances harmful to health and safety:

- **Hindmarch v Chemrock Cryogenics UK Ltd** ET Case No.2500983/06: H was a highly skilled employee in a niche area of work – lining petrochemical tanks – who could be required by CC Ltd to work anywhere in the world. In August 2005 he refused to go to Qatar, insisting that because of the state of alert relating to terrorist attacks, he would not work in any Muslim country. He claimed that his subsequent dismissal was automatically unfair by virtue of S.100(1)(c). The tribunal held that H had made a generalised assumption about the safety of UK nationals working in Muslim countries. Although he believed there was a higher risk, that belief, having been reached without any reference to the safety and security measures CC Ltd would have put in place, was not based on reasonable grounds.

Potentially harmful to third parties. Section 100(1)(c) protects employees who bring to their employer's attention by reasonable means circumstances connected with their work which they reasonably believed were harmful or potentially harmful. In Brendon v BNFL Flurochemicals Ltd EAT 766/95 the question arose as to whether S.100 is confined to health and safety in the workplace, or whether it protects employees who express concern about potential damage to third parties outside the workplace, such as consumers of a company's products or the general public. The question arose when B, a sales executive for a company selling a variety of chemicals, was dismissed for his poor sales performance but alleged that the real reason was his concern over a health and safety matter. One of the chemicals produced by the company was used in many countries in the course of eye operations. The chemical was prohibited in the United States, however, because it was thought to cause blindness. B suspected that a customer who had ordered a quantity of the chemical intended to export it illegally to the United States and he was concerned about the risk the chemical posed for American eye patients. B devoted a lot of time to investigating the potential side-effects of the chemical and it was around this time that his sales began to fall. When his employer dismissed him he claimed that his dismissal was automatically unfair. The tribunal dismissed B's claim and he appealed. **11.31**

The EAT accepted that it was arguable that S.100 might stretch beyond hazards in the workplace and that an employee might legitimately be concerned about something which happened elsewhere. However, it did not decide the point. Instead, it upheld the tribunal's decision that B had been dismissed on account of his poor sales record and that health and safety matters played no part. The EAT pointed out that S.100(1)(c) refers to an employee raising health and safety matters with the employer 'by reasonable means'. It was unlikely that the provision entitled B to devote so much time to his health and safety concerns that his work suffered and his sales fell.

A tribunal took the view that S.100(1)(c) did cover complaints about hazards to third parties in the Lines v Johnson t/a County Coaches ET Case No.2500359/96. In **11.32**

457

that case L was dismissed because he refused to drive a 29-seater bus to transport 33 passengers. A tribunal found the dismissal unfair under S.100(1)(c). The employer had required L to use the bus in contravention of the Public Service Vehicles (Passenger) Regulations 1984, the purpose of which is to ensure the safety of passengers. Similarly, in Barton v Wandsworth Council ET Case No.11268/94 a different tribunal held that an ambulance driver's concerns for the safety of patients following a reduction in the quality of the escort service provided to assist patients in ambulances was a concern that could be protected by the health and safety provisions of the ERA.

It seems unlikely that the legislation was not intended to protect employees bringing to their employer's attention matters which affected the health or safety of others outside the workplace. The point which the EAT made clear in the BNFL case, however, is that while S.100(1)(c) probably does protect an employee who brings the matter to the employer's attention, it may not protect acts which go beyond that. Once an employee has informed the employer of the potential risk, it is unlikely that he or she will be protected *under this subsection* for pursuing the matter further. However, S.100(1)(d) and (e) are more wide-ranging than S.100(1)(c) in that they protect an employee who walks off the job or actually does something to avert danger or protect others – so long as the danger is 'serious and imminent' and the steps taken are not inappropriate or negligent (see below).

Even if S.100(1)(c) were restricted to matters of health and safety in the workplace, an employee bringing concerns about health and safety outside the workplace to the employer's attention would very likely be covered by the automatically unfair dismissal provision in S.103 ERA, which governs 'protected disclosures' – see 'Section 100(1)(e)' below, and Chapter 13.

11.33   Some cases brought under S.100(1)(c):

- **Stephanou v Teaching Personnel Ltd** ET Case No.1200183/97: the office premises at which S worked were devastated by fire. When S had finished helping his employer clear up he tried to go back to his telephone sales duties. However, because there was no heating and all the windows were open to disperse the smoke and fumes, S asked to leave early because he was so cold. Although it was clear that H, the director to whom he spoke, was not pleased about the request, he granted permission. However, later that evening H called to dismiss S. The tribunal found that S was dismissed for protesting about having to stay at work in conditions that posed a risk to health and safety. There was no nominated safety representative and his protest therefore fell within S.100(1)(c)

- **Hobell v J Todd t/a Todd Opticians** ET Case No.61769/94: H was dismissed after one week's employment as an optical receptionist. She had made it clear to her employer that she was dissatisfied with arrangements for lunch times. There were no settled breaks – she was expected to eat her

458

lunch while working – and she could go out only if this was convenient to others. The employer's response was to the effect that if she did not like the job she did not have to stay. H then wrote to the employer setting out her belief that the Shops Act 1950 and health and safety legislation entitled her to a fixed lunch-hour. The employer dismissed her on receiving the letter. The tribunal held that the dismissal was automatically unfair. H had clearly been dismissed because of the letter in which she had quite reasonably brought to her employer's attention her belief that the lunch-time arrangement was harmful or potentially harmful to her health and safety

- **Akinbobola v Swirl Court Services** ET Case No.28720/96: a representative of the workforce attended a meeting with the employer at which the provision of protective equipment was discussed. The employees' understanding was that an agreement had been reached whereby they were not required to carry out work for which protective equipment was necessary but not available. On one occasion, A was sent home without pay when he refused to work with chemicals from a container which contained no explanatory label without goggles and gloves. On another occasion, he refused to pick up litter from an underground railway tunnel unless he was provided with a torchlight and litter picker. They were not provided and he was dismissed for 'his failure to work on many occasions'. The tribunal held that his dismissal was unfair under S.100(1)(c).

Section 100(1)(d)

11.34

This subsection protects employees who left, proposed to leave, or refused to return to their place of work in circumstances of danger which they reasonably believed to be serious and imminent and which they could not reasonably have been expected to avert.

Reasonable belief. In Begum v Sunlight Services Group Ltd ET Case No.2304046/97 a tribunal had to consider the reasonableness of an employee's belief that her working conditions fell within the scope of S.100(1)(d). B worked in the 'clean' room of her employer's laundry business. Her job was to pack laundered surgical gowns. The 'clean' room was a controlled environment and its air conditioning system was unable to cope with extremes of temperature. B and her colleagues had to stand to work and were expected to stay until the workload for the day had been processed. During a period of very hot weather, B and her colleagues asked whether they could be allowed to open their protective gowns or open the door to the clean room because the heat and humidity was making them feel unwell and they had been allowed to do so in a previous year during intense heat. A supervisor refused and passed on the request to a manager, C. B did not speak good English. Through her colleagues she explained to C that the heat was intolerable and that unless something was done they would go home before the end of the shift. C told them that if they went home they would be doing so for good. She took no steps to investigate

11.35

459

the complaint and did not check the temperature. B and others did not fully understand the extent of C's ultimatum and left because they considered conditions unsafe. They were dismissed.

After they had left, the temperature was found to be 74°F, equal to or just below the employer's recommended maximum temperature. There was no thermometer in the room. The tribunal found that B had a reasonable belief that the heat and humidity constituted a serious and imminent danger; because she had no means of objectively checking the temperature and her manager had refused to do so, her only way of judging the temperature was by her own assessment and she felt it was too hot to work and it was making her feel ill.

11.36   **Serious and imminent danger.** Claims brought under S.100(1)(d) will fail if the employee concerned is unable to show that he or she acted in circumstances of danger which he or she reasonably believed to be serious and imminent. What amounts to a serious and imminent danger is a question of fact and will vary from case to case.

In Harvest Press Ltd v McCaffrey 1999 IRLR 778, EAT, M complained about the behaviour of H, a colleague with whom he shared the night shift. Upon finding out about M's complaint, H became very abusive. M, concerned for his safety, went home, telephoned his manager and refused to return to work unless H was removed or dismissed. The following day, the employer spoke to H about the incident and telephoned M to inform him that by walking out in the middle of a shift he was taken to have resigned. A tribunal subsequently found that M had been dismissed in circumstances that fell within S.100(1)(d). In upholding this decision, the EAT commented that S.100(1)(d) was intended to be wide, the word 'danger' being used without limitation. There was no reason to restrict circumstances of danger to those generated by the workplace itself. The EAT gave a number of examples involving the presence or absence of other employees that could fall within S.100(1)(d), in addition to that provided by the facts of the case itself:

- premises becoming unsafe as a result of an unskilled and untrained employee working on dangerous processes in the workplace, where the danger of a mistake extends to those working with him or her

- the absence of a person with specific safety responsibilities where dangerous processes were being carried on

- a foolhardy employee determined to indulge in horseplay persistently adopting dangerous practices in the workplace.

The EAT concluded that S.100(1)(d) covered any danger, however originating. A sensible employer would have spoken to M to form a view as to whether his concerns were genuine and acted accordingly.

In the Begum case, discussed above, the tribunal applied the Oxford dictionary definition of 'danger', which reads: 'liability or exposure to harm or injury; risk, peril'. In the tribunal's opinion, there was therefore no need for the danger to be life-threatening. Because there was no way for the danger in that case to be objectively assessed, the employees' subjective feelings were enough to establish reasonable belief that the danger was serious and imminent. **11.37**

It is important to realise that circumstances of danger may change over a period of time. In Balfour Kilpatrick Ltd v Acheson and ors 2003 IRLR 683, EAT, a tribunal found that there had been circumstances of danger that the employees reasonably believed to be serious and imminent sufficient to justify a mass walk-out on the day those circumstances arose. The employees were engaged in electrical work on a building site. The site was on marshy ground susceptible to flooding and the portakabins in which working clothes were kept were inadequately heated. Heavy rain led to wide areas of standing water, increasing the risk of exposure to Weil's disease carried by rats on the site. There were also concerns about the dangers of working with electricity in the wet conditions. Moreover, protective clothing and boots were soaking wet. The men were justified in walking out and refusing to work in these circumstances. However, four days later the men were still refusing to work and it was this refusal that led to their dismissal. The tribunal found that the weather had improved and the clothing and boots had largely dried. The men were no longer reasonable in their belief that danger was still serious and imminent. There was no challenge to this finding before the EAT.

The following cases, some of which were decided under the similar wording contained in S.100(1)(e) (see below), give useful examples of 'serious and imminent' danger: **11.38**

- **Hoyle v Nottingham Ambulance Service NHS Trust** ET Case No.2601392/98: H, an ambulance driver in the patient transport service, raised a number of concerns with his employer in a series of confrontational letters. He claimed he faced a danger in loading stretchered patients into ambulances without ramps and in following a schedule that he believed encouraged drivers to break the speed limit. The employer acknowledged there was a problem and was taking steps to deal with it. In the meantime, H was instructed to raise any further concerns with the safety representative. Instead, H made complaints to the Health and Safety Executive and to the police. A tribunal found that H did not believe the risk was serious and imminent. The risk of harm was avoidable by H taking care and seeking assistance where necessary. The transfer schedules were only a guide and were not an encouragement to break the speed limit

- **Dent v Greater Reading Omnibus Co Ltd** ET Case No.2700330/97: D was a bus driver. When his indicators failed, D stopped the bus to report the

461

failure and refused to drive it any further. D was dismissed, either expressly or constructively. A tribunal found that the condition of the bus gave rise to a circumstance of danger and that D reasonably believed that danger to be serious and imminent

- **Dodd v Blue Star Engineering Ltd** ET Case No.31942/94: D worked in the electronics department but because of a shortfall of work she was transferred to work on a machine known as a grinding master. D refused to operate the machine because it was a dusty and dirty job and the position in which she had to stand was dangerous because of the continual passing of men carrying aluminium strips. D was sent home to think over her decision. The following day D still refused and her employment was terminated. The tribunal noted that D had not complained to the safety representative and decided that D's only real complaint was that the machine was dirty. The tribunal held that this did not constitute circumstances of danger within S.100

- **Ballard v Rushlake Services Ltd** ET Case No.1101336/98: B worked for a small company engaged in the removal of asbestos from premises. On one particular job, he became concerned that P, the employer's managing director, was setting up the work in a way different to the method statement that had been submitted to the Health and Safety Executive (HSE). P instructed the employees to work in a way that reduced costs and he disregarded the HSE guidelines as impractical when B drew his attention to them. B felt he was unable to work safely and called in the HSE. He was dismissed. A tribunal found that B had a reasonable belief that he was working in circumstances of serious and imminent danger. It heard evidence to that effect from the HSE officer called to the job site.

11.39 Section 100(1)(e)

This subsection protects employees who, in circumstances of danger which they reasonably believed to be serious and imminent, took (or proposed to take) appropriate steps to protect themselves or other persons from the danger. The cases discussed above under S.100(1)(d) on the question of 'serious and imminent' danger apply equally to this subsection. In Masiak v City Restaurants (UK) Ltd 1999 IRLR 780, EAT, the Appeal Tribunal held that 'other persons' can include members of the public and is not restricted to other employees or workers of the employer. Therefore it was open to M, who walked out of his employer's restaurant having refused to cook food that he considered to be a potential health hazard, to bring a claim for automatic unfair dismissal under S.100(1)(e).

Whether an employee has taken, or proposed to take, appropriate steps for the purposes of this final ground is to be judged by reference to all the circumstances, including his or her knowledge and the facilities and advice available to him or her at the time – S.100(2). A tribunal that rules there is no serious and imminent danger without hearing evidence will therefore err in law – Masiak (above). If, however, an employer shows that it was, or would have been, so negligent of the employee to take the steps that he or she took, or proposed to take, that a reasonable employer might have dismissed him or her, then the employee's dismissal will not be regarded as automatically unfair – S.100(3). In these circumstances, the fairness of the dismissal will be determined according to the usual test under S.98(4).

The test under S.100(2) will obviously be one of proportionality – i.e. whether the employee's response was in proportion to the danger posed. But the test does allow for some subjectivity in so far as the appropriateness of the steps taken must be gauged according to the employee's perception of the danger and his or her understanding of the situation. It would be no defence, therefore, for an employer to say that he had taken steps to remedy the situation if the employee was unaware of this. In the Begum case (discussed under 'Section 100(1)(d)' above), the tribunal found that S.100(1)(e) also applied to the situation that B found herself in. The fact that there was no means of objective assessment of the temperature and that the employer did not investigate the complaint meant that it was reasonable for B to leave the premises. S.100(3) did not apply since B was not endangering anyone's life by leaving the premises and there was no active machinery that might have caused harm as a result of B leaving when she did. **11.40**

Informing the employer. Words were written into S.100(1)(e) by the EAT in Balfour Kilpatrick Ltd v Acheson and ors 2003 IRLR 683, EAT, to bring S.100 into line with EU Directive No.89/391, which obliges employees to 'immediately inform the employer and/or the workers with specific responsibility for the safety and health of workers of any work situation they have reasonable grounds for considering represents a serious and immediate danger to safety and health and of any shortcomings in the protection arrangements'. This was done to fill a lacuna in the scope of subsection (c), which provides that, when raising a health and safety concern, employees should go through a safety committee or representative wherever possible, rather than directly to the employer. According to the EAT, in order to ensure that S.100 was compatible with the Directive, subsection (e) should read: 'in circumstances of danger which the employee reasonably believed to be serious and imminent, he took (or proposed to take) appropriate steps to protect himself or other persons from the danger *or to communicate these circumstances by any appropriate means to the employer*' – see under 'Section 100(1)(c) – appropriate channels' above for further details. **11.41**

Protected disclosures. An employee may be tempted to 'blow the whistle' on an employer by referring a health and safety matter to an outside body, such as the Health and Safety Executive, or even a newspaper. An employee dismissed in these circumstances might be able to bring a claim under this subsection, although a tribunal would have to consider whether he or she had taken **11.42**

463

'appropriate steps' to protect him or herself or other persons from danger. What is perhaps more likely is that the employee would bring a claim under S.103A ERA, which protects whistleblowers who are dismissed for making a 'protected disclosure'. One of the categories of disclosure covered by that provision is that which tends to show 'that the health or safety of any individual has been, is being or is likely to be endangered'. This right, which is subject to qualifications, exists entirely independently of the rights contained in S.100 and is in many ways wider than the protection conferred by that provision. More details can be found in Chapter 13.

12 Dismissal for asserting a statutory right

Assertion of a statutory right

Requirement of good faith

Reason for dismissal

12.1

Under S.104 of the Employment Rights Act 1996 (ERA), an employee's dismissal is automatically unfair if the reason or principal reason for the dismissal was that:

- the employee brought proceedings against the employer to enforce a relevant statutory right – S.104(1)(a), or

- the employee alleged that the employer had infringed a relevant statutory right – S.104(1)(b).

It is also automatically unfair to select an employee for redundancy for one of the reasons specified in S.104(1) where the reason (or principal reason) for the dismissal was redundancy but the redundancy situation applied equally to one or more other employees in the same undertaking who held positions similar to that held by the employee and who were not dismissed – S.105(1) and (7).

It is immaterial whether the employee actually had the statutory right in question or whether the right had been infringed, but the employee's claim to the right and its infringement must have been made in good faith – S.104(2). Furthermore, it is sufficient that the employee made it reasonably clear to the employer what the right claimed to have been infringed was; it is not necessary actually to specify the right – S.104(3).

12.2

An employee may bring a claim of unfair dismissal for asserting a statutory right whatever his or her length of service – the one-year qualifying period normally required to bring an unfair dismissal claim does not apply.

In a claim brought under S.104, there are three main requirements:

- the employee must have asserted a relevant statutory right

- the assertion must have been made in good faith, and

- the assertion must have been the reason or principal reason for the dismissal.

These requirements are considered in turn below.

12.3 Assertion of a statutory right

The first requirement is that the employee must have asserted a relevant statutory right, either by bringing proceedings against the employer to enforce such a right, or by alleging that the employer has infringed such a right – S.104(1).

12.4 Relevant statutory rights

Section 104 does not apply to all statutory rights but only to the 'relevant' statutory rights referred to in S.104(4). These include 'any right conferred by this Act [i.e. the ERA] for which the remedy for its infringement is by way of a complaint or reference to an employment tribunal' – S.104(4)(a). This means that when a new employment right is inserted into the ERA it automatically becomes a relevant statutory right, provided of course that the remedy for infringement of that right is by way of a complaint to an employment tribunal. The relevant statutory rights covered by S.104(4)(a) are:

- the right to receive a written statement of employment particulars, a statement of changes to particulars or an itemised pay statement – Ss.1, 4 and 8 ERA

- protection of wages rights – Ss.13, 15, 18 and 21 ERA

- the right to a guarantee payment – S.28 ERA

- protection from detriment rights (jury service; health and safety; Sunday working; working time; trustees of occupational pension schemes; employee representatives; paid time off for study or training; protected disclosures; maternity, paternity and parental leave; time off for dependants; tax credits; flexible working; and study and training) – Ss.43M–47F ERA

- the right to time off for public duties – S.50 ERA

- the right of redundant employees to paid time off to look for work or arrange training – Ss.52 and 53 ERA

- the right to paid time off for ante-natal care – Ss.55 and 56 ERA

- the right to time off for dependants – S.57A ERA

- the right of pension scheme trustees to paid time off – Ss.58 and 59 ERA

- the right of employee representatives to paid time off – Ss.61 and 62 ERA

- the right to paid time off for a young person for study or training – Ss.63A and 63B ERA

- the right to make a request in relation to study and training, and have it properly considered by the employer – S.63D and 63F ERA

- the right to remuneration on suspension on medical grounds – S.64 ERA
- the right to alternative work and remuneration for maternity suspension – Ss.67 and 68 ERA
- the right to parental leave – S.76 ERA
- the right to have an application for flexible working properly considered – Ss.80G and 80H ERA
- the right to receive a written statement of reasons for dismissal – S.92 ERA
- the right not to be unfairly dismissed – S.94 ERA
- the right to a redundancy payment – S.135 ERA.

A number of additional relevant statutory rights are listed in paragraphs (b) to (e) of S.104(4). These are:

12.5

- the right to minimum notice – S.86 ERA (this right is not caught by the catch-all provision of S.104(4)(a) because the remedy for infringement is a claim for damages for wrongful dismissal)
- the right not to suffer unauthorised deductions from wages in respect of union subscriptions – S.68 Trade Union and Labour Relations (Consolidation) Act 1992 (TULR(C)A)
- the right not to suffer unauthorised deductions from wages in respect of a union political fund – S.86 TULR(C)A
- the right not to be offered an inducement in relation to union membership or activities – S.145A TULR(C)A
- the right not to be offered an inducement in relation to collective bargaining – S.145B TULR(C)A
- the right not to be subjected to a detriment on grounds related to union membership or activities – S.146 TULR(C)A
- the right of union officials to paid time off for union duties – Ss.168 and 169 TULR(C)A
- the right of union learning representatives to paid time off for learning and training activities – Ss.168A and 169 TULR(C)A
- the right of union members to time off for union activities – S.170 TULR(C)A
- any of the rights conferred by the Working Time Regulations 1998 SI 1998/1833 (the Working Time Regulations 1998); the Merchant Shipping (Working Time: Inland Waterways) Regulations 2003 SI 2003/3049; the Fishing Vessels (Working Time: Sea-fishermen) Regulations 2004 SI 2004/1713; or the Cross-border Railway Services (Working Time) Regulations 2008 SI 2008/1660

467

- the rights conferred by the Transfer of Undertakings (Protection of Employment) Regulations 2006 SI 2006/246.

12.6 To establish a claim of automatic unfair dismissal under S.104 it is crucial that the right asserted falls within one of the above lists. There are a number of employment rights that do not appear above, including the right to be accompanied under S.10 of the Employment Relations Act 1999, and a claim under S.104 cannot therefore be brought in respect of them. Similarly, a claim under S.104 cannot be brought in respect of any of the anti-discrimination rights contained in the various discrimination statutes and statutory instruments (consolidated into the Equality Act 2010 from a date to be determined). However, employees who bring a discrimination, harassment or equal pay claim are protected from less favourable treatment (including dismissal) at the hands of their employer as a result under the statutory 'victimisation' provisions contained in the anti-discrimination legislation – see, for example, IDS Employment Law Handbook, 'Sex Discrimination' (2008) Chapter 6.

12.7 **Inclusion of TUPE rights.** A little-known but significant recent amendment to S.104(4) was the inclusion of the rights conferred by the Transfer of Undertakings (Protection of Employment) Regulations 2006 SI 2006/246 (TUPE). The rights under the previous incarnation of the Regulations, the Transfer of Undertakings (Protection of Employment) Regulations 1981 SI 1981/1794, were not included.

There are two reasons why this change is significant. First, prior to the 2006 amendment, an employee dismissed for asserting a right to the same rate of pay as he or she enjoyed prior to a transfer would need to establish both a right under TUPE *and* a relevant statutory right under the ERA. For example, in Capitol Security Services Ltd v Blake EAT 961/97 the EAT remitted a claim to a tribunal to consider whether an employee alleging an infringement of his 'statutory right to have his terms and conditions of service maintained' under TUPE was in fact also alleging infringement of his right not to suffer unauthorised deductions from pay under S.13 ERA (a relevant statutory right for the purposes of S.104(4)).

12.8 Secondly, the inclusion of TUPE rights in S.104(4) affords a degree of TUPE protection to employees who have less than one year's continuous employment. As discussed in Chapter 10, Reg 7(1) TUPE specifies that where there is a transfer of an undertaking and the transfer, or a reason connected with it that is not an economic, technical or organisational reason entailing changes in the workforce, is the reason or principal reason for the dismissal, that dismissal will be automatically unfair. However, unlike most other forms of automatically unfair dismissal, TUPE dismissals are subject to a one-year qualifying period. This is not the case for unfair dismissal claims under S.104, which can be brought from the first day of employment.

For details of the rights afforded to employees under TUPE, see IDS Employment Law Handbook, 'Transfer of Undertakings' (2007).

Asserting the right

An employee asserts a relevant statutory right in one of two ways: by bringing tribunal proceedings to enforce the right – S.104(1)(a), or by alleging that the employer has infringed the right – S.104(1)(b). As we will see below, the majority of cases are brought under the latter provision. First, however, two examples of cases brought under S.104(1)(a):

- **Budzynska v Resource Management Holdings Ltd t/a Malla Technical Recruitment Consultancy** ET Case No.6005608/99: B was employed by an employment agency to work for one of its clients, Haden Young. In January 1999 B claimed that she was entitled to paid holidays. Having failed to receive a satisfactory response she brought tribunal proceedings, which were settled through Acas. As a result of the settlement B's basic rate of pay was increased, which meant that when national insurance contributions were taken into account, the total cost of her services to the agency was 96p an hour more than it was charging Haden Young. The agency tried to renegotiate the arrangement with Haden Young and when this proved impossible it terminated B's contract. A tribunal found that the principal reason for her dismissal was that she had brought a claim under the Working Time Regulations 1998 and held that her dismissal was therefore automatically unfair under S.104(1)(a)

- **Stanford v City Centre Restaurants (UK) Ltd** ET Case No.2306191/03: S was employed as a waiter by CCR Ltd at one of its restaurants in June 2003 after an informal interview. He had been employed at another of its restaurants until March that year and had brought an unfair dismissal claim against the company. When the HR director discovered this, he told S that he could only continue in his job if he dropped the claim, and further added that the claim was weak and would leave S with hefty legal bills. When S refused to withdraw the claim, he was dismissed with immediate effect. The tribunal found that the reason for dismissal was that S had brought an unfair dismissal claim against CCR Ltd.

As mentioned above, the majority of cases decided to date have been brought under S.104(1)(b), which covers the situation where an employee alleges that the employer has infringed his or her relevant statutory right. The leading case is Mennell v Newell and Wright (Transport Contractors) Ltd 1997 ICR 1039, CA, where M, an HGV driver, refused to sign a draft contract that would have allowed his employer to make deductions from his wages on termination of employment in order to recoup training costs. He was told that he would be sacked if he did not sign. He persisted in his refusal and was dismissed. M claimed that he had been unfairly dismissed for asserting his statutory right to protection against unlawful deductions from wages, contained in S.13 ERA. A

469

tribunal dismissed the claim on the basis that there had been no infringement of S.13, only the possibility of such an infringement in the future. The EAT overturned the tribunal's decision, holding that, in the light of S.104(2), it was sufficient that the employee had alleged in good faith that the employer had infringed a relevant statutory right; there was no requirement that the employer had actually infringed the right in question. While this was enough to determine the appeal, the EAT went one step further, stating that if the employer 'sought by threat of dismissal to impose a variation of the contract of employment to incorporate a term which negated the employee's statutory right not to suffer a deduction of wages without his freely given consent, that is, or might be, an infringement of his statutory right at the time when the threat is made, bearing in mind the words of [S.104(2)]'.

The case subsequently came before the Court of Appeal, which agreed with the EAT that S.104 is not confined to cases where a statutory right has actually been infringed. It is sufficient if the employee has alleged that the employer has infringed a statutory right, and that the making of that allegation was the reason or the principal reason for the dismissal. The allegation need not be specific, provided it has been made reasonably clear to the employer what right was claimed to have been infringed. Further, the allegation need not be correct, either as to the entitlement to the right or as to its infringement, provided the claim was made in good faith. The important point is that the employee must have made an allegation of the kind protected by S.104; if he or she had not, the making of such an allegation could not have been the reason for his or her dismissal. To that extent, the Court upheld the EAT's decision. However, the Court decided that, on the facts of the case, M had not alleged an infringement by his employer of his statutory rights, since he was unable to say when, where, to whom or in what terms he had made the allegation. The most he was able to say was that he had told management that he would sign the agreement only if the clause relating to the repayment of training expenses was amended, and this was not sufficient for the purposes of S.104(1)(b). The employer's appeal was allowed on that basis.

12.11 **Actual or threatened infringement?** The Court of Appeal's judgment in Mennell makes it clear that an employer does not actually need to have infringed a statutory right in order for the claim to succeed. However, despite the EAT's suggestion that an employer's threat to make an unauthorised deduction from wages may amount to an actual infringement of S.13 ERA, it would seem that it is still necessary for the employee to have *alleged that the employer has actually infringed* a statutory right. Based on a strict interpretation of the wording of S.104, an allegation that the employer has merely proposed or threatened to infringe such a right is not sufficient.

In Burke v Thames and Chiltern Trust Ltd ET Case No.2700367/99 B, a case worker in a care home, complained to his employer about the number of hours that he and other staff were going to have to work in the coming month. He was subsequently summarily dismissed. B claimed that he had been dismissed for asserting a statutory right in relation to the Working Time Regulations 1998. The tribunal held that the wording of S.104(1)(b) required an allegation that the employer *had infringed* a statutory right. This meant that the alleged breach must relate to a past and not a future event. B's allegation about a roster that he was going to have to work in the future was about something that he feared would happen rather than something that had happened and it was therefore not open to the tribunal to find that he was dismissed for asserting a statutory right under S.104(1)(b).

However, tribunals have not universally adopted this approach. In Callaghan v McDougall and anor t/a New Horizon Recruitment ET Case No.1900295/99, for example, C was employed as a minibus driver. The day after he started work, C was given a standard form contract to sign. This included a section requiring C to signify his agreement to opt out of the 48-hour limit on the working week laid down in the Working Time Regulations 1998. C completed the rest of the contract but refused to sign the opt-out clause. When he was again asked to sign the opt-out he refused on the ground that he was working for a basic weekly wage and was not willing to work over the 48-hour limit. C was told that his employment would come to an end unless he signed. C refused and left his employment. He claimed that he had been dismissed for asserting a statutory right not to work more than a 48-hour week under the 1998 Regulations. The tribunal found that C believed in good faith that he had this right and that it would be infringed. It followed that he had been unfairly dismissed for asserting a statutory right.

What constitutes an allegation of infringement? The employee's case in Mennell v Newell and Wright (Transport Contractors) Ltd (above) ultimately failed because the Court of Appeal held that the fact that he told his employer that he would only sign the agreement if it were amended was not enough to amount to an allegation that his statutory right had been infringed. This raises the question as to what exactly the employee must allege in order to rely on S.104(1)(b). Ultimately this will be a question of fact for the tribunal to decide in each case. In the following cases, the tribunal found that an employee's allegations did amount to an assertion that the employer had infringed a statutory right:

- **Albion Hotel (Freshwater) Ltd v Silva and anor** 2002 IRLR 200, EAT: Mr and Mrs S were employed as managers of a hotel. Under their contracts of employment they were entitled to an annual bonus calculated by reference to the 'per person average bed night cost'. The hotel did not fare well under their management and when the bonus was due the employer made no payment. At a meeting between Mr and Mrs S and two company directors, Mr and Mrs S asserted that a bonus was due to them and the directors stated that no bonus was likely to be payable on the figures they had available. Mr and Mrs S continued to demand payment of the bonus and complained that it had not been paid. They were subsequently

12.12

12.13

471

dismissed for 'poor management'. The tribunal found that the reason for their dismissal was in fact their assertion that a substantial bonus was due to them. Accordingly, the tribunal found that the employer had dismissed them for asserting that the employer had infringed a statutory right – namely the right not to have an unlawful deduction made from wages under S.13 ERA. The EAT upheld this aspect of the tribunal's decision

- **Hutton v Wright** ET Case No.2103491/00: H was employed as a bar worker. One Sunday, she agreed to stay past her usual finishing time of midnight after her co-worker had to leave. When H prepared to leave, her employer, W, tried to stop her by telling her that there were still customers to serve. H pointed out to W that she was entitled to go home as she was only paid until midnight and by then it was 12.20 a.m. W told H that she had to stay until he said she could go. H said that she was prepared to stay if she was paid. W refused to pay her. H left and was dismissed. Before leaving, she had told W that he could not dismiss her for asking to be paid for the hours that she had worked. H brought a claim that she had been dismissed for asserting a statutory right. The tribunal held that the principal reason for her dismissal was her refusal to stay at work without being paid and that W's failure to pay her for time worked was an unlawful deduction from wages within the meaning of S.13(1) ERA, which was a statutory right. H was dismissed for asserting that right and the dismissal was therefore automatically unfair under S.104.

12.14   In Fraser v Carter Refrigeration and Retail Services Ltd ET Case No.2202270/00, on the other hand, the employee's complaints were not sufficient to satisfy S.104(1)(b). F worked for CRR as a duty refrigeration engineer operating from home. He responded to customers' calls to attend their premises to service their refrigerators during normal working hours. In addition, one week in five he was on emergency call-out outside normal working hours. Following complaints by a couple of customers that he had arrived late to their call-out requests, CRR gave F a final written warning. Similar customer complaints followed. At a meeting to discuss the complaints F explained to CRR that the reason he had not responded to one of the calls was that he had slept through his alarm as a result of having worked 37 hours over a weekend period without an adequate break. F was subsequently dismissed. He claimed that he had been dismissed for asserting his rights under health and safety legislation and under the Working Time Regulations 1998. The tribunal held that F's comments to his managers that he was fatigued on account of lack of sleep were not sufficient to amount to an allegation that CRR had infringed his statutory rights.

12.15   **Request for information.** It appears that a simple request for information relating to a statutory right does not of itself amount to an assertion. In Angel v Pitts-Tucker and Co ET Case No.3202086/97 A wrote a memo to her employer saying that she would like to know her benefits and asking for clarification on sick pay, wage reviews and bonuses. She was dismissed. The tribunal held that her memo was 'merely a request for information' and did not amount to an allegation that a relevant statutory right had been infringed.

Ultimately, however, whether or not an employee's request amounts to an assertion of a statutory right will be a question of fact for the tribunal to decide in each case. The EAT in Albion Hotel (Freshwater) Ltd v Silva and anor (above) recognised that there is a 'somewhat fine distinction between asking for a bonus (which would not be regarded as an assertion of a breach of the statutory right) and asking persistently, which might amount to an assertion of breach of a statutory right'.

Details of the allegation   12.16

Section 104(3) expressly states that it is sufficient that the employee made it reasonably clear to the employer what the right claimed to have been infringed was; it is not necessary for the employee actually to specify the right. Clearly, an employee is not required to cite the section number of the right in question, or quote the precise statutory wording. However, it must still be made reasonably clear to the employer what right the employee is relying on.

In Armstrong v Walter Scott Motors (London) Ltd EAT 766/02 A worked as a car salesman. He wrote a letter to his employer to complain about a term in the staff handbook which provided that he would not accrue leave entitlement during the first year of employment. A wrote: 'I find this requirement morally indefensible in this day and age. I find it astonishing and infuriating that such a requirement was ever enforced, and fail to understand how any employee could be expected to work for a full year without taking leave.' He went on to request that he be allowed to take paid leave. A was dismissed and brought a claim for unfair dismissal under S.104 ERA. The tribunal decided unanimously that A had been dismissed because he had written the letter of complaint. However, the majority of the tribunal went on to find that A had not alleged, within S.104(1)(b), that his employer had infringed a statutory right. The majority considered that A had not suggested that his employer had failed to comply with 'any statutory right, as opposed to contractual arrangement or moral obligation'. More was required to make it reasonably clear to the employer what right was infringed. On appeal, the EAT stated that, in its view, A had made it 'reasonably clear to his employer that he had a right, in common with all others, not to have to wait for a year in order to take his holiday'. The EAT noted further that A did indeed have this right under the Working Time Regulations 1998, and that the right was being infringed. The EAT concluded that A had alleged that his employer was infringing his right to paid holiday under the Regulations. It followed, in the light of the tribunal's finding that A had been dismissed because he had written his letter of complaint, that A had been unfairly dismissed under S.104 ERA for asserting a statutory right.

473

12.17 In Jimenez v Nelabrook Ltd EAT 614/97, on the other hand, J repeatedly asked her employer for her correct tax code in an attempt to ascertain whether tax was being paid on her behalf. Her employer dismissed her. J claimed that she had been dismissed for asserting her statutory right to an itemised pay statement under S.8 ERA. A tribunal found that J had not sought an itemised pay statement: the principal reason for the dismissal was the fact that she had requested information about her tax code. It concluded that she had not been dismissed for asserting a statutory right. J appealed to the EAT, who held that, in the light of the Court of Appeal's judgment in Mennell v Newell and Wright (Transport Contractors) Ltd (above), the crucial question was whether J was able to identify any occasion on which she had alleged that her employer had infringed her rights under S.8. Although S.104(3) made it clear that it was not necessary for J to refer specifically to S.8, the EAT thought that at the very least it was incumbent on her to ask for the details that would have been contained in an itemised pay statement. On the tribunal's findings of fact, she had not done so, and accordingly she had not asserted a statutory right. Her appeal was therefore dismissed.

12.18 **Timing of allegation**
In order to be able to bring a claim under S.104 the employee's assertion that the employer has infringed a relevant statutory right must be made *prior* to dismissal. In Capitol Security Services Ltd v Blake EAT 961/97 B argued that his main complaint was of a change in pay arrangements which amounted to an unauthorised reduction in pay contrary to S.13 ERA. The EAT noted that, since the proceedings referred to in S.104(1)(a) or the allegation referred to in S.104(1)(b) must be the reason for the dismissal, they or it must precede the dismissal. The very proceedings before the tribunal itself cannot therefore be relied upon, nor allegations made in initiating or prosecuting those proceedings. As the tribunal in the instant case had made no findings of fact as to whether there were any allegations relating to pay prior to dismissal, the EAT remitted the matter to the tribunal so that the necessary facts could be established.

A similar point arose in Wilcox v Select Products Ltd ET Case No.1601394/99. W was employed as a shift worker by SP Ltd. He had worked a 12-hour shift on a number of occasions without complaint. However, one Saturday after coming off shift at 6 a.m. he was asked by his manager to work another 12-hour shift starting at 6 p.m. the same day. W refused and was dismissed. Following W's dismissal, a Citizens Advice Bureau drafted a letter for him to give to his employer stating, among other things, that he was owed a week's pay in lieu of notice. W later claimed that he had been dismissed for asserting a statutory right. The tribunal held that W's refusal to work a further 12-hour shift did not amount to an allegation that a statutory right had been infringed. Since he had made no other allegation prior to his dismissal his claim under S.104 had to fail.

474

Requirement of good faith

Section 104(2) provides that it is immaterial whether or not the employee actually has the relevant statutory right or whether the right has been infringed. However, the subsection goes on to state that the employee's claim to the right and that it has been infringed must be made in good faith. It follows that an employee's genuine but mistaken belief that he or she has the statutory right in question will suffice.

This point is illustrated by Callaghan v McDougall and anor t/a New Horizon Recruitment ET Case No.1900295/99. The tribunal held that C, a minibus driver, had been dismissed for asserting a statutory right under the Working Time Regulations 1998 and his dismissal was therefore automatically unfair. It was irrelevant, for the purposes of S.104(1), that C might have fallen within the category of 'transport workers', which was then excluded from the scope of the Regulations. His claim to the right and his belief that it would be infringed had been made in good faith and, therefore, by virtue of S.104(2), he could bring a claim under S.104.

Section 104(2) also covers the situation where the employee has the right in question but there has been no actual infringement by the employer. The Court of Appeal's judgment in Mennell v Newell and Wright (Transport Contractors) Ltd 1997 ICR 1039, CA, makes it clear that the employer does not actually need to have infringed a statutory right in order for the claim to succeed. It is sufficient that the employee genuinely believes that an infringement has occurred.

For example, in Philip Hodges and Co v Crush EAT 1061/95 C agreed to a reduction in salary in the face of a threat of dismissal by her employer. After C's earnings had been reduced, a law centre adviser wrote to her employer on her behalf claiming that she had suffered unlawful deductions from her wages contrary to S.13 ERA. Following discussions with her employer, during which C again asserted that what had happened was unlawful, she was dismissed. The letter of dismissal specifically referred to the fact that she had taken outside legal advice. A tribunal found that C had agreed to the variation in contract and that consequently no unauthorised deductions had taken place. However, it held that the reason for C's dismissal was that she had asserted a relevant statutory right. On the employer's appeal, the EAT upheld the tribunal's finding that the reason for the dismissal was one that fell within S.104. In the EAT's opinion, the fact that the employee had authorised the reduction in her salary and that there had therefore been no unlawful deductions was irrelevant. The tribunal had found that the claim that the employer had made unlawful deductions was made in good faith and this was sufficient to bring S.104 into play.

The question of whether an employee has acted in good faith in asserting that his or her statutory right has been infringed is one of fact for the tribunal to

475

determine in each case. In Albion Hotel (Freshwater) Ltd v Silva and anor (above) the tribunal took the view that Mr and Mrs S's allegations were 'completely exaggerated' and that they had 'little hesitation in adding to their evidence matters which are self-serving'. However, the tribunal concluded that, in making a claim for a substantial bonus, Mr and Mrs S were acting in good faith, 'however misguided they may have been'. The EAT refused to interfere with this finding. The question of whether or not the employees acted in good faith in making their claim that they were entitled to a bonus and had been denied it was one of fact for the tribunal. The tribunal had taken into account the fact that the employees may have been misguided in claiming that they were entitled to a bonus, but concluded that they had nonetheless done so in good faith. The tribunal was not required to make a finding as to whether any bonus was in fact due to the employees. It was sufficient for the tribunal to find that the employees believed in good faith that a bonus was due. It followed that it was irrelevant that, given the poor trading of the hotel under their management, the employees may not in fact have been due a bonus at all.

12.22 Reason for dismissal

The final requirement under S.104 is that the assertion of the relevant statutory right must be the reason, or the principal reason, for the employee's dismissal. The burden of proof is on the employee to establish the reason for dismissal, on the balance of probabilities. Where the parties advance different reasons, it is for the tribunal to decide, as a question of fact, which reason caused (or principally caused) the dismissal.

In JP Fitzpatrick (Cable TV) Ltd v Whicker EAT 1165/97 W found it difficult to carry out her job during her basic working hours and accordingly regularly worked overtime. On one occasion she put in an application for 45 minutes' overtime, which was refused partly on the basis that she was not performing well. W complained that she was not being paid what she was owed and that she would not work unpaid overtime. This amounted to an assertion of a statutory right. She subsequently decided not to work any overtime, which meant that some of her work remained unfinished. A few days later W's employer terminated her employment, saying that she did not fit in. Before the tribunal, W claimed that she had been dismissed for asserting a statutory right. Her employer advanced other reasons for her dismissal, including that W was inefficient and deliberately left work unfinished. The EAT upheld the tribunal's finding that W had been dismissed for asserting a statutory right. The fact that W had asserted a statutory right, coupled with her dismissal eight days later, called for an explanation from the employer. Having rejected each of the reasons put forward by the employer, the tribunal correctly inferred that the reason or principal reason for dismissal was that advanced by W. Furthermore, the EAT held that there was a sufficient causative link between the assertion of the statutory right

476

and the dismissal. Having complained that she had not been paid for overtime worked, W resolved to operate a personal overtime ban. Her employer felt this showed a lack of cooperation on W's part, which explained the employer's comment that W did not 'fit in'. It was for this reason that she was dismissed.

Three further examples: **12.23**

- **Dance v Mitie Cleaning (North) Ltd** ET Case No.2508310/04: D had been employed by MC Ltd to work at Nissan's premises at a rate of £6.33 an hour. Following a complaint by Nissan, which made it clear that the company was no longer prepared to have D working at its premises, he was moved to other work as a janitor and his pay reduced to £6.17 an hour. D successfully brought a claim for unlawful deductions from wages over the reduction, following which MC Ltd decided it could not afford to employ him at the higher rate. He was called to a meeting, dismissed and offered re-engagement at the lower rate. Before the tribunal, MC Ltd argued that there was 'some other substantial reason' for the dismissal; namely, that Nissan no longer wanted D working on its premises. However, the tribunal disagreed, finding that the real reason for dismissal was that MC Ltd did not want to pay D at the higher rate in respect of which he had asserted a statutory right. The dismissal was therefore automatically unfair under S.104

- **Seddon v Furnstyle Ltd** ET Case No.1800912/99: S, a furniture assembler, led a delegation of employees arguing for various employment rights – including those under the Working Time Regulations 1998 – shortly after commencing employment. His employer had never heard of the 1998 Regulations and was put out that a new employee was raising such matters. S was dismissed a few days later. He was told: 'You're a craftsman, making quality furniture, but you're a personality, an individual, and there's no place for you in my team.' Before the tribunal, the employer argued that S had been dismissed because he could not assemble furniture quickly enough. Considering all the evidence, including the fact that S was a skilled craftsman and that the employer could produce no direct evidence as to his inability to work at the speed required, the tribunal had no difficulty drawing the inference that the reason for S's dismissal was that he had asserted statutory rights under the Working Time Regulations

- **Martins v Autoclean** ET Case No.5000800/99: M was employed as a car washer. He was unhappy about the way his employer treated him and contacted a Citizens Advice Bureau. The CAB wrote a letter on his behalf to his employer requesting, among other things, arrears of wages and a statement of particulars of employment. M was dismissed on the day the letter was received. His employer claimed that M was dismissed – for swearing at a customer – before the letter had been read. However, following his dismissal, M had asked another employee, who had been present at his dismissal interview, why he had been dismissed and was told

477

that he was considered to be a disloyal employee because he had taken his grievance to an outside body. The tribunal held that had M been dismissed for swearing, as the employer contended, he would have had no reason to enquire as to why he had been dismissed. There was also no reason to suppose that M's ex-colleague had lied about the reason for dismissal. The tribunal concluded that M had been unfairly dismissed for asserting a statutory right.

12.24 Each case turns on its own facts, however. In Nicol v Nightingale Group Ltd ET Case No.2900161/98 the employer succeeded in establishing that the reason for dismissal was not the fact that the employee had asserted a relevant statutory right. N's employer believed she was helping a colleague to advance a claim for compensation for personal injuries that was not entirely genuine. As a result, foreseeing a question mark over her continued employment, payment for a training course was withheld. The agreement with regard to the training fees provided that, should N leave employment, the course fees would be deducted from her final pay or would otherwise be repayable by her. N complained about the non-payment while her employer continued to investigate matters relating to the personal injuries claim and she was dismissed on 26 December. N claimed that she was dismissed because she had asserted her right to receive her pay in full. A tribunal found that she was dismissed because her employer had doubts about her loyalty, not because of her assertion of a statutory right. Her unfair dismissal claim failed.

In Budzynska v Resource Management Holdings Ltd t/a Malla Technical Recruitment Consultancy ET Case No.6005608/99 the tribunal applied the 'but for' test to establish the true reason for dismissal: but for the employee's allegation of an infringement, would he or she have been dismissed? In that case B's employer argued that the principal reason for her dismissal was that it was no longer economic to employ her. However, the tribunal found that but for B's claim for paid holiday and the fact that she had thereby secured an increase in pay, she would not have been dismissed. The principal reason for her dismissal was therefore the bringing of her claim alleging a breach of the Working Time Regulations 1998.

12.25 **Constructive dismissal**
It can be particularly difficult for a tribunal to determine whether an allegation that a statutory right has been infringed is the reason for dismissal in cases where the employee has resigned and claimed constructive dismissal. The employee must demonstrate that he or she resigned in response to the employer's repudiatory breach of contract, and that the employer's actions related to the employee's assertion of a statutory right. Two contrasting examples:

• **McMahon and Waters v Millington t/a Poppy** ET Case Nos.2901530–31/99: M and W were employed as mobile cleaners. They repeatedly raised

478

concerns with their employer about pay statements, deductions for tax and national insurance contributions, and holiday pay. The employer promised to do something, but never gave the claimants a satisfactory reply. After three months of inaction on the part of their employer, M and W resigned and claimed constructive dismissal for a reason relating to the assertion of a statutory right. The tribunal found that M and W's complaints amounted to the assertion of a statutory right. They were entitled to take their employer's protracted inaction as a refusal to deal with their complaints, which entitled them to resign and claim constructive dismissal. As the reason for their resignations was their assertion of a statutory right, the tribunal held that they had been automatically unfairly dismissed under S.104

- **Scott v Lowe** EAT 780–81/98: S resigned after her wages cheque bounced on two separate occasions. She argued that she had been constructively dismissed under S.104 for asserting that she had suffered an unlawful deduction from her wages. However, the tribunal rejected her claim, holding that the principal reason for S's resignation was her entirely legitimate concern that her employer's financial position was such that there was some doubt as to whether she would be promptly paid in full on subsequent occasions. It emphasised that S.104 does not protect an employee who suffers an unlawful deduction from wages, but only an employee who is dismissed because there has been an allegation of such an unlawful deduction. The EAT refused to intervene, holding that the tribunal's approach could not be faulted.

Multiple reasons for dismissal 12.26

It is important to note that a claim under S.104 may succeed even if there is more than one reason for the dismissal. S.104(1) expressly states that it is sufficient that the *principal* reason for dismissal is the assertion of a relevant statutory right. In Callaghan v Park Welding and Fabrication Co Ltd ET Case No.1800087/96 C was recruited as a sheet-metal worker. He started work on a trial basis at an hourly rate of £4.50 but was told that his hourly rate would increase by 25p a month until it reached the level of £5.50 an hour. After one month C was given a rise of 25p an hour but at the end of the second month he was refused a further increase because his employer was dissatisfied with his performance. C became disillusioned and his performance deteriorated. He left a letter on his manager's desk asking for a written statement of terms and conditions and demanding the pay rise to which he believed he was entitled. The letter stated that the refusal to award a pay increase amounted to an unlawful deduction from wages contrary to S.13 ERA. Later that afternoon, C was invited to a meeting with his manager and a decision was taken to dismiss him. The tribunal found that the reason for the dismissal was a combination of C's written request to his employer and the employer's disappointment in C's performance. On the balance of probabilities, however, and bearing in mind that the employer had received C's letter a matter of hours before deciding to dismiss him, the tribunal found that the contents of the letter were the principal reason for the dismissal. Accordingly, the dismissal was automatically unfair under S.104.

12.27 Where there are mixed reasons for the dismissal, tribunals will not necessarily find that the principal reason is the one falling within S.104. Three examples:

- **Sivagurunathan v Harpalani t/a Harpers** ET Case No.3200838/00: S was employed from 14 July 1999 as a paralegal. He maintained that he was taken on with a view to a training contract so that he could qualify as a solicitor. On 24 November S wrote to his employer concerning three issues: he said he was entitled by law to 20 days' paid holiday a year; he wanted a pay increase as a matter of urgency; and he was not prepared to work for much longer without a training contract. S was dismissed and subsequently claimed that he was dismissed for asserting his rights under the Working Time Regulations 1998. The tribunal dismissed the application. It thought that S was dismissed because of financial pressures and because of his request for a training contract. The request for paid holiday had some bearing, but it was not the principal reason for dismissal by any means

- **Foxall v Cygnet Security Services Ltd** ET Case No.3101928/97: F sent a letter to his employer, setting out various demands. The tribunal recognised that one of these demands, which related to the right to written details of employment, concerned a statutory right under the ERA. However, the tribunal decided that because F had made many other demands that did not concern a breach of a statutory right, he was unable to prove that the principal reason for his dismissal was the demand for written particulars of employment. Accordingly, S.104 did not apply

- **Copeman v Metcalfe t/a The Three Horseshoes** ET Case No.1500634/05: C's employment transferred to M in February 2005 when M took over the pub in which she worked. C originally worked 19.5 hours a week but soon after the takeover M asked her to change her contracted hours. He also informed her that he would not be responsible for paying her maternity pay when she took maternity leave (she was pregnant at the time). C became very worried about the situation and gave M a medical certificate saying she was suffering from stress and should remain off work for a week. She was then told that her role was no longer required and was given £100 in lieu of notice. The tribunal held that C was dismissed for a combination of reasons – her refusal to change her hours, her sick leave so soon after M took over and her assertion that she was entitled to be paid maternity pay. However, the tribunal was not satisfied that the foremost reason was C's assertion of a statutory right, and so her unfair dismissal claim under this head failed.

480

Manner in which complaints made   12.28

Where an employee raises his or her complaint in a vigorous or aggressive manner, the employer could argue that it was not the nature of the complaint or allegation that led to the dismissal but, rather, the manner in which the complaint was made. This is a difficult distinction to make, particularly as the allegation is so bound up with the behaviour in question, but a tribunal may sometimes accept the argument that it was really the manner of complaint that caused the dismissal.

Three examples:

- **Hummerston v Akhter Computers Ltd** ET Case No.3200086/98: H, who worked as a computer assembler, received a salary, profit-related pay and a monthly bonus that was dependent on performance at work and attendance. Each month H's bonus payments varied. In September, representatives of a client came to inspect the factory, one of whom was disabled. While they were being shown around, H made noises described by his manager as akin to monkey noises. H was given a first written warning about his behaviour and poor conduct. When H did not receive a bonus in respect of that month he raised the issue with his manager, who explained to him that he was not receiving a bonus because of his poor conduct. H exploded into a torrent of abuse against the manager, who told H to leave and take four weeks' notice. The tribunal held that withholding the bonus was an unlawful deduction – it had never been made clear to H that it could be withdrawn for misconduct – but that the principal reason for his dismissal was the abusive manner in which he raised his concerns about the bonus with his manager. Therefore, his dismissal was not in response to his asserting a statutory right and was not automatically unfair

- **Smith v Strongvalue Ltd t/a Stirk House Hotel** ET Case No.2403598/99: S's employer was generally dissatisfied with her demeanour and attitude. During the three weeks of her employment she had to work more than 48 hours a week on average. She complained about the work rota and said she was not willing to work more than 48 hours a week. She was dismissed. The tribunal held that although there was a strong likelihood (amounting almost to a certainty) that she would have been dismissed in any event within a short period, the principal reason for her dismissal was her complaint about working hours. She was unfairly dismissed for asserting a statutory right

- **Greenwood v Picnic Anywhere Ltd** ET Case No.1101660/08: G submitted a grievance in which she stated that she had spoken to her local Citizens Advice Bureau and had been informed that she was entitled to holiday and sick pay. Her employer responded that, due to the 'adversarial tone' of G's grievance, it had no choice but to dismiss her. The tribunal concluded that the reason for dismissal was not the tone of the grievance but the substance of it – G had asserted her right to paid annual leave and had been unfairly dismissed for that reason.

481

13 Whistleblowing dismissals

Disclosure of information

Qualifying disclosures

Method of disclosure

Reason for dismissal

Injury to feelings

13.1

Under S.103A of the Employment Rights Act 1996 (ERA), an employee will be regarded as unfairly dismissed if the reason, or principal reason, for the dismissal is that the employee had made a 'protected disclosure'. It is also automatically unfair to select an employee for redundancy if the reason or principal reason for which the employee was selected for redundancy was that the employee had made a protected disclosure – S.105(6A).

The provisions on protected disclosures were inserted into the ERA by the Public Interest Disclosure Act 1998 (PIDA) to protect workers who disclose information about an alleged wrongdoing in certain defined circumstances. This is commonly referred to as 'whistleblowing', and we use that term throughout this chapter. It is important to note from the outset that, despite the title of the PIDA, the scope of the whistleblowing provisions is not limited to disclosures that are in the 'public interest'.

An employee may bring a claim under S.103A whatever his or her length of service, as the one-year qualifying period normally required to bring an unfair dismissal claim does not apply. In addition, interim relief is available in S.103A (see Chapter 19) and there is no cap on the compensation that a tribunal may award (see Chapter 18).

13.2

While S.103A itself is a straightforward legislative provision, it only applies where there has been a protected disclosure within the meaning of Ss.43A–43L (contained in Part IVA ERA), which are notoriously complex provisions. Briefly, for a disclosure to gain statutory protection, it must satisfy the following three conditions:

- it must be a 'disclosure of information'

- it must be a 'qualifying' disclosure – i.e. one that, in the reasonable belief of the worker making it, tends to show that one or more of six 'relevant failures' has occurred or is likely to occur

- it must be made in accordance with one of six specified methods of disclosure.

483

We consider these conditions in turn below, before examining the requirement that the disclosure must be the reason for dismissal. Finally, we briefly consider the rules relating to injury to feelings awards in detriment claims, which may be of relevance where the employee claims both unfair dismissal and detriment on account of having made a protected disclosure.

Note that employees (and other workers) are also protected from suffering a *detriment* as a result of making a protected disclosure (see S.47B ERA). There is substantial overlap between the two provisions, particularly when it comes to causation, and many of the cases considered in this chapter were in fact decided under S.47B rather than S.103A. One major difference between the two is that while S.47B applies to all workers, S.103A is confined to employees. However, as Ss.43A–43L refer to 'workers', we have adopted the same terminology in this chapter to avoid confusion. It must be stressed, however, that the right to claim unfair dismissal under S.103A only applies to employees as defined (see further Chapter 2 under 'Employees only').

13.3 Disclosure of information

Although the word 'disclosure' is not itself defined in the ERA, it is clear that the phrase 'disclosure of information' in S.43B is intended to have a wide reach and that an employee simply has to communicate the information by some effective means in order for the communication to constitute a disclosure of that information. There is no requirement in the legislation, for example, that the disclosure must be in writing. Indeed, the EAT has confirmed that handing over a video recording amounts to a disclosure – Aspinall v MSI Mech Forge Ltd EAT 891/01.

The word 'disclosure' is often associated with the revelation of information that was formerly unknown or secret, but the statutory scheme intends a wider meaning than this, as is apparent from S.43L(3). This provides that 'any reference in this Part [i.e. the protected disclosure provisions of Part IVA] to the disclosure of information shall have effect, in relation to any case where the person receiving the information is already aware of it, as a reference to bringing the information to his attention'. Accordingly, protection is not denied simply because the information being communicated was already known to the recipient.

13.4 **Misconduct is not a part of disclosure.** In Bolton School v Evans 2007 ICR 641, CA, the Court of Appeal rejected as 'highly artificial' the contention that the whole of an employee's conduct in disclosing information – including any misconduct – must be regarded as part and parcel of the disclosure itself. A teacher did not therefore enjoy the protection of the whistleblowing provisions when hacking into his employer's computer system in order to expose its vulnerabilities. This case is considered further under 'Reason for dismissal' below.

484

Requirement that claimant convey facts. A recent decision of the EAT 13.5
suggests that tribunals should scrutinise the communication alleged to amount
to a protected disclosure to see whether it actually discloses any *information*.
In Cavendish Munro Professional Risks Management Ltd v Geduld 2010 ICR
325, EAT, G was a director, minority shareholder and employee of CMPRM
Ltd. Following friction between G and the other two directors, he was removed
as a director of the company. He then consulted solicitors, who wrote to
CMPRM Ltd expressing concerns as to the fairness and lawfulness of G's
treatment and threatening legal action if no acceptable resolution could be
found. Shortly thereafter, G was dismissed. An employment tribunal found that
the solicitor's letter amounted to a protected disclosure since, in G's reasonable
belief, it tended to show that CMPRM Ltd was failing to comply with its
obligations to G. On appeal, the employer argued that the letter simply voiced
concerns and therefore did not amount to a 'disclosure of information'.

The EAT noted the lack of any previous appellate authority on the meaning of
'disclosure of information', and observed that S.43F, which concerns disclosure
to a prescribed person (see 'Method of disclosure' below), draws a distinction
between 'information' and the making of an 'allegation'. In the Appeal
Tribunal's view, the ordinary meaning of giving information is to 'convey
facts'. The solicitor's letter had not conveyed any facts; it simply expressed
dissatisfaction with G's treatment. For that reason, it did not amount to a
disclosure of information and could not be a protected disclosure.

Prior to the Geduld decision, it was widely assumed that solicitors' letters sent in
the context of an employer/employee dispute would generally amount to
protected disclosures. Post-Geduld, it seems that many such communications will
not enjoy statutory protection. The key factor is that information, in the form of
facts, must be disclosed for the whistleblowing provisions to be engaged: a mere
allegation will not suffice, although a letter or verbal communication that
conveys facts *and* makes an allegation could amount to a protected disclosure. To
demonstrate the practical distinction between giving information and making an
allegation, the EAT in Geduld posited the following example: 'Communicating
"information" would be "The wards have not been cleaned for the past two
weeks. Yesterday, sharps were left lying around". Contrasted with that would be
a statement that "you are not complying with Health and Safety requirements".
In our view this would be an allegation not information.'

Qualifying disclosures 13.6

The first step in establishing that a disclosure enjoys protection under the ERA
is showing that it meets the qualifying criteria in S.43B. A qualifying disclosure
is any disclosure of information which, in the reasonable belief of the worker,
tends to show one or more of the following:

485

- that a criminal offence has been committed, is being committed or is likely to be committed – S.43B(1)(a)

- that a person has failed, is failing or is likely to fail to comply with any legal obligation to which he or she is subject – S.43B(1)(b)

- that a miscarriage of justice has occurred, is occurring or is likely to occur – S.43B(1)(c)

- that the health or safety of any individual has been endangered, is being endagered or is likely to be endangered – S.43B(1)(d)

- that the environment has been damaged, is being damaged or is likely to be damaged – S.43B(1)(e)

- that information tending to show any matter falling within any one of the above has been, is being or is likely to be deliberately concealed – S.43B(1)(f).

13.7 If a worker makes a disclosure of information about any matter that does not fall into one (or more) of the above categories then he or she will not be entitled to protection in respect of that disclosure. Each of the six categories in S.43B(1) involves some form of malpractice or wrongdoing and they are collectively referred to in the statutory provisions as the 'relevant failures'.

There are two situations in which a disclosure of information will not constitute a 'qualified disclosure', even if it relates to one of the specified relevant failures. These are:

- where the person making the disclosure commits an offence by making it – S.43B(3)

- where the disclosure of information is one in respect of which legal professional privilege could be claimed in legal proceedings and is made by the person to whom the information was disclosed in the course of obtaining legal advice – S.43B(4).

13.8 **Place where relevant failure occurs.** Section 43B(2) states that it is immaterial where the relevant failure occurred, is occurring or would occur. Nor is it material whether the national law applying to any such failure is that of the United Kingdom or of any other country or territory. It follows that the particular circumstances forming the basis of a qualifying disclosure can occur anywhere in the world. A worker may disclose to his employer, for example, that a foreign supplier is in alleged breach of a legal obligation not to employ child labour. So long as all the other prerequisites are met, such a disclosure would be a qualifying disclosure within the meaning of S.43B(1).

However, it should be noted that although the location of a relevant failure is not geographically limited, the right to protection against unfair dismissal for having made a protected disclosure is confined to employees working in Great Britain and Northern Ireland.

Failings need not be those of the employer. Following Hibbins v Hesters Way Neighbourhood Project 2009 ICR 319, EAT, it is clear that a qualifying disclosure can relate to the failings of someone other than the employer. In that case, H saw a police appeal for information about the identity and whereabouts of a named suspect in a rape case and recognised him as a student who had recently applied to join one of HWNP's courses. She telephoned the police and provided them with the student's address and mobile phone number. An employment tribunal did not consider this to be a protected disclosure, as it did not relate to any wrongdoing or failure by the respondent employer. However, on appeal the EAT took a different view. It considered that the identification of the wrongdoer as 'a person' in S.43B(1) expanded the reach of the legislation to include all legal persons and not just the employer. Thus, the Appeal Tribunal continued, 'there is no limitation whatsoever on the people or the entities whose wrongdoings can be [the] subject of qualified disclosures'.

13.9

Reasonable belief

13.10

The requirement that the worker should believe that the information disclosed tends to show that a relevant failure has occurred, is occurring or is likely to occur is not a particularly onerous one. It is clear from the wording of S.43B(1) that the test is, in essence, a subjective one, although there is an objective element to it. The statutory language is cast in terms of 'the *reasonable* belief of *the worker making the disclosure*' (our stress), not 'the belief of a reasonable worker'. Thus, the focus is on what the worker in question believed rather than what anyone else might or might not have believed in the same circumstances. In consequence, the worker's personality and individual circumstances have to be taken into account when judging whether he or she had a 'reasonable belief'.

However, the statutory test is not 100 per cent subjective. If that were the case, the worker would only have to show that he or she genuinely believed that the relevant failure to which the disclosure relates had occurred. But S.43B(1) requires a *reasonable* belief of the worker making the disclosure, not a *genuine* belief. This suggests that there has to be some substantiated basis for the worker's belief. Rumours, unfounded suspicions, uncorroborated allegations and the like will not be enough. For example, in Starforth v Eagle Pest Control Services (UK) Ltd ET Case No.2510727/06, S – a pest control technician – told his employer that it could be a breach of health and safety regulations for him to spray an area with insecticide in order to eradicate fleas unless he had personally seen the fleas or had obtained evidence of their existence through monitoring. Although the tribunal accepted that S had a genuine belief in what he was saying, it was not a reasonable belief. Among other things, none of the documents that S had relied on categorically stated that identification of the relevant pest must be made personally before an insecticide is used. Further, he

487

had failed to take into account that there was only a negligible risk to health and safety.

13.11 **Likelihood of occurrence**
Under S.43B(1) a disclosure can qualify for statutory protection if it tends to show that a relevant failure is *likely* to occur. The Court of Appeal considered the meaning of 'likely' in this context in Kraus v Penna plc and anor 2004 IRLR 260, CA. That case concerned a disclosure that was alleged to fall within S.43B(1)(b), but the Court was satisfied that the same approach could be taken to the meaning of 'likely' in all of subsections (a) to (f). In the Court's view 'likely' should be construed 'as requiring more than a possibility, or a risk, that an employer (or other person) might fail to comply with a relevant legal obligation'. Instead, 'the information disclosed should, in the reasonable belief of the worker at the time it is disclosed, tend to show that it is *probable or more probable than not* that the employer will fail to comply with the relevant legal obligation' (our emphasis). Although aspects of the Kraus decision have subsequently met with disapproval from another division of the Court of Appeal in Babula v Waltham Forest College 2007 ICR 1026, CA (see below under 'Criminal offences'), this particular aspect of the decision was not challenged.

It should, however, be noted that in a disability discrimination case – SCA Packaging Ltd v Boyle 2009 ICR 1056, HL – the House of Lords took a different view on the meaning of the word 'likely' to that of the Court of Appeal in Kraus. In their Lordships' opinion, the word 'likely' in the context of the Disability Discrimination Act 1995 (repealed and replaced by the Equality Act 2010 from a date to be appointed) means 'could well happen' rather than 'more likely than not'. As that case concerned the application of the DDA rather than the whistleblowing provisions in the ERA, and the House of Lords accepted that the word 'likely' can have different meanings in different legislative provisions, it has not overturned the Kraus decision as such. However, a worker denied the protection of the whistleblowing provisions on the basis that, for example, there was only a 40 per cent probability that the relevant failure would occur might wish to refer to Baroness Hale's comments in the Boyle judgment in any appeal, where she considered statutory guidance which stated that it is likely that an event will happen if it is more probable than not that it will happen: 'This curious statement appears to have got "likely" and "probable" the wrong way round. It is probable that an event will happen if it is more likely than not that it will do so. Probability denotes a degree of likelihood greater than 50 per cent. Likelihood, on the other hand, is a much more variable concept.'

13.12 **Criminal offences**
Any disclosure which, in the reasonable belief of the worker making it, tends to show that a criminal offence has been committed (or is being committed or is likely to be committed) amounts to a qualifying disclosure – S.43B(1)(a).

488

The main point of contention under this head is the extent to which the worker is expected to have knowledge of the criminal law. However, this matter appears to have been largely resolved following Babula v Waltham Forest College 2007 ICR 1026, CA, where the Court of Appeal made it clear that a worker will still be able to avail him or herself of the statutory protection even if he or she was in fact mistaken as to the existence of any criminal offence or legal obligation on which the disclosure was based. Accordingly, G was entitled to bring his claim that he had been dismissed on account of his public disclosure of the likelihood of his predecessor committing an offence of inciting religious hatred, even though at the relevant time no such criminal offence existed. It was sufficient that the worker had reasonably believed such an offence or legal obligation to exist.

In reaching this decision, the Court of Appeal overruled a statement of principle in Kraus v Penna plc and anor 2004 IRLR 260, CA, to the effect that a worker's reasonable belief is only relevant to the information he or she is disclosing and not to the existence of the legal obligation the employer is alleged to have breached and that, if the employer was as a matter of law under no legal obligation, then a worker cannot claim the protection of the legislation by claiming that he or she reasonably believed that the employer was under such an obligation. The Court of Appeal in Babula took the view that this constituted an unwarranted gloss on the wording of the statute, since there is 'nothing in S.43B(1) which requires the whistleblower to be right'. The Court added that this less restrictive construction was supported by strong policy considerations, since the purpose of the statutory provisions was to encourage responsible whistleblowing. As Lord Justice Wall, who gave the leading judgment, put it: 'To expect employees on the factory floor or in shops and offices to have a detailed knowledge of the criminal law sufficient to enable them to determine whether or not particular facts which they reasonably believe to be true are capable, as a matter of law, of constituting a particular criminal offence seems to me both unrealistic and to work against the policy of the statute.'

Legal obligations   13.13

Any disclosure which, in the reasonable belief of the worker making it, tends to show that a breach of a legal obligation has occurred (or is occurring or is likely to occur) amounts to a qualifying disclosure – S.43B(1)(b). This is by far the most common category of relevant failure relied upon by workers making protected disclosure claims, and case law has shown that its scope is wider than might first be assumed.

The scope of S.43B(1)(b) is broad: it would seem to cover not only statutory requirements but also any obligation imposed under the common law (e.g. negligence, nuisance and defamation), as well as contractual obligations (including those under a contract of employment – see below) and the requirements of administrative law.

489

13.14 **Identifying the legal obligation.** Decisions of the EAT indicate that, in relying on a breach of legal obligation as a basis for making a protected disclosure, it is necessary for the worker to identify the particular legal obligation which is alleged to have been breached. In Fincham v HM Prison Service EAT 0925/01 and 0991/01 Mr Justice Elias observed: '[T]here must in our view be some disclosure which actually identifies, albeit not in strict legal language, the breach of legal obligation on which the [worker] is relying.'

A similar point was made in Everett Financial Management Ltd v Murrell EAT 552–3/02 and 952/02. In that case a group of equity dealers had held a meeting with various directors at which they apparently voiced concern over the way in which the business was being conducted. The following day the employees wrote to the directors seeking reassurance that the company was not engaged in any unlawful activity that would be in contravention of any Securities and Investments Board principle or regulation. One of the employees eventually resigned and claimed that he had suffered a detriment on account of having made a protected disclosure. The tribunal accepted that the employees' letter had been a qualifying disclosure within the meaning of S.43B(1)(b) but the EAT overturned that finding on appeal. The letter did not disclose any information detailing a breach of legal obligation. Although it plainly referred to what may or may not have been a qualifying disclosure in respect of the meeting held between the employees and the directors, it was not, on its own, capable of being a qualifying disclosure.

13.15 **Breach of employment contract.** In Parkins v Sodexho Ltd 2002 IRLR 109, EAT, it was confirmed that S.43B(1)(b) can potentially cover any disclosure relating to a breach by an employer of an employee's contract of employment. Surprise has been expressed in some quarters about this wide interpretation of 'legal obligation', since it seems to permit workers to make complaints in a far broader range of circumstances than was anticipated at the time the PIDA was enacted. In particular, it enables a worker to 'blow the whistle' and gain the special protection which flows from this in respect of matters that are of no direct concern to anyone other than the worker and the employer.

It is doubtful that a simple complaint of 'you are breaching my contract of employment' would amount to a qualifying disclosure, however, since the EAT in Cavendish Munro Professional Risks Management Ltd v Geduld 2010 ICR 325, EAT (see above under 'Disclosure of information') emphasised that to be a disclosure of information, a communication must convey some facts, rather than state a mere allegation. Presumably, though, a complaint that the employer is in breach of contract which sets out the factual basis for that allegation – such as 'I have not received my commission for the month of June and this is in breach of my contract of employment' – would amount to a disclosure of information.

It is important to bear in mind here the distinction between a breach of employment law and a breach of good industrial relations practice. In Goode v Marks and Spencer plc EAT 0442/09, for example, G sought to establish that he had made a

490

qualifying disclosure when sending an e-mail to *The Times* outlining M&S's plans to change its enhanced redundancy scheme to the detriment of its employees. However, both the tribunal and the EAT considered that the disclosure could not qualify under S.43B(1)(b) because it did not disclose information showing any existing or likely breach of a legal obligation: the redundancy scheme was clearly stated as discretionary and nothing in the disclosure indicated that M&S would not properly inform and consult the workforce.

Miscarriages of justice   13.16

Any disclosure which, in the reasonable belief of the worker, tends to show that a miscarriage of justice has occurred, is occurring or is likely to occur, is a qualifying disclosure – S.43B(1)(c).

It is uncertain what is meant by the term 'miscarriage of justice'. It is not defined in the statutory provisions governing protected disclosures or, for that matter, in any other legal context. Clearly, this category of relevant failure covers perjury and the deliberate omission to disclose evidence to the defence, but in most cases disclosures about such matters would in any event be protected under S.43B(1)(a) and/or (b) on the ground that they relate to the commission of a criminal offence or breach of legal obligation.

Endangerment of health and safety   13.17

Any disclosure which, in the reasonable belief of the worker, tends to show that the health or safety of any individual has been, is being or is likely to be endangered is a qualifying disclosure – S.43B(1)(d). As discussed in Chapter 11, S.43B(1)(d) goes further than the protection accorded by S.100(1)(e) ERA, which renders unlawful any dismissal where 'in circumstances of danger which the employee reasonably believed to be serious and imminent, he took (or proposed to take) appropriate steps to protect himself or other persons from the danger'. While it is true that that protection applies whether or not the perceived danger is to the employee personally or to others (including members of the public – see Masiak v City Restaurants (UK) Ltd 1999 IRLR 780, EAT), it can only be gained where there is a *serious or imminent prospect of danger*. In contrast, no such requirement applies to the whistleblowing protection. To come within S.43B(1)(d), the only limitation is that the worker must have a reasonable belief that health and safety has been endangered, or is being endangered or is likely to be endangered: there is no test of seriousness or imminence.

Similarly, S.43B(1)(d) is of wider scope than the protection under S.100(1)(c), which provides that dismissal is automatically unfair where the reason for dismissal is that the employee brought to the employer's attention, by reasonable means, circumstances connected with his or her work which he or she reasonably believed were harmful or potentially harmful to health or safety. As explained in Chapter 11, this protection only applies where there is either

——— 491

no health and safety representative or safety committee or it was not reasonably practicable for the employee to raise the matter by those means. No such limitation applies to S.43B(1)(d).

13.18 Given the wider scope of S.43B(1)(d), employees dismissed after raising health and safety concerns would often be best served by framing their claims around a protected disclosure, and pleading a breach of S.100 in the alternative. It should not, however, be assumed that just because a claimant asserts that he or she believed there was a risk to health and safety, the tribunal will agree. An example:

- **Smith and ors v Ministry of Defence** ET Case No. 1401537/04: S and a group of fellow security guards had expressed distaste at working with a colleague, T, who had previously been convicted of indecently assaulting a child. S also raised concerns that T might come into contact with children at the staff nursery, which was situated outside the site about 50 metres from one of the guard points. Dissatisfied with the response they received from the MoD, S and his colleagues took the matter to the press and were dismissed for gross misconduct. The tribunal considered that there was only a theoretical possibility that T, as one of 75 or 80 guards, might be on duty at the guard post nearest the nursery at the time of a fire evacuation and need to assist with the children. Another concern – that T might have the opportunity to 'groom' a child – was based on nothing more than an uninformed and generalised assumption. The guard post and the nursery were physically wholly separate. Although the claimants were convinced of a danger to the children, their belief was not 'reasonable' because there was no rational or reasoned basis for it. The disclosures did not, therefore, qualify for protection.

13.19 **Statutory obligation to disclose.** It is relevant to point out here that employees themselves are under a duty to report certain concerns they may have about health and safety issues. Reg 14(2) of the Management of Health and Safety at Work Regulations 1999 SI 1999/3242 provides that every employee shall inform his or her employer or an appropriate employee representative of any work situation which a person with training and instruction would reasonably consider represented a serious and immediate danger to health and safety or any matter which such a person would reasonably consider represented a shortcoming in the employer's protection arrangements for health and safety. The employee's concerns must be connected to his or her own health and safety or arise out of or in connection with his or her own activities at work. The duty only arises if the concern is one that has not previously been reported to the employer or to any employee representative. This statutory obligation in effect requires employees to make disclosures which would then be protected under S.43B(1)(d).

492

Environmental damage

13.20

Any disclosure which, in the reasonable belief of the worker, tends to show that the environment has been, is being, or is likely to be damaged, is a qualifying disclosure – S.43B(1)(e).

No definition of 'environment' is given for these purposes, but clearly the word is intended to have a wide compass. There is no requirement for any particular level of damage to be inflicted on the environment in order for a disclosure to amount to a 'qualifying disclosure'. Undoubtedly, the case of a worker at a chemical plant who discovers that the company is regularly polluting local rivers would be covered. But it is difficult to establish the point at which environmental concerns would be so minor that disclosure about them would not be covered. Would, for example, a disclosure about a company that refuses to implement a recycling scheme for waste paper be a qualifying disclosure within the terms of S.43B(1)(e)? It seems unlikely, but no case has yet arisen to help determine the parameters of this category.

It should be remembered that S.43B(2) specifically provides that it is immaterial whether a relevant failure occurred or is likely to occur in the United Kingdom or elsewhere – see under 'Place where relevant failure occurs' above. This may have particular relevance in the context of environmental disclosures where, for example, a worker's concern relates to damage to the environment of another country by a company with an international sphere of operations.

Concealment of information

13.21

Any disclosure which, in the reasonable belief of the worker, tends to show 'that information tending to show any matter falling within any one of the [other five categories of relevant failure] has been, or is likely to be deliberately concealed' is a qualifying disclosure – S.43B(1)(f).

This category of relevant failure concerns cover-ups and suppression of evidence. It has the effect of bringing within the scope of protection any disclosure of information that relates not only to substantive wrongdoing and malpractice, but also information tending to show that there has been (or is likely to be) a cover-up or deliberate concealment of that information. It is important to emphasise the word 'deliberate' in this context. S.43B(1)(f) would not cover the inadvertent destruction or mislaying of documents or evidence.

Method of disclosure

13.22

The mere fact that a disclosure is a qualifying disclosure within the meaning of S.43B ERA is not sufficient to confer statutory protection on a worker who blows the whistle at work. The disclosure must also be made in the correct manner. The seven permissible methods of disclosure are set out in Ss.43C–43H. These are:

- disclosure to the employer – S.43C(1)(a)

493

- disclosure to the person responsible for the relevant failure – S.43C(1)(b)

- disclosure to a legal adviser – S.43D

- disclosure to a Minister of the Crown – S.43E

- disclosure to a prescribed person – S.43F

- external disclosure in other cases – S.43G

- disclosure of exceptionally serious failures – S.43H.

As explained below, the statutory provisions construct a tiered disclosure regime. The tiers are defined by the comparative ease with which a worker gains protection depending on the person or body to whom the disclosure is made. A worker who makes a qualifying disclosure to his or her employer, a legal adviser or a Minister of the Crown will have fewer hoops to jump through in order to secure protection than someone who makes a disclosure to a complete outsider. Between these extremes lies an intermediate tier covering disclosure to any third party whom the worker believes to be responsible for the relevant failure and disclosure to a person or body who has been statutorily prescribed by an order made by the Secretary of State for the purpose of receiving protected disclosures about specific types of malpractice or wrongdoing.

13.23 **Good faith**

Apart from disclosures to legal advisers made in accordance with S.43D (see below), all qualifying disclosures must be made in 'good faith' – Ss.43C, 43E–43H. A failure to show good faith will mean that the disclosure is not protected. Unfortunately, the meaning of this all-important requirement is not spelled out anywhere in the relevant statutory provisions. However, it is clearly directed towards an assessment of the motives of the worker in making the disclosure.

In legal terms, 'good faith' has long been equated with 'acting honestly' or 'acting with honest motives'. Thus the intention behind imposing a requirement of good faith is presumably to ensure that the worker's motivation for disclosing the information is an honest one. If the worker's main intention or desire is to cause harm or to advance a personal grudge, or there is some other ulterior motive, then he or she will not be protected.

13.24 **Grudges, personal antagonism and ulterior motives.** The leading case on the good faith requirement is Street v Derbyshire Unemployed Workers' Centre 2004 ICR 213, EAT. There the claimant, who was an administrator at an unemployment advice centre, wrote to the treasurer of the local authority making detailed allegations of corruption against a senior manager at the centre. She also wrote a letter in similar vein to an elected councillor. Following an investigation into the claimant's allegations, the accused manager was fully exonerated. The employer commenced disciplinary proceedings against the applicant, which culminated in her dismissal for breach of trust and confidence. Her claim of

494

unfair dismissal under S.103A foundered on the fact that she was found to have lacked the necessary good faith when making the disclosures to the two external parties. The tribunal found that the claimant's principal motivation was personal antagonism towards the senior manager. On appeal, the EAT ruled that the tribunal had been entitled to reach this conclusion. In so holding, the Appeal Tribunal pointed out that there were few areas in which the judgment of an employment tribunal is more fact-sensitive than in assessing the issue of good faith in the context of protected disclosures. In the EAT's words: 'It is not... the purpose of the Public Interest Disclosure Act to allow grudges to be promoted and disclosures to be made in order to advance personal antagonism. It is, as the [Act's title] implies, to be used in order to promote the public interest. The advancement of a grudge is inimical to that purpose.'

13.25 The EAT's ruling that the advancement of a grudge is inimical to the purpose of the PIDA provisions has been subject to criticism by those who believe it is important that malpractice and wrongdoing are brought to light regardless of the motivation of the person making the disclosure. However, in the absence of an amendment to the statutory provisions, the good faith requirement cannot be sidestepped because of the importance of the information being disclosed, and tribunals have no option but to examine a claimant's motives where bad faith is alleged. The task for tribunals is particularly difficult where – as is often the case – the claimant has mixed motives. In such circumstances, the tribunal must attempt to work out the principal, or dominant, motivation for the claimant's disclosure. Two cases where the tribunal found that disclosures were not made in good faith:

- **Ray v Fish Brothers (Swindon) Ltd** ET Case No.1400838/08: R suggested to a female colleague, M, that she (M) had suffered sexual harassment as a result of a comment made by a male colleague, N, to the effect that she should take off her wet trousers and hang them over a radiator to dry. M told R that N had not made the remark, and in any event she did not consider she was being sexually harassed. Despite this response, R complained to his manager that M had been sexually harassed by N. The manager investigated but took no further action, considering there was nothing to R's complaints. R then complained about the sexual harassment to the group HR manager, who again found no substance in the complaints. When R was subsequently disciplined for having deliberately made malicious allegations, he claimed that he had been subjected to a detriment for having made a protected disclosure. However, the tribunal considered that R's predominant motive in making the allegations was not his desire to protect M or alert the company to a potentially dangerous situation, but his dislike of N. It followed that his disclosure was not made in good faith and did not enjoy statutory protection

- **Smith and ors v Ministry of Defence** ET Case No.1401537/04: S and six colleagues had made disclosures to the press indicating that a security guard with whom they worked was a convicted sex offender and was working in

495

a role where he might have to evacuate children from a nursery in the event of a fire. The tribunal concluded that it was primarily the claimants' strong revulsion at having to work with T that governed their actions. If they had been primarily concerned for the children's safety, they would not have taken their concerns to the press. They would have used the MoD's whistleblowing or grievance procedure, or approached the nursery or Ofsted. The tribunal noted that for good faith to be present in a disclosure to the press, there would need to be features which were lacking in this case, such as a high degree of urgency or an inability to raise concerns properly through other avenues.

13.26   **Burden of proof and weight of evidence.** The question of whether there is a burden of proof in respect of the good faith requirement, and if so where that burden lies, was not specifically dealt with in Street v Derbyshire Unemployed Workers' Centre 2004 ICR 213, EAT. However, in Lucas v Chichester Diocesan Housing Association Ltd EAT 0713/04 the EAT pointed towards there being a burden on the employer but did not definitively decide the issue, instead offering views on the approach tribunals should take to the evidence of bad faith. In that case, L had raised concerns about financial irregularities in the way a manager, M, was running a project. M expressed anger about the allegations and a week later L's hours and earnings were reduced. She raised the concerns again, following which she was dismissed because her 'strained relationship' with colleagues was having an adverse effect on the project. The tribunal dismissed L's claim under S.103A on the basis that she had made the allegations to spite M rather than to promote the public interest and had therefore failed to satisfy the good faith requirement.

On appeal, the EAT stated that, where it is argued that a disclosure was not made in good faith, a tribunal 'must consider all the evidence and decide for itself whether the dominant or predominant motive is an ulterior one'. The evidence supporting the argument that the disclosure was made in bad faith must be cogent, since 'bad faith is a surprising and unusual feature of working relationships'. As in all cases where improper motivation is alleged, the allegation should be made explicit in advance and should be put squarely to the claimant. In particular, the chronology of events and the impression given by witnesses are very important in such cases.

Turning to the facts of the case, the Appeal Tribunal concluded that there had been no grounds for the tribunal's finding that L's disclosures had not been made in good faith. The contention that L had been motivated by personal antagonism had neither been mentioned in the employer's response nor put to L in cross-examination at the hearing. Moreover, with regard to the argument that L's action had been motivated by spite towards M owing to the reduction in her hours, L had not been informed of that reduction until after she had first made the relevant disclosures. In the EAT's view, the disclosures had clearly been based on the very real and, as it turned out, substantiated financial irregularities that L had encountered.

The question of where the burden of proof lies was returned to in Bachnak v Emerging Markets Partnership (Europe) Ltd EAT 0288/05 where the EAT, having considered the Lucas judgment, rejected the contention that the burden of proof in respect of good/bad faith is a neutral one. It concluded that it is for the respondent to prove that the disclosure was made in bad faith.

Disclosure to employer 13.27

A qualifying disclosure that is made to the worker's employer will be a protected disclosure so long as it is made in good faith – S.43C(1)(a). The requirement of good faith is discussed in detail in the section immediately above. As mentioned previously, S.43C(1)(a) disclosures – along with disclosures to legal advisers under S.43D and disclosures made by employees of statutory bodies to a Minister of the Crown under S.43E – are subject to the least stringent conditions so far as the worker is concerned.

Meaning of employer. Although protection from unfair dismissal under S.103A 13.28 is only afforded to 'employees', it is necessary for present purposes to briefly consider the extended definitions of 'worker' and 'employer' that apply to Part IVA ERA (the protected disclosure provisions). The reason for this is that, following BP plc v Elstone and anor 2010 ICR 879, EAT (see below under 'Reason for dismissal'), it is possible for an employee to be unfairly dismissed for having made a protected disclosure to a previous employer. Such an employee would qualify for protection from unfair dismissal even if, at the time he or she made the disclosure, she was a worker under the extended definition, not an employee.

A 'worker' under S.230(3) ERA includes employees, apprentices, and individuals who provide personal services under any contract, whether of employment or otherwise, as long as the party to whom the personal service is provided is not a client or customer. S.43K(1) provides that, for the purposes of the protected disclosure provisions, the term 'worker' also includes individuals who are not covered by S.230(3) but who fall into one of the following categories:

- agency and similar workers: any individual who is or was introduced by a third party (i.e. agency) and the terms of his or her engagement are or were substantially determined not by the individual but by the third person or the client of the third person or both – S.43K(1)(a)

- homeworkers, freelancers and similar individuals: any individual whose workplace is not under the control or management of the employer but who would fall within the ordinary definition of 'worker' in S.230(3) were it not for the requirement that he or she personally perform the work or services for the employer – S.43K(1)(b)

- health workers: any individual who works or worked as a person performing services under a contract entered into by him or her with a Primary Care Trust (in England), a Local Health Board (in Wales), or a Health Board (in Scotland) – S.43K(1)(ba), (bb) and (ca)

- National Health Service practitioners: any individual who provides general medical services, general dental services, general ophthalmic services or pharmaceutical services under arrangements made with a Primary Care Trust, Local Health Board or Health Board – S.43K(1)(c)

- trainees: any individual who is not an employee under a contract of employment but who is nevertheless provided with work experience as part of a training course or programme or is provided with training for employment (or both), except in cases where the course is run by an 'educational establishment' (which includes any university, college or school) – S.43K(1)(d) and (3).

13.29 Section 43K(2) provides a corresponding definition of 'employer'. In the case of agency workers, it includes the person who substantially determines or determined the terms on which the worker was engaged; for health workers and NHS professionals it includes the Primary Care Trust, Local Health Board or Health Board; and in the case of trainees, it includes the person providing the work or training. This extended definition may be relevant in determining whether, in a particular case, a disclosure was made to the worker's employer. In Douglas v Birmingham City Council and ors EAT 0518/02, for example, a disclosure made by a classroom assistant to the school board of governors was held to be a disclosure by a worker to her employer having regard to the extended definitions that apply to the words 'worker' and 'employer' under Part IVA.

There is some doubt as to whom, within a company or organisation, a disclosure should be made in order for it to be regarded as having been made to the worker's employer. The statutory provisions are silent on this issue. However, a sensible construction of S.43C(1)(a) would surely be that a disclosure made to any person senior to the worker with express or implied authority over the worker should be regarded as having been made to the employer. A disclosure made to a junior colleague or even one of equal status, on the other hand, would be unlikely to be covered. Where a dispute arises as to whether a disclosure was made to the appropriate person, the employment tribunal would undoubtedly pay close attention to the provisions of any relevant whistleblowing policy.

13.30 **Disclosure to persons designated by a whistleblowing policy.** By virtue of S.43C(2), a worker who, in accordance with an authorised procedure, makes a qualifying disclosure to a person other than his or her employer is to be treated for the purposes of Part IVA as making the qualifying disclosure to the employer. The intention behind this is to enable an employer, via a whistleblowing policy, to designate a person or body as having authority to receive qualifying disclosures and the legal effect of a disclosure made in accordance with such designation will be the same as that of a disclosure made directly to the employer.

Does subject matter have to relate to the employer? Nothing in the statutory provisions requires a qualifying disclosure to relate to the conduct of the employer in order for that disclosure to come within S.43C(1)(a). It is axiomatic that it is far less likely that an employer would victimise a worker for making a disclosure about matters of no direct or indirect concern to the employer. But if a worker were to be subject to victimisation in these circumstances, he or she would not lose the protection of the statutory provisions simply because the relevant failure about which the disclosure was made was not that of the employer.

13.31

Disclosure to person responsible for relevant failure

13.32

Section 43C(1)(b) provides that 'a qualifying disclosure is made in accordance with this section if the worker makes the disclosure... where the worker reasonably believes that the relevant failure relates solely or mainly to (i) the conduct of a person other than his employer, or (ii) any other matter for which a person other than his employer has legal responsibility, to that other person'. Although this provision is very closely allied to disclosures made to the employer under S.43C(1)(a), it is, in reality, a separate means by which a qualifying disclosure can be made. The focus is on a third party who is responsible (or perceived to be so by the worker) for the relevant failure about which the disclosure is made.

As with disclosures to the employer, disclosures under S.43C(1)(b) must be made in good faith. There is, however, an additional requirement: the worker must 'reasonably believe' that the relevant failure relates to the conduct of the third party or another matter for which that party has legal responsibility.

To our knowledge, the only appellate decision concerning the application of S.43C(1)(b) is Premier Mortgage Connections Ltd v Miller EAT 0113/07. In that case M claimed that she had been unfairly dismissed under S.103A for having informed a former director of PMC Ltd of her concerns that substantial sums of money were being wrongly appropriated to another organisation in which one of the remaining directors was involved. An employment tribunal found, among other things, that the disclosure was protected because it concerned events that took place when the former director had legal responsibility for financial matters at PMC Ltd. The employer appealed, arguing that the statutory provisions do not go so far as to cover disclosure to persons who once had legal responsibility for a relevant failure.

On appeal, the EAT considered that S.43C(1)(b) 'is directed to protecting a disclosure which the employee reasonably believes is made to the person who

13.33

499

has ongoing legal responsibility for dealing with it at the time the disclosure is made. The language of the statute is in the present tense.' Thus, it is outside the scope of the statutory provisions to disclose relevant failings to a person who once had, but no longer has, legal responsibility for that failing. Turning to the matter of reasonable belief, the EAT thought it appropriate for tribunals to construe this requirement subjectively, in line with the construction given in Babula v Waltham Forest College 2007 ICR 1026, CA, to the phrase 'in the reasonable belief of the worker' that appears in S.43B(1) (see under 'Qualifying disclosures' above). It was apparent that the tribunal had not considered whether, at the time she made the disclosures, M reasonably believed that the former director was still legally responsible for the relevant failure, and so the case was remitted for it to consider that matter.

It is clear from the EAT's decision in the Premier Mortgage case that a tribunal should not make its own assessment of whether a worker could have held a reasonable belief that the third party was solely or mainly responsible for the relevant failure. S.43C(1)(b) focuses on the *actual* worker's belief, and so long as there is some rational basis for the worker believing that a third party was responsible for the relevant failure, that should be enough to confer protection on the worker, irrespective of whether that belief was correct.

13.34 ## Disclosure to legal adviser

Where a disclosure is made 'in the course of obtaining legal advice', it will be protected under S.43D. There is no requirement in these circumstances for disclosure to be made 'in good faith', making this particular method of disclosure unique in this regard. The reason for this is obvious. Anyone is entitled to consult a legal adviser regarding his or her rights and it would be a gross infringement of that entitlement if a worker were to be inhibited from doing so due to his or her motives. Disclosures are liable to be made in the course of giving instructions to a legal adviser where the worker specifically seeks advice concerning a whistleblowing problem. S.43D therefore ensures that if a worker suffers victimisation at the hands of the employer merely for making a disclosure to a legal adviser, he or she will be entitled to the statutory protection conferred by the whistleblowing provisions.

The term 'legal adviser' only appears in the heading of S.43D, and there is no statutory definition of 'legal advice' for these purposes. Clearly disclosures to qualified lawyers, made in the course of obtaining legal advice (as opposed to a non-professional context), are covered by S.43D. The situation is less clear, however, in respect of CAB workers or non-legally-qualified advisers. It would seem risky to assume that disclosures to any kind of lay adviser would automatically be protected under S.43D. Notably, Government Ministers who piloted the Public Interest Disclosure Bill through Parliament were adamant that trade union officials who give advice

500

to their members would not fall within S.43D if qualifying disclosures were made to them in the course of giving such advice.

Disclosure to Minister of the Crown

13.35

Section 43E provides that where a worker's employer is an individual appointed by a Minister of the Crown under any enactment, or a body whose members are so appointed, a qualifying disclosure will be protected if it is made in good faith to a Minister of the Crown. The good faith requirement has been discussed in detail under 'Good faith' above. To come within S.43E, a disclosure could presumably be made to any appropriate person within the Minister's department.

The scope of S.43E embraces public bodies and individuals appointed under statute. Such persons/bodies include the utility regulators, statutory quangos (i.e. executive non-departmental public bodies and NHS bodies), the National Lottery Regulator, the Equality and Human Rights Commission and statutory tribunals. Permitting disclosures to be made to a Minister recognises the fact that, in reality, sponsoring ministerial departments retain substantial control and influence over statutory bodies and individuals appointed under statute. It is appropriate, therefore, to allow workers to make disclosures concerning malpractice and wrongdoing to the Minister as an alternative to (or in addition to) making disclosures to their employer.

Disclosure to prescribed persons

13.36

Section 43F provides that qualifying disclosures made in good faith to a prescribed person will be protected under the statutory scheme. This method of making protected disclosures comprises something of a halfway house between internal disclosures made to a worker's own employer on the one hand and external disclosures made to an outside body such as the police or the press on the other. The conditions are, as a result, more stringent than those applying to internal disclosures but substantially less onerous than apply in the case of external disclosures.

A qualifying disclosure to a prescribed person or body is protected under S.43F so long as the worker meets all of the following conditions:

- the disclosure is made in good faith
- it is made to a person prescribed in an order made by the Secretary of State
- the worker reasonably believes that the relevant failure falls within any description of matters in respect of which that person is so prescribed
- the worker reasonably believes that the information disclosed, and any allegation contained in it, is substantially true.

If these conditions are met, then protection will be conferred in respect of the disclosure even if the worker has not previously made the disclosure to his or

501

her employer. Where, however, a worker has raised his or her concerns internally with the employer first, a tribunal is likely to take into account the employer's response in assessing the reasonableness of the worker's belief in the veracity of the allegation.

13.37 Attention should be drawn to the words 'substantially true' used in S.43F. The word 'substantially' appears to require the worker to believe on a rational basis that the majority of the information contained within the disclosure is true. If he or she reasonably believes that only elements of the allegation are accurate, the worker may well find it difficult to convince a tribunal that this condition has been met. The same would be true if the worker's allegation was to the effect that there was habitual malpractice or wrongdoing on a large number of occasions. If the worker's evidence deals only with one or two such occasions, there is a danger that the tribunal will conclude that he or she did not reasonably believe that the allegation was substantially true. This would not matter in the case of an internal disclosure to the employer, since such a belief is not a precondition for making a protected disclosure under S.43C(1)(a). It does matter, however, where the disclosure is made to a prescribed person pursuant to S.43F.

It is important to note that a qualifying disclosure to a prescribed person or body will only be protected if the disclosure is directed to the *appropriate* person or body, depending on the subject matter of the disclosure. Each of the prescribed bodies and persons set out in the relevant statutory list (details of which are given below) has a corresponding list of matters in respect of which it is prescribed. In effect, each body has a 'jurisdiction' over specific matters and a worker is only entitled to make a disclosure to a specific person or body if the relevant failure falls within that jurisdiction.

13.38 **Prescribed persons.** The Schedule to the Public Interest Disclosure (Prescribed Persons) Order 1999 SI 1999/1549 (as amended by the Public Interest Disclosure (Prescribed Persons) (Amendment) Order 2009 SI 2009/2457) lists all prescribed persons and matters in respect of which those persons are prescribed. Among the 50 bodies and persons listed are the Audit Commission; the Certification Officer; the Charity Commissioners; the Civil Aviation Authority; the Commissioners of Customs and Excise and the Inland Revenue; the Director of the Serious Fraud Office; the Environment Agency; the Food Standards Agency; the Financial Services Authority; the Children's Commissioner; the Health and Safety Executive; the Information Commissioner; the Pensions Regulator; the Office of Fair Trading; the Rail Regulator; the Secretary of State for Business, Innovation and Skills; the Secretary of State for Transport; the Treasury; and local authorities responsible for the enforcement of health and safety, food standards and consumer protection legislation.

Given that the bodies listed in the Schedule are liable to undergo changes of name or be replaced by different bodies with similar functions, the 1999 Order makes provision for any successor body automatically to become prescribed for the purposes of S.43F. Thus, the final category of person prescribed is 'a person ("person A") carrying out functions, by virtue of legislation, relating to relevant failures falling within one or more matters within a description of matters in respect of which another person ("person B") is prescribed by this Order, where person B was previously responsible for carrying out the same or substantially similar functions and has ceased to be so responsible'.

One question that has arisen is whether a worker can rely on S.43F where the disclosure was made to a regulator who was added to the list after the disclosure was made. This matter was addressed by the Court of Session in Miklaszewicz v Stolt Offshore Ltd 2002 IRLR 344, Ct Sess (Inner House). In that case, the claimant made a disclosure of information concerning a tax scam to tax inspectors several years before the Revenue was designated a 'prescribed person' for the purposes of S.43F. The Court of Session held that the disclosure was nevertheless a 'protected disclosure' under that provision because the statutory provisions protecting workers from being dismissed for making protected disclosures bite not on the original act of making the disclosure but on the act of the employer in dismissing the worker. Therefore, provided that the person to whom the disclosure was made has been prescribed for the purposes of S.43F by the date of the dismissal, the criteria for claiming unfair dismissal for having made a protected disclosure under S.103A will have been satisfied. **13.39**

It should be noted that the police are *not* on the list of prescribed bodies or persons. Therefore, a worker who discloses an allegation of criminal wrongdoing to the police will not be making a protected disclosure pursuant to S.43F. In order for such a disclosure to be protected, the worker would have to satisfy the stringent conditions for external disclosures to outside bodies specified in S.43G or, if the matter concerns an 'exceptionally serious failure', the slightly less stringent conditions set out in S.43H. These are discussed below.

External disclosure in other cases
13.40

The range of persons (or organisations) to whom an external disclosure can be made is vast. It includes the police, the press, MPs, union officials, professional bodies, non-prescribed regulators (i.e. those who are not prescribed persons under S.43F), relatives of patients at risk, shareholders, non-executive directors, contracting parties to commercial contracts and pressure groups.

Where a worker decides to make a disclosure to an external organisation, the most stringent rules apply. In order to gain protection under the Act, he or she will have to satisfy five conditions set out in S.43G:

- the worker must have made the qualifying disclosure in good faith – S.43G(1)(a)

- he or she must reasonably believe that the information disclosed, and any allegation contained in it, is substantially true – S.43G(1)(b)

503

- the worker must not have made the disclosure for the purposes of personal gain – S.43G(1)(c)

- one of the conditions in S.43G(2) must have been met (see below) – S.43G(1)(d), and

- in all the circumstances of the case, it must be reasonable to make the disclosure – S.43G(1)(e).

13.41 In effect, these five conditions fall into three distinct categories. The first three relate to the quality of evidence underpinning the worker's belief that a relevant failure has occurred and to his or her motives for making the disclosure. The fourth condition requires that one of three grounds for making an external disclosure applies. And the fifth imposes an overarching requirement that, having regard to all the circumstances of the case, the making of the disclosure to an outside party was a reasonable thing to do.

The requirements of good faith and the worker's reasonable belief are identical to those in respect of disclosure to prescribed persons (considered under 'Good faith' and 'Disclosure to prescribed persons' above), and do not warrant further analysis here. The remaining three requirements are considered in turn below.

13.42 **Personal gain.** A unique requirement in respect of external disclosures is that the employee must not have disclosed the information for the purposes of gain – S.43G(1)(c). This provision is aimed at discouraging cheque-book journalism by seeking to ensure that the worker's primary motives for making a disclosure are the public good, rather than personal gain. It should be noted, however, that S.43G(1)(c) does not outlaw personal gain per se. The issue is not whether the worker made a personal gain but whether his or her *purpose* in making the disclosure was to make a personal gain. If the whistleblower happens to be paid for making a disclosure to the press but he or she can show that the purpose of the disclosure was, say, to highlight criminal activities or health and safety fears, then protection for that disclosure will not necessarily be lost. In any case, payments in these cases are often made at the worker's request to his or her family or to a charity. In these circumstances, can it be said that the worker's motive was to personally gain from the disclosure?

In any event, any statutory reward payable in respect of disclosure has to be disregarded – S.43L(2). Occasionally, provision is made in legislation to enable statutory agencies to make payments as a reward for useful information supplied. The Inland Revenue, for example, operates such a practice. Any such payment would not prejudice a worker's protection under S.43G even if the prospect of the reward was the main motivating factor behind the disclosure.

One final point to note: S.43G(1)(c) simply states that a worker must not make the disclosure for purposes of personal gain. This leaves open the question of how to treat mixed motives. What if the worker's motives are to gain personally from the disclosure *and* to bring to light something which it would be in the public's interest to know? In the absence of guidance from the courts on this matter, we are of the view that the approach for determining the 'personal gain' issue should be the same as that for determining whether the worker has acted in good faith when making the disclosure. Thus, where there are mixed motives, the worker would be denied statutory protection under S.43G only if it were shown that his or her *primary* motivation for making the disclosure was to gain personally from it.

Satisfying one of the additional conditions in S.43G(2). Section 43G(1)(d) requires that *one* of three additional conditions specified in S.43G(2) be met. These additional conditions are that:

13.43

- at the time of the disclosure, the worker reasonably believes that he or she will be subjected to a detriment by raising the concern with the employer in accordance with S.43C or a prescribed person in accordance with S.43F – S.43G(2)(a)

- where no person is prescribed in accordance with S.43F in relation to the relevant failure, the worker reasonably believes that it is likely that evidence will be concealed or destroyed if he or she makes a disclosure to the employer – S.43G(2)(b)

- the worker has previously made a disclosure of substantially the same information, either (i) to his or her employer or (ii) to a prescribed person for the purposes of S.43F – S.43G(2)(c).

The first two conditions concern the situation where the worker perceives a threat – either to himself or to relevant evidence – and will require a tribunal to consider whether the worker reasonably believed in that threat. It seems fair to assume that the test of reasonableness in these circumstances is largely subjective – see under 'Disclosure to person responsible for relevant failure' above. The third condition does not import any test of reasonableness, and instead hinges on the worker being able to demonstrate that the information is not being disclosed for the first time. In Bruckner v Rail Training International Ltd ET Case No.3300396/08, for example, B had raised as a grievance with his employer the issue of his place of work as stated in his employment contract – it listed the office of his employer's former accountants. When his grievance was rejected, he sent a redacted version of his employment contract, including the stated place of work, to the accountants. The tribunal was satisfied that he was disclosing information which was substantially the same as he had originally disclosed to the employer.

13.44

'Reasonable in all the circumstances'. Assuming the worker has successfully jumped through all the various hoops imposed up to this point by S.43G(1), there is one final overriding requirement that must be met. It must be shown that, in all the circumstances of the case, it was reasonable for the worker to have made the external disclosure – S.43G(1)(e).

13.45

505

The assessment of reasonableness in this context is a matter for the tribunal, based on its own objective judgment. In reaching its decision, there are six criteria it must take into account. These are:

- the identity of the person to whom the disclosure is made – S.43G(3)(a)

- the seriousness of the relevant failure – S.43G(3)(b)

- whether the relevant failure is continuing or is likely to recur – S.43G(3)(c)

- whether the disclosure is made in breach of a duty of confidentiality owed by the employer to any other person – S.43G(3)(d)

- in the case of a previous disclosure to the worker's employer or a prescribed person, the response of the employer or prescribed person – S.43G(3)(e); and

- in the case of a previous disclosure to the worker's employer, whether the worker complied with an internal procedure authorised by the employer – S.43G(3)(f).

In Bruckner v Rail Training International Ltd (above), the tribunal found that it was reasonable in all the circumstances for an employee to have made a disclosure to his employer's former accountants, tending to show that the employer was falsely listing their offices as his place of work. The accountants were closely linked to the relevant failing; the failing on the part of the employer was serious; no duty of confidentiality prevented the employee from making the disclosure; the employer had no internal procedure to speak of; and the response of the employer to the original disclosure clearly demonstrated that the relevant failure (the listing of a false address) was likely to continue.

13.46 Exceptionally serious failures

The stringent rules on external disclosures to non-prescribed persons are relaxed somewhat in cases concerning 'exceptionally serious' failures – see S.43H. For a qualifying disclosure to fall within this section, the following conditions must be met:

- the worker must make the disclosure in good faith – S.43H(1)(a)

- he or she must reasonably believe that the information disclosed, and any allegation contained in it, is substantially true – S.43H(1)(b)

- the worker must not have made the disclosure for the purposes of personal gain – S.43H(1)(c)

- the relevant failure must be of an exceptionally serious nature – S.43H(1)(d), and

- in all the circumstances of the case, it must be reasonable to make the disclosure – S.43H(1)(e).

Section 43H(2) goes on to provide that, in determining for the purposes of S.43H(1)(e) whether it was reasonable for the worker to make the disclosure, regard must be had, in particular, to the identity of the person to whom the disclosure was made. (This contrasts with S.43G above, where a tribunal considering the disclosure of failures which are not exceptionally serious must have regard to six factors in determining whether it was reasonable for the worker to make the disclosure.)

Meaning of 'exceptionally serious'. There is no statutory guidance as to what is meant by an 'exceptionally serious failure'. The wording implies something that is of extreme public concern, and it is clear that successful cases under this section will be rare. An example of an exceptionally serious failure might be where a disclosure is made to the police regarding sexual abuse at a children's home, or to a newspaper about reckless or negligent maintenance of railway track. Two cases: **13.47**

- **Collins v The National Trust** ET Case No.2507255/05: C was employed by the National Trust as head warden of part of a coastal strip. This area included a piece of land which had been transferred to the Trust by the local Council. In 1999, the Trust discovered that the transferred land was contaminated with asbestos and a dispute arose between the Council and the Trust as to who was legally liable for action to be taken in respect of the site. A draft report was prepared by the Council concluding that the site was a potential hazard to the public and recommended that remedial work be carried out. The Trust informed its staff that a 'holding' statement would be released to the press, and that all enquiries should be referred to a specific individual. However, C decided to leak the report to a local newspaper and he was subsequently dismissed for breaching the Trust's press protocol. The tribunal held that C had made a qualifying disclosure which was protected by S.43H. The relevant failures – namely, the damage to the environment, the endangerment of public health and safety and the concealment of information – were of an exceptionally serious nature. Furthermore, in the tribunal's view, it had been reasonable for C to make the disclosure to the press, as this enabled the public to obtain further specialist advice about the problem

- **Bolkavac v DynCorp Aerospace Operations (UK) Ltd** ET Case No.3102729/01: B worked as a police monitor, under the control of the United Nations, in Bosnia. She became deeply concerned about the trafficking of women and girls for prostitution by organised criminal gangs and believed that police monitors and their superiors were not taking the problem seriously. As a result she sent a memo to about 50 people working for her employer and for the United Nations about the issue containing graphic details. She also implied in the memo that many of its recipients were habitués of brothels. B was subsequently dismissed and she claimed that her memo was a protected disclosure and she had been dismissed because of it. A tribunal upheld her claim. It ruled that B's concerns had to be set in the context of a grave

507

humanitarian situation involving the exploitation and enslavement of women by criminals. The tribunal had no hesitation in finding that the failure of some elements of the UN administration to get an adequate grip on the situation and do something about it was of an exceptionally serious nature satisfying the requirements of S.43H. B had made the disclosure in good faith, had reasonably believed the content of it to be true and had not made it for personal gain. As to whether, in all the circumstances of the case, it was reasonable for B to make the disclosure, the tribunal noted that she had not continued to raise the matter with her employer or with senior officials in the UN's International Police Task Force because they had either already been alerted to her concerns or had intimated that they did not share her views about the seriousness of the issue. The tribunal concluded that, in the circumstances of the case, it had been reasonable for B to make an external disclosure to a wide audience and that the disclosure was protected under S.43H. She was subsequently awarded £110,000 by way of compensation.

13.48 A decision that went the other way was Holbrook v Queen Mary's Sidcup NHS Trust ET Case No.1101904/06. H had been employed as a junior radiographer. In January 2006, he was on duty when two patients were brought into accident and emergency with injuries sustained from a road traffic accident. One of the patients was a police officer in uniform and H formed the impression that the officer had been drinking. H dialled 999 and anonymously reported his suspicion to the police. He was eventually dismissed for breaching patient confidentiality. The tribunal rejected H's claim that his qualifying disclosure was protected under S.43H. This was because it was not reasonable in the circumstances for him to have made the disclosure. Among other things, he had not consulted with more senior staff before making the disclosure, which was, in the tribunal's opinion, 'a serious error of judgement'.

13.49 ## Reason for dismissal

As stated at the outset of this chapter, S.103A ERA provides that a dismissal will be automatically unfair 'if the reason (or, if more than one, the principal reason) for the dismissal is that the employee made a protected disclosure'. It is important to note that this protection is accorded to 'employees' only – i.e. individuals who have entered into or work or worked under a contract of employment – S.230(1) ERA. This includes apprentices working under a contract of apprenticeship – S.230(2) – but not other types of 'worker' as defined under the protected disclosure provisions.

Workers who are not employees are limited to bringing claims under S.47B, i.e. claims that they have suffered a detriment on the ground of making a protected disclosure. However, unlike employees, they can claim that a dismissal

508

constitutes a 'detriment' for these purposes. Employees are prohibited from doing so by virtue of S.47B(2).

While a S.103A claim depends on there having been an employment relationship between the claimant and respondent, the protected disclosure need not have had any direct connection to the employer. The statutory language of S.103A would, for example, appear to cover an employee who makes a protected disclosure regarding environmental damage by company A, and is then dismissed by his employer, company B, which is angered by the tightening of the regulatory climate in the wake of the employee's disclosure. This is demonstrated by the following case, which was brought under the detriment provisions in S.47B:

13.50

- **BP plc v Elstone and anor** 2010 ICR 879, EAT: while employed by P Ltd, E made a number of disclosures concerning health and safety to senior BP managers regarding BP contracts that he was involved with. In 2008, he was dismissed by P Ltd for gross misconduct on the ground that he had disclosed confidential information. Three days later, he joined BP as a consultant. However, while he was in discussion about further consultancy work, BP told him that it was no longer prepared to engage him at all because it had learned from P Ltd that he had been dismissed for disclosing confidential information. He brought a detriment claim against BP, arguing that the decision not to offer him further work was reached on the ground that he had made a protected disclosure. In the view of both the tribunal and the EAT, the legislation clearly states that protected disclosures can only occur where there is an employment relationship (within the wider definition of employment). However, both were agreed that there is nothing in the statutory wording that suggests that this must be the same employment relationship in which the employee was subjected to the detriment. Furthermore, given the aims of the legislation – to encourage responsible whistleblowing and protect whistleblowers – there can be no grounds for a court or tribunal to insert such a requirement.

Causation

13.51

Although the wording of Ss.47B and 103A is different, both only render the employer's action unlawful where that action was done because the employee or worker had made a protected disclosure. In effect, both sections require a test of causation to be satisfied.

This all-important element of causation is likely to be the focus of most protected disclosure claims where the disclosure has been made internally to the employer. As we saw above under 'Method of disclosure', the hurdles that have to be overcome in respect of such disclosures are comparatively low compared with disclosures to external persons or bodies. As a result, it is relatively easy for an employee to make protected disclosures in the course of his or her employment even if, at the time, neither the employee nor the employer appreciates that this has happened. Take, for example, a disciplinary hearing being conducted into an allegation that the employee has committed an act of misconduct. If, during that hearing, the

509

employee were to disclose in good faith that a senior manager was fiddling his expenses, that would be likely to amount to a protected disclosure. But would this mean that any action subsequently taken against the employee would be unlawful under S.47B or S.103A? The answer depends on whether the qualifying disclosure was the cause of the detriment or dismissal complained of.

13.52 **Unconscious and conscious reasons for dismissal.** Whistleblower protection is analogous to the victimisation provisions in discrimination legislation, in that both seek to prohibit action taken on the ground of a protected act. This has led courts and tribunals considering claims under Ss.47B and 103A to turn to the substantial body of case law concerning causation under the victimisation provisions for guidance. In Chief Constable of West Yorkshire Police v Khan 2001 ICR 1065, HL – a claim concerning victimisation contrary to S.2(1)(a) of the Race Relations Act 1976 – Lord Nicholls stated that the causation exercise for tribunals is not legal, but factual. A tribunal should ask 'why did the alleged discriminator act as he did? What, consciously or unconsciously, was his reason?'

The Khan approach was expressly approved for the purposes of S.103A in Trustees of Mama East African Women's Group v Dobson EAT 0219–20/05. D had been employed as a teacher by the employer, a charity. She was informed by one of her students that another student – the sister of S, the manager of the college where D taught – had mistreated children in a crèche run by the charity. D reported the allegations to another employee and subsequently brought the matter to the attention of the manager. S conducted an investigation during which she spoke to her sister, other students and parents, as well as the student who, according to D, had made the initial allegations. S concluded that there was no evidence of mistreatment.

13.53 S called D to a disciplinary meeting and informed her that she had acted unprofessionally in reporting unfounded allegations and would be dismissed. In a letter confirming her dismissal for gross misconduct, the trustees identified three reasons for her dismissal: that she had made false allegations; that she had failed to follow proper procedures in reporting those allegations; and that she had breached confidentiality by not reporting the allegations to S in the first instance. An employment tribunal was satisfied that D had made a protected disclosure and that the reason for dismissal was the making of that disclosure. The charity appealed, maintaining that the reason for D's dismissal was not her disclosure, but the reasons set out in the dismissal letter.

In the EAT's view, establishing the reason for dismissal in a S.103A claim requires the tribunal to determine the decision-making process in the mind of the dismissing officer. This requires the tribunal to consider the employer's conscious and unconscious reason for acting as it did. The EAT was satisfied that the tribunal had followed this approach, looked at the reasons advanced by the trustees in the dismissal letter, and made a firm conclusion that the reason for the dismissal was that a protected disclosure had been made. In addition, the Appeal Tribunal agreed with D's submission that it would be contrary to the purpose of the whistleblowing legislation if an employer could put forward an explanation for dismissal which was not the disclosure itself, but something intimately connected with it, in order to avoid liability.

Multiple disclosures. When faced with a case in which the claimant alleges that he or she has made multiple protected disclosures, a tribunal should ask itself whether, taken as a whole, the disclosures were the reason for the dismissal. This was confirmed in El-Megrisi v Azad University (IR) in Oxford EAT 0448/08, where the EAT overturned a tribunal's decision on the basis that it had isolated the last of a series of disclosures, concluded that it was not the reason for dismissal, and gone on to find that the dismissal was because E was an 'obstructive nuisance' who objected to 'questionable' tasks. On the facts of the case, it was clear that the employer's negative view of E was formed because she had made protected disclosures, and that these disclosures, taken cumulatively, were the reason for dismissal.   **13.54**

Disclosing own misconduct. A number of regulatory bodies grant immunity to whistleblowers in respect of their own misconduct. However, no immunity is provided for in the ERA. Accordingly, where an employee discloses information that tends to show, among other things, that he or she has committed misconduct, a subsequent dismissal on the ground of that misconduct will be unlikely to fall foul of S.103A. An example: **13.55**

- **Scarsbrook v London Borough of Waltham Forest** ET Case No.3203294/06: S and a number of colleagues had made a series of protected disclosures about the conduct of two of their managers, G and W. One of the complaints was that G had told S to claim for 23 hours' overtime each month in lieu of any formal acting-up allowance during the absence of a colleague on suspension. This led to an investigation by the Council's anti-fraud team, which, noting that G and W had subsequently left the Council's employment and therefore could not be disciplined, recommended that S be disciplined for having submitted false overtime claims and falsifying fixed penalty notices and trade waste figures. Following a disciplinary hearing, S was dismissed for gross misconduct, whereupon she claimed to have been unfairly dismissed under S.103A. While the tribunal accepted that the information that led to the anti-fraud investigation might not have come to light had S not made her protected disclosure, it did not view this as meaning that she was dismissed because she had made a protected disclosure

Burden of proof   **13.56**

The burden of proof in whistleblowing cases applies in the same way as for most other forms of automatically unfair dismissal and is outlined in Chapter 10 under 'Different rules applicable to automatically unfair dismissals'. Thus, it is for the employer to prove the reason for dismissal. Usually, the employer

511

seeks to discharge this burden by showing that, where dismissal is admitted, the reason for it was one of the potentially fair reasons in S.98(1) and (2) ERA. It will therefore normally be the employee who argues that the real reason for dismissal was an automatically unfair reason. In these circumstances, the employee acquires an evidential burden to show – without having to prove – that there is an issue which warrants investigation and which is capable of establishing the competing automatically unfair reason that he or she is advancing. However, once the employee satisfies the tribunal that there is such an issue, the burden reverts to the employer, who must prove, on the balance of probabilities, which one of the competing reasons was the principal reason for dismissal – Maund v Penwith District Council 1984 ICR 143, CA.

There is an important qualification to the position as described above. Where the employee lacks the requisite one year's continuous service to claim ordinary unfair dismissal, he or she will acquire the burden of proving, on the balance of probabilities, that the reason for dismissal was an automatically unfair reason – Smith v Hayle Town Council 1978 ICR 996, CA, and Tedeschi v Hosiden Besson Ltd EAT 959/95.

13.57 The burden of proof under S.103A was directly addressed in Kuzel v Roche Products Ltd 2008 ICR 799, CA, a case in which the claimant, K, did have the requisite one year's continuous service to claim ordinary unfair dismissal. K brought a claim under S.103A, arguing that she had been dismissed because she had made protected disclosures regarding various regulatory issues. R Ltd's response was that K had been dismissed for 'some other substantial reason': namely, the alleged breakdown in her relationship with her manager, D, and another colleague. The tribunal found that K had been dismissed because D had lost his temper and had failed to follow the HR director's advice. Since this did not amount to a potentially fair reason under S.98 ERA, it followed that the dismissal was unfair. However, the tribunal found that K had not been dismissed for making protected disclosures contrary to S.103A. It stated that there was no evidence supporting K's claim that it was her zeal in pursuing the regulatory issues that led to her dismissal. Indeed, it found that there was evidence of D encouraging and supporting K in the actions she was taking, even if there was a difference in style and approach.

On appeal to the Court of Appeal, Lord Justice Mummery – giving the only reasoned judgment – reiterated that the principles in the Maund and Smith cases (see above) apply to S.103A claims and emphatically rejected the contention that the burden of proof was on K to prove that her making of protected disclosures was the reason for her dismissal. However, Mummery LJ was in agreement with the EAT that, once a tribunal has rejected the reason for dismissal advanced by the employer, it is not bound to accept the reason put forward by the claimant. Though in many cases a tribunal will accept the claimant's reason, there will be cases where, having considered all the evidence, the tribunal concludes that the true reason for dismissal is one which has not been advanced by either party.

512

Drawing inferences. Often there will be a dearth of direct evidence as to an **13.58** employer's motives in deciding to dismiss an employee. Given the importance of establishing a sufficient causal link between the making of the protected disclosure and the dismissal complained of, it may be appropriate for a tribunal in these circumstances to draw inferences as to the real reason for the employer's action on the basis of its principal findings of fact. In Kuzel (above), Mummery LJ endorsed this approach, stating that a tribunal assessing the reason for dismissal can draw 'reasonable inferences from primary facts established by the evidence or not contested in the evidence'. An example:

- **Leonard v Serviceteam Ltd** ET Case No.2306083/01: L, who was employed as a plumber, was required to remedy defects in Council-owned properties in accordance with a service contract between his employer, S Ltd, and the local authority. He became embroiled in a dispute with a senior manager, K, about whether or not he was entitled to leave premises at which he had been working because a tenant had become aggressive. K claimed that L was in breach of contract by deserting the premises and alleged that, during the discussions on the matter, L had resigned. L categorically denied this and tried to resolve the situation by going to more senior levels of management. Initially, a senior HR manager took his part, but his support was withdrawn shortly after L wrote to the company implicating K in a detailed allegation of corruption. The upshot was that S Ltd concluded that L had resigned from his employment. When considering L's claim that he had been unfairly dismissed contrary to S.103A, a tribunal found that he had made a qualifying disclosure in good faith. Turning to the question of whether the principal reason for dismissal was that he had made that disclosure, the tribunal observed that the crucial question was what had caused the HR manager's change of heart. In the tribunal's assessment, S Ltd had failed to provide any explanation as to why the manager had changed his mind about L; and in the absence of any cogent evidence, it was appropriate to infer that the true reason was the content of the letter S Ltd had received and in particular the allegations of corruption made in respect of K. That being the reason why L's contract was terminated, it followed that his dismissal was automatically unfair.

Note, however, that unlike discrimination claims, while it may be appropriate for a tribunal to draw inferences from its findings of fact, a tribunal will never be *obliged* to draw such inferences. In Kuzel, Mummery LJ stated: 'The statutory structure of the unfair dismissal legislation is so different from that of the discrimination legislation that an attempt at cross fertilisation or legal transplants runs a risk of complicating rather than clarifying the legal concepts... there simply is no need to resort to the discrimination legislation in order to ascertain the operation of the burden of proof in unfair dismissal cases.'

513

13.59 **Manner of disclosure**

Tribunals are likely to encounter particular problems when grappling with issues of causation where the employer claims that the dismissal was not imposed by reason of the protected disclosure itself but because of the manner in which the disclosure was made – i.e. that the dismissal was for the potentially fair reason of misconduct. The fact that an employee uses, for example, intemperate language in making a disclosure does not preclude the disclosure from qualifying for protection – see 'Method of disclosure' above. However, where the employer's defence rests on the reason why the particular action against the employee was taken, a tribunal will have to undertake the difficult task of determining whether the employer's reaction to the way in which a disclosure was made can be distinguished from its reaction to the act of making the disclosure.

This problem lay at the heart of the EAT's decision in Hossack v Kettering Borough Council EAT 1113/01. In that case a local authority employed H as a policy research officer to the Conservative Group on the Council. Her line manager, who was the leader of the Conservative Group, had upbraided her on several occasions for acting and speaking as if she were an elected Conservative councillor without clearing her remarks or actions with him first. The problem reached its height when H took it upon herself to contact the district auditor and disclose matters to him that had been specifically deleted by her line manager from a report that she been commissioned to write. As a result she was dismissed and informed that the reasons for dismissal were her lack of judgement and understanding of her role and her clear intention to ignore the formal reporting relationship between herself and her line manager. A tribunal rejected H's claims of detriment and unfair dismissal under Ss.47B and 103A.

On appeal, H argued that, since it was accepted that she had made a protected disclosure, it was not open to the employer to discipline or dismiss her for the 'manner' in which the disclosure was made. To do so would undermine the provisions as to how a disclosure must be made in order for it to gain protection. In her view, so long as there was no evidence of her acting maliciously or in bad faith, her actions as a whole in making the disclosure were protected, which meant that her dismissal for the tone or manner in which she made the disclosure flouted the legislative protection. The EAT roundly rejected this argument. It was not an accurate analysis of the employer's behaviour to assert that H was dismissed for the manner in which she had made the disclosure. The employment tribunal had clearly found that the reason for dismissal was H's inability to differentiate between her role as a research officer (for which she had been employed by the Council) and the role of a member of the Conservative Group or its Leader (which was no part of her job). In the EAT's view, 'the manner in which the [employee] went about the protected disclosure was a manifestation of her inability to understand her advisory role'.

13.60 In Bolton School v Evans 2007 ICR 641, CA, E, a teacher working for the school, had become concerned that a new computer system could be hacked into by students and that this could lead to unauthorised disclosures of confidential

514

information in contravention of the school's obligations under the Data Protection Act 1998. E raised his concerns with two members of staff and the school's Head of ICT agreed that the system should be tested. After decoding the passwords with the help of a former student, E then hacked into the computer system to demonstrate its security failings. Afterwards he informed the headmaster of his actions but failed to tell ICT services, which on discovering the intrusion shut down the entire system, causing losses of £1,000. The headmaster concluded that E had hacked into the system without authority and issued him with a written warning. E resigned, claiming that he had been subjected to a detriment and unfairly constructively dismissed for making a protected disclosure; namely, that he alerted the school to potential breaches of the DPA.

In upholding E's claim, the tribunal concluded that although he had been disciplined for breaking into the computer system, this conduct was not distinct from the disclosure of the information itself, but part and parcel of it. The EAT overturned that finding and E appealed to the Court of Appeal, arguing that the reference to 'any disclosure of information' in S.43B(1)(b) should be given a wide meaning, including both verbal and non-verbal means of communication. In his view, his entire course of conduct – including hacking into the computer system – should be regarded as a continuing act of disclosure. However, the Court of Appeal was not persuaded by E's argument. In its view, there was no reason to think that Parliament intended the word 'disclosure' in S.43B to be given anything other than its ordinary meaning; and the construction of that provision advocated by E was 'highly artificial'. Put simply, E was disciplined for his actions in hacking into the system, and not for informing the school that its system was insecure. Even if E's whole course of conduct amounted to a continuing act of disclosure, said the Court, the fact remained that the school's principal reason for disciplining him was its belief that he had, at the same time as making the disclosure, committed an act of misconduct. In the Court's view, this meant that E's claim under S.103A would fail in any event, as the disclosure was not the reason for the constructive dismissal. The Court observed that, although tribunals should generally be careful when an employer alleges that an employee was dismissed because of acts related to the disclosure and not because of the disclosure itself, in this case the school had had no ulterior motive for its decision to discipline E.

Constructive dismissal   13.61

It is not surprising that many protected disclosure cases brought under S.103A are constructive dismissal cases, given the strained relations that often result when an employee blows the whistle. If the employer reacts in a hostile, provocative or insensitive manner towards an employee who makes a protected disclosure, then it is easy to see how this can lead to claims that the employer has breached the fundamental term of mutual trust and confidence that is implied into every contract of employment.

515

Claimants who allege that they have been unfairly constructively dismissed for making a protected disclosure often also plead a claim of detriment under S.47B. This represents something of a fall-back position in the event that the tribunal finds that the employee resigned for a reason other than the treatment meted out in response to the protected disclosure. An example:

• **Musker v Bowling Green Court (Chester) Ltd** ET Case No.2102073/08: M was employed as a duty manager of sheltered accommodation. She raised concerns that BGC Ltd was offering to provide personal services to residents, which would have been unlawful as BGC Ltd was not registered for those purposes with the Commission for Social Care Inspection. Following M's actions, attitudes towards her changed, and on one occasion another duty manager launched such a verbal attack on M that she went home. She resigned two days later, claiming that she could not continue to work in such a hostile climate, but withdrew the resignation following a grievance hearing. M's relationship with her colleagues did not improve, and she resigned for a second time two months later, claiming that she had been subjected to a detriment and constructively dismissed for having made a protected disclosure. The tribunal was satisfied that the disclosure was protected and that M had suffered a detriment by her colleagues' 'cold' attitude after the disclosure. However, it did not consider that this treatment amounted to a fundamental breach of contract, and so M's constructive dismissal claim was not made out. She was, however, awarded compensation of £4,000 for injury to feelings on account of the detriment she had suffered.

As the case above shows, it is possible to claim compensation for injury to feelings in respect of an unlawful detriment under S.47B, another reason why claimants often choose to include such a complaint in their tribunal claim.

13.62 ## Injury to feelings

In a successful claim under S.103A, there is no cap on the compensation that a tribunal may award – S.124(1A). However, it was reaffirmed by the House of Lords in Dunnachie v Kingston upon Hull City Council 2004 ICR 1052, HL, that compensation for non-financial losses such as injury to feelings cannot be awarded as part of the compensatory award in unfair dismissal cases.

The Dunnachie decision does not necessarily put paid to a claimant's hopes of recovering compensation for injury to feelings, however, as it was confirmed by the EAT in Virgo Fidelis Senior School v Boyle 2004 IRLR 268, EAT, that injury to feelings awards can be made in claims of detriment under S.47B, using the guidelines applicable to awards in discrimination cases set out by the Court of Appeal in Vento v Chief Constable of West Yorkshire Police (No.2) 2003 IRLR 102, CA (and updated in Da'Bell v National Society for the Prevention of Cruelty to Children EAT 0227/09) – see IDS Employment Law Handbook, 'Sex Discrimination' (2008), Chapter 15.

In Melia v Magna Kansei Ltd 2006 ICR 410, CA, M had made a protected disclosure in the form of a grievance about his manager's behaviour in May 2001. In June, MK Ltd took steps to isolate M from his colleagues, changed the security code to the office in which he worked, and instructed security not to allow him access to the workplace. Thereafter, the conduct of the company's investigation of M's grievance led him to conclude that the outcome had been pre-determined against him. He resigned in November and brought successful claims under S.47B and S.103A. In assessing compensation, the tribunal noted that the right not to suffer a detriment under S.47B(1) is excluded by S.47B(2) where the detriment amounts to dismissal. This led it to conclude that the cut-off point for awarding M a sum in respect of injury to feelings was June 2001, as by this stage the employer's actions had amounted to a fundamental breach of contract that would have entitled M to resign and claim constructive dismissal. The EAT upheld the tribunal's decision, but the Court of Appeal took a different view.

13.63

According to the Court of Appeal, the tribunal and the EAT in the instant case had erred in holding that the words 'amount to dismissal' in S.47(B)(2) exclude not only actual dismissal but also the behaviour of the employer which amounts to constructive dismissal, with the result that compensation for the period in which the employer's conduct was in fundamental breach of contract fell to be determined under the unfair dismissal compensation provisions. In the Court of Appeal's view, it is not the employer's conduct of itself that amounts to dismissal in a constructive dismissal case, but the employee's termination of the contract, meaning the claimant's effective date of dismissal was 9 November 2001, the date he resigned in response to his employer's repudiatory breach. Thus the loss for which the claimant could be compensated under the unfair dismissal provisions, being the loss sustained in consequence of the dismissal, was that which he suffered after 9 November 2001 and the detriment sustained *before* that date was not taken out of the scope of S.47B. Accordingly, the claimant was entitled to receive an award for injury to feelings in respect of the whole period up to 9 November 2001.

14 Remedies

When a tribunal finds that a complaint of unfair dismissal is well founded, it **14.1** must decide the appropriate remedy. There are three remedies for unfair dismissal. These, in the order in which tribunals should consider them, are:

- reinstatement – i.e. an order that the employee be reinstated in his or her old job with no financial loss

- re-engagement – i.e. an order that the employee be re-engaged in a job comparable to that from which he or she was dismissed, or in other suitable employment

- compensation – i.e. a monetary award to the employee.

The sequence in which a tribunal must consider these remedies is strict. Thus, when an employee wishes to be re-employed but the tribunal decides not to make an order for reinstatement, it must then move on to consider re-engagement and, failing that, compensation – Ss.112(4) and 116(1) and (2) Employment Rights Act 1996 (ERA). As a result, although the EAT has recommended in the past that a claimant plead both forms of re-employment 'in the alternative' – Arab-British Chamber of Commerce v Saleh EAT 394/88 – this should not really be necessary in practice.

In Telcon Metals Ltd v Henry EAT 287/87 Mr Justice Popplewell emphasised **14.2** that employers would be wrong to think that reinstatement and re-engagement are remedies which tribunals should be slow to consider. On dismissing an employee unfairly, an employer should not imagine that it can simply pay out money to be rid of that employee. Popplewell J stressed that reinstatement and re-engagement are the primary remedies which the legislation directs tribunals to consider before awarding compensation. In reality, though, re-employment orders are very rare. According to the Employment Tribunal and EAT statistics for 2008/09, tribunals upheld 3,935 claims of unfair dismissal, but only made seven orders for reinstatement or re-engagement.

In some cases it is possible for a tribunal to make what amounts to a *declaration* that the employee was unfairly dismissed, but decline to couple this with a reinstatement or re-engagement order or an award of compensation. This might be appropriate where the employee was wholly responsible for his or her dismissal (although the dismissal was nonetheless technically unfair). Or it might occur where gross misconduct by the employee only came to light after the dismissal. In either case, a tribunal can decide that it would not be just and

519

equitable in the circumstances to award any compensation to the employee – see Chapters 15 and 18.

This chapter explains employment tribunals' powers to make reinstatement and re-engagement orders and also describes in outline the types of monetary award that can be made. Chapter 15 deals with basic awards, Chapters 16–18 with compensatory awards and Chapter 19 with additional awards (available where an employer fails to comply with a reinstatement or re-engagement order) and interim relief orders (to keep an employee's contract in being pending the hearing of a claim that he or she was unfairly dismissed on one of the protected grounds specified in S.128(1)(b) ERA).

14.3 ## Reinstatement and re-engagement

Reinstatement under S.113 ERA is the first remedy that a tribunal should consider and it is only if it decides that reinstatement is *not* a suitable remedy that it should go on to consider the alternative remedy of re-engagement – S.116(1) and (2). When a tribunal upholds an unfair dismissal complaint, S.112(2) provides that it must explain its powers to make reinstatement or re-engagement orders under S.113 and ask the claimant if he or she wishes such an order to be made. The remedies the claimant seeks should be stated on the claim form (ET1). However, even if the claimant made no specific request for reinstatement or re-engagement on this form, he or she will not be barred from doing so at the tribunal hearing.

Although the requirements of S.112 are mandatory, a tribunal's failure to explain its powers of reinstatement or re-engagement to the claimant will not necessarily render its decision on compensation a nullity. In Cowley v Manson Timber Ltd 1995 ICR 367, CA, the Court of Appeal held that it all depends on whether the employee has suffered prejudice or injustice as a result of the failure to comply with S.112. In that case the Court ruled that the employee had suffered no injustice – he had been represented at the hearing, his ET1 had stated that he wanted compensation only, and neither he nor his representative had suggested at the hearing that he wished to be re-employed. Nonetheless, failure by a tribunal to explain its powers to award reinstatement or re-engagement should make the EAT more ready to remit the case on the question of remedies where it cannot be shown that the claimant suffered no prejudice or injustice – Constantine v McGregor Cory Ltd 2000 ICR 938, EAT.

14.4 When explaining its powers in line with S.112(2), a tribunal is not obliged to use the terms 'reinstatement' and 're-engagement'. Given the informality of employment tribunal proceedings and the frequent appearance of parties without legal representation, it can often be more appropriate for a tribunal to explain its powers in lay terms. So long as the tribunal has explained both the nature of the orders available to it and the circumstances in which they may be

520

made, and has asked the claimant whether he or she wishes the tribunal to make such an order, S.112(2) will have been complied with – Bass v Travis Perkins Trading Company Ltd EAT 0352/07.

The EAT has recognised that it is unnecessary in some situations to follow S.112 to the letter – e.g. where the claimant has settled into new employment (Richardson v Walker EAT 312/79), or has contributed 100 per cent to a dismissal that is unfair only on technical grounds (Pratt v Pickfords Removals Ltd EAT 43/86). Tribunals have a discretion whether or not to grant an order for re-employment. However, if a claimant asks for reinstatement (or re-engagement) and the tribunal decides against making a re-employment order, it must give reasons for this – Plumley v AD International Ltd EAT 592/82. Reasons for rejection need not be elaborate, however. If, for example, there is substantial contributory conduct on the part of the employee, it may be sufficient to say: 'Having regard to the decision we have come to on the question of contribution, it would not be just to make a reinstatement order.'

Reinstatement   14.5
The contents of a reinstatement order are prescribed by statute and tribunals have no discretion to vary the statutory requirements. A reinstatement order must require that *the employer shall treat the complainant in all respects as if he or she had not been dismissed* and must specify:

- the amount payable by the employer in respect of pay and other benefits lost by the employee between the date the employment ended and the date of reinstatement

- the rights and privileges, including seniority and pension rights, which must be restored to the employee. Note that the restoration of pension rights may require the employee to fulfil certain conditions – in Whelan v Sutcliffe Catering West Ltd ET Case No.1027/88, for example, an order was made dependent on the employee refunding to the pension scheme the lump sum and pension payments received

- the date by which the reinstatement order must be complied with – S.114(2).

The amount payable to the employee must take into account any improvement in terms and conditions – e.g. a pay increase – that the employee would have received had he or she not been dismissed – S.114(3). As a quid pro quo, the tribunal is also required to take into account any sums received by the employee between dismissal and reinstatement (for more details, see 'Arrears of pay' below).

Re-engagement   14.6
If the tribunal decides not to make an order for reinstatement, then, as already mentioned, it must go on to consider re-engagement – S.116(2). This is a more flexible remedy than reinstatement and tribunals have a

521

wide discretion as to the terms of a re-engagement order. The only real statutory restriction on this discretion is that the re-engagement must be on terms which are, *so far as is reasonably practicable, as favourable as an order for reinstatement* (unless there has been contributory conduct, which is discussed below) – S.116(4). Note, however, that in Rank Xerox (UK) Ltd v Stryczek 1995 IRLR 568, EAT, the EAT held that a tribunal had erred in ordering the re-engagement of an employee in a position which would have amounted to a promotion – the position included a substantially higher salary than the employee had enjoyed prior to his dismissal, and also a company car. The EAT stated that it is not permissible for a tribunal to order re-engagement on terms that are significantly more favourable than those which the employee would have obtained had reinstatement been ordered.

Under S.115(1), re-engagement of an employee need only be in *employment comparable to that from which he or she was dismissed or other suitable employment*. In contrast with a reinstatement order, re-engagement need not be with the same employer but may be with a successor – i.e. another employer who has taken over the business, or with an associated employer such as another company in the same group. A somewhat unusual example of re-engagement is provided by Department of Health v Bruce and anor EAT 14/92. B was employed at the time of her dismissal by the DSS, which had been part of the Department of Health and Social Security until that department was split into the DSS and the DH. The tribunal ordered that B be re-engaged, but with the DH rather than the DSS. The EAT held that the tribunal was wrong to find that the Civil Service was one 'inalienable whole' for the purpose of determining B's employer. Nevertheless, the majority of the appeal tribunal (the chairman dissenting) took the view that the special relationship between the two new departments justified the order of re-engagement with the DH.

14.7 Although tribunals have considerable latitude as to the nature of the terms they order for re-engagement, they *must* specify terms under the following heads:

- the identity of the employer – i.e. whether re-engagement is with the same employer or with a successor or an associated employer

- the nature of the employment

- remuneration

- any arrears of pay and other benefits awarded for the period between dismissal and re-engagement

- any rights and privileges, including seniority and pension rights, to be restored to the employee

- the date by which re-engagement must take place – S.115(2).

522

In British Telecommunications plc v Thompson EAT 883–4/95 an order for **14.8** the re-engagement of an employee who was suffering from a stress-related illness stated that the employer had to comply within 14 days of the date when the employee's doctor certified that he was fit for work. The EAT held that the order was invalid because there was no specified date of return.

In Pirelli General Cable Works Ltd v Murray 1979 IRLR 190, EAT, the EAT ruled that a tribunal had not discharged its statutory obligations by simply ordering re-engagement on terms to be agreed between the parties. Similarly, in Stena Houlder Ltd v Keenan EAT 543/93 the tribunal ordered re-engagement of an employee 'in employment comparable to that from which he was dismissed or other suitable employment as agreed between the parties and on terms and conditions and remuneration also to be agreed'. The EAT held that the order was invalid because it failed to specify either the nature of the employment or the rate of remuneration as required by S.115. The Appeal Tribunal could understand how the tribunal had come to make such an order since the employer had accepted at the hearing that, if re-engagement were to be ordered, suitable arrangements could be made for the re-employment of the employee. Moreover, when the order was read in conjunction with the tribunal's statement of reasons, there emerged sufficiently clear guidance as to what the nature of the re-employment would be. But the order has to be read by itself and it must be sufficiently specific as to leave no doubt as to what steps are required to comply with it.

That said, the EAT has stated that it is undesirable for a tribunal to order re-engagement in respect of a specific job, as distinct from identifying the nature of the proposed employment. There might, however, be some circumstances where identifying a particular job is appropriate, such as where there is only one post in which a claimant could be re-engaged, but generally such an approach will not be permissible – Rank Xerox (UK) Ltd v Stryczek 1995 IRLR 568, EAT.

If the terms of a re-engagement order are silent or ambiguous on an **14.9** important issue, the tribunal is entitled to review the order and fill out its terms. In Electronic Data Processing Ltd v Wright 1986 IRLR 8, EAT, the tribunal had omitted to state the location at which re-engagement was to take place – because this is not one of the statutory particulars to be specified – and was unaware that the employer operated at more than one location. The EAT ruled that the tribunal could review the order and specify one particular location.

Finally, in Lilley Construction Ltd v Dunn 1984 IRLR 483, EAT, the Appeal Tribunal advised tribunals not to make 'offer directions' – i.e. directions to employers to make re-engagement offers to employees. The EAT doubted whether tribunals had any jurisdiction to make such orders and also pointed

523

to the confusion that could be caused if the employee refused an offer of re-engagement stemming from a tribunal direction of dubious validity.

14.10   **Costs**

Note that under rule 39 of the Employment Tribunal Rules of Procedure (contained in Schedule 1 to the Employment Tribunals (Constitution and Rules of Procedure) Regulations 2004 SI 2004/1861), a tribunal must make a costs order against a legally represented respondent where, in an unfair dismissal case, a hearing has been postponed or adjourned and (a) the claimant informed the respondent not less than seven days before the hearing that he or she wanted to be reinstated or re-engaged, and (b) the postponement or adjournment was caused by the respondent failing, without a special reason, to provide reasonable evidence as to the availability of the job from which the claimant was dismissed, or of comparable or suitable employment.

14.11   **Arrears of pay**

As already noted, a tribunal making a re-employment order (i.e. an order for either reinstatement or re-engagement) must specify any amount payable by the employer in respect of any benefit which the employee might reasonably be expected to have received but for the dismissal – Ss.114(2)(a) and 115(2)(d). The largest part of this award will, of course, be arrears of pay between the date of dismissal and the date of re-employment. The award must be based on what the employee would *actually have earned* during the period between dismissal and re-employment. This may not necessarily correspond with what he or she was earning before dismissal because that employee may have been employed in a seasonal business with fluctuating opportunities for overtime, commission, etc. Tribunals should investigate these matters and adjust their awards accordingly – Coakley v Hutchison's Coaches (Overtown) Ltd EAT 247/85. In Foot v Ministry of Defence ET Case No.4153/84 there was an interval of seven months between F's dismissal and his reinstatement, during which time F had been fit for three months but then unfit for four months. The tribunal therefore made a monetary award of three months' full pay (including overtime) and four months' sick pay.

It should be noted that, where an employee is re-engaged on different terms, salary or arrears of pay for the period between dismissal and re-engagement should be based on the salary *before dismissal* and not on the salary after re-engagement – Electronic Data Processing Ltd v Wright 1986 IRLR 8, EAT.

14.12   Under S.114(3), an order for reinstatement must require that the employee is treated as benefiting from any improvements in terms and conditions which he or she would have benefited from but for the dismissal from the date on which such improvements came into effect. However, the Court of Appeal confirmed in O'Laoire v Jackel International Ltd (No.2) 1991 ICR 718, CA, that this only applies to benefits from contractual improvements in the terms and conditions of employment that have arisen in the interim period.

524

There is no limit to the amount of back pay and benefits that can be awarded to cover an employee's monetary loss between dismissal and the tribunal's order. In particular, the ceiling of £65,300 that currently applies to a compensatory award for unfair dismissal has no application in the context of such orders (see also 'Enforcement of order' below). Certain sums, however, are to be deducted from these awards. They are:

- wages in lieu of notice or ex gratia payments made by the employer

- remuneration received from another employer

- any other benefits the tribunal thinks appropriate in the circumstances – Ss.114(4) and 115(3).

Sums awarded under Ss.114(2) or 115(2) cannot be reduced on the ground that **14.13** the employee has failed to mitigate his or her loss – see City and Hackney Health Authority v Crisp 1990 IRLR 47, EAT, where the employer had sought a reduction on the ground that the employee could have brought her claim sooner. The sums can, however, be reduced to take account of the claimant's contributory conduct – see below under 'Contributory conduct'.

In obiter remarks in an earlier hearing of the O'Laoire case mentioned above (O'Laoire v Jackel International Ltd 1990 ICR 197, CA), Lord Donaldson advised that reinstatement orders should not specify a lump sum to be paid to the employee in respect of arrears of pay because, in theory at least, reinstatement could take place before the date by which it must take place under the reinstatement order. Instead, Lord Donaldson thought that the order should specify the amounts payable by reference to rates of pay or other applicable formulae so that the appropriate calculations of the amount owed to the employee could be made when the actual date of reinstatement was known. Furthermore, no financial provision should be made as to what is to happen if reinstatement takes place *after* the date specified in the tribunal's order as, once this date has passed, any purported reinstatement would be a breach by the employer of the terms of the reinstatement order and therefore invalid. Although Lord Donaldson's comments were concerned with reinstatement orders under what is now S.114(2), they would presumably apply equally to re-engagement orders under S.115(2).

Employee preventing compliance
14.14

A re-employment order will only be made at the employee's request or with his or her agreement. It would be unusual, therefore, for an employee to prevent the order from being complied with. If, however, he or she does so *unreasonably*, S.117(8) states that the tribunal will take that conduct into account as a failure on the employee's part to mitigate his or her loss when making an award of compensation. In Miller v Liquidator for Matthew Primrose and Co Ltd EAT 17/77 the employee did not return to work after a tribunal had made a reinstatement order. The working atmosphere had

525

deteriorated and the employer subsequently went into liquidation. The EAT held that the employee's refusal to comply with the reinstatement order was not unreasonable in the circumstances.

14.15   Factors to be taken into account

When considering whether to make an order for reinstatement or re-engagement, tribunals have a specific duty under S.116 to consider:

- whether the *employee wants* an order to be made and, in the case of re- engagement, what sort of order he or she wants – S.116(1)(a) and (3)(a). (Many employees do not wish to be re-employed with the same company and in such cases tribunals can move directly to considering compensation)

- whether it is *practicable* for the employer to comply. In the case of re- engagement, the test of practicability is extended to successors of the employer and to associated employers – S.116(1)(b) and (3)(b)

- whether it would be just to make either type of order where the *employee's conduct* caused or contributed to some extent to his or her dismissal and if so, in the case of re-engagement, on what terms – S.116(1)(c) and (3)(c).

14.16   The requirements of S.116 are mandatory to the extent that tribunals must take the factors listed therein into account when considering whether or not to grant a re-employment order – Kelvin International Services v Stephenson EAT 1057/95. However, tribunals are not limited to these considerations and they have a 'general discretion' to take into account a wide range of other factors, including the consequences for industrial relations if the order is complied with – Port of London Authority v Payne and ors 1994 ICR 555, CA. For instance, in Securicor Ltd v Smith EAT 252 and 302/87 the treatment meted out to a third party employee – who had been reinstated after his dismissal was revoked – was held to be a valid consideration for the tribunal when assessing whether reinstatement would be an appropriate remedy in S's case. And in Cowen v Rentokil Initial Facility Services (UK) Ltd t/a Initial Transport Services EAT 0473/07 the EAT considered that the refusal by the employee of a previous offer of re-engagement by the employer, and the fact that the post offered had subsequently been filled, were both potentially relevant factors for the tribunal to take into account. However, the offer and refusal in that case had taken place amidst 'without prejudice' negotiations and therefore attracted legal professional privilege. In those circumstances, the tribunal should not have been referred to the fact that an offer had been made.

14.17   Practicability

'Practicability' is by far the most important factor for tribunals to take into account when considering whether to make a re-employment order. It is a question of fact for the tribunal, which has discretion to decide whether or not to make a re-employment order. It follows that any appeal against a decision

526 ───────────────────────────────────────

will only succeed if the tribunal has taken into account the wrong considerations, ignored the right considerations, or reached a legally perverse decision. In Clancy v Cannock Chase Technical College and anor 2001 IRLR 331, EAT, the EAT reiterated that it will only rarely interfere with a tribunal's findings on the issue of practicability and will do so only if the tribunal's decision is perverse in the circumstances. Where a tribunal has directed itself properly on the law and has heard evidence on the issue of practicability, a plea of perversity will be hard to get off the ground. In the words of Mr Justice Lindsay, then President of the EAT: 'Of all the subjects properly to be left as the exclusive province of an employment tribunal as the "industrial jury", few can be more obviously their territory than the issue of "practicability" within S.116(1)(b) and... S.116(3)(b).'

Although it is a high hurdle to overcome, there are, of course, cases where the perversity argument succeeds. In Scottish Police Services Authority v McBride EAT 0020/09, for example, M, a fingerprint specialist, had been unfairly dismissed after the Authority came to the view that her involvement in a high-profile failed prosecution meant that her work could no longer be relied on in court. The tribunal ordered that M be re-engaged as a 'non-court-going' fingerprint specialist. On appeal by the Authority, the EAT considered that, given the background of conflict and mistrust between M and the Authority, not to mention M's desire to return to full 'court-going' duties, it was perverse of the tribunal to conclude that a re-engagement order was practicable.

When assessing practicability, the EAT has stated that tribunals should not **14.18** try to analyse in too much detail the application of the word 'practicable' but should look at the circumstances of each case and take a 'broad common sense view' – Meridian Ltd v Gomersall and anor 1977 IRLR 425, EAT. It should be borne in mind, however, that the test is one of 'practicability' not 'expediency'. In Qualcast (Wolverhampton) Ltd v Ross 1979 ICR 386, EAT, the Appeal Tribunal remitted the question of reinstatement to the tribunal for reconsideration, refusing to accept the tribunal's decision to decline an order for reinstatement because it had not considered it expedient to make such an order.

It is important to note that there are two stages at which a tribunal may have to assess the question of practicability. The first arises when the tribunal considers whether to make an order for reinstatement or re-engagement at the remedies hearing, having found the employer liable for unfair dismissal. The second arises later but only if the employer refuses to comply with a re-employment order, in which case a second remedies hearing will be necessary. At this second hearing the onus is on the employer to show – on the balance of probabilities – that complying with the order was impracticable. The EAT ruled in Timex Corporation v Thomson 1981 IRLR 522, EAT, that a *lesser emphasis* on practicability is required at the first stage, when the tribunal has only to *take into account* the consideration of practicability and does not need to make a final

527

determination on the issue. This was endorsed by the Court of Appeal in Port of London Authority v Payne and ors 1994 ICR 555, CA. The Court stated in that case that at the first stage, prior to making an order, the tribunal need only make a provisional determination or assessment on the evidence before it as to whether it is practicable for the employer to reinstate or re-engage the employee. It is only at the second stage, where the employer has not complied with the order and seeks to show that it was not practicable to do so, that a tribunal must make a final determination on practicability.

14.19 **Effect on business.** Reinstating a dismissed employee should never necessitate redundancies or significant overstaffing. In Freemans plc v Flynn 1984 ICR 874, EAT, the EAT rejected the argument that the effect of a re-engagement order was to place a duty on the employer to find a place for the dismissed employee irrespective of whether there were vacancies. This placed too high a duty on employers. That reasoning was followed in Cold Drawn Tubes Ltd v Middleton 1992 IRLR 160, EAT, where the EAT emphasised that 'it would be contrary to the spirit of the legislation to compel redundancies, and it would be contrary to common sense and to justice to enforce over manning', although in Highland Fish Farmers Ltd v Thorburn and anor EAT 1094/94 the EAT found that Mr Justice Tucker in the Middleton case was drawing attention to a very important consideration, but not purporting to lay down an absolute rule. (Note, also, the special provisions on employing a permanent replacement, below.)

In Port of London Authority v Payne and ors (above) the Court of Appeal stressed that the test is one of practicability, not possibility. In that case a tribunal rejected the employer's argument that a lack of vacancies had made it impracticable to comply with re-engagement orders. The tribunal took the view that the employer should have invited applications for voluntary severance from the existing workforce. The Court of Appeal held that the tribunal had applied too high a standard. Although tribunals should carefully scrutinise the reasons advanced by employers, due weight should be given to their commercial judgement. 'The employer cannot be expected to explore every possible avenue which ingenuity might suggest. The employer does not have to show that reinstatement or re-engagement was *impossible*. It is a matter of what is practicable in the circumstances of the employer's business at the relevant time.' Two examples:

- **United States Navy v Coady** EAT 275/94: C was purportedly dismissed for redundancy. A tribunal found that no redundancy situation in fact existed; the employer had simply replaced C with someone it considered better at the job. The tribunal ordered reinstatement, despite the employer's objection that this would cause overstaffing. The EAT upheld the decision. The services of the employee were not redundant and reinstatement would simply put matters back to where they were before the dismissal. Any resulting overstaffing would be the result, not of the reinstatement, but of the way in which the employer had gone about the management of the club

528

in which C worked and the termination of his employment. It might be inexpedient for the employer to reinstate C, but it was not impracticable

- **Carpenter v ABB Industrial Systems Ltd** COET 3088/179: C, an engineer, was unfairly dismissed for redundancy. The employer failed to comply with the tribunal's order for reinstatement on the ground that it would have forced the company to make someone else redundant. However, during the course of the tribunal hearing, it emerged that the company had in fact, since the first practicability hearing, taken on a contract engineer from an agency and that this worker was still there. The tribunal held that, in the circumstances, reinstatement was certainly practicable.

In Cruickshank v London Borough of Richmond EAT 483/97 C was successful in his unfair dismissal claim. On his ET1 he had sought reinstatement and he reiterated that wish at the remedies hearing before the tribunal. However, less than one month before the hearing on liability the employer had 'deleted' C's post. On remitting the case to the tribunal on the question of remedies, the EAT directed it to consider in particular whether the deletion of M's post was done solely to frustrate the possibility of his reinstatement. **14.20**

Replacements. Employing a permanent replacement for a dismissed employee will not of itself make re-employment impracticable. S.116(5) and (6) state that, in deciding whether to make a re-employment order, a tribunal must ignore the employment of a replacement unless the employer shows: **14.21**

- that it was not practicable to arrange for the dismissed employee's work to be done without engaging a permanent replacement, or

- that before engaging a permanent replacement a reasonable period had gone by without word from the dismissed employee as to whether he or she wanted re-employment and there was no reasonable alternative to hiring a permanent replacement.

(Much the same applies to the consideration of practicability at the second stage following an employer's non-compliance with an order – S.117(7).) In practice, this may mean that a large employer with significant resources will find it harder to rely on the S.116(6) exception than a smaller, less well-resourced employer, with the potentially anomalous result that the large employer might be forced to dismiss the permanent replacement.

Relationship with colleagues. The personal relationship between the employee and his or her colleagues is clearly a relevant factor that will affect the question of practicability and/or the tribunal's exercise of its discretion. Re-employment is unlikely to be on the cards if relations at work have become irretrievably soured. For example, in Intercity East Coast Ltd v McGregor EAT 473/96 the acrimonious relationship between the employee and his supervisor had been an important factor leading up to the dismissal, to which the employee had been found to have contributed by 20 per cent. **14.22**

529

The EAT held that it was 'not practicable to order two parties to reunite when war has broken out'. In Baldwin v KLM Royal Dutch Airlines ET Case No.67019/95, by contrast, a tribunal ordered the reinstatement of B even though he had been dismissed for assaulting a colleague, H. The tribunal found that B was a good employee and that the assault was a one-off incident. Although H had said that he could no longer work with B, the tribunal did not think that his views should provide a veto on the employee's return to work. In Thamesdown Borough Council v Turrell EAT 459/97, however, the EAT overturned a tribunal decision to order reinstatement in circumstances where a reorganisation that resulted in the deletion of T's job had been completed by the time of the final hearing on remedies and where there was a real threat of industrial action if T returned to work because his colleagues had lost trust and confidence in him.

14.23   **Trust and confidence.** As the Turrell case demonstrates, a breakdown of trust and confidence between employer and employee may be sufficient to render re-employment impracticable. In Wood Group Heavy Industrial Turbines Ltd v Crossan 1998 IRLR 680, EAT, for example, the employer genuinely believed that C had been dealing drugs at work and the EAT held that this was enough to render his re-engagement impracticable. And in Central and North West London NHS Foundation Trust v Abimbola EAT 0542/08 the Appeal Tribunal concluded that a tribunal had been wrong to exclude from its consideration of practicability both the dishonesty of the claimant at the remedies hearing and the fact that, in the light of one proven instance of assault and three unproven allegations, the respondent could no longer be expected to trust the claimant.

Tribunals should, however, be careful not to hold against the employee allegations made in the course of litigation and should be wary of assessing an employee's attitude solely from his or her performance during the litigation – Cruickshank v London Borough of Richmond EAT 483/97. In Mills v Norwich Systems and Accounting ET Case No.29275/95 a tribunal was unconvinced by the employer's claim that the experience of contesting the unfair dismissal claim had left a legacy of bitterness which rendered reinstatement impracticable. The tribunal added that it was surprised to hear such an argument advanced by a company that employed over 140 people. As this suggests, the question of personality clashes is closely bound up with the size of employer or employment unit. In Enessy Co SA t/a The Tulchan Estate v Minoprio and anor 1978 IRLR 489, EAT, the employees were a married couple employed as cooks in a small hotel. The EAT took the obiter view that it was one thing to order reinstatement where the employee works in a factory or other substantial organisation, but it would only be in exceptional circumstances that it would be appropriate to force upon a reluctant employer the reinstatement of employees with whom he would have to work in a close relationship unless the tribunal was persuaded by powerful evidence that such an arrangement would succeed.

530

In London Borough of Greenwich v Dell EAT 1166/94 a tribunal found that a **14.24** caretaker employed by a local authority was unfairly dismissed on account of his political activities on behalf of the British National Party. The tribunal found that it would be impracticable to reinstate the employee in his former position on a multiracial housing estate but ordered the authority to re-engage him in a post where he would not have any contact with ethnic minorities. The EAT overturned the tribunal's decision, stating that the notion of the employee being appointed to some segregated post free of any contact with racial minorities was offensive to a local authority which advocated racial equality.

Lack of trust on the employee's part may also make re-employment impracticable. In Nothman v London Borough of Barnet (No.2) 1980 IRLR 65, CA, for example, the Court of Appeal held that the employee's allegations of a long-standing conspiracy by colleagues to oust her from her job made it impracticable to order reinstatement.

Capability and ill health. Issues of capability and ill health will also be **14.25** relevant to the question of practicability. In SMT Sales and Service Co Ltd v Irwin EAT 485/79 the EAT held that it would not be practicable for the company to re-engage a senior manager in whom it had genuinely lost confidence, whether the reasons for doing so were well founded or not. In Hemmings v Redland Bricks Ltd ET Case No.9432/96, on the other hand, the employer argued that, although the employee had satisfactory appraisals and no disciplinary record, there had in fact been serious shortcomings in her performance. No action had been taken on these shortcomings because they would have been difficult to prove. The tribunal said that in the circumstances it could not be expected to attach much weight to these alleged shortcomings and reinstatement was ordered.

In British Telecommunications plc v Thompson EAT 883–4/95 T was dismissed following a stress-related illness. A tribunal ordered re-engagement to be complied with once T was fit to return to full-time employment. The EAT held that, apart from making the order invalid, the fact that the tribunal was unable to specify a date for re-engagement also betrayed the real reason why re-engagement was not in fact practicable. The EAT also expressed surprise that the tribunal had considered it appropriate for such a vulnerable employee to return to a senior post in a highly stressful business. In another case, McGarry v British Railways Board EAT 63/91, the EAT held that a tribunal was entitled to hold that reinstatement was impracticable, even though the tribunal had not heard any evidence specifically on that point. The tribunal had been given the whole history of M's employment, which showed that M had suffered from recurrent periods of unfitness for work and that it was very doubtful that he would be fit for any form of work within the company. In such circumstances it was not necessary for the tribunal to hear evidence from the employer in order to entitle it to decide that re-engagement was manifestly impracticable.

531

14.26 **Training.** Tribunals have been known to take an employee's training into account when deciding on practicability. In Blackhurst v St Helens and Knowsley Health Authority ET Case No.8102/85, for example, a tribunal ordered the reinstatement of a claimant who had five months of his training course as a nurse to run. Tribunals have also been considerate to apprentices in similar circumstances.

14.27 **Security checks.** The need for an employer to carry out security screening checks for a reinstated or re-engaged employee will not necessarily make a re-employment order impracticable. In Ojo v G4S Security Services (UK) Ltd ET Case No. 2200328/09 the employer argued that, since it would have to submit O to a Criminal Records Bureau (CRB) check as if he were a new employee – a process that can take up to 3 months – it was not practicable for him to be re-engaged. However, the tribunal disagreed, finding that a company of the respondent's size could re-engage O on full-pay, but either assign him no duties or assign him to duties that did not require a CRB check.

14.28 **Risk to public.** The existence of a duty owed to the public will not necessarily determine the issue of practicability. Even where an employer genuinely believes that a dismissed employee could pose a risk to the public, re-employment will not automatically be impracticable. A tribunal will, however, judge each case on its merits and clearly a serious offence such as sexual assault will present a greater obstacle to practicability than the theft of, say, £2. For example, in ILEA v Gravett 1988 IRLR 497, EAT, a tribunal was justified in refusing to grant an order for the re-employment of a swimming instructor who was dismissed for indecent exposure and indecent assault and later convicted of these offences. This should be contrasted with the case of petty theft by a gas meter inspector in British Gas plc v Turton EAT 292 and 319/88.

14.29 **Contributory conduct**

Tribunals are required by statute to consider whether it would be just to make a reinstatement or re-engagement order where the employee caused or contributed to some extent to the dismissal – S.116(1)(c) and (3)(c). Contributory conduct will also be highly relevant to the question of practicability – e.g. where the employee's misconduct has soured the working relationship. In Kelvin International Services v Stephenson EAT 1057/95 the EAT allowed an appeal against a tribunal's order of reinstatement on the ground that no consideration had been given to the question of conduct. The case concerned a dismissal for suspected theft where the mutual trust and confidence between employer and employee had broken down. The question of whether the employee's conduct had contributed to the dismissal was therefore highly material both to the issue of practicability and to the question of whether it was just to order reinstatement.

There is no reason in principle why a tribunal should not make a re-employment order even where there is a large degree of contributory conduct, provided that it

532 ───

forms a reasonable view that the circumstances warrant it. In Automatic Cooling Engineers Ltd v Scott EAT 545/81, for instance, the EAT upheld a re-engagement order (in favour of an apprentice) in a case where contribution had been assessed at 75 per cent.

However, in United Distillers Ltd v Harrower EAT 1151/96 the EAT took the view that it could not be practicable to reinstate an employee where the conduct related to an established and admitted act of *dishonesty*. In Boots Company plc v Lees-Collier 1986 IRLR 485, EAT, on the other hand, the Appeal Tribunal declined to overturn a tribunal's decision to reinstate an employee, even though his employer remained convinced that he was guilty of theft. In United Distillers and Vintners Ltd v Brown EAT 1471/99 the EAT upheld a tribunal decision to order the reinstatement of an employee who had been found to have contributed to his dismissal by 10 per cent. However, the EAT stressed the importance of the tribunal's finding that issues of honesty were not at stake and that trust and confidence between the employee and the employer were intact. In cases where the contribution assessment was high, however, the EAT cautioned that it may be necessary for a tribunal to consider whether or not the employer could genuinely trust the employee again, although each case would depend on its own facts.

14.30

In the case of re-engagement, tribunals must also take contributory conduct into account when considering the terms of the order. However, even where there has been significant contributory fault, the EAT has counselled against ordering re-engagement of a senior employee in a demoted position – Atlantic Steam Navigation Co Ltd v Murdoch EAT 234/83. Contrast this with Johnson Matthey plc v Watters EAT 0236–38/08, in which the EAT held that a tribunal had been entitled to order that an employee be re-engaged at one point lower in the grade scale than his original role, to take account of his 20 per cent contribution to the dismissal.

In practice, tribunals often take the employee's conduct into account by reducing or even eliminating an award of back pay, etc, for the period between dismissal and re-engagement. An example:

14.31

- **Gray v University of Warwick** ET Case No.1302304/09: the tribunal found that G had been unfairly dismissed but that he had made a 20 per cent contribution to his dismissal by his own misconduct. The University opposed a reinstatement order, arguing that it had lost trust and confidence in G. However, the tribunal noted that G was no more culpable than three of his colleagues who had not been dismissed, and the only reason he had been dismissed and they had not was that G had an unrelated 'live' warning on his personnel file. Any loss of trust and confidence 'flowed from a flawed investigation and disciplinary process' and could not be relied on by the University to resist a reinstatement order. However, the sum in arrears due to G from the date of his dismissal to the date of his reinstatement order was reduced by 20 per cent to take account of his contributory conduct.

14.32 **Protected industrial action.** Note that, in the case of an unfair dismissal for participation in protected industrial action, S.239(4)(a) of the Trade Union and Labour Relations (Consolidation) Act 1992 provides that a tribunal shall not make any order for reinstatement or re-engagement until after the conclusion of the protected industrial action by any employee in relation to the relevant dispute.

14.33 Enforcement of order

The remedy for an employer's failure to abide by a reinstatement or re-engagement order depends on whether there has been partial compliance or complete non-compliance. If the employer reinstates or re-engages the employee but the terms of the order are not fully complied with (i.e. there has been partial compliance), S.117(1) provides that the tribunal will make an award of compensation to the employee. The amount of the award will be such as the tribunal thinks fit having regard to the loss sustained by the employee as a result of the employer's failure to comply fully with the order – S.117(2).

If there is a total failure to comply on the employer's part – i.e. the employer refuses to reinstate or re-engage the employee – the tribunal will go on to assess the employee's compensation for unfair dismissal in the normal way. (If the employee unreasonably prevented compliance, this should be taken into account as a failure by him or her to mitigate his or her losses – S.112(8).) The tribunal will also make an *additional award* unless the employer can show that it was not practicable to comply with the order – S.117(3). The question of practicability is discussed above. Additional awards are dealt with in Chapter 19. Note that at this stage, it is not open to the employee to seek a further order for re-employment – Mabirizi v National Hospital for Nervous Diseases 1990 ICR 281, EAT.

14.34 It used to be the case that, where the employee was highly paid or there had been a long delay between the date of dismissal and the date of the tribunal's hearing, the amount of arrears of pay which the employer would have to pay in pursuance of a tribunal's order for re-employment meant that it was cheaper for the employer to refuse to comply (or only partially comply) with the order. This was because the compensation that a tribunal could award on account of the employer's partial compliance or total non-compliance was subject to the same statutory limit as applied to compensatory awards. (This limit is currently £65,300 but prior to 25 October 1999 was only £12,000.) In O'Laoire v Jackel International Ltd 1990 ICR 197, CA, the claimant's actual losses consequent on the dismissal exceeded £100,000, but the maximum which the tribunal could award him at that time was £12,185. When the matter reached the Court of Appeal, Lord Donaldson noted that 'the present maximum level of award... can positively discourage employers from complying with an order for reinstatement, contrary to the interests of

534

Parliament, and in addition causes injustice to higher paid employees'. This anomaly was later removed and S.124(3) ERA now provides that, in the case of partial compliance, the statutory limit may be lifted by such amount as is necessary to enable the award fully to reflect the amount specified as arrears of pay and benefits in the original reinstatement or re- engagement order. Similarly, in the case of total non-compliance, the statutory limit may be exceeded by the extent necessary to enable the aggregate of the compensatory and additional awards fully to reflect the amount of arrears of pay and benefits specified in the original order – S.124(4).

Note, however, that, in cases of total non-compliance with a reinstatement order made under S.114, i.e. where an additional award is made under S.117(3)(b) as well as a compensatory award under S.117(3)(a), the statutory limit should only be exceeded to the extent of the S.114 loss (i.e. the loss incurred between dismissal and when reinstatement should have occurred) *less* the additional award – Selfridges Ltd v Malik 1998 ICR 268, EAT. This is because the S.114 loss is not a free-standing head of damage to be awarded whether or not reinstatement is complied with. The S.114 loss is only payable in respect of a reinstatement order which *has* been complied with. If there is total non-compliance, then the S.114 loss forms part of the compensatory award. The same principle applies to loss under S.115 where an employer totally fails to comply with a re-engagement order. This approach has since been endorsed by the EAT in Midland Mainline v Wade EAT 1382/01 and, more recently, by the Court of Appeal in Parry v National Westminster Bank plc 2005 IRLR 193, CA.

It is for the tribunal to decide whether or not the employer has complied properly with the order. In Electronic Data Processing Ltd v Wright 1986 IRLR 8, EAT, W was unfairly dismissed for redundancy and a tribunal made an order that she be re-engaged in a lower-paid trainee's position. W had been employed in Sheffield but the employer offered her a post in Manchester. The tribunal decided that this was not a proper offer of re-engagement. This was upheld by the EAT on the basis that the tribunal was entitled to interpret its own order. If the terms of the order had been ambiguous, it would have been open to the tribunal to give effect to its original intentions by filling out the terms of the order to stipulate that re-engagement must be in Sheffield. **14.35**

The distinction between *non-compliance* and a *failure 'fully' to comply* is an important one since, as noted above, it is only in cases of total non-compliance that an additional award is payable under S.117(3)(b). In some cases, however, the line between the two may be hard to draw – for example, where the employee is re-engaged but not in the type of post ordered by the tribunal. The question of whether there had been partial compliance or non-compliance with a reinstatement order was considered in the following case:

- **Artisan Press v Srawley and anor** 1986 ICR 328, EAT: S and P were unfairly dismissed from their jobs as security staff. A tribunal made reinstatement

535

orders, with which the employer purported to comply. However, S and P were in fact re-employed as cleaners with some minor security functions so that their jobs were significantly different from those they had performed before dismissal. The tribunal held that the employer had failed to comply with the reinstatement order. On appeal, the employer argued that there had only been a failure to comply 'fully' with the order and that compensation should have been awarded under what is now S.117(1) and not S.117(3). However, the EAT held that 'reinstatement' means treating the employee in all respects as if he or she has not been dismissed. If an employee is 'reinstated' in a different job on less favourable terms, then he or she has not been reinstated at all and there has been a total failure to comply with the reinstatement order. The tribunal's award was therefore correct.

14.36 The EAT went on to say that a failure to comply 'fully' with a reinstatement order must refer to ancillary matters that may be specified in the order and not to the terms of the order itself. For example, an order will specify the date by which the employee is to be reinstated. If the employer is two weeks late in taking the employee back but does reinstate the employee properly in his or her old job with no change to terms and conditions, that would seem to be only a failure to comply fully with the order and would properly be compensated for by an award of two weeks' pay rather than an additional award (but note Lord Donaldson's later conflicting obiter remarks in the Court of Appeal in O'Laoire v Jackel International Ltd 1990 ICR 197, CA, as to the validity of purported re-employment after the deadline for compliance – see 'Arrears of pay' above).

14.37 ## Compensation

Despite the emphasis on re-employment orders in the ERA, in practice the only remedy awarded in the vast majority of successful unfair dismissal claims is monetary compensation. Most awards of compensation fall under two main heads:

- the *basic award* (see S.118(1)(a)), normally calculated in exactly the same way as a redundancy payment and intended to compensate the employee for loss of job security – see Chapter 15 for details

- the *compensatory award* (see S.118(1)(b)), intended to compensate the employee for financial loss suffered as the result of the unfair dismissal (subject to a current maximum of £65,300). There is no formula for calculating a compensatory award other than what the tribunal considers 'just and equitable' – see Chapters 16–18 for details.

In addition to the basic and compensatory awards, there are two other forms of compensation that may come into play in exceptional cases, specifically in relation to cases where re-employment has been ordered:

536

- an *additional award* under S.117(3)(b) – such an award need not be directly related to the employee's loss but may be penal, where the tribunal has made a reinstatement or re-engagement order but the employer has totally failed to comply with that order (see under 'Reinstatement and re-engagement – enforcement of order' above and Chapter 19).

- an award of four weeks' pay (unless this would result in injustice to the employer) where the employee is regarded as unfairly dismissed because of the employer's failure to follow the statutory retirement procedure (see Chapter 9) and an order for reinstatement or re-engagement is made – S.112(5) and (6). Note that this award should be deducted from any later award of compensation made under S.117(1) (where the employer only partially complies with the re-employment order) or S.117(3)(a) (where there has been total non-compliance with the order) – Ss.117(2a) and 123(8).

'Special awards', which used to be available under S.118(2) and (3) where **14.38** dismissal was for a trade union or health and safety reason or for a reason connected with the employee's role as an occupational pension scheme trustee or employee representative and the employee had asked for reinstatement or re-engagement were abolished by the Employment Relations Act 1999 in relation to dismissals on or after 25 October 1999.

In addition to the awards mentioned above, tribunals have the power to make *interim relief orders* in certain circumstances. An interim relief order is a mechanism for keeping an employee's contract alive – normally through what is, in effect, an order for suspension on full pay – pending a full tribunal hearing. These orders are only available to employees who claim to have been dismissed on one of the specified statutory grounds benefiting from special protection under S.128(1) ERA – see Chapter 19 for more detail.

Finally, it should be noted that S.126 ERA *prohibits double recovery of losses* under the ERA, the Sex Discrimination Act 1975, the Race Relations Act 1976, the Disability Discrimination Act 1995, the Employment Equality (Sexual Orientation) Regulations 2003 SI 2003/1661, the Employment Equality (Religion or Belief) Regulations 2003 SI 2003/1660 or the Employment Equality (Age) Regulations 2006 SI 2006/1031 in respect of the same complaint. (Note that the anti-discrimination legislation is due be incorporated into the Equality Act 2010 from a date to be appointed.)

15 Basic awards

Calculation of basic award

Reductions in basic award

Settlements and ex gratia payments

Order of deductions

In the majority of successful unfair dismissal claims the remedy will be an **15.1** award of monetary compensation made up – ordinarily – of a basic award and a compensatory award – S.118(1)(a) and (b) Employment Rights Act 1996 (ERA). The basic award is designed to compensate an employee for the *loss of job security* caused by the unfair dismissal by awarding him or her a sum almost exactly equivalent to a statutory redundancy payment. The compensatory award is intended to reflect the actual losses that the employee suffers as a consequence of being unfairly dismissed.

This chapter explains how a basic award is calculated (for details of how the underlying unit of a 'week's pay' is made up, see IDS Employment Law Handbook, 'Wages' (2003), Chapter 11). It also deals with the circumstances in which a tribunal may reduce or eliminate a basic award and considers how far ex gratia payments made by employers may affect liability for paying a basic award. Interest on tribunal awards is dealt with in Chapter 16. Compensatory awards are dealt with in Chapters 16–18.

Calculation of basic award

15.2

The basic award is calculated in units of a week's pay as defined in Ss.220–229 ERA – for details see IDS Employment Law Handbook, 'Wages' (2003), Chapter 11. The total will usually depend on the employee's age and length of continuous service and the relevant amount of a week's pay. There are, however, some exceptions to this rule. The first is where the reason for the dismissal (or selection for redundancy) was a trade union reason (so that the dismissal was automatically unfair under S.152(1) or S.153 of the Trade Union and Labour Relations (Consolidation) Act 1992 (TULR(C)A)), in which case a minimum basic award applies under S.156 – see IDS Employment Law Handbook, 'Trade Unions' (2000), Chapter 10.

The second exception arises if the dismissal was for one of the inadmissible reasons set out in S.120 ERA, namely:

- dismissal for carrying out health and safety activities or being a health and safety representative under S.100(1)(a) or (b) ERA – S.120(1)

539

- dismissal for being a working time representative for the purposes of the Working Time Regulations 1998 SI 1998/1833 under S.101A(d) ERA – S.120(1)

- dismissal for being a trustee of the occupational pension scheme under S.102(1) ERA – S.120(1)

- dismissal for being an employee representative for collective redundancy consultation purposes (under Chapter II of Part IV TULR(C)A) or for consultation with regard to a transfer of an undertaking (under the Transfer of Undertakings (Protection of Employment) Regulations 1981 SI 1981/1794) under S.103 ERA – S.120(1)

- dismissal by reason of retirement where the employer has failed to comply with the statutory retirement procedure under S.98ZG ERA – S.120(1A)

- dismissal relating to trade union 'blacklists' under S.104F – S.120(1C).

15.3 Where S.120(1) applies (i.e. in respect of the first four types of dismissal listed above), the basic award is subject to a current *minimum* of £4,700 (normally increased each year in April) – S.156(1) TULR(C)A and S.120(1) ERA. Where S.120(1C) applies (i.e. 'blacklisting' dismissals), the basic award must not be less than £5,000. If the basic award calculated normally would be higher than these figures, then the employee should be awarded the higher amount subject to the normal maximum – see 'Formula for calculating basic award' below. These statutory minima apply before any reduction is made under S.122 – see 'Reductions to basic award' below.

Where S.120(1A) applies (i.e. retirement dismissals), the tribunal must increase the basic award to *four weeks' pay* if the amount of the basic award, before any deduction under S.122(3A) or (4) is made (see 'Reductions in basic award' below), is less than four weeks' pay. However, the tribunal has discretion under S.120(1B) not to increase the basic award if to do so would result in injustice to the employer.

A final exception to the normal rule arises where the employee has been dismissed because of redundancy but he or she is not entitled to a redundancy payment – having unreasonably refused an offer of suitable alternative employment or unreasonably walked out of such employment during a trial period. In such circumstances the basic award will be two weeks' pay – S.121.

15.4 **Formula for calculating basic award**
To calculate the basic award, a statutory formula is applied. The employee's years of continuous employment are counted backwards from the effective date of termination (EDT). The EDT is the date on which the employment contract ended unless the employer dismissed the employee with no notice or with inadequate notice, in which case the EDT is postponed to the date on which the statutory (not contractual) minimum notice under S.86 ERA would have

540 ───────────────────────────

expired – S.97(2) ERA (see IDS Employment Law Handbook, 'Contracts of Employment' (2009), Chapter 11). *A maximum of 20 years' continuous employment can be counted* – S.119(3). The amount of the award is:

- 1½ weeks' pay for each year in which the employee was 41 years old or older – S.119(2)(a) ERA

- one week's pay for each year in which the employee was below the age of 41 but not younger than 22 – S.119(2)(b)

- half a week's pay for each year in which the employee was below the age of 22 – S.119(2)(c).

There is *no lower age limit* for a basic award. Years of service in which an employee was below the age of 18 do count for a basic award (even though they do not at present count for a statutory redundancy payment, which, in most other respects, is calculated in the same way as a basic award). Note, however, that it is illegal to employ a child below the age of 13 unless this is authorised by Byelaw – see S.18 of the Children and Young Persons Act 1933.

Age discrimination. Given that the formula for calculating the basic award relies on age-based factors, the Government reviewed the scheme prior to the coming into force of the Employment Equality (Age) Regulations 2006 SI 2006/1031 on 1 October 2006. In its *Coming of Age* consultation document, published in July 2005, it expressed an intention to remove the three age bands for calculating redundancy payments and basic awards. In the end, however, the Government decided to retain these bands, despite the fact that the multiplier based on age bands would appear to amount to direct discrimination, and the multiplier based on length of service seems indirectly discriminatory. In the context of the redundancy scheme, the Government opined that there were three groups benefiting from payments under the scheme – younger, prime age and older workers – which each represent a distinct economic category. At one end of the spectrum, younger workers tend not to be out of work for long and only experience a small fall in pay when switching jobs. Older workers, on the other hand, face difficulties in finding new jobs, experience a substantial fall in pay if they do find new employment, and are much more likely to become long-term unemployed. As a result, the Government felt that the practice of applying different 'multipliers' to different age bands so as to give greater financial assistance to older workers is justified.

15.5

Calculation date

15.6

For the purposes of calculating the basic award, the calculation date (i.e. the date on which a week's pay is calculated) is:

- the employee's last day of work, if the notice given is less than the statutory minimum period of notice laid down in S.86 ERA

- where the notice is the same as or more than the statutory minimum, the date as determined by ascertaining the statutory minimum period applicable and calculating the latest day when the employer would have needed to give that notice in order for the employee's contract to have been terminated on the day that he or she actually left work – S.226(3) ERA.

The current ceiling on the amount of a week's pay is £380 and anything earned in excess of this is disregarded. This figure is usually adjusted upwards every April. Since a maximum of 20 years' service can count and the pay ceiling is £380, the *maximum possible basic award* at present is £11,400. To obtain this an employee would have to earn at least £380 per week and be able to show 20 years' service during which he or she was not below the age of 41. (Note that where the employee's wage is actually lower than the national minimum wage (NMW) under the National Minimum Wage Act 1998, then the NMW must be used to calculate a week's pay, not the employee's actual wage – Paggetti v Cobb 2002 IRLR 861, EAT).

15.7 ## Reductions in basic award

There are five grounds on which a tribunal may reduce a basic award:

- where the employee has unreasonably refused an offer of reinstatement – S.122(1) ERA

- where the employee's conduct before dismissal makes a reduction just and equitable – S.122(2)

- where the employee has been awarded any amount in respect of the dismissal under a designated dismissal procedures agreement – S.122(3A)

- where the employee has been dismissed for redundancy and has received a redundancy payment – S.122(4)

- where the employee has been unfairly dismissed for a reason relating to a trade union 'blacklist' under S.104F ERA and has received a basic award in respect of the same dismissal under S.156 TULR(C)A – S.122(5).

There is no overarching requirement that it should be just and equitable to make a basic award – Belcher and ors v Great Bear Distribution Ltd EAT 0453/05, and reductions in the basic award can only be made where expressly permitted by statute – Cadbury Ltd v Doddington 1977 ICR 982, EAT. As a result, these are the only permissible grounds for reducing basic awards. Unlike the compensatory award, a basic award cannot, for example, be reduced to take into account the applicant's failure to mitigate his or her loss – Lock v Connell Estate Agents 1994 IRLR 444, EAT, or be subject to a 'Polkey' deduction – Taylor and ors v John Webster, Buildings Civil Engineering 1999 ICR 561, EAT, and Market Force (UK) Ltd v Hunt 2002

542 ────────────────────────────────────

IRLR 863, EAT. Furthermore, the provisions allowing tribunals to adjust awards by up to 25 per cent where either party has unreasonably failed to comply with the Acas Code of Practice on Disciplinary and Grievance Procedures do not apply to basic awards – see S.124A ERA.

Since the basic award is not intended to compensate for direct financial loss, it is not open to a tribunal to reduce or eliminate it because an employee has suffered no financial loss through his or her dismissal. It is the compensatory award that is meant to make good financial loss. The basic award compensates for loss of job security. Two illustrations: **15.8**

- **Cadbury Ltd v Doddington** 1977 ICR 982, EAT: a tribunal found D's dismissal, after a long sickness absence, procedurally unfair but awarded no compensation because D would not have been fit to return to work anyway. The EAT said that this was not a ground for reducing the basic award but only for withholding a compensatory award

- **Yates v Bletchington Park Holdings Ltd** ET Case No.22676/83: Y resigned over withdrawal of company car facilities. A tribunal found that this was an unfair constructive dismissal. In fact, the day after she resigned Y had started a new job which carried both the same salary and a company car. She had suffered no direct financial loss but the tribunal held nevertheless that she was entitled to a basic award.

Unreasonable refusal of reinstatement offer

15.9

An unreasonable refusal of an offer of reinstatement only applies as a ground for reducing a basic award – by what is just and equitable – if the offer would have had the effect of reinstating the employee in all respects as if he or she had not been dismissed – S.122(1). Refusal of an offer made on different terms and conditions, even if the refusal is unreasonable, will not be grounds for reducing the basic award under this head (although it may well be grounds for reducing the compensatory award as constituting a failure by the employee to mitigate his or her loss – see Chapter 18).

In McDonald v Capital Coaches Ltd EAT 140/94 M was summarily dismissed for misconduct. Soon afterwards, the employer wrote to him stating that, since his record prior to the events leading to his dismissal was very good, the company would like him to come into work 'to discuss any problems… and see if these can be resolved amicably'. M declined and brought tribunal proceedings. The tribunal found the dismissal unfair but reduced M's basic award to nil under S.122(1). The EAT held that the tribunal had erred in construing the employer's letter as an offer of reinstatement. It was no more than an invitation to have a chat about the situation surrounding M's dismissal. For S.122(1) to apply, the offer must be one that can be accepted as such in a legal sense, not just in layperson's terms.

In Parkes v Banham Patent Locks Ltd EAT 207/96 Mr Justice Mummery recommended that tribunals adopt the following step-by-step approach to **15.10**

543

S.122(1). First, has the employer made an offer? Secondly, if that offer were to be accepted, would it have the effect of reinstating the employee as if he or she had not been dismissed? If so, did the employee refuse the offer? If the employee did refuse the offer, did he or she act reasonably or unreasonably in so doing? And, finally, if the employee acted unreasonably in refusing the offer, the tribunal must ask whether, and to what extent, it is just and equitable to reduce the basic award. The EAT also confirmed that there was no reason why S.122(1) should not apply to offers of reinstatement following a constructive dismissal. (For the avoidance of confusion, it is important to bear in mind that the issue here is an *offer* by the employer to reinstate the employee, not an order by the tribunal to reinstate the employee under S.114 ERA – see Chapter 14 for details of such orders.)

The question of reasonableness was considered by the Court of Appeal in Wilding v British Telecommunications plc 2002 ICR 1079, CA, in the context of compensatory awards, offers of re-employment and mitigation of loss. Lord Justice Potter stated that the test of unreasonableness is an objective one based on the totality of the evidence and, in applying that test, the circumstances in which the offer was made and refused, the attitude of the employer, the way in which the former employee had been treated and all the surrounding circumstances should be taken into account.

15.11   An example:

- **Cockram v Honda of UK Manufacturing Ltd** ET Case No.1400708/08: C was unfairly dismissed for breaching the company's smoking ban. Within three weeks he found another job in a completely different field of work on a broadly comparable wage but involving longer working hours. The new job provided a stakeholder pension, rather than the final salary pension scheme he had enjoyed with H Ltd. After the merits hearing the company's solicitor made an offer of reinstatement. C did not reply to the offer and it remained open at the date of the remedies hearing. At that hearing C stated that he was depressed about what had happened to him and that he could not go through it again. He said it made him feel physically sick even to think about it. He also said he was a loyal worker and was grateful to his new company for employing him. The tribunal held that, although the offer was made at a late stage, H Ltd had openly accepted the tribunal's decision and had sought to take appropriate steps to put the matter right. It had also apologised to C. There was no evidence that C would find it impossible to return to work for the company and as a result he was found to have unreasonably refused the offer of reinstatement and his award was limited to the basic award, reduced by 25 per cent for his unreasonable refusal.

Note that an employee's refusal to accept an offer of an alternative job made *before* he or she is dismissed could in certain circumstances warrant a reduction in the basic award on the ground of the employee's conduct under S.122(2) –

544

see below. This happened in Fulton v RMC Russell plc EAT 0055/03, where the EAT refused to interfere with a tribunal's finding that F's basic award should be reduced by 50 per cent under S.122(2) to reflect his conduct after he failed to apply for a different job and was subsequently dismissed.

Employee's conduct

15.12

A reduction on the ground of the employee's conduct can be made where 'the tribunal considers that any conduct of the complainant before the dismissal (or, where the dismissal was with notice, before the notice was given) was such that it would be just and equitable to reduce or further reduce the amount of the basic award to any extent' – S.122(2). (But note that this section does *not* apply where the reason for dismissal was *redundancy* unless the selection was for an inadmissible reason entitling the employee to a minimum basic award, in which case special provisions apply – see 'Redundancy cases' below.) It is the conduct of the employee alone which should be considered here, not that of any other employee – Parker Foundry Ltd v Slack 1992 ICR 302, CA; or, for that matter, the employer.

The wording of S.122(2) makes it clear that, unlike deductions from the compensatory award for contributory fault, it is unnecessary that the employee's conduct should have caused or contributed to the dismissal. Indeed, the misconduct may only come to light after the dismissal. In Hutchinson v Arkon Group Ltd and anor ET Case No.56347/92 the employer demoted H, who then resigned and brought a successful claim of unfair constructive dismissal. After H left, the employer discovered that he had, while still in the company's employ, set up a rival business. The tribunal held that this breach of trust and confidence warranted a 100 per cent reduction in the basic award. Note, however, that the misconduct must have taken place before the dismissal – where the dismissal was summary – or before notice was given, where the dismissal was with notice – see, for example, Belcher and ors v Great Bear Distribution Ltd EAT 0453/05 and Mullinger v Department for Work and Pensions EAT 0515/05. In Bell v Service Engines (Newcastle) Ltd ET Case No.3456/85 B was unfairly dismissed but committed various thefts from his employer during his notice period, for which he was convicted and fined. The tribunal decided that it was not just and equitable to make any compensatory award but it was constrained by the wording of S.122(2) to make a basic award in full.

An employee's unacceptable conduct should not be ignored simply because it is connected with a 'background or underlying illness'. In Sinclair v Wandsworth Council EAT 0145/07 the tribunal found that the employer's failure to apply its alcohol policy when dismissing S for being drunk at work rendered the dismissal unfair. However, the EAT held that the tribunal had erred in deciding that actions arising from S's alcoholism could not amount to contributory conduct for the purposes of S.122. If the tribunal was right on this point, then totally unacceptable conduct in the workplace could be excused by reference to

15.13

545

underlying illness. In reaching this conclusion, the EAT referred to an earlier case, Edmund Nuttall Ltd v Butterfield 2006 ICR 77, EAT, in which another division of the EAT held that the fact that the matters causing an employee's dismissal arose as a result of his mental illness did not mean that his award for unfair dismissal could not be reduced. In the Council's view, the same logic should apply with regard to S's alcoholism.

One question that has arisen in a number of cases is the extent to which tribunals are justified in treating the basic award and the compensatory award differently in respect of deductions for misconduct. In RSPCA v Cruden 1986 ICR 205, EAT, the EAT held that a tribunal was not necessarily bound to reduce the basic and compensatory awards in precisely the same proportions. The EAT pointed out that deductions for contributory conduct are a matter for the tribunal's discretion and that the wording of the two provisions is not identical. It added, however, that in light of the similarity between the provisions, it was likely to be only in exceptional circumstances that the deductions from the basic award and the compensatory award would differ. In Charles Robertson (Developments) Ltd v White and anor 1995 ICR 349, EAT, a tribunal made a 100 per cent reduction in the compensatory award on account of contributory conduct but reduced the basic award by only 50 per cent. The tribunal took the view that it would not be just and equitable to reduce the basic award to nil because the employees, in being dismissed without a fair hearing, had been deprived of an important right. The EAT upheld the decision on the basis that a discrepancy in reductions to the two awards was not wrong in principle. The two provisions are worded differently and different considerations apply to each. Similarly, in Optikinetics Ltd v Whooley 1999 ICR 984, EAT, the EAT noted that under S.122(2) a tribunal had a wide discretion whether or not to reduce the basic award on the ground of conduct and could choose not to do so. By contrast, this would not be a permissible option in relation to the compensatory award where a reduction for contributory conduct is mandatory. However, in the majority of cases, the reduction for conduct will be the same for both awards. If a tribunal does reduce the basic and compensatory awards by different proportions, it should give its reasons for doing so – Sterling Granada Contract Services Ltd v Hodgkinson EAT 894/95.

15.14   One situation in which the deductions from the two awards may well differ is where the tribunal not only makes a finding of contributory conduct but also decides that it would be just and equitable under S.123(1) to reduce the compensatory award to reflect the chance that the employee would have been dismissed even if a fair procedure had been followed. (Details of these 'no difference' dismissals are discussed in Chapter 18.) In Rao v Civil Aviation Authority 1994 ICR 495, CA, the Court of Appeal pointed out that in such cases the same misconduct may result in the basic award being reduced by a higher percentage deduction than the compensatory award. This is because the tribunal, in deciding the extent to which the employee's compensatory award should be reduced for contributory conduct under S.123(6), is entitled to take into account the amount by which the award has already been reduced on just and equitable grounds under S.123(1).

Tribunals will only be able to make a reduction under S.122(2) if they have sufficient evidence before them of the misconduct in question. In Western Leisure v Flynn and anor EAT 375/92 the circumstances were such that the employer knew that one of two employees was guilty of dishonesty and so decided to dismiss both. A tribunal held the dismissals to be unfair because the employer had failed to carry out a proper investigation. The tribunal nevertheless reduced the compensatory awards to nil on the ground that, had a proper investigation been carried out, the employees would inevitably have been dismissed. The employer appealed, arguing that the tribunal should also have declined to make any basic award to the employees. The EAT pointed out that the employees' compensatory awards had not been reduced on account of contributory conduct under S.123(6) but under the 'just and equitable' provision in S.123(1). The employer had put forward no evidence of dishonesty against either employee and the tribunal could not be expected to conduct its own investigation into whether one or other, or both, of the employees had in fact been dishonest.

Redundancy cases. As already noted, a reduction for misconduct under S.122(2) can only be made in limited circumstances in redundancy cases. These are where a minimum basic award applies under S.120(1). A minimum basic award applies to dismissals for certain inadmissible reasons (see above under 'Calculation of basic award'). Where this minimum award applies in a case of selection for redundancy for an inadmissible reason listed in S.120(1), a reduction may be made under S.122(2) *but only* by the amount by which the minimum award of £4,700 exceeds the normal basic award – S.156 TULR(C)A and S.122(3) ERA. Take, for example, a case where the normal basic award would have been £2,000 but, because the selection for redundancy was for an inadmissible reason, it is raised to the minimum £4,700 threshold. If the tribunal then decides to reduce compensation by 50 per cent, it can only apply this reduction to the difference between £4,700 and £2,000 (i.e. 50 per cent of £2,700). The employee will receive £3,350 after the reduction, instead of the £2,350 that he or she would have received if the reduction had been applied to the full amount of the basic award.

15.15

Trade union dismissals. Where the dismissal or selection for redundancy was for trade union reasons, the tribunal must disregard conduct leading to the dismissal that was a breach of a contractual term relating to union membership. Tribunals must also disregard a refusal to pay, or to allow deductions from pay to be made in favour of, somebody other than a union (a charity, for example) – S.155 TULR(C)A. The House of Lords confirmed in Tracey and ors v

15.16

Crosville Wales Ltd 1997 ICR 862, HL, that, in this context, tribunals must ignore any industrial action in which the applicant participated. The House of Lords did, however, agree with the Court of Appeal that there were limited circumstances in which conduct could, in theory, be taken into account, namely, where there was individual blameworthy conduct additional to, or separate from, the mere act of participation in industrial action. Transport and General Workers' Union v Howard 1992 ICR 106, EAT, is an example of a case in which confrontational conduct by the employee during industrial action was held to be sufficiently independent (rather than collective) to be considered contributory fault, justifying a reduction.

15.17 Designated dismissal procedures agreements

Section 122(3A) was inserted into the ERA by the Employment Rights (Dispute Resolution) Act 1998. It provides that where the employee has already received a payment under a designated dismissal procedures agreement, a tribunal should reduce a basic award by an amount that it considers just and equitable having regard to that payment.

Section 110 ERA sets out the stringent requirements for such agreements which, if met, effectively displace the protection against unfair dismissal set out in S.94 ERA and substitute a collective regime for dismissal with recourse to arbitration in case of disputes. As the consent of the Secretary of State is required for a designated dismissal procedures agreement to take effect, such agreements are rare in practice.

15.18 Receipt of a redundancy payment

Any redundancy payment received by an employee must be deducted from the basic award – S.122(4) ERA. In most cases this will extinguish the basic award altogether but where the employee began employment before the age of 18 the basic award may be higher than a statutory redundancy payment. If the amount of the basic award is lower than the redundancy payment, the excess is deductible from the compensatory award – S.123(7).

'Redundancy payment' in this context is not confined to a statutory redundancy payment but includes *any* payment made by the employer on the ground of redundancy. Thus it would cover corresponding payments made to civil servants and NHS employees who are excluded from the statutory redundancy scheme. It would also cover certain ex gratia payments – see below. Note, however, that for S.122(4) to apply, the dismissal must in fact have been by reason of redundancy. In Boorman v Allmakes Ltd 1995 ICR 842, CA, B was dismissed and given an ex gratia payment of £5,000 which was stated to incorporate his statutory redundancy entitlement. A tribunal found that B was not in fact redundant and went on to hold that his dismissal was unfair. Despite the ex gratia payment that B had received, the tribunal made a basic award of £2,079. The Court of Appeal upheld the award on the ground that, since B's dismissal was not a result of redundancy, S.122(4) did not apply. (See also Varig Brazilian Airways v Tully EAT 1014/96, Hannigan v Scottish and Newcastle Retail Ltd EAT 1109/95.)

Another example: **15.19**

- **Ashman v Sainsbury's Supermarkets Ltd** ET Case No.2201620/08: C was dismissed at a time when other members of the team in which she worked were made redundant. Her role was not redundant, but she was unable to carry it out as she suffered from severe RSI and would have had to be dismissed on capability grounds in any event, so her employer decided that it would be kinder to make her redundant at the same time as her colleagues. The tribunal held that the dismissal was unfair because the employer had failed to prove a fair reason for dismissal, but found that C would have been dismissed fairly in any event and so no compensatory award was made. C was awarded a basic award in full since the dismissal was not on the ground of redundancy, even though C had received a redundancy payment.

Trade union blacklists   **15.20**
Section 122(5) provides that where an employee has been unfairly dismissed for a reason relating to the use of a trade union 'blacklist' under S104F ERA and has received a basic award in respect of the same dismissal under S.156 TULR(C)A, the amount of the basic award under the ERA will be reduced accordingly. S.156 TULR(C)A applies a minimum basic award in cases of dismissal on grounds related to trade union membership or activities under S.152 or S.153 TULR(C)A. There is obviously considerable overlap between these provisions and S.104F ERA, in effect giving 'blacklisted' employees two causes of action in respect of the same dismissal. Where an employee successfully claims under both Acts, S.122(5) ensures that he or she does not receive a basic award in respect of each claim, thereby preventing double recovery.

Settlements and ex gratia payments   **15.21**

Any agreement to forgo a statutory employment right is void under S.203 ERA. Thus an attempt by an employer to settle an unfair dismissal claim will be void and the agreement will not preclude the employee from pursuing a claim even if he or she accepts the money. There are, however, a number of exceptions to this rule, of which three are relevant in the present context: (i) where the settlement is formally incorporated in a tribunal decision; (ii) where it is reached under the auspices of an Acas conciliator in accordance with S.203(2)(e); or (iii) where it satisfies the conditions for compromise agreements contained in S.203(3) (see further Chapter 2 under 'Settlements and contracting out').

If an ex gratia payment does not fall within any of these exceptions, there is nothing to prevent the employee pressing ahead with an unfair dismissal claim.

549

The ex gratia payment will then be offset against any compensatory award (since it will go towards lessening the employee's direct financial loss) and, possibly, against any additional award, if one is made, but it will not necessarily be treated as meeting any liability for a basic award (see below).

15.22   The leading case is Chelsea Football Club and Athletic Co Ltd v Heath 1981 ICR 323, EAT. In that case H was unfairly dismissed and then given a cheque for £7,500 by the employer which was described simply as 'ex gratia compensation'. The tribunal held that none of the statutory grounds for reducing a basic award (see above) applied. Although, therefore, £7,500 exceeded the maximum amount which it could have awarded H at that time, the tribunal proceeded to make a basic award of £1,920. On appeal, the EAT pointed out that the employer's argument was not that there should be a reduction in the basic award but rather that it should not be ordered to pay one at all because it had already paid the basic award as part of the £7,500. The EAT said that whether or not a severance payment should be treated as extinguishing liability for a basic award was a 'question of construction'. If an employer stated clearly that a severance payment was intended to meet any possible liability for basic or compensatory awards that might be made by a tribunal, then it would have no further liability (provided the payment was large enough). However, when the employer simply makes a *general* payment – particularly one expressed as being 'ex gratia' – it will run the risk of a tribunal treating that payment as if it did not refer to unfair dismissal liability at all.

The message for employers is clear. Any severance payment to a dismissed employee should expressly be stated to cover all possible liability arising out of the employee's complaint to a tribunal. In the Chelsea FC case, the EAT did in fact set aside the tribunal award. Use of the word 'compensation' seems to have tipped the scales and the EAT accepted that the employer's intention was to compensate H for rights arising from his dismissal. In Pomphrey of Sittingbourne Ltd v Reed EAT 457/94, however, R was paid 12 weeks' salary in lieu of notice on the termination of his employment. Following the tribunal's finding of unfair dismissal, the company sought to argue that, in view of the long period that R had been off sick by the time of his dismissal, there had been no contractual obligation to make any payment in lieu of notice and, therefore, the payment should be offset against the basic award. The EAT held that, regardless of whether contractually obliged to do so, the company had made a payment that was expressly stated to be a payment in lieu of notice. It could not later change its mind and have the payment appropriated to the basic award.

15.23   In Boorman v Allmakes Ltd 1995 ICR 842, CA, the employer made an ex gratia payment that was expressed to include the employee's statutory redundancy entitlement. A tribunal found that the dismissal was not in fact on account of redundancy and made a basic award of £2,079. The Court of Appeal rejected the employer's argument that the ex gratia payment included the payment of £2,079, either as a basic award or a redundancy payment. A payment expressed to be ex gratia and to incorporate a statutory redundancy entitlement could not be construed as incorporating a payment to which the employee would only be entitled had he or she been unfairly dismissed.

Note that if an ex gratia payment is set off against the basic award, any surplus that remains should be applied against the compensatory award (see the Chelsea FC case above and Chapter 18). Any remaining surplus should be carried over to be set off against an additional award, if one is made (see Darr and anor v LRC Products Ltd 1993 IRLR 257, EAT, and Chapter 19).

Ideally, from an employer's perspective, any severance payment should be endorsed by an Acas conciliator (if Acas has been involved in promoting a settlement) or should satisfy the conditions for compromise agreements contained in S.203(3). This would prevent the employee pursuing an unfair dismissal claim later and sidestep the issue of whether the payment could be interpreted as extinguishing a basic award. Settlements and compromise agreements are considered in greater detail in Chapter 2.

Order of deductions   15.24

By analogy with compensatory awards, it would seem that ex gratia payments should be deducted from the basic award before any other reductions (for contributory conduct or on any other ground set out above) are applied. However, an employer who has made a statutory or contractual redundancy payment is entitled to have this deducted last (i.e. after all other deductions have been made) – see further Chapter 18.

16 Compensatory awards: types of loss

Nature and maximum amount of award

Immediate loss

Future loss

Expenses

Loss of statutory rights

Pension loss

Interest

Drafting schedules of loss

16.1

The second (and usually the largest) element of the compensation awarded in cases of unfair dismissal is the compensatory award. Unlike the basic award, which is calculated by reference to a statutory formula that bears little relation to the employee's real financial loss, the compensatory award is intended to reflect the actual losses that the employee suffers as a consequence of being unfairly dismissed. To this end, employment tribunals are directed by statute to award 'such amount as the tribunal considers just and equitable in all the circumstances, having regard to the loss sustained by the complainant in consequence of the dismissal in so far as that loss is attributable to action taken by the employer' – S.123(1) Employment Rights Act 1996 (ERA).

When assessing what the employee has actually lost as a consequence of being unfairly dismissed, the tribunal looks at the net remuneration that the employee would have continued to receive if the dismissal had not occurred. This raises a number of questions: does the employee have to give credit for a severance payment received from the employer? Must credit be given for earnings received from a new employer? For which lost benefits will the employee be compensated? At which point in time will the employee's losses no longer be attributable to the dismissal? Before such questions can be answered, there are some general points concerning the amount and nature of the compensatory award that should be noted.

Nature and maximum amount of award

16.2

Section 123 ERA, as set out above, requires an employment tribunal to have regard to the loss incurred by the employee as a result of the dismissal, but other factors apart from actual loss can be taken into account. The objective is to award what the tribunal considers to be a 'just and equitable' amount. It follows that the compensatory award can, in appropriate cases, be something other than a precise arithmetical computation of the employee's losses.

Certain general points, however, apply to limit the otherwise wide discretion a tribunal has to adopt a broad-brush approach to the calculation of the compensatory award. These limits are discussed below.

16.3   Unfairness must have made a difference

The fundamental limit to the compensation that a tribunal may award on a finding of unfair dismissal is that it must only cover loss that flows from the unfair dismissal. Thus, if a tribunal finds that the employee would have been dismissed in any event, and on the same day, the compensatory award will generally be nil – in such circumstances the unfairness makes no difference. An example:

- **Ros and Angel t/a Cherry Tree Day Nursery v Fanstone** EAT 0273/07: F had been summarily dismissed on the day her resignation had been due to take effect, and her employer had refused to supply her with a reference, leading her prospective new employer to withdraw its job offer. The tribunal, having found the dismissal unfair, awarded a sum of £4,000 to reflect the immediate and future loss of earnings that F would experience as a result of the dismissal. On appeal, the EAT set aside the award of compensation. The losses were not attributable to the dismissal, since F would have departed at the end of the day on which she was dismissed. Rather, the losses – at their highest – were attributable to the refusal to provide a reference, something for which a tribunal cannot award compensation.

If a tribunal finds that the unfairness merely hastened a dismissal that would have occurred at a later date, then, in addition to the basic award, it should only award compensation covering the period between when the dismissal did occur and when it considers it would have occurred had the employer acted fairly. In King and ors v Eaton Ltd (No.2) 1998 IRLR 686, Ct Sess (Inner House), the Court of Session stated that while it may not always be appropriate to classify a case as one of 'procedural' or 'substantive' unfairness, such a distinction can assist a tribunal in reaching a hypothetical view on what might have happened had the unfairness not occurred. In cases where the employer's only failing was procedural, it may be fairly straightforward to establish what would have happened had a fair procedure been adopted, and to award compensation accordingly. Where the failing is more substantive in nature, it may be more difficult to determine what would have happened.

It is clear from the above that a tribunal is entitled to limit the compensatory award in a case where, had a proper dismissal procedure been applied, dismissal would have occurred in any event albeit at a later date. But whereas

554 ───────────────────────────────────

the King case (above) suggests that this kind of reduction is confined mainly to cases of procedural failings, decisions in subsequent cases have in fact extended the capacity to limit the compensatory award in this way to where the unfairness is substantive rather than purely procedural. For example, in Lambe v 186K Ltd 2005 ICR 307, CA, the Court of Appeal held that a tribunal had been entitled to find on the evidence that, despite both the process of selection for redundancy and the lack of consultation being unfair, the claimant would have been dismissed in any event after a period of seven weeks' consultation. The tribunal had therefore been justified in limiting the compensation which the claimant received to seven weeks of loss.

Where a tribunal considers that there is only a chance that, had there been no unfairness, the dismissal would have occurred in any event, it may reduce the compensation by a percentage that reflects its assessment of that chance. This is known as a 'Polkey reduction', after the case of Polkey v AE Dayton Services Ltd 1988 ICR 142, HL, and is addressed at length in Chapter 18 under 'Polkey reductions'.

Statutory cap 16.4

As the tribunal is seeking to ascertain the employee's true losses, there is no limit placed on the amount of a week's pay, as there is with the calculation of the basic award. If the employee's net earnings were £1,000 a week, then this is the amount on which the tribunal will base its calculations. (Note, however, that if the employer is paying the employee an amount less than the national minimum wage, the tribunal is obliged to ensure that, in calculating a week's pay, it takes the national minimum wage into account – Paggetti v Cobb 2002 IRLR 861, EAT.)

In theory, at least, there is no limit on the period over which losses can be assessed (but see below on the effects of obtaining new employment and the employee's duty to mitigate his or her loss). S.124(1) does, however, place a statutory limit on the size of a compensatory award, which takes effect once all the calculations, including deductions, have been made. The limit – which is subject to review every year – currently stands at £65,300 (as from 1 February 2010).

Exceptions to statutory limit 16.5

As we saw in Chapter 10, S.124(1A) ERA removes the statutory limit on the compensatory award in certain circumstances. There is now no statutory maximum on the compensatory award that can be made where the reason for the dismissal was that the employee:

- carried out or proposed to carry out activities in connection with preventing or reducing risks to health and safety at work, having been designated by the employer to do so (S.100(1)(a) ERA)

555

- performed or proposed to perform the functions of a health and safety representative, or member of a safety committee, either in accordance with arrangements established by statute or after being recognised as such by the employer (S.100(1)(b))

- took part, or proposed to take part, in consultation with the employer pursuant to the Health and Safety (Consultation with Employees) Regulations 1996 SI 1996/1513 or in an election of safety representatives within the meaning of those Regulations, whether as a candidate or otherwise (S.100(1)(ba))

- brought to the employer's attention, by reasonable means, circumstances connected with his or her work which he or she reasonably believed were harmful or potentially harmful to health or safety (S.100(1)(c))

- in circumstances of danger which he or she reasonably believed to be serious and imminent and which he or she could not reasonably be expected to avert, left, proposed to leave or (while the danger persisted) refused to return to his or her place of work or any dangerous part of his or her place of work (S.100(1)(d))

- in circumstances of danger took, or proposed to take, appropriate steps to protect him or herself or other persons from danger which he or she reasonably believed to be serious and imminent (S.100(1)(e))

- made a protected disclosure (S.103A), or

- was selected for redundancy and the reason for selection was one of the above reasons (S.105(3) and (6A)).

Furthermore, in limited circumstances the compensatory award can be increased by an additional award – see Chapter 19 for details.

16.6 **Compensation, not punishment**
The compensatory award is strictly limited to making good the employee's financial loss. In no sense should the tribunal seek to bring into its calculations any consideration of what would be 'just' in order to punish the employer or reflect its disapproval of the employer's employment practices. Nor should its award reflect any feelings of sympathy for the employee or the tribunal's view of what a fair severance payment would be – see Lifeguard Assurance Ltd v Zadrozny and anor 1977 IRLR 56, EAT.

The principle that the purpose of the compensatory award is confined to compensating only proven financial loss and is not in any sense to be used to penalise the employer was confirmed by the EAT in Morgans v Alpha Plus Security Ltd 2005 IRLR 234, EAT. In that case, the Appeal Tribunal, presided over by Mr Justice Burton, rejected the contention that invalidity benefits received by the unfairly dismissed employee did not have to be offset in full

556

from the compensatory award. In support of this conclusion, the EAT relied upon the House of Lords' ruling in Dunnachie v Kingston upon Hull City Council 2004 ICR 1052, HL, to the effect that compensation under S.123 ERA is not recoverable in respect of non-economic losses. In the course of giving judgment, Burton J stated: 'If there is no loss, no compensation can be recovered even for the most unfair of unfair dismissals... but the basic award marks the disapproval of the tribunal.'

Manner of dismissal

16.7

Following the ruling of the National Industrial Relations Court in Norton Tool Co Ltd v Tewson 1972 ICR 501, NIRC, it was settled law, for over 30 years, that compensation for unfair dismissal covers economic loss alone and that a tribunal should not normally take account of the manner of dismissal (including injury to feelings) when assessing compensation under S.123 ERA unless there was cogent evidence that the manner of the dismissal had caused actual financial loss.

However, uncertainty as to the Norton Tool rule arose as a result of comments made in the House of Lords by Lord Hoffmann in Johnson v Unisys Ltd 2001 ICR 480, HL. In that case, the House of Lords decided that the implied term of mutual trust and confidence did not apply to the manner of dismissal, so no damages could be recovered at common law where the manner of dismissal caused psychiatric damage and consequential loss of earnings. Part of the House of Lords' reasoning was that a common law right should not be developed which would effectively cover the same ground as the statutory right not to be unfairly dismissed. During his judgment, Lord Hoffmann suggested that 'in an appropriate case' unfair dismissal compensation could cover not just financial loss but also 'distress, humiliation, damage to reputation in the community or to family life'.

Lord Hoffmann's comments led to a spirited debate as to whether, in unfair dismissal cases, tribunals should set aside the Norton Tool rule and make awards for non-pecuniary losses in appropriate circumstances. It was not clear whether Lord Hoffmann's remarks were part of the binding ratio of his judgment or were merely obiter – i.e. incidental to his decision and reasoning. After a fair amount of confusion, the matter was finally resolved by a further decision of the House of Lords in Dunnachie v Kingston upon Hull City Council 2004 ICR 1052, HL. That was a case where the employee won his claim of unfair (constructive) dismissal on the basis that he had been subjected to a prolonged campaign of bullying and undermining by his erstwhile manager. A tribunal found that, in failing to deal with the matter, his employer's actions had reduced him to a 'state of overt despair', and it awarded the claimant £10,000 to reflect the injury to his feelings in addition to his financial losses on the basis that Lord Hoffmann's remarks in Johnson permitted such an award.

557

16.8 When the case eventually reached the House of Lords their Lordships unanimously ruled that S.123 ERA precludes the award of non-economic loss. Lord Steyn, who gave the main judgment with which the other Law Lords all agreed, explained his reasoning as follows:

- the remarks of Lord Hoffmann in Johnson v Unisys Ltd were, in fact, merely obiter dicta and not essential to his decision in that case. Therefore, the fact that two other Law Lords in Johnson expressed agreement with Lord Hoffmann's decision was not to be taken as indicating their approval of his remarks concerning Norton Tool

- S.123(1) ERA, which governs the position on the compensatory award, stipulates that a tribunal may award such amount as it 'considers just and equitable in all the circumstances having regard to the loss sustained by the complainant'. 'Loss', in this context, is confined to financial losses. It precludes – as the NIRC held in Norton Tool – the award of non-economic losses such as injury to feelings.

As Sir John Donaldson had explained in the Norton Tool case, the phrase 'just and equitable' gives tribunals a degree of flexibility as regards the informality of their procedures, so that precise and detailed proof of every item of loss does not necessarily have to be demanded of a complainant. But it does not permit tribunals to award additional sums that do not amount to 'loss' as defined.

16.9 ## Stigma damages

On a related point, as a result of the House of Lords' decision in Malik and anor v Bank of Credit and Commerce International SA (in compulsory liquidation) 1997 ICR 606, HL, damages for wrongful dismissal (breach of contract) may include losses resulting from difficulties that the employee experiences in the labour market in securing new employment as a result of the employer's poor reputation at the time of dismissal. In that case, the claimant employees had been 'tarnished' by the corrupt and dishonest means by which the employer had operated BCCI – that tarnish taking the form of damage to their reputations in the labour market, with resultant harm being done to their prospects of future employment even though they themselves were entirely innocent of corruption or dishonesty. The House of Lords held that the losses flowing from the damage to the employees' reputations was recoverable in a claim for breach of contract on the ground that the company had, by its conduct, breached the term of implied trust and confidence. Losses to reputation were, in Lord Nicholls' phrase, 'continuing financial losses' – as distinct from 'premature termination losses' – inasmuch as the repercussions of the damage to reputation continued to cause loss after the employment relationship had ended. Such losses were recoverable in claims for breach of contract (and, presumably, unfair constructive dismissal) – subject to proof that a breach of the implied term has occurred, that the damage to reputation was actually caused by the breach, and that the employee had taken steps to mitigate his loss.

The issue of stigma damages was given further consideration by the Court of Appeal in Abbey National plc and anor v Chagger 2010 ICR 397, CA, a case which seems to confirm, albeit by indirect means, that stigma damages are recoverable in unfair dismissal claims. C had successfully argued that his selection for redundancy was both an unfair dismissal and an act of race discrimination. He contended that compensation should reflect his decreased chances of finding other employment after leaving AN plc due to the 'stigma' of having brought race discrimination proceedings. AN plc argued that such damages are not appropriate, since any employer refusing to recruit an employee on the basis that the employee has brought discrimination proceedings against a former employer would be committing an act of unlawful victimisation under S.2 of the Race Relations Act 1976. Lord Justice Elias, giving judgment for the Court, examined the Malik decision and concluded that, while the stigma in C's case was of a different nature, the House of Lords' reasoning applied to it just as much as it did to the stigma of a failed and disgraced former employer. The pivotal issue was whether the fact that the third party's conduct would be unlawful should change matters. In Elias LJ's view, there are a number of public policy reasons why it should not. Among them is the fact that a third party employer could lawfully refuse to recruit an employee who had brought unfair dismissal proceedings against his or her former employer – there is no equivalent to the victimisation provisions in respect of unfair dismissal. Elias LJ stated that it would be 'unsatisfactory and somewhat artificial if tribunals were obliged to discount stigma loss in the context of discrimination law but not in other contexts'.

Implicit in Elias LJ's reasoning is the notion that stigma damages are potentially available in unfair dismissal claims (and, for that matter, all employment tribunal claims in which there is an element of future loss). However, he went on to point out that the effect of any stigma is not a separate head of damage, but rather a factor to be taken into consideration when a tribunal calculates the degree of future loss that the claimant will experience (see further below under 'Future loss').

'Deemed losses' and the Norton Tool rule

16.10

Although, as stated above, the House of Lords in Dunnachie v Kingston upon Hull City Council 2004 ICR 1052, HL, approved Sir John Donaldson's statement in Norton Tool Co Ltd v Tewson 1972 ICR 501, NIRC, that the compensatory award should be used only to compensate proven financial loss, one other aspect of the NIRC's ruling did not receive much attention from their Lordships. This was its decision that an employee who had been unfairly dismissed without notice, and who had taken up fresh employment during what would have been the notice period, was entitled to receive a sum equivalent to notice pay as part of his unfair dismissal compensation without giving credit for the monies he had earned from the new employment. This aspect of Norton Tool was followed by the EAT in TBA Industrial Products Ltd v Locke 1984 IRLR 48, EAT, and approved, although obiter (i.e. not binding), by the Court

559

of Appeal in Addison v Babcock FATA Ltd 1987 ICR 805, CA. In the light of Dunnachie, the question obviously arose whether the Norton Tool principle remained good law, and this fell to be considered by different divisions of the EAT in Morgans v Alpha Plus Security Ltd 2005 IRLR 234, EAT, and Voith Turbo Ltd v Stowe 2005 IRLR 228, EAT.

The issue that lay at the heart of the Morgans case was whether incapacity benefits received by the employee during the period covered by the compensatory award should be deducted from that award. The EAT, presided over by its then President Mr Justice Burton, held that the social security benefits did have to be deducted in full, reasoning that in the light of Dunnachie v Kingston upon Hull City Council (above), there was no room for the rule in Norton Tool that an employee can be 'treated' as having suffered loss if no actual loss has occurred. In reaching this conclusion, Burton J relied heavily on the similar legal reasoning he adopted in Hardy v Polk (Leeds) Ltd 2004 IRLR 420, EAT, when holding that an employee who mitigated the loss caused by his summary dismissal by finding new employment during what would have been his notice period was required to offset his earnings from that new employment against the compensatory award.

16.11 However, a different view was taken by the EAT in Voith, presided over by His Honour Judge McMullen. In that case, which concerned exactly the same issue as Hardy v Polk, the EAT expressed the view that the decisions of Burton J in that case and in the Morgans case flew in the face of the established 'good industrial practice' promoted by NIRC in Norton Tool. The EAT specifically cited Norton Tool as justification for not requiring an employee who had been paid in lieu of notice to give credit for monies earned from fresh employment during the notice period.

Neither the Morgans nor the Voith case progressed to the Court of Appeal, but the scope of Norton Tool was eventually given detailed consideration in Langley and anor v Burlo 2007 ICR 390, CA. That case concerned B, who had been unfairly and wrongfully dismissed from her role as a nanny at a time when she was recovering from a car accident. Due to her injuries, B would have been unable to work during her eight-week contractual notice period, and under the terms of her contract would only have been entitled to statutory sick pay. In assessing B's compensatory award, the tribunal did not take account of the eight weeks' notice period since it had already awarded eight weeks' pay in respect of the wrongful dismissal. The award for wrongful dismissal was overturned on appeal, but in her cross-appeal B contended that the principle in Norton Tool – that, since it is good industrial practice to give full pay in lieu of notice to an employee who is dismissed without notice, an employee's compensation should include a sum equivalent to the pay in lieu of notice which she should have had, irrespective of whether she has found other work during the notice period – should be extended to cases where the employee is unable to work his or her notice period due to sickness.

560

The EAT accepted that good industrial practice was as B had described it, but it held, by a majority, that the Norton Tool principle was no longer a legitimate basis for awarding full compensation for the notice period. The Appeal Tribunal stated that the principle had been undermined by the House of Lords' decision in the Dunnachie v Kingston upon Hull City Council (above) that S.123 permits only the award of sums which reflect the loss resulting from the dismissal and that it is not legitimate to award sums which are additional to such loss.

16.12

When the case reached the Court of Appeal, the result was the same – B was not entitled to full pay for the extent of her notice period – but the reasoning was very different. Unlike the EAT, the Court considered that Norton Tool remains good law, observing that it had neither been expressly nor impliedly overruled by Dunnachie. However, the Court stated that the authority of Norton Tool is restricted to the narrow point that, since it is good industrial practice for an employer who has dismissed an employee without notice to make a full payment in lieu of notice, a tribunal in assessing compensation for dismissal should not subject this payment to any deduction for sums earned in other employment during the notice period. There are no grounds for extending the principle to cover other facets of good industrial relations practice which, if applied to the award of compensation under S.123, would result in an award greater than the loss caused to the employee as a consequence of the dismissal. As a result, B had only been entitled to statutory sick pay during her notice period.

While there was undoubtedly a degree of logic to the reasoning that Dunnachie put paid to any flexibility on the part of tribunals to treat anything other than actual financial loss as comprising 'loss' for the purposes of S.123 ERA, the Court in Burlo was clearly swayed by the fact that the Norton Tool principle has been applied in tribunals for over 30 years and, in the words of Lord Justice Mummery, 'has not been shown to have worked unfairly'. Until such time as the Supreme Court says otherwise, courts and tribunals should continue to apply the narrow Norton Tool principle in calculating compensation for wages in lieu of notice in unfair dismissal cases.

So the Norton Tool exception to the principle that the compensatory award should be based solely on actual loss remains valid. However, as the Burlo case makes clear, the scope of the exception will be tightly defined. This is fully apparent from the Court of Appeal's subsequent decision in Stuart Peters Ltd v Bell 2009 ICR 1556, CA, where it was held that the Norton Tool principle does not apply to claims of unfair constructive dismissal. In the Stuart Peters case the claimant, B, had been unfairly constructively dismissed without being paid her six months' contractual notice pay. In awarding compensation, the tribunal relied on the Norton Tool principle and did not give credit for the earnings from three months of temporary work that the claimant had performed during the notice period. The EAT upheld this

16.13

decision, but the Court of Appeal saw things differently. Lord Justice Elias, who gave the leading judgment, stressed that the Norton Tool principle is not simply designed to give full compensation during what would have been the notice period had the contract been terminated with notice. Rather, it is designed to uphold expectations that will result from the application of good industrial relations practice where the employer has chosen to terminate the contract. Its purpose is to ensure that an employer who fails to comply with good industrial relations practice is not in a better position than he would have been in if he had followed the practice. Even if the employer genuinely believes that he is entitled to dismiss summarily for gross misconduct, he must take the consequences of getting his assessment wrong.

Lord Justice Elias then contrasted this situation with that of a constructive dismissal, where entirely different considerations arise. If the employee resigns in response to the employer's alleged repudiatory breach of contract, there is no general – let alone appropriate – practice of making a payment in lieu of notice. In fact, the employer will usually dispute that there has been a repudiatory breach at all – he is purporting to keep the contract alive and is willing to continue to pay the wages. Elias LJ emphasised that it is not that a different legal rule operates in such circumstances, simply that there is a difference in good practice, which leads to a different result. Even if this means that the employer avoids the application of the Norton Tool principle where he commits a breach of contract, this is simply the effect of the principle being rooted in good practice rather than 'wider considerations of justice or logic'.

16.14   **Tribunals' discretion**

In some cases it will be possible to assess compensation with a high degree of accuracy. For example, where the employee promptly obtains a new job that pays more than the old one, the losses will be limited to the short period of unemployment between the two jobs. In other cases – e.g. where the claimant is still unemployed when the tribunal comes to assess compensation, or where a new job pays *less* than the old one – the tribunal will be forced to adopt a far more speculative approach to assessing likely periods of unemployment or likely future earnings.

So far as possible, tribunals should use the facts that are at their disposal in order to reach an accurate assessment of compensation. But the fact that they will often be compelled to adopt a broad-brush approach has long been recognised by the courts. In Norton Tool Co Ltd v Tewson 1972 ICR 501, NIRC, for example, Sir John Donaldson recognised that what is now S.123(1) gives tribunals a good deal of discretion when assessing compensatory awards and said that the award was 'not to be assessed by adopting the approach of a conscientious and skilled cost accountant or actuary'.

562

The extent of this discretion means that an appeal against a tribunal's assessment of compensation is unlikely to meet with much success unless it can be shown that the tribunal misdirected itself in law or made a decision that no reasonable tribunal could have made. The appeal courts may even be prepared to overlook minor errors in the tribunal's calculations – Fougère v Phoenix Motor Co Ltd 1976 ICR 495, EAT.

There are limits to the tribunals' discretion, however. In the Norton Tool case Sir John Donaldson stated that the object of the compensatory award is 'to compensate, and compensate fully, but not to award a bonus' and went on to say that tribunals must exercise their discretion 'judicially and upon the basis of principle', and that they should break down a compensatory award into heads of compensation so that the parties can follow how the compensation was assessed. These are outlined below.

Heads of compensation   16.15

The heads of compensation normally used by tribunals are:

- immediate loss of earnings – i.e. loss between the dismissal and the hearing at which the tribunal decides on compensation

- future loss of earnings – i.e. estimated loss after the hearing

- expenses incurred as a consequence of the dismissal

- loss of statutory employment protection rights – this covers, for example, the fact that an unfairly dismissed employee will be unable to bring another unfair dismissal claim until he or she has had a year's continuous employment in a new job

- loss of pension rights.

It is the employee's duty to provide evidence of his or her losses. In the words of Mr Justice Bristow in Adda International Ltd v Curcio 1976 IRLR 425, EAT, 'the tribunal must have something to bite on, and if an applicant produces nothing for it to bite on, he will have only himself to thank'. Claimants must therefore be fully prepared to show evidence of loss under each head of damage because the tribunal will not be required to take any particular point into account on compensation unless the claimant produces evidence in support. Very often, tribunals now require claimants to provide a 'schedule of loss' to the respondent as part of the case management process leading up to a tribunal hearing – see the section 'Drafting a schedule of loss' at the end of this chapter. Tribunals have a duty, however, to enquire into each head of compensation – Tidman v Aveling Marshall Ltd 1977 IRLR 218, EAT. A tribunal should also briefly explain the manner and reasoning by which it arrived at its figures. The very discipline of setting out and explaining the heads of compensation is seen as a way of both guarding

563

against and highlighting any errors, while also steering the tribunal towards a reasonable figure.

Before going on to explain the methods by which the various heads of compensation are assessed, and the circumstances in which a compensatory award may be reduced, it is worth noting the comments of His Honour Judge Hull QC in Garage Equipment Maintenance Co Ltd v Holloway EAT 582/94, where he pointed out that the kind of precise argument that goes into assessing damages at common law in personal injury claims is inappropriate in cases of unfair dismissal. Matters of compensation raise extremely difficult questions of logic and causation, but it is clear both from the wide wording of S.123(1) and from countless decided cases that tribunals are enjoined to use a very broad-brush approach. This approach may have its drawbacks: it will inevitably mean that a great many imponderables which could be investigated at length will be put to one side and a very general view taken, 'but it does have the advantage that it is relatively simple and straightforward'. Common sense and a just approach are more important than an over-adherence to strict logic.

16.16 Immediate loss

The employee's 'immediate loss' is the loss incurred between the effective date of termination of the contract of employment and the date when the tribunal assesses the loss (i.e. at the remedies hearing). Subject to what is said below about the employee obtaining new employment, immediate loss is assessed up to this date even if the final compensation hearing is subject to considerable delay because of protracted appeals on the issue of liability – Gilham and ors v Kent County Council (No.3) 1986 ICR 52, EAT.

This period covered by 'immediate loss' as defined above is also the period that is subject to the recoupment provisions under the Employment Protection (Recoupment of Jobseeker's Allowance and Income Support) Regulations 1996 SI 1996/2349. These provisions put in place a procedure whereby the employer is directed to deduct from compensation awarded to the employee any sums received by the employee of Jobseeker's Allowance or Income Support. The employer is then obliged to pay over such sums to the Department for Work and Pensions as a way of enabling the DWP to recoup the social security payments it has made during the relevant period. In an unfair dismissal case the recoupment provisions potentially apply to that part of the compensatory award covering lost earnings up to the conclusion of proceedings but not any award the tribunal may make for future loss. For more detail on the Recoupment Regulations, see Chapter 20.

In contrast to the basic award (see Chapter 15), for the purposes of the compensatory award, loss is assessed by reference to the net pay that the employee would have earned but for the dismissal. The award is intended to compensate the employee only for actual loss stemming from the dismissal. Therefore, as part of the general rule that sums received in mitigation of loss should be offset against the losses claimed, the employee must give credit where he or she receives pay in lieu of notice or an ex gratia payment from the employer (see, for example, DCM Optical Clinic plc v Stark EAT 0124/04). The employee must also give credit for earnings from any new employment obtained since dismissal (subject to an exception regarding the notice period that is considered below).

New employment

16.17

An important point arises concerning the situation where an employee obtains new employment in the period between the date of dismissal and the date on which the tribunal assesses compensation.

The Ging rule: new earnings required to be offset. The general rule is that a tribunal should offset the employee's new earnings against his or her losses to discover what the overall loss has been during this period – Ging v Ellward Lancs Ltd 1978 ITR 265, EAT. So, taking the example of a dismissed employee who obtains a better-paid job after a period of unemployment, the compensation will be based on his or her old pay for the period of unemployment, *less* what has since been earned *in excess* of the old salary in the new job. (If the new job pays *less* than the old, then the employee can be compensated for the difference between the old and the new pay.)

16.18

However, this approach can produce some unacceptable results. It is not hard to imagine a situation where the employee's new salary, coupled with a delay in the tribunal proceedings, would mean that losses between dismissal and the date when the employee started the new job were cancelled out by the time of the tribunal hearing. Such a result is seen as undesirable, partly because the amount of compensation should not depend so greatly on a random factor like the timing of the tribunal hearing, and partly because the dismissed employee is penalised for obtaining new, well-paid work.

Exceptions to the Ging rule. An exception to the rule in Ging was first developed in relation to the situation where the employee is deemed to have entered new *permanent* employment before the tribunal hearing on compensation. In Courtaulds Northern Spinning Ltd v Moosa 1984 ICR 218, EAT, the hearing did not take place until more than three years after the dismissal date. For 18 months of those three years, M had worked for a new employer. He was then made redundant. In this case the respondent's liability was held to have ceased when M entered the new job because, according to the EAT, it was an equivalent permanent job. Thus, neither M's earnings in the new job nor his renewed losses when he became unemployed again before the hearing were taken into account. (It may be worth noting here, however, that the measure by which the EAT identified the new employment as being

16.19

565

permanent was the fact that it had lasted long enough for M to have acquired new employment protection rights.)

The fact that S.123(1) ERA requires tribunals to award such sums as they consider just and equitable leaves some scope for them to use their discretion to circumvent the more undesirable aspects of the Ging decision. This has been confirmed in two Scottish cases. In Lytlarch Ltd t/a Viceroy Restaurant v Reid EAT 269/90 the EAT, while acknowledging the general rule in Ging, said that the rule may not necessarily apply where there is a long delay between dismissal and the compensation hearing. And in Fentiman v Fluid Engineering Products Ltd 1991 IRLR 150, EAT, the Appeal Tribunal added that the Ging method of calculation will not necessarily be appropriate in circumstances where new earnings are considerably higher than the old and where a significant period of time has passed between the employee starting the new job and the date of the tribunal's assessment of compensation. In that case a period of 39 weeks in the new job was considered to be sufficiently 'permanent' to justify limiting the assessment of the claimant's compensation to the date when he started the new job. In both these cases the EAT confirmed that the Ging rule remains the general rule, but exceptions have now clearly been established.

Even so, this is a matter that could do with further clarification by the courts because we seem to be left with a rather rigid 'all or nothing' approach. If Ging does apply, new earnings will be fully offset up to the tribunal hearing. If it does not apply, assessment of losses will abruptly cease at the point when the employee obtains a new job. Note that where the employee's new job pays *less* than the old one, assessment of losses based on the difference between those earnings can continue over a substantial period.

16.20   An attempt to provide clarification of this difficult issue was made by the EAT in Whelan and anor v Richardson 1998 ICR 318, EAT. In that case an employee was unfairly dismissed from her job which paid her £72 per week. She found employment in another job which paid £52 per week and which lasted 18 weeks. She then got a job paying £96 per week. She was still in that job when, some 15 months after her dismissal, the tribunal held a hearing to assess her loss. The assessment was made by calculating the wages which she would have received from the date of dismissal to the date she started the higher-paid job, and then deducting the money she earned during her 18 weeks' temporary employment in the lower-paid job. The EAT upheld the tribunal's calculation, stating that it had been correct to treat as the cut-off point the date that the employee secured permanent employment that was at least as well paid as the original job. The EAT laid down a series of propositions to be applied when assessing an employee's loss:

- the assessment of loss must be judged on the basis of the facts as they appear at the date of the remedies hearing

- where the employee has been unemployed during the period from the dismissal to the date of the remedies hearing, then, subject to the duty to mitigate, the employee will recover what he or she would have earned during that period had he or she not been dismissed. The tribunal should also consider for how long the loss is likely to continue

- where the employee has found alternative work that pays less than the job from which he or she was dismissed, the employee will be compensated in the same manner as described in the previous proposition, save that the new, lower income will be deducted from the loss of earnings

- if, at the date of the remedies hearing, the employee has found alternative permanent employment which pays at least as much as the job from which he or she was dismissed, then the tribunal should only assess the employee's loss from the date of dismissal to the date on which he or she started the new job. The dismissing employer cannot rely on the employee's increased earnings to reduce the loss sustained prior to taking the new employment.

Earnings from temporary new employment. As for the question of whether employment taken by the employee following his or her dismissal is in fact temporary or permanent, that is for the tribunal to decide. The EAT in Whelan and anor v Richardson (above) added that a dismissed employee should not be discouraged from taking temporary employment because of a fear that the employer will not be liable for losses which continue after the temporary employment comes to an end.

However, in Dench v Flynn and Partners 1998 IRLR 653, CA, the Court of Appeal held that an employer's liability for the loss suffered by an unfairly dismissed employee does not necessarily cease once the employee commences new employment of a permanent nature at a salary equivalent to or higher than that which the employee previously enjoyed. The Court acknowledged that in many cases the loss consequent upon unfair dismissal will cease on such an event. But to regard the obtaining of equivalent permanent employment as always putting an end to the attribution of the loss to the unfair dismissal can in some cases lead to an award that is not just and equitable. This was particularly so where the new employment appears to be permanent when entered into but which, through no fault of the employee's, proves to be of only a short duration. The Court of Appeal ruled that, in such a case, the reason why any subsequent employment did not last will be an important consideration. If the employee simply resigned for no good reason or was dismissed for incompetence or misconduct, for example, it is likely that a tribunal would take the view that any losses that the employee had subsequently suffered were attributable to his or her own behaviour and were not in consequence of the original unfair dismissal.

16.21

16.22 **Self-employment and earnings from insecure employment.** It is not just earnings from a subsequent employer that may be taken into account. Some employees, for example, become *self-employed* after being unfairly dismissed. In such cases their earnings will be set off against their losses in the usual way. However, an issue arises when the claimant's earnings from being self-employed are highly variable. In Islam Channel Ltd v Ridley EAT 0083/09 the claimant had not sustained an immediate loss of earnings after dismissal because she had obtained freelance work that paid her approximately £5,000 more than she would have earned but for the dismissal. However, having noted that the work was inherently insecure and that, by the date of the hearing, R had begun to sustain a monthly loss, the tribunal awarded a sum for future loss without giving any credit for the £5,000 excess earned during the period of immediate loss. Upholding this decision, the EAT noted that, as a result of Dench (above), it is clear that the obtaining of higher paid work will not always break the chain of causation. The tribunal in the instant case had exercised its discretion to award compensation that was 'just and equitable', a discretion that affords tribunals the room to adopt different approaches to the fundamentally different tasks of assessing immediate and future loss. The EAT added that, if it were wrong on that point, the tribunal's decision not to give credit for the £5,000 could be viewed as a reflection of the risk that what freelance work R still had could dry up during the period of future loss.

16.23 **Higher education grants.** In Justfern Ltd v D'Ingerthorpe and ors 1994 IRLR 164, EAT, the question arose of whether a £4,000 educational grant that the employee had received following his dismissal should be taken into account in determining his loss. A tribunal declined to offset the grant on the ground that it would not be just and equitable for the employer to benefit from the employee's efforts to improve himself. The EAT held that the grant was sufficiently remote from the matter of the compensatory award to justify the tribunal's decision.

16.24 **Duty to mitigate losses.** It should be noted that the final amount of compensation that an employee receives depends to a great extent on whether he or she has taken reasonable steps to mitigate his or her loss. Accepting a lower-paid job, becoming self-employed, or even pursuing a course of study may or may not amount to reasonable mitigation of loss. This issue is considered in detail in Chapter 18, under 'Failure to mitigate losses'.

16.25 **Social security benefits**
Social security benefits are another potential source of income for a dismissed employee. The first point to note is that any unemployment benefit – i.e. what is currently termed 'Jobseeker's Allowance' and 'Income Support' – which the employee receives after being unfairly dismissed is not offset against the employee's immediate losses but is instead subject to the recoupment procedure

– see Chapter 20. The effect on the compensatory award of receipt of other welfare benefits is more problematic, as we shall see below.

Incapacity benefits. There has historically been a degree of uncertainty surrounding the question of whether employees who are in receipt of state invalidity benefits (now termed incapacity benefits) following dismissal should have these benefits deducted from the compensatory award. In Hilton International Hotels (UK) Ltd v Faraji 1994 ICR 259, EAT, the Appeal Tribunal took the view that sums received by an employee by way of invalidity benefit following his or her unfair dismissal are not to be offset against the compensatory award. Although this meant that an employee might receive more in compensation than he or she would have received if he or she had remained in employment, the EAT pointed out that the right to invalidity benefit arises as a result of the national insurance scheme and is dependent to some degree upon the amount of payments made to that scheme by the employee. Accordingly, invalidity benefit could properly be classified as an insurance benefit. As such, it came within the well-established common law principle that the proceeds of insurance constitute an exception to the general principle that an injured party should be awarded such sum as will place him or her in the position he or she would have been in but for the injury. This meant that the value of such benefits did not fall to be offset against the employee's loss of earnings when calculating the compensatory award.

16.26

In Puglia v C James and Sons 1996 ICR 301, EAT, by contrast, the EAT took the view that the Hilton decision had been reached without the assistance of all the relevant authorities and should not be followed. In particular, the EAT referred to Sun and Sand Ltd v Fitzjohn 1979 ICR 268, EAT, in which it had been held that, unless there was a provision in the contract of employment entitling the employee to receive full wages or salary in addition to sick pay, the amount of any sickness benefit received by the employee during the period covered by the compensatory award should be deducted from the award.

In Rubenstein and anor t/a McGuffies Dispensing Chemists v McGloughlin 1996 IRLR 557, EAT, the Appeal Tribunal declined to follow either the Faraji or the Puglia decisions. It stated that there was no need for an 'all or nothing' approach. The obligation under S.123(1) ERA to award what is just and equitable in all the circumstances conferred on a tribunal a good deal of flexibility in the matter. The EAT concluded that tribunals should treat the employer and employee equally by deducting one half of the invalidity benefit received by an employee from his or her compensatory award.

The EAT's most recent pronouncement on the subject came in Morgans v Alpha Plus Security Ltd 2005 IRLR 234. In that case the Appeal Tribunal conducted a thoroughgoing review of all the previous case law and concluded that incapacity benefits received by the claimant from the date of his unfair dismissal to the date of the remedies hearing should be deducted in full from his

16.27

569

immediate losses. In so holding, the EAT reached the same conclusion as that reached in the Puglia case (above). Mr Justice Burton supported his reasoning by citing the House of Lords' decision in Dunnachie v Kingston upon Hull City Council 2004 ICR 1052, HL, in which their Lordships had laid to rest the 'heresy' that S.123 enables a dismissed employee to recover more than his or her actual economic losses. In Burton J's view, this meant that there was no longer room for the approach taken by the NIRC in Norton Tool Co Ltd v Tewson 1972 ICR 501, NIRC, under which an employee could be *treated* as having suffered a loss where he or she recovers less than he or she would have received in accordance with good industrial practice.

The EAT in Morgans concluded that it is not possible to disregard the receipt of monies from third party sources such as the DSS following dismissal. To do so would put the claimant in a better position than he or she would have been in had he or she remained in employment, which would not accord with S.123. In the words of Burton J: 'Loss which is in fact recouped by receipt of monies from third parties is simply not a loss suffered, and in our judgment such receipts cannot be disregarded.' The EAT accordingly upheld the employment tribunal's decision to the effect that the claimant's actual economic loss should be reduced by the total amount of incapacity benefits received.

16.28   As we saw above under 'Nature and amount of award – "deemed losses" and the Norton Tool rule', the Court of Appeal in Langley and anor v Burlo 2007 ICR 390, CA, held that the Norton Tool rule still applies, but only to the narrow situation where an employee has been dismissed without notice and has found further employment during the notice period. The Court rejected the extension of the rule to other aspects of good industrial practice, and so it is difficult to see how, in the absence of a further judgment from the Court of Appeal or Supreme Court overruling Morgans, a tribunal has any choice but to deduct in full from the compensatory award any incapacity benefits received by the employee.

One further point to note about incapacity benefits is that the fact that a claimant is in receipt of such benefits does not prevent the tribunal making an award for loss of earnings. In Sheffield Forgemasters International Ltd v Fox; Telindus Ltd v Brading 2009 ICR 333, EAT, the Appeal Tribunal noted that the Social Security (Incapacity for Work) (General) Regulations 1995 SI 1995/311 provide for situations where a claimant is *deemed* to be incapable of work and so eligible to receive incapacity benefit. As a result, the receipt of incapacity benefit cannot be considered a conclusive indication that a claimant is or was unable to work during a given period. It therefore remains open to a tribunal to award loss of earnings for the same period, though credit would obviously need to be given for any sums received by way of incapacity benefit. Note that 'employment and support allowance' has replaced incapacity benefit for new claimants from October 2008. However, given that the eligibility criteria are substantially the same, it is likely that the approach taken by the EAT in the above case would be equally applicable to the new scheme.

Housing benefit. In Savage v Saxena 1998 ICR 357, EAT, the Appeal Tribunal had to consider whether or not housing benefit should be taken into account when assessing the compensatory award. The majority of the EAT held that the starting point in assessing compensation was S.123(1), which, as previously stated, provides that the compensatory award 'shall be such amount as the tribunal considers just and equitable in all the circumstances having regard to the loss sustained by the complainant in consequence of the dismissal in so far as that loss is attributable to action taken by the employer'. Under the common law principles governing the assessment of compensation, account must be taken of sums to which the injured party would not have been entitled had it not been for the injury. However, the majority of the EAT thought that housing benefit did not fall within that rule because it was not sufficiently proximate to the loss sustained in consequence of the dismissal in so far as that loss is attributable to the employer's actions. The payment of housing benefit results from the inability of a claimant to meet reasonable housing needs from his or her resources. Further, it is paid in respect of the needs of the household, not the individual. In that respect it differs markedly from invalidity benefit.

16.29

The EAT also noted that the Housing Benefit (General) Regulations 1987 SI 1987/1971 contained provisions whereby the authorities may recover housing benefit when employees are awarded unfair dismissal compensation. Accordingly, the fact that a tribunal did not take housing benefit into account when assessing unfair dismissal compensation would not result in double recovery for the employee, since the award would be subject to the 'claw-back' provisions. On the other hand, there was no provision under the Regulations for the authorities to take the tribunal's method of calculating the compensatory award into account, so that if the tribunal were to reduce the compensatory award by the amount of housing benefit received, the right to claw back housing benefit would still apply. That outcome would not be just and equitable, because the defaulting employer would obtain a benefit and the employee would be doubly penalised. The EAT concluded by a majority that the tribunal had erred in taking housing benefit into account when assessing the employee's compensation.

Early retirement schemes

16.30

Sums that an employee receives under a scheme for early retirement or retirement on the ground of ill health will not normally be deducted from a compensatory award should the employee subsequently claim unfair dismissal. This is because such sums are the fruits of money set aside in the past in respect of past work. This forms an exception to the general rule in cases of unfair and wrongful dismissal that financial benefits which the employee would not have received but for the dismissal are deducted from

571

damages for lost earnings. The payments here represent an entitlement over and above the pay that the employer would have provided but for the dismissal – see Smoker v London Fire and Civil Defence Authority; Wood v British Coal Corporation 1991 ICR 449, HL.

16.31 **Remoteness of loss**

Section 123(1) ERA states that in assessing compensation a tribunal must only consider losses that are attributable to action taken by the employer. This leaves scope for the employer to argue that, after a certain point, the employee's losses become too remote from the original dismissal for the employer to continue to remain liable (i.e. the chain of causation has been broken). For example, an unfairly dismissed employee may work in a new job for a considerable period of time before leaving or being dismissed again. When the hearing into the question of compensation for the original unfair dismissal subsequently takes place, the first employer may seek to argue that the employee's losses incurred since leaving the second job are no longer attributable to the earlier dismissal and that liability to pay compensation therefore ceases at the point when the new job was obtained. It was precisely this argument that succeeded in Courtaulds 1984 IRLR 43, EAT, discussed above under 'New employment'.

It will be appreciated that Ging v Ellward Lancs Ltd 1978 ITR 265, EAT, and Courtaulds Northern Spinning Ltd v Moosa (see under 'New employment' above) are to some extent a mirror image of each other. It will sometimes be to the advantage of the employer if his liability to pay compensation continues right up to the tribunal hearing (thereby allowing the employee's superior new earnings to be offset, so far as possible, against his or her losses). On the other hand, in circumstances like those in the Courtaulds case – i.e. where the employee is no longer in the new employment by the time of the tribunal hearing and is therefore suffering renewed losses – the employer is likely to seek to establish that liability ceased when the employee obtained new employment. In Mabey Plant Hire Ltd v Richens, unreported 6.5.93, CA, the Court of Appeal decided that where an employee is unfairly dismissed and, before the assessment of compensation, obtains alternative employment which *could* have been permanent but which ends for reasons unrelated to the first employer, the chain of causation between the dismissal by the first employer and the employee's full loss of earnings is broken.

The question of remoteness of loss is considered in more detail under 'Future loss' below. It should be noted that the question of whether the respondent employer remains liable to pay compensation after the employee has obtained, and then left, new employment is also very much a question of whether the employee has mitigated his or her loss – see Chapter 18 under 'Failure to mitigate losses'.

572

New earnings, notice pay and the notice period

16.32

Before we consider in detail how to assess an employee's loss, there is one more preliminary matter to be considered. An employee's notice entitlement may affect those matters that fall to be offset against his or her losses. There are three situations for consideration here:

- where the employer dismisses unfairly and without giving notice or pay in lieu of notice

- where the employer dismisses unfairly and without giving notice, but does give pay in lieu of notice

- where the employee resigns without notice and successfully claims constructive dismissal.

In any of these scenarios, the employee may find other work during what would have been the notice period. From this point on, the employee actually suffers either no net loss of earnings or only a reduced loss.

No payment in lieu. Where an employer dismisses an employee without notice and without pay in lieu of notice, the general rule is that the employee is entitled to include net pay for the statutory or contractual notice period in his or her claim for immediate loss from the dismissal – Norton Tool Co Ltd v Tewson 1972 ICR 501, NIRC. This is because good industrial practice requires employers to make payments in lieu of notice when they dismiss employees with no, or inadequate, notice.

16.33

New employment during notice period. An employee who has been dismissed without notice is entitled to claim notice pay in full despite having found paid employment during the notice period. In the Norton Tool case the National Industrial Relations Court (the predecessor of the EAT) took the view that, had the employee, in accordance with good industrial practice, been paid his wages in lieu at the time of dismissal, he would not have had to make any repayment upon obtaining new employment while the notice period was still running. His compensation, therefore, did not fall to be reduced by any sums earned during the notice period. This was followed in TBA Industrial Products Ltd v Locke 1984 IRLR 48, EAT, and approved, although obiter (i.e. not binding), by the Court of Appeal in Addison v Babcock FATA Ltd 1987 ICR 805, CA. And, as we saw above under 'Nature and amount of award – "deemed losses" and the Norton Tool rule', the Court of Appeal in Langley and anor v Burlo 2007 ICR 390, CA, expressly held that the Norton Tool rule still applies in this narrow context.

16.34

The general rule that an employee does not have to give credit for any wages earned during the notice period when claiming notice pay seems, however, to be subject to exceptions. The employer may be able to argue that notice pay should be offset against actual earnings where, for example, the notice period is very long and the employee's prospects of re-employment are very high (see

573

the Babcock case), or where the contract is for a fixed term with a substantial unexpired portion. In Isleworth Studios Ltd v Rickard 1988 ICR 432, EAT, the Appeal Tribunal took the view that the 'Norton principle' did not extend to the situation where an employee made substantial gains from new earnings following the summary termination of his fixed-term contract with a lengthy period left to run.

One very clear exception to the Norton Tool principle is where there has been a constructive dismissal. In Stuart Peters Ltd v Bell 2009 ICR 1556, CA, the Court of Appeal explained that the Norton Tool rule exists to ensure that an employer who does not follow good industrial relations practice is not put in a more advantageous position than if he had followed such practice. There is, the Court explained, no industrial practice of making a full payment in lieu of notice where termination is triggered by the employee, since an employer will generally dispute that there has been a breach of contract and will regard the employee as simply having resigned. As a result, a tribunal calculating compensation for an unfair constructive dismissal should take full account of any sums earned during the notice period and set these off against the sum in respect of notice pay to which the employee is entitled.

16.35 **Credit for payments in lieu.** Where an employer has dismissed an employee without notice but has made a payment in lieu of notice, the employee must give credit for the notice money already paid – Addison v Babcock FATA Ltd (above). If this were not so, the employee would receive double remuneration for the statutory notice period.

The position, however, may be different in Scotland, where the authorities are somewhat confused on the matter. In Finnie v Top Hat Frozen Foods 1985 IRLR 365, EAT, the Scottish EAT (which is technically not bound by decisions of the Court of Appeal) reached the conclusion that payments in lieu of notice do not fall to be offset against the award for immediate loss. But in Heggie v Uniroyal Englebert Tyres Ltd 1999 IRLR 802, Ct Sess (Inner House) – a decision of the Court of Session concerning the order in which various deductions including one for contributory fault should be made – it was implied that a payment in lieu should be taken into account when calculating immediate loss. It would, however, seem prudent for those practising in Scotland to assume that credit for payments in lieu of notice should be given by a tribunal, particularly as this accords with the principle in Dunnachie v Kingston upon Hull City Council 2004 ICR 1052, HL (a House of Lords decision that binds Scottish courts), that compensation for unfair dismissal should reflect an employee's actual loss.

16.36 **Credit to be given for gross payments.** As previously stated, when calculating the compensatory award, it is the employee's *net*, rather than gross, loss that has to be considered. The same rule applies to payments in lieu of notice. If an employer pays an employee a payment in lieu of notice based on the employee's gross pay, the entire sum has to be offset against any award of compensation. The employee cannot argue that only the net sum falls to be deducted, and that the difference between the net and the gross sum represents a windfall which is not to be taken into account when calculating immediate loss – see MBS Ltd v Calo 1983 IRLR 189, EAT, and Warnock v Marshalls of Cambridge Aerospace Ltd EAT 0250/03.

Waiver of notice. An employee can waive the right to statutory notice – S.86(3) ERA. Waiver will mean that the employee also loses the right to receive a payment in lieu of notice because the termination of the employment contract without notice will no longer amount to a breach of contract for which damages would be due – Trotter v Forth Ports Authority 1991 IRLR 419, Ct Sess (Outer House). Where an employee who waives the notice entitlement is subsequently unfairly dismissed, he or she will be entitled to compensation for losses incurred from the date of dismissal in the normal way. However, any new earnings during the notional notice period clearly will be offset against the employee's overall losses.

16.37

Termination payments

16.38

Termination payments made by the employer – be they made on an ex gratia basis or paid in the form of contractual redundancy payments – are an important factor in the calculation of loss. The general approach is that any ex gratia payment should be set off against the losses incurred by the employee – Horizon Holidays Ltd v Grassi 1987 IRLR 371, EAT; DCM Optical Clinic plc v Stark EAT 0124/04. But, as we shall see, redundancy payments are a special case to which specific rules apply.

General guidance as to the correct approach to be adopted for taking account of severance payments (including redundancy packages) was given by the EAT in Darr and anor v LRC Products Ltd 1993 IRLR 257, EAT. In that case an employment tribunal failed to give adequate reasons for declining to make a compensatory award, stating simply that the severance payment that the employee had received on being dismissed for redundancy more than covered any compensation that the tribunal would or could have awarded. The EAT stated that the tribunal should first have assessed the employee's loss of earnings over the appropriate period, then deducted the part of the severance payment which was not already apportioned to the basic award and, finally, have applied the statutory maximum to the net sum. The tribunal's reasons were insufficient to show that it had adopted the correct approach or made the necessary calculations.

Treatment of ex gratia payments. Outside of the specific statutory provisions dealing with redundancy payments (see below), the general flexibility accorded to the calculation of the compensatory award by virtue of S.123(1) ERA permits the taking into account of ex gratia payments to be approached differently according to circumstance. In Addison v Babcock

16.39

FATA Ltd 1987 ICR 805, CA, the employee had been given an ex gratia payment when he was unfairly dismissed for redundancy. However, the tribunal found that he would have been dismissed in any event some 15 months later along with the rest of the workforce and that he would have received an ex gratia payment at that time. It was therefore conceded before the Court of Appeal that the ex gratia payment was demonstrably part of the employee's future loss, so that he would not be properly compensated if it were deducted from the part of the compensatory award representing immediate loss. This exception was extended in Roadchef Ltd v Hastings EAT 593/87. There, a redundancy dismissal, although procedurally unfair, was found to be inevitable because a proper consultation period would merely have delayed dismissal by four weeks. The tribunal held that an ex gratia payment that the employer had added to the redundancy payment should not be deducted from the compensatory award of four weeks' pay because there was no reason to suppose that the extra payment would not have been granted if the dismissal had been delayed by proper consultation.

16.40 Note that in Rushton v Harcros Timber and Building Supplies Ltd 1993 IRLR 254, EAT, however, the EAT explicitly declined to follow the line of authority outlined above. In that case the employee was made redundant and received statutory redundancy pay of £4,730 and an additional ex gratia payment of £5,320. The dismissal was held to be unfair for lack of warning but the tribunal declined to award any compensation on the grounds that the basic award was extinguished by the redundancy payment and any compensatory award was more than covered by the ex gratia payment. The employee argued that he should have been awarded the four weeks' pay he would have earned if a fair amount of warning had been given and that the ex gratia payment should not have been deducted from that amount. The EAT upheld the tribunal's decision on the ground that there was no evidence to suggest that the employee would have received the same ex gratia payment following a fair dismissal. The EAT went on, however, to express the view that credit should always be given for severance payments made by the employer. It stated that the manifest purpose of the specific redundancy payment deduction provision in S.123(7) ERA – discussed below – is to encourage employers who find it necessary to dismiss for redundancy to be generous in making ex gratia payments. The frequency and levels of such payments would be reduced if employers had to take into account the possibility of a tribunal award over and above the ex gratia payment, however generous that payment may be.

In Simrad Ltd v Scott 1997 IRLR 147, EAT, the question arose of whether a sum which the employer had lent the employee during her employment could be offset against the compensatory award. The loan was an unusual one in that it was made to the employee on the understanding that it would be repaid by her working overtime. The EAT pointed out that an ex gratia payment is usually a payment arising directly from the dismissal. It also pointed out that, in dismissing the employee, the employer had denied her the means by which it had been agreed that the loan would be repaid. The EAT therefore concluded that it would not be just and equitable to offset the loan against the employee's compensatory award.

Treatment of redundancy payments. By virtue of S.122(4)(b) ERA, the **16.41** amount paid by the employer by way of a redundancy payment serves to reduce the employer's liability for the basic award in circumstances where a dismissal is found to be unfair – see further Chapter 15, under 'Reductions in basic award – receipt of a redundancy payment'. S.123(7) ERA then further provides that 'if the amount of any payment made by the employer to the employee on the ground that the dismissal was by reason of redundancy (whether in pursuance of Part XI [ERA] or otherwise) exceeds the amount of the basic award, that excess goes to reduce the amount of the compensatory award'. Thus, if the employer's redundancy scheme is more generous than the statutory redundancy scheme and the dismissal is subsequently judged by a tribunal to be unfair, the part of the redundancy payment that corresponds to a statutory redundancy payment will normally extinguish entitlement to a basic award, with the excess then serving to reduce the compensatory award.

A crucial point in respect of S.123(7) is that Parliament has specifically stipulated that any excess should be offset against the *compensatory award*, not against the claimant's *losses*. In Digital Equipment Co Ltd v Clements (No.2) 1998 ICR 258, CA, the Court of Appeal explained that this means that, unlike with ex gratia payments and factors that might reduce an employee's losses, the deduction should come *after* any Polkey reductions or adjustments for contributory fault (see Chapter 18, under 'Offsetting enhanced redundancy payments').

Where the employer pays the employee what is described as a 'redundancy payment' but it transpires that the payment is mislabelled because no genuine redundancy situation arises, it would seem to be the case that S.127(3) does not apply. As we saw above, that provision defines a 'redundancy payment' as 'any payment made by the employer to the employee on the ground that the dismissal was by reason of redundancy (whether in pursuance of Part XI or otherwise)'. It is noteworthy that exactly the same wording appears in S.122(4)(b), which, as previously stated, requires that the amount of a basic award to be reduced by the amount of any redundancy payment already paid to the employee. In Boorman v Allmakes Ltd 1995 ICR 842, CA, the Court of Appeal, having considered the meaning of this wording, held that S.122(4)(b) only applies if the dismissal was in fact by reason of a genuine redundancy (i.e. as defined in Part XI of the ERA). Given that this wording is identical to that in S.123(7), it is highly arguable that the two provisions should be interpreted consistently, leading to the conclusion that S.123(7) also only applies to payments made in the context of genuine redundancies. If that is so, then where a payment is mislabelled as a redundancy payment, the tribunal should

577

approach it in the same way as if it were an ex gratia termination payment – i.e. it should give credit for the payment when calculating the 'net loss' the claimant has incurred, before any deductions or adjustments are made. Where, however, an enhanced redundancy payment is paid in the context of a genuine redundancy, it should be left out of account when calculating the claimant's full losses. Then, once these have been ascertained and the nominal compensatory award calculated on the basis of them, the redundancy payment should be deducted from the award in accordance with S.123(7). (For details about the correct stages at which various adjustments/deductions to and from the compensatory award have to be made, see Chapter 18, under 'Order of adjustments and deductions'.)

16.42   **Calculation of immediate loss**

We have seen that immediate loss relates to the net remuneration that would have been received had the employee not been dismissed. We have also seen that credit must usually be given for any new earnings, etc. We now consider how tribunals assess exactly what an employee has lost. (Remember, there is no rigid formula or maximum amount for calculating a 'week's pay'. The only limit is the overall limit on the size of a compensatory award, currently standing at £65,300 – see under 'Nature and maximum amount of award' above.)

First, it should be noted that remuneration for these purposes is not limited to basic pay but can cover any regular bonuses or fringe benefits that an employee may have been receiving in the job. This is not restricted to benefits that are explicitly authorised by the contract: what counts is take-home pay, plus other contractual or non-contractual benefits that the employee would expect to receive in the period under review. Having said this, if the remuneration is disputed, the tribunal will obviously use the contract as the main means to identify the employee's entitlement – Kinzley v Minories Finance Ltd 1988 ICR 113, EAT.

In addition to basic pay and regular bonus payments, the following are taken into account when assessing immediate loss:

- overtime, whether contractual or not, where there is a reasonable expectation that it would have been worked – Mullet v Brush Electrical Machines Ltd 1977 ICR 829, EAT

- tips, whether they are paid direct to the employee by customers or shared out among employees from a tronc, provided tax is deducted – Palmanor Ltd t/a Chaplins Night Club v Cedron 1978 IRLR 303, EAT

- pay increases that the employee would have received during the relevant period, even if the employee had no contractual right to an increase – Leske v Rogers of Saltcoats (ES) Ltd EAT 520/82. Compensation can be awarded for increases that the employee would probably have received, although it may be made subject to a reduction to reflect the tribunal's

578

view of the likelihood of this happening – York Trailer Co Ltd v Sparkes 1973 ICR 518, NIRC

- a backdated pay increase if it is backdated to a date before the dismissal and would have been awarded to the employee – Leske v Rogers of Saltcoats (ES) Ltd (above)

- expenses, provided these are regular, and only to the extent that they represent a profit or 'perk' in the hands of the employee over and above what is spent purely on the employer's behalf – S and U Stores Ltd v Wilkes 1974 ICR 645, NIRC. The fact that benefits of this kind are taxed will help to indicate that they form part of the employee's remuneration and should therefore be compensated. In contrast, tax-free 'benefits' tend to suggest that the sums were intended merely to reimburse genuine expenses incurred on the employer's behalf and are therefore not remuneration. (Note that if an allowance for expenses is merely a device to give the employee some tax-free remuneration the whole contract may be illegal and unenforceable – see the section on 'Illegality' in Chapter 2.)

Expectation of enhanced redundancy payment. A dismissed employee may **16.43** be able to receive compensation for a thwarted expectation that he or she would receive a more generous redundancy payment than the statutory entitlement. In Lee v IPC Business Press Ltd 1984 ICR 306, EAT, the Appeal Tribunal confirmed that the expectation of receiving an especially favourable redundancy payment is something that may be lost as a result of unfair dismissal and is something that should be compensated by the tribunal where appropriate. (The EAT thought that this could include cases where the expectation was based on a non-contractual agreement that was 'binding in honour' only.)

Note, however, that S.123(3) ERA provides that the loss of any entitlement or potential entitlement to a redundancy payment (statutory or contractual) or any expectation of such a payment should be compensated only to the extent to which it exceeds the basic award.

In MacCulloch v Imperial Chemical Industries Ltd EAT 0275/09 M had been paid an enhanced redundancy payment when she was dismissed. Having found her dismissal unfair, the tribunal held that she would have been dismissed in any event at a later date, but that she would have been entitled to a more generous enhanced redundancy payment. The tribunal offset the amount of the payment that M had received against her losses, and went on to deduct from M's compensatory award the amount by which her redundancy payment had exceeded the basic award. On appeal, the EAT rejected this approach. What the tribunal should have done was to include in the calculation of loss a sum that reflects the payment the claimant *would* have received, minus the amount of a basic award. Only once the losses had been calculated, and any other adjustments or deductions made, should the tribunal have deducted from the

579

compensatory award the amount by which the redundancy payment that the employee *did* receive exceeded the basic award.

Finally, note also that special rules apply to the order of deductions under S.123. This topic is dealt with in Chapter 18, under 'Order of adjustments and deductions'.

16.44   **Fringe benefits and benefits in kind**
The assessment of loss is not confined to pay received by the employee in the form of money. Fringe benefits and benefits in kind can also be counted so long as they were received on a regular basis and were not one-off payments – Mullet v Brush Electrical Machines Ltd 1977 ICR 829, EAT. Here we look at how tribunals assess the value of such benefits. Note also that any increase in benefits which the employee would have enjoyed but for the dismissal should also be taken into account – York Trailer Co Ltd v Sparkes 1973 ICR 518, NIRC.

16.45   **Loss of a company car.** This is an obvious item of loss. However, there is no general rule as to how such loss to the employee should be assessed because of the wide range of terms and conditions on which employees are supplied with company cars. Business use of a car and reimbursement of associated expenses should be disregarded: it is only the loss of a car for *private* purposes that should be compensated – Texet Ltd v Greenhough EAT 410/82. Many tribunals in practice adopt a broad-brush approach and award a conventional figure of £50–150 per week for the value of the car, depending on the type of car and the basis upon which it was supplied (in particular, the level of private, as opposed to business, use). Other more detailed methods for valuing the loss of private use of a company car are:

- using the annual tables produced by the AA and RAC, which set out the worth and running costs of different capacities of car. AA estimates were used in the wrongful dismissal case of Shove v Downs Surgical plc 1984 ICR 532, QBD, where, after reducing the estimated running costs by the ratio of business use to private use, the judge arrived at a figure of £10,000 for the loss of a company Daimler over a 30-month period

- using the car benefit assessments prepared by the HM Revenue and Customs for taxation purposes. Use of the Revenue's scales was, however, rejected in Shove v Downs Surgical plc (above) on the ground that they simply represented a valuation for tax purposes and not an assessment of the benefit to the employee. Note that the basis upon which car benefit is assessed for taxation purposes has undergone radical revision since the Shove case. Since April 2002, a new system for assessing taxable benefit has applied under which a percentage reduction to the car's list price is applied depending on the carbon dioxide emissions of the vehicle. This may, however, make the use of Inland Revenue scales even less helpful in

580

assessing the actual value of the loss of private use of the vehicle for compensation purposes

- taking account of actual car transactions carried out by the employee. In Nohar v Granitstone (Galloway) Ltd 1974 ICR 273, NIRC, N lost his company car when he was dismissed, bought himself a new car and then resold it at a loss when he found another job with a company car. The NIRC allowed the award to cover most of the loss on resale and the cost of taxing and insuring N's car while he owned it

- taking account of the cost of hiring a car. This can produce a reasonable result in circumstances like those in the Nohar case (above) where the period for assessment is relatively short. However, the employee's compensation may be assessed too highly by this method because the hire costs will include the hire company's profits.

16.46   Free fuel for private use of a company car is also a taxable benefit, the loss of which should be compensated. Since 6 April 2003, the taxable value of this benefit has been calculated using the same percentage figure as that used to calculate the taxable benefit of the car (see above) applied to an amount set each year in the Chancellor of the Exchequer's Budget. Other car-related benefits such as free maintenance, road tax and insurance are also relevant considerations. If, unusually, a private mileage allowance is payable to the employee as a benefit, the Revenue classifies this as earnings, so this would also potentially be a recoverable head of loss.

The Revenue's company car and car fuel calculator is available online (at www.hmrc.gov.uk/calcs/cars.htm). This may assist in calculating the value of car-related losses for the purposes of assessing this element of the compensatory award.

16.47   **Free or subsidised accommodation.** This benefit may be valued by estimating its worth on the open market, perhaps with the help of an estate agent or surveyor. Alternatively, it can be valued by comparing it with the cost of the employee's new accommodation. In Denyer v Cowdray Estate ET Case No.2830/89 D, a golf-course keeper, was effectively ousted from premises of which he was service tenant when he was unfairly dismissed. Looking at the accommodation benefit that D had lost and at the value of the council accommodation that he subsequently obtained, the employment tribunal assessed D's annual loss at £1,300. (Note that much will depend here on the period of future loss determined by the tribunal – e.g. if the employee has prospects of obtaining more lucrative employment, the tribunal will limit the period for which compensation is awarded – see below.)

Where a dismissed employee remains in free or subsidised accommodation, the value of this may be offset against the losses incurred as a result of losing the job. In Gibbons v Smith ET Case No.16284/81 G's free use of a cottage cancelled out any immediate losses. However, the tribunal did make an award for future loss to cover the rent that G would have to pay once a possession order took effect. In cases where the employer obtains an order stating that the ex-employee must pay rent until a possession order takes effect, the sums paid may be recovered by the employee as part of his or her compensatory award – Jackson v Shavington Social Club and Institute Ltd ET Case No.18471/80.

16.48 **Other benefits.** The loss of free meals, free medical or life insurance, low interest loans and mortgages, profits under a profit-share scheme and private health care are all examples of other benefits that can be taken into account when assessing an employee's immediate losses. The value of these benefits can usually be assessed straightforwardly by taking the difference between the cost to the employee of the benefit before dismissal and the cost on the open market after dismissal. If the employer wishes to argue for a different basis of assessment, this must be done at the tribunal hearing as it will be too late to raise the matter on appeal – UBAF Bank Ltd v Davis 1978 IRLR 442, EAT.

Tribunals are used to making informed guesses when calculating the compensatory award and will place a value even on those benefits that are very difficult to quantify. In Casey v Texas Homecare Ltd EAT 632/87 the EAT held that a tribunal was wrong to decline to estimate the value to the employee of a share option scheme on the ground that it was too 'speculative and indefinite' a matter. Having sufficient evidence on which to rely, the EAT arrived at a figure of £1,000 after making deductions from its original figure to take account of the possibility that share prices might fall and the fact that the employee had received accelerated payment of the benefit through the compensatory award.

16.49 **Loss of national insurance contributions.** This can form part of the dismissed employee's losses. Normally an unemployed person will continue to make contributions because deductions are made from Jobseeker's Allowance and Income Support. However, where the individual is unemployed as a result of being unfairly dismissed, he or she is not entitled to claim benefit during the period in respect of which the *future* element of a compensatory award applies. The halting of national insurance contributions during this period may eventually cause loss to the employee if the contributions are interrupted long enough to have an effect on his or her entitlement to benefits. In Allen v Key Markets Ltd ET Case No.10088/83 a tribunal treated a break in contributions of 52 weeks – i.e. the period covered by the award for future loss – as substantial enough to justify an extra £4.30 being added to the compensatory award for each of those 52 weeks. This would allow the employee to make his own contributions.

Note that loss of rights under an occupational pension scheme is considered separately in Chapter 17.

Future loss

16.50

Immediate loss can normally be assessed fairly accurately since the tribunal will have information before it on the employee's actual earnings (if any) following dismissal and on what the employee's earnings would have been in the old job. However, assessment of the employee's future loss is, by its very nature, a far more speculative exercise. There may, of course, be no future loss – e.g. where the employee has already obtained reasonably secure and equally lucrative new employment – but where this is not the case the tribunal will have to look into the future and attempt to guess how long the employee's losses will continue and how much they are likely to be.

Question of fact. Since tribunal findings on the question of future loss are largely a matter of informed guesswork, they will normally be difficult to challenge on appeal. In Sandown Pier Ltd v Moonan EAT 399/93 a tribunal held that a 50-year-old employee was likely to remain unemployed for 15 years. While making it fairly clear that it would not have reached the same conclusion, the EAT noted that the tribunal's finding was supported by some evidence – the employee lived in an area of high unemployment and had already made a number of vain attempts to find work – and held that there were therefore no grounds for overturning the decision.

16.51

There will be situations, however, where the EAT finds fault with the tribunal's approach and remits the matter of compensation, either to the same or to a fresh tribunal. In NCP Services Ltd v Topliss EAT 0147/09 the Appeal Tribunal held that a tribunal calculating future loss in a case that has been remitted by the EAT should make its decision on the basis of facts known at the date of the remitted hearing, rather than limiting itself to facts known at the time of the original hearing. This, the EAT explained 'has the result of substituting certainty for that which was uncertain though estimated on the best available evidence' and is preferable to substituting a hypothetical situation that bears no relation to current reality.

Tribunal's duty to give its assessment of future loss. Although the employment tribunal is entitled to take a broad-brush approach to ascertaining the extent of future loss, it is still under a duty to give full reasons for its decision. In Lancaster Fibre Technology Ltd v Walshaw EAT 1028/02 a tribunal held that 'we think we have to come to a figure which is not a mathematical figure reflecting all those difficulties and the figure that we have come to for all those losses, trying to reflect as far as we can all those difficulties, is £20,000'. The EAT noted that the tribunal failed to give any indication in its decision as to what period it was considering as appropriate for the calculation of future loss or what, if any, multiplier in respect of future loss it had in mind. The EAT therefore remitted the case to a fresh tribunal on the issue of future loss. Similarly, in Thornett v Scope (below) the Court of Appeal

16.52

583

remitted the matter of future loss, holding that while there was material before the tribunal which might have justified limiting T's losses to six months, the reasons for the tribunal's decision did not emerge with sufficient clarity to permit its determination to be upheld. There was, for example, no analysis in the tribunal's decision as to how T's employment was expected to have ended after six months.

Like immediate loss, future loss is assessed by reference to the employee's *net* earnings in the job from which he or she was dismissed. However, these earnings will not be treated as static and account will be taken of possible future pay increases (or decreases) – York Trailer Co Ltd v Sparkes 1973 ICR 518, NIRC.

16.53 **Circumstances in which future losses occur**
There are three basic situations in which the tribunal will have to consider the question of future loss:

- where the employee has found a new job that pays as least as well as the old one by the time of the tribunal hearing on compensation. In this situation, there will usually be no future loss, so the tribunal can restrict compensation for loss of earnings to 'immediate loss' – see above. (Note, however, the Court of Appeal's caution in Dench v Flynn and Partners 1998 IRLR 653, CA, that it will not always be just and equitable to treat the acquisition of permanent alternative employment as breaking the chain of causation for attribution of loss. In particular, if the employment ends unexpectedly after a relatively short duration, the tribunal should consider the reasons for and effect of this when assessing the appropriate award for future loss)

- where the employee has found a new job that does not pay as well as the old one. Here, there may be evidence that earnings in the new job will increase to the old level in the foreseeable future. Based, as far as possible, on such evidence, tribunals simply have to guess how long it will take the employee to catch up to the old level of earnings and make an award for the difference up to that time. However, it may be that the new earnings will never reach the old level. Despite this, tribunals usually set a limit on the continuing loss, unless the employee's prospects are particularly dim (see below)

- where the employee has not yet found a new job. In such a case, tribunals simply have to do the best they can from their knowledge of the employee and of the local labour market to assess how long the employee is likely to be out of work and how much he or she is likely to earn when a job is eventually found.

In theory, an award for a period of future loss could cover the remainder of the employee's working life in an appropriately extreme case. In Morganite Electrical Carbon Ltd v Donne 1988 ICR 18, EAT, the Appeal Tribunal rejected the argument that a period of 82 weeks was excessive. In practice,

584 ————————————————————

however, most tribunals seem to settle on a figure somewhere between 13 and 39 weeks. For a high-earning employee, a substantial period of future loss is likely to run up against the statutory cap on the compensatory award that applies in most cases of unfair dismissal. Career-long loss is discussed below.

Unemployment benefits and recoupment. Note that, unlike immediate loss, the future loss element of the compensatory award is *not* subject to the recoupment provisions because the employee will not be eligible to claim either Jobseeker's Allowance (JSA) or Income Support (IS) for the period covered by an award for future loss. The effect of the Jobseeker's Allowance Regulations 1996 SI 1996/207 and the Income Support (General) Regulations 1987 SI 1987/1967 is that any lump sum award for future loss of earning will be treated as 'earnings' over the period to which it applies, for the purposes of assessing a claimant's eligibility for JSA or IS under the Jobseeker's Act 1995 and the Social Security Act 1986 respectively. A tribunal need not, therefore, concern itself that the claimant may enjoy an element of double recovery during the period of future loss. 16.54

Evidence and speculation 16.55
Future loss generally presents tribunals with greater problems than immediate loss as, rather than assessing what has happened and whether the employer bears responsibility, the tribunal is attempting to predict what might happen, and will often have scant evidence to go on. If the employer seeks to contend that the employee would or might have ceased to be employed in any event had fair procedures been followed, or alternatively would not have continued in employment indefinitely, it is for the employer to adduce any relevant evidence on which it wishes to rely – Software 2000 Ltd v Andrews and ors 2007 ICR 825, EAT.

The nature of the predictive task faced by tribunals was examined fairly recently by the Court of Appeal in Thornett v Scope 2007 ICR 236, CA. In that case, the tribunal had made a finding that, had she not been unfairly dismissed, the claimant would only have remained in her role for a further six months due to ongoing disagreements with her colleagues. On appeal, the EAT held that the tribunal should not have launched itself upon 'a sea of speculation' and should have accepted that it could not, on the evidence before it, 'sensibly recreate the world as it might have been'. Given the evidence about how the claimant and her colleagues could work together, the EAT considered that it was wrong to place a limitation in time as to the duration of the relationship and to reduce the losses accordingly. However, when the case reached the Court of Appeal, Lord Justice Pill stated that deciding compensation for future loss of earnings will 'almost inevitably involve a consideration of uncertainties'. There may be cases in which evidence to the contrary is so sparse that a tribunal should work on the basis that loss of earnings would have continued indefinitely but where there is evidence that this may not have been so, that evidence must be taken into account.

585

16.56 Applying this reasoning, Pill LJ found that there was evidence in the instant case which, taken at its lowest, created a risk that the claimant's employment would not have continued indefinitely. Accordingly, he disagreed with the EAT's conclusion that the tribunal had erred in embarking on a speculative venture. In his Lordship's view, 'any assessment of a future loss, including one that the employment will continue indefinitely, is by way of prediction and inevitably involves a speculative element. Judges and tribunals are familiar with making predictions based on the evidence they have heard. The tribunal's statutory duty may involve making such predictions and tribunals cannot be expected, or even allowed, to opt out of that duty because their task is a difficult one and may involve speculation.'

However, it is important, observed Pill LJ, that when a tribunal reaches a conclusion as to what is likely to have happened had the employment been allowed to continue, the reasons for that conclusion and the factors relied on are sufficiently stated. In the instant case, while there was material before the tribunal which might have justified the six-month limit on future losses, the reasons for the tribunal's decision did not emerge with sufficient clarity to permit its determination to be upheld. There was, for example, no analysis in the tribunal's decision as to how T's employment was expected to have ended after six months: whether by disciplinary action, a breakdown of attempts to work together which would have permitted a fair dismissal, or resignation by the claimant.

The Thornett decision was followed by the EAT in the Software 2000 case (above) in which Mr Justice Elias (as he then was) accepted that there will be circumstances where the nature of the evidence which the employer wishes to adduce, or on which it seeks to rely, is so unreliable that the tribunal may take the view that the whole exercise of seeking to reconstruct what might have been is so riddled with uncertainty that no sensible prediction based on that evidence can properly be made. Whether that is the position is a matter of impression and judgement for the tribunal. But in determining this, the tribunal must direct itself properly by recognising that it should have regard to any material and reliable evidence which might assist it in fixing just compensation, even if there are limits to the extent to which it can confidently predict what might have been; and it must appreciate that a degree of uncertainty is an inevitable feature of the exercise.

16.57 ## Career-long loss

In Kingston Upon Hull City Council v Dunnachie (No.3) 2003 IRLR 843, EAT, the EAT considered the extent to which tribunals are entitled to rely on the 'Ogden Tables' – which are issued by the Government Actuary's Department and which allow for an actuarial adjustment of compensation for future loss in personal injury cases – in helping to assess future loss in unfair dismissal cases. (The 6th edition of these Tables was published by the Government Actuary's Department in May 2007.) The EAT concluded that reliance on such tables is appropriate only where it is established that the claimant is likely to suffer a

586

career-long future loss of earnings. The tribunal should determine whether on the balance of probabilities this is the case by comparing 'old job facts' and 'new job facts'. 'Old job facts' include personal factors (such as health, family situation and location); economic factors (such as the introduction of new technology and the possibility of lay-offs or redundancies); whether the claimant would have taken early retirement or considered a second career; and whether it is likely that the claimant's earnings in the old job would have remained stable. 'New job facts' include an assessment of whether and when the claimant is likely to obtain a new job; whether this will entail a pay cut; if so, whether the claimant will eventually obtain better paid employment; and the claimant's prospects of securing promotion or a pay rise in the new job.

In the subsequent case of Birmingham City Council v Jaddoo EAT 0448/04 the **16.58** EAT reiterated the point made in Dunnachie that use of the Ogden Tables is only ever appropriate where a tribunal is satisfied that the loss caused by the actions of the employer is likely to be sustained by the employee across the remainder of his or her career. In Jaddoo the EAT's President, Mr Justice Burton, specifically remarked that great caution should be exercised by a tribunal in relation to a conclusion as to the existence of lifelong loss where the claimant is as young as 31 or 32, as was so in that particular case. Whenever an assessment of career-long loss is made, Burton J also emphasised, allowance has to be made within the tribunal's calculations for the duty of the employee to take reasonable steps to mitigate his or her loss.

The EAT also held in the Dunnachie case that the Ogden Tables are relevant only once the tribunal has determined a figure for estimated annual future loss and an estimated period of loss lasting until retirement. It is unlikely that a tribunal will arrive at a single annual figure for estimated loss. In some cases one figure in respect of the first one or two years and then a lower figure in respect of later periods will be appropriate. Whenever it is appropriate to use the Ogden Tables, the tribunal should adopt the discount rate in force under the Damages Act 1996 (currently 2.5 per cent) to take account of accelerated receipt of compensation (see further under 'Discount for accelerated receipt' below). Once the tribunal has applied the Ogden Table multipliers, it is generally inappropriate for it then to apply a large percentage discount for contingencies, since such contingencies should have been taken into account at the outset in order to arrive at the multiplicand (the figure for estimated annual loss) and period of loss.

Employee's health and fitness   **16.59**
The health and fitness of the employee, both before and after the dismissal, are important factors in the assessment of future loss. In Fougère v Phoenix Motor Co Ltd 1976 ICR 495, EAT, the Appeal Tribunal found that a tribunal wrongly based its assessment of F's future loss on the likely period of unemployment for an average employee in good health. F, however, was 58 and suffering from a

────────────────────────────────────── **587**

hernia and bronchitis which, the EAT said, were highly relevant factors. On the one hand, F's unemployment was likely to be extended by his circumstances; on the other, the employer might have dismissed him fairly on the ground of incapacity in the not too distant future. Either way, the tribunal should have taken F's personal circumstances into account and the EAT remitted the case for it to do so.

In Curtis v James Paterson (Darlington) Ltd 1973 ICR 496, NIRC, the tribunal lowered its assessment of the claimant's future loss because his ill health would probably have led to absences and therefore lower wages even if he had not been dismissed. In contrast, the tribunal in Wilson v Glenrose (Fishmerchants) Ltd and ors EAT 444/91 found that the fact that the claimant's workmates had known about his back problem and had helped him with any heavy lifting work meant that he would have been able to hold his job until retirement age had he not been dismissed.

The task for tribunals is assessing the contribution of ill-health to an employee's losses is different in respect of immediate and future loss. In Seafield Holdings Ltd (t/a Seafield Logistics) v Drewett 2006 ICR 1413, EAT, the claimant had suffered from a long-standing medical condition that was exacerbated by conduct on the part of her employer that led her to resign and claim unfair constructive dismissal. Following her dismissal, the claimant's condition left her unable to work. In awarding compensation, the tribunal adopted a 'but for' approach, concluding that, but for the actions of the employer, the claimant would have been able to return to work. Allowing the employer's appeal in part, the EAT was satisfied that a 'but for' approach was appropriate for determining the employee's loss between the date of dismissal and the tribunal hearing (i.e. her immediate losses). However, it concluded that such an approach is wholly unsuitable for the task of determining future loss. Instead, tribunals should make an estimate of the chance that, had the employer not acted in the way it did, the employee's illness would still have prevented him or her from working.

16.60 Where an employee becomes unfit for work following his or her dismissal, this may well be considered an intervening act, after which the employee's losses are no longer attributable to the dismissal – see discussion on 'Remoteness of loss' below. The situation will be different, however, if the employee suffers ill health as a direct result of the unfair dismissal. In Devine v Designer Flowers Wholesale Florist Sundries Ltd 1993 IRLR 517, EAT, an employee's dismissal caused her to suffer anxiety and depression, which rendered her unfit for work. The EAT stated that the fact that the employee's incapacity was caused by the unfair dismissal did not necessarily mean that she was entitled to compensation for the whole period of incapacity. It was for the tribunal to decide how far an employee's losses are attributable to action taken by the employer and to arrive at a sum that is just and equitable. The tribunal may want to consider, for example, whether the illness would have manifested itself in any event. It is also

588

important to ascertain the extent to which the illness was actually caused by the dismissal, as opposed to the manner in which the dismissal was carried out. (It should be noted that the House of Lords has reconfirmed in Dunnachie v Kingston upon Hull City Council 2004 ICR 1052, HL, that non-economic loss – e.g. for manner of dismissal – is not recoverable under S.123(1).)

In Dignity Funerals Ltd v Bruce 2005 IRLR 189, Ct Sess (Inner House), the Court of Session agreed with the Scottish EAT that the tribunal had erred in failing to give any satisfactory reason for its decision to make no compensatory award for the period between dismissal and the date of the tribunal hearing. The claimant, who had been dismissed for gross misconduct, was diagnosed with reactive depression, a condition from which he had also suffered for five years before dismissal. The Court of Session noted, referring to the Devine case (above), that the tribunal should have decided 'whether the depression in the period after the dismissal was caused to any material extent by the dismissal itself; whether, if so, it had continued to be so caused for all or part of the period up to the hearing; and, if it was still caused at the date of the hearing, for how long it would continue to be so caused'. In the absence of any proper basis of findings of fact, however, the EAT should not have substituted its own figure for the compensatory award, but rather should have remitted the issue to the tribunal for consideration.

(On the vexed question of whether invalidity (incapacity) benefits received by an employee during the period covered by the compensatory award should be offset, see the discussion under 'Immediate loss – social security benefits' above.)

Constructive dismissal. The issue of how ill health impacts on future loss can prove particularly troublesome in cases of constructive dismissal. In GAB Robins v Triggs 2008 ICR 529, CA, the claimant had been bullied and overworked by her manager, leading to anxiety, depression and a lengthy sickness absence. She had exhausted her entitlement to full sick pay when she resigned and claimed constructive dismissal. Having found her dismissal unfair, the employment tribunal determined that it was appropriate to award a sum in respect of future loss of earnings, even though the claimant had been signed off work at the time of her dismissal and her entitlement to sick pay had run out by the time her resignation took effect. The employer appealed unsuccessfully to the EAT, which agreed with the tribunal that the employer's repudiatory conduct had to be considered as part of a cumulative sequence of events that led to the employee's acceptance of the fundamental breach of her employment contract. As such, the ill health and subsequent reduced earning capacity that the claimant suffered as a result of that conduct had to be treated as a consequence of her dismissal, giving rise to compensation under S.123 ERA. On further appeal, the Court of Appeal expressed a degree of 'instinctive sympathy' with the approach of the employment tribunal and the EAT, but held that it offended the principle that loss must flow from the dismissal. While the employer's repudiatory conduct is an essential condition of constructive

16.61

dismissal, it is not that conduct, but rather the employee's acceptance of the breach, which effects the dismissal. Damage – in the instant case, the claimant's anxiety and depression – caused by the repudiatory conduct is damage in respect of which an employee has already accrued a cause of action at common law, and does not fall within the remit of S.123.

In light of the GAB Robbins decision, claimants wishing to recover damages for future loss caused by repudiatory conduct that led to a constructive dismissal must pursue a claim for damages for breach of contract (or possibly negligence) in the county courts or High Court. While such a claim will generally be more expensive to bring than an employment tribunal claim, it does have the advantage that losses will not be subject to the statutory cap (see above under 'Nature and maximum amount of award – statutory cap'), and is subject to a substantially longer time limit – three years in a personal injury claim as opposed to three months in an unfair dismissal claim.

16.62 **Assessing future loss: other considerations**
The following are the some of the main factors that an employment tribunal will take into account when making its assessment of future loss.

16.63 **Local labour market.** The tribunal will be expected to use its industrial knowledge and understanding of the local labour market. In Welburn v Luxihomes Ltd COET 3088/232 the tribunal noted that the employee lived in a holiday resort and that most of the work in the area was seasonal. It assessed her future loss for a period of 45 weeks until the next holiday season began. In times of high unemployment and recession, awards for future loss are likely to be greatest as tribunals take a less optimistic view of the time it will take for an employee to obtain equivalent new employment.

16.64 **Personal circumstances of the employee.** These must be taken into account. In Haslam v Manchetts Cleaning Supplies Ltd COET 3130/19, for example, the tribunal found that the employee might have difficulty in obtaining a new job because she lived in a country area without a car. And in Malcolm v Balmstore Ltd t/a Thompson's Bakery COET 3169/50 the employee was a young Afro-Caribbean with no formal qualifications and poor communication skills, although he had worked with adequate skill and confidence at a specialist West Indian bakery until his dismissal. The tribunal thought it likely that he would have great difficulty finding other employment. In Gerbaldiv Jones t/a Milton Business Products ET Case No.14248/95 a tribunal found that the employer's failure to give a dismissed employee a reference despite her excellent work record would hamper her attempts to find a job. It assessed her period of future loss at 52 weeks.

Clearly, the age, experience and level of qualification of an employee are all important factors. An apprentice dismissed before his or her period of training has been completed will have higher losses as a result of the early termination of

590

the apprenticeship – see FC Shepherd and Co Ltd v Jerrom 1986 ICR 802, CA. It is also an unfortunate fact that older people are particularly likely to experience difficulties obtaining equivalent new employment, even after the introduction of the Employment Equality (Age) Regulations 2006 SI 2006/1031. Tribunals will sometimes take the view that older employees will be unlikely to find another appropriate job and, so far as the statutory maximum allows, try to award compensation up to normal retiring age. (Compensation may even be awarded beyond normal retiring age if the evidence shows that the employee would have stayed on past that age – Barrel Plating and Phosphating Co Ltd v Danks 1976 IRLR 262, EAT.) Two examples:

- **Kerley v New Forest Bakeries Ltd (in liquidation) and ors** ET Case No.7405/83: K was a 59-year-old baker with no experience in any other trade. The tribunal thought that his prospects of obtaining employment before retirement were 'virtually nil' and went straight to the maximum figure for his compensatory award

- **Machan v New Longmoor Club** ET Case No.10876/87: M was a 53-year-old cleaner. The tribunal thought that the average age of office cleaners was well over 50 and that there was a 60 per cent staff turnover in the trade, so that jobs were continuously available for which age was no barrier. It awarded nothing for future loss because M should be able to obtain a job comparable to her previous one almost immediately.

Self-employment, retraining and study. Some employees become self-employed after being dismissed. Tribunals will take account of earnings from self-employment and – subject to the employee showing that self-employment was a reasonable way of mitigating losses – compensation can be awarded in order to make up any difference between the employee's new and old earnings. **16.65**

If the new earnings from self employment are already higher than those from the old job by the time the tribunal comes to calculate compensation, the excess will be deducted from the immediate loss in the normal way. However, it will not always be safe to assume that there will be no award for future loss. In Islam Channel Ltd v Ridley EAT 0083/09 the claimant, R, had found freelance work after being dismissed as a television journalist. In the 49 weeks between the date of dismissal and the remedies hearing, she had earned roughly £5,000 more from the freelance work than she would have earned had she remained employed. However, all of this 'profit' came from the first 30 weeks of that period: for the last 19 weeks, the frequency of freelance work had dropped off and R was earning around £500 a month less than in her previous job. Upon finding that R had been unfairly dismissed, the tribunal declined to award any immediate loss of earnings as R had not incurred any loss during the relevant period. Turning to future loss, the tribunal noted that the new freelance work was inherently insecure and proceeded to award R £6,149, representing one year's future loss (a period which it described as 'modest') at just over £512 a month. Further, it decided that the claimant need not give credit for the £5,000 'profit' earned during the period of immediate loss.

Before the EAT, the employer argued that credit had to be given for the £5,000. To do otherwise, it contended, would be to land R with a windfall and unfairly punish the employer. The Appeal Tribunal noted that, as a result of the Court of Appeal's decision in Dench v Flynn and Partners 1998 IRLR 653, CA, the obtaining of new work does not act as an 'automatic guillotine' to sever the causal link between the dismissal and any future losses the claimant may experience. It was therefore open to the tribunal, in assessing what would be 'just and equitable' compensation, to treat losses sustained after the first 30 weeks of the freelance work as flowing from the dismissal. On the question of whether credit should be given for the 'profit' earned during the period of immediate loss, the EAT stated that, as an alternative to treating immediate and future losses as one and deducting any sums earned in mitigation, it is open to a tribunal in seeking to settle on just and equitable compensation to draw a line between past and future losses. In addition, the EAT stated that, if it were wrong that a tribunal has the discretion to separate past and future losses, there was an alternative way in which the tribunal could have assessed compensation which would have led to substantially the same result. Given its finding that R's new job was inherently insecure, the tribunal could have required R to give credit for the £5,000 excess she had earned prior to the remedies hearing, but increased her award for future loss based on an assessment of the risk of losing the new job. Had the tribunal assessed that risk at 20 per cent and increased R's compensation accordingly, it would have reached approximately the same overall figure. The EAT acknowledged that this was an exercise conducted after the event but stated that it supported the conclusion that the tribunal's award was just and equitable.

16.66 Some examples of compensation being awarded to employees who became self-employed after dismissal:

- **Oliver v Panayi t/a Criss Hair Dressers** ET Case No.7637/78: a dismissed hairdresser established her own salon. A tribunal awarded a year's net loss of previous earnings to allow for the build-up of the business to the point where she would be as well off as in her previous employment

- **Sparkes v ET Barwick Mills Ltd** ET Case No.41388/76: a dismissed employee decided to set up on his own as a commission agent. A tribunal awarded two years' interest on the capital borrowed to set up the business as part of compensation for future loss. Since he had previously had a company car, it also awarded the employee the down-payment on a car he thought necessary for his new business

- **Glen Henderson Ltd v Nisbet** EAT 34/90: N was unfairly dismissed for redundancy. She then went on a five-week business enterprise course with a view to becoming self-employed. Thereafter she was self-employed. A tribunal awarded her compensation for the time she was on the course and one year's future loss on the basis of her self-employed earnings. This decision was upheld by the EAT

- **Pacific Direct Ltd v Riaz** EAT 0072/02: R was unfairly dismissed following her failure to accept a new commission structure. She then set up her own business, working from home. By October 2001, when the tribunal hearing took place, R had generated £10,300 from the start of the year. However, due to a fire at her flat during the summer, she had been unable to generate any income in June, July or August, though she had been pursuing her business since then and was actively seeking other work. The tribunal found that she was entitled to recover loss of earnings on a basis of an income of £30,000 from January 2001 for a period of 15 months, from which the £10,300 already earned would be deducted. The employer's appeal on the basis that the fire at R's flat should have broken the chain of causation was dismissed. In the EAT's view, the tribunal had taken this setback into account but did not regard it as terminating the loss consequent upon the dismissal that was attributable to the employer's action. It was a permissible approach to decide that R had reasonably mitigated her loss but would not achieve the same earnings level as before until April 2002.

In the Nisbet case (above), the EAT considered that the claimant's five-week course was merely part of her mitigation of loss through her decision to become self-employed. But employees who embark upon a training course following dismissal may well be considered to have voluntarily removed themselves from the job market, with the result that the employer is no longer liable for their losses. In Holroyd v Gravure Cylinders Ltd 1984 IRLR 259, EAT, for example, the employee decided to take a 12-month postgraduate university course after his dismissal. A tribunal refused to extend his compensation past the date on which he began the course. On appeal to the EAT, Lord McDonald said that it had been correct to do so. The employee had decided to take himself out of the labour market for 12 months and so should not be compensated for that period. Any suggestion of continuing future loss after the end of the course was 'so remote as to be incapable... of calculation'.

16.67

Similarly, in Simrad Ltd v Scott 1997 IRLR 147, EAT, the Appeal Tribunal directed a tribunal to ignore all losses directly arising from the employee's decision to retrain as a nurse. However, the EAT clarified in Khanum v IBC Vehicles Ltd EAT 685/98 that the Simrad case did not create a rule of law that embarking upon a course of further education necessarily breaks the chain of causation. The EAT also said that the fact that it may have been reasonable for an employee to go to college did not determine the issue either way. The issue for the tribunal is whether the decision to undertake the course is a direct result of the dismissal. Given that the tribunal had found that the claimant had no choice but to attend university, the EAT said that the loss she suffered in doing so must be a direct result of her dismissal. (Both this case and the Simrad case are discussed in more detail under 'Remoteness of loss' below.)

16.68 **Mitigation.** Note that the amount awarded for future loss is greatly affected by the question of what steps it is reasonable to expect the employee to take to mitigate his or her losses. For instance, if the dismissed employee has accepted a much lower-paid job than the previous one, the tribunal is unlikely to award the full difference in pay for either immediate or future loss unless the employee can show that, in the circumstances, it was reasonable to accept such a low-paid job. We consider this question in more detail in Chapter 18, under 'Failure to mitigate losses'.

16.69 ## Discount for accelerated receipt

As any award for future years is payable by the employer up front in a single lump sum, a discount rate is usually applied (unless the award is fairly small) to take into account the benefit to the employee of receiving the money early, on the assumption that the money can then be invested to yield growth. The Court of Appeal confirmed in the case of Bentwood Bros (Manchester) Ltd v Shepherd 2003 ICR 1000, CA, that tribunals should not ignore the fact that the employee has the benefit of receiving immediately money he or she would otherwise have had to wait for and should therefore apply a discount for accelerated receipt. However, in that particular case, the tribunal applied a single deduction of 5 per cent of the total compensation designed to compensate two and a half years' future earnings and ten years' pension payments. The Court of Appeal held that, in doing this, the tribunal had failed to recognise that the conventional investment rate of 5 per cent, referred to in textbooks such as Harvey on Industrial Relations and Employment Law, was intended to be an annual rate. The Court also held that 5 per cent was arguably on the high side, given that until recently 4.5 per cent was the statutory discount rate applicable in personal injury cases and that this had since been reduced to 2.5 per cent. The question of the appropriate rate to apply as a discount for accelerated receipt was therefore remitted to the tribunal for reconsideration. The tribunal subsequently concluded that 3 per cent was the appropriate discount for accelerated receipt.

In Benchmark Dental Laboratories Group Ltd v Perfitt EAT 0304/04 the EAT considered two matters of general interest with regard to discount from the compensatory award for accelerated receipt. The first concerned the appropriate discount rate. The EAT pointed out that the rate prescribed for use in personal injury cases is set by the Lord Chancellor pursuant to S.1 of the Damages Act 1996. The Damages (Personal Injuries) Order 2001 SI 2001/2301 currently prescribes 2.5 per cent as the assumed rate of return on investment of awards of personal injury damages. Although employment tribunals are not bound by this discount, the EAT observed that it is good practice for them to adopt it.

The second issue concerned the application of that rate to the particular circumstances of the case. The employment tribunal found that the employee had been unfairly dismissed and subject to disability discrimination. It further found that, at the age of 57, the period of the employee's loss would be likely to continue until his retirement age, i.e. eight years. It calculated his actual financial loss as being £121,864 and then applied a 2.5 per cent discount for accelerated payment to that entire sum, resulting in an award of £118,818. On appeal, the EAT ruled that the tribunal had erred by applying the 2.5 per cent discount to the entire period of loss. That was because receipt of the entire sum was not accelerated to the same extent equally across the whole period: the benefit to the employee of early receipt was far greater in respect of that part of the award for lost earnings at the end of the period. Taking a broad-brush approach, the EAT held that one appropriate way of calculating the discount for accelerated receipt in the instant case was to apply a total discount of 10 per cent to half the award, since it was the second half of the award in respect of which early receipt was most accelerated. This would represent a discount of 2.5 per cent multiplied by half the number of years covered by the compensation award (in this case, four). If greater sophistication was required, the parties should refer the tribunal to appropriate compensation tables, such as the Ogden tables (see below). But the EAT made it clear that in the absence of a more sophisticated approach, a tribunal would not err in law by applying a discount for accelerated receipt on the basis of the broad considerations set out above.

16.70 Note that where a multiplier and multiplicand are being used (e.g. where the Ogden Tables are being used to assess career-long loss of earnings), the formula may already incorporate a discount for accelerated receipt. However, as has previously been explained, the EAT in Kingston Upon Hull City Council v Dunnachie (No.3) 2003 IRLR 843, EAT, emphasised that the use of Ogden Tables in unfair dismissal cases will be rare – see under 'Career-long loss' above. Turning to consider how tribunals should use the Ogden Tables whenever they are appropriate, the EAT pointed out that the tables were of use only once the tribunal had determined a figure for estimated annual loss (i.e. the multiplicand). In the EAT's view, it was unlikely that a tribunal would arrive at a single annual figure for estimated loss. In some cases one figure in respect of the first one or two years and then a lower figure in respect of later periods would be appropriate. The EAT was of the view, however, that where an employee was close to retirement a tribunal could adopt a single multiplicand and then apply the Ogden Tables and a discount for (i) contingencies and (ii) accelerated receipt. So far as the latter is concerned, a tribunal should adopt the prevailing rate of return specified under the Damages Act 1996 (currently 2.5 per cent). Once a tribunal had applied a multiplier from a relevant Ogden Table, it was inappropriate for it then to apply a large percentage discount for generalised contingencies since, if there were contingencies justifying something in the order of a 50 per cent discount, it was

595

likely that the assessment that the employee was likely to sustain career-long loss would have been unjustified in the first place.

16.71 **'Decelerated' payment.** In Melia v Magna Kansei Ltd EAT 0339/04 the issue arose as to whether an employee could recover as part of the compensatory award the obverse of accelerated receipt, namely any loss that flows from being denied the opportunity to invest compensation prior to the conclusion of the tribunal proceedings. The EAT in Melia termed such loss 'a premium for decelerated payment', although this masks the fact that, in reality, such loss comprises pre-judgment interest. The question of whether tribunals are able to make such an award is discussed below under 'Interest'.

16.72 **Remoteness of loss**

Section 123(1) ERA expressly states that the loss suffered by the employee must be attributable to action taken by the employer. We have seen in the case of Courtaulds Northern Spinning Ltd v Moosa 1984 ICR 218, EAT (see under 'Immediate loss' above), how an employer may successfully argue that the employee's losses are no longer attributable to the employer's action. That case concerned an employee who worked in new employment for 18 months but was then dismissed again before the tribunal hearing of the original claim. The EAT held that the original employer's liability ceased when the employee entered the new employment.

In Mabey Plant Hire Ltd v Richens, unreported 6.5.93, CA, an employee got a new job at a lower rate of pay for which he was overqualified. He was dismissed from that job a few months later on account of a clash of personalities and a failure to comply with company regulations. The Court of Appeal held that the new employment could have been permanent and that it came to an end for reasons unrelated to any action taken by the original employer. The chain of causation was therefore broken and any future loss was restricted to the difference between the employee's original salary and the salary he would have continued to earn with the second employer but for the second dismissal.

In other cases, however, a tribunal may conclude that the employee's loss after a second dismissal is still attributable to the first dismissal – for example, where the period of new employment is short. In Dundee Plant Co Ltd v Riddler EAT 377/88 the employee found a new job but gave it up after three months when it proved unsuitable (reasonably, said the tribunal). The EAT upheld the tribunal's finding that the employer's liability did not terminate when the employee found the new job. And in Witham Weld v Hedley EAT 176/95 the employee gained new employment immediately after her dismissal but it proved to be unsuitable and she left after four weeks. The EAT stated that 'a reasonable but unsuccessful attempt to mitigate does not cut the chain between the wrongdoing and loss which on ordinary principles of causation flowed from it'.

596

The Court of Appeal came to a similar conclusion in the case of Dench v Flynn and Partners 1998 IRLR 653, CA, overturning a tribunal decision that the claimant was not entitled to compensation after she had taken up new employment, even though the new job had been terminated after only two months. The Court took the sensible view that, contrary to the EAT's approach in Whelan and anor v Richardson 1998 ICR 318, EAT, there is no hard-and-fast rule as to whether permanent alternative employment breaks the chain of causation for loss. The tribunal's only duty is to award what is just and equitable in the circumstances and the tribunal must consider the effect of the unfair dismissal and the effect of the termination of any subsequent employment.

There is obviously a very close connection here between the issue of remoteness and the question of whether an employee has taken reasonable steps to mitigate his or her losses. In cases like Holroyd v Gravure Cylinders Ltd (above) (see 'Self-employment, retraining and study') and Dundee Plant Co Ltd v Riddler (immediately above) the question of whether the employees' actions in entering a training course, on the one hand, and leaving a new job, on the other, were reasonable mitigation of loss is almost identical to the question of whether their ongoing losses were still attributable to the actions of the employers. In other words, if the employee's attempts to mitigate loss are considered reasonable, the chain of causation is unlikely to be broken and the losses sustained by the employee will still be attributable to the original dismissal. But if the employee's actions following dismissal are considered to be unreasonable, they may well constitute a *novus actus interveniens* – or 'intervening act' – following which the employee's losses can no longer be said to be attributable to the dismissal by the employer. **16.73**

Notwithstanding their similarity, however, issues of remoteness and mitigation need to be kept separate. In Wilson v Glenrose (Fishmerchants) Ltd and ors EAT 444/91 an employee who had poor prospects of obtaining new employment chose to claim sickness benefits for two years before becoming 'unemployed'. The EAT held that the tribunal was wrong to award no future loss on the ground that causation between the employee's dismissal and his current unemployment had been broken by his claiming sickness benefit. It should first have considered whether claiming for that period was, in the circumstances, a reasonable action in mitigation of loss.

Change of career. A radical approach to the question of how far an employee's losses are attributable to actions of the employer – and the relationship between this question and that of mitigation – was adopted by the EAT in the case of Simrad Ltd v Scott 1997 IRLR 147, EAT. In that case the employee was dismissed from her job as an electronics technician and decided to retrain as a nurse. The tribunal found that it was reasonable in her circumstances to seek to change careers in this way and assessed her future loss for a period of 15 months. On appeal, the EAT stated that the approach a tribunal should adopt consists of three stages. First, the tribunal must quantify the losses claimed. **16.74**

Secondly, it must consider the extent to which any or all of those losses are attributable to action taken by the employer. Thirdly, the tribunal must consider whether, in all the circumstances, it is just and equitable to make the relevant award. It is largely at this third stage that the question of mitigation arises since, while the facts relating to mitigation will frequently bear upon the question of causative link, it is essentially an equitable plea to be judged in the context of reasonableness.

Having set out this approach, the EAT formed the opinion that the tribunal had erred by missing out the second stage and merely asking itself whether the employee acted reasonably in deciding on a career change. The EAT stated that, if an element of loss fails the 'attribution test' at stage two, it cannot be awarded on just and equitable grounds at stage three. The EAT went on to hold that the employee's decision to embark upon a nursing career was not sufficiently linked to the original dismissal. Although it would not have happened but for the dismissal, her decision to become a nurse was too remote 'both in time and content' to be properly attributable to the employer's conduct. Accordingly, all losses directly arising from the decision to become a nurse had to be ignored for compensation purposes.

The Simrad approach has proved to be quite influential. It was cited in Leonard and ors v Strathclyde Buses Ltd 1998 IRLR 693, EAT, in which the employees were forced to sell their shares in SB Ltd back to the company when they were dismissed. SB Ltd was soon after taken over by another company, which paid significantly more for the shares than SB Ltd had done. The employees claimed as part of their compensation the enhanced value which they would have received for their shares but for their dismissals. The EAT stated that it was not enough for the employees to establish that, but for their dismissals, they would have received more for their shares. The increase in value of the shares had occurred as a result of the intervention of a third party and was not, therefore, attributable to the conduct of the employer.

16.75 The Simrad case was also cited in Jones v Lingfield Leisure plc EAT 712/97. In that case a fitness trainer was employed at a leisure centre and also ran a number of additional classes on a self-employed basis. Because she was employed at the centre, she did not have to pay the fee that other self-employed instructors paid to the centre. She was unfairly dismissed and claimed as part of her compensation the loss of the self-employed earnings. The EAT upheld a tribunal ruling that these losses were too remote. In the EAT's view, the compensatory award is not meant to compensate an employee for losses arising out of the discontinuance by the employee of a business that she was carrying out while employed by the employer. The EAT was prepared to accept, however, that the fact that the claimant had not paid any fee to the centre for her classes might constitute a lost fringe benefit for which she could claim.

However, in Khanum v IBC Vehicles Ltd EAT 685/98 the EAT sought to temper the significance of the decision in the Simrad case, emphasising that the outcome in that case had turned very much on its own facts and that it did not create a rule of law to the effect that embarking upon a course of further education necessarily breaks the chain of causation. The claimant, an apprentice robotics technician, qualified in electronics to ONC and HNC level, had told her employer that she was interested in taking a degree course. The claimant's subsequent dismissal for attending a university open day was found to be unfair. At the remedies hearing, the tribunal learnt that the employee had been diagnosed as suffering from depression shortly before her dismissal. After the dismissal, she had made several unsuccessful job applications. Her former employer dominated the local automobile industry and there was evidence (which the tribunal accepted) that she had been 'blacklisted'. Ten months after dismissal, the employee started a degree course in computer systems engineering. The tribunal decided that it was sensible and laudable for her to take the course, but that her decision to do so 'inevitably' broke the chain of causation between her dismissal and her financial loss. On appeal, the EAT overturned the tribunal's conclusions in view of the fact that the employee had had no choice but to attend university. The EAT identified three special factors governing her case. The first was that she had completed an apprenticeship for a specialist job in the car industry. The second was that her employer's dominant position in that industry could prevent the employee from pursuing her chosen career and there was evidence that it had blacklisted her. And the third was that she was unfairly and unlawfully dismissed. Taking those factors together, it was reasonably foreseeable that the employee would or might have had to retrain in a different career as a result of her dismissal. The EAT further noted that the tribunal had not considered whether it would have been 'just and reasonable' to award compensation to the claimant. In view of the tribunal's findings as to the difficulties she experienced in obtaining employment and her state of health, it was clear that the tribunal had not directed itself properly on the third stage identified in the Simrad case (i.e. whether it was just and equitable to make the award).

In assessing the period for which to award compensation for future loss, the tribunal will also take account of other contingencies that may intervene to break the link between the dismissal and the employee's ongoing losses – e.g. where the evidence shows that the employee would shortly have left the old job of his or her own accord or where the employee would have been dismissed fairly at a later date. For instance, in James W Cook and Co (Wivenhoe) Ltd v Tipper and ors 1990 ICR 716, CA, the claimant was one of a number of employees unfairly dismissed shortly before the shipyard where they worked was closed. The Court of Appeal limited the employees' compensation to losses up to the date when the shipyard closed, at which point they would have been dismissed in any case.

16.76

In Garage Equipment Maintenance Co Ltd v Holloway EAT 582/94 the employee gained new employment in October 1992 at a slighter lower salary, which was subsequently reduced by £8,000 in April 1993. In the assessment of his future loss, the tribunal awarded him the difference between the salary in his former job and that in his new job, taking into account the £8,000 reduction. On appeal, the original employer argued that the reduction in salary that the employee suffered in his new job was not the result of its actions and that the tribunal had in effect made it compensate him for something for which it, as former employer, bore no responsibility. The EAT rejected the appeal, holding that the tribunal was entitled to take a broad-brush approach and that there had been no error of law.

16.77 **Loss of private income.** It will be an issue of fact for a tribunal to determine whether or not loss of the ability to generate private income associated with the lost employment will be recoverable as part of the award for future loss. In Jones v Lingfield Leisure plc 1999 EWCA Civ 1456, CA, a duty manager at a leisure club was allowed to give classes as an instructor and fitness trainer at the premises, which generated a substantial private income. Following her dismissal, an employment tribunal concluded that it was only empowered to compensate the employee for her loss as an employee, and therefore any loss which the employee might have suffered by losing her ability to work on her own account at her ex-employer's premises was not a matter within its jurisdiction. That finding was upheld by the EAT and the Court of Appeal. However, the Court of Appeal noted that it was not excluding the possibility that there could be a situation where the opportunity to earn other money in a self-employed capacity, using the employer's facilities, could come within S.123 ERA when quantifying future loss.

In Schlesinger v Swindon and Marlborough NHS Trust EAT 0072/04 the claimant was a consultant gynaecologist working under a part-time contract that allowed him to work within the private sector as well. He therefore also worked at a private hospital. He was suspended following his arrest and subsequently dismissed. A tribunal decided that his dismissal was unfair and awarded compensation of £12,918. The employee appealed in relation to the tribunal's refusal to make an award in respect of loss of private income. In light of S.123, there were two tests to be considered, namely: (i) whether the loss was attributable to the employer's action, and (ii) if so, whether the amount claimed was just and equitable in all the circumstances. The EAT held that there were no grounds for interfering with the tribunal's decision. While it was accepted that the contract allowed the employee to take on private work, it had been a matter for the particular specialist as to whether he did or did not take on that work. In the instant case, there was not a sufficient contractual link to allow the employee to claim loss of private income.

16.78 **Tax rebates**
Where an employee is dismissed and then unemployed for a time, he or she may become entitled to a tax rebate. The general rule is that such matters are not to

600

be taken into account by a tribunal when assessing the compensatory award because consideration of detailed tax calculations would introduce unnecessary complications into a system that is supposed to be simple and informal – Adda International Ltd v Curcio 1976 IRLR 425, EAT. However, in MBS Ltd v Calo 1983 IRLR 189, EAT, the Appeal Tribunal, while endorsing the above principle, suggested that it might be proper for tax rebates to be offset against the employee's losses where high earners were involved and the sums in question could be substantial.

Interestingly, the employees in Lucas and ors v Laurence Scott Electromotors Ltd 1983 IRLR 61, EAT, managed to recover compensation for *loss* of a tax rebate. Here the employees were dismissed in March 1981 in circumstances that meant that they would have been fairly dismissed in July 1981. The employees remained unemployed for the whole of the financial year starting from April 1981. Had the employees been dismissed in July rather than in March, they would have been entitled to a rebate when they ceased working for the rest of that financial year. The tribunal's decision that this loss was attributable to the employer's action was upheld on appeal by the EAT.

Expenses

16.79

Section 123(2)(a) ERA expressly states that assessment of an employee's loss shall be taken to include any expenses reasonably incurred by the complainant in consequence of the dismissal. These may include:

- sums reasonably spent in looking for a new job – e.g. telephone calls, postage and the cost of attending interviews

- removal expenses if the employee has to move out of tied accommodation or move to a different area in order to secure another job.

Home removal costs. In Daykin v IHW Engineering Ltd ET Case No.01838/83 the claimant had to sell his house and move into a council flat while looking for work. The tribunal awarded him removal expenses and also solicitors' conveyancing charges and estate agents' commission on the sale of the house. The employee had satisfied the tribunal that the sale of the house was a direct consequence of his dismissal.

16.80

School fees. In Derrick v DeVilbiss Co Ltd ET Case No.15631/83 the claimant found a new job in another area after his dismissal. He had settled his daughter in a private school and was anxious to leave her there until she took her GCE exams. He decided to move and leave his daughter as a boarder and claimed £1,800 for extra school fees and expenses. The tribunal thought it was an inevitable result of his dismissal that the claimant would either incur extra

16.81

travelling expenses through long-distance commuting to his new job or extra school fees. It therefore awarded the £1,800 in full.

16.82 **Business set-up costs.** Expenses incurred by ex-employees in setting themselves up in business on their own account may also be awarded if the tribunal considers that this is a reasonable way of mitigating the loss arising from dismissal. In Gardiner-Hill v Roland Berger Technics Ltd 1982 IRLR 498, EAT, the Appeal Tribunal considered a claim by an ex-managing director for £500 worth of expenses in setting up a consultancy service to be reasonable.

16.83 **Legal costs.** The legal fees involved in bringing an unfair dismissal claim cannot be included in a compensatory award – Nohar v Granitstone (Galloway) Ltd 1974 ICR 273, NIRC. This is because the award of legal costs and expenses to parties at tribunal hearings is governed strictly by the Employment Tribunals (Constitution and Rules of Procedure) Regulations 2004 SI 2004/1861, which provides that costs can be awarded only in limited circumstances – see IDS Employment Law Handbook, 'Employment Tribunal Practice and Procedure' (2006), Chapter 18, for more detail on the power to award costs.

16.84 ## Loss of statutory rights

An employee who has been unfairly dismissed will – unless reinstated or re-engaged – lose a number of statutory employment protection rights that are dependent on the employee having remained in employment for a qualifying period. Most notably, the employee will lose the right not to be unfairly dismissed until he or she has worked long enough for a new employer – i.e. for a year – to qualify for the right again. It is commonplace for tribunals to award a nominal sum to reflect the loss of these rights – see, for example, SH Muffett Ltd v Head 1986 IRLR 488, EAT. That decision, itself now nearly 20 years old, was made during the time in which the qualifying period for claiming unfair dismissal was raised from one to two years. Furthermore, the EAT decided in that case to increase substantially the nominal sum awardable from £20 (at which it had stood since being set by the National Industrial Relations Court in Norton Tool Co Ltd v Tewson 1972 ICR 501, NIRC) to £100, on the basis that the pound had undergone considerable devaluation in the interim. The EAT also noted that the figure of £100 should be reviewed within three to four years. In fact, the figure awarded by tribunals has remained fairly static since that time and appears largely unrelated to inflation and the retail prices index.

Loss of rights to statutory notice can also be compensated. This may be a serious loss for a long-serving employee who has, for example, worked for 12 years and become entitled to the statutory maximum of 12 weeks' notice, since it will take him or her 12 years with a new employer to recover his or her position. In Daley v AE Dorsett (Almar Dolls Ltd) 1982 ICR 1, EAT, it was held that in such a case it would be reasonable to award net pay for half the statutory notice period to compensate for loss of an intangible benefit. Thus, an employee with 12 years' service should get six weeks' net pay. In Annansingh v AW Lawson and Co Ltd EAT 733/85 a tribunal awarded an employee only £20 for loss of statutory rights, although he had been continuously employed for 24 years. The EAT held that the minimum figure the tribunal should have awarded under this head was six weeks' pay – i.e. half the employee's statutory notice entitlement.

However, the Daley case was qualified in SH Muffett Ltd v Head (above), **16.85** where the EAT added that only in exceptional cases should the tribunal award pay for half of the statutory notice period; less would usually be more appropriate. In Arthur Guinness Son and Co (GB) Ltd v Green 1989 ICR 241, EAT, for example, the EAT reduced the award of ten weeks' pay a tribunal had made to an employee with 28 years' service to a mere four weeks.

It is now fairly common practice for tribunals to award between £200 and £300 as a global sum for both loss of protection from unfair dismissal and loss of the accrued right to statutory notice.

Note that an employee may receive no award for loss of statutory rights if the tribunal is satisfied that the employee would shortly have been fairly dismissed from his or her employment anyway – Puglia v C James and Sons 1996 ICR 301, EAT. However, in Tyson v Concurrent Systems Inc Ltd EAT 0028/03 the EAT held that a tribunal cannot simply omit to deal with a claim for compensation for loss of statutory rights and it therefore awarded £200 under this head of loss.

Pension loss   16.86

One of the most significant losses that an employee is likely to sustain as a result of being unfairly dismissed is that of pension rights, particularly where the employee was a member of a final salary (defined benefits) occupational pension scheme. Until fairly recently, such losses tended to be calculated in a rough-and-ready way, since the statutory cap on the compensatory award frequently got in the way of tribunals awarding anything like the full losses involved. However, following the raising of the cap from £12,000 to £55,000 in October 1999, and the subsequent annual inflation indexing of that figure so that it stands (as from 1 February 2010) at £65,300, the scope for awarding substantial sums by way of pension loss has increased significantly. As a consequence, the approach that tribunals adopt to the calculation of such loss has become more sophisticated.

It would be idle to pretend that the calculation of pension loss is a simple matter. This is acknowledged in the revised guidance that was issued by a committee of tribunal chairmen in 2003. The committee's booklet, entitled 'Guidelines on Compensation for Loss of Pension Rights' (3rd edition), suggests that in assessing pension loss as a component of the compensatory award, one of two approaches – the 'simplified approach' or the 'substantial loss' approach – should be adopted by tribunals.

The tribunal guidelines, together with a detailed analysis of the different types of pension loss, are discussed in detail in Chapter 17.

16.87 One point that should be mentioned here, however, is that it is not open to a tribunal to separate the issue of causation in respect of pension loss from the causation of the employee's other losses. In Aegon UK Corporate Services Ltd v Roberts 2010 ICR 596, CA, the claimant, R, had been a member of a final salary pension scheme before she was unfairly dismissed. Soon after dismissal, she found another job with JR Ltd which paid her more than she had previously earned. However, the new job came with a defined contribution pension scheme that was much less valuable and, by the time the tribunal came to assess compensation, R had lost the new job. With regard to causation, the tribunal decided that, so far as remuneration was concerned, the termination of the new job amounted to an intervening cause of loss and so her loss of earnings beyond that point could not be attributed to A Ltd. However, with regard to pension loss, the tribunal took the view that such loss could continue even though the claimant obtained permanent employment paying an equivalent or higher salary. It considered that the loss of R's final salary pension was a 'unique type of benefit' which she did not obtain on joining JR Ltd and which she would be unlikely to obtain in any other employment. The tribunal therefore decided that the pension loss should not be 'thrown in' with other benefits and treated as part of the total remuneration package, and awarded R over £37,000.

The EAT agreed with the tribunal that a break in the chain of causation does not have to apply for all purposes and in respect of each benefit. It further took the view that the tribunal was entitled to treat pension benefits as a 'very significant factor', the loss of which could not be quantified in purely monetary terms. The case progressed to the Court of Appeal, which held that a pension does not have any special status in the calculation of future loss, but is simply part of the overall remuneration package and must be assessed in monetary terms. A tribunal does not have leeway to apply different principles of causation to different aspects of the remuneration package. Thus, having found that there was no shortfall in remuneration because, even taking account of the pension loss, the overall package with JR Ltd was more favourable than it had been with A Ltd, the tribunal was not entitled to award R pension loss.

Interest

16.88

Following the enactment of the Employment Tribunals (Interest) Order 1990 SI 1990/479 ('the Interest Order 1990'), tribunals have the power to award interest on the compensation they award. However, it should be noted that interest only begins to accrue when the tribunal's monetary award remains unpaid for *42 days after promulgation of the award*. The tribunal promulgates an award when the documentary confirmation of that part of its decision is recorded as having been sent to the parties.

Interest still accrues from the same date even if the tribunal's decision is subject to review or appeal but, if the result of the review or appeal is to vary the amount payable, interest accrues on the amount as varied.

With regard to appeals to the EAT, much will depend on whether the appeal process was commenced before or after promulgation of the award by the tribunal. If the appeal is brought against a tribunal decision which already contained a promulgated award, then interest will begin to accrue 42 days after that original decision was promulgated. But if the appeal is against a tribunal decision which did not contain an order for payment of compensation, then interest will only begin to accrue 42 days after the appellate court promulgates an order for compensation (if this ever happens). The same principle operates where further appeals are pursued. Again, where an appeal results in the amount of compensation being varied, any interest will accrue on the amount as varied.

The remitting of a case for a fresh tribunal hearing may affect the accrual of interest in one of three ways:

16.89

- where the original tribunal's decision on compensation was not promulgated to the parties, any interest will only begin to accrue 42 days after the new tribunal has promulgated the award

- where the original tribunal's decision on compensation was promulgated and the case is remitted to a new tribunal on a question which does not affect the assessment of compensation, interest still accrues from 42 days after the original award was promulgated

- where the original tribunal's decision on compensation was promulgated, but the amount of compensation is eventually altered on a remit, interest will accrue on the new, varied amount of compensation, but from 42 days after the original award was promulgated.

Computation of interest

16.90

Interest is based on any part of the compensation which remains unpaid 42 days after the relevant promulgation (for which see above). Any interest payable will be simple interest accruing from day to day – Art 3(1) of the

605

Interest Order 1990. Article 4 of that Order stipulates that the rate of interest is that specified in S.17 of the Judgments Act 1838. The rate at the time of writing (which has remained unchanged since 1 April 1993) is 8 per cent. Should the rate alter, the relevant rate is the rate specified by S.17 of the 1838 Act as at the date of promulgation of the tribunal's decision.

Certain sums are to be disregarded when determining the amount of the monetary award upon which interest will accrue. These are:

- any award by the tribunal of costs or expenses

- any part of the monetary award which is subject to recoupment (see Chapter 20)

- any part of the award which the payer – i.e. the employer – is required, under statutory provision, to deduct and pay over to the tax authorities in respect of tax or national insurance contributions.

16.91 **Pre-judgment interest**

In High Court proceedings, the Court is empowered under the Supreme Court Act 1981 to award not only post-judgment interest but also interest backdated to such date as it concludes is appropriate. This can be as far back as the date when the debt accrued. Employment tribunals have no such express power in unfair dismissal cases. However, in Melia v Magna Kansei Ltd EAT 0339/04 the question arose whether an employee could, in fact, recover such a sum as a head of loss under the compensatory award on the basis of what is 'just and equitable'. In that case, the tribunal had made a deduction of 2.5 per cent on account of accelerated receipt of the award covering pension loss and loss of future earnings. The claimant argued that if it was just and equitable to make such a deduction, it should surely be just and equitable to include as a head of loss the obverse, namely 'a premium for decelerated or delayed payment'. On appeal, the EAT could find no case authority prohibiting such an award and reasoned that 'in a case where, as here, a deduction of 2.5 per cent per annum is made from a calculation in order to make an allowance for accelerated payment, so there ought to be an increase or premium of 2.5 per cent per annum in respect of what one might loosely call "decelerated" or "delayed" payment; if the one is doable within the ordinary concept of common law damages or, here, of just and equitable compensation, so should the latter'.

The EAT went on to observe that the rate of the premium should be the same as that applied for accelerated receipt. The current standard rate in personal injuries is 2.5 per cent – the rate that the tribunal applied in the instant case – and it is that rate which another division of the EAT recommended tribunals to adopt in Benchmark Dental Laboratories Group Ltd v Perfitt EAT 0304/04 – see under 'Accelerated receipt' above. The EAT acknowledged that this was considerably less than the annual rate of interest on judgment debts, but given that an award for 'decelerated receipt' would, in the EAT's view, only be applicable in a case where a corresponding deduction for accelerated receipt has been made, 'it is simple fairness to apply the same rate both ways'.

Drafting schedules of loss   16.92

A schedule of loss is a claimant's statement of the loss he or she has suffered as a result of the employer's actions. The employment tribunal will usually order the claimant to produce such a schedule at an early stage in proceedings as part of general case management directions. Both parties and the tribunal are then clear as to what the claimant is seeking, which may encourage settlement. The schedule usually sets out the claimant's losses at the time of drafting, which may, of course, increase by the time of the hearing if the claimant has not found a new job. It should therefore be updated just prior to the hearing.

In an unfair dismissal claim, the claimant will need to set out details of the basic and compensatory awards. As we have seen in Chapter 15, the former is calculated according to the claimant's age, length of service and week's pay (currently capped at £380). This chapter demonstrates, however, that the details of compensatory award the claimant is seeking will form the bulk of the drafting work. Ideally, the individual elements of immediate loss – loss of earnings, benefits, pension contributions, etc – should be set out first. A sum for loss of statutory rights can be included at this stage (see above under 'Loss of statutory rights'). The schedule should then set out any pay the employee received in lieu of notice and any sums received from the employer by way of a redundancy, severance or ex gratia payment. A claimant will also need to provide details of the extent to which he or she has mitigated losses by finding new employment or claiming incapacity benefit. Note, however, that if the employee was dismissed without notice, no credit need be given for sums earned during what would have been the notice period. If the claim is likely to involve an award of future loss that will see a reduction for accelerated payment, the schedule should include a percentage premium on the award for immediate loss to take account of decelerated payment. This percentage should be the same as the discount of accelerated payment (see below).

When considering future losses, a general rule of thumb is that, barring exceptional   16.93
circumstances, the tribunal is unlikely to make an award that continues for more than two years at most. More usual is a period of six months to a year (from the date of the hearing). The claimant can be expected to be put to proof in verifying the nature and scale of any losses, so claims for future loss should be realistic. The typical way to express future loss of earnings is by assessing the weekly loss and multiplying that by the number of weeks for which the loss is expected to continue. The schedule should also include any anticipated future loss relating to benefits and pensions. As with immediate loss, any sums in mitigation should be included – these will be the sums that the claimant expects to receive from other employment

607

or incapacity benefits. To take account of the fact that the claimant will receive the award for future loss all at once, rather than spread out over a number of years, the sum claimed for future loss should be reduced by the same percentage by which the sum claimed for immediate loss was increased.

Once the total losses have been set out in the schedule of loss, it is necessary next to consider any deductions or adjustments that should be made. The types of adjustment and deduction that can be made in an unfair dismissal claim, along with the order in which they should be made, are explored in detail in Chapter 18. Claimants often dispute, or do not own up to, the applicability of deductions and adjustments that may be unfavourable to their case. However, if it is obvious that such an adjustment will be made, it is better to include it in the schedule and increase its overall credibility with the tribunal. Note that, where the claimant has received a redundancy payment (contractual or statutory), the final deduction should be the extent to which the payment exceeds the amount of the basic award.

Unless the claim is one of those to which the statutory cap of, currently, £65,300 does not apply (see under 'Nature and maximum amount of award – statutory cap' above), the total amount claimed should not exceed the cap. It would, however, seem prudent to list the full extent of the losses and then apply the cap, as this is likely to make the tribunal's task in calculating compensation somewhat easier.

16.94 If the unfair dismissal claim is accompanied by a complaint of discrimination (e.g. based on the allegation that a dismissal was both unfair and discriminatory on, say, the ground of race), then the claimant will want to consider any additional financial loss, injury to feelings, personal injury, aggravated damages (where the employer has behaved in a 'high handed, malicious, oppressive or insulting manner') and interest. Such sums should be clearly demarked from the compensation for unfair dismissal, since there is no guarantee that the tribunal will uphold both complaints.

From the employer's point of view, it is good practice to prepare a counter-schedule, particularly where the basis for calculation or the heads of loss are disputed. This will help narrow the issues in dispute and may encourage settlement. It is also the ideal place for a respondent to raise the issue of any deductions or adjustments that it thinks should be made to compensation. The employer should also ask the claimant to provide evidence of his or her attempts to mitigate loss. Remember, it is for the claimant to prove his or her loss but for the respondent to prove the claimant's failure to mitigate that loss.

As a general rule, the more accurate the claimant's schedule of loss, the fewer holes the employer will be able to pick in it, so that while the schedule should put the claimant's losses at their highest, it should not be fanciful. If wholly unrealistic, it may come back to haunt the claimant at a later stage. In particular, it may result in a loss of credibility, which may weaken the claimant's case in a general sense so far as the tribunal is concerned.

17 Compensatory awards: pension loss

Principles of loss

Tribunal guidelines

Types of pension

The 'simplified loss' approach

The 'substantial loss' approach

Where an employee who is a member of an occupational pension scheme is unfairly **17.1** dismissed, the loss of his or her pension rights can form one of the most important elements of the compensatory award. Sometimes the benefits of belonging to a pension scheme will form a significant part of the remuneration package and losses under this head will consequently be substantial. It often used to be the case (before the statutory limit on compensatory awards was substantially increased from £12,000 to £50,000 in October 1999) that it was obvious, even before the tribunal had finished its calculations, that the employee's total losses had exceeded the statutory limit. In such cases tribunals would frequently dispense with the need for complex actuarial calculations of pension loss. However, since the increase of the statutory cap in October 1999, and the subsequent annual inflation indexing of that figure (which is currently set at £65,300), the scope for awarding significant sums by way of pension loss has increased substantially. As a consequence, tribunals have had to adopt a more sophisticated approach to the assessment of pension loss involving far more precise calculations of the monetary value of the pension rights that the employee has lost.

Further complications have arisen as a result of the changing nature of pension provision in this country. The last decade has seen the closure of the vast majority of private sector final salary (defined benefit) pension schemes to new members, meaning that an employee who belonged to such a scheme prior to dismissal is unlikely to obtain an equivalent pension in any future employment. It is therefore increasingly common for claimants to seek compensation for a sustained period of pension loss.

Principles of loss

17.2

While the process for calculating pension loss can be very different to that for calculating loss of earnings, the fundamental principles are the same: the tribunal should award such amount as it considers just and equitable in all

609

the circumstances, having regard to the loss sustained by the complainant in consequence of the dismissal in so far as that loss is attributable to action taken by the employer – S.123 Employment Rights Act 1996 (ERA) (see Chapter 16). The fact that an employment tribunal, rather than a civil court, is tasked with calculating the loss should not be overlooked. The discretion and flexibility afforded to tribunals by the 'just and equitable' formula in S.123 is substantial, and means that tribunals can adopt a relatively broad-brush approach to calculating pension loss that might not be acceptable in, for example, a High Court personal injury claim. Successful appeals are therefore rare and will generally involve a misdirection as to the law or perversity in a tribunal's decision.

17.3 Relationship with loss of earnings

For practical reasons, pension loss is generally dealt with by tribunals as a separate head of loss, distinct from immediate and future loss of earnings. However, the Court of Appeal has recently emphasised that, in reality, a pension is merely part of an employee's remuneration package – Aegon UK Corporate Services Ltd v Roberts 2009 IRLR 1042, CA. In that case the tribunal found that the claimant was unlikely to ever again enjoy membership of a final salary pension scheme. However, it also found that, even taking into account her pension loss, the remuneration package she received in the new job was more favourable than that which she had enjoyed with the respondent. The tribunal considered that, upon the claimant gaining new employment, the chain of causation had been broken in respect of the loss of earnings, but it nevertheless awarded a sum to reflect the loss of a final salary pension. Although the EAT endorsed this approach, Lord Justice Elias in the Court of Appeal stated that pensions do not enjoy any special status in the calculation of loss, are essentially part of the remuneration package (albeit in a deferred form), and must be assessed according to the same principles as loss of earnings. The tribunal had erred in applying a different standard of causation to pension loss, and the EAT had been wrong to class a final salary pension as an 'unquantifiable benefit' that justified different treatment: tribunals must translate pension loss into monetary terms, no matter how difficult and speculative the exercise, otherwise assessing loss would be impossible.

Although the Aegon decision makes it clear that a tribunal cannot apply different standards of causation to pension loss and loss of earnings, a tribunal is not bound to find that both types of loss will end at the same time. In Bentwood Bros (Manchester) Ltd v Shepherd 2003 ICR 1000, CA, the tribunal awarded compensation for loss of earnings for a period of two and a half years, but went on to award compensation for pension loss for a period of ten years. Although the Court of Appeal was surprised by the finding that the claimant would never again gain pensionable employment, that finding was supported by evidence and was therefore neither perverse nor an error of law.

Burden of proof   17.4

In an unfair dismissal case, the burden of proving loss lies firmly on the employee, so if he or she claims loss of pension rights as an element of compensation it is up to him or her to prove what that loss is – Copson and anor v Eversure Accessories Ltd 1974 ICR 636, NIRC. In that case the National Industrial Relations Court (the predecessor to the EAT) said that tribunals should help claimants in appropriate cases: if it is apparent that there is a pension scheme and that its details are relevant, the tribunal should tell the employee that he or she is entitled to apply for an order requiring the employer to disclose those details. In Tidman v Aveling Marshall Ltd 1977 IRLR 218, EAT, the EAT went further and said that it is the duty of the tribunal to enquire into possible heads of compensation and to raise the issue of pension rights: while proof of loss still rests with the claimant, tribunals should be generous with unrepresented claimants.

Tribunals and appellate courts may be less sympathetic to claimants who are legally represented or who ought to understand their pension scheme, however. For example, in Cawthorn and Sinclair Ltd v Hedger 1974 ICR 146, NIRC, the NIRC thought that the assessment by a tribunal of H's pension loss was ungenerous but refused to change it. As Sir Hugh Griffiths said: 'The burden of proving a loss lies upon the employee. He had made scant attempt to discharge it in this case.' H had been the Chief Accountant and could have been expected to be familiar with the company pension scheme.

Tribunal guidelines   17.5

Although no *statutory* guidance is given as to how the calculation of pension loss is to be made, tribunals may refer to guidelines prepared by a committee of employment judges in consultation with the Government Actuary's Department, first issued in 1990. The revised third edition, entitled 'Employment Tribunals – Compensation for loss of pension rights', was published in 2003. This booklet – referred to as the 'tribunal guidelines' throughout this chapter – has proved highly valuable for tribunals and representatives alike and is available from The Stationery Office (www.tso.co.uk/bookshop) and the Employment Tribunals website (www.employmenttribunals.gov.uk).

However, although the original tribunal guidelines received the general approval of the EAT in Benson v Dairy Crest Ltd EAT 192/89 and the method of assessing pension loss has been gratefully adopted by tribunals, it should be stressed that they remain only guidelines and, as such, have no statutory force. In Bingham v Hobourn Engineering Ltd 1992 IRLR 298, EAT, the Appeal Tribunal held that the tribunal did not commit an error of law when it failed to follow exactly the scheme recommended in the then

611

extant guidelines. Mr Justice Knox said the booklet was a 'valuable guide', but added that the factors in each case should be evaluated to see what adjustment should be made or whether, in the circumstances, the guidelines were a safe guide at all.

And more recently, in Port of Tilbury (London) Ltd v Birch and ors 2005 IRLR 92, EAT, the EAT ruled that a tribunal had erred in preferring, without detailed explanation, the 'simplified approach' recommended in the third edition of the tribunal guidelines instead of the alternative approaches advocated by the legal representatives of the parties in that case. The EAT observed: 'The point about the [tribunal guidelines] is that [they] may assist an employment tribunal when there is little forthcoming from the parties as to how to approach what is recognised to be a difficult area, that is to say assessing a proper compensation of loss of pension rights... [W]here the parties or one of the parties puts forward credible evidence and submissions on that matter, it seems to us that the first duty of the tribunal is to consider that evidence and those submissions in order to ascertain whether a fair and equitable assessment of the loss of pension rights can be worked out on that basis. If it cannot, the employment tribunal must adequately explain why not. To say... that it rejects the parties' submissions entirely on the basis that it is not one suggested in the booklet is in our view an error of law.'

17.6   The need for a tribunal to set out its reasoning on the issue of pension loss was again emphasised in Greenhoff v Barnsley Metropolitan Borough Council 2006 ICR 1514, EAT. In overturning a tribunal's award of pension loss on the basis that it had failed to explain why it had adopted the approach it did in preference to either of the approaches set out in the tribunal guidelines, the EAT suggested that tribunals could avoid many of the problems that arise in such cases by:

- identifying all possible benefits that the employee could obtain under the pension scheme

- setting out the terms of the pension scheme relevant to each benefit

- considering in respect of each such possible benefit, first, the advantages and disadvantages of applying the 'simplified approach' or the 'substantial loss approach' (see further below) and also any other approach that might be considered appropriate by the tribunal or the parties

- explaining why it adopted a particular approach and rejected any other possible approach; and

- setting out its conclusions and explaining the compensation arrived at in respect of each head of claim so that the parties and the EAT can then ascertain if it has made an error.

612

Types of pension   17.7

Before we consider the different types of pension loss that may occur when an employee is dismissed, it is helpful to look at the various types of pension available. Very generally, an occupational pension scheme is a scheme dependent on contributions by the employer and (usually) the employee that provides for a pension on retirement at a level over and above that provided by the state scheme.

The state scheme   17.8

The state scheme is made up of the following components:

- basic state pension – a flat-rate pension (i.e. independent of earnings levels) payable to all who attain the state pension age provided that certain contribution requirements have been met

- SERPS – the state earnings-related pension scheme (also known as the additional state pension), which varies according to an employee's earnings between the lower and upper earnings limit on which he or she paid full national insurance contributions between April 1978 and March 2002

- S2P – the state second pension brought in to replace SERPS from April 2002. The main reason for the change was to provide a more generous pension provision for people earning less than the lower earnings limit. Eventually, the S2P is designed to be a second flat-rate pension benefit.

It is possible for employers to *contract out* of SERPS any employees who are members of an occupational pension scheme that satisfies certain criteria. It is also possible for individual employees to opt out of SERPS and/or their employers' schemes and to operate their own personal pension scheme. Some employers make contributions to personal schemes. The tribunal guidelines recommend the assumption that there is no loss of basic state pension on dismissal. The onus is then on the employee to prove otherwise. However, if a dismissed employee who is not in a contracted-out occupational or personal pension scheme is dismissed, he or she may lose the second state pension element for the period of unemployment and this is an area of potential loss that should be covered.

In October 2003, the 'Minimum Income Guarantee' (under which those aged 60 or over with combined income and savings of less than £12,000 had their income increased to the minimum income guarantee) was replaced by the 'Pension Credit system'. This replicates the minimum income guarantee but reduces the effect of the clawback provisions regarding income from other sources by lowering the rate to 40 per cent from 100 per cent, as was the case under the old system.

613

17.9 Types of occupational scheme

There are two basic types of occupational pension scheme: 'final salary' schemes and 'money purchase' schemes. These are also called 'defined benefit' schemes and 'defined contribution' schemes respectively – names that more clearly indicate their nature.

17.10   **Final salary schemes.** Under defined benefit schemes, the pension benefits received on retirement are based on a proportion of pensionable pay as at retirement multiplied by the number of years of pensionable service. Typically, benefits are calculated at 1/60th or 1/80th of final salary for each year of pensionable service. Thus, if an employee retires on a salary of £30,000 pa after 25 years' pensionable service and the scheme is based on 1/60th of final salary, he or she will receive an annual pension of 25/60 x £30,000 = £12,500.

The employer's contributions to a final salary scheme are not fixed: the employer simply undertakes to put into the scheme whatever is necessary to provide the scheme's members with the final predefined benefits. The employer's contributions are not earmarked for the benefit of any individual employee and individual pensions will not necessarily be directly related to the employee's and the employer's contributions. Typically, an employer's contributions to a 'good' occupational pension scheme – i.e. one that provides a level of benefit significantly better than SERPS or S2P – will, if it is a contributory scheme, be 20 per cent of the total payroll of scheme members. The employees' contributions, if any, are usually around 5 per cent of salary.

Final salary schemes come in different shapes and sizes. The essential point, however, is that they are based on predefined rules relating to the employee's earnings and years of pensionable service and not to contributions to the pension fund (whether from employee or employer). Final salary schemes are becoming increasingly rare due to the cost to the employer and the difficulties in budgeting accurately as to the employer's liability for such an open-ended commitment. As a result, over recent years, many employers have diluted the fraction of final salary payable or have closed their final salary schemes to new members. In some cases, employers have even closed the final salary scheme to existing members and have opted to offer money purchase schemes instead.

17.11   Although non-funded schemes (such as some that exist in the public sector) may seem different to normal final salary schemes because they lack a fund, the tribunal guidelines assert that membership of such a scheme should be treated in the same way as a normal final salary scheme, since the level of employer contributions is usually pegged as though it were funded. Deferred pensions from such schemes, though, do seem to be more generous.

Additional Voluntary Contributions (AVCs) allow an employee to top up his or her occupational pension, normally on a money purchase basis (irrespective of whether the scheme itself is final salary) and losses arising

614 ————————————————————————

under this head should therefore be treated in the same way as money purchase schemes. As AVCs are usually only made by the employee, they have little impact on future pension loss, but as they are not transferable (unlike free-standing AVCs), the tribunal guidelines state that there may be a loss in the form of charges for setting up a replacement scheme. Some public sector schemes allow members to buy *extra years* and, in such cases, working out final salary loss will need to take those extra years into account.

Money purchase schemes. Defined contributions schemes are quite different to final salary schemes. The contributions by either employer or employee, or both, are at predetermined rates and are earmarked for the individual employee. The ultimate benefits are dependent on the value of the fund built up during the employee's membership of the scheme. The amount of the pension will vary in accordance with factors such as the success of the scheme's investment policy and interest rates current at retiring age. So, if an employee has been in a scheme for 25 years, it is necessary to look at the total contributions by employer and employee, calculate the present value of those contributions, and then work out what annuity this sum will purchase.

17.12

It is comparatively easy to calculate an employee's loss arising from premature exclusion from a money purchase scheme. What has been contributed already remains invested for the benefit of the employee and what he or she loses is simply the prospective value of further contributions that would have been made by the employer. This is subject to any penalty for early leaving, but such penalty will be quantifiable under the rules of the scheme.

Other pension options. The employer and employee can agree for both or either of them to make contributions to a private pension policy with a pension provider (often an individual life insurance company) of the employee's choice. This allows the employee to control the investment decisions in respect of the pension fund. In appropriate cases, such a personal pension plan vehicle can be used to contract out of SERPS and S2P. Clearly, the use of such schemes may be unwieldy for a large organisation wanting to make pension provision for its entire workforce.

17.13

To ensure better pension provision, the Welfare Reform and Pensions Act 1999 made it compulsory for all employers (unless there are fewer than five employees or there is already a suitable pension scheme in place) to offer their employees, as a minimum, access to a *stakeholder scheme* providing money purchase benefits. There is no obligation on the employer, however, to make contributions to such a scheme.

Life assurance cover. Life assurance benefits are commonly provided by pension schemes and the tribunal guidelines advise that this head of loss could be compensated by awarding an amount equal to the cost to the employee of replicating the cover on the open market.

17.14

17.15 **Future reform**

In recognition of the fact that many employees in the private sector currently have no private pension provision, the Pensions Act 2008 provides for the automatic enrolment of 'jobholders' (a wide category that includes employees, workers and agency workers aged between 16 and 75) into a workplace pension scheme. Furthermore, the Act also requires that employers make contributions of at least 3 per cent of 'qualifying earnings' (all earnings between £5,035 and £33,540). These measures have yet to be brought into force, but a Department for Work and Pensions consultation, 'Workplace Pension Reform – Completing the Picture', issued in September 2009, reiterated that the plan is for a phased introduction over five years, starting in 2012.

Although many of the jobholders covered by the 2008 Act will be workers or agency workers, rather than employees, and therefore unable to claim unfair dismissal, it is likely that a large number of employees will gain pension rights for the first time as a result of the reforms. The likely effect of this will be to make pension loss a more common element of compensation for unfair dismissal, since the vast majority of dismissed employees will be losing out on pension contributions. At the same time, however, the reforms will make it easier for respondents to resist submissions that the claimant will never again find pensionable employment.

17.16 # The 'simplified loss' approach

The tribunal guidelines offer two alternative methods to assessing pension loss. They suggest that the one likely to be appropriate in the majority of cases is what is termed, in the guidelines, the 'simplified approach'. This method, which is retained from previous editions of the guidelines but was formerly called the 'contributions method', continues to have considerable support. In brief, the simplified approach takes the tribunal through three stages, requiring calculations under three distinct heads of pension loss. The third edition of the tribunal guidelines also introduced a new method – termed the 'substantial loss approach' – which is akin to the method for assessing pension loss in cases of personal injury. This also entails three separate calculations, but is likely to be relevant only in complex cases requiring actuarial input where there is potential career-long loss. This alternative method is discussed in detail under 'The "substantial loss" approach' below.

The simplified approach, as set out in the tribunal guidelines, involves making separate calculations in respect of the following:

● loss of enhancement of accrued pension rights – i.e. rights that had already accrued at the date of dismissal

616 ───

- loss of pension rights which would have accrued during the period between the date of dismissal and the date of the tribunal hearing

- loss of future pension rights that would have accrued between the hearing date and the date of retirement.

Each of these three calculations is discussed separately below.

Calculating loss of enhancement of accrued rights   17.17

As a result of dismissal, the employee may have lost the benefit of further enhancement of the rights that have already accrued under the pension scheme. If the scheme is a *money purchase scheme*, calculation of loss in this respect does not present a particular problem because the sums invested on behalf of the employee up to dismissal remain invested and will hopefully continue to increase in value. There may be a penalty for leaving the scheme early but this will be easily quantifiable.

Things are much more complicated if the scheme is a *final salary scheme*. To explain what the employee stands to lose, it is first necessary to explain the concept of a *deferred pension*. This is what a member of a final salary scheme becomes entitled to if he or she leaves the scheme early – e.g. where the employee is dismissed before reaching retirement age. A deferred pension is a pension payable in the future on what would have been the employee's retirement date but calculated with reference to the employee's earnings and service at the date of dismissal. So, if the scheme is based on 1/60th of final salary for each year, and the employee has ten years' pensionable service, the entitlement will be to 10/60ths of the employee's earnings at the date of dismissal. If those earnings were £30,000, this will mean a basic deferred pension of £5,000 a year.

The problem that arises is that the simplified approach uses the employee's salary at the date employment terminated as the 'final' salary. In fact, the employee *might* have remained with the employer and retired with a substantially higher final salary, significantly more years of service and, consequently, a much more valuable pension. In this sense the employee stands to lose a considerable amount. Suppose the same employee had worked for another ten years and then retired normally on a salary of £45,000 (a fairly modest rate of increase by current standards). His or her pension would have been 20/60ths x £45,000 = £15,000, £7,500 of which would relate to the first ten years of service. So, by enforced early leaving the employee has lost £2,500 a year between retirement and death – the difference between £7,500 and £5,000 – even on the assumption that he or she moves into a new job with identical salary, pension scheme and salary progression.

In order to provide a measure of protection to employees in these   17.18
circumstances, the Pension Schemes Act 1993 requires that the deferred pension be revalued in line with increases to the cost of living index up to retirement age

617

(when the deferred pension becomes payable) subject to a maximum increase of 5 per cent per annum over the accumulation period. (Note that the annual rate of increase after retirement age will depend on the rules of the scheme.) However, as the tribunal guidelines point out, the modest protection against inflation provided by the 1993 Act does not necessarily prevent loss of enhancement of accrued pension rights in the way outlined above because the employee's salary is likely to have increased at a faster rate than 5 per cent (and at a faster rate than inflation). In other words, loss relating to the accrued rights is still likely to occur and the compensatory award must reflect this.

Under Part IV of the Pension Schemes Act 1993, an individual can require his ex-employer to transfer the value of his accrued pension either to a comparable scheme operated by the new employer or to a personal pension scheme, where compatible. The guidelines remark, however, that there is a common fallacy that an employee who requests such a transfer suffers no financial loss. In fact, in most cases in the private sector (though not necessarily in the public sector), the transfer value will be assessed on the basis of the value of the deferred pension alone, which means, of course, that loss of accrued rights will still need to be compensated.

17.19   Many imponderables arise when assessing loss of accrued rights. For example, the employee might have received a wage rise and a better pension through being promoted. On the other hand, the company might have gone into liquidation or the employee might have been fairly dismissed or resigned from the job at a later date. Once again, the tribunal is asked to look to the future and to attempt to estimate how far and for how long losses incurred by the employee are attributable to the unfair dismissal. Helpfully, in view of these exigencies, the tribunal guidelines provide a revised and simplified actuarial method for conducting the initial valuation of losses relating to accrued rights. Once losses have been calculated using this method, the tribunal can make deductions to take account of the various contingencies that may have caused the employee to withdraw from the scheme for a reason other than unfair dismissal.

The guidelines recommend two ways of dealing with the loss of enhancement of accrued rights, depending on the circumstances. These are:

- awarding no compensation at all

- using the new simplified actuarial method.

17.20   **No compensation.** There are certain categories of case in which it is thought right not to make any award of compensation in respect of accrued pension rights, although there may well be compensation payable in respect of loss between dismissal and the tribunal hearing and future loss. These are where:

- the employee is within five years of normal retiring age (the previous guidelines limited this exception to private sector schemes but the current version makes no such distinction)

- the tribunal finds that employment would have ended in any event within a year.

(There is a potential third category which is absent from the revised guidelines – i.e. inflation-proofed public sector schemes that are not subject to the 5 per cent formula.)

The first of the above categories assumes that little or no loss of enhancement will occur in so short a space of time. However, this is based on the assumption that the statutory indexation of 5 per cent is reasonable. Where price increases run at substantially more than 5 per cent, this assumption may need to be reviewed. Additionally, earnings seem to rise faster than prices, so inflation-proofing based solely on price increases may not correspond to anticipated increases in salary.

Actuarial method. The tribunal guidelines contain a simplified actuarial method, produced by the Government Actuary's Department, to assess the losses relating to accrued rights that are incurred by employees with more than five years to go until retirement. The method consists of a table of multipliers based on the employee's age, normal retirement age, sex, and whether the scheme is a public or private sector one (see Appendix 4 to the guidelines). The appropriate multiplier is applied to the deferred pension to which the employee is entitled. The resulting figure represents the initial assessment of the employee's losses for loss of enhancement of accrued rights from which any appropriate deductions should then be made.

17.21

Taking the example of a male private sector employee who was 51 years old when dismissed, whose normal retirement age would have been 60, and who is entitled to a deferred pension of £6,000: the appropriate multiplier from the table will be 1.99. Therefore, the initial assessment of losses relating to the employee's accrued rights will be just under £12,000. This is not the end of the matter, however. The table assumes that the employee would not have left the employment for any reason other than death or disability. Employees do, of course, frequently leave their employment for other reasons. It is to take account of possibilities such as this that the tribunal may subsequently reduce the figure – see below under 'Deductions for the "withdrawal factor"'.

The Government Actuary's Department table makes various *assumptions* (which take into account both inflation and taxation considerations). If these assumptions are inappropriate, then adjustments will have to be made to the method used. These assumptions are that:

- private sector pensions are based on a defined amount of pension (usually 1/60th of final salary) of which part can be taken as a lump sum. Public sector schemes have a lump sum payable in addition to the pension – equal to three years of pension payments at the initial rate

619

- there is a widow(er)'s pension at 50 per cent of the employee's rate

- the maximum possible amount is taken as a lump sum

- post-retirement, pensions increase annually in line with the Retail Prices Index (up to 5 per cent in the private sector)

- contracting-out is ignored.

17.22 **Deductions for the 'withdrawal factor'.** The tribunal guidelines expressly state that the table of multipliers assumes that the employee would not have left his or her employment before retirement for any reason other than death or disability. As mentioned previously, there may be a number of factors in a particular case which make this assumption incorrect. As we have seen, a tribunal is likely to make deductions from the figure that is produced by the actuarial calculation to take account of any of the multitude of reasons which might have caused the employee to leave the employment at a later date even if he or she had not been unfairly dismissed. The Government Actuary's Department used to provide a table of age-based reduction factors to take account of the likelihood of withdrawal before normal retiring age. However, the tribunal guidelines conclude that it is inappropriate to set a percentage 'withdrawal factor' calculation by reference to a table and that this percentage is best left to the discretion of the tribunal which has had the benefit of hearing the case and seeing the parties. (It should be noted that the appropriate reduction is not the same as the likelihood that the employee would have left employment anyway: if he or she had stayed for a few more years, the accrued pension would still have been enhanced.) Two cases, decided when the old table of reduction factors was in use, illustrate the general principle:

- **Hearne v Manpower Ltd** COET 1353/213: a tribunal had failed to apply a withdrawal factor at all to the assessment of past loss and the EAT remitted the case. The Table 2 factor would have been 20 per cent for H, who was 43, but the employer argued strongly for a withdrawal factor of 50 per cent because of very high turnover and mobility of labour in this particular industry. The tribunal agreed that a higher withdrawal factor would be warranted for many employees in this business – but not for H. On his employment record, H was a 'stayer', who had voluntarily changed his job only once, so it used 20 per cent as the factor

- **TBA Industrial Products Ltd v Locke** 1984 IRLR 48, EAT: a tribunal applied a high withdrawal factor of 70 per cent because it thought there was a high degree of probability that L would have been fairly dismissed in any event, either for redundancy or because of his unsatisfactory work performance. It then further reduced L's overall compensatory award by an additional 70 per cent to reflect L's conduct contributing to his dismissal. L argued on appeal that this meant that he was being penalised twice over for his poor work performance. The EAT, however, said that the tribunal had been quite correct because it had taken L's performance into account for two distinct purposes – assessing the present value of L's future pension rights and reducing his compensation because of his contribution to his own dismissal.

Note that the guidelines stress that no calculation of the value of accrued rights is necessary if the tribunal is adopting the 'substantial loss' approach to assessing future loss (as this head of loss is already built into the actuarial calculation). This approach is discussed in detail later in this chapter.

Calculating loss between dismissal and remedies hearing

17.23

If the pension is a *money purchase scheme*, assessing the loss between the dismissal and the hearing is simply a matter of calculating the value of the additional contributions which the employer would have made to the employee's pension during this time. An early leaver may also be required to pay a penalty and this loss, which is easily quantifiable, should be factored in.

The position in relation to assessing losses arising from early departure from a *final salary scheme* is more complex because the employer's contributions towards an individual's pension are not predetermined. What the employee has actually lost is the prospective right to a pension based on his or her final salary on retirement. The loss is therefore the difference between the deferred pension (inclusive of cost of living rises and other benefits) which the employee is entitled to and the pension and other benefits which would have been received had the dismissal not taken place.

In terms of assessing the value of the loss of final salary pension rights between dismissal and the remedies hearing, the tribunal guidelines recognise that the actual loss is the difference between the actual deferred pension received and the slightly higher one for which the employee would have qualified had he or she remained employed for that extra period. However, for the sake of simplicity (and in the interests of what the authors of the guidelines believe is most just and equitable to both parties), the guidelines advocate looking not at the additional contingent benefits that would have accrued but rather at the contributions that the employer would have made to the pension fund during this period. The guidelines therefore recommend basing compensation for the period between the dismissal and the remedies hearing on the notional contributions that the employer would have made towards the employee's pension had the employee still been in employment. The weekly loss figure is then simply multiplied by the number of weeks between the dismissal and the hearing.

As the guidelines recognise, this is not a technically correct approach **17.24** because, where the scheme in question is final salary, the employer does not in fact make a specific contribution to each individual employee's pension: instead it makes a contribution to the general pension fund that represents

621

a percentage of the total pensionable wage bill. The actual percentage payable under the scheme is normally shown in the scheme's actuarial report. The proportion of this percentage that is attributable to the individual employee usually increases with age. While in a simple case it might be considered unnecessary to try to allow for this, not to do so can make a difference of as much as 25 per cent to the multiplicand. Accordingly, in more complex cases or in those in which age is an issue, tribunals should apply the factors in Tables 1 and 2 of Appendix 7 to the guidelines in order to make the appropriate adjustment.

Tribunals should always be sensitive to arguments in a particular case that, owing to the nature of the scheme in question or the claimant's personal circumstances, losses are more or less substantial during this period than the broad-brush method discussed above allows for. In Forshaw v Forshaw Ltd EAT 0462/03 the EAT allowed an appeal on the basis that the tribunal had failed to consider the claimant's argument that he had lost 'notional contributions' to a small self-administrated pension scheme (effectively a hybrid scheme in which benefits were calculated on a money purchase basis) even though no actual contributions had been made to the scheme during the period in question.

17.25 The following points should also be noted:

- pensionable pay may not be the same as actual pay. Pensionable pay may be restricted to basic pay and may exclude fluctuating payments such as bonuses, commission and overtime. It will be up to the employer to produce evidence to challenge the assumption that gross pay is equivalent to pensionable pay

- the percentage contributed by the employer may not be known. In this case a standard figure of 20 per cent of payroll (15 per cent from the employer and 5 per cent from the employee) should be assumed, according to the tribunal guidelines

- the percentage currently contributed by the employer may be anomalous – e.g. because of a 'contributions holiday'. The guidelines recommend that calculations take no account of such anomalies

- pension provision is not part of pay for the purposes of the Recoupment Regulations and this element of compensation is not therefore subject to recoupment of social security benefits (see Chapter 20).

Finally, and importantly, the guidelines stress that, as with the calculation of the value of accrued rights, calculating loss between dismissal and the remedies hearing is not necessary if the tribunal is adopting the 'substantial loss' approach to assessing future loss (as this head of loss is already built into the actuarial calculation). This approach is discussed in detail later in this chapter.

Calculating loss of future pension rights

17.26

The employee's loss on dismissal may include loss of benefits that would have accrued under the employer's pension scheme if he or she had continued to be in the same employment beyond the date of the hearing. Where the period of loss of future earnings is unlikely to exceed two years, the tribunal guidelines recommend using employer's contributions (or notional contributions in the case of final salary schemes) as the basis for calculating compensation for loss of future pension rights (i.e. the same basis as for calculating losses from dismissal to the date of the remedies hearing set out above). Where pension loss beyond two years is being claimed, the substantial loss formula rather than the simplified approach should normally be adopted – Orthet Ltd v Vince-Cain 2005 ICR 374, EAT.

The guidelines also advise that the simplified approach should only be used in circumstances where the tribunal decides that, when the applicant finds employment, it will be either with a comparable pension scheme or at a higher salary to offset the absence of such a scheme. The guidelines note that tribunals have tended in many cases to find that claimants will obtain comparable employment within a fairly short period, ranging from three months to two years.

Where the lost pension is a money purchase scheme, the guidelines state that the future loss during the relevant period (i.e. from the date of the tribunal hearing until the estimated date when the claimant will enter new employment with equivalent pension provision) is calculated by aggregating the contributions that the employer would have made during this period (bearing in mind that they are tax-free). A discount for accelerated receipt should then be made.

Where the lost pension was a final salary scheme, the same approach should be adopted using the notional contributions approach (the same as set out above under 'Loss between dismissal and hearing'). Again, a deduction for accelerated receipt must be made. Any contributions holiday or other anomaly should be ignored and, as before, account should be taken of the difference in contributions applicable for older claimants.

17.27

Where there is no pension scheme or the employee was in a scheme which was not contracted out, losses may still arise as a result of S2P not accruing. A chart to calculate the value of this loss, using a simple formula, is set out in Appendix 3 to the tribunal guidelines.

The simplified approach does not deal specifically with the situation where the employee has *already* found a new job. In these circumstances, there are two possibilities:

- there is a pension scheme in the new job. In this case, the tribunal will have to evaluate this new scheme against the old one. A simple method will be to compare the employer's contributions under the new scheme with the

623

employer's contributions under the old scheme and to treat the difference as the loss (or profit)

- there is no pension scheme in the new job. In this case, any continuing loss of earnings will have to be increased by the continuing loss of the previous employer's pension contributions.

If earnings in the new job are higher than in the old, this may compensate for the loss of pension rights. This was the case in Burrill and ors v Rhodes Gill and Co Ltd ET Case No.12772/75 where an increase in the employee's earnings was held to adequately cover the loss of the employer's contributions. If, however, the new earnings are lower, the tribunal may be able to estimate when they will rise to a sufficiently high level to compensate for the absence of a pension scheme. The same logic applies to the situation where the employee elects to become self-employed after being dismissed (and such action is found to be reasonable mitigation of his or her loss).

17.28 Finally, two further points should be made about future loss generally. First, such loss may include the lost opportunity of joining a pension scheme where the employee is dismissed from a job that is covered by a scheme that has a qualifying period or age and the employee has not yet qualified. Entitlement will probably depend upon whether or not the employee is considered a 'stayer'. In Samuels v Clifford Chance EAT 559/90 employees did not qualify for the occupational pension scheme until they had completed five years' service at the firm. S was unfairly dismissed after two and a half years' service and the tribunal therefore had to assess the likelihood that she would, but for her dismissal, have remained with the firm for the further two and a half years necessary to qualify. The tribunal looked at S's curriculum vitae, which showed that she had never in fact stayed with one employer for as long as five years. It also heard her own testimony as to her intentions prior to her dismissal. The tribunal came to the conclusion that there was no guarantee that she would have stayed in CC's employ for five years and declined to make any award in respect of loss of pension rights. On appeal, the EAT upheld the tribunal's decision. (It should be noted, however, that substantial qualifying periods in respect of membership of occupational pension schemes are, these days, unusual.)

Secondly, tribunals tend to restrict awards for future loss to a period of months rather than years (and this is in line with the guidelines' recommendation of a fixed period of up to two years in most cases). But this is not always so, as the following case shows:

- **Hearne v Manpower Ltd** COET 1353/213: H was unfairly dismissed at the age of 43. He rapidly found a job in the same industry but with no occupational pension scheme. It was agreed that his pension loss was £563 a year. The employer argued that only two years' loss should be awarded because of the high labour turnover in the industry and the chance that H would soon find another job with a pension scheme. H argued that he was

624 ————————————————————————

a natural 'stayer' who would not change jobs at his age and that the award should therefore be of 22 years' loss – i.e. to retiring age. The tribunal agreed that H was unlikely to move and that he had no foreseeable prospects of a pension scheme. It thought, however, that compensating him up to retiring age was pushing matters too far because of imponderables and it settled for a ten-year multiplier to apply to his annual loss.

It is important to note that the above calculations for future loss should not be applied if the 'substantial loss' approach is being adopted (as this head of loss is already built into the actuarial calculation). The appropriate method if such circumstances apply is set out below.

The 'substantial loss' approach   17.29

Generally speaking, the tribunal guidelines advocate that the use of the substantial loss approach be restricted to those cases where the claimant was a long-standing employee in a stable job whose age means he or she would be unlikely to be looking to move. More specifically, the circumstances that would suggest use of the substantial loss approach (because they involve quantifiable ongoing losses) include findings by the tribunal as follows:

- permanent new employment by the date of the remedies hearing, but little chance of moving on to better paid employment in the future

- no permanent new employment, and on the balance of probabilities, no new employment likely before state pension age (usually severe disability cases)

- no permanent new employment, but likely to find alternative employment in time, which involves valuing loss to retirement and beyond before applying a reduction for the percentage chance that the claimant would not have remained in the original career until retirement (Ministry of Defence v Cannock and ors 1994 ICR 918, EAT).

Ogden tables and multipliers. The guidelines also note that the Ogden tables,   17.30
which are prepared by the Government Actuary's Department for use in personal injury cases, are also occasionally used by tribunals for assessing future loss of earnings – see Chapter 16 under 'Future loss – career-long loss'. In Kingston Upon Hull City Council v Dunnachie (No.3) 2003 IRLR 843, EAT, the EAT approved the use of the Ogden tables in circumstances where career-long loss of earnings was being assessed. However, it stated: 'Nothing that we have said in the course of this judgment (or indeed that was addressed to us in argument) impinges on the question of the applicability of the use of Ogden Tables in relation to pension loss, where different questions may arise.' The issue was therefore left open until the EAT in Evans v Barclays Bank plc EAT 0137/09 held that a tribunal had not erred by using the Ogden tables in preference to the guidelines when assessing the career-long loss a claimant had

experienced upon being dismissed from a role that carried with it a final salary pension scheme.

However, while Ogden tables *may* be used by a tribunal in determining the degree of pension loss (in the sense that it is not an error of law for a tribunal to use them), it is submitted that the more appropriate tables for a tribunal to use would be the tables of multipliers for pension loss set out in the appendices to the tribunal guidelines. Like the Ogden tables, these are prepared by the Government Actuary's Department. However, unlike the Ogden tables, they have been expressly designed by the Actuary for the purpose of assessing long-term or complex pension loss.

17.31 **Calculation of long-term loss**

To calculate the loss figure, the following equation is used:

$$\text{loss of pension rights} = A \text{ minus } B \text{ minus } C$$

where

A = value of prospective final salary rights up to normal retirement age in former employment (had the dismissal not occurred). The relevant period of service is from commencement of employment through to normal retirement age.

B = value of accrued final salary pension rights to date of dismissal. The relevant period of service is up to the date of dismissal only.

C = value of prospective final salary rights to normal retirement age in new employment. The relevant period of service is from commencement in the new job until normal retirement age in the new job.

Note that C will have no value if the claimant is unlikely to find pensionable employment again or has joined a money purchase or stakeholder scheme. Loss of employer contributions is already factored into the equation but will need to be taken into account when assessing loss of earnings in order to work out whether or not there is a continuing loss of earnings. Also, note that, in the interests of simplicity, guaranteed minimum pension or top-up pension rights are ignored.

For both A and B, the annual amount of pension is worked out on the basis of pensionable earnings in the year up to dismissal (or according to the rules of the scheme in question). In each case, the annual pension must be worked out using the scheme rules.

Once the annual amounts have been established, these are then multiplied by the appropriate multiplier corresponding to the claimant's age set out in Tables 1 – 4 of Appendix 5 to the guidelines (for A and C) and Tables 1 – 4 of Appendix 6 (for B). In the case of A and B the relevant age is as at the date of dismissal. In the case of C the relevant age is as at the date of commencing the new job.

626

'Withdrawal factor' deductions   17.32

When a figure has been arrived at using this formula, the tribunal should assess and then deduct the amount of any 'withdrawal factors'. The guidelines offer no useful tables in this regard and the decision as to what deduction to make is at the tribunal's discretion, taking into account factors such as the age, work record, status and health of the claimant and the strength of the former employer's business. The guidelines state that the Government Actuary's Department is opposed to the use of a blanket percentage chance or withdrawal factor (as derived from Clancy v Cannock Chase Technical College and anor 2001 IRLR 331, EAT) as there may be specific facts which allow the tribunal to adopt a more sophisticated approach to the withdrawal factor. If, for example, the percentage chance of losing the old job was higher than that in the new job, this should be reflected by using different percentage reduction figures for A and B (which relate to the old job) and C (which relates to the new job).

Other considerations   17.33

If the claimant was obliged to contribute to the scheme in his or her former employment, the fact that he or she is relieved of this financial burden should be taken into account by deducting any employee contributions from net earnings before applying the appropriate multiplier. As a corollary to this, if the claimant is joining a contributory scheme, this financial outlay should be accommodated by ensuring that this value is included in C. If the claimant's new employment allows for the accrual of S2P, the value of this (see Table 3.2 in Appendix 3 to the guidelines) should be deducted from the resultant value of A minus B.

The guidelines recommend (though not strictly within the substantial loss approach) that where the lost pension is a money purchase scheme and the new job pays less and has no equivalent pension scheme, the employer's contributions should be added to the continuing loss of earnings before applying the relevant multiplier from the Ogden tables. Note, however, that this approach using the Ogden tables is only applicable if there is long-term loss. If not, then the simplified approach should be used.

Finally, the guidelines emphasise that the substantial loss approach automatically builds in compensation for loss of enhancement of accrued rights, loss of pension rights from dismissal to the remedies hearing and future pension loss, so these do not need to be calculated separately as they do for the simplified approach set out above.

18 Compensatory awards: adjustments and reductions

Payments received by employee

Failure to mitigate losses

'Just and equitable' reductions

'Polkey reductions'

Adjustments for breach of Acas Code of Practice

Adjustments for failure to provide written particulars

Contributory conduct

Offsetting enhanced redundancy payments

Application of statutory cap

Order of adjustments and deductions

The first task of an employment tribunal, when assessing the compensatory **18.1** award, is to calculate the actual loss sustained by the employee. In calculating such loss, credit has to be given for any payment already paid by the employer to the employee in respect of the dismissal in the form of an ex gratia payment or payment in lieu of notice. This ensures that the employee is not awarded a head of compensation in respect of which he or she has already been compensated ('double recovery') – see Chapter 16 under 'Immediate loss'.

A different rule applies in the case of enhanced redundancy payments. As explained under 'Payments received by employee' below, any payment made by the employer on account of redundancy in excess of the statutory payment falls to be taken into account in calculating the compensatory award, but only after all other relevant deductions have been made.

Once the total loss has been calculated, the tribunal will turn its attention to **18.2** considering whether to make any other appropriate adjustment or deduction. In this regard, there are various circumstances in which the amount of the compensatory award is liable to be reduced or increased according to specific statutory provisions. Briefly, these circumstances are:

- where the employee fails to take reasonable steps to mitigate his or her losses – S.123(4) ERA

- where the tribunal considers it 'just and equitable' to award a lesser amount than would otherwise be appropriate (which embraces so-called 'Polkey

629

reductions', where the employee would have been dismissed in any event had the procedural failings which rendered the dismissal unfair not occurred) – S.123(1) ERA

- where the employee has caused or contributed to his or her dismissal – i.e. is guilty of 'contributory conduct' – S.123(6) Employment Rights Act 1996.

- where the employer or employee has failed to comply with the provisions of the Acas Code of Practice on Disciplinary and Grievance Procedures – S.207A Trade Union and Labour Relations (Consolidation) Act 1992

- where the employer has failed to provide full and accurate written particulars of employment and the employment tribunal makes a finding to this effect in the course of proceedings for unfair dismissal – S.38 Employment Act 2008.

18.3   (A further head under which an employee's compensation can effectively be reduced is that of 'recoupment' of unemployment benefits (i.e. Jobseeker's Allowance and Income Support). Recoupment is explained in Chapter 20. Other benefits that are not subject to recoupment – such as disability allowance – may fall to be deducted as a payment received by the employee. These are dealt with in Chapter 16, under 'Immediate loss – social security benefits')

Each of the five types of statutory adjustment/deduction listed above are discussed in detail in the following sections of this chapter. However, an important general point needs to be made first.

18.4   **Importance of order in which adjustments/deductions are made.** Where more than one adjustment or deduction has to be made from the total compensatory award, the order in which those adjustments/deductions are made can have a crucial effect on the resulting compensation figure. This is particularly so where one of the relevant adjustments or deductions is in the nature of a percentage increase or decrease as opposed to a specific sum. If the point at which that percentage is applied occurs before other deductions or adjustments have been made, the effect of that deduction will be greater than if it is applied after other specific monetary deductions have been made. To illustrate this point, let us assume that a tribunal assesses an employee's total loss at £20,000 but orders two deductions from that sum to be made, namely: (i) a 25 per cent deduction on account of the employee's contribution towards dismissal; and (ii) a deduction of an ex gratia payment of £4,000 paid by the employer. If the contribution deduction is applied first, followed by the ex gratia payment deduction, the resulting award would be £11,000 (i.e. £20,000 – 25 per cent = £15,000 – £4,000 = £11,000). If the reverse order for the deductions is applied, the resulting figure would be £12,000 (i.e. £20,000 – £4,000 = £16,000 – 25 per cent = £12,000). As can be seen, the order in which the relevant deductions are made affects the resulting award by plus or minus £1,000.

630 ────────────────────────────────────

It is similarly the case that the stage at which any adjustment for breach of the Acas Code of Practice on Disciplinary and Grievance Procedures can have a significant impact on 'quantum' – i.e. the amount of compensation awarded. Since the adjustment can be up to plus or minus 25 per cent of the total compensatory award, the order in which this adjustment is made – especially if made in conjunction with other deductions or adjustments – is of considerable significance.

The exact order in which deductions should be made from the compensatory award is considered under 'Order of adjustments and deductions' below. Suffice it to say here that the order in which the various deductions and adjustments are discussed in this chapter reflects the order in which they have to be made (if applicable) when calculating the compensatory award.

Payments received by employee 18.5

In Chapter 16, under 'Immediate loss – termination payments', we saw that when an employment tribunal calculates the degree of loss experienced by a dismissed employee it should give credit for any sums received by way of an ex gratia payment. Similarly, the tribunal should give credit for any sums paid out by way of incapacity benefit (see Chapter 16 under 'Immediate loss – social security benefits'). Much of the case law in this area has described such sums as being offset against, or deducted from, the *compensatory award*, but in our view such terminology is not entirely accurate. Rather, these sums are offset against a claimant's *losses* to determine the 'net loss' – the starting point for the compensatory award, prior to any adjustments or deductions.

However, a different approach must be taken in respect of enhanced redundancy payments in so far as the payments exceed the amount of the basic award. These are not covered by the general principles governing compensation but instead by a specific provision, S.123(7) ERA – as discussed under 'Off-setting enhanced redundancy payments' below.

Note that unemployment benefits – Jobseeker's Allowance and Income Support – should not be factored into the calculation of loss, nor should they be deducted by the tribunal. Instead, they are subject to the recoupment procedure outlined in Chapter 20.

Failure to mitigate losses 18.6

Claims for damages at common law are subject to the rule that claimants must take reasonable steps to mitigate their losses. This rule is given statutory force in its application to the compensatory award in unfair dismissal cases by S.123(4) ERA, which provides that: 'In ascertaining the loss [sustained by the claimant] the tribunal shall apply the same rule concerning the duty of a person

631

to mitigate his loss as applies to damages recoverable under the common law of England and Wales or (as the case may be) Scotland.' The test is simply whether the employee's conduct – e.g. in taking or refusing a particular source of income – is reasonable on the facts of each case – Yetton v Eastwoods Froy Ltd 1966 3 All ER 353, QBD.

18.7 General principles

The duty to mitigate in accordance with S.123(4) ERA does not arise unless and until the employee has actually been dismissed. A refusal to agree to a transfer during the currency of employment would not, therefore, constitute a failure to mitigate loss unless the offer of the transferred employment remained after the employee had been dismissed – see McAndrew v Prestwick Circuits Ltd 1988 IRLR 514, EAT.

18.8 **Correct approach to making deductions for failure to mitigate.** When calculating the compensatory award, the calculation should initially be based on the assumption that the employee has taken all reasonable steps to reduce his or her loss. If the employee in fact failed to take such steps – e.g. by turning down suitable new employment – the compensatory award should be reduced so as to cover only those losses that would have been incurred even if the employee had taken the appropriate steps. A useful approach to this matter was suggested by Sir John Donaldson in Archbold Freightage Ltd v Wilson 1974 IRLR 10, NIRC: the dismissed employee's duty to mitigate his or her loss will be fulfilled if he or she can be said to have acted as a reasonable person would do if he or she had no hope of seeking compensation from his or her previous employer.

In Savage v Saxena 1998 ICR 357, EAT, the EAT recommended a three-step approach to determining whether an employee has failed to mitigate his or her losses:

- identify what steps should have been taken by the claimant to mitigate his or her loss

- find the date upon which such steps would have produced an alternative income

- thereafter reduce the amount of compensation by the amount of income which would have been earned.

18.9 This approach is easy to follow in a case where an employee has not found new employment by the date of the remedies hearing. However, step two above will need to be adjusted if, by the date of the hearing, the employee has secured an alternative income but at a lower rate than that which he or she enjoyed under the old job. In such a case, as the EAT makes clear in Glasgow City Council v Rayton EAT 0005/07, it will be necessary for the tribunal to establish the date on which the employee would have secured the same or better-paid employment.

632

Where a tribunal finds that an employee is found by an employment tribunal to have failed to mitigate his or her losses, it should not simply reduce the whole compensatory award by a percentage. Instead, it should attempt to estimate from the available evidence exactly when the employee should have got a suitable job. The tribunal should then take into account the earnings that it thinks would have been earned from that point onwards and reduce the compensation accordingly – Peara v Enderlin Ltd 1979 ICR 804, EAT. In Ladbroke Racing Ltd v Connolly EAT 160/83 the EAT added that the tribunal should estimate the amount of earnings the employee would have received had appropriate steps been taken and, if the employee would still have earned less than in the original job, further compensation can be awarded for the partial loss incurred thereafter.

Tribunals must be careful not to impose arbitrary cut-off dates in this regard, up to which full loss of earnings is awarded and then nothing else for ongoing loss. In Mears v Lloyd Green and Co EAT 0707/02 the claimant succeeded in her appeal against a tribunal decision to impose a three-month cut-off period for full loss of earnings based on its findings that the claimant had been unwise in mentioning to employment agencies her pending tribunal proceedings against the respondent, as that was an irrelevant factor to take into account. A similar conclusion was reached by the EAT in Glasgow City Council v Rayton (above), where the tribunal, having decided that the employee had failed to mitigate, appeared to use the date of the remedies hearing as a cut-off date. Saying that the claimant was not entitled to be compensated for loss of earnings from that date was not the same thing as identifying when a proper mitigatory course of action would have made a difference to the employee's earning position. In so holding, the EAT rejected the contention that it was permissible for the tribunal to apply the remedies hearing date as a cut-off pursuant to its broad discretion to award 'just and equitable' compensation under S.123(1) ERA in the absence of clear reasons why that date was relevant to the issue of mitigation.

Focus must be on the individual's particular circumstances. Whether an **18.10** employee has done enough to fulfil the duty to mitigate depends on the circumstances of each case and is to be judged subjectively – Johnson v Hobart Manufacturing Co Ltd EAT 210/89. For instance, an employer cannot argue that a younger or fitter employee would have found new work sooner: the question is whether the employee in question has taken reasonable steps to minimise his or her losses – Fougère v Phoenix Motor Co Ltd 1976 ICR 495, EAT. But it is not the case that the tribunal should simply accept the subjective view of the claimant: while this certainly has to be taken into account, the tribunal's task is to consider all the circumstances in deciding whether the claimant has acted unreasonably in failing to find fresh employment or some alternative means of mitigating the losses as a result of having been unfairly dismissed – Beijing Ton Ren Tang (UK) Ltd v Wang EAT 0024/09.

It follows that much will depend on variables such as local levels of unemployment, whether the employee's skills are readily transferable to other

633

available employment, and the personal characteristics of the employee. For example, older employees, pregnant employees and people in poor health are particularly likely to have problems obtaining new employment. In Bennett v Tippins EAT 361/89 the claimant was unfairly dismissed from her job as a waitress on account of her pregnancy. The employer argued that her compensation should be reduced because she had failed to get another job despite the great shortage of bar and restaurant staff in her area. The EAT, however, stated that T's pregnancy made the general availability of jobs irrelevant since employers are reluctant to take on staff who are pregnant.

18.11   It has been recognised by the EAT that the issues that need to be taken on board by a tribunal when determining whether and to what extent an employee has failed to mitigate his or her loss are tricky and that mitigation 'is a notoriously difficult area for a tribunal to have to deal with' – per Elias J in Patel v Cummings Hoar Cummings EAT 0605/07. In that case the EAT upheld a tribunal's decision that an unfairly dismissed accountant should have found equivalent paid employment within 12 months. The tribunal had properly taken into account such factors as the employee's failure to consider jobs outside accountancy and his failure to maximise self-employed earnings following his dismissal.

It may not be reasonable to expect an employee to take the first job that comes along, especially one with lower pay than the employee might reasonably expect to receive. In particular, a skilled or highly educated employee does not necessarily have to lower his or her sights immediately as regards the kind of job he or she is prepared to apply for in seeking new employment – Orthet Ltd v Vince-Cain 2005 ICR 374, EAT. On the other hand, undue delay in accepting something in the vain hope of a better offer may result in compensation being reduced. It should always be borne in mind that employees can, of course, claim any partial loss arising from acceptance of suitable, though less well-paid, employment, as discussed above under 'Correct approach to making deductions for failure to mitigate'.

18.12   The effect of the dismissal on the individual employee may well be a relevant matter in determining whether there has been a failure to mitigate. In Beijing Ton Ren Tang (UK) Ltd v Wang (above) the EAT held that an employment tribunal had correctly found that it would not have been reasonable to expect the claimant to have got herself straight back into the job market given her circumstances. She had been recruited in China to carry out a particular job for 12 months and had expected to return to China after that; she had been greatly shocked by her sudden dismissal, spoke no English, felt isolated, and did not know the country outside London. On these facts, the EAT ruled that the tribunal had been entitled to find that the employee had not failed to mitigate her loss even though she had not sought new employment for the 17-week period from the date of her dismissal until the date she would, in any event, have returned to China.

A similar view might well be taken in circumstances where a claimant has, say, been traumatically dismissed on discriminatory grounds and feels unable to contemplate returning to a work environment for a substantial period. On a similar basis, it may be that the fact that the employee has been discriminatorily dismissed has an impact on the length of time he or she will be on the labour market. In Abbey National plc and anor v Chagger 2010 ICR 397, CA, the Court of Appeal recognised this. Since the employee will not be looking for new employment at a time of his or her own choosing, his or her prospects may be adversely affected and he or she may have been stigmatised by bringing tribunal proceedings, which also have an adverse effect on the chances of obtaining new employment. In consequence of factors such as these, the discriminatory dismissal may well alter the employee's subsequent career path and thus significantly delay the point at which it can reasonably be said that the employee should have found an alternative income.

Burden of proof. The onus lies on the employer as the party who is alleging **18.13** that the employee has failed to mitigate his or her losses – Fyfe v Scientific Furnishings Ltd 1989 ICR 648, EAT. It follows that tribunals are under no duty to consider the question of mitigation unless the employer raises it and adduces some evidence of failure to mitigate.

Sufficiency of tribunal's reasons. A tribunal will be expected to give clear reasons **18.14** for its decision regarding mitigation. The failure to do so may well make the decision vulnerable on appeal. In C and A Pumps Ltd v Thompson EAT 0218/06, for example, an employment tribunal was found to have erred in law when it awarded the employee full loss for six months despite evidence that he could and should have found alternative employment within four to six weeks. The tribunal had failed to set out its reasons on this matter sufficiently. The EAT speculated that the tribunal might have had in mind that the employee had been suffering from stress and that it had been reasonable for him not to start looking for work during the first six months after he was dismissed. But the tribunal had not spelled out either the condition from which the employee was suffering or its effect on his ability to find new employment. Furthermore, the tribunal had also awarded the employee 26 weeks' partial loss at £150 a week without any explanation of the basis on which these figures were arrived at. They appeared to derive from the tribunal's general awareness about the type of alternative employment that might have been available, but it was wholly unclear what that was and why a person with the employee's qualifications and experience should only have taken a job at a level that entailed an ongoing loss of £150. The EAT concluded that the tribunal had given inadequate consideration to the issue of mitigation in its decision and remitted the case to the same tribunal for reconsideration.

Failure to utilise internal appeal against dismissal
18.15

There has been some controversy over the question of whether the failure to pursue internal appeal procedures following dismissal can constitute a failure to mitigate

635

loss. In Hoover Ltd v Forde 1980 ICR 239, EAT, the EAT held that it could, but the opposite view was taken by the EAT in Scotland in William Muir (Bond 9) Ltd v Lamb 1985 IRLR 95, EAT. Both these decisions were considered in Lock v Connell Estate Agents 1994 IRLR 444, EAT, where the EAT took the view that the William Muir decision was to be preferred. In the opinion of His Honour Judge Hull, the suggestion that an employee may be under a duty to mitigate his or her loss by appealing to the employer was a strange one. 'The employer has made up his mind to dismiss the applicant, presumably after taking proper thought and carrying out the procedural duties of fairness as well as considering the merits. If the decision was a careful and responsible one, then the prospect of it being reversed on appeal must be remote. The prospect may be even more remote in the unlikely event that the decision has been an irresponsible and hasty one; in that event, what possible confidence can the employee have in the integrity of the employer?' HHJ Hull also pointed out that to place employees under an obligation to mitigate in this way could cause extreme inconvenience for tribunals assessing compensation, since they may be drawn into hearing extensive evidence from both sides on the likelihood that the appeal would have been successful. Therefore, a failure to invoke internal procedures before dismissal will not amount to a failure to mitigate by the employee.

Note, however, that as from 6 April 2009 employment tribunals have been entitled under S.207A TULR(C)A to penalise employees (as well as employers) for failure to comply with any provision of the Acas Code of Practice on Disciplinary and Grievance Procedures that is relevant to certain specified claims (which include unfair dismissal) – see under 'Adjustments for breach of Acas Code of Practice' below. Para 25 of the Code specifically states that: 'Where an employee feels that disciplinary action taken against them is wrong or unjust they should appeal against that decision.' Although there has thus far been no appellate case law on S.207A, it is possible that tribunals may, in certain circumstances, conclude that an employee's failure to utilise an internal appeal against dismissal justifies making a reduction in the compensatory award of up to 25 per cent under that section.

18.16   **Refusal of offer of re-employment**
An unreasonable refusal of an offer of re-employment may amount to a failure to mitigate. It should be borne in mind, however, that the duty to mitigate only arises after dismissal, so refusing offers made *before* employment was terminated cannot amount to a failure to mitigate – Savoia v Chiltern Herb Farms Ltd 1981 IRLR 65, EAT. A refusal is more likely to be reasonable if the employee has been badly treated by the employer – Fyfe v Scientific Furnishings Ltd 1989 ICR 648, EAT. And an employee's refusal to accept an offer of reinstatement in the old job is less likely to be reasonable than a refusal to accept an offer of re-engagement in a different job, but everything is subject to the reasonableness test. Some examples:

- **Comeau v Hart and anor** ET Case No.32364/86: a dismissal was held to be unfair because the employer had taken too much account of the conduct of the husband of the employee when dismissing her. The employer had later recanted and indicated that she could be reinstated in her old job. Her rejection of this offer was held to be unreasonable: she should have recognised that immediate dismissal was an understandable reaction to her husband's threatening behaviour and she should have avoided further loss by resuming employment

- **Baillie Brothers v Pritchard** EAT 59/89: an employee acted reasonably in refusing alternative employment offered some months after his dismissal: the new job paid less and the use of a van for travelling to and from work was lost, as was the employee's statutory protection against unfair dismissal

- **Cocking v Moulinex Swan Holdings** Ltd EAT 1233/94: about three weeks after his dismissal for redundancy, C was offered re-engagement. He declined because he had committed himself to setting up a business with someone else. The EAT upheld the tribunal's decision that the refusal was unreasonable. The offer was of suitable alternative employment with an employer with whom there had been no falling-out, and C's commitment to the proposed business venture was not such as to prevent him withdrawing from it in order to mitigate his loss.

In the case of Wilding v British Telecommunications plc 2002 ICR 1079, CA (a **18.17** disability discrimination case), W was offered re-employment with BT on a part-time basis, shortly after BT had lodged an appeal against a tribunal finding that he had been discriminated against on the ground of disability. W rejected the offer of re-employment and set out a number of grounds for so doing, including the fact that he viewed BT's appeal against the decision on liability as inconsistent with its offer of re-employment; the manner of his dismissal; the injury to feelings he had suffered; and the way in which his appeal against dismissal had been conducted, along with various other grounds. A tribunal concluded that W had acted unreasonably in refusing BT's offer and had therefore failed to mitigate his loss. The EAT agreed, as did the Court of Appeal, which rejected the notion that the test for mitigation is a purely objective one. In the Court's view, it also requires the tribunal to look at all the circumstances of the case, including the subjective reasons that the complainant has given for turning down the offer. It followed that where the claimant has given a full explanation as to why he turned down the offer, the ultimate question for the tribunal was whether he acted unreasonably in doing so. The answer to this should be determined after taking into account the history and all the circumstances of the case, including the claimant's state of mind, and remembering that the burden of proof and the standard of reasonableness to be applied is not too high.

Although a refusal to accept redeployment or a transfer before the dismissal cannot amount to a failure to mitigate, continuing to reject such offers after the dismissal has been executed may do so. This may be the case even if the employer's attempts to force this change on the employee were the very reason the dismissal was unfair in the first place – Pearson v Leeds Polytechnic Students' Union EAT 182/84.

18.18 Even where the employer's conduct has justified the employee resigning and claiming unfair constructive dismissal, inflexibility on the part of an employee, or a refusal to listen to the employer's attempts to explain, may amount to a failure to mitigate. In Coote v McAlpine Humberoak Ltd ET Case No.20948/ 83 a manager resigned after being questioned about thefts in a way that made him believe he was no longer trusted. Although this amounted to unfair dismissal, his refusal to meet or hear any explanation from management was a failure to mitigate and no compensatory award was made.

In another case, an offshore oil worker elected to resign and become self-employed after a unilateral cut in his overtime was imposed. He later became unemployed. Despite a finding of unfair constructive dismissal, this course of action was held to be an unreasonable failure to mitigate. Although becoming self-employed can be a good mitigation of loss (see below), here a long-serving employee had given up a good salary and pension at a time when the oil industry was depressed and prospects were poor. The employee should have reconsidered his position and accepted the modified terms and no compensation for future loss was therefore awarded – Plewinski v McDermott Engineering London EAT 465/88. In Touchstone Productions Ltd v Patrick EAT 1216/95, on the other hand, it was held to be wholly unrealistic to expect an employee who had been physically assaulted by one of his managers to accept an offer of re-engagement.

Note that, where a tribunal has ordered the reinstatement or re-engagement of an employee (see Chapter 14), the employee will be taken to have failed to mitigate his or her loss if he or she unreasonably prevents the order from being complied with – S.117(8) ERA.

18.19 **Seeking new employment**

Remaining unemployed unnecessarily or taking low-paid employment when higher-paid work is available will clearly amount to a failure to mitigate and a tribunal will cut the employee's compensation accordingly. However, the kind of work a dismissed employee should seek varies greatly between individuals and from area to area. High levels of unemployment can play their part in what constitutes reasonable mitigation. For instance, difficulties in obtaining suitable employment might justify the acceptance of lower-paid employment than would otherwise have been reasonable. One London teacher was unfairly dismissed when school populations were declining and there were job shortages in the South-East. The only offer came from Wales, at a lower salary and minus London weighting. The tribunal held it reasonable for her to accept this and awarded her a full year's net difference between the two salaries – Collen v Lewis and anor ET Case No.33173/83.

Conversely, high unemployment can also work to reduce compensation where a dismissed employee unrealistically refuses lower-paid employment. Breach of the mitigation rule in this way is particularly likely if the employee has already made fruitless attempts to get better-paid work over a reasonable period. It has even been suggested that the value of having a job during times of high unemployment may make a job refusal unreasonable even where the money offered is less than state benefits – Daley v AE Dorsett (Almar Dolls Ltd) 1982 ICR 1, EAT.

Is registering for employment sufficient mitigation? Simply signing on at a Jobcentre (now rebranded Jobcentre Plus) was held to be insufficient mitigation of loss in Burns v George Boyd (Engineering) Ltd EAT 458/84. At the very least, regular visits to the Jobcentre seem to be required – Bristol Garage (Brighton) Ltd v Lowen 1979 IRLR 86, EAT. In practice, tribunals are likely to expect more than this and claimants would be well advised to keep copies and records of job applications and interviews in order to rebut any charges that they have failed to take reasonable steps to mitigate their losses. **18.20**

Abandoning new employment. The duty to mitigate will not be allowed to operate oppressively. For instance, it may be reasonable for an employee to give up a new job which proves unsuitable – e.g. because it involves too high a degree of responsibility, or too much travelling for that particular employee – see Dundee Plant Co Ltd v Riddler EAT 377/88, where an employee gave up a new job after three months because of the unacceptable amount of travelling involved. **18.21**

Registering as sick or disabled. It may be reasonable mitigation of loss for an employee to register as sick or disabled, but this should not be regarded as all that has to be done in mitigation unless the circumstances warrant it – Plessey Military Communications Ltd v Brough EAT 518/84. **18.22**

Accepting part-time employment. In Ahunanya v Scottish and Southern Energy plc EAT 0540/08 the EAT upheld an employment tribunal's decision that an employee who had been dismissed from a full-time job failed to mitigate his loss from the point at which he accepted part-time employment. There was evidence to show that the employee had applied for only one other job in addition to the part-time job vacancy, and that part-time employment now suited his personal circumstances. The tribunal was therefore entitled, said the EAT, to award the employee his full loss (uprated to the national minimum wage hourly rate in view of the employer's failure to pay this) until the date the employee began working in the part-time job, but then not to award any further loss on the ground that the employee had failed to mitigate from that date onwards. **18.23**

Temporary employment. In some circumstances, it is possible that the chain of causation between an unfair dismissal and the losses flowing from that dismissal is not broken by the acceptance of temporary new employment. This may be so whether the new employment in question was always intended to be **18.24**

639

temporary or just worked out that way. In Dench v Flynn and Partners 1998 IRLR 653, CA, the Court of Appeal rejected the contention that the loss flowing from an unfair dismissal automatically comes to an end once permanent employment has been obtained. Lord Justice Beldam, with whose judgment the two other judges agreed, said that it was wrong to conclude in every case that the taking of new employment necessarily broke the chain of causation.

In Cowen v Rentokil Initial Facility Services UK Ltd t/a Initial Transport Services EAT 0473/07 the EAT relied on Beldam LJ's comments in the Dench case to overturn a tribunal's decision that an employee's losses ended when he accepted new employment that turned out to be temporary. The tribunal had incorrectly assumed that the obtaining of permanent employment necessarily broke the chain of causation. In that case, the new employment was very different from the employee's former job and it came to an end because he was unable to satisfy the new employer that he was the right man for the job. Moreover, it was obvious when the job was taken up that it might only last for the probationary period, and that is in fact what happened. In those circumstances, the EAT felt justified in concluding that the chain of causation had not been broken and that compensation should be calculated as including a period of loss subsequent to the termination of the employee's new job.

18.25 In Cowen, Mr Justice Elias made it clear that the EAT's decision in that case should not be interpreted as suggesting that just because a new job is of relatively short duration will inevitably mean that causation is not broken. It all depends on the circumstances of the case. The reason why an employee loses the second job may have a bearing on the question. So, for example, if the reason for the employee's dismissal from the alternative job was culpable misconduct on his or her part, that might well break the chain of causation. Elias J cautioned tribunals, however, not to become embroiled in satellite litigation as to the precise circumstances in which the second dismissal took place.

Clearly, the length of time that an employee remains in the new employment may also be an important factor. For example, an employee who was dismissed 18 months after starting new employment was not, according to the EAT in Courtaulds Northern Spinning v Moosa 1984 IRLR 43, EAT, entitled to claim ongoing loss against the first employer following the termination of his second job.

18.26 **Effect on compensation where employee finds higher-paid employment.** Where an employee successfully mitigates his or her loss by finding new employment at a salary or wage that is higher than that enjoyed in the old job, the question arises as to what effect this has on his compensation. In particular, does the higher payment have to be offset against the employee's losses for the purpose of the compensatory award? This issue is dealt with in detail in Chapter 16, under 'Immediate loss – new employment'.

Becoming self-employed   18.27

Dismissed employees may become self-employed instead of seeking other jobs and this can amount to reasonable mitigation of loss, especially where the individual is not young or is in a specialised trade where employment openings are few. In such cases profits may not be immediately forthcoming so that losses from dismissal tend to be heavier than where an employee simply seeks and obtains work with another employer. In Gardiner-Hill v Roland Berger Technics Ltd 1982 IRLR 498, EAT, a managing director spent 80 per cent of his time between dismissal and the tribunal hearing trying to set up his own company. The employer argued that this had prevented him from looking for salaried work and so the 'lost earnings' element of his compensatory award should be reduced accordingly. Reversing the tribunal's decision, the EAT held that the employee's duty is to take such steps as are reasonable in the circumstances. This case concerned a 55-year-old managing director with 16 years' experience in a specialist business. In seeking to market his expertise and experience in his own business he had acted prudently.

An employee may also be awarded expenses incurred in setting up a business. In United Freight Distribution Ltd v McDougall EAT 218/94 an employee decided to set up his own business following his dismissal. The tribunal found this to be a reasonable course of action and it also reimbursed him the £550 legal fees which he had incurred in selling his house and another £2,500 which he had borrowed from his father. The EAT upheld the award of £550, stating that the tribunal had clearly considered the legal fees to be a reasonable expense incurred in the setting up of the business. In respect of the £2,500 loan, however, the tribunal had failed to establish what the employee had spent the money on and the EAT remitted the case for the tribunal to consider the matter further.

Opting for retraining or further education   18.28

Some employees decide to go on a training or re-education course after being dismissed to aid their eventual search for employment. Taking oneself off the employment market in this way may well amount to a failure to mitigate, although in some cases the tribunal may decide that an employee acted reasonably in seeking retraining. In Hibiscus Housing Association Ltd v McIntosh EAT 0534/08 the EAT held that it is certainly not the law that an employee who seeks higher or further education after having been unfairly dismissed thereby fails to mitigate his or her loss. But nor is it the case that, even if there is no failure to mitigate, once the employee embarks upon the course he or she is entitled to pursue it to the very end at the employer's expense. On the facts of the particular case, the EAT upheld an employment tribunal's decision that it was not unreasonable for the employee to take up a part-time university course alongside obtaining part-time employment in the circumstances, especially given that her former employer had declined to offer a satisfactory job reference.

641

In Sealey v Avon Aluminium Co Ltd EAT 516/78 the claimant was compensated for the loss of 52 weeks' pay although for 29 of these he was back at college. His compensation was reduced only by so much of the maintenance element of his grant as was attributable to 29 weeks out of the 52. Similarly, in Glen Henderson Ltd v Nisbet EAT 34/90 the employee followed the advice from her Jobcentre to go on a five-week business enterprise course with a view to becoming self-employed. The tribunal found this behaviour reasonable and awarded her compensation for loss of earnings while she was on the course and also one year's future loss on the basis of her self-employed earnings. The EAT upheld the tribunal's decision.

18.29   In Layte v Tavern Wholesaling Ltd ET Case No.56291/95 a former office manager made efforts to gain alternative employment following her dismissal, then decided to take a two-year course in business and finance studies. A tribunal held that, having regard to the level of remuneration in her previous job and the state of the employment market generally in her area, this was a reasonable course for her to take.

Note that where a tribunal finds that an employee has failed to mitigate his or her loss it should not necessarily treat that failure as bringing the period of compensation to an end. Thus, where an employee's decision to embark upon a course is held to be unreasonable, the tribunal should judge when the employee ought to have obtained fresh employment at a similar level – Mullarkey v Up the Creek Ltd EAT 263/95. In practice, however, tribunals often do treat the date the course started as the cut-off point, presumably because the course is considered to be an intervening act, after which the employee's losses are too remote to be attributable to the unfair dismissal.

18.30   The Mullarkey case demonstrates the confusion that often exists between questions of mitigation and remoteness of loss. The tribunal in that case found the employee's decision to embark on a full-time course to be a reasonable act of mitigation. It nevertheless decided to award her no compensation from the date her course started because any losses suffered from that date onwards were a result of her own actions and were not caused by the dismissal. The EAT held this to be wrong. If the employee's actions were reasonable mitigation, then they could not have broken the chain of causation. But for the unfair dismissal, the employee would not have embarked on the course and would still have been in salaried employment with the employer.

This is to be contrasted with Simrad Ltd v Scott 1997 IRLR 147, EAT, where the EAT, in spite of a tribunal finding that the employee acted reasonably in retraining as a nurse, held that her losses from the date she started her course were too remote to be attributable to the actions of the employer. In our view, the Mullarkey approach is to be preferred on this point. Only if the employee's decision was unreasonable could it plausibly be considered to be an intervening act that relieves the employer of any further liability for the employee's losses.

In Tchoula v ICTS (UK) Ltd 2000 ICR 1191, EAT, a tribunal found that T, a security guard who had been victimised on the ground of race, had mitigated his loss by retraining in the IT sector. The EAT sympathised with ICTS's argument on appeal that it should not be responsible for funding T's change of career. However, the question for the EAT was whether the employment tribunal's finding that T had mitigated his loss was perverse. The EAT did not think that it was. It was open to the tribunal to find that it was reasonable for T to retrain in the IT sector and that it was reasonably foreseeable that such a course would be necessary as a result of T's unlawful dismissal. The tribunal was entitled to accept T's evidence that he did not pursue work in the security field as he would have needed a clean record to do so and because of his dismissal by ICTS he did not have such a record.

In Khanum v IBC Vehicles Ltd EAT 685/98 the EAT held that an employment tribunal should have allowed the claimant to recover losses incurred after embarking on her course of study as she had not failed to mitigate her loss. The claimant's former employer had dominated the local automobile industry in which she had worked and there was evidence that she had been 'blacklisted'. In the light of this, it had been reasonable for the claimant to enrol for a degree course. In so concluding, the EAT distinguished the decision in Simrad Ltd v Scott (above) and rejected the employer's contention that the decision in that case established a general rule of law that, for the purposes of compensation, the chain of causation is necessarily broken where an employee goes on to further education after being dismissed. Similarly, in Orthet Ltd v Vince-Cain 2005 374, EAT, the EAT upheld a tribunal conclusion that the claimant's decision to undertake a four-year undergraduate course in dietetics, when her efforts to find another suitably senior position in retail management failed, amounted to reasonable mitigation. The employee had childcare responsibilities which meant that she required reasonable flexibility in her working hours, which would not have been accommodated had she set her sights lower at a store management position (rather than a more senior position) in retail. It was therefore reasonable for her to seek to maintain that flexibility in any new work which she found. The EAT approved the tribunal's award based on loss of earnings for nine months in each of the four years of the course, giving credit for work during vacations.

Mitigation during the notice period 18.32

In Norton Tool Co Ltd v Tewson 1972 ICR 501, NIRC, the National Industrial Relations Court held that an employee is entitled to unfair dismissal compensation covering the period from the date of his or her dismissal to the date when notice – had it been properly given – would have expired, even though the employee has entered fresh employment during that period. The NIRC reasoned that it was 'just and equitable' (within the meaning of what is now S.123(1) ERA) to treat the employee as having suffered a loss in so far as he had received less than he should have done had the employer acted in accordance with 'good industrial practice' by giving notice or making a payment in lieu.

18.31

643

There were highly respectable arguments presented in subsequent decisions that called into question the validity of the so-called Norton Tool principle. In particular, it was argued – and in some cases accepted – that the principle offended the cardinal rule that the compensatory award should be based only on the employee's actual losses.

18.33 However, the validity of the principle seemed to be settled when it was approved by the Court of Appeal in Addison v Babcock FATA Ltd 1987 ICR 805, CA. In that case the Court refused to extend the Norton Tool principle to the situation in which the employee has received a full payment in lieu of notice from the employer and subsequently seeks to recover compensation in respect of exactly the same notice period as part of an unfair dismissal compensatory award. The Court held that a notice payment is not an independent right to which an employee is entitled in addition to, and apart from, any compensation from the ex-employer for lost earnings during the period of notice. Accordingly, the employee had to give credit for the notice payment by offsetting it against such part of a compensatory award as covers the notional notice period. It logically followed that the Norton Tool principle should not be extended to allow an employee to reap the benefit of a double payment in respect of the same period of loss – namely, a payment in lieu of notice on the one hand, and a compensatory award covering lost earnings during the notice period on the other. Subject to this, however, the Court of Appeal did approve the Norton Tool principle as being correct so long as it remains confined to its proper ambit – i.e. earnings from new employment during the notice period. Any such earnings did not fall to be deducted from the compensatory award.

The position thus seemed to be nicely settled until the House of Lords handed down its seminal decision in Dunnachie v Kingston Upon Hull City Council 2004 ICR 1052, HL. There, it was held that the general provision governing the calculation of the compensatory award – S.123(1) ERA – permits only the award of sums in unfair dismissal cases that reflect the actual loss resulting from the dismissal. This meant that it is not legitimate to award sums that are additional to such loss (e.g. injury to feelings caused by the dismissal). At the time of their Lordships' decision, many commentators considered that the Norton Tool principle could not survive the House of Lords' ruling. In the event, however, it appears to have done precisely that. For in the later case of Langley and anor v Burlo 2007 ICR 390, CA, the Court of Appeal took the view that the Dunnachie decision should not be regarded as authority for the proposition that Norton Tool was no longer good law, since the issue of whether the principle remained valid had not arisen for specific consideration in that case. In the Court of Appeal's view, the Norton Tool principle survived 'and should be applied by tribunals unless and until there is another decision which is directly in point'.

18.34 Even so, the Court of Appeal in Burlo did make it clear that the Norton tool principle has a narrow compass. In particular, it could not be applied in a way that resulted in an award of compensation *greater* than the loss caused to the employee as a consequence of the dismissal. It followed that a claimant was not entitled to receive, as part of her compensatory award, full pay for her notice period in circumstances where she would not have been able to work during her notice as a result of a physical injury and her contract expressly provided that she would be paid only statutory sick pay in periods of incapacity for work. Even if it were true that good industrial practice requires that an employee who is summarily dismissed while unfit for work through sickness should receive pay in lieu of notice at the normal rate of pay, that precept could not be prayed in aid in the assessment of the claimant's compensation. If the claimant had not been dismissed she would have received statutory sick pay during her period of absence. Therefore statutory sick pay was the correct measure of her weekly loss during the notice period and the compensatory award had to be calculated on that basis.

It follows from this that the Norton Tool principle has a limited compass: it applies where an employee has been deprived of his or her full contractual notice, remains fit and able to work, and secures new employment during the notional notice period. In such a case, the employee's new earnings do not have to be set off against his or her losses when calculating the compensatory award. Furthermore, in a case where the employer makes a payment in lieu of notice and the employee secures new employment during the notice period, though the employee will not be entitled to receive compensation for unfair dismissal for lost earnings in respect of the notice period, his or her earnings from the new employment will be ignored. In other words, the employee will not have to give credit for those earnings by offsetting them against the losses on which compensation for unfair dismissal is awarded.

For a more detailed discussion of the application of the Norton Tool principle in assessing loss upon which the compensatory award is based, see Chapter 16, under 'Nature and maximum amount of award – "deemed losses" and the Norton Tool rule'. And for further discussion of the specific effect the Norton Tool principle has on the treatment of new earnings during notice periods for compensatory award purposes, see Chapter 16, under 'Immediate loss – new earnings, notice pay and the notice period'.

Application in constructive dismissal cases. In Stuart Peters Ltd v Bell 2009   **18.35**
ICR 1556, CA, the Court of Appeal, while approving the workings of the Norton Tool principle as described above, held that it did not apply to constructive dismissal cases. In Lord Justice Elias's judgment, there is no industrial relations practice of making a full payment in lieu of notice where termination is triggered by the employee. As a result, an employee who succeeds in a claim of unfair constructive dismissal is entitled to compensation in respect of the entire notice period. However, account must be taken of earnings received from any new employment during that period by off-setting these against the losses which form the basis for the assessment of the compensatory award.

645

18.36 'Just and equitable' reductions

As explained in the introduction to Chapter 16, S.123(1) ERA provides that the compensatory award shall be 'such amount as the tribunal considers just and equitable in all the circumstances having regard to the loss sustained by the complainant in consequence of the dismissal'. Under this subsection the employment tribunal can effectively reduce the compensatory award (but not the basic award) to reflect general considerations of fairness.

The cases where tribunals may decide that it is just and equitable to reduce compensation under this head can be divided roughly into two groupings:

- where, by the time of the tribunal hearing, the employer can show that the employee is guilty of misconduct that would have merited dismissal, even if the employer did not know about that misconduct at the time of the dismissal

- where, albeit that the dismissal has been rendered unfair solely because of procedural failings in the dismissal procedure, the tribunal is satisfied that the employee could nevertheless have been fairly dismissed at a later date or if the employer had followed a proper procedure.

18.37 The second of these bases for reducing the compensatory award is commonly known as a 'Polkey reduction' (or deduction) after the case in which the House of Lords confirmed that such a reduction was possible. In practice, it is now by far the most common basis on which reductions in the compensatory award are made by tribunals. As previously stated, a Polkey reduction is merely a sub-category of the reductions tribunals may make when calculating the amount that is 'just and equitable' to award employees who have been unfairly dismissed after having regard to their actual losses. But in view of the considerable amount of case law and judicial guidance that so-called Polkey reductions have attracted, we discuss these reductions in a separate section of this chapter below. First, however, we look at the other common form of 'just and equitable' reduction.

18.38 Misconduct not known to employer at date of dismissal

What happens if an employer dismisses an employee on grounds that are held by a tribunal to be inadequate (and thus unfair) but discovers only after the employee has been dismissed that the employee was guilty of misconduct that would have formed the basis for a fair dismissal had the employer known about it at the time? Clearly, such misconduct cannot be said to have 'caused or contributed' to the dismissal so as to justify a reduction in the compensatory award for contributory fault under S.123(6) ERA, since the conduct in question was not in the mind of the employer at the time of dismissal. But can the misconduct be taken into account on some other basis? The answer is that, although the unfairness of the dismissal will be unaltered by misconduct that comes to light after the dismissal, the tribunal is entitled to take it into account in accordance with the general statutory provision governing the calculation of the compensatory award –

646

S.123(1) ERA. The inclusion of the words 'such amount as is just and equitable' in that provision implicitly allows a tribunal to take into account a factor such as the employee's wrongdoing in order to limit or reduce the amount of the compensatory award that would otherwise have been awarded.

A leading example of this principle being applied is the House of Lords' decision in W Devis and Sons Ltd v Atkins 1977 ICR 662, HL. In that case, the employee was the manager of an abattoir who was dismissed because the employer was not satisfied with his methods of making purchases. Several weeks later, the employer received information suggesting that the employee had been dishonestly dealing in live animals. A tribunal ruled the employee's dismissal to be unfair but decided, in the light of the subsequently discovered information, that it was not just and equitable to make any award. The House of Lords, upholding the tribunal's decision, said it was clear that, on the basis of the information that subsequently came to light, the employee could have been fairly dismissed if the employer had known about this conduct. The fact that the employee had not suffered any injustice meant that, applying what is now S.123(1), it was not just and equitable that he should receive any award.

Limits on power to make 'just and equitable' reductions. There are, 18.39 however, limits on the tribunal's power to reduce the compensatory award under S.123(1) on account of misconduct not known to the employer at the time dismissal takes place. First and foremost, it is well established that S.123(1) applies only to pre-termination conduct that does not come to light until after the dismissal: post-termination conduct, on the other hand, cannot be taken into account as a basis for a reduction – Soros and anor v Davison and anor 1994 ICR 590, EAT. In Soros, an employment tribunal held that the employees had been unfairly dismissed at a hearing on liability. Following that hearing, but prior to the hearing on remedy, the employees sold information about their former employer to a national newspaper. The employer applied for a stay on the remedy hearing until a High Court action for breach of confidentiality had been heard. The tribunal refused the application on the ground that the alleged breaches of duty were not relevant to the issue of remedies for unfair dismissal because they occurred after the employees had been dismissed. The EAT agreed, stating that the calculation of the compensatory award for unfair dismissal under S.123(1) is only concerned with events that occur during the currency of the contract of employment.

In Mullinger v Department for Work and Pensions EAT 0515/05 the EAT relied on the Soros case as authority for ruling that misconduct on the part of the employee occurring after his employment had ended could not form the basis for a reduction in the compensatory payment awardable to him for unfair dismissal. In that case, in support of the argument that it would be 'just and equitable' to reduce compensation under S.123(1), counsel for the employer posited some extreme hypothetical examples, such as where an employee faced with a letter of dismissal becomes so incensed that he assaults or even kills the messenger who delivers the

647

letter. Perhaps a more realistic scenario might be where a dismissed employee re-enters his former employer's premises and sabotages the computer system. Even when faced with examples of this kind, the EAT was unimpressed with the submission that S.123(1) allows the employee's actions to be taken into account when calculating the compensatory award. Mr Justice Langstaff stated: 'We would merely observe that if it is the case that there is some financial consequence to an employer of some action taken by a former employee after his employment has ceased then there are remedies in law which an employer may be able to take advantage of. It does not seem to us to be at all unjust to leave the employer to those remedies. It does seem to us to strain the language of the statute, to be inconsistent with Soros, and to establish a principle with uncertain boundaries if we were to accede to [counsel for the employer's] submission.' (Note that, although the Mullinger case was appealed further – Mullinger v Department for Work and Pensions 2007 EWCA Civ 1334, CA – the Court of Appeal was not called upon to consider the particular observations of Langstaff J above, whose judgment on other aspects was upheld.)

18.40   A second limitation on the ability of tribunals to take into account misconduct unknown to the employer at the time of dismissal is that, although tribunals are entitled to take a view as to what is just and equitable to award in all the circumstances, they must do so after 'having regard to the loss sustained by the complainant'. In effect, this ensures that considerations of justice and equity do not extend so far as empowering tribunals to award compensation simply on a 'feels fair' basis, with no regard being paid to the actual financial losses sustained by the employee as a result of having been unfairly dismissed. The interplay between 'justice and equity' on the one hand, and 'having regard to the loss sustained' on the other, was clearly explained by Mr Justice Tudor Evans in the Soros case (above) when commenting on the principle established by the House of Lords in Devis v Atkins. He observed: 'In our opinion, the House of Lords in [the Devis case] held that when assessing compensation for unfair dismissal, a tribunal should have regard to the loss sustained in consequence of the dismissal but should then ask itself whether it is just and equitable that the employee should be compensated, fully or at all, for that loss, bearing in mind the circumstances [of the particular case].'

The constraint to have regard to the actual losses of the complainant is illustrated by the EAT's decision in Abbey Motors (Hemel Hempstead) Ltd v Carta EAT 403/95. There, the employee deliberately misled the tribunal when he told it that he had not been able to find work during the 18 months following his dismissal. The employer produced evidence that he had earned £2,000 since that date. The tribunal decided to reduce C's compensatory award by double the amount of his post-dismissal earnings (although this still resulted in his receiving the maximum compensatory award applicable at that time). The employer appealed, arguing that the award should have been reduced to nothing to reflect the employee's behaviour. The EAT, however, in upholding the tribunal's decision, held that the tribunal was entitled to take account of the veracity of witnesses in respect of calculating the loss actually sustained and to adjust the amount of the award where, as in this case, the employee had tried to mislead the tribunal. But a nil award would not have been appropriate because it is clear from S.123(1) that a tribunal is not entitled to assess compensation without any regard to the actual loss sustained by the employee in consequence of the dismissal.

18.41
A possible further limitation on tribunals' power to make a reduction under S.123(1) applies in respect of misconduct that could have been relied on and was known to the employer at the time of dismissal but which formed no part of the employer's decision to dismiss. It would seem from the Court of Appeal's decision in Devonshire v Trico-Folberth Ltd 1989 ICR 747, CA, that it is not just and equitable for a tribunal to take account of such misconduct as a basis for reducing the compensatory award. In that case the employee was dismissed on account of her absence record. She appealed against this decision and the appeal panel decided that she should not be dismissed for her attendance record but that her employment should be terminated on medical grounds. A tribunal found that the dismissal on medical grounds was unfair but that if the employee had been dismissed on the original ground the dismissal would have been fair. It awarded compensation of £9,057. The employer appealed, claiming that it was not just and equitable to make the compensatory award as the dismissal would have been fair if it had given a different reason for it. Both the EAT and the Court of Appeal rejected the employer's contention. The employer had specifically chosen not to rely on the employee's attendance as a reason for dismissal and therefore could not rely on it when attempting to reduce her compensatory award.

The distinguishing factor for the Court of Appeal seems to have been that, factually speaking, the case was not one of subsequently discovered conduct (as was the case in Devis): rather, the employer had made a conscious decision not to dismiss on the ground of attendance. Nevertheless, the decision is hard to reconcile with the actual reasoning in Devis v Atkins. If compensation can be reduced on the basis of facts coming to light after the dismissal that would have justified the dismissal, the same logic would seem to apply where circumstances existed at the time of the dismissal which, if the employer had relied on them, would have made for a fair dismissal. This seems to have been the view taken by the EAT in McNee v Charles Tennant and Co Ltd EAT 338/90. In that case the employee was also originally dismissed for poor attendance, but this reason was changed to medical reasons on internal appeal. The EAT upheld a tribunal's decision not to make a compensatory award on the ground that the employee could have been dismissed fairly on several previous occasions for his absence record.

Considerations of fairness remain paramount
18.42
Even in a case of misconduct occurring prior to dismissal but only coming to the employer's attention after dismissal, tribunals must be careful not to leap to the conclusion that it is invariably just and equitable to reduce the

649

compensatory award in the light of the misconduct. In Panama v London Borough of Hackney 2003 IRLR 278, CA, the Court of Appeal enjoined tribunals always to have regard to the consideration of overall fairness in such cases, which it described as being 'paramount'.

In the Panama case, the employment tribunal was held to have erred in holding that an unfairly dismissed employee was not entitled to compensation because evidence of fraudulent conduct that came to the employer's attention shortly after the dismissal meant that the employee would have been fairly dismissed in any event. Although the tribunal was asking itself a hypothetical question as to what would have happened if the employer had known of the allegations of fraud, it still had to approach the issue on the basis of whether a dismissal would have been fair or unfair, bearing in mind the statutory test for establishing the reasonableness of the decision to dismiss set out in S.98(4) ERA and the well known guidelines in British Home Stores Ltd v Burchell 1980 ICR 303, EAT (see the introduction to Chapter 6, 'Conduct'). In the particular case, a dismissal on the ground of fraud would not have been fair because the employer had failed to carry out a reasonable investigation into the allegations of fraud and therefore did not have reasonable grounds for its belief that the employee was guilty of dishonesty. There was therefore no basis for making any deduction from the claimant's compensatory award on the ground that 'it was just and equitable' to do so.

18.43 'Polkey reductions'

The other main category of cases in which employment tribunals often make 'just and equitable' reductions under S.123(1) ERA is where the unfairly dismissed employee could have been dismissed fairly at a later date or if a proper procedure had been followed. Ever since the House of Lords' landmark decision in Polkey v AE Dayton Services Ltd 1988 ICR 142, HL, 'procedural unfairness' cases – in which the dismissal is held to be unfair purely on procedural grounds but compensation is reduced to reflect the likelihood that the employee would still have been dismissed in any event had a proper procedure been followed – are by far the most common type of reduction made by employment tribunals.

18.44 The 'Polkey principle'

The House of Lords' decision in the Polkey case ended what had become known as the 'no difference rule'. That rule meant that where there was a proven procedural irregularity in an otherwise fair dismissal – e.g. failure to warn or consult before a redundancy, or failure to allow the employee to state his or her case before a misconduct dismissal – but it could be shown that carrying out the proper procedure would have made 'no difference', then the dismissal would be fair. The House of Lords overturned this rule in all cases, except those where it would be 'utterly useless' or 'futile' to carry out the

650 ⸺

required procedure. This meant that the reasonableness of the employer's action in dispensing with normal procedural requirements remained highly relevant to the question of whether the dismissal was fair, but the question of whether such a procedure would have made any difference was no longer a relevant consideration. The practical upshot was undoubtedly an increase in the number of findings of unfair dismissal.

Although the House of Lords held that it should not be open to an employer to argue that 'no difference' dismissals should be regarded as fair, it was prepared to accept that the 'no difference rule' should live on as regards compensation. The basic principle stems from the earlier decision of the House of Lords in W Devis and Sons Ltd v Atkins 1977 ICR 662, HL (previously discussed under 'Just and equitable awards – misconduct not known to employer at date of dismissal' above). In that case Viscount Dilhorne asserted that 'it cannot be just and equitable that a sum should be awarded in compensation when in fact the employee has suffered no injustice by being dismissed'. This approach was taken up in the Polkey case, where the House of Lords ruled that the question of whether the employee ultimately suffered any injustice – i.e. whether the procedural irregularities really made any difference – was to be taken into account when assessing compensation.

Current status of the rule in Polkey. In the autumn of 2004, the legislative landscape against which compensation for unfair dismissal in general operates profoundly changed with the introduction of statutory disciplinary and dismissal procedures (DDPs). The effect was to render dismissals automatically unfair in cases where employers failed to comply with certain basic procedures, and to impose virtually automatic uplifts to the resulting compensation of between 10 and 50 per cent. However, the statutory provisions further provided that so long as an employer complied with the relevant statutory DDPs, any failure to follow due procedure over and above what the DDPs required would not render the dismissal unfair provided that the employer could show that it would have decided to dismiss the employee in any event, regardless of the breach of procedure. The effect of this provision was to enact a limited reversal of the rule in Polkey by reinstating the 'no difference' rule that the Polkey case overturned.

18.45

As it turned out, these new statutory provisions were to have a short shelf life. Following widespread criticism about their complexity and the fact that they had served to make internal dispute mechanisms within the workplace far too formal, they were repealed with effect from 6 April 2009. Although transitional provisions providing for the DDPs to continue to operate apply to dismissals effected before that date, the law as it applies to unfair dismissal compensation in respect of any dismissal where the effective date of termination falls on or after 6 April 2009 is now virtually identical to how it was before the advent of the DDPs. The one significant change is the introduction of a statutory provision – S.207A TULR(C)A – allowing for the compensatory award to be

651

increased or reduced by up to 25 per cent for any failure by the employer or employee to comply with the Acas Code of Practice on Disciplinary and Grievance Procedures. This adjustment is discussed in detail under 'Adjustments for breach of Acas Code of Practice' below. Suffice it to say here, however, that the principle in Polkey flourishes now as strongly as it did before the advent of the statutory DDPs.

18.46 **Types of case to which Polkey principle applies**
In the Polkey case itself the reason for dismissal was never in dispute, as both sides accepted that the real reason was redundancy. The issue was simply whether the complete lack of prior warning and consultation had rendered the dismissal unfair. But it is reasonably clear from the House of Lords' decision that their Lordships did not intend their ruling to be limited to any specific reason for dismissal. Whether an employer dismisses for redundancy, misconduct, incapability or for another permissible reason, it will not be able to elude a finding of unfair dismissal by pleading that a failure of procedure made no difference to the outcome of the dismissal process. But in all such cases, tribunals will be entitled, when assessing the compensatory award payable in respect of the unfair dismissal, to consider whether a reduction should be made on the ground that the lack of a fair procedure made any practical difference to the decision to dismiss.

Accepting that the Polkey principle potentially applies to all types of case irrespective of the reason for dismissal, its precise scope has nevertheless been called into question on certain other bases, as we shall see below.

18.47 **Cases where reason for dismissal is in dispute.** In Gover and ors v Propertycare Ltd 2006 ICR 1073, CA, it was contended that it was not open to apply the Polkey principle to a case where the reason for dismissal was found by an employment tribunal to be different from that on which the employer relied when dismissing. In Gover, two employees resigned and claimed unfair constructive dismissal following the unilateral imposition by their employer of detrimental changes to their commission terms. A tribunal found that the dismissal was unfair in view of the complete lack of consultation about the change to the employees' terms and conditions. However, the tribunal went on to find that, even if there had been proper consultation as a result of which the employer had made its proposed change of commission terms far more reasonable, the employees would have remained intransigent and would still have refused those terms. In those circumstances, the tribunal applied a Polkey reduction by limiting the period of the compensatory award to four months – the period of time it would have taken, in the tribunal's view, for the employer to conduct proper consultation. The employees appealed, contending that the tribunal's speculation about what would have happened during consultation and the reaction of the employer at the end of this process fundamentally altered the reason for the dismissal. They claimed that it was not open to the tribunal to apply a Polkey reduction based on that degree of speculation and on a set of hypothetical circumstances that bore no relation to the actual dismissal which had taken place.

In rejecting the employees' contention, the Court of Appeal held that the Polkey principle is not limited to the same or similar facts as concerned the Polkey case itself. In particular, it does not apply only to cases where the employer has a valid reason for dismissal but has acted unfairly in its mode of reliance on that reason, so that any fair dismissal would have been for exactly the same reason. Lord Justice Buxton observed that the Polkey principle was merely an example of the general application of the requirements of S.123(1) ERA in awarding what is just and equitable having regard to the loss sustained by the complainant. In any event, on the particular facts of the instant case, his Lordship pointed out that the real dismissal and the hypothesised dismissal (i.e. the one based on what would have occurred had there been proper consultation) both entailed a refusal by the employees to accept changes to their terms. The reason for dismissal was therefore basically the same.

The facts of the Gover case are similar, in many ways, to those in Henderson **18.48** and ors v Mite Olscot Ltd EAT 0030/07. In that case employees were dismissed ostensibly for redundancy, having refused to agree to changes in their terms and conditions. An employment tribunal ruled that their dismissals were unfair on the basis that the real explanation for the decision to dismiss was not redundancy but that the employees delayed in accepting the changes to their terms and conditions. However, it declined to award a compensatory award because, as it transpired that the employer had ceased to trade on the same day as the dismissals, it was clear that the employees would have been dismissed in any event, so they had not suffered any loss. In the alternative, the tribunal reasoned that the employees were authors of their misfortune because the closure of the employer's business would not have occurred had they not dug their heels in about agreeing to changes to their pay terms. In those circumstances, it was not 'just and equitable' within the meaning of S.123(1) ERA to award compensation for loss.

On appeal to the EAT, the employees contended that the tribunal had erred by making a Polkey reduction in view of the fact that the employer's asserted reason for dismissal – redundancy – was found not to have been the real reason. The Appeal Tribunal, however, held that both planks of the tribunal's reasoning in declining to make a compensatory award had been correct. This was not a case where any issue of a Polkey reduction arose given that the closure of the business had coincided with the date of the dismissals and it had been shown that the dismissals would have occurred by reason of the closure in any event. As a result, the employees had sustained no loss on the basis of which they should have been compensated, and therefore there was no compensatory award from which to make any reduction. Additionally, the EAT ruled that the

653

tribunal's alternative reasoning – that it was just and equitable not to make any compensatory award – was one that was reasonably open to it in the circumstances. In so holding, the EAT implicitly rejected the employee's contention that a Polkey reduction can never be made where it transpires that the real reason for dismissal is different from that relied upon by the employer when dismissing.

In O'Donoghue v Redcar and Cleveland Borough Council 2001 IRLR 615, CA, the Court of Appeal held that where an employee had been found to have been unfairly dismissed on sex discriminatory grounds, the employment tribunal had been entitled to deploy Polkey-type reasoning to limit the period of loss. On the evidence, the tribunal concluded that the employee would have been dismissed in any event within six months by reason of her antagonistic and intransigent attitude.

18.49   **Cases where observance of a proper procedure would have delayed dismissal.** Even before the Polkey decision, an unfairly dismissed employee's compensation was sometimes limited to the period between dismissal and the time the employment would have been fairly terminated in any case (see, for example, Young's of Gosport Ltd v Kendell 1977 ICR 907, EAT). The most typical examples of this today are cases of redundancy dismissals that are unfair owing to lack of consultation but where a proper consultation would merely have delayed a fair dismissal. In such cases it will not be appropriate for the tribunal to award nil compensation because loss has clearly been sustained during the notional consultation period. In Mining Supplies (Longwall) Ltd v Baker 1988 ICR 676, EAT, B was found to have been unfairly dismissed for redundancy as there had not been appropriate consultation with him on his selection. The tribunal awarded him six weeks' pay for his compensatory award as it decided that this was how much time the necessary consultations would have taken, after which he would inevitably have been selected for redundancy anyway. The EAT upheld the decision to award compensation but reduced the amount. There was no principle that if the tribunal found that consultation would make no difference, no compensatory award should be made. However, each case depended on its own facts. In this case two weeks' pay was a reasonable amount to award for the time consultation would have taken.

However, the EAT took a different approach in Elkouil v Coney Island Ltd 2002 IRLR 174, EAT. In that case, a tribunal found that redundancy consultation should have begun ten weeks before dismissal. It further found that, as consultation would have prolonged E's employment by two weeks, E should be awarded a compensatory award equal to two weeks' pay. The EAT overturned this because if consultation had commenced when it should have, E would have had the benefit of looking for a new job ten weeks earlier than he actually did. This should have been reflected in a compensatory award of ten weeks.

18.50   In Walker and ors v Dysch Rosen Shoes Ltd and anor EAT 341–42/90 W was dismissed for a reason connected with the imminent transfer of the undertaking in which he worked. The tribunal held that even if the dismissal was for an 'economic, technical or organisational reason' (and thus not automatically unfair under the TUPE Regulations), it was still unfair in this case owing to procedural failings. The tribunal then reduced the compensatory award by 90 per cent on the ground that W's dismissal was inevitable because the new employer was clearly determined to dismiss him. The EAT said that the tribunal was wrong on this point: in assessing compensation, it should have gone on to consider whether W would have been dismissed fairly by his new employer (following proper procedures, etc). The EAT held that full compensation should be awarded for the period in which proper consultation would have taken place. The likelihood of a (fair) dismissal being inevitable (because consultation would have made no difference) was to be taken into account from this point on.

The same logic may apply in other types of case where a fair procedure would have delayed an otherwise inevitable dismissal. For example, Slaughter v C Brewer and Sons Ltd 1990 ICR 730, EAT, concerned an ill-health dismissal. Although the EAT remitted the case to a tribunal to hear further evidence on compensation, it canvassed the possibility that 'a dismissal may be unfair on procedural grounds yet it may be quite apparent from the medical evidence that an applicant was, at the date of dismissal, quite incapable of carrying out her or his proper function. In another case there may have been insufficient medical evidence, hence unfairness, but the subsequent investigation would have shown that the dismissal was inevitable. In such a case a possible view might be that such an investigation would have taken some days or weeks and that compensation should cover that period.'

It should be pointed out, however, that there is a difference between the nature of the procedural requirements in a redundancy case and those in, say, a case of dismissal for incapability. In the former, a reasonable consultation period will usually be between two and four weeks, so it will be quite reasonable to award full compensation for that period even if the dismissal was inevitable. In cases of incapability, however, an employer's failure to allow the employee an opportunity to improve before dismissing may represent a very considerable period by which a proper procedure would have delayed the dismissal. In such cases the tribunal may be more likely to seek to reduce the compensation by the relevant percentage figure from the outset – see the pre-Polkey case of Winterhalter Gastronom Ltd v Webb 1973 ICR 245, NIRC.

Cases of 'substantive' as opposed to 'procedural' unfairness. It has been 18.51
suggested in several cases that the Polkey principle applies only to cases where the unfairness of the dismissal derives from procedural failings rather than substantive injustice. The basic reasoning underlying this view is that it is only appropriate to speculate about what would have happened or might have happened in the context of procedural failings, since only in such cases is it feasible to construct the world as it might have been by positing what the fate of the employee would have been if the procedural failures had not occurred.

655

In contrast, it is far more difficult and, so the argument goes, neither just nor equitable to speculate about what would or might have been the position where an employee has been dismissed in circumstances that are substantively unfair – for example, because of the employer's lack of a reasonably held and genuine belief in the employee's misconduct, or, in a redundancy case, because of the inherent unfairness of the redundancy selection.

It is clear that the courts have struggled with the proposition that Polkey only applies to procedural unfair dismissals, but, after some doubt, they seem to have come down decisively in favour of rejecting it. Initially, the argument did hold sway. In Steel Stockholders (Birmingham) Ltd v Kirkwood 1993 IRLR 515, EAT, the EAT expressly stated that the Polkey principle did not apply where the decision to dismiss was substantively unfair. On the facts of the case before it, the Appeal Tribunal held that no reduction should be made since the reason the employee's redundancy dismissal was unfair was that the employer had adopted an artificially narrow pool for selection, thereby denying the employee the right to be compared with all the other employees who were involved in the employer's reorganisation. This was no mere procedural irregularity: rather, the employer's failure impugned the very basis for the dismissal itself and thus caused it to be substantively unfair. Accordingly, there were no grounds for assessing what might have happened had the employer adopted an appropriate pool for selection.

18.52   The chief problem with this decision, as other cases eventually made clear, is that the distinction between what is 'procedural' and what is 'substantive' is very difficult to draw. In O'Dea v ISC Chemicals Ltd 1996 ICR 222, CA, the Court of Appeal described the decision in Steel Stockholders (above) as 'controversial', and held the procedural/substantive distinction made in that case to be unwarranted. In O'Dea the tribunal had found the employee to have been dismissed for redundancy and not, as the employee claimed, by reason of his trade union activities. It went on to hold that the employee's dismissal was unfair because of a serious breach of procedure and reduced his compensatory award by 80 per cent to reflect the fact that he had only a one-in-five chance of being retained by the employer even if it had adopted a fair procedure. Upholding that decision when it reached the Court of Appeal, Lord Justice Peter Gibson observed: 'I do not regard it as helpful to characterise the defect as procedural or substantive nor in my view should the [employment] tribunal be expected to do so, though in fact in the present case the [employment] tribunal did repeatedly describe the defect as procedural. The fact of the matter is that the applicant lost only a one-in-five chance of being retained, and I can see no arguable case that he should have been compensated on the same footing as if he was bound to have been retained but for his trade union activities.'

However, although the Steel Stockholders decision should no longer be considered good law, there are a number of cases that warn against an over-zealous use of Polkey reductions. For example, in Chloride Ltd v Cain and anor EAT 564/94, EAT, a tribunal found that there had been a complete lack of consultation by the employer, no objective selection criteria and no consideration of possible alternative employment. The EAT rejected the employer's argument that the tribunal, in assessing compensation, should have reduced the award to reflect the chance that the employees could have been fairly dismissed if a proper procedure had been adopted. While the EAT accepted that the Steel Stockholders decision was wrong, it shared that decision's antipathy 'towards an employer who has used unfair criteria seeking to maintain subsequently that a different and fair basis of selection would or might have led to the same result'. The EAT stated that the tribunal was entitled to decide that the employer had used unfair criteria in selecting an employee for redundancy and that the overall justice and equity of the case was not much affected by the fact that other criteria might have been adopted. And in Eclipse Blinds Ltd v Bill EAT 818/92 the EAT stressed that the task of the tribunal was to take into account all the circumstances rather than to isolate one factor, such as whether consultation would have made any difference.

In King and ors v Eaton Ltd (No.2) 1998 IRLR 686, Ct Sess (Inner House), the Court of Session held that, in considering the question of what would have happened had the unfairness not occurred ('the hypothetical question', to use the phrase used by the EAT in Fisher v California Cake and Cookie Ltd 1997 IRLR 212, EAT), making a distinction between the 'merely' procedural and the more genuinely substantive will often be of some practical use. If there has been a merely procedural lapse or omission, it may be relatively straightforward to envisage what the course of events might have been if procedures had stayed on track. If, on the other hand, what went wrong was more fundamental, and seems to have gone 'to the heart of the matter', it may well be difficult to envisage what would have happened in the hypothetical situation of the unfairness not having occurred. In that case, the tribunal cannot be expected to 'embark on a sea of speculation'.

18.53

It may well be thought that the observations made by the Court of Session above offer a commonsense approach towards the issue of making Polkey reductions. The approach advocates the avoidance of too formulaic an application of the procedural/substantive distinction, while making it clear that in the case of seriously flawed dismissal procedures a tribunal cannot be expected to speculate about what might have happened had the employer acted totally differently. Even so, in subsequent decisions the Court of Appeal has downplayed the relevance of the distinction between procedural and substantive unfairness, as the case below illustrates.

In O'Donoghue v Redcar and Cleveland Borough Council 2001 IRLR 615, CA, a claimant unsuccessfully contended before the Court of Appeal that it was not open to a tribunal – in the light of the King decision – to make a finding on the inevitability of her dismissal, since her dismissal had been found to be

18.54

substantively unfair. The tribunal in that case had held that the claimant had been both unfairly dismissed and victimised, but that she would have been fairly dismissed in any event within six months because of her unacceptable attitude towards colleagues and the complaints that had arisen as a result of her behaviour. Accordingly, it limited her compensation to the period of six months during which her employment would have continued. The Court of Appeal rejected the employee's appeal, stating that: 'If the facts are such that an [employment] tribunal, while finding that an employee/applicant has been dismissed unfairly (whether substantively or procedurally), concludes that, but for the dismissal, the applicant would have been bound soon thereafter to be dismissed (fairly) by reason of some course of conduct or characteristic attitude which the employer reasonably regards as unacceptable but which the employee cannot or will not moderate, then it is just and equitable that compensation for the unfair dismissal should be awarded on that basis. We do not read Polkey or King v Eaton Ltd as precluding such an analysis...'

Taking their cue from this, more recent decisions of the appellate courts have moved away from a detailed discussion of the procedural/substantive issue and have shifted the focus on to whether and when tribunals come under an absolute duty to consider making a Polkey reduction whenever there is evidence to suggest that the employee might have been fairly dismissed, either when the unfair dismissal actually occurred or at some later date – see Gover v Propertycare Ltd 2006 ICR 1073, CA; Thornett v Scope 2007 ICR 236, CA, and Software 2000 Ltd v Andrews and ors 2007 ICR 825, EAT. While all these cases recognise the wisdom of the remarks made by Lord Prosser in the King case (see above), it is clear that the courts are increasingly reluctant to support the view that there is a clear dividing line between procedural and substantive unfairness, still less that such a line should be used to determine when it is and is not appropriate to make a Polkey reduction. This issue, along with the cases mentioned above, is further discussed below, under 'Tribunals' duty to consider making a Polkey reduction'.

18.55 Finally, it is interesting to note, with reference back to the King case, that the appellate courts will interfere with a Polkey percentage assessment by a tribunal on the ground that the unfairness of the dismissal was so unjust as to preclude any speculation about whether the employee could and would have been fairly dismissed at some later date. In Davidson v Industrial and Marine Engineering Services Ltd EAT 0071/03 the EAT quashed a tribunal's decision to make a 60 per cent Polkey reduction on the basis that the process adopted by the employer was so fundamentally flawed that it was impossible to assess the percentage chance of the claimant still being dismissed had a fair procedure been followed. A similar conclusion was reached by the EAT in Scotland in Manzie v Optos plc EAT S/0029/04, where the EAT quashed a finding of a 50 per cent Polkey reduction on the ground that it could not conceive how it could be said that dismissal could have been considered likely. The EAT ruled that the way in which the employee had been treated by the employer 'offends practically every aspect of fairness that can be imagined'.

Polkey reductions and redundancy. Although, as we have seen, the Polkey principle potentially covers all types of dismissal, it features particularly prominently in redundancy cases. Indeed, the EAT has held that an employment tribunal will be regarded as having erred in law if it fails to consider whether it is just and equitable to award full compensation in a case where the employer has failed to consult before a redundancy – Hepworth Refractories Ltd v Lingard EAT 555/90.

18.56

Where, in a redundancy case, the tribunal finds that a proper procedure might have led to an offer of *alternative employment*, it should identify the job that would have been offered and base its assessment of the employee's losses on the wages that would have been earned in that alternative job. Take the example of an employee who earned £400 per week before being made redundant without sufficient consultation. If the tribunal subsequently finds that proper consultation would have given the employee a 50 per cent chance of securing alternative employment with the employer in a post paying £300 per week, then the employee's losses for the purpose of calculating the compensatory award should be assessed at £150 per week (50 per cent of £300 per week) – see Red Bank Manufacturing Co Ltd v Meadows 1992 IRLR 209, EAT.

The above approach is illustrated by the case of Thompson Wholesale Foods v Norris EAT 800/92. There, the claimant was dismissed for redundancy but the tribunal found that his dismissal was unfair for lack of consultation and that, had the consultation been carried out, there was a chance that the employee would have accepted alternative employment in a job with lower pay. The employment tribunal awarded N compensation for a period of one year from the date of his dismissal, calculated at the rate of his pre-dismissal earnings. The EAT held that this was wrong: the tribunal should have assessed the chance that the outcome would have been different if a fair procedure had been followed and should also have determined the rate of pay that the employee would have been likely to receive in any new position.

18.57

One question that may arise in the context of considering whether alternative employment would have been offered and accepted by an employee if a fair consultation process had been undertaken is on whom the burden of proof lies to show that such employment would have been accepted by the employee and on what terms. In Virgin Media Ltd v Seddington and anor EAT 0539/08 the EAT held that the burden falls on the employee to show what job, or kind of job, he or she believes was available and to provide supporting evidence that such employment would have been accepted. This case is discussed in more detail in the section below.

─── 659

18.58   **Tribunals' duty to consider making a Polkey reduction**

A question of considerable practical importance is: in what circumstances does an employment tribunal have to consider whether to make a Polkey reduction? In King and ors v Eaton Ltd (No.2) 1998 IRLR 686, Ct Sess (Inner House), Lord Prosser (giving the lead judgment of the Court of Session) observed: '[T]he matter will be one of impression and judgement, so that a tribunal will have to decide whether the unfair departure from what should have happened was of a kind which makes it possible to say, with more or less confidence, that the failure makes no difference, or whether the failure was such that one cannot sensibly reconstruct the world as it might have been.' In many cases since, this statement has been expressly approved. However, at the same time as making this statement, Lord Prosser also accepted that a useful distinction might be drawn between procedural and substantive unfairness, and suggested that, in cases where dismissals are unfair owing to substantive unfairness, it might sometimes be a step too far for them to speculate about what could or would have been the case if the employee had not been fairly dismissed by the employer. We have already seen that this distinction is no longer one that finds judicial support. Instead, the Court of Appeal and the EAT have suggested that, regardless of the type of case or nature of the unfairness, employment tribunals will be expected to consider making a Polkey reduction whenever there is evidence to support the view that the employee might have been dismissed if the employer had acted fairly.

18.59   **Degree of speculation expected of tribunals.** In Gover and ors v Propertycare Ltd 2006 ICR 1073, CA, Lord Justice Buxton expressly approved the way in which His Honour Judge McMullen at EAT level had formulated the basis for considering whether or not a Polkey reduction should be made. In that case, the employment tribunal held that the compensatory award of employees who had been unfairly dismissed for refusing to agree to changes in their terms and conditions should be limited to four months' losses. That was the period of time the tribunal said it would have taken to conduct proper consultation about the proposed changes, at the end of which the employees would have been fairly dismissed, as it was likely, in the tribunal's view, that the employer would have offered more reasonable terms but the employees would have continued to reject these. On appeal, upholding the tribunal's Polkey reduction, HHJ McMullen observed: 'The tribunal [was] doing what it [was] engaged to do: to draw upon its industrial experience of circumstances such as this and to construct, from evidence not from speculation, a framework which is a working hypothesis about what would have occurred had the [employer] behaved differently and fairly... The criticism advanced by [counsel] is that in seeking to construct the hypothesis the tribunal had so many pieces of the jigsaw missing that the only correct approach was to disallow any kind of Polkey reduction, We do not accept that proposition because the findings, based upon a careful analysis of the material which it had before it, and drawing upon its experience, do indicate that it was satisfied that there was material sufficient to make a judgement.'

660 ───────────────────────────────────

The Court of Appeal's approval of HHJ McMullen's formulation suggests that tribunals may be required to hypothesise about 'what ifs' and 'maybes' in their deliberations as to remedy to a far greater extent than was previously understood. This impression has been reinforced by subsequent decisions of the Court of Appeal and the EAT, as discussed below.

18.60 In Thornett v Scope 2007 ICR 236, CA, an employee was dismissed when she refused to relocate after being suspended from work for bullying and harassing a colleague. An employment tribunal held that her dismissal was unfair, but it limited the compensatory award to six months' loss on the basis that if the employer had encouraged the parties in the dispute to try to work together this would have been bound to have resulted in failure after six months. On appeal, the EAT held that the tribunal had erred by launching itself upon 'a sea of speculation' and should have accepted that it could not, on the evidence before it, 'sensibly recreate the world as it might have been'. Given the evidence about how the parties could work together, it was wrong to place a limitation in time as to the duration of the relationship and to reduce the losses accordingly.

However, on further appeal, the Court of Appeal overturned the EAT's judgment and reinstated the decision of the employment tribunal. It held that a tribunal's task when assessing compensation for future loss of earnings will almost inevitably involve a consideration of uncertainties. Any assessment of future loss is by way of prediction and therefore involves a speculative element. A tribunal's statutory duty may involve making such predictions and tribunals cannot be expected, or even allowed, to opt out of that duty merely because their task is a difficult one and may involve speculation. Although there may be cases in which evidence to the contrary is so sparse that a tribunal should approach the question on the basis that loss of earnings would have continued indefinitely, whenever there is any evidence at all that it may not have been the case this must be taken into account. Applying this reasoning to the facts of the particular case, the tribunal had been entitled to limit the unfairly dismissed employee's compensation to a period of six months on the ground that her employment would in any event have ended within six months of her dismissal.

18.61 In Software 2000 Ltd v Andrews and ors 2007 ICR 825, EAT, Mr Justice Elias, the then President of the EAT, reviewed all the authorities on the application of Polkey, including the Gover and Scope cases (above), and summarised the principles to be extracted from them. These included:

- in assessing compensation for unfair dismissal, the employment tribunal must assess the loss flowing from that dismissal, which will normally involve an assessment of how long the employee would have been employed but for the dismissal

- if the employer contends that the employee would or might have ceased to have been employed in any event had fair procedures been adopted, the tribunal must have regard to all relevant evidence, including any evidence from the employee (for example, to the effect that he or she intended to retire in the near future)

- there will be circumstances where the nature of the evidence for this purpose is so unreliable that the tribunal may reasonably take the view that the exercise of seeking to reconstruct what might have been is so riddled with uncertainty that no sensible prediction based on the evidence can properly be made. Whether that is the position is a matter of impression and judgement for the tribunal

- however, the tribunal must recognise that it should have regard to any material and reliable evidence that might assist it in fixing just and equitable compensation, even if there are limits to the extent to which it can confidently predict what might have been; and it must appreciate that a degree of uncertainty is an inevitable feature of the exercise. The mere fact that an element of speculation is involved is not a reason for refusing to have regard to the evidence

- a finding that an employee would have continued in employment indefinitely on the same terms should only be made where the evidence to the contrary (i.e. that employment might have been terminated earlier) is so scant that it can effectively be ignored.

18.62 These principles have been consistently applied by the EAT in later cases, including Butler v GR Carr (Essex) Ltd EAT 0128/07; Wilson UK Ltd v Turton and anor EAT 0348/08; and Allied Distillers Ltd v Handley and ors EAT 0020–21/08. Of particular note is Elias J's observation that tribunals *must* have regard to any material and reliable evidence that might assist it in fixing just and equitable compensation even if there are limits to the extent to which it can confidently predict what might have been. At another point in his judgment, Elias J made it clear just how limited the scope is for tribunals to evade the task of making a Polkey reduction on the ground that determining what could or would have happened is just too speculative: 'The question is not whether the tribunal can predict with confidence all that would have occurred; rather it is whether it can make any assessment with sufficient confidence about what is likely to have happened, using its common sense, experience and sense of justice. It may not be able to complete the jigsaw but may have sufficient pieces for some conclusions to be drawn as to how the picture would have developed. For example, there may be insufficient evidence, or it may be too unreliable, to enable a tribunal to say with any precision whether an employee would, on the balance of probabilities, have been dismissed, and yet sufficient evidence for the tribunal to conclude that on any view there must have been some realistic chance that he would have been. Some assessment must be made of that risk when calculating the compensation even though it will be a difficult and to some extent speculative exercise.'

The way in which Elias J's guidance is likely to affect matters in practice is apparent from the outcome of the employer's appeal in the Software 2000 case itself. The employment tribunal had found that the claimants had been unfairly dismissed because the criteria that had been used to select them for redundancy were too subjective and had been improperly applied. The employer submitted that, even if the selection exercise had been properly conducted, the claimants would still have been dismissed. However, the tribunal declined to make a Polkey reduction on the grounds that the selection procedure was so flawed that it was impossible to say what the outcome would have been. On appeal, applying its own guidance to the facts as found, the EAT ruled that the tribunal had erred in law. In particular, it had ignored valid evidence that to some extent would have helped it to decide whether the employees would – absent the procedural failings – have been dismissed in any event. For example, two of the claimants, P and T, had received the lowest scores (44 and 48 respectively) out of a total pool of 22 employees. The 'break mark' had been set at 60, and the next lowest scored employee had been given a score of 59. The employer had conceded that T had been scored too low on one of the more acceptable criteria it had used in the redundancy exercise. But even accepting that, T would still have fallen well short of the break mark, alongside P, who had an even lower score. The EAT accepted that this was plainly evidence (among other examples) that the tribunal should have considered, and it was erroneous to have simply ignored that evidence or treated it as being too unreliable.

In the cases below, the EAT similarly concluded that employment tribunals fell into error by declining to consider making Polkey reductions on the ground that the exercise would be too speculative:

18.63

- **Secor Consulting Ltd v Meffen** EAT 0180/05: M, a highly paid employee responsible for securing lucrative accounts for S Ltd's consultancy business, was dismissed for redundancy after his failure to find sufficient new business to justify his salary. An employment tribunal found his dismissal unfair for lack of consultation. S Ltd contended that if proper dismissal procedures had been applied, M would either have been dismissed or would have accepted alternative employment at a lower salary. The tribunal accepted that it was a distinct possibility that M might have been offered (and accepted) continued employment at a lower salary, but it declined to make a Polkey reduction on this basis since it had 'no means of deciding at what level to place a hypothetical alternative salary'. On appeal, the EAT (by a majority) held that the tribunal had erred. Whether or not M would have accepted alternative employment or agreed to do the same job at a lower salary were matters that had been specifically raised by S Ltd. Moreover, it had adduced evidence as to what alternative employment options existed and the salaries applicable to those options. In these circumstances, the tribunal had an obligation, difficult though it was, to consider on the evidence before it what the percentage chance was that M

663

would have accepted an alternative job offer and at what level of salary. The case was remitted to enable this exercise to be undertaken

- **CEX Ltd v Lewis** EAT 0013/07: An employment tribunal found that L had been unfairly dismissed after being made redundant following a flawed procedure that involved no consultation. C Ltd had also not followed the statutory dismissal procedures applicable at that time. In consequence, the tribunal awarded a 10 per cent uplift in compensation due to the failure to observe the statutory procedures, but declined to make a Polkey reduction on the ground that, even if a proper consultation had occurred, there was a 100 per cent chance that L would have retained his job. On appeal, the EAT referred to the guidance given in Software 2000 Ltd v Andrews (see above), and in particular the point made in that case that a finding that an employee would have continued in employment indefinitely on the same terms should only be made where the evidence to the contrary (i.e. that employment might have been terminated earlier) is so scant that it can effectively be ignored. In this case there was evidence before the tribunal that L would still have been dismissed if proper consultation had taken place, and the tribunal had not found that evidence to be so unreliable or of so little substance that it could be ignored. Therefore, it had erred in law in finding that there was a 100 per cent certainty that L would have been retained

- **Wilson UK Ltd v Turton and anor** EAT 0348/08: T and L were unfairly dismissed by reason of redundancy owing to the complete lack of a proper procedure in selecting them from among a pool of five employees. The employment tribunal decided not to make any Polkey reduction because it reasoned that, as any one of the five employees could have performed the work of the others, and in view of the fundamental flaws in the procedure, it could not be certain that both T and L would inevitably have been selected for redundancy if a fair procedure had been followed. On appeal, the EAT held that the tribunal had erred. That the failure to consult was a fundamental defect did not preclude consideration of any assessment of the outcome if proper consultation had taken place. The tribunal's reasoning revealed that it was looking for 'certainty' of outcome rather than 'possibility'. Citing the guidance given by Elias J in the Software 2000 case (above), the EAT observed that certainty is not what is required when dealing with the possibilities inherent in a Polkey reduction. There were two important factors upon which such a reduction could, and indeed should, have been based in this case: (i) the tribunal had found that there was a genuine redundancy situation (making it inevitable that two of the five employees within the pool would have been dismissed had a proper procedure been followed); and (ii) both T and L had formed part of the pool. These factors were sufficient to trigger a Polkey reduction of some kind and the case was therefore remitted to enable the tribunal to reconsider its decision on this point.

Is tribunal under duty to consider Polkey of its own motion? In Boulton and   **18.64**
Paul Ltd v Arnold 1994 IRLR 532, EAT, the EAT held that the tribunal, having
found that the employer had adopted redundancy selection criteria that were
intrinsically unfair and different from those that had been agreed upon, was not
under any obligation to consider of its own motion whether the compensatory
award should have been reduced to reflect the possibility that the employee
might in any event have been dismissed under a fair procedure. However, that
decision contradicts the later one in Fisher v California Cake and Cookie Ltd
1997 IRLR 212, EAT, where it was held that in addressing the hypothetical
question as to whether adopting a fair procedure would have achieved the same
result, a tribunal must conduct its own investigation into the matter and reach
its own conclusion. In the EAT's view, where the tribunal determines that there
is any evidence at all to support the contention that dismissal might have
occurred in any event, it is necessary for it to go on to address the question of
whether the dismissal would or would not have occurred as a matter of
probability expressed in percentage terms. In many cases, the failure to address
this question will render the tribunal's approach flawed.

We would suggest that the approach adopted in the Fisher case sits more easily
with the flurry of recent cases – Gover, Scope and Software 2000 (all discussed
above) – which emphasise that if there is any evidence at all that the employee
would have been dismissed in any event, a tribunal cannot shirk its obligation
to consider making a Polkey reduction simply by saying that the exercise is too
speculative. Clearly, the upshot of any Polkey consideration will depend on the
actual evidence before the tribunal and, in this regard, an employer who wishes
to argue that the employee might have been dismissed in any event should
present the tribunal with some evidence to that effect. But essentially the duty
falls on to the tribunal to construct a 'working hypothesis' (to use HHJ
McMullen's phrase in Gover) as to what could or would have occurred. If the
tribunal fails to do this off its own bat it is likely to be regarded as having made
an error of law.

Burden of proof. In Britool Ltd v Roberts and ors 1993 IRLR 481, EAT, the   **18.65**
EAT stated that the burden of proving that an employee would have been
dismissed in any event was on the employer. While it is for the employee to show
what loss he or she has suffered as a result of the dismissal, this burden is not a
heavy one since the fact that there has been an unfair dismissal in itself creates a
prima facie loss. Accordingly, so long as the employee can put forward an
arguable case that he or she would have been retained were it not for the unfair
procedure, the evidential burden shifts to the employer to show that the dismissal
might have occurred even if a correct procedure had been followed. Thus, on the
facts of the case, the EAT held that the tribunal had not erred in declining to make
a Polkey reduction. Although the dismissed employee had performed very badly
in the employer's selection procedure, that procedure had been found to be unfair

— 665

and the employer had not adduced any evidence that a fair procedure would equally have led to the employee's dismissal.

In Virgin Media Ltd v Seddington and anor EAT 0539/08, the question arose whether a tribunal had erred in declining to make a Polkey reduction following a finding of unfair redundancy. It was clear from the evidence that the employees were unquestionably redundant and so would inevitably have lost their jobs even if a fair procedure had been applied. In those circumstances, the EAT held that the relevant consideration was whether, if the employer had acted fairly, the employees would have been offered and accepted alternative employment and, if so, on what terms. When undertaking a Polkey exercise in this form, the Appeal Tribunal observed that the burden does not necessarily fall entirely on the employer to adduce evidence about what would have happened. The employer may well have the initial burden of showing that there was no suitable employment that the employee could or would have accepted and for providing appropriate evidential support for that assertion. But once the employer raises a prima facie case to this effect, the burden shifts onto the employee to show what actual or type of job he or she believes was available and to provide supporting evidence that such employment would have been accepted.

18.66 On the facts of the particular case, the EAT conceded that it was not easy to judge whether the burden had shifted on to the employees. A list of available jobs had been put before the tribunal and it would have been easy for the claimants to flesh out the vague generalities made about these in their witness statements by identifying particular jobs on the list which they would or might have accepted. But it was also arguable that the employer had not itself done enough to put the issue into play. The case was therefore remitted to the tribunal to determine whether a Polkey reduction issue arose and, if appropriate, to determine the level of reduction.

The EAT in Seddington also made the more general point that reliance on burden of proof in borderline cases was inherently unsatisfactory. Mr Justice Underhill observed: 'In the field of compensation in particular, there may often be uncertainty as to precisely who has to prove what, and in what degree of detail, before the burden shifts to the other party. Parties would be well advised to make clear well in advance of any hearing what their case is on any point of importance, irrespective of the burden of proof, and be prepared to adduce appropriate evidence (and if necessary seek appropriate disclosure). It is not right that tribunals should have to consider the [Polkey] issue on the basis of inadequate evidence – or, in extreme cases, decline to decide it at all – because the parties have failed to anticipate it or because each has thought that the burden was on the other.'

18.67 **Requirement to provide adequate reasons.** In Whitehead v Robertson Partnership EAT 0331/01 the EAT stressed the importance of employment tribunals adequately explaining their reasons for making a Polkey reduction. In the EAT's view, it was incumbent upon the tribunal to demonstrate its analysis of the hypothetical question by explaining its conclusions on the following:

- what potentially fair reason for dismissal, if any, might emerge as a result of a proper investigation and disciplinary process?

- depending on the principal reason for any future hypothetical dismissal, would dismissal for that reason be fair or unfair?

- even if a potentially fair dismissal was available, would the employer in fact have dismissed the employee as opposed to imposing some lesser penalty, and if so, would that have ensured the employee's continued employment?

The need for tribunals to articulate the evidential and factual bases for their conclusions is apparent from the EAT's decision in Photo Corporation (UK) Ltd v Truelove EAT 0054/04. In that case T, a loyal and hardworking employee of 15 years' standing, became involved with an ex-colleague. When the ex-colleague began working for a competitor, T was immediately suspended from work due to confidentiality concerns. She resigned and claimed unfair constructive dismissal. A tribunal awarded her a compensatory award and chose not to make a Polkey reduction. On appeal, the EAT remitted the question of a Polkey reduction to the tribunal on the basis that the tribunal should have considered the inevitability of T's dismissal. The tribunal, reconsidering the issue, 'guestimated' that there was a 66 per cent chance that T would have retained her employment had a fair procedure been followed, and therefore applied this reduction to her compensatory award. **18.68**

When the matter returned to the EAT on further appeal, the Appeal Tribunal accepted that the tribunal had been right to come up with a hypothetical answer, but noted that the answer should be one that was reasoned and based on the facts. The tribunal had given no clue as to why it had reached the 66 per cent figure. The question that the tribunal should have asked itself was: if proper and full consultation had taken place, would a solution have been reached to resolve the employer's concerns about leakage of confidential information that would have allowed T to remain in her post or an alternative post? The EAT concluded that the tribunal was bound to decide that, following a three-week consultation period (as the tribunal had decided would have been appropriate), there was a 100 per cent chance that T would have been dismissed. The EAT therefore substituted this finding in place of the tribunal's and accordingly reduced T's compensatory award to nil.

Amount of reduction

In any case where the employer has dismissed for a substantively fair reason but has failed to follow a fair procedure, the compensatory award (but not the basic award) may be reduced – potentially to nil – so long as it can be shown that a fair procedure would have resulted in a dismissal anyway. The logic for a nil award (or to express it differently, a 100 per cent reduction) is that any **18.69** procedural failure that served to render the dismissal unfair made absolutely no difference: the outcome would have been exactly the same even if a fair procedure had been adopted. The phrase 'exactly the same' in this context means that the employee would have been fairly dismissed on the same date as he or she was unfairly dismissed.

So, for example, in Cormack v Saltire Vehicles Ltd EAT 209/90 a car mechanic was dismissed for misconduct after he left one vehicle in a dangerous condition and failed to carry out an MOT test properly on another. He was refused an internal appeal, despite having a contractual right to one. The employment tribunal found his dismissal unfair as a result of this breach of procedure, but held that it was not just and equitable to make a compensatory award as the employer had, in all other respects, acted reasonably, and a fuller appeal procedure would ultimately have made no difference at all. The EAT upheld this decision on appeal.

18.70 The obverse finding – that had a proper procedure been carried out there was a 100 per cent likelihood of the employee not only retaining his or her employment but doing so on exactly the same terms and conditions – will lead the tribunal to conclude that it is not just and equitable to reduce the compensatory award to any extent at all. Such a finding is tantamount to concluding that the employee would have remained employed indefinitely by the employer. But one only has to ask how many of us have such security of tenure in our jobs to realise that absolute certainty will be rare. Accordingly, a 100 per cent finding that a claimant's employment would not at any point have been fairly terminated should only be made if the evidence to the contrary is so scant that it can be effectively ignored – Software 2000 Ltd v Andrews and ors 2007 ICR 825, EAT.

18.71 **No 'all or nothing' approach.** In the Polkey case, Lord Bridge was at pains to point out that there is no need for an 'all or nothing' approach when making an appropriate reduction. He cited with approval the case of Sillifant v Powell Duffryn Timber Ltd 1983 IRLR 91, EAT, in which Mr Justice Browne-Wilkinson pointed out that 'if the… tribunal thinks there is a doubt whether or not the employee would have been dismissed, this element can be reflected by reducing the normal amount of compensation by a percentage representing the chance that the employee would still have lost his employment'. Thus it would be quite reasonable to make a 20 per cent award if, for example, there is only a one in five chance that a fair procedure would have made any difference to the outcome.

The following are examples of this approach being put into practice:

- **Akram v Rieter Automotive Carpets Ltd** EAT 1319/95: A was made redundant and refused an offer of alternative employment. A tribunal found that the dismissal was procedurally unfair but awarded no compensation on the ground that a proper procedure would have made no difference. The

EAT held that the decision not to make an award was inconsistent with the tribunal's finding that, if a proper procedure had been adopted, there was a chance that A would have accepted the alternative job offer. The case was therefore remitted for the tribunal to calculate the compensatory award on the basis of the percentage chance of A accepting the alternative work

- **Wolesley Centers Ltd v Simmons** 1994 ICR 503, EAT: W's dismissal for redundancy was unfair because there had been no consultation or warning and no attempt to find alternative employment. In assessing compensation, the tribunal chose not to make a Polkey reduction because it took the view that 'on a balance of probabilities' the employee would not have been dismissed had a proper procedure been followed. The EAT held that the tribunal had fallen into the error of adopting an 'all or nothing' approach. In cases where it is reasonably clear that the employee would not have been dismissed following a fair procedure, there is no need for a percentage assessment of the chance of a different outcome. But it was clear from the tribunal's reference to the 'balance of probabilities', and its acknowledgement that the recession would have made it difficult for the employer to find the employee an alternative position, that the tribunal considered the issue in this case to be far from clear-cut. Accordingly, it should have assessed the chance that the employee would have been retained had the employer behaved fairly.

Is a 'percentage approach' to reductions always appropriate? An employment **18.72** tribunal's assessment of whether a proper procedure would have made any difference is usually made on a percentage basis. So if, for example, a tribunal assesses in an unfair redundancy case that there was a 20 per cent likelihood that the employee would not have been selected for redundancy had a proper consultation process taken place, the tribunal should award full compensation for the period over which consultation should notionally have occurred. It should then apply an 80 per cent reduction to the compensation for losses beyond this point. The following case confirms this approach, while also demonstrating the high level of speculation often required of the tribunal in such cases:

- **Walker and ors v Dysch Rosen Shoes Ltd and anor** EAT 341–42/90: W was dismissed for a reason connected with the imminent transfer of the undertaking in which he worked. The tribunal held that even if the dismissal was for an 'economic, technical or organisational reason' (and thus not automatically unfair under the relevant TUPE Regulations), it was still unfair in this case owing to procedural failings. The tribunal then reduced the compensatory award by 90 per cent on the ground that W's dismissal was inevitable because the new employer was clearly determined to dismiss him. The EAT said that the tribunal was wrong on this point: in assessing compensation, it should have gone on to consider whether W would have been dismissed fairly by his new employer (following proper procedures, etc). The EAT held that full compensation should be awarded for the period

669

in which proper consultation would have taken place. The likelihood of a (fair) dismissal being inevitable (because consultation would have made no difference) was to be taken into account from this point on.

18.73 Making a percentage reduction is not, however, the correct method of proceeding where a tribunal categorically finds that the employee would have been dismissed in any event at the end of the period during which fair procedures were applied. In such a case the compensatory award will properly be confined to compensating the employee for the losses he or she has sustained during the time it would have taken for a fair procedure to be completed. A percentage reduction is not appropriate because there is an absolute cut-off date representing the date when the employee would have been dismissed – fairly – in any event. Up until that date, he or she would be entitled to recover full losses since these are directly attributable to the unfair dismissal. But from that date forwards, he or she suffers no further loss at all. This approach was approved by the Court of Appeal in O'Donoghue v Redcar and Cleveland Borough Council 2001 IRLR 615, CA.

However, as the Akram and Wolesley Centers cases (discussed above) demonstrate, this straightforward 'limiting the loss period' approach is not feasible where the tribunal is far less certain as to whether employment would have continued had the employee not been unfairly dismissed. In such circumstances it will still be appropriate for a tribunal to apply a percentage approach to its assessment of likelihood. So, for example, in an incapability dismissal context, a tribunal might conclude there was a 75 per cent chance that the employee's performance would not have sufficiently improved over, say, a three-month review period. In other words, after three months there was only a 25 per cent chance of the employee avoiding a fair dismissal. In those circumstances, assuming the employee's net salary was £1,000 a month and that he was entitled to one month's notice, the correct calculation of the compensatory award would be:

- 3 x £1,000 (i.e. salary over the notional performance review period) plus

- 1 x £1,000 (i.e. salary during the notional notice period) plus

- 25 per cent x £1,000 (i.e. £250) x as many months/years as the tribunal feels is just and equitable to reflect the employee's ongoing loss.

It is the last-mentioned head of loss that reflects the Polkey reduction.

18.74 **Reduction applies to all heads of compensatory award.** In Hope v Jordan Engineering Ltd EAT 0545/07 the question arose whether the Polkey reduction applied to all heads of loss comprising the compensatory award, including, for example, compensation for loss of statutory rights or long notice. In this particular case, the tribunal had applied a 100 per cent reduction to an employee's compensatory award on the basis that, even if a fair redundancy procedure had been applied, she would have been dismissed in any event. The

EAT ruled that this reduction covered all heads of the compensatory award. Giving the Appeal Tribunal's judgment, His Honour Judge Peter Clark remarked: 'It seems to us that there is no warrant in Polkey v AE Dayton Services Ltd... for the proposition that any head of [the] compensatory award escapes the Polkey deduction. Once a tribunal finds that it is a 100 per cent Polkey deduction case, there is no purpose in carrying out an assessment of loss under the compensatory award.'

Driving home this point, HHJ Clark, when turning to the uplift of between 10 and 50 per cent that should notionally have been applied to the compensatory award in order to penalise the employer for breaching the statutory dismissal and disciplinary procedures that then applied, observed: 'If there is no compensatory award as here, no uplift falls to be applied... That makes sense to us. 10–50 per cent of 0 still equals 0.' Notwithstanding the repeal of the statutory procedures, these comments may have continuing validity in view of the power under S.207A TULR(C)A to adjust the compensatory award upwards or downwards in respect of flagrant breaches of the Acas Code of Practice on Disciplinary and Grievance Procedures. For further details, see under 'Adjustments for breach of Acas Code of Practice' below.

Relationship with contributory conduct
18.75

The legal basis for making Polkey reductions under S.123(1) ERA and reductions on account of employees' contributory conduct under S.123(6) ERA are very different (the latter are discussed in detail immediately below). In particular, the evidence that is germane to whether or not an employee has 'caused or contributed' to his or her dismissal may not be the same as that relevant to assessing what is 'just and equitable' to award the complainant having regard to the loss sustained in consequence of the unfair dismissal. An unwary tribunal can easily fall into the trap of blurring the line between the two different types of reduction.

In some cases, an employment tribunal may have good grounds for making both types of reduction. For example, it might find that there was a 50 per cent chance that the employee would have been dismissed even if a fair procedure had been followed and also that the employee was 20 per cent to blame for the dismissal in the first place. In Rao v Civil Aviation Authority 1994 ICR 495, CA, the Court of Appeal rejected the contention that the making of both deductions would amount to a double penalty for the employee. The Court held that the proper approach of tribunals in these circumstances is first to assess the loss sustained by the employee in accordance with S.123(1), which will include the percentage deduction to reflect the chance that he or she would have been dismissed in any event. The tribunal should then make the deduction for contributory fault.

However, in deciding the extent of the employee's contributory conduct and the amount by which it would be just and equitable to reduce the award for that

671

reason under S.123(6), the Court made it clear in the Rao case that the tribunal should bear in mind that there has already been a deduction under S.123(1). This point was considered and further elucidated in Cox v Camden London Borough Council 1996 ICR 815, EAT. There, the EAT explained that the rationale was that where a percentage reduction has already been made on account of contributory fault, this may have some influence on the percentage reduction a tribunal chooses when applying a 'just and equitable' reduction under S.123(1) ERA (e.g. when applying Polkey).

18.76 ## Adjustments for breach of Acas Code of Practice

On 1 October 2004 provisions contained in the Employment Act 2002 were brought into force that made it obligatory to comply with certain statutory dismissal and disciplinary procedures (DDPs). A failure to comply with these would have a significant impact on the amount of the compensatory award that a claimant might hope to receive following a finding of unfair dismissal. In particular, tribunals were obliged, in appropriate circumstances, to increase the compensatory award by at least 10 per cent and up to a maximum of 50 per cent where a DDP had not been completed and the failure was attributable to the employer.

The way in which these statutory procedures worked in practice attracted a high level of criticism. Suffice it to say that, following a Government-commissioned review, the statutory provisions were repealed with effect from 6 April 2009 and were replaced by a much less prescriptive regime aimed at encouraging dispute resolution in the workplace. This new regime centres on the Acas Code of Practice on Disciplinary and Grievance Procedures ('the Code'), as explained below.

18.77 ### Relevance of the Code

Although the Acas Code has been in existence since 1977, its provisions were amended and expanded to coincide with the legislative changes just mentioned. Crucially, for present purposes, the potential for adjusting the compensatory award has been retained in order to penalise serious breaches of the Code. The scope of such adjustments are discussed in detail below. For details of the contents of the Code and when it applies, see Chapter 3, under 'Fairness of internal procedure – the Acas Code of Practice'.

In accordance with S.207 of the Trade Union and Labour Relations (Consolidation) Act 1992 (TULR(C)A), the revised Code is admissible in any employment tribunal proceedings and the tribunal is obliged to take into account any relevant provision of the Code when determining those proceedings. A breach of the Code does not in itself give rise to legal proceedings; but a failure by either party to abide by its provisions will be taken into account by a tribunal as evidence when determining a relevant claim.

672

Accompanying the Code (which is 11 pages long) is an 82-page non-statutory guide, 'Discipline and grievances at work' ('the Acas guide'). This provides more detailed advice and guidance, much of which was taken from the 2004 version of the Code. It is designed to complement the Code and contains a number of sample disciplinary and grievance procedures. However, tribunals are not obliged to take this Guide into account when reaching a decision. Both Code and Guide are available on the Acas website (www.acas.org.uk/drr).

Impact of the Code on unfair dismissal claims. With specific regard to unfair dismissal, the Code impacts on claims in relation to both liability and remedy. The employer's compliance with the Code is a factor to be taken into account when determining the reasonableness of the dismissal in accordance with the statutory test of reasonableness under S.98(4) ERA. If the dismissal is found to be unfair, compliance by both employer and employee is then taken into account when determining whether there should be an adjustment to any compensatory award made under S.207A(2) or (3) TULR(C)A. Compliance is also relevant to the question of compensation where the disciplinary procedures result in a claim being brought under one of the other jurisdictions listed in Schedule A2 to the TULR(C)A, e.g. a claim for unlawful detriment or wrongful or discriminatory dismissal. **18.78**

With regard to the provisions of the Code dealing with grievances (as opposed to disciplinary procedures), these do not impose liability on the employer because no claim specifically arises from an employer's failure to follow a fair procedure in and of itself. However, a breach of these provisions may be relevant to both parties in relation to the adjustment of any award made by a tribunal in respect of a successful claim brought by the employee. This is because an alleged failure to deal adequately with a grievance could be evidence of, for example, discrimination. Equally, a failure to deal adequately with a grievance may amount to a breach of contract leading to a constructive dismissal claim.

Full details of the Code can be found in IDS Employment Law Supplement, 'Disciplinary and Grievance Procedures' (June 2009).

Increase/reduction in compensatory award
18.79

Section 207A(2) TULR(C)A provides that: 'If, in any proceedings to which this section applies, it appears to the employment tribunal that – (a) the claim to which the proceedings relate concerns a matter to which a relevant Code of Practice applies, (b) the employer has failed to comply with that Code in relation to that matter, and (c) the failure was unreasonable, the employment tribunal may, if it considers it just and equitable in all the circumstances to do so, increase any award it makes to the employee by no more than 25%'.

An identical provision in respect of any failure to comply by an employee is set out in S.207(A)(3). This reflects the fact that the Code is aimed at

673

encouraging compliance by both employers *and* employees, so an employee's failure to follow the Code in respect of disciplinary action commenced by the employer or in respect of a grievance raised by him or her is as likely to lead to a compensation adjustment as a failure by the employer to follow the correct procedures.

18.80 The all-important list of proceeding (or 'jurisdictions') to which Ss.207A(2) and (3) apply are set out in Schedule A2 TULR(C)A. Unfair dismissal is included in the list, along with other types of proceedings such as discrimination complaints, unauthorised deductions from wages, breach of the Working Time Regulations 1998 and breach of contract claims arising on or outstanding at the date of termination of employment. S.207(A)(6) empowers the Secretary of State to add or subtract jurisdictions to or from the list.

Section 207A(4) TULR(C)A makes it clear that the reference in S.207A(2) and (3) to 'a relevant Code of Practice' is to any Code which 'relates exclusively or primarily to procedure for the resolution of disputes'. The only Code that currently applies under this provision is the revised Acas Code of Practice on Disciplinary and Grievance Procedures.

18.81 **Adjustment only applies to compensatory award.** By virtue of S.124A ERA, it is clear that any adjustment made in accordance with S.207A TULR(C)A applies to the compensatory award only. In other words, the adjustment – whether taking the form of an uplift in favour of the employee or a reduction in favour of the employer – does not apply to the basic award, protective award or any other type of compensation awardable by a tribunal.

18.82 **Unreasonable failure to comply.** The potential for adjustment to the compensatory award under S.207A TULR(C)A only applies if the employer's or employee's failure to comply with the provisions of the Code is 'unreasonable'. This implies that a failure to follow the reasonable standards may be reasonable. That said, it seems likely that, in unfair dismissal cases, adjustments will be fairly common. This is because, as mentioned above, a failure to follow the Code is relevant to the question of liability as well as remedy and may render the dismissal procedurally unfair under S.98(4) ERA on the ground that the employer has not acted reasonably in all the circumstances. It is difficult to envisage a situation in which a tribunal could find that an employer has acted unreasonably in failing to comply with the Code when deciding on liability but then go on to hold that that failure was reasonable when it comes to deciding whether there should be an uplift in compensation. And if it does, can it really be said that the dismissal was unfair in the first place? It seems that remedies hearings generally are likely to become more protracted in future as parties put forward arguments concerning the reasonableness or otherwise of a failure to follow the Code.

18.83 **Tribunal's discretion: 'just and equitable'.** Where there has been an unreasonable failure to comply with the Code, the tribunal may increase or reduce the award where it 'considers it just and equitable in all the circumstances to do so'. This terminology is very similar to that used under the old statutory dispute resolution procedures, so tribunals may well rely on case law decided under that regime when deciding the amount of adjustment, if any. Some of these cases are discussed below.

In Butler v GR Carr (Essex) Ltd EAT 0128/07 His Honour Judge McMullen was reluctant to set out general principles for establishing the amount of any adjustment to penalise breaches of the statutory provisions, stressing that it is for the tribunal to do what it considers just and equitable in the circumstances and that there are 'unlimited matters' to be considered. However, in Lawless v Print Plus EAT 0333/09, the current President of the EAT, Mr Justice Underhill, was much more forthcoming about the considerations that were relevant when determining whether, and to what extent, compensatory awards should be uplifted to penalise employers' failures. His Lordship pointed out that although the phrase 'just and equitable in all the circumstances' connoted a broad discretion, the relevant circumstances were confined to those which were related in some way to the failure to comply with the statutory procedures. We would suggest that similar reasoning applies, mutatis mutandis, to breaches of the Acas Code.

So, for example, the uplift ought not be used by a tribunal to mark its disapproval of the employer's conduct in respect of unrelated matters – see Aptuit (Edinburgh) Ltd v Kennedy EAT 0057/06. The EAT adopted similar reasoning in Drewett v Penfold EAT 0395/09 when holding that an employment tribunal had erred in limiting an uplift to 20 per cent solely because the employer (a sole trader) had been going through a distressing family situation after the loss of his wife. The tribunal made it clear that, but for that consideration, it would have awarded a higher percentage uplift. The EAT ruled that this factor was irrelevant because (a) it was a circumstance outwith the employer's role as an employer and the employment relationship generally; and (b) it was not a circumstance surrounding, related to or causally resulting in the failure to complete the statutory procedure. The EAT substituted a finding of 50 per cent uplift (the maximum awardable for breach of the statutory procedures).

18.84 In the Lawless case (above) Underhill J acknowledged that the relevant circumstances to be taken into account by tribunals when considering uplifts would vary from case to case but would always include the following:

- whether the procedures were applied to some extent or were ignored altogether

- whether the failure to comply with the procedures was deliberate or inadvertent, and

- whether there were circumstances that mitigated the blameworthiness of the failure to comply.

Furthermore, the size and resources of the employer were capable of amounting to a relevant factor in the tribunal's consideration of whether an uplift was

675

appropriate and, if so, how much. Relevance would depend on whether that factor aggravated or mitigated the culpability and/or seriousness of the employer's failure. But it should not be thought that failures by small businesses were always to be thought of as venial.

18.85 **Level of uplift.** Under the now-repealed statutory DDPs, tribunals had a discretion to award uplifts in favour of employees of up to 50 per cent. Save where there were exceptional circumstances, the minimum uplift was 10 per cent. This contrasts with the current position in respect of breaches of the Acas Code where the maximum limit is 25 per cent. As yet, there is very little case law to help establish the approach tribunals should adopt towards these uplifts. But the general view is that, given the much reduced ceiling, the EAT and higher courts are likely to be even less willing to interfere in the amount of an uplift awarded by tribunals than they were before under the old procedures. Even in respect of these, the EAT had made it clear that it would be slow to interfere with decisions on the level of uplift – see Home Office v Khan and anor EAT 0257/07 (a decision that was unsuccessfully appealed to the Court of Appeal on a separate point).

Nevertheless, the legal bases on which the EAT did from time to time interfere with tribunals' decisions on this issue are instructive, in that they may well provide useful guidance for tribunals when dealing with breaches of the Code. One point that emerges forcefully and consistently is that tribunals are expected to give clear, albeit brief, reasons to explain why they alighted on one particular percentage as opposed to another when awarding an uplift.

18.86 In McKindless Group v McLaughlin 2008 IRLR 678, EAT, Lady Smith set out what was quite a prescriptive approach to how tribunals should approach uplifts in the context of the DDPs. She made it clear that the discretion accorded to tribunals to go beyond the minimum 10 per cent should only be exercised by reference to particular facts or circumstances surrounding the failure to complete the statutory procedure that made it just and equitable that the employer should be penalised further. There was no room for exercising the discretion where there was no evidence from which the tribunal could make findings of fact as to the circumstances surrounding the dismissal and how and why it was that the failure to complete the statutory procedure occurred. The mere failure to carry out any stage of the three-stage statutory procedure would not necessarily point to an uplift beyond the minimum. It would depend on the circumstances of the failure, including the level of culpability concerned. Furthermore, the employer was not, in Lady Smith's view, obliged to explain the failure. This meant that the evidential burden was firmly on the employee to place material before the tribunal in support of any argument that uplift should be greater than 10 per cent.

On the facts of the McKindless case, the employment tribunal had awarded an employee a 50 per cent uplift in his compensatory award on account of the employer's complete failure to carry out the DDP. The tribunal was persuaded to award the maximum uplift because the employer had conceded only at a late stage that the employee's dismissal was automatically unfair owing to its failure to comply with the statutory procedure. Had the employer conceded earlier, it was possible that the case would have settled. On appeal, the EAT held that this was an entirely irrelevant consideration. As the tribunal had not given any additional reason for awarding the 50 per cent uplift, the EAT allowed the employer's appeal and substituted an uplift of 10 per cent.

It is clear from both the McKindless case and other EAT decisions that one **18.87** important factor in determining the level of an uplift is the degree of culpability on the part of the defaulting party. In Virgin Media Ltd v Seddington and anor EAT 0539/08 the EAT overturned a 40 per cent uplift awarded partly on the basis that, in awarding this, the tribunal had not expressly considered the issue of culpability at all. The obverse happened in Lawless v Print Plus (discussed above). There, the EAT held that where there had been wholesale failure to comply with the statutory procedures, aggravated by the employer's deliberate and intemperate refusal to permit an appeal (which was the third stage of the three-stage statutory DDPs), the starting point for the tribunal's consideration of the appropriate uplift should have been at or close to the top of the scale (i.e. 50 per cent). Although the small scale of the employer's business and the haste with which the decision to dismiss had been taken were both relevant factors, the tribunal had given too much weight to them when awarding an uplift of only 10 per cent given the degree of culpability on the employer's part. The EAT accordingly substituted a 40 per cent uplift.

In other cases, where it is clear that tribunals have specifically addressed the **18.88** matter of culpability, the EAT has been content to uphold the levels of uplift awarded. For example, in Metrobus Ltd v Cook EAT 0490/06 the Appeal Tribunal upheld an uplift of 40 per cent for a 'blatant' breach of the statutory procedure, accepting the tribunal's view that the provision was 'more penal than compensatory in nature'. A similar approach was taken by another division of the EAT in CEX Ltd v Lewis EAT 0013/07, when it held that the reason for the employer's failure to complete a statutory disciplinary procedure was ignorance rather than deliberate disregard, and this entitled a tribunal to limit the uplift to the 10 per cent minimum adjustment under the statutory procedures.

A further matter that might influence the level of uplift is the size of the total compensation awarded. In Abbey National plc and anor v Chagger 2010 ICR 397, CA, an employment tribunal awarded almost £2.8 million to a claimant found to have been both unfairly dismissed and discriminated against on the ground of his racial origins. The tribunal awarded an uplift of only 2 per cent, utilising a specific provision in the Employment Act 2002 to award less than the normal minimum of

677

10 per cent for non-compliance with the statutory procedures if there were 'exceptional circumstances' for doing so. In this particular case the tribunal had calculated that a 10 per cent uplift would have resulted in the employer being penalised to the extent of almost £300,000 in respect of its procedural failings. In the tribunal's view, the size of the award made the circumstances of this case exceptional. On appeal, both the EAT and the Court of Appeal upheld the tribunal's decision on this point. Lord Justice Elias, giving the judgment of the Court of Appeal, observed that 'we do not think Parliament would have intended the sums awarded to be wholly disproportionate to the nature of the breach'.

18.89 Although the Chagger case was concerned with a specific statutory provision governing the now defunct statutory procedures, it arguably established the broader principle that a tribunal can take into account the overall level of compensation when considering what adjustment to make. In that case, it will continue to be justified for a tribunal to take this consideration into account when setting the level of uplift (if any) which it deems to be just and equitable to award for breach of the Acas Code.

18.90
Adjustments for failure to provide written particulars

Section 38 of the Employment Act 2002 states that tribunals must award compensation to an employee where, upon a successful claim being made under any of the tribunal jurisdictions listed in Schedule 5, it becomes evident that the employer was in breach of his duty to provide full and accurate written particulars under S.1 ERA 1996 – Ss.38(1)–(3) EA 2002. This duty is covered in full in IDS Employment Law Handbook, 'Contracts of Employment' (2009), Chapter 3.

The list of jurisdictions set out in Schedule 5 is fairly extensive and includes unfair dismissal. S.38 does not give employees a free-standing right to claim compensation for failure to provide full and accurate written particulars. The right to compensation is dependent upon a successful claim being brought by the employee under one of the jurisdictions listed in Schedule 5. However, an award under S.38 is not dependent on a claim having been brought under S.11 ERA for a breach by the employer of the duty imposed by S.1. It is sufficient that the tribunal make a finding at the hearing that the employer was in breach of S.1 at the time the main proceedings were begun.

The crucial date for determining whether the employer was in breach of the rules on written particulars is the date on which the main proceedings were begun by the employee – S.38(2)(b) and (3)(b) EA 2002.

18.91 **Amount of award.** The tribunal must award the 'minimum amount' of two weeks' pay and may, if it considers it just and equitable in the circumstances, award the 'higher amount' of four weeks' pay – S.38(2), (3) and (4) EA 2002. The tribunal does not have to make any award under S.38 if there are exceptional circumstances which would make an award or increase unjust or inequitable – S.38(5) EA 2002.

An award made under S.38 is on top of any award the tribunal may already have made in respect of the main claim, but is not dependent on the making of any such award. The tribunal can still make an award for failure to give written particulars where it has found in favour of the employee in the main claim but has not awarded compensation – S.38(2).

A 'week's pay' is calculated in accordance with Ss.220–229 ERA and is limited to the maximum under S.227 (currently £380) – S.38(6) EA 2002. The date of calculation is either the date on which main proceedings were commenced or, if the employee was no longer employed at that date, the effective date of termination of employment – S.38(7) EA 2002. For details of how to calculate a week's pay for these purposes, see IDS Employment Law Handbook, 'Wages' (2003), Chapter 11. **18.92**

In an unfair dismissal claim, any S.38 increase is applied to the compensatory award *before* the application of the statutory maximum (currently £65,300) – S.124A ERA. For more detail on the order in which deductions and increases are made to compensatory awards, see under 'Order of adjustments and deductions' below.

Contributory conduct
18.93

Section 123(6) ERA states that: '[W]here the tribunal finds that the dismissal was to any extent caused or contributed to by any action of the complainant, it shall reduce the… compensatory award by such proportion as it considers just and equitable having regard to that finding.' This ground for making a reduction is commonly referred to as 'contributory conduct' or 'contributory fault' – the latter being the term used extensively in the context of damages for tort, where plaintiffs are similarly liable to have their damages awards reduced on account of actions of their own that contributed to the injury or wrong suffered.

Differences between compensatory and basic award reductions. Under the ERA 1996, there is an equivalent provision for reduction of the basic award – see S.122(2). However, the actual statutory language used in respect of that particular reduction differs from that used in S.122(6) regarding reductions in the compensatory award. In the light of this difference of wording, the EAT in Optikinetics Ltd v Whooley 1999 ICR 984, EAT, held that S.122(2) gives tribunals a wide discretion whether or not to reduce the basic award on the ground of *any* kind of conduct on the employee's part that occurred prior to the **18.94**

679

dismissal and that this discretion allowed a tribunal to choose, in an appropriate case, to make no reduction at all. This contrasts with the position under S.122(6) where, to justify any reduction at all on account of an employee's conduct, the conduct in question must be shown to have caused or contributed to the employee's dismissal. In that sense, the capacity to make reductions to the compensatory award is more restrictive than in respect of the basic award.

Once that restriction has been overcome, however, and conduct has been found that qualifies for a reduction of the compensatory award under S.123(6), a tribunal has no option but to make such a reduction, since the relevant provision stipulates that the tribunal '*shall* reduce the amount of the compensatory award' (our emphasis). Its discretion lies only in the amount of the reduction, which must be 'such proportion as it considers just and equitable' having regard to the finding that the employee caused or contributed to his or her dismissal. These aspects of S.122(6) are discussed in more detail under 'General principles' below. In contrast, far greater latitude is given to tribunals as to whether or not to make reductions in the basic award even where contributory conduct is found to have occurred. This means that, while the percentage deduction for conduct will usually be the same for both the basic and the compensatory award, this will not always be the case.

For further discussion of the principles governing reductions from the basic award on grounds of contributory conduct under S.122(1) ERA, and for a detailed discussion of the case law on whether and to what extent it is permissible to make different levels of contributory conduct reductions to the basic and compensatory awards, see Chapter 15 under 'Reductions in basic award'.

18.95 **When is a reduction for contributory conduct appropriate?** In Nelson v BBC (No.2) 1980 ICR 110, CA, the Court of Appeal said that three factors must be satisfied if the tribunal is to find contributory conduct:

- the relevant action must be culpable or blameworthy
- it must have actually caused or contributed to the dismissal
- it must be just and equitable to reduce the award by the proportion specified.

Each of these factors is discussed in detail under separate headings later in this chapter. The first two factors focus on the nature of the conduct that is said to have caused or contributed to the unfairly dismissed employee's dismissal. The third factor in effect deals with quantum: by how much should the tribunal reduce the compensatory award once it has found that such a reduction is appropriate. Before turning to these matters, however, it is appropriate to examine the general principles that apply to reductions made under S.123(6) ERA.

18.96 **General principles**
Before discussing in detail the kind of conduct capable of giving rise to a reduction of the compensatory award on the ground of the employee's

680

contributory conduct/fault, we first set out some of the general principles that apply to the making of such a reduction.

Duty on tribunals to consider contributory conduct. What is clear from recent case authorities is that S.123(6) ERA imposes an absolute duty on employment tribunals to consider the issue of contributory fault in any case where it was possible that there was blameworthy conduct on the part of the employee. This is so regardless of whether the issue was raised by the parties – Swallow Security Services Ltd v Millicent EAT 0297/08. Whether or not this duty is triggered will depend on the findings of fact made by the tribunal and, in particular, whether those findings reveal proven conduct attributable to the employee that potentially caused his or her dismissal or contributed in any way to it. On the facts of the Swallow case, the EAT ruled that the employment tribunal had erred when it failed to consider the issue of contributory fault given its findings that the employee had knowingly taken holiday leave in excess of her entitlement and extended the period of unauthorised absence by reporting sick. Although her dismissal nominally for redundancy was found to be a shame and therefore unfair, the EAT ruled that the employee's conduct in taking excess holiday leave and then going off sick was potentially 'blameworthy' or 'culpable', and that, as such, the tribunal should have considered whether that conduct contributed to the dismissal and therefore justified a reduction in the employee's compensatory award under S.123(6).

18.97

A similar conclusion was reached by another division of the EAT in Sodexho Defence Services Ltd v Steele EAT 0378 and 0380/08. In that case, the EAT went on to observe that whether it is appropriate for the tribunal to consider the issue of contributory conduct at the liability or remedies hearing (if held separately) was a matter of judgement for the particular tribunal. That said, it was crucial that by the time the issue of remedy is being considered, the parties are aware of the findings of fact made by the tribunal because these will be needed in order to address matters that are relevant to whether the employee caused or contributed to his or her dismissal.

Distinction between findings relating to fairness and contributory conduct. As long ago as 1984, the EAT was cautioning tribunals to mark a clear distinction between considerations relevant to an investigation of fairness of dismissal on the one hand, and those relevant to an investigation of contributory fault on the other – Iggesund Converters Ltd v Lewis 1984 ICR 544, EAT. The latter requires clear findings of fact as to what (if any) blameworthy conduct on the employee's part the employer knew about at the time of dismissal. The question of fairness, on the other hand, entails the tribunal considering whether, in all the circumstances, the employer's decision to dismiss fell within the band of reasonable responses.

18.98

The need to draw a sharp distinction between these matters was made even more powerfully by the Court of Appeal in London Ambulance Service NHS

Trust v Small 2009 IRLR 563, CA. In that case an ambulance paramedic was dismissed following a complaint from the daughter of a patient on whom the employee had attended during an emergency home call-out. In particular, the employee was accused of making an inappropriate remark and failing to administer pain relief. The employment tribunal ruled that the dismissal was unfair as it fell outside the band of reasonable responses but that the employee had contributed to the extent of 10 per cent towards his dismissal. This low level of contribution was based on the tribunal's specific finding that the inappropriate remark was made with the best of intentions and the failure to give pain relief constituted an honest if mistaken belief as to whether it was correct to administer it. The EAT rejected the employer's appeal against the finding of unfair dismissal, and the employer appealed.

Before the Court of Appeal the employer contended that the employment tribunal had wrongly substituted its own view of the reasonableness of the decision to dismiss for that of the employer. In so doing, it had allowed itself to be influenced by its findings on the contributory fault issue. Lord Justice Mummery, giving the judgment of the Court, agreed. He accepted that the tribunal had been bound to make findings of fact about the employee's conduct for the purposes of deciding the extent to which his conduct contributed to his dismissal. But that was a different issue from whether the employer had unfairly dismissed the employee for misconduct. Contributory fault only arose for decision if it was established that the dismissal was unfair. The contributory fault decision was one for the tribunal to make on the evidence that it heard, and was not one for the employer to make. This made it different from the actual decision to dismiss, which was a decision for the employer to make. It was not the role of the tribunal to conduct a rehearing of the facts that formed the basis for the decision to dismiss, still less to substitute its decision for that of the employer. In this case, the tribunal had failed to keep the issues and relevant facts pertaining to the two distinct issues separate.

18.99 **Conduct of employer or other employees irrelevant.** Only the blameworthy conduct of the employee is relevant when considering whether compensation should be reduced under S.123(6) ERA, not that of the employer or other employees. In Parker Foundry Ltd v Slack 1992 ICR 302, CA, the claimant's dismissal for fighting at work was held to be unfair on procedural grounds but his compensation was then reduced by 50 per cent for contributory fault. The claimant appealed against this reduction, saying that the tribunal should have taken account of the fact that the other employee involved in the fight had merely been suspended from work. The EAT rejected this argument: although the consistency of treatment of the two was relevant to the fairness of the dismissal, it was not a matter for the tribunal to consider when assessing contributory fault. The tribunal had found that both employees were 50 per cent to blame for the fight so it was entitled to find that the claimant, by his

682

conduct, had contributed to his dismissal to that extent. The Court of Appeal subsequently upheld this decision.

Similarly, in Salmon v Ribble Motor Services Ltd EAT 51/91 an employment tribunal found an employee's dismissal for organising a union meeting during working hours, which resulted in an unofficial stoppage, to be unfair on procedural grounds but held that by his involvement in the meeting he had contributed to his dismissal by 60 per cent. The EAT held that the fact that two other employees who had been equally responsible for calling the meeting had not been dismissed gave no grounds for overturning the tribunal's finding on contribution.

More recently, in Sandwell and anor v Westwood EAT 0032/09, an **18.100** employment tribunal's disinclination to make a reduction for contributory fault solely because of the employer's own inept conduct was held on appeal to be misconceived. The tribunal had stated that, but for the employer's ineptitude, it would have made a finding that the claimant had contributed to her dismissal to the tune of 20 per cent. The EAT ruled that the tribunal had erred by regarding the employer's conduct as being a relevant consideration to the decision not to make a reduction on account of contributory fault. Also, when intimating that it would have made a reduction but for the employer's conduct, the tribunal had erred by not sufficiently identifying the conduct of the employee it had in mind as the basis for making the putative reduction, and by failing to explain the rationale for setting the reduction at 20 per cent. The case was remitted to the tribunal to allow it to rectify these errors.

In Live Nation (Venues) Ltd and ors v Hussain EAT 0234–6/08 an employment tribunal gave two reasons for refusing to make a contributory fault reduction. The first was that, in its estimation, there was no blameworthy conduct on the part of the claimant that had caused or contributed to his dismissal. The second was that, in any event, the employer's own conduct in dismissing the claimant – about which the tribunal was highly critical – meant that it was not just and equitable to make any reduction in any case. On appeal, the EAT accepted that the second of these reasons amounted to an error of law because the conduct of the employer was immaterial. The focus should have been exclusively on the conduct of the employee. However, the tribunal's error did not affect its principal conclusion that there was no blameworthy conduct so as to trigger a finding of contributory fault.

Employee's actions post-dismissal irrelevant. By definition, deductions can **18.101** only be made under S.123(6) in respect of actions by the employee that took place *prior* to the dismissal and of which the employer had knowledge when the decision to dismiss was taken. This is because the employee's conduct must be shown to have actually caused or contributed to the employer's decision to dismiss. In Nawaz v John Haggas Ltd EAT 838/83 the employee's compensation for unfair dismissal was reduced by 20 per cent because of his

683

failure to make any representations about his dismissal before presenting his tribunal application. The EAT said this was an error of law because conduct after dismissal cannot be contributory conduct within the meaning of S.123(6): the tribunal was confusing contributory conduct and mitigation of loss – as to which see below, under 'Failure to mitigate losses'.

The proposition that post-dismissal conduct cannot constitute a basis for making a reduction on the ground of contributory fault was affirmed in Mullinger v Department for Work and Pensions EAT 0515/05. In that case, an employee was found to have been unfairly dismissed but the tribunal made a reduction of 75 per cent for contributory conduct based on two separate considerations: (i) the employee's misuse of office computer equipment while still in employment; and (ii) his intransigence in refusing to return official documents after his employment had been terminated. In setting the level of contribution, the tribunal acknowledged that the second of these considerations was not a factor in the employee's dismissal. Nevertheless, the tribunal felt that it was a factor 'that must be taken into account in considering what is, in all the material circumstances, just and equitable'. On appeal, the EAT ruled that the tribunal had erred in law by taking account of misconduct that the employee only perpetrated after his dismissal. Such conduct had no bearing on the issue of contribution, and the case was therefore remitted to a fresh tribunal to decide the extent (if any) of the employee's contribution based solely on the misconduct that had been perpetrated prior to dismissal. The Court of Appeal subsequently upheld the EAT's decision to remit on this basis – Mullinger v Department for Work and Pensions 2007 EWCA Civ 1334, CA.

18.102 The more problematic issue arising in the Mullinger case was whether post-dismissal misconduct can ever legitimately lead to a reduction in the overall compensatory award on some other statutory basis. The employer's contention was that, even if post-dismissal conduct could not properly form the basis for a finding of contributory fault under S.123(6), there was no reason why, in the exercise of its discretion to award 'such amount as is just and equitable' under S.123(1) ERA, a tribunal should not take account of such conduct for this purpose. For reasons fully elaborated under 'Just and equitable amount' below, the EAT rejected this interpretation of S.123(1). In its view, there was no scope for adjusting compensation on account of an employee's misconduct if this occurs after the date of dismissal. This was in contrast to misconduct occurring before that of dismissal but which is only discovered by the employer after that date. The EAT made it clear that conduct of the latter kind can be taken into account in considering what is just and equitable to award by way of a compensatory award. The EAT's observations on S.123(1) were, in effect, obiter, and were not considered by the Court of Appeal when the case was unsuccessfully appealed by the employer.

18.103 **Is finding of contributory conduct a bar to reinstatement?** Section 116(1) and (3) ERA specifically state that, in determining whether to order the reinstatement or re-engagement of an unfairly dismissed employee, an employment tribunal should have regard to three specific factors. One of these is whether it would be just to order reinstatement/re-engagement where the employee has caused or contributed to some extent to his or her dismissal. The EAT has made it clear that the test of whether conduct amounts to contributory fault for the purposes of S.116(1) and (3) is exactly the same as that for determining whether a reduction in the compensatory award should be made under S.123(6) – see Boots Company plc v Lees-Collier 1986 ICR 728, EAT.

Clearly, the fact that there is contributory fault does not present an absolute bar to the capacity of a tribunal to order re-employment: if this were the case, S.116(1) and (3) would have said so. But contributory fault is patently a factor that must to be taken into account when a tribunal exercises its discretion over re-employment orders – the implication being that where an employee has caused or contributed to the dismissal this may well make re-employment less likely. The *extent* of any contribution will properly be a relevant consideration in this regard. In Thornton v British Telecommunications plc ET Case No.1700376/08 an employment tribunal ordered the employee to be reinstated despite it finding that he had made a 15 per cent contribution to his dismissal. That level of contribution – which was made because of the employee's attitude towards time-keeping rules that he found to be irksome – did not preclude an order for reinstatement in the tribunal's view. By way of contrast, in Pathak v Next Directory Ltd ET Case No.1902284/08 a tribunal declined to order reinstatement in respect of an employee found to have contributed 50 per cent towards her dismissal. The tribunal felt in this case that such a level of contribution made reinstatement inappropriate.

'Culpable or blameworthy conduct'

18.104

As stated at the start of this chapter, for conduct to be the basis for a finding of contributory fault under S.123(6) ERA, it has to have the characteristic of culpability or blameworthiness. This was firmly established by the Court of Appeal in Nelson v British Broadcasting Corporation (No.2) 1980 ICR 110, CA, where Lord Justice Brandon explained that, in view of the wording of what is now S.123(6), it could never be just and equitable to reduce a successful complainant's compensation unless the conduct on his or her part was culpable or blameworthy. Put another way, if a person is blameless, it can neither be just nor equitable to reduce his or her compensation on the ground that he or she caused or contributed to the dismissal.

Conduct by the employee capable of causing or contributing to dismissal is not limited to actions that amount to breaches of contract or that are illegal in nature. In the Nelson case (above) the Court said that it could also include conduct that was 'perverse or foolish', 'bloody-minded' or merely 'unreasonable in all the circumstances'. Whether the conduct is unreasonable will depend on the facts. The most typical forms of blameworthy conduct are

685

'misconduct' in the conventional sense – e.g. disloyalty, dishonesty, taking a holiday without permission or acting in competition with the employer. But S.123(6) can cover wider forms of conduct where, for example, the employee manages to aggravate a situation, or precipitate the dismissal. Some examples of less obvious forms of 'blameworthy conduct':

• refusing to reveal the names of fellow employees involved in misconduct – Simpson v British Steel Corporation EAT 594/83

• walking out of a meeting which had been set up to resolve the employee's difficulties regarding her terms and conditions of employment – Wall v Brookside Metal Co Ltd EAT 579/89

• responding aggressively when the employer issued a final warning – Daykin v IHW Engineering Ltd ET Case No.01838/83.

18.105   There are, of course, limits to how far tribunals will view conduct as 'blameworthy'. In Glenrose (Fish Merchants) Ltd v Chapman and ors EAT 467/91, for example, the EAT upheld a tribunal's decision that a number of employees who had refused to work overtime in protest at what they understood to be a unilateral variation of contract imposed by their employer had not, in the circumstances, contributed to their dismissals, even though they were effectively acting in breach of contract. And in Doyle-Davidson v Ormerods Ltd ET Case No.48770/94 an employee was dismissed for refusing to sign a new contract with less favourable terms, for writing to the employer in aggressive language, and for being provocative in the way she completed her time sheets. A tribunal refused to accept that she had been guilty of contributory conduct and accordingly it made no reduction in her compensation. The employee was entitled to express her reservations about the proposed changes and the language in her letter was not unreasonable. Nor was it unreasonable for her to make a point about her working hours when completing time sheets.

18.106   **Knowledge that conduct is wrong.** The fact that an employee did not know that what he or she was doing was wrong will not necessarily save him or her from a finding of contributory conduct. In Allen v Hammett EAT 245/81 the claimant employee, acting entirely on the advice of his solicitor, refused to return a cheque that had been paid to him in error by his employer. This refusal eventually led to his dismissal, which was judged to be unfair by the tribunal, which nevertheless reduced his award by 60 per cent for contributory conduct. Before the EAT, the employee argued that because he had acted in good faith upon his solicitor's advice, his conduct could not be regarded as culpable or blameworthy under the Nelson test. The EAT, however, while sympathetic to the employee's position, stated that it was a general principle of law that a person is held responsible for the actions of his or her agents. The tribunal had been entitled to make the reduction it had. The employee's remedy lay in legal action against his solicitor for negligence.

Tribunals will usually be alive to the particular circumstances in which misconduct on an employee's part occurs, especially if mitigating circumstances explain the conduct in question despite the fact that the employee knows he or she has done wrong. In Peled-Hada and anor v Windsor Great Perk Ltd ET Case No.2700087–8/08, two employees claimed they were too ill to come into work, though this was untrue. This was one of a number of incidents that directly led to their dismissals. They were found to have been unfairly dismissed but the tribunal let them off the hook so far as a finding of contributory conduct was concerned. It recognised that they had been working under great stress – employees and suppliers had not been paid owing to the employer's financial difficulties and court bailiffs had entered the premises on more than one occasion. In these circumstances, although the tribunal made it clear that it was not condoning the employees' actions, it concluded that their conduct had not reached the required threshold to trigger a reduction in their compensation award.

Employee's failure to explain his/her actions. An employee's failure to give the employer an explanation for his or her conduct can contribute to a dismissal. In Kwik Save Stores Ltd v Clerkin EAT 295/96 a tribunal accepted the claimant's contention that his dismissal for allegedly falsifying the clocking-off cards of employees was unfair because he had in fact only been carrying out what he had thought to be standard company procedure. However, the tribunal found that his failure to raise this defence to his actions at the disciplinary hearing contributed to his dismissal by 40 per cent. And in Blair v British Steel plc ET Case No.9271/95 the employee was dismissed for playing football while off sick. The tribunal held that the dismissal was unfair for lack of investigation into the incident. But it reduced the compensatory award by 80 per cent because the employee, although represented by skilled advisers at his disciplinary hearings, had omitted to draw the employer's attention to the full circumstances of his absence, the potentially therapeutic nature of playing football, or the need for a medical opinion.

18.107

Refusal to participate in a disciplinary process. In Vassoo v Gambro Healthcare UK Ltd and ors ET Case No.2300615/07 an employment tribunal declined to make a contributory fault reduction in respect of the employee's refusal to participate in the disciplinary process prior to dismissal. The tribunal held that this failure could not be said to be 'blameworthy'. Employees are entitled to say that they do not wish to ask or answer questions in the context of a disciplinary hearing. The tribunal observed that although such action may make it more likely that disciplinary allegations will be upheld, it cannot be said to amount to blameworthy conduct justifying a reduction in the compensation awarded. Similar thinking applies in respect of the failure by employees to utilise internal appeals – see under 'Failure to utilise internal appeal' below.

18.108

Conduct during disciplinary process. Whereas there is – according to the employment tribunal's decision in the Vassoo case (see above) – no room at all

18.109

for a finding of contributory fault where an employee refuses to cooperate with a disciplinary procedure, there appears to be more room to find contributory fault in respect of the manner in which an employee conducts him or herself during a disciplinary process. That said, the case law suggests that the scope for such a finding remains limited – see British Steel Corporation v Williams EAT 776/82 and Sidhu v Superdrug Stores plc EAT 0244/06. In the latter case, an employment tribunal made a 90 per cent reduction in the employee's compensatory award because he could have done far more to assist himself during the course of two disciplinary hearings by probing the evidence submitted by the employer to support the allegation of gross misconduct and by attempting to call witnesses at the disciplinary hearing. On appeal, the EAT cautioned that a finding of contributory conduct in such a case was only appropriate if the tribunal is sure that the employee has caused or contributed to his or her dismissal by some aspect of his or her conduct during the disciplinary process. Although the EAT did not say so expressly, the implication is that such conduct will be rare.

The outcome in the Sidhu case can be contrasted with the EAT's decision in Bell v Governing Body of Grampian Primary School EAT 0142/07. There, the EAT upheld an employment tribunal's decision that the employee's sarcastic and aggressive behaviour during the disciplinary process justified a reduction in the compensatory award for contributory fault. In that case, it was specifically found by the tribunal that the employee's conduct had been in the mind of the employer when deciding to dismiss, and that, had the employee behaved more acceptably, the chances were that a lesser disciplinary penalty would have been imposed.

18.110 Likewise, in Perkin v St George's Healthcare NHS Trust 2006 ICR 617, CA, the Court of Appeal appeared to uphold an employment tribunal's finding of a 100 per cent contribution based on the manner in which the employee had behaved during a disciplinary inquiry. However, despite a lengthily reasoned principal judgment from Lord Justice Wall, the Court undertook very little analysis of S.123(6) and in particular of how the conduct – which was based on the employee's personality and accusatory management style – had actually caused or contributed to the employee's dismissal within the meaning of S.123(6).

In contrast, Wall LJ's reasoning in upholding the tribunal's alternative finding of a 100 per cent 'Polkey reduction' from the employee's compensatory award was far more extensive. A reduction on this ground is permissible if the unfairness of the dismissal lies solely in procedural failings on the part of the employer and it can be shown that the employee would have been dismissed in any event even if such failings had not occurred – for further details see under 'Polkey reductions' below. The employment tribunal had observed that the manner in which the employee had conducted himself during the disciplinary hearing was illustrative of the difficulties the employer had faced when dealing with the employee throughout his employment. In the Court of Appeal's view, the tribunal had been entitled to have regard to the fact that the employee had attacked the honesty, financial probity and integrity of his colleagues during the disciplinary proceedings and had doggedly insisted on maintaining his stance in relation to those attacks even though they were manifestly unfounded. The Court ruled that the tribunal was entitled to conclude that it would have been impossible for the employee to remain a member of the employer's senior executive team and that, had a proper disciplinary process been undertaken, it would have ended with the same result. Accordingly, it had been open to the tribunal to make a reduction in the compensatory award of 100 per cent under the Polkey principle.

Failure to utilise internal appeal. An employee's failure to make use of an internal appeals procedure to reverse a decision to dismiss cannot normally be considered under S.123(6) ERA because it is not conduct that can in any way be said to have contributed to the dismissal. Only if the dismissal did not occur until *after* the appeal can such conduct be taken into account – see Hoover Ltd v Forde 1980 ICR 239, EAT. **18.111**

Unreasonable refusal to accept suitable alternative employment. An employee's refusal to accept an offer of re-engagement from the employer made after the dismissal will not justify a reduction in compensation for contributory conduct under S.123(6), but may be considered in the context of mitigation – see below, under 'Failure to mitigate losses'. Note, however, that by virtue of S.122(1) ERA, the unreasonable refusal of an offer of re-engagement can specifically serve to reduce a basic award (see Chapter 15 under 'Reductions in basic award'). **18.112**

Ill-health and capability dismissals. The issue of contributory fault typically arises in cases where misconduct was the reason for dismissal. In cases of dismissal for incapability or ill health the 'conduct' in question is likely to be beyond the employee's control, so the element of blameworthiness or culpability is lacking. In Slaughter v C Brewer and Sons Ltd 1990 ICR 730, EAT, the EAT affirmed that, for this reason, dismissals on the ground of ill health will rarely give rise to a finding of contributory conduct. Much the same applies to capability dismissals. In Kraft Foods Ltd v Fox 1978 ICR 311, EAT, the EAT stated that if an employee is incompetent or incapable and cannot measure up to the job, it is wrong to say that this can be a factor contributing to the dismissal. 'The whole point about contribution,' the EAT continued, 'is that it is something by way of conduct on the part of the employee over which he has control.' **18.113**

In some cases where an employee is judged to have been unfairly dismissed on the ground of capability owing to the lack of an adequate performance review procedure, the tribunal proceeds to limit the compensatory award in accordance with its discretion under S.123(1) ERA to award 'such amount as [it] considers

689

just and equitable having regard to the loss sustained by the complainant'. The basis for limiting the award in this way is often that the tribunal is satisfied that the adoption of a fair procedure would, at best, only have delayed the inevitable, in that the employee would have been dismissed in any event. In Plumley v AD International Ltd EAT 592/82 the EAT held that, where compensation is limited because an employee's performance is unlikely to improve, it should not be further reduced for contributing to his or her own dismissal.

18.114 One possible circumstance in which contribution in the context of an ill-health or capability dismissal might be appropriate is where the employee has blatantly and persistently refused to obtain medical reports, undergo a medical examination or ignored medical advice. In Hague v Clean Factory and Office Services Ltd ET Case No.5942/95 the claimant ignored his GP's advice to stay off work on account of a viral infection. The infection affected his ability to do his job properly. A client complained about the employee's work, by which time he had been forced to take sick leave. He was held to have been unfairly dismissed but was found to have contributed to his dismissal by not taking his GP's advice.

The Hague case can be contrasted with that of Claymore Graphics Ltd v Simpson EAT 450/99, in which the employee became sick with stress and depression. His doctor predicted he would recover fully in 4–6 weeks. While he was unwell, the employee went into the office outside working hours, smoked in a no-smoking area, and left a colleague an abusive note, for which he was summarily dismissed in absentia as he was too ill to attend the hearing. A tribunal found the dismissal unfair because it was clear that the employee's conduct might well have had its origins in his mental state, and even if it did not, he was not well enough to answer the disciplinary charges. The tribunal ruled that any reasonable employer would have waited 4–6 weeks until the employee had recovered before deciding whether disciplinary action was appropriate. On appeal, the EAT upheld the tribunal's decision on the basis that the employee's misconduct could well have been attributable to stress and depression and that it could be 'involuntary in the sense of attributable to a problematic mental state'. This was all the more reason for not classifying it as contributory conduct.

Cases of genuine incapability should be distinguished from those in which the incapability was the employee's own fault, in the sense that he or she was lazy, negligent or idle, or did not try to improve. In reality, such cases are more akin to misconduct than genuine incapability and the degree of contribution may be considerable. For example, in Chauhan and anor v Man Truck and Bus UK Ltd EAT 931/94 the tribunal accepted that the employee's dismissal raised issues of incapability in that he was not really up to the job. Nevertheless, the tribunal assessed contribution at 75 per cent on account of his lack of initiative and failure to make a proper effort.

690 ———————————————————————————————————

Mental illness and alcoholism. The fact that an employee's conduct or **18.115** capability is explicable by a mental illness or mental condition is unlikely, without more, to constitute a sound basis for making a finding of contributory conduct. A person's mental state is not, on the whole, culpable or blameworthy conduct over which that person has any control. However, where a mental condition leads to pre-planned misconduct, the position may well be different.

In Edmund Nuttall Ltd v Butterfield 2006 ICR 77, EAT, the employee's duties entailed extensive travel by car. On his way home from a business trip, he committed two offences of indecent exposure and one of dangerous driving. The following day, he was admitted to hospital after having suffered a nervous breakdown. The employee was subsequently convicted in the criminal courts and sentenced to a three-year Community Rehabilitation Order with a condition of medical treatment, He was also disqualified from driving for two years. It transpired that he had been exposing himself to females over an 18-month period. At a later date, the employer found out about the employee's conviction and this led to his eventual dismissal for gross misconduct. He brought claims of disability discrimination and unfair dismissal, both of which were upheld by an employment tribunal. In respect of compensation for unfair dismissal, the tribunal held that the employee had not been guilty of culpable conduct and accordingly there was no basis for making a reduction for contributory fault under S.123(6) ERA.

On appeal, the EAT overturned the tribunal's decision with regard to both the **18.116** finding that the employee had been discriminated against on the ground of disability and that he had not contributed to his dismissal. Although the Appeal Tribunal upheld the finding of unfair dismissal, it concluded that the employment tribunal's decision that the employee was not guilty of culpable or blameworthy conduct was perverse. In the EAT's view, while it was entirely proper that the degree of culpability was reflected in the tribunal's findings as to the employee's mental state, the fact that he had committed pre-planned offences of a criminal nature and then concealed the true position (including his convictions) from the employer was plainly culpable conduct that merited a reduction in the compensatory award under S.123(6). The case was remitted to a different tribunal to consider what the extent of that reduction should be.

A similar ruling in a different context was reached by the EAT in Sinclair v Wandsworth Council EAT 0145/07. In that case the employee (who admitted that he was an alcoholic) was dismissed when he was found to be under the influence of alcohol at work in breach of the employer's alcohol policy. His dismissal was held to be unfair because he had not been given sufficient details of the policy and, in particular, the steps he was expected to take to avoid disciplinary action in respect of his condition. In awarding compensation, although the tribunal did find contributory fault to the extent of 25 per cent on grounds unrelated to the employee's alcoholism, it specifically refused to increase the percentage reduction further on account of the employee's breach

691

of the alcohol policy. It took the view that alcoholism was an illness and so could not be categorised as culpable or blameworthy conduct. On appeal, the EAT overturned the tribunal's decision on this point, ruling that it was not the case that unacceptable conduct can be excused by reference to a background or underlying illness. The fact was that the employer had been faced with such conduct in the workplace. The case was remitted to the same tribunal to decide whether and by how much to increase the finding of contributory fault beyond 25 per cent.

18.117 **Personality clashes.** In Bell v Governing Body of Grampian Primary School EAT 0142/07 a school teacher was found to have been unfairly dismissed owing to the employer's failure to comply with the then applicable statutory dismissal procedures. The employment tribunal went on to make a 75 per cent reduction in the employee's compensatory award on account of the blame it laid at the employee's door for his dismissal. The contributory conduct in question took several forms, including the making of what were described as 'silly' comments to the head teacher when he queried remarks the employee had made about a parent who had complained about the employee; the aggressive manner in which the employee had conducted himself during the disciplinary process; 'trying to be clever' in the retorts he gave to questions during the disciplinary process; and soliciting other teachers to bring a grievance against the head teacher.

On appeal, the EAT emphasised that when making a reduction under S.123(6) ERA, the tribunal must be satisfied that there is actual culpable or blameworthy conduct on the part of the employee, which must go beyond an issue of personality, disposition or a tendency towards unhelpfulness. That said, in the instant case, the Appeal Tribunal concluded that this was not a case in which the employment tribunal had found simple instances of non-participation in the disciplinary process or unhelpfulness. On the facts, it had been entitled to find that the employee's conduct had operated on the mind of the employer and had been part of the background that had induced the disciplinary panel to uphold the allegations made against him and to choose to deal with the matter by way of dismissal.

18.118 **Statutorily protected conduct.** A finding of contributory fault would be wholly inappropriate where the conduct in question was statutorily protected behaviour – e.g. where the employee had not disclosed a 'spent' criminal conviction – Property Guards Ltd v Taylor and anor 1982 IRLR 175, EAT.

18.119 **Industrial pressure to dismiss.** Employment tribunals are specifically prohibited from taking account of industrial pressure to dismiss an employee when deciding on the fairness of a dismissal – S.107 ERA. Industrial pressure in this context comprises calling, organising, procuring or financing a strike or other industrial action, or threatening to do so. Nor can such industrial pressure be taken into account when assessing the compensatory award – S.123(5). In other words, employers cannot plead for a reduction in compensation because they faced industrial action if they did not dismiss the employee. However, under the contributory conduct provision of S.123(6), the compensation for any unfair dismissal may be reduced if the employee in some way brought about both the industrial pressure and the subsequent unfair dismissal.

In Colwyn Borough Council v Dutton 1980 IRLR 420, EAT, for example, the employee was a dustcart driver whose colleagues refused to go out with him following several careless driving incidents. Although industrial pressure was the reason for his dismissal, the EAT said that the employee's careless driving was a factor and his compensation should be reduced accordingly. And in Sulemanji v Toughened Glass Ltd and anor 1979 ICR 799, EAT, an employee's uncooperative attitude towards resolving a dispute with other workers was found to be contributory conduct justifying a 100 per cent reduction.

Industrial action. Special provisions apply to dismissals for participating in official industrial action. Full details of these rules are contained in IDS Employment Law Handbook, 'Industrial Action' (2010), Chapter 8. Basically, under S.238 TULR(C)A an employee who is dismissed while participating in official industrial action cannot bring a claim of unfair dismissal unless at least one other employee who was also taking part in the action was either not dismissed or was (in contrast to the claimant) re-engaged within three months. In Courtaulds Northern Spinning Ltd v Moosa 1984 IRLR 43, EAT, the EAT held that the policy behind these special provisions was that an employment tribunal should be prevented from going into the rights or wrongs of an industrial dispute. It followed, said the EAT, that an employee's participation in industrial action could not constitute contributory conduct.

18.120

In Tracey and ors v Crosville Wales Ltd 1997 ICR 862, HL, the House of Lords held that it was impossible to allocate blame for industrial action to any individual employee, particularly in cases where the collective blame for the industrial action is shared by employees who have been re-engaged. This conclusion merely reflected the fact that any reduction in compensation should be just and equitable. The House of Lords agreed with the conclusions of the Court of Appeal. In particular, it agreed with Lord Justice Waite's comments on the limited circumstances in which conduct could in theory be taken into account; namely, where there was individual blameworthy conduct additional to, or separate from, the mere act of participation in industrial action. According to the Court of Appeal, the question that tribunals must ask themselves is: 'Have these applicants been responsible, in addition to mere participation in the relevant industrial action, for any conduct of their own contributing to the dismissal which was sufficiently blameworthy to make it just and equitable to reduce their compensation?' The Court said, for example, that if the leaders of the industrial action were dismissed, their particular activities as leaders could properly be examined and the tribunal would be

693

entitled to make a deduction for contributory fault if it found that the conduct had been overhasty or inflammatory.

18.121   The House of Lords' decision has the virtue of clarifying the point that normally an individual who has demonstrated that he or she has been unfairly dismissed when participating in industrial action – not an easy task itself due to the procedural rules that apply in such cases – should not have his or her compensation for that dismissal reduced on the ground that he or she contributed to the dismissal by participating in industrial action. But the acknowledged exception to this rule where the employee's conduct is 'individual blameworthy conduct additional to or separate from the mere act of participation in industrial action' raises the obvious question as to what type of conduct falls within this exception.

The EAT's decision in Transport and General Workers' Union v Howard 1992 ICR 106, EAT, is one example of a case in which confrontational conduct by the employee during industrial action was held to be sufficiently independent (rather than collective) to be considered contributory fault, justifying a reduction. Furthermore, in Gosling v Ford Motor Co Ltd EAT 221/90 a tribunal's decision to reduce the employee's compensation by 75 per cent for contributory fault was upheld by the EAT. In that case the employee had substantially contributed to his own dismissal by his unjustifiable conduct in inciting industrial action (regardless of the merits of the industrial action) and by his refusal to sign an undertaking that he would not be involved in any unconstitutional action. A similar conclusion was reached in Crowther v British Railways Board EAT 762 and 1118/95, where the EAT decided that the employee's actions in inciting industrial action outside the normal procedures for the industry could amount to conduct justifying a reduction in his compensation.

18.122   The decisions above – particularly Gosling and Crowther – raise the possibility that the person who incites industrial action will be more likely to have his or her compensation reduced than a mere participant in the action. While, from one perspective, this certainly has a degree of logic about it, from another it is potentially a dangerous finding to make. The organisers of industrial action are those who are more likely to be victimised for this activity and, as such, surely should not be unduly penalised if UK law is to genuinely protect the right to organise lawful industrial action. Therefore, it might be fair to say that so long as an individual is acting within the scope of normal procedures for calling industrial action and is not offending against the criminal law, the exception to the general rule acknowledged by the House of Lords should not be invoked. It is submitted that, in interpreting this exception, the realities of the situation – particularly the often heated nature of industrial disputes – will have to be borne in mind.

18.123   **Union membership, activities and use of union services.** Where the reason for dismissal or selection for redundancy is shown to have been for trade union reasons, in considering whether to reduce the compensatory award on the ground of an employee's conduct, a tribunal must completely disregard conduct leading to the dismissal that comprises a breach (or proposed breach) of an arrangement or contractual term requiring the employee (a) to be or become a member of a union or cease to be a member; (b) to take part or not take part in union activities; or (c) not to make use of the services of a union – S.155(2) TULR(C)A.

Tribunals must also disregard a refusal to pay, or to allow deductions from pay to be made in favour of, somebody other than a union (e.g. a charity) – S.155(4) TULR(C)A. A similar disregard applies where the conduct in question comprises: (a) the refusal by the employee of an offer by the employer the main purpose of which is to induce the employee not to be or seek to become a member of a trade union, make use of its services or participate in its activities; or (b) the refusal by the employee of an offer that has the intended result that the employee's terms and conditions will not (or will no longer be) determined by collective agreement negotiated by the union – S.155(2A) TULR(C)A.

Causal link between conduct and dismissal

18.124

In order for a deduction to be made under S.123(6) ERA, a causal link between the employee's conduct and the dismissal must be shown to exist. This means that the conduct must have taken place before the dismissal; the employer must have been aware of the conduct; and the employer must then have dismissed the employee at least partly in consequence of that conduct. An employment tribunal cannot simply point to some misbehaviour by the employee and reduce compensation on that count. In Hutchinson v Enfield Rolling Mills Ltd 1981 IRLR 318, EAT, the employee was seen at a demonstration in Brighton while absent from work through ill health. A tribunal found that he had been unfairly dismissed but assessed his contribution at 100 per cent because of his generally obstreperous attitude. On appeal, the EAT held that, while the employee's attendance at the demonstration was capable of constituting contributory conduct, his attitude had no bearing on the dismissal and so the tribunal had erred in reducing the award for contributory fault.

In Smith and anor v McPhee and anor EAT 338–339/89 conduct that at first glance seemed clearly to have contributed to the dismissal was held not to have done so when the real reason for dismissal became apparent. M, a hotel barmaid, had filled a lemonade bottle with caustic soda for her own use but accidentally left it on the bar overnight. The next morning the employer herself used the bottle to clean a sink and then put it back on the bar. Later on another barmaid mistook it for lemonade with the result that an unfortunate customer suffered severe burns to his mouth. M was promptly dismissed for leaving the item on the bar. The tribunal came to the conclusion that M had not in reality been dismissed on account of her own conduct but in order to divert attention away from the employer's own careless behaviour and thus protect the reputation of the hotel. The EAT upheld the tribunal's decision that, since the real reason for M's dismissal was not her conduct but

695

the need for a scapegoat, the dismissal was unfair and her conduct, though reprehensible, had not in fact contributed to that dismissal.

18.125 **Conduct contributing to but not the sole reason for dismissal.** When considering the issue of contributory fault, tribunals are entitled to rely on a broad view of the employee's conduct, including behaviour which, although not relating to the main reason for dismissal, nonetheless played a material part in the dismissal. In Robert Whiting Designs Ltd v Lamb 1978 ICR 89, EAT, the employee was dismissed for lack of competence but the EAT found that his improper bonus claims were factors contributing to his dismissal. And in Arthur v Pronto Services (UK) Ltd ET Case No.5175/95 the employee, an accident-prone driver, crashed a company vehicle through his own negligence. When his employer threatened to deduct the repair cost from his pay, he counter-threatened to bring a claim of unlawful deduction from his wages and was promptly dismissed. A tribunal found that the reason for the employee's dismissal was that he had asserted a statutory right and that the dismissal was therefore automatically unfair under S.104 ERA. However, it held that he had contributed to his dismissal by his negligent driving.

Similarly, in BSW Ltd v Brown EAT 0835/04 B was the principal shareholder of the company as well as its employee. He was dismissed after it was discovered that he had committed the company to a lease for premises without authority. An employment tribunal, in ruling that B had been unfairly dismissed, found that the real reason for dismissal was that the company's chairman had already resolved to dismiss B and that the issue of the lease merely provided a cover under which to carry out the dismissal. However, the tribunal reduced B's compensatory award by 50 per cent on account of his conduct concerning the lease. On appeal, the EAT upheld the tribunal's decision. The lease issue had been a factor in the company's mind to the extent that it was the primary ground advanced by the employer as explaining the dismissal. This was so even though the real reason was camouflaged and overtaken by the legitimate reason concerning the employee's conduct over the lease.

18.126 **Failure to establish a potentially fair reason for dismissal.** The fact that an employer has failed to establish a potentially fair reason for dismissal within the terms of S.98(1)(b) and (2) ERA does not preclude a finding of contributory conduct. In Chauhan and anor v Man Truck and Bus UK Ltd EAT 931/94 the tribunal rejected the employer's claim that an employee had been dismissed for 'some other substantial reason' and held that it had failed to establish that the dismissal came under any of the permissible reasons listed in S.98(2) ERA. It nevertheless ruled that the employee's poor performance had contributed to the dismissal by 75 per cent, a finding upheld on appeal by the EAT.

18.127 **Constructive dismissal.** It used to be considered highly unlikely that a tribunal could legitimately make a finding of contributory conduct in a constructive

696

dismissal case. This was because it was felt that if the tribunal were to find contributory conduct it would be difficult to conclude that the employer's conduct was sufficiently serious to constitute the fundamental breach of contract required to give rise to a constructive dismissal. In Holroyd v Gravure Cylinders Ltd 1984 IRLR 259, EAT, Lord McDonald went so far as to say that it would only be in 'exceptional' cases that a finding of contributory conduct would accompany one of constructive dismissal. However, that statement has been modified in subsequent cases.

In Morrison v Amalgamated Transport and General Workers' Union 1989 IRLR 361, NICA, the employee was suspended without pay and resigned. The suspension was held to be in fundamental breach of contract and M succeeded in her claim of unfair constructive dismissal. However, the tribunal reduced her compensation by 40 per cent because she had by her conduct 'provoked and precipitated' the employer's unlawful reaction. The employee appealed against the reduction, citing the Holroyd case (above) to the effect that the tribunal had failed to identify any exceptional circumstances justifying a finding of contributory conduct in a constructive dismissal case. The Northern Ireland Court of Appeal, however, stated that Lord McDonald's dictum should not be taken as a statement of legal principle. It was simply an observation that contributory conduct will be comparatively rare where the employee has been constructively dismissed. The Court went on to point out that, since it was open to a tribunal to declare a constructive dismissal fair, there could be no inconsistency in its holding that the employee contributed to the dismissal in the first place.

If contribution is to apply, there must be a connection between the employee's **18.128** conduct and the fundamental breach. In British Rail Staff Association (Newcastle Central Branch) v Robson EAT 4/89 and 12/89 R, a club stewardess, overheard a meeting of the club committee at which she thought she was being unfairly criticised. She complained to the committee about what she had heard but nothing was done to put matters right. The tribunal found that the failure of the committee to clear up the matter had destroyed the necessary degree of confidence and trust between the parties. It held that R had been unfairly constructively dismissed. However, the tribunal reduced her award by one third to reflect the fact that the chain of events had been started by R's improper behaviour in listening in upon the private deliberations of the committee. The EAT upheld the employee's appeal against the finding of contributory conduct. It stated that however blameworthy R's eavesdropping might have been, it had in no way caused or compounded that behaviour of her employer which entitled her to treat herself as being constructively dismissed. It therefore ruled that the tribunal had been wrong in law to make any reduction.

By way of contrast, in Polentarutti v Autokraft Ltd 1991 ICR 757, EAT, a sufficient causal connection was found to have been established between the constructive dismissal and the contributory conduct of the employee. In that case P had, in the course of an afternoon's work, machined 24 hub-caps, of which 23 were found to be defective. Subsequently the employer refused to pay P for some overtime work and he resigned and brought a claim for unfair constructive dismissal. An employment tribunal upheld P's claim but reduced his award by two thirds because he had contributed to his dismissal. On appeal, P argued that there was an insufficient connection between his shoddy workmanship and A Ltd's repudiatory breach of contract. The EAT accepted that the employer's breach was not caused solely by P's poor workmanship but stated that a tribunal does not require a direct causal link in order to make a reduction. All that is required is that the action of the employee to some extent contributed to the dismissal. In the present case, said the EAT, there was ample evidence upon which the tribunal could find a sufficient link to justify its finding of contributory conduct.

Constructive dismissal cases often entail the build-up of separate incidents that culminate in a 'final straw' in response to which the employee resigns and claims constructive dismissal. The EAT in Garner v Grange Furnishing Ltd 1977 IRLR 206, EAT, has made it clear that in such cases the employee's own conduct may be found to have contributed to the dismissal, and, in order to assess the level of the contribution, the tribunal should look broadly at the conduct over the whole period and not just at the culminating incidents.

18.129   ## Amount of reduction – 'just and equitable' proportion
Once the element of contributory fault has been established, the amount of any reduction is a matter of fact and degree for the tribunal's discretion. In this regard, it is useful to provide a reminder of the wording of S.123(6) ERA, which is: 'Where the tribunal finds that the dismissal was to any extent caused or contributed to by any action of the complainant, it shall reduce the amount of the compensatory award *by such proportion as it considers just and equitable* having regard to that finding' (our emphasis). It is important to note that the just and equitable consideration in the context of contributory conduct applies only to the proportion (i.e. the percentage amount) by which the tribunal reduces the award. It does not apply to whether or not to make a reduction in the first place, or entitle the tribunal to take into account matters other than conduct that is causative or contributory to the dismissal – see Parker Foundry Ltd v Slack 1992 ICR 302, CA, per Balcombe LJ. Once a tribunal has found, on the evidence, that an employee has to some extent caused or contributed to his or her dismissal, it 'shall' (i.e. must) reduce the award. The only discretion then left to it is by how much.

It should also be noted that in cases where there are no grounds for making a reduction on account of contributory fault under S.123(6) – e.g. because the 'culpability' element is lacking in, say, a capability dismissal – the

698 ────────────────────────────────

compensatory award, but not the basic award, may still be reduced under S.123(1) ERA on the basis that it is just and equitable to do so. One example would be where a dismissal was unfair on procedural grounds in circumstances in which the evidence showed that the employee was indeed incapable of performing the job. Another would be where an employer only discovers the fact that an employee has committed an act of misconduct after he or she has been dismissed even though that act occurred before the date of dismissal. Although neither scenario would provide the basis for a finding of contributory fault, a tribunal would be entitled to take into account the justice and equity of the situation when assessing the overall compensatory award under S.123(1). See further under 'Just and equitable reductions' above.

Guidance on the amount of reduction. In Hollier v Plysu Ltd 1983 IRLR 260, EAT, the EAT suggested that the contribution should be assessed broadly and should generally fall within the following categories: wholly to blame (100 per cent); largely to blame (75 per cent); employer and employee equally to blame (50 per cent); slightly to blame (25 per cent).

18.130

Although this suggestion provides useful guidance, tribunals retain their discretion and findings of 90 per cent or 10 per cent are occasionally made. This is despite the obiter remarks of Lord MacDonald in Yorke v Brown EAT 262/84 to the effect that the assessment of an employee's contribution as low as 10 per cent is almost *de minimis* and that tribunals should in general apportion responsibility for the dismissal on a broader basis or not at all. In Alexander v Ellwood Glass Ltd ET Case No.28122/95 the employee was dismissed after informing the employer that he needed six weeks' unpaid leave to look after his wife following an operation. A tribunal found that no reasonable employer would have dismissed in those circumstances. Nevertheless, it went on to hold that the employee must have known that his wife was going to need looking after and that his failure to plan or discuss the time off with the employer at an earlier stage contributed to the dismissal by 10 per cent.

Since the assessment of contribution is a matter of discretion for the tribunal, few appeals succeed on this point. The EAT will only interfere if the tribunal has erred in law or made a perverse decision. In Foster v Somerset County Council 2004 EWCA Civ 222 the Court of Appeal (applying Hollier v Plysu Ltd above) held that the EAT's decision to reduce a 100 per cent reduction for contributory fault to 90 per cent, in circumstances where it did not find the tribunal's decision on contribution to be perverse, was an error of law. And in LA Recruitment and Management Services Ltd v MacKinnon EAT 0020/04, the EAT, while confirming that a tribunal's decisions regarding the degree of contribution will rarely be interfered with on appeal, observed that such interference may

699

be more appropriate where the gap between what the claimant seeks by way of compensation and what the tribunal actually awards is very substantial.

18.131 The following are some examples of where the EAT has felt it to be justified to interfere with the amount of contribution as found by tribunals below:

- **Coalter v Walter Craven Ltd** EAT 314/79: a funeral receptionist was unfairly dismissed after failing to notice when two bodies were mixed up and placed in the wrong coffins. The tribunal assessed her contributory conduct at 50 per cent but the EAT reduced it to 25 per cent, pointing out that it was her first mistake and that she had been given no clear written instructions as to her duties

- **Cornelius v London Borough of Hackney** EAT 1061/94: an in-house auditor was unfairly dismissed for disclosing confidential information concerning internal corruption to the councillor chairing the investigating committee and to union representatives. The tribunal found him to be 50 per cent responsible for his dismissal on the basis that he should have passed the documents to management. The EAT found the tribunal's decision perverse and held that C had not contributed to his dismissal at all. It was his duty to uncover corruption and he had not acted out of any improper motive

- **Nairne v Highland and Islands Fire Brigade** 1989 IRLR 366, Ct Sess (Inner House): a high-ranking fire officer who needed to drive as part of his job was dismissed following a second disqualification for a drink-driving offence. The EAT increased the contribution from 25 per cent to 75 per cent. This decision was upheld by the Court of Session.

18.132 **Nil awards (100 per cent contribution).** As already noted, the power of tribunals to reduce compensation extends to finding a 100 per cent 'contribution'. The ability to reduce compensation to this degree was first recognised by the National Industrial Relations Court (the precursor of the EAT) in Maris v Rotherham Corporation 1974 IRLR 147, NIRC. Following that decision, the EAT in England and Scotland were for a time divided on the extent to which 100 per cent deductions were, in practice, permissible, but the divergence came to an end in 1977 with the House of Lords' decision in W Devis and Sons Ltd v Atkins 1977 ICR 662, HL. In that case their Lordships unanimously decided that there was no inconsistency in finding that an employee was unfairly dismissed and that he or she contributed 100 per cent to this dismissal, so reducing the compensatory award to nil.

While it has been clear since the Devis case that 100 per cent deductions are possible, they remain rare and there is ample case authority that both recognises this and encourages that this remains so. In Moreland v David Newton (t/a Aden Castings) EAT 435/92 the EAT said that a reduction of 100 per cent is

700

unusual and a tribunal must fully justify such a course of action by reference to facts and reasons in its decision.

The most likely situation in which a 100 per cent reduction will be ordered is where the tribunal considers that an employee's misconduct was such that dismissal was wholly justified but nonetheless feels compelled to find the dismissal unfair because of procedural flaws in the dismissal procedure. Even then, a finding of 100 per cent contribution will not automatically follow, since the question of the appropriate level of contribution remains, as we have seen, one for the tribunal's discretion. Three examples:

18.133

- **Smith v Lodge Bros (Funerals) Ltd** EAT 92/88: S was dismissed for being absent from work without informing his employer. A tribunal found his dismissal unfair because he had been dismissed by letter and given no opportunity to state his case but it went on to reduce his compensation by 100 per cent. On appeal, S argued that it was legally impossible to reduce compensation by 100 per cent when the employer had been guilty of a major procedural defect. The EAT rejected this argument. It said that the tribunal had expressly found that S's conduct had caused the dismissal while the employer's conduct, although wrong, had not caused the dismissal in any shape or form

- **Ardyne Scaffolding Ltd v Rennie** EAT 688/93: R was dismissed after returning to work drunk following a Christmas lunch. A tribunal found that the employer had handled the dismissal unfairly but reduced the compensatory award by 75 per cent on account of the employee's conduct. The EAT rejected the employer's argument that, since R's conduct was the sole occasion for the dismissal, the tribunal should have made a much higher assessment of the employee's contribution

- **Palmer v Clark and Symonds Ltd** EAT 388/98: P worked as a receptionist for a car repair company and her job was to obtain insurance excess charges direct from customers. While P was on holiday, her employer carried out an investigation. Eight customers had paid P cash but there was no record of their payments in the company's books. P was arrested on return from holiday and never returned to work. The tribunal found unfair dismissal but awarded compensation subject to 100 per cent contribution. P's appeal on the basis that the tribunal had failed to consider what outcome might have followed from a fair procedure was rejected by the EAT because, in any event, the result would have remained the same and P would still have been subject to the 100 per cent reduction.

Although it can be gleaned from the above cases that the EAT will rarely interfere with a tribunal's decision regarding the amount of contribution, a finding of 100 per cent contributory fault has to be firmly based on logic that is consistent with the tribunal's findings of fact. If such findings accept some measure of fault on both sides regarding the cause of the dismissal, or if the

18.134

701

dismissal is contributed to by a mixture of blameworthy and non-blameworthy conduct on the part of the employee, it is difficult to see how a 100 per cent reduction could, in principle, be justified.

This point is illustrated by the EAT's decision in Langston v Department for Business Enterprise and Regulatory Reform EAT 0534/09. In that case, the complainant was a senior employee with specialist knowledge of nuclear and explosion issues. His post attracted a high level of security clearance. However, while attending a conference abroad, his colleagues became concerned about his unusual behaviour, which included unfounded allegations that his room had been broken into and that money and personal effects had been stolen. He was later diagnosed by the employer's medical adviser as having suffered an 'acute transient psychotic disorder', which occurred in parallel with the employee being highly stressed as the result of the demands of his job. The medical adviser reported that a repeat episode could not be ruled out in the future. As a result, the employee's security clearance was revoked. For a while, the employer sought to find suitable alternative employment, but these efforts were overtaken by the need to make redundancies, and the employee eventually became a casualty of these.

18.135 An employment tribunal found that the employee had been unfairly dismissed because the real reason for his dismissal was not redundancy but the decision to delete his post, which itself was linked to the removal of his personal security clearance. His dismissal for 'some other substantial reason' was held to be automatically unfair because the employer failed to carry out the statutory dismissal procedures applicable to most dismissals at the time. However, the tribunal went on to make a finding of 100 per cent contribution against the employee on account of his 'bizarre and misjudged' conduct at the conference, which, in the tribunal's view, had destroyed the employer's trust and confidence in him. The EAT allowed the employee's appeal on the ground that the tribunal had failed to consider whether the conduct relied on as the basis for the contributory fault finding was within the control of the employee and was 'culpable or blameworthy', as it was required to be – see under 'Culpable or blameworthy conduct' above. Had the tribunal properly addressed that matter, then in the context of the facts as found it could not have properly concluded that a 100 per cent reduction, or anywhere near it, was appropriate. The EAT therefore remitted the case to a new tribunal to consider afresh the extent to which (if any) the employee's conduct had contributed to his dismissal.

In effect, the Langston case illustrates the proposition that, for a 100 per cent contribution finding to be permissible, the employee's conduct must be found to be the sole reason for the dismissal. This proposition is confirmed by the obiter remarks of Mr Justice Elias in Kelly-Madden v Manor Surgery 2007 ICR 203, EAT. This is not the same thing as saying that just because there is fault on the employer's part means that a 100 per cent finding is impossible. If that were the case, no such finding would be permissible in any case where the employer has been guilty of procedural errors that led to a finding that the dismissal was unfair. Reflecting on what he had said in the Kelly-Madden case, Elias J in Ingram v Bristol Street Parts EAT 0601/06 clarified the role that procedural fault on the part of the employer might have in this context. He observed that sometimes procedural failings by the employer will be causally relevant to the dismissal itself, in which case a finding of 100 per cent contribution would not be justified. But if the employee's blameworthy conduct was found to be the sole factor resulting in the dismissal, then a 100 per cent finding could be justifiable.

The 'Polkey effect'. In the section on 'Polkey reductions' above, we discuss in detail the effects on the calculation of compensation of the House of Lords' decision in Polkey v AE Dayton Services Ltd 1988 ICR 142, HL. That case established that, based on the wording of what is now S.123(1) ERA, tribunals are entitled to reduce the amount of the compensatory award in circumstances where dismissal is found to be unfair by reason of procedural failures by the employer. The amount of any such reduction depends on an assessment by the tribunal of the likelihood that, had the procedural irregularities not occurred, the employee would have still been dismissed. Where a reduction is made on this basis, there may also be an element of contributory fault in respect of which a separate and additional reduction is made. The precise relationship between S.123(1) and 123(6) is considered under 'Polkey reductions' above.

18.136

Tribunal's duty to provide sufficient reasons

18.137

It should be noted that, although the wording of S.123(6) is mandatory – an employment tribunal '*shall* reduce the amount of the compensatory award' – the tribunal is nonetheless obliged to give its reasons for making (or not making) a reduction – Nairne v Highland and Islands Fire Brigade 1989 IRLR 366, Ct Sess (Inner House). In South West Trains v Miles EAT 0039/03, the EAT held that a tribunal considering contribution ought, if it is going to find no contribution at all, to make a clear finding with proper reasons that the employee was neither blameworthy nor culpable. Extending that theme, in Mars UK Ltd t/a Masterfoods v Parker EAT 0412/06 the EAT doubted that there would be many cases where it would be sufficient for a tribunal simply to declare that an employee did not contribute to his or her dismissal without explaining why: only if it is obvious from the remainder of its full reasoned decision why there was no contributory fault would such a minimalist approach be permissible.

On the other hand, if the tribunal does find contributory fault, it must be satisfied that the employee did actually commit the acts that contributed to the dismissal and should explain why this is so. In London Borough of Lewisham v James EAT 0581–2/03 the EAT stated that 'it is quite plain that

703

S.123(6) is not satisfied by reference to a finding simply that an employer had reasonable belief in the conduct. The conduct which is to form the basis of a deduction for contributory fault, whatever it is, must be established, proved and identified by the tribunal.'

In Cornwall County Council and anor v McCabe EAT 147/97 M, a teacher, was dismissed following allegations by two female pupils that he had fondled them. A tribunal found the dismissal to be unfair due to a woefully inadequate investigation, but nonetheless reduced M's award by 20 per cent for contributory conduct. The EAT set aside the deduction: there was nothing in the tribunal's decision to show what misconduct M had actually committed. A 'no smoke without fire' approach was not acceptable.

18.138 **Allowing relevant evidence to be given.** Tribunals must be careful not to exclude evidence that may be relevant to showing that the employee contributed to his or her dismissal simply because of the overwhelming case that the employee was unfairly dismissed. In PJ and ME Egan t/a Dell Care Home v Owen EAT 0035/08 it was obvious on the face of the employer's own admissions that it had completely failed to conduct a sufficient investigation into allegations of misconduct against the employee. For that reason, the employment tribunal found that the employee had been unfairly dismissed. The tribunal proceeded to refuse to hear three witnesses whom the employer wished to call for the purpose of proving the truth behind at least some of the allegations that had caused the employee to be dismissed. On appeal, the EAT ruled that this was an error of law. Though the evidence that the employer wished to call was not material to the question of fairness of the dismissal, it was relevant both to considerations of contribution under S.123(6) and the amount of the compensatory award under S.123(1), and therefore should not have been excluded.

18.139 **Separation of findings relevant to unfairness and contribution.** As we have seen, tribunals are expected to separate in their minds findings relevant to the issue of the fairness of dismissal from those relevant to contributory fault and other aspects of compensation – see the discussion of London Ambulance Service NHS Trust v Small 2008 IRLR 563, CA, under 'General principles' above. In that case Lord Justice Mummery advised that, as a general rule, it would be good practice for tribunals to keep their findings on these matters separate. Although some facts may be relevant to more than one issue, the legal elements of the different issues and the role of the tribunal in adjudicating them are not necessarily the same. Making separate and sequential findings of fact on discrete issues might therefore help to avoid errors of law, even if this leads to a degree of duplication.

Since the decision in Small, the Court of Appeal has had a further opportunity to consider the way in which tribunals should approach evidence relevant to the fairness of dismissal on the one hand, and that

704

relevant to contributory fault on the other. In Salford Royal NHS Foundation Trust v Roldan 2010 IRLR 721, CA, Lord Justice Elias, giving the only reasoned judgment of the Court of Appeal, accepted that Mummery LJ in Small had said it would be helpful, when looking at questions of fairness, contributory fault and 'Polkey reductions', etc, for tribunals to set out separately their relevant findings of fact with respect to each issue. But Elias LJ considered that Mummery LJ had not been laying down any fixed rule about this and that, in any event, his observations did not amount to a requirement that witnesses should give their evidence on these matters in a 'compartmentalised' way. In particular, it was not appropriate in the normal run of things for witnesses to give evidence first on liability and then separately to give similar (if not identical) evidence dealing with the question of contributory fault. This was especially true where the tribunal has made it clear in advance of the hearing that the parties will be expected to adduce evidence as to liability and remedy at the same hearing. But even where there is a split hearing on issues of liability and remedy, it was not the case that tribunals are required to hear all witnesses twice: such a notion would only add to the length and cost of hearings without having any obvious benefit. Elias LJ observed that it was important that the parties clarify with the tribunal precisely what issues the tribunal wishes to have determined at which stage. If there is any doubt about whether a party needs to adduce evidence on a particular point or whether it should be left to a later hearing, that matter ought to be raised with the tribunal.

The outcome in the Roldan case was that the Court of Appeal reinstated an **18.140** employment tribunal's decision not only that the employee had been unfairly dismissed but that there should be no reduction made to her compensation on account of contributory fault. The case concerned S, an experienced registered nurse, who was accused by a relatively inexperienced nurse of mistreating a vulnerable patient by, among other things, throwing wet wipes at his face and making an abusive 'V' sign gesture. The employment tribunal, however, found her dismissal to be unfair, principally for lack of a sufficient investigation. At the subsequent remedies hearing, the tribunal refused to allow the nurse who had witnessed the alleged incidents to be recalled to give evidence relevant to the issue of contributory fault. On appeal, the EAT overturned the tribunal's decision on liability and also concluded that the tribunal had erred in shutting out evidence pertaining to contributory conduct. Citing the Court of Appeal's decision in the Small case, the EAT held that the tribunal should have allowed the junior nurse to be recalled to provide further evidence pertaining to the question of whether S's conduct had contributed to her dismissal. However, on further appeal, the Court of Appeal overturned the EAT's decision on both the liability and the contributory fault issues for the reasons discussed above.

705

18.141 Offsetting enhanced redundancy payments

Section 123(7) ERA makes special provision in respect of the setting off of redundancy payments. It provides that if the amount of any redundancy payment made by the employer exceeds the amount of the basic award, 'that excess goes to reduce the amount of the *compensatory award*' (our emphasis). Thus, if the employer's redundancy scheme is more generous than the statutory scheme and the dismissal is subsequently judged by a tribunal to be unfair, the part of the redundancy payment that corresponds to the statutory entitlement will normally extinguish entitlement to a basic award (see Chapter 15 under 'Reductions in basic award'), with the excess then serving to reduce the compensatory award.

In Digital Equipment Co Ltd v Clements (No.2) 1997 ICR 237, EAT, the employee had received a contractual redundancy payment which exceeded his statutory entitlement by £20,685. The EAT held that an excess redundancy payment should be treated no differently from any other payment made upon termination of employment. Accordingly, the EAT deducted the £20,685 from the assessment of the employee's losses before applying a 50 per cent Polkey reduction. However, when the case reached the Court of Appeal – reported at Digital Equipment Co Ltd v Clements (No.2) 1998 ICR 258, CA – the Court held that this was wrong. Enhanced redundancy payments must be subtracted from the compensatory award *after* the percentage deduction. In its view, 'Parliament has drawn a clear distinction in the treatment of the excess of redundancy payments... and the other elements which go to make up the loss'.

18.142 The distinction is that S.123(7) specifically provides that excess redundancy payments should be deducted from the compensatory award itself, rather than being treated as part of the calculation of the employee's losses which go to make up the amount of the compensatory award. The correct approach, therefore, is first to assess the employee's loss, making any proportional reductions to ensure that the compensation is just and equitable, and then to deduct from the resulting compensatory award the excess redundancy payment. This method, said the Court, accords with the clear intention of S.123(7) that employers should receive full credit for redundancy payments which are larger than required by statute.

It is important to note that S.123(7) only applies to redundancy payments, both statutory and contractual. Thus, if there is no genuine redundancy situation, a payment labelled as a redundancy payment would fall to be offset against the claimant's losses in the same way as an ex gratia termination payment.

18.143 Provided a redundancy payment is genuine, a tribunal should effectively take no account of it until it has calculated the measure of loss and applied any other deductions and adjustments. In MacCulloch v Imperial Chemical Industries Ltd EAT 0275/09 a tribunal fell into error by offsetting an enhanced redundancy payment against the claimant's losses, and then deducting the amount of the

706

payment that exceeded the basic award from the claimant's compensatory award. The EAT explained that, in circumstances such as the instant case where a tribunal determines that, but for the dismissal, the claimant would have received a larger enhanced redundancy payment at a later date, the correct approach is to include in the calculation of loss a sum that reflects the payment the claimant *would* have received, minus the amount of a basic award to which the claimant would have been entitled at the later date. Only once the losses have been calculated, and any other adjustments or deductions made, should the tribunal deduct from the compensatory award the amount by which the redundancy payment that the employee *did* receive exceeds the basic award.

Application of statutory cap

18.144

All relevant adjustments and deductions have to be made *before* the application of the statutory cap on compensation. In most cases of unfair dismissal a statutory ceiling is placed on the amount of the compensatory award (currently £65,300 as from 1 February 2010), although there are a few exceptions where no such ceiling is imposed – see Chapter 16 under 'Nature and maximum amount of award'. Whenever the statutory cap does apply, it is only if the total figure for the compensatory award exceeds the prevailing maximum once all relevant adjustments and deductions have been made that the tribunal should reduce the level of its award to the prevailing maximum – see Walter Braund (London) Ltd v Murray 1991 IRLR 100, EAT. So, for example, if the employee's losses amount to £90,000 and the tribunal assesses his or her contribution towards the dismissal at 25 per cent, a 25 per cent reduction should be applied to the £90,000 to leave £67,500. Since this exceeds the statutory maximum, the compensatory award would then be reduced to the prevailing statutory maximum. It would be wrong first to apply the statutory maximum of (currently) £65,300 and then reduce it by 25 per cent to arrive at a figure of £48,975.

Order of adjustments and deductions

18.145

Having considered the different types of deduction that may be made from the compensatory award, it is important to be aware of the order in which adjustments and deductions – if applicable – should be made. Sometimes a tribunal, in assessing the compensatory award, may have to make a deduction of an ex gratia payment made by the employer as well making a percentage deduction for contributory conduct under S.123(6) ERA and/or a reduction to reflect what is 'just and equitable' under S.123(1) ERA. Where this happens, the question arises as to which deduction should be made first.

707

To take a simple example: a tribunal assesses the employee's losses, before any deductions, at £10,000. It also finds that the employer made an ex gratia payment of £2,000 that must be offset against those losses and that the employee contributed 50 per cent to the dismissal. If the tribunal first deducts the £2,000 ex gratia payment, then applies the 50 per cent deduction for contributory fault to the remaining £8,000, the employee will come away with £4,000. If, however, the tribunal does the calculation the other way round, applying the 50 per cent deduction first to arrive at a figure of £5,000 and then offsetting the £2,000 payment, the employee will end up with the lesser sum of £3,000. Clearly, therefore, the order in which the calculation is done can make a considerable difference to the amount of the final compensatory award.

18.146 **General principles.** Faced with a number of conflicting EAT decisions on the matter, the then President of the EAT, Mr Justice Morison, decided to lay down guidelines for tribunals to follow. In Digital Equipment Co Ltd v Clements (No.2) 1997 ICR 237, EAT, Morison J held that the correct approach is first to offset any contractual or ex gratia termination payments (including a payment in lieu of notice) in order to arrive at the employee's 'net loss', then to make any proportionate reduction necessary to reflect contributory fault or, in a case of a procedurally unfair dismissal, the chance that the employee would have been dismissed in any event (see under 'Polkey reductions' above). The EAT stated that it was important to bear in mind the difference between a proportionate reduction of an award and a deduction or set-off. A deduction in the latter sense takes place as part of the calculation of the award, which then falls to be proportionately reduced to reflect contributory conduct or a Polkey reduction. Similarly, said the EAT, a deduction for failure to mitigate should be made before any such percentage reduction.

Considerable support for this approach has since come from the Court of Appeal in Ministry of Defence v Wheeler and ors 1998 IRLR 23, CA, where a similar view was taken as to the order of deductions. Furthermore, in Heggie v Uniroyal Englebert Tyres Ltd 1999 IRLR 802, Ct Sess (Inner House), the Inner House of the Court of Session confirmed that any payment in lieu of notice should be deducted before any proportionate deduction for contributory conduct on the employee's part.

Where a tribunal has to make both a Polkey reduction and a reduction for contributory conduct, it will make no difference to the final amount which percentage is applied first. However, in Rao v Civil Aviation Authority 1994 IRLR 240, CA, the Court of Appeal held that an employment tribunal should first make the Polkey reduction under S.123(1). The size of that reduction may well have a significant bearing on what further reduction falls to be made for contributory conduct under S.123(6).

708

Off-setting enhanced redundancy payments. It is crucial to note, however, that different considerations apply to the setting-off of redundancy payments. As we have seen under 'Payment received by employees' above, S.123(7) ERA specifically provides that, if the amount of any redundancy payment made by the employer exceeds the amount of the basic award, 'that excess goes to reduce the amount of the compensatory award'. In the Digital Equipment case (above), the employee had received a contractual redundancy payment which exceeded his statutory entitlement by £20,685. The EAT held that an excess redundancy payment should be treated no differently from any other payment made upon termination of employment. Accordingly, following the guidelines set out above, the EAT deducted the £20,685 from the assessment of the employee's losses before applying a 50 per cent Polkey reduction. However, when the case reached the Court of Appeal – Digital Equipment Co Ltd v Clements (No.2) 1998 ICR 258, CA – the Court held that this was wrong. Enhanced redundancy payments must be subtracted from the compensatory award after the percentage deduction. In its view, 'Parliament has drawn a clear distinction in the treatment of the excess of redundancy payments... and the other elements which go to make up the loss'.

18.147

The distinction is that S.123(7) specifically provides that excess redundancy payments should be deducted from the compensatory award itself, rather than be treated as part of the calculation of the employee's losses which go to make up the amount of the compensatory award. The correct approach, therefore, is first to assess the employee's loss, making any proportional reductions to ensure that the compensation is just and equitable, and then to deduct from the resulting compensatory award the excess redundancy payment. This method, said the Court, accords with the clear intention of S.123(7) that employers should receive full credit for redundancy payments which are larger than required by statute.

Section 207A TULR(C)A and S.38 EA 2002 adjustments. The question arises whether any adjustment to the compensatory award pursuant to the new statutory provision for making adjustments of up to 25 per cent in respect of breaches of the Acas Code of Practice on Disciplinary and Grievance Procedures has to be made before or after any reduction on account of: (i) payment by the employer to the employee of an ex gratia payment or payment in lieu of notice; (ii) failure to mitigate; (iii) a 'just and equitable' reduction in accordance with S.123(1) ERA (including a Polkey reduction to reflect the chance that dismissal would have occurred even if the proper procedure had been followed); (iv) contributory fault; (v) payment of an enhanced redundancy payment in excess of the amount of the basic award; and (vi) adjustment made under S.38 EA 2002 in respect of a failure to provide full and accurate written particulars of employment.

18.148

In respect of each of the reductions mentioned in (i), (ii) and (iii), any percentage adjustment for breach of the Acas Code should be made *after* any such

709

reduction has first been made in accordance with the guidance set out in Digital Equipment v Clements (above).

18.149   In respect of (iv) and (v), S.124A ERA stipulates that: 'Where an award of compensation for unfair dismissal falls to be reduced or increased – (a) under S.207A of the TULR(C)A 1992... or (b) increased under S.38 of the [EA 2002]... the adjustment... shall be applied *immediately before* any reduction under S.123(6) or (7)' (our emphasis). This means that any reduction on account of contributory fault or payment of an enhanced redundancy payment must be made immediately after the adjustment for breach of the Acas Code or the increase of up to four weeks' pay for a failure to provide written particulars of employment is applied.

Regarding (vi), S.207A(5) TULR(C)A provides that: 'Where an award falls to be adjusted under [S107A for breach of the Acas Code] *and* under S.38 EA 2002, the adjustment under [S.107A] shall be made *before* the adjustment under [S.38]' (our emphasis). In other words, the appropriate adjustment for breach of the Acas Code is made before any adjustment in respect of the employer's failure to provide accurate written particulars.

18.150   **Statutory ceiling on compensatory award.** If the statutory cap on the compensatory award (currently £65,300) applies, the cap must be applied after all deductions and other adjustments have been made. The circumstances in which the cap does and does not apply are discussed in Chapter 16 under 'Nature and maximum amount of award'.

18.151   **Summary of principles**

The correct order for deductions is as summarised below with regard to the rules discussed above. The summary reflects the Court of Appeal's comments in the Digital Equipment case (above), but duly modified to include, at the appropriate point, adjustments that fall to be made under S.107A TULR(C)A in respect of breaches of the Acas Code.

To calculate the compensatory award, it is first necessary to ascertain the employee's total loss in consequence of the dismissal, in so far as that loss is attributable to the employer's actions – S.123(1) ERA. Deductions and adjustments (if applicable) should then be made strictly in the following order:

- deduction of any payment already made by the employer as compensation for the dismissal (e.g. an ex gratia payment or payment in lieu of notice) but not any enhanced redundancy payment

- deduction of sums earned by way of mitigation, or to reflect the employee's failure to take reasonable steps in mitigation – S.123(4)

- 'just and equitable' reductions based on S.123(1) ERA, including reductions in accordance with the principle in Polkey v AE Dayton Services Ltd 1988 ICR 142, HL

710

- increase or reduction (adjustment) of up to 25 per cent where the employer or employee failed to comply with a material provision of the Acas Code of Practice on Disciplinary and Grievance Procedures – S.207A TULR(C)A

- adjustment of up to four weeks' pay in respect of the employer's failure to provide full and accurate written particulars – S.38 EA 2002

- percentage reduction for the employee's contributory fault – S.123(6) ERA

- deduction of any enhanced redundancy payment to the extent that it exceeds the basic award (liability for the basic award will also have been set off by the statutory redundancy payment under S122(4)) – S.123(7) ERA

- application of the statutory cap (£65,300 at the time of writing) – S.124 ERA.

19 Additional awards and interim relief

Additional awards

Interim relief

In most cases in which an employee succeeds in an unfair dismissal complaint before a tribunal, his or her remedy will be an award of financial compensation. In the great majority of cases this will consist of a basic award and a compensatory award, as discussed in the four preceding chapters. However, as explained in Chapter 14, the tribunal must first consider whether it is appropriate to grant reinstatement or re-engagement of the employee. In the rare cases that it does so, two further awards may be made:

19.1

- an *additional award* under S.117(3)(b) of the Employment Rights Act 1996 (ERA) where the employer has totally failed to comply with the tribunal's order to reinstate or re-engage the employee (and has been unable to show the tribunal that it was impracticable to do so)

- an *award of four weeks' pay* (unless this would result in injustice to the employer) under S.112(5) and (6) ERA where the employer has failed to comply with the statutory retirement procedure under S.98ZG (see Chapter 9) and an order for reinstatement or re-engagement is made. Note that this award should be deducted from any later award of compensation made under S.117(1) (where the employer only partially complies with the re-employment order) or S.117(3)(a) (where there has been total non-compliance with the order) – Ss.117(2A) and 123(8).

Note that 'special awards' – which used to be available under S.118(2) and (3) ERA where the dismissal was for one of a number of automatically unfair reasons (e.g. trade union activities, membership or non-membership) and the employee had asked for reinstatement or re-engagement – were repealed by the Employment Relations Act 1999. As a corollary, the amount that can be awarded by a tribunal by way of an additional award under S.117(3)(b) ERA was significantly increased from between 13–26 weeks' pay to between 26–52 weeks' pay (see 'Additional awards' below for more detail). At the same time, the Employment Relations Act 1999 inserted a new S.124(1A) into the ERA which removes the statutory limit on the compensatory award (currently £65,300) in some (though not all) cases which would previously have benefited from a special award under S.118(2) and (3) – see Chapter 16.

713

This chapter explains the circumstances in which an additional award may be made and also considers the special remedy of interim relief, which may be available in certain cases between the date of dismissal and the date of the tribunal's full hearing of the unfair dismissal complaint.

Additional awards

19.2

If an order for reinstatement or re-engagement has been made but the employer has not complied with it at all (for an analysis of the distinction between total and partial non-compliance, see Chapter 14 under 'Reinstatement and re-engagement – enforcement of order'), the tribunal *must* make an additional award on top of the normal basic and compensatory awards unless the employer satisfies the tribunal that it was not practicable to comply with the order – S.117(4)(a) ERA. The question of practicability is discussed in Chapter 14.

Size of award

19.3

Under S.117(3)(b) ERA, tribunals have considerable discretion as to how much to grant by way of additional award but the award must be of an amount *not less than 26 weeks' pay and not more than 52 weeks' pay*. These limits were introduced by the Employment Relations Act 1999 and replaced the previous two-tier system under which an additional award of between 13 and 26 weeks' pay was available for non-compliance with a re-employment order in an ordinary unfair dismissal case and a higher additional award of between 26 and 52 weeks' pay applicable where the dismissal amounted to an act of unlawful sex, race or disability discrimination.

A week's pay is calculated in accordance with Ss.220–229 ERA – for details see IDS Employment Law Handbook, 'Wages' (2003), Chapter 11. A week's pay in this context is subject to a current maximum of £380 (a figure which is normally increased each year). Thus, the minimum possible additional award is currently £9,880, while the maximum is £19,760.

The calculation date (i.e. the date on which the employee's pay is ascertained) is the date the employer's notice was given (not the date on which it expired): if no notice was given, it is the effective date of termination of the contract – S.226(2) ERA.

19.4

The EAT has pointed out that tribunals have a wide discretion in fixing an additional award within the statutory limits, although it has said that 'some sort of proper assessment and balancing must take place'. A tribunal that simply announced a maximum additional award without any explanation had misapplied the law by not carrying out any sort of reasoned exercise to determine what the figure should be – Morganite Electrical Carbon Ltd v Donne 1988 ICR 18, EAT. The EAT in that case also held that a tribunal may not, in an effort to ensure compliance, simply decree in advance that it will

714

make the maximum additional award if the employer fails to comply with a re-employment order. The way in which the tribunal exercises its discretion should properly take into account the true purpose of an additional award. In the words of Judge Knox in Mabirizi v National Hospital for Nervous Diseases 1990 ICR 281, EAT, 'the compensation is not intended to be a precisely calculated substitute for financial loss but rather a general solatium to be arrived at by fixing the appropriate point on the scale which Parliament has fixed'.

Factors that may be taken into account include:

- the conduct of the employer in refusing to comply with the re-employment order, and

- the extent to which the compensatory award has met the actual loss suffered by the employee.

These are two rather different considerations. The first views the award as a penalty on an unmeritorious employer; the second concentrates on compensation to the employee. In practice, both factors are commonly taken into account by tribunals. Below are some examples of cases in which an additional award was made. (However, it should be noted that all of these cases bar one pre-date the changes made by the Employment Relations Act 1999 and were therefore decided when the two-tier system for additional awards (see above) was still in place so that the maximum additional award that could be made in a normal unfair dismissal case was 26 weeks' pay): **19.5**

- **Bowden v Crest Nicholson Operations Ltd** ET Case No.1100186/03: B was employed as regional managing director until his dismissal. The employer admitted that the dismissal was unfair but opposed B's application for re-engagement, maintaining that it was not practicable to re-employ him. Bearing in mind B's conciliatory attitude and his willingness to work with others constructively, the tribunal rejected this argument, holding that, taking into account both the operation of the company and also that of associated employers, it was practicable to place B in comparable or other suitable employment. It found that the employer failed to comply with the order without good reason, and awarded the maximum additional award of 52 weeks' pay

- **Goodall v University of Lincolnshire and Humberside** ET Case No.1801296/98: on Monday morning G, a caretaker, reported a substantial amount of damage to the premises after it had been used for a Christmas party on the previous Friday night. However, the duty caretaker on the night in question had stated that there was no damage at the end of the night. A tribunal found G's subsequent dismissal unfair and ordered reinstatement but the University refused to agree. A number of staff did not accept that the tribunal's decision: they believed that if G

715

was exonerated, they must be being blamed; and other members of the caretaking staff said they could no longer work with him. The tribunal decided that there had been a wilful refusal to reinstate for no other reason than a desire to uphold the original decision. However, it accepted that the employer's concerns were genuine, albeit misconceived. For that reason, it awarded 22 weeks' additional award, rather than the maximum 26 weeks

- **Travers v Chief Constable, Dorset Constabulary** ET Case No.3103759/98: T was dismissed for being under the influence of alcohol at work. It was submitted that she had a drink problem and was taking steps to deal with it. The tribunal found the dismissal to be unfair. No reasonable employer would have dismissed without endeavouring to assist the employee. The Chief Constable was ordered to reinstate T but refused, claiming there had been a breach of trust and confidence. The tribunal rejected that contention – the Constabulary had failed to offer T any help not because of any breach of trust but because it did not want her back in her old job. This was a blatant case of failure to take an award of reinstatement seriously. The tribunal awarded the maximum additional award

- **Motherwell Railway Club v McQueen and anor** 1989 ICR 418, EAT: when making additional awards of 20 weeks' pay to Mr and Mrs M, the tribunal took into account the fact that, unknown to the employer, Mr M had been certified unfit for work. On appeal, the EAT rejected the employer's argument that no additional award should have been made since Mr M's health made reinstatement impossible. It pointed out that it was because the employer made no attempt to comply with the reinstatement order that the facts about Mr M's illness did not come to light. Since the employer had done nothing to show that reinstatement was not practicable at the time, the tribunal was bound to make an award. It was correct to penalise the employer by more than the minimum, but less than the maximum

- **Initial Textile Services v Ritchie** EAT 358/89: R was unfairly dismissed (a fact conceded by ITS). The tribunal found no significant contribution on her part and made a reinstatement order, against which ITS appealed unsuccessfully. It refused to reinstate R and the tribunal made a maximum award of 26 weeks' pay. ITS argued before the EAT that the tribunal should have made a minimum award of only 13 weeks' pay because it had lost confidence in R as an employee and R had already been fully compensated by her compensatory award. The EAT, however, thought that more than the minimum was called for: the employer had conceded unfairness, reinstatement was practicable, and there had been no contribution by the employee. But the tribunal had not taken all the circumstances into account – in particular, that R had been fully compensated – and the EAT therefore reduced the additional award to one of 20 weeks' pay.

In Mabirizi v National Hospital for Nervous Diseases 1990 ICR 281, EAT, the **19.6** hospital failed to produce evidence at the remedies hearing to the effect that reinstatement would be impracticable and the tribunal ordered that M should be reinstated. The hospital failed to comply with the order. However, when fixing the additional award payable to M, the tribunal took account of evidence given by the hospital that it had lost trust and confidence in M as it had concerns that, while off sick, M had been working elsewhere. Therefore its failure to reinstate her had not been mere wilful refusal. The employee appealed unsuccessfully to the EAT. As put rather colourfully by Judge Knox: 'The Act… expressly contemplates that an employer should be able both to try to persuade the industrial tribunal… that reinstatement would be impracticable and to try to persuade the industrial tribunal after the event of non-compliance… that it was not practicable to comply with the order. One process looks forward, the other looks back and although it may be that a cherry that is rejected at the first bite will be likely to be regarded as indigestible at the second, there is in our view no doubt at all that two bites are allowed.' Therefore, a tribunal is entitled, when deciding the appropriate level of additional award, to take into account the employer's genuinely felt objection to reinstatement, irrespective of its earlier finding on the question of practicability.

In the Mabirizi case, the EAT also confirmed that a tribunal is entitled to take into account any failure on the claimant's part to mitigate his or her loss when considering the additional award. However, this should not be used as a factor resulting in a quantifiable reduction in the sum to which the employee would otherwise be entitled. This is because additional awards are *not subject to deduction* in the same way as compensatory awards. For example, an additional award cannot be reduced to take account of the employee's contributory conduct. It will, of course, be fairly rare for a tribunal to order re-engagement in the first place where there is any significant degree of contributory conduct, but tribunals did so in Ayub v Vauxhall Motors Ltd 1978 IRLR 428, ET, and Gordon v Greater Glasgow Health Board SCOET S/1920/84, both cases in which the employee was held to have contributed by 50 per cent to the dismissal. Since re-engagement was practicable but refused by the employers in both cases, the tribunals were obliged to make additional awards: in each case they made 19-week awards – about halfway between 13 and 26 weeks (the limits then applicable) – to reflect the employee's responsibility for the dismissal.

Note that, as an exception to the general rule, an ex gratia payment by the **19.7** employer may be set off against the additional award. In Darr and anor v LRC Products Ltd 1993 IRLR 257, EAT, a tribunal declined to make any basic, compensatory or additional award on the ground that the employer had made a severance payment that more than covered any compensation the tribunal would have awarded. The EAT remitted the case because the tribunal had failed to give adequate reasons as to how it had come to that conclusion. Nevertheless, the

717

EAT said that there was no reason in law why a severance payment should not be offset against the additional award. The matter would turn on whether, as a matter of construction, the payment was offered and accepted on the understanding that it was in satisfaction of any compensation, including any additional award, that might be awarded as a result of the dismissal.

It is worth reiterating that an additional award is only available where the employer has *totally* failed to comply with the tribunal's order to re-employ – i.e. has refused to reinstate or re-engage the employee. It is not available where the employer has taken the employee back but has only partially complied with the terms of the order. For the compensation available in cases of partial compliance with the order – and a discussion of the distinction between partial and total non-compliance – see Chapter 14.

19.8   **Additional awards and arrears of pay.** As explained in Chapter 14, in making a reinstatement or re-engagement order, a tribunal will usually make an award of back pay and other benefits that the employee, but for the dismissal, would have received in the period from dismissal to the date the order is complied with. If the order is not complied with, the employee receives compensation in the normal way – i.e. a basic and a compensatory award, as explained in the four preceding chapters – and, if the employer fails to establish that it was not practicable to comply, an additional award (as set out above). Since the compensatory award is subject to a statutory cap (currently £65,300), it used to be the case (before the cap was increased substantially from £12,000 to £50,000 in October 1999) that, if the employee was highly paid or a long period of time had elapsed between the dismissal and the tribunal hearing, it could be financially advantageous for the employer not to comply with the tribunal's order. That is, the arrears of pay that the employer would have to pay in complying with the order would amount to more than the combined amount of any compensatory and additional awards that the tribunal could make for non-compliance. This loophole has now been closed and S.124(4) ERA provides that the statutory limit on the compensatory award may be exceeded to the extent necessary to enable the aggregate of the compensatory and additional awards fully to reflect the amount of arrears of pay and benefits specified in the original order.

Note, however, that, where an additional award is made under S.117(3)(b) and a compensatory award under S.117(3)(a), the statutory limit should only be exceeded to the extent of the loss incurred between dismissal and when re-employment should have occurred less the additional award – Selfridges Ltd v Malik 1998 ICR 268, EAT. This is because back pay, etc, is not a free-standing head of damage to be awarded whether or not re-employment is complied with. It is only payable in respect of a re-employment order which has been complied with. If there is total non-compliance with the order, then loss forms part of the compensatory award. See Chapter 14 under 'Reinstatement and re-engagement – enforcement of order' for more details.

718 ─────────────────────────────────

Interim relief

19.9

Interim relief is a remedy available to employees who claim to have been dismissed for one of a number of inadmissible reasons (see 'Availability of interim relief' below). The statutory provisions are set out in Ss.161–166 of the Trade Union and Labour Relations (Consolidation) Act 1992 (TULR(C)A) and Ss.128–132 ERA.

Purpose of interim relief

19.10

Interim relief is an emergency interlocutory procedure designed, in appropriate cases, to ensure the preservation of the status quo pending the hearing of the unfair dismissal complaint. It is only available in specified categories of cases (as listed below) deemed by statute to be deserving of such protection and should be sought promptly by the claimant, who must apply for interim relief no later than seven days after dismissal.

If the employee complies with the tightly defined application procedure and satisfies a tribunal at a special hearing that he or she is likely to succeed at a full hearing in showing that the dismissal was for one of the relevant inadmissible reasons, then interim relief prevents the dismissal from taking full effect before the full hearing. This is because the tribunal may make a reinstatement or re-engagement order pending the full hearing or, alternatively, a continuation of contract order which will have the effect of keeping the employee suspended on full pay until the full tribunal hearing.

Availability of interim relief

19.11

Under S.161(1) TULR(C)A, an employee alleging unfair dismissal on any of the grounds set out in S.152 TULR(C)A can claim interim relief. S.152(1) provides that the dismissal of an employee will be automatically unfair if the reason for it (or, if more than one, the principal reason) was that the employee:

- was, or proposed to become, a member of an independent trade union, or

- had taken part, or proposed to take part, in the activities of an independent trade union at an appropriate time, or

- had made use, or proposed to make use, of trade union services at an appropriate time, or

- had failed to accept an offer made by the employer of inducements relating to trade union membership or activities or to collective bargaining, or

- was not a member of any trade union, or of a particular trade union, or of one of a number of particular trade unions, or had refused, or proposed to refuse, to become or remain a member.

719

(Note that interim relief is not available in cases of selection for redundancy for trade union reasons under S.153 TULR(C)A.)

19.12 Under S.128(1) ERA, an employee alleging unfair dismissal can claim interim relief if the reason (or principal reason) for the dismissal was that he or she:

- carried out (or proposed to carry out) any designated health and safety activities (S.100(1)(a))

- performed (or proposed to perform) any functions as a health and safety representative or as a member of a safety committee (S.100(1)(b))

- performed (or proposed to perform) any functions or activities as a working time representative or as a candidate for such a role (S.101A(1)(d))

- performed (or proposed to perform) any functions as a trustee of a relevant occupational pension scheme (S.102(1))

- performed (or proposed to perform) any functions or activities as an employee representative (or candidate for such a role) for the purposes of consultation on collective redundancies (under Chapter II of Part IV TULR(C)A) or a proposed transfer of an undertaking (under Regs 9, 13 and 15 of the Transfer of Undertakings (Protection of Employment) Regulations 2006 SI 2006/246) (S.103 ERA)

- made a protected disclosure under the Public Interest Disclosure Act 1998 (S.103A ERA)

- was dismissed for a reason connected with the statutory trade union recognition procedures contained in Schedule A1 to the TULR(C)A (para 161(2) of Schedule A1)

- was selected for dismissal for a reason relating to a trade union blacklist prohibited under the Employment Relations Act 1999 (Blacklists) Regulations 2010 SI 2010/493 (S.104F(1) ERA).

19.13 In addition, S.12(5) of the Employment Relations Act 1999 provides that interim relief may be sought where the reason (or principal reason) for the dismissal was that the worker exercised (or sought to exercise) the right under S.10 of that Act to be accompanied at a disciplinary or grievance hearing, or accompanied or sought to accompany another worker (whether of the same employer or not) to such a hearing. Similarly, under Reg 18(5) of the Employee Study and Training (Procedural Requirements) Regulations 2010 SI 2010/155 interim relief may be available where the reason (or principal reason) for the dismissal was that the person exercised (or sought to exercise) the right under Reg 16 to be accompanied at a meeting to consider a request to enter into study or training, or accompanied or sought to accompany an employee to such a meeting. In either case, the provisions of Ss.128–132 ERA will apply.

720

Note that interim relief is not available in cases of selection for redundancy for any of these inadmissible reasons. This means that where there is a genuine redundancy situation, claimants will be hard pushed to persuade a tribunal that they were in fact dismissed for the inadmissible reason – and are therefore entitled to interim relief under S.128 – and not by reason of redundancy. For instance, in McConnell and anor v Bombardier Aerospace/Short Brothers plc (No.2) 2009 IRLR 201, NICA, the Northern Ireland Court of Appeal held that a tribunal had been entitled to find that it had no jurisdiction to hear the claimants' application for interim relief. Although the claimants maintained that they were dismissed because of their trade union and health and safety representative activities, the tribunal correctly found that the reason (or principal reason) for their dismissals was redundancy. Accordingly, interim relief was not available.

In what follows, the first statutory reference will be to the TULR(C)A, followed by the relevant ERA reference.

Application procedure

19.14

Time is of the essence because the employee must present an application for interim relief, together with the claim form (ET1) claiming unfair dismissal for one of the inadmissible reasons, by the end of the *seven* days immediately following the effective date of termination – S.161(2)/S.128(2). If an employee is dismissed on a Monday, the application must therefore be presented by the following Monday. Tribunals have no jurisdiction to extend this time limit for any reason.

The application should state that the dismissal was unfair for one of the inadmissible reasons and state what the alleged reason was. However, tribunals do have discretion to allow subsequent amendment of a timeous application. In Barley and ors v Amey Roadstone Corporation Ltd 1977 ICR 546, EAT, for example, the applications were in time and they referred to interim relief and unfair dismissal but they did not in terms claim that the claimants had been dismissed for trade union reasons or state what those reasons were. The EAT held that the applications were not nullities and that they could be corrected outside the seven-day time limit.

Certificate required in cases of trade union membership/activities. When a claimant is claiming to have been dismissed because of actual or proposed union membership or participation in union activities, he or she must also produce (within the seven-day time limit) a certificate from an authorised union official – S.161(3) TULR(C)A. (No certificate is required if the employee is claiming that the dismissal was because of actual or proposed non-membership of a union. Nor is there any analogous provision requiring any sort of certificate under S.128 ERA, S.12(5) of the Employment Relations Act 1999 or Reg 18(5) of the Employee Study and Training (Procedural Requirements) Regulations 2010 SI 2010/155).

19.15

Section 161(3) sets out precise requirements for the official's certificate. It must:

- be in writing and be signed by an authorised official of the independent union of which the employee was a member or which he or she was proposing to join

- state that at the date of dismissal the employee was or proposed to become a member of the union

- state that there appear to be reasonable grounds for supposing that the reason (or principal reason) for the employee's dismissal was one alleged in the unfair dismissal complaint – i.e. a S.152 reason (see above).

'Authorised official' in this context means an official of the union who is 'authorised by [the union] to act for the purposes of this section' – S.161(4). The employee himself (or herself) may be an authorised official. In Farmeary v Veterinary Drug Co Ltd 1976 IRLR 322, ET, F was a GMWU recruitment officer who signed his own certificate as 'For the purpose of the Act... Authorised District Officer'. He failed, however, to produce any evidence of specific authorisation from the union to sign interim relief certificates and the tribunal refused to accept his argument that under the union's rules a district officer had a general authorisation to act on behalf of the union within his or her district.

19.16 What constitutes authorisation was considered by the EAT in Sulemany v Habib Bank Ltd 1983 ICR 60, EAT, which laid down the following rules:

- nothing in S.161 requires the certificate to state on its face that the signatory is a duly authorised official of the union

- where a certificate is signed by a union official a tribunal should, in the absence of any challenge to the contrary, proceed on the basis that the official is duly authorised

- if authorisation is challenged, the onus lies on the official to show that he or she had express or implied authority to sign the certificate.

In the Sulemany case the official who signed the certificate merely stated to the tribunal that his authority to sign the certificate was 'self-evident' from the fact that he signed as a negotiating officer of the union concerned. The EAT said that this was not good enough: the official had failed to provide any *evidence* sufficient to satisfy the tribunal that he was duly authorised. In Pickering v Equal Opportunities Commission ET Case No.2401664/96 the certificate from P's trade union accompanying the application for interim relief stated: 'In accordance with S.161(3), I hereby certify that: (1) [P] was a fully paid up member of the CPSA on the date of her departure from the EOC. (2) That she was CPSA's Branch Secretary in the EOC. (3) That management's decision not to grant [P] unpaid leave to undertake a union scholarship and thus forcing her to leave her job with the EOC appears to be reasonable grounds for supporting

722

her application to an [employment] tribunal.' The tribunal dismissed the application. Although the certificate supported P's claim, it did not appear to have given the certification required by S.161(3).

Express authorisation is preferable but a tribunal may be willing to imply authorisation from other functions performed by an official. For example, in Hird v ITS Rubber Ltd ET Case No.5463/87 a district secretary had no specific authorisation to sign interim relief certificates but he did have authority to conduct tribunal cases on behalf of union members and to authorise expenditure on tribunal litigation. The tribunal was prepared to imply that he had authority to sign certificates for the purposes of S.161. In the absence of contrary evidence, the tribunal is entitled to assume that a full-time union official – for example, a regional officer – has the requisite authority – Stone v Charrington and Co Ltd 1977 ICR 248, EAT. However, such authority is unlikely to be implied in the case of a shop steward or work representative, although a person in such a role could be given express authority to sign certificates by the relevant union. **19.17**

A certificate purporting to be signed by an authorised union official 'shall be taken to be signed by him unless the contrary is proved' – S.161(5). In Tee v Power Brakes Ltd ET Case No.27767/83 a certificate was signed on behalf of an authorised official by his secretary using her own name. The tribunal rejected it, although it said that it might have reached a different conclusion if the secretary had been authorised to act on behalf of the union.

The certificate should state that 'there appear to be *reasonable grounds* for supposing' (our stress) that the employee was dismissed because of union membership or activities. In Sulemany v Habib Bank Ltd (above) the certificate merely stated: 'I confirm that I have grounds for [supposing] that the principal reason for dismissal of the above-named is that given in paragraph 13 of the attached form [E]T1.' The EAT said that the certificate could be read in conjunction with the ET1 (i.e. the claim form) and that the latter clearly set out the employee's allegations about the reason for his dismissal. It also held that on a commonsense view the certificate would not be invalidated because it only referred to 'grounds' instead of 'reasonable grounds'.

This was in line with an earlier decision in Bradley v Edward Ryde and Sons 1979 ICR 488, EAT, in which the EAT stressed that too great a concentration on technicality was to be avoided in considering interim relief certificates. This was another case in which there was 'substantial compliance' with S.161 if the certificate was read together with the employee's unfair dismissal complaint. Since the union official clearly intended the two documents to be linked (although he did not expressly say so), the EAT held that the requirements of S.161 had been met. **19.18**

Tribunals will want to be satisfied, however, that the official has given proper consideration to the matter and is not merely rubber-stamping allegations

723

contained in an ET1. In Edge v TI Richards and Ross Ltd ET Case No.27871/83 a certificate merely said: 'I would request interim relief… on the basis that he has been dismissed for trade union activities.' The tribunal pointed out that the certificate did not contain any appraisal or judgement of the reason for dismissal and held that it did not meet the requirements of S.161(3).

Note that in Stone v Charrington and Co Ltd (above), the EAT mentioned, per curiam, that once given, the certificate cannot be revoked or withdrawn by the union official (except in special cases; for instance, where the employee is guilty of fraud). Any mistake made by the official can, however, be rectified at the hearing of the application for interim relief.

19.19 Prompt determination of application

Once a valid and timeous application for interim relief has been made, the tribunal is required to determine the issue as soon as is practicable – S.162(1)/ S.128(3). It must give the employer at least seven days' notice of the hearing, together with a copy of the application and, where relevant, of any accompanying certificate – S.162(2)/S.128(4). The tribunal is not allowed to postpone a hearing of an application for interim relief unless special circumstances justify such a course of action – S.162(4)/S.128(5).

19.20 Joinder of third parties in union membership cases

Under S.160 TULR(C)A, either the claimant or the employer can join a third party to the proceedings, with the result that the tribunal can order that party to pay some or all of the compensation awarded. This provision applies where it is claimed that the employer was pressured into dismissing the claimant by actual or threatened industrial action by a third party and the pressure was exercised because the claimant was not a union member. If a request to add a third party under S.160 is made before the date of the hearing, joinder will automatically be granted and, provided the request is made three or more days before that date, the tribunal must provide that third party with a copy of the application (and any certificate) as soon as is reasonably practicable, together with notice of the date, time and place of the interlocutory hearing – Ss.160(2) and 162(3). Joinder is discretionary if sought at a later time but will be automatically refused if sought after the tribunal has awarded compensation or made a re-employment order – S.160(2).

19.21 Likelihood of success

Once the employee has successfully surmounted the procedural hurdles to making an application for interim relief, the tribunal must go on to decide whether it is likely that he or she will succeed at a full hearing of the unfair dismissal complaint – S.163(1)/S.129(1). It is worth pointing out at the outset that this does not require the tribunal to make any findings of fact. Rather, as the tribunal reminded itself in Ryb v Nomura International plc ET Case No.3202174/09, it must make a decision as to the likelihood of the claimant's

724

success at a full hearing of the unfair dismissal complaint based on the material before it, which will usually consist of the parties' pleadings, the witness statements and any other relevant documentary evidence. As the tribunal put it, the basic task and function is to make 'a broad assessment on the material available to try to give the tribunal a feel and to make a prediction about what is likely to happen at the eventual hearing before a full tribunal'. This was so regardless of the volume or complexity of the material before it. Accordingly, in Raja v Secretary of State for Justice EAT 0364/09 the EAT held that the employment judge had erred in holding that interim relief applications were not suitable in cases involving complicated, long-running disputes and should be restricted to simple factual conflicts. In so finding, the judge had added an additional criterion for which there was no statutory or judicial authority. Once the claimant complied with the procedural requirements of S.128, he or she was entitled as a right to have the application heard by a tribunal. That said, where there were hundreds of pages of documentation before the tribunal, the EAT suggested that it was advisable for the tribunal to ask the parties to direct its attention to the parts relevant to the interim relief application.

19.22 When considering the 'likelihood' of the claimant succeeding at tribunal, the correct test to be applied is whether he or she has a 'pretty good chance of success' at the full hearing – Taplin v C Shippam Ltd 1978 ICR 1068, EAT. In that case, the EAT expressly ruled out alternative tests such as a 'real possibility' or 'reasonable prospect' of success or a 51 per cent or better chance of success. According to the EAT, the burden of proof in an interim relief application was intended to be greater than that at the full hearing, where the tribunal need only be satisfied on the 'balance of probabilities' that the claimant has made out his or her case – i.e. the '51 per cent or better' test. Some examples:

- **Daniels v E Ivor Hughes Educational Foundation** ET Case No.3317706/06: D began working for the employer – a private school – as a teacher in September 2005. D raised issues about the behaviour of certain pupils, including bullying and threats of violence, with the head teacher and referred a particularly serious incident to the police. At around the same time the employer decided that there were matters about D's behaviour that needed investigating. After an investigation he was called to a disciplinary hearing and dismissed. He claimed he was dismissed for making protected disclosures and made an application for interim relief. The tribunal acceded to his application, finding that the employer had made no mention of any concerns about D's behaviour before he made the protected disclosures. Given the timing of the disciplinary hearing and dismissal, the tribunal believed that there was a 'pretty good chance' of D's claim being upheld

- **Pickles v Peter Reed (Textiles) Ltd** ET Case No.1116/96: P was asked early in 1995 to become shop steward, in place of the previous steward who had retired. He refused and no steward was appointed or elected. However,

P acted as 'quasi' steward, distributing ballot papers and union literature as and when required. Later in 1995 the employer decided one redundancy was necessary and selected P on the basis of his disciplinary record. The tribunal dismissed P's application for interim relief as he had failed to persuade it that he had 'a pretty good chance' of succeeding in his claim that he was dismissed by reason of his union activities

- **Grainger v Wellman Graham Ltd** ET Case No.1400579/99: G was senior steward for MSF. So long as he did not hold formal meetings or act in a disruptive fashion he was allowed to talk to members about union business at any time during working hours. He believed bullying was a problem at work and identified a team leader, S, as a principal perpetrator. He decided to hold a meeting, outside working hours and on union premises, to discuss the issue. The employer gained the impression that G was coercing employees to attend the meeting and he was called to a disciplinary meeting at which he was dismissed. His application for interim relief was granted as the tribunal decided that most of the matters relied on by the employer as justifying the dismissal could properly be categorised as improper ways of carrying out legitimate union duties – organising and publicising a union meeting and persuading people to attend. There was therefore a 'pretty good chance' that a tribunal would conclude that the principal reason for G's dismissal was his conduct of trade union activities at a proper time

- **Knight and anor v CC and RJ Emerson Ltd** ET Case Nos.1901155/98 and 1901157/98: a tribunal held that there were many reasons to suggest that the employer wanted to get rid of K because of his union membership: the coincidence of the build-up of the dispute between them and the date K joined the union was a powerful argument to suggest that it may have been the reason for dismissal. However, the employer's stated reason for dismissal was that K had falsified travelling expenses. K said that he had made a genuine mistake but the tribunal found that he had been caught out in a conscious fiddle. Although the dismissal was likely to be found unfair, and there was a significant chance that the reason for the dismissal would be held to be K's union membership, the Taplin test had not been satisfied and the application for interim relief was therefore dismissed.

19.23   In trade union cases an employer's hostility to unions has often been treated as a persuasive factor in applications for interim relief. In Lorenz v Excelsior Packers ET Case No.25037/84, for example, the employer refused to recognise the TGWU even though 40 out of 46 workers were members. There was also evidence that union members had been threatened with dismissal if they took part in union activities and that the employer refused to allow Acas onto its premises. This background helped the tribunal to conclude that the claimant was likely to succeed in his claim that he was dismissed because of union membership.

726 —————————————————————

Similarly, if the employer advances an implausible alternative reason for dismissal, the tribunal may find that it is likely to be a cover-up for a true, inadmissible reason. In Griffin and anor v Unipack Ltd ET Case Nos.15506–07/77 the claimants were dismissed for leaving the premises to make a phone call to a union official and the employer argued that this was a straightforward dismissal for misconduct. The tribunal thought that this was spurious since leaving the premises for a few minutes fell far short of warranting instant dismissal. Since there was also evidence of the employer's hostility towards unions, interim relief was granted. And in O'Brien v Thames Water Utilities Ltd ET Case No.23918/95 a shop steward was dismissed for gross misconduct after a three-month period of surveillance and monitoring by the employer had produced eight charges of misconduct against him. The tribunal noted that there was no warrant in the employer's disciplinary code for the kind of monitoring and accumulation of charges that had occurred. The employer had clearly identified the employee as a troublemaker on account of his trade union activities and had 'banked up' a number of charges over a period of time so as to justify his dismissal. Interim relief was granted.

Tribunal powers

19.24

Where a tribunal is satisfied that interim relief should be granted, it must explain its powers to the parties and, in particular, must ask the employer whether it is willing to reinstate or re-engage the employee pending a full hearing or a settlement – S.163(2)/S.129(2) and (3). Different considerations apply to reinstatement and re-engagement:

- if the employer is willing to reinstate (i.e. to treat the employee in all respects as if he or she had not been dismissed), the tribunal must make a reinstatement order – S.163(4)/S.129(5)

- if the employer is willing to re-engage the employee in another job on terms and conditions not less favourable than those that would have applied but for the dismissal, then the tribunal must ask the employee if he or she is willing to accept re-engagement on those terms and conditions. If the employee is willing, the tribunal must make an order to that effect

- if the employee is unwilling and the tribunal considers that the refusal is reasonable, then it must make a continuation of contract order (see below). If the tribunal considers that the employee's refusal is unreasonable, however, then it will make no order at all – i.e. the employee will derive no benefit from the interim relief proceedings – S.163(5)/S.129(6), (7) and (8).

If the employer is not willing to re-employ the employee, as is often the case in practice, then the tribunal must make a continuation of contract order – S.163(6)/S.129(9)(b).

19.25 **Continuation of contract**

A continuation of contract order (CCO) *must* be made if the employer refuses to re-employ or if the employee reasonably refuses an offer of re-engagement. An unreasonable refusal on the employee's part will result in no order at all. It is not clear what the appropriate test for reasonableness is in this context, although it is likely to be an objective test – i.e. would a reasonable employee have refused in similar circumstances?

A CCO must also be made if the employer fails to attend the interim relief hearing (and the employee is successful at the hearing) – S.163(6)/S.129(9)(a). In effect a CCO is an order for suspension on full pay, together with any other benefits (such as pension rights) derived from the employment – S.164(1)/S.130(1). The order will include back pay from the date of dismissal and must specify an amount, corresponding to what the employee could reasonably have been expected to earn, to be paid in respect of each normal pay period – S.164(2)/S.130(2). Furthermore, it appears that the tribunal has power to specify the method of payment. In Blitz v Vectone Group Holding Ltd EAT 0306/09 the EAT ordered the employer, who repeatedly failed to pay B's monthly salary on time by providing him with cheques that took time to clear, to make any future payments by bank transfer.

Payments made by the employer to the employee – e.g. pay in lieu of notice – go towards discharging a CCO – S.164(5) and (6)/S.130(5) and (6). Similarly, pay received from another employer will be offset. In Williams v G and R Cadwallader Ltd COET 1889/31 the employee got a new job at comparable pay within two weeks of dismissal. The tribunal limited the CCO award to two weeks' pay because of the new earnings: the employee could not expect to be earning under the original contract if he was in fact working for somebody else.

19.26 A CCO continues in force *until the determination or settlement of the complaint* – S.164(1)/S.130(1). This will include any appeal from the tribunal's decision. In Zucker v Astrid Jewels Ltd 1978 ICR 1088, EAT, Z succeeded at an interim relief hearing and the tribunal made a CCO. However, she lost her case at the full tribunal hearing and the CCO appeared to have lapsed from the date the decision was announced. Z appealed to the EAT, which allowed the appeal and remitted the case for a rehearing by a fresh tribunal. It was understood that Z had by that time obtained new employment. The EAT said that the CCO should not have lapsed when it did – because Z's complaint had not been finally determined – but should have continued until the date when she found other employment and should have been revoked with effect from that date.

Any payments made under a CCO are *not* recoverable in the event of the employee losing his or her unfair dismissal claim at the full hearing. Nor can a CCO be stayed in anticipation of the employee losing the claim. In Initial Textile Services v Rendell EAT 383/91 R submitted a claim to a tribunal

728

alleging that he had been unfairly dismissed for his involvement in trade union activities. Owing to a listing error, the interim relief hearing did not take place until more than four months after the date the claim was lodged. At that hearing the tribunal was satisfied that it was likely that R would establish that he had been dismissed for his involvement in trade union activities and made a CCO for £217 per week and awarded £3,605 back pay. Anxious to avoid payment of such a large sum, the employer appealed against the tribunal's decision on the ground of perversity. However, since the appeal might not be heard for several months, it lodged an interlocutory (i.e. interim) appeal asking the EAT to stay the CCO pending the hearing of the full appeal on the ground that the money due for payment under the order would be irrecoverable in the event of R losing his claim.

The EAT dismissed this application, having failed to identify any error made by the tribunal which would definitely result in a successful appeal. The EAT also doubted whether it had the power to stay an interim relief order pending appeal because it would not be clear until the appeal was heard whether there would be a valid ground for allowing that appeal. Finally, the statutory provisions were clearly intended to be stringent provisions designed to protect 'the work of shop stewards in the trade union movement'. Turning to those provisions, the EAT noted that once a tribunal has concluded that an employee is likely to establish that he or she was dismissed for a S.152 reason, the employer has the opportunity to re-employ the employee. In the event of that not happening, the tribunal is obliged to make an order under S.164, including back pay and wages, until the matter is finally settled. The EAT was bound by these provisions and could find no reason to stay the CCO. Accordingly, the appeal was dismissed but with a recommendation that the unfair dismissal claim should take place as a matter of extreme urgency and be heard by a differently constituted tribunal.

Transfer of undertakings. In Dowling v ME Ilic Haulage and anor 2004 ICR 1176, EAT, the EAT held that, in the event of a relevant transfer of undertaking for the purposes of the Transfer of Undertakings (Protection of Employment) Regulations 2006 SI 2006/246 (TUPE), liability for a CCO does not pass from the transferor to the transferee employer. This case is discussed in detail in IDS Employment Law Handbook, 'Transfer of Undertakings' (2007), Chapter 3. But, in short, the EAT essentially reached this conclusion on the basis that, upon dismissal, the employee's contract of employment comes to an end and is replaced with a statutory and unilateral 'contract' between the parties, in that the employee receives pay but has no corresponding obligation to provide services. According to Mr Justice Burton, then President of the EAT, an individual who is the subject of a CCO is an ex-employee and there is no subsisting employment contract to which TUPE can apply, so as to transfer the rights and liabilities under it to the new employer. **19.27**

With respect, this interpretation seems fraught with difficulties and does not seem to accord with the purpose of the interim relief provisions. A CCO clearly envisages a continuation of the employment relationship and the effect of any such order is generally understood to be that the individual remains the employer's employee, albeit that he or she is suspended on full pay. It would seem that TUPE would operate in these circumstances. However, until we have authority to this effect, Dowling remains the only case specifically on the point.

19.28 **Change of circumstances**

If either party considers that there has been a relevant change of circumstances since the making of an interim relief order, that party may apply to the tribunal for revocation or variation of the order – S.165(1)/S.131(1). This would happen typically if the employee has found new employment or has decided to leave the job market by, for example, starting a full-time course of further education.

An application to revoke or vary a CCO need not be made to the tribunal which originally made the order but may be made to any tribunal. In British Coal Corporation v McGinty 1987 ICR 912, EAT, a tribunal made a CCO after interim relief proceedings. The substantive unfair dismissal hearing began several weeks later before a different tribunal. The hearing was protracted and, after it had been in progress for some months, the employer applied for the CCO to be revoked. The second tribunal thought that it lacked jurisdiction to entertain the application and that this could only be done by the tribunal which made the original CCO. The EAT ruled that this was wrong and that such an application could be heard by any tribunal having jurisdiction to hear cases from the locality. The EAT also made the point that it is undesirable that a tribunal which had made (or refused to make) an interim relief order should conduct the full hearing of the unfair dismissal claim. This is because the tribunal could well be thought to have come to a provisional view of the merits of the case – i.e. to have prejudged the issue before the full hearing.

19.29 **Failure to comply**

If the employer fails to comply with a tribunal's order of reinstatement or re-engagement pending the full hearing, the tribunal will, on the application of the employee, make a CCO and also order the employer to pay such amount of compensation as it considers just and equitable, having regard to the infringement of the employee's right to be reinstated in pursuance of the order and to any loss suffered by the employee in consequence of the non-compliance – S.166(1)/S.132(1) and (2).

The employee can also make an application to the tribunal if the employer has failed to comply with a CCO – S.166(3)/S.132(4). If the non-compliance consists of a failure to pay the proper amount ordered under S.164(2)/S.130(2), the tribunal will determine the amount outstanding and order the employer to

730 ──────────────────────────────────────

pay it. This amount will be in addition to any compensation for unfair dismissal that the employee may receive at the full hearing – S.166(4)/S.132(5). If the non-compliance is in regard to any other aspect of the order, the tribunal will award the employee such compensation as it considers just and equitable in all the circumstances having regard to any loss suffered by the employee in consequence of the non-compliance – S.166(5)/S.132(6).

20 Recoupment

An employee who has been dismissed may well need to draw social security benefits in order to alleviate the financial hardship that the dismissal will cause. A subsequent finding by an employment tribunal that the dismissal was unfair may lead to an award of compensation that is aimed at removing that hardship altogether. This raises two issues. How is an employment tribunal, in fixing the level of compensation, to allow for the fact that the dismissed employee has been in receipt of social security payments? And how is Jobcentre Plus (the executive agency of the Department for Work and Pensions that administers such payments) to treat that employee's past and potential claims for such benefits?

20.1

Jobseeker's Allowance and Income Support

20.2

In relation to awards made in respect of *future* loss – i.e. losses that the claimant is projected to sustain subsequent to the conclusion of tribunal proceedings – the position is relatively straightforward. By virtue of the Jobseeker's Allowance Regulations 1996 SI 1996/207 and the Income Support (General) Regulations 1987 SI 1987/1967, a compensatory award for unfair dismissal will be treated as 'earnings' over the period to which it applies for the purpose of assessing a claimant's eligibility for Jobseeker's Allowance (JSA) or Income Support (IS) under the Jobseeker's Act 1995 and the Social Security Act 1986 respectively. There will therefore be no element of double recovery if a tribunal awards compensation for loss of future earnings and the tribunal is not required to consider JSA or IS when calculating such loss. See Chapter 16 on the calculation of future loss generally.

So far as loss incurred *before* the hearing is concerned, the position is governed by the Employment Protection (Recoupment of Jobseeker's Allowance and Income Support) Regulations 1996 SI 1996/2349 (the 'Recoupment Regulations'), as amended. The procedure is that the tribunal assesses loss without regard to JSA or IS and Jobcentre Plus recoups from the employer the amount of JSA or IS paid to the employee over the relevant period. The employer, in turn, deducts these benefits from the amount due before paying the tribunal's award to the employee. The employee receives the same amount as before, with no double recovery, but the employer takes full responsibility for the loss inflicted on the employee and receives no subsidy from the social security system.

733

20.3 Other social security benefits

The Recoupment Regulations do not cover other social security benefits, such as Incapacity Benefit, Employment and Support Allowance and Housing Benefit, and there has been widespread confusion and inconsistency in the way such benefits are treated by tribunals. The current consensus appears to be that credit in respect of such benefits must be given by the employee – see Chapter 16 under 'Immediate loss – social security benefits'.

20.4 Scope of Recoupment Regulations

The Recoupment Regulations only apply to the following types of tribunal award:

- guarantee payments
- awards made under a collective agreement for guaranteed remuneration in a case where there is an exemption order excluding the right to statutory guarantee payments
- payments of remuneration for a period of suspension on medical or maternity grounds
- payments accompanying orders for reinstatement or re-engagement in unfair dismissal cases (see Chapter 14)
- compensatory awards covering immediate loss in unfair dismissal cases (see Chapter 16)
- additional awards of compensation in unfair dismissal cases where a reinstatement or re-engagement order has not been complied with (see Chapter 19)
- payments made in respect of interim relief orders and orders for continuation of contract (see Chapter 19)
- protective awards (see further 'Protective awards' below)
- payments ordered on an employer's default in paying a protective award – Reg 3(1) and the Schedule to the Regulations.

20.5 **Redundancy and discrimination claims.** The Recoupment Regulations do not apply to statutory redundancy payments as these are calculated by reference to past service and are not intended to cover the same period as the social security payments. Nor do they cover compensation for discrimination, even when the discrimination complained of takes the form of a dismissal and the tribunal's award is similar to a compensatory award in an unfair dismissal case. In such cases tribunals will prevent double recovery by deducting from the award of compensation an amount corresponding to the amount of social security benefit already paid.

734

Settlement of claims. The Recoupment Regulations only apply to monetary **20.6** awards actually made by tribunals. They do not apply to settlements arrived at by the parties. This may act as an incentive to both employees and employers to settle claims, since any payment under the settlement will not be subject to recoupment of social security benefits received. This incentive will be strongest in cases where the employee was on low wages because recoupment may have the effect of removing most, if not all, of the award. Take the case of an employee who receives £2,000 by way of JSA between dismissal and the date set for the tribunal hearing, but who would have earned £4,000 in that period if he or she had stayed in employment. Success before the tribunal would mean £4,000 being awarded for loss of earnings so far, but £2,000 of this would be subject to recoupment, leaving the employee with only £2,000 compensation for immediate loss. If there was no significant element of future loss, this might make an offer of settlement from the employer of £3,000 very attractive to the employee because there would be no recoupment, and he or she would therefore be £1,000 better off. The employer in turn would save £1,000 by settling the case in advance because there is no obligation to pay any sum to Jobcentre Plus.

Calculating the monetary award and 'prescribed element' **20.7**
In applying the Recoupment Regulations, a tribunal must first assess the total monetary award without taking any account of JSA or IS – Reg 4(1). It must then calculate and specify in its decision the following particulars:

- the total monetary award

- the amount of the 'prescribed element'

- the period to which the 'prescribed element' relates

- the amount, if any, by which the total monetary award exceeds the 'prescribed element' – Reg 4(3).

The prescribed element. The Schedule to the Recoupment Regulations sets out, in **20.8** respect of each type of award to which the Regulations applies, the 'prescribed element' of the award that is subject to recoupment of JSA or IS. In every instance, the prescribed element is that part of the monetary award covering the employee's losses up to the conclusion of the tribunal proceedings. Thus, in an unfair dismissal case the prescribed element will be that part of the award that covers lost earnings up to the conclusion of proceedings but not any award the tribunal may make for 'future loss'. In the case of guarantee payments, suspension pay or protective awards the prescribed element will be the entire award.

The 'conclusion of tribunal proceedings' is the date on which the tribunal announces its decision on compensation or, if the decision is not given orally, the date on which its written decision is sent to the parties – Reg 2(3). If there is more than one tribunal hearing – e.g. because of intervening appeals – the conclusion of proceedings is the date of the final hearing – Reg 2(5). In Tipton

735

v West Midlands Co-operative Society Ltd EAT 859/86 a tribunal found the claimant's dismissal unfair and made a reinstatement order in September 1982, the dismissal having taken effect in February 1982. After appeals to the EAT, the Court of Appeal and the House of Lords the case returned to the tribunal, which made an award of compensation (instead of reinstatement) in October 1986. This was subject to a further appeal to the EAT, heard in September 1987, which resulted in a further remit to the tribunal with instructions to settle the amount of the prescribed element. Tribunal proceedings were not concluded until the final hearing on remit, so the period covered by the prescribed element in this case was over five years.

20.9 **Effect where there has been a failure to mitigate.** If a compensatory award is subject to a cut-off point before the date of the hearing on account of the employee's failure to mitigate, then recoupment can only apply to the period covered by the compensatory award. In Homan v AI Bacon Co Ltd EAT 1154/94 and 236/95 the period between the date of the claimant's dismissal and the date of the tribunal's decision was just over ten months. However, the tribunal ruled that the claimant had failed to mitigate her loss during that period and therefore limited her compensatory award to six months. For the purposes of recoupment, however, the tribunal defined the period of the prescribed element as equating to the period between the dismissal and the tribunal's decision (i.e. ten months). On appeal, the EAT held that this was wrong. The prescribed element, the EAT made clear, deals only with the element in the compensatory award attributable to actual financial loss, which means that the only period to which it can apply is the period in respect of which compensation is actually awarded. Accordingly, the period of the prescribed element in the instant case was six rather than ten months.

Similarly, in Bramley v Tesco Ltd EAT 776/77 a tribunal awarded only four weeks' pay as compensation and the EAT held that the Department of Employment could recoup only four weeks' JSA.

20.10 **Effect of contributory fault or application of statutory cap.** If the amount of the compensatory award is reduced either because of the employee's contributory fault or because it exceeds the prevailing statutory limit, the prescribed element must be reduced proportionately – Reg 4(2). In Mason v Wimpey Waste Management Ltd and anor 1982 IRLR 454, EAT, a tribunal assessed the claimant's monetary loss at £7,712, of which £5,918 was referable to the period from the date of dismissal to the conclusion of tribunal proceedings. The statutory maximum for a compensatory award was then £5,200, so the tribunal took this to be the prescribed element since the whole sum clearly referred to the period between dismissal and the final tribunal hearing. The EAT held that it should have reduced £5,918 – the 'original' prescribed element – by the same proportion as the reduction from £7,712 to £5,200 for the total compensatory award, which would have produced a revised figure for the prescribed element of £3,991. This was beneficial to the claimant, since it is only the prescribed element that is subject to recoupment.

736

Application of recoupment where no JSA or IS received. A tribunal's duties in respect of recoupment do not apply if it is satisfied that the claimant has neither received nor claimed JSA or IS in respect of the relevant period – Reg 4(8).

20.11

Recoupment procedure

20.12

When a tribunal has made an oral announcement of a monetary award that includes a prescribed element, the Secretary of the Tribunals must notify Jobcentre Plus of the particulars – Reg 4(5). He or she must also send a copy of the written decision to Jobcentre Plus as soon as reasonably practicable after sending copies to the parties – Reg 4(6).

Service of recoupment notice. An employer should not pay the employee the prescribed element of the monetary award until Jobcentre Plus has served a recoupment notice, or given written notification that it does not intend to serve a notice – Reg 7(2). (If the employer does make the payment, it will still be liable to pay the recoupable amount to Jobcentre Plus – Reg 8(9).) Jobcentre Plus should serve the notice or notification on the employer within 21 days of the tribunal's announcement of its decision or within nine days of the decision being sent to the parties, whichever is the later, or as soon as practicable thereafter – Reg 8(5) and (6). If the tribunal's decision is reserved, the 21-day period runs from the date it is sent to the parties – Reg 8(6)(b). A copy of the recoupment notice must also be sent to the employee and, if requested, to the Secretary of the Tribunals – Reg 8(4).

20.13

A recoupment notice operates as an instruction to the employer to pay the 'recoupable amount' to Jobcentre Plus from out of the prescribed element of the monetary award – the recoupable amount being the amount of the JSA or IS paid to the employee during the period to which the prescribed element relates – Reg 8(8). Payment to Jobcentre Plus completely discharges the employer's obligations to the employee to pay the amount equivalent to the recoupable amount by way of the monetary award – Reg 8(10). However, such payment does not affect the employer's obligation to pay any balance of the monetary award to the employee – Reg 8(8).

Tribunal's duty to explain recoupment procedure. Regulation 4(4) stipulates that where a tribunal at the hearing announces to the parties its decision to make a monetary award, it must at the same time inform the parties of the amount of any prescribed element included in that award and must explain the effect of the recoupment procedure outlined above. There is, however, a limit to how far this duty extends. In Kwakye-Manu v City of Hackney Health Authority EAT 329/95 the EAT rejected the argument that the tribunal must explain the effect of the Recoupment Regulations in its written decision. The duty under Reg 4(4) is confined to an oral explanation at the time of the hearing, and the purpose of that explanation is simply to alert the parties to the fact that recoupment applies. In any

20.14

737

event, a failure to comply with that duty does not amount to a misdirection in law vitiating the tribunal's award of compensation.

Strangely, however, in the specific case of protective awards, although the same duty to explain arises in respect of any oral announcement made at the hearing, the Recoupment Regulations also impose a duty on the tribunal to explain in its written decision to the employer the latter's duties with regard to the recoupment and the effect of the recoupment procedure – Reg 5(2). A number of other special rules apply to protective awards in respect of recoupment, which are discussed in the final section of this chapter.

20.15 ## Challenging recoupment

An employee who has received a copy of a recoupment notice and who disagrees with the amount specified in it may notify Jobcentre Plus in writing that he or she disagrees with its assessment: this should be done within 21 days, subject to possible extension by Jobcentre Plus for 'special reasons' – Reg 10(1). Where such a notice is served on Jobcentre Plus, its officials will make a decision as to the amount of JSA or IS actually paid in respect of the 'prescribed element' period – Reg 10(2). Jobcentre Plus is entitled to revise any decision made pursuant to Reg 10(2), either of its own motion or on application by a party to the tribunal proceedings – Reg 10(2A). An employee is entitled to appeal to the First-tier Tribunal against any decision made by Jobcentre Plus under Reg 10(2) or (2A) – Reg 10(2B).

If, as a result of the employee's complaint Reg 10(1), it turns out that Jobcentre Plus has recovered too much from the employer, it is required to pay the difference to the employee – Reg 10(3).

In circumstances where Jobcentre Plus has made a recoupment of JSA or IS from the employer but the original tribunal decision is subsequently varied following a rehearing or varied or set aside on appeal, Jobcentre Plus must repay the employer or, as the case may be, pay the employee the amount that should have been paid having regard to the decision on rehearing or appeal – Reg 10(4).

20.16 ## Protective awards

A protective award is an award of pay made to employees affected by their employer's failure to consult properly over collective redundancies – see IDS Employment Law Handbook, 'Redundancy' (2008), Chapter 11. There are some additional procedural requirements that apply to the recoupment procedure for protective awards and to claims by individuals that protective awards have not been paid.

When a tribunal makes a protective award, whether orally or in a reserved written decision, the Secretary of the Tribunals must 'forthwith' give Jobcentre Plus the following particulars:

738 ————————————————————————

- the date of the hearing where the decision was announced orally, or the date the decision was sent to the parties
- the location of the tribunal
- the name and address of the employer
- the description of the employees concerned
- the dates of the protected period – Reg 5(1).

The tribunal must also explain orally, if giving an oral decision, or in its written decision, what the employer is required to do – Reg 5(2). The employer must within ten days of the tribunal's decision (or, if that is not reasonably practicable, as soon as is reasonably practicable) tell Jobcentre Plus in writing: **20.17**

- the name, address and National Insurance number of each employee to whom the award relates
- the date (or proposed date) of termination of employment for each such employee – Reg 6.

The employer should not make any payment under a protective award until a recoupment notice, or a notification that it does not intend to serve a recoupment notice, has been received from Jobcentre Plus – Reg 7(2). Jobcentre Plus must serve a recoupment notice or notification on the employer within 21 days of receipt of the required information from the employer – Reg 8(7). However, the delay in payment by the employer does not prevent an employee from complaining to a tribunal under S.192 of the Trade Union and Labour Relations (Consolidation) Act 1992 that the employer has failed to pay remuneration due under a protective award – Reg 7(3).

21 Written reasons for dismissal

Entitlement

Employer's obligation

Grounds for complaint

Remedies

By virtue of S.92 of the Employment Rights Act 1996 (ERA) a dismissed **21.1** employee with one year's continuous employment is entitled, on request, to a written statement from his or her employer giving particulars of the reasons for dismissal. If an employer unreasonably fails to provide a written statement within 14 days of a request being made, or if the reasons given are inadequate or untrue, the employee concerned may seek redress from an employment tribunal under S.93. If a written statement is provided in accordance with S.92, the employee in question may rely on it as evidence in a claim of unfair dismissal or in any other legal proceedings – S.92(5).

Entitlement   **21.2**

An employee's right under S.92 arises in any of the following circumstances:

- where an employer gives notice of dismissal – S.92(1)(a)

- where an employer dismisses without notice – S.92(1)(b), or

- where the employee is employed under a limited-term contract and the contract terminates by virtue of the limiting event without being renewed under the same contract – S.92(1)(c). (A 'limited-term' contract is explained in Chapter 1 under 'Non-renewal of limited-term contracts'.)

The right cannot apply to cases of constructive dismissal, since it is the employee who takes the initiative in such cases by terminating the contract.

There may be circumstances where the employee claims to have been dismissed **21.3** but the employer denies this – see, for example, Hogg v Dover College 1990 ICR 39, EAT (discussed in Chapter 1 under 'Express dismissal – ambiguous conduct'). Where an employer seeks to avoid liability under S.92 by denying that there has been a dismissal within the terms of that section, the tribunal must first decide whether or not a dismissal has taken place – Brown v Stuart Scott and Co 1981 ICR 166, EAT. The test is objective: whether there was in fact a dismissal, not whether the employer subjectively believed that there was – Broomsgrove v Eagle Alexander Ltd 1981 IRLR 127, EAT. It is up to the employee to show that a relevant dismissal has occurred. But even if the

741

employee is successful in showing this, the employer's genuine and reasonable belief that there has been no dismissal may render a failure to supply written reasons reasonable, meaning that the employer can escape liability – see 'Employer's obligation – unreasonable failure' below.

21.4 Qualifying employees

There is no upper age limit on the right to request written reasons for dismissal and it applies even where the reason for dismissal is retirement in accordance with S.98(2)(ba) ERA (see Chapter 9). However, the armed forces, share fishermen and police officers do not qualify for the right – Ss.192, 199, 200 ERA. Nor does it apply where, in the opinion of a Minister of the Crown, disclosure of the information would be contrary to the interests of national security – S.202 ERA.

As a general rule, S.92 does not assist employees who do not have one year's continuous service on the effective date of termination (EDT) of the employment contract – S.92(3). The EDT for these purposes is the date on which notice expires or, where the contract is terminated without notice, the date on which the termination takes effect – S.92(6)(a) and (b). In relation to an employee who is employed under a limited-term contract which terminates by virtue of the limiting event without being renewed under the same contract, the EDT is the date on which the termination takes effect – S.92(6)(c).

21.5

Usually, therefore, an employee's period of continuous service ends when the employment contract ends. However, S.92(7) provides for an artificial postponement of the EDT where the employer terminates the contract of employment without notice or with less than the *statutory minimum* notice. In such a case the EDT for the purposes of calculating continuous service will be the date on which the statutory minimum notice would have expired had it been given. (For a detailed discussion of how to calculate the EDT see IDS Employment Law Handbook, 'Contracts of Employment' (2009), Chapter 11.)

There are two **exceptions** to the one-year continuous employment rule in S.92(3), which are contained in S.92(4) and (4A). These provide that an employee who is dismissed while pregnant or during ordinary or additional maternity leave or adoption leave is entitled to receive written reasons irrespective of his or her length of service and without having to make a request. This does not apply to paternity or parental leave, or to any other automatically unfair reasons for dismissal.

21.6 Request

Section 92(2) stipulates that, subject to S.92(4) and (4A), an employer is under no obligation to provide a written statement unless a request has been made by the employee. S.92(4) and (4A) provide that, where an employee is dismissed while pregnant or during ordinary or additional maternity or adoption leave, he or she is entitled to receive written reasons without having to make a request.

742

An employee's request for written reasons may be made either orally or in writing at any time after dismissal, or within the notice period if the employer dismisses with notice. Guidance as to what constitutes a request for written reasons was provided by the EAT in HT Greenwood Ltd t/a Greenwood Savings and Loans v Miller EAT 499/87. In that case an employee's solicitors wrote to their client's former employer requesting a number of documents, including a 'statutory letter dismissing her and giving her reason for dismissal'. The EAT stated that the letter was arguably too vague to constitute a S.92 request, finding that the provision envisages that a request will be 'a separate and specific statement or at any rate a clearly defined sentence'.

Other than in pregnancy or maternity/adoption leave cases under S.92(4) and (4A), if an employer provides an employee with written reasons for dismissal *without* having received a specific request from the employee, a tribunal is not empowered to consider whether the reasons provided are inadequate or untrue for the purposes of a S.93 claim – Catherine Haigh Harlequin Hair Design v Seed 1990 IRLR 175, EAT. An employee in these circumstances would have to make a formal request for written reasons, despite the fact that they had already been supplied, in order to be able to argue at an employment tribunal that they were inadequate or untrue. **21.7**

Employer's obligation **21.8**

Once a request has been made the employer is obliged to provide a written statement giving particulars of the reasons for dismissal within 14 days. Written reasons must be sent or given either directly to the employee in question or to his or her authorised agent. The employer should not simply send written reasons to the tribunal, despite the fact that the tribunal will pass them on to the employee. In Rowan v Machinery Installations (South Wales) Ltd 1981 IRLR 122, EAT, the EAT held that where an employee had brought an unfair dismissal claim it was not sufficient for the employer to include the written reasons for dismissal in the response form.

There has been some debate as to whether an employer fulfils its obligations simply by putting a written statement of reasons into the post. In Kennedy v JGS Bell 'Jim's Inn' EAT 103/78 the EAT suggested that the posting of a written statement was sufficient to comply with what is now S.92. The EAT added, however, that a prudent employer would send written reasons by recorded delivery and that any employer who failed to do so would run the risk of having its evidence on that point rejected. In Keen v Dymo Ltd 1977 IRLR 118 an employment tribunal held that there was a breach where the written reasons had been sent by second class post within the time limit but arrived one day late: they had to arrive with the employee before the end of the 14th day in order to comply. Certainly, an employer would be well advised to take steps to ensure that a statement of written reasons actually reaches the employee in question.

21.9 In practice, of course, an employer should not wait for a dismissed employee to request written reasons for dismissal before providing them. Giving an employee a written explanation for any disciplinary action was described as a core principle of reasonable behaviour in the 2004 version of the Acas Code of Practice on Disciplinary and Grievance Procedures, although the current 2009 version does not put it quite so strongly. Para 17 of the 2009 Code states that after a disciplinary meeting the employer should decide whether or not disciplinary or any other action is justified and inform the employee accordingly in writing. Para 21 goes on to provide that following a decision to dismiss, the employee should be informed as soon as possible of the reasons for the dismissal. Furthermore, the Acas Guide on Discipline and Grievances at Work, which supplements the Code but has no statutory standing, still states that it is good practice to give written reasons for all dismissals. A failure to comply with the Code (where it applies) is relevant to the question of liability for unfair dismissal (see Chapter 3 under 'Fairness of internal procedure – the Acas Code of Practice') and compensation (see Chapter 18).

21.10 Grounds for complaint

Section 93(1) specifies two grounds on which a dismissed employee can make a complaint to a tribunal. The first is that his or her employer has unreasonably failed to provide a written statement of reasons for dismissal within 14 days of the employee's request. The second is that the particulars given by the employer in purported compliance with its obligations are inadequate or untrue.

The two grounds for complaint are separate, although an employee is entitled to claim in the alternative – Arlett v AMK (Property Management) Ltd EAT 475/81. The distinction between the two grounds is important. If an employee can show that written reasons were given but that they were inadequate or untrue, he or she is entitled to compensation regardless of whether or not the employer has acted reasonably in failing to provide adequate or true reasons.

21.11 Unreasonable failure
There are two questions to be considered under this head: (i) was there a failure to provide written reasons? and (ii) if so, was that failure unreasonable?

21.12 **Was there a failure?** Prior to reform by the TURERA in 1993, an employer would only be caught by S.93 if he refused to provide written reasons. Although a refusal could be either explicit or by conduct, it certainly had to include some element of deliberate or intentional withholding of the reasons for dismissal. A mere failure to provide written reasons within the 14-day time limit did not automatically amount to a refusal. Under the current provisions, however, a refusal is not required. An employer is potentially in breach of S.93 if it fails to

744

provide written reasons. The current provision seems to be fairly straightforward. It will usually be clear whether or not an employer has failed to provide written reasons within the time limit.

Was the failure unreasonable? Once an employee has shown that his or her employer has failed to provide written reasons, the next hurdle is to prove that the failure was unreasonable. Whether or not the employee succeeds will depend on the facts of the individual case. In Daynecourt Insurance Brokers Ltd v Iles 1978 IRLR 335, EAT, the EAT stated that the test of reasonableness was objective and that tribunals should have regard to 'the behaviour to be expected of the reasonable employer' in reaching their decision. In that case, an employee under police investigation for theft requested written reasons for dismissal from his employer. The employer ignored the request in reliance on a general direction from the police not to answer correspondence or deal with any matter related to the investigation. The tribunal decided that the employer should have sought the advice of the police on this specific matter and that, accordingly, the refusal to provide written reasons was unreasonable. The EAT upheld the tribunal's decision.

21.13

The fact that an employee knows perfectly well why he or she has been dismissed will not of itself render an employer's failure to provide written reasons reasonable. This is because one purpose of S.92 is to enable employees to have some documentation to produce to third parties – McBrearty v Thomson t/a Highfield Mini-Market EAT 653/90. However, an employee's knowledge of the reasons for dismissal may be relevant if exceptional circumstances exist, although it is difficult to predict when this will be the case. In Petch v DHSS EAT 851/86 the EAT held that an employer's refusal to provide written reasons was reasonable where the employee knew the reasons for dismissal and where the provision of written reasons would have prejudiced the employee's retirement arrangements.

Finally, as mentioned above under 'Entitlement', a failure to supply written reasons can, in some circumstances, be justified by an employer's mistaken belief that no dismissal in fact took place. In Broomsgrove v Eagle Alexander Ltd (above) the EAT held that an objective test must be applied: did the employer genuinely and reasonably believe that no dismissal had occurred? However, in Brown v Stuart Scott and Co (above) a different division of the EAT suggested that an employer's conscientious belief that there had been no dismissal would suffice. The apparent discrepancy may be explained by the fact that in the latter case the employee was claiming that the employer did not honestly believe that there had been a dismissal. Given that the statute refers to an 'unreasonable' failure, we would submit that the proper test is the objective one propounded by the EAT in Broomsgrove.

21.14

Inadequate reasons

21.15

Section 92 requires an employer to give 'particulars of the reasons for... dismissal'. This raises the question of how much detail will be considered adequate to comply with the duty. In Earl v Valleythorn Ltd EAT 376/81 the EAT said that an employer was not required to give 'full particulars of each act relied upon as constituting conduct giving rise to the dismissal' and held that it had been sufficient for the employer to state that the employee had been dismissed for 'dishonesty'. Further, in Walls v City Bakeries EAT 759/86 the EAT held that an employer's reference to 'grounds of gross industrial misconduct concerning the incidents that took place on Saturday 26th October, 1985' had been sufficiently specific and that there had been no need for the employer to state that the employee had been dismissed for 'attempted theft'.

Nevertheless, it is generally accepted that employers are obliged to do more than simply indicate which of the 'potentially fair' reasons for dismissal listed in S.98 ERA is applicable. It is clear that S.92 intends employers to be clear about the underlying reasons for dismissal rather than simply to use the technical label given to such reasons.

21.16   There has been some debate as to whether an employer may answer an employee's request for written reasons by referring to existing documents. In Kent County Council v Gilham and ors 1985 IRLR 16, CA, the Court of Appeal held that a letter which referred to two earlier documents, copies of which were enclosed, contained adequate particulars of the reasons for dismissal. The Court distinguished the EAT's earlier decision in Horsley Smith and Sherry Ltd v Dutton 1977 IRLR 172, EAT, that a letter which simply referred to an interview and letter prior to dismissal was inadequate on the ground that in that case, the employer had not given any written reasons to the employee. Accordingly, if an employer wishes to explain the reasons for a dismissal by reference to another document, the employer should provide a copy of that document together with the written statement.

If a tribunal finds a reference to an earlier document to be inadequate, it is nevertheless possible for it to hold that the employer's failure to provide written reasons was reasonable in the circumstances. In Marchant v Earley Town Council 1979 ICR 891, for example, the EAT held that an employer's refusal to provide written reasons was not unreasonable where the employer's sole reason for refusal was the belief that the information had already been supplied in writing.

21.17   **Untrue reasons**

It is often difficult for an employee to prove that the reasons given for dismissal are untrue. To do so, he or she must point to inconsistent conduct or statements by the employer, or show that the facts surrounding the dismissal are such that the employer could not genuinely have believed in the reason put forward. In practice, if an employee believes that the reasons for dismissal put forward by his or her employer are untrue, he or she is more likely to bring an unfair dismissal or discrimination claim either in addition to, or instead of, a claim under S.93.

The written reasons given by the employer have to be 'true' in the sense that they must be the reasons which the employer actually relied on in dismissing the employee. It is clear that an employee is not entitled under S.93 to complain that the employer was mistaken in believing these reasons to be true in fact or that these reasons did not justify dismissal. That issue is the sole preserve of unfair dismissal claims. In Harvard Securities plc v Younghusband 1990 IRLR 17, EAT, the employer stated that the reason for dismissing an employee was that he had improperly divulged to a third party confidential information relating to the business of the company. The employee argued that this was an 'untrue' reason because the information could not properly be regarded as confidential. The EAT rejected this argument, adding that the aim of what is now S.92 is to require employers to state truthfully from the outset the reason on which they relied. Whether or not they were justified in dismissing the employee for that reason was irrelevant. A similar conclusion was reached in Lynes v Devon County Council EAT 618/96 where the EAT held that the truth to be established under S.93 was not the truth of the complaints relied upon by the employer but the truth that those complaints were really the reasons that the employer had in mind when dismissing.

Remedies

21.18

Where a complaint under S.93 is well founded the tribunal has two remedies at its disposal. First, it may make a declaration as to what it finds were the employer's reasons for dismissing the employee. Secondly, it must order that the employer pay the employee a sum equal to two weeks' pay. The tribunal has no discretion in the latter instance either to refuse to make an award or over how much to award. A week's pay is calculated by reference to Ss.220–229 ERA (see IDS Employment Law Handbook, 'Wages' (3rd Ed), Chapter 11). There is no maximum limit on a week's pay for this purpose.

Time limit

21.19

A complaint that an employer has not complied with S.92 must be brought within three months of the EDT unless it is not reasonably practicable for the complaint to be brought within that time. It should be noted that the EDT for this purpose will be the actual date of dismissal and will not be artificially postponed by virtue of S.92(7). (For a detailed discussion of how to calculate the EDT see IDS Employment Law Handbook, 'Contracts of Employment' (2009), Chapter 11.)

Case list

(Note that employment tribunal cases are not included in this list.)

A

C

D

E

H

M

N

765

S

T

U

V

Index

investigations, 6.142
mitigating circumstances, 6.148
off-duty conduct, 6.150
reasonableness of dismissal, 6.143–6.149
threats, 6.149

Final salary schemes
pension loss, 17.10–17.11

Final written warnings
see **Warnings**

First written warnings
see **Warnings**

Fit notes
ill health, 5.14, 5.67

Flouting company rules
disobedience, dismissal for, 6.60–6.63

Flouting specific instructions
disobedience, dismissal for, 6.59

Flouting working practices
disobedience, dismissal for, 6.60–6.63

Foreign employment
exclusion from right to claim
EU-derived rights, enforcement of, 2.34–2.36
general rule, 2.32–2.33
introduction, 2.1

Fraudulent conduct
dismissal for, 6.127, 6.130–6.131

Fringe benefits
immediate loss, calculation of
accommodation, 16.47
company car, 16.45–16.46
generally, 16.44
national insurance contributions, 16.49
other benefits, 16.48

Frustration of contract
exclusion from place of work by third party, 1.62
generally, 1.58
illness of employee, 1.59–1.60, 5.6
imprisonment of employee, 1.61

Fundamental breach
see **Breach of contract**

Future dismissal
warnings, 1.18

Future loss
compensatory awards
accelerated receipt, discount for, 16.69–16.70
assessment of, 16.62–16.68
career-long loss, 16.57–16.58
circumstances resulting in, 16.53
constructive dismissal, 16.61
decelerated receipt, 16.71
employee's health and fitness, 16.59–16.61
evidence, 16.55–16.56
fact, question of, 16.51
generally, 16.50
mitigation of, 16.68
Ogden Tables and multipliers, 16.58
private income, 16.77
recoupment, 16.54
remoteness, 16.72–16.77
retraining, 16.65–16.67
speculation, 16.55–16.56
tax rebates, 16.78
tribunal's duty to assess, 16.52
unemployment benefits, 16.54

G

Good faith
asserting statutory rights, 12.19–12.21
whistleblowing, 13.23

Grievances
hearings for misconduct, raised during, 6.211
procedural fairness, 3.60–3.62

Gross incompetence
warnings on capability, 4.42

Gross misconduct
investigations, and, 6.179

Gross unsuitability
warnings on capability, 4.42

Grudges
whistleblowing, 13.24–13.25

H

Heads of compensation
compensatory awards, 16.15

Health and safety dismissals
alcohol, 6.76–6.77